CROSS-FUNCTIONAL CONNECTIONS

MARKETING MISCUES

CRITICAL THINKING CASES

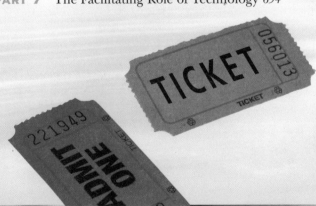

Marketing

LAMB, HAIR, MCDANIEL

8

Charles W. Lamb, Jr.

M.J. Neeley Professor of Marketing
M.J. Neeley School of Business
Texas Christian University

Joseph F. Hair, Jr.

Alvin C. Copeland Endowed
Chair of Franchising and Director,
Entrepreneurship Institute
Louisiana State University

Carl McDaniel

Chair, Department of Marketing
College of Business Administration
University of Texas at Arlington

THOMSON

SOUTH-WESTERN

Australia · Canada · Mexico · Singapore · Spain · United Kingdom · United States

Marketing, 8e
Charles W. Lamb, Jr., Joseph F. Hair, Jr., and Carl McDaniel

VP/Editorial Director:
Jack W. Calhoun

VP/Editor-in-Chief:
Dave Shaut

Senior Publisher:
Melissa Acuña

Executive Editor:
Neil Marquardt

Developmental Editor:
Jamie Gleich Bryant

Marketing Manager:
Nicole Moore

Production Editor:
Amy McGuire

Manager of Technology, Editorial
Vicky True

Technology Project Editor:
Pam Wallace

Web Coordinator:
Karen Schaffer

Senior Manufacturing Coordinator:
Diane Lohman

Production House:
Pre-Press Company, Inc.

Printer:
Quebecor World Dubuque

Art Director:
Michelle Kunkler

Cover and Internal Designer:
Ann Small
a small design studio

Cover Image:
© John Lund/CORBIS

Photography Manager:
Deanna Ettinger

Photo Researcher:
Terri Miller

ASIA (including India)
Thomson Learning
5 Shenton Way
#01-01 UIC Building
Singapore 068808

CANADA
Thomson Nelson
1120 Birchmount Road
Toronto, Ontario
Canada M1K 5G4

AUSTRALIA/NEW ZEALAND
Thomson Learning Australia
102 Dodds Street
Southbank, Victoria 3006
Australia

UK/EUROPE/MIDDLE
EAST/AFRICA
Thomson Learning
High Holborn House
50-51 Bedford Road
London WC1R 4LR
United Kingdom

LATIN AMERICA
Thomson Learning
Seneca, 53
Colonia Polanco
11560 Mexico
D.F. Mexico

SPAIN (includes Portugal)
Thomson Paraninfo
Calle Magallanes, 25
28015 Madrid, Spain

**To Jamie Gleich Bryant,
World's Greatest Developmental Editor.**

—Charles W. Lamb, Jr.
—Joseph F. Hair, Jr.
—Carl McDaniel

Brief Contents

Contents

PART 1
The World of Marketing   1

PART 2
Analyzing Marketing Opportunities   147

PART 3
Product Decisions 303

PART 4
Distribution Decisions 389

ABOUT THIS EDITION

You are holding a textbook that has experienced a dramatic increase with each edition in the number of colleges and university student-users. It is now one of the world's leading marketing textbooks. We are very grateful to the hundreds of professors around the world that have selected our text to give college students their first exposure to the dynamic world of marketing. We are honored that a majority of professors stay with our text edition after edition. Our research gives us an indication why this is true. Students find *Marketing*, by Lamb, Hair, and McDaniel, the most exciting, readable, and enjoyable text of their college career.

SO WHAT'S NEW?

If you are already familiar with *Marketing*, you may be asking, "So what's new?" The answer is quite a bit.

New Content

In addition to the dozens of new examples in each chapter, we have added new topical content and revised and updated existing material throughout the book.

PART 1   We have retained the proven format of Chapter 1 (An Overview of Marketing) and added a new Career Appendix to introduce students to various aspects of a career in marketing, like types of marketing jobs, pay scales, preparation for interviewing, and what to expect the first year on the job. Chapter 2 (Strategic Planning for Competitive Advantage) has been streamlined and now culminates with a Marketing Plan Appendix to help students better understand the level of detail needed in a strategic marketing plan. A thoroughly revised Chapter 3 (Social Responsibility, Ethics, and the Marketing Environment) tackles the issue of sustainability and offers new content on demographics, including new material on women as principal economic decision makers. We have completely revised the sections on Generation Y, Generation X, baby boomers, and older consumers, and on marketing to Hispanic Americans, African Americans, and Asian Americans. The chapter contains new material on purchasing power and household income distribution across the United States. Chapter 4 (Developing a

Global Vision) has been greatly revised to reflect constant changes in the global marketplace. We have updated the section on the impact of globalization on trade. There is new content on the effects of purchasing power across nations and the global distribution of wealth. Three new sections on the World Bank, the International Monetary Fund, and the effects of exchange rates are highly relevant for today's global marketer.

PART 2   Chapter 5 (Consumer Decision Making) has new material on how consumers use cutoffs to narrow product choices, and Chapter 6 (Business Marketing) has a completely revised section on business marketing on the Internet. Chapter 7 (Segmenting and Targeting Markets) now includes information on dynamic segmentation, the practice of one-to-one marketing (getting down to a market segment of only one consumer), privacy issues related to one-to-one marketing, and the role of the Internet in marketing to individual consumers. Chapter 8 (Decision Support Systems and Marketing Research) addresses virtual focus groups in a new section and has a new and detailed exhibit comparing the costs of collecting data using traditional methods versus using the Internet.

PART 3   Chapter 10 (Developing and Managing Products) adds tips for successful product development and information on the differences between product adoption habits across different nations. Chapter 11 (Services and Nonprofit Organization Marketing) contains the latest projections for service sector employment.

PART 4   Companies everywhere are working to squeeze inefficiencies out of their supply chains, so in Chapter 12 (Supply Chain Management) we give students an introduction to radio-frequency-identification (RFID) tags, the latest technology in distribution. Chapter 13 (Retailing) has updated the hottest retailing trends and now includes a section on firm-customer interactivity and m-commerce. There is also a new exhibit listing resources for franchising.

PART 5   Chapter 15 (Advertising and Public Relations) contains new statistics on which media marketers are using most for their advertising. There is also new material about a new trend in Internet marketing called "advergaming." Electronic couponing gets a new look in Chapter 16 (Sales Promotion and

Personal Selling), which also contains new material on the efforts of many companies to revive dying customer loyalty through frequent-shopper programs. In this chapter, we also look at the rise of co-branded credit cards as a sales promotion tool.

PART 6 Chapter 17 (Pricing Concepts) has more detailed descriptions on calculating retail prices and markups. It also includes a revised section on the impact of Internet auctions on pricing. New content on the impact of competition on pricing is included in Chapter 18 (Setting the Right Price).

PART 7 Chapter 19 (Internet Marketing) is completely revised for every edition of *Marketing* to reflect the constantly evolving world of Internet marketing and e-commerce. We have streamlined Chapter 20 (Customer Relationship Management), including clearer descriptions of each concept, so that students can get a better grasp of this complex topic.

New Visual Learning Objective Summaries

Through our years teaching, we know that not all students learn the material the same way. Some can read books and understand the concepts just from their verbal presentation. Other students need to rewrite the material in their own words in order to understand it completely. Still others learn best from diagrams and exhibits.

For this reason, every learning objective topic in the Eighth Edition concludes with a graphic depiction of the material discussed. These pieces of art, called **Review Learning Objectives**, are designed to give students a picture of the content, which they can use to help them recall the material. For example, Learning Objective 4 in Chapter 4 discusses the various ways of entering the global marketing place. The detailed discussion of everything from exporting to direct investment ends with the following review:

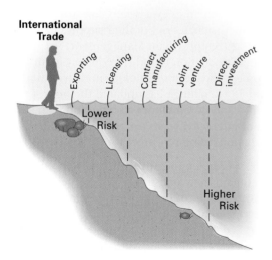

These reviews are not meant to repeat every nuance of the chapter content. Rather, they are meant to provide visual cues that prompt the student to recall the salient points in the chapter. Our new visual reviews do not replace our end-of-chapter review summaries. (Some students will prefer the written summary to the visual summary.) But what we now offer is a choice that meets an individual student's needs.

New Marketing in Entertainment Boxes

In this edition of *Marketing*, we have developed a **Marketing in Entertainment** box for each chapter. These short boxes give students a concentrated example of how chapter concepts can be found in the entertainment industry. Although not all students have had experience working in the world of business, nearly all can relate to examples about entertainment. Using examples from this industry will enhance students' understanding.

We take a wide view of this important industry, from television and film, to publishing (for example, books and magazines), fine art (like theater and circus), Internet, video gaming, and nonmedia entertainment (like tailgating). We also take a look at companies that create the equipment, computer hardware, and software that power our entertainment choices. At the end of each chapter, students will find a detailed exercise on the **Marketing in Entertainment** box to help them arrive at a deeper understanding of how marketing is operating in the entertainment choices they make every day.

New Application Exercises

If you are familiar with *Marketing*, you may recall that we have had an Application for Small Business for many years. For this edition, we wanted something new and exciting for this feature to generate enthusiasm with both students and instructors.

Now, the end of each chapter contains a new application exercise that gives students the opportunity to work with marketing concepts in various real-world contexts. We incorporate activities (rather than questions) to help students appreciate the width and depth of the marketing industry. These exercises come from instructors around the country who have contributed their teaching ideas to our unique supplement **Great Ideas in Teaching Marketing** since the First Edition.

For this edition, we asked a panel of 35 judges to review every Great Idea we have ever published. After reviewing over 1,000 ideas, we decided to use the winning entries as the basis for the new application exercise. Activities are designed to help students get into marketing by creating an ethnic dining guide, playing a world geography game, drafting a plan to revive the Hydrox cookie brand, collecting a list of 100 new products and graphing the distribution of new product types, comparing two retail stores according to their retailing mixes, researching the complete supply chain for a product of their choosing, creating an advertising campaign for a product using the rules from the Hasbro game Taboo, role playing a televised interview after a marketing crisis, and much more.

New Career Exercises

Many students who take principles of marketing may not be aware of the numerous career opportunities open to marketing majors. Even though we talk about marketing careers in Chapter 1 (Learning Objective 5) and have followed that introduction with a detailed Career Appendix, we know that job hunting is a serious concern for many students—of all disciplines. Our new **Career Exercises** at the end of each chapter aim to give students the opportunity to explore careers in a variety of marketing disciplines.

Each Career Exercise relates to the content covered in the chapter. For example, after Chapter 2 (Strategic Planning for Competitive Advantage), students are led through a personal SWOT analysis. In Chapter 11 (Services and Nonprofit Organization Marketing), students are shown how to research nonprofit organizations through Guidestar.org, a database of over 850,000 registered nonprofits, and Give.org, the division of the Better Business Bureau that concentrates exclusively on nonprofit groups and charities. If students work these exercises throughout the semester, they will feel comfortable looking for marketing jobs now, and will know what resources are available throughout their careers.

New Videos from Popular Movies

For the Eighth Edition of *Marketing*, we have replaced our medium-length videos with a new and innovative type of video. Joseph Champoux, the leading educator in teaching through film, has carefully selected a film clip for every chapter. Scenes from *The Family Man, Bowfinger, About a Boy, Lost in Translation, Casino, Intolerable Cruelty,* and other films help students see the world of marketing from a new perspective. These clips are a great way to conclude teaching the chapter because they require students to draw the connections and articulate the relationship between the movie and the chapter concepts. By thinking metaphorically—rather than just literally—about the concepts, students gain a deeper understanding of marketing. Clips are available on DVD for professors and through Xtra! for students.

New Still Shaky

The only thing familiar about this feature is the name. We have kept our study tip at the end of each chapter, but we have added a resource list to it. Because students often look for additional review opportunities, we have created a simple checklist that shows students what support materials are available for the chapter and where to find them—on Xtra! (**http://lambxtra .swlearning.com**), at our Web site (**http://lamb .swlearning.com**), or in the *Grademaker Study Guide.*

CLASSIC FEATURES HAVE BEEN UPDATED AND ENHANCED

Looking Forward

Each chapter begins with a new, current, real-world story about a marketing decision or situation facing a company. These vignettes, called **Looking Forward**, have been carefully prepared to stimulate student interest in the topics to come in the chapter and can be used to begin class discussion. A special section before the chapter summary called **Looking Back** answers the teaser questions posed at the beginning of the chapter and helps illustrate how the chapter material relates to the real world of marketing. In the Eighth Edition, you'll read about companies like Coach, DuPont, In-n-Out, JCPenney, Porsche, Starbucks, Virgin Mobile, and XM Satellite Radio.

Global Perspectives Boxes

Today most businesses compete not only locally and nationally, but globally as well. Companies that may have never given a thought to exporting now face competition from abroad. Thinking globally should be a part of every manager's tactical and strategic planning. Accordingly, we address this topic in detail early in Chapter 4. We have also integrated numerous global examples within the body of the text and identified them with the icon shown in the margin. Global marketing is fully integrated throughout the book, cases, and videos, as well.

Our **Global Perspectives** boxes, which appear in nearly every chapter, provide expanded global examples of the marketing issues facing companies in Africa, Asia, Europe, North America, and South America. Each box concludes with thought-provoking questions carefully prepared to stimulate class discussion. You'll read about South American food being exported to the United States, how Disneyland Paris became Europe's number one tourist attraction, and what Wal-Mart is doing to be successful in Japan, among other topics.

Ethics in Marketing Boxes

In this edition we continue our emphasis on ethics. The **Ethics in Marketing** boxes, complete with questions focusing on ethical decision making, have been revised in each chapter. This feature offers provocative examples of how ethics comes into play in many marketing decisions. Is it ethical to target teens at school? Should banks track customers' credit ratings? Are J.D. Power and Associates' initial car quality ratings reliable? What about limiting a country's ability to capitalize on its natural resources? Or mixing pharmaceutical ads with medical research? Students will consider these and many other hotly debated ethical questions.

Review and Applications

To help students focus their study time, we continue to group end-of-chapter discussion and writing questions with their related learning objective summary. Questions are numbered according to the learning objective to which they correspond. For example, the summary point for Chapter 10 Learning Objective 2 has four related questions. They are numbered 2.1, 2.2, 2.3, and 2.4. This organization helps students identify questions pertinent to the learning objective they are studying, allowing each chapter to function as a series of content blocks that can be read over multiple study sessions.

Ethics Exercise

In today's business environment, ethics are extremely important. In recent years, there have been numerous scandals and trials that stem from a lack of ethical judgment. Although some might say that these occurrences are the work of a few bad apples spoiling the bunch, it is clear that ethical decision making plays a very important role in a company's success and prosperity. An **Ethics Exercise** appears at the end of every chapter. A brief scenario presents students with a situation in which the right thing to do may or may not be crystal clear. To help students make appropriate ethical decisions, we always refer students back to the American Marketing Association's Code of Ethics, found on-line at **http://www.marketingpower.com**. This gives students a resource for the exercise and helps reinforce the ethical standards that marketers should uphold. Over the course of the book, regularly consulting the Code will show students the limitations to a code of ethics. It will also reinforce the importance of not simply consulting existing rules of conduct, but of developing an ethical personality.

Entrepreneurship Case

Entrepreneurship, whether in the newest dot com or in America's largest corporations, is what fueled the greatest period of expansion in American history. Ten chapters have new entrepreneurship cases highlighting the challenges facing entrepreneurs in the 21st century. These cases focus on a wide variety of companies, like Look-Look (a marketing research company specializing in cool spotting), RockStar Games (maker of video games for mature audiences), Playbill (publisher of programs for fine arts events), and MTV, among others.

But we also recognize that entrepreneurial activities take place across the *Fortune* 500, so we profile industry giants like Apple and its new Garage Band software, Best Buy, and Valvoline. All have used a highly entrepreneurial approach in various parts of their business. Your students will find these cases an exciting and challenging aspect of each chapter.

Watch It

Video is a valuable teaching tool, so this edition has retained its comprehensive video package that combines short, medium, and long segments. **Watch It** gives students a brief description of the long (Feature Presentation) and medium (Encore Presentation) segments relating to that chapter. For instance, in Chapter 9 (Product Concepts), the Feature Presentation is a segment about Fluker Cricket Farms in Baton Rouge, Louisiana, and the Encore Presentation is scene from *Josie and the Pussycats*. Students are prepared for video viewing in or out of class by reading the **Watch It** at the end of the chapter.

Not mentioned in the Watch It but available to the professor are short, 30-second ads embedded in the PowerPoint presentation slides for each chapter. Over forty ads aired during the recent Super Bowl have been selected to illustrate key chapter concepts. Viewing the commercials in the context of the class pushes students to analyze the content, appeals, and execution of the ads.

Each type of video helps students deepen their understanding of marketing concepts, allowing them to consider the subject from multiple directions.

Marketing Miscues

Mistakes can have tough consequences, but they also offer a great lesson. This is especially true in marketing. At the end of each part you will find new cases that describe good and bad ideas that couldn't make it in the rough and tumble marketplace. Often amusing and always interesting, these cases about Scholastic Book Publishers losing touch with its primary market, Google's troubles with trademark infringement, Major League Baseball's snafu with using Spiderman-themed bases, and Disney's flop *The Alamo*, will help your students avoid the same mistakes made by these well-known companies. After all, making smart decisions is at the heart of successful marketing.

Critical Thinking Cases

Our society has an enormous capacity for generating data, but our ability to use the data to make good decisions has lagged behind. In the hope of better preparing the next generation of business leaders, many educators are beginning to place greater emphasis on developing critical thinking skills.

Marketing, Eighth Edition, contributes to this effort with a more challenging comprehensive case at the end of each of the seven major parts—all of them new for this edition. **Critical Thinking Cases** feature well-known brands like Twister, Knott's Berry Farm, Vivendi Universal Games, and easyCinema.

OUR PEDAGOGY IS DESIGNED WITH YOUR STUDENTS IN MIND

All of our new and exciting content is anchored by the cornerstone of our text, our fully **Integrated Learning System (ILS)**. The text and all major supplements are organized around the learning objectives that appear at the beginning of each chapter, so *Marketing* is both easy to teach from and to learn.

A numbered icon like the one shown in the margin identifies each objective in each chapter and appears next to its related material throughout the text, Instructor's Manual, Test Bank, PowerPoint, and Study Guide. In addition, we consider multiple learning styles in the organization of our text pedagogy.

Integrated Learning System Is More Important than Ever

Since the First Edition, the **Integrated Learning System** has been one of the hallmarks of *Marketing*. In the Eighth Edition, the Integrated Learning System is more important than ever because the collegiate environment has changed for both students *and* instructors.

Changing Psychographics
In the past, students focused almost exclusively on their studies. Many of today's students, however, do not have this luxury. They work, commute, volunteer, and may even have families to raise. For students with active lifestyles, study time often comes in blocks of minutes rather than blocks of hours. This can make it hard to read a chapter in a single sitting. In fact, it can take anywhere from two to five sittings to completely read through a chapter once. With all the starting and stopping of studying, it can be hard to retain the chapter concepts.

Changing Demographics
Of the nearly 2 million high school students that enter college in the fall, 82 percent regularly use a computer. Most, if not all, have a shorter attention span than previous cohorts of students due to their immersion in a highly visualized culture. Today's students are used to receiving information in bullet points and other abbreviated formats. As an example of this, watch a pop music video. You will experience literally hundreds of images during a 3- to 4-minute song. Video directors piece together frames of imagery, which often appear for no more than a few seconds, and which result in the inter-splicing of images that creates virtually unconscious visual stimulation.

The changing psychographics and demographics are affecting more than the student population. Growing enrollments coupled with stabilizing (at best) or reduced (at worse) budgets mean than student-teacher ratios are higher than ever. Budget considerations are causing universities to reduce the number of tenured faculty and increasingly rely on part-time, adjunct, and non-tenure-track teachers. This means that colleges and universities have increasing numbers of new faculty each semester. And without effective teaching tools, new faculty may be ill-equipped to face the challenges of teaching today's time-pressed, media-focused students.

New Model Meets Needs of New Environment
Traditional pedagogical models assume that students have the ability to focus exclusively on studies and that professors have the ability to focus exclusively on class preparation, delivery, and evaluation. We propose an alternative model that meets the needs of today's students and professors without diminishing the importance of the material being studied.

Our unique **Integrated Learning System** model has proven to be of such tremendous value to professors that South-Western College Publishing is now using the system with basic textbook packages in other business disciplines. ILS breaks each chapter into cohesive blocks of content organized around the learning objectives, which are placed in the margin throughout the chapter. A visual learning summary (explained above) concludes the presentation of each learning objective. Students know exactly where a learning objective begins and where it ends. At the end of the chapter, review questions are located after the appropriate summary point. Students can answer the questions that relate to the material they have just read.

Likewise, all supplements are organized by learning objective. For students, the *Grademaker Study Guide* indicates the different types of review questions for each objective. Students can divide the material in each chapter into manageable chunks, read it, review it, and practice it successfully.

The same organization underpins the Test Bank; all 3,500 testing items are grouped by chapter and by learning objective so that professors can design tests that reflect the content focused on in class. Each of the more than 975 PowerPoint slides is identified by the corresponding learning objective. New instructors using *Marketing* and its supplements will find a support system to get them started and feeling confident from the first day. Experienced instructors using *Marketing* and its supplements will benefit from an intuitive approach to organizing classes, evaluation, and grading.

Our Text Pedagogy Excites and Reinforces Learning

Pedagogical features are meant to reinforce learning, but that doesn't mean that they have to be boring. We have created teaching tools within the text itself that will excite student interest as well as teach. Not one of our features is casually included: each has been designed and written to meet a specific learning need, level, or style.

- **Cross-Functional Connections:** No marketer is an island. Marketing professionals work with every functional area of the company. The Cross-Functional Connections that open every part explore the give and take between marketing and all other business functions. Solutions to the topical questions are provided at the end of each part so that students can test their understanding of how marketing is integrated with the other functions of business.

- **Opening Vignettes, Revisited at Chapter Conclusions:** Each chapter begins with a new, current, real-world story about a marketing decision or situation facing a company. A special section called **Looking Back** answers the teaser questions posed in **Looking Forward** and helps illustrate how the chapter material relates to the real world of marketing.

- **Use It Now:** Students are often heard to comment, "Yes, I can use this information when I graduate and get into my career, but what take-away value can I get right now?" Use It Now addresses this concern by covering a topic related to the chapter that the student can put to work today. For example, in Chapter 4 (Developing a Global Vision), Use It Now tells students how to find a job overseas and also offers tips on changing money abroad.

- **Terms:** Key terms appear in boldface in the text, with definitions in the margins, making it easy for students to check their understanding of key definitions. A complete alphabetical list of key terms appears at the end of each chapter as a study checklist, with page citations for easy reference.

- **Review and Applications:** The end of each chapter contains a section titled Review and Applications, a summary that distills the main points of the chapter. Chapter summaries are organized around the learning objectives so that students can use them as a quick check of their understanding of chapter concepts. Discussion questions and activities are under the learning objective to which they pertain.

- **Writing Questions:** To help students improve their writing skills, we have included writing exercises in the review section at the end of each chapter. These exercises are marked with the icon shown here. The writing questions are designed to be brief so that students can accomplish writing assignments in a short time and instructors' grading time is minimized.

- **End of Chapter Team Activities:** The ability to work collaboratively is a key to success in today's business world. End-of-chapter team activities, identified by the icon shown here, give students opportunities to learn to work together by engaging in consensus building and problem solving.

- **InfoTrac Exercises:** Not all students have mastered the research skills they will need to use during their college and later careers. To give students some direction, we have created exercises that require them to use Gale Research Group's InfoTrac database of over 12 million articles from nearly 4,000 periodicals. Access to InfoTrac's College Edition comes free with this textbook.

- **Application Exercise:** These activities are based on winning teaching ideas from the "Best of the Great Ideas in Teaching Marketing" contest held in conjunction with the publication of the Eighth Edition. Developed by professors across the country, these exercises allow students to explore the principles of marketing in greater detail through engaging and enjoyable activities.

- **Career Exercise:** Finding a job is uppermost in the mind of most students. To help them experience the great possibilities of a career in marketing, we have designed special career exercises, which provide resources and enrichment exercises to help students develop their marketing career potential.

- **Ethics Exercise:** Short ethical dilemmas help students practice doing the right thing. Questions following each scenario prompt students to make an ethical decision and refer them to the AMA Code of Ethics.

- **Entrepreneurship Case:** All chapters contain an entrepreneurship case with questions to help students work through problems facing real small business companies today.

All components of our comprehensive support package have been developed to help you prepare lectures and tests as quickly and easily as possible. We provide a wealth of information and activities beyond the text to supplement your lectures, as well as teaching aids in a variety of formats to fit your own teaching style.

WE INTEGRATE TECHNOLOGY IN A MEANINGFUL WAY

From the beginning, we have integrated new technologies into our Integrated Learning System in a meaningful way. The Eighth Edition continues this tradition by adding new and exciting content to our technology materials. We have also enhanced and refined popular media supplements to bring concepts alive in the classroom.

NOW

MarketingNow for *Marketing, 8e,* is an online assessment-driven and student-centered tutorial that provides students with a personalized learning plan. Based on a diagnostic Pre-Test, a customized learning path is generated for individual students that targets their study needs and helps them to visualize, organize, practice, and master the material in the text. Media resources enhance problem-solving skills and improve conceptual understanding. An access code access to MarketingNow for *Marketing,* 8e, can be bundled with new textbooks.

Xtra!

Our new Xtra! (**http://lambxtra.swlearning.com**) is like no other. We have included extra content modules on competitive intelligence and multicultural marketing. Each chapter has an **Ask the Author** segment in which one of the authors responds to frequently asked questions (FAQs) about the marketing topics discussed in the given chapter. For Xtra!, we have revised the Marketing Planning Worksheets to make them easier to use, plus we have retained our exhibit worksheets for the tables and diagrams in the text. Students can print out the worksheets and, following the instructions on the sheet, fill in the diagram or table. They can then check their recall of important topics using the actual text exhibit. Other self-assessment tools include a quiz for each chapter that contains questions similar to what students will see on exams and in the *Grademaker Study Guide.* To help students decide whether or not they need additional review, an abridged chapter from the *Grademaker* is also on Xtra! And lastly, Xtra! features a student version of the PowerPoint presentation.

Fresh Internet Activities and Real-Time Examples

 The Internet continues to be a powerful resource for teaching and learning. Each chapter of *Marketing* contains numerous examples of the Internet's role in marketing, designated throughout the text by the icon in the margin. In addition, we regularly offer opportunities for students to use the Internet to further their study of chapter content. **Online** activities with URLs appear in the margins throughout each chapter and are tied either to organizations mentioned in the text or to the concepts being discussed.

Because each activity calls for student effort and feedback, you can use these mini-exercises as additional assignments or quizzing opportunities. We have kept the best exercises from the Seventh Edition and added over eighty new ones. Knowing how fast the Internet changes, we have a made a concerted effort to create exercises and to direct students to sites that have staying power and that will not become obsolete by the end of the semester. Links to all URLs in the book are located on the text's Internet site at **http://lamb.swlearning.com**.

New Internet Marketing Chapter

E-commerce changes at the speed of light. We completely rewrite Chapter 19, Internet Marketing, with each new edition to keep pace with the dynamic world of e-commerce. We explain how the Internet has affected the traditional marketing mix, marketing objectives, and marketing strategies. We also examine the metrics Internet marketers are using to measure the success of their marketing campaigns. Our Internet Marketing chapter is located at the text's Web site at **http://lamb.swlearning.com** and contains all of the features of our print chapters with the added bonus of direct links to company examples and sources of information.

Who Wants to Be a Marketer?

When we debuted **Who Wants to Be a Marketer?** with the Sixth Edition, we did not anticipate how popular it would become. Developed by John Drea of Western Illinois University, this exciting supplement to the Eighth Edition of *Marketing* by Lamb, Hair, and McDaniel is an in-class, computer-based game. Who Wants to Be a Marketer? is a fun and exciting way to review terminology and concepts with students. This easy-to-use game requires only Microsoft PowerPoint and a method (such as a data projector) to display the screen to the entire class. The original game has two rounds of fifty original questions per chapter, for a total of 1,500 questions!

For the Eighth Edition, we have created a second version of Who Wants to Be a Marketer? that is compatible with using clickers. Rather than a single question and response theme, the new version uses multiple-choice questions to help students review. Students can use clickers to answer quiz questions formatted similar to the popular game "Who Wants to Be a Millionaire." Both versions of Who Wants to Be a Marketer? are available only for adopters of *Marketing* by Lamb, Hair, and McDaniel.

We Offer a Robust, Comprehensive Web Site

Lamb, Hair, and McDaniel's Web site contains a wide array of supplementary products for instructors to use to enhance their course material and presentations, and to guide students down the path to a clear understanding of the concepts presented within the text.

It also offers Web pages dedicated to students' needs and geared toward helping them succeed. The instructor's site includes: a sample chapter from the Test Bank and the *Grademaker Study Guide*; the entire Instructor Manual, *Great Ideas in Teaching Marketing*; the entire PowerPoint presentation with hyperlinks in viewable and printable formats; case updates for all the end-of-chapter and end-of-part cases (one update per case per semester); and Who Wants to Be a Marketer?. The abundant student materials include:

- The **Interactive Study Center** contains materials for every chapter of *Marketing, 8e:* chapter summary points; crossword puzzles of marketing terminology; Internet Applications which contain **Online** margin activities plus **Use It Now, Review Exercises,** and **Career Exercises** from the text that have an Internet component; and interactive quizzes with a self-assessment for each chapter.
- A downloadable set of **PowerPoint slides** and the order form for the *Grademaker Study Guide*, plus an abridged sample chapter from the study guide, can be found on the Student Resources page.
- **Chapter 19** on Internet Marketing.
- The **Marketing Plan Project** features a real small business. Students can review the case and develop a marketing plan for a real company struggling with various marketing issues. In conjunction with questions keyed to every chapter, instructors can use the Marketing Plan Project as a comprehensive case. Without the questions, the case provides the basis for a student project, which can be submitted at its completion to the profiled company via the publisher as part of the Marketing Plan Project Contest. Guidelines and contest rules appear on the Marketing Plan Project page at **http://lamb.swlearning.com**.

INNOVATIVE AND VALUABLE INSTRUCTOR SUPPLEMENTS

Instructor Resource CD-ROM

Managing your classroom resources is now easier than ever. The new Instructor Resource CD-ROM contains all key instructor supplements—Instructor's Manual, Test Bank, and PowerPoint.

PowerPoint CD-ROM

To take full advantage of the new features of the *Marketing, 8e*, PowerPoint presentation, you'll want to use the customizable PowerPoint CD-ROM. Many of the hundreds of full-color images provided with this new edition of *Marketing* contain valuable teaching notes to help guide you through your lecture. In addition, hyperlinks to the **Online** activities in the chapter margins

are embedded in each chapter of slides so that you can maximize your use of these activities during class time. Short 30-second television ads from recent Super Bowl broadcasts are also embedded in the slide presentation and are viewable only through the PowerPoint CD-ROM. All you need is Windows to run the PowerPoint viewer and an LCD panel for classroom display.

Triple Option Video Package

The video package to accompany *Marketing, 8e,* is the most comprehensive and innovative in our history. We provide you with three options for video use: Each chapter has a combination of thirty-second clips (short) embedded in the instructor's PowerPoint CD-ROM presentation, two- to four-minute movie clips (medium) for classroom viewing, and a 10- to 15-minute clip (long) for both classroom viewing and home viewing via Xtra! There are more than 40 short clips plus 20 medium clips and 17 long segments.

The short clips consist of television ads that were originally broadcast during the **Super Bowl** games. The long clips (Feature Presentation) are excerpted footage from various episodes of the 30-minute **Small Business School (SBS)** program broadcast nationwide on PBS. And the medium clips (Encore Presentation) show scenes from popular feature films that should be used after students have read the chapter and worked the end-of-chapter exercises.

A final note about the Feature Presentation: Each chapter has a designated SBS segment as the lead segment for that chapter, but because the SBS programs cover all aspects of business, SBS segments raise more issues than just those presented in the assigned chapter. For example, the lead segment for Chapter 1 is on Wahoo's Fish Taco, a uniquely Californian restaurant, but the content in the Wahoo's Fish Taco segment also relates to material in Chapter 5 (Consumer Decision Making), Chapter 7 (Segmenting and Targeting Markets), Chapter 13 (Retailing), and Chapter 15 (Advertising and Public Relations). The rich SBS videos will help reinforce what you've learned by showing you people who are doing marketing every day—and not according to thematic units. The multifaceted SBS videos give you maximum flexibility in how you use the videos. Combined with the short and medium option videos, the possibilities are endless!

A Value-Added Instructor Manual Like No Other

Our Instructor's Manual is the core of our **Integrated Learning System**. For the Eighth Edition of *Marketing*, we have made our popular Instructor's Manual even more valuable for new and experienced instructors alike. Here is a list of the new features that will reduce class preparation time:

- Suggested syllabi for 12- and 16-week terms.
- A pedagogy grid for each chapter briefly laying out 1) all the options the professor has in the chapter, and 2) what key points in the chapter each feature addresses. The features included on the grid are Looking Forward, the boxed features, Use It Now, Application Exercise, Ethics Exercise, Career Exercise, Entrepreneurship Case, and each video option.
- Three suggested lesson plans for each chapter: a lecture lesson plan, a small-group work lesson plan, and a video lesson plan.

We have retained the proven features like the detailed chapter outline, lists of support material, additional class activities, and solutions for all Review and Applications, Entrepreneurship, Marketing Miscues, and Critical Thinking Cases in the book. There are also teaching tips on setting up each of the Application Exercises. Our manual is truly "one-stop shopping" for instructors teaching any size marketing course.

Comprehensive Test Bank and Windows Testing Software

Our enhanced Test Bank is organized around the learning objectives. It is available in print and new Windows software formats (ExamView testing software).

With ExamView, you can choose to prepare tests that cover all learning objectives or that emphasize only those you feel are most important. This updated Test Bank is one of the most comprehensive on the market, with over 3,500 true/false, multiple-choice, scenario, and essay questions. Our testing database, combined with the ease of ExamView, takes the pain out of exam preparation.

WebTutor™ Advantage on Blackboard™ or Web CT™

WebTutor™ Advantage puts you ahead of the game in providing online course management for instructors and online learning for students. It contains all of the interactive study guide components that you could ever want and many valuable technology—oriented additions you never thought you'd get! WebTutor™ Advantage also contains e-lectures—this valuable student resource combines the robust PowerPoint presentation with narration. WebTutor™ Advantage also contains the Small Business School digitized videos and pedagogy, Ask the Authors video FAQs, and the Who Wants to Be a Marketer? game.

WebTutor™ ToolBox

Preloaded with content and available via a free access code when packaged with this text, WebTutor™ ToolBox pairs all the content of this text's rich Book Companion Web site with sophisticated course man-

agement functionality. You can assign materials (including online quizzes) and have the results flow automatically to your grade book. WebTutor™ ToolBox is ready to use as soon as you log on—or you can customize its preloaded content by uploading images and other resources, adding Web links, or creating your own practice materials. Students only have access to student resources on the Web site. Instructors can enter an access code for password-protected Instructor Resources.

Other Outstanding Supplements

- **Transparency Acetates:** To supplement the Power-Point presentation, 200 transparency acetates are available. They include figures and diagrams from *Marketing, 8e,* as well as synopses of important text content. Images are tied to the **Integrated Learning System** through the Instructor's Manual lecture outlines. Transparencies and their discussion prompts appear within the learning objective content where they apply. In addition, if you need more acetates than the 200 in our package, our PowerPoint presentation is available in printable format on the instructor and student resource pages of the Lamb, Hair, and McDaniel Web site (**http://lamb.swlearning.com**). View the slides and create your own acetates tailored to your particular course needs.
- **Handbook for New Instructors: Getting Started with Great Ideas**: This helpful supplement has been completely revised for the Eighth Edition. It was specifically designed for instructors preparing to teach their first course in principles of marketing. And we have bolstered our helpful hints on everything from developing a course outline to grading, with winning general teachings from our "Best of the Great Ideas in Teaching Marketing" contest. To give you a complete resource for teaching ideas, we have included all of the winning entries, nearly one hundred in all, at the end of the Handbook. You'll find great teaching ideas for every chapter, plus a wealth of general tips. If you're new, let professors from around the country help you get started teaching principles of marketing!
- **Great Ideas in Teaching Marketing:** We have begun collecting Great Ideas on our instructor's resource page on the Lamb, Hair, and McDaniel Web site. In this way, we can accept submissions year-round. Great Ideas in Teaching Marketing will still be published with each new edition of *Marketing* as part of the **Handbook for New Instructors**. You can also review all current great ideas by chapter at **http://lamb.swlearning.com**.
- *Wall Street Journal* **Edition:** South-Western and WSJ have teamed up to offer you the option of a WSJ package. If you are interested in ordering

Marketing, 8e with WSJ, please contact your local representative. This package includes a card entitling learners to receive a subscription to *The Wall Street Journal* and WSJ.com, giving them access to many articles used as examples in this textbook. This *Wall Street Journal* edition makes it easy to relate marketing concepts to daily news stories. Instructors with 10 or more students who redeem their subscription offers will receive their own free subscription.

• **Custom Publishing**: Thomson Custom Publishing now offers the fastest and easiest way to customize your course materials. Make your classroom unique—select the content that best suits your needs and deliver it the way you want. You can customize our print or electronic materials, create an e-book, or publish your own material. For more information about options or to locate your local Thomson Custom Publishing representative, visit **http://www.thomsoncustom.com**. To build a custom text online, visit Thomson's digital library at **http://www.textchoice2.com**. This site allows you to preview content and create a custom project online. You can arrange text chapters or database selections or upload your own material to create the perfect learning solution for your course.

INNOVATIVE AND VALUABLE STUDENT SUPPLEMENTS

Marketing, 8e, provides an excellent vehicle for learning the fundamentals. For students to gain a true understanding of marketing, however, it's best if they can apply the principles they are learning in the classroom. And it's best if they have study aids that address their particular learning style. Our student supplements meet the needs of a variety of learning styles from visual to auditory, from hands-on to abstract conceptualization.

Grademaker Study Guide

The **Grademaker Study Guide** has been greatly updated for this edition. As part of the **Integrated Learning System**, the study guide questions are linked to the learning objectives by numbered icons. A student having difficulty with the material found in Chapter 5, Learning Objective 2, can quickly go to this learning objective in the *Grademaker* and find numerous questions and aids to master that material. Every chapter includes application questions in a variety of formats to help students to master concepts. Study guide questions are designed to be similar in type and difficulty level to the Test Bank questions. By careful review of the *Grademaker*, students can dramatically improve their test scores.

Each *Grademaker* chapter opens with a self-assessment pre-test to help students identify areas where they need the most review, followed by chapter outlines with definitions, vocabulary practice, true/false, multiple choice, agree/disagree, and essay questions. This edition of the *Grademaker* also has marketing scenarios and marketing applications. Each scenario presents a marketing situation and is followed by a series of questions that ask students to evaluate the situation presented. The new applications require students to put marketing concepts to work, such as in the creation of a print advertisement for the chapter on Advertising and Public Relations (Chapter 15).

NOW

As described above, this dynamic, online learning tool is assessment-driven and student-centered to provide students with a personalized learning plan. Results from a diagnostic pre-test generate a customized learning path for each individual student.

Xtra!

As described above, **Xtra!** is like no other interactive content that has ever accompanied *Marketing*. Videos, exhibit worksheets, supplemental content modules, quizzes, and PowerPoint slides are the powerful Xtra! study tools we have created especially for this edition. Xtra! is the most powerful electronic learning tool ever created for marketing students. It is located at **http://lambxtra.swlearning.com**.

InfoTrac™

Packaged free with every new copy of *Marketing, 8e*, is a password for the InfoTrac database by Gale Research. InfoTrac enables students to connect with the real world of management through academic journals, business and popular magazines and newspapers, and a vast array of government publications. We used InfoTrac in creating the end-of-chapter exercises and cases; students can use InfoTrac for marketing plan projects and review questions.

The Business and Company Resource Center

Now you can give your students FREE access to a dynamic database of information and resources. The Business & Company Resource Center supplies online access to a wide variety of global business information, including competitive intelligence, career and investment opportunities, business rankings, company histories, and much more. Unlike other online resources, this comprehensive database offers ever-changing research results, providing accurate and up-to-date company and industry intelligence for thousands of companies. View a guided tour of the Business & Company Resource Center at **http://www.gale.com/BusinessRC**. *For college and university adopters only.*

Cadotte: Experience Marketing at the Marketplace

This simulation will challenge students to make tough marketing decisions in a competitive, fast-paced market where the customers are demanding and the competition is working hard to increase market share. Theory comes alive as students learn to manage a new business venture, increase profit, improve customer satisfaction, and capture dominant market share.

MEET THE AUTHORS

Charles W. Lamb, Jr.

Charles W. Lamb, Jr., is the M.J. Neeley Professor of Marketing, M.J. Neeley School of Business, Texas Christian University. He served as chair of the department of marketing from 1982 to 1988 and again from 1997 to 2003. He is currently chair of the Department of Information Systems and Supply Chain Management and president of the Academy of Marketing Science.

Lamb has authored or co-authored more than a dozen books and anthologies on marketing topics and over 150 articles that have appeared in academic journals and conference proceedings.

In 1997, he was awarded the prestigious Chancellor's Award for Distinguished Research and Creative Activity at TCU. This is the highest honor that the university bestows on its faculty. Other key honors he has received include the M.J. Neeley School of Business Research Award and selection as a Distinguished Fellow of the Academy of Marketing Science and a Fellow of the Southwestern Marketing Association.

Lamb earned an associate degree from Sinclair Community College, a bachelor's degree from Miami University, an MBA from Wright State University, and a doctorate from Kent State University. He previously served as assistant and associate professor of marketing at Texas A & M University.

Joseph F. Hair, Jr.

Joseph Hair is Alvin C. Copeland Endowed Chair of Franchising and Director, Entrepreneurship Institute, Louisiana State University. Previously, Hair held the Phil B. Hardin Chair of Marketing at the University of Mississippi. He has taught graduate and undergraduate marketing and marketing research courses.

Hair has authored 30 books, monographs, and cases and over 60 articles in scholarly journals. He also has participated on many university committees and has chaired numerous departmental task forces. He serves on the editorial review boards of several journals.

He is a member of the American Marketing Association, Academy of Marketing Science, Southern Marketing Association, and Southwestern Marketing Association. He was the 2004 recipient of the Academy of Marketing Science Excellence in Teaching Award.

Hair holds a bachelor's degree in economics, a master's degree in marketing, and a doctorate in marketing, all from the University of Florida. He also serves as a marketing consultant to businesses in a variety of industries, ranging from food and retailing to financial services, health care, electronics, and the U.S. Departments of Agriculture and Interior.

Carl McDaniel

Carl McDaniel is a professor of marketing at the University of Texas–Arlington, where he has been chairman of the marketing department since 1976. He has been an instructor for more than 20 years and is the recipient of several awards for outstanding teaching. McDaniel has also been a district sales manager for Southwestern Bell Telephone Company. Currently, he serves as a board member of the North Texas Higher Education Authority, a billion dollar financial institution.

In addition to *Marketing*, McDaniel has co-authored numerous textbooks in marketing and business. McDaniel's research has appeared in such publications as the *Journal of Marketing, Journal of Business Research, Journal of the Academy of Marketing Science*, and *California Management Review.*

McDaniel is a member of the American Marketing Association, the Academy of Marketing Science, and the Society for Marketing Advances. In addition to his academic experience, McDaniel has business experience as the co-owner of a marketing research firm. Recently, McDaniel served as senior consultant to the International Trade Centre (ITC), Geneva, Switzerland. The ITC's mission is to help developing nations increase their exports. He has a bachelor's degree from the University of Arkansas and his master's degree and doctorate from Arizona State University.

Acknowledgments

This book could not have been written and published without the generous expert assistance of many people. First we wish to thank Julie Baker, Texas Christian University, for her contributions to several chapters. We would also like to recognize and thank Vicky Crittenden, Boston College, and Bill Crittenden, Northeastern University, for contributing the Cross-Functional Connections that open each part. Vicky also did and excellent job on the Critical Thinking cases and Marketing Miscues. We must also thank Jeffrey Gleich for contributing all of the new Entrepreneurship cases.

We also wish to thank each of the following persons for their work on the best supplement package that is available today. Our gratitude goes out to: Susan Peterson of Scottsdale Community College for her detailed update of the Study Guide; Thomas and Betty Pritchett of Kennesaw State University for revising our comprehensive Test Bank and for writing the quizzes that appear in other parts of the package; Deborah Baker of Texas Christian University revised the PowerPoint™ presentation and added the wonderful teaching notes, hyperlinks, and videos to her already complete slide presentation; Jeffery Gleich for the excellent video teaching notes; and John Drea of Western Illinois University who created the fun classroom review game, "Who Wants to Be a Marketer?"

Administrative assistant Fran Eller at TCU typed the manuscript, provided important quality control, and helped keep the project (and us) on schedule. Jeannette Hood, UTA administrative assistant, played a major role in managing the marketing office so that Carl could write. Their dedication, hard work, and support were exemplary.

Our deepest gratitude goes to the team at Thomson Learning that has made this text a market leader. Jamie Gleich Bryant, our developmental editor, is world-class in her abilities and dedication. Amy McGuire, our production editor, helped make this text a reality. A special thanks goes to Neil Marquardt, our executive editor, and Melissa Acuña, our Publisher, for their suggestions and support.

Finally, we are particularly indebted to our reviewers:

Barry Ashmen
Bucks County Community College

Thomas S. Bennett
Gaston Community College

Ken Bell
Ellsworth Community College

Larry Borgen
Normandale Community College

P. J. Forrest
Mississippi College

Daniel J. Goebel
University of Southern Mississippi

Mark Green
Simpson College

Richard A. Halberg
Houghton College

Dorothy R. Harpool
Wichita State University

Thomas J. Lang
University of Miami

Ronald E. Michaels
University of Central Florida

Monica Perry
University of North Carolina, Charlotte

William Rech
Bucks County Community College

Dick Rose
University of Phoenix (deceased)

James V. Spiers
Arizona State University

Jeffrey Schmidt
University of Illinois

Wayne Alexander
Moorhead State University

Linda Anglin
Mankato State University

Thomas S. Bennett
Gaston Community College

For the Eight Edition of *Marketing*, we held a contest called "The Best of the Great Ideas in Teaching Marketing," in which we compiled all of the great teaching ideas ever submitted to the supplement **Great Ideas in Teaching Marketing**. More than 1,000 ideas were categorized according to the chapter for which they worked best, and then a panel of 35 judges awarded a Winner, Runner-Up, and Honorable Mention for each chapter *and* for hundreds of general teaching ideas. Some of these winning ideas are the basis for the **Application Exercise** at the end of each chapter, and all can be found in the **Handbook for New Instructors: Getting Started with Great Ideas.** And the winners are . . .

(The institution listed represents where the scholar was teaching at the time he or she submitted the winning idea. When two names appear on the same line, it indicates collaborators on the same idea. In some chapters there were ties for first, second, and third place.)

Winners

Chapter 1	Stephen Baglione, Saint Leo University
	Ira S. Kalb, University of Southern California
Chapter 2	Robert O'Keefe, Philip R. Kemp, and J. Steven Kelly, DePaul University
	Michael Hartford, Morehead State University
Chapter 3	Raymond F. Keyes, Boston College
Chapter 4	Gregory J. Baleja, Alma College
	John L. Beisel, Pittsburgh State University
Chapter 5	P.J. Forrest, Mississippi College
	Mark Andrew Mitchell, University of South Carolina, Spartanburg
Chapter 6	Elizabeth J. Wilson, Louisiana State University
Chapter 7	Barbara Coleman, Augusta College
Chapter 8	Kay Blythe Tracy, Gettysburg College

	Deborah C. Calhoun, College of Notre Dame of Maryland
Chapter 9	Deborah Reed Scarfino, William Jewel College
Chapter 10	Deborah Reed Scarfino, William Jewel College
Chapter 11	Kay Blythe Tracy, Gettysburg College
Chapter 12	Debra Decelles, Anthony Rossi, Susan Sunderline, John Gardner, State University of New York College–Brockport
Chapter 13	David M. Blanchette, Rhode Island College
	Amy R. Hubbert, University of Nebraska at Omaha
Chapter 14	Gary M. Donnelly, Casper College
Chapter 15	Gary M. Donnelly, Casper College
Chapter 16	John Ronchetto, University of San Diego
Chapters 17 & 18	Vaughn Judd, Auburn University, Montgomery
Chapter 19	Mandeep Singh, Western Illinois University
Chapter 20	Keith Absher, University of North Alabama
General Tips	William G. Browne, Oregon State University
	Roy E. Nicely, Valdosta State College
	Michael Luthy, Bellarmine College
	Ed Cerny, University of South Carolina
	Leonard R. Geiser, Goshen College
	Shirine Mafi, Otterbein College
	Stacia Wert-Gray, University of Central Oklahoma, and Gordon T. Gray, Oklahoma City University
	Theresa B. Flaherty, Old Dominion University
	Dwayne D. Gremler, University of Idaho
	Paula J. Haynes, University of Tennessee at Chattanooga
	Michael B. Septon, Missouri Western State College

Runner Up

Chapter 1	Nancy Ryan McClure, University of Central Oklahoma, and James L. Thomas, Jacksonville State University

Rich Brown, Freed-Hardeman University

Chapter 2 Martha E. Hardesty, College of St. Catherine

Pat LeMay Burr, University of Incarnate Word, and Richard M. Burr, Trinity University

Chapter 3 Gregory P. Turner, College of Charleston

Chapter 4 Jacqueline J. Kacen, University of Michigan–Dearborn

David J. Brennan, Webster University

Chapter 5 Barbara-Jean Ross, Louisiana State University, and Laura A. Williams, Tulane University

Tom Hickey, Oswego State University of New York

Chapter 6 Richard Turshen, Pace University

Chapter 7 Marcel L. Berard, Community College of Rhode Island

Chapter 8 Matthew D. Shank and Fred Beasley, Northern Kentucky University

Elwin Myers, Texas A & M University

Chapter 9 Robert J. Brake, Concordia University

Chapter 10 Barbara Ross-Wooldridge, University of Texas at Tyler

Karen L. Stewart, Richard Stockton College

Chapter 11 Allan C. Reddy, Valdosta State University

Chapter 12 John L. Beisel, Pittsburgh State University

Chapter 13 Chris Pullig, Louisiana State University

John T. Drea and Mandeep Singh, Western Illinois University

Chapter 14 Lynn R. Godwin, University of St. Thomas

Nancy M. Can, Community College of Philadelphia

Chapter 15 Richard M. Lei, Northern Arizona University

S. J. Garner, Eastern Kentucky University

Chapter 16 Julie M. Pharr, Tennessee Technological University

Chapters 17 & 18 Philip R. Kemp, DePaul University

Laura Balus, Central Community College

Chapter 19 Judy Strauss and Raymond Frost, Central Connecticut State University

Chapter 20 Debbie Easterling, University of Maryland–Eastern Shore

General Tips Chuck Nielson, Louisiana State University

Christine A. Bell, Albright College

Teri Shaffer, Southeastern Louisiana State University

Charles E. Michaels, Jr., University of South Florida, and John Perrachione, Truman State University

Debbie Easterling, Bentley College

Reginald A. Graham, Eastern Montana College

Charles S. Madden, Baylor University

Donna H. Green, University of Windsor

Leon Winer, Pace University

Carolyn Y. Nicholson, Stetson University

L. Jean Harrison-Walker, University of Houston–Clear Lake

Honorable Mention

Chapter 1 Deanna R. D. Mader and Fred H. Mader, Marshall University

Sheri Carder, Lake City Community College

Chapter 2 PJ Forrest, Mississippi College

Chapter 3 Mark Andrew Mitchell, University of South Carolina, Spartanburg

Chapter 4 William C. Moncrief, Texas Christian University

Andrew Banasiewicz, Louisiana State University

Chapter 5 Anita Jackson, Central Connecticut State University

Al Rosenbloom, Benedictine University

Chapter 6 Gregory B. Turner, College of Charleston

Shirine Mafi, Otterbein College

Chapter 7 Kim McKeage, University of Maine

Chapter 8   Michael C. Murphy and Jon Shapiro, Rogers University

Gregory S. Martin, University of West Florida

Chapter 9   Alice Griswold, Clarke College

Robert D. Winsor, Loyola Marymount University

Chapter 10   Taylor W. Meloan, University of Southern California

Chapter 11   Jacqueline K. Eastman, Valdosta State University

Chapter 12   Monica Perry and Thomas Stevenson, University of North Carolina–Charlotte

Chapter 13   Mark B. Houston, Bowling Green State University, and Beth A. Walker, Arizona State University

Karen L. Stewart, Richard Stockton College

Chapter 14   David M. Blanchette, Rhode Island College

Chapter 15   Jack K. Mandel, Nassau Community College

Stephen B. Castleberry, University of Minnesota, Duluth

Chapter 16   Kathleen M. Bailey, Loyola University of New Orleans

Chapters   Keith Absher, University of North
17 & 18   Alabama

William Brannen, Creighton University

Chapter 19   Trina Sego, Rensselaer at Hartford

Chapter 20   Patrick A. Okonkwo and G. Dean Kortge, Central Michigan University

General   Christine A. Bell, Albright College
Tips
Murugappan Natesan, University of Alberta, and N. Chinna Natesan, Southwest Texas State University

Judith J. Leonard, Eastern Kentucky University

Sandra L. Lueder, Southern Connecticut State University

Robert A. Compton, Valley Forge Military College

James H. Glenn and Cornelia J. Glenn, Owensboro Community College

James A. Seaman, Central Ohio State University

Daniel L. Sherrell, Louisiana State University

Kristen B. Hovsepian, Ashland University

Scott Roberts and Joseph Anderson, Northern Arizona University

And we must thank our 35 judges for their careful reading and ranking of so many great teaching ideas. Their efforts made the Eighth Edition and its teaching package stronger, and we appreciate the time required to thoughtfully review over 1,000 ideas.

Roshan (Bob) D. Ahuja
Xavier University

Barry L. Bayus
University of North Carolina–Chapel Hill

Deirdre Bird
Providence College

L. Michelle Bobbitt
Bradley University

Meg Clark
Cincinnati State Technical and Community College

Irvine Clarke III
James Madison University

Brian I. Connett
California State University, Northridge

Ronald Decker
University of Wisconsin, Eau Claire

Jana G. Goodrich
Pennsylvania State University

David M. Hardesty
University of Miami

James W. Harvey
George Mason University

R. Vish Iyer
University of Northern Colorado

Anupam Jaju
George Mason University

Mathew Joseph
Georgia College and State University

Vaughn Judd
Auburn University–Montgomery

Bernard P. Lake
Kirkwood Community College

Ron Lennon
Barry University

James L. Macke
Cincinnati State Technical and Community
College

Bronna McNeely
Midwestern State University

Jamie M. Ressler
Palm Beach Atlantic University

Lawrence Ross
Florida Southern College

Jan Napoleon Saykiewicz
Duquesne University

Don Self
Auburn University, Montgomery

Peggy O. Shields
University of Southern Indiana

Lois J. Smith
University of Wisconsin–Whitewater

James Ward
Arizona State University

Jim Wenthe
Georgia College and State University

Arch G. Woodside
Boston College

SAMPLE FROM CHAPTER 1 OF THE STUDY GUIDE

LEARNING OBJECTIVES

1   Define the term "marketing"

Marketing is an organizational function and a set of processes for creating, communicating, and delivering value to customers and for managing customer relationships in ways that benefit the organization and its stakeholders.

2   Describe four marketing management philosophies

Four competing philosophies strongly influence the role of marketing and marketing activities within an organization. These philosophies are commonly referred to as production, sales, marketing, and societal marketing orientations.

    The production orientation focuses on internal efficiency to achieve lower prices for consumers. It assumes that price is the critical variable in the purchase decision.

    A sales orientation assumes that buyers resist purchasing items that are not essential and that consumers must be persuaded to buy.

    The marketing orientation is based on an understanding that a sale predominantly depends on the customer's decision to purchase a product and on the customer's perception of the value of that product. Responsiveness to customer wants is the central focus of the marketing orientation.

    The societal marketing orientation holds that the firm should strive to satisfy customer needs and wants while meeting organizational objectives and preserving or enhancing both the individual's and society's long-term best interests.

3   Discuss the differences between sales and market orientations

Selling Orientation	*Marketing Orientation*
Organization's focus is inward on the firm's needs	Focus is outward on the wants and preferences of customers
Business is defined by its goods and services offered	Business is defined by benefits sought by customers
Product is directed to everybody	Product is directed to specific groups (target markets)
Primary goal is profit through maximum sales volume	Primary goal is profit through customer satisfaction
Goals are achieved through intensive promotion	Goals are achieved through coordinated marketing

4   Describe several reasons for studying marketing

Marketing provides a delivery system for a standard of living, which is a monumental task in a society such as the United States, where a typical family consumes 2.5 tons of food per year. No matter what an individual's area of concentration in business, the terminology and fundamentals of marketing are important for communicating with others in the firm.

    Between one-fourth and one-third of the entire civilian work force in the United States performs marketing activities. Marketing offers career opportunities in areas such as professional selling, marketing research, advertising, retail buying, distribution management, product management, product development, and wholesaling.

    As a consumer of goods and services, everyone participates in the marketing process every day. By understanding marketing, one can become a more sophisticated consumer.

Answer the following questions to see how well you understand the material. Re-take it after you review to check yourself.

1. Marketing is defined as:

2. What five conditions must be satisfied for any kind of exchange to take place?

3. List and briefly describe four marketing management philosophies are:

4. List five ways in which a marketing orientation is different from a sales orientation.

5. Name four reasons for studying marketing.

CHAPTER OUTLINE

1   Define the term "marketing"

I.   What Is Marketing?

     A.   Marketing is a philosophy or a management orientation that stresses the importance of customer satisfaction, as well as the set of activities used to implement this philosophy.

     B.   The American Marketing Association definition of marketing:

        Marketing Marketing is an organizational function and a set of processes for creating, communicating, and delivering value to customers and for managing customer relationships in ways that benefit the organization and its stakeholders.

     C.   The Concept of Exchange

        The concept of **exchange** means that people give up something in order to receive something that they would rather have.

1. The usual medium of exchange is money. Exchange can also be through barter or trade of items or services.

2. Five conditions must be satisfied for an exchange to take place:

   a. There must be at least two parties.
   b. Each party has something that might be of value to the other party.
   c. Each party is capable of communication and delivery.
   d. Each party is free to accept or reject the exchange offer.
   e. Each party believes it is appropriate or desirable to deal with the other party.

3. Exchange may not take place even if all of these conditions exist, but these conditions are necessary for exchange to be possible.

2   Describe four marketing management philosophies

II. Marketing Management Philosophies

Four competing philosophies strongly influence an organization's marketing activities. These philosophies are commonly referred to as production, sales, marketing, and societal orientations.

A. Production Orientation

The **production orientation** focuses on internal capabilities of the firm rather than on the desires and needs of the marketplace. The firm is concerned with what it does best, based on its resources and experience, rather than with what consumers want.

B. Sales Orientation

A **sales orientation** assumes that more goods and services will be purchased if aggressive sales techniques are used and that high sales result in high profits.

C. Market Orientation

1. The **marketing concept** states that the social and economic justification for an organization's existence is the satisfaction of customer wants and needs while meeting organizational objectives.

2. The marketing concept involves:

    a. Focusing on customer wants and needs so the organization can differentiate its product(s) from competitors' offerings

    b. Integrating all the organization's activities, including production, to satisfy these wants and needs

    c. Achieving long-term goals for the organization by satisfying customer wants and needs legally and responsibly.

3. A **market orientation** involves obtaining information about customers, competitors, and markets; examining the information from a total business perspective; determining how to deliver superior customer value; and implementing actions to provide value to customers.

4. Understanding your competitive arena and competitor's strengths and weaknesses is a critical component of market orientation.

     5.   Market-oriented companies are successful coordinating all business functions to deliver customer value.

  D.   Societal Marketing Orientation

      1.   The **societal marketing orientation** states that an organization exists not only to satisfy customer wants and needs and to meet organizational but also to preserve or enhance individual's and society's long-term best interests.

      2.   This orientation extends the marketing concept to serve three bodies   rather than two: customers, the organization itself, and society as a whole

3   Discuss the differences between sales and market orientations

III.   Differences Between Sales and Market Orientations

  A.   The Organization's Focus

      1.   Sales-oriented firms tend to be inward-looking. They focus on satisfying their own needs rather than those of customers.

      2.   Market-oriented firms derive their competitive advantage from an external focus. Departments in these firms coordinate their activities and focus on satisfying customers.

  B.   Customer Value

      1.   **Customer value** is the ratio of benefits to the sacrifice necessary to obtain those benefits.

      2.   Creating customer value is a core business strategy of many successful firms.
      3.   Marketers interested in customer value

          a.   Offer products that perform
          b.   Give consumers more than they expect
          c.   Avoid unrealistic pricing
          d.   Give the buyer facts
          e.   Offer organization-wide commitment in service and after-sales support

  C.   Customer Satisfaction

      Customer satisfaction is the feeling that a product has met or exceeded the customer's expectations. The organizational culture focuses on delighting customers rather than on selling products.

  D.   Building Relationships

      Relationship marketing involves forging long-term partnerships with customers and contributing to their success.

      Most successful relationship marketing strategies involve the following features:

      1.   Customer-oriented personnel: employees' attitudes and actions are geared toward the customers' best interests.
      2.   Training: employees receive specialized training in building relationships with customers.

The World
of Marketing

CREATING CUSTOMER VALUE THROUGH EFFECTIVE CROSS-FUNCTIONAL INTERACTIONS

Three levels of strategy form a "hierarchy of strategy" within a company: corporate strategy, business strategy, and functional strategy. Corporate- and business-level strategies are supported by individual functional strategies that bring together the various activities necessary to create customer value. The speed of change in today's business world has led to functional-level managers becoming empowered to make decisions that will give their companies a competitive edge in a rapidly evolving, digitized marketplace. For example, to speed decision making and empower the management team, Gaylord Entertainment, a diversified hospitality and entertainment company that includes the Gaylord Hotels and the Grand Ole Opry, reduced its management layers and now focuses upon cross-functional teams in its core branded businesses of hospitality, attractions, and entertainment.

Traditionally, the need for functional expertise has resulted in workers who are experts in specialized portions of the organization's tasks. For example, a functional-level marketing strategist resolves questions concerning what products deliver customer satisfaction and value, what price to charge, how to distribute the products, and what type of marketing communication activities will have the desired impact. On the other hand, the functional-level manufacturing strategist decides what products manufacturing can make, at what rate to produce, and how to make the products (e.g., labor or capital intensive). Since such functional activities require expertise in only one functional area, managers have traditionally been trained to manage "vertically."

Such vertical activities have led to the creation of corporate silos in business. An employee working in a silo generally does not understand the importance of his or her functional processes in providing the final product or service to the customer. This vertical focus has resulted in departments comprised of functional specialists who have tended to talk only with each other. For example, marketers talk to other marketing folks, operational discussions take place on the shop floor among manufacturing engineers, development team members talk within their research and development groups, and financial analysts and accountants talk to each other.

Individual functional-level strategies resulting from such departmentalization are the center of much intraorganizational conflict. For example, conflict between the marketing group and the production schedule is common. Marketing tends to want output increased or decreased immediately. But the production schedule, once made, is often seen as very inflexible. Though such functional excellence is sufficient for success in a relatively stable business environment, such rigidity in functional groups does not meet the demands of a dynamic, global marketplace.

Although crossing functional boundaries (referred to as managing "horizontally") requires a significant level of coordination among business functions, today's business environment has put considerable pressure on functional groups to work together more harmoniously. For example, it is imperative that marketing managers take a keen interest in financial issues and that operational managers have a better understanding of the firm's customers. The CEO of ARAMARK, a supplier of food service to entertainment events such as the Olympic Games, credits the company's problem-solving success to its ability to integrate perspectives from a broad range of disciplines. As such, managing the process, and not the function, must be incorporated into organizational philosophies.

As businesses have moved into the twenty-first century, we have seen a dramatic rush to get products into the marketplace at a much faster pace than ever before. At the same time, customers are much more demanding about what they want in these products. The bottom line is that customers want customized products delivered immediately. To compete in this fast-paced environment, companies have turned to management processes such as cross-functional teams, job rotations, skills training, and even total elimination of functional groups.

Many have witnessed the flight demonstrations of the U.S. Navy's Blue Angels or the Air Force's Thunderbirds. Before being assigned to fly with one of these teams, each pilot has demonstrated superior flying skills. Nevertheless, the success of the final product, the flight show, is not due just to the many highly skilled pilots. The spectators see a carefully choreographed show that required input from many functional groups. Operationally, the capabilities of both pilots and airplanes have to be known. From the marketer's perspective, the show has to be exciting enough to justify the spectator's effort to find parking or a good viewing location. These issues are not unlike the cross-functional issues encountered by NASCAR. NASCAR executives have to continually attract new fans while simultaneously coordinating the interests of many internal stakeholders. Since flight demonstrations and NASCAR compete with each other and with all other entertainment choices, the internal mechanisms that get the right product to the consumer must all be working in harmony.

Unfortunately, successful cross-functional interactions do not come easy in most companies and are often mired in conflict. Reasons for conflict between and among functional areas include divergent personalities, physical separation, data differences, and suboptimal reward systems.

Marketing people tend to be extroverted and interact easily with others, whereas R&D and manufacturing people are frequently introverted and work well with individual work processes and output. In addition to having different personalities, marketers and their product management colleagues in R&D and manufacturing are often housed in different locations, which is surprising considering that the overlapping effects that all three groups have on a company's product.

The marketing department is typically located in the company's headquarters, which may be in the heart of a major business district, with sales located strategically close to customers. The manufacturing group is typically located in low-wage areas or low-rent districts, possibly close to suppliers. The manufacturing group may even be in a different country. It becomes easy for each department to "do its own thing," particularly if the groups are separated by language differences as well as time zones.

Another major source of conflict between marketing and its R&D and manufacturing counterparts is the type of data collected and used in decision making. Technical specialists in R&D and manufacturing have a difficult time understanding how marketers can work without "hard" data. It is difficult to mesh marketing's attitudinal data with data on cycle times or tensile strength. For example, while marketing's forecasts are rarely 100 percent accurate, manufacturing can determine the precise costs associated with production processes.

Not surprisingly, marketing's reward system based on increased sales is often in direct conflict with manufacturing's and R&D's reward systems that are driven by cost reduction. Marketing's ability to increase sales may be driven by offering consumers depth in the product line. Unfortunately, increased depth leads to more changeover over the production lines, which, in turn, drives up the cost of production.

A major challenge for marketers has been to develop mechanisms for reducing conflict between the marketing department and other business functions. In addition to managing the process and not the function via cross-functional teams, marketers have begun using the vast information technology infrastructure to facilitate interactions across functions. For example, retailers are now able to transmit orders via the electronic highway, directly to a supplier's computer. The supplier's computer automatically sends the order to the shop floor, while simultaneously reconciling the order with the retail store's credit history. This reduction in the need for human intervention not only speeds up the transaction process, but also reduces the chance for error and conflict across functional groups.

Recognition of the customer's role in the organization and empowering employees are both necessary for success in today's business environment. Rapidly changing technology has made the cross-functional communication process much easier. Teamwork and an information technology infrastructure, in an environment that encourages and rewards better communication among all business functions, will ultimately result in a more satisfied, loyal customer.

Questions

1. How do marketing, manufacturing, finance, accounting, and human resources overlap? What does each of these functions do that results in this overlap?

2. Why is cross-functional coordination necessary to have a customer-oriented firm?

3. What roles do teamwork and technology play in cross-functional coordination?

1

An Overview of Marketing

LEARNING OBJECTIVES

1 Define the term *marketing*

2 Describe four marketing management philosophies

3 Discuss the differences between sales and market orientations

4 Describe several reasons for studying marketing

All boaters have heard the cliché. The two best days in boating are the day you buy your boat and the day you sell it. But a company called MarineMax is aiming to change that. Here's how.

Clearwater, Florida–based Marine-Max sells boats—so many that it's the world's largest recreational boating retailer. On the surface, achieving this position might appear to be the result of the company's aggressive acquisitions strategy. But the real power behind the company's success is its focus on "the total boating experience."

Though selling a product, MarineMax uses a sailor's eye to focus on the full range of customer needs. The result is a company that surrounds its products with a remarkable array of services designed to eliminate traditional boating hassles. The goal, says a company official, is to make "boat ownership a real pleasure, every day."

For example, the company's service program, MarineMax Care, reduces dock-side cursing by ensuring that every boat is maintained and even fully fueled. The company also provides hands-on training for all new "Captains," including fundamental operation, safety, docking, right down to tying to the cleat. MarineMax takes on all aspects of the boating life cycle: financing, insurance, and delivery of a fully equipped vessel that's fueled and ready to cruise. MarineMax even saves its owners the trouble of having their crafts customized. If a customer names a new boat, MarineMax will have that name painted on the transom when it's delivered. MarineMax also operates a nationwide brokerage, so when a customer wants to upgrade or sell, MarineMax can handle those transactions, too.

MarineMax believes it's selling a relationship, not just a product, and relationship building begins in the prepurchase phase. For example, the company encourages potential customers to take a test run before buying. Similarly, the company organizes frequent, festive demo days where prospective customers are invited for food, music, and an opportunity to try out a variety of boats. By getting behind the wheel of an 18 footer, or a 25 footer, customers can get a feel for what's right for them.

Postsale, the company seeks to continue the relationship. Beyond insurance, maintenance, training, and brokerage programs, MarineMax organizes hundreds of "Getaways" annually. Led by a MarineMax-piloted craft, these are opportunities for owners to take escorted trips they might not otherwise have the opportunity to do. Ranging from weekend runs to two-week voyages to the Bahamas, these events are enormously popular, and openings are filled fast.

Company officials confirm that their focus is on the boating experience, not just selling boats. In fact, once MarineMax gets a customer, it tends to keep that customer for as long as they're in boating. Moreover, positive customer experiences have translated into powerful word-of-mouth advertising: the company's existing customers are often some of its best salespeople. In the end, MarineMax is selling boating more than it is selling boats. And, by doing everything it can to meet the needs of its customers, the company has experienced great success.[1]

Explain MarineMax's philosophy of business. What does it mean that Marine-Max is selling a relationship, not just a product?

Describe the term *marketing*

What does the term *marketing* mean to you? Many people think it means the same as personal selling. Others think marketing is the same as personal selling and advertising. Still others believe marketing has something to do with making products available in stores, arranging displays, and maintaining inventories of products for future sales. Actually, marketing includes all of these activities and more.

Marketing has two facets. First, it is a philosophy, an attitude, a perspective, or a management orientation that stresses customer satisfaction. Second, marketing is a set of activities used to implement this philosophy. This is the marketing process.

The American Marketing Association's definition encompasses both perspectives: "**Marketing** is an organizational function and a set of processes for creating, communicating, and delivering value to customers and for managing customer relationships in ways that benefit the organization and its stakeholders.[2] In this chapter, we will focus mostly on the marketing orientation—the marketing concept—and on how it differs from other competing philosophies.

THE CONCEPT OF EXCHANGE

Exchange is a key concept in the definition of marketing. The concept of **exchange** is quite simple. It means that people give up something to receive something they would rather have. Normally, we think of money as the medium of exchange. We "give up" money to "get" the goods and services we want. Exchange does not require money, however. Two persons may barter or trade such items as baseball cards or oil paintings.

An exchange can take place only if the following five conditions exist:

1. There must be at least two parties.
2. Each party has something that might be of value to the other party.
3. Each party is capable of communication and delivery.
4. Each party is free to accept or reject the exchange offer.
5. Each party believes it is appropriate or desirable to deal with the other party.[3]

marketing
An organizational function and a set of processes for creating, communicating, and delivering value to customers and for managing customer relationships in ways that benefit the organization and its stakeholders.

exchange
The idea that people give up something to receive something they would rather have.

Exchange will not necessarily take place even if all these conditions exist. They are, however, necessary for exchange to be possible. For example, you may place an advertisement in your local newspaper stating that your used automobile is for sale at a certain price. Several people may call you to ask about the car, some may test-drive it, and one or more may even make you an offer. All five conditions are necessary for an exchange to exist. But unless you reach an agreement with a buyer and actually sell the car, an exchange will not take place. Notice that marketing can occur even if an exchange does not occur. In the example just discussed, you would have engaged in marketing even if no one bought your used automobile.

REVIEW LEARNING OBJECTIVE 1

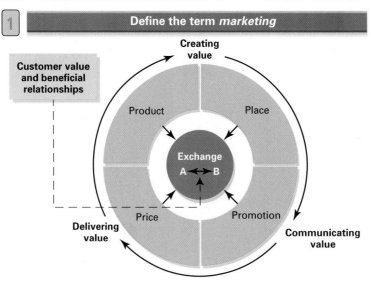

1 Define the term *marketing*

Customer value and beneficial relationships

Creating value

Product   Place

Exchange
A ⟷ B

Price   Promotion

Delivering value

Communicating value

2 MARKETING MANAGEMENT PHILOSOPHIES

Describe four marketing management philosophies

Four competing philosophies strongly influence an organization's marketing activities. These philosophies are commonly referred to as production, sales, market, and societal marketing orientations.

PRODUCTION ORIENTATION

A **production orientation** is a philosophy that focuses on the internal capabilities of the firm rather than on the desires and needs of the marketplace. A production orientation means that management assesses its resources and asks these questions: "What can we do best?" "What can our engineers design?" "What is easy to produce, given our equipment?" In the case of a service organization, managers ask, "What services are most convenient for the firm to offer?" and "Where do our talents lie?" Some have referred to this orientation as a *Field of Dreams* orientation, referring to the movie line, "If we build it, they will come." The furniture industry is infamous for its disregard of customers and for its slow cycle times. This has always been a production-oriented industry.

Are production-oriented firms ever successful? Find out by watching the video FAQ on Xtra!

There is nothing wrong with assessing a firm's capabilities; in fact, such assessments are major considerations in strategic marketing planning (see Chapter 2). A production orientation falls short because it does not consider whether the goods and services that the firm produces most efficiently also meet the needs of the marketplace. Sometimes what a firm can best produce is exactly what the market wants. For example, the research and development department of 3M's commercial tape division developed and patented the adhesive component of Post-it Notes a year before a commercial application was identified. In other situations, as when competition is weak or demand exceeds supply, a production-oriented firm can survive and even prosper. More often, however, firms that succeed in competitive markets have a clear understanding that they must first determine what customers want and then produce it, rather than focusing on what company management thinks should be produced.

SALES ORIENTATION

A **sales orientation** is based on the ideas that people will buy more goods and services if aggressive sales techniques are used and that high sales result in high profits. Not only are sales to the final buyer emphasized but intermediaries are also encouraged to push manufacturers' products more aggressively. To sales-oriented firms, marketing means selling things and collecting money.

The fundamental problem with a sales orientation, as with a production orientation, is a lack of understanding of the needs and wants of the marketplace. Sales-oriented companies often find that, despite the quality of their sales force, they cannot convince people to buy goods or services that are neither wanted nor needed.

Some sales-oriented firms simply lack understanding of what is important to their customers. Many so-called dot-com businesses that came into existence in the late 1990s are no longer around because they focused on the technology rather than the customer.

Kimberly Knickle couldn't have been happier when she signed up with on-line grocer Streamline.com. Streamline installed a refrigerator in her garage to make deliveries when she wasn't home, picked up the dry cleaning, delivered stamps, and dropped off parcel shipments. The best part was the customer service. When something went wrong, Streamline instantly credited her account. She could always get someone on the phone. As the company gained a larger customer base, however, the deliveries became inconsistent, telephone customer

production orientation
A philosophy that focuses on the internal capabilities of the firm rather than on the desires and needs of the marketplace.

sales orientation
The idea that people will buy more goods and services if aggressive sales techniques are used and that high sales result in high profits.

service put her on hold more often, and the company overcharged her several times. The big blow came when it revamped its Web site: in the past, she could place an order for 30 items quickly, but the company switched to a new system that checked inventory in real time, slowing down the interface tremendously. "The grocery store is two minutes away," Knickle says. "In 25 minutes, I could get two-thirds of my shopping done at the store. This was supposed to make my life easier."[4]

MARKET ORIENTATION

The **marketing concept** is a simple and intuitively appealing philosophy that articulates a market orientation. It states that the social and economic justification for an organization's existence is the satisfaction of customer wants and needs while meeting organizational objectives. It is based on an understanding that a sale does not depend on an aggressive sales force, but rather on a customer's decision to purchase a product. What a business thinks it produces is not of primary importance to its success. Instead, what customers think they are buying—the perceived value—defines a business. The marketing concept includes the following:

Satisfying customer needs and wants is the cornerstone of the marketing concept. Hamid Hashmi understands this marketing fundamental. He is CEO of the Muvico Theater in Boca Raton, Florida, which boasts 20 theaters ranging from 100 to 450 seats, a full-service bar, a 230+ seat restaurant, and a day-care center available to customers as well as the company's 350 employees.

© AP/WIDE WORLD PHOTOS

- Focusing on customer wants and needs so that the organization can distinguish its product(s) from competitors' offerings
- Integrating all the organization's activities, including production, to satisfy these wants
- Achieving long-term goals for the organization by satisfying customer wants and needs legally and responsibly

Firms that adopt and implement the marketing concept are said to be market oriented. Achieving a **market orientation** involves obtaining information about customers, competitors, and markets; examining the information from a total business perspective; determining how to deliver superior customer value; and implementing actions to provide value to customers.[5] It also entails establishing and maintaining mutually rewarding relationships with customers.

Understanding your competitive arena and competitors' strengths and weaknesses is a critical component of market orientation. This includes assessing what existing or potential competitors might be intending to do tomorrow as well as what they are doing today. Western Union failed to define its competitive arena as telecommunications, concentrating instead on telegraph services, and was eventually outflanked by fax technology. Had Western Union been a market-oriented company, its management might have better understood the changes taking place, seen the competitive threat, and developed strategies to counter the threat.[6] (See the Online exercise at the top of the page to find out more about Western Union's situation.)

marketing concept
The idea that the social and economic justification for an organization's existence is the satisfaction of customer wants and needs while meeting organizational objectives.

market orientation
A philosophy that assumes that a sale does not depend on an aggressive sales force but rather on a customer's decision to purchase a product. It is synonymous with the marketing concept.

Although Yoplait is not founded upon a societal marketing orientation in the same way as, say, the Sierra Club, the company still communicates to its customers its concern about women's health. For each pink lid redeemed by a Yoplait customer, the company donates 10 cents to the Susan G. Komen Breast Cancer Foundation.

SOCIETAL MARKETING ORIENTATION

One reason a market-oriented organization may choose not to deliver the benefits sought by customers is that these benefits may not be good for individuals or society. This philosophy, called a **societal marketing orientation**, states that an organization exists not only to satisfy customer wants and needs and to meet organizational objectives but also to preserve or enhance individuals' and society's long-term best interests. Marketing products and containers that are less toxic than normal, are more durable, contain reusable materials, or are made of recyclable materials is consistent with a societal marketing orientation. Duracell and Eveready battery companies have reduced the levels of mercury in their batteries and will eventually market mercury-free products. Turtle Wax car wash products and detergents are biodegradable and can be "digested" by waste treatment plants. The company's plastic containers are made of recyclable plastic, and its spray products do not use propellants that damage the ozone layer in the earth's upper atmosphere. Whether a product serves individuals' best interests is not always clear, as the "Ethics in Marketing" box describes.

FAQs

Why haven't more firms adopted the societal marketing orientation? Find out by watching the video FAQ on Xtra!

societal marketing orientation
The idea that an organization exists not only to satisfy customer wants and needs and to meet organizational objectives but also to preserve or enhance individuals' and society's long-term best interests.

REVIEW LEARNING OBJECTIVE 2

2 | Describe four marketing management philosophies

Orientation	Focus
Production	What can we make or do best?
Sales	How can we sell more aggressively?
Marketing	What do customers want and need?
Societal	What do customers want and need, and how can we benefit society?

3 DIFFERENCES BETWEEN SALES AND MARKET ORIENTATIONS

Discuss the differences between sales and market orientations

The differences between sales and market orientations are substantial. The two orientations can be compared in terms of five characteristics: the organization's focus, the firm's business, those to whom the product is directed, the firm's primary goal, and the tools used to achieve those goals.

Ethics in Marketing Ethics in Marketing
hics in Marketing Ethics in Marketing Ethics in Marketing Ethics in Marketing Ethics in Market
hics in Marketing Ethics in Marketing Ethics in Marketing **ETHICS IN MARKETING** Ethics in Marketing Ethics in Market
hics in Marketing Ethics in Marketing Ethics in Marketing Ethics in Marketing Ethics in Market
hics in Marketing Ethics in Marketing Ethics in Marketing
Ethics in Marketing

> NICOTINE LOLLIPOPS

Hundreds of independent druggists across the United States are producing suckers under brand names such as NicoStop, NicoPop, and Likatine—all spiked with nicotine, and all produced under the radar screen of the Food and Drug Administration. The high-octane pops, in flavors such as cherry, grape, apricot, and tequila sunrise, are the latest attempt to quench Americans' craving for nicotine and the dopamine buzz it provides. "Trying to stop smoking? It's as easy as having a lollipop!!!" exclaims Tom Jones Drug in Garner, North Carolina, on a Web site advertising nicotine lollipops.

No one is tallying sales in this cottage industry, but it's clear that they are growing fast. One supplier to pharmacists says sales of the nicotine used in lollipops increased 20-fold from 2000 to 2001. Many pharmacists also are concocting nicotine-spiked hard candy, gummy lozenges, and even lip balm, selling them in stores and on the Internet.

The lollipops are drawing fire from critics and putting druggists into the crosshairs of regulators. An FDA spokesperson said the agency "is looking into" the legality of the lollipops and declined to elaborate.

Tobacco-control activists say the suckers are dangerous because children can easily get their hands on them and end up hooked on nicotine. It is possible to buy the lollipops online with no prescription or proof of age required.

Pharmacists say the chances of children buying the lollipops are remote. For one thing, they are expensive, selling for $2 or $3 a pop. They also say they sell the pops only to customers who have a doctor's prescription. The Compounder, an Aurora, Illinois pharmacy, labels its lollipops, "This is NOT candy. NOT FOR CHILDREN."

Underage use isn't the only concern, however. Nicorette gum, nicotine patches, nasal sprays, and other smoking-cessation products from big drug companies have received FDA approval only after rigorous testing to prove they are safe and also effective in helping people overcome cigarette addiction. The lollipops haven't passed such tests. Nicotine is addictive, but it doesn't cause the diseases associated with smoking.

Still, many pharmacists say their concoctions are superior to patches and gums. One reason is that smokers put the lollipop in their mouth, get a hit of nicotine, and remove it, just as they do with a cigarette. Another reason, pharmacists say, is that the nicotine compound used in the lollipops, known as nicotine salicylate, is more readily absorbed, with a taste that is more easily masked than the nicotine found in gums and patches, known as nicotine polacrilex.

But nicotine salicylate hasn't been proved safe and effective for use as a medicine and isn't approved by the FDA. Nor is it listed in the U.S. Pharmacopoeia, a compendium of recognized drugs and ingredients used in the pharmaceutical industry.

The FDA has insisted that makers of smoking-cessation aids avoid making their products taste too good so they aren't abused. When GlaxoSmithKline wanted to make Nicorette gum more minty, the FDA at first refused. "They were worried about introducing anything that tasted better," says Kenneth R. Strahs, head of smoking-control research and development for the company. "They were worried about abuse, especially by young people." Glaxo had to conduct a lengthy "abuse liability" study to show the FDA that the new flavor wouldn't make it more likely to be addictive.[7]

Are marketers of nicotine lollipops practicing a societal marketing orientation? Why or why not? What concerns should people have about these products?

THE ORGANIZATION'S FOCUS

Personnel in sales-oriented firms tend to be "inward looking," focusing on selling what the organization makes rather than making what the market wants. Many of the historic sources of competitive advantage—technology, innovation, economies of scale—allowed companies to focus their efforts internally and prosper. Today, many successful firms derive their competitive advantage from an external, market-oriented focus. A market orientation has helped companies such as Dell, Inc., the Royal Bank of Canada, and Southwest Airlines outperform their competitors. These companies put customers at the center of their business in ways most companies do poorly or not at all.[8] As Genesys Telecommunications Laboratories, Inc.'s chief executive told a large gathering of customers, "You are my bosses. You pay for my house, my car, my salary, and my kid's school."[9] He went on to say that customer care is a company's most important responsibility.

A sales orientation has led to the demise of many firms including Streamline.com, the Digital Entertainment Network, and Urban Box Office. As one technology industry analyst put it, "no one has ever gone to a Web site because they heard there was great Java running."[10] Kmart illustrates the problems companies experience when they lose their customer focus. After the company filed for Chapter 11 bankruptcy, one industry analyst concluded that "they [Kmart] need to define themselves more clearly and know who their customer is."[11] Another stated that "it focused on going up against Wal-Mart products and prices, but didn't consider the customer."[12]

Philip Morris
How does Philip Morris handle the sensitive issues associated with marketing tobacco? What kind of information does its Web site provide about smoking and its negative effects on health? How do you think Philip Morris is able to justify such marketing tactics? After checking around the site, do you think that approach makes the company more or less trustworthy?
http://www.philipmorris.com/

Online

Customer Value

Customer value is the ratio of benefits to the sacrifice necessary to obtain those benefits. The automobile industry illustrates the importance of creating customer value. To penetrate the fiercely competitive luxury automobile market, Lexus adopted a customer-driven approach, with particular emphasis on service. Lexus stresses product quality with a standard of zero defects in manufacturing. The service quality goal is to treat each customer as one would treat a guest in one's home, to pursue the perfect person-to-person relationship, and to strive to improve continually. This pursuit has enabled Lexus to establish a clear quality image and capture a significant share of the luxury car market.

Customer value is not simply a matter of high quality. A high-quality product that is available only at a high price will not be perceived as a good value, nor will bare-bones service or low-quality goods selling for a low price. Instead, customers value goods and services that are of the quality they expect and that are sold at prices they are willing to pay. Value can be used to sell a Mercedes Benz as well as a $3 Tyson frozen chicken dinner.

Delivering customer value means elevating the customer experience, improving customer satisfaction, and paying close attention to customer feedback and attitudes. The firm constantly changes itself in order to deliver more value to customers. The firm may have one or more customer advisory boards to capture real data and suggestions. It's also likely to seek out customer insight through quality improvement initiatives.[13]

Marketers interested in customer value

- *Offer products that perform:* This is the bare minimum requirement. Consumers have lost patience with shoddy merchandise.
- *Give consumers more than they expect:* Christopher Zane, owner of Zane's Cycles, one of the ten largest bicycle shops in the United States, suggests removing the bar rather than raising it. Zane's Cycles offers lifetime free service, lifetime parts warranties, and 90-day price protection. The price protection plan is important to demonstrate to customers that they are getting free lifetime parts and services along with the lowest price available for the brands and models that they buy.[14]
- *Avoid unrealistic pricing:* E-marketers are leveraging Internet technology to redefine how prices are set and negotiated. With lower costs, e-marketers can often offer lower prices than their brick-and-mortar counterparts. The enormous popularity of auction sites such as eBay and Amazon.com and the customer-bid model used by Priceline illustrates that online customers are interested in bargain prices. Many are not willing to pay a premium for the convenience of examining the merchandise and taking it home with them.

customer value
The ratio of benefits to the sacrifice necessary to obtain those benefits.

- *Give the buyer facts:* Today's sophisticated consumer wants informative advertising and knowledgeable salespeople. Web sites that don't provide enough information are among the top ten things that "irk" Internet shoppers most.

- *Offer organization-wide commitment in service and after-sales support:* People fly Southwest Airlines because the airline offers superior value. Although passengers do not get assigned seats or meals (just peanuts or crackers) when they use the airline, its service is reliable and friendly and costs less than most major airlines. All Southwest employees are involved in the effort to satisfy customers. Pilots tend to the boarding gate when their help is needed, and ticket agents help move luggage. One reservation agent flew from Dallas to Tulsa with a frail, elderly woman whose son was afraid she couldn't handle the change of planes by herself on her way to St. Louis.

According to a Datamonitor study, "U.S. online businesses lose more than $6 billion in potential e-commerce sales annually due to lack of customer service at their Web sites."[15] Another report revealed that while 38 percent of studied companies responded to customer e-mails in six hours or less, a whopping 24 percent sent no response at all![16] Service quality is explored in more detail in Chapter 11.

Customer Satisfaction

Customer satisfaction is customers' evaluation of a good or service in terms of whether it has met their needs and expectations. Failure to meet needs and expectations results in dissatisfaction with the good or service.[17] Keeping current customers satisfied is just as important as attracting new ones and a lot less expensive. Firms that have a reputation for delivering high levels of customer satisfaction do things differently from their competitors. Top management is obsessed with customer satisfaction, and employees throughout the organization understand the link between their job and satisfied customers. The culture of the organization is to focus on delighting customers rather than on selling products.

Staples, the office supply retailer, offers great prices on its paper, pens, fax machines, and other office supplies, but its main strategy is to grow by providing customers with the best solutions to their problems. Its approach is to emulate customer-intimate companies like Home Depot and Airborne Express. These companies do not pursue one-time transactions: They cultivate relationships.

One industry that understands the importance of customer satisfaction is the common carrier industry. FedEx has built its reputation on fulfilling its promise of reliable package delivery. This ad for FedEx connects the idea of its reputation for customer satisfaction with the high reputation its customers have for satisfying *their* customers.

Building Relationships

Attracting new customers to a business is only the beginning. The best companies view new customer attraction as the launching point for developing and enhancing a long-term relationship. Companies can expand market share in three ways: attracting new customers, increasing business with existing customers, and retaining current customers. Building relationships with existing customers directly addresses two of the three possibilities and indirectly addresses the other.

Relationship marketing is a strategy that entails forging long-term partnerships with customers. It begins with developing a clear understanding of who your customers are, what they value, what they want to buy, and how they prefer to interact with you and be served by you.[18] Companies then build relationships with customers by offering value and providing customer satisfaction. They are rewarded with repeat sales and referrals that lead to increases in sales, market share, and profits. Costs also fall because serving existing customers is less expensive than attracting new ones.

customer satisfaction
Customers' evaluation of a good or service in terms of whether it has met their needs and expectations.

relationship marketing
A strategy that entails forging long-term partnerships with customers.

Relationships at the House of Mouse

One organization that knows how to build and maintain relationships with its customers is Walt Disney World, which has launched a new program to help visitors maximize their visit to the park. Visitors can pick up a Pal Mickey doll at the gate and then receive messages that help take the hassle out of the guest experience. For example, park employees can tell you through Pal Mickey or your cell phone when the firework display will begin or where in the Magic Kingdom your child's favorite character will be at a certain time. Disney's information technology unit is also working on GPS technology software for the park. Guests could use the technology to find out, for example, how many people are waiting for the bus to a specific hotel or resort. The same information would go to the bus drivers, allowing them to modify the bus schedule to accommodate fluctuating crowd sizes. All of these technological innovations are meant to ensure that a visit to Walt Disney World doesn't become so chaotic that it damages the positive relationship that Disney strives to have with all of its customers.[19]

FAQs

Aren't the goals of relationship marketing and personal selling contradictory? Find out by watching the video FAQ on Xtra!

empowerment
Delegation of authority to solve customers' problems quickly—usually by the first person that the customer notifies regarding a problem.

A new form of relationship marketing that has emerged in the last few years is called one-to-one marketing. As the name suggests, *one-to-one marketing* is an individualized marketing method that utilizes customer information to build long-term, personalized, and profitable relationships with customers. The goals of this approach are to reduce costs, increase customer satisfaction, and increase revenue by building and maintaining customer loyalty. Customers also benefit from stable relationships with suppliers. Business buyers have found that partnerships with their suppliers are essential to producing high-quality products while cutting costs. Customers remain loyal to firms that provide them greater value and satisfaction than they can expect from competing firms.

Most successful relationship marketing strategies, including one-to-one marketing, depend on customer-oriented personnel, effective training programs, employees with authority to make decisions and solve problems, and teamwork.

Customer-Oriented Personnel For an organization to be focused on building relationships with customers, employees' attitudes and actions must be customer oriented. An employee may be the only contact a particular customer has with the firm. In that customer's eyes, the employee is the firm. Any person, department, or division that is not customer oriented weakens the positive image of the entire organization. For example, a potential customer who is greeted discourteously may well assume that the employee's attitude represents the whole firm.

The Role of Training Leading marketers recognize the role of employee training in customer service and relationship building. Edward Jones Company, ranked number one among *Fortune*'s "100 Best Companies to Work For," for two straight years, spends 3.8 percent of its payroll on training, with an average of 146 hours for every employee. New brokers get more than four times that much.[20] It is no coincidence that the public companies on this list such as Southwest Airlines and Cisco Systems perform much better than other firms in their respective industries. All new employees at Disneyland and Walt Disney World must attend Disney University, a special training program for Disney employees. They must first pass Traditions 1, a daylong course focusing on the Disney philosophy and operational procedures. Then they go on to specialized training. Similarly, McDonald's has Hamburger University. At American Express's Quality University, line employees and managers learn how to treat customers. There is an extra payoff for companies such as Disney and McDonald's that train their employees to be customer oriented. When employees make their customers happy, the employees are more likely to derive satisfaction from their jobs. Having contented workers who are committed to their jobs leads to better customer service and greater employee retention.

Empowerment In addition to training, many marketing-oriented firms are giving employees more authority to solve customer problems on the spot. The term used to describe this delegation of authority is **empowerment**. Employees develop ownership attitudes when they are treated like part-owners of the business and are expected to act the part. These employees manage themselves, are more likely to work hard, account for their own performance and the company's, and take prudent risks to build a stronger business and sustain the company's success. FedEx customer service representatives are trained and empowered to resolve customer problems. Although the average FedEx transaction costs only $16, the customer service representatives are empowered to spend up to $100 to resolve a customer problem.

After John Yokoyama, owner of Pike Place Fish in Seattle's historic Farmer's Market, committed to empowering his employees, his cost of doing business dropped from 77 percent to 54 percent—a 43 percent increase in gross profit. Yokoyama attributes this success to each individual in the company taking personal responsibility for company profitability. "They like to win. They take it personally. They set new records nearly every month."[21]

Empowerment gives customers the feeling that their concerns are being addressed and gives employees the feeling that their expertise matters. The result is greater satisfaction for both customers and employees.

Teamwork Many organizations, such as Southwest Airlines and Walt Disney World, that are frequently noted for delivering superior customer value and providing high levels of customer satisfaction assign employees to teams and teach them team-building skills. **Teamwork** entails collaborative efforts of people to accomplish common objectives. Job performance, company performance, product value, and customer satisfaction all improve when people in the same department or work group begin supporting and assisting each other and emphasize cooperation instead of competition. Performance is also enhanced when people in different areas of responsibility such as production and sales or sales and service practice teamwork, with the ultimate goal of delivering superior customer value and satisfaction.

THE FIRM'S BUSINESS

A sales-oriented firm defines its business (or mission) in terms of goods and services. A market-oriented firm defines its business in terms of the benefits its customers seek. People who spend their money, time, and energy expect to receive benefits, not just goods and services. This distinction has enormous implications.

Because of the limited way it defines its business, a sales-oriented firm often misses opportunities to serve customers whose wants can be met through only a wide range of product offerings instead of specific products. For example, in 1989, 220-year-old Britannica had estimated revenues of $650 million and a worldwide sales force of 7,500. Just five years later, after three consecutive years of losses, the sales force had collapsed to as few as 280 representatives. How did this respected company sink so low? Britannica managers saw that competitors were beginning to use CD-ROM to store huge masses of information but chose to ignore the new computer technology, as well as an offer to team up with Microsoft.

It's not hard to see why parents would rather give their children an encyclopedia on a compact disc instead of a printed one. The CD-ROM versions were either given away or sold by other publishers for under $400. A full 32-volume set of *Encyclopaedia Britannica* weighs about 120 pounds, costs a minimum of $1,500, and takes up four and one-half feet of shelf space. If Britannica had defined its business as providing information instead of publishing books, it might not have suffered such a precipitous fall.

Customer-intimate companies achieve great success by building longtime relationships with their customers. Home Depot is an industry benchmark in this respect. Here, employee Juan Cruz loads plywood for a customer preparing her home against an impending hurricane.

© AP/WIDE WORLD PHOTOS

teamwork
Collaborative efforts of people to accomplish common objectives.

Adopting a "better late than never" philosophy, Britannica has made its complete 32-volume set available free on the Internet. The company no longer sells door-to-door and hopes to return to profitability by selling advertising on its Web site.

Answering the question "What is this firm's business?" in terms of the benefits customers seek, instead of goods and services, has at least three important advantages:

- It ensures that the firm keeps focusing on customers and avoids becoming preoccupied with goods, services, or the organization's internal needs.
- It encourages innovation and creativity by reminding people that there are many ways to satisfy customer wants.
- It stimulates an awareness of changes in customer desires and preferences so that product offerings are more likely to remain relevant.

Market orientation and the idea of focusing on customer wants do not mean that customers will always receive everything they want. It is not possible, for example, to profitably manufacture and market automobile tires that will last for 100,000 miles for $25. Furthermore, customers' preferences must be mediated by sound professional judgment as to how to deliver the benefits they seek. As one adage suggests, "People don't know what they want—they only want what they know." Consumers have a limited set of experiences. They are unlikely to request anything beyond those experiences because they are not aware of benefits they may gain from other potential offerings. For example, before the Internet, many people thought that shopping for some products was boring and time consuming, but could not express their need for electronic shopping.

THOSE TO WHOM THE PRODUCT IS DIRECTED

A sales-oriented organization targets its products at "everybody" or "the average customer." A market-oriented organization aims at specific groups of people. The fallacy of developing products directed at the average user is that relatively few average users actually exist. Typically, populations are characterized by diversity. An average is simply a midpoint in some set of characteristics. Because most potential customers are not "average," they are not likely to be attracted to an average product marketed to the average customer. Consider the market for shampoo as one simple example. There are shampoos for oily hair, dry hair, and dandruff. Some shampoos remove the gray or color hair. Special shampoos are marketed for infants and elderly people. There is even shampoo for people with average or normal hair (whatever that is), but this is a fairly small portion of the total market for shampoo.

A market-oriented organization recognizes that different customer groups want different features or benefits. It may therefore need to develop different goods, services, and promotional appeals. A market-oriented organization carefully analyzes the market and divides it into groups of people who are fairly similar in terms of selected characteristics. Then the organization develops marketing programs that will bring about mutually satisfying exchanges with one or more of those groups.

Paying attention to the customer isn't exactly a new concept. Back in the 1920s, General Motors began designing cars for every lifestyle and pocketbook. This was a breakthrough for an industry that had been largely driven by production needs ever since Henry Ford promised any color as long as it was black. Chapter 7 thoroughly explores the topic of analyzing markets and selecting those that appear to be most promising to the firm. This chapter's "Global Perspectives" box describes one company's effort to adapt its orientation to a new market.

THE FIRM'S PRIMARY GOAL

A sales-oriented organization seeks to achieve profitability through sales volume and tries to convince potential customers to buy, even if the seller knows that the customer and product are mismatched. Sales-oriented organizations place a higher premium on making a sale than on developing a long-term relationship with a customer. In contrast, the ultimate goal of most market-oriented organizations is to make a profit by creating customer value, providing customer satisfaction, and building long-term relationships with customers. The exception is so-called nonprofit organizations that exist to achieve goals other than profits. Nonprofit organizations can and should adopt a market orientation. Nonprofit organization marketing is explored further in Chapter 11.

> TOUGH MARKET

 On Wal-Mart Stores, Inc.'s new global battlefield, the obstacles are huge. Japan is one of the world's quirkiest and most difficult retail markets. Until a few years ago, laws restricted store size and operating hours to protect small, inefficient retailers. In urban areas, steep real estate prices have forced retailers to build multilevel outlets that resemble department stores and sell a mix of food, apparel, and household items. Big discount stores have emerged only recently in new suburban communities.

Japanese customers often demand the freshest food and orderly stores, with short checkout lines and an abundance of clerks to do everything from answering questions to keeping fruit displays tidy. Then there's Japan's complex and expensive distribution system, a labyrinth of wholesalers and transport companies with long-term business ties to suppliers. Under these ties, suppliers will sell only to certain wholesalers, who sell to other wholesalers and so on. A product might go through three or more hands before reaching a retailer.

Wal-Mart spent four years studying the market and concluded it needed a local partner. In Seiyu, Japan's fifth-largest supermarket chain, it found an established chain with plentiful, well-situated—if shabby—outlets and a sorry balance sheet. The 40-year-old company had expanded into scores of different businesses during Japan's boom, and the bust left it saddled with debt and starved for cash. Wal-Mart bought a 6 percent stake in Seiyu with the option of increasing it to 67 percent by 2007.

Wal-Mart says it will soon announce plans for new stores, possibly including supercenters—large stores that combine a grocery store with extensive general merchandise. But its main focus now is on making existing stores more efficient. Wal-Mart is showing wholesalers and suppliers how to lower their prices by shaving costs and forecasting demand. A new computer system will soon allow manufacturers to track their product sales at Seiyu by item, hour, and gross margin, which would enable them to manufacture and deliver goods more efficiently.

One goal is eventually to bypass the network of suppliers and wholesalers. With the economy weak for so long, suppliers are beginning to break ranks and sell to retailers, if that means they can earn some extra money.

Wal-Mart's best effort so far is the four-story Seiyu store in Futamatagawa that it recently renovated. Newly widened aisles boast taller display fixtures. Trademark yellow smiley faces look down on tables piled with large dog-food bags, jumbo rice sacks, and other fast-moving merchandise. Some customers say they are only mildly impressed, however. "I think it is easier to find things," says Yuka Nakagone, a 28-year-old housewife shopping the food aisles. "But I don't think the items have changed very much." Wal-Mart says sales are up 15 percent since the remodeling, even though only about 500 of the store's 50,000 items are being sold at Wal-Mart's famous rock-bottom rates.[22]

Do you think that Wal-Mart will be able to successfully implement the same business model in Japan that it has used in the United States? What might be the major hurdles? What marketing management philosophy does Wal-Mart appear to be following in Japan?

TOOLS THE ORGANIZATION USES TO ACHIEVE ITS GOALS

Sales-oriented organizations seek to generate sales volume through intensive promotional activities, mainly personal selling and advertising. In contrast, market-oriented organizations recognize that promotion decisions are only one of four basic marketing mix decisions that have to be made: product decisions, place (or distribution) decisions, promotion decisions, and pricing decisions. A market-oriented organization recognizes each of these four components as important. Furthermore, market-oriented organizations recognize that marketing is not just a responsibility of the marketing department. Interfunctional coordination means that skills and resources throughout the organization are needed to deliver superior customer service and value.

A WORD OF CAUTION

This comparison of sales and market orientations is not meant to belittle the role of promotion, especially personal selling, in the marketing mix. Promotion is the means by which organizations communicate with present and prospective customers about the merits and characteristics of their organization and products. Effective promotion is an essential part of effective marketing. Salespeople who work for market-oriented organizations are generally perceived by their customers to be problem solvers and important links to supply sources and new products. Chapter 16 examines the nature of personal selling in more detail.

REVIEW LEARNING OBJECTIVE 3

3	Discuss the differences between sales and market orientations				
	What is the organization's focus?	**What business are you in?**	**To whom is the product directed?**	**What is your primary goal?**	**How do you seek to achieve your goal?**
Sales Orientation	Inward, upon the organization's needs	Selling goods and services	Everybody	Profit through maximum sales volume	Primarily through intensive promotion
Market Orientation	Outward, upon the wants and preferences of customers	Satisfying customer wants and needs and delivering superior value	Specific groups of people	Profit through customer satisfaction	Through coordinated marketing and interfunctional activities

4 WHY STUDY MARKETING?

Describe several reasons for studying marketing

Now that you understand the meaning of the term *marketing*, why it is important to adopt a marketing orientation, how organizations implement this philosophy, and how one-to-one marketing is evolving, you may be asking, "What's in it for me?" or "Why should I study marketing?" These are important questions, whether you are majoring in a business field other than marketing (such as accounting, finance, or management information systems) or a nonbusiness field (such as journalism, economics, or agriculture). There are several important reasons to study marketing: Marketing plays an important role in society, marketing is important to businesses, marketing offers outstanding career opportunities, and marketing affects your life every day.

MARKETING PLAYS AN IMPORTANT ROLE IN SOCIETY

The total population of the United States exceeds 280 million people. Think about how many transactions are needed each day to feed, clothe, and shelter a population of this size. The number is huge. And yet it all works quite well, partly because the well-developed U.S. economic system efficiently distributes the output of farms and factories. A typical U.S. family, for example, consumes 2.5 tons of food a year. Marketing makes food available when we want it, in desired quantities, at accessible locations, and in sanitary and convenient packages and forms (such as instant and frozen foods).

MARKETING IS IMPORTANT TO BUSINESSES

The fundamental objectives of most businesses are survival, profits, and growth. Marketing contributes directly to achieving these objectives. Marketing includes the following activities, which are vital to business organizations: assessing the wants and satisfactions of present and potential customers, designing and managing product offerings, determining prices and pricing policies, developing distribution strategies, and communicating with present and potential customers.

All businesspeople, regardless of specialization or area of responsibility, need to be familiar with the terminology and fundamentals of accounting, finance, management, and marketing. People in all business areas need to be able to communicate with specialists in other areas. Furthermore, marketing is not just a job done by people in a marketing department. Marketing is a part of the job of everyone in the organization. As David Packard of Hewlett-Packard put it: "Marketing is far too important to be left only to the marketing department." Marketing is not a department so much as a companywide orientation. Therefore, a basic understanding of marketing is important to all businesspeople.

MARKETING OFFERS OUTSTANDING CAREER OPPORTUNITIES

Between a fourth and a third of the entire civilian workforce in the United States performs marketing activities. Marketing offers great career opportunities in such areas as professional selling, marketing research, advertising, retail buying, distribution management, product management, product development, and wholesaling. Marketing career opportunities also exist in a variety of nonbusiness organizations, including hospitals, museums, universities, the armed forces, and various government and social service agencies. (See Chapter 11.)

As the global marketplace becomes more challenging, companies all over the world and of all sizes are going to have to become better marketers. For a comprehensive look at career opportunities in marketing and a variety of other useful information about careers, read the Career Appendix at the end of this chapter, work the career exercise at the end of every chapter, and visit our Web site at **http://lamb.swlearning.com**.

MARKETING AFFECTS YOUR LIFE EVERY DAY

Marketing plays a major role in your everyday life. You participate in the marketing process as a consumer of goods and services. About half of every dollar you spend pays for marketing costs, such as marketing research, product development, packaging, transportation, storage, advertising, and sales expenses. By developing a better understanding of marketing, you will become a better-informed consumer. You will better understand the buying process and be able to negotiate more effectively with sellers. Moreover, you will be better prepared to demand satisfaction when the goods and services you buy do not meet the standards promised by the manufacturer or the marketer.

REVIEW LEARNING OBJECTIVE 4

4 | Describe several reasons for studying marketing

Why Study Marketing?

- Important to society
- Important to business
- Good career opportunities

+

Marketing affects you every day!

This book is divided into 20 chapters organized into seven major parts. The chapters are written from the marketing manager's perspective. Each chapter begins with a brief list of learning objectives followed by "Looking Forward," a brief story about a marketing situation faced by a firm or industry. At the end of each of these opening vignettes, thought-provoking questions link the story to the subject addressed in the chapter. Your instructor may wish to begin chapter discussions by asking members of your class to share their views about the questions.

The examples of global marketing highlighted in most chapters will help you understand that marketing takes place all over the world, between buyers and sellers in different countries. These and other global marketing examples throughout the book, marked with the icon shown in the margin, are intended to help you develop a global perspective on marketing.

Marketing ethics is another important topic selected for special treatment throughout the book. Chapters include highlighted stories about firms or industries that have faced ethical dilemmas or have engaged in practices that some consider unethical. Questions are posed to focus your thinking on the key ethical issues raised in each story.

Small business examples are highlighted with icons. Every chapter also includes an "Entrepreneurship Case" related to small business. This material illustrates how entrepreneurs and small businesses have used the principles and concepts discussed in the book to grow and prosper.

End-of-chapter materials begin with a final comment on the chapter-opening vignette called "Looking Back." This is followed by "Use It Now," a feature designed how you can use what you learned in the chapter right now in your everyday life. Then comes a summary of the major topics ("Review and Applications"), with discussion and writing questions (writing questions are identified with the icon in the margin) related to the topics. The questions include specific Internet and team activities, which are identified by appropriate icons. The online icon is also placed throughout the text to identify examples relating to technology. A set of exercises, including application, ethics, and career exercises, is next. Then come the "Entrepreneurship Case" and "Watch It," a section describing the different videos that supplement the chapter. Immediately following "Watch It" is a feature called "Still Shaky," which lets you know what additional resources are available to help you master chapter content.

Marketing 8e is also supported by InfoTrac College Edition. Several chapters throughout the book will give you the opportunity to refine your research skills through exercises specifically designed for InfoTrac. These exercises will be flagged by the icon at the left. All these features are intended to help you develop a more thorough understanding of marketing and enjoy the learning process.

The remaining chapters in Part 1 introduce you to the activities involved in developing a marketing plan, the dynamic environment in which marketing decisions must be made, ethics and social responsibility, and global marketing. Part 2 covers consumer decision making and buyer behavior; business marketing; the concepts of positioning, market segmentation, and targeting; and the nature and uses of marketing research and decision support systems. Parts 3 through 6 examine the elements of the marketing mix—product, place (distribution), promotion, and pricing. Part 7 contains two chapters. The first examines Internet marketing, and the second focuses on customer relationship management.

LOOKING BACK

Look back at the story at the beginning of this chapter about MarineMax. You should now find the assignment at the end of the story fairly easy. MarineMax is the world's largest recreational boat retailer because it focuses on identifying and satisfying customer needs rather than selling boats. As the Chief Marketing Officer put it, "the real power behind the company's success is a focus on 'the total boating experience.'"

Relationship marketing is a strategy that entails forging long-term partnerships with customers. MarineMax's goal is not to sell boats to people, congratulate them on their new purchase, and send them on their way. It does what it can to assure a positive experience by delivering every boat fully fueled, training "new Captains," offering insurance and other after-the-sale services, organizing trips, and even helping owners sell their boats when they are ready to move up to newer or bigger craft. MarineMax truly focuses on providing customer satisfaction and building and maintaining long-term relationships with recreational boaters. Though not mentioned specifically in the story, MarineMax builds and maintains these relationships using one-to-one marketing.

USE IT NOW

Lisa Imm, age 25, an assistant marketing manager at Commtouch, Inc., a global provider of Web-based e-mail, was looking to change fields—from database marketing to Internet marketing. But she had no idea how her current skills would transfer. Bottom line: She needed to network, and fast.

She didn't hit the party circuit or attend career fairs. Instead, she joined the e-mail list for Silicon Valley Web Grrls (**www.webgrrls.com**), a networking group for women who work in the technology sector. "I instantly had access to more than 1,000 people without physically having to meet them," Imm says. "The list is my virtual Rolodex."

Imm used the network not only to tap into what jobs were available but also to get valuable advice when she was considering offers: "People wrote back saying, 'I wouldn't work for that company, and this is why.' It was like having 100 personal recruiters and career counselors." A month after gathering information from the Web Grrls community and other sources, Imm landed her job.

What's her advice for others looking to take advantage of the power of a cyber-schmooze? First, be sure to join a group with credentials: "You can refer to the group on your résumé. Many times in an interview people will say, 'Wow! I've used that group too!' It's a great conversation starter." Also, give as generously as you receive. "If you don't respond to people when you've got the advice that they need, then you won't get much out of it."[23]

REVIEW AND APPLICATIONS

1 **Define the term** *marketing***.** Marketing is an organizational function and a set of processes for creating, communicating, and delivering value to customers and for managing customer relationships in ways that benefit the organization and its stakeholders.

1.1 What is the AMA? What does it do? How do its services benefit marketers?
ONLINE http://www.marketingpower.com

1.2 INFOTRAC COLLEGE EDITION Log on to InfoTrac at **http://www.infotrac-college.com** and conduct a keyword search for "marketing." Read a couple of the articles. Based on what you have learned in this chapter, how do these articles describe or relate to marketing?

2 **Describe four marketing management philosophies.** The role of marketing and the character of marketing activities within an organization are strongly influenced by its philosophy and orientation. A production-oriented organization focuses on the internal capabilities of the firm rather than on the desires and needs of the marketplace. A sales orientation is based on the beliefs that people will buy more products if aggressive sales techniques are used and that high sales volumes produce high profits. A market-oriented organization focuses on satisfying customer wants and needs while meeting organizational objectives. A societal marketing orientation goes beyond a market orientation to include the preservation or enhancement of individuals' and society's long-term best interests.

2.1 **WRITING** Your company president has decided to restructure the firm to make it more market oriented. She is going to announce the changes at an upcoming meeting. She has asked you to prepare a short speech outlining the general reasons for the new company orientation.

2.2 Donald E. Petersen, former chairman of the board of Ford Motor Company, remarked, "If we aren't customer driven, our cars won't be either." Explain how this statement reflects the marketing concept.

2.3 Give an example of a company that might be successfully following a production orientation. Why might a firm in this industry be successful following such an orientation?

3 **Discuss the differences between sales and market orientations.** First, sales-oriented firms focus on their own needs; market-oriented firms focus on customers' needs and preferences. Second, sales-oriented companies consider themselves to be deliverers of goods and services, whereas market-oriented companies view themselves as satisfiers of customers. Third, sales-oriented firms direct their products to everyone; market-oriented firms aim at specific segments of the population. Fourth, although the primary goal of both types of firms is profit, sales-oriented businesses pursue maximum sales volume through intensive promotion, whereas market-oriented businesses pursue customer satisfaction through coordinated activities.

3.1 A friend of yours agrees with the adage "People don't know what they want—they only want what they know." Write your friend a letter expressing the extent to which you think marketers shape consumer wants.

3.2 **WRITING** Your local supermarket's slogan is "It's your store." However, when you asked one of the stock people to help you find a bag of chips, he told you it was not his job and that you should look a littler harder. On your way out, you noticed a sign with an address for complaints. Draft a letter explaining why the supermarket's slogan will never be credible unless the employees carry it out.

4 **Describe several reasons for studying marketing.** First, marketing affects the allocation of goods and services that influence a nation's economy and standard of living. Second, an understanding of marketing is crucial to understanding most businesses. Third, career opportunities in marketing are diverse, profitable, and expected to increase significantly during the coming decade. Fourth, understanding marketing makes consumers more informed.

4.1 **WRITING** Write a letter to a friend or family member explaining why you think that a course in marketing will help you in your career in some field other than marketing.

TERMS

customer satisfaction 12	marketing 6	relationship marketing 12
customer value 11	marketing concept 8	sales orientation 7
empowerment 13	market orientation 8	societal marketing orientation 9
exchange 6	production orientation 7	teamwork 14

APPLICATION EXERCISE

Understanding the differences among the various marketing management philosophies is the starting point for understanding the fundamentals of marketing.[24] From reading the chapter, you may be convinced that the marketing orientation is the most appealing philosophy and the one best suited to creating a competitive advantage. Not all companies, however, use the marketing orientation. And even companies that follow it may not execute well in all areas.

Activities

1. Visit your local grocery store and go through the cereal, snack-food, and dental hygiene aisles. Go up and down each aisle slowly, noticing how many different products are available and how they are organized on the shelves.

2. Count the varieties of product in each product category. For example, how many different kinds of cereal are on the shelves? How many different sizes? Do the same for snack food and toothpaste.

3. Now try to find a type of product in the grocery store that does not exhibit such variety. There may not be many. Why do you think there are enough kinds of cereals to fill an entire aisle (and then some), but not enough different types of, say, peanut butter to fill an entire aisle? Can this difference be explained in terms of marketing management philosophy (peanut butter manufacturers do not follow the marketing concept) or by something else entirely?

4. Have you ever wanted to see a particular kind of cereal or snack food on the shelf? Think of product varietals (like lemon-flavored toothpaste or chocolate-covered popcorn) that you have never seen on the shelf but would be interested in trying if someone would make it. Write a letter or send an e-mail to an appropriate company, suggesting that it add your concept to its current product line.

ETHICS EXERCISE

In today's business environment, ethics are extrememly important. In recent years, there have been numerous scandals and trials that stem from a lack of ethical judgment. For this reason, we are including an ethical exercise in every chapter. A brief scenario will present you with a situation in which the right thing to do may or may not be crystal clear, and you will need to decide the ethical way out of the dilemma. To help you with these decisions, we will always refer you back to the AMA's Code of Ethics, found online at **http://www.marketingpower. com**. This will give you a resource for the exercise and will also help reinforce the ethical standards that marketers should uphold.

Rani Pharmaceuticals is the maker of several popular drugs used to treat high blood pressure and arthritis. Over time, the company has developed a positive relationship with many of the patients who use its medications through a quarterly newsletter that offers all the latest information on new medical research findings and general health and fitness articles. The company has just been acquired by a group of investors who also own Soothing Waters Hot Tubs and Spas. The marketing director for Soothing Waters would like to use Rani's mailing list for a direct-mail promotion.

Questions

1. What should Rani Pharmaceuticals do?

2. Does the AMA Code of Ethics address the use of customer information by multiple divisions of the same company? Go to **http://www.marketingpower.com** and review the code. Then, write a brief paragraph on how the AMA Code of Ethics relates to Rani Pharmaceuticals' dilemma.

CAREER EXERCISE

Getting started in a career can be a daunting task. To help you explore the many options in the field of marketing, we have created a set of exercises that will connect you to online resources with valuable information on the different possibilities. For example, the exercise for Chapter 8 will help you explore a career in marketing research. Over the course of the book, you will have the opportunity to work with most, if not all, of the available marketing careers to see which interests you and suits you best. We start by presenting a general overview of the avenues that a career in marketing could follow. As you go through the following Web sites, make notes on anything you find interesting. Doing this will help you begin formulating ideas about a marketing career.

Research to Get Started

1. To get a feel for common types of marketing jobs, go to the AMA's Web site at **http://www.marketingpower.com**. When you register on the job postings page, you will be able to consult the marketing "help wanted" ads. Peruse the database of ads and see what's out there. What sounds interesting to you? Are there any jobs or job descriptions that don't interest you at all? Start to make a list of ideas that you would like to investigate further.

2. Another wonderful resource for general career information is the *Wall Street Journal*'s Career Journal. Available online at **http://www.careerjournal.com**, the Career Journal provides a great forum for job seekers. When you type "marketing" in the search engine, you can view the job postings for marketing careers. You can even refine your search as you pinpoint areas of marketing that are most interesting. All in all, the Career Journal is a great place to start a job hunt.

3. If an advanced degree in business is part of your long-term career strategy, you may want to consult **http://www.gmat.com** to read about the Graduate Management Admission Test, view sample test questions, and consult resources for mapping and financing your MBA degree.

Go to **http://lamb.swlearning.com** for other sites of interest as you begin plotting your career map, including salary calculators and career planning resources.

ENTREPRENEURSHIP CASE

NOODÉ SKINCARE LLC. 1-888-972-3477

A NOODÉ FOR A NEW GENERATION

When Seth Ratner launched Noodé (pronounced "newday") in spring 2001, he had a very clearly articulated marketing strategy—and a hefty first-year sales goal of $1.7 million. Nine months after rollout, Ratner's plan seemed to be working quite well: his skin-care company and product line had already topped the $1 million mark and showed no signs of slowing.

Formerly of Zirh Skin Nutrition, a male skin-care line that was acquired by Shisheido, Ratner recognized an underserved market in young people ages 15 to 29, a group he named "Generation Me." A combination of Generation X and Generation Y, Generation Me had long been ignored by the more recognized skin-care companies, which tended to make products to help older consumers fight wrinkles and recondition aging skin. No serious, conservatively priced, high-end skin-care solutions existed for young skin problems, such as oily skin, combination skin, and acne. That is, not until Noodé.

Noodé's 12-product line was developed by a group of dermatologists focusing on prevention and maintenance rather than repair. Although the products are serious skin care, their names all tie into the Generation Me market: Clean Me face wash, Scrub Me Gently facial scrub, Make Me Soft facial moisturizer, Help Me acne cream, Renew Me face peel, Make Me Moist body lotion, Rub Me massage oil, Wash Me Everywhere body wash, Scrub Me Harder body scrub, Heal and Protect Me face and body cream for calming and reducing redness, and the newest product, Shield Me sunscreen gel with SPF 15. Noodé intends to focus exclusively on skin care—and not branch out into cosmetics—so that it will not lose its message of serious skin care.

So with only 11 products when the line was launched (Shield Me was added one year later), how did Noodé ring up so many sales in such a short period of time? The starting point was zeroing in on the Generation Me market. Ratner wanted to identify what 15- to 29-year-olds wanted. He found that they are consumers concerned about "me" and want products exclusively for "me." Once the target market was clearly identified, Ratner built a product line to meet its needs and wants. That is why none of the flagship products contained sun protection. Generation Me likes to look tan, and Noodé products are geared toward a youthful market. The new Shield Me product seems to send a conflicting message, but the SPF 15 gives only enough protection to avoid burning during daily activities. Also appealing to the target market is the product packaging. Colorful products packaged in clear bottles with funky writing attract interest. Creamier products are sold in an innovative style of packaging referred to as a "tottle," a tube and a bottle combined, which prevents accidental discharge of the product.

Once the market and product were ready, Noodé introduced them in high-end retailers like Henri Bendel, Bloomingdale's, Fred Segal, and Nordstrom. The idea was to build relationships with stores, train store personnel, and make brochures, literature, and samples available to store customers. Noodé cosponsored a Teen Appreciation Day at Bloomingdale's during the back-to-school season with Ralph fragrances, Tony & Tina cosmetics, and *Lucky* magazine. Teens received free facials and makeovers during the event, which generated a month's worth of sales for Noodé in a single day. The cost of sponsorship was minimal.

Keeping promotion costs minimal has been a key tactic for Ratner. Rather than roll out his new product and company with a pricey national advertising campaign, he chose to use catalog inserts, postcards, in-store support combined with a heavy sampling program, and store events like the Teen Appreciation Day. Low promotion costs help Noodé make the most of its pricing strategy. Price points range from $15 for the Rub Me and Scrub Me products to $20 for the Help Me acne product.

In a market full of high-priced products aimed at older consumers, Noodé is certainly poised to be a long-term success. Noodé brings together a fun, cool skin-care line (that's still serious and effective) with the niche market it's designed to serve.[25]

Questions

1. Review the definition of marketing on page 6. Using the information from the case, identify each of Noodé's activities that correspond to the elements of the definition.

2. Based on what you have read in the case, describe Noodé's marketing management philosophy.

3. How does Noodé maintain its outward organization focus?

WATCH IT

At the end of every chapter, "Watch It" will tell you about the different video options that accompany the text and support the chapter content. Each chapter will have a combination of 30-second clips (Preview) embedded in the instructor's PowerPoint presentation, a 10- to 15-minute clip (Feature Presentation) for classroom viewing, and 2- to 4-minute clips (Encore Presentation) for classroom viewing. The Preview clips contain television ads that were originally broadcast during Super Bowl games. The Feature Presentation clips are excerpts from various episodes of the 30-minute Small Business School (SBS) program nationally broadcast on PBS. And the Encore Presentation clips are taken from popular Hollywood movies and offer a unique and fun perspective on marketing topics.

Because the SBS program covers all aspects of business, SBS segments raise more issues than just those presented in a single chapter. For example, the lead segment for Chapter 1 about Wahoo's Fish Taco, a uniquely Californian restaurant, also relates to material in Chapter 5 (Consumer Decision Making), Chapter 7 (Segmenting and Targeting Markets), Chapter 13 (Retailing), and Chapter 15 (Advertising and Public Relations). The rich SBS videos will help reinforce what you've learned by introducing you to people who are doing marketing every day—and not according to thematic units.

Read the descriptions and get ready to watch it!

FEATURE PRESENTATION

Wahoo's Fish Taco

To give you insight into Chapter 1, Small Business School will introduce you to a company that shows the marketing concept in action. Entrepreneurs Wing Lam, Ed Lee, and Mingo Lee built their experience as avid surfers in Baja into a successful restaurant concept, Wahoo's Fish Taco. Wahoo's now operates 22 stores employing 300 people, and each store pulls in over $1 million in revenue from an extremely fanatic and loyal customer base. The company has prospered from using a market-oriented strategy that provides a specific experience to their core customers of surfers, skateboarders, and snowboarders. Geared for the person with an active lifestyle, the food is great tasting, very healthy, and served quickly. The restaurants themselves are designed to feel like the surfer hangouts Wing, Ed, and Mingo frequented while in Baja, and the comfortable atmosphere encourages customers to linger for as long as they like. The video explores how Wahoo's unfailing commitment to customer service and its customer-centric operations strategy combine to create the perfect marketing recipe.

What to Watch for and Ask Yourself

1. Explain how customers are the starting and focal point of Wahoo's business.

2. Wahoo's has some unique products, promotion strategies, and distribution strategies. How do these strategies support the company's market-oriented marketing philosophy?

3. List the major points of Wahoo's operations strategy and tactics, and describe how together they reflect the marketing concept.

ENCORE PRESENTATION

The Jerk

As an encore to reviewing and studying the overview of marketing presented in this chapter, watch the scene from *The Jerk*. It features Steve Martin in his first starring role as Navin Johnson, an insecure fellow trying to get a successful start at a St. Louis gas station. The scene is an edited sequence from The New Phone Book segment that appears in the first twenty-six minutes of the film. Does Navin quickly identify Stan Fox's (Bill Macy) customer needs and desires about his falling eyeglasses? How does Navin get customer information so he can design a product solution? Does he exceed those needs with his innovative solution? Does the product appear to offer superior customer value? Why or why not?

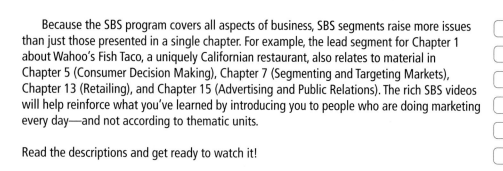

SmallBusinessSchool ▫
the Series on PBS stations and the Web

Still Shaky?

If you're having trouble with the concepts in this chapter, consider using some of the following study resources. You can review the videos, or test yourself with materials designed for all kinds of learning styles.

- [x] **Xtra! (http://lambxtra.swlearning.com)**
  - [x] Quiz
  - [x] Feature Videos
  - [x] Encore Videos
  - [x] FAQ Videos
  - [x] Exhibit Worksheets
  - [x] Marketing Plan Worksheets
  - [ ] Content
- [x] **http://lamb.swlearning.com**
  - [x] Quiz
  - [x] PowerPoint slides
  - [x] Marketing News
  - [x] Review Exercises
  - [x] Links
  - [x] Marketing Plan Contest
  - [x] Career Exercise
  - [x] Use It Now
- [x] **Study guide**
  - [x] Outline
  - [x] Vocab Review
  - [x] Test Questions
  - [x] Marketing Scenario

Need More? Here's a tip. Use your textbook more like a notebook and less like a reference book. The margins are a great place for writing questions on content you don't understand, highlighting important concepts, and adding examples to help you remember the material. Writing in your book makes it a more comprehensive resource for marketing and a better study tool. For example, if you write review questions in the margins, you can quiz yourself by covering the chapter content with a piece of paper and revealing each section to see if you really understand.

Careers in Marketing

One of the most important decisions in your life is choosing a career. Not only will your career choice affect your income and lifestyle, but it also will have a major impact on your happiness and self-fulfillment.

You can use many of the basic concepts of marketing introduced in this book to get the career you want by marketing yourself. The purpose of marketing is to create exchanges that satisfy individual as well as organizational objectives, and a career is certainly an exchange situation for both you and an organization. The purpose of this appendix is to help you market yourself to prospective employers by providing some helpful tools and information.

Available Careers

Marketing careers have a bright outlook into the next decade. The U.S. Bureau of Labor Statistics estimates that employment in marketing fields will grow between 21 and 35 percent through 2012. Many of these increases will be in the areas of sales, public relations, retailing, advertising, marketing research, and product management.

- *Sales:* There are more opportunities in sales than in any other area of marketing. Sales positions vary greatly among companies. Some selling positions focus more on providing information; others emphasize locating potential customers, making presentations to committees, and closing the sale. Because compensation is often in the form of salary plus commission, there are few limits on the amount of money a person can make and therefore great potential. Sales positions can be found in many organizations, including manufacturing, wholesaling, retailing, insurance, real estate, financial services, and many other service businesses.

- *Public relations:* Public relations firms help create an image or a message for an individual or organization and communicate it effectively to a desired audience. All types of firms, profit and non-profit organizations, individuals, and even countries employ public relations specialists. Communication skills, both written and oral, are critical for success in public relations.

- *Retailing:* Retail careers require many skills. Retail personnel may manage a sales force or other personnel, select and order merchandise, and be responsible for promotional activities, inventory control, store security, and accounting. Large retail stores have a variety of positions, including store or department manager, buyer, display designer, and catalog manager.

- *Advertising:* Many organizations employ advertising specialists. Advertising agencies are the largest employers; however, manufacturers, retailers, banks, radio and television stations, hospitals, and insurance agencies all have advertising departments. Creativity, artistic talent, and communication skills are a few of the attributes needed for a successful career in advertising. Account executives serve as a liaison between the advertising agency and the client. Account executives must have a good knowledge of business practices and possess excellent sales skills.

- *Marketing management:* Marketing managers develop the firm's detailed marketing strategy. With the help of subordinates, including *market research managers* and *product development managers,* they determine the demand for products and services offered by the firm and its competitors. In addition, they identify potential markets—for example, business firms, wholesalers, retailers, government, or the general public. Marketing managers develop pricing straegy with an eye towards maximizing the firm's share of the market and its profits while ensuring that the firm's customers are satisfied. In collaboration with sales, product development, and other managers, they monitor trends that indicate the need for new products and services and oversee product development. Marketing managers work with advertising and promotion managers to promote the firm's products and services and to attract potential users..

- *Marketing research:* The most rapid growth in marketing careers is in marketing research. Marketing research firms, advertising agencies, universities, private firms, nonprofit organizations, and governments provide growing opportunities in marketing research. Researchers conduct industry research, advertising research, pricing and packaging research, new-product testing, and test marketing. Researchers are involved in one or more stages of the research process, depending on the size of the organization conducting the research. Marketing research requires knowledge of statistics, data processing and analysis, psychology, and communication.

- *Product management:* Product managers coordinate all or most of the activities required to market a product. Thus, they need a general knowledge of all aspects of marketing. Product managers are responsible for the successes and failures of a product and are compensated well for this responsibility. Most product managers have previous sales experience and skills in communication. The position of product manager is a major step in the career path of top-level marketing executives.

Starting in a marketing job is also one of the *best routes to the top* of any organization. More CEOs come from sales and marketing backgrounds than from any other field. As examples, Lee Iacocca (Chrysler), Phil Lippincott (Scott Paper), John Akers (IBM), John Sparks (Whirlpool), and Bruno Bich (Bic Pen) came up through sales and marketing. Typically, a college graduate enters the marketing field in a sales position, then moves to sales supervisor, and next sales manager at the district, regional, and national levels. Individuals who prefer to advance through the ranks of marketing management can usually make a career move into product or brand management or another marketing headquarters job after serving for a couple of years in the initial sales position.

Probably the most difficult part of job hunting is deciding exactly what type of work you would like. Many students have had no working experience other than summer jobs, so they are not sure what career to pursue. Too often, college students and their parents rush toward occupational fields that seem to offer the highest monetary payoff or are currently "hot," instead of looking at the long run over a 40- to 50-year working life. One straightforward approach to deciding what type of job to undertake is to do a "self-analysis." This involves honestly asking yourself what your skills, abilities, and interests really are and then identifying occupational fields that match up well with your personality profile. Some students prefer to take various vocational aptitude tests to help identify their interests and abilities. Your college's placement office or psychology department can inform you about the availability of these tests. You may find it useful to develop a FAB (feature–advantage–benefit) matrix that shows what your skills are, why they offer an advantage, and how they would benefit an employer. Exhibit 1 shows an example.

Your First Marketing Assignment

Marketing yourself to a prospective employer will usually be your first big marketing assignment. With your services (as represented by your qualifications, education, training, and personal characteristics) as the product, you must convince prospective employers that they should buy your services over those of many other candidates for the job. All the steps of the marketing and sales process apply: identifying opportunities, developing yourself as a product, prospecting for potential employers, planning your approach to them, approaching with a résumé and cover letter, making your sales presentation and demonstrating your qualifications in a personal interview, dealing with objections or giving reasons why the employer should hire you over other candidates, attempting to close the sale by enthusiastically asking for the job and employing appropriate closing techniques, and following up by thanking the prospective employer for the interview and reinforcing a positive impression.

EXHIBIT 1

The FAB Matrix

Need of Employer This job requires . . .	Feature of Job Applicant I have . . .	Advantage of Feature This feature means that . . .	Benefit to Employer You will . . .
• Frequent sales presentations to individuals and groups.	• Taken 10 classes that required presentations.	• I require limited or no training in making presentations.	• Save on the cost of training and have an employee with the ability and confidence to be productive early.
• Knowledge of personal computers, software, and applications.	• Taken a personal computer course and used Lotus in most upper-level classes.	• I can already use Word, Excel, dBase, SAS, SPSS, and other software.	• Save time and money on training.
• A person with management potential.	• Been president of a student marketing group and social fraternity president for two years.	• I have experience leading people.	• Save time because I am capable of stepping into a leadership position as needed.

Prospecting for a Potential Employer

After you have determined what you're selling (your skills, abilities, interests, and so forth) and identified the type of job you think you would like, you might begin your personal selling process by looking at the *College Placement Annual* at your college placement office. The *College Placement Annual* provides a variety of information about prospective employers and lists the organizations according to the types of jobs they have available—for example, advertising, banking, marketing research, and sales. Another very important source is an online search on the Internet. Other sources of information about prospective employers include directories such as those published by Dun and Bradstreet, Standard & Poor's, and trade associations; the annual American Marketing Association membership directory (company listings); the Yellow Pages of telephone books in cities where you would like to live and work; and classified sections of the *Wall Street Journal* or city newspapers. Before contacting a particular company, look up its annual report and stock evaluation (from *Value Line* or various other sources) in your college library to learn as much as possible about the company and its prospects for the future. You might also obtain a list of articles on the company from the *Business Periodicals Index (BPI)*.

College Placement Office
Use your college placement office to find out which companies are going to be interviewing on campus on what dates; then sign up for interviews with those companies that seem to best match your job skills and requirements. Usually, the college placement office has books, pamphlets, or files that will give you leads on other prospective employers that may not be interviewing on campus that term.

Job-Hunting Expenses
Although campus interviews are convenient, students seldom get a job without follow-up interviews with more senior managers—usually at company headquarters. These additional interviews generally take a full day and may involve long-distance trips. You should be forewarned that job hunting can be expensive. Printing your résumé, typing cover letters, buying envelopes and stamps, making long-distance telephone calls, incurring travel expenses, and buying new clothing will require a sizable outlay of money. Even though most companies eventually reimburse you for expenses incurred on a company visit, they seldom pay in advance. Reimbursement can take several weeks, so you may encounter some cash-flow problems over the short run.

The Internet

The Internet is the fastest growing medium for job searching today. Many companies are using the Internet to assist them in their recruiting efforts. Some companies are even conducting initial interviews online via video-conferencing. Just as some companies post jobs on a bulletin board, companies can list job opportunities on job posting Web sites. Some of the more popular job search Web sites are listed in Exhibit 2. These sites also contain information about résumé writing, interviewing, and tips that you can use to secure the job that you want.

Employment Agencies

Although many employment agencies receive fees from employers for providing good job candidates, others charge job seekers huge fees (sometimes thousands of dollars) for helping them find jobs. Therefore, make sure you fully understand the fee arrangement before signing up with an employment agency. Some employment agencies may not be worth your time and/or money because they use a programmed approach to helping you write your résumé and cover letter and prospect for potential employers. Potential employers have seen these "canned" formats and approaches so many times that your personal advertisement (your résumé and cover letter) will be almost indistinguishable from others.

The Hidden Job Market

It has been estimated that nearly 90 percent of available jobs are never advertised and never reach employment agency files, so creative resourcefulness often pays off in finding the best jobs. Consider every reasonable source for leads. Sometimes your professors, deans, or college administrators can give you names and contact persons at companies that have hired recent graduates.

Do not be bashful about letting other people know that you are looking for work. Classmates, friends, and business associates of your family may be of help not only directly but also indirectly, acting as extra pairs of eyes and ears alert to job opportunities for you.

Planning Your Approach (the Preapproach)

After conducting your self-analysis and identifying potential employers looking for people with your abilities and interests, you need to prepare your *résumé* (or personal advertisement). Your résumé should focus on your achievements to date, your educational background, your work experience, and your special abilities and interests. Some students make the mistake of merely listing their assigned responsibilities on different jobs without indicating what they accomplished on the job. If you achieved something on the job, say it—for example, "Helped computerize office files," "Increased sales in my territory by 10 percent," "Received a 15 percent raise after three months on the job," or "Promoted to assistant store manager after four months." When looking for a job, remember that employers are looking for *a track record of achievement,* so you must distinguish yourself from those who may have had the same assigned job responsibilities as you did but performed poorly. If your work experience is minimal, consider a "skills" résumé, in which you emphasize your particular abilities, such as

organizing, programming, or leadership skills, and give supporting evidence whenever you can. Examples of various types of résumés can be found in the *College Placement Annual* and in various other job-hunting publications (ask your college business reference librarian to direct you). Exhibit 2 lists some Web sites where you can learn about résumé formats.

Remember that there is no one correct format for your résumé. A little tasteful creativity can help differentiate your résumé from countless look-alike résumés. If you are a young college graduate, your résumé will usually be only one page long, but do not worry about going to a second page if you have something important to present. One student so blindly followed the one-page résumé rule that he left out having served in the military—service that is usually viewed very positively by prospective employers, especially if it involved significant leadership responsibilities or work experience.

If you know what job you want, you may want to put your *job objective* near the top of your résumé. If you are not sure what job you want or want to send out the same résumé for several different jobs, then you can describe your job objective in your *cover letter.* A key element in the cover letter is convincing the prospective employer to grant you an interview. Thus, you must talk in terms of the employer's interests, not just your own. You are answering the question: "Why should we hire you?" You may need to send a letter with your résumé enclosed to a hundred or more companies to obtain five to ten interviews, so do not be discouraged if you get replies from only a few companies or are told by many companies that they have no job opportunities at present. You will probably need only a few interviews and just one job offer to get your career started.

Review some of the publications and sources mentioned in the previous section on prospecting (e.g., *College Placement Annual,* Dun and Bradstreet directories, and annual reports) to learn as much as you can about your prospective employer so that you can tailor your cover letter. Remember, the employer is thinking in terms of the company's needs, not yours. For one example of a résumé, see Exhibit 3. A cover letter is illustrated in Exhibit 4.

Making Your Approach

Prospective employers can be approached by mail, telephone, the Internet, or personal contact. Personal contact is best, but this usually requires that you know someone with influence who can arrange an interview for you. Of course, a few enterprising students have devised elaborate and sometimes successful schemes to get job interviews. For example, we know of one young man who simply went to the headquarters of the company he wanted to work for and asked to see the president. Told that the president of the company could not see him, the student said that he was willing to wait until the president had time. This audacious individual went back three different days until the president finally agreed to see him, perhaps mainly out of curiosity about what sort of young man would be so outrageous in his job search.

Fortunately for this young man, he had a lot to offer and was able to communicate this to the president, so he was hired. This unorthodox approach shows how far people have gone to impress potential employers, and if you feel comfortable doing it, then go ahead. A personal contact within the company certainly can win you some special attention and enable you to avoid competing head-on with the large number of other candidates looking for a job. Most students, however, start their approach in the traditional way by mailing their résumé and cover letter to the recruiting department of the company. More recently, students have begun to e-mail their résumés, and some companies are requiring this as a means of screening out applicants who are not computer literate. Unless your résumé matches a particular need at that time, it will probably be filed away for possible future reference or merely discarded. To try to get around the system, some students send their letter by express mail or mailgram or address it to a key executive, with "Personal" written on the

EXHIBIT 3

Sample Résumé

RACHEL E. SANFORD
2935 Mountain View Road
Ellington, PA 19401
(216) 567-0000

JOB OBJECTIVE	Sales representative for a consumer-products company
EDUCATION	Graduated *cum laude* with BS in Marketing Management (June 2005), University of Southern Pennsylvania. Career-related courses included Selling and Sales Management, Public Speaking, Business Writing, Public Relations, Marketing Research, Computer Programming, and Multivariate Data Analysis.
ACTIVITIES AND HONORS	President, Student Marketing Association; Vice president, Chi Omega Sorority; Captain, women's varsity tennis team; sportswriter for the *Campus View* student newspaper. Named to Who's Who among American College Students, 2003–2004. On Dean's List all four years. Overall grade point average = 3.65.

WORK EXPERIENCE

Summer 2003	*Sales* representative, Peabody Manufacturing Company. Sold women's blouses to boutiques and small department stores in southeastern Pennsylvania. Exceeded assigned sales quota by 20%; named "outstanding" summer employee for 2003.
Summer 2002	Buyer, Hamm's Department Stores, Inc., Midway, Pa. Developed purchase plan, initiated purchase orders, monitored and controlled expenditures for nearly $2 million worth of women's clothing. Made monthly progress reports (written and oral) to Hamm's Executive Committee. Received 15% bonus as #2 buyer in the six stores of the Hamm's chain in special "Back to School" purchasing competition.
Summer 2001	*Retail* clerk, Hamm's Department Stores, Inc., Midway, Pa. After 3 months, received 10% pay raise and promotion to evening salesclerk supervisor over seven part-time salesclerks. Devised new inventory control system for handbags and accessories that cut costs over $50,000 annually.
Summer 2000	*Cosmetics salesperson,* Heavenly Charm, Inc., Midway, Pa. Sold $63,000 worth of Heavenly Charm cosmetics door to door. Named #1 salesperson in the sales region. Offered full-time job as sales supervisor.
INTERESTS	Tennis, golf, public speaking, short story writing, and reading biographies.

envelope. These students believe that bypassing the company's personnel office will increase the likelihood that their cover letter and résumé will be read by someone with authority to hire. Other students send their résumé on a CD or DVD, and one student in Louisiana sent a King Cake to the recipient of the résumé, while another sent a packet of Louisiana spices. Using gimmicks, no matter how creative, to get a job interview will offend some executives and thus cause you to be rejected from consideration for a job. But you can probably also be sure that a few executives will admire your efforts and grant you an interview.

Only you know how comfortable you feel with different approaches to obtaining a job interview. We advise you not to use an approach that is out of character for you and thus will make you feel awkward and embarrassed.

Making Your Sales Presentation

Your personal sales presentation will come during the interview with the prospective employer's recruiters or interviewers. Like any presentation, it requires thorough preparation and an effective follow-up, as well as a solid performance during the interview itself.

Pre-Interview Considerations

Preparing for the interview is crucial. You will already have gathered information on the company, as suggested in the preceding sections; you should review it now. Exhibit 5 shows a pre-interview checklist that can help you prepare. In addition, the self-assessment test in Exhibit 6 can help you determine if you're ready for the interview.

Keep the following in mind in preparing for your interview:

- Find out the exact place and time of the interview.
- Be certain you know the interviewer's name and how to pronounce it if it looks difficult.
- Do some research on the company with which you are interviewing— talk to people and read the company literature to know what its products or services are, where its offices are located, what its growth has been, and how its prospects look for the future.
- Think of two or three good questions that you would like to ask during your interview.
- Plan to arrive at the designated place for your interview a little early so that you will not feel rushed and worried about being on time.
- Plan to dress in a manner appropriate to the job for which you are interviewing.

A guide for the interview conversation itself is to prepare nine positive thoughts before you go in for the interview:

- Three reasons why you selected the employer to interview
- Three reasons you particularly like the employer
- Three assets you have that should interest the employer

EXHIBIT 4

Sample Cover Letter

Rachel E. Sanford
2935 Mountain View Road
Ellington, PA 19401

Mr. Samuel Abramson
District Sales Manager
Hixson Appliance Company
Philadelphia, PA 19103

Dear Mr. Abramson:

Hixson has been a familiar name to me ever since I was barely able to see over my mother's kitchen counter. Virtually every appliance we had was a Hixson, so I know firsthand what fine quality products you sell. My career interest is in sales, and there is no company that I would rather work with than Hixson Appliance.

I will be graduating this June from Southern Pennsylvania University with a BS in marketing management, and I would like you to consider me for a job as a sales representative with your company. As you can see in my enclosed résumé, I have successfully worked in sales jobs during three of the last four summers. My college course electives (e.g., public speaking, business writing, and public relations) have been carefully selected with my career objective in mind. Even my extracurricular activities in sports and campus organizations have helped prepare me for working with a variety of people and competitive challenges.

Will you please grant me an interview so that I can convince you that I'm someone you should hire for your sales team? I'll call you next Thursday afternoon to arrange an appointment at your convenience.

Look forward to meeting you soon.

Sincerely,

Rachel E. Sanford

Enclosure

EXHIBIT 5

Before the Interview

- **Practice**
  - ✓ Questions you may be asked
  - ✓ Questions you want to ask about the position and organization
  - ✓ Role-playing an interview
- **Self-assessment**
  - ✓ Goals
  - ✓ Skills, abilities, accomplishments
  - ✓ Work values (important factors you look for in a job)
  - ✓ Experiences
  - ✓ Personality
- **Research**
  - ✓ Obtain company literature
  - ✓ Write or visit the organization
  - ✓ Talk to people familiar with the organization
- **Obtain references**
- **Plan ahead**
  - ✓ Attire to be worn to the interview
  - ✓ Directions to the interview site
  - ✓ Time of arrival (get there with at least 5–10 minutes to spare)

Try to make a positive impression on everyone you encounter in the company, even while waiting in the lobby for your interview. Sometimes managers will ask their receptionists and secretaries for an opinion of you, and your friendliness, courtesy, professional demeanor, personal habits, and the like will all be used to judge you. Even the magazines you choose to read while waiting can be a positive or negative factor. For instance, it will probably be less impressive if you leaf through a popular magazine like *People* or *Sports Illustrated* than if you read something more professional such as *Business Week* or the *Wall Street Journal*.

During the Interview

During the interview, do not be merely a passive respondent to the interviewer's questions. Being graciously assertive by asking reasonable questions of your own will indicate to the interviewer that you are alert, energetic, and sincerely interested in the job. The personal interview is your opportunity to persuade the prospective employer that you should be hired. To use a show business analogy, you will be onstage for only a short time (during the personal interview), so try to present an honest but positive image of yourself. Perhaps it will help you to be alert and enthusiastic if you imagine that you are being interviewed on television. Exhibit 7 lists a number of questions that are frequently asked during interviews.

Sometimes prospective employers will ask you to *demonstrate* certain abilities by having you write a timed essay about some part of your life, sell something (such as a desk calculator) to the interviewer, or respond to hostile questions. Be calm and confident during any such unorthodox interviewing approaches and you will make a good impression. Remember, most employers want you to perform well because they are looking for the best people they can find in a given time frame for the money they have to offer.

EXHIBIT 6

Self-Assessment Test

How assertive are you (or will you be) as you interview for a position? Listed below are questions that will help you to evaluate yourself: answer yes or no to the questions, being honest with yourself. If you have five or fewer yes answers, you still have some work to do. A good score is seven or more yes answers.

Yes	No	
——	——	Have you made an effort to research the company before the interview?
——	——	Have you prepared several questions that you want to ask?
——	——	If an interviewer asks a personal question unrelated to the job, will you be able to tactfully call this to his attention?
——	——	If an interviewer gives you a hypothetical job-related problem, do you have confidence in your ability to respond in a timely and succinct manner?
——	——	If the interviewer seems distracted or uninterested during your interview, will you be able to steer the interview back on track and gain her attention?
——	——	When you meet the interviewer, will you be the first to introduce yourself and begin the conversation?
——	——	If the interviewer continually interrupts when you are responding to questions or giving information about yourself, can you politely handle this?
——	——	If the interviewer never gives you the opportunity to talk about yourself and you have only five minutes remaining in the interview, have you thought about phrases or ways to redirect the interview and regain control of the process?
——	——	When the interviewer is beginning to close the interview, are you prepared to ask questions about how you stand, what the determining factors are for candidate selection, and by what date you will have an answer?

EXHIBIT 7

Some Questions Frequently Asked during a Job Interview

- Of the jobs you've had to date, which one did you like best? Why?
- Why do you want to work for our company?
- Tell me what you know about our company.
- Do any of your relatives or friends work for our company? If so, in what jobs?
- Tell me about yourself, your strengths, weaknesses, career goals, and so forth.
- Is any member of your family a professional marketer? If so, what area of marketing?
- Why do you want to start your career in marketing?
- Persuade me that we should hire you.
- What extracurricular activities did you participate in at college? What leadership positions did you have in any of these activities?
- What benefits have you derived from participation in extracurricular activities that will help you in your career?
- Where do you see yourself within our company in five years? In ten years? Twenty years?
- What is your ultimate career goal?
- What do you consider your greatest achievement to date?
- What is your biggest failure to date?
- What is (was) your favorite subject in school? Why?
- Are you willing to travel and possibly relocate?
- How would the people who know you describe you?
- How would you describe yourself?
- What do you like most about marketing?
- What do you like least about marketing?
- If we hire you, how soon could you start work?
- What is the minimum we would have to offer you to come with us?
- What goals have you set for yourself? How are you planning to achieve them?
- Who or what has had the greatest influence on the development of your career interests?

EXHIBIT 7

Some Questions Frequently Asked during a Job Interview *(continued)*

- What factors did you consider in choosing your major?
- Why are you interested in our organization?
- What can you tell me about yourself?
- What two or three things are most important to you in a position?
- What kind of work do you want to do?
- What can you tell me about a project you initiated?
- What are your expectations of your future employer?
- What is your GPA? How do you feel about it? Does it reflect your ability?
- How do you resolve conflicts?
- What do you feel are your strengths? Your weaknesses? How do you evaluate yourself?
- What work experience has been the most valuable to you and why?
- What was the most useful criticism you ever received, and who was it from?
- Can you give an example of a problem you have solved and the process you used?
- Can you describe the project or situation that best demonstrates your analytical skills?
- What has been your greatest challenge?
- Can you describe a situation where you had a conflict with another individual and explain how you dealt with it?
- What were the biggest problems you have encountered in college? How have you handled them? What did you learn from them?
- What are your team-player qualities? Give examples.
- Can you describe your leadership style?
- What interests or concerns you about the position or the company?
- In a particular leadership role you had, what was the greatest challenge?
- What idea have you developed and implemented that was particularly creative or innovative?
- What characteristics do you think are important for this position?
- How have your educational and work experiences prepared you for this position?
- Can you take me through a project where you demonstrated skills?
- How do you think you have changed personally since you started college?
- Can you tell me about a team project that you are particularly proud of and discuss your contribution?
- How do you motivate people?
- Why did you choose the extracurricular activities you did? What did you gain? What did you contribute?
- What types of situations put you under pressure, and how do you deal with the pressure?
- Can you tell me about a difficult decision you have made?
- Can you give an example of a situation in which you failed and explain how you handled it?
- Can you tell me about a situation when you had to persuade another person of your point of view?
- What frustrates you the most?
- Knowing what you know now about your college experience, would you make the same decisions?
- What can you contribute to this company?
- How would you react to having your credibility questioned?
- What characteristics are important in a good manager? How have you displayed one of these characteristics?
- What challenges are you looking for in a position?
- What two or three accomplishments have given you the most satisfaction?
- Can you describe a leadership role of yours and tell why you committed your time to it?
- How are you conducting your job search, and how will you make your decision?
- What is the most important lesson you have learned in or out of school?
- Can you describe a situation where you had to work with someone who was difficult? How was the person difficult, and how did you handle it?
- We are looking at a lot of great candidates; why are you the best person for this position?
- How would your friends describe you? Your professors?
- What else should I know about you?

EXHIBIT 8

Sample Interview Questions to Be Asked by Job Candidates

- Where is the organization going? What plans or projects are being developed to maintain or increase its market share? Have many new product lines been decided upon recently? Is the sales growth in the new product line sustainable?

- Who are the people with whom I will be working? May I speak with some of them?

- May I have a copy of the job description?

- What might be a typical first assignment?

- Do you have a performance appraisal system? How is it structured? How frequently will I be evaluated?

- What is the potential for promotion in the organization? In promotions, are employees ever transferred between functional fields? What is the average time to get to _____ level in the career path? Is your policy to promote from within, or are many senior jobs filled by experienced people from outside? Do you have a job posting system?

- What type of training will I receive? When does the training program begin? Is it possible to move through your program faster? About how many individuals go through your internship program?

- What is the normal routine of a (an) _____ like? Can I progress at my own pace, or is it structured? Do employees normally work overtime?

- How much travel is normally expected? Is a car provided to traveling personnel?

- How much freedom is given to new people? How much discipline is required? How much input does the new person have? How much decision-making authority is given to new personnel?

- How frequently do you relocate employees? Is it possible to transfer from one division to another?

- What is the housing market for a single person in _____ (city)? Is public transportation adequate?

- How much contact with and exposure to management is there?

- How soon should I expect to report to work?

If you are given intelligence, aptitude, or psychological tests, you should try to be honest so that you do not create unrealistic expectations that you will not be able to fulfill. It is just as important that you do not create a false impression and begin with a company that is not right for you as it is to secure employment in the first place. Many experts say that it is not very difficult to "cheat" on aptitude or psychological tests if you are able to "play the role" and provide the answers that you know the company wants to read. Usually, the so-called safe approach in most personality and preference (interest) tests is to not take extreme positions on anything that is not clearly associated with the job you are applying for. For sales jobs, it is probably safe to come across as highly extroverted and interested in group activities, but it may not be safe to appear to be overly interested in literature, music, art, or any solitary activity. In addition, the "right" answers tend to indicate a conservative, goal-oriented, money-motivated, and gregarious personality.

Dealing with Objections. Sometimes interviewers will bluntly ask, "Why should we hire you?" This requires that you think in terms of the employer's needs and present in concise form all your major "selling points." Also, sometimes the interviewer may bring up reasons why you are not the ideal candidate. For example, he or she may say: (1) "We're really looking for someone with a little more experience"; (2) "We'd like to get someone with a more technical educational background"; or (3) "We need someone to start work within two weeks." These kinds of statements are similar to *objections* or requests for additional information. In other words, the interviewer is saying, "Convince me that I shouldn't rule you out for this reason." To overcome such objections, you might respond to each, respectively, along the following lines:

(1) "I've had over a year's experience working with two different companies during my summer vacations, and I've worked part-time with a third company all during college. I'm a fast learner, and I've adapted well to each of the three companies, so I feel that my working experience is equivalent to that of someone who has had three or four years' experience with the same company."

(2) "Although I didn't choose to earn a technical undergraduate degree, I've taken several technical courses in college, including basic engineering courses, chemistry, physics, and two years of math. I'm very confident that I can quickly learn whatever is necessary technically to do the job, and my real strength is that my education has been a blend of technical and managerial courses."

(3) "Well, I do have one more term of school, so I couldn't start full-time work in two weeks, but perhaps we could work out an arrangement in which I could work part-time—maybe Friday, Saturday, and Sunday or on weekends until I graduate."

Good "salespeople" do not allow an objection to block a sale. Providing reasonable solutions or alternative perspectives can often overcome objections or, at least, allow room for further negotiation toward a compromise solution.

How to Act during the Interview. The following can help you behave appropriately during the interview:

- *Think positive.* Be enthusiastic, interested, knowledgeable, and confident.
- *Take few notes.* It is acceptable to take notes during the interview, but limit them to things that are essential to remember. You want to focus more on listening and observing rather than writing.
- *Relate to the interviewer.* Build positive rapport with the interviewer. Listen and observe; relate yourself to the employer or position.
- *Watch your body language.* Be aware of nervousness (fidgeting, shaking leg, tapping, etc.). Project confidence (eye contact, firm handshake, upright posture).
- *Be aware of the questions the employer asks.* Answer with information relevant to the position. Provide a direct answer; avoid being long-winded.

- *Think about the questions you ask.* They should indicate that you know something about the job. Avoid questions that could easily be answered elsewhere (through research). Obtain information you need to know to be satisfied with the job (interviewing is a two-way process). Salary and benefit questions should be asked after the job is offered.
- *Achieve effective closure.* Ask when the employer expects to make a decision. Restate your interest and ability to perform the job. Show confidence and enthusiasm (smile, end with a firm handshake). Obtain the employer's business card, if possible (it may be useful when writing a thank-you letter).

Interview Questions. Too many employment applicants spend all their time preparing for the questions employers will ask them. Too often, they fail to ask vital questions that would help them learn if a job is right for them. Failing to ask important questions during the interview often leads to jobs that offer neither interest nor challenge. Too often, uninformed applicants accept positions hoping that they will develop into something more meaningful and rewarding later. Exhibit 8 suggests questions that you may want to ask.

Closing the Sale

Although it is not likely that a prospective employer will offer you a job immediately after the job interview, you should nevertheless let the interviewer know that you definitely want the job and are confident that you will do an excellent job for the employer. You will need to use your best judgment on how to best do this.

In each stage of the personal selling process, you should be looking for feedback from the interviewer's body language and voice inflections or tone.

Following Up the Interview

Within a few days after any job interview, whether you want the job or not, it is business courtesy to write thank-you letters to interviewers. In these letters you can reinforce the positive impression you made in the interview and again express your keen interest in working for the company. If you do not hear from the company within a few weeks, it may be appropriate to write another letter expressing your continuing interest in the job and asking for a decision so that you can consider other options if necessary. As a possible reason for this follow-up letter, you might mention an additional personal achievement since the interview, give a more detailed answer to one of the interviewer's questions, or perhaps send a newspaper or magazine article of interest. A neat, well-written, courteous follow-up letter gives you a chance not only to make a stronger impression on the interviewer but also to exhibit positive qualities such as initiative, energy, sensitivity to others' feelings, and awareness of business protocol.

Many applicants fail to write a thank-you letter after an interview, yet many employers say that the deciding factor between several similar job candidates is often the thank-you note. The thank-you letter should be typewritten. If the interviewer is a very technology-driven person, a thank-you e-mail may also be appropriate. However, the personal touch of a typewritten and hand-signed letter leaves a better impression.

Be sure to write a follow-up letter in all of the following situations:

- *After two or three weeks of no reply*
- *When a job has been refused:* Express your regret that no job is available and ask if you might be considered in the future. Also, ask how you could improve yourself to better fit what the company is looking for.
- *After an interview:* Express your thanks for the interviewer's time and courtesy. Answer any unanswered questions and clarify any misconceptions.

- *To accept a job (even if previously done in person or on the phone):* State your acceptance. Reiterate the agreement, the time for beginning work, and the like. Do not start asking for favors.
- *To refuse a job offer:* Graciously decline the offer. Be warm and interested and indicate that you appreciate the offer.

Follow-up letters are also appropriate after you have received replies to both solicited and unsolicited letters of inquiry. Always make certain that your letters possess the attitude, quality, and skill of a professional.

On the Job

Working Conditions

Advertising, marketing, promotions, public relations, and sales managers work in offices close to those of top managers. Long hours, including evenings and weekends, are common. About 44 percent of advertising, marketing, and public relations managers work more than 40 hours per week. Substantial travel may also be involved. For example, attendance at meetings sponsored by associations or industries is often mandatory. Sales managers travel to local, regional, and national offices and to various dealers and distributors. Advertising and promotions managers may travel to meet with clients or representatives of communications media. At times, public relations managers travel to meet with special interest groups or government officials. Job transfers between headquarters and regional offices are common, particularly among sales managers.

Moving Up the Ladder

Most advertising, marketing, promotions, public relations, and sales management positions are filled by promoting experienced staff or related professional personnel. For example, many managers are former sales representatives, purchasing agents, buyers, or product, advertising, promotions, or public relations specialists. In small firms, where the number of positions is limited, advancement to a management position usually comes slowly. In large firms, promotion may occur more quickly.

Although experience, ability, and leadership are emphasized for promotion, advancement can be accelerated by participation in management training programs conducted by many large firms. Many firms also provide their employees with continuing education opportunities, either in-house or at local colleges and universities, and encourage employee participation in seminars and conferences, often provided by professional societies. In collaboration with colleges and universities, numerous marketing and related associations sponsor national or local management training programs. Staying abreast of what is happening in your industry and getting involved in related industry associations can be important for your career advancement.

Your Early Working Career

Even though you want to choose a company that you will stay with throughout your working life, it is realistic to recognize that you will probably work for three, four, or more companies during your career. If you are not fully satisfied with your job or company during the first few years of your full-time working life, remember that you are building experience and knowledge that will increase your marketability for future job opportunities. Keep a positive outlook and do the best you can in all job assignments—and your chance for new opportunities will come. Do not be too discouraged by mistakes that you may make in your career; nearly every successful person has made and continues to make many mistakes. View these mistakes largely as *learning experiences,* and they will not be too traumatic or damaging to your confidence.

Good luck in your marketing career!

2

Strategic Planning for Competitive Advantage

LEARNING OBJECTIVES

1 Understand the importance of strategic marketing and know a basic outline for a marketing plan

2 Develop an appropriate business mission statement

3 Describe the criteria for stating good marketing objectives

4 Explain the components of a situation analysis

5 Identify sources of competitive advantage

6 Identify strategic alternatives

7 Discuss target market strategies

8 Describe the elements of the marketing mix

9 Explain why implementation, evaluation, and control of the marketing plan are necessary

10 Identify several techniques that help make strategic planning effective

When a hamburger chain based in California called In-N-Out opened its doors in Phoenix, cars stacked up for blocks, and customers lined up in the streets. In San Francisco, lines snaked out the door for weeks after In-N-Out opened there for the first time. When the company introduced outlet number 171 north of Los Angeles, drivers pulled up hours in advance, waiting for the restaurant to open.

In-N-Out, a no-frills hamburger chain, is no ordinary company. Its burgers are made with freshly ground beef served on buns baked daily with sides of hand-cut potatoes. Food is top quality, prepared to each customer's order. Along with burgers and fries, In-N-Out offers sodas and ice cream shakes. That's it—no chicken, no salads, no pseudo-pie desserts, no toys for the kids.

Industry consultants note that efforts intended to attract more customers, such as expanded menus, special promotions, and playgrounds for children, often don't pull their weight. Doing very few things, but doing them well, makes for the kind of operational simplicity that McDonald's abandoned long ago. And high quality allows for premium pricing. Customers gladly pay $4.60 for a Double-Double combo, compared with about $4.00 for a Big Mac value meal.

Research shows that customers don't even mind waiting up to 15 minutes during the lunch rush, which is a typical wait at In-N-Out for that time of day.

Surprisingly, the chain beats other burger makers in speed-of-service ratings. Meaning: Delays don't hurt when the food is worth waiting for.

The founders of In-N-Out began selling burgers the same year that brothers Dick and Mac McDonald opened their first restaurant. Today, the companies couldn't be more different. According to Economic, a Chicage-based restaurant consultant, In-N-Out is getting a far greater return on its investment than its global competitor. With less than 200 stores, In-N-Out's sales reach only $285 million annually, compared to the $20.8 billion generated by the 31,108 McDonald's locations around the globe. But In-N-Out's average single store sales of $1.7 million beat McDonald's $1.6 million per store sales and more than doubled the industry average. "It's remarkable," says Ron Paul, Economics' president. "They have a narrower menu, there is no kid's menu, slower service, and they make more money than McDonald's."

Today's burgers are the same as those served by In-N-Out's founder. The last change on the menu was in 1996, when Dr. Pepper was added to the selection of soft drinks. The chain protects its secret sauce recipe, never giving out any information about the ingredients. Staying mum helps to foster cult status, one of In-N-Out's most valuable assets. Other

elements contributing to cult status include being talked up by celebrities such as Lucy Liu, being placed in a Coen brothers' movie (*The Big Lebowski*), and being praised by chef Julia Child. In-N-Out relies on word of mouth—it does its talking with food and lets everybody else shout. The company is low key with its ads too, relying mostly on billboards and radio.

In-N-Out has grown slowly. The first restaurant was opened in 1948; the second one came three years later. By 1976, the chain still had just 18 outlets. Even today, In-N-Out has only 180 outlets in three states, adding about 10 stores per year. Most of the chain's restaurants are clustered in southern California, with a few in northern California, Arizona, and Nevada.

In 2002, In-N-Out's sales were up nearly 10 percent; in contrast, McDonald's U.S. sales were flat, and Burger King's decreased 3.4 percent. Former CEO Steve Tanner notes that In-N-Out executives need only "pay attention to what the customer wants, and then give it to them. Nobody else in the food business does that."[1]

What are the elements of In-N-Out's marketing strategy? How would you describe its competitive advantage? Why do you think the burger chain is so successful?

Online

In-N-Out Burger

What simple idea does In-N-Out want visitors to its Web site to understand? How does that differentiate In-N-Out from its competition? Visit the Web sites of McDonald's and Burger King too and compare the three companies' strategies for communicating a value proposition. Whose is easiest to understand? Whose is most appealing?

http://www.in-n-out.com

http://www.mcdonalds.com

http://www.burgerking.com

Understand the importance of strategic marketing and know a basic outline for a marketing plan

Strategic planning is the managerial process of creating and maintaining a fit between the organization's objectives and resources and the evolving market opportunities. The goal of strategic planning is long-run profitability and growth. Thus, strategic decisions require long-term commitments of resources.

A strategic error can threaten a firm's survival. On the other hand, a good strategic plan can help protect and grow the firm's resources. For instance, if the March of Dimes had decided to focus on fighting polio, the organization would no longer exist. Most of us view polio as a conquered disease. The March of Dimes survived by making the strategic decision to switch to fighting birth defects.

Strategic marketing management addresses two questions: What is the organization's main activity at a particular time? How will it reach its goals? Here are some examples of strategic decisions:

- The decision of Sears to buy Lands' End, a successful clothing catalog and online retail business, for $1.9 billion. The move could upgrade Sears' image and increase its presence in the catalog business and on the Internet. Lands' End clothing will enjoy greater retail distribution in Sears stores.[2]
- PepsiCo's introduction of Pepsi Edge and Coca-Cola's introduction of C2, both of which boast half the carbs, sugar, and calories of regular colas but with more flavor than diet sodas.[3]
- Kmart Corporation's decision to file for Chapter 11 bankruptcy and close almost 300 stores in 2002, potentially jeopardizing its exclusive relationship with profitable brands such as Disney and Joe Boxer.[4]
- S. C. Johnson's introduction of Shout Color Catchers, a laundry sheet for the washer that collects loose dyes and prevents clothes from bleeding color onto other laundry items.[5]

All these decisions have affected or will affect each organization's long-run course, its allocation of resources, and ultimately its financial success. In contrast, an operating decision, such as changing the package design for Post's cornflakes or altering the sweetness of a Kraft salad dressing, probably won't have a big impact on the long-run profitability of the company.

How do companies go about strategic marketing planning? How do employees know how to implement the long-term goals of the firm? The answer is a marketing plan.

strategic planning
The managerial process of creating and maintaining a fit between the organization's objectives and resources and evolving market opportunities.

Strategic planning is critical to business success. In a strategic move to regain market share as a retailing giant, Sears purchased Land's End, one of the most successful catalog retailers in the United States.

© AP/WIDE WORLD PHOTOS

EXHIBIT 2.1

Elements of Marketing Plan

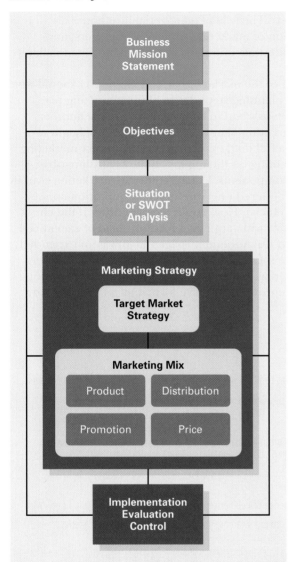

WHAT IS A MARKETING PLAN?

Planning is the process of anticipating future events and determining strategies to achieve organizational objectives in the future. **Marketing planning** involves designing activities relating to marketing objectives and the changing marketing environment. Marketing planning is the basis for all marketing strategies and decisions. Issues such as product lines, distribution channels, marketing communications, and pricing are all delineated in the **marketing plan**. The marketing plan is a written document that acts as a guidebook of marketing activities for the marketing manager. In this chapter, you will learn the importance of writing a marketing plan and the types of information contained in a marketing plan.

WHY WRITE A MARKETING PLAN?

By specifying objectives and defining the actions required to attain them, a marketing plan provides the basis by which actual and expected performance can be compared. Marketing can be one of the most expensive and complicated business activities, but it is also one of the most important. The written marketing plan provides clearly stated activities that help employees and managers understand and work toward common goals.

Writing a marketing plan allows you to examine the marketing environment in conjunction with the inner workings of the business. Once the marketing plan is written, it serves as a reference point for the success of future activities. Finally, the marketing plan allows the marketing manager to enter the marketplace with an awareness of possibilities and problems.

MARKETING PLAN ELEMENTS

Marketing plans can be presented in many different ways. Most businesses need a written marketing plan because the scope of a marketing plan is large and can be complex. Details about tasks and activity assignments may be lost if communicated orally. Regardless of the way a marketing plan is presented, some elements are common to all marketing plans. These include defining the business mission and objectives, performing a situation analysis, delineating a target market, and establishing components of the marketing mix. Exhibit 2.1 shows these elements, which are also described further below. Other elements that may be included in a plan are budgets, implementation timetables, required marketing research efforts, or elements of advanced strategic planning. An example of a thumbnail marketing plan sketch appears in Exhibit 2.2.

planning
The process of anticipating future events and determining strategies to achieve organizational objectives in the future.

marketing planning
Designing activities relating to marketing objectives and the changing marketing environment.

marketing plan
A written document that acts as a guidebook of marketing activities for the marketing manager.

FAQs

It takes too long to write a detailed marketing plan. Can I get away with a brief outline? Find out by watching the video FAQ on Xtra!

WRITING THE MARKETING PLAN

The creation and implementation of a complete marketing plan will allow the organization to achieve marketing objectives and succeed. However, the marketing plan is only as good as the information it contains and the effort, creativity, and thought that went into its creation. Having a good marketing information system and a wealth of competitive intelligence (covered in Chapter 8) is critical to a thorough and accurate situation analysis. The role of managerial intuition is also important in the creation and selection of marketing strategies. Managers must weigh any information against its accuracy and their own judgment when making a marketing decision.

Note that the overall structure of the marketing plan (Exhibit 2.1) should not be viewed as a series of sequential planning steps. Many of the marketing plan elements are decided on simultaneously and in conjunction with one another. Similarly, the summary sample marketing plan (Exhibit 2.2) does not begin to cover the intricacies and detail of a full marketing plan. Further, every marketing plan has a different content, depending on the organization, its mission, objectives, targets, and marketing mix components. Visualize how the marketing plan in Exhibit 2.2 would differ if the firm offered only wireless communication connectivity services (not the physical products). How would the plan differ if the target market consisted of *Fortune* 500 firms with large sales forces instead of executives?

The marketing plan outline in the Appendix (pages 65–67) is an expanded set of questions that can guide the formulation of a marketing plan. However, this outline should not be regarded as the only correct format for a marketing plan. Many organizations have their own distinctive format or terminology for

EXHIBIT 2.2

Sample Summary Marketing Plan

Business Mission	Ultracel is in the business of providing advanced communications technology and communications convenience to mobile users.
Marketing Objective	To achieve 20 percent, in dollar volume, of the wireless telephone market by year-end, 2006.
Situation Analysis	
Strengths	Well-funded organization, highly skilled workforce with low turnover, excellent relationships with suppliers, product differential and sustainable competitive advantage of patented color screen and Internet connectivity.
Weaknesses	Company name not well known, small firm with no manufacturing cost advantages, no long-term contracts with distributors, inexperience in the wireless communications market.
Opportunities	Explosive growth of wireless phone users, worldwide acceptance of cellular technology, newly expanded digital networks.
Threats	Heavy competition; technology is incompatible with current analog systems; not everyone can afford the systems, potential governmental regulation.
Target Market Selection	Young, mobile executives in North America and Europe, with incomes over $200,000 per year; frequent travelers; computer-dependent individuals.
Marketing Mix	
Product	Personal digital telephone. Brand name: Ultracel-4000. Features: simultaneous voice/data communication, Internet access, operation within buildings, linkups to data subscription and e-mail services, computer data storage, color screen, lightweight, 500-hour battery, 3-year unlimited warranty on parts and labor, 24-hour technical support, leather or titanium carrying case.
Place	Available through electronics retailers, upscale computer retailers, or via Web order company direct; products transported via airplane and temperature-controlled motor carrier.
Promotion	Fifty manufacturer's representatives for selling force, with 25 percent commissions; advertising in print media, Internet Web sites, cable television, and outdoor billboards; sales promotion in the form of introductory product rebates, technology trade shows; public relations efforts to news media and sponsorship of world-championship sporting events.
Price	Retail price of $299; assuming mild price sensitivity and future price wars. Lease option available; corporate discounts of 20 percent for volume purchases.
Implementation	First quarter: Complete marketing research on price, design promotional campaign, sign contracts with manufacturer's reps. Second quarter: Public relations campaign, product introduction at trade shows, rollout of advertising. Third quarter: Test market international markets.

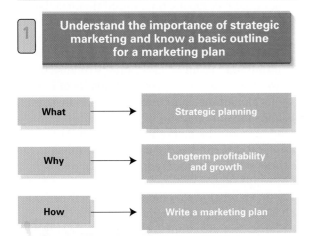

1. Understand the importance of strategic marketing and know a basic outline for a marketing plan

What	→	Strategic planning
Why	→	Longterm profitability and growth
How	→	Write a marketing plan

creating a marketing plan. Every marketing plan should be unique to the firm for which it was created. Remember that although the format and order of presentation should be flexible, the same types of questions and topic areas should be covered in any marketing plan.

As you can see by the extent of the marketing plan outline in the Appendix, creating a complete marketing plan is not a simple or quick effort. However, it can be instructive to create summary marketing plans such as the sample summary plan shown in Exhibit 2.2 to get a quick idea of what a firm's marketing strategy is all about.

2 DEFINING THE BUSINESS MISSION

Develop an appropriate business mission statement

FAQs

Are there really any implications of having a poorly-stated mission statement? Find out by watching the video FAQ on Xtra!

mission statement
A statement of the firm's business based on a careful analysis of benefits sought by present and potential customers and analysis of existing and anticipated environmental conditions.

marketing myopia
Defining a business in terms of goods and services rather than in terms of the benefits that customers seek.

The foundation of any marketing plan is the firm's **mission statement,** which answers the question, "What business are we in?" Business mission definition profoundly affects the firm's long-run resource allocation, profitability, and survival. The mission statement is based on a careful analysis of benefits sought by present and potential customers and analysis of existing and anticipated environmental conditions. The firm's mission statement establishes boundaries for all subsequent decisions, objectives, and strategies. The American Marketing Association's mission statement is shown in Exhibit 2.3.

A mission statement should focus on the market or markets the organization is attempting to serve rather than on the good or service offered. Otherwise, a new technology may quickly make the good or service obsolete and the mission statement irrelevant to company functions. Business mission statements that are stated too narrowly suffer from **marketing myopia**—defining a business in terms of goods and services rather than in terms of the benefits that customers seek. In this context, *myopia* means narrow, short-term thinking. For example, Frito-Lay defines its mission as being in the snack-food business rather than in the corn chip business. The mission of sports teams is not just to play games but to serve the interests of the fans. AT&T does not sell telephones or long-distance services; it markets communications technology.

Alternatively, business missions may be stated too broadly. "To provide products of superior quality and value that improve the lives of the world's consumers" is probably too broad a mission statement for any firm except Procter & Gamble. Care must be taken when stating what business a firm is in. For example, the

EXHIBIT 2.3

American Marketing Association's Mission Statement

The American Marketing Association is an international professional organization for people involved in the practice, study, and teaching of marketing. Our principal roles are:

- To always understand and satisfy the needs of marketers so as to provide them with products and services that will help them be better marketers.
- To empower marketers through information, education, relationships, and resources that will enrich their professional development and careers.
- To advance the thought, application, and ethical practice of marketing.

SOURCE: http://www.marketingpower.com/about/ama/mission/, November 1, 2004.

2 Develop an appropriate business mission statement

Q: What business are we in?

A: Business mission statement

    → Too narrow → marketing myopia

        Too broad → no direction

        Just right → focus on markets served and benefits customers seek

strategic business unit (SBU)
A subgroup of a single business or collection of related businesses within the larger organization.

marketing objective
A statement of what is to be accomplished through marketing activities.

mission of Ben & Jerry's centers on three important aspects of its ice cream business: (1) Product: "To make, distribute and sell the finest quality all natural ice cream and related products in a wide variety of innovative flavors made from Vermont Dairy products;" (2) Economic: "To operate the company on a sound financial basis of profitable growth, increasing value for our shareholders, and creating career opportunities and financial rewards for our employees;" and (3) Social: "To operate the company in a way that actively recognizes the central role that business plays in the structure of society by initiating innovative ways to improve the quality of life of a broad community—local, national, and international."[6] By correctly stating the business mission in terms of the benefits that customers seek, the foundation for the marketing plan is set. Many companies are focusing on designing more appropriate mission statements because these statements are frequently displayed on the World Wide Web.

The organization may need to define a mission statement and objectives for a **strategic business unit (SBU)**, which is a subgroup of a single business or collection of related businesses within the larger organization. A properly defined SBU should have a distinct mission and specific target market, control over its resources, its own competitors, and plans independent of the other SBUs in the organization. Thus, a large firm such as Kraft General Foods may have marketing plans for each of its SBUs, which include breakfast foods, desserts, pet foods, and beverages.

SETTING MARKETING PLAN OBJECTIVES

Describe the criteria for stating good marketing objectives

Before the details of a marketing plan can be developed, objectives for the plan must be stated. Without objectives, there is no basis for measuring the success of marketing plan activities. For example, in 2001, Hewlett-Packard's net income was $408 million—an 89 percent one-year growth rate. Sales and the number of employees also grew during this period. Sounds great, doesn't it? Actually, these figures failed to meet objectives, and in 2002, H-P executives were denied their bonuses.[7]

A **marketing objective** is a statement of what is to be accomplished through marketing activities. To be useful, stated objectives should meet several criteria. First, objectives should be realistic, measurable, and time specific. It is tempting to state that the objective is "to be the best marketer of ferret food." However, what is "best" for one firm might be sales of one million pounds of ferret food per year, and to another firm, "best" might mean dominant market share. It may also be unrealistic for start-up firms or new products to command dominant market share, given other competitors in the marketplace. Finally, by what time should the objective be met? A more realistic objective would be "To achieve 10 percent dollar market share in the specialty pet food market within 12 months of product introduction."

Second, objectives must also be consistent with and indicate the priorities of the organization. Specifically, objectives flow from the business mission statement to the rest of the marketing plan.

© AP/WIDE WORLD PHOTOS

Facing increased competition in the toy market from general retailers like Wal-Mart and Target, Toys "R" Us is increasingly relying on contributions to the company's bottom line from its SBUs. Baby's "R" Us created the first one-stop shopping venue for infant needs and has become the biggest money-maker for Toys "R" Us.

EXHIBIT 2.4

Examples of Marketing Objectives

Poorly Stated Objectives	Well-Stated Objectives
Our objective is to be a leader in the industry in terms of new-product development.	Our objective is to spend 12 percent of sales revenue between 2005 and 2006 on research and development in an effort to introduce at least five new products in 2006.
Our objective is to maximize profits.	Our objective is to achieve a 10 percent return on investment during 2005, with a payback on new investments of no longer than four years.
Our objective is to better serve customers.	Our objective is to obtain customer satisfaction ratings of at least 90 percent on the 2005 annual customer satisfaction survey, and to retain at least 85 percent of our 2005 customers as repeat purchasers in 2006.
Our objective is to be the best that we can be.	Our objective is to increase market share from 30 percent to 40 percent in 2005 by increasing promotional expenditures by 14 percent.

REVIEW LEARNING OBJECTIVE 3

3 **Describe the criteria for stating good marketing objectives**

Realistic, measureable, and time-specific objectives consistent with the firm's objectives:

1. Communicate marketing manangement philosophy

2. Provide management direction

3. Motivate employees

4. Force executives to think clearly

5. Allow for better evaluation of results

FAQs

How can a company identify its own strengths, weaknesses, opportunities and threats without being very biased? Find out by watching the video FAQ on Xtra!

Exhibit 2.4 shows some well-stated and poorly stated objectives. Notice how well they do or do not meet the above criteria.

Carefully specified objectives serve several functions. First, they communicate marketing management philosophies and provide direction for lower-level marketing managers so that marketing efforts are integrated and pointed in a consistent direction. Objectives also serve as motivators by creating something for employees to strive for. When objectives are attainable and challenging, they motivate those charged with achieving the objectives. Additionally, the process of writing specific objectives forces executives to clarify their thinking. Finally, objectives form a basis for control; the effectiveness of a plan can be gauged in light of the stated objectives.

4 CONDUCTING A SITUATION ANALYSIS

Explain the components of a situation analysis

Before specific marketing activities can be defined, marketers must understand the current and potential environment that the product or service will be marketed in. A situation analysis is sometimes referred to as a **SWOT analysis**; that is, the firm should identify its internal strengths (S) and weaknesses (W) and also examine external opportunities (O) and threats (T).

When examining internal strengths and weaknesses, the marketing manager should focus on organizational resources such as production costs, marketing skills, financial resources, company or brand image, employee capabilities, and available technology. For example, a potential weakness for AirTran Airways (formerly Valu-Jet) is the age of its airplane fleet, which could project an image of danger or low quality. Other weaknesses include high labor turnover rates and limited flights.

SWOT analysis
Identifying internal strengths (S) and weaknesses (W) and also examining external opportunities (O) and threats (T).

Explain the components of a situation analysis

| I N T E R N A L | **Strengths**
• production costs
• marketing skills
• financial resources
• image
• technology
Weaknesses |
| E X T E R N A L | **Opportunities**
• social
• demographic
• economic
• technological
• political/legal
• competitive
Threats |

A potential strength is the low operating costs of the airline, which translate into lower prices for consumers. Another issue to consider in this section of the marketing plan is the historical background of the firm—its sales and profit history.

When examining external opportunities and threats, marketing managers must analyze aspects of the marketing environment. This process is called **environmental scanning**—the collection and interpretation of information about forces, events, and relationships in the external environment that may affect the future of the organization or the implementation of the marketing plan. Environmental scanning helps identify market opportunities and threats and provides guidelines for the design of marketing strategy. The six most often studied macroenvironmental forces are social, demographic, economic, technological, political and legal, and competitive. These forces are examined in detail in Chapter 3. For example, H&R Block, a tax preparation service, benefits from complex changes in tax codes that motivate citizens to have their tax returns prepared by a professional. Alternatively, tax-simplification or flat-tax plans would allow people to easily prepare their own returns.

5 COMPETITIVE ADVANTAGE

Identify sources of competitive advantage

Performing a SWOT analysis allows firms to identify their competitive advantage. A **competitive advantage** is a set of unique features of a company and its products that are perceived by the target market as significant and superior to the competition. It is the factor or factors that cause customers to patronize a firm and not the competition. There are three types of competitive advantages: cost, product/service differentiation, and niche strategies.

COST COMPETITIVE ADVANTAGE

Cost leadership can result from obtaining inexpensive raw materials, creating an efficient scale of plant operations, designing products for ease of manufacture, controlling overhead costs, and avoiding marginal customers. DuPont, for example, has an exceptional cost competitive advantage in the production of titanium dioxide. Technicians created a production process using low-cost feedstock, giving DuPont a 20 percent cost advantage over its competitors. The cheaper feedstock technology is complex and can be accomplished only by investing about $100 million and several years of testing time, however. Having a **cost competitive advantage** means being the low-cost competitor in an industry while maintaining satisfactory profit margins.

A cost competitive advantage enables a firm to deliver superior customer value. Chaparral Steel, for example, is the leading low-cost U.S. steel producer because it uses only scrap iron and steel and a very efficient continuous-casting process to make new steel. In fact, Chaparral is so efficient that it is the only U.S. steel producer that ships to Japan.

Costs can be reduced in a variety of ways.

- *Experience curves:* **Experience curves** tell us that costs decline at a predictable rate as experience with a product increases. The experience curve effect encompasses a broad range of manufacturing, marketing, and administrative costs. Experience curves reflect learning by doing, technological advances, and economies of scale. Firms like Boeing and Texas Instruments use historical experience curves as a basis for predicting and setting prices. Experience

environmental scanning
Collection and interpretation of information about forces, events, and relationships in the external environment that may affect the future of the organization or the implementation of the marketing plan.

competitive advantage
The set of unique features of a company and its products that are perceived by the target market as significant and superior to the competition.

cost competitive advantage
Being the low-cost competitor in an industry while maintaining satisfactory profit margins.

experience curves
Curves that show costs declining at a predictable rate as experience with a product increases.

© AP/WIDE WORLD PHOTOS

One way companies can create competitive advantage through cost leadership is by reducing labor costs. Increasingly in the toy industry, this labor reduction comes from outsourcing manufacturing operations. Mattel, the brand holder of Barbie dolls and related products, makes around 4.23 million Barbie dolls annually at this factory in China's Guangdong Province, or 35 percent of the global Barbie production.

curves allow management to forecast costs and set prices based on anticipated costs as opposed to current costs.

- *Efficient labor:* Labor costs can be an important component of total costs in low-skill, labor-intensive industries such as product assembly and apparel manufacturing. Many U.S. manufacturers such as Nike, Levi Strauss, and Liz Claiborne have gone offshore to achieve cheaper manufacturing costs. Many American companies are also outsourcing activities such as data entry and other labor-intensive jobs.

- *No-frills goods and services:* Marketers can lower costs by removing frills and options from a product or service. Southwest Airlines, for example, offers low fares but no seat assignments or meals. Low prices give Southwest a higher load factor and greater economies of scale, which, in turn, mean even lower prices such as Southwest's "Friends Fly Free" promotions.

- **GLOBAL** *Government subsidies:* Governments may provide grants and interest-free loans to target industries. Such government assistance enabled Japanese semiconductor manufacturers to become global leaders.

- **GLOBAL** *Product design:* Cutting-edge design technology can help offset high labor costs. BMW is a world leader in designing cars for ease of manufacture and assembly. Reverse engineering—the process of disassembling a product piece by piece to learn its components and obtain clues as to the manufacturing process—can also mean savings. Reverse engineering a low-cost competitor's product can save research and design costs. Japanese engineers have reversed many products, such as computer chips, coming out of Silicon Valley.

- *Reengineering:* Reengineering entails fundamental rethinking and redesign of business processes to achieve dramatic improvements in critical measures of performance. It often involves reorganizing from functional departments such as sales, engineering, and production to cross-disciplinary teams.

- *Production innovations:* Production innovations such as new technology and simplified production techniques help lower the average cost of production. Technologies such as computer-aided design and computer-aided manufacturing (CAD/CAM) and increasingly sophisticated robots help companies like Boeing, Ford, and General Electric reduce their manufacturing costs.

- *New methods of service delivery:* Medical expenses have been substantially lowered by the use of outpatient surgery and walk-in clinics. Airlines, such as Delta, are lowering reservation and ticketing costs by encouraging passengers to use the Internet to book flights and by providing self-check-in kiosks at the airport.

PRODUCT/SERVICE DIFFERENTIATION COMPETITIVE ADVANTAGE

Because cost competitive advantages are subject to continual erosion, product/service differentiation tends to provide a longer lasting competitive advantage. The durability of this strategy tends to make it more attractive to many top managers. A **product/service differentiation competitive advantage** exists when a firm provides something unique that is valuable to buyers beyond simply offering a low price. Examples include brand names (Lexus), a strong dealer network (Caterpillar Tractor for construction work), product reliability (Maytag appliances), image (Neiman Marcus in retailing), or service (FedEx). A great example of a company that has a strong product/service competitive advantage is Dell, Inc. Dell takes orders straight from customers and builds each customer's personal computer to demand. This means that the customers get exactly what they want.

Dell also gives its customers fast, convenient service that other companies can't match, including three-day delivery of PCs with all their custom software preloaded. No other computer company has been able to do what Dell does.[8]

NICHE COMPETITIVE ADVANTAGE

A **niche competitive advantage** seeks to target and effectively serve a single segment of the market (see Chapter 7). For small companies with limited resources that potentially face giant competitors, niching may be the only viable option. A market segment that has good growth potential but is not crucial to the success of major competitors is a good candidate for developing a niche strategy.

Many companies using a niche strategy serve only a limited geographic market. Buddy Freddy's is a very successful restaurant chain but is found only in Florida. Migros is the dominant grocery chain in Switzerland. It has no stores outside that small country.

Block Drug Company uses niching by focusing its product line on tooth products. It markets Polident to clean false teeth, Poligrip to hold false teeth, and Sensodyne toothpaste for persons with sensitive teeth. The Orvis Company manufactures and sells everything that anyone might ever need for fly fishing. Orvis is a very successful nicher.

BUILDING SUSTAINABLE COMPETITIVE ADVANTAGE

The key to having a competitive advantage is the ability to sustain that advantage. A **sustainable competitive advantage** is one that cannot be copied by the competition. Dell, Inc., discussed earlier, is a good example of a company that has a sustainable competitive advantage. Others include Rolex (high-quality watches), Nordstrom department stores (service), and Southwest Airlines (low price). In contrast, when Datril was introduced into the pain-reliever market, it was touted as being exactly like Tylenol, only cheaper. Tylenol responded by lowering its price, thus destroying Datril's competitive advantage and ability to remain on the market. In this case, low price was not a sustainable competitive advantage. Without a competitive advantage, target customers don't perceive any reason to patronize an organization instead of its competitors. The "Ethics in Marketing" box describes what is happening in the deregulated electric utility market in Texas as companies try to gain competitive advantage using price.

The notion of competitive advantage means that a successful firm will stake out a position unique in some manner from its rivals. Imitation of competitors indicates a lack of competitive advantage and almost ensures mediocre performance. Moreover, competitors rarely stand still, so it is not surprising that imitation causes managers to feel trapped in a seemingly endless game of catch-up. They are regularly surprised by the new accomplishments of their rivals.

Companies need to build their own competitive advantages rather than copy a competitor. The sources of tomorrow's competitive advantages are the skills and

product/service differentiation competitive advantage
The provision of something that is unique and valuable to buyers beyond simply offering a lower price than the competition's.

niche competitive advantage
The advantage achieved when a firm seeks to target and effectively serve a small segment of the market.

sustainable competitive advantage
An advantage that cannot be copied by the competition.

ETHICS IN MARKETING

> COMPETITION HEATS UP FOR TEXAS UTILITIES

Two years after Texas's electricity market was deregulated, competition among rival electric utility companies is heating up. TXU Energy, bashed by competitors' advertising for raising rates twice in one year, sent letters to their customers telling them about "lower pricing for TXU Energy Customers." The letter stated that beginning November 1, 2003, TXU's average rates would drop from 10.2 cents per kilowatt-hour to 8.9 cents. Actually, the lower rate from November through May was automatic, left over from the old regulated system that required TXU and other monopoly utilities to charge higher rates during warmer months, when air conditioners increase demand and costs, and lower their rates during cooler months, when residential usage typically falls.

TXU's letter did not mention that the rates of its main competitor in North Texas, Reliant Resources of Houston, would also be lowered, to 8.3 cents per kilowatt-hour. Neither did it point out that the rates would go back up in May or June. TXU says that its competitors are comparing TXU's peak prices with their own year-round prices—a tactic that TXU claims is not fair. The so-called summer peak rate is the rate most commonly referred to in media reports—and now advertising—as a utility's standard rate.

The letter was the first step in TXU's marketing campaign to counter its competitors' pricing.

Competitors, whose advertising has reminded TXU customers of the utility's two recent rate increases, are crying foul at TXU's letter. They argue that TXU is, in the words of Pat Hammond of Reliant Resources, "comparing apples and oranges" when it implies that rates have fallen. TXU executives have identified Reliant as their chief rival in the Fort Worth–Dallas market, TXU's home turf. Reliant has taken about 100,000 customers from TXU since deregulation opened the market.

This new aggressiveness contrasts sharply with the marketing in 2002, the first year of deregulation, when rivals rarely mentioned one another. Carl Bracy, TXU's senior vice president for residential and small business marketing, notes, "We're trying to feel our way along in developing marketing strategies. We have to focus on providing value for the customer. I'm disappointed that some of our competitors now seek to address TXU directly rather than talking about what they can do for customers."[9]

Do you think TXU's pricing and advertising strategies are ethical? What about its competitors' strategies? Defend your answer.

REVIEW LEARNING OBJECTIVE 5

5 | **Identify sources of competitive advantage**

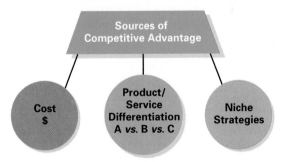

To create sustainable competitive advantage, don't copy someone else, build your own:

Sources of Competitive Advantage

- **Cost $**
- **Product/ Service Differentiation A vs. B vs. C**
- **Niche Strategies**

assets of the organization. Assets include patents, copyrights, locations, and equipment and technology that are superior to those of the competition. Skills are functions such as customer service and promotion that the firm performs better than its competitors. Travelocity, for example, is known for its ease of online travel reservations. Marketing managers should continually focus the firm's skills and assets on sustaining and creating competitive advantages.

Remember, a sustainable competitive advantage is a function of the speed with which competitors can imitate a leading company's strategy and plans. Imitation requires a competitor to identify the leader's competitive advantage, determine how it is achieved, and then learn how to duplicate it.

6 STRATEGIC DIRECTIONS

Identify strategic alternatives

The end result of the SWOT analysis and identification of a competitive advantage is to evaluate the strategic direction of the firm. Selecting a strategic alternative is the next step in marketing planning.

STRATEGIC ALTERNATIVES

To discover a marketing opportunity, management must know how to identify the alternatives. One method for developing alternatives is Ansoff's strategic opportunity matrix (see Exhibit 2.5), which matches products with markets. Firms can explore these four options:

- *Market penetration:* A firm using the **market penetration** alternative would try to increase market share among existing customers. If Kraft General Foods started a major campaign for Maxwell House coffee, with aggressive advertising and cents-off coupons to existing customers, it would be following a penetration strategy. McDonald's sold the most Happy Meals in history with a promotion that included Ty's Teeny Beanie Babies. Customer databases, discussed in Chapters 8 and 20, help managers implement this strategy.
- *Market development:* **Market development** means attracting new customers to existing products. Ideally, new uses for old products stimulate additional sales among existing customers while also bringing in new buyers. McDonald's, for example, has opened restaurants in Russia, China, and Italy and is eagerly expanding into Eastern European countries. Coca-Cola and Pepsi have faster growth in their new foreign markets than at home. In the nonprofit area, the growing emphasis on continuing education and executive development by colleges and universities is a market development strategy.
- *Product development:* A **product development** strategy entails the creation of new products for present markets. Dell added four printers for home and business use, as well as replacement ink cartridges and toner, to its product mix. Coach, a company whose core product is fashionable handbags, has radically expanded its products to include gloves, jewelry, watches, men's and women's apparel and footwear, and luggage.[11]

    Managers following the product development strategy can rely on their extensive knowledge of the target audience. They usually have a good feel for what customers like and dislike about current products and what existing needs are not being met. In addition, managers can rely on established distribution channels.
- *Diversification:* **Diversification** is a strategy of increasing sales by introducing new products into new markets. For example, LTV Corporation, a steel producer, diversified into the monorail business. Sony practiced a diversification

---

Marketing... in Entertainment

Hallmark of Successful Marketing

In December 1951, Hallmark, the creator and manufacturer of greeting cards, stationery, and gifts, began sponsoring its Hall of Fame signature series of television films. Hallmark films soon earned a reputation for high quality and dedication to family-oriented programming. Hallmark was the first sponsor to receive an Emmy award, and since its inception, its series of telefilms has won a record 78 Emmys. A quarter of all Academy Award–winning actors have appeared in Hallmark productions. But Hallmark has recently changed from a product development strategy (making high-quality telefilms) to a market development strategy (developing new customers for its established telefilm series). In conjunction with Crown Media, Hallmark launched the Hallmark Channel on cable and satellite television. More recently, Hallmark has decided to scale back advertising (from 12 minutes per hour to 4) and offer title sponsorships instead. For example, a Hallmark telefilm sponsored by DaimlerChrysler would be called a "Chrysler Movie Event." Chrysler would buy the four minutes of available advertising per hour and be allowed product placement in the film. As a sponsor, Chrysler would also potentially benefit from cross-platform opportunities, such as the opportunity for placements in Hallmark's Gold Crown stores and its Gold Crown mailer that goes out to 144 million people each month. Although still in the sponsorship game, Hallmark is now at the other end.[10]

---

market penetration
A marketing strategy that tries to increase market share among existing customers.

market development
A marketing strategy that entails attracting new customers to existing products.

product development
A marketing strategy that entails the creation of new products for current customers.

diversification
A strategy of increasing sales by introducing new products into new markets.

EXHIBIT 2.5

Ansoff's Strategic Opportunity Matrix

	Present Product	New Product
Present Market	**Market penetration:** McDonald's sells more Happy Meals with Disney movie promotions.	**Product development:** McDonald's introduces salad shakers and McWater.
New Market	**Market development:** McDonald's opens restaurants in China.	**Diversification:** McDonald's introduces line of children's clothing.

heavily moisturized hair without the heavily part. Dove shampoos and conditioners, with Weightless Moisturizers, leave hair smooth without weighing it down. Moisture and lift—the best of both worlds.

COURTESY OF UNILEVER PHOTOGRAPH BY ROBIN BROADBENT

Companies pursue a product development strategy when they create new products for present markets. Dove has leveraged what it knows about its customers and created new moisturizing shampoos and conditioners.

strategy when it acquired Columbia Pictures; although motion pictures are not a new product in the marketplace, it was a new product for Sony. Coca-Cola manufactures and markets water-treatment and water-conditioning equipment, which has been a very challenging task for the traditional soft drink company. A diversification strategy can be risky when a firm is entering unfamiliar markets. On the other hand, it can be very profitable when a firm is entering markets with little or no competition.

SELECTING A STRATEGIC ALTERNATIVE

Selecting which alternative to pursue depends on the overall company philosophy and culture. The choice also depends on the tool used to make the decision. Companies generally have one of two philosophies about when they expect profits. They either pursue profits right away or first seek to increase market share and then pursue profits. In the long run, market share and profitability are compatible goals.

Many companies have long followed this credo: Build market share, and profits will surely follow. Historically, this was true for Detroit automakers, who consistently sacrificed short-term profits to achieve market share (e.g., high-dollar incentives to increase sales of new cars). Under the leadership of Bill Ford, however, Ford Motor has abandoned its quest for dominant market share. In a departure from the status quo, Ford now stresses profitability by selling fewer cars at higher prices using fewer incentives.[12] The "Global Perspectives" box describes the strategy used by Chinese electronics maker SVA to enter the U.S. market.

REVIEW LEARNING OBJECTIVE 6

6	**Identify strategic alternatives**

Market development	= ↑ customers
Market penetration	= ↑ share
Product development	= ↑ products
Diversification	= ↑ new products + ↑ new markets

> CAN CHINESE BRANDS MAKE IT ABROAD?

Chinese companies, dominating global manufacturing because of their low-cost labor, supply the world's biggest brands and retailers' private labels with products ranging from toys to televisions. But the Chinese government is now encouraging some of the biggest companies to sell their own branded products abroad for several reasons: the Chinese market is highly competitive and puts constant pressure on prices; branded products can be more profitable than OEM (original-equipment manufacturer) products; and competing in foreign markets forces companies to innovate and improve, helping them to shed their image as producers of cheap goods.

The Chinese companies that have a track record in low-cost, high-quality manufacturing and show marketing savvy on the local level are most likely to succeed in establishing brands in overseas markets. In general, Chinese manufacturers have relied on a fully integrated model in the domestic market. They start by using foreign technology and then try to develop their own technology and products. Most of these companies have their own distribution networks and large, cheap sales forces. Attempting to use this model in developed markets would be expensive, time consuming, and/or beyond the skills of management. The Chinese have no overseas distribution channels or service networks, little promotional or advertising knowledge, and limited pricing skills.

For the last two years, SVA, a Shanghai-based electronics company, has marketed its branded products, such as the plasma televisions it sells in U.S. retail chains like Costco Wholesale. The company mass-produces quality products at low cost and now records annual sales of $4 billion.

SVA made several important choices when it entered the U.S. market. First, it decided to rely largely on distributors that offer promotion and service assistance to manufacturers. This strategy gives the company a chance to learn about the U.S. market and the time to develop its own overseas marketing capabilities.

Second, SVA chose to work with distributors on trade-level promotional activities, including attendance at industry conferences, rather than spend millions of dollars to build brand awareness. Distributors find SVA attractive because it enables them to offer customers low-cost products.

Third, the company decided to avoid the low-end color TV market where it would have faced intense competition from other Chinese companies selling on an OEM basis. Instead, it put its efforts into upmarket products such as plasma displays and TFT-LCD monitors and televisions. Sales of these products are growing quickly and they face relatively little competition from other Chinese companies. SVA wants to be perceived as providing products that offer value for the money to technology-savvy customers who are not put off by the absence of well-known brand names.

Finally, SVA recognized from the start that it needed a local team to run its U.S. business. Besides recruiting U.S.-based executives and giving them an equity stake in the venture, it hired former Sony production managers from Japan to help it control its manufacturing quality and is working with international firms to improve the design of its offerings. Consumer focus groups help the company refine its product lineup for the U.S. market. The result has been some initial sales success, with 2003 revenue expected to reach $80 million.[13]

What is SVA's competitive advantage? What strategic alternative is SVA using to grow its business?

7 DESCRIBING THE TARGET MARKET

Discuss target market strategies

Marketing strategy involves the activities of selecting and describing one or more target markets and developing and maintaining a marketing mix that will produce mutually satisfying exchanges with target markets.

marketing strategy
The activities of selecting and describing one or more target markets and developing and maintaining a marketing mix that will produce mutually satisfying exchanges with target markets.

TARGET MARKET STRATEGY

A market segment is a group of individuals or organizations that share one or more characteristics. They therefore may have relatively similar product needs. For example, parents of newborn babies need products such as formula, diapers, and special foods. The target market strategy identifies the market segment or segments on which to focus. This process begins with a **market opportunity analysis (MOA)**—the description and estimation of the size and sales potential of market segments that are of interest to the firm and the assessment of key competitors in these market segments. After the firm describes the market seg-

market opportunity analysis (MOA)
The description and estimation of the size and sales potential of market segments that are of interest to the firm and the assessment of key competitors in these market segments.

While traditional clothing lines and retailers are seeing only modest sales gains, Quiksilver, a specialty retailer targeting youths lured by the look of skateboarders and surfers, has been riding a wave of hot sales. Following a niche strategy has enabled Quiksilver to target and effectively serve a single segment of the market.

ments, it may target one or more of them. There are three general strategies for selecting target markets. Target market(s) can be selected by appealing to the entire market with one marketing mix, concentrating on one segment, or appealing to multiple market segments using multiple marketing mixes. The characteristics, advantages, and disadvantages of each strategic option are examined in Chapter 7. Target markets could be smokers who are concerned about white teeth (the target of Topol toothpaste), people concerned about sugar and calories in their soft drinks (Diet Pepsi), or college students needing inexpensive about-town transportation (Yamaha Razz scooter).

Any market segment that is targeted must be fully described. Demographics, psychographics, and buyer behavior should be assessed. Buyer behavior is covered in Chapters 5 and 6. If segments are differentiated by ethnicity, multicultural aspects of the marketing mix should be examined. (A comprehensive module on multicultural marketing is on Xtra!.) If the target market is international, it is especially important to describe differences in culture, economic and technological development, and political structure that may affect the marketing plan. Global marketing is covered in more detail in Chapter 4.

REVIEW LEARNING OBJECTIVE 7

7 | **Discuss target market strategies**

Target Market Options

Entire Market	Multiple Markets	Single Market

8 THE MARKETING MIX

Describe the elements of the marketing mix

marketing mix
A unique blend of product, place, promotion, and pricing strategies designed to produce mutually satisfying exchanges with a target market.

four Ps
Product, place, promotion, and price, which together make up the marketing mix.

The term **marketing mix** refers to a unique blend of product, place (distribution), promotion, and pricing strategies (often referred to as the **four Ps**) designed to produce mutually satisfying exchanges with a target market. The marketing manager can control each component of the marketing mix, but the strategies for all four components must be blended to achieve optimal results. Any marketing mix is only as good as its weakest component. For example, the first pump toothpastes were distributed over cosmetic counters and failed. Not until pump toothpastes were distributed the same way as tube toothpastes did the products succeed. The best promotion and the lowest price cannot save a poor product. Similarly, excellent products with poor placing, pricing, or promotion will likely fail.

Successful marketing mixes have been carefully designed to satisfy target markets. At first glance, McDonald's and Wendy's may appear to have roughly identical marketing mixes because they are both in the fast-food hamburger business. However, McDonald's has been most successful with targeting parents with young children for lunchtime meals, whereas Wendy's targets the adult crowd for lunches and dinner. McDonald's has playgrounds, Ronald McDonald the clown, and children's Happy Meals. Wendy's has salad bars, carpeted restaurants, and no playgrounds.

Variations in marketing mixes do not occur by chance. Astute marketing managers devise marketing strategies to gain advantages over competitors and best serve the needs and wants of a particular target market segment. By manipulating elements of the marketing mix, marketing managers can fine-tune the customer offering and achieve competitive success.

PRODUCT STRATEGIES

Typically, the marketing mix starts with the product "P." The heart of the marketing mix, the starting point, is the product offering and product strategy. It is hard to design a place strategy, decide on a promotion campaign, or set a price without knowing the product to be marketed.

The product includes not only the physical unit but also its package, warranty, after-sale service, brand name, company image, value, and many other factors. A Godiva chocolate has many product elements: the chocolate itself, a fancy gold wrapper, a customer satisfaction guarantee, and the prestige of the Godiva brand name. We buy things not only for what they do (benefits) but also for what they mean to us (status, quality, or reputation).

Products can be tangible goods such as computers, ideas like those offered by a consultant, or services such as medical care. Products should also offer customer value. Product decisions are covered in Chapters 9 and 10, and services marketing is detailed in Chapter 11.

PLACE (DISTRIBUTION) STRATEGIES

Place, or distribution, strategies are concerned with making products available when and where customers want them. Would you rather buy a kiwi fruit at the 24-hour grocery store within walking distance or fly to Australia to pick your own? A part of this place "P" is physical distribution, which involves all the business activities concerned with storing and transporting raw materials or finished products. The goal is to make sure products arrive in usable condition at designated places when needed. Place strategies are covered in Chapters 12 and 13.

PROMOTION STRATEGIES

Promotion includes advertising, public relations, sales promotion, and personal selling. Promotion's role in the marketing mix is to bring about mutually satisfying exchanges with target markets by informing, educating, persuading, and reminding them of the benefits of an organization or a product. A good promotion strategy, like using the Dilbert character in a national promotion strategy for Office Depot, can dramatically increase sales. Good promotion strategies do not guaran-

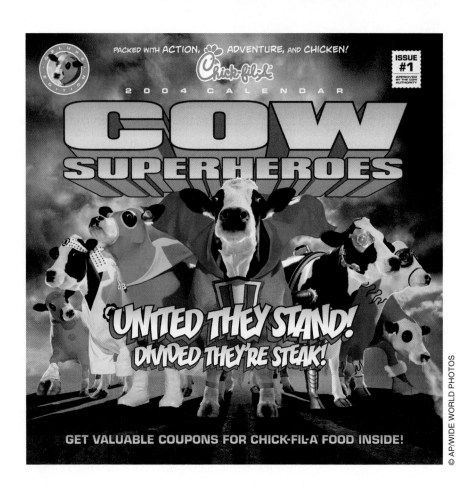

GET VALUABLE COUPONS FOR CHICK-FIL-A FOOD INSIDE!

The role of promotion is to inform, persuade, and remind. Chik-Fil-A's popular "Eat Mor Chikin" cows have been the subject of outdoor advertising, television advertising, and even a yearly calendar that contains over $20 worth of coupons for free food.

Describe the elements of the marketing mix

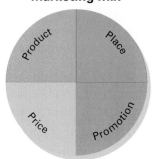

Marketing Mix

tee success, however. Despite massive promotional campaigns, the movies *The Alamo* and *The Ladykillers* had disappointing box-office returns. Each element of the promotion "P" is coordinated and managed with the others to create a promotional blend or mix. These integrated marketing communications activities are described in Chapters 14, 15, and 16. Technology-driven aspects of promotional marketing are covered in Chapters 19 and 20.

PRICING STRATEGIES

Price is what a buyer must give up to obtain a product. It is often the most flexible of the four marketing mix elements—the quickest element to change. Marketers can raise or lower prices more frequently and easily than they can change other marketing mix variables. Price is an important competitive weapon and is very important to the organization because price multiplied by the number of units sold equals total revenue for the firm. Pricing decisions are covered in Chapters 17 and 18.

 FOLLOWING UP ON THE MARKETING PLAN

Explain why implementation, evaluation, and control of the marketing plan are necessary

IMPLEMENTATION

Implementation is the process that turns marketing plans into action assignments and ensures that these assignments are executed in a way that accomplishes the plans' objectives. Implementation activities may involve detailed job assignments, activity descriptions, timelines, budgets, and lots of communication. Although implementation is essentially "doing what you said you were going to do," many organizations repeatedly experience failures in strategy implementation. Brilliant marketing plans are doomed to fail if they are not properly implemented. These detailed communications may or may not be part of the written marketing plan. If they are not part of the plan, they should be specified elsewhere as soon as the plan has been communicated.

EVALUATION AND CONTROL

After a marketing plan is implemented, it should be evaluated. **Evaluation** entails gauging the extent to which marketing objectives have been achieved during the specified time period. Four common reasons for failing to achieve a marketing objective are unrealistic marketing objectives, inappropriate marketing strategies in the plan, poor implementation, and changes in the environment after the objective was specified and the strategy was implemented.

Once a plan is chosen and implemented, its effectiveness must be monitored. **Control** provides the mechanisms for evaluating marketing results in light of the plan's objectives and for correcting actions that do not help the organization reach those objectives within budget guidelines. Firms need to establish formal and informal control programs to make the entire operation more efficient.

Perhaps the broadest control device available to marketing managers is the **marketing audit**—a thorough, systematic, periodic evaluation of the objectives, strategies, structure, and performance of the marketing organization. A marketing audit helps management allocate marketing resources efficiently. It has four characteristics:

- *Comprehensive:* The marketing audit covers all the major marketing issues facing an organization and not just trouble spots.
- *Systematic:* The marketing audit takes place in an orderly sequence and covers the organization's marketing environment, internal marketing system, and specific marketing activities. The diagnosis is followed by an action plan with both short-run and long-run proposals for improving overall marketing effectiveness.
- *Independent:* The marketing audit is normally conducted by an inside or outside party who is independent enough to have top management's confidence and to be objective.
- *Periodic:* The marketing audit should be carried out on a regular schedule instead of only in a crisis. Whether it seems successful or is in deep trouble, any organization can benefit greatly from such an audit.

Although the main purpose of the marketing audit is to develop a full profile of the organization's marketing effort and to provide a basis for developing and revising the marketing plan, it is also an excellent way to improve communication and raise the level of marketing consciousness within the organization. It is a useful vehicle for selling the philosophy and techniques of strategic marketing to other members of the organization.

---

implementation
The process that turns marketing plans into action assignments and ensures that these assignments are executed in a way that accomplishes the plans' objectives.

evaluation
Gauging the extent to which the marketing objectives have been achieved during the specified time period.

control
Provides the mechanisms for evaluating marketing results in light of the plan's objectives and for correcting actions that do not help the organization reach those objectives within budget guidelines.

marketing audit
A thorough, systematic, periodic evaluation of the objectives, strategies, structure, and performance of the marketing organization.

REVIEW LEARNING OBJECTIVE 9

 Explain why implementation, evaluation, and control of the marketing plan are necessary

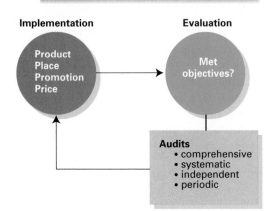

EFFECTIVE STRATEGIC PLANNING

Identify several techniques that help make strategic planning effective

Effective strategic planning requires continual attention, creativity, and management commitment. Strategic planning should not be an annual exercise, in which managers go through the motions and forget about strategic planning until the next year. It should be an ongoing process because the environment is continually changing and the firm's resources and capabilities are continually evolving.

Sound strategic planning is based on creativity. Managers should challenge assumptions about the firm and the environment and establish new strategies. For example, major oil companies developed the concept of the gasoline service station in an age when cars needed frequent and rather elaborate servicing. They held on to the full-service approach, but independents were quick to respond to new realities and moved to lower-cost self-service and convenience-store operations. The majors took several decades to catch up.

Perhaps the most critical element in successful strategic planning is top management's support and participation. For example, Michael Anthony, CEO of Brookstone, Inc. and the Brookstone buying team, rack up hundreds of thousands of frequent flyer miles searching the world for manufacturers and inventors of unique products that can be carried in its retail stores, catalogs, and Internet site. Anthony has codeveloped some of these products and has also been active in remodeling efforts for Brookstone's 250 permanent and seasonal stores.

REVIEW LEARNING OBJECTIVE 10

 Identify several techniques that help make strategic planning effective

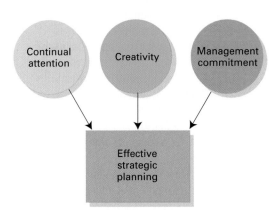

LOOKING BACK

Look back at the story about In-N-Out at the beginning of this chapter. In-N-Out has used several marketing strategy elements to increase its sales. Product strategies include offering fresh, top-quality hamburgers and french fries, a secret sauce, a simple menu, and fast service. The restaurant distributes its products and services in only three states. Promotion strategies include publicity, such as being talked about by celebrities like Lucy Liu and Julia Child, and movie placements. This publicity results in word of mouth. In-N-Out also uses billboard and radio advertising. The pricing strategy is to charge more than the typical fast-food restaurant, based on the higher quality food it serves.

The foundation of In-N-Out's competitive advantage is the fresh, high-quality food that is prepared to the customer's order. The company is so successful because it offers a consistently good product that is differentiated in the fast-food market. In-N-Out is a niche marketer that sticks to what it does best and does not get sidetracked by products and services that might pull attention away from the main focus of the business.

USE IT NOW

How do the elements of a marketing plan apply to you personally? Put yourself in the situation of looking for a new job. In this scenario, you are marketing yourself. Let's look at the pieces of a marketing plan to see how to plan for your own marketing.

First, what is your mission? Are you looking only for part-time or temporary experience to enhance your résumé, or a career stepping-stone, or a full-time, long-term career choice? This mission will help set the stage for the rest of your plan. Next, what are your objectives? Do you need to find a job within the next 30 days, or are you more flexible? Are there specific job activities that you would like to perform? These job activities could be stated in the objectives portion of your résumé. Be sure the objectives are very specific; general objectives are of little use to you or an employer.

It's now time for your SWOT analysis. Be very honest in your self-assessment of weaknesses and strengths because these issues often come up during job interviews. What about opportunities and threats in the marketplace? Who is your competition? Do you have a competitive advantage? Consider any special leadership skills, international travel, computer experience, team projects, communications efforts, and other attributes. Any competitive advantage you possess should be noted in the cover letter of your résumé and your job interview. The "Career Exercise" on pages 60–61 will help you conduct a personal SWOT analysis.

What is your target market? Are you only looking for jobs with big, established organizations or small entrepreneurial firms? Companies in a particular industry? Do you have any geographic preferences? When you figure out your target, compile a list of firms that meet your requirements and describe them. The more you know about your target market potential employers, the more prepared you will be in an interview.

You are the product. How can you best present yourself? Think of your own packaging with regard to dress, appearance, mannerisms, and speech. What about place? Are you willing to travel or relocate? Or do you need an employer close to home? How will you travel to the employer? Is telecommuting an option? How will you promote yourself? A carefully constructed cover letter, résumé, business card, and personal Web site can all help communicate your skills to a potential employer. Think carefully about pricing issues, including salary, commission, bonuses, overtime, flexible time, insurance, and other benefits. What is a fair price for you? What is a normal price for a company of that size in that industry to offer?

Have you set up an implementation plan for applying to companies? Contacting them for potential interviews? Working on your wardrobe and interviewing skills? Remember to send thank you notes for your interviews as a control measure. When job offers come in, how will you evaluate them? If job offers don't come in, can you find out why and control for those aspects?

As you can see, marketing plan elements can apply to marketing an organization or an individual. And writing down a marketing plan can greatly assist in the search for the perfect strategy or job!

REVIEW AND APPLICATIONS

1 **Understand the importance of strategic marketing and know a basic outline for a marketing plan.** Strategic marketing planning is the basis for all marketing strategies and decisions. The marketing plan is a written document that acts as a guide-book of marketing activities for the marketing manager. By specifying objectives and defining the actions required to attain them, a marketing plan provides the basis on which actual and expected performance can be compared.

Although there is no set formula for a marketing plan or a single correct outline, basic factors that should be covered include stating the business mission, setting objectives, performing a situation analysis of internal and external environmental forces, selecting target market(s), delineating a marketing mix (product, place, promotion, and price), and establishing ways to implement, evaluate, and control the plan.

1.1 Your cousin wants to start his own business, and he is in a hurry. He has decided not to write a marketing plan because he thinks that preparing such a document would take too long. He says he doesn't need a formal proposal because he has already received funding from your uncle. Explain why it is important for him to write a plan anyway.

1.2 After graduation, you decide to take a position as the marketing manager for a small snack-food manufacturer. The company, Shur Snak, is growing, and this is the first time that the company has ever employed a marketing manager. Consequently, there is no marketing plan in place for you to follow. Outline a basic marketing plan for your boss to give her an idea of the direction you want to take the company.

2 **Develop an appropriate business mission statement.** The mission statement is based on a careful analysis of benefits sought by present and potential customers and analysis of existing and anticipated environmental conditions. The firm's mission statement establishes boundaries for all subsequent decisions, objectives, and strategies. A mission statement should focus on the market or markets the organization is attempting to serve rather than on the good or service offered.

2.1 How can a new company best define its business mission statement? Can you find examples of good and bad mission statements on the Internet? How might you improve the bad ones?

2.2 Thinking back to question 1.2, write a business mission statement for Shur Snak. What elements should you include? Evaluate the mission statement you wrote against some of those you found online in question 2.1.

3 **Describe the criteria for stating good marketing objectives.** Objectives should be realistic, measurable, and time specific. Objectives must also be consistent and indicate the priorities of the organization.

3.1 Building on our Shur Snak example, imagine that your boss has stated that the marketing objective of the company is to do the best job of satisfying the needs and wants of the customer. Explain that although this objective is admirable, it does not meet the criteria for good objectives. What are these criteria? What is a specific example of a better objective for Shur Snak?

4 **Explain the components of a situation analysis.** In the situation (or SWOT) analysis, the firm should identify its internal strengths (S) and weaknesses (W) and also examine external opportunities (O) and threats (T). When examining external opportunities and threats, marketing managers must analyze aspects of the marketing environment in a process called environmental scanning. The six most often studied macroenvironmental forces are social, demographic, economic, technological, political and legal, and competitive. During the situation analysis, it is crucial that the marketer identify a competitive advantage and establish that it is a sustainable competitive advantage.

4.1 Competition in the private courier sector is fierce. UPS and FedEx dominate, but other companies, such as Airborne, Emery, and even the United States Postal Service (USPS), still have a decent chunk of the express package delivery market. Perform a mini-situation analysis on one of the companies listed below by stating one strength, one weakness, one opportunity, and one threat. You may want to consult the following Web sites as you build your grid:

UPS   http://www.ups.com
FedEx   http://www.fedex.com
Airborne   http://www.airborne.com
Emery   http://www.emeryworldwide.com
USPS   http://www.usps.gov

5 **Identify sources of competitive advantage.** A competitive advantage is a set of unique features of a company and its products that are perceived by the target market as significant and superior to the competition. There are three types of competitive advantages: cost, product/service differentiation, and niche strategies. Sources of cost competitive advantages include experience curves, efficient labor, no-frills goods and services, government subsidies, product design, reengineering, product innovations, and new methods of service delivery. A product/service differentiation competitive advantage exists when a firm provides something unique that is valuable to buyers beyond just low price. Niche competitive advantages come from targeting unique segments with specific needs and wants. The goal of all these sources of competitive advantage is to be sustainable.

5.1 Break into small groups and discuss examples (at least two per person) of the last few products you have purchased. What specific strategies were used to achieve competitive advantage? Is that competitive advantage sustainable against the competitors?

6 **Identify strategic alternatives.** The strategic opportunity matrix can be used to help management develop strategic alternatives. The four options are market penetration, product development, market development, and diversification.

6.1 Based on your SWOT analysis, decide what the strategic growth options are for the company you chose in question 4.1.

6.2 Review the "Marketing in Entertainment" box on Hallmark. Create a strategic opportunity matrix for the company based on the information in the box. If there are gaps, suggest ways the company can fill them.

7 **Discuss target market strategies.** The target market strategy identifies which market segment or segments to focus on. This process begins with a market opportunity analysis (MOA), which describes and estimates the size and sales potential of market segments that are of interest to the firm. In addition, an assessment of key competitors in these market segments is performed. After the market segments are described, one or more may be targeted by the firm. The three strategies for selecting target markets are appealing to the entire market with one marketing mix, concentrating on one segment, or appealing to multiple market segments using multiple marketing mixes.

7.1 You are given the task of deciding the marketing strategy for a transportation company. How do the marketing mix elements change when the target market is (a) low-income workers without personal transportation, (b) corporate international business travelers, or (c) companies with urgent documents or perishable materials to get to customers?

8 **Describe the elements of the marketing mix.** The marketing mix (or four Ps) is a blend of product, place, promotion, and pricing strategies designed to produce mutually satisfying exchanges with a target market. The starting point of the marketing mix is the product offering. Products can be tangible goods, ideas, or services. Place (distribution) strategies are concerned with making products available when and where customers want them. Promotion includes advertising, public relations, sales promotion, and personal selling. Price is what a buyer must give up to obtain a product and is often the easiest to change of the four marketing mix elements.

8.1   Choose three or four other students and make up a team. Create a marketing plan to increase enrollment in your school. Describe the four marketing mix elements that make up the plan.

9 **Explain why implementation, evaluation, and control of the marketing plan are necessary.** Before a marketing plan can work, it must be implemented; that is, people must perform the actions in the plan. The plan should also be evaluated to see if it has achieved its objectives. Poor implementation can be a major factor in a plan's failure. Control provides the mechanisms for evaluating marketing results in light of the plan's objectives and for correcting actions that do not help the organization reach those objectives within budget guidelines.

9.1 Have your school enrollment marketing plan team (from question 8.1) develop a plan to implement, evaluate, and control the marketing strategy.

9.2 I N F O T R A C° COLLEGE EDITION Using InfoTrac and the *Wall Street Journal*'s archive at **http://wsj.com**, trace the history of Kimberly-Clark's marketing plan and strategy for Cottonelle Fresh Rollwipes (premoistened toilet paper). Once you have a basic understanding of the product development and launch history, evaluate the plan set in motion by Kimberly-Clark. Does the company consider the product (and hence the plan) a success? Has the product been well received in the market? Are competitors moving in to take away market share with their own versions? Write a brief report giving a two-sentence synopsis of the product history and then describing what went right with the plan and what went wrong (if anything). If you identify flaws in the plan, say what the company could have done to avoid those problems.

10 **Identify several techniques that help make strategic planning effective.** First, management must realize that strategic planning is an ongoing process and not a once-a-year exercise. Second, good strategic planning involves a high level of creativity. The last requirement is top management's support and cooperation.

10.1 What techniques can make your school enrollment marketing plan more effective?

TERMS

competitive advantage 44
control 54
cost competitive advantage 44
diversification 48
environmental scanning 44
evaluation 54
experience curves 44
four Ps 51
implementation 54
market development 48

market opportunity analysis (MOA) 50
market penetration 48
marketing audit 54
marketing mix 51
marketing myopia 41
marketing objective 42
marketing plan 39
marketing planning 39
marketing strategy 50
mission statement 41

niche competitive advantage 46
planning 39
product development 48
product/service differentiation competitive advantage 46
strategic business unit (SBU) 42
strategic planning 38
sustainable competitive advantage 46
SWOT analysis 43

APPLICATION EXERCISE

As you now know from reading the chapter, an important part of the strategy-making process involves scanning the environment for changes that affect your marketing efforts. This exercise is designed to introduce you to the business press and to help you make the connection between the concepts you learn in the classroom and real-world marketing activities.[14]

Activities

1. Find a current article of substance in the business press (the *Wall Street Journal,* the *Financial Times, Fortune, BusinessWeek, Inc.,* etc.) that discusses topics you have covered in this course. Although this is only Chapter 2, you will be surprised by the amount of terminology you have already learned. If you are having trouble finding an article, read through the table of contents at the beginning of the book to familiarize yourself with the names of concepts that will be presented later in the course. Read your article carefully, making notes about relevant content.

2. Write a one-paragraph summary of the key points in your article; then write a list of the terms or concepts critical to understanding the article. Provide definitions of those terms. If you are unfamiliar with a term or concept that is central to the article, do some research in your text-book or see your professor during office hours. Relate these key points to the concepts in your text by citing page numbers.

3. Explain the environments that are relevant to the situation presented in the article. (Chapter 3 contains a full list of environmental factors.)

4. How are the strategic elements of target market and marketing mix relevant to the article?

(You may find this exercise useful throughout the semester, as reading material from outside the text will reinforce the concepts you are learning in your course. The business press is also the place to find fully contextual examples that can aid in understanding difficult material.)

ETHICS EXERCISE

Abercrombie & Fitch, a retail clothing chain based in New Albany, Ohio, launched a line of thong underwear for preteen girls. Words like "eye candy" and "wink wink" were printed on the front of the skimpy underwear that some argued would fit girls aged five to ten. Abercrombie is known for its provocative ads and sexually oriented catalogs. Supporters of the strategy claim that producing thong-style underwear for the age 10 to 16 crowd is a good move; critics think that the line is tasteless and that marketing it to young girls is contemptuous.

Questions

1. Is marketing adult-styled undergarments to a younger audience unethical?

2. Would Abercrombie have been in the spotlight had the sexy words been omitted from the product?

3. What does the AMA Code of Ethics have to say about using sex to market products to adult consumers? To younger consumers? Read the code at **http://www.marketingpower.com** and then write a brief paragraph on how the code relates to this situation.

CAREER EXERCISE

One way to have a better idea of how marketing strategy works is to use it in your career planning. For example, you might conduct a personal SWOT analysis, create a career marketing plan, or simply do some environmental scanning in the general business environment and any industries in which you might like to work.

Activities

1. To begin your personal SWOT analysis, assume you have just completed your college education and are ready to apply for a job as a marketing manager of a small- to medium-sized

firm. A personal SWOT analysis will help you determine if your current situation matches your overall strategy. Gather information about your strengths and weaknesses by analyzing your personal interests and learning more about your personality style. Most college placement offices have software to help students identify their interests and personality styles and then match that information to certain career paths. This type of assessment can help ensure that you do not choose a career path that is incongruent with your personality and interests.

2. Probably the hardest portion of the personal SWOT analysis will be identifying personal weaknesses. Compare the skills, abilities, knowledge, and experience you need to be a successful marketer with your personal inventory in order to identify potential weaknesses and develop a plan to minimize or overcome them. Remember that most annual evaluations will include both strengths and weaknesses, so don't forget to include this valuable information in your analysis.

3. Identify opportunities by looking at various employment possibilities for entry-level managers at this particular time. In this part of the analysis, it helps to match personal strengths with opportunities. For example, if you have experience in manufacturing, you may choose to initially apply only to manufacturing-type businesses.

4. The last step of the analysis involves identifying potential threats. Threats are barriers that can prevent you from obtaining your goals, such as an economic recession that reduces the number of job openings for entry-level managers. By knowing what the barriers are and by assembling proactive plans to help deal with them, you can reduce the possibility that your strategy will become ineffective. Not only can focusing on a personal SWOT analysis be a practical way to prepare for an actual marketing strategy analysis, but it also allows you to learn more about yourself and your long-term plans.

ENTREPRENEURSHIP CASE

© AP/WIDE WORLD PHOTOS

CIRQUE DU SOLEIL: THE FIRE WITHIN

A 27-foot-long bronze clown shoe is the only indication that there is something otherworldly within the concrete walls of the large, rather nondescript building. Located in Montreal, the building is home to what many feel is the most successful entertainment company in the world—Cirque du Soleil.

The company's massive headquarters houses practice rooms the size of airplane hangars where cast members work on their routines. More than 300 seamstresses, engineers, and makeup artists sew, design, and build custom materials for exotic shows with stage lives of 10 to 12 years. In fact, the production staff often invents materials, such as the special waterproof makeup required for the production of *O*, a show performed mostly in a 1.5 million-gallon pool of water that was also specially designed and engineered by Cirque employees. Another key inhouse resource is Cirque's team of 32 talent scouts and casting staff that recruits and cultivates performers from all over the world. The department maintains a database of 20,000 names, any of whom could be called at any time to join the members of Cirque's cast, who number 2,700 and speak 27 languages.

Shows with exotic names like *Mystère, La Nouba, O, Dralion, Varekai,* and *Zumanity* communicate through style and tone that they are intended to do more than just amuse. Cirque designs productions with distinct personalities that are meant to evoke awe, wonder, inspiration, and reflection. As one cast member put it, "The goal of a Cirque performer is not just to perform a quadruple somersault, but to treat it as some manifestation of a spiritual, inner life. Like in dance, the goal is . . . to have a language, a conversation, with the audience."

Audiences have responded. Even with ticket prices that start at $45 and can run as high as $360, the company sells about 97 percent of all its seats at every show. For Cirque, that translates to about $500,000 a week in sales and yearly profits of $100 million on gross revenues of $500 million.

Incredibly, every one of the 15 shows that Cirque has produced over its 20-year history has returned a profit. In contrast, 90 percent of the high-budget Broadway shows that strive to reach the same target market fail to break even. Cirque's statistics, however, are eye-popping. *Mystère,* which opened at the Treasure Island hotel and casino in Las Vegas in 1993 and still runs today, cost $45 million to produce and has returned over $430 million; *O,* which opened at the Bellagio hotel and casino in 1998, cost $92 million to produce and has already returned over $480 million. Though the company splits about half of its profits with its hotel and casino partners, those same partners sometimes absorb up to 75 percent of Cirque's production costs.

At the helm of this incredible business machine is the dynamic duo of Franco Dragone and Daniel Lamarre. Dragone, a Belgian, is the creative force behind most of the company's nine current productions, and Lamarre, a former television executive, presides over show and new venture development. Together, they have transformed a one-tour, one-residence circus company into an entertainment powerhouse with five simultaneous world tours; four permanent facilities in Las Vegas—Treasure Island, the Bellagio, New York–New York, and the MGM Grand—all of which are part of the Mirage family of casinos; another permanent theater at Disney World; and a series of shows on the cable television channel Bravo that has already won an Emmy.

Lamarre claims that his business is successful because he and his staff "let the creative people run it." He guides the company with an invisible hand, making sure that business policies do not interfere with the creative process; it is Dragone and his team of creative and production personnel, not a predetermined budget, that defines the content, style, and material requirements for each project. Because of their sound planning, Cirque du Soleil can claim that it is one of the world's elite businesses, as well as one of the world's elite entertainment companies.[15]

Questions

1. Based on what you have read in the case, outline a rudimentary SWOT analysis for Cirque du Soleil.

2. List and describe at least three keys to Cirque du Soleil's competitive advantage.

3. Explain how Cirque du Soleil implements, evaluates, and controls the elements of its marketing plan.

WATCH IT

SmallBusinessSchool ▣
the Series on PBS stations and the Web

FEATURE PRESENTATION

Nicole Miller Fashion House

To give you insight into Chapter 2, Small Business School goes to New York City to visit the Nicole Miller Fashion House. This video segment explores how founders Bud Konheim and Nicole Miller implement a marketing strategy based on the four Ps. The Nicole Miller Company has devised a strategy to target its products toward a very specific market. Nicole and her designers create clothes and accessories for women who want to cultivate a stylish and youthful look, but who don't want to pay premium prices for high-end couture. Even though Bud and Nicole use a value pricing technique for their lines, Nicole's signature clothes and accessories have a unique, upscale appeal.

In order to best understand her customers, Nicole started offering her full line of fashions exclusively through Nicole Miller Boutiques. There are thirty Nicole Miller Boutiques in all, fifteen owned by Nicole Miller Company, and fifteen owned by licensees. That distribution strategy has exposed the full range of Nicole's designs to potential customers, and it has given the brand the strength it needed to later stand alongside major fashion labels offered in luxury department stores like Neiman Marcus, Saks Fifth Avenue, and Nordstrom.

What to Watch for and Ask Yourself

1. Fashionable dresses and handbags are among the tangible items that Nicole Miller sells, but what is she selling that's intangible?

2. Describe how Nicole Miller's pricing and distribution strategy work to support her product strategy.

3. What type of competitive advantage does Nicole Miller have—cost, product differentiation, or niche? Or is it a combination of any of these?

ENCORE PRESENTATION

U-571

Now that you have worked through the chapter, you may be ready to "think outside the box" about strategy. As an encore to your work, watch the film clip from *U-571,* starring Harvey Keitel and Matthew McConaughey. This action-packed World War II thriller shows a U.S. submarine crew's efforts to retrieve an Enigma encryption device from a disabled German submarine. After the crew gets the device, a German vessel torpedoes and sinks their submarine. The survivors must now use the disabled German submarine to escape from the enemy with their prize.

How are the concepts of competitive advantage, situation analysis, and strategic objective illustrated in the clip?

STILL SHAKY?

If you're having trouble with the concepts in this chapter, consider using some of the following study resources. You can review the videos, or test yourself with materials designed for all kinds of learning styles.

☑ **Xtra! (http://lambxtra.swlearning.com)**

☑ Quiz	☑ Feature Videos	☑ Encore Videos	☑ FAQ Videos
☑ Exhibit Worksheets	☑ Marketing Plan Worksheets	☐ Content	

☑ **http://lamb.swlearning.com**

☑ Quiz	☑ PowerPoint slides	☑ Marketing News	☑ Review Exercises
☑ Links	☑ Marketing Plan Contest	☐ Career Exercise	☐ Use It Now

☑ **Study guide**

☑ Outline	☑ Vocab Review	☑ Test Questions	☑ Marketing Scenario

Need More? Here's a tip. Try to explain the key concepts in this chapter to a friend or family member who is not taking the class with you. This will help you identify areas where you need to review—and how much.

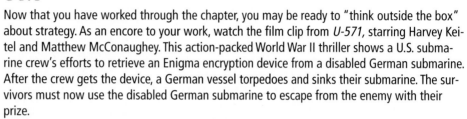

Marketing Plan Appendix

As you read in Chapter 2, there is more than one correct format for a marketing plan. Many organizations have their own distinctive format or terminology for creating a marketing plan, and every marketing plan should be unique to the firm for which it was created. The format and order of presentation, therefore, must be flexible. This appendix presents only one way to organize a marketing plan. The outline is meant to give you a more detailed look at what you need to include, topics you need to cover, and the types of questions you must answer in any marketing plan. But, depending on the product or service for which you are drafting a plan, this set of questions may only be the starting point for more industry-specific issues you need to address.

If you are assigned a marketing plan as a course requirement, this appendix can help you organize your work. In addition, Xtra! contains worksheets that guide you through the process of marketing planning. The worksheets can be completed electronically or printed out and filled in by hand. If you are having trouble coming up with a company to serve as the basis of your plan, consider using the unique small business which is profiled at **http://lamb.swlearning.com**. Follow the Marketing Plan Project link to find out about a company that is either struggling to create a marketing plan, experiencing difficulties executing it, or working through a challenging marketing transition. The highlighted company changes periodically to ensure that the topics are relevant.

One company that you may find interesting to use as the basis of your project is called Metronaps. Use InfoTrac (**http://infotrac-college.com**) to locate an article written by Lucas Conley for the May 2004 issue of *Fast Company*. The article, titled "*This* Close," recounts the struggles of entrepreneur Arshad Chowdhury and his patent-pending Napod. While an MBA student at Carnegie Mellon University, Chowdhury began charging $1 for 40 minutes of rest on a collection of lawn chairs. By the fifth day of his venture, he was filling every seat. Now, Chowdhury is trying to establish napping centers across the United States, but he is encountering a number of marketing obstacles, not the least of which is deciding upon a brand name. The company started as NapCentre, then changed to Blink PowerNaps, and has seemed to settle on Metronaps. The information in Conley's article should be sufficient to launch you into the questions outlined below, and the $20,000 Napod, designed by a Formula-One prototype team, should make an interesting focus for your marketing plan assignment.

I. Business Mission

- What is the mission of the firm? What business is it in? How well is its mission understood throughout the organization? Five years from now, what business does it wish to be in?
- Does the firm define its business in terms of benefits its customers want rather than in terms of goods and services?

II. Objectives

- Is the firm's mission statement able to be translated into operational terms regarding the firm's objectives?
- What are the stated objectives of the organization? Are they formally written down? Do they lead logically to clearly stated marketing objectives? Are objectives based on sales, profits, or customers?
- Are the organization's marketing objectives stated in hierarchical order? Are they specific so that progress toward achievement can be measured? Are the objectives reasonable in light of the organization's resources? Are the objectives ambiguous? Do the objectives specify a time frame?
- Is the firm's main objective to maximize customer satisfaction or to get as many customers as possible?

III. Situation Analysis (SWOT Analysis)

- Has one or more competitive advantages been identified in the SWOT analysis?
- Are these advantages sustainable against the competition?

A. Internal Strengths and Weaknesses

- What is the history of the firm, including sales, profits, and organizational philosophies?
- What is the nature of the firm and its current situation?
- What resources does the firm have (financial, human, time, experience, asset, skill)?
- What policies inhibit the achievement of the firm's objectives with respect to organization, resource allocation, operations, hiring, training, and so on?

B. External Opportunities and Threats

- *Social:* What major social and lifestyle trends will have an impact on the firm? What action has the firm been taking in response to these trends?
- *Demographics:* What impact will forecasted trends in the size, age, profile, and distribution of population have on the firm? How will the changing nature of the family, the increase in the proportion of women in the workforce, and changes in the ethnic composition of the population affect the firm? What action has the firm taken in response to these developments and trends? Has the firm reevaluated its traditional products and expanded the range of specialized offerings to respond to these changes?
- *Economic:* What major trends in taxation and income sources will have an impact on the firm? What action has the firm taken in response to these trends?

- *Political, Legal, and Financial:* What laws are now being proposed at international, federal, state, and local levels that could affect marketing strategy and tactics? What recent changes in regulations and court decisions affect the firm? What political changes are taking place at each government level? What action has the firm taken in response to these legal and political changes?
- *Competition:* Which organizations are competing with the firm directly by offering a similar product? Which organizations are competing with the firm indirectly by securing its prime prospects' time, money, energy, or commitment? What new competitive trends seem likely to emerge? How effective is the competition? What benefits do competitors offer that the firm does not? Is it appropriate for the firm to compete?
- *Technological:* What major technological changes are occurring that affect the firm?
- *Ecological:* What is the outlook for the cost and availability of natural resources and energy needed by the firm? Are the firm's products, services, and operations environmentally friendly?

IV. Marketing Strategy

A. Target Market Strategy

- Are the members of each market homogeneous or heterogeneous with respect to geographic, sociodemographic, and behavioral characteristics?
- What are the size, growth rate, and national and regional trends in each of the organization's market segments?
- Is the size of each market segment sufficiently large or important to warrant a unique marketing mix?
- Are market segments measurable and accessible to distribution and communication efforts?
- Which are the high- or low-opportunity segments?
- What are the evolving needs and satisfactions being sought by target markets?
- What benefits does the organization offer to each segment? How do these benefits compare with benefits offered by competitors?
- Is the firm positioning itself with a unique product? Is the product needed?
- How much of the firm's business is repeat versus new business? What percentage of the public can be classified as nonusers, light users, or heavy users?
- How do current target markets rate the firm and its competitors with respect to reputation, quality, and price? What is the firm's image with the specific market segments it seeks to serve?
- Does the firm try to direct its products only to specific groups of people or to everybody?
- Who buys the firm's products? How does a potential customer find out about the organization? When and how does a person become a customer?
- What are the major objections given by potential customers as to why they do not buy the firm's products?
- How do customers find out about and decide to purchase the product? When and where?
- Should the firm seek to expand, contract, or change the emphasis of its selected target markets? If so, in which target markets, and how vigorously?

- Could the firm more usefully withdraw from some areas where there are alternative suppliers and use its resources to serve new, unserved customer groups?
- What publics other than target markets (financial, media, government, citizen, local, general, and internal) represent opportunities or problems for the firm?

B. Marketing Mix

- Does the firm seek to achieve its objective chiefly through coordinated use of marketing activities (product, place, promotion, and pricing) or only through intensive promotion?
- Are the objectives and roles of each element of the marketing mix clearly specified?

1. Product

- What are the major product/service offerings of the firm? Do they complement each other, or is there unnecessary duplication?
- What are the features and benefits of each product offering?
- Where are the firm and each major product in the life cycle?
- What are the pressures among various target markets to increase or decrease the range and quality of products?
- What are the major weaknesses in each product area? What are the major complaints? What goes wrong most often?
- Is the product name easy to pronounce? Spell? Recall? Is it descriptive, and does it communicate the benefits the product offers? Does the name distinguish the firm or product from all others?
- What warranties are offered with the product? Are there other ways to guarantee customer satisfaction?
- Does the product offer good customer value?
- How is customer service handled? How is service quality assessed?

2. Place/Distribution

- Should the firm try to deliver its offerings directly to customers, or can it better deliver selected offerings by involving other organizations? What channel(s) should be used in distributing product offerings?
- What physical distribution facilities should be used? Where should they be located? What should be their major characteristics?
- Are members of the target market willing and able to travel some distance to buy the product?
- How good is access to facilities? Can access be improved? Which facilities need priority attention in these areas?
- How are facility locations chosen? Is the site accessible to the target markets? Is it visible to the target markets?
- What are the location and atmosphere of retail establishments? Do these retailers satisfy customers?
- When are products made available to users (season of year, day of week, time of day)? Are these times most appropriate?

3. Promotion

- How does a typical customer find out about the firm's products?
- Does the message the firm delivers gain the attention of the intended target audience? Does it address the wants and needs of the target market, and does it suggest benefits or a means for satisfying these wants? Is the message appropriately positioned?
- Does the promotion effort effectively inform, persuade, educate, and remind customers about the firm's products?
- Does the firm establish budgets and measure effectiveness of promotional efforts?

a. Advertising

- Which media are currently being used? Has the firm chosen the types of media that will best reach its target markets?
- Are the types of media used the most cost-effective, and do they contribute positively to the firm's image?
- Are the dates and times the ads will appear the most appropriate? Has the firm prepared several versions of its advertisements?
- Does the organization use an outside advertising agency? What functions does the ad agency perform for the organization?
- What system is used to handle consumer inquiries resulting from advertising and promotions? What follow-up is done?

b. Public Relations

- Is there a well-conceived public relations and publicity program? Does the program have the ability to respond to bad publicity?
- How is public relations normally handled by the firm? By whom? Have those responsible nurtured working relationships with media outlets?
- Is the firm using all available public relations avenues? Is an effort made to understand each of the publicity outlet's needs and to provide each with story types that will appeal to its audience in readily usable forms?
- What does the annual report say about the firm and its products? Who is being effectively reached by this vehicle? Does the benefit of the publication justify the cost?

c. Personal Selling

- How much of a typical salesperson's time is spent soliciting new customers as compared to serving existing customers?
- How does the sales force determine which prospect will be called on and by whom? How is the frequency of contacts determined?
- How is the sales force compensated? Are there incentives for encouraging more business?
- How is the sales force organized and managed?
- Has the sales force prepared an approach tailored to each prospect?

- Has the firm matched sales personnel with the target market characteristics?
- Is there appropriate follow-up to the initial personal selling effort? Are customers made to feel appreciated?
- Can database or direct marketing be used to replace or supplement the sales force?

d. Sales Promotion

- What is the specific purpose of each sales promotion activity? Why is it offered? What does it try to achieve?
- What categories of sales promotion are being used? Is sales promotion directed to the trade, the final consumer, or both?
- Is the effort directed at all the firm's key publics or restricted to only potential customers?

4. Price

- What levels of pricing and specific prices should be used?
- What mechanisms does the firm have to ensure that the prices charged are acceptable to customers?
- How price sensitive are customers?
- If a price change is put into effect, how will the number of customers change? Will total revenue increase or decrease?
- Which method is used for establishing a price: going rate, demand oriented, or cost based?
- What discounts are offered, and with what rationale?
- Has the firm considered the psychological dimensions of price?
- Have price increases kept pace with cost increases, inflation, or competitive levels?
- How are price promotions used?
- Do interested prospects have opportunities to sample products at an introductory price?
- What methods of payment are accepted? Is it in the firm's best interest to use these various payment methods?

V. Implementation, Evaluation, and Control

- Is the marketing organization structured appropriately to implement the marketing plan?
- What specific activities must take place? Who is responsible for these activities?
- What is the implementation timetable?
- What other marketing research is necessary?
- What will be the financial impact of this plan on a one-year projected income statement? How does projected income compare with expected revenue if the plan is not implemented?
- What are the performance standards?
- What monitoring procedures (audits) will take place and when?
- Does the firm seem to be trying to do too much or not enough?
- Are the core marketing strategies for achieving objectives sound? Are the objectives being met, and are the objectives appropriate?
- Are enough resources (or too many resources) budgeted to accomplish the marketing objectives?

3

Social Responsibility, Ethics, and the Marketing Environment

LEARNING OBJECTIVES

1 Discuss corporate social responsibility

2 Describe the role of ethics and ethical decisions in business

3 Discuss the external environment of marketing, and explain how it affects a firm

4 Describe the social factors that affect marketing

5 Explain the importance to marketing managers of current demographic trends

6 Explain the importance to marketing managers of multiculturalism and growing ethnic markets

7 Identify consumer and marketer reactions to the state of the economy

8 Identify the impact of technology on a firm

9 Discuss the political and legal environment of marketing

10 Explain the basics of foreign and domestic competition

AP/WIDE WORLD PHOTOS

Paul Tebo is no one's idea of a revolutionary. A mild-mannered, gray-haired, 59-year-old chemical engineer, he has worked at DuPont for 35 years. He used to run the firm's $3 billion-a-year petrochemicals division, an operation that once tarred the industrial giant with a reputation as America's worst polluter. Today, Tebo is in the soy milk business. As an advocate for social responsibility and DuPont's corporate vice president for safety, health, and environment, he's trying to help transform DuPont from an oil-and-chemicals company into an eco-friendly life-sciences firm. Hence, his interest in making things out of a renewable resource like soy. The new corporate mission? A revolutionary idea called sustainable growth.

Sustainable growth is about building an economy that generates wealth while helping to save the planet. DuPont set out in that direction a decade ago by pledging to reduce waste, emissions, and energy usage; the idea then was to curb pollution and cut costs. More recently, DuPont has ventured into uncharted territory: its new goal is to own a collection of businesses that can go on forever without depleting natural resources. So, for example, the

company spun off its massive Conoco oil-and-gas unit five years ago and used the proceeds to buy Pioneer Hi-Bred International, whose seeds produce not only food for people and livestock but renewable materials for commercial uses—turning corn into stretch T-shirts, for example.

When DuPont makes a strategic decision, Tebo says, the company poses a question he thinks should be on every twenty-first-century CEO's agenda: "How do you bring the economics together with the environmental and the societal needs so that they are all part of your business strategies?"

At DuPont, which got its start in 1802 making gunpowder, that now means producing soy protein, creating biodegradable material for plastic tableware, and hiring the former executive director of Greenpeace as a high-level consultant.

DuPont is at the cutting edge—and maybe over the edge—of the movement to make corporations more socially responsible. But poke around any number of *Fortune* 500 companies, and you'll find people grappling with a host of unexpected issues, from renewable energy to global poverty. UPS's fleet, for instance,

includes 1,800 alternative-fuel vehicles, while FedEx just announced a plan to convert all its trucks to hybrid electric-diesel engines. Nike has removed vinyl, which has been linked to cancer, from almost all its footwear. It also developed a program with Delta Air Lines, called Eco-Class, which invests in projects that offset emissions created when Nike employees take business trips. To preserve biodiversity, Starbucks is buying more organic and shade-grown coffee, which minimizes disruption of rain forests; it is also buying more "fair-trade" coffee, which gives the owners of family farms an agreed-upon price for their harvest. Just recently ten major banks, including Citigroup and Barclays, agreed to meet environmental and social impact standards when financing public works projects, such as dams and power plants, particularly in developing nations.[1]

Do socially responsible companies tend to be more or less profitable than others? Are DuPont, UPS, and Nike acting in the stockholders' best interests with their socially responsible activities? How do uncontrollable factors in the environment affect these and other companies? We'll look at these issues and more in chapter 3.

Discuss corporate social responsibility

corporate social responsibility
Business's concern for society's welfare.

sustainability
The idea that socially responsible companies will outperform their peers by focusing on the world's social problems and viewing them as opportunities to build profits and help the world at the same time.

pyramid of corporate social responsibility
A model that suggests corporate social responsibility is composed of economic, legal, ethical, and philanthropic responsibilities and that the firm's economic performance supports the entire structure.

Corporate social responsibility is a business's concern for society's welfare. This concern is demonstrated by managers who consider both the long-range best interests of the company and the company's relationship to the society within which it operates. The newest theory in social responsibility is called **sustainability**. This refers to the idea that socially responsible companies will outperform their peers by focusing on the world's social problems and viewing them as opportunities to build profits and help the world at the same time. It is also the notion that companies cannot thrive for long (i.e., lack sustainability) in a world where billions of people are suffering and are desperately poor. Thus, it is in business's interest to find ways to attack society's ills. Only business organizations have the talent, creativity, and executive ability to do the job.

Skeptics say business should focus on making a profit and leave social and environmental problems to nonprofit organizations (like the World Wildlife Federation or the Sierra Club) and government. Economist Milton Friedman believes that the free market, and not companies, should decide what is best for the world. He asks, "If business people do have a social responsibility other than making maximum profits for stockholders, how are they to know what it is?"[2]

Friedman argues that to the degree that business executives spend more money than they need to—to purchase delivery vehicles with hybrid engines, or to pay higher wages in developing countries, or even to donate company funds to charity—they are spending shareholders' money to further their own agendas. Better to pay dividends and let the shareholders give the money away, if they choose.

Proponents of corporate social responsibility say that's a false dichotomy. Smart companies, they say, can prosper and build shareholder value by tackling global problems. Barbara Waugh, a lifelong social activist who works for Hewlett-Packard, says, "After working to change the world through politics, education, government, and the churches, I believe I can have more impact through the corporate sector."[3] As a result of her efforts, H-P has begun a three-year project designed to create jobs, improve education, and provide better access to government services in the Indian state of Kuppam, which has a population of 320,000. Working with the local government, as well as a branch of H-P Labs based in India, the company is studying how to provide the rural poor with access to government records, schools, health information, crop prices, and the like. The hope is to stimulate small tech-based businesses. (An example: Village photographers, with solar-powered digital cameras and printers, now take pictures for government ID cards, saving residents a trip to the city.) At a minimum, this effort builds goodwill and the H-P brand in India; at best, it will help the company discover new, profitable lines of business. Similar efforts are under way in poor cities and rural areas of the United States and in South Africa.[4]

One theorist suggests that total corporate social responsibility has four components: economic, legal, ethical, and philanthropic.[5] The **pyramid of corporate social responsibility** portrays economic performance as the foundation for the other three responsibilities. At the same time that it pursues profits (economic responsibility), however, a business is expected to obey the law (legal responsibility); to do what is right, just, and fair (ethical responsibilities); and to be a good corporate citizen (philanthropic responsibility). These four components are distinct but together constitute the whole. Still, if the company doesn't make a profit, then the other three responsibilities are moot.

You see kids waiting for a bus.

We see a neighborhood waiting for a dentist.

So we brought the dentist to them. Working in partnership with dental programs from across the country, Crest is reaching out to kids and neighborhoods with a fleet of vans that are actual traveling dentist offices. These vans have kept over 73,000 appointments since October 2001, and that's just a start. Because we'll go to any length to get kids on the road to healthy, beautiful smiles for life.

Crest

Healthy, beautiful smiles for life.

THE PROCTER & GAMBLE COMPANY. USED BY PERMISSION

Even though there is debate about the role of social responsibility in business, many companies are finding ways to incorporate socially responsible practices that also increase shareholder value. This ad for Crest promotes the company's sponsorship of traveling dentist programs, in which fully equipped vans visit economically depressed neighborhoods across the United States.

1 Discuss corporate social responsibility

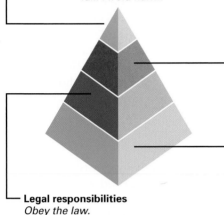

Philanthropic responsibilities
Be a good corporate citizen.
Contribute resources to the
community; improve the
quality of life.

Ethical responsibilities
Be ethical.
Do what is right, just, and
fair. Avoid harm.

Legal responsibilities
Obey the law.
Law is society's codification
of right and wrong. Play by
the rules of the game.

Economic responsibilities
Be profitable.
Profit is the foundation
on which all other
responsibilities rest.

A current study ranked (in order) Home Depot, Johnson & Johnson, DaimlerChrysler, Anheuser-Busch, and McDonald's as having the highest level of social responsibility in America.[6] Yet, does being socially responsible create additional demand for the company's goods and services? The answer is quite complex. In some cases, it is "yes," and in others, "no." For example, one factor is the issue on which the company focuses, such as health, education, or charitable giving and how this is perceived by the target market. Other factors are product/service quality and how the target market perceives the importance of social responsibility.[7]

In summary, the evidence that corporate social responsibility drives profit and growth is inconclusive. There's also the difficulty of defining social responsibility. Socially responsible investment funds have generally tracked the broader stock market. Since its inception in 1991, the Domini Social Equity fund, the oldest and largest such fund, has gained an average of 8.66 percent annually, while the Standard & Poors's 500 has gained 9 percent. On the other hand, a recent study by Governance Metrics International, which rates companies on their governance policies, labor practices, environmental activities, and litigation history, found that stocks of the top-ranked firms significantly outperformed the market, while low-rated companies trailed the indexes.[8] For now, about the most one can say is that there doesn't seem to be a financial penalty for embracing socially responsible programs.

Paul Tebo of DuPont (discussed in "Looking Forward") sees the question differently. Tebo argues that both the world and the company are better off because of the progress DuPont has made. It has dramatically reduced greenhouse gas emissions and hazardous waste, even after accounting for the sale of Conoco, and its waste-treatment costs are down. Looking ahead, DuPont wants to generate 25 percent of revenues from renewable resources by 2010. (In 2003 the figure was 14 percent.)[9]

2 ETHICAL BEHAVIOR IN BUSINESS

Describe the role of ethics and ethical decisions in business

Social responsibility and ethics go hand in hand. **Ethics** refers to the moral principles or values that generally govern the conduct of an individual or a group. Ethics can also be viewed as the standard of behavior by which conduct is judged. Standards that are legal may not always be ethical, and vice versa. Laws are the values and standards enforceable by the courts. Ethics consists of personal moral principles and values rather than societal prescriptions.

Defining the boundaries of ethicality and legality can be difficult. Often, judgment is needed to determine whether an action that may be legal is an ethical or unethical act. Also, judgment is required to determine if an unethical act is legal or illegal. For example, the courts are still trying to determine the legality of various unethical acts committed by corporate executives at Global Crossing, Enron, WorldCom, and Tyco. On the other hand, the secretly arranged $139.5 million compensation package for Dick Grasso, former chairman of the New York Stock Exchange, was unethical but perhaps not illegal. It did, however, cost him his job.[10] The new New York Stock Exchange Board of Directors and the New York State Attorney General are suing Grasso to recover the excessive payment.

Morals are the rules people develop as a result of cultural values and norms. Culture is a socializing force that dictates what is right and wrong. Moral standards may also reflect the laws and regulations that affect social and economic behavior. Thus, morals can be considered a foundation of ethical behavior.

ethics
The moral principles or values that generally govern the conduct of an individual.

morals
The rules people develop as a result of cultural values and norms.

Morals are usually characterized as good or bad. "Good" and "bad" have different connotations, including "effective" and "ineffective." A good salesperson makes or exceeds the assigned quota. If the salesperson sells a new stereo or television set to a disadvantaged consumer—knowing full well that the person can't keep up the monthly payments—is the salesperson still a good one? What if the sale enables the salesperson to exceed his or her quota?

"Good" and "bad" can also refer to "conforming" and "deviant" behaviors. A doctor who runs large ads offering discounts on open-heart surgery would be considered bad, or unprofessional, in the sense of not conforming to the norms of the medical profession. "Bad" and "good" are also used to express the distinction between criminal and law-abiding behavior. And finally, different religions define "good" and "bad" in markedly different ways. A Muslim who eats pork would be considered bad, as would a fundamentalist Christian who drinks whiskey.

Morality and Business Ethics

 Today's business ethics actually consists of a subset of major life values learned since birth. The values businesspeople use to make decisions have been acquired through family, educational, and religious institutions.

Ethical values are situation specific and time oriented. Nevertheless, everyone must have an ethical base that applies to conduct in the business world and in personal life. One approach to developing a personal set of ethics is to examine the consequences of a particular act. Who is helped or hurt? How long lasting are the consequences? What actions produce the greatest good for the greatest number of people? A second approach stresses the importance of rules. Rules come in the form of customs, laws, professional standards, and common sense. Consider these examples of rules:

- Always treat others as you would like to be treated.
- Copying copyrighted computer software is against the law.
- It is wrong to lie, bribe, or exploit.

The last approach emphasizes the development of moral character within individuals. Ethical development can be thought of as having three levels:[12]

- *Preconventional morality,* the most basic level, is childlike. It is calculating, self-centered, and even selfish, based on what will be immediately punished or rewarded. Fortunately, most businesspeople have progressed beyond the self-centered and manipulative actions of preconventional morality.
- *Conventional morality* moves from an egocentric viewpoint toward the expectations of society. Loyalty and obedience to the organization (or society) become paramount. At the level of conventional morality, an ethical marketing decision would be concerned only with whether it is legal and how it will be viewed by others. This type of morality could be likened to the adage "When in Rome, do as the Romans do."
- *Postconventional morality* represents the morality of the mature adult. At this level, people are less concerned about how others might see them and more

concerned about how they see and judge themselves over the long run. A marketing decision maker who has attained a postconventional level of morality might ask, "Even though it is legal and will increase company profits, is it right in the long run? Might it do more harm than good in the end?"

ETHICAL DECISION MAKING

How do businesspeople make ethical decisions? There is no cut-and-dried answer. Some of the ethical issues managers face are shown in Exhibit 3.1. Studies show that the following factors tend to influence ethical decision making and judgments:[13]

Unethical Practices Marketing Managers May Have to Deal With

- Entertainment and gift giving
- False or misleading advertising
- Misrepresentation of goods, services, and company capabilities
- Lies told customers in order to get the sale
- Manipulation of data (falsifying or misusing statistics or information)
- Misleading product or service warranties
- Unfair manipulation of customers
- Exploitation of children and/or disadvantaged groups
- Stereotypical portrayals of women, minority groups, and senior citizens
- Invasion of customer privacy
- Sexually oriented advertising appeals
- Product or service deception
- Unsafe products or services
- Price deception
- Price discrimination
- Unfair remarks and inaccurate statements about competitors
- Smaller amounts of product in the same-size packages

- *Extent of ethical problems within the organization:* Marketing professionals who perceive fewer ethical problems in their organizations tend to disapprove more strongly of "unethical" or questionable practices than those who perceive more ethical problems. Apparently, the healthier the ethical environment, the more likely that marketers will take a strong stand against questionable practices.
- *Top-management actions on ethics:* Top managers can influence the behavior of marketing professionals by encouraging ethical behavior and discouraging unethical behavior.
- *Potential magnitude of the consequences:* The greater the harm done to victims, the more likely that marketing professionals will recognize a problem as unethical.
- *Social consensus:* The greater the degree of agreement among managerial peers that an action is harmful, the more likely that marketers will recognize a problem as unethical.
- *Probability of a harmful outcome:* The greater the likelihood that an action will result in a harmful outcome, the more likely that marketers will recognize a problem as unethical.
- *Length of time between the decision and the onset of consequences:* The shorter the length of time between the action and the onset of negative consequences, the more likely that marketers will perceive a problem as unethical.
- *Number of people to be affected:* The greater the number of persons affected by a negative outcome, the more likely that marketers will recognize a problem as unethical.

ETHICAL GUIDELINES

Many organizations have become more interested in ethical issues. One sign of this interest is the increase in the number of large companies that appoint ethics officers—from virtually none five years ago to almost 25 percent of large corporations now. In addition, many companies of various sizes have developed a **code of ethics** as a guideline to help marketing managers and other employees make better decisions. In fact, a national

code of ethics
A guideline to help marketing managers and other employees make better decisions.

study found that 60 percent of the companies maintained a code of ethics, 33 percent offered ethics training, and 33 percent employed an ethics officer.[14] Some of the most highly praised codes of ethics are those of Boeing, Hewlett-Packard, Johnson & Johnson, and the Norton Company.

Creating ethics guidelines has several advantages:

- It helps employees identify what their firm recognizes as acceptable business practices.
- A code of ethics can be an effective internal control on behavior, which is more desirable than external controls like government regulation.
- A written code helps employees avoid confusion when determining whether their decisions are ethical.
- The process of formulating the code of ethics facilitates discussion among employees about what is right and wrong and ultimately leads to better decisions.

Businesses, however, must be careful not to make their code of ethics too vague or too detailed. Codes that are too vague give little or no guidance to employees in their day-to-day activities. Codes that are too detailed encourage employees to substitute rules for judgment. For instance, if employees are involved in questionable behavior, they may use the absence of a written rule as a reason to continue behaving that way, even though their conscience may be saying no. The checklist in Exhibit 3.2 is an example of a simple but helpful set of ethical guidelines. Following the checklist will not guarantee the "rightness" of a decision, but it will improve the chances that the decision will be ethical.

Although many companies have issued policies on ethical behavior, marketing managers must still put the policies into effect. They must address the classic "matter of degree" issue. For example, marketing researchers must often resort to deception to obtain unbiased answers to their research questions. Asking for a few minutes of a respondent's time is dishonest if the researcher knows the interview will last 45 minutes. Not only must management post a code of ethics, but it must also give examples of what is ethical and unethical for each item in the code. Moreover, top management must stress to all employees the importance of adhering to the company's

EXHIBIT 3.2

Ethics Checklist

- Does the decision benefit one person or group but hurt or not benefit other individuals or groups? In other words, is my decision fair to all concerned?

- Would individuals or groups, particularly customers, be upset if they knew about my decision?

- Has important information been overlooked because my decision was made without input from other knowledgeable individuals or groups?

- Does my decision presume that my company is an exception to a common practice in this industry and that I therefore have the authority to break a rule?

- Would my decision offend or upset qualified job applicants?

- Will my decision create conflict between individuals or groups within the company?

- Will I have to pull rank or use coercion to implement my decision?

- Would I prefer to avoid the consequences of my decision?

- Did I avoid truthfully answering any of the above questions by telling myself that the risks of getting caught are low or that I could get away with the potentially unethical behavior?

In an effort to ensure that employees know how to act in an ethical manner, many companies have a code of ethics or ethical guidelines. Companies from Boeing to Tower Records use games to practice ethical decision making. There is even a game based on the popular cartoon character, Dilbert.

© TERRI MILLER/E-VISUAL COMMUNICATIONS INC. © WORKING VALUES, LTD., DILBERT © UNITED FEATURE SYNDICATE, INC.

code of ethics. Without a detailed code of ethics and top management's support, creating ethical guidelines becomes an empty exercise.

Ethics training is an excellent way to help employees put good ethics into practice. Raytheon, one of the world's largest defense contractors, requires all its employees to attend formal classroom ethics awareness training each year. In addition, all employees must complete online scenario-based ethics and business conduct training annually.[15] At Niagara Mohawk, an electric and natural gas utility, an Ethics and Compliance Office manages a company-wide ethics program that includes a code of conduct detailing employee responsibilities to avoid conflicts of interest. Niagara Mohawk recently won the Better Business Bureau's International Torch Award for business ethics.[16]

REVIEW LEARNING OBJECTIVE 2

2	Describe the role of ethics and ethical decisions in business

MORALITY		
Preconventional	Conventional	Post-Conventional
What's in it for me?	Everyone else is doing it!	Is this good in the long run?
Will I get caught?	When in Rome . . .	
ETHICAL CLIMATE		
TOP MANAGEMENT ETHICS		
MAGNITUDE OF CONSEQUENCES		
SOCIAL CONSENSUS		
PROBABILITY OF HARM		
LENGTH OF TIME BETWEEN DECISION AND IMPACT		
NUMBER OF PEOPLE AFFECTED		
ETHICAL TRAINING		

3 THE EXTERNAL MARKETING ENVIRONMENT

Discuss the external environment of marketing, and explain how it affects a firm

All managerial decision making should be grounded in a good ethical base. In other words, proper ethics should permeate every managerial action. Perhaps the most important decisions a marketing manager must make relate to the creation of the marketing mix. Recall from Chapters 1 and 2 that a marketing mix is the unique combination of product, place (distribution), promotion, and price strategies. The marketing mix is, of course, under the firm's control and is designed to appeal to a specific group of potential buyers. A **target market** is a defined group that managers feel is most likely to buy a firm's product.

Over time, managers must alter the marketing mix because of changes in the environment in which consumers live, work, and make purchasing decisions. Also, as markets mature, some new consumers become part of the target market; others drop out. Those who remain may have different tastes, needs, incomes, lifestyles, and buying habits than the original target consumers.

Although managers can control the marketing mix, they cannot control elements in the external environment that continually mold and reshape the target market. Exhibit 3.3 shows the controllable and uncontrollable variables that affect the target market, whether it consists of consumers or business purchasers. The uncontrollable elements in the center of the diagram continually evolve and create changes in the target market. In contrast, managers can shape and reshape the marketing mix, depicted on the left side of the exhibit, to influence the target market. That is, managers react to changes in the external environment and attempt to create a more effective marketing mix.

target market
A defined group most likely to buy a firm's product.

EXHIBIT 3.3

Uncontrollable Elements in the External Environment Create Opportunities and Threats for a Firm's Marketing Mix

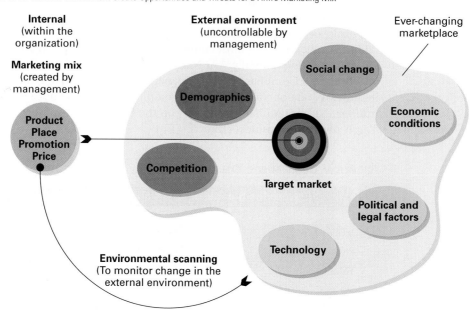

UNDERSTANDING THE EXTERNAL ENVIRONMENT

Unless marketing managers understand the external environment, the firm cannot intelligently plan for the future. Thus, many organizations assemble a team of specialists to continually collect and evaluate environmental information, a process called *environmental scanning*. The goal in gathering the environmental data is to identify future market opportunities and threats.

For example, as technology continues to blur the line between personal computers, television, and compact disc players, a company like Sony may find itself competing against a company like Dell. Research shows that children would like to find more games bundled with computer software, while adults are more likely to desire various word-processing and business-related software. Is this information an opportunity or a threat to Dell marketing managers?

ENVIRONMENTAL MANAGEMENT

No one business is large or powerful enough to create major change in the external environment. Thus, marketing managers are basically adapters rather than agents of change. For example, despite the huge size of General Motors and Ford, these companies are continually challenged to meet the competitive push by the Japanese for an ever-growing share of the U.S. automobile market. Competition is basically an uncontrollable element in the external environment.

 A firm is not always completely at the mercy of the external environment, however. Sometimes a firm can influence external events. For example, extensive lobbying by FedEx enabled it to acquire virtually all of the Japanese routes that it has sought. Japan had originally opposed new cargo routes for FedEx. The favorable decision was based on months of lobbying by FedEx at the White House, at several agencies, and in Congress for help in overcoming Japanese resistance. When a company implements strategies that attempt to shape the external environment within which it operates, it is engaging in **environmental management**.

FAQs

Isn't it true that if you build a really great product, you don't have to worry about the external environment? Find out the answer by watching the video FAQ on Xtra!

---

environmental management
When a company implements strategies that attempt to shape the external environment within which it operates.

The factors within the external environment that are important to marketing managers can be classified as social, demographic, economic, technological, political and legal, and competitive.

REVIEW LEARNING OBJECTIVE 3

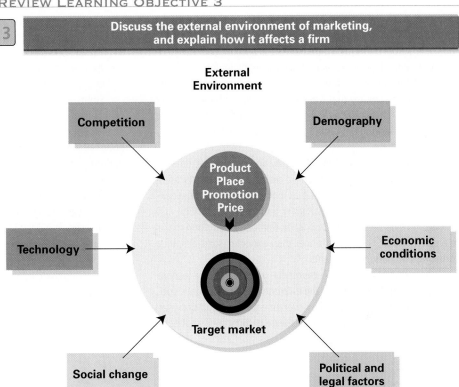

| 3 | Discuss the external environment of marketing, and explain how it affects a firm |

External Environment

Competition

Demography

Product
Place
Promotion
Price

Technology

Economic
conditions

Target market

Social change

Political and
legal factors

4 SOCIAL FACTORS

Describe the social factors that affect marketing

Social change is perhaps the most difficult external variable for marketing managers to forecast, influence, or integrate into marketing plans. Social factors include our attitudes, values, and lifestyles. Social factors influence the products people buy, the prices paid for products, the effectiveness of specific promotions, and how, where, and when people expect to purchase products.

AMERICAN VALUES

A *value* is a strongly held and enduring belief. During the United States' first 200 years, four basic values strongly influenced attitudes and lifestyles:

- *Self-sufficiency:* Every person should stand on his or her own two feet.
- *Upward mobility:* Success would come to anyone who got an education, worked hard, and played by the rules.
- *Work ethic:* Hard work, dedication to family, and frugality were moral and right.
- *Conformity:* No one should expect to be treated differently from everybody else.

These core values still hold for a majority of Americans today. A person's values are key determinants of what is important and not important, what actions to take or not to take, and how one behaves in social situations.

FAQs

Since social factors are illusive and hard to measure, can't you just ignore them in planning the marketing mix? Find out the answer by watching the video FAQ on Xtra!

FOR JAPANESE GIRLS, UNIFORMS ARE NOW TOO COOL FOR SCHOOL

Browsing in Tokyo's trendy 109 department store, 16-year-olds Sumie Tanaka and Saki Sanao are wearing what look like typical Japanese school uniforms: white blouses, navy-blue pleated miniskirts, knee-high socks, and matching penny loafers.

But the outfits aren't the teenagers' real school uniforms. They are uniform-like clothes that the two girls from the Tokyo suburb of Saitama have specifically picked out to wear on their shopping trip. "Everyone is wearing uniforms," says Tanaka. "They're cute and easy to coordinate."

Once seen as a symbol of conformity and oppression, the school uniform has become ultra-chic among Japanese girls. Many are wearing uniforms, or clothes that look like uniforms, on weekends and after school. Some girls wear uniforms even though their schools have no dress code. Ozakishoji Company, a uniform maker in western Japan, is seeing stronger-than-expected sales despite a shrinking population of students.

After years of riding the cutting edge of Japan's fickle fashion waves, schoolgirls are seen as the ultimate arbiters of what's cool, and their tastes are monitored by everyone from fashion designers to electronics companies. Schoolgirls were behind the rise of pop icons such as Hello Kitty and were early and enthusiastic users of text messaging over cell phones.

The uniform's popularity may be a sign of anxiety about growing up. Japan's long economic slump has severely constrained career opportunities for the young, especially for women.

Eighteen-year-old Eri Ishida, a student at Chiba Keisai High School east of Tokyo, says she dreads the day she will no longer be able to put on her navy-blue miniskirt, white blouse, and burgundy bow. "When I think that this is my last chance to wear a school uniform, I want to stay in school longer," says Ishida, who plans to study fashion design after she graduates next March.

Uniforms weren't always so cool. Decades ago, the school uniform was widely reviled as the most visible symbol of the strict control schools exercised over students. In addition to imposing inflexible dress codes, many schools forbid students to wear makeup and jewelry.[17]

Do you think conformity is a major value among American teenagers and young adults? Do you think that uniforms will be a hot fashion item in the United States? How do American values shape American fashion trends? Give an example.

AP/WIDE WORLD PHOTOS

One social factor that has recently had an important impact on the marketing of food products is the popularity of the Atkins diet. Since the diet restricts intake of carbohydrates, manufacturers of breads, cereals, and snack foods, like Frito Lay, have retooled product offerings and promotional messages to appeal to this growing market segment and to maintain demand for their products.

A person's values are typically formed through interaction with family, friends, and other influencers such as teachers, religious leaders, and politicians. The changing environment can also play a key role in shaping one's values. For example, people born during the 1970s and 1980s tend to be more comfortable with technology and its importance in the home than persons born in the 1950s. A change in values in Japan has meant a rush toward conformity, as the Global Perspectives box explains.

Values also influence our buying habits. Today's consumers are demanding, inquisitive, and discriminating. No longer willing to tolerate products that break down, they are insisting on high-quality goods that save time, energy, and often calories. U.S. consumers rank the characteristics of product quality as (1) reliability, (2) durability, (3) easy maintenance, (4) ease of use, (5) a trusted brand name, and (6) a low price. Shoppers are also concerned about nutrition and want to know what's in their food, and most are also environmentalists.

THE GROWTH OF COMPONENT LIFESTYLES

People in the United States today are piecing together **component lifestyles**. A lifestyle is a mode of living; it is the way people decide to live their lives. In other words, they are choosing products and services that meet diverse needs and interests rather than conforming to traditional stereotypes.

In the past, a person's profession—for instance, banker—defined his or her lifestyle. Today, a person can be a banker and also a gourmet, fitness enthusiast, dedicated single parent, and Internet guru. Each of these lifestyles is associated with different goods and services and represents a target audience. For example, for the gourmet, marketers offer cooking utensils, wines, and exotic foods through magazines like *Bon Appetit* and *Gourmet*. The fitness enthusiast buys Adidas equipment and special jogging outfits and reads *Runner* magazine. Component lifestyles increase the complexity of consumers' buying habits. The banker may own a BMW but change the oil himself or herself. He or she may buy fast food for lunch but French wine for dinner, own sophisticated photographic equipment and a low-priced home stereo, and shop for socks at Kmart or Wal-Mart and suits or dresses at Brooks Brothers. The unique lifestyles of every consumer can require a different marketing mix.

THE CHANGING ROLE OF FAMILIES AND WORKING WOMEN

Component lifestyles have evolved because consumers can choose from a growing number of goods and services, and most have the money to exercise more options. The growth of dual-income families has resulted in increased purchasing power. Approximately 63 percent of all females between 16 and 65 years old are now in the workforce. Today, more than 9 million women-owned businesses in the United States generate $3.6 trillion in revenues.[18] The phenomenon of working women has probably had a greater effect on marketing than has any other social change.

As women's earnings grow, so do their levels of expertise, experience, and authority. Working-age women are not the same group businesses targeted 30 years ago. They expect different things in life—from their jobs, from their spouses, and from the products and services they buy. Not all companies understand this notion. Even though women spend about $55 billion of the total $95 billion spent on consumer electronics, experts say companies continue to assume women aren't very interested in high-tech products or respond only to "technology-made-simple" themes.[19] Gateway, for example, produced a laptop in pink and had it featured in the popular movie *Legally Blond 2*. Some observers feel that this type of campaign will backfire. Most women in business today are just as tech-savvy as their male counterparts, or more so. They resent being viewed as "clueless." "I've corresponded with thousands of women and I can tell you, they are just as offended as I am," says Aliza Sherman, creator of several Web sites for women and author of *Powertools for Women in Business*. "It's insulting to think in order to appeal to women you have to turn it pink and simplify it," she says.[20]

component lifestyles
The practice of choosing goods and services that meet one's diverse needs and interests rather than conforming to a single, traditional lifestyle.

A/P/WIDE WORLD PHOTOS

Single women are now the second largest group of homebuyers after couples. Reflecting this trend are the changing demographics of customers at Home Depot and Lowes, which both indicate that about half of the purchases made in their stores are by women. As a result, both companies have made adjustments to how they market to women.

Single working women are now the second largest group of home buyers after couples. Both Home Depot and Lowe's estimate that about half of all purchases in their stores are made by women.[21] In addition, married women often influence buying decisions made as a couple or when the husband shops alone. Currently, all Home Depot stores offer classes and clinics that are open to both men and women. Several years ago the company began offering women-only classes in some stores as an alternative to "Monday Night Football." In 2002, it required all of its stores to hold a women-only woodworking course that was "very successful," says Kim McKesson, a merchandising executive for the Atlanta-based chain.[22]

In a recent survey, two-thirds to three-quarters of women said they are making many major economic decisions either independently or equally with a spouse. Few of the women said they left important marketplace decisions to others.[23]

Cost is a more important consideration in decisions made by women, whereas quality is relatively more important to men. This difference has important ramifications for managers creating a new marketing mix. When it comes to big-ticket, long-term items, women remain active in the decision-making process, though a plurality say they are more likely to make these decisions with a spouse. Life experience is an important factor in women's independence in long-term planning; married women over age 55 are more likely to make these decisions on their own than their younger counterparts are. Single women, of course, make more of their own decisions.[24]

REVIEW LEARNING OBJECTIVE 4

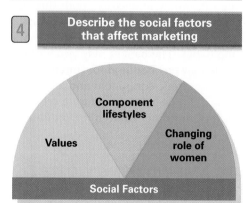

4 | Describe the social factors that affect marketing

5 DEMOGRAPHIC FACTORS

Explain the importance to marketing managers of current demographic trends

Another uncontrollable variable in the external environment—also extremely important to marketing managers—is **demography**, the study of people's vital statistics, such as their age, race and ethnicity, and location. Demographics are significant because the basis for any market is people. Demographic characteristics are strongly related to consumer buyer behavior in the marketplace.

We turn our attention now to a closer look at age groups, their impact, and the opportunities they present for marketers. The cohorts have been given the names of Generation Y, Generation X, and baby boomers. You will find that each cohort group has its own needs, values, and consumption patterns.

GENERATION Y

Those designated by demographics as **Generation Y** were born between 1979 and 1994. They are about 60 million strong, more than three times as large as Generation X. And though Generation Y is much smaller than the baby boom, which lasted nearly 20 years and produced 78 million children, its members are plentiful enough to put their own footprints on society.

The marketing impact of Generation Y has been immense. Companies that sell toys, videos, software, and clothing to kids have boomed in recent years. Nine of the ten best-selling videos of all time are animated films from Walt Disney. Club Med, the French vacation company, now earns half its U.S. revenues from family resorts. The members of Generation Y were born into a world vastly different from the one their parents entered. The changes in family, the workforce, technology, and demographics in recent decades will no doubt affect their attitudes, but often in unpredictable ways.

Gen Yers appear to be a "notoriously fickle" consumer group, demanding the latest trends in record time. Communicators wanting to reach Gen Y teens have "to embrace that type of fast change." A critical consumer group, they "don't like a hard sell." They are "brand and fashion-conscious," but as one advertising manager has learned, you have to get the "merchandise in front of them without being in their face."[25]

demography
The study of people's vital statistics, such as their age, race and ethnicity, and location.

Generation Y
People born between 1979 and 1994.

EXHIBIT 3.4

The Magic 21

41%	Share of 21-year-olds who currently live with mom and/or dad.
60%	Share of college students who plan to move back home after graduation.
1 in 4	Odds that a 21-year-old was raised by a single parent.
70%	Share of 21-year-olds who have a full- or part-time job.
$2,241,141	Amount the average 21-year-old will spend between now and the end of his/her life.
$208,953	Amount the average 21-year-old will spend on cars during his or her life.
93%	Share of 21-year-olds who have a credit card today.
43%	Share of 21-year-olds who have a tattoo or a body piercing.
$3,000	Credit card debt of the average 21-year-old.
2	Number of children the average 21-year-old woman will have in her lifetime.
78%	Share of 21-year-olds who have never married.
19%	Share of 21-year-olds who are married.
5.8	Years until the average 21-year-old man marries for the first time.
4.1	Years until the average 21-year-old woman marries for the first time.
10	Years until the average 21-year-old buys his or her first home.

SOURCE: John Fetto, "Twenty-One, and Counting," *American Demographics*, September 2003, 48.

Many Gen Yers have recently turned 21 or will do so in the next few years—about 4.3 million of them in 2005. Twenty-one-year-olds tend to be a special challenge in the marketplace. Gen Yers tend to be skeptical consumers who, after years of exposure to saturation marketing, are hardened to traditional advertising tactics. They're much less brand loyal than previous generations and are more accepting of generic labels. A survey by Miami-based Market Segment Research found that 18- to 24-year-olds are more likely than other consumers to buy a product on the spur of the moment and change brands if the mood strikes. Only one in five looks for a particular brand, compared with the one in three 60-year-olds who shops for specific brands. "Twenty-one-year-olds are in a period of transition," says Marshal Cohen, president of NPDFashionworld in Port Washington, New York. "They believe that what's in today is gone tomorrow. So they're not ready to make any strong brand attachments."[26] Some key characteristics of 21-year-olds are shown in Exhibit 3.4.

One thing 21-year-olds are attached to is technology. Telecommunications, television, and the Internet are so ubiquitous in their lives that they bounce seamlessly from one to another, sometimes consuming several media simultaneously. One of those media is typically a cell phone. Two companies that are in sync with Gen Yers are Boost Mobile and Virgin Mobile. Boost is adding 40,000 customers a month, almost all Gen Yers. Virgin is signing up about 2,000 per day. The handsets themselves aren't the big sell; although some come in funky colors or are co-branded with edgy outfits like women's surf-gear maker Roxy, the phones are similar to others. But both Boost and Virgin eschew traditional distribution channels, focusing instead on selling in surf shops, record stores, and other places where kids hang out. Credit checks and binding contracts are out, so the companies rely on pay-as-you-go plans. Rather than receive a monthly bill, customers can purchase prepaid chunks of airtime, in increments ranging from $20 to $50, at places like 7-Eleven or Target.[27]

GENERATION X

Generation X—people born between 1965 and 1978—consists of 40 million consumers. It is the first generation of latchkey children—products of dual-career households or, in roughly half of the cases, of divorced or separated parents. Gen Xers have been bombarded by multiple media since their cradle days; thus, they are savvy and cynical consumers.

With careers launched and families started, Gen Xers are at the stage in life when suddenly a host of demands are competing for their time—and their budgets. As a result, Gen X spending is quite diffuse: food, housing, transportation. Time is at a premium for harried Gen Xers, so they're outsourcing the tasks of daily life, which include everything from domestic help to babysitting. Xers spend 78 percent more than average on personal services, more than any other age group, and therefore spend 15 percent less than average on housekeeping supplies.[28]

About 65 percent of Gen X women have children, and most Gen X couples have set up households. With Gen Xers now heading their own households,

Generation X
People born between 1965 and 1978.

Generation X is not nearly as large as either Generation Y or the baby boom generation. Still, it represents a lucrative market, since its members spend a larger-than-average share of their incomes on restaurant meals, clothing, and electronics.

baby boomers
People born between 1946 and 1964.

companies have the opportunity to tailor messages to a new generation in its prime spending years. Some brands that Gen X helped popularize are beginning to adjust their marketing to reflect this new stage in their customers' lives. For example, ads for handbag designer Kate Spade showed children leaping out of station wagons and tumbling around in pajamas, while Kenneth Cole ads showed children swinging on tires.

Meanwhile, other brands have expanded their offerings to include Gen X babies; Tommy Hilfiger and DKNY have both launched children's lines. And Crate & Barrel opened a Gen X–specific retail offshoot, CB2. While Crate & Barrel is more mature and sophisticated, CB2 is more urban, edgy, hip.[29]

Why does tailoring the merchandise to particular age groups matter? One reason is that each generation enters a life stage with its own tastes and biases, and tailoring products to what customers value is key to sales.

BABY BOOMERS—AMERICA'S MASS MARKET

Baby boomers represent 42 percent of all U.S. households and control 50 percent of all consumer spending.[30] This group totals nearly 78 million people, so it's useful to divide boomers into two subgroups: the Younger Boomers, ages 41 to 49 in 2005, whose spending is still directed by their children; and the Older Boomers, ages 50 to 59 in 2005, who are in their empty nesting years. For Younger Boomers, the home is still the castle, and family is the priority. For the first time at this stage of life, a majority (69 percent) of householders own their homes instead of renting them.[31] So it's no surprise that the Younger Boomers are directing a larger share of their budgets to their homes than any other age group. Spending on kids is also shaping the Younger Boomer's budget. This household devotes a significant amount of money to keeping the growing family busy. They spend 11 percent more than average on pets, toys, and playground equipment.[32]

Now that the kids are grown, Older Boomers are directing their funds to upgrading their homes in small ways, spending 50 percent more than average on housewares, such as china and silverware, for example.[33] They're also taking a new look at their wardrobes, spending 13 percent more than average on adult women's apparel and 11 percent more than average on adult men's apparel. Looking for a way to show off their new clothes, Older Boomers are also planning vacations; they spend 23 percent more than the average household on hotels and vacation homes.[34]

OLDER CONSUMERS: NOT JUST GRANDPARENTS

The generation prior to the baby boomers have already crossed the 60-year threshold that many demographers use to define the "mature market." Yet today's mature consumers are wealthier, healthier, and better educated than those of earlier generations. Though better off than earlier generations, many lost a substantial amount of their nest eggs in the recent $8 trillion stock market meltdown. As a result, many plan to continue working until their 70s or even their 80s.[35] The main reason is the need for more money.

When aging boomers finally retire, fixed incomes will mean tighter budgets. But while spending among seniors reflects this reality, they are far from being out of the consumer marketplace. Seniors spend money maintaining what they've already accumulated. Preserving the home, for example, eats up a large share of the budget—86 percent more than in the average household.[36] Given the amount of time they now spend at home, these consumers also direct a larger chunk of their budgets to food to be eaten there. For example, they spend 50 percent more than average on fresh fruits and vegetables, 33 percent more than average on fresh milk and cream, and 25 percent more than average on baked goods.

Businesspeople who want to actively pursue the mature market must understand it. Aging consumers create some obvious opportunities. For example, JCPenney's Easy Dressing clothes feature Velcro fasteners for women with arthritis or other ailments who may have difficulty with zippers or buttons. By 2025, consumers over 65 will be the largest growth market by far. Between 2000 and 2025, the number of people in this age group will double to over 70 million.[37]

AMERICANS ON THE MOVE

The average U.S. citizen moves every six years—a trend that has implications for marketing. A large influx of people into an area creates many new opportunities for all types of businesses. Conversely, significant out-migration from a city or town may force many of its businesses to move or close down and markets to dry up. The six states experiencing the greatest population increases due to interstate migration are Florida, Georgia, North Carolina, Virginia, Washington, and Arizona. The cities with the greatest projected population growth from 1995 to 2005 are Houston, Washington, D.C., Atlanta, San Diego, Phoenix, Orlando, and Dallas.[38]

In addition to migration within its borders, the United States experiences immigration from other countries. The six states with the highest levels of immigration from abroad are California, New York, New Jersey, Illinois, Texas, and Massachusetts. The presence of large numbers of immigrants in an area creates a need for markets that cater to their unique needs and desires.

REVIEW LEARNING OBJECTIVE 5

5

Explain the importance to marketing managers of current demographic trends

Age	Gen Y	Gen X	Baby Boom	Seniors
	1979–1984 60 million	1965–1978 40 million	1946–1964 78 million	Before 1946 70 million

6 GROWING ETHNIC MARKETS

Explain the importance to marketing managers of multiculturalism and growing ethnic markets

By 2007, Hispanics will wield more than $900 billion in spending power, an increase of 315 percent since 1990. By that same year, African Americans' spending will top the $850 billion mark, and Asian Americans' spending power will have soared 287 percent since 1990, to $455 billion—far outpacing total U.S. growth in buying power.[39]

In 2003, Hispanics overtook African Americans to become America's largest minority group with 12.5 percent of the population. In 2004, African Americans made up 12.3 percent of the population and Asian Americans 3.6 percent.[40] America's growing ethnic diversity is having a profound impact on marketing.

Companies across the United States have recognized that diversity can result in bottom-line benefits. More than ever, diversity is emerging as a priority goal for visionary leaders who embrace the incontestable fact that the United States is becoming a truly multicultural society. Data from the 2000 U.S. Census

Multicultural marketing has found great success on the Internet. Numerous sites, like iMinorities.com, provide information and services targeted toward a variety of minority groups.

confirmed that minorities now constitute one-third of the nation's population and control $1 trillion in annual spending—an increase of more than $420 billion since 1990, according to the Selig Center for Economic Growth at the University of Georgia.[41] For marketers seeking to tap this bulging consumer purse, the latest census data reveal a multicultural marketplace that's more diverse than ever.

MARKETING TO AFRICAN AMERICANS

Many firms are creating new and different products for the African American market. Often entrepreneurial African Americans are the first to realize unique product opportunities. For example, when Yla Eason couldn't find an African American superhero doll to buy for her son, she founded Olmec Corporation. Now this New York–based toy manufacturer is a $2 million company, marketing more than 60 kinds of African American and Hispanic dolls. Eason has a distribution partnership with Hasbro.

Several companies owned by African Americans—such as Soft Sheen, M&M, Johnson, and ProLine—target the African American market for health and beauty aids. Huge corporations like Revlon, Gillette, and Alberto-Culver have either divisions or major product lines for this market as well. Alberto-Culver's hair-care line for this segment includes 75 products. In fact, hair-care items are the largest single category in the African American health and beauty aid industry. Maybelline with its Shades of You product line has the largest share (28 percent) of the African American health and beauty aid market.

The promotional dollars spent on African Americans continue to rise. One reason is the relationship that blacks have with certain media. For example, African Americans spend considerable time with radio (an astounding 4 hours a day versus 2.8 hours for other groups), and urban audiences have an intensely personal relationship with the medium. Pepsi used radio to raise the level of Mountain Dew awareness and its market share in urban markets. Artists like Busta Rhymes personify the image of Mountain Dew and create the lyrics and the vibe that sells the product.[42]

Never before have there been so many black media choices. ABC Radio Network's Tom Joyner reaches an audience of 7 million in 100 markets, and Doug Banks is heard by 1.5 million listeners in 36 markets. BET, the black cable TV network, has 62 million viewers.[43] The 32-year-old *Essence* magazine reaches one-third of all black females ages 18 to 49.

MARKETING TO HISPANIC AMERICANS

The term *Hispanic* encompasses people of many different backgrounds. Nearly 60 percent of Hispanic Americans are of Mexican descent. The next largest group, Puerto Ricans, make up just under 10 percent of Hispanics. Other groups, including Central Americans, Dominicans, South Americans, and Cubans, account for less than 5 percent of all Hispanics.[44]

The diversity of the Hispanic population and the language differences create many challenges for those trying to target this market. Hispanics, especially recent immigrants, often prefer products from their native country. Therefore, many retailers along the southern U.S. border import goods from Mexico. In New York City, more than 6,000 *bodegas* (grocery stores) sell such items as plantains, chorizo (pork sausage), and religious candles to Puerto Rican Americans. The *bodegas* also serve as neighborhood social centers. Fresh produce is usually very important to Hispanics because of their tradition of shopping every day at open-air produce markets in their native country.

Many Hispanics are loyal to the brands found in their homeland. If these are not available, Hispanics will choose brands that reflect their native values and culture. Research shows that Hispanics often are not aware of many mainstream U.S. brands. In general, Hispanics tend to be very brand loyal.[45]

The total advertising budget for Hispanics in 2004 was over $2.2 billion. Hispanic consumers, in general, think very positively about companies that advertise in Spanish.

The number of TV, radio, and cable channels aimed at Hispanic Americans continues to expand. Four national Hispanic radio networks air Spanish-language programming over 600 stations. An estimated 80 percent of Hispanics listen to radio. The second most popular radio station in Los Angeles is KWKW, "*La Mexicana*."[46] As for television, there are three Spanish-language networks: Univision, Telemundo, and Galavision.

Mainstream retailers have also been actively targeting the Hispanic market. Wal-Mart and Mervyn's have hired ethnic specialists and tested ethnic promotional campaigns. Those moves have spurred retailers like JCPenney and Sears to boost ethnic ad budgets. JCPenney spends about $6 million per year on Hispanic marketing, for Spanish-language TV commercials, brochures and credit applications in Spanish, and Hispanic fashion shows.

MARKETING TO ASIAN AMERICANS

Asian Americans, who represent only 4.2 percent of the U.S. population, have the highest average family income of all groups. Census data put the figure at $51,200, more than $10,000 above the average U.S. household. Between 1990 and 2001, Asian Americans' purchasing power jumped 124 percent to $254 billion—more than that of any other minority group—and is expected to continue to grow. Sixty percent of all Asian Americans have at least a bachelor's degree.[47]

Because Asian Americans are younger and better educated and have higher incomes than average, they are sometimes called a "marketer's dream." As a group, Asian Americans are more comfortable with technology than the general population is. They are far more likely to use automated teller machines, and many more of them own DVD players, compact disc players, microwave ovens, home computers, and telephone answering machines.

A number of products have been developed specifically for the Asian American market. For example, Kayla Beverly Hills salon draws Asian American consumers because the firm offers cosmetics formulated for them. Anheuser-Busch's agricultural products division sells rice to Asian Americans, who are rice connoisseurs. The company developed eight varieties of California-grown rice, each with a different label, to cover a range of nationalities and tastes.

Nonetheless, cultural diversity within the Asian American market complicates promotional efforts. "There really isn't one Asian American market," says Nancy Shimamoto of San Francisco–based Hispanic & Asian Marketing Research, Inc., a division of Cheskin.[48] Instead, she says, marketers must recognize the cultural and linguistic differences that exist among the Chinese American, Filipino, Japanese, Vietnamese, Korean, Indian, and Pakistani markets. "There is absolutely no common language or culture, and to find the ties that bind is extraordinarily difficult," she says.[49]

Although Asian Americans embrace the values of the larger U.S. population, they also hold on to the cultural values of their particular subgroup. Consider language. Many Asian Americans, particularly Koreans and Chinese, speak their native tongue at home. Filipinos are far less likely to do so. Or consider big-ticket purchases. In Japanese American homes, the husband alone makes the decision on such purchases nearly half the time; the wife decides only about 6 percent of the time. In Filipino families, however, wives make these decisions a little more often than their husbands do, although by far the most decisions are made by husbands and wives jointly or with the input of other family members.[50]

Asian Americans like to shop at stores owned and managed by other Asian Americans. Small businesses such as flower shops, grocery stores, and appliance stores are often best equipped to offer the products that Asian Americans want. For example, at first glance the Ha Nam supermarket in Los Angeles's Koreatown might be any other grocery store. But next to the Kraft American singles and the State Fair corn dogs are jars of whole cabbage kimchi. A snack bar in another part of the store cooks up aromatic mung cakes, and an entire aisle is devoted to dried seafood.

Some entrepreneurs are building large enclosed malls that cater to Asian consumers. At the Aberdeen Centre near Vancouver, British Columbia, nearly 80 percent of the merchants are Chinese Canadians, as are 80 percent of the customers. The mall offers fashions made in Hong Kong, a shop for traditional Chinese medicines, and a theater showing Chinese movies. Kung fu martial-arts demonstrations and Chinese folk dances are held in the mall on weekends.

ETHNIC AND CULTURAL DIVERSITY

Multiculturalism occurs when all major ethnic groups in an area—such as a city, county, or census tract—are roughly equally represented. Because of its current demographic transition, the trend in the United States is toward greater multiculturalism.

San Francisco County is the most diverse county in the nation. The proportions of major ethnic groups are closer to being equal there than anywhere else. People of many ancestries have long been attracted to the area. Elsewhere, however, a careful examination of the statistics from the latest U.S. Census Bureau reveals that the nation's minority groups, especially Hispanics and Asians, are heavily clustered in selected regions and markets. Rather than witnessing the formation of a homogeneous national melting pot, we are seeing the creation of numerous mini-melting pots, while the rest of America remains much less diverse.

In a broad swath of the country, the minority presence is still quite limited. America's racial and ethnic patterns have taken on distinctly regional dimensions. Hispanics dominate large portions of counties in a span of states stretching from California to Texas. Blacks are strongly represented in counties of the South as well as selected urban areas in the Northeast and Midwest. The Asian presence is relatively small and highly concentrated in a few scattered counties, largely in the West. And Native Americans are concentrated in select pockets in Oklahoma, the Southeast, the upper Midwest, and the West. Multiethnic counties are most prominent in California and the Southwest, with mixes of Asians and Hispanics, or Hispanics and Native Americans.

FAQs

Isn't multiculturalism more a myth than a reality? Find out the answer by watching the video FAQ on Xtra!

multiculturalism
When all major ethnic groups in an area—such as a city, county, or census tract—are roughly equally represented.

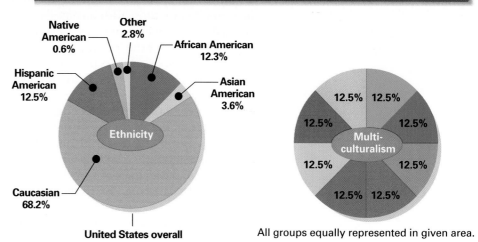

6 Explain the importance to marketing managers of multiculturalism and growing ethnic markets

United States overall

All groups equally represented in given area.

7 ECONOMIC FACTORS

Identify consumer and marketer re-actions to the state of the economy

In addition to social and demographic factors, marketing managers must understand and react to the economic environment. The three economic areas of greatest concern to most marketers are the distribution of consumer income, inflation, and recession.

RISING INCOMES

As disposable (or after-tax) incomes rise, more families and individuals can afford the "good life." Fortunately, U.S. incomes have continued to rise, although at a rather slow pace. After adjustment for inflation, the median household income in the United States in 2005 was approximately $42,700. This means half of all U.S. households earned less and the other half earned more.[51]

Education is the primary determinant of a person's earning potential. For example, only 1 percent of those with a high school education earn over $100,000 annually. By comparison, 13 percent of college-educated workers earn six figures or more.[52] Along with "willingness to buy," or "ability to buy," income is a key determinant of target markets. A marketer who knows where the money is knows where the markets are. If you are seeking a new store location for Dollar General, a retail chain that caters to lower-income consumers, you would probably concentrate on the South and Midwest because most households with annual incomes of less than $45,000 are concentrated in these areas.[53]

The middle class consists of households with incomes between $45,000 and $74,999. They include 25.8 million of the approximately 56 million total households in the United States.[54] Exhibit 3.5 reveals the location of America's middle class. The massive size of this group, and its purchasing power, makes it absolutely essential for most marketers. For example, the middle class is the target market for the South Carolina Tourism Board, which promotes the

EXHIBIT 3.5

Where America's Middle Class Lives

The Massive Middle-Class Market

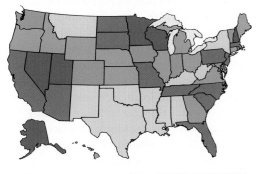

Percent of Households with Annual Income Between $45,000 and $74,999	19.8%–23.2%
	23.2%–24.7%
	24.7%–25.9%
	25.9%–26.8%
	26.8%–28.5%

SOURCE: "The Massive Middle-Class Market," *American Demographics,* December 2002/January 2003, 38.

state as a drive-to vacation destination. To narrow the market, the agency built a comprehensive demographic and geographic profile and ran a coupon in Sunday newspaper supplements in key metros. The result: 11,000 requests in one day for information, the largest one-day response the organization had ever had.

The near-affluent, those with incomes of $75,000 to $99,999, are primarily concentrated along the East and West Coasts. The affluent, those with household incomes of $100,000 to $199,999, are concentrated in the Northeast and in the mid-Atlantic states. Because of its proximity to the New York City and Philadelphia metros, New Jersey has the largest share of households earning $100,000 or more.[55]

The upper echelon is defined as households with annual incomes of $200,000+. A group that accounts for only 2 percent of all U.S. households usually doesn't warrant much attention from marketers. But this 2 percent is obviously the exception. Commanding the biggest bucks in America, this small, select group of households includes the titans of U.S. earning and spending. When Bill Gates and Oprah filled out their income tax forms, this was undoubtedly their income bracket.

Those in the upper echelon share a lot demographically with their slightly less wealthy counterparts, who earn between $100,000 and $199,999, but the two groups aren't exactly the same. For one thing, while both tend to be concentrated in the power centers of America—New York, Washington, and San Francisco—the superwealthy also have homes in sunny, leisure locales, such as Naples and West Palm Beach in Florida and Santa Barbara in California. Another difference is that the superrich tend to be older—more than one-third are over 55, which suggests that they likely receive income from other sources besides a weekly paycheck. By contrast, the largest group among the affluent is still of working age, a more sprightly 45 to 54.[56]

PURCHASING POWER

Rising incomes don't necessarily mean a higher standard of living, however. Increased standards of living are a function of purchasing power. **Purchasing power** is measured by comparing income to the relative cost of a set standard of goods and services in different geographic areas, usually referred to as the cost of living. Another way to think of purchasing power is income minus the cost living (i.e., expenses). In general, a cost of living index takes into account housing, food and groceries, transportation, utilities, health care, and miscellaneous expenses such as clothing, services, and entertainment. Homefair's salary calculator uses these metrics when it figures the cost of living index in Akron, Ohio as being nearly half the cost of living in New York City. This means that a worker living in New York must earn nearly $90,000 to have the same standard of living as someone making $45,000 in Akron. Monstermoving.com uses a cost of living index that also includes property and income taxes, as well as auto insurance costs. Not surprisingly, Monstermove.com's comparative figures on the cost of living in both places are even more dramatic. The cost of living in New York City measures 397 percent higher than in Akron! So, a worker making $45,000 in Akron would need to make $223,916 in New York to have the same standard of living!

When income is high relative to the cost of living, people have more discretionary income. That means they have more money to spend on non-essential items (in other words, on wants rather than needs). This information is important to marketers for obvious reasons. Consumers with high purchasing power can afford to spend more money without jeopardizing their budget for necessities, like food, housing, utilities, and so forth. They also have the ability to purchase higher priced necessities, for example, a more expensive car, a home in a more expensive neighborhood, or a designer handbag versus a purse from a discount store.

purchasing power
A comparison of income versus the relative cost of a set standard of goods and services in different geographic areas.

INFLATION

Inflation is a general rise in prices, often accompanied by a lack of increase in wages, which results in decreased purchasing power. Fortunately, the United States has had a low rate of inflation for over a decade. During the early and mid-2000s, the U.S. inflation rate has been less than 3 percent. This relatively low rate has been attributed to several factors including Federal Reserve actions, the recession of 2001, and the productivity of the economy. Relatively high unemployment rates have also helped hold real wage gains in check.[57]

In times of low inflation, businesses seeking to increase their profit margins can do so only by increasing their efficiency. If they significantly increase prices, no one will purchase their goods or services.

In more inflationary times, marketers use a number of pricing strategies to cope. (See Chapter 18 for more on these strategies.) But in general, marketers must be aware that inflation causes consumers to either build up or diminish their brand loyalty. In one research session, a consumer panelist noted, "I used to use just Betty Crocker mixes, but now I think of either Betty Crocker or Duncan Hines, depending on which is on sale." Another participant said, "Pennies count now, and so I look at the whole shelf, and I read the ingredients. I don't really understand, but I can tell if it's exactly the same. So now I use this cheaper brand, and honestly, it works just as well." Inflation pressures consumers to make more economical purchases. Nevertheless, most consumers try hard to maintain their standard of living.

In creating marketing strategies to cope with inflation, managers must realize that, despite what happens to the seller's cost, the buyer is not going to pay more for a product than the subjective value he or she places on it. No matter how compelling the justification might be for a 10 percent price increase, marketers must always examine its impact on demand. Many marketers try to hold prices level as long as is practical.

RECESSION

A **recession** is a period of economic activity characterized by negative growth, which reduces demand for goods and services. During recession, the growth rates of income, production, and employment all fall to below zero percent. For example, in a true recession, you wouldn't receive a smaller raise than in previous years, but you would get a pay cut. The slowdown in the high-tech sector, overextended consumer credit, and the terrorist attacks on America resulted in the economy slipping into a recession in 2001. The problems of inflation and recession go hand in hand, yet recession requires different marketing strategies:

- *Improve existing products and introduce new ones:* The goal is to reduce production hours, waste, and the cost of materials. Recessions increase the demand for goods and services that are economical and efficient, offer value, help organizations streamline practices and procedures, and improve customer service.
- *Maintain and expand customer services:* In a recession, many organizations postpone the purchase of new equipment and materials. Sales of replacement parts and other services may become an important source of income.
- *Emphasize top-of-the-line products and promote product value:* Customers with less to spend will seek demonstrated quality, durability, satisfaction, and capacity to save time and money. High-priced, high-value items consistently fare well during recessions.

inflation
A general rise in prices, often accompanied by a lack of increase in wages, which results in decreased purchasing power.

recession
A period of economic activity characterized by negative growth, which reduces demand for goods and services.

| 7 | **Identify consumer and marketer reactions to the state of the economy** |

	Low	**Middle Class**	**Near Affluent**	**Affluent**	**Upper Class**
Income	< $45,000 per year	$45,000 – $75,000 per year	$75,000 – $99,999 per year	$100,000 – $199,999 per year	$200,000 + per year
	19.4%	≈ 50% of population	13.1%	15.6%	2% of population
	Less ←	College Education		→ More	
Location	South & Midwest	Midwest	East & West Coasts	Northeast Mid-Atlantic	Washington D.C. San Francisco New York City
Inflation	High	Low			Zero
Economic Activity	Recession		Growth		

8 TECHNOLOGICAL FACTORS

Identify the impact of technology on a firm

ONLINE

Sometimes new technology is an effective weapon against inflation and recession. New machines that reduce production costs can be one of a firm's most valuable assets. The power of a personal-computer microchip doubles about every 18 months. Our ability, as a nation, to maintain and build wealth depends in large part on the speed and effectiveness with which we invent and adopt machines that lift productivity. For example, coal mining is typically thought of as unskilled, backbreaking labor. But visit Cyprus Amax Mineral Company's Twenty-mile Mine near Oak Creek, Colorado, and you will find workers with push-button controls who walk along massive machines that shear 30-inch slices from an 850-foot coal wall. Laptop computers help miners track equipment breakdowns and water quality.

The United States excels at both basic and applied research. **Basic research** (or *pure research*) attempts to expand the frontiers of knowledge but is not aimed at a specific, pragmatic problem. Basic research aims to confirm an existing theory or to learn more about a concept or phenomenon. For example, basic research might focus on high-energy physics. **Applied research**, in contrast, attempts to develop new or improved products. The United States has dramatically improved its track record in applied research. For example, the United States leads the world in applying basic research to aircraft design and propulsion systems.

Recall that we are referring here to technology that is external to the firm. Of course, developing new technology internally is a key to creating and maintaining a long-term competitive advantage. Nonetheless, external technology is important to managers for two reasons. First, by acquiring the technology, the firm may be able to operate more efficiently or create a better product. Second, a new technology may render your existing products obsolete. The debut of George Eastman's Kodak camera 116 years ago marked the birth of film-based photography. In 2003, for the first time digital cameras outsold traditional cameras that use film. You can imagine the profound impact that this shift is having

basic research
Pure research that aims to confirm an existing theory or to learn more about a concept or phenomenon.

applied research
An attempt to develop new or improved products.

8 | **Identify the impact of technology on a firm**

Basic Research → Applied Research → Technology Advances

↓ ↓ ↓

Marketing Mix

on Kodak, which generates 40 percent of its revenue from sales of consumer film and photo-finishing products and services. Experts say, though, that if Kodak had studied external technology over the last ten years, it would have seen this coming.[58]

Companies today must seek out technology that will make them better competitors. New technology is having a mind-boggling impact. American factories are making 41 percent more today with 8 percent fewer hours of labor than they did ten years ago.[59] Information technology and the Internet continue to transform business in a magnitude equal to the invention of the electric light and the steam engine. Entire sales, production, and delivery processes are now linked electronically across borders and time zones. Real-time market sales data from electronic data terminals (cash registers) enable marketing managers to respond to demand changes in an instant.

9 POLITICAL AND LEGAL FACTORS

Discuss the political and legal environment of marketing

Business needs government regulation to protect innovators of new technology, the interests of society in general, one business from another, and consumers. In turn, government needs business, because the marketplace generates taxes that support public efforts to educate our youth, pave our roads, protect our shores, and so on. The private sector also serves as a counterweight to government. The decentralization of power inherent in a private-enterprise system supplies the limitation on government essential for the survival of a democracy.

Every aspect of the marketing mix is subject to laws and restrictions. It is the duty of marketing managers or their legal assistants to understand these laws and conform to them, because failure to comply with regulations can have major consequences for a firm. Sometimes just sensing trends and taking corrective action before a government agency acts can help avoid regulation. The tobacco industry failed to do this. As a result, Joe Camel and the Marlboro Man are fading into the sunset along with other strategies used to promote tobacco products.

The challenge is not simply to keep the marketing department out of trouble, however, but to help it implement creative new programs to accomplish marketing objectives. It is all too easy for a marketing manager or sometimes a lawyer to say "no" to a marketing innovation that actually entails little risk. For example, an overly cautious lawyer could hold up sales of a desirable new product by warning that the package design could prompt a copyright infringement suit. Thus, it is important to have a thorough understanding of the laws established by the federal government, state governments, and regulatory agencies to govern marketing-related issues.

FEDERAL LEGISLATION

Federal laws that affect marketing fall into several categories. First, the Sherman Act, the Clayton Act, the Federal Trade Commission Act, the Celler-Kefauver Antimerger Act, and the Hart-Scott-Rodino Act were passed to regulate the competitive environment. Second, the Robinson-Patman Act was designed to regulate pricing practices. Third, the Wheeler-Lea Act was created to control false advertising. These key pieces of legislation are summarized in Exhibit 3.6. The primary federal laws that protect consumers are shown in Exhibit 3.7.

EXHIBIT 3.6

Primary U.S. Laws That Affect Marketing

LEGISLATION	IMPACT ON MARKETING
Sherman Act of 1890	Makes trusts and conspiracies in restraint of trade illegal; makes monopolies and attempts to monopolize a misdemeanor.
Clayton Act of 1914	Outlaws discrimination in prices to different buyers; prohibits tying contracts (which require the buyer of one product to also buy another item in the line); makes illegal the combining of two or more competing corporations by pooling ownership of stock.
Federal Trade Commission Act of 1914	Creates the Federal Trade Commission to deal with antitrust matters; outlaws unfair methods of competition.
Robinson-Patman Act of 1936	Prohibits charging different prices to different buyers of merchandise of like grade and quantity; requires sellers to make any supplementary services or allowances available to all purchasers on a proportionately equal basis.
Wheeler-Lea Amendments to the FTC Act of 1938	Broadens the Federal Trade Commission's power to prohibit practices that might injure the public without affecting competition; outlaws false and deceptive advertising.
Lanham Act of 1946	Establishes protection for trademarks.
Celler-Kefauver Antimerger Act of 1950	Strengthens the Clayton Act to prevent corporate acquisitions that reduce competition.
Hart-Scott-Rodino Act of 1976	Requires large companies to notify the government of their intent to merge.

EXHIBIT 3.7

Primary U.S. Laws Protecting Consumers

Federal Food and Drug Act of 1906	Prohibits adulteration and misbranding of foods and drugs involved in interstate commerce; strengthened by the Food, Drug, and Cosmetic Act (1938) and the Kefauver-Harris Drug Amendment (1962).
Federal Hazardous Substances Act of 1960	Requires warning labels on hazardous household chemicals.
Kefauver-Harris Drug Amendment of 1962	Requires that manufacturers conduct tests to prove drug effectiveness and safety.
Consumer Credit Protection Act of 1968	Requires that lenders fully disclose true interest rates and all other charges to credit customers for loans and installment purchases.
Child Protection and Toy Safety Act of 1969	Prevents marketing of products so dangerous that adequate safety warnings cannot be given.
Public Health Smoking Act of 1970	Prohibits cigarette advertising on TV and radio and revises the health hazard warning on cigarette packages.
Poison Prevention Labeling Act of 1970	Requires safety packaging for products that may be harmful to children.
National Environmental Policy Act of 1970	Established the Environmental Protection Agency to deal with various types of pollution and organizations that create pollution.
Public Health Cigarette Smoking Act of 1971	Prohibits tobacco advertising on radio and television.
Consumer Product Safety Act of 1972	Created the Consumer Product Safety Commission, which has authority to specify safety standards for most products.
Child Protection Act of 1990	Regulates the number of minutes of advertising on children's television.
Children's Online Privacy Protection Act of 1998	Empowers the FTC to set rules regarding how and when marketers must obtain parental permission before asking children marketing research questions.
Aviation Security Act of 2001	Requires airlines to take extra security measures to protect passengers, including the installation of stronger cockpit doors, improved baggage screening, and increased security training for airport personnel.
Homeland Security Act of 2002	Protects consumers against terrorist acts. Created the Department of Homeland Security.
Do Not Call Law of 2003	Protects consumers against unwanted telemarketing calls.
Can-Spam Act of 2003	Protects consumers against unwanted email, or Spam.

STATE LAWS

State legislation that affects marketing varies. Oregon, for example, limits utility advertising to 0.5 percent of the company's net income. California has forced industry to improve consumer products and has also enacted legislation to lower the energy consumption of refrigerators, freezers, and air conditioners. Several states, including New Mexico and Kansas, are considering levying a tax on all in-state commercial advertising.

Federal Trade Commission

As a marketing manager, how would you use the FTC Web site in designing a new marketing campaign?

http://www.ftc.gov

Online

REGULATORY AGENCIES

Although some state regulatory bodies actively pursue violations of their marketing statutes, federal regulators generally have the greatest clout. The Consumer Product Safety Commission, the Federal Trade Commission, and the Food and Drug Administration are the three federal agencies most directly and actively involved in marketing affairs. These agencies, plus others, are discussed throughout the book, but a brief introduction is in order at this point.

The sole purpose of the **Consumer Product Safety Commission (CPSC)** is to protect the health and safety of consumers in and around their homes. The CPSC has the power to set mandatory safety standards for almost all products that consumers use (about 15,000 items). The CPSC consists of a five-member committee and about 1,100 staff members, including technicians, lawyers, and administrative help. The commission can fine offending firms up to $500,000 and sentence their officers to up to a year in prison. It can also ban dangerous products from the marketplace.

The **Federal Trade Commission (FTC)** also consists of five members, each holding office for seven years. The FTC is empowered to prevent persons or corporations from using unfair methods of competition in commerce. It is authorized to investigate the practices of business combinations and to conduct hearings on antitrust matters and deceptive advertising. The FTC has a vast array of regulatory powers (see Exhibit 3.8). Nevertheless, it is not invincible. For example, the FTC had proposed to ban all advertising to children under age 8, to ban all advertising of the sugared products that are most likely to cause tooth decay to children under age 12, and to require dental health and nutritional advertisements to be paid for by industry. Business reacted by lobbying to reduce the FTC's power. The two-year lobbying effort resulted in passage of the FTC

Consumer Product Safety Commission (CPSC)
A federal agency established to protect the health and safety of consumers in and around their homes.

Federal Trade Commission (FTC)
A federal agency empowered to prevent persons or corporations from using unfair methods of competition in commerce.

EXHIBIT 3.8

Powers of the Federal Trade Commission

REMEDY	PROCEDURE
Cease-and-Desist Order	A final order is issued to cease an illegal practice—and is often challenged in the courts.
Consent Decree	A business consents to stop the questionable practice without admitting its illegality.
Affirmative Disclosure	An advertiser is required to provide additional information about products in advertisements.
Corrective Advertising	An advertiser is required to correct the past effects of misleading advertising. (For example, 25 percent of a firm's media budget must be spent on FTC-approved advertisements or FTC-specified advertising.)
Restitution	Refunds are required to be given to consumers misled by deceptive advertising. According to a 1975 court-of-appeals decision, this remedy cannot be used except for practices carried out after the issuance of a cease-and-desist order.
Counteradvertising	The FTC proposed that the Federal Communications Commission permit advertisements in broadcast media to counteract advertising claims (also that free time be provided under certain conditions).

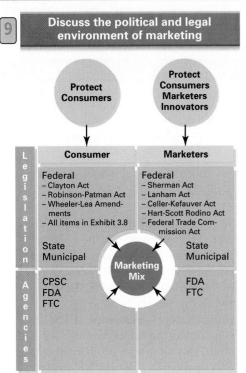

Improvement Act of 1980. The major provisions of the act are as follows:

It bans the use of unfairness as a standard for industrywide rules against advertising. All the proposals concerning children's advertising were therefore suspended, because they were based almost entirely on the unfairness standard. It requires oversight hearings on the FTC every six months. This congressional review is designed to keep the commission accountable. Moreover, it keeps Congress aware of one of the many regulatory agencies it has created and is responsible for monitoring.

Businesses rarely band together to create change in the legal environment as they did to pass the FTC Improvement Act. Generally, marketing managers react only to legislation, regulation, and edicts. It is usually less costly to stay attuned to the regulatory environment than to fight the government. If marketers had toned down their hard-hitting advertisements to children, they might have avoided an FTC inquiry altogether. The FTC also regulates advertising on the Internet as well as Internet abuses of consumer privacy (discussed in Chapter 8). The **Food and Drug Administration (FDA)**, another powerful agency, is charged with enforcing regulations against selling and distributing adulterated, misbranded, or hazardous food and drug products. In the last decade it took a very aggressive stance against tobacco products and is now paying attention to the fast-food industry.

10 COMPETITIVE FACTORS

Explain the basics of foreign and domestic competition

The competitive environment encompasses the number of competitors a firm must face, the relative size of the competitors, and the degree of interdependence within the industry. Management has little control over the competitive environment confronting a firm.

COMPETITION FOR MARKET SHARE AND PROFITS

As U.S. population growth slows, costs rise, and available resources tighten, firms find that they must work harder to maintain their profits and market share regardless of the form of the competitive market. Take, for example, the competition among airlines. In the aftermath of September 11, 2001, the airline industry imploded. Proud competitors, such as United Airlines, declared bankruptcy. American Airlines, the world's largest airline, teetered on the brink of going under. Survival in such a horrific environment meant drastically cutting costs and squeezing out revenue wherever possible. Yet two competitors not only survived, but earned a profit. Southwest Airlines made money and avoided layoffs with its efficient strategy based on one type of plane and lower labor costs. Jet Blue, a discounting newcomer, doubled its fleet during 2002, the worst downturn in aviation history, and turned a profit.

Food and Drug Administration (FDA)
A federal agency charged with enforcing regulations against selling and distributing adulterated, misbranded, or hazardous food and drug products.

Competition in the consumer packaged-goods industry is as difficult as any in America. For example, growth is very low in the $7.6 billion cold cereal market. To increase sales and profits, a company must take market share from a competitor. In 2002, sales of Special K Red Berries helped Kellogg bump General Mills from the number one spot in the U.S. cold cereal business. In 2003, General Mills added freeze-dried berries to Cheerios, the nation's top-selling cereal brand, and narrowed Kellogg's lead. Kellogg fired back with more fruit cereals: Fruit Harvest, a sweet, crunchy brand that comes in berry and apple versions, and Kashi Organic Promise Strawberry

---

Online

Food and Drug Administration
What topics are currently receiving attention in FDA News? What effect has the attention had on market share?
http://www.fda.gov

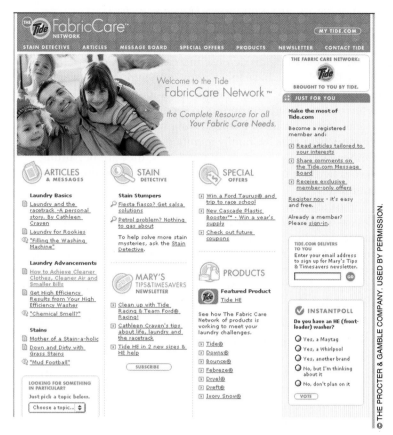

Competition is a driving force in the marketing environment, including laundry. Tide has become one of America's brand icons, in part by continually improving its product and increasing its market share. How competitive is the world of detergent? The formula for Tide is covered by 44 patents.

Fields, which is aimed at the health-food market. Other manufacturers have jumped in: Kraft Food's Post unit has come up with Honey Bunches of Oats with Real Strawberries. Steve Sanger, chief executive of Minneapolis-based General Mills, likens the berry explosion to the introduction of sugar-sweetened cereals in the 1950s. "In my 29 years here, I don't think we introduced a cereal product that got a 2 percent market share in the first month," he says of the launch of Cheerios Berry Burst.[60]

In recent years, nobody has played the competitive game better than Procter & Gamble's Tide. While the rest of the industry stagnated, Tide's sales climbed by 41 percent, to $1.8 billion over the past five years. It now owns 40 percent of the market. Its strategy? First, Tide spends more than $100 million a year promoting its brand name by advertising on television, billboards, subways, buses, magazines, and the Internet. It sponsors a NASCAR race car and youth soccer leagues. It holds nationwide publicity stunts, such as its recent Dirtiest Kid in America contest. Tide has made itself an American brand icon—right up there with Coke and McDonald's.

But the real genius of Tide's strategy is its relentless stream of new and improved products. Each year P&G spends close to $2 billion on research and development, a large portion of which goes toward developing new formulations of Tide. There's Tide With Bleach, Tide Free (which has no fragrance), Tide WearCare (which purports to keep fabrics vibrant longer), Tide Kick (whose package includes a nozzle to rub detergent directly into fabrics), and Tide HE (high-efficiency) for use in front-loading washers. In all, Tide has spawned more than 60 variations of itself.[61]

GLOBAL COMPETITION

General Mills and Procter & Gamble are savvy international competitors conducting business throughout the world. Many foreign competitors also consider the United States to be a ripe target market. Thus, a U.S. marketing manager can no longer focus only on domestic competitors. In automobiles, textiles, watches, televisions, steel, and many other areas, foreign competition has been strong. In the past, foreign firms penetrated U.S. markets by concentrating on price, but today the emphasis has switched to product quality. Nestlé, Sony, Rolls Royce, and Sandoz Pharmaceuticals are noted for quality, not cheap prices.

Global competition is discussed in much more detail in Chapter 4.

THE IMPACT OF TERRORISM ON BUSINESS

Though we hate to call terrorism "an uncontrollable variable in the external environment," it must be acknowledged that terrorism has had a profound impact on American business and commerce around the globe. The horrendous events of September 11, 2001, created a feeling of uncertainty among both businesses and consumers. The effects on the tourism and airline industries were particularly severe. Most importantly, however, the American system worked. The resiliency, flexibility, and strength built into the American political and economic systems carried the country through its darkest times since World War II. By public demand, government returned to its traditional role as guardian of the country's safety. In turn, government spending on defense increased by a larger percentage than in any year since 1982. Now we have more regulation and more government intervention in business and the economy than at any time since the 1970s.

Concern about terrorism caused consumers to spend more time at home, preparing food at home, entertaining at home, buying home furnishings, and even spending more money on gifts for family members.[62] As the events of September 11 fade in consumers' memories, they are beginning to resume their old purchase habits and are showing renewed optimism.

Businesses have lost revenue and experienced increased costs as a result of terrorism. For example, international and domestic shipping costs have risen due to increased security measures. Wal-Mart, the world's biggest corporation, has turned to technology to reduce employee travel to troubled areas. For example, Wal-Mart's retail buyers are using the following to interact with suppliers:

- *Videoconferencing:* Wal-Mart improved studio lighting and auxiliary cameras to show products in greater detail to its suppliers in China.
- *Digital photography:* In working out details on a new children's sandal, one buyer photographed materials at a toy store and e-mailed them to China.
- *E-mail:* Suppliers are bidding on contracts via e-mail.
- *Computer-assisted design:* Product designs and modifications are being shared over the Internet.[63]

 REVIEW LEARNING OBJECTIVE 10

10 Explain the basics of foreign and domestic competition

Highly Competitive Marketplace

Mature Industries

Slow growth/ No growth

Can only increase market share by taking it from a competitor.

LOOKING BACK

Look back at the story about DuPont at the beginning of the chapter. The evidence that corporate social responsibility drives profits and growth is inconclusive.

DuPont, UPS, and Nike may or may not be acting in the stockholders' interests in the short run. If their socially responsible activities result in lower returns to shareholders, the answer is that

they are not. Also, making the planet a better place to live is in everyone's best interest in the long run. Uncontrollable factors in the environment create threats and opportunities for all companies.

Are you at the preconventional, conventional, or postconventional stage of ethical development? If you determine that you are at the preconventional level, you should begin striving for a more mature ethical outlook. This may mean taking an ethics course, reading a book on ethics, or engaging in a lot of introspection about yourself and your values. A person with preconventional ethics will probably have a difficult time succeeding in today's business world.

ETHICS: A PART OF EVERYDAY LIFE

Realize that ethics plays a part in our lives every day. We all must answer questions such as these:

- How do I balance the time and energy obligations of my work and my family?
- How much should I pay my employees?
- What should I do with the child of my husband's first marriage who is disrupting our new family?
- How am I spending my money?
- Should I "borrow" a copy of my friend's software?
- If I know my employee is having troubles at home, should I treat her differently?
- What should I do if I know a neighbor's child is getting into serious trouble?
- How do I react to a sexist or racist joke?

Too many people make decisions about everyday questions without considering the underlying moral and ethical framework of the problems. They are simply swept along by the need to get through the day. Our challenge to you is to always think about the ethical consequences of your actions. Make doing so a habit.

Waiting for dramatic events before consciously tackling ethical considerations is like playing a sport only on the weekend. Just as a weekend warrior often ends up with pulled muscles and poor performance, people who seldom consider the ethical implications of daily activities won't have the coordination to work through the more difficult times in their lives. Don't let this happen to you.

KNOW YOUR ETHICAL VALUES

 To get a better idea of your own level of ethical development, take an ethics test. Go to **http://www.worldbank.org/wbi/corpgov/eastasia/m5/m5selftest.htm.** Check your responses against those of others and read their comments. This test will give you better insight into yourself. A short discussion is provided after each question.

WORK FOR A SOCIALLY RESPONSIBLE FIRM

When you enter the job market, make certain that you are going to work for a socially responsible organization. Ask a prospective employer how the company gives back to society. If you plan to work for a large company, check out *Fortune*'s current list of America's most admired corporations. (It appears around March 1.)

If you plan to work for a multinational firm, examine *Fortune*'s list of the most globally admired corporations, which appears in October. The list is broken down by industry and includes 10 to 15 companies in each industry. Working for an ethical, socially responsible organization will make you proud of the place where you work.

REVIEW AND APPLICATIONS

1   **Discuss corporate social responsibility.** Responsibility in business refers to a firm's concern for the way its decisions affect society. Social responsibility has four components: economic, legal, ethical, and philanthropic. These are intertwined, yet the most fundamental is earning a profit. If a firm does not earn a profit, the other three responsibilities are moot. Most businesspeople believe they should do more than pursue profits. Although a company must consider its economic needs first, it must also operate within the law, do what is ethical and fair, and be a good corporate citizen. The concept of sustainability is that socially responsible companies will outperform their peers by focusing on the world's social problems and viewing them as an opportunity to earn profits and help the world at the same time.

1.1   Describe at least three situations in which you would not purchase the products of a firm even though it is very socially responsible.

1.2 A firm's only responsibility to society is to earn a fair profit. Comment.

1.3 Is sustainability a viable concept for America's businesses?

2 **Describe the role of ethics and ethical decisions in business.** Business ethics may be viewed as a subset of the values of society as a whole. The ethical conduct of businesspeople is shaped by societal elements, including family, education, religion, and social movements. As members of society, businesspeople are morally obligated to consider the ethical implications of their decisions.

Ethical decision making is approached in three basic ways. The first approach examines the consequences of decisions. The second approach relies on rules and laws to guide decision making. The third approach is based on a theory of moral development that places individuals or groups in one of three developmental stages: preconventional morality, conventional morality, or postconventional morality.

Many companies develop a code of ethics to help their employees make ethical decisions. A code of ethics can help employees identify acceptable business practices, can be an effective internal control on behavior, can help employees avoid confusion when determining whether decisions are ethical, and can facilitate discussion about what is right and wrong.

2.1 **WRITING** Write a paragraph discussing the ethical dilemma in the following situation and identifying possible solutions: An insurance agent forgets to get the required signature from one of her clients who is buying an automobile insurance policy. The client acknowledges the purchase by giving the agent a signed personal check for the full amount. To avoid embarrassment and inconvenience, the agent forges the client's signature on the insurance application and sends it to the insurance company for processing.

2.2 Discuss the relationship between ethics and social responsibility.

2.3 Indecency in the media was a hotly debated issue in 2004. Review the "Marketing in Entertainment" box on CBS' social responsibility report. Do you think it is ethical to create programming that contains vulgar language, legitimizes rude behavior, or contains gratuitous sex and violence? Is it socially responsible? How could a media company create such programming and still act ethically and responsibly? Is it possible to reconcile these two seemingly divergent concepts?

3 **Discuss the external environment of marketing, and explain how it affects a firm.** The external marketing environment consists of social, demographic, economic, technological, political and legal, and competitive variables. Marketers generally cannot control the elements of the external environment. Instead, they must understand how the external environment is changing and the impact of that change on the target market. Then marketing managers can create a marketing mix to effectively meet the needs of target customers.

3.1 What is the purpose of environmental scanning? Give an example.

3.2 **TEAM** Form six teams and make each one responsible for one of the uncontrollable elements in the marketing environment. Your boss, the company president, has asked each team to provide one-year and five-year forecasts of the major trends the firm will face. The firm is in the telecommunications equipment industry. It has no plans to become a telecommunications service provider like, for example, SBC and AT&T. Each team should use the library, the Internet, and other data sources to make its forecasts. Each team member should examine a minimum of one data source. The team members should then pool their data and prepare a recommendation. A spokesperson for each team should present the findings to the class.

4 **Describe the social factors that affect marketing.** Within the external environment, social factors are perhaps the most difficult for marketers to anticipate. Several major social trends are currently shaping marketing strategies. First, people of all ages have a broader range of interests, defying traditional consumer profiles. Second, changing gender roles are bringing more women into the workforce and increasing the number of men who shop. Third, a greater number of dual-career families has created demand for time-saving goods and services.

4.1 Every country has a set of core values and beliefs. These values may vary somewhat from region to region of the nation. Identify five core values for your area of the country. Clip magazine advertisements that reflect these values and bring them to class.

4.2 Give an example of component lifestyles based upon someone you know.

5 **Explain the importance to marketing managers of current demographic trends.** Today, several basic demographic patterns are influencing marketing mixes. Because the U.S. population is growing at a slower rate, marketers can no longer rely on profits from generally expanding markets. Marketers are also faced with increasingly experienced consumers among the younger generations such as Gen X and Gen Y. And because the population is also growing older, marketers are offering more products that appeal to middle-aged and elderly consumers.

5.1 Baby boomers in America are aging. Describe how this might affect the marketing mix for the following:

a. Bally's Health Clubs

b. McDonald's

c. Whirlpool Corporation

d. The state of Florida

e. Target Stores

5.2 WRITING You have been asked to address a local Chamber of Commerce on the subject of "Generation Y." Prepare an outline for your talk.

5.3 How should Ford Motor Company market differently to Generation Y, Generation X, and baby boomers?

6 **Explain the importance to marketing managers of multiculturalism and growing ethnic markets.** Multiculturalism occurs when all major ethnic groups in an area are roughly equally represented. Growing multiculturalism makes the marketer's task more challenging. America is not a melting pot but numerous mini-melting pots. Hispanics are the fastest growing segment of the population followed by African Americans. Many companies are now creating departments and product lines to effectively target multicultural market segments. Companies have quickly found that ethnic markets are not homogeneous.

6.1 WRITING Go to the library and look up a minority market such as the Hispanic market. Write a memo to your boss that details the many submarkets within this segment.

6.2 INFOTRAC COLLEGE EDITION Go to the library and the Internet and find examples of large companies directing marketing mixes to each major ethnic group. You may find it useful to research material using InfoTrac.

7 **Identify consumer and marketer reactions to the state of the economy.** Marketers most frequently target marketing mixes to America's huge middle class. Of course, many goods and services are also targeted to upper-income consumers and lower-income consumers as well. During a time of inflation, marketers generally attempt to maintain level pricing to avoid losing customer brand loyalty. During times of recession, many marketers maintain or reduce prices to counter the effects of decreased demand; they also concentrate on increasing production efficiency and improving customer service.

7.1 Explain how consumers' buying habits may change during a recessionary period.

7.2 Periods of inflation require firms to alter their marketing mix. Suppose a recent economic forecast predicts that inflation will be almost 10 percent during the next 18 months. Your company manufactures hand tools for the home gardener. Write a memo to the company president explaining how the firm may have to alter its marketing mix.

8 **Identify the impact of technology on a firm.** Monitoring new technology is essential to keeping up with competitors in today's marketing environment. The United States excels in basic research and, in recent years, has dramatically improved its track record in applied research. Information technology and the Internet have been driving increased U.S. productivity for the past decade. Without innovation, U.S. companies can't compete in global markets.

8.1 Give three examples of how technology has benefited marketers. Also, give several examples of firms that have been hurt because they did not keep up with technological changes.

9 **Discuss the political and legal environment of marketing.** All marketing activities are subject to state and federal laws and the rulings of regulatory agencies. Marketers are responsible for remaining aware of and abiding by such regulations. Some key federal laws that affect marketing are the Sherman Act, Clayton Act, Federal Trade Commission Act, Robinson-Patman Act, Wheeler-Lea Amendments to the FTC Act, Lanham Act, Celler-Kefauver Antimerger Act, and Hart-Scott-Rodino Act. Many laws have been passed to protect the consumer as well. The Consumer Product Safety Commission, the Federal Trade Commission, and the Food and Drug Administration are the three federal agencies most involved in regulating marketing activities.

9.1 The Federal Trade Commission and other governmental agencies have been both praised and criticized for their regulation of marketing activities. To what degree do you think the government should regulate marketing? Explain your position.

9.2 Can you think of any other areas where consumer protection laws are needed?

10 **Explain the basics of foreign and domestic competition.** The competitive environment encompasses the number of competitors a firm must face, the relative size of the competitors, and the degree of interdependence within the industry. Declining population growth, rising costs, and shortages of resources have heightened domestic competition. September 11 had a major negative impact on many industries such as tourism and the airlines. Meanwhile, dwindling international barriers are bringing in more foreign competitors and offering expanding opportunities for U.S. companies abroad.

10.1 Explain how the nature of competition is changing in America.

10.2 Might there be times when a company becomes too competitive? If so, what could be the consequences?

TERMS

applied research 90
baby boomers 82
basic research 90
code of ethics 73
component lifestyles 79
Consumer Product Safety Commission (CPSC) 93
corporate social responsibility 70
demography 80

environmental management 76
ethics 71
Federal Trade Commission (FTC) 93
Food and Drug Administration (FDA) 94
Generation X 81
Generation Y 80
inflation 89
morals 71
multiculturalism 86

purchasing power 88
pyramid of corporate social responsibility 70
recession 89
sustainability 70
target market 75

APPLICATION EXERCISE

Demographic factors play a large role in shaping the external marketing environment. One of those demographic factors is culture. The importance of cultural understanding cannot be overstated, especially in today's global marketplace and our own multicultural country. In general, Americans tend to be ethnocentric; that is, they are quick to prejudge other cultural norms as wrong (or of less significance) because they differ from American practices.

One way to be exposed to another culture is by examining the foods typical of that culture. In this exercise, you will need to work in a team to create a guide to ethnic dining in your city or area. The finished guide will be descriptive in nature; it is not meant to be a rating guide.[64]

Activities

1. Identify ethnic dining categories for inclusion in your guide. Once you have identified categories for your area, make a list of restaurants for each category.

2. You will need to create a data collection form so that the same information is collected from each restaurant. For example, you will want to include the name, address, and phone number for each restaurant. Think of other information that would be helpful.

3. Divide up the restaurant list your team generated in activity 1 so that each team member is responsible for collecting information from a certain number of restaurants. Consider dividing the list geographically so that each team member can visit an assortment of ethnic restaurants. If your budget allows, eat at a few of the restaurants in addition to collecting the information. After you have all the information, meet to review and compare your findings.

4. Was there a meal or type of food that you particularly liked? Disliked? Which type of ethnic restaurant seemed most foreign to you? Why do you think that was?

ETHICS EXERCISE

Jane Barksdale has designed a line of clothing targeted toward Hispanic Americans. The items are sold only by catalog and on the Internet. She thinks that she can increase sales by claiming in ads that the firm is owned by a Hispanic American and all the employees are Hispanic Americans. She is not Hispanic American nor are most of the employees. She needs a high level of sales to pay her bank loan and remain in business.

Questions

1. Should she claim that she is Hispanic American?

2. Does the AMA Code of Ethics address this issue? Go to **http://www.marketingpower.com** and review the code. Then, write a brief paragraph on what the AMA Code of Ethics contains that relates to Jane Barksdale's dilemma.

CAREER EXERCISE

Although there may seem to be only a few career trails to pursue for the topics addressed in this chapter, if you consider possibilities beyond working for a *Fortune* 500 company, you may come up with some ideas.

Activities

1. Working at any of the government agencies listed in the chapter will keep you in touch with marketing, but from the control side. Go to the Web site of the Consumer Products Safety Commission at **http://www.cpsc.gov**, the Federal Trade Commission at **http://www. ftc.gov**, and the Food and Drug Administration at **http://www.fda.gov**.

Each site gives detailed information on employment opportunities with the agency. Although some will be technical, such as chemist positions at the FDA, you may find some interesting openings that involve regulating marketing activities. If you are truly interested in government work, you can sign up for a newsletter at **http://www.federaljobsearch.com** to get the latest federal job postings free via e-mail.

2. Another career tip comes from the "Use It Now" feature, which discusses working for a socially responsible company. Web sites like Business-Ethics.com (**http://www. businessethics.com**) provide rankings of socially responsible companies. You can also find lists of socially responsible companies by researching socially responsible investing. Financial analysts provide information to clients who want to focus some of their investment portfolio on companies that pursue socially responsible business objectives. This information can help you compile a list of socially responsible companies to work for. Use your favorite Internet search engine to locate sites keyed to "socially responsible investing." You may need to examine the components of some mutual funds to get detailed lists.

3. To put the external environment into the context of your career path, try envisioning what the external environment will look like for your job search. One way to do this is through environmental scanning. Probably the foremost company in this area is Kiplinger. *The Kiplinger Letter* is a weekly subscription newsletter that contains a wealth of information in easy-to-read, semibulleted format. You can subscribe online, but if you don't want to pay for the weekly consolidated environmental assessment, you can still go to the company's Web site at **http://www.kiplinger.com** to view a wealth of information on numerous topics. Type "career" into the site's search engine and read a sampling of the many articles on career-related issues. You may even want to consult Kiplinger's Jobs page periodically to see if a position opens up at business's premier environmental scanning company.

ENTREPRENEURSHIP CASE

© ARNOLD TURNER/WIREIMAGE.COM

ROCKSTAR GAMES: CAUGHT IN THEIR OWN VICE?

In Oakland, California, police arrest a gang of teens who now face charges for five homicides, several carjackings, and a slew of armed robberies. Roughly 2,000 miles away in Tennessee, stepbrothers Joshua and William Buckner, ages 14 and 16, are arrested and plead guilty to reckless homicide, aggravated assault, and reckless endangerment for fatally shooting one motorist and critically wounding a second.

The tie that binds these seemingly unrelated crimes is a video game—Rockstar Games' *Grand Theft Auto: Vice City*. When questioned about their crimes, both sets of perpetrators cited boredom and a desire to emulate the action of the main character in *Vice City* as the cause of their violent behavior.

In *Vice City*, players assume the role of Tommy Vercetti, an ex-con who loses cocaine and money in a botched drug deal. To recoup his losses, he must accomplish various missions in an attempt to ascend the hierarchy of *Vice City*'s underworld. The game awards points to players for mass shootings, graphic rapes, liaisons with prostitutes, car thefts, and drug sales. The violence is extreme and often grotesque. In one mission, players controlling Vercetti can earn points for raping a woman in the back of a stolen car and them deciding whether to kick her to death, cut her to pieces with a machete, or fatally shoot her.

Its graphic violence and sexually explicit material have earned *Vice City* an M rating from the Entertainment Software Rating Board, which indicates to consumers that the game is intended only for gamers aged 17 or older. Younger gamers, however, are playing the game in large numbers, and critics, parents, and politicians are horrified to find that children are being exposed to a game that glorifies such behavior. Racism rears its head in the game too, as Vercetti at one point is instructed by a narrator to "shoot the Haitians."

The backlash against Rockstar Games has been significant. Haitian and Cuban groups have filed suit against the company in Florida, where state legislators have proposed a bill that would increase the fines levied against retailers who rent or sell M-rated video games to minors. The lawmakers note that several small towns and cities have already passed such legislation.

In New York, Rockstar's racial insensitivity aroused the ire of state Attorney General Eliot Spitzer, New York City Mayor Michael Bloomberg, and the Anti-Defamation League. Their pressure persuaded Rockstar to remove the racially offensive line from all future copies of the game. Other than that, Rockstar has officially declined to comment any on any other inquiries for almost a year. The Interactive Entertainment Merchants Association, an industry group including giant retailers such as Wal-Mart and Blockbuster, Inc., has reacted by adopting procedures intended to stop the sale of mature and adult video games to minors.

Despite the negative reactions, the game has gained mass-market acceptance. *Vice City* alone accounted for nearly half of Rockstar's $1.04 billion in revenue in 2003—a year when revenue for all M-rated video games actually declined from $910 million to $833 million. Rockstar currently dominates the adult segment of the market with the ten M-rated games it produces. Players of the game say its plot lines are pure fantasy, and the chief operating officer of Rockstar Games, Terry Donovan, defends his company by claiming that if the popular HBO television series *The Sopranos* was a video game, it would be *Grand Theft Auto*.

His customers, he asserts, are young male professionals who are willing to spend serious money on intense simulation-type games that provide primal stress release. Donovan and many others believe that the M rating is enough to alert parents to the games' adult content and that legislation from the government infringes on freedom of speech. At the moment, the popular counterargument is that like drugs, alcohol, and pornography, the games represent a threat to the psychological development of young people and should be controlled as such.[65]

Questions

1. Describe the technological, social, and political forces acting on the video game industry.

2. How is Rockstar responding to its environmental conditions? Do you agree with Rockstar's approach? Why or why not?

3. Do you think Rockstar Games' chief operating officer, Terry Donovan, displays adequate concern for corporate social responsibility? Explain.

WATCH IT

SmallBusinessSchool ▫
the Series on PBS stations and the Web

FEATURE PRESENTATION

Record Technologies

To give you insight into Chapter 3, Small Business School introduces you to Record Technologies Incorporated (RTI), a company that blossomed just as its product was seemingly made obsolete. In this video segment, you'll learn why Record Technology has chosen to stand by its choice to produce vinyl records in a marketing environment that has been revolutionized by digital technology. Though CDs and MP3s have become the format of choice for most music listeners, RTI has found that high quality vinyl recordings are still popular with ardent audiophiles, who are willing to spend as much as $20,000 for a phonograph turntable and $25 to $30 for a single record. Don MacInnis, the company's owner, has developed a strategy to serve that market niche. His company and its 37 dedicated employees manufacture the highest quality vinyl records in the world and sell them to musicians and record producers. Don combines top-quality products with unparalleled service in order to make his business stand out from the rest—a synthesis that has given his company the strength to survive one of the biggest revolutions in any industry at any time.

What to Watch for and Ask Yourself

1. Which uncontrollable factor in the external environment affected RTI's business the most? Were there any others?

2. How did RTI adjust its marketing mix to cope with the environmental changes they faced?

3. Which part of the marketing mix is the most important for RTI to manage in order to survive in its environment?

ENCORE PRESENTATION

Jaws

Now that you have finished studying Chapter 3, you may be ready to think metaphorically about marketing ethics and external environments. As an encore to your work, watch the film clip from *Jaws*, starring Roy Scheider, Richard Dreyfuss, and Robert Shaw. You are probably familiar with the movie's plot: A giant great white shark terrorizes an east coast community's beaches. In this scene, the community's police chief, mayor, and others disagree on how to handle the situation. Special effects add much shock value to an early Steven Spielberg directorial effort—his sixth feature film.

Which ethical decision-making concepts are illustrated in this clip? Can you see how it relates to marketing?

JAWS/CORBIS

STILL SHAKY?

If you're having trouble with the concepts in this chapter, consider using some of the following study resources. You can review the videos, or test yourself with materials designed for all kinds of learning styles.

☑ **Xtra! (http://lambxtra.swlearning.com)**

☑ Quiz ☑ Feature Videos ☑ Encore Videos ☑ FAQ Videos

☑ Exhibit Worksheets ☑ Marketing Plan Worksheets ☑ Content

☑ **http://lamb.swlearning.com**

☑ Quiz ☑ PowerPoint slides ☑ Marketing News ☐ Review Exercises

☑ Links ☑ Marketing Plan Contest ☑ Career Exercise ☑ Use It Now

☑ **Study guide**

☑ Outline ☑ Vocab Review ☑ Test Questions ☑ Marketing Scenario

Need More? Here's a tip. Create your own diagram of the marketing environment and compare it to the example in the chapter. Read a selection of business articles and list the factors at play in each of the articles you read. Visit the Xtra! Web site at **http://lambxtra.swlearning.com** for a wealth of review and mastery activities.

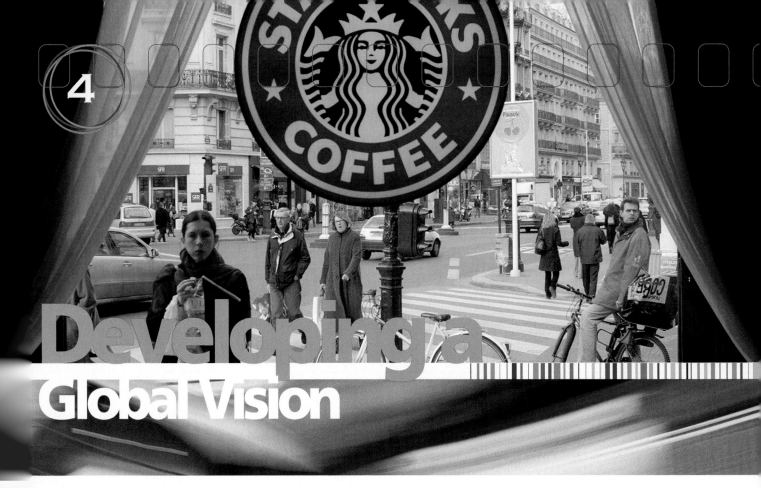

4

Developing a
Global Vision

LEARNING OBJECTIVES

1 Discuss the importance of global marketing

2 Discuss the impact of multinational firms on the world economy

3 Describe the external environment facing global marketers

4 Identify the various ways of entering the global marketplace

5 List the basic elements involved in developing a global marketing mix

6 Discover how the Internet is affecting global marketing

Could French philosopher Jean-Paul Sartre have found inspiration sipping from a paper cup of steaming Starbucks java? After much thought, the U.S. coffee empire announced that it would open its first store in France, a country where family-run cafés are the favorite hangout for everyone from truck drivers to philosophers. "It is with the utmost respect and admiration for the café society in France that we announce our entry into the market," Starbucks Chairman Howard Schultz said in a statement. Authors, philosophers, and artists have made French coffeehouse culture distinctive, he said, adding that he believed Starbucks "will fit well into the French café tradition."

The first French Starbucks opened in a high-tourist area of central Paris near the Opéra Garnier. Coffee is a centuries-old experience in France, and many traditions—like kaffeeklatsch in smoky bistros with grumpy service from bow-tied garçons—die hard. Sartre, the existentialist philosopher, was known for engaging in high-minded discourse in the smoky rooms of Les Deux Magots, a Left Bank café.

But would the late thinker, a frequent café goer, have enjoyed the experience if he couldn't light up his trademark pipe? Starbucks in Paris are smoke-free. "It's something we debated for a long time," says Franck Esquerre, managing director of Starbucks France. "In the stores, we're going to be nonsmoking to preserve the quality of the coffee. But in some cases, if we have outside seating, people can smoke."

The company may also have to combat a French perception that American coffee is watered down: they call it "jus de chaussettes," or juice wrung from soggy socks. The takeout concept is not new to France, however. The homegrown espresso bar chain Columbus Coffee, which started in 1994, has more than 20 locations in the capital. But harried commuters toting paper cups of coffee are nonetheless a rare sight.

Starbucks already has more than 1,600 shops outside North America in countries ranging from New Zealand to Kuwait, but arguably none has such deeply ingrained coffee-drinking habits as France. Add the country's tough labor laws, scarce urban real estate, a widespread suspicion of multinationals, and recent geopolitical tensions between Paris and Washington—and success in France looks daunting. However, Starbucks is following a previously trodden route. Thirty years ago, another big multinational, McDonald's, opened its first restaurant in Strasbourg in eastern France. Now the U.S. fast-food chain has nearly 1,000 outlets in France and is profitable, though it is plagued by labor disputes and image problems.[1]

What are some of the other variables in the international external environment besides culture that Starbucks should consider when entering France? Is it possible to market products the same way all over the world? Is globalization the wave of the future in international marketing?

REWARDS OF GLOBAL MARKETING

Today, global revolutions are under way in many areas of our lives: management, politics, communications, technology. The word *global* has assumed a new meaning, referring to a boundless mobility and competition in social, business, and intellectual arenas. No longer just an option, **global marketing**—marketing that targets markets throughout the world—has become an imperative for business.

U.S. managers must develop a global vision not only to recognize and react to international marketing opportunities but also to remain competitive at home. Often a U.S. firm's toughest domestic competition comes from foreign companies. Moreover, a global vision enables a manager to understand that customer and distribution networks operate worldwide, blurring geographic and political barriers and making them increasingly irrelevant to business decisions. In summary, having a **global vision** means recognizing and reacting to international marketing opportunities, being aware of threats from foreign competitors in all markets, and effectively using international distribution networks.

Over the past two decades, world trade has climbed from $200 billion a year to over $7 trillion. Countries and companies that were never considered major players in global marketing are now important, some of them showing great skill.

Today, marketers face many challenges to their customary practices. Product development costs are rising, the life of products is getting shorter, and new technology is spreading around the world faster than ever. But marketing winners relish the pace of change instead of fearing it.

An example of a young company with a global vision that has capitalized on new technology is Ashtech in Sunnyvale, California. Ashtech makes equipment to capture and convert satellite signals from the U.S. government's Global Positioning System. Ashtech's chief engineer and his team of ten torture and test everything built by Ashtech—expensive black boxes of chips and circuits that use satellite signals to tell surveyors, farmers, mining machine operators, and others where they are with great accuracy. Over half of Ashtech's output is exported. Its biggest customer is Japan.

Adopting a global vision can be very lucrative for a company. Gillette, for example, gets about two-thirds of its revenue from its international division. About 70 percent of General Motors' profits come from operations outside the United States. Although Cheetos and Ruffles haven't done very well in Japan, the potato chip has been quite successful. PepsiCo's (owner of Frito-Lay) overseas snack business brings in more than $3.25 billion annually.

Another company with a global vision is Pillsbury. The Pillsbury Doughboy is used in India to sell a product that the company had just about abandoned in America: flour. Pillsbury (owned by General Mills) has many higher margin products such as microwave pizzas in other parts of the world, but it discovered that in this tradition-bound market, it needed to push the basics.

Even so, selling packaged flour in India has been almost revolutionary, because most Indian housewives still buy raw wheat in bulk, clean it by hand, store it in huge metal hampers, and, every week, carry some to a neighborhood mill, or *chakki*, where it is ground between two stones.

To help reach those housewives, the Doughboy himself has gotten a makeover. In TV advertising, he presses his palms together and bows in the traditional Indian greeting. He speaks six regional languages.

Global marketing is not a one-way street, whereby only U.S. companies sell their wares and services throughout the world. Foreign competition in the domestic market used to be relatively rare but now is found in almost every industry. In fact, in many industries U.S. businesses have lost significant market share to imported products. In electronics, cameras, automobiles, fine china, tractors, leather goods, and a host of other consumer and industrial products, U.S. companies have struggled at home to maintain their market shares against foreign competitors.

global marketing
Marketing that targets markets throughout the world.

global vision
Recognizing and reacting to international marketing opportunities, being aware of threats from foreign competitors in all markets, and effectively using international distribution networks.

IMPORTANCE OF GLOBAL MARKETING TO THE UNITED STATES

Many countries depend more on international commerce than the United States does. For example, France, Britain, and Germany all derive more than 19 percent of their gross domestic product from world trade, compared to about 12 percent for the United States. Nevertheless, the impact of international business on the U.S. economy is still impressive:

- The United States exports about a fifth of its industrial production and a third of its farm products.[2]
- One of every 16 jobs in the United States is directly or indirectly supported by exports.
- U.S. businesses export over $731 billion in goods to foreign countries every year, and almost a third of U.S. corporate profits comes from international trade and foreign investment.[3]
- Exports account for 22 percent of America's growth in economic activity.[4]
- The United States is the world's leading exporter of grain, selling more than $20 billion of this product a year to foreign countries, or about one-third of all agricultural exports.[5]
- Chemicals, office machinery and computers, automobiles, aircraft, and electrical and industrial machinery make up almost half of all nonagricultural exports.

These statistics might seem to imply that practically every business in the United States is selling its wares throughout the world, but nothing could be further from the truth. About 85 percent of all U.S. exports of manufactured goods are shipped by 250 companies; less than 10 percent of all manufacturing businesses, or around 25,000 companies, export their goods on a regular basis.[6] Most small- and medium-sized firms are essentially nonparticipants in global trade and marketing. Only the very large multinational companies have seriously attempted to compete worldwide. Fortunately, more of the smaller companies are now aggressively pursuing international markets.

FAQs

Isn't global marketing important only to large multinational corporations? Find out the answer by watching the video FAQ on Xtra!

THE FEAR OF TRADE AND GLOBALIZATION

The protests during meetings of the World Trade Organization, the World Bank, and the International Monetary Fund (the three organizations are discussed later in the chapter) showed that many people fear world trade and globalization. What do they fear? The negatives of global trade are as follows:

- Millions of Americans have lost jobs due to imports, production shifts abroad, or from outsourcing of tech jobs. Most find new jobs—that often pay less.
- Millions of others fear losing their jobs, especially at those companies operating under competitive pressure.
- Employers often threaten to outsource jobs if workers do not accept pay cuts.
- Service and white-collar jobs are increasingly vulnerable to operations moving offshore.

The United States is not the only country that has experienced some negative effects from globalization. Developing countries such as Mauritius have also found that global trade offers both advantages and disadvantages.

When Mauritius won independence from Britain in 1968, this tiny island off the coast of Madagascar had little to offer the world except sugar cane and white-sand beaches. So the government decided to embrace the global economy with low taxes and relaxed labor laws. And the global economy embraced it right back. Clothing companies rushed to set up textile factories

AP/WIDE WORLD PHOTOS

Estela Pacheco sews pajamas for Wal-Mart at a textile factory located 15 miles from San Salvador, El Salvador. Frustrated by stalled international free trade talks, El Salvador is leading negotiations to create a giant trade bloc across the Americas in an effort to bring more industrial jobs to the country.

on the island—and, improbably, Mauritius became a powerhouse. Median household income nearly doubled in the 1990s to roughly $380 a month in 2002, making it one of the most prosperous nations in Africa. Its textile business grew so rapidly—turning out clothes for such global brands as Gap and Calvin Klein—that employers had to import workers from China and India to staff their production lines.

In 2002, with help from beneficial trade agreements, Mauritius exported $913 million in clothing to the U.S. and Europe. The literacy rate on Mauritius is among the highest in Africa, and the government is stable and democratic.

But now this poster child for globalization is starting to see the downside of free trade. As trade barriers ease around the world, China and India are flooding the world's markets with their own textiles and undercutting Mauritius's prices by drawing on their own vast pools of cheap labor. Since the late 1990s, thousands of Mauritians have been cast out of the textile factories as they have closed or downsized. The unemployment rate among Mauritians, who are mostly ethnic Indians, crept up to 9.8% in 2003 from less than 3% a decade ago, and many expect it to continue to rise.[7]

The story of Mauritius shows the heightened expectations that success in globalization brings—and the perils of relying too heavily on one industry. The nation has broadened into tourism and financial services over the years, but the garment industry still employs directly or indirectly nearly one in five working Mauritians.

BENEFITS OF GLOBALIZATION

Globalization relies on competition to drive down prices and increase product and service quality. Business goes to the countries that operate most efficiently and/or have the technology to produce what is needed. As just described, jobs were created in Mauritius because of its low-cost labor (as opposed, for example, to the United States). When even lower cost labor was identified in China and India, however, Mauritius lost jobs, but new jobs were created in China and India.

In summary, globalization expands economic freedom, spurs competition, and raises the productivity and living standards of people in countries that open themselves to the global marketplace. For less developed countries, globalization offers access to foreign capital, global export markets, and advanced technology while breaking the monopoly of inefficient and protected domestic producers. Faster growth, in turn, reduces poverty, encourages democratization, and promotes higher labor and environmental standards. Though government officials may face more difficult choices as a result of globalization, their citizens enjoy greater individual freedom. In this sense, globalization acts as a check on governmental power by making it more difficult for governments to abuse the freedom and property of their citizens.

A few specific examples of the benefits of globalization include:

• In China and the rest of East Asia, more people rose out of poverty between 1990 and 2000 than the entire population of the United States. The main reason was global trade.[8]

- General Electric recently hired 6,000 people in India, bringing its headcount there to 10,000, to handle accounting, claims processing, customer service and credit evaluation, and research for GE around the world. GE plans to hire thousands more.
- More than 2,000 Moroccans are helping Spanish and French consumers from call centers near Rabat and Tangiers built by outsourcers and a unit of Spain's phone giant, Telefonica. India, the Philippines, Jamaica, Estonia, Hungary, and the Czech Republic also are establishing themselves as low-cost call center sites. Ireland used to be a call center favorite, but wages there are now on a par with those in the rest of Europe. Based on your authors' experiences, if you call a Microsoft or Dell service center, you may be speaking to someone in India.

REVIEW LEARNING OBJECTIVE 1

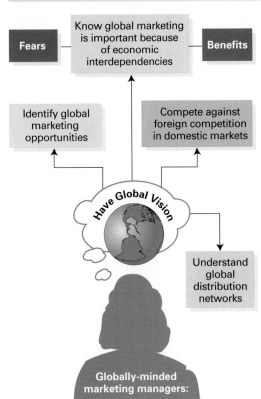

1 Discuss the importance of global marketing

Know global marketing is important because of economic interdependencies

Fears

Benefits

Identify global marketing opportunities

Compete against foreign competition in domestic markets

Have Global Vision

Understand global distribution networks

Globally-minded marketing managers:

THE IMPACT OF TERRORISM ON GLOBAL TRADE

The terrorist attacks on America on September 11, 2001, changed forever the way the world conducts business. The immediate impact was a shrinkage of global trade. Nevertheless, the world's major markets are too vitally integrated for globalization to stop, even though the process may be slower and costlier.

Companies are paying more for insurance and to provide security for overseas staff and property. Heightened border inspections slow movements of cargo, forcing companies to stock more inventory. For example, rules established in late 2003 require all transportation companies to alert the Bureau of Customs and Border Protection by computer or fax about the contents and recipients of international cargo before it is loaded at a foreign port or reaches the United States. This "automated notification" system is intended to give Customs officials more time to zero in on suspicious shipments and intercept them.[9]

Tighter immigration policies curtail the liberal inflows of skilled and blue-collar workers that allowed companies to expand while keeping wages in check. Meanwhile, greater concern about political risk is causing companies to greatly narrow their horizons when making new investments. The impact of terrorism will lessen over time, but multinational firms will always, now, be on guard.

2 MULTINATIONAL FIRMS

Discuss the impact of multinational firms on the world economy

multinational corporation
A company that is heavily engaged in international trade, beyond exporting and importing.

The United States has a number of large companies that are global marketers. Many of them have been very successful. A company that is heavily engaged in international trade, beyond exporting and importing, is called a **multinational corporation**. Multinational corporations move resources, goods, services, and skills across national boundaries without regard to the country in which the headquarters is located. The leading multinational firms in the world are listed in Exhibit 4.1.

Multinationals often develop their global business in stages. In the first stage, companies operate in one country and sell into others. Second-stage multinationals set up foreign subsidiaries to handle sales in one country. In the third stage, they operate an entire line of business in another country. The fourth stage has evolved

EXHIBIT 4.1

The World's Largest Multinational Corporations

Rank	Company	Country	Revenue ($ Millions)
1	Wal-Mart Stores	U.S.	263,009.0
2	BP	Britain	232,571.0
3	ExxonMobil	U.S.	222,883.0
4	Royal Dutch/Shell Group	Netherlands/Britain	201,728.0
5	General Motors	U.S.	195,324.0
6	Ford Motor	U.S.	164,505.0
7	DaimlerChrysler	Germany	156,602.2
8	Toyota Motor	Japan	153,111.0
9	General Electric	U.S.	134,187.0
10	Total	France	118,441.4
11	Allianz	Germany	114,949.9
12	ChevronTexaco	U.S.	112,937.0
13	AXA	France	111,912.2
14	ConocoPhillips	U.S.	99,468.0
15	Volkswagen	Germany	98,636.6
16	Nippon Telegraph & Telephone	Japan	98,229.1
17	ING Group	Netherlands	95,893.3
18	Citigroup	U.S.	94,713.0
19	International Business Machines	U.S.	89,131.0
20	American International Group	U.S.	81,303.0
21	Siemens	Germany	80,501.0
22	Carrefour	France	79,773.8
23	Hitachi	Japan	76,423.3
24	Hewlett-Packard	U.S.	73,061.0
25	Honda Motor	Japan	72,263.7

SOURCE: "The World's Largest Corporations," *Fortune*, July 26, 2004, 163.

primarily due to the Internet and involves mostly high-tech companies. For these firms, the executive suite is virtual. Their top executives and core corporate functions are in different countries, wherever the firms can gain a competitive edge through the availability of talent or capital, low costs, or proximity to their most important customers.

A good example of a fourth-stage company is Trend Micro, an Internet antivirus software company.[10] Its top executives, engineers, and support staff are spread around the world so that they can respond quickly to new virus threats—which can start anywhere and spread like wildfire. The main virus response center is in the Philippines, where 250 ever-vigilant engineers work evening and midnight shifts as needed. Six other labs are scattered from Munich to Tokyo.

Trend Micro's financial head-quarters is in Tokyo, where it went public; product development is in PhD-rich Taiwan; and most of its sales are in Silicon Valley—inside the giant American market. When companies fragment this way, they are no longer limited to the strengths, or hobbled by the weaknesses, of their native lands.

Such fourth-stage multinationals are being created around the world. They include business-intelligence-software maker Business Objects, with headquarters in France and San Jose, California; Wipro, a tech-services supplier with headquarters in India and Santa Clara, California; and computer-peripherals maker Logitech International, with headquarters in Switzerland and Fremont, California.

Many multinational corporations are enormous. For example, Wal-Mart's annual sales are larger than the gross domestic product of all but 30 nations in the world. A multinational company may have several worldwide headquarters, depending on where certain markets or technologies are. Britain's APV, a maker of food-processing equipment, has a different headquarters for each of its world-wide businesses. ABB Asea Brown Boveri, the European electrical engineering giant based in Zurich, Switzerland, groups its thousands of products and services into 50 or so business areas. Each is run by a leadership team that crafts global business strategy, sets product development priorities, and decides where to make its products. None of the teams work out of the Zurich headquarters; instead, they are scattered around the world. Leadership for power transformers is based in Germany, electric drives in Finland, and process automation in the United States.

The role of multinational corporations in developing nations is a subject of controversy. Multinationals' ability to tap financial, physical, and human resources from all over the world and combine them economically and

cs in MarketingEthics in Marketing Ethics in Marketing Ethics in Marketing Ethics in Marketing
cs in MarketingEthics in Marketing Ethics in Marketing Ethics in Marketing Ethics in Marketin
cs in MarketingEthics in Marketing Ethics in Marketing Ethics in Marketing Ethics in Marketin

ETHICS IN MARKETING

cs in MarketingEthics in Marketing Ethics in Marketing Ethics in Marketing Ethics in Marketin
Ethics in Marketing
Ethics in Marketing

> EXXONMOBIL TELLS CHAD'S GOVERNMENT: YOU EARNED THE ROYALTIES, BUT YOU CAN'T HAVE THEM

In 1994, exploratory drilling in Chad by Exxon (now Exxon-Mobil) determined that there were at least a billion barrels of oil underground. This amount was sufficient for the company to build a pipeline from the land-locked country to the ocean and still earn a satisfactory profit. Yet Exxon's excitement was tempered by the huge political risk. The project's path has not been smooth in this country of ox carts and camel caravans. Chad, a nation of eight million people about twice the size of Texas, is one of the ten poorest countries in the world, according to figures from the United Nations. In the past three decades, it has experienced at least as many political coups. Its president, Idriss Deby, came to power in a military coup in 1990 and since then has twice been elected in votes tainted by charges from international observers of fraud and oppression of opposition parties.

Exxon was highly aware of what happened in Angola where Western oil companies had remained partners with the government even as it pursued a civil war that killed and maimed tens of thousands of people. Chad, being particularly poor and contentious, looked like another oil nightmare waiting to happen.

Consequently, Exxon decided to bring in the World Bank. For Exxon, the equation was simple. Poor countries have little choice but to stay on good terms with the World Bank—their main lender. If Exxon had the bank as a partner, Chad might be less likely to renege on the deal later. The World Bank insisted that Chad's oil profits be steered into development projects, under international scrutiny. Convincing Deby's government to give up some sovereignty over Chad's oil income was not easy, but the World Bank wielded a big stick: if the government didn't agree to strict auditing, the World Bank told Chad, the bankers would walk, and the oil would likely stay buried forever.[11]

Do you think that it is ethical to deny the sovereign government of Chad the right to decide how the country should use its oil royalties? In 2000, ChevronTexaco paid Chad $25 million for the right to join ExxonMobil's consortium. Technically, the fee was not for royalties, since no oil had been pumped at that time. Deby spent part of the money on military equipment. What, if anything, should the World Bank and ExxonMobil do? Should Chad's share of the money go only for schools, roads, water filtration systems, and other infrastructure?

profitably can be of benefit to any country. They also often possess and can transfer the most up-to-date technology. Critics, however, claim that often the wrong kind of technology is transferred to developing nations. Usually, it is **capital-intensive** (requiring a greater expenditure for equipment than for labor) and thus does not substantially increase employment. A "modern sector" then emerges in the nation, employing a small proportion of the labor force at relatively high productivity and income levels and with increasingly capital-intensive technologies. In addition, multinationals sometimes support reactionary and oppressive regimes if it is in their best interests to do so. Other critics say that the firms take more wealth out of developing nations than they bring in, thus widening the gap between rich and poor nations. The petroleum industry has been heavily criticized in the past for its actions in some developing countries. The "Ethics in Marketing" box explains how ExxonMobil is trying to avoid such criticism in its huge project in the African nation of Chad.

GLOBAL MARKETING STANDARDIZATION

Traditionally, marketing-oriented multinational corporations have operated somewhat differently in each country. They use a strategy of providing different product features, packaging, advertising, and so on. However, Ted Levitt, a Harvard professor, described a trend toward what he referred to as "global marketing," with a slightly different meaning.[12] He contended that communication and technology have made the world smaller so that almost all consumers everywhere want all the things they have heard about, seen, or experienced. Thus, he saw the emergence of global markets for standardized consumer products on a huge scale, as opposed to segmented foreign markets with different products. In this book, global marketing is defined as individuals and organizations using a global vision

FAQs

Does global marketing standardization really work? Find out the answer by watching the video FAQ on Xtra!

capital-intensive
Using more capital than labor in the production process.

Coca-Cola Company

How does Coca-Cola's mission statement reflect its commitment to global markets? Does the site as a whole reflect this commitment?

http://www.cocacola.com/

Colgate-Palmolive

Compare Colgate-Palmolive's site with Coca-Cola's site. Which more strongly conveys a global image?

http://www.colgate.com/

Online

to effectively market goods and services across national boundaries. To make the distinction, we can refer to Levitt's notion as **global marketing standardization**.

Global marketing standardization presumes that the markets throughout the world are becoming more alike. Firms practicing global marketing standardization produce "globally standardized products" to be sold the same way all over the world. Uniform production should enable companies to lower production and marketing costs and increase profits.

Levitt cited Coca-Cola, Colgate-Palmolive, and McDonald's as successful global marketers. His critics point out, however, that the success of these three companies is really based on variation, not on offering the same product everywhere. McDonald's, for example, changes its salad dressings and provides self-serve espresso for French tastes. It sells bulgogi burgers in South Korea and falafel burgers in Egypt. It also offers different products to suit tastes in Germany (where it offers beer) and Japan (where it offers sake). Further, the fact that Coca-Cola and Colgate-Palmolive sell some of their products in more than 160 countries does not signify that they have adopted a high degree of standardization for all their products globally. Only three Coca-Cola brands are standardized, and one of them, Sprite, has a different formulation in Japan. Some Colgate-Palmolive products are marketed in just a few countries. Axion paste dishwashing detergent, for example, was formulated for developing countries, and La Croix Plus detergent was custom made for the French market. Colgate toothpaste is marketed the same way globally, although its advanced Gum Protection Formula is used in only 27 nations.

Nevertheless, some multinational corporations are moving toward a degree of global marketing standardization. 3M markets some of its industrial tapes the same way around the globe. Procter & Gamble calls its new philosophy "global planning." The idea is to determine which product modifications are necessary from country to country while trying to minimize those modifications. P&G has at least four products that are marketed similarly in most parts of the world: Camay soap, Crest toothpaste, Head and Shoulders shampoo, and Pampers diapers. However, the smell of Camay, the flavor of Crest, and the formula of Head and Shoulders, as well as the advertising, vary from country to country.

REVIEW LEARNING OBJECTIVE 2

2 **Discuss the impact of multinational firms on the world economy**

- Human Resources
- Physical Resources
- Financial Resources

MNC

Growth Revenue Profits

Global Marketing

3 EXTERNAL ENVIRONMENT FACING GLOBAL MARKETERS

Describe the external environment facing global marketers

global marketing standardization
Production of uniform products that can be sold the same way all over the world.

A global marketer or a firm considering global marketing must consider the external environment. Many of the same environmental factors that operate in the domestic market also exist internationally. These factors include culture, economic and technological development, political structure and actions, demographic makeup, and natural resources.

CULTURE

Central to any society is the common set of values shared by its citizens that determines what is socially acceptable. Culture underlies the family, the educational system, religion, and the social class system. The network of social organizations generates overlapping roles and status positions. These values and roles have a tremendous effect on people's preferences and thus on marketers' options. Inca Kola, a fruity, greenish yellow carbonated drink, is the largest selling soft drink in Peru. Despite being compared to "liquid bubble gum," the drink has become a symbol of national pride and heritage. The drink was invented in Peru and contains only fruit indigenous to the country.

Culture is a major factor marketers face when marketing products globally. Inca Kola, the largest selling soft drink in Peru, is a symbol of national heritage. Here a firefighter is delivering a case of the beverage to police engaged in a hostage stand-off.

FAQs

Is there one uncontrollable factor in the global environment that is more important than the others? Find out the answer by watching the video FAQ on Xtra!

Culture may influence product preferences as in Inca Kola or influence the marketing mix in other ways. A U.S. luggage manufacturer found out that culture also affects thinking and perception. The company designed a new Middle East advertising campaign around the image of its luggage being carried on a magic flying carpet. A substantial part of a group in a marketing research study thought they were seeing advertising for Samsonite *carpets*. Green Giant learned that it could not use its Jolly Green Giant in parts of Asia where a green hat worn by a man signifies that he has an unfaithful wife.

Language is another important aspect of culture. Marketers must take care in translating product names, slogans, production instructions, and promotional messages so as not to convey the wrong meaning. For example, Mitsubishi Motors had to rename its Pajero model in Spanish-speaking countries because the term describes a sexual activity. Toyota Motors' MR2 model dropped the number 2 in France because the combination sounds like a French swearword. The literal translation of Coca-Cola in Chinese characters means "bite the wax tadpole."

Each country has its own customs and traditions that determine business practices and influence negotiations with foreign customers. In many countries, personal relationships are more important than financial considerations. For instance, skipping social engagements in Mexico may lead to lost sales. Negotiations in Japan often include long evenings of dining, drinking, and entertaining, and only after a close personal relationship has been formed do business negotiations begin. The Japanese go through a very elaborate ritual when exchanging business cards. An American businesswoman was unaware of this important cultural tradition. She came into a meeting and tossed some of her business cards across the table at a group of stunned Japanese executives. One of them turned his back on her and walked out. The deal never went through.

Making successful sales presentations abroad requires a thorough understanding of the country's culture. Germans, for example, don't like risk and need strong reassurance. A successful presentation to a German client will emphasize three points: the bottom-line benefits of the product or service, that there will be strong service support, and that the product is guaranteed. In southern Europe, it is an insult to show a price list. Without negotiating, you will not close the sale. The English want plenty of documentation for product claims and are less likely to simply accept the word of the sales representative. Scandinavian and Dutch companies are more likely to approach business transactions as Americans do than are companies in any other country.[13]

Fortunately, some habits and customs seem to be the same throughout much of the world. A study of 37,743 consumers from 40 different countries found that 95 percent brushed their teeth daily. Other activities that majorities worldwide engage in include reading a newspaper, listening to the radio, taking a shower, and washing their hair.

ECONOMIC AND TECHNOLOGICAL DEVELOPMENT

A second major factor in the external environment facing the global marketer is the level of economic development in the countries where it operates. In general, complex and sophisticated industries are found in developed countries, and more basic industries are found in less developed nations. Average family incomes are higher in the more developed countries compared to the less developed markets. Larger incomes mean greater purchasing power and demand not only for consumer goods and services but also for the machinery and workers required to produce consumer goods.

According to the World Bank, the combined gross national income (GNI) of the 234 nations for which data are available is approximately $31.3 trillion. Divide that up among the world's 6.1 billion inhabitants, and you get just $5,170 for every man, woman, and child on Earth. The United States accounts for a third of the income earned worldwide, or $9.9 trillion—more than any other single country. If America's GNI were divided equally among its 284 million residents, each American would receive $34,870—6.7 times the world average. Even so, Americans are still not the richest people on the planet. That title goes to the residents of Luxembourg, where the per capita GNI is $41,770 (see Exhibit 4.2).[14]

In low-income countries where the annual GNI per capita is $745 or less, the average life expectancy is only 58.9 years, compared with 77.5 years in the United States. Eighty out of every 1,000 newborns die in low-income countries each year, versus only seven in the United States. Just 59.8 percent of children are immunized against measles in those nations, compared with 91 percent of children stateside. And there are only 6 computers per 1,000 residents; in America there are 625.[15]

Just because a country has a low GNI per capita doesn't mean that everyone is poor. In fact, some of these countries have large and growing pockets of wealth. The average Bentley automobile costs around $600,000. Bentley opened showrooms in China in May 2002 and sold 50 cars in its first eight months, compared with 80 in Japan for all 2002. Chinese consumers also buy about 30 Ferraris and 70 Maseratis per year—an indication of the speed at which China's young entrepreneurs are garnering wealth. Chinese buyers of superluxury cars tend to be younger than in other markets—typically, they are 35 to 50 years old and have made their money in real estate or with their own companies.[16]

EXHIBIT 4.2

Where the Global Money Is and Is Not

Country	GNI per Capita*	Index**
Luxembourg	$41,770	0.8
Switzerland	$36,970	0.9
United States	$34,870	1.0
Canada	$21,340	1.6
Greece	$11,780	3.0
Mexico	$ 5,540	6.3
Chile	$ 4,350	8.0
Malaysia	$ 3,640	9.6
Brazil	$ 3,060	11.4
Morocco	$ 1,180	29.6
China	$ 890	39.2
Indonesia	$ 680	51.3
India	$ 460	75.8
Kenya	$ 340	102.6
Sierra Leone	$ 140	249.10

*GNI per capita refers to a country's gross national income divided by the total population of the country.

**The U.S. average is 1. For example, the GNI per capita of the United States is 8 times that of Chile.

SOURCE: World Bank.

POLITICAL STRUCTURE AND ACTIONS

Political structure is a third important variable facing global marketers. Government policies run the gamut from no private ownership and minimal individual freedom to little central government and maximum personal freedom. As rights of private property increase, government-owned industries and centralized planning tend to decrease. But rarely will a political environment be at one extreme or the other. India, for instance, is a republic with elements of socialism, monopoly capitalism, and competitive capitalism in its political ideology.

A recent World Bank study found that the least amount of business regulation fosters the strongest economies.[17] The least regulated and most efficient economies are concentrated among countries with well-established common-law traditions, including Australia, Canada, New Zealand, the United Kingdom, and the United States. On a par with the best performers are Singapore and Hong Kong. Not far behind are Denmark, Norway, and Sweden, social democracies that recently streamlined their business regulation.

The countries with the most inefficient across-the-board regulations and political structures are Bolivia, Burkina Faso, Chad, Costa Rica, Guatemala, Mali, Mozambique, Paraguay, the Philippines, and Venezuela.

Legal Considerations

Closely related to and often intertwined with the political environment are legal considerations. In France, nationalistic sentiments led to a law that requires pop music stations to play at least 40 percent of their songs in French (even though French teenagers love American and English rock and roll).

Many legal structures are designed to either encourage or limit trade. Here are some examples:

- *Tariff: a tax levied on the goods entering a country.* In 2002, the United States imposed a stiff tariff, ranging from 8 to 30 percent of the value, on steel imports in an effort to protect about 5,000 U.S. jobs.[18]

- *Quota: a limit on the amount of a specific product that can enter a country.* The United States has strict quotas for imported textiles, sugar, and many dairy products. Several U.S. companies have sought quotas as a means of protection from foreign competition. For example, Harley-Davidson convinced the U.S. government to place quotas on large motorcycles imported to the United States. These quotas gave the company the opportunity to improve its quality and compete with Japanese motorcycles.

- *Boycott: the exclusion of all products from certain countries or companies.* Governments use boycotts to exclude companies from countries with which they have a political dispute. Several Arab nations boycotted Coca-Cola because it maintained distributors in Israel.

- *Exchange control: a law compelling a company earning foreign exchange from its exports to sell it to a control agency, usually a central bank.* A company wishing to buy goods abroad must first obtain foreign currency exchange from the control agency. Generally, exchange controls limit the importation of luxuries. For instance, Avon Products drastically cut back new production lines and products in the Philippines because exchange controls prevented the company from converting pesos to dollars to ship back to the home office. The pesos had to be used in the Philippines. China restricts the amount of foreign currency each Chinese company is allowed to keep from its exports. Therefore, Chinese companies must usually get the government's approval to release funds before they can buy products from foreign companies.

Marketing... in Entertainment

Exporting Culture

Australia and the United States have concluded negotiations on a free trade agreement, but not without serious hurdles. One main point of contention involved entertainment media, such as film and television. The policy divide was simply one of culture versus commerce. Whereas the Australians view their television and film media as cultural vehicles, Hollywood views TV shows and movies as vehicles for profit. The Australian Film Alliance and the Media, Entertainment, and Arts Alliance aligned to block free trade (in other words, tax-free imports) of American cultural media because, so the Australians claim, the market has failed to create a level playing field. Exports of Aussie television programming hit an all-time low recently, just as imports of American programming hit an all-time high, creating a visual media trade deficit of $440 million with the United States alone. To compound the problem, only 20 percent of movie tickets sold in Australia are for locally produced films. This conflict is not unique to Australia. Europe also has a cultural media trade deficit with the United States, even though European countries limit imports of film, television programming, and music.[19]

- *Market grouping (also known as a common trade alliance): occurs when several countries agree to work together to form a common trade area that enhances trade opportunities.* The best-known market grouping is the European Union (EU), which will be discussed in more detail later. The EU, which was known as the European Community before 1994, has been evolving for more than four decades, yet until recently, many trade barriers existed among its member nations.
- *Trade agreement: an agreement to stimulate international trade.* Not all government efforts are meant to stifle imports or investment by foreign corporations. The Uruguay Round of trade negotiations is an example of an effort to encourage trade, as was the grant of most favored nation (MFN) status to China. The largest Latin American trade agreement is **Mercosur**, which includes Argentina, Bolivia, Brazil, Chile, Paraguay, and Uruguay. The elimination of most tariffs among the trading partners has resulted in trade revenues of over $16 billion annually. The economic boom created by Mercosur will undoubtedly cause other nations to seek trade agreements on their own or to enter Mercosur. The European Union hopes to have a free trade pact with Mercosur in the future.

Uruguay Round

The **Uruguay Round** is an agreement that has dramatically lowered trade barriers worldwide. Adopted in 1994, the agreement has been signed by 148 nations.[20] It is the most ambitious global trade agreement ever negotiated. The agreement has reduced tariffs by one-third worldwide—a move that is expected to raise global income by $235 billion annually. Perhaps most notable is the recognition of new global realities. For the first time an agreement covers services, intellectual property rights, and trade-related investment measures such as exchange controls.

The Uruguay Round made several major changes in world trading practices:

- *Entertainment, pharmaceuticals, integrated circuits, and software:* The rules protect patents, copyrights, and trademarks for 20 years. Computer programs receive 50 years' protection and semiconductor chips receive 10 years'. But many developing nations were given a decade to phase in patent protection for drugs. France, which limits the number of U.S. movies and TV shows that can be shown, refused to liberalize market access for the U.S. entertainment industry.
- *Financial, legal, and accounting services:* Services came under international trading rules for the first time, creating a vast opportunity for these competitive U.S. industries. Now it is easier for managers and key personnel to be admitted to a country. Licensing standards for professionals, such as doctors, cannot discriminate against foreign applicants. That is, foreign applicants cannot be held to higher standards than domestic practitioners.
- *Agriculture:* Europe is gradually reducing farm subsidies, opening new opportunities for such U.S. farm exports as wheat and corn. Japan and Korea are beginning to import rice. But U.S. growers of sugar and citrus fruit have had their subsidies trimmed.
- *Textiles and apparel:* Strict quotas limiting imports from developing countries are being phased out, causing further job losses in the U.S. clothing trade. But retailers and consumers are the big winners, because past quotas have added $15 billion a year to clothing prices.
- *A new trade organization:* The **World Trade Organization (WTO)** replaced the old **General Agreement on Tariffs and Trade (GATT)**, which was created in 1948. The old GATT contained extensive loopholes that enabled countries to avoid the trade-barrier reduction agreements—a situation similar to obeying the law only if you want to! Today, all WTO members must fully comply with all agreements under the Uruguay Round. The WTO also has an effective dispute settlement procedure with strict time limits to resolve disputes.

Mercosur
The largest Latin American trade agreement, which includes Argentina, Bolivia, Brazil, Chile, Paraguay, and Uruguay.

Uruguay Round
An agreement to dramatically lower trade barriers worldwide; created the World Trade Organization.

World Trade Organization (WTO)
A trade organization that replaced the old General Agreement on Tariffs and Trade (GATT).

General Agreement on Tariffs and Trade (GATT)
A trade agreement that contained loopholes that enabled countries to avoid trade-barrier reduction agreements.

The latest round of WTO trade talks began in Doha, Qatar, in 2001. For the most part, the periodic meetings of WTO members under the Doha round have been very contentious. Typically, the discussions find developing countries on one side of the argument and the rich developed countries on the other. Recent negotiations in Cancún, Mexico, collapsed when the developing nations, led by Brazil, India, and China, demanded that the United States and the European Union drop agricultural tariffs and slash domestic agricultural subsidies faster and deeper than either was willing to do. The $300 billion a year in domestic subsidies to farmers encourages huge amounts of excess production.[21] This, in turn, depresses global agricultural prices and makes it difficult, or impossible, for developing countries to compete. Since the breakdown in Cancún, the WTO is considering ways to simplify the consensus decision-making model that has made it almost impossible for the 148-nation group to agree.[22]

The trend toward globalization has resulted in the creation of additional agreements and organizations: the North American Free Trade Agreement, the Free Trade Agreement of the Americas, the European Union, the World Bank, and the International Monetary Fund.

North American Free Trade Agreement

At the time it was instituted, the **North American Free Trade Agreement (NAFTA)** created the world's largest free trade zone. Ratified by the U.S. Congress in 1993, the agreement includes Canada, the United States, and Mexico, with a combined population of 360 million and economy of $6 trillion.

Canada, the largest U.S. trading partner, entered a free trade agreement with the United States in 1988. Thus, many of the new long-run opportunities for U.S. business under NAFTA have been in Mexico, America's second largest trading partner. Tariffs on Mexican exports to the United States averaged just 4 percent before the treaty was signed, and most goods entered the United States duty-free. Therefore, the main impact of NAFTA was to open the Mexican market to U.S. companies. When the treaty went into effect, tariffs on about half the items traded across the Rio Grande disappeared. The pact removed a web of Mexican licensing requirements, quotas, and tariffs that limited transactions in U.S. goods and services. For instance, the pact allowed U.S. and Canadian financial-services companies to own subsidiaries in Mexico for the first time in 50 years.

The real question is whether NAFTA can continue to deliver rising prosperity in all three countries. America has certainly benefited from cheaper imports and more investment opportunities abroad. Over the years, Mexico has also made huge economic gains due to NAFTA. The U.S.-Mexico cross border trade now averages over $650 million a day.[23] Over $1 billion in trade flows daily between the United States and Canada.[24] During the 1990s, many Canadian manufacturers switched from producing a broad cross section of products to higher value niche products that were less prone to competitive pressures such as wood products, clothing, and transportation equipment.

Although Mexico has thrived under NAFTA, its prospects are not as bright as in the past. Its advantage as a low-cost producer is being lost to countries such as India and China. American businesses complain that Mexico has a dysfunctional judicial system, unreliable power supplies, poor roads, high corporate tax rates, and unfriendly labor relations.[25] This has given companies pause when considering investing in Mexico. Mexico still has a lot to offer, but it must improve its infrastructure.

Free Trade Area of the Americas

The goal of the **Free Trade Area of the Americas (FTAA)** is to establish a free trade zone similar to NAFTA throughout the Western Hemisphere. If ratified by all member nations, the FTAA would become the largest trading zone in the world, consisting of 800 million people in 34 countries in both North and South

North American Free Trade Agreement (NAFTA)
An agreement between Canada, the United States, and Mexico that created the world's largest free trade zone.

Free Trade Area of the Americas (FTAA)
A regional trade agreement that, when signed, will create a regional trading zone encompassing 34 countries in North and South America.

America with a combined gross domestic product of $11 trillion! Similar to NAFTA, the FTAA pledges to support trade "without barriers, without subsidies, without unfair practices, and with an increasing stream of productive investments."[26] Leaders from the 34 countries have agreed to finish FTAA negotiations in 2005. If that occurs, over the next decade nontariff barriers would be removed, tariffs would gradually be reduced to zero, rules for investing and financial markets would be standardized, and a process would be established to handle trade disputes. For more information about the FTAA, see **http://www.ftaa-alca.org**. For more information about Mercosur, see **http://www.mercosur.org/english/default.htm**.

EXHIBIT 4.3

The Expanded European Union

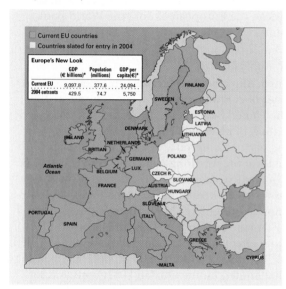

*:The € is the symbol for the euro, the currency used in most EU countries.
SOURCES: Eurostat; International Monetary Fund.

European Union

One of the world's most important free trade zones is the **European Union**, which now encompasses most of Europe. In 2004, the EU expanded from 15 members (Austria, Belgium, Denmark, Finland, France, Germany, Greece, Iceland, Italy, Luxembourg, the Netherlands, Portugal, Spain, Sweden, and the United Kingdom) to 25 members with a combined population of 450 million (see Exhibit 4.3). The new members are Cyprus, the Czech Republic, Estonia, Hungary, Latvia, Lithuania, Malta, Poland, Slovakia, and Slovenia. The new entrants differ in several ways from the older members. Eight of the new members are former Soviet satellites and remain saddled with inefficient government offices, state-controlled enterprises, and large, protected farm sectors. Most economists predict that it will take 50 years or longer before productivity and living standards in the new entrants catch up to those in western Europe.[27]

Nonetheless, the primary goal of the EU is to create a unified European market. Common foreign, security, and defense policies are also goals, as well as European citizenship—whereby any EU citizen can live, work, vote, and run for office anywhere in the member countries. The EU is creating standardized trade rules and coordinated health and safety standards. Duties, customs procedures, and taxes have also been also standardized. A driver hauling cargo from Amsterdam to Lisbon can now clear four border crossings by showing a single piece of paper. Before the formation of the EU, the same driver would have carried two pounds of paper to cross the same borders. The overall goal is to end the need for a special product for each country—for example, a different Braun electric razor for Italy, Germany, France, and so forth. Goods marked GEC (goods for EC) can be traded freely, without being retested at each border.

Some economists have called the EU the "United States of Europe." It is an attractive market, with purchasing power almost equal to that of the United States. But the EU will probably never be a United States of Europe. For one thing, even in a united Europe, marketers will not be able to produce a single Europroduct for a generic Euroconsumer. With more than 15 different languages and individual national customs, Europe will always be far more diverse than the United States. Thus, product differences will continue. It will be a long time, for instance, before the French begin drinking the instant coffee that Britons enjoy. Preferences for washing machines also differ: British homemakers want front-loaders, and the French want top-loaders; Germans like lots of settings and high spin speeds; Italians like lower speeds. Even European companies that think they understand Euroconsumers often have difficulties producing "the right product." Atag Holdings NV, a diversified Dutch company whose main business is kitchen appliances, was confident it could cater to both the "potato" and "spaghetti" belts—marketers' terms for consumer preferences in northern and southern Europe. But Atag quickly discovered that preferences vary much more than that. For example, on its ovens, burner shape and size, knob and clock placement, temperature range, and colors vary greatly from country to country. Although Atag's kitchenware unit has lifted foreign sales to 25 percent of its total from 4 percent in the mid-1990s, it now believes that its range of designs and speed in delivering them, rather than the magic bullet of a Europroduct, will keep it competitive.

An entirely different type of problem facing global marketers is the possibility of a protectionist movement by the EU against outsiders. For example, European automakers have proposed holding Japanese imports at roughly their current 10 percent market share. The Irish, Danes, and Dutch don't make cars and have unrestricted home markets; they would be unhappy about limited imports of Toyotas and Datsuns. But France has a strict quota on Japanese cars to protect Renault and Peugeot. These local carmakers could be hurt if the quota is raised at all.

American businesses have recently been stung by aggressive antitrust and other regulatory actions taken by the European Commission, the EU's executive branch. By EU law, the Commission must review any merger or acquisition involving any company with significant revenues in the EU. The biggest action to date was denying the merger of General Electric with Honeywell, both U.S. firms. Recently, the European Commission set its sights on Microsoft. The Commission claims that Microsoft is illegally leveraging its Windows operating system monopoly to gain unfair advantage in the server and audiovisual software markets. Possible penalties include unbundling MediaPlayer from Windows, forcing Microsoft to reveal details of how it links Windows PCs and servers, or even fining Microsoft 10 percent of its yearly revenues.[28] The EU also has strict privacy laws. The Commission recently ruled that the office phone numbers of General Motors' European employees were "personal information" and could not be published in the firm's global internal employee phone book.[29] For more information about the EU, go to **http://europa.eu.int/index-en.htm**.

The World Bank and International Monetary Fund

Two international financial organizations are instrumental in fostering global trade. The **World Bank** offers low-interest loans to developing nations. Originally, the purpose of the loans was to help these nations build infrastructure such as roads, power plants, schools, drainage projects, and hospitals. Now the World Bank offers loans to help developing nations relieve their debt burdens. To receive the loans, countries must pledge to lower trade barriers and aid private enterprise. In addition to making loans, the World Bank is a major source of advice and information for developing nations. The United States has granted the organization $60 million to create knowledge databases on nutrition, birth control, software engineering, creating quality products, and basic accounting systems.

The **International Monetary Fund (IMF)** was founded in 1945, one year after the creation of the World Bank, to promote trade through financial cooperation and eliminate trade barriers in the process. The IMF makes short-term loans to member nations that are unable to meet their budgetary expenses. It operates as a lender of last resort for troubled nations. In exchange for these emergency loans, IMF lenders frequently extract significant commitments from the borrowing nations to address the problems that led to the crises. These steps may include curtailing imports or even devaluing the currency.

DEMOGRAPHIC MAKEUP

The three most densely populated nations in the world are China, India, and Indonesia. But that fact alone is not particularly useful to marketers. They also need to know whether the population is mostly urban or rural, because marketers

World Bank
An international bank that offers low-interest loans, advice, and information to developing nations.

International Monetary Fund (IMF)
An international organization that acts as a lender of last resort, providing loans to troubled nations, and also works to promote trade through financial cooperation.

may not have easy access to rural consumers. In Belgium about 90 percent of the population lives in an urban setting, whereas in Kenya almost 80 percent of the population lives in a rural setting. Belgium is thus the more attractive market. Just as important as population is personal income within a country. Exhibit 4.2 showed gross national income per capita in selected countries.

Another key demographic consideration is age. There is a wide gap between the older populations of the industrialized countries and the vast working-age populations of developing countries. This gap has enormous implications for economies, businesses, and the competitiveness of individual countries. It means that while Europe and Japan struggle with pension schemes and the rising cost of health care, countries like China, Brazil, and Mexico can reap the fruits of what's known as a demographic dividend: falling labor costs, a healthier and more educated population, and the entry of millions of women into the workforce.

The demographic dividend is a gift of falling birthrates, and it causes a temporary bulge in the number of working-age people. Population experts have estimated that one-third of East Asia's economic miracle can be attributed to a beneficial age structure. But the miracle occurred only because the governments had policies in place to educate their people, create jobs, and improve health.

The big question is whether China, India, Brazil, Mexico, and other developing nations can do the same. "It's a one-time-only chance for developing countries to benefit from their favorable age structure" and close the wealth gap with their richer counterparts, says Joseph Chamie, director of the United Nations population division.[30]

NATURAL RESOURCES

A final factor in the external environment that has become more evident in the past decade is the shortage of natural resources. For example, petroleum shortages have created huge amounts of wealth for oil-producing countries such as Norway, Saudi Arabia, and the United Arab Emirates. Both consumer and industrial markets have blossomed in these countries. Other countries—such as Indonesia, Mexico, and Venezuela—were able to borrow heavily against oil reserves in order to develop more rapidly. On the other hand, industrial countries like Japan, the United States, and much of western Europe experienced rampant inflation in the 1970s and an enormous transfer of wealth to the petroleum-rich nations. But during much of the 1990s, when the price of oil fell, the petroleum-rich nations suffered. Many were not able to service their foreign debts when their oil revenues were sharply reduced. The U.S. dependence on foreign oil will likely remain high.

Petroleum is not the only natural resource that affects international marketing. Warm climate and lack of water mean that many of Africa's countries will remain importers of foodstuffs. The United States, on the other hand, must rely on Africa for many precious metals. Japan depends heavily on the United States for timber and logs. A Minnesota company manufactures and sells a million pairs of disposable chopsticks to Japan each year. The list could go on, but the point is clear. Vast differences in natural resources create international dependencies, huge shifts of wealth, inflation and recession, export opportunities for countries with abundant resources, and even a stimulus for military intervention.

REVIEW LEARNING OBJECTIVE 3

[3] **Describe the external environment facing global marketers**

Natural Resources
• dependence
• independence

Cultural
• values
• language
• customs
• traditions

Demography
• urban v. rural
• young v. old
• purchasing power

Global Marketing Mix

Economic Development

Political Structure
• tariffs
• quotas
• boycotts
• exchange controls
• market groupings
• trade agreements

Technological Development

Identify the various ways of entering the global marketplace

A company should consider entering the global marketplace only after its management has a solid grasp of the global environment. Some relevant questions are "What are our options in selling abroad?" "How difficult is global marketing?" and "What are the potential risks and returns?" Concrete answers to these questions would probably encourage the many U.S. firms not selling overseas to venture into the international arena. Foreign sales could be an important source of profits.

Companies decide to "go global" for a number of reasons. Perhaps the most important is to earn additional profits. Managers may feel that international sales will result in higher profit margins or more added-on profits. A second stimulus is that a firm may have a unique product or technological advantage not available to other international competitors. Such advantages should result in major business successes abroad. In other situations, management may have exclusive market information about foreign customers, marketplaces, or market situations not known to others. While exclusivity can provide an initial motivation for international marketing, managers must realize that competitors can be expected to catch up with the firm's information advantage. Finally, saturated domestic markets, excess capacity, and potential for economies of scale can also be motivators to "go global." Economies of scale mean that average per-unit production costs fall as output is increased.

Many firms form multinational partnerships—called strategic alliances—to assist them in penetrating global markets; strategic alliances are examined in Chapter 6. Five other methods of entering the global marketplace are, in order of risk, exporting, licensing, contract manufacturing, the joint venture, and direct investment (see Exhibit 4.4).

EXPORTING

When a company decides to enter the global market, exporting is usually the least complicated and least risky alternative. **Exporting** is selling domestically produced products to buyers in another country. A company, for example, can sell directly to foreign importers or buyers. Exporting is not limited to huge corporations such as General Motors or 3M. Indeed, small companies account for 96 percent of all U.S. exporters, but only 30 percent of the export volume.[31] The United States is the world's largest exporter.

exporting
Selling domestically produced products to buyers in another country.

EXHIBIT 4.4

Risk Levels for Five Methods of Entering the Global Marketplace

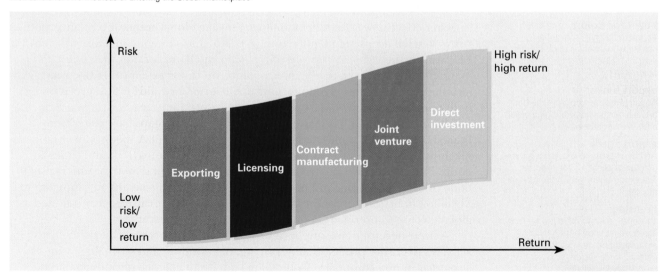

The U.S. Commercial Service within the Department of Commerce promotes itself as "Your Global Business Partner." It offers trade specialists in more than a hundred U.S. cities and 80 countries to help beginning exporters, as well as those already engaged in global marketing, increase their business. The primary services offered by the U.S. Commercial Service are marketing research, locating qualified buyers and partners, trade events, and global business consulting. These services are explained in more detail in Exhibit 4.5.

Recently, the U.S. Commercial Service launched a joint venture with IBM called BuyUSA.com. The Internet service offers one-on-one export counseling provided by the U.S. Commercial Service. In addition, the site provides Web-based sales leads to exporters. A U.S. exporter fills out a questionnaire on its product offerings and receives access to qualified foreign buyers. We suggest that you go to the Web site and take the BuyUSA tour and demo to learn more about how the U.S. Commercial Service aids American firms wanting to "go global." For those interested in international business, a nongovernmental Web site that offers links to hundreds of useful sites is available from the International Federation of International Trade Associations (**http://fita.org**).

Instead of selling directly to foreign buyers, a company may decide to sell to intermediaries located in its domestic market. The most common intermediary is the export merchant, also known as a **buyer for export**, which is usually treated like a domestic customer by the domestic manufacturer. The buyer for export assumes all risks and sells internationally for its own account. The domestic firm is involved only to the extent that its products are bought in foreign markets.

A second type of intermediary is the **export broker**, who plays the traditional broker's role by bringing buyer and seller together. The manufacturer still retains title and assumes all the risks. Export brokers operate primarily in agricultural products and raw materials.

Export agents, a third type of intermediary, are foreign sales agents-distributors who live in the foreign country and perform the same functions as domestic manufacturers' agents, helping with international financing, shipping, and so on. The U.S. Department of Commerce has an agent-distributor service that helps about 5,000 U.S. companies a year find an agent or distributor in virtually any country of the world. A second category of agents resides in the manufacturer's country but represents foreign buyers. This type of agent acts as a hired purchasing agent for foreign customers operating in the exporter's home market.

LICENSING

Another effective way for a firm to move into the global arena with relatively little risk is to sell a license to manufacture its product to someone in a foreign country. **Licensing** is the legal process whereby a licensor allows another firm to use its manufacturing process, trademarks, patents, trade secrets, or other proprietary knowledge. The licensee, in turn, pays the licensor a royalty or fee agreed on by both parties.

Because licensing has many advantages, U.S. companies have eagerly embraced the concept, sometimes in unusual ways. Caterpillar, the producer of heavy machinery, has licensed Wolverine World Wide to make "CAT" brand shoes and boots. Europeans have latched onto CAT gear as the new symbol of American outdoor culture. CAT is one of Europe's hottest brands, which translates into almost $1 billion in licensing revenues.[32] CAT also granted Overland Appean Limited a global license to produce CAT apparel.

A licensor must make sure it can exercise sufficient control over the licensee's activities to ensure proper quality, pricing, distribution, and so on. Licensing may also create a new competitor in the long run, if the licensee decides to void the

buyer for export
An intermediary in the global market who assumes all ownership risks and sells globally for its own account.

export broker
An intermediary who plays the traditional broker's role by bringing buyer and seller together.

export agent
An intermediary who acts like a manufacturer's agent for the exporter. The export agent lives in the foreign market.

licensing
The legal process whereby a licensor agrees to let another firm use its manufacturing process, trademarks, patents, trade secrets, or other proprietary knowledge.

EXHIBIT 4.5

Assistance Provided by the U.S. Commercial Service

Marketing Research

COUNTRY COMMERCIAL GUIDES

provide overviews for doing business in more than 120 countries with information on market conditions, best export prospects, financing, finding distributors, and legal and cultural issues.

INDUSTRY SECTOR ANALYSES

offer succinct international market information on specific industries that can help determine market potential, market size, and competitors for a firm's products and services.

INTERNATIONAL MARKET INSIGHTS

report on current conditions in specific country markets and identify upcoming opportunities for generating sales.

WEBCASTS

present market opportunities and insights on how to do business in specific countries. They are available on **http://www.usatrade.gov**.

FLEXIBLE MARKET RESEARCH

provides timely, customized, reliable answers to a company's inquiries about a market and its receptivity to its products and services.

Locating Qualified Buyers and Partners

MATCHMAKER TRADE DELEGATIONS

let managers meet face-to-face with qualified business prospects in two to four promising export markets. The program includes comprehensive country briefings, logistical support, and follow-up counseling.

INTERNATIONAL PARTNER SEARCHES

deliver detailed company information on up to five prescreened potential partners that have expressed an interest in a company's products and services.

GOLD KEY

arranges one-on-one appointments with carefully selected potential business partners in a targeted export market.

INTERNATIONAL COMPANY PROFILES

provide affordable, fast credit checks and background information on potential international buyers and other business partners.

TRADE OPPORTUNITY PROGRAM

provides daily worldwide trade leads from companies seeking to purchase or represent a firm's products or services. These leads are reviewed by our trade specialists and commercial officers.

GOLD KEY USA

helps international buyers locate the best U.S. suppliers. Counseling before and after business meetings is part of this service.

VIRTUAL MATCHMAKERS

give sales managers the opportunity to meet with groups of prescreened international business prospects and get answers to your market questions in an interactive video conference focusing on your industry.

VIDEO GOLD KEY

enables sales managers to meet with individual potential business partners throughout the world without leaving the United States. Available now in more than 100 U.S. and international locations.

Trade Events

COMMERCIAL NEWS USA

promotes a firm's products and services to more than 400,000 international buyers. A great way to reach a targeted audience eager to buy U.S. products and services, this magazine has a proven track record of high response rates and sales results.

SHOW TIME

provides in-depth counseling at major trade shows from a team of market and industry specialists who know the local and regional markets.

CATALOG EXHIBITIONS

showcase a firm's product and service literature in fast-growing export markets around the world.

SINGLE COMPANY PROMOTIONS

provide meeting space and carefully screened invitation lists to help a company present successful seminars featuring its products and services.

INTERNATIONAL BUYER PROGRAM

recruits and brings more than 125,000 international end-users and distributors to visit top U.S. trade shows. The Commercial Service helps organize meetings and provide matchmaking services and business counseling to help generate sales.

U.S. PAVILIONS

put your company in the best international trade shows with access to thousands of buyers. One-on-one matching at the show with potential buyers arranged by the commercial service's team of market and industry specialists can help generate sales and long-term business relationships at these high-volume shows.

Consulting

- Determine the best markets for a firm's products and services.
- Develop an effective export strategy.
- Evaluate international competitors.
- Identify and comply with legal and regulatory issues.
- Locate export financing.
- Settle disputes.
- Win contract bids.
- Learn about cultural and business protocol.

SOURCE: U.S. Commercial Service.

license agreement. International law is often ineffective in stopping such actions. Two common ways of maintaining effective control over licensees are shipping one or more critical components from the United States or locally registering patents and trademarks to the U.S. firm, not to the licensee. Garment companies maintain control by delivering only so many labels per day; they also supply their own fabric and collect the scraps, and do accurate unit counts.

Franchising is a form of licensing that has grown rapidly in recent years. More than 400 U.S. franchisors operate more than 40,000 outlets in foreign countries, bringing in sales of over $9 billion.[33] Over half of the international franchises are for fast-food restaurants and business services. New Horizons Computer Learning Centers has been franchising internationally since 1992. It now has locations in 50 countries. Most of the inquiries New Horizons receives about franchise opportunities come through the U.S. Commercial Service's Gold Key program (see Exhibit 4.5).[34]

CONTRACT MANUFACTURING

Firms that do not want to become involved in licensing or to become heavily involved in global marketing may engage in **contract manufacturing**, which is private-label manufacturing by a foreign company. The foreign company produces a certain volume of products to specification, with the domestic firm's brand name on the goods. The domestic company usually handles the marketing. Thus, the domestic firm can broaden its global marketing base without investing in overseas plants and equipment. After establishing a solid base, the domestic firm may switch to a joint venture or direct investment.

Recently, particularly in China, contract manufacturers have been making overruns and selling the excess production directly to either consumers or retailers. New Balance, for example, found that a contract manufacturer was producing extra running shoes and selling them to nonauthorized retailers. The retailers were selling the knock-off New Balance shoes for $20, while authorized retailers were trying to sell the same shoe for $60. Recently, New Balance changed its relationship with its suppliers. It cut the number of factories it uses in China to six and monitors them more closely. It has also begun using high-tech shoe labels to better spot counterfeits and keep control of its own production.

Other companies have experienced similar problems. Unilever discovered that one of its suppliers in Shanghai had been making excess cases of soap and selling them directly to retailers. Procter & Gamble says one of its Chinese suppliers sold empty P&G shampoo bottles to another company, which filled them with counterfeit shampoo. P&G fired the supplier.[35]

JOINT VENTURE

Joint ventures are somewhat similar to licensing agreements. In a **joint venture**, the domestic firm buys part of a foreign company or joins with a foreign company to create a new entity. A joint venture is a quick and relatively inexpensive way to go global and to gain needed expertise.[36] For example, Robert Mondavi Wineries entered into a joint venture with Baron Philippe de Rothschild, owner of Bordeaux's First Growth chateau, Mouton-Rothschild. They created a wine in California called Opus One. It was immediately established as the American vanguard of quality and price. Mondavi has entered other joint ventures with the Frescobaldi family in Tuscany and with Errazuriz in Chile.

Recently, General Motors entered into a joint venture with Avtovaz, a Soviet-era auto manufacturer in Russia, to produce a car to be called the Chevrolet Niva. Russia is expected to be one of the top ten growth markets for cars during this decade, and GM wants to be a player. The assembly and engineering will be done at low cost in Russia. GM is providing $333 million and technology. Avtovaz offers skilled workers and a distribution system.

contract manufacturing
Private-label manufacturing by a foreign company.

joint venture
When a domestic firm buys part of a foreign company or joins with a foreign company to create a new entity.

Joint ventures can be very risky. Many fail; others fall victim to a takeover, in which one partner buys out the other. Sometimes joint venture partners simply can't agree on management strategies and policies. For example, Procter & Gamble and its Vietnamese partner couldn't agree on what to do next in their unprofitable joint venture. Consumer-products giant P&G wanted to inject more cash into the business; but because Phuong Dong Soap & Detergent, its state-owned partner, said it couldn't provide the cash to match it, P&G offered to buy out the Vietnamese stake. So far Phuong Dong has flatly refused to sell, and Ministry of Planning and Investment officials have described such an option as "impossible."

In a successful joint venture, both parties gain valuable skills from the alliance. In the General Motors–Suzuki joint venture in Canada, for example, both parties have contributed and gained. The alliance, CAMI Automotive, was formed to manufacture low-end cars for the U.S. market. The plant, run by Suzuki management, produces the Chevrolet Equinox. Through CAMI, Suzuki has gained access to GM's dealer network and an expanded market for parts and components. GM avoided the cost of developing low-end cars and obtained models it needed to revitalize the lower end of its product line and its average fuel-economy rating. The CAMI factory is one of the most productive plants in North America. There GM has learned how Japanese carmakers use work teams, run flexible assembly lines, and manage quality control.

DIRECT INVESTMENT

Active ownership of a foreign company or of overseas manufacturing or market-ing facilities is **direct foreign investment**. Direct foreign investment by U.S. manufacturers is currently about $50 billion annually. Direct investors have either a controlling interest or a large minority interest in the firm. Thus, they have the greatest potential reward and the greatest potential risk.[37]

For example, Mexico has attracted top U.S. candy manufacturers looking for cheap labor, cheap sugar, and a youthful Mexican market with a sweet tooth. American confectioners are also using Mexico as a platform to export back into the U.S. market, more than tripling Mexican candy sales in the United States to around $150 million a year from less than $50 million in 1993, the year before NAFTA went into effect. That sales surge is behind the shrinking candy workforce north of the border. All of the Big Three U.S. candy makers—Mars, Inc., Tootsie Roll Industries, and Hershey Foods—operate plants in Mexico.[38]

Direct investment by American companies in China has also mushroomed. Coca-Cola has invested $1.1 billion in 31 bottling plants and two concentrate plants. Kodak has plowed $1.2 billion into five manufacturing plants and more than 8,000 outlets. Motorola has spent $3.4 billion on two manufacturing plants. Another giant, Procter & Gamble, has invested over $1 billion in five plants for food, personal-care, and household consumer goods.[39] And the list goes on. The booming mass market in China has created tremendous profit opportunities for global competitors. In 2004, General Motors' most profitable market was China.

Common carriers like FedEx are good examples of companies using direct investment abroad. The company has operations worldwide to support its global package delivery services. In this ad, FedEx uses the tag line, "Yeah . . . we go there" to illustrate the reach of its international network.

direct foreign investment
Active ownership of a foreign company or of overseas manufacturing or marketing facilities.

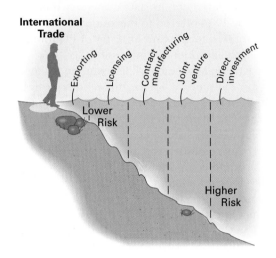

Sometimes firms make direct investments because they can find no suitable local partners. Also, direct investments avoid the communication problems and conflicts of interest that can arise with joint ventures. Other firms simply don't want to share their technology, which they fear may be stolen or ultimately used against them by creating a new competitor. Texas Instruments has historically been one of the latter companies.

A firm may make a direct foreign investment by acquiring an interest in an existing company or by building new facilities. It might do so because it has trouble transferring some resource to a foreign operation or getting that resource locally. One important resource is personnel, especially managers. If the local labor market is tight, the firm may buy an entire foreign firm and retain all its employees instead of paying higher salaries than competitors.

The United States is a popular place for direct investment by foreign companies. In 2005, the value of foreign-owned businesses in the United States was more than $500 billion.

5 THE GLOBAL MARKETING MIX

List the basic elements involved in developing a global marketing mix

To succeed, firms seeking to enter into foreign trade must still adhere to the principles of the marketing mix. Information gathered on foreign markets through research is the basis for the four Ps of global marketing strategy: product, place (distribution), promotion, and price. Marketing managers who understand the advantages and disadvantages of different ways of entering the global market and the effect of the external environment on the firm's marketing mix have a better chance of reaching their goals.

The first step in creating a marketing mix is developing a thorough understanding of the global target market. Often this knowledge can be obtained through the same types of marketing research used in the domestic market (see Chapter 8). However, global marketing research is conducted in vastly different environments. Conducting a survey can be difficult in developing countries, where telephone ownership is growing but is still not common and mail delivery is slow or sporadic. Drawing samples based on known population parameters is often difficult because of the lack of data. In some cities in South America, Mexico, Africa, and Asia, street maps are unavailable, streets are unidentified, and houses are unnumbered. Moreover, the questions a marketer can ask may differ in other cultures. In some cultures, people tend to be more private than in the United States and will not respond to personal questions on surveys. For instance, in France, questions about one's age and income are considered especially rude.

PRODUCT AND PROMOTION

With the proper information, a good marketing mix can be developed. One important decision is whether to alter the product or the promotion for the global marketplace. Other options are to radically change the product or to adjust either the promotional message or the product to suit local conditions.

One Product, One Message

The strategy of global marketing standardization, which was discussed earlier, means developing a single product for all markets and promoting it the same way all over the world. For instance, Procter & Gamble uses the same product and promotional themes for Head and Shoulders in China as it does in the United States. The advertising draws attention to a person's dandruff problem, which stands out in a nation of black-haired people. Head and Shoulders is now the best-selling shampoo in China despite costing over 300 percent more than local brands. Buoyed by its success with Head and Shoulders, P&G is using the same product and same promotion strategy with Tide detergent in China. It also used another common promotion tactic that has been successful in the United States. The company spent half a million dollars to reach agreements with local washing machine manufacturers, which now include a free box of Tide with every new washer.

Global media—especially satellite and cable TV networks like CNN International, MTV Networks, and British Sky Broadcasting—make it possible to beam advertising to audiences unreachable a few years ago. Eighteen-year-olds in Paris often have more in common with 18-year-olds in New York than with their own parents. Almost all of MTV's advertisers run unified, English-language campaigns in the 28 nations the firm reaches. The audiences buy the same products, go to the same movies, listen to the same music, and sip the same colas. Global advertising merely works on that premise. Although teens throughout the world prefer movies above all other forms of television programming, they are closely followed by music videos, stand-up comedy, and then sports.

Global marketing standardization can sometimes backfire. Procter & Gamble decided to use the same name and promotion strategy for dishwashing liquids around the world. So, in Germany, the name of P&G's dishwashing liquid changed from Fairy to Dawn—the name it sells under in the United States. But since German consumers did not know what "Dawn" was, sales for the brand plummeted.

Unchanged products may fail simply because of cultural factors. The game *Trivial Pursuit* failed in Japan. It seems that getting the answers wrong can be seen as a loss of face. Any type of war game tends to do very poorly in Germany, even though Germany is by far the world's biggest game-playing nation. A successful game in Germany has plenty of details and thick rulebooks. *Monopoly* remains the world's favorite board game; it seems to overcome all cultural barriers. The game is available in 25 languages, including Russian, Croatian, and Hebrew.

Mattel, Scrabble
Hasbro, Monopoly
Visit Mattel's Scrabble site and Hasbro's Monopoly site. Which game has a more international presence on the Internet? Does this surprise you? Why?
http://www.mattelscrabble.com/
http://www.monopoly.com/

Online

GILLES BASSIGNAC/GAMMA

A one-product, one-message strategy does not work for all products. Parker Brothers' *Monopoly*, however, uses this strategy very successfully. A French Riviera version of the popular game debuted at the Cannes film festival. Depicted here is the Russian gameboard.

Product Invention

In the context of global marketing, product invention can be taken to mean either creating a new product for a market or drastically changing an existing product. For the Japanese market, Nabisco had to remove the cream filling from its Oreo cookies because Japanese children thought they were too sweet. Ford thinks it can save billions on its product development costs by developing a single small-car

Disneyland Resort Paris

How does Disney vary its park information to suit specific cultural tastes? Compare the presentation of theme park information for the U.S., Tokyo, and Paris resorts. What similarities and differences do you notice?

http://disney.go.com

Online

chassis and then altering its styling to suit different countries. Campbell Soup invented a watercress and duck gizzard soup that is now selling well in China. It is also considering a cream of snake soup. Frito-Lay's most popular potato chip in Thailand is shrimp flavored. Popular ice cream flavors in Japan include pickled orchid, eel, fish, sea slug, whale meat, soft-shelled turtle, and cedar chips.[40] Dormont Manufacturing Company makes a simple gas hose that hooks up to deep-fat fryers and similar appliances. Sounds like something that could be sold globally, right? Wrong—in Europe differing national standards mean that a different hose is required for each country. Minutiae such as the color of the plastic coating or how the end pieces should be attached to the rest of the hose and the couplings themselves create a myriad of design problems for Dormont Manufacturing.

Coca Cola's Thums Up cola outsells Coke by a four-to-one margin in India. Coke sells a pear-flavored drink in Turkey and a berry drink in Germany. Now Coke is developing soft drinks for tastes around the world.

Consumers in different countries use products differently. For example, in many countries, clothing is worn much longer between washings than in the United States, so a more durable fabric must be produced and marketed. For Peru, Goodyear developed a tire that contains a higher percentage of natural rubber and has better treads than tires manufactured elsewhere in order to handle the tough Peruvian driving conditions. Rubbermaid has sold millions of open-top wastebaskets in America; Europeans, picky about garbage peeking out of bins, want bins with tight lids that snap into place.

Successful global marketers have discovered that the path to profitability is through tailoring products to various tastes and desires. A Japanese salesclerk displays a package of flounder and spinach stew, a jar of white bait porridge, and a wild duck cream stew, all produced by America's leading baby-food maker, Gerber. The Japanese baby-food market has tripled in the past fifteen years, and more than four hundred infant entries jostle for spots on Japan's jam-packed supermarket shelves.

AP/WIDE WORLD PHOTOS

Product Adaptation

Another alternative for global marketers is to slightly alter a basic product to meet local conditions. Sometimes it is as simple as changing the package size. In India, Unilever sells single-use sachets of Sunsilk shampoo for 2 to 4 cents. Unilever's Rexona brand deodorant sticks sell for 16 cents and up. They are big hits in India, the Philippines, Bolivia, and Peru—where Unilever has grabbed 60 percent of the deodorant market. A nickel-size Vaseline package and a tube containing enough Close Up toothpaste for 20 brushings sell for about 8 cents each. In Nigeria, Unilever sells 3-inch-square packets of margarine that don't need refrigeration.[41]

Sometimes power sources and/or voltage must be changed on electronic products. It may be necessary, for example, to change the size and shape of the electrical plug. In other cases, the change may be a bit more radical. In India, people often lack reliable access to electricity or can't afford batteries. So, Freeplay Energy Group of London created a radio that is charged by cranking a handle.

After the initial failure of Disneyland Paris in 1992, Disney quickly learned not to ignore the local culture. For example, the company failed to consider even basic local customs such as serving wine with meals. A complete cultural makeover has made the park Europe's biggest tourist attraction, even more popular than the Eiffel Tower.[42] Disney's new Walt Disney Studios park, outside Paris, blends Disney entertainment and attractions with the history and culture of European film since French camera-makers helped invent the motion picture in the late 1800s. A big stunt show, designed by French stuntman Remy Julienne, features cars and motorcycles that race through a village modeled after the French resort town of St. Tropez.

Message Adaptation

Another global marketing strategy is to maintain the same basic product but alter the promotional strategy. Bicycles are mainly pleasure vehicles in the United States. In many parts of the world, however, they are a family's main mode of transportation. Thus, promotion in these countries should stress durability and efficiency. In contrast, U.S. advertising may emphasize escaping and having fun.

Harley-Davidson decided that its American promotion theme, "One steady constant in an increasingly screwed-up world," wouldn't appeal to the Japanese market. The Japanese ads combine American images with traditional Japanese ones: American riders passing a geisha in a rickshaw, Japanese ponies nibbling at a Harley motorcycle. Waiting lists for Harleys in Japan are now six months long.

When Britney Spears took her "In the Zone" tour to South Korea, she posed for photographs in traditional South Korean costume. This photo shows the mixing of the American message (the photo in the background) with the South Korean message (the pose in the foreground).

AP/WIDE WORLD PHOTOS

Global marketers find that promotion is a daunting task in some countries. For example, commercial television time is readily available in Canada but severely restricted in Germany. Product placement (prominently featuring brand names in exchange for payment) on television shows is prohibited in Great Britain. Until recently, marketers in Indonesia had only one subscription TV channel with few viewers (120,000 out of a nation of more than 200 million people). Because of this limited television audience, several marketers, such as the country's main Toyota dealer, had to develop direct-mail campaigns to reach their target markets.

Some cultures view a product as having less value if it has to be advertised. In other nations, claims that seem exaggerated by U.S. standards are commonplace. Germany does not permit advertisers to state that their products are "best" or "better" than those of competitors, a description commonly used in U.S. advertising. The hard-sell tactics and sexual themes so common in U.S. advertising are taboo in many countries. Procter & Gamble's advertisements for Cheer detergents were voted least popular in Japan because they used hard-sell testimonials. The negative reaction forced P&G to withdraw Cheer from the Japanese market. In the Middle East, pictures of women in print advertisements have been covered with censors' ink.

Language barriers, translation problems, and cultural differences have generated numerous headaches for international marketing managers. Consider these examples:

- A toothpaste claiming to give users white teeth was especially inappropriate in many areas of Southeast Asia, where the well-to-do chew betel nuts and black teeth are a sign of higher social status.
- Procter & Gamble's Japanese advertising for Camay soap nearly devastated the product. In one commercial, a man meeting a woman for the first time immediately compared her skin to that of a fine porcelain doll. Although the ad had worked in other Asian countries, the man came across as rude and disrespectful in Japan.
- A teenager careening down a store aisle on a grocery cart in a Coca-Cola ad was perceived as too rebellious in Singapore.

PLACE (DISTRIBUTION)

Solving promotional, price, and product problems does not guarantee global marketing success. The product still has to get adequate distribution. For example, Europeans don't play sports as much as Americans do, so they don't visit sporting-goods stores as often. Realizing this, Reebok started selling its shoes in about 800 traditional shoe stores in France. In one year, the company doubled its French sales. Harley-Davidson had to open two company-owned stores in Japan to get distribution for its Harley clothing and clothing accessories.

The Japanese distribution system is considered the most complicated in the world. Imported goods wind their way through layers of agents, wholesalers, and retailers. For example, a bottle of 96 aspirins costs about $20 because the bottle passes through at least six wholesalers, each of whom increases the selling price. As a result, the Japanese consumer pays the world's most exorbitant prices. These distribution channels seem to be based on historical and traditional patterns of socially arranged trade-offs, which Japanese officials claim are very hard for the government to change. Today, however, the system seems to be changing because of pressure from the Japanese consumer. Japanese shoppers are now placing emphasis on low prices in their purchasing decisions. The retailer who can cut distribution costs and therefore the retail price gets the sale. For example, Kojima, a Japanese electronics superstore chain like the U.S. chains Circuit City and Best Buy, had to bypass General Electric's Japanese distribution partner Toshiba to import its merchandise at a good price. Toshiba's distribution system required refrigerators to pass through too many hands before they reached the retailer. Kojima went directly to GE headquarters in the United States and persuaded the company to sell it refrigerators, which were then shipped directly to Kojima. It is now selling GE refrigerators for about $800—half the price of a typical Japanese model.

Some distribution strategies that are common in other countries are illegal in the United States. At the Tony Roma's restaurant in Mexico City, nearly everything is "Made in the USA," from the Idaho potatoes to the Blue Ridge barbecue sauce. But you won't find a Budweiser or a Miller Lite at any of the U.S. chain's 15 Mexican franchises. The only beer on tap is brewed by Mexican giant Grupo Modelo SA, maker of the top-selling U.S. beer import, Corona Extra, and one of two domestic beer companies. "We used to offer 28 different kinds of beer, including American beers," says food manager José Luis Rojas. "But Modelo gave us money to sell only its beer."[43] That kind of tie-up—illegal in the United States—is common in restaurants, corner stores, and stadiums throughout Mexico, where Modelo and its rival Fomento Economico Mexicano SA, known as Femsa, have a 99 percent market share between them.

In many developing nations, channels of distribution and the physical infrastructure are inadequate. To combat these problems, companies are using creative strategies. Colgate-Palmolive has introduced villagers in India to the concept of brushing teeth by rolling into villages with video vans that show half-hour infomercials on the benefits of toothpaste. The company received more than half of its revenue in that nation from rural areas in 2004. Until recently, the rural market was virtually invisible, due to a lack of distribution. Unilever's Indian subsidiary, Hindustan Lever, began door-to-door sales of its cosmetics, toothpastes, and detergents in 2000. It plans to have over a million direct-sales consultants by 2008. Hindustan Lever contributes about 10 percent of Unilever's revenue.[44] Similarly, an available labor supply has enabled Amway to build a 90,000-person direct-sales force in China with sales of over $720 million annually.[45]

Distribution in China is very difficult. Only 1 percent of China's roads are Western-standard expressways, and airfreight accounts for less than 1 percent of all freight volume.[46] Therefore, the main modes of transport are truck and train. But in a fragmented trucking industry with few major companies, multinationals have difficulty telling which companies are reliable. In the rail system, theft is a major problem. Distribution consultants are beginning to spring up to help multinationals navigate the complicated system.

Certainly, not all global distribution is inefficient or primitive. Kia Motors uses high-profile components in its Sorento SUV to enhance sales overseas. Many of the car's 30,000 parts are shipped to the Hwaseong, South Korea vehicle assembly plant from around the world. Here are the steps in the assembly of the car's CD player:

1. Panasonic Automotive sources optical pickup units, which read the CDs, in China. They are then shipped to Thailand.
2. The mechanical structure and electronic components are added in Thailand, and then the units are shipped to a Matsushita Communication Industrial plant in Reynosa, Mexico.
3. The units are trucked to a Delco Electronics plant in Matamoros, Mexico, where they are assembled into an audio system.
4. The audio systems are trucked to California and shipped to South Korea.
5. The players are fitted into the Sorento in Hwaseong, South Korea.
6. The Sorentos are shipped to the United States.[47]

PRICING

Once marketing managers have determined a global product and promotion strategy, they can select the remainder of the marketing mix. Pricing presents some unique problems in the global sphere. Exporters must not only cover their production costs but also consider transportation costs, insurance, taxes, and tariffs. When deciding on a final price, marketers must also determine what customers are willing to spend on a particular product. Marketers also need to ensure that their foreign buyers will pay them. Because developing nations lack mass purchasing power, selling to them often poses special pricing problems. Sometimes a product can be simplified in order to lower the price. The firm must not assume that low-income countries are willing to accept lower quality, however. Although the nomads of the Sahara are very poor, they still buy expensive fabrics to make their clothing. Their survival in harsh conditions and extreme temperatures requires this expense. Additionally, certain expensive luxury items can be sold almost anywhere.

Exchange Rates

The exchange rate is the price of one country's currency in terms of another country's currency. If a country's currency *appreciates*, less of that country's currency is needed to buy another country's currency. If a country's currency *depreciates*, more of that currency will be needed to buy another country's currency.

How do appreciation and depreciation affect the prices of a country's goods? If, say, the U.S. dollar depreciates relative to the Japanese yen, U.S. residents have to pay more dollars to buy Japanese goods. To illustrate, suppose the dollar price of a yen is $0.012 and that a Toyota is priced at 2 million yen. At this exchange rate, a U.S. resident pays $24,000 for a Toyota ($0.012 × 2 million yen = $24,000). If the dollar depreciates to $0.018 to one yen, then the U.S. resident will have to pay $36,000 for a Toyota.

As the dollar depreciates, the prices of Japanese goods rise for U.S. residents, so they buy fewer Japanese goods—thus, U.S. imports may decline. At the same time, as the dollar depreciates relative to the yen, the yen appreciates relative to the dollar. This means prices of U.S. goods fall for the Japanese, so they buy more U.S. goods—and U.S. exports rise.

Currency markets operate under a system of **floating exchange rates**. Prices of different currencies "float" up and down based on the demand for and the supply of each currency. Global currency traders create the supply of and demand for a particular country's currency based on that country's investment, trade potential, and economic strength.

Recently, manufacturers, politicians, and labor representatives have accused China of keeping its currency artificially low to boost exports and thereby causing American manufacturers to close U.S. plants. Since 1994 Chinese exports to the United States have more than tripled.[48] However, trade relations between the two countries are very complex. Ten of China's top 40 exporters are U.S.

floating exchange rates
Prices of different currencies move up and down based on the demand for and the supply of each currency.

companies including Dell and Motorola. What's more, retailers Wal-Mart Stores and Target count on low-priced goods from China to help meet U.S. consumer demand for affordable products. This, in turn, helps America hold down inflation. Thus, the United States and China have created a mutually beneficial economic synergy.

Purchasing Power

As you learned in Chapter 3, *purchasing power* is measured by comparing the relative cost of a standard set of goods and services in different geographic locations.

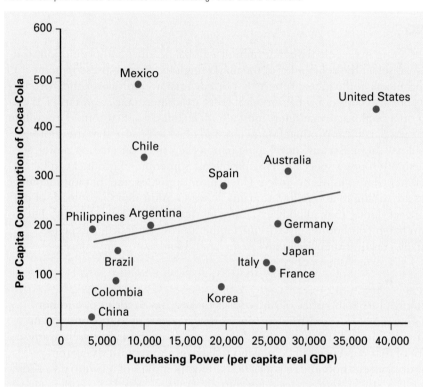

EXHIBIT 4.6

How Consumption of Coca-Cola Varies with Purchasing Power around the World

SOURCES: "GDP—Per Capita." *The World Factbook*, [Online] available at http://www.odci.gov/cia/publications/factbook/fields/2004.html, 25 September 2003; "Operations Review: Selected Market Results," *The Coca-Cola Company 2000 Annual Report*, [Online] available at http://www2.coca-cola.com/investors/annualreport/2002/or_smr.htm, 28 June 2003.

Purchasing power is also an important factor in global marketing. A bottle of Coke costs $2.30 in Tokyo. Because a bottle of Coke costs only about $1.00 in the United States, the average American would have more purchasing power than the average Japanese. Purchasing power is surprisingly strong in countries like Mexico, India, and China, which have low average levels of income. This is because basic living expenses, such as food, shelter, and transportation, are very inexpensive in those countries, so consumers still have money to spend after paying for necessities. (Recall the discussion of cost of living from Chapter 3.) To illustrate, the average Chinese household spends only 5 percent of its income on basic living expenses whereas the average American household spends 45 to 50 percent. Because basic living expenses are minimal in China, Mexico, and India, purchasing power is strong, and millions of Chinese, Mexican, and Indian consumers increasingly have extra money to spend on what they want, in addition to what they need.

Consequently, countries with high and growing levels of purchasing power are good choices for companies looking for attractive global markets. As Exhibit 4.6 shows, Coke has found that the per capita consumption of Coca-Cola, or how many bottles of Coke a person drinks per year rises directly with purchasing power. For example, in eastern Europe, as countries began to embrace capitalism after the fall of communism, per capita consumption of Coke increased from 20 to 31 Cokes in just two years, and now, more than a decade later, it is at 46 Cokes per year.[49]

Dumping

Dumping is generally considered to be the sale of an exported product at a price lower than that charged for the same or a like product in the "home" market of the exporter. This practice is regarded as a form of price discrimination that can potentially harm the importing nation's competing industries. Dumping may occur as a result of exporter business strategies that include (1) trying to increase an overseas market share, (2) temporarily distribut-

dumping
The sale of an exported product at a price lower than that charged for the same or a like product in the "home" market of the exporter.

ing products in overseas markets to offset slack demand in the home market, (3) lowering unit costs by exploiting large-scale production, and (4) attempting to maintain stable prices during periods of exchange rate fluctuations.

Historically, the dumping of goods has presented serious problems in international trade. As a result, dumping has led to significant disagreements among countries and diverse views about its harmfulness. Some trade economists view dumping as harmful only when it involves the use of "predatory" practices that intentionally try to eliminate competition and gain monopoly power in a market. They believe that predatory dumping rarely occurs and that antidumping rules are a protectionist tool whose cost to consumers and import-using industries exceeds the benefits to the industries receiving protection.

Countertrade

Global trade does not always involve cash. Countertrade is a fast-growing way to conduct global business. In **countertrade**, all or part of the payment for goods or services is in the form of other goods or services. Countertrade is thus a form of barter (swapping goods for goods), an age-old practice whose origins have been traced back to cave dwellers. The U.S. Department of Commerce says that roughly 30 percent of all global trade is countertrade. In fact, both India and China have made billion-dollar government purchasing lists, with most of the goods to be paid for by countertrade.

One common type of countertrade is straight barter. For example, PepsiCo sends Pepsi syrup to Russian bottling plants and in payment gets Stolichnaya vodka, which is then marketed in the West. Another form of countertrade is the compensation agreement. Typically, a company provides technology and equipment for a plant in a developing nation and agrees to take full or partial payment in goods produced by that plant. For example, General Tire Company supplied equipment and know-how for a Romanian truck tire plant. In turn, General Tire sold the tires it received from the plant in the United States under the Victoria brand name. Pierre Cardin gives technical advice to China in exchange for silk and cashmere. In these cases, both sides benefit even though they don't use cash.

REVIEW LEARNING OBJECTIVE 5

5 List the basic elements involved in developing a global marketing mix

Global Marketing Mix

PRODUCT + PROMOTION	PLACE (Distribution)	PRICE
One Product, One Message	Channel Choice	Dumping
Product Invention	Channel Structure	Countertrade
Product Adaptation	Country Infrastructure	Exchange Rates
Message Adaptation		Purchasing Power

6 THE IMPACT OF THE INTERNET

Discover how the Internet is affecting global marketing

In many respects "going global" is easier than it has ever been before. Opening an e-commerce site on the Internet immediately puts a company in the international marketplace. Sophisticated language translation software can make any site accessible to persons around the world. Global shippers such as UPS, FedEx, and DHL help solve international e-commerce distribution complexities. E4X, Inc., offers software to ease currency conversions. Sites that use E4X's software can post prices in U.S. dollars, then ask their customers what currency they wish to use for payment. If the answer is a currency other than dollars, E4X takes over the transaction and translates the price into any of 22 currencies, collects the payment from the customer, and pays the site in dollars, just as though it were any other transaction. Customers never realize they're dealing with a third party.

Nevertheless, the promise of "borderless commerce" and the new "Internet economy" are still being restrained by the old brick-and-mortar rules, regulations, and habits. For example, Americans spend an average of $6,500 per year by credit

countertrade
A form of trade in which all or part of the payment for goods or services is in the form of other goods or services.

Online

REVIEW LEARNING OBJECTIVE 6

 6 Discover how the Internet is affecting global marketing

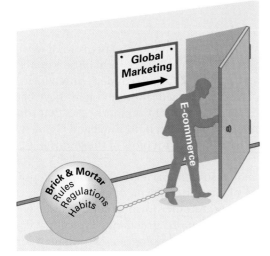

card whereas Japanese spend less than $2,000. Many Japanese don't even have a credit card. So how do they pay for e-commerce purchases? 7-Eleven Japan, with over 8,000 convenience stores, has come to the rescue. eS-Books, the Japanese Web site partner of Yahoo! Japan, lets shoppers buy books and videos on the Internet, then specify to which 7-Eleven the merchandise is to be shipped. The buyer goes to that specific store and pays cash for the e-purchase.

The e-commerce site for the American clothing retailer Lands' End in Germany is not allowed to mention its unconditional refund policy because German retailers, which normally do not allow returns after 14 days, sued and won a court ruling blocking mention of it.

Scandinavians, like the Japanese, are reluctant to use credit cards, the currency of the Internet, and the French have an *horreur* of revealing the private information that Net retailers often request. French Web sites tend to be decidedly French. For example, FNAC, the largest French video, book, and music retailer, offers a daily "cultural newspaper" at its site. A trendy Web site in France will have a black background, while bright colors and a geometrical layout give a site a German feel. Dutch surfers are keen on video downloads, and Scandinavians seem to have a soft spot for images of nature.

Whatever their preferences in Web design, Europeans have shown themselves interested in saving money through Internet shopping. One of the hot test e-commerce sites in Europe, LetsBuyIt.com in Sweden, is about nothing but bargains.

LOOKING BACK

Look back at the story about Starbucks in France. Besides cultural factors, other uncontrollable variables in the global external environment include economic and technological, political, and demographic variables as well as natural resources.

Most products cannot be marketed exactly the same way all over the world. Different cultures, languages, levels of economic development, and distribution channels in global markets usually require either new products or modified products.

Pricing, promotion, and distribution strategies must often be altered as well. There is no doubt that international markets will become even more important in the future.

USE IT NOW

STUDY THE ROLE OF A GLOBAL MANAGER

 As business becomes more global, chances are that you may become a global manager. Start learning right now what this means and if it's right for you. The life of a global manager can be hectic. One way to see if you might be cut out to be a global manager is to spend some time abroad. The ideal situation is to find a job overseas during the summer months. This experience will help you decide if you want to be a global manager. Also, it will look good on your résumé. One source of international jobs information is **http://www.internationaljobs.org/**. Also, go to Google and type in "effective global manager." Read several articles about what it takes to be a global manager.

TRAVEL ABROAD

Employers worldwide look favorably on people who have taken time out for traveling. They've shown that they're able to organize a trip and look after their security and finances. Experience with different cultures, confidence in meeting people, and self-reliance are very important skills to have.

STA Travel (**http://www.statravel.com**) with 300 branches worldwide, specializes in student and youth travel. Students and those under age 26 with certain youth identification cards get discounts of up to a third off the published prices of airfares, hotels, city tours, around-the-world tickets, and overland tours.

Busabout (**http://www.busabout.com**) is a novel way for young travelers to explore Europe by road. Buses link 70 cities with service every one to two days in each direction allowing you the freedom to stop off for as long as you like along the way. The buses are nonsmoking and air-conditioned with an on-board guide to book your travel selections and accommodations as you go.

Hostels or budget hotels range from $15 to $30 a night. You decide when and where to start, stop off, or end the trip. Thus, you might buy a cheap "open-jaw" ticket (flying in to one city, departing from another). Arrive in Athens, for example, and return from London, or fly to Madrid and leave from Rome.

You can buy two types of passes at a 10 percent discount for students or those under 26. A Consecutive Pass allows unlimited travel in the Busabout network, from two weeks to seven months. A Flexipass allows you to choose the number of traveling days within a time frame, ranging from 10 days in two months to 30 days in four months.

A rail pass is another great way to get around Europe. Go to **http://railpass.com** for more information.

CHANGING MONEY ABROAD

If you travel, work, or study abroad, you are going to need to change U.S. dollars into foreign currency. Making mistakes when changing money can cost you 10 to 20 percent of your bankroll. Here are a few tips about changing money abroad.

1. Know the exchange rate between U.S. dollars and the currencies of the countries you plan to visit before you go. Go to **http://www.cnnfn.com/markets/currencies** for the latest quotations. Keep up with the changing rates by reading *USA Today International* or the *International Herald Tribune* every day.
2. Avoid changing money at airports, train stations, and hotels. These places usually have the worst rates. Ask local people where they change money. Locals know where the best rates are.
3. Try to bargain with the clerk. Sometimes you can do better than the posted rate simply by asking.
4. Rather than making several small transactions, make one large exchange. This will often get you a better rate.
5. Don't change more than you will need. You'll pay another fee to change the foreign currency back to U.S. dollars.
6. Use a credit card. Typically, any major credit card will give you a better rate than a change booth or bank. Sometimes the spread is substantial, so minimize cash and use credit.
7. Traveler's checks usually have a worse exchange rate than cash. In other words, a $100 American Express traveler's check will give you less in exchange than a $100 bill. If your traveler's checks are lost or stolen, however, they will be replaced, so the peace of mind is usually worth the added expense.
8. Use your American ATM card to withdraw cash at foreign money machines. If your card is part of a global network, such as Cirrus or Plus, you may be able to withdraw money for a nominal fee at a reasonable exchange rate.

1 **Discuss the importance of global marketing.** Businesspeople who adopt a global vision are better able to identify global marketing opportunities, understand the nature of global networks, and compete against foreign competition in domestic markets.

1.1 What is meant by "having a global vision"? Why is it important?

1.2 Isolationists have suggested that America would be much better off economically and politically if we just "built a wall" around the country and didn't deal with outsiders. Do you agree? Why or why not?

2 **Discuss the impact of multinational firms on the world economy.** Multinational corporations are international traders that regularly operate across national borders. Because of their vast size and financial, technological, and material resources, multinational corporations have a great influence on the world economy. They have the ability to overcome trade problems, save on labor costs, and tap new technology.

2.1 Rubbermaid, the U.S. manufacturer of kitchen products and other household items, is considering moving to global marketing standardization. What are the pros and cons of this strategy?

2.2 Do you believe that multinationals are beneficial or harmful to developing nations? Why? What could foreign governments do to make them more beneficial?

3 **Describe the external environment facing global marketers.** Global marketers face the same environmental factors as they do domestically: culture, economic and technological development, political structure and actions, demography, and natural resources. Cultural considerations include societal values, attitudes and beliefs, language, and customary business practices. A country's economic and technological status depends on its stage of industrial development, which, in turn, affects average family incomes. The political structure is shaped by political ideology and such policies as tariffs, quotas, boycotts, exchange controls, trade agreements, and market groupings. Demographic variables include the size of a population and its age and geographic distribution.

3.1 Many marketers now believe that teenagers in the developed countries are becoming "global consumers." That is, they all want and buy the same goods and services. Do you think this is true? If so, what has caused the phenomenon?

3.2 Renault and Peugeot dominate the French market but have no presence in the U.S. market. Why do you think that this is true?

3.3 WRITING Suppose that you are the marketing manager for a consumer-products firm that is about to undertake its first expansion abroad. Write a memo to your staff reminding them of the role culture will play in the new venture. Give examples.

3.4 WRITING Suppose that your state senator has asked you to contribute a brief article to her constituents' newsletter that answers the question, "Will there ever be a United States of Europe'?" Write a draft of your article, and include reasons why or why not.

3.5 TEAM Divide into six teams. Each team will be responsible for one of the following industries: entertainment; pharmaceuticals; computers and software; financial, legal, or accounting services; agriculture; and textiles and apparel. Interview one or more executives in each of these industries to determine how the WTO and NAFTA have affected and will affect their organizations. If a local firm cannot be contacted in your industry, use the library and the Internet to prepare your report.

3.6 What are the major barriers to international trade? Explain how government policies may be used to either restrict or stimulate global marketing.

3.7 INFOTRAC COLLEGE EDITION   Review the "Marketing in Entertainme nt" box on Australia's attempt to restrict imports of U.S. media programming. What other c ountries impose similar restrictions on U.S. films and television programs? Use InfoTrac and the *Wall Street Journal Online* to conduct your research. Or use your favorite search engine to find links keyed to terms like "movie quota," "film quota," and "television quota." Write a summary of your findings.

---

4 **Identify the various ways of entering the global marketplace.** Firms use the following strategies to enter global markets, in descending order of risk and profit: direct investment, joint venture, contract manufacturing, licensing, and exporting.

4.1 Candartel, an upscale manufacturer of lamps and lampshades in America, has decided to "go global." Top management is having trouble deciding how to develop the market. What are some market entry options for the firm?

4.2 Explain how the U.S. Commercial Service can help companies wanting to enter the international market.

4.3 What are some of the advantages and potential disadvantages of entering a joint venture?

---

5 **List the basic elements involved in developing a global marketing mix.** A firm's major consideration is how much it will adjust the four Ps—product, promotion, place (distribution), and price—within each country. One strategy is to use one product and one promotion message worldwide. A second strategy is to create new products for global markets. A third strategy is to keep the product basically the same but alter the promotional message. A fourth strategy is to slightly alter the product to meet local conditions.

5.1 The sale of cigarettes in many developed countries either has peaked or is declining. However, the developing markets represent major growth markets. Should U.S. tobacco companies capitalize on this opportunity?

5.2 Describe at least three situations where an American company might want to keep the product the same but alter the promotion. Also, give three examples where the product must be altered.

5.3 Explain how exchange rates can affect a firm's global sales.

---

6 **Discover how the Internet is affecting global marketing.** Simply opening a Web site can open the door for international sales. International carriers, like UPS, can help solve logistics problems. Language translation software can help an e-commerce business become multilingual. Yet cultural differences and old-line rules, regulations, and taxes hinder rapid development of e-commerce in many countries.

6.1 Describe how "going global" via the Internet presents opportunities and challenges.

6.2 Give several examples of how culture may hinder "going global" via the Internet.

TERMS

buyer for export 124
capital-intensive 113
contract manufacturing 126
countertrade 135
direct foreign investment 127
dumping 134
export agent 124
export broker 124
exporting 123

floating exchange rates 133
Free Trade Area of the
   Americas (FTAA) 119
General Agreement on Tariffs and Trade
   (GATT) 118
global marketing 108
global marketing standardization 114
global vision 108
International Monetary Fund (IMF) 121

joint venture 126
licensing 124
Mercosur 118
multinational corporation 111
North American Free Trade Agreement
   (NAFTA) 119
Uruguay Round 118
World Bank 121
World Trade Organization (WTO) 118

APPLICATION EXERCISE

To be effective as a marketer, it is important to know geography. How will you be able to decide whether to expand into a new territory (domestic or foreign) if you don't know where it is and something about its culture, currency, and economy? If you can't place the European countries on a blank map, or if you can't label the lower 48 states without a list to help you, you're not alone. In one study, students incorrectly located over 50 percent of European countries and over 25 percent of the states in the Unites States. To help you brush up on your geography, we've compiled some tools that you will find useful.[50]

Activities

1. To review domestic geography, go to **http://www.50states.com/tools/usamap.htm** and print the blank map of the United States. Label the map. For a challenge, add the state capitals to the map.

2. Once you have successfully labeled the U.S. map, you may be ready to try labeling a world map. If so, go to **http://www.clickandlearn.com** and view the free, printable, blackline maps. Under the category of world maps, choose the blackline detail map. This shows country outlines, whereas the basic blackline outline map shows only the continents. You will notice that there are also blackline maps for each continent, so if taking on the entire world is too daunting, start with more manageable blocks.

3. To be a global marketer, it is not enough to know where countries are located. You will need to know about the culture, the main exports, the currency, and even the main imports. Select a half-dozen or so countries with which you are unfamiliar, and research basic geographical information about them.

ETHICS EXERCISE

Moore Electronics sells automated lighting for airport runways. The government of an eastern European country has offered Moore a contract to provide equipment for the 15 major airports in the country. The official in charge of awarding the contract, however, is demanding a 5 percent kickback. He told Moore to build this into the contract price so that there would be no cost to Moore. Without the kickback, Moore loses the contract. Such kickbacks are considered a normal way of doing business in this country.

Questions

1. What should Moore do?

2. Does the AMA Code of Ethics address this issue? Go to **http://www.marketingpower.com** and review the code. Then write a brief paragraph on what the AMA Code of Ethics contains that relates to Moore's dilemma.

CAREER EXERCISE

If you'd like to explore a career that has global potential, you will first want to learn more about what is happening in the area of global marketing. The easiest way to do this is to read the contents of the Global Marketing Discussion List, posted at **http://glreach.com/eng/ed/gmd.php3** and **http://glreach.com/eng/index.php3**. This list, which is a part of Global Reach, is a good place to start learning more about issues relevant to global marketers. If it offers a newsletter, consider subscribing. That way you'll be on top of the trends and concerns affecting global marketing.

Once you have determined that working on a global level is definitely for you, you will need to consult global job-location resources. A good one is the Global Career Center (**http://www.globalcareercenter.com**), which allows you to search jobs available by country, post a résumé, and more.

Activities

1. A career in global marketing will be greatly enhanced if you speak more than one language. When the schedule for next term's classes comes out, review the languages offered at your school. Ask to visit some introductory classes in a language that interests you.

2. Investigate a global internship using your favorite search engine. Make a list of five internships that sound interesting. Contact the companies for further information.

ENTREPRENEURSHIP CASE

© AP/WIDE WORLD PHOTOS

 MTV: ROCKING THE WORLD ONE NATION AT A TIME

To most people, MTV is as American as apple pie, baseball, and freedom of speech. It is a cultural icon to every American who grew up in the 1980s or 1990s, and it is easily the most palpable influence on the behavior of the demographic it targets with its programming. A closer look at MTV's business, however, reveals that its true significance is its ability to translate its formula for success into the many languages of the world. The network now owns 33 distinct channels that broadcast shows in 18 languages to 1.8 billion viewers in over 160 countries.

MTV Networks International, a subsidiary of MTV that actually dwarfs its parent, took its first steps on foreign soil with MTV Europe in 1987 and soon thereafter became Europe's largest television network. With a blueprint for success in hand, the large subsidiary turned its attention to the global youth market, which today includes over 2.5 billion people between the ages of 10 and 34. As it watched demand for television sets and paid programming services explode in rapidly developing markets, such as China, Latin America, and India, MTV was poised to capitalize.

Large and diverse markets, however, are difficult to understand and expensive to penetrate. Initially, MTV simply tried to export a standardized version of its American programming, but it quickly discovered that teens from around the world—while they do enjoy American music—are mostly interested in what's happening in their own regions. MTV responded by undertaking the costly and complex task of producing localized content for specific markets. Now, veejay selection, programming, and service offerings are all unique in any given market.

Digital television and interactive services are very popular in Europe, so MTV UK developed a service that allows viewers to obtain information on CDs, check concert dates, and vote for their favorite performers during the MTV European Music Awards directly from their TV sets. In Asia, a virtual animated veejay named LiLi can interact with viewers in five different languages. Controlled by an actor behind the image, LiLi can also interview guests and provide popular culture tips. Brazilian viewers, who also tend to be huge soccer fans, enjoy *Rockgol*, an MTV-produced soccer championship contested by Brazilian record industry executives and musicians.

MTV Japan, a joint venture between MTV Networks and local investment firm H&Q Asia Pacific, operates in the world's second largest music market and one of the world's most advanced mobile telecommunications markets. Identifying those two trends, MTV Japan developed a service that lets subscribers use their mobile phones to download entertainment news and new music or vote for their favorite veejay.

The development cycle is long for such detailed international projects, but MTV Networks International president Bill Roedy is a patient man. He spent ten years working with Chinese officials for the right to air MTV programming for just six hours a day. The payoff? Forty cable providers now carry MTV Mandarin into 60 million Chinese homes. Roedy is also sensitive to foreign leaders' fears that their culture will be "Americanized" by MTV. Before his networks enter markets with extreme cultural differences, such as Israel, Singapore, Cuba, or China, Roedy meets with key political figures to allay their fears. "We've had very little resistance once we explain that we're not in the business of exporting American culture," he notes.[51]

Questions

1. Identity the key environmental challenges MTV has faced in its effort to expand globally, and discuss how MTV has overcome them.

2. What is MTV's global market entry strategy? Discuss whether you agree with MTV's approach, and identify its advantages and disadvantages.

3. Discuss MTV's global product strategy.

WATCH IT

SmallBusinessSchool
the Series on PBS stations and the Web

FEATURE PRESENTATION

Automated Food Systems

To give you insight into the concepts in Chapter 4, Small Business School introduces you to Glen and Wanda Walser and their company, Automated Food Systems, which designs and manufactures machinery that makes corn dogs. The Walsers market the machine to owners of vending stands at large fairs, to large food companies that distribute their packaged corn dogs in supermarkets, and to distributors who sell food-processing equipment. Automated Food Systems' machines now make 95 percent of the 2.5 billion corn dogs produced in the United States each year. This video segment explores how the company took its successful domestic product to a global market. After designing a machine capable of making over 16,000 corn dogs an hour, the Walsers discovered that variations on the corn dog are eaten by many cultures in many countries around the world. A key point from the video is how Automated Food Systems used its cultural knowledge and resources, like the U.S. Department of Commerce, to identify and access various global markets.

What to Watch for and Ask Yourself

1. How have the Walsers used a global vision to identify opportunities? How have they adapted their business approach to serve those markets?

2. Identify the global target market for Automated Food Systems' product, and briefly describe at least three elements of the marketing mix used to reach it.

3. Which of the global environmental factors is the most important for Automated Food Systems to consider?

4. What strategy has Automated Food Systems adopted for entering the global market? Is it low risk or high risk? Briefly explain its strategy.

ENCORE PRESENTATION

Lost in Translation

Now that you have a sense about the issues marketers must consider before entering foreign markets, you may be better able to appreciate how drastic cultural differences can be. The film *Lost in Translation,* starring Scarlett Johansson and Bill Murray, illustrates these differences expertly. Based on director Sophia Coppola's Academy Award winning screenplay, this film was shot entirely on location in Japan. It offers extraordinary views of various parts of Japanese culture that are not available to you without a visit.

If you're having trouble with the concepts in this chapter, consider using some of the following study resources. You can review the videos, or test yourself with materials designed for all kinds of learning styles.

☑ **Xtra! (http://lambxtra.swlearning.com)**

| ☑ Quiz | ☑ Feature Videos | ☑ Encore Videos | ☑ FAQ Videos |
| ☑ Exhibit Worksheets | ☑ Marketing Plan Worksheets | ☐ Content | |

☑ **http://lamb.swlearning.com**

| ☑ Quiz | ☑ PowerPoint slides | ☑ Marketing News | ☐ Review Exercises |
| ☑ Links | ☑ Marketing Plan Contest | ☑ Career Exercise | ☑ Use It Now |

☑ **Study guide**

| ☑ Outline | ☑ Vocab Review | ☑ Test Questions | ☑ Marketing Scenario |

Need More? Here's a tip. Work out any Review and Applications questions that your professor didn't assign as homework. Visit your professor or TA during office hours to check your answers.

MARKETING MISCUE

Scholastic Stumbles even with Market Access

Scholastic Corporation bought the rights to the Harry Potter book series in 1997. Since then, the company has sold over 80 million copies of Harry Potter books, generating sales of more than $500 million. Despite the publication of *Harry Potter and the Order of the Phoenix* in June 2003, Standard & Poor's placed Scholastic on its CreditWatch list in July 2003 because of the company's weaker-than-anticipated operating performance and discretionary cash flow for fiscal year 2003. Already, in May 2003, Scholastic had begun cutting 4 percent of its workforce (approximately 400 employees), citing lagging retail sales and an overall weak economy.

Scholastic is a leading reading entertainment publisher for the children's market. Yet industry analysts have suggested that Scholastic has not exploited the special advantages of its access to young readers. Specializing in children's books, Scholastic is a prominent name in the academic marketplace, but the company appears to have dropped the ball when it comes to building relationships with teachers and schools. Instead, some have suggested that the company has opted to focus on direct marketing via catalogs cluttered with junky offerings.

Has Scholastic relied too much on magic instead of literacy concerns in its marketing efforts? Although the Harry Potter books lead to an immediate, large increase in book sales, such sales do not provide for steady long-term growth. Instead, the company risks becoming dependent on the next blockbuster book by writers such as J. K. Rowling. Analysts wonder if Scholastic would have been better off in a rather tepid marketplace if it had followed a strategy of promoting literacy skills. The fear is that Scholastic's lack of market focus has allowed children's books competitors, such as Simon & Schuster and Houghton Mifflin, to get a head start in promoting literacy.

Experts say that reading is the fundamental skill on which all formal education depends. The following statistics are particularly alarming in today's society:

- 20 percent of elementary students in the United States have significant problems learning to read.
- 40 percent of fourth graders in the United States cannot read at a basic level.
- 20 percent of elementary students do not read fluently enough to engage in independent reading.
- 33 percent of weak readers are from college-educated families.

Not surprisingly, given these statistics, reading failure is the overwhelming reason that children are retained, assigned to special education, given long-term remedial services, and/or drop out of school.

State and local budget cuts have made the financial position of many public schools extremely precarious. As a result, purchases of Scholastic's educational books by teachers and sales of its children's books to libraries have declined. Unfortunately, Scholastic did not seize the opportunity to penetrate a market in which it has historically had a strong foothold. Given the educators' focus on literacy and the decrease in educational purchases, industry experts wonder why Scholastic has not focused its marketing energies upon increasing interest in book fairs and book clubs.

At book fairs, parents and children are able to purchase quality children's books at reasonable prices with the hosting school receiving a percentage of the profit. The profit is then used to purchase resource materials, obtain books for the school's library, or fund special school projects. Hosting or supporting a school's book club encourages students to read. Readers are more likely to purchase books for home libraries, possibly even through a school's book fair.

With reading at the forefront of early childhood education and with more than 100,000 school book fairs annually and book clubs in many elementary and junior high schools, Scholastic may have an untapped market opportunity in its unparalleled access to young readers and their teachers. But does Scholastic have the marketing savvy needed to restore the company to profitability in a tough economic environment where political interest in boosting literacy is growing at the same time budgets are being cut?[1]

Questions

1. What are the major external hurdles that Scholastic faces in its struggle to survive in a lackluster marketplace?

2. What type of relationships does Scholastic need to develop to be successful with book fairs and book clubs?

Vivendi Universal Games: Theft of Source Code for *Half-Life 2*

September 2003 was not a good month for game developers at Valve Corporation. First, the previously announced shipping date of September 30 for a much-anticipated computer game, *Half-Life 2*, was pushed back, and the company now aimed for a holiday release of the game. Next, one week after the announced shipping delay, the company reported that someone had hacked into managing director and founder Gabe Newell's computer and stolen the engine code for *Half-Life 2*. While slippage in release dates is not uncommon in the gaming industry, the problems at Valve hit Vivendi Universal Games, the game's publisher, at a time when this games division of Vivendi Universal S.A. was already tagged as one of the corporation's poorest performers.

The Gaming Industry

Electronic games are a favorite pastime for many and generate an estimated $10.3 billion worldwide. According to researchers at the National Institute on Media and the Family, 87 percent of the students surveyed in grades 4 through 12 reported that they played video games regularly. The study also found that games are more popular among boys (96 percent play) than girls (78 percent play).

Though the games' popularity continues to grow, this growth has been accompanied by considerable bad press. The electronic game industry has been subject to two major criticisms: (1) that playing violent video games will lead to aggressive behavior in the gamer and (2) that electronic games, along with television and computers, are leading contributors to a sedentary lifestyle and, thus, to the epidemic of childhood obesity. It is estimated that today's young people spend almost 40 hours a week in front of some kind of electronic equipment.

Despite these concerns, sales of game-related equipment and services have surpassed Hollywood box-office sales. Sales of one popular video game, *Madden NFL 2004,* have exceeded $200 million. Digital interactive home entertainment has seen annual growth rates of 40 percent. By 2002, mobile gaming had become the top wireless data traffic in Europe.

Vivendi Universal S.A.

Vivendi Universal S.A. (**http://www. vivendiuniversal. com**), a diversified media group headquartered in Paris, operates in five sectors: telecommunications (Cegetal Group, Vivendi Telecom International); music (Universal Music Group); television and film (Vivendi Universal Entertainment, Canal+ Group); Internet (Vivendi Universal Net); and games (Vivendi Universal Games). Vivendi Universal Games (VU Games) is the smallest of the Vivendi operating units.

Vivendi Universal Games (**http://www.vugames.com**) is the producer of educational software such as Knowledge Adventure's JumpStart series. VU Games is also world renowned for its Blizzard Entertainment game studio, which produced the *Warcraft, Diablo*, and *StarCraft* games. Though considered a major force in the gaming industry, VU Games was experiencing sales and financial woes in 2003. Sales in the first half of 2003 were 29 percent below same-period sales in 2002, resulting in a loss of $62 million on sales of $286 million. However, VU Games' 2002 revenues had been slightly higher than 2001 revenues. VU Games' 2002/2003 share of the U.S. and European markets was estimated at 7 percent of total sales. The company's 2004 launch of *World of Warcraft* was to be the company's entrée into online gaming. Asia, the company's strongest area for market penetration, was thought to be especially interested in online gaming.

Competitors

VU Games' major competitors include the following:

- Electronic Arts, the industry leader with games such as *NFL Street, James Bond, Harry Potter, Medal of Honor*, and *Sim City*.
- Konami Corporation, with *Yu-Gi-Oh!, Metal Gear Solid, Silent Hill, Castlevania,* and the *Disney Sports* series.
- Capcom, with products including *Resident Evil, Street Fighter, Breath of Fire*, and *Mega Man*.
- Ubisoft, with *Tom Clancy's Splinter Cell Pandora Tomorrow, Rayman, Prince of Persia,* and *Myst*, as well as a relatively new entrant *Uru: Ages Beyond Myst*, which is targeted toward women.
- Microsoft Game Studios, with offerings such as *Counter-Strike, Halo, Amped 2, Zoo Tycoon,* and *Wheel of Fortune*.

The Quintessential Twenty-First Century Crime

Founded in 1996, Valve Corporation is an entertainment software company that debuted with *Half-Life*, released in November 1998. In September 2003, a hacker began accessing Gabe Newell's e-mail account at Valve. The hacker designed a program that slipped unnoticed into Newell's e-mail account and spied on everything typed on Newell's keyboard. Unfortunately, the engine code for *Half-Life 2* was the hacker's target.

Half-Life 2 was one of the most anticipated games of 2003. Excitement was driven by the new technology that Valve had created for the game. Dubbed "Source," the game's new graphics engine determines how the player is affected by the virtual world. "Source" enabled the game to have three highly desirable features: (1) the game breaks the mold of first-person perspective games, (2) the game engine allows faster and more detailed graphics and online play with other players, and (3) the game is the first mainstream game that gamers can download directly from the Internet.

In only a few weeks, however, the hacker had collected at least one-third of the game's code and was able to release a rudimentary but playable version of *Half-Life 2* on the Internet. Not only was the source code for *Half-Life 2* compromised, but the code had already been licensed to Troika, the developer of *Vampire the Masquerade: Bloodlines* to be published by Activision. With Valve and VU Games thrust into a chaotic virtual nightmare, the release of *Half-Life 2* was pushed back once again with the company announcing yet another new release date of April 2004. Though consumers did not endorse the code theft, there was considerable anger about the delayed release. Had VU Games and Valve created too much buzz, too early, about *Half-Life 2*?[2]

Questions

1. What types of downstream effects might the theft have on Valve's licensing business?

2. Is there anything that the electronic game industry, as a whole, can do to prevent repeat occurrences of such theft?

3. What is marketing's role in this situation?

CROSS-FUNCTIONAL CONNECTIONS SOLUTIONS

Questions

1. How do marketing, manufacturing, finance, accounting, and human resources overlap? What does each of these functions do that results in this overlap?

   The overlap among all functional areas within a firm occurs because all work to provide the final product or service to the consumer. Each functional area contributes in different ways to delivering the desired product to the end customer. Marketing, manufacturing, finance, accounting, and human resources work from the idea that the customer is most important and that the goal is to produce a product that meets the changing needs of consumers. Marketing and manufacturing tend to come into direct contact with the company's customers and products. Finance, accounting, and human resources tend to work on the periphery and may never come into contact with the physical aspects of the product and may never meet the end user of the product or service. By working together and utilizing each area's expertise and knowledge, however, the different areas can create an integrated production process aimed at satisfying the customer.

2. Why is cross-functional coordination necessary to have a customer-oriented firm?

   Historically, everyone assumed that the customer belonged to the marketing department. We know now that this is not true. Everyone in the organization must understand the customer's wants and needs in order to satisfy these needs. Without the customer, there would be no need for an organization. For example, no customers would mean no products to develop or manufacture, no accounts receivable, and no need for employees. From the customer's perspective, good or bad products belong to the entire company—not just one particular function. Customers will not keep coming back if the company produces only low-quality merchandise—even if the marketing group has some of the best marketers in the world. Likewise, a high-quality product will not be successful in the marketplace if the product is positioned inaccurately, advertised inappropriately, priced too high or too low, or not available in the right outlets. Therefore, it is imperative that the business functions work together to send the same message to the marketplace.

3. What roles do teamwork and technology play in cross-functional coordination?

   Technology has created a digitized marketplace in which business decisions have to be made quickly in order for the firm to remain competitive. Customer demands increase in this fast-paced market, making it necessary for all functional areas to work together to deliver products to market quickly. In working as a team, functional areas partner in the production/delivery process, sharing relevant information with one another, as well as eliminating wasted time spent when working independently in departments.

Suggested Readings

Walter J. Michalski and Dana G. King, *40 Tools for Cross-Functional Teams: Building Synergy for Breakthrough Creativity*, (New York: Productivity Press, 1998).

Glenn M. Parker, *Cross Functional Teams: Working with Allies, Enemies, and Other Strangers*, (Hoboken, NJ: Jossey Bass Wiley, 2003).

Andrew Spanyi, "Strategic Achievement," *Industrial Engineer*, March 2003, 40–43.

PART

2

Analyzing
Marketing
Opportunities

INFORMATION INTEGRATION FACILITATES MARKET KNOWLEDGE

Understanding customers is at the heart of the information-gathering process. Whether it is determining individual buying behavior, sharpening the company's target marketing skills, or understanding competitive actions, information is the key to success. The traditional perception of information gathering is that it is the "job" of the marketing department. However, many companies have come to realize that the market belongs to the entire company—making it everyone's responsibility to understand the marketplace.

MTV Networks understands clearly the need for information integration as a means to better understanding its target audience. The network thrives on being a trendy, hip entertainment provider. It uses cultural anthropologists to acquire information about target viewers and to disseminate this market research information within the network's organizational structure. These cultural anthropologists gather information from the target audience by visiting their homes, talking with them on the streets, and observing them as they go about their daily lives. Internally, the programming, marketing, and scheduling departments share this marketplace information. The ultimate goal is to bring the thoughts and feelings of MTV's target audience into the organization's mainstream, functional processes.

The information debate between marketing and other business functions centers on the qualitative-versus-quantitative format of functional data. The data collected by marketers are perceived to be qualitative and abstract in contrast to the quantitative data utilized by other functional areas. It has been difficult to get engineers and accountants to understand that marketing data are statistically valid and are useful in making company-wide decisions.

Aside from the need for a general cross-functional sharing of data, information gathering and dissemination processes need to be formally integrated across functions in four major areas:

1. Benchmarking studies
2. Customer satisfaction studies
3. Data mining
4. Forecasting

Benchmarking is the process of comparing a firm's performance in various activities against the performance of other companies that have completed similar activities.

A benchmarking study could focus on cross-company comparisons of purchasing processes, inventory management, product development cycles, hiring practices, payroll processes, order fulfillment, and overall performance of various marketing activities. Gathering information on a firm's competitors during a benchmarking study requires an extensive amount of secondary research. Recently, cross-functional "shadow teams" have been formed to assist in better benchmarking of competitive activities. These shadow teams integrate internal information with all externally available information on specific competitors.

Benchmarking in the entertainment industry is reaching new heights as companies in all facets of entertainment gauge success in various areas of stakeholder satisfaction. For example, companies such as Silicon Graphics provide advanced technology solutions for state-of-the-art digital imaging. In benchmarking studies, Silicon Graphics has set records in technical computing performance. TravelCLICK (**http://www.travelclick.net**), a leading provider of digital media and data solutions to the worldwide travel industry, recently developed a quarterly benchmarking report that will allow hotel chains to track booking performance on the Internet. The company's reports provide pricing and booking performance by including benchmarked companies such as British Airways, Fairmont Hotels & Resorts, SAS, USAirways, Marriott Hotels, and Hilton Hotels. Organizations such as the Hollywood Entertainment District and the Christian Film & Television Commission conduct economic benchmarking.

Customer satisfaction is driven by issues related to all functions within the firm. Companies such as Sterling Research Group, Inc. and Deloitte & Touche offer customer satisfaction tracking programs for a wide range of entertainment-related businesses. Entertainment companies (for example, JFV Entertainment) post customer satisfaction measures on their Web sites. Therefore, a valid *customer satisfaction study* should gather information that can be shared with manufacturing (regarding satisfaction with speed of delivery), research and development (regarding satisfaction with product quality), human resources (regarding satisfaction with complaint handling), and finance/accounting (regarding satisfaction with credit policies). All of these functional areas need to have input into the design of such studies.

The digital age has led to considerable *data mining*. E-commerce capabilities allow companies to gather and analyze customer information in a matter of minutes, rather than having to wait for results from months-long data-gathering processes. This use of technology is where considerable cross-functional interactions must occur. For example, casino operators Harrah's Entertainment, MGM Mirage, and Foxwoods Resorts gather and store a wealth of consumer information—information that has to be effectively disseminated to the appropriate individuals at exactly the right time.

Forecasting crosses the boundaries of multiple business functions. For example, marketing may offer a discount on a particular price. The impact of this price discount is felt simultaneously in many functional areas. A key functional partner in a price discount is manufacturing. The production plan will have to accommodate the expected increase in product sales and the oftentimes below-average product sales immediately after the discount period. While price is easy for marketers to change, manufacturing's plans cannot be changed overnight. The impact of a price change may be felt in the company's production schedule, the level of finished goods inventory, and the availability of raw materials. Unfortunately, marketing's ability to make price changes quickly has been the cause of much conflict between marketing and manufacturing.

Much of a firm's financial planning is driven by the company's sales forecast. Marketing has historically had a reputation of being too optimistic in its projections. Consequently, financial planners have been known to take the sales forecast with "a grain of salt," and planning has often evolved around a lower-than-predicted level of sales. Marketing, then, views financial planners as too conservative and complains that they base their plans on internal data that are not driven by the marketplace.

Predicting worldwide demand has become a forecasting challenge for many companies. Martin Professional, Inc. is a producer and distributor of computer-controlled lighting, speaker systems, and smoke machines for indoor and outdoor entertainment events. The company employs a demand planning manager (DPM), whose job is to ensure that market intelligence is included in the organization's planning process, thus driving customer satisfaction, inventory turnover, and overall company profitability. The company's internal systems allow for the dissemination of real-time forecasts, enabling synchronization of production and inventory with customer demand.

Marketplace information is a key driver in all decisions made by a company. Therefore, it is imperative that all functional areas participate in the gathering and dissemination of information. The importance of information is reflected in the executive position of chief knowledge officer that is now being staffed in many companies. Without a doubt, success in today's global environment is dependent upon all functional areas understanding the firm's customers and competitors.

Questions

1. Why has information historically been perceived as "owned" by the marketing department?

2. What data differences exist across functions?

3. What is the job of a chief knowledge officer?

5

Consumer Decision Making

LEARNING OBJECTIVES

1 Explain why marketing managers should understand consumer behavior

2 Analyze the components of the consumer decision-making process

3 Explain the consumer's postpurchase evaluation process

4 Identify the types of consumer buying decisions and discuss the significance of consumer involvement

5 Identify and understand the cultural factors that affect consumer buying decisions

6 Identify and understand the social factors that affect consumer buying decisions

7 Identify and understand the individual factors that affect consumer buying decisions

8 Identify and understand the psychological factors that affect consumer buying decisions

© EVAN AGOSTINI / GETTY IMAGES

Identifying changes in consumer behavior often requires picking up a small blip on a marketer's radar that over time becomes more and more obvious. Virgin Mobile USA realized that Generation Y consumers were not responding to the mobile phone advertising and calling plans offered by AT&T, Cingular, and Verizon. It took advantage of Gen Yers' discontent with the current product and service offerings in the wireless phone market by creating marketing campaigns and calling plans aimed directly at this group of consumers. According to Dan Schulman, CEO of Virgin Mobile USA, the company is "wholly focused on and attuned to the needs, desires, and lifestyles of young Americans."

One problem mainstream mobile companies were encountering was branding. Many Gen Yers associated existing brands, like Nextel, with their parents. Therefore, Virgin Mobile repositioned its line of phones with a new slogan: "Live without a plan. The phone of choice for hipsters, slackers, and many people in between." The slogan is designed to convey that Virgin Mobile subscribers will not have to sign a contract, pay monthly bills, or deal with hidden fees. Other benefits include free voice-mail and off-peak calls without extra charges. Another reason that Virgin Mobile's pay-as-you-go plan appeals to Gen Yers is that many of them do not have the credit card required to activate a phone. The pay-as-you-go plan also allows them to assert more control over their minutes. The service is reasonably priced at $2.50 for the first ten minutes of each day and then 10 cents for each additional minute. Convenience is also

important to Gen Yers. Virgin Mobile subscribers can reload their "Top-Up airtime cards" at more than 38,000 locations nationwide, including 7-Eleven, virginmobileusa.com, Sprint stores, and Target.

To further entice Gen Yers, some Virgin handsets are cobranded with MTV; all of them bear hip names such as the Party Animal, Slider, Vox, and Rave. The handsets and accessories are available in over 9,000 U.S. locations, including small independent businesses like surf shops, mega-retailers such as Target, and mobile phone stores like Sprint.

Virgin Mobile offers other value-added benefits such as rings from popular artists like Mystikal, Linkin Park, and JayZ; movie theme rings; and the "rescue ring," which is a preprogrammed incoming call to help you "escape from a bad date." Over 40 percent of subscribers use *MTV, which allows users to access music news and gossip, play games, vote for videos, and text message the popular MTV show, *Total Request Live.* In addition to providing MTV content, Virgin Mobile launched a game dubbed "American Oddball," a play on the *American Idol* hit TV show, that allows subscribers to send free text messages to Virgin Mobile answering bizarre questions about the show.

Text messaging is popular with Virgin Mobile subscribers. More than 60 percent of them send over 25 text messages per month—a total of 150 million text messages in a little less than a year. These numbers are high, considering

that the average consumer receives only about 12 text messages per month.

Virgin Mobile's campaign has been a big success. The company recently enrolled its one millionth subscriber—a remarkable achievement considering that the product was launched only one and a half years earlier. Of those subscribers, 70 percent were under 30 years old, a clear indication that Virgin Mobile is reaching Gen Yers. Every day Virgin Mobile is signing up 2,000 more young adults.

Not only is Virgin Mobile attracting customers, but it is focusing on their needs and desires in terms of postpurchase services. In a study by Market Strategies, Inc., Virgin Mobile rated 95 percent in customer satisfaction. Another independent study rated Virgin Mobile USA number one in customer satisfaction among all prepaid wireless services.[1]

Virgin Mobile clearly has been successful in anticipating changes in the mobile phone service purchasing patterns of Generation Y consumers. Which mobile phone company do you have service from and what made you choose them? If you get your phone from a carrier other than Virgin Mobile, what makes your current plan more appealing, and what might motivate you to switch? What factors are likely to affect mobile phone service purchasing decisions of Gen Yers in the future? Questions like these will be considered as you read this chapter on the consumer decision-making process and its influences.

Online

Virgin Mobile   Sprint PCS   T-Mobile

Describe the special service offerings available at Virgin Mobile's Web site that are designed to influence the decision making of its target market. Would those services appeal to traditional cellular customers? For comparison, check out the Web sites of T-Mobile and Sprint and describe how they differ from Virgin Mobile's site.

http://www.virginmobileusa.com   http://www.sprintpcs.com   http://www.tmobile.com

THE IMPORTANCE OF UNDERSTANDING CONSUMER BEHAVIOR

Explain why marketing managers should understand consumer behavior

Consumers' product and service preferences are constantly changing. In order to address this constant state of flux and to create a proper marketing mix for a well-defined market, marketing managers must have a thorough knowledge of consumer behavior. **Consumer behavior** describes how consumers make purchase decisions and how they use and dispose of the purchased goods or services. The study of consumer behavior also includes an analysis of factors that influence purchase decisions and product use.

Understanding how consumers make purchase decisions can help marketing managers in several ways. For example, if a manager knows through research that gas mileage is the most important attribute for a certain target market, the manufacturer can redesign the product to meet that criterion. If the firm cannot change the design in the short run, it can use promotion in an effort to change consumers' decision-making criteria. In the opening vignette, you learned that Virgin Mobile realized that Gen Yers were looking for more flexibility and convenience and more value-added services than traditional mobile phone plans offered. As a result, it designed a highly successful marketing strategy that more closely matched targeted consumers' needs, wants, and desires by offering more freedom and convenience.

REVIEW LEARNING OBJECTIVE 1

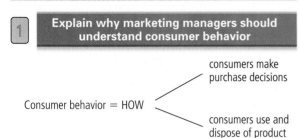

THE CONSUMER DECISION-MAKING PROCESS

Analyze the components of the consumer decision-making process

When buying products, consumers generally follow the **consumer decision-making process** shown in Exhibit 5.1: (1) need recognition, (2) information search, (3) evaluation of alternatives, (4) purchase, and (5) postpurchase behavior. These five steps represent a general process that can be used as a guideline for studying how consumers make decisions. It is important to note that this guideline does not assume that consumers' decisions will proceed in order through all of the steps of the process. In fact, the consumer may end the process at any time; he or she may not even make a purchase. Explanations as to why a consumer's progression through these steps may vary are offered at the end of the chapter in the section on the types of consumer buying decisions. Before addressing this issue, however, we will describe each step in the process in greater detail.

NEED RECOGNITION

consumer behavior
Processes a consumer uses to make purchase decisions, as well as to use and dispose of purchased goods or services; also includes factors that influence purchase decisions and product use.

consumer decision-making process
A five-step process used by consumers when buying goods or services.

need recognition
Result of an imbalance between actual and desired states.

stimulus
Any unit of input affecting one or more of the five senses: sight, smell, taste, touch, hearing.

The first stage in the consumer decision-making process is need recognition. **Need recognition** occurs when consumers are faced with an imbalance between actual and desired states. For example, have you ever gotten blisters from an old running shoe? Or maybe you have seen a TV commercial for a new sports car and wanted to buy it. Need recognition is triggered when a consumer is exposed to either an internal or an external **stimulus**. *Internal stimuli* are occurrences you experience, such as hunger or thirst. For example, you may hear your stomach growl and then realize that you are hungry. *External stimuli* are influences from an outside source such as someone's recommendation of a new restaurant, the color of an automobile, the design of a package, a brand name mentioned by a friend, or an advertisement on television or radio.

A marketing manager's objective is to get consumers to recognize an imbalance between their present status and their preferred state. Advertising and sales promotion often provide this stimulus. Surveying buyer preferences provides marketers with information about consumer wants and needs that can be used to

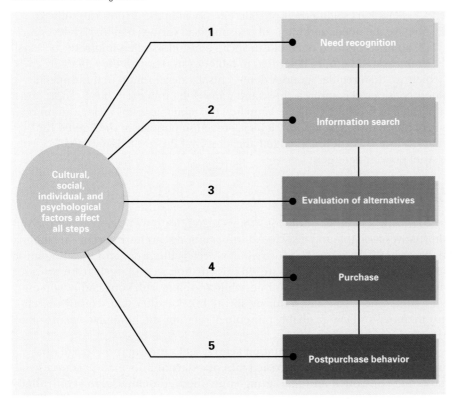

Exhibit 5.1

1 Need recognition
2 Information search
3 Evaluation of alternatives
4 Purchase
5 Postpurchase behavior

Cultural, social, individual, and psychological factors affect all steps

tailor products and services. For example, Procter & Gamble frequently surveys consumers regarding their wants and needs. P&G recently used the Internet to test market its new Crest Whitestrips home-bleaching kit. The test revealed that 80 percent of potential buyers were women between the ages of 35 and 54, identifying the best target market for the product. The company was then able to fine-tune its marketing plan before launching the product nationwide.[2] In another example of how far P&G will go to learn about market trends, the company recently began videotaping consumers at home in its own version of reality TV to learn things about them that surveys do not reveal.[3]

Marketing managers can create wants on the part of the consumer. A **want** exists when someone has an unfulfilled need and has determined that a particular good or service will satisfy it. When college students move in to their own apartment or dorm room for the first time, they often need to furnish it and want new furniture rather than hand-me-downs from their parents. A want can be for a specific product, or it can be for a certain attribute or feature of a product. In this example, the college students not only need home furnishings, but also want items that reflect their personal sense of style. Similarly, consumers may want ready-to-eat meals, drive-through dry-cleaning service, and Internet shopping to fill their need for convenience.

Another way marketers create new products and services is by observing trends in the marketplace. IKEA, the home furnishing giant, watches the home decor trends and then creates affordable, trendy furniture. For example, marketers at IKEA realized that Generation Y consumers prefer furniture that is stylish, easy to clean, multifunctional, and portable. As a result, IKEA uses "bold orange, pink and green colors." The wood boasts a lacquered finish that can be wiped clean and doesn't need polish. IKEA also offers a space-saving, multifunction desk that can be converted into a dining table; it has wheels so that it can be easily moved.[4]

Consumers recognize unfulfilled wants in various ways. The two most common occur when a current product isn't performing properly and when the consumer is about to run out of something that is generally kept on hand. Consumers may also recognize unfulfilled wants if they become aware of a product whose features make it seem superior to the one currently used. Such wants are usually created by advertising and other promotional activities. For example, Cingular offers FastForward, a service for mobile phone customers that forwards incoming wireless calls to a landline phone. The required adaptor serves a dual function as a mobile phone charger and a forwarding device. In addition to offering simplicity and convenience, the new service appeals to consumers who want to save money and mobile phone minutes.[5] Similarly, aware of the popularity of MP3s and consumers' desire to take their music with them, more than a dozen car stereo

want
Recognition of an unfulfilled need and a product that will satisfy it.

manufacturers such as Sonicblue and Kenwood have added MP3 capabilities to their products. Other companies are also hoping to fulfill consumer needs with small portable MP3 players such as the iPod by Apple Computer.[6]

Marketers selling their products in global markets must carefully observe the needs and wants of consumers in various regions. Unilever hit on an unrecognized need of European consumers when it introduced Persil Tablets, premeasured laundry detergent in tablet form. Though the tablets are more expensive than regular laundry detergents, Unilever found that European consumers considered laundry a chore and wanted the process to be as simple and uncomplicated as possible. Unilever launched the tablets as a less messy and more convenient alternative. The laundry tablets proved so popular in the United Kingdom that Unilever's Persil brand edged ahead of rival Procter & Gamble's best-selling Ariel powder detergent.[7]

INFORMATION SEARCH

After recognizing a need or want, consumers search for information about the various alternatives available to satisfy it. An information search can occur internally, externally, or both. An **internal information search** is the process of recalling information stored in the memory. This stored information stems largely from previous experience with a product. For example, while traveling with your family, you encounter a hotel where you stayed during spring break earlier that year. By searching your memory, you can probably remember whether the hotel had clean rooms and friendly service.

In contrast, an **external information search** seeks information in the outside environment. There are two basic types of external information sources: nonmarketing-controlled and marketing-controlled. A **nonmarketing-controlled information source** is not associated with marketers promoting a product. These information sources include personal experiences (trying or observing a new product); personal sources (family, friends, acquaintances, and coworkers who may recommend a product or service); and public sources, such as Underwriters Laboratories, *Consumer Reports*, and other rating organizations that comment on products and services. For example, if you are in the mood to go to the movies, you may search your memory for past experiences at various cinemas when determining which one to go to (personal experience). To choose which movie you will see, you may rely on the recommendation of a friend or family member (personal sources). Alternatively, you may read the critical reviews in the newspaper or online (public sources). Marketers gather information on how these information sources work and use it to attract customers. For example, car manufacturers know that younger customers are likely to get information from friends and family, so they try to develop enthusiasm for their products via word of mouth.

On the other hand, a **marketing-controlled information source** is biased toward a specific product, because it originates with marketers promoting that product. Marketing-controlled information sources include mass-media advertising (radio, newspaper, television, and magazine advertising), sales promotion (contests, displays, premiums, and so forth), salespeople, product labels and packaging, and the Internet. Many consumers, however, are wary of the information they receive from marketing-controlled sources, arguing that most marketing campaigns stress the attributes of the product and don't mention the faults. These sentiments tend to be stronger among better educated and higher income consumers. For instance, in spite of extensive advertising highlighting its philanthropic activities, Philip Morris Companies continues to have a poor reputation among consumers. In fact, after a survey revealed that an extensive image campaign had not changed consumer opinion about the company, Philip Morris decided to change its corporate name to Altria to shift the focus away from the Philip Morris brand and onto the company's other brands like Kraft Foods and

internal information search
The process of recalling past information stored in the memory.

external information search
The process of seeking information in the outside environment.

nonmarketing-controlled information source
A product information source that is not associated with advertising or promotion.

marketing-controlled information source
A product information source that originates with marketers promoting the product.

The Benefits of Tea

Brain
May help prevent the affects of brain-degenerative diseases

Cancer
Studies have shown that tea inhibits the growth of cancers

Immune System
Helps maintain a healthy immune system

Bones and Joints
May prevent and relieve joint inflammation

Teeth
May prevent cavities and bad breath

Heart and Blood Vessels
A USDA study reports that tea prevents the buildup of bad cholesterol

Liver
May help defuse the effects of harmful toxins

Weight
Stimulates the body's metabolism

From Head to Toe

Courtesy of Celestial Seasonings® For more information on the health benefits and research related to tea, visit www.celestialseasonings.com.

AP/WIDE WORLD PHOTOS

Whereas non-marketing controlled information is neutral, marketing-controlled information is biased toward a specific product. This ad from Celestial Seasonings seems to cut through both types: it proclaims the benefits of tea in general, but since the company name is on the ad as a sponsor, the information cannot be considered completely unbiased. Or can it?

FAQs

What do customers consider when they are comparing goods and services to the competition? Find out by watching the video FAQ on Xtra!

Miller Beer. In another example, surveys showed that consumers were skeptical about quality assurance advertisements made by Bridgestone's Firestone Tires in the wake of the company's massive tire recall.[8]

The extent to which an individual conducts an external search depends on his or her perceived risk, knowledge, prior experience, and level of interest in the good or service. Generally, as the perceived risk of the purchase increases, the consumer enlarges the search and considers more alternative brands. For example, suppose that you want to purchase a surround sound system for your home stereo. The decision is relatively risky because of the expense and technical nature of the stereo system, so you are motivated to search for information about models, prices, options, compatibility with existing entertainment products, and capabilities. You may decide to compare attributes of many speaker systems because the value of the time expended finding the "right" stereo will be less than the cost of buying the wrong system. In contrast, more than 60 percent of bar patrons don't know what they will drink until seconds before they place their order, challenging the marketers of alcoholic beverages to find ways of "educating" potential customers on the spot.[9]

A consumer's knowledge about the product or service will also affect the extent of an external information search. If the consumer is knowledgeable and well informed about a potential purchase, he or she is less likely to search for additional information. In addition, the more knowledgeable the consumer is, the more efficiently he or she will conduct the search process, thereby requiring less time to search. For example, a novice computer user will spend considerable time and energy in the information search because it is a first-time purchase. In contrast, an expert computer user will be able to make a better decision more quickly because of his or her experience and knowledge about computers.

Another closely related factor that affects the extent of a consumer's external search is confidence in one's decision-making ability. A confident consumer not only has sufficient stored information about the product but also feels self-assured about making the right decision. People lacking this confidence will continue an information search even when they know a great deal about the product. Consumers with prior experience in buying a certain product will have less perceived risk than inexperienced consumers. Therefore, they will spend less time searching and limit the number of products that they consider.

A third factor influencing the external information search is product experience. Consumers who have had a positive prior experience with a product are more likely to limit their search to only those items related to the positive experience. For example, when flying, consumers are likely to choose airlines with which they have had positive experiences, such as consistent on-time arrivals. They will avoid airlines with which they had a negative experience, such as lost luggage.

Product experience can also play a major role in a consumer's decision to make a high-risk purchase. For example, TiVo, the maker of personal video recorders, found that due to the expensive and complex nature of its product, advertising was only moderately effective in generating sales. Instead, personal experience is the most important factor in the decision to purchase a PVR.[10]

Finally, the extent of the search undertaken is positively related to the amount of interest a consumer has in a product. A consumer who is more interested in a product will spend more time searching for information and alternatives. For example, suppose you are a dedicated runner who reads jogging and fitness magazines and catalogs. In searching for a new pair of running shoes, you may enjoy reading about the new brands available and spend more time and effort than other buyers in deciding on the right shoe.

The consumer's information search should yield a group of brands, sometimes called the buyer's **evoked set** (or **consideration set**), which are the consumer's most preferred alternatives. From this set, the buyer will further evaluate the alternatives and make a choice. Consumers do not consider all brands available in a product category, but they do seriously consider a much smaller set. For example, from the many brands of pizza available, consumers are likely to consider only the alternatives that fit their price range, location, take-out/delivery needs, and taste preferences. Having too many choices can, in fact, confuse consumers and cause them to delay the decision to buy or, in some instances, cause them to not buy at all.

EVALUATION OF ALTERNATIVES AND PURCHASE

After getting information and constructing an evoked set of alternative products, the consumer is ready to make a decision. A consumer will use the information stored in memory and obtained from outside sources to develop a set of criteria. These standards help the consumer evaluate and compare alternatives. One way to begin narrowing the number of choices in the evoked set is to pick a product attribute and then exclude all products in the set that don't have that attribute. For example, assume Jane and Jill, both college sophomores, are looking for their first apartment. They need a two-bedroom apartment, reasonably priced, and located near campus. They want the apartment to have a swimming pool, washer and dryer, and covered parking. Jane and Jill begin their search with all apartments in the area and then systematically eliminate possibilities that lack the features they need. Hence, if there are 50 alternatives in the area, they may reduce their list to just 10 apartments that possess all of the desired attributes.

Another way to narrow the number of choices is to use cutoffs. Cutoffs are either minimum or maximum levels of an attribute that an alternative must pass to be considered. Suppose Jane and Jill set a maximum of $1,000 to spend on combined rent. Then all apartments with rent higher than $1,000 will be eliminated, further reducing the list of apartments from ten to eight. A final way to narrow the choices is to rank the attributes under consideration in order of importance and evaluate the products based on how well each performs on the most important attributes. To reach a final decision on one of the remaining eight apartments, Jane and Jill may decide proximity to campus is the most important attribute. As a result, they will choose to rent the apartment closest to campus.

If new brands are added to an evoked set, the consumer's evaluation of the existing brands in that set changes. As a result, certain brands in the original set may become more desirable. Suppose Jane and Jill find two apartments located equal distance from campus, one priced at $800 and the other at $750. Faced with this choice, they may decide that the $800 apartment is too expensive given that a comparable apartment is cheaper. If they add a $900 apartment to the list, however, then they may perceive the $800 apartment as more reasonable and decide to rent it.

evoked set (consideration set)
A group of brands, resulting from an information search, from which a buyer can choose.

The goal of the marketing manager is to determine which attributes have the most influence on a consumer's choice. Several attributes may collectively affect a consumer's evaluation of products. A single attribute, such as price, may not adequately explain how consumers form their evoked set. Moreover, attributes the marketer thinks are important may not be very important to the consumer. For example, if you are buying a new notebook computer, you will first have to determine which computers are in your price range. But, in making a final decision, you may also consider weight, screen size, software included, processor speeds, CD and DVD drives, service packages, and reputation.

A brand name can also have a significant impact on a consumer's ultimate choice. In one online survey, Johnson & Johnson was found to have the best corporate reputation among American companies, benefiting from its heritage as the premier maker of baby powder and shampoo. Respondents uniformly cited the familiarity and comfort they feel in using J&J products on their children. When faced with dozens of products on the drugstore shelf, consumers naturally gravitate toward J&J products. By providing consumers with a certain set of promises, brands in essence simplify the consumer decision-making process so consumers do not have to rethink their options every time they need something.[11]

Following the evaluation of alternatives, the consumer decides which product to buy or decides not to buy a product at all. If he or she decides to make a purchase, the next step in the process is an evaluation of the product after the purchase.

REVIEW LEARNING OBJECTIVE

2 | Analyze the components of the consumer decision-making process

INDIVIDUAL

CULTURAL

| Need Recognition **1** | → | Information Search **2** | → | Evaluate Alternatives **3** | → | Purchase **4** |

SOCIAL

PSYCHOLOGICAL

3

Explain the consumer's postpurchase evaluation process

cognitive dissonance
Inner tension that a consumer experiences after recognizing an inconsistency between behavior and values or opinions.

POSTPURCHASE BEHAVIOR

When buying products, consumers expect certain outcomes from the purchase. How well these expectations are met determines whether the consumer is satisfied or dissatisfied with the purchase. For example, if a person bids on a used car stereo from eBay and wins, he may have fairly low expectations regarding performance. If the stereo's performance turns out to be of superior quality, then the person's satisfaction will be high because his expectations were exceeded. Conversely, if the person bid on a new car stereo expecting superior quality and performance, but the stereo broke within one month, he would be very dissatisfied because his expectations were not met. Price often influences the level of expectations for a product or service.

For the marketer, an important element of any postpurchase evaluation is reducing any lingering doubts that the decision was sound. This is particularly important because 75 percent of all consumers say they had a bad experience in the last year with a product or service they purchased.[12] When people recognize inconsistency between their values or opinions and their behavior, they tend to feel an inner tension called **cognitive dissonance**. For example, suppose a person who

Consumer Decision Making Chapter 5 **157**

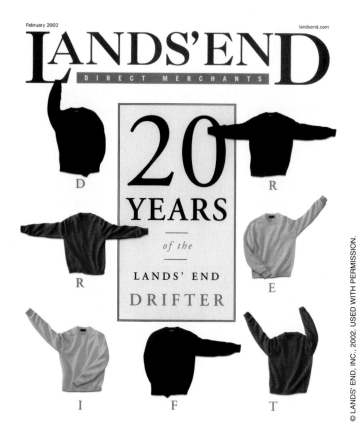

One way companies reduce the effects of cognitive dissonance is by offering comprehensive money-back guarantees or refund policies. Lands' End was a pioneer in this area and still offers a lifetime guarantee of all its merchandise.

REVIEW LEARNING OBJECTIVE

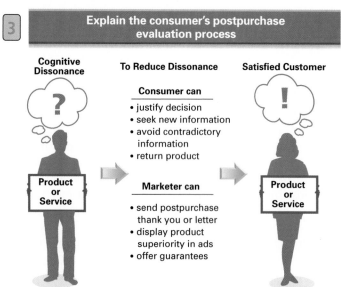

normally tans in a tanning bed decides to try a new "airbrush" tanning method, called a "Hollywood" or "mystic" tanning. Mystic tanning costs $30 to $50, significantly more than "fake tanner" or a tanning bed. The person may feel inner tension or anxiety prior to spending more on the tan, which is a feeling of dissonance. This feeling occurs because she knows the product has some disadvantages, such as being expensive, and some advantages, such as being free of harmful ultraviolet rays. In this case, the disadvantage of higher cost battles the advantage of no harmful UV rays.[13]

Consumers try to reduce dissonance by justifying their decision. They may seek new information that reinforces positive ideas about the purchase, avoid information that contradicts their decision, or revoke the original decision by returning the product. Consumers using the "mystic tanning" mentioned above may ask several friends about their experiences, do online research, and talk with the tanning booth representative to obtain additional information about the procedure to ensure satisfaction, thereby reducing dissonance. In some instances, people deliberately seek contrary information in order to refute it and reduce dissonance. Dissatisfied customers sometimes rely on word of mouth to reduce cognitive dissonance, by letting friends and family know they are displeased.

Marketing managers can help reduce dissonance through effective communication with purchasers. For example, a customer service manager may slip a note inside the package congratulating the buyer on making a wise decision. Postpurchase letters sent by manufacturers and dissonance-reducing statements in instruction booklets may help customers feel at ease with their purchase. Advertising that displays the product's superiority over competing brands or guarantees can also help relieve the possible dissonance of someone who has already bought the product. In the tanning example, the tanning salon may offer a 100 percent money-back guarantee. The mystictan.com Web site explains the procedure and even shows endorsements from the Dallas Cowboys cheerleaders. Because the company offers this additional information and communicates effectively with its customers, they are more likely to understand the procedure and the expected results; hence, it is likely that the outcome will meet or exceed their expectations rather than being disappointing.[14]

Identify the types of consumer buying decisions and discuss the significance of consumer involvement

All consumer buying decisions generally fall along a continuum of three broad categories: routine response behavior, limited decision making, and extensive decision making (see Exhibit 5.2). Goods and services in these three categories can best be described in terms of five factors: level of consumer involvement, length of time to make a decision, cost of the good or service, degree of information search, and the number of alternatives considered. The level of consumer involvement is perhaps the most significant determinant in classifying buying decisions. **Involvement** is the amount of time and effort a buyer invests in the search, evaluation, and decision processes of consumer behavior.

Frequently purchased, low-cost goods and services are generally associated with **routine response behavior**. These goods and services can also be called low-involvement products because consumers spend little time on search and decision before making the purchase. Usually, buyers are familiar with several different brands in the product category but stick with one brand. Consumers engaged in routine response behavior normally don't experience need recognition until they are exposed to advertising or see the product displayed on a store shelf. Consumers buy first and evaluate later, whereas the reverse is true for extensive decision making. A consumer who has previously purchased a whitening toothpaste and was satisfied with it will probably walk to the toothpaste aisle and select that same brand without spending 20 minutes examining all other alternatives.

Limited decision making typically occurs when a consumer has previous product experience but is unfamiliar with the current brands available. Limited decision making is also associated with lower levels of involvement (although higher than routine decisions) because consumers do expend moderate effort in searching for information or in considering various alternatives. But what happens if the consumer's usual brand of whitening toothpaste is sold out? Assuming that toothpaste is needed, the consumer will be forced to choose another brand. Before making a final decision, the consumer will likely evaluate several other brands based on their active ingredients, their promotional claims, and the consumer's prior experiences.

Consumers practice **extensive decision making** when buying an unfamiliar, expensive product or an infrequently bought item. This process is the most complex type of consumer buying decision and is associated with high involvement on the part of the consumer. This process resembles the model outlined in Exhibit 5.1. These consumers want to make the right decision, so they want to know as much as they can about the product category and available brands. People usually experience cognitive dissonance only when buying high-involvement products. Buyers use several criteria for evaluating their options and spend much time seeking information. Buying a home or a car, for example, requires extensive decision making.

The type of decision making that consumers use to purchase a product does not necessarily remain constant. For instance, if a routinely purchased product no longer satisfies, consumers may practice limited or extensive

EXHIBIT 5.2

Continuum of Consumer Buying Decisions

	Routine	Limited	Extensive
	⟵————————⟶		
Involvement	low	low to moderate	high
Time	short	short to moderate	long
Cost	low	low to moderate	high
Information Search	internal only	mostly internal	internal and external
Number of Alternatives	one	few	many

involvement
The amount of time and effort a buyer invests in the search, evaluation, and decision processes of consumer behavior.

routine response behavior
The type of decision making exhibited by consumers buying frequently purchased, low-cost goods and services; requires little search and decision time.

limited decision making
The type of decision making that requires a moderate amount of time for gathering information and deliberating about an unfamiliar brand in a familiar product category.

extensive decision making
The most complex type of consumer decision making, used when buying an unfamiliar, expensive product or an infrequently bought item; requires use of several criteria for evaluating options and much time for seeking information.

decision making to switch to another brand. And people who first use extensive decision making may then use limited or routine decision making for future purchases. For example, when a family gets a new puppy, they will spend a lot of time and energy trying out different toys to determine which one the dog prefers. Once the new owners learn that the dog prefers a bone to a ball, however, the purchase no longer requires extensive evaluation and will become routine.

FACTORS DETERMINING THE LEVEL OF CONSUMER INVOLVEMENT

The level of involvement in the purchase depends on the following five factors:

- *Previous experience:* When consumers have had previous experience with a good or service, the level of involvement typically decreases. After repeated product trials, consumers learn to make quick choices. Because consumers are familiar with the product and know whether it will satisfy their needs, they become less involved in the purchase. For example, a consumer purchasing cereal has many brands to choose from—just think of any grocery store cereal aisle. If the consumer always buys the same brand because it satisfies his hunger, then he has a low level of involvement. When a consumer purchases cereal for the first time, however, it likely will be a much more involved purchase.
- *Interest:* Involvement is directly related to consumer interests, as in cars, music, movies, bicycling, or electronics. Naturally, these areas of interest vary from one individual to another. A person highly involved in bike racing will be very interested in the type of bike she owns and will spend quite a bit of time evaluating different bikes. If a person wants a bike only for recreation, however, he may be fairly uninvolved in the purchase and just look for a bike from the most convenient location.
- *Perceived risk of negative consequences:* As the perceived risk in purchasing a product increases, so does a consumer's level of involvement. The types of risks that concern consumers include financial risk, social risk, and psychological risk. First, financial risk is exposure to loss of wealth or purchasing power. Because high risk is associated with high-priced purchases, consumers tend to become extremely involved. Therefore, price and involvement are usually directly related: As price increases, so does the level of involvement. For example, someone who is purchasing a new car for the first time will spend much more time and effort making this purchase than someone who has purchased several new cars. Second, consumers take social risks when they buy products that can affect people's social opinions of them (for example, driving an old, beat-up car or wearing unstylish clothes). Third, buyers undergo psychological risk if they feel that making the wrong decision might cause some concern or anxiety. For example, some consumers feel guilty about eating foods that are not healthy, such as regular ice cream rather than fat-free frozen yogurt.
- *Situation:* The circumstances of a purchase may temporarily transform a low-involvement decision into a high-involvement one. High involvement comes into play when the consumer perceives risk in a specific situation. For example, an individual might routinely buy low-priced brands of liquor and wine. When the boss visits, however, the consumer might make a high-involvement decision and buy more prestigious brands.
- *Social visibility:* Involvement also increases as the social visibility of a product increases. Products often on social display include clothing (especially designer labels), jewelry, cars, and furniture. All these items make a statement about the purchaser and, therefore, carry a social risk.

MARKETING IMPLICATIONS OF INVOLVEMENT

Marketing strategy varies according to the level of involvement associated with the product. For high-involvement product purchases, marketing managers have several responsibilities. First, promotion to the target market should be extensive and informative. A good ad gives consumers the information they need for making the purchase decision, as well as specifying the benefits and unique advantages of owning the product. For example, Philips Magnavox, the leading manufacturer of high-definition, flat-screen televisions, features a print ad that not only provides extensive product information, such as size parameters and screen alternatives (wide or standard), but also appeals to consumers' sense of style and their need to save space. Most importantly, the ad's tag line is aimed at both men and women as a couple: "The Philips High-Definition Flat TV as seen from two points of view. His. And Hers."[15]

Purchasing online involves added risk for many consumers, even in limited decision-making situations. To overcome the challenges of getting shoppers to complete purchases online, Landsend.com created a virtual three-dimensional model that customers can use to try on clothes. It also offers an online "personal shopper" to help customers identify items they might like. Purchase rates have been 26 percent higher among online shoppers who use the model and 80 percent higher among customers who use the personal shopper.[16]

For low-involvement product purchases, consumers may not recognize their wants until they are in the store. Therefore, in-store promotion is an important tool when promoting low-involvement products. Marketing managers focus on package design so the product will be eye-catching and easily recognized on the shelf. Examples of products that take this approach are Campbell's soups, Tide detergent, Velveeta cheese, and Heinz ketchup. In-store displays also stimulate sales of low-involvement products. A good display can explain the product's purpose and prompt recognition of a want. Displays of health and beauty aid items in supermarkets have been known to increase sales many times above normal. Coupons, cents-off deals, and two-for-one offers also effectively promote low-involvement items.

PHILIPS

Let's make things better

The Philips High-Definition Flat TV as seen from two points of view. His. And Hers.
Now there's a TV for both you and your better half. One that offers a larger-than-life image without taking up your whole living room. Philips Flat TVs are available in a wide range of screen sizes ranging from 15" to 50" in standard and widescreen formats. With a depth of less than 4.5 inches, Flat TVs not only save space, the incredible high-definition picture is flat-out amazing. And the design is enough to enhance any room. So any way you look at it, a Philips Flat TV will give you maximum impact with minimal disruption of your home. And, quite possibly, your marriage.

See More with Less TV. Experience More with Philips HD Flat TV.

Learn more about Philips Flat TV at www.flattv.philips.com.

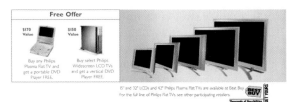

As the level of purchasing involvement increases, so does the marketing manager's responsibility to provide extensive and informative promotional materials to potential customers. This ad for Philips' high-definition flat TV appeals to both men and women with detailed copy that is also a tool for reducing cognitive dissonance.

EXHIBIT 5.3

Factors That Affect the Consumer Decision-Making Process

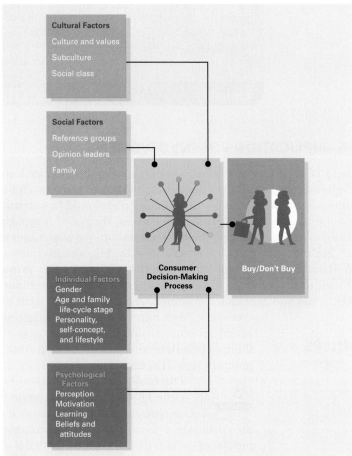

Cultural Factors
Culture and values
Subculture
Social class

Social Factors
Reference groups
Opinion leaders
Family

Individual Factors
Gender
Age and family
 life-cycle stage
Personality,
 self-concept,
 and lifestyle

Psychological Factors
Perception
Motivation
Learning
Beliefs and
 attitudes

Consumer Decision-Making Process

Buy/Don't Buy

REVIEW LEARNING OBJECTIVE

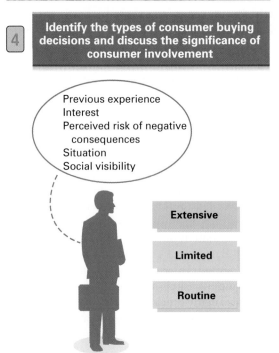

4 **Identify the types of consumer buying decisions and discuss the significance of consumer involvement**

Previous experience
Interest
Perceived risk of negative
 consequences
Situation
Social visibility

Extensive

Limited

Routine

Linking a product to a higher-involvement issue is another tactic that marketing managers can use to increase the sales of a low-involvement product. For example, many food products are no longer just nutritious but also low in carbohydrate, fat, or cholesterol. Although packaged food may normally be a low-involvement product, reference to health issues raises the involvement level. To take advantage of aging baby boomers' interest in healthier foods, an advertisement from H.J. Heinz linked its ketchup with a growing body of research that suggests lycopene, an antioxidant found in tomatoes, can reduce the risk of prostate and cervical cancer.[17] Similarly, food products, such as Silk soy milk and Gardenburger meatless burgers, both of which contain soy protein, tout their health benefits in reducing the risk of coronary heart disease, preventing certain cancers, and reducing the symptoms of menopause. Soy-based products, long shunned in the United States for their taste, have seen their sales skyrocket as a result of these health claims.[18]

FACTORS INFLUENCING CONSUMER BUYING DECISIONS

The consumer decision-making process does not occur in a vacuum. On the contrary, underlying cultural, social, individual, and psychological factors strongly influence the decision process. They have an effect from the time a consumer perceives a stimulus through postpurchase behavior. Cultural factors, which include culture and values, subculture, and social class, exert the broadest influence over consumer decision making. Social factors sum up the social interactions between a consumer and influential groups of people, such as reference groups, opinion leaders, and family members. Individual factors, which include gender, age, family life-cycle stage, personality, self-concept, and lifestyle, are unique to each individual and play a major role in the type of products and services consumers want. Psychological factors determine how consumers perceive and interact with their environments and influence the ultimate decisions consumers make. They include perception, motivation, learning, beliefs, and attitudes. Exhibit 5.3 summarizes these influences.

5 CULTURAL INFLUENCES ON CONSUMER BUYING DECISIONS

Identify and understand the cultural factors that affect consumer buying decisions

The first major group of factors that influence consumer decision making is comprised of cultural factors. Cultural factors exert the broadest and deepest influence over a person's consumer behavior and decision making. Marketers must understand the way people's culture and its accompanying values, as well as their subculture and social class, influence their buying behavior.

EXHIBIT 5.4

Components of American Culture

COMPONENT	EXAMPLES
Values	Success through hard work
	Emphasis on personal freedom
Language	English as the dominant language
Myths	Santa Claus delivers presents to good boys and girls on Christmas Eve.
	Abraham Lincoln walked a mile to return a penny.
Customs	Bathing daily
	Shaking hands when greeting new people
	Standard gratuity of 15 percent at restaurants
Rituals	Thanksgiving Day dinner
	Singing the "Star Spangled Banner" before baseball games
	Going to religious services on the appropriate day
Laws	Child labor laws
	Sherman Anti-Trust Act guarantees competition
Material artifacts	Diamond engagement rings
	Cell phones

SOURCE: Adapted from *Consumer Behavior* by William D. Wells and David Prensky. Copyright © 1996 by John Wiley & Sons, Inc. Reprinted by permission of John Wiley & Sons, Inc. All Rights Reserved.

CULTURE AND VALUES

Culture is the essential character of a society that distinguishes it from other cultural groups. The underlying elements of every culture are the values, language, myths, customs, rituals, and laws that shape the behavior of the culture, as well as the material artifacts, or products, of that behavior as they are transmitted from one generation to the next. Exhibit 5.4 lists some defining components of American culture.

Culture is pervasive. Cultural values and influences are the ocean in which individuals swim, and yet most are completely unaware that it is there. What people eat, how they dress, what they think and feel, and what language they speak are all dimensions of culture. It encompasses all the things consumers do without conscious choice because their culture's values, customs, and rituals are ingrained in their daily habits.

Culture is functional. Human interaction creates values and prescribes acceptable behavior for each culture. By establishing common expectations, culture gives order to society. Sometimes these expectations are coded into laws. For example, drivers in our culture must stop at a red light. Other times these expectations are taken for granted. For example, grocery stores and hospitals are open 24 hours whereas banks are open only during bankers' hours.

Culture is learned. Consumers are not born knowing the values and norms of their society. Instead, they must learn what is acceptable from family and friends. Children learn the values that will govern their behavior from parents, teachers, and peers. As members of our society, they learn to shake hands when they greet someone, to drive on the right-hand side of the road, and to eat pizza and drink Coca-Cola.

Culture is dynamic. It adapts to changing needs and an evolving environment. The rapid growth of technology in today's world has accelerated the rate of cultural change. Television has changed entertainment patterns and family communication and has heightened public awareness of political and other news events. Automation has increased the amount of leisure time we have and, in some ways, has changed the traditional work ethic. Cultural norms will continue to evolve because of our need for social patterns that solve problems.

In the United States, our rapidly increasing diversity is causing major shifts in culture. For example, the growth of the Hispanic community is influencing American food, music, clothing, and entertainment. Additionally, African

culture
The set of values, norms, attitudes, and other meaningful symbols that shape human behavior and the artifacts, or products, of that behavior as they are transmitted from one generation to the next.

©AP/WIDE WORLD PHOTOS

Increases in the minority populations are changing the marketing implications of culture. Avon has responded to those changes by creating multicultural beauty advisory boards which help in product development, aggressively recruiting minority sales women, and revamping promotional materials to reflect the demographics of the United States. Avon's CEO Andrea Jung is pictured here with Serena Williams. The Williams sisters are spokespersons for Avon's new color cosmetics.

value
The enduring belief that a specific mode of conduct is personally or socially preferable to another mode of conduct.

American culture has been embraced by the mainstream. Indeed, African American women make up one of the fastest growing segments of the American population. The projected growth rate of this segment is 8 percent compared to 4 percent for the total U.S. population. Additionally, "one in two married black women is the primary decision maker in buying a house, versus one in four married white women." Traditionally, marketers have not taken advantage of the opportunity to market to African American women. Now, however, many companies are taking note of this rapidly growing segment of the population. For example, Kraft's Honey Bunches of Oats cereal developed an advertising campaign that focused on black women. Research showed that African American women do not like to eat cereal when others are around, so the print ad shows a black woman eating a bowl of cereal alone with the caption "Take a breather. This moment is yours. Just you and your bowl of Honey Bunches of Oats."[19] Avon has hired Venus and Serena Williams, sisters and tennis stars, to be spokespersons for its color cosmetics and a new jewelry line. But they are doing more than just promoting Avon products. They are also recruiting African American sales representatives. In addition to featuring the famous tennis stars, Avon has used a multicultural beauty advisory board to develop new products for African American women. In fact, Avon is revamping all its promotional materials to reflect the demographics of the United States.[20]

The most defining element of a culture is its **values**—the enduring beliefs shared by a society that a specific mode of conduct is personally or socially preferable to another mode of conduct. People's value systems have a great effect on their consumer behavior. Consumers with similar value systems tend to react alike to prices and other marketing-related inducements. Values also correspond to consumption patterns. For example, Americans place a high value on convenience. This value has created lucrative markets for products such as breakfast bars, energy bars, and nutrition bars that allow consumers to eat on the go.[21] Values can also influence consumers' TV viewing habits or the magazines they read. For instance, people who strongly object to violence avoid crime shows, and those who oppose pornography do not buy *Hustler*. Core American values—those considered central to the American way of life—are presented in Exhibit 5.5.

The personal values of target consumers have important implications for marketing managers. When marketers understand the core values that underlie the attitudes that shape the buying patterns of America's consumers and how these values were molded by experiences, they can target their message more effectively. For example, the personal value systems of older consumers, baby boomers, Generation Xers, and Generation Yers are quite different. The key to understanding older consumers, or everyone born before 1945, is recognizing the impact of the Great Depression and World War II on their lives. Facing these two immense challenges shaped a generation characterized by discipline, self-denial, financial and social conservatism, and a sense of obligation. Boomers, those individuals nurtured in the bountiful postwar period between 1945 and 1964, believe they are entitled to the wealth and opportunity that seemed endless in their youth. Generation Xers are very accepting of diversity and individuality. They are also a very entrepreneurial-driven generation, ready to tackle life's challenges for themselves rather than as part of a crowd.[22] Gen Yers are more serious and socially conscious than Gen Xers. Some of the

EXHIBIT 5.5

Core American Values

Success	Americans admire hard work, entrepreneurship, achievement, and success. Those achieving success in American society are rewarded with money, status, and prestige. For example, Bill Gates, once a nerdy computer buff, built Microsoft Corporation into an internationally known giant. Gates is now one of the richest people in the world.
Materialism	Americans value owning tangible goods. American society encourages consumption, ownership, and possession. Americans judge others based on their material possessions; for example, the type of car they own, where they live, and what type of clothes they wear.
Freedom	The American culture was founded on the principle of religious and political freedom. The U.S. Constitution and the Bill of Rights assure American citizens the right to life, liberty, and the pursuit of happiness. These freedoms are fundamental to the legal system and the moral fiber of American culture. The Internet, for example, is built on the principle of the right to free speech. Lawmakers who have attempted to limit the material available on the Internet have met with tough opposition from proponents of free speech. Spam has become such a major problem in recent years, however, that individuals are becoming more favorable to laws restricting spam even if they limit spammers' free speech.
Progress	Technological advances, as well as advances in medicine, science, health, and the quality of products and services, are important to Americans. Each year, for example, more than 20,000 new or improved consumer products are introduced on America's supermarket shelves.*
Youth	Americans are obsessed with youth and spend a good deal of time on products and procedures that make them feel and look younger. Americans spend millions each year on health and beauty aids, health clubs, and healthy foods. Media and advertising encourage the quest for youth by using young, attractive, slim models, such as those in ads from fashion designer Calvin Klein.
Capitalism	Americans believe in a free enterprise system characterized by competition and the chance for monetary success. Capitalism creates choices, quality, and value for Americans. Laws prohibit monopolistic control of a market and regulate free trade. Americans encourage small business success, such as that found by Apple Computer, Wal-Mart, and McDonald's, all of which started as small enterprises with a better idea that toppled the competition.

*Data obtained from the Food Marketing Institute Web site at www.fmi.org, 2004.

SOURCE: From *Consumer Behavior* by William D. Wells and David Prensky. Copyright © 1996 John Wiley & Sons, Inc. Reprinted by permission of John Wiley & Sons, Inc. All Rights Reserved.

defining events of their lives include Columbine, the O. J. Simpson trial, the Clinton impeachment, and the 2000 presidential election. They grew up with cable television, computers, debit cards, and cell phones, making them the most well connected generation to date—a fact that has important implications for word-of-mouth influence.[23]

Gen Yers are notorious for being one of the most difficult market segments to reach. They are the "most unpredictable, advertising-saturated and marketing-skeptical group of adults America has ever seen,"[24] and they also have a tendency to ignore media. When Toyota launched its new car, the Scion, the marketing department put the car on display outside coffee shops and raves to encourage word-of-mouth marketing. From its approximately $12,500 price to its design, the vehicle is focused on Gen Yers' lifestyle. The seats fully recline for a nap between classes; a 15-volt outlet allows students to connect their computer, and the audio system reads MP3 files. The importance of these features to Gen Yers is underscored by a study conducted by MTV. It asked Gen Yers how many hours a day they spent Web surfing, chatting with friends, and downloading music. Surprisingly, the survey revealed that these consumers are spending more than 24 hours a day on these activities—a result that can be explained by Gen Yers' ability to multitask. They can download music, watch TV, and talk to friends via instant messaging all at the same time.

Values represent what is most important in people's lives. Therefore, marketers watch carefully for shifts in consumers' values over time. For example, millions of Americans have an interest in spirituality, as evidenced by the soaring sales of books with religious or spiritual themes and the popularity of television shows with similar themes. Similarly, after the September 11 terrorist attacks, when many people were fearful and concerned about self-protection, gun sales soared as did the sale of drugs to cure anthrax.

McDonald's has responded to cultural differences like no other company. It introduced Teriyaki burgers in Japan, falafel burgers in Egypt, and created a Spam, eggs, and rice breakfast platter for Hawaiians.

PHIL MISLINSKI/GETTY IMAGES

subculture
A homogeneous group of people who share elements of the overall culture as well as unique elements of their own group.

UNDERSTANDING CULTURE DIFFERENCES

 Underlying core values can vary across cultures. Most Americans are more concerned about their health than their weight. But for many Brazilian women, being thin is more important than being healthy. In fact, a recent survey found that 75 percent of Brazilian women over the age of 20 who wanted to lose weight had taken prescription diet drugs for obesity even though less than one-third of the women were obese and the drugs presented the risk of side effects such as heart and lung damage. In contrast, most Chinese women do not place a high value on thinness and show little concern about being overweight.[25]

 Without understanding a culture, a firm has little chance of selling products in it. Like people, products have cultural values and rules that influence their perception and use. Culture, therefore, must be understood before the behavior of individuals within the cultural context can be understood. Colors, for example, may have different meanings in global markets than they do at home. In China, white is the color of mourning and brides wear red. In the United States, black is for mourning and brides wear white. American designers at Universal Studios found they had much to learn about Japanese culture when planning a new theme park for Japan. Surveys showed that many of their original ideas to create Japanese attractions would not appeal to Japanese consumers who were hoping for an authentic American theme park that catered to their cultural differences. After extensive surveys and product testing, the result was a Universal Studios theme park with a more orderly clockwise layout, Japanese-style American food, and a Jurassic Park water slide designed to prevent riders from getting wet.[26]

Language is another important aspect of culture that global marketers must deal with. They must take care in translating product names, slogans, and promotional messages into foreign languages so as not to convey the wrong message. Consider the following examples of blunders made by marketers when delivering their message to Spanish-speaking consumers: General Motors discovered too late that Nova (the name of an economical car) literally means "doesn't go" in Spanish; Coors encouraged its English-speaking customers to "Turn it loose," but the phrase in Spanish means "Suffer from diarrhea"; and when Frank Perdue said, "It takes a tough man to make a tender chicken," Spanish speakers heard "It takes a sexually stimulated man to make a chicken affectionate."

As more companies expand their operations globally, the need to understand the cultures of foreign countries becomes more important. Though marketers expanding into global markets generally adapt their products and business formats to the local culture, some fear that increasing globalization, as well as the proliferation of the Internet, will result in a homogeneous world culture of the future. U.S. companies in particular, they fear, are Americanizing the world by exporting bastions of American culture, such as McDonald's fast-food restaurants, Starbucks coffeehouses, Microsoft software, and American movies and entertainment. Read more about this issue in the "Global Perspectives" box.

SUBCULTURE

A culture can be divided into subcultures on the basis of demographic characteristics, geographic regions, national and ethnic background, political beliefs, and religious beliefs. A **subculture** is a homogeneous group of people who share elements of the overall culture as well as cultural elements unique to their own group. Within sub-

Global Perspectives Global Perspectives Global Perspectives Global Perspectives Global Perspectiv
Global Perspectives Global Perspectives Global Perspectives Global Perspectives Global Perspectiv
bal Perspectives Global Perspectives Global Perspectives Global Perspectives Global Perspectives Global Perspectives Global Perspectiv
Global Perspectives Global Perspectives Global Perspectives Global Perspectives Global Perspectives Global Perspectiv
al Perspectives Global Perspectives GLOBAL PERSPECTIVES Global Perspectives Global Perspectiv
Global Perspectives Global Perspectives Global Perspectives Global Perspectives Global Perspectives Global Perspective
Global Perspectives Global Perspectives Global Perspectives Global Perspectives

> IS GLOBALIZATION CHANGING CULTURES?

Over 150 years ago, Karl Marx and Friedrich Engels described the present day phenomenon of *globalization* when they wrote that people would "find new wants requiring for their satisfaction the products of distant lands and climes." Indeed, as Marx and Engels postulated, "modern industry has established the world market," which today we call *globalization*.

Globalization is not a new concept. Humans have been weaving commercial and cultural connections since the beginning of civilization. Today, computers, the Internet, cellular phones, cable television, and cheaper air transportation have accelerated and complicated these connections. Yet the basic dynamic remains the same: As people cross borders and oceans moving goods and services, their ideas move with them. And cultures change. The difference today is the speed at which these changes take place.

Examples of the fusion of cultures can be found around the world. In a Starbucks in Texas, Italian espresso is served by Hispanic Americans listening to classical music. The classic American Barbie doll comes in 30 nationalities. Students at a high school in Los Angeles speak 32 different native languages. Harley-Davidson outsells Japanese motorcycles in Japan every year. Internet gamers in the United States compete with gamers all over the world from their Sony Playstations. In certain areas of the United States, many promotions and product packages feature both Spanish and English. *Cosmopolitan* magazine, the racy American fashion publication,

is read by some 260,000 Chinese women every month. Revlon adapted the color palette and composition of its cosmetics to suit the Indian skin and climate. Diners across the United States enjoy Japanese sushi, Thai dishes, and Indian food. Many cable channels including TNT, MTV, CNN, and ESPN are available in countries all over the world.

Nevertheless, globalization has become a worrisome issue for many cultures. Sociologists and anthropologists have expressed concern that cultural cloning will be the result of what they regard as the "cultural assault" of ubiquitous Western multinationals such as McDonald's, Coca-Cola, Disney, and Nike; cable channels such as MTV; and even the English language itself. France, in particular, worries that American films and television will replace traditional French entertainment. Indians worry that American junk food, television, films, blue jeans, pornography, and Christian missionaries will ruin traditional Indian values. Australians fear what they call American "cultural imperialism." Others, however, say that cultural change is an inevitable part of national evolution. They argue that cultures take what they want from other cultures and adapt it to their needs. Instead of cultures becoming more uniform, both old and new will tend to transform each other.[27]

What do you think? Are different cultures becoming more alike? If so, is this bad? If cultures are becoming more alike, how does this affect global marketing strategies?

---

cultures, people's attitudes, values, and purchase decisions are even more similar than they are within the broader culture. Subcultural differences may result in considerable variation within a culture in what, how, when, and where people buy goods and services.

In the United States alone, countless subcultures can be identified. Many are concentrated geographically. People belonging to the Mormon religion, for example, are clustered mainly in Utah; Cajuns are located in the bayou regions of southern Louisiana. Hispanics are more predominant in those states that border Mexico, whereas the majority of Chinese, Japanese, and Koreans are found in the Pacific region of the United States.

Other subcultures are geographically dispersed. For example, computer hackers, people who are hearing or visually impaired, Harley-Davidson bikers, military families, university professors, and gays may be found throughout the country. Yet they have identifiable attitudes, values, and needs that distinguish them from the larger culture. For instance, Nokia Corporation sells phones that flash or vibrate for people with hearing problems while other companies, such as Nike and Pfizer, have aired commercials featuring people with various disabilities.[28] Similarly, Burger King has had good results in Chicago targeting people who work unusual hours and crave dinner-type food in the morning by advertising and offering burgers in the morning instead of waiting until 10:30 A.M. like most of its competitors.[29]

Online

Grateful Dead

What kind of marketing program could you design to attract the subculture of Grateful Dead followers? Visit the GD Online Store to see how marketers are currently doing this. What other elements of the site could help you design a successful program?

http://www.dead.net

If marketers can identify subcultures, they can then design special marketing programs to serve their needs. According to the U.S. Census Bureau, the Hispanic population is the largest and fastest growing subculture, increasing at a rate of four times that of the general population. To tap into this large and growing segment, marketers have been spending a larger percentage of their marketing budgets advertising to Hispanics. Companies like Procter & Gamble, Anheuser-Busch, Hershey Foods, and Chuck E. Cheese all have Hispanic marketing campaigns, as do major league sports teams like the Texas Rangers and the Dallas Mavericks. The campaigns often feature both English and Spanish advertising and appeal to cultural pride.[31]

Other companies have been successful in targeting much smaller subcultures that are often overlooked. For example, Shaklee Corporation, a multilevel marketing company, has targeted subcultures such as the Amish, Mennonites, and Hasidic Jews. To recruit salespeople in these subcultures, Shaklee caters to their special needs. For example, Amish and Mennonite salespeople can earn a "bonus buggy" instead of the more traditional new car. To accommodate Hasidic customers, Shaklee toughened standards on its kosher products.[32]

SOCIAL CLASS

The United States, like other societies, does have a social class system. A **social class** is a group of people who are considered nearly equal in status or community esteem, who regularly socialize among themselves both formally and informally, and who share behavioral norms.

A number of techniques have been used to measure social class, and a number of criteria have been used to define it. One view of contemporary U.S. status structure is shown in Exhibit 5.6.

As you can see from Exhibit 5.6, the upper and upper middle classes comprise the small segment of affluent and wealthy Americans. The upper social classes are more likely than other classes to contribute something to society—for example, by volunteer work or active participation in civic affairs. In terms of consumer buying patterns, the affluent are more likely to own their own home and purchase new cars and trucks and are less likely to smoke. The very rich flex their financial muscles by spending more on vacation homes, vacations and cruises, and housekeeping and gardening services. The most affluent consumers are more likely to attend art auctions and galleries, dance performances, operas, the theater, museums, concerts, and sporting events. Marketers often pay attention to the super-wealthy. For example, the Mercedes-Benz Maybach 62, touted as the "world's most luxurious car," is aimed at this group. Priced at $353,000, the car features electronic doors, reclining seats with footrests, and a champagne cooler.[33]

The majority of Americans today define themselves as middle class, regardless of their actual income or educational attainment. This phenomenon is most likely due to the fact that working-class Americans tend to aspire to the middle-class lifestyle while some of those who do achieve affluence may downwardly aspire to respectable middle-class status as a matter of principle. Attaining goals and achieving status and prestige are important to middle-class consumers. People falling into the middle class live in the gap between the haves and the have-nots. They aspire to the lifestyle of the more affluent but are constrained by the economic realities and cautious attitudes they share with the working class.

The working class is a distinct subset of the middle class. Interest in organized labor is one of the most common attributes among the working class. This group

social class
A group of people in a society who are considered nearly equal in status or community esteem, who regularly socialize among themselves both formally and informally, and who share behavioral norms.

EXHIBIT 5.6

U.S. Social Class

Upper Classes		
Capitalist class	1%	People whose investment decisions shape the national economy; income mostly from assets, earned or inherited; university connections
Upper middle class	14%	Upper-level managers, professionals, owners of medium-sized businesses; college-educated; family income nearly twice national average
Middle Classes		
Middle class	33%	Middle-level white-collar, top-level blue-collar; education past high school typical; income somewhat above national average
Working class	32%	Middle-level blue-collar, lower-level white-collar; income slightly below national average
Lower Classes		
Working poor	11–12%	Low-paid service workers and operatives; some high school education; below mainstream in living standard but above poverty line
Underclass	8–9%	People who are not regularly employed and who depend primarily on the welfare system for sustenance; little schooling; living standard below poverty line

SOURCE: Adapted from Richard P. Coleman, "The Continuing Significance of Social Class to Marketing," *Journal of Consumer Research*, December 1983, 267; Dennis Gilbert and Joseph A. Kahl, *The American Class Structure: A Synthesis* (Homewood, IL: Dorsey Press, 1982), ch. 11.

EXHIBIT 5.7

Social Class and Education

Percentage of adults in self-identified social classes who have a bachelor's degree or higher

Social Class	Percent
Upper	61
Middle	34
Lower	20

SOURCE: "The New Working Class," *American Demographics*, January 1998, 51–55.

often rates job security as the most important reason for taking a job. The working-class person depends heavily on relatives and the community for economic and emotional support. The emphasis on family ties is one sign of the group's intensely local view of the world. They like the local news far more than do middle-class audiences who favor national and world coverage. They are also more likely to vacation closer to home.

Lifestyle distinctions between the social classes are greater than the distinctions within a given class. The most significant separation between the classes is the one between the middle and lower classes. It is here that the major shift in lifestyles appears. Members of the lower class typically fall at or below the poverty level in terms of income. This social class has the highest unemployment rate, and many individuals or families are subsidized through the welfare system. Many are illiterate, with little formal education. Compared to more affluent consumers, lower-class consumers have poorer diets and typically purchase very different types of foods when they shop.

Social class is typically measured as a combination of occupation, income, education, wealth, and other variables. For instance, affluent upper-class consumers are more likely to be salaried executives or self-employed professionals with at least an undergraduate degree. Working-class or middle-class consumers are more likely to be hourly service workers or blue-collar employees with only a high school education. Educational attainment, however, seems to be the most reliable indicator of a person's social and economic status (see Exhibit 5.7). Those with college degrees or graduate degrees are more likely to fall into the upper classes, while those people with some college experience but no degree fall closest to traditional concepts of the middle class.

Marketers are interested in social class for two main reasons. First, social class often indicates which medium to use for advertising. Suppose an insurance company seeks to sell its policies to middle-class families. It might advertise during the local evening news because middle-class families tend to watch more television than other classes do. If the company wants to sell more policies to upscale individuals, it might place a print ad in a business publication like the *Wall Street Journal*. The Internet, long the domain of more educated and affluent families, is be-

5 **Identify and understand the cultural factors that affect consumer buying decisions**

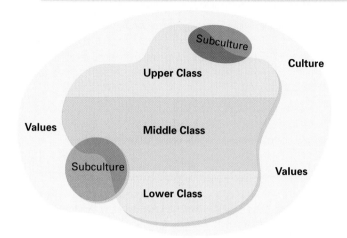

coming an important advertising outlet for advertisers hoping to reach blue-collar workers and homemakers. As the middle class rapidly adopts the medium, marketers are having to do more research to find out which Web sites will reach their audience.

Second, knowing what products appeal to which social classes can help marketers determine where to best distribute their products. For example, a survey of consumer spending in the Washington, D.C. area reveals a stark contrast between Brie-eaters and Velveeta-eaters. The buyers of Brie, the soft and savory French cheese, are concentrated in the upscale neighborhoods of Northwest D.C. and the western suburbs of Montgomery County, Maryland, and Fairfax County, Virginia, where most residents are executives, white-collar professionals, or politicians. Brie fans tend to be college-educated professionals with six-figure incomes and an activist spirit. In contrast, aficionados of Velveeta, processed cheese marketed by Kraft, are concentrated in the middle-class, family-filled suburbs of Prince George's County and the predominantly black D.C. neighborhoods. Velveeta buyers tend to be married with children, high school educated, and employed at modestly paying service and blue-collar jobs.[34]

6 SOCIAL INFLUENCES ON CONSUMER BUYING DECISIONS

Identify and understand the social factors that affect consumer buying decisions

Most consumers are likely to seek out the opinions of others to reduce their search and evaluation effort or uncertainty, especially as the perceived risk of the decision increases. Consumers may also seek out others' opinions for guidance on new products or services, products with image-related attributes, or products where attribute information is lacking or uninformative. Specifically, consumers interact socially with reference groups, opinion leaders, and family members to obtain product information and decision approval.

REFERENCE GROUPS

reference group
A group in society that influences an individual's purchasing behavior.

primary membership group
A reference group with which people interact regularly in an informal, face-to-face manner, such as family, friends, or fellow employees.

secondary membership group
A reference group with which people associate less consistently and more formally than a primary membership group, such as a club, professional group, or religious group.

aspirational reference group
A group that someone would like to join.

norm
A value or attitude deemed acceptable by a group.

All the formal and informal groups that influence the buying behavior of an individual are that person's **reference groups.** Consumers may use products or brands to identify with or become a member of a group. They learn from observing how members of their reference groups consume, and they use the same criteria to make their own consumer decisions.

Reference groups can be categorized very broadly as either direct or indirect (see Exhibit 5.8). Direct reference groups are face-to-face membership groups that touch people's lives directly. They can be either primary or secondary. **Primary membership groups** include all groups with which people interact regularly in an informal, face-to-face manner, such as family, friends, and coworkers. In contrast, people associate with **secondary membership groups** less consistently and more formally. These groups might include clubs, professional groups, and religious groups.

Consumers also are influenced by many indirect, nonmembership reference groups they do not belong to. **Aspirational reference groups** are those a person would like to join. To join an aspirational group, a person must at least conform to the norms of that group. (**Norms** are the values and attitudes deemed acceptable

EXHIBIT 5.8

Types of Reference Groups

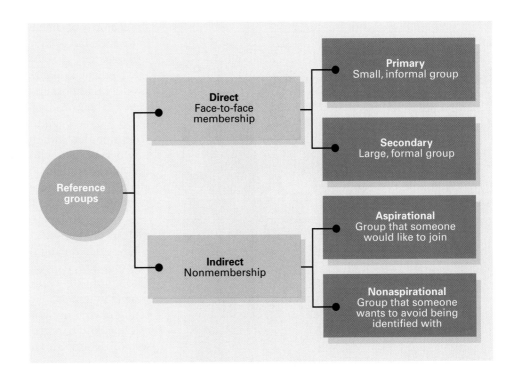

by the group.) Thus, a person who wants to be elected to public office may begin to dress more conservatively, as other politicians do. He or she may go to many of the restaurants and social engagements that city and business leaders attend and try to play a role that is acceptable to voters and other influential people. Similarly, teenagers today may dye their hair and experiment with body piercing and tattoos. Athletes are an aspirational group for several market segments. To appeal to the younger market, Coca-Cola signed LeBron James to an endorsement contract. James, the number one pick in the NBA draft, went to the pros straight from high school. Coca-Cola hopes this influential person will encourage consumers to drink Coke because they would like to identify with the basketball star.[35]

Nonaspirational reference groups, or dissociative groups, influence our behavior when we try to maintain distance from them. A consumer may avoid buying some types of clothing or car, going to certain restaurants or stores, or even buying a home in a certain neighborhood in order to avoid being associated with a particular group.

The activities, values, and goals of reference groups directly influence consumer behavior. For marketers, reference groups have three important implications: (1) they serve as information sources and influence perceptions; (2) they affect an individual's aspiration levels; and (3) their norms either constrain or stimulate consumer behavior. For example, Teenage Research Unlimited, an Illinois research firm devoted to uncovering what's cool in the teen market, recently identified four loose groups of today's teens based on their interests in clothes, music, and activities. Tracking these groups reveals how products become cool and how groups influence the adoption of cool products by other groups. According to Teenage Research Unlimited, a trend or fad often starts with "Edge" teens who have the most innovative tastes. These teens are on the cutting edge of fashion and music, and they wear their attitude all over their bodies in the form of tattoos, body piercing, studded jewelry, or colored tresses. Certain fads embraced by Edgers will spark an interest in the small group of teens called "Influencers," who project the look other teens covet. Influencers also create their own trends like rap music, baggy jeans, and pro sports clothes. Once a fad is embraced and adopted by Influencers, the look becomes cool and desirable. "Conformers" and "Passives" comprise

nonaspirational reference group
A group with which an individual does not want to associate.

Japanese teenage girls have long provided the marketing litmus test companies need before launching new products. Perhaps their success in this area is due to the fact that they are caught in a pivotal clash between a tradition of collectivism and a growing sense of individualism.

the majority of the teen population, but they will not embrace a fad until it gets its seal of approval from the Influencers.[36]

Understanding the effect of reference groups on a product is important for marketers as they track the life cycle of their products. Retailer Abercrombie & Fitch noticed it was beginning to lose its target audience of college students when its stores began attracting large numbers of high school students trying to be more like the college students. To solve the problem, A&F created its Hollister store chain specifically for high school students.[37]

GLOBAL In Japan, companies have long relied on the nation's high school girls to give them advice during product testing. Fads that catch on among teenage girls often become big trends throughout the country and among Japanese consumers in general. Food manufacturers frequently recruit Tokyo schoolgirls to sample potato chip recipes or chocolate bars. Television networks survey high school girls to fine-tune story lines for higher ratings on prime-time shows. Other companies pay girls to keep diaries of what they buy. In 1995, Warner-Lambert hired high school girls to help choose a new gum flavor. After extensive chewing and comparing, the girls settled on a flavor that became Trickle, now Japan's best-selling bubble gum.[38]

OPINION LEADERS

Reference groups frequently include individuals known as group leaders, or **opinion leaders**—those who influence others. Obviously, it is important for marketing managers to persuade such people to purchase their goods or services. Many products and services that are integral parts of Americans' lives today got their initial boost from opinion leaders. For example, DVDs and SUVs (sport utility vehicles) were purchased by opinion leaders well ahead of the general public. Exhibit 5.9 lists some products and services for which individuals often seek the advice of an opinion leader before purchasing.

Opinion leaders are often the first to try new products and services out of pure curiosity. They are typically self-indulgent, making them more likely to explore unproven but intriguing products and services. Technology companies have found that teenagers, because of their willingness to experiment, are key opinion leaders for the success of new technologies. For example, text messaging became popular with teenagers before it gained widespread appeal. As a result, many technology companies include it in their marketing programs targeted to teens. Similarly, Jet Blue Airways, Redken, FreshLook Color Contacts, and Bombay Sapphire gin advertise on *Fashion Week TV*. The show reaches 20,000 viewers described as "fashion insiders and media and socialite attendees." In addition to their commercials, these advertisers are featured in *Fashion Week* programs and VIP lounges. One VIP lounge showcased airline seats and flight attendants both outfitted in Jet Blue regalia. The flight attendants wore FreshLook Contacts and served Bombay Sapphire martinis. By reaching opinion leaders, these companies hope to start a trend that will carry into the mass market.[39]

Opinion leadership is a casual, face-to-face phenomenon and usually inconspicuous, so locating opinion leaders can be a challenge. Thus, marketers often try to create opinion leaders. They may use high school cheerleaders to model

opinion leader
An individual who influences the opinions of others.

© PETER M. WILSON/CORBIS

EXHIBIT 5.9

Words of Wisdom: Opinion Leaders' Consumer Clout Extends Far Beyond Their Own Purchases

	Average Number of People to Whom Opinion Leaders Recommended Products* in the Past Year	Millions of Recommendations Made
Restaurant	5.0	70
Vacation destination	5.1	44
TV show	4.9	45
Car	4.1	29
Retail store	4.7	29
Clothing	4.5	24
Consumer electronics	4.5	16
Office equipment	5.8	12
Stock, mutual fund, CD, etc.	3.4	12

*Among those who recommended the product at all.

SOURCE: Roper Starch Worldwide, Inc., New York, NY. Adapted from "Maximizing the Market with Influentials," *American Demographics*, July 1995, 42.

new fall fashions or civic leaders to promote insurance, new cars, and other merchandise. Revatex, the maker of JNCO jeans, sponsors extreme-sports athletes who appeal to the teen market. It also gives free clothes to trendsetters among teens in the hopes they will influence others to purchase the brand. JNCO outfits big-name DJs in the rave scene, as well as members of hip, alternative bands favored by the teen crowd. Similarly, the Web site of New York retailer Alloy Online (**http://www. alloyonline. com**) offers style tips, quizzes on topics like "What is your ideal guy type?" and gossip about teen idols like Britney Spears. It encourages teens to offer feedback about their likes and dislikes in a section called "Dig or Dis."[40] The "Ethics in Marketing" box questions how much marketers should target teenagers.

On a national level, companies sometimes use movie stars, sports figures, and other celebrities to promote products, hoping they are appropriate opinion leaders. Nike, for example, signed golf superstar Tiger Woods as a spokesperson for its products. The company hopes that consumers will see an affinity between the values that Woods represents and the values that Nike represents—earned success, discipline, hard work, achievement, and integrity. Nike also believes that the quality of Woods's golf game will be associated with the quality and value of its products. One year after Woods began appearing in ads and on the fairway with Nike's new line of golf balls, the company's market share tripled.[42]

The effectiveness of celebrity endorsements depends largely on how credible and attractive the spokesperson is and how familiar people are with him or her. Endorsements are most likely to succeed if an association between the spokesperson and the product can be reasonably established. For example, comedian Bill Cosby failed as an endorser for financial products but succeeded with such products as Kodak cameras and Jell-O gelatin. Consumers could not mentally link Bill Cosby with serious investment decisions but could associate him with leisure activities and everyday consumption. Additionally, in selecting a celebrity endorser, marketers must consider the broader meanings associated with the endorser. Although the endorser may have certain attributes that are desirable for endorsing the product, he or she may also have other attributes that are inappropriate.

A marketing manager can also try to use opinion leaders through group sanctioning or referrals. For example, some companies sell products endorsed by the American Heart Association or the American Cancer Society. Marketers also seek endorsements from schools, churches, cities, the military, and fraternal organizations as a form of group opinion leadership. Salespeople often ask to use opinion leaders' names as a means of achieving greater personal influence in a sales presentation.

FAMILY

The family is the most important social institution for many consumers, strongly influencing values, attitudes, self-concept—and buying behavior. For example, a family that strongly values good health will have a grocery list distinctly different from that of a family that views every dinner as a gourmet event. Moreover, the family is responsible for the **socialization process**, the passing down of cultural

socialization process
How cultural values and norms are passed down to children.

> ## SHOULD MARKETERS TARGET TEENS AT SCHOOL?

Marketers focus on identifying unmet needs, developing products and services to meet those needs, and finding a way to sell products to those consumers. Although the process sounds simple, sometimes the way a product is marketed arouses considerable criticism.

For example, manufacturers know that kids, teenagers, and Gen Yers are the biggest consumers of soft drinks and snack foods. Companies, such as Coca-Cola and PepsiCo, also know that brand loyalty for these products usually develops during the teen years. Thus, it is critical to the manufacturers' long-term success to convince teens to choose their brand. To achieve this objective, both Coca-Cola and PepsiCo have entered into long-term, exclusive contracts with schools to distribute their products through vending machines. These contracts have been criticized because 25 percent of American children are obese or at risk for obesity and there are three times as many overweight high school students today as there were 20 years ago. Some critics attribute the increase in obesity to the greater availability of soft drinks and snack foods in schools.

Some evidence suggests that these products are displacing healthier foods in students' diets. For example, a study published by the *American Journal of Health Promotion* showed a decrease in the "consumption of breakfast, fruits, vegetables and milk as [students] moved from elementary to junior high and middle school. Between the third to the eighth grades, fruit consumption fell by 41 percent and vegetable consumption dropped by 25 percent. Soft drink consumption tripled, often at the expense of healthier alternatives, such as milk and fruit juice." Still other critics blame soft drinks for tooth decay, and one study even linked soft drink consumption to fractured bones in high school girls.

The heavy criticism has prompted Coca-Cola and PepsiCo to create healthy new products as well as market existing nutritious products to young Americans. PepsiCo launched its Health Is Power (HIP) School Resource Guide, which provides educators and administrators with the tools to successfully integrate PepsiCo products into schools. Moreover, the HIP guide offers tips on teaching kids how to make healthy food and beverage choices and integrate fitness into their daily activities.

Although Coca-Cola has taken some steps in addressing the obesity issue, it has not been nearly as active as PepsiCo. Still Coca-Cola and its bottlers have made a commitment to guidelines governing school beverage distribution that can be voluntarily adopted by schools.[41]

So what do you think? Should Coca-Cola and PepsiCo be able to target kids and teens at school? Should the companies eliminate the soft drinks and snack food in school vending machines altogether?

values and norms to children. Children learn by observing their parents' consumption patterns, and so they will tend to shop in a similar pattern.

Decision-making roles among family members tend to vary significantly, depending on the type of item purchased. Family members assume a variety of roles in the purchase process. *Initiators* are the ones who suggest, initiate, or plant the seed for the purchase process. The initiator can be any member of the family. For example, Sister might initiate the product search by asking for a new bicycle as a birthday present. *Influencers* are those members of the family whose opinions are valued. In our example, Mom might function as a price-range watchdog, an influencer whose main role is to veto or approve price ranges. Brother may give his opinion on certain makes of bicycles. The *decision maker* is the member of the family who actually makes the decision to buy or not to buy. For example, Dad or Mom is likely to choose the final brand and model of bicycle to buy after seeking further information from Sister about cosmetic features such as color and imposing additional criteria of his or her own, such as durability and safety. The *purchaser* (probably Dad or Mom) is the one who actually exchanges money for the product. Finally, the *consumer* is the actual user—Sister, in the case of the bicycle.

Marketers should consider family purchase situations along with the distribution of consumer and decision-maker roles among family members. Ordinary marketing views the individual as both decision maker and consumer. Family marketing adds several other possibilities: Sometimes more than one family member or all family members are involved in the decision; sometimes only children are involved in the decision; sometimes more than one consumer is involved; and sometimes the decision maker and the consumer are different people. Exhibit 5.10 represents the patterns of family purchasing relationships that are possible.

EXHIBIT 5.10

Relationships among Purchasers and Consumers in the Family

		Purchase Decision Maker		
		Parent(s) Only	Child/Children Only	Some or All Family Members
Consumer	Parent(s)	golf clubs cosmetics wine	Mother's Day card	Christmas gifts minivan
	Child/ Children	diapers breakfast cereal	candy small toys	bicycle
	Some Family Members	videos long-distance phone service	children's movies	computers sports events
	All Family Members	clothing life insurance	fast-food restaurant	swim club membership vacations

SOURCE: From "Pulling the Family's Strings" by Robert Boutillier, *American Demographics,* August 1993. © 1993 PRIMEDIA Intertec, Stamford, CT. Reprinted with permission.

Children can have great influence over the purchase decisions of their parents. In many families, with both parents working and short on time, children are encouraged to participate. In addition, children in single-parent households become more involved in family decisions at an earlier age. Children are especially influential in decisions about food and eating out. Therefore, food companies listen closely to what children want. Children also are more interested in entertainment than food. Therefore, McDonald's and Burger King spend about $4 billion annually on toys for their kid meals; Quaker Oatmeal now features hidden treasures; Heinz ketchup is available in funky purple; and Parkay margarine comes in shocking pink and electric blue. Both the ketchup and the margarine come in squeezable bottles designed to allow small hands to create pictures. Promotions for food products aimed at children include a Web site that illustrates how to build a fort with french fries and books that teach children to count using Cheerios, M&Ms, and Oreos.[43] Children influence purchase decisions for many more products and services than food. Even though they are usually not the actual purchasers of such items, children often participate in decisions about toys, clothes, vacations, recreation, automobiles, and many other products.

REVIEW LEARNING OBJECTIVE

6 | **Identify and understand the social factors that affect consumer buying decisions**

Reference Groups	Direct		Indirect	
	Primary	Secondary	Aspirational	Non-Aspirational

Opinion Leaders	People you know	Celebrities

Family	Socialization Process		
	Initiators	Decision Makers	Consumers
	Influencers		Purchasers

7 INDIVIDUAL INFLUENCES ON CONSUMER BUYING DECISIONS

Identify and understand the individual factors that affect consumer buying decisions

A person's buying decisions are also influenced by personal characteristics that are unique to each individual, such as gender; age and life-cycle stage; and personality, self-concept, and lifestyle. Individual characteristics are generally stable over the course of one's life. For instance, most people do not change their gender, and the act of changing personality or lifestyle requires a complete reorientation of one's life. In the case of age and life-cycle stage, these changes occur gradually over time.

GameGirlz
GameSpot
What kinds of games are available at the Game-Girlz Web site? How do the games "for" girls differ from the games "for" boys at GameSpot?

http://www.game-girlz.com
http://www.gamespot.com

Online

GENDER

Physiological differences between men and women result in different needs, such as health and beauty products. Just as important are the distinct cultural, social, and economic roles played by men and women and the effects that these have on their decision-making processes. For example, in addition to the many networks with programming targeted to women, a new one has been launched for men—Spike TV, which calls itself the "first network for men." Two new magazines are geared to men who like to shop: *Cargo*, the first to be released, is modeled after *Lucky*, a women's shopping magazine; *Vitals*, dubbed a "luxury shopping magazine" for men, was launched at the end of 2004.[44]

 Indeed, men and women do shop differently. Studies show that men and women share similar motivations in terms of where to shop—that is, seeking reasonable prices, merchandise quality, and a friendly, low-pressure environment—but they don't necessarily feel the same about shopping in general. Most women enjoy shopping. Their male counterparts claim to dislike the experience and shop only out of necessity. Further, men desire simple shopping experiences, stores with less variety, and convenience. Stores that are easy to shop in, are near home or office, or have knowledgeable personnel appeal more to men than to women.[45] The Internet appeals to men who find its ease of use a more enjoyable way to shop for clothing and gifts. Many Internet retailers are designing their sites to attract male gift buyers. Banana Republic's Web site prompts customers purchasing gifts to choose a price range. The site then returns five to six different suggestions. To help its male shoppers, intimate apparel retailer Victoria's Secret lets women create password-protected wish lists and then zap them to their significant others to ensure there's no mistaking colors or sizes.

Trends in gender marketing are influenced by the changing roles of men and women in society. For instance, as women around the world are working and earning more, many industries are attracting new customers by marketing to women. The video game industry, which has traditionally targeted 18- to 22-year-old men with games featuring guns and explosions, is beginning to develop new games based on popular female characters like Barbie and Nancy Drew aimed at capturing female customers. In South Korea, major credit card companies are now targeting working women by offering credit card benefits attractive to women such as discounts at department and bridal stores and disfigurement insurance for plastic surgery.[46]

The changing roles of women are also forcing companies that have traditionally targeted women to develop new strategies. Revlon stopped using glamorous supermodels to promote its products because it felt traditional "Cindy Crawford" ads "conveyed a man's view of women, not a woman's."[47] The company attempted to modernize its image by using new unknown models in ads highlighting universal truths about being a woman, such as a woman checking her reflection in the frozen food section of the grocery store. But the campaign did not work, and after seven months Revlon began using well-known models again with the new positioning statement "Be Unforgettable." The focus of the new campaign was on product benefits and promoting the Revlon brand name. It is often difficult for marketers to know how to respond as gender roles evolve and change.

AGE AND FAMILY LIFE-CYCLE STAGE

The age and family life-cycle stage of a consumer can have a significant impact on consumer behavior. How old a consumer is generally indicates what products he or she may be interested in purchasing. Consumer tastes in food, clothing, cars,

AP/WIDE WORLD PHOTOS

As the proportion of children in the U.S. population swells, this market segment is becoming increasingly important to marketers wanting to influence the kids who influence their parents' purchasing habits. Heinz's colored ketchups in the E-Z Squirt bottles are designed to do just that.

Create a day you'll treasure forever
614 pages to inspire you!

dream dresses
- ELEGANT
- FAIRY-TALE
- SEXY

"WOW!" FLOWERS
25 NEW COLOR COMBINATIONS

talk-of-the-town weddings
DETAILS YOUR GUESTS WILL NEVER FORGET

MAKEUP THAT LASTS
look great in every photo

Candlelight
Bask in the glow of a romantic reception

FROM THE PUBLISHERS OF VOGUE & GLAMOUR

AP/WIDE WORLD PHOTOS

Age and position in the family life cycle can affect consumer behavior. Since many women use the same products and brands as they did when they got married, marketers use magazines like *Bride's* to influence consumer behavior for products unrelated to a wedding, for example appliances and homekeeping products.

furniture, and recreation are often age related. For example, researchers from *American Demographics* magazine and the research firm Encino examined the correlation between television shows and the age of viewers. As expected, the target audience of many TV shows directly coincided with the viewers. *American Juniors* on Fox was most popular with the 13–16 age range, *8 Simple Rules for Dating My Teenage Daughter* on ABC was most popular with the 17–20 age range, and *Big Brother 4* on CBS was most popular with the 21–25 age range. Similarly, there are very few general audience magazines. Almost all are targeted to a specific age and/or ethnic group.[48]

Related to a person's age is his or her place in the family life cycle. As Chapter 7 explains in more detail, the *family life cycle* is an orderly series of stages through which consumers' attitudes and behavioral tendencies evolve through maturity, experience, and changing income and status. Marketers often define their target markets in terms of family life cycle, such as "young singles," "young married with children," and "middle-aged married without children." For instance, young singles spend more than average on alcoholic beverages, education, and entertainment. New parents typically increase their spending on health care, clothing, housing, and food and decrease their spending on alcohol, education, and transportation. Households with older children spend more on food, entertainment, personal care products, and education, as well as cars and gasoline. After their children leave home, spending by older couples on vehicles, women's clothing, health care, and long-distance calls typically increases. For instance, the presence of children in the home is the most significant determinant of the type of vehicle that's driven off the new car lot. Parents are the ultimate need-driven car consumers, requiring larger cars and trucks to haul their children and all their belongings. It comes as no surprise then that for all households with children, SUVs rank either first or second among new-vehicle purchases followed by minivans.[49]

Marketers should also be aware of the many nontraditional life-cycle paths that are common today and provide insights into the needs and wants of such consumers as divorced parents, lifelong singles, and childless couples. Three decades ago, traditional families comprised of married couples with children under 18 accounted for nearly a majority of U.S. households. Today, traditional families make up only 23 percent of all households, while people living alone or with nonfamily members represent more than 30 percent. Furthermore, according to the U.S. Census Bureau, the number of single-mother households grew by 25 percent over the last decade. The shift toward more single-parent households is part of a broader societal change that has put more women on the career track. Although many marketers continue to be wary of targeting nontraditional families, Charles Schwab targeted single mothers in a recent advertising campaign featuring Sarah Ferguson, the Duchess of York and a divorced mom. The idea was to appeal to single mothers' heightened awareness of the need for financial self-sufficiency.[50]

PERSONALITY, SELF-CONCEPT, AND LIFESTYLE

Each consumer has a unique personality. **Personality** is a broad concept that can be thought of as a way of organizing and grouping how an individual typically

personality
A way of organizing and grouping the consistencies of an individual's reactions to situations.

EXHIBIT 5.11

Some Common Personality Traits

• Adaptability	• Deference
• Need for affiliation	• Defensiveness
• Aggressiveness	• Emotionalism
• Need for achievement	• Orderliness
• Ascendancy	• Sociability
• Autonomy	• Stability
• Dominance	• Self-confidence

self-concept
How consumers perceive themselves in terms of attitudes, perceptions, beliefs, and self-evaluations.

ideal self-image
The way an individual would like to be.

real self-image
The way an individual actually perceives himself or herself.

reacts to situations. Thus, personality combines psychological makeup and environmental forces. It includes people's underlying dispositions, especially their most dominant characteristics. Although personality is one of the least useful concepts in the study of consumer behavior, some marketers believe that personality influences the types and brands of products purchased. For instance, the type of car, clothes, or jewelry a consumer buys may reflect one or more personality traits. Personality traits like those listed in Exhibit 5.11 may be used to describe a consumer's personality.

Self-concept, or self-perception, is how consumers perceive themselves. Self-concept includes attitudes, perceptions, beliefs, and self-evaluations. Although self-concept may change, the change is often gradual. Through self-concept, people define their identity, which in turn provides for consistent and coherent behavior.

Self-concept combines the **ideal self-image** (the way an individual would like to be) and the **real self-image** (how an individual actually perceives himself or herself). Generally, we try to raise our real self-image toward our ideal (or at least narrow the gap). Consumers seldom buy products that jeopardize their self-image. For example, someone who sees herself as a trendsetter wouldn't buy clothing that doesn't project a contemporary image.

Human behavior depends largely on self-concept. Because consumers want to protect their identity as individuals, the products they buy, the stores they patronize, and the credit cards they carry support their self-image. No other product quite reflects a person's self-image as much as the car he or she drives. For example, many young consumers do not like family sedans like the Honda Accord or Toyota Camry and say they would buy one for their mom, but not for themselves. Likewise, younger car buyers may avoid minivans because they do not want to sacrifice the youthful image they have of themselves just because they have new responsibilities. To combat decreasing sales, marketers of the Nissan Quest minivan decided to reposition it as something other than a "mom mobile" or "soccer mom car." They chose the ad copy "Passion built it. Passion will fill it up," followed by "What if we made a minivan that changed the way people think of minivans?"[51]

By influencing the degree to which consumers perceive a good or service to be self-relevant, marketers can affect consumers' motivation to learn about, shop for, and buy a certain brand. Marketers also consider self-concept important because it helps explain the relationship between individuals' perceptions of themselves and their consumer behavior.

An important component of self-concept is *body image*, the perception of the attractiveness of one's own physical features. For example, individuals who have cosmetic surgery often experience significant improvement in their overall body image and self-concept. Moreover, a person's perception of body image can be a stronger reason for weight loss than either good health or other social factors.[52] With the median age of Americans rising, many companies are introducing products and services aimed at aging baby boomers who are concerned about their age and physical appearance. Sales of hair-coloring products for men, for instance, have more than doubled over the last decade, and television and print advertisements aimed at getting men to dye the gray out of their hair have tripled. Similarly, many companies including PepsiCo with Tropicana juices and Eli Lilly with its Cialis product are repositioning their products to focus on lifestyle. Bank of America is featuring Harley-riding seniors in its advertisements for its private-bank marketing campaign, and high-end anti-aging creams are flying off department store shelves. Finally marketers are also seeing boomers respond to products aimed at younger audiences. For instance, new Starwood "W" Hotels, designed and advertised to attract a young, hip crowd, are attracting large numbers of boomers.[53]

Personality and self-concept are reflected in lifestyle. A **lifestyle** is a mode of living, as identified by a person's activities, interests, and opinions. *Psychographics* is the analytical technique used to examine consumer lifestyles and to categorize consumers. Unlike personality characteristics, which are hard to describe and measure, lifestyle characteristics are useful in segmenting and targeting consumers. Lifestyle and psychographic analysis explicitly addresses the way consumers outwardly express their inner selves in their social and cultural environment.

Many companies now use psychographics to better understand their market segments. For many years, marketers selling products to mothers conveniently assumed that all moms were fairly homogeneous and concerned about the same things—the health and well-being of their children—and that they could all be reached with a similar message. But recent lifestyle research has shown that there are traditional, blended, and nontraditional moms, and companies like Procter & Gamble and Pillsbury are using strategies to reach these different types of mothers. Psychographics is also effective with other segments. Gap, one of the leading retailers in advertising a lifestyle, consistently uses celebrities to market each season's line. In an attempt to bring back baby boomers and their children, Gap signed Madonna and Missy Elliot for its fall line. The ad featured cord jeans for women in 30- and 60-second TV spots. To further entice consumers, a limited edition CD remix was offered in stores and online.[54] Psychographics and lifestyle segmentation are discussed in more detail in Chapter 7.

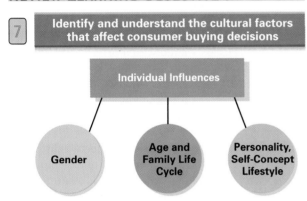

REVIEW LEARNING OBJECTIVE 7

7 Identify and understand the cultural factors that affect consumer buying decisions

Individual Influences

Gender

Age and Family Life Cycle

Personality, Self-Concept Lifestyle

8 PSYCHOLOGICAL INFLUENCES ON CONSUMER BUYING DECISIONS

Identify and understand the psychological factors that affect consumer buying decisions

An individual's buying decisions are further influenced by psychological factors: perception, motivation, learning, and beliefs and attitudes. These factors are what consumers use to interact with their world. They are the tools consumers use to recognize their feelings, gather and analyze information, formulate thoughts and opinions, and take action. Unlike the other three influences on consumer behavior, psychological influences can be affected by a person's environment because they are applied on specific occasions. For example, you will perceive different stimuli and process these stimuli in different ways depending on whether you are sitting in class concentrating on the instructor, sitting outside of class talking to friends, or sitting in your dorm room watching television.

PERCEPTION

The world is full of stimuli. A stimulus is any unit of input affecting one or more of the five senses: sight, smell, taste, touch, hearing. The process by which we select, organize, and interpret these stimuli into a meaningful and coherent picture is called **perception**. In essence, perception is how we see the world around us and how we recognize that we need some help in making a purchasing decision.

People cannot perceive every stimulus in their environment. Therefore, they use **selective exposure** to decide which stimuli to notice and which to ignore. A typical consumer is exposed to more than 2,500 advertising messages a day but notices only between 11 and 20.

The familiarity of an object, contrast, movement, intensity (such as increased volume), and smell are cues that influence perception. Consumers use these cues

lifestyle
A mode of living as identified by a person's activities, interests, and opinions.

perception
The process by which people select, organize, and interpret stimuli into a meaningful and coherent picture.

selective exposure
The process whereby a consumer notices certain stimuli and ignores others.

FAQs

Which is more important in the purchase decision, perception or reality? Find out by watching the video FAQ on Xtra!

to identify and define products and brands. The shape of a product's packaging, such as Coca-Cola's signature contour bottle, for instance, can influence perception. Color is another cue, and it plays a key role in consumers' perceptions. Packaged foods manufacturers use color to trigger unconscious associations for grocery shoppers who typically make their shopping decisions in the blink of an eye. Red, for instance, used on packages of Campbell's soups and SunMaid raisins, is associated with prolonged and increased eating. Green is associated with environmental goodness and healthy, low-fat foods. Healthy Choice entrées and SnackWells cookies use green. Premium products, like Sheba cat food and Ben & Jerry's ice cream, use black and gold on their packaging to convey their use of superior ingredients.[55] The shape and look of a product's packaging can also influence perception. Ivory Soap recently began packaging about one-third of its product in special packaging based on the original late nineteenth-century design. The company hopes to take advantage of a consumer trend toward simplifying life by emphasizing the brand's heritage and image of purity.[56]

What is perceived by consumers may also depend on the stimuli's vividness or shock value. Graphic warnings of the hazards associated with a product's use are perceived more readily and remembered more accurately than less vivid warnings or warnings that are written in text. "Sexier" ads excel at attracting the attention of younger consumers. Companies like Calvin Klein and Guess use sensuous ads to "cut through the clutter" of competing ads and other stimuli to capture the attention of the target audience.

Two other concepts closely related to selective exposure are selective distortion and selective retention. **Selective distortion** occurs when consumers change or distort information that conflicts with their feelings or beliefs. For example, suppose a college student buys a Sonicblue Rio MP3 player. After the purchase, if the student gets new information about an alternative brand, such as an Apple iPod, he or she may distort the information to make it more consistent with the prior view that the Sonicblue Rio is just as good as the iPod, if not better. Business travelers who fly often may distort or discount information about airline crashes because they must use air travel constantly in their jobs.

Selective retention is remembering only information that supports personal feelings or beliefs. The consumer forgets all information that may be inconsistent. After reading a pamphlet that contradicts one's political beliefs, for instance, a person may forget many of the points outlined in it. Similarly, consumers may see a news report on suspected illegal practices by their favorite retail store, but soon forget the reason the store was featured on the news.

Which stimuli will be perceived often depends on the individual. People can be exposed to the same stimuli under identical conditions but perceive them very differently. For example, two people viewing a TV commercial may have different interpretations of the advertising message. One person may be thoroughly engrossed by the message and become highly motivated to buy the product. Thirty seconds after the ad ends, the second person may not be able to recall the content of the message or even the product advertised.

Marketing Implications of Perception

Marketers must recognize the importance of cues, or signals, in consumers' perception of products. Marketing managers first identify the important attributes, such as price or quality, that the targeted consumers want in a product and then design signals to communicate these attributes. For example, consumers will pay more for candy in expensive-looking foil packages. But shiny labels on wine bottles signify less expensive wines; dull labels indicate more expensive wines. Marketers also often use price as a signal to consumers that the product is of higher quality than competing products. Gibson Guitar Corporation briefly cut prices on many of its guitars to compete with Japanese rivals Yamaha and Ibanez but found instead that it sold more guitars when it charged more for them. Consumers perceived that the higher price indicated a better quality instrument.[57]

selective distortion
A process whereby a consumer changes or distorts information that conflicts with his or her feelings or beliefs.

selective retention
A process whereby a consumer remembers only that information that supports his or her personal beliefs.

Of course, brand names send signals to consumers. The brand names of Close-Up toothpaste, DieHard batteries, and Caress moisturizing soap, for example, identify important product qualities. Names chosen for search engines and sites on the Internet, such as Yahoo!, Amazon.com, and Excite, are intended to convey excitement, intensity, and vastness. Companies might even change their names to send a message to consumers. As today's utility companies increasingly enter nonregulated markets, many are shaking their stodgy "Power & Light & Electric" names in favor of those that let consumers know they are not just about electricity anymore, such as Reliant Resources, Entergy, and Cinergy.

Consumers also associate quality and reliability with certain brand names. Companies watch their brand identity closely, in large part because a strong link has been established between perceived brand value and customer loyalty. Brand names that consistently enjoy high perceived value from consumers include Kodak, Disney, National Geographic, Mercedes-Benz, and Fisher-Price. Naming a product after a place can also add perceived value by association. Brand names using the words Santa Fe, Dakota, or Texas convey a sense of openness, freedom, and youth, but products named after other locations might conjure up images of pollution and crime.

Marketing managers are also interested in the *threshold level of perception*: the minimum difference in a stimulus that the consumer will notice. This concept is sometimes referred to as the "just-noticeable difference." For example, how much would Sony have to drop the price of a DVD player before consumers recognized it as a bargain—$25? $50? or more? One study found that the just-noticeable difference in a stimulus is about a 20 percent change. For example, consumers will likely notice a 20 percent price decrease more quickly than a 15 percent decrease. This marketing principle can be applied to other marketing variables as well, such as package size or loudness of a broadcast advertisement.[58]

Another study showed that the bargain-price threshold for a name brand is lower than that for a store brand. In other words, consumers perceive a bargain more readily when stores offer a small discount on a name-brand item than when they offer the same discount on a store brand; a larger discount is needed to achieve a similar effect for a store brand.[59] Researchers also found that for low-cost grocery items, consumers typically do not see past the second digit in the price. For instance, consumers do not perceive any real difference between two comparable cans of tuna, one priced at $1.52 and the other at $1.59, because they ignore the last digit.[60]

Besides changing such stimuli as price, package size, and volume, marketers can change the product or attempt to reposition its image. Realtors, for example, have changed a property's address to enhance its image. In fact, one San Francisco real estate company almost lost a major deal when one of its potential clients refused to move into an office whose address was 444 Market Street because of the association of the number four with death in the Chinese community. The company saved the deal by renovating the lobby to include a new entrance and changing the building's address to One Front Street.[61] But marketers must be careful when adding features. How many new services will discounter Target Stores need to add before consumers perceive it as a full-service department store? How many sporty features will General Motors have to add to a basic two-door sedan before consumers start perceiving it as a sports car?

Marketing managers who intend to do business in global markets should be aware of how foreign consumers perceive their products. For instance, in Japan, product labels are often written in English or French, even though they may not translate into anything meaningful. Many Japanese associate foreign words on product labels with the exotic, the expensive, and high quality.

Marketers have often been suspected of sending advertising messages subconsciously to consumers in what is known as *subliminal perception*. The controversy began in 1957 when a researcher claimed to have increased popcorn and Coca-Cola sales at a movie theater after flashing "Eat popcorn" and "Drink Coca-Cola" on the screen every five seconds for 1/300th of a second, although the audience did not consciously recognize the messages. Almost immediately consumer protection groups became concerned that advertisers were brainwashing consumers, and this practice was pronounced illegal in California and Canada. Although the researcher later admitted to making up the data and scientists have been unable to replicate the study since, consumers are still wary of hidden messages that advertisers may be sending.

MOTIVATION

By studying motivation, marketers can analyze the major forces influencing consumers to buy or not buy products. When you buy a product, you usually do so to fulfill some kind of need. These needs become motives when aroused sufficiently. For instance, suppose this morning you were so hungry before class that you needed to eat something. In response to that need, you stopped at McDonald's for an Egg McMuffin. In other words, you were motivated by hunger to stop at McDonald's. **Motives** are the driving forces that cause a person to take action to satisfy specific needs.

Why are people driven by particular needs at particular times? One popular theory is **Maslow's hierarchy of needs**, shown in Exhibit 5.12, which arranges needs in ascending order of importance: physiological, safety, social, esteem, and self-actualization. As a person fulfills one need, a higher level need becomes more important.

The most basic human needs are *physiological*—that is the needs for food, water, and shelter. Because they are essential to survival, these needs must be satisfied first. Ads showing a juicy hamburger or a runner gulping down Gatorade after a marathon are examples of appeals to satisfy the physiological needs of hunger and thirst.

Safety needs include security and freedom from pain and discomfort. Marketers sometimes appeal to consumers' fears and anxieties about safety to sell their products. For example, aware of the aging population's health fears, the retail medical imaging centers AmeriScan and HealthScreen America advertise that they offer consumers a full body scan for early detection of health problems such as coronary disease and cancer. On the other hand, some companies or industries advertise to allay consumer fears. For example, in the wake of the September 11 terrorist attacks, the airline industry found itself having to conduct an image

motive
A driving force that causes a person to take action to satisfy specific needs.

Maslow's hierarchy of needs
A method of classifying human needs and motivations into five categories in ascending order of importance: physiological, safety, social, esteem, and self-actualization.

EXHIBIT 5.12

Maslow's Hierarchy of Needs

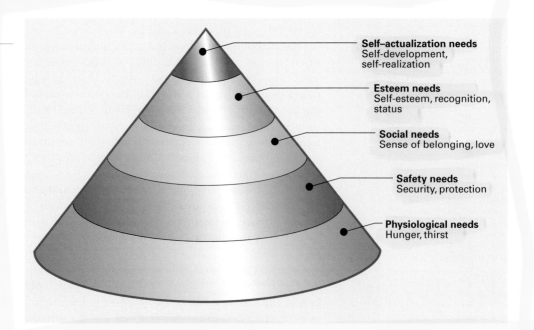

- **Self-actualization needs**
  Self-development, self-realization
- **Esteem needs**
  Self-esteem, recognition, status
- **Social needs**
  Sense of belonging, love
- **Safety needs**
  Security, protection
- **Physiological needs**
  Hunger, thirst

Respect yourself
IN THE MORNING.™

Nutri-Grain
Muffin Bars

NEW WHOLESOME MUFFIN BARS | HEARTY NOT HEAVY

Self-esteem needs include self-respect, prestige, recognition, and even fame. Although Nutri Grain is advertising a food product (physiological needs), the need to taking care of your physical appearance (social needs, self-esteem needs) is communicated through the image and the tag line, "Respect yourself in the morning."

campaign to reassure consumers about the safety of air travel.[62]

After physiological and safety needs have been fulfilled, *social needs*—especially love and a sense of belonging—become the focus. Love includes acceptance by one's peers, as well as sex and romantic love. Marketing managers probably appeal more to this need than to any other. Ads for clothes, cosmetics, and vacation packages suggest that buying the product can bring love. The need to belong is also a favorite of marketers, especially those marketing products to teens. Shoes and clothing brands such as Nike, adidas, Tommy Hilfiger, Gap, JNCO, and Abercrombie & Fitch score high with teenagers as "cool" brands. Teens who wear these labels feel and look like they belong to the in-crowd.

Love is acceptance without regard to one's contribution. Esteem is acceptance based on one's contribution to the group. *Self-esteem needs* include self-respect and a sense of accomplishment. Esteem needs also include prestige, fame, and recognition of one's accomplishments. Mont Blanc pens, Mercedes-Benz automobiles, and Neiman-Marcus stores all appeal to esteem needs. Most high-end spas and health clubs appeal to consumers' self-esteem needs. Like exclusive country clubs, clubs such as Chicago's East Bank Club are designed to make members feel proud of their commitment to fitness while also giving them a sense of social accomplishment. In fact, the clubs can be so effective that even during an economic recession, patrons will not give up their membership because to do so would be a public admission of financial problems.[63]

GLOBAL Asian consumers, in particular, are strongly motivated by status and appearance. Asians are always conscious of their place in a group, institution, or society as a whole. The importance of gaining social recognition turns Asians into some of the most image-conscious consumers in the world. Status-conscious Asians will not hesitate to spend freely on premium brands, such as BMW, Mercedes-Benz, and the best Scotch whiskey and French cognac. Indeed, marketers of luxury products such as Gucci, Louis Vuitton, and Prada find that demand for their products is so strong among image-conscious consumers that their sales are generally unaffected by economic downturns. In some cases, companies have been able to make up for sluggish European and U.S. sales by raising prices and volume in Asia.

The highest human need is *self-actualization*. It refers to finding self-fulfillment and self-expression, reaching the point in life at which "people are what they feel they should be." Maslow felt that very few people ever attain this level. Even so, advertisements may focus on this type of need. For example, American Express ads convey the message that acquiring its card is one of the highest attainments in life. Similarly, Microsoft appealed to consumers' needs for self-actualization when it chose "Yes, You Can" as the Windows XP slogan. And the U.S. Armed Forces' slogan urges young people to "Be all that you can be."

LEARNING

learning
A process that creates changes in behavior, immediate or expected, through experience and practice.

Almost all consumer behavior results from **learning**, which is the process that creates changes in behavior through experience and practice. It is not possible to observe learning directly, but we can infer when it has occurred by a person's actions. For example, suppose you see an advertisement for a new and improved cold medicine. If you go to the store that day and buy that remedy, we infer that you have learned something about the cold medicine.

There are two types of learning: experiential and conceptual. *Experiential learning* occurs when an experience changes your behavior. For example, if you try the new cold medicine when you get home and it does not relieve your symptoms, you may not buy that brand again. *Conceptual learning*, which is not acquired through direct experience, is the second type of learning. Assume, for example, that you are standing at a soft drink machine and notice a new diet flavor with an artificial sweetener. Because someone has told you that diet beverages leave an aftertaste, you choose a different drink. You have learned that you would not like this new diet drink without ever trying it.

Reinforcement and repetition boost learning. Reinforcement can be positive or negative. If you see a vendor selling frozen yogurt (stimulus), buy it (response), and find the yogurt to be quite refreshing (reward), your behavior has been positively reinforced. On the other hand, if you buy a new flavor of yogurt and it does not taste good (negative reinforcement), you will not buy that flavor of yogurt again (response). Without positive or negative reinforcement, a person will not be motivated to repeat the behavior pattern or to avoid it. Thus, if a new brand evokes neutral feelings, some marketing activity, such as a price change or an increase in promotion, may be required to induce further consumption. Learning theory is helpful in reminding marketers that concrete and timely actions are what reinforce desired consumer behavior.

Repetition is a key strategy in promotional campaigns because it can lead to increased learning. Most marketers use repetitious advertising so that consumers will learn what their unique advantage is over the competition. Generally, to heighten learning, advertising messages should be spread over time rather than clustered together.

A related learning concept useful to marketing managers is stimulus generalization. In theory, **stimulus generalization** occurs when one response is extended to a second stimulus similar to the first. Marketers often use a successful, well-known brand name for a family of products because it gives consumers familiarity with and knowledge about each product in the family. Such brand-name families spur the introduction of new products and facilitate the sale of existing items. Jell-O frozen pudding pops rely on the familiarity of Jell-O gelatin; Clorox bathroom cleaner relies on familiarity with Clorox bleach; and Ivory shampoo relies on familiarity with Ivory soap. Microsoft entered the video game industry, hoping that the Microsoft brand would guarantee sales for the Xbox. Initial response to the Xbox was strong based on Microsoft's reputation, but the company has had to work hard to make real progress in an industry dominated by other brand giants Sony and Nintendo. Branding is examined in more detail in Chapter 9.

GLOBAL   Another form of stimulus generalization occurs when retailers or wholesalers design their packages to resemble well-known manufacturers' brands. Such imitation often confuses consumers, who buy the imitator thinking it's the original. U.S. manufacturers in foreign markets have sometimes found little, if any, brand protection. In South Korea, Procter & Gamble's Ivory soap competes head-on with the Korean brand Bory, which has an almost identical logo on the package. Consumers dissatisfied with Bory may attribute their dissatisfaction to Ivory, never realizing that Bory is an imitator. Counterfeit products are also produced to look exactly like the original. For example, counterfeit Levi's jeans made in China are hot items in Europe, where Levi Strauss has had trouble keeping up with demand. The knockoffs look so much like the real thing that unsuspecting consumers don't know the difference—until after a few washes, when the belt loops fall off and the rivets begin to rust.

stimulus generalization
A form of learning that occurs when one response is extended to a second stimulus similar to the first.

The opposite of stimulus generalization is **stimulus discrimination**, which means learning to differentiate among similar products. Consumers may perceive one product as more rewarding or stimulating. For example, some consumers prefer Coca-Cola and others prefer Pepsi. Many insist they can taste a difference between the two brands.

Save Harry (Potter)
Center for Science in the Public Interest
Identify the beliefs and attitudes of the supporters of SaveHarry.com. Can you think of any way to turn these negative beliefs about product attributes into positive ones? Should Coke respond? If so, how?
http://www.saveharry.com
http://www.cspinet.org

Online ◀ ▶

With some types of products—such as aspirin, gasoline, bleach, paper towels—marketers rely on promotion to point out brand differences that consumers would otherwise not recognize. This process, called *product differentiation*, is discussed in more detail in Chapter 7. Usually, product differentiation is based on superficial differences. For example, Bayer tells consumers that it's the aspirin "doctors recommend most."

BELIEFS AND ATTITUDES

Beliefs and attitudes are closely linked to values. A **belief** is an organized pattern of knowledge that an individual holds as true about his or her world. A consumer may believe that Sony's camcorder makes the best home videos, tolerates hard use, and is reasonably priced. These beliefs may be based on knowledge, faith, or hearsay. Consumers tend to develop a set of beliefs about a product's attributes and then, through these beliefs, form a *brand image*—a set of beliefs about a particular brand. In turn, the brand image shapes consumers' attitudes toward the product.

An **attitude** is a learned tendency to respond consistently toward a given object, such as a brand. Attitudes rest on an individual's value system, which represents personal standards of good and bad, right and wrong, and so forth; therefore, attitudes tend to be more enduring and complex than beliefs.

 For an example of the nature of attitudes, consider the differing attitudes of consumers around the world toward the practice of purchasing on credit. Americans have long been enthusiastic about charging goods and services and are willing to pay high interest rates for the privilege of postponing payment. To many European consumers, doing what amounts to taking out a loan—even a small one—to pay for anything seems absurd. Germans especially are reluctant to buy on credit. Italy has a sophisticated credit and banking system well suited to handling credit cards, but Italians prefer to carry cash, often huge wads of it. Although most Japanese consumers have credit cards, card purchases amount to less than 1 percent of all consumer transactions. The Japanese have long looked down on credit purchases but acquire cards to use while traveling abroad.

If a good or service is meeting its profit goals, positive attitudes toward the product merely need to be reinforced. If the brand is not succeeding, however, the marketing manager must strive to change target consumers' attitudes toward it. Changes in attitude tend to grow out of an individual's attempt to reconcile long-held values with a constant stream of new information. This change can be accomplished in three ways: changing beliefs about the brand's attributes, changing the relative importance of these beliefs, and adding new beliefs.

Changing Beliefs about Attributes

The first technique is to turn neutral or negative beliefs about product attributes into positive ones. For example, many consumers believe that it is easier and

stimulus discrimination
A learned ability to differentiate among similar products.

belief
An organized pattern of knowledge that an individual holds as true about his or her world.

attitude
A learned tendency to respond consistently toward a given object.

How did you know you liked water before you tried it?

Lactose free, high in protein, with a surprisingly good taste. *Don't be so stubborn.*

COURTESY OF WHITE WAVE

cheaper to take traditional film to be developed than it is to print their own digital photos. To change this belief, Sony Corporation has begun setting up kiosks in retail outlets that let consumers print their digital photos. The kiosks eliminate the need for consumers to purchase their own high-quality printer. Similarly, companies like Sageport and It's Never 2 Late are trying to change senior citizens' belief that computers are too complicated for them to learn. Sageport offers seniors an appliance that gives them Internet access without the need to operate a PC, and It's Never 2 Late is adapting software and hardware with larger type, fewer options, and more graphics to make it easier for seniors to use a PC.

Changing beliefs about a service can be more difficult because service attributes are intangible. Convincing consumers to switch hairstylists or lawyers or to go to a mall dental clinic can be much more difficult than getting them to change brands of razor blades. Image, which is also largely intangible, significantly determines service patronage. For example, Tomra, a Norwegian recycling giant, hopes to increase the number of Americans who recycle by changing their perception that recycling is an unsavory chore. By building new rePlanet recycling kiosks in communities as an alternative to neighborhood recycling centers, Tomra is offering Americans a clean, convenient, service-oriented way to be responsible citizens.[64] Service marketing is explored in detail in Chapter 11.

To increase sales, a company must change negative attitudes about its product held by those who are not buying it. One way to accomplish this is to change the beliefs about the product's attributes, such as taste. This ad for Silk soymilk does just that with its catchy question, and the follow-up, "Don't be so stubborn."

Changing the Importance of Beliefs

The second approach to modifying attitudes is to change the relative importance of beliefs about an attribute. Cole Haan, originally a men's shoe outfitter, used boats and cars in their ads for years to associate the brand with active lifestyles, an important attribute for men. Now that they are selling women's products, such as handbags and shoes, some of their new ads use models and emphasize how the products look, an important attribute for women. They are hoping the new ads will change customers' perceptions and beliefs about them as a store that only sells men's products.[65]

Marketers can also emphasize the importance of some beliefs over others. For example, DaimlerChrysler's Jeep unit positions it as being rugged but promotes its luxury features. The newest Grand Cherokees have even more off-road capability, but very few owners ever take them off-road. Luxury features include a climate-control system with infrared beams that track drivers' and passengers' skin temperature to automatically adjust air conditioning and heat, his and her key rings that remember settings for power seats and mirrors, a system to reprogram radio stations for different drivers, and many other comforts.

Adding New Beliefs

The third approach to transforming attitudes is to add new beliefs. Although changes in consumption patterns often come slowly, cereal marketers are betting that consumers will eventually warm up to the idea of cereal as a snack. A print ad for Ralston Purina's Cookie-Crisp cereal features a boy popping the sugary nuggets into his mouth while he does his homework. Boxes of Kellogg's Cracklin' Oat Bran boast that the cereal tastes like oatmeal cookies and makes "a great snack . . . anytime." Similarly, commercials for Quaker Oats 100% Natural cereal promote eating it straight from the box. James River Corporation, the manufacturer of Dixie paper products, is also attempting to add new beliefs about the uses of its paper plates and cups with an advertising campaign aimed at positioning its product as a "home cleanup replacement." Commercials pitch Dixie paper plates as an alternative to washing dishes after everyday meals.

 U.S. companies attempting to market their goods overseas may need to help consumers add new beliefs about a product in general. Coca-Cola and PepsiCo have both found it challenging to sell their diet cola brands to consumers in India partly because diet foods of any kind are a new concept there, a country where malnutrition was widespread not too many years ago. Indians also have deep-rooted attitudes that anything labeled "diet" is meant for a sick person, such as a diabetic. As a general rule, most Indians are not diet-conscious, preferring food prepared in the traditional manner that tastes good. Indians are also suspicious of the artificial sweeteners used in diet colas. India's Health Ministry has required warning labels on cans and bottles of Diet Coke and Diet Pepsi saying "Not Recommended for Children."[66]

REVIEW LEARNING OBJECTIVE 8

8 **Identify and understand the individual factors that affect consumer buying decisions**

Perception	Selective Exposure	
	Selective Retention	Selective Distortion

Motivation	Needs				
	Physiological	Safety	Social	Esteem	Self-Actualization

Learning	Stimulus Generalization	Stimulus Discrimination

Beliefs & Attitudes	Changing Beliefs about Attributes	Changing Importance of Beliefs	Adding New Beliefs

LOOKING BACK

Reflecting on the chapter material, you should now be able to see how cultural, social, individual, and psychological factors affect the consumer decision-making process. Purchase decisions are influenced by many factors, from opinion leaders to peer groups. Individuals have unique values and opinions based upon the environment in which they have grown up. Marketers hoping to reach different segments must understand each segment's needs and wants, as well as the influnces that shape them, vary. Consumer behavior is a fascinating and often intricate process. An appreciation of consumer behavior and the factors that influence it will help you identify target markets and design effective marketing mixes. In the opening vignette, you saw how Virgin Mobile designed a targeted marketing strategy to successfully appeal to the Gen Y mobile phone market.

USE IT NOW

FIND PRODUCT RATINGS

Consumer Reports Online (**http://www. consumerreports.org**) is your one-stop source for information on hundreds of products you might be interested in purchasing, such as cars and trucks, appliances, electronics, household products, home office equipment, money and investing, health and food products, personal products, and leisure activities. The section on cars and trucks, for instance, offers a wealth of advice for those thinking of buying a new or used car, or seeking safety and maintenance tips. The site includes comparison ratings, reliability reports, negotiation advice, a personal car selector, information on car equipment and accessories, as well as exclusive ratings on auto-buying Web sites. Consumers Union, publisher of *Consumer Reports*, is a nonprofit consumer advocacy group with over 60 years of product testing. The group doesn't accept any outside advertising or support from product manufacturers, so the information you find is as unbiased as possible, but you have to pay for it as a subscriber.

FIND THE BEST PRICE

Narrowed down your purchase decision to a single brand or a small set of alternative brands? Now find the best price on the Web with the use of a "shopping bot," a search engine that will systematically search the Web to find the lowest price from online retailers and auction sites. Visit CNET Shopper at **http://www.cnet.com** to search for the lowest price on computer systems and accessories, cameras, handheld personal assistants, software, and games. Or visit Shop-Best.com (**http://www.shopbest.com**) for a shopping bot that can find the best price for an even broader selection of merchandise. ShopBest.com offers over 20 shopping departments, including apparel, computer hardware and software, art, furniture, music, movies, housewares, and toys.

REVIEW AND APPLICATIONS

1 **Explain why marketing managers should understand consumer behavior.** Consumer behavior describes how consumers make purchase decisions and how they use and dispose of the products they buy. An understanding of consumer behavior reduces marketing managers' uncertainty when they are defining a target market and designing a marketing mix.

1.1 The type of decision making a consumer uses for a product does not necessarily remain constant. Why? Support your answer with an example from your own experience.

2 **Analyze the components of the consumer decision-making process.** The consumer decision-making process begins with need recognition, when stimuli trigger awareness of an unfulfilled want. If additional information is required to make a purchase decision, the consumer may engage in an internal or external information search. The consumer then evaluates the additional information and establishes purchase guidelines. Finally, a purchase decision is made.

2.1 Visit Carpoint's Web site at **http://carpoint.msn.com/home/New.asp**. How does the site assist consumers in the evaluation stage of choosing a new car? Develop your own hypothetical evoked set of three or four car models and present your comparisons. Which vehicle attributes would be most important in your purchase decision?

3 **Explain the consumer's postpurchase evaluation process.** Consumer postpurchase evaluation is influenced by prepurchase expectations, the prepurchase information search, and the consumer's general level of self-confidence. Cognitive dissonance is the inner tension that a consumer experiences after recognizing a purchased product's disadvantages. When a purchase creates cognitive dissonance, consumers tend to react by seeking positive reinforcement for the purchase decision, avoiding negative information about the purchase decision, or revoking the purchase decision by returning the product.

3.1 Recall an occasion when you experienced cognitive dissonance about a purchase. In a letter to a friend, describe the event and explain what you did about it.

3.2 Review the "Marketing in Entertainment" box on *Snitch*. Since this highly targeted publication is free, do *Snitch*'s marketing managers need to worry about the post-purchase evaluation process? Does *Snitch* have a paper in your area? Identify and collect samples of free publications in your area. Group the publications according to common traits. Then determine what factors would influence a consumer to pick one up. In other words, what factors influence the consumer "buying" decision of a free newspaper?

4 **Identify the types of consumer buying decisions and discuss the significance of consumer involvement.** Consumer decision making falls into three broad categories. First, consumers exhibit routine response behavior for frequently purchased, low-cost items that require very little decision effort; routine response behavior is typically characterized by brand loyalty. Second, consumers engage in limited decision making for occasional purchases or for unfamiliar brands in familiar product categories. Third, consumers practice extensive decision making when making unfamiliar, expensive, or infrequent purchases. High-involvement decisions usually include an extensive information search and a thorough evaluation of alternatives. In contrast, low-involvement decisions are characterized by brand loyalty and a lack of personal identification with the product. The main factors affecting the level of consumer involvement are previous experience, interest, perceived risk of negative consequences (financial, social, and psychological), situation, and social visibility.

4.1 Describe the three categories of consumer decision-making behavior. Name typical products for which each type of consumer behavior is used.

5 **Identify and understand the cultural factors that affect consumer buying decisions.** Cultural influences on consumer buying decisions include culture and values, subculture, and social class. Culture is the essential character of a society that distinguishes it from other cultural groups. The underlying elements of every culture are the values, language, myths, customs, rituals, laws, and the artifacts, or products, that are transmitted from one generation to the next. The most defining element of a culture is its values—the enduring beliefs shared by a society that a specific mode of conduct is personally or socially preferable to another mode of conduct. A culture can be divided into subcultures on the basis of demographic characteristics, geographic regions, national and ethnic background, political beliefs, and religious beliefs. Subcultures share elements of the overall culture as well as cultural elements unique to their own group. A social class is a group of people who are considered nearly equal in status or community esteem, who regularly socialize among themselves both formally and informally, and who share behavioral norms.

5.1 WRITING You are a new marketing manager for a firm that produces a line of athletic shoes to be targeted to the college student subculture. In a memo to your boss, list some product attributes that might appeal to this subculture and the steps in your customers' purchase processes, and recommend some marketing strategies that can influence their decision.

6 **Identify and understand the social factors that affect consumer buying decisions.** Social factors include such external influences as reference groups, opinion leaders, and family. Consumers seek out others' opinions for guidance on new products or services and products with image-related attributes or because attribute information is lacking or uninformative. Consumers may use products or brands to identify with or become a member of a reference group. Opinion leaders are members of reference groups who influence others' purchase decisions. Family members also influence purchase decisions; children tend to shop in similar patterns as their parents.

6.1 Family members play many different roles in the buying process: initiator, influencer, decision maker, purchaser, and consumer. Identify the person in your family who might play each of these roles in the purchase of a dinner at Pizza Hut, a summer vacation, Froot Loops breakfast cereal, an Abercrombie & Fitch sweater, golf clubs, an Internet service provider, and a new car.

7 **Identify and understand the individual factors that affect consumer buying decisions.** Individual factors that affect consumer buying decisions include gender; age and family life-cycle stage; and personality, self-concept, and lifestyle. Beyond obvious physiological differences, men and women differ in their social and economic roles and that affects consumer buying decisions. How old a consumer is generally indicates what products he or she may be interested in purchasing. Marketers often define their target markets in terms of consumers' life-cycle stage, following changes in consumers' attitudes and behavioral tendencies as they mature. Finally, certain products and brands reflect consumers' personality, self-concept, and lifestyle.

7.1 Assume you are involved in the following consumer decision situations: (a) renting a video to watch with your roommates, (b) choosing a fast-food restaurant to go to with a new friend, (c) buying a popular music compact disc, (d) buying jeans to wear to class. List the individual factors that would influence your decision in each situation and explain your responses.

8 **Identify and understand the psychological factors that affect consumer buying decisions.** Psychological factors include perception, motivation, learning, values, beliefs, and attitudes. These factors allow consumers to interact with the world around them, recognize their feelings, gather and analyze information, formulate thoughts and opinions, and take action. Perception allows consumers to recognize their consumption problems. Motivation is what drives consumers to take action to satisfy specific consumption needs. Almost all consumer behavior results from learning, which is the process that creates changes in behavior through experience. Consumers with similar beliefs and attitudes tend to react alike to marketing-related inducements.

8.1 **ONLINE** How do beliefs and attitudes influence consumer behavior? How can negative attitudes toward a product be changed? How can marketers alter beliefs about a product? Give some examples of how marketers have changed negative attitudes about a product or added or altered beliefs about a product.

8.2 **INFOTRAC COLLEGE EDITION** How can nonmarketing periodicals help you understand consumer behavior? Using InfoTrac (**http://www.infotrac-college.com**), research articles from such publications as the *Journal of Psychology, Journal of American Ethnic History, Psychology Today, Race and Class, Working Women, Society*, and others. Select and read three articles that explore different topics (i.e., do not select three articles on psychology). Then, make a list of factors you think could affect consumer purchasing behavior. Include with each factor a way marketers could use this information to their benefit.

TERMS

APPLICATION EXERCISE

Principles of consumer behavior are evident in many areas of marketing. Perhaps the easiest place to see this critical foundation of marketing activity is in print ads.[67]

Activities

1. Review the main concepts in this chapter and create a checklist that itemizes them. Then, comb through your favorite magazines and newspapers for advertisements that illustrate each concept. To get a wide variety of ads, you will need to look through several magazines. If you don't have many magazines at your disposal, go to the campus library periodical room. Photocopy the ads you select to support this chapter.

2. Because pictures can help reinforce understanding, consider doing this exercise for each chapter in the book. At the end of the semester, you will have a portfolio of ads that illustrate the concepts in the entire book, which can help you study. Simply look through your portfolio and try to recall the concepts at work in each advertisement. This exercise can be a prelude to a longer study session for comprehensive exams.

ETHICS EXERCISE

EyeOnU operates a Web filter service for public schools and libraries to protect students from inappropriate material on the Internet. Like the industry as a whole, the company's market share has been stagnant for the past two years. Looking for new sources of revenue, the company is considering selling the data it has collected about student surfing habits to marketers trying to learn more about students' behavior on the Web. The data are anonymous, but privacy advocates are concerned about the precedent of selling information about children to marketers.

Questions

1. What should EyeOnU do? Should it protect the student's data, or should it take the opportunity to create new revenues?

2. Does the AMA Code of Ethics address this issue? Go to **http://www.marketingpower. com** and review the code. Then, write a brief paragraph on how the AMA Code of Ethics relates to EyeOnU's dilemma.

CAREER EXERCISE

Starting a career that focuses on identifying and researching consumer behavior will inevitably involve locating companies that specialize in recognizing trends, both general and specific. To get an idea of what these companies provide to the marketing industry, go to **http://www.trendsinstitute.com** and read some of the posted reports and current research activities. Perhaps the largest organization, other than the federal government, that tracks consumer behaviors—among other indices—is the Conference Board. You can see some of the CB's work at its Web site, **http://www.consumerspendingtrends.com**, or go to its home page at **http://www. conference-board.org**. Although employment opportunities are not listed online, contact information is available.

Activities

1. Go to **http://www.marketingresearchjobs.com** and enter "consumer research" or "consumer psychology" into the site's search engine. Review five listings and make a list of recurring job requirements. Based on what you discover, do you think that a job in this field will require a special minor? If so, what?

2. Visit KnowThis.com and check out its list of consumer behavior companies (**http://www. knowthis.com/research/companies/psychographic.htm**). Identify four to five companies that specialize in consumer research and write a brief description of each company (location, sales, clients, number of employees, and the like). Are the companies nearly identical except for their geography? If not, note some of the distinctions.

© INDEX STOCK IMAGERY/SW PRODUCTION

BUCKING THE TREND: IS 'FAMILY' THE NEXT THEME RESTAURANT?

In 1995, attorney and real estate investor Stephen Waite sparked a revitalization in Albany, New York, when he opened his Big House Brewing Company in a century-old vacant downtown building. The extremely successful restaurant and pub set off a chain reaction of development and improvement projects that have transformed downtown Albany into a very different place, especially after five o'clock. Waite then turned his attention to an entirely new type of restaurant concept, this time in Clifton Park, an Albany suburb.

Waite and his new business partner, Eric Shilling, want to create a family-friendly restaurant with miniature golf in the summer and outdoor ice skating in the winter, plus clowns and magicians the whole year round. Providing recreational activities in conjunction with family dining is not a new trend: places like Chuck E. Cheese and Dave & Buster's have been doing it for years. But what Waite and Shilling know will set their establishment apart is the fact that it is a unique facility. The restaurant menu will incorporate dishes made with locally grown products, like local apples. Having dishes that are indigenous to the area will set the restaurant apart from the bevy of national chain restaurants and attractions that make up the American suburban landscape. In fact, the new complex will not be located near a strip mall or commercial area. The proposed site is a wooded six-acre plot near the community sports complex and local schools.

Waite and Shilling's whole project is bucking the trend of locating chains near other chains to drive traffic, forecasting that people are getting tired of chains. In fact, there is some evidence that Americans are getting tired of the sameness that pervades their culture. Even companies once thought of as innovators, like Hard Rock Café and Gap, are struggling to some degree as consumers' attention fades. Some former innovators, like Planet Hollywood, are now defunct. In some cases, consumers have stayed away because they are weary of the theme; in some cases it's because consumers demand higher quality than the theme restaurants provide. Amex conducted a series of seminars that examined consumer dining trends. Panelists included people from the marketing research discipline and chefs and owners of major restaurants like Bobby Flay. One trend panelists identified was that of authenticity. Another was that consumers want an experience. But do theme restaurants provide the experience consumers seek?

With ten consecutive years of growth, the National Restaurant Association looked to top $408 billion in sales for 2002. And despite the hard times at many theme-based retailers (not just restaurants), Waite and Shilling are not alone in looking for the next successful theme. McDonald's opened its second-largest outlet in Columbus, Ohio's Easton Town Center. Not just a restaurant, this McDonald's includes an interactive miniature drive-thru for kids, a karaoke booth for customers to record CDs, a separate area where adults can eat, a merchandise area where customers can purchase McDonald's apparel and souvenirs, and a McTreat Center that sells ice cream treats, cookies, pastries, and imported Lavazza specialty coffee.

Although family-oriented dining is not new, it may very well be the new trend in theme restaurants. And even though Waite and Shilling want their family entertainment venue to be distinct from the chains in the nearby area, they are already looking at turning their idea into a regional chain, should it be as successful as they anticipate. [68]

Questions

1. What type of consumer buying decision best describes dining at Waite and Shilling's new family restaurant and entertainment complex? Is it different than the decision made to dine at McDonald's new Edu-Tainment restaurant? At a regular McDonald's restaurant? How?

2. List the factors that would influence a consumer to spend his or her dining budget at a family entertainment-themed restaurant. Include cultural, social, individual, and psychological factors on your list.

3. What influences on consumer decision making do you think are contributing to the declining performance of once-popular theme chains, like the Hard Rock Café, The Gap, the Disney Store, and the Warner Bros. Store? Based on the factors you identify, do you think that opening a new theme restaurant is wise? Why or why not?

SmallBusinessSchool ◼
the Series on PBS stations and the Web

FEATURE PRESENTATION

Cowgirl Enterprises

To give you insight into Chapter 5, Small Business School introduces you to Donna Baase and her company, Cowgirl Enterprises, maker of organically made and cleverly marketed skincare products. The company sells environmental conscientiousness and an independent image to the woman who is a cowgirl at heart. Donna sincerely hopes that educating people and exposing them to products such as Cowgirl Cream, Trail Boss Bars, and Cowgirl Lip Balm will raise awareness about what plants and herbs can do for the human body. Her customers are wildly enthusiastic, and success has taken her products to beauty and personal-care stores in Colorado, New Mexico, and beyond. Spas and gift stores are popular outlets for the earthy products in eye-catching boxes, which the company also sells through its mail-order catalog and Web site.

What to Watch for and Ask Yourself

1. What kinds of images does the name, Cowgirl Enterprises, evoke?

2. Donna Baase says, "It's about the archetype of a cowgirl. And to me, it has to do with independence, resourcefulness, staying in the saddle, taking the reins . . . making use of the natural resources around us." What type of influence on the purchase decision is she talking about? Explain.

3. Is the decision to buy Cowgirl products routine, limited, or extended?

4. According to Maslow's theory, buying a Cowgirl product satisfies which type of need?

ENCORE PRESENTATION

The Family Man (I)

See the theories in Chapter 5 at work in this clip from *The Family Man,* starring Nicolas Cage (Jack) and Tea Leone (Kate). In the selected scene, Jack is still trying to adapt to his new life as husband, father, and tire salesman. He walks into the men's department of a mall department store and begins to admire the suits. How does this scene relate to the many factors that affect the consumer decision-making process shown in Exhibit 5.1? Can you describe Jack's decision using terms and concepts from the chapter?

STILL SHAKY?

If you're having trouble with the concepts in this chapter, consider using some of the following study resources. You can review the videos, or test yourself with materials designed for all kinds of learning styles.

☑ **Xtra! (http://lambxtra.swlearning.com)**

| ☑ Quiz | ☑ Feature Videos | ☑ Encore Videos | ☑ FAQ Videos |
| ☑ Exhibit Worksheets | ☑ Marketing Plan Worksheets | ☐ Content | |

☑ **http://lamb.swlearning.com**

| ☑ Quiz | ☑ PowerPoint slides | ☑ Marketing News | ☑ Review Exercises |
| ☑ Links | ☑ Marketing Plan Contest | ☑ Career Exercise | ☑ Use It Now |

☑ **Study guide**

| ☑ Outline | ☑ Vocab Review | ☑ Test Questions | ☑ Marketing Scenario |

Need More? Here's a tip. Imagine you are the professor, and make up your own test for Chapter 5. What are the main topics and key concepts that students should know? If you work with a study group, exchange practice tests. Work them individually then "grade" them collectively. This way you can discuss trouble spots and answer each other's questions.

6

Business Marketing

LEARNING OBJECTIVES

1 Describe business marketing

2 Describe the role of the Internet in business marketing

3 Discuss the role of relationship marketing and strategic alliances in business marketing

4 Identify the four major categories of business market customers

5 Explain the North American Industry Classification System

6 Explain the major differences between business and consumer markets

7 Describe the seven types of business goods and services

8 Discuss the unique aspects of business buying behavior

W. W. Grainger is one of the largest business distributors in the world. With nearly 600 locations throughout North America, 1,900 customer service associates, and a robust product line (tools, pumps, motors, safety and material handling products, and lighting, ventilation, and cleaning items), Grainger is the leading distributor of products that allow organizations of all types to keep their facilities and equipment running smoothly. Grainger's objective is to grow by capturing market share in the highly fragmented North American facilities maintenance market. For the longer term, the company is focused on these goals:

1. *Accelerate sales growth and increase market share by*
   - capturing a greater share of the business of existing accounts;
   - targeting high-potential customer segments.
2. *Increase operating leverage through*
   - accelerating sales growth;
   - targeting high-potential customer segments;
   - reconfiguring the logistics network to improve efficiency and customer service;
   - enhancing internal processes with technology.
3. *Improve return on invested capital by*
   - growing those business units that earn more than the cost of capital;
   - improving the profitability of business units that earn less than the cost of capital.

Its large sales force and its catalog containing 220,000 products allow Grainger to meet customer needs in a highly responsive manner. With its 600 branch locations, it can deliver products to customers within hours of a call. The company's major strategic focus is on offering a multichannel approach for purchasing maintenance and operating supplies. This involves providing consistent service through its branches, service centers, and distribution centers. Investments in sales training and a revamped logistics/distribution network are at the heart of this effort. Grainger was recently cited by one distributor industry magazine as "the strongest brand in the industrial distribution industry—because customers believe Grainger can get them what they need when they need it. You can find a Grainger catalog in virtually every purchasing agent's office in North America." In 2002, Grainger was ranked 350th on the *Fortune* 500 list and was included on *Fortune*'s list of "Most Admired Companies."[1]

What role would the Internet play in Grainger's strategy, given the firm's past success, the nature of its product line (rather stodgy basic industrial items), and the firm's organization (a 220,000-item catalog, a 1,900-person sales force, and 600 branch locations)? Even though it provides only very brief descriptions, with 220,000 items a Grainger catalog is massive—weighing several pounds. In the past, Grainger executives, worrying that the catalog would get too heavy for the average person to lift, limited product descriptions to a couple of lines. How could the Internet help Grainger address this issue? Can you cite an example?

Online

Grainger

Visit Grainger's Web site and look for ways that Grainger has made Internet shopping more efficient and effective than standard catalog shopping. What are the potential benefits for its customers? What are the potential benefits for Grainger?

http://www.grainger.com

1 WHAT IS BUSINESS MARKETING?

Describe business marketing

Business marketing is the marketing of goods and services to individuals and organizations for purposes other than personal consumption. The sale of a personal computer to your college or university is an example of business marketing. Business products include those that are used to manufacture other products, become part of another product, aid the normal operations of an organization, or are acquired for resale without any substantial change in form. The key characteristic distinguishing business products from consumer products is intended use, not physical characteristics. A product that is purchased for personal or family consumption or as a gift is a consumer good. If that same product, such as a personal computer or a cell phone, is bought for use in a business, it is a business product.

The size of the business market in the United States and most other countries substantially exceeds that of the consumer market. In the business market, a single customer can account for a huge volume of purchases. For example, General Motors' purchasing department spends more than $85 billion per year on goods and services. This is more than the gross domestic product of Ireland, Portugal, Turkey, or Greece.[2] Companies such as General Electric, DuPont, and IBM spend over $60 million per day on business purchases.[3]

REVIEW LEARNING OBJECTIVE 1

| 1 | Describe business marketing |

CONSUMER   BUSINESS

cupboards   oven   cupboards   coffee pot   oven

folder and pen   Teddy bear   photocopier   folder and pen

2 BUSINESS MARKETING ON THE INTERNET

Describe the role of the Internet in business marketing

ONLINE

It is hard to imagine that commercial use of the Internet began as recently as the mid-1990s.[4] In 1995, the commercial Web sites that did exist were static. Only a few had data-retrieval capabilities. Frames, tables, and styles were not available. Security of any sort was rare, and streaming video did not exist.

business marketing
The marketing of goods and services to individuals and organizations for purposes other than personal consumption.

GLOBAL

What a difference a decade has made! U.S. businesses spent about $482 billion on online transactions with other businesses in 2003, up 242 percent from $141 billion in 2001. By comparison, consumers spent only $71 billion online in 2002.[5] This unbelievable growth rate is not restricted to the United States. Business commerce on the Internet in Europe is expected to triple from $314 billion in 2003

EXHIBIT 6.1

Internet Sites Specifically for Small Businesses

http://www.allbusiness.com   AllBusiness provides entrepreneurs with the knowledge and tools to start, manage, and grow their business. The site links to hundreds of how-to articles and provides expert answers to questions.

http://www.bcentral.com   Microsoft bCentral offers small-business solutions such as assistance in establishing an online business presence, enhancing sales or services, or managing business operations. The site also contains practical tips, advice, and links to how-to articles.

http://office.com   Office.com offers practical information on how to start or run a business and how to transform an existing company into an e-business. Users access over 500 databases for news that affects their companies or industries. Office.com is one of the ten most visited business Web sites on the Internet.

http://www.quicken.com/small_business/   This site offers information on starting, running, and growing a small business. It also provides links to a variety of other Quicken sites that are useful to small-business owners and managers.

to $1 trillion in 2006.[6] Productivity gains from U.S. business use of the Internet are expected to reach $450 billion per year by 2005.[7] These gains are not restricted to large companies. Exhibit 6.1 identifies some popular Internet sites that cater to small businesses.

Leading-edge business marketers are using the Internet to transform the way they do business. The Internet provides a powerful platform for conveying information, conducting transactions, delivering innovative services, building customer and supplier relationships, gathering marketing research data, reducing costs and prices, and integrating the entire supply chain from suppliers to end users.[8]

THREE ILLUSTRATIONS

Carrier Corporation, the resins division of General Electric Company, and Dell, Inc.'s operations in Ireland illustrate how companies are using the Internet to transform the way they do business, benefiting suppliers, customers, and the companies themselves.

At Carrier, the world's largest manufacturer of air conditioners, company officials claim to have reduced costs by $100 million annually by buying and selling on the Internet.[9] Carrier now sells over $1 billion worth of products through its Web site. International sales and service results have been particularly remarkable.

The time required for Brazilian customers to place an order with Carrier and get confirmation has dropped from six days to six minutes. Inventory turnover has increased from 17 to 24 times per year. And 77 percent of the Brazilian customers report that they are "satisfied" or "highly satisfied" with the service they are receiving.[10] A similar initiative in Korea has resulted in 50 percent of all sales passing through the Web site and orders being delivered in 18 days compared to 33 days in the past.[11]

In 1997, General Electric's resins division launched an e-commerce site that was affectionately named GEPolymerland. Employees thought it sounded like a magical place, like Disneyland or Never-Never Land. It has produced what some might call magical results. Sales made through the Web site increased 12-fold from 1999 to 2000 and grew from $1.2 billion in 1999 to $3 billion in 2001.[12]

GE's goals for the site are reducing costs and helping customers streamline their buying. Since 95 percent of online orders go straight into GEPolymerland's information-management system without human intervention, the site cuts GE's costs and speeds up orders. There are savings on customer service costs, too. Answering a technical question by telephone might cost $80, but if the customer accesses the same information using a search tool, the cost is only 50 cents.[13]

Journal of the American Medical Association

Visit the Web site for the *Journal of the American Medical Association* and look up its "Principles Governing Advertising." What does the document say about digital advertising? Do you agree with the stated policy? Why or why not? Rate the viability of this publication as a vehicle for business marketing.

http://jama.ama-assn.org

Online

GLOBAL Dell's computer factory on the outskirts of Limerick, on the western coast of Ireland, supplies custom-built PCs to business customers all over Europe. As orders come into the factory via Dell's Web site and call centers, the company relays to its suppliers details of which components it needs, how many, and when. All the bits and pieces—hard drives, motherboards, modems, and so on—roll in to big bays at the back of the building and roll out as completed computers just a few hours later. A leading pioneer in electronic commerce, Dell now sells over $50 million worth of computers from its Web site each day! Because Dell's suppliers have real-time access to information about orders through Dell's corporate extranet, they can deliver just enough of the right parts to keep the production line moving smoothly. By plugging suppliers directly into its customer database, Dell ensures that they will instantly know about any changes in demand. And by plugging its customers into its supply chain via its Web site, Dell enables them to track the progress of their order from the factory to their office door, thus saving on telephone and fax inquiries. The Internet's universal connectivity has enabled Dell to create a three-way "information partnership" with its suppliers and customers by treating them as collaborators. Together, they find ways of improving efficiency and share the benefits across the entire chain of supply and demand.

Dell is just one of thousands of business marketers that have integrated the Internet and electronic commerce into their corporate strategies. E-commerce not only speeds up and automates a company's internal processes, but just as importantly, it spreads the efficiency gains to the business systems of its suppliers and customers. E-commerce seamlessly moves data and information over open and closed networks, bringing together previously separate groups inside the organization and throughout the supply chain. By integrating suppliers and customers in this way, the Internet and e-commerce provide a powerful set of tools that are ideally suited to the business-to-business arena.[14]

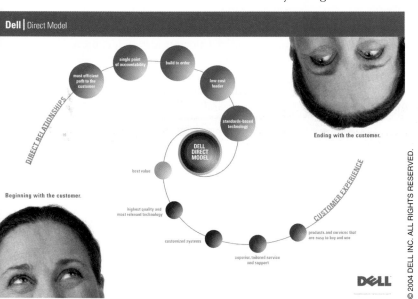

Dell is just one of thousands of business marketers that have integrated the Internet into their business strategies. But at Dell, the Internet is the cornerstone of how it serves consumers and businesses of all sizes. The strategy has reaped great success. In fact, competitors think twice about launching a price war against Dell, whose Internet business model has enabled the company to become the industry's most efficient computer systems company.

POTENTIAL UNREALIZED

ONLINE Despite the growth of e-commerce, most business buying and selling is still done off-line. One recent study found that only 18 percent of business marketers with an online presence sell online at all. Another study found that corporate purchasing agents make a mere 20 percent of purchases online. As one person put it, "if you are buying a stapler, you have no problems clicking around online. If you're buying 15,000 staplers, you want to talk to someone."[15] What are the 82 percent of business marketers that have a presence on the Internet but are not selling goods and services offering? Most provide product information and promotion. Some answer questions. Others provide contact and ordering information. Some are engaging in activities that may be considered unethical. The "Ethics in Marketing box" in this chapter is one illustration. Business Internet marketing represents trillions of dollars of sales potential per year. It has currently reached only a fraction of its potential.

> DRUG ADS AND MEDICAL RESEARCH: DO THEY BELONG TOGETHER?

Breaking a longstanding taboo in medical publishing against mixing ads and medical research, drug makers are experimenting with several controversial tactics online for promoting prescription drugs to physicians. "Open up to the possibilities," beckons an Internet ad for Pulmicort Turbuhaler, a prescription steroid medicine for asthma. The ad shows a large pair of lungs, and a father and child heading along a golden path under clear, blue skies.

What's surprising about the ad is where it appears: in the middle of a clinical paper, written by physicians, about research on treating asthma. The ad-studded research paper is posted on eMedicine.com, Inc., which provides peer-reviewed reference material on disease to physicians. The site is courting drug companies by providing desirable ad placements for their drugs.

Keeping commercial messages far away from scientific research has been a commandment of medical marketing to physicians. The rule's proponents argue that it is crucial to preserving the integrity of research. "Placement of advertising adjacent to editorial content on the same topic is prohibited," the American Medical Association states flatly in one edict.

People in the field say eMedicine.com has sparked quite a controversy by permitting drug advertisers to penetrate the scientific content of published research so deeply with their messages.

There's nothing illegal about mixing ads with research, however. The Food and Drug Administration regulates drug claims made in advertising and prohibits companies from implying that products can treat diseases for which they haven't been approved. But there's no specific agency prohibition against placing ads in the middle of scientific editorial content.

In the ultracompetitive world of drug marketing, advertisers are eager to bond with doctors. In fact, some drug companies have begun creating "virtual detailing" programs, in which physicians can learn about drugs online. Drug makers also are catering to busy physicians with "interactive grand rounds," continuing education programs on medicine delivered over the Internet and on hand-held personal digital assistants.

Ad agencies are thrilled to have new options to present to pharmaceutical clients, which in the past might have been blocked from linking their brands so closely with editorial research. One reason for the excitement is that the Internet allows marketers to catch doctors at the exact moment when they are thinking about a particular disease.[16]

Discuss the pros and cons of drug companies advertising to physicians in online medical journals. Is this any different from advertising in print journals? Explain why drug companies' marketing to physicians is considered business marketing.

REVIEW LEARNING OBJECTIVE 2

2 Describe the role of the Internet in business marketing

Business Internet Uses

THEN   **Revenue Generation**
Basic Marketing Communication

and

NOW   **Reduce costs**
Build partnerships and alliances
Build and support branding

---

3 RELATIONSHIP MARKETING AND STRATEGIC ALLIANCES

Discuss the role of relationship marketing and strategic alliances in business marketing

As Chapter 1 explained, relationship marketing is a strategy that entails seeking and establishing ongoing partnerships with customers. Relationship marketing has become an important business marketing strategy as customers have become more demanding and competition has become more intense. Building long-term relationships with customers offers companies a way to build competitive advantage. For

example, the FedEx Powership program includes a series of automated shipping, tracking, and invoicing systems that save customers time and money while solidifying their loyalty to FedEx. This produces a win-win situation. FedEx has a satisfied loyal customer, and the customer saves time and money shipping products to its customers.

STRATEGIC ALLIANCES

A **strategic alliance**, sometimes called a *strategic partnership*, is a cooperative agreement between business firms. Strategic alliances can take the form of licensing or distribution agreements, joint ventures, research and development consortia, and partnerships. They may be between manufacturers, manufacturers and customers, manufacturers and suppliers, and manufacturers and channel intermediaries.

Business marketers form strategic alliances to leverage what they have (technology, financial resources, access to markets) by combining these assets with those of other firms. Sometimes the alliance partners' assets are complementary. For example, UPS has developed strategic alliances with Ford, Nike, and Daimler-Chrysler to employ its information-technology expertise to track shipments and handle online orders. Ford uses UPS to track the more than four million cars and trucks it produces annually. Dealers log onto an Internet site to find out exactly where their orders are in the distribution system, much the way customers already can track UPS packages on the Internet using a tracking number.

Some alliances are formed with multiple partners to achieve increased productivity and lower costs for all participants. For example, Dow Chemical launched a program called MyAccount@Dow in 1999. Initially a pilot test serving 200 customers, primarily in Latin America, it now has more than 8,000 registered users in 35 countries, captures 40 percent of the company's total sales volume in Latin America, and (as of late 2001) reportedly generated about $100 million in revenues a month. The program allows customers to review their account histories, check the availability of products, and manage their order-delivery schedules. Such capabilities give the supplier, in turn, a clearer picture of its customers' inventory levels and buying patterns—information that permits the supplier to manage its own inventory more efficiently and to book customers' orders with greater certainty. The program, which is linked to Dow's internal systems, tracks all interactions with customers—by telephone, fax, or computer—cutting the company's cost per transaction to about $1, from $50 to $100. Overall, the company claims to have wrested more than $30 million a year in productivity improvements from its self-service system.[17]

What makes programs like Dow's successful? Increasing productivity and lowering costs are important. So are customer relationships built on trust (and supported by nondisclosure agreements) if, for example, suppliers are to be able to monitor a customer's sales and inventory levels, forecast product demand, and assure the delivery of goods and services as needed.[18]

Not all so-called exchanges are successful, particularly when participants lack trust in their trading partners and benefits are not shared. General Motors, Ford, DaimlerChrysler, Nissan Motor Company, and Renault SA created an Internet automobile parts exchange, called Covisint, that was expected to account for $300 billion in sales per year. The auto manufacturers assumed that if they built a Web site, trading volume would follow. But the industry is characterized by mistrust between buyers and sellers. After a decade of being forced to accept price concessions, suppliers were in no hurry to participate. The manufacturers didn't help by boasting that Covisint would squeeze an additional 30 percent in savings out of vendors.[19]

Strategic alliances are at the heart of business marketing. Nobody knows this better than UPS. Its alliance with Office Depot makes UPS services available to the multitude of businesspeople who shop the supply superstore.

strategic alliance (strategic partnership)
A cooperative agreement between business firms.

RELATIONSHIPS IN OTHER CULTURES

 Although the terms *relationship marketing* and *strategic alliances* are fairly new, and popularized mostly by American business executives and educators, the concepts have long been familiar in other cultures. Businesses in countries such as Mexico, China, Japan, Korea, and much of Europe rely heavily on personal relationships. Chapter 20 explores customer relationship management in detail.

In Japan, for example, exchange between firms is based on personal relationships that are developed through what is called *amae*, or indulgent dependency. *Amae* is the feeling of nurturing concern for, and dependence upon, another. Reciprocity and personal relationships contribute to *amae*. Relationships between companies can develop into a **keiretsu**—a network of interlocking corporate affiliates. Within a keiretsu, executives may sit on the boards of their customers or their suppliers. Members of a keiretsu trade with each other whenever possible and often engage in joint product development, finance, and marketing activity. For example, the Toyota Group keiretsu includes 14 core companies and another 170 that receive preferential treatment. Toyota holds an equity position in many of these 170 member firms and is represented on many of their boards of directors.

Many American firms have found that the best way to compete in Asian countries is to form relationships with Asian firms. For example, Fuji-Xerox markets copiers in Japan and other Asian countries. Whirlpool has spent over $200 million buying controlling interests in competing firms in China and in India. The "Global Perspectives" box in this chapter describes the relationship between JCPenney and TAL Apparel Ltd., a Hong Kong–based company.

keiretsu
A network of interlocking corporate affiliates.

Global Perspectives

GLOBAL PERSPECTIVES

> MADE TO MEASURE: INVENTORY MANAGEMENT AT JCPENNEY VIA HONG KONG

 On a Saturday afternoon in August, Carolyn Thurmond walked into a JCPenney store in Atlanta's Northlake Mall and bought a white Stafford wrinkle-free dress shirt for her husband, size 17 neck, 34/35 sleeve. On Monday morning, a computer technician in Hong Kong downloaded a record of the sale. By Wednesday afternoon, a factory worker in Taiwan had packed an identical replacement shirt into a bundle to be shipped back to the Atlanta store.

This speedy process is part of a streamlined supply chain and production system for dress shirts that was years in the making. In an industry where the goal is speedy turnaround of merchandise, Penney stores now hold almost no extra inventory of house-brand dress shirts. Less than a decade ago, Penney would have had thousands of them warehoused across the United States, tying up capital and slowly going out of style.

Penney is conspicuously absent from the entire program, which is designed and operated by TAL Apparel Ltd., a closely held Hong Kong shirt maker. TAL collects point-of-sale data for Penney's shirts directly from its stores in North America, then runs the numbers through a computer model it designed. The Hong Kong company then decides how many shirts to make, and in what styles, colors, and sizes. The manufacturer sends the shirts directly to each Penney store, bypassing the retailer's warehouses—and corporate decision makers.

TAL, a no-name giant, makes one in eight dress shirts sold in the United States. Its close relationship with U.S. retailers is part of a power shift taking place in global manufacturing. As retailers strive to cut costs and keep pace with consumer tastes, they are coming to depend more on suppliers that can respond swiftly to their changing needs. with TAL has rushed in, even starting to take over such critical areas as sales forecasting and inventory management.

Rodney Birkins Jr., vice president for sourcing of JCPenney Private Brands, Inc., describes the added efficiency Penney has been able to achieve TAL as "phenomenal." Just a decade ago, Penney would routinely hold up to six months of inventory in its warehouses and three months' worth at stores. Now, for the shirt lines that TAL handles, "it's zero," Mr. Birkins says. With decisions made at the factory, TAL can respond instantly to changes in consumer demand: stepping up production if there is a spike in sales or dialing it down if there's a slump. The system "directly links the manufacturer to the customer," says Mr. Birkins. "That is the future."[20]

In essence, Penney's has outsourced its inventory management to TAL. What conditions do you think were necessary for this to happen? How does the arrangement between Penney's and TAL benefit consumers?

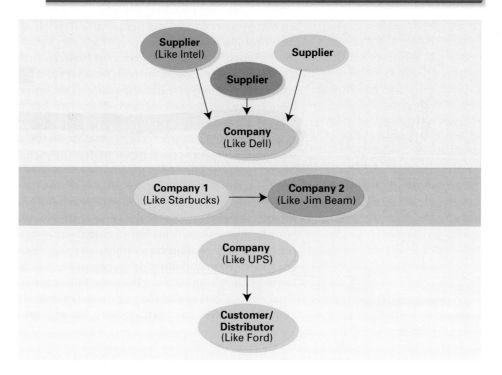

| 3 | Discuss the role of relationship marketing and strategic alliances in business marketing |

4 MAJOR CATEGORIES OF BUSINESS CUSTOMERS

Identify the four major categories of business market customers

The business market consists of four major categories of customers: producers, resellers, governments, and institutions.

PRODUCERS

The producer segment of the business market includes profit-oriented individuals and organizations that use purchased goods and services to produce other products, to incorporate into other products, or to facilitate the daily operations of the organization. Examples of producers include construction, manufacturing, transportation, finance, real estate, and food service firms. In the United States there are over 13 million firms in the producer segment of the business market. Some of these firms are small, and others are among the world's largest businesses.

Producers are often called **original equipment manufacturers** or **OEMs**. This term includes all individuals and organizations that buy business goods and incorporate them into the products that they produce for eventual sale to other producers or to consumers. Companies such as General Motors that buy steel, paint, tires, and batteries are said to be OEMs.

RESELLERS

original equipment manufacturers (OEMs)
Individuals and organizations that buy business goods and incorporate them into the products that they produce for eventual sale to other producers or to consumers.

The reseller market includes retail and wholesale businesses that buy finished goods and resell them for a profit. A retailer sells mainly to final consumers; wholesalers sell mostly to retailers and other organizational customers. There are approximately 1.5 million retailers and 500,000 wholesalers operating in the United States. Consumer-product firms like Procter & Gamble, Kraft General Foods, and Coca-Cola sell directly to large retailers and retail chains and through wholesalers to smaller retail units. Retailing is explored in detail in Chapter 13.

Business product distributors are wholesalers that buy business products and resell them to business customers. They often carry thousands of items in stock and employ sales forces to call on business customers. Businesses that wish to buy a gross of pencils or a hundred pounds of fertilizer typically purchase these items from local distributors rather than directly from manufacturers such as Empire Pencil or Dow Chemical.

A few years ago, many people thought that the Internet would eliminate the need for distributors. Why would customers pay distributor markups when they could buy directly from manufacturers with a few mouse clicks? The answer is that many business customers, especially small firms, depend on relationships with knowledgeable distributors for information and advice that is not available to them online.

The producer segment of the business market includes manufacturing, like this globe production line, as well as construction, finance, transportation, real estate, and others.

GOVERNMENTS

A third major segment of the business market is government. Government organizations include thousands of federal, state, and local buying units. They make up what may be the largest single market for goods and services in the world.

Contracts for government purchases are often put out for bid. Interested vendors submit bids (usually sealed) to provide specified products during a particular time. Sometimes the lowest bidder is awarded the contract. When the lowest bidder is not awarded the contract, strong evidence must be presented to justify the decision. Grounds for rejecting the lowest bid include lack of experience, inadequate financing, or poor past performance. Bidding allows all potential suppliers a fair chance at winning government contracts and helps ensure that public funds are spent wisely.

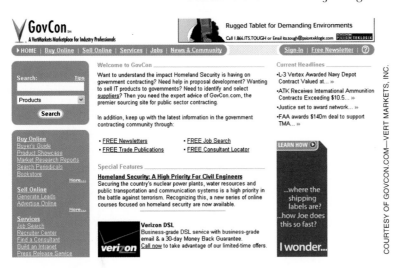

Federal Government

Name just about any good or service and chances are that someone in the federal government uses it. The U.S. federal government buys goods and services valued at over $590 billion per year, making it the world's largest customer.

Although much of the federal government's buying is centralized, no single federal agency contracts for all the government's requirements, and no single buyer in any agency purchases all that the agency needs. We can view the federal government as a combination of several large companies with overlapping responsibilities and thousands of small independent units.

One popular source of information about government procurement is *Commerce Business Daily*. Until recently, businesses hoping to sell to the federal government found the document unorganized, and it often arrived too late to be useful. The online version (**http://www.cbd-net.com**) is more timely and lets contractors find leads using keyword searches. *Doing Business with the General Services Administration, Selling to the Military*, and *Selling to the U.S. Air*

For doing business with the federal government, there is no better online resource than govcon.com. Users can check industry news, consult government databases, and view active contracts.

Force are other examples of publications designed to explain how to do business with the federal government.

State, County, and City Government

Selling to states, counties, and cities can be less frustrating for both small and large vendors than selling to the federal government. Paperwork is typically simpler and more manageable than it is at the federal level. On the other hand, vendors must decide which of the over 82,000 government units are likely to buy their wares. State and local buying agencies include school districts, highway departments, government-operated hospitals, and housing agencies.

INSTITUTIONS

The fourth major segment of the business market is institutions that seek to achieve goals other than the standard business goals of profit, market share, and return on investment. This segment includes schools, hospitals, colleges and universities, churches, labor unions, fraternal organizations, civic clubs, foundations, and other so-called nonbusiness organizations. Xerox offers educational and medical institutions the same prices as government agencies (the lowest that Xerox offers) and has a separate sales force that calls on these customers.

REVIEW LEARNING OBJECTIVE 4

4 | Identify the four major categories of business market customers

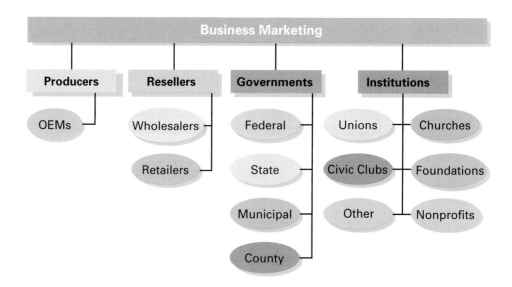

5 THE NORTH AMERICAN INDUSTRY CLASSIFICATION SYSTEM

Explain the North American Industry Classification System

North American Industry Classification System (NAICS)
A detailed numbering system developed by the United States, Canada, and Mexico to classify North American business establishments by their main production processes.

 The **North American Industry Classification System (NAICS)** is an industry classification system introduced in 1997 to replace the standard industrial classification system (SIC). NAICS (pronounced *nakes*) is a system for classifying North American business establishments. The system, developed jointly by the United States, Canada, and Mexico, provides a common industry classification system for the North American Free Trade Association (NAFTA) partners. Goods- or service-producing firms that use identical or similar production processes are grouped together.

FAQs

Why was NAICS created to replace the SIC system? Find out more by watching the video FAQ on Xtra!

NAICS is an extremely valuable tool for business marketers engaged in analyzing, segmenting, and targeting markets. Each classification group is relatively homogeneous in terms of raw materials required, components used, manufacturing processes employed, and problems faced. The more digits in a code, the more homogeneous the group is. Therefore, if a supplier understands the needs and requirements of a few firms within a classification, requirements can be projected for all firms in that category. The number, size, and geographic dispersion of firms can also be identified. This information can be converted to market potential estimates, market share estimates, and sales forecasts. It can also be used for identifying potential new customers. NAICS codes can help identify firms that may be prospective users of a supplier's goods and services.

Exhibit 6.2 provides an overview of NAICS. Exhibit 6.3 illustrates the six-digit classification system for two of the 20 NAICS economic sectors: manufacturing and information. The hierarchical structure of NAICS allows industry data to be summarized at several levels of detail. To illustrate:

- The first two digits designate a major economic sector such as agriculture (11) or manufacturing (31–33).
- The third digit designates an economic subsector such as crop production or apparel manufacturing.
- The fourth digit designates an industry group, such as grain and oil seed farming or fiber, yarn, and thread mills.
- The fifth digit designates the NAICS industry, such as wheat farming or broadwoven fabric mills.
- The sixth digit, when used, identifies subdivisions of NAICS industries that accommodate user needs in individual countries.[21]

For a complete listing of all NAICS codes, see **http://www.census.gov/epcd/www/naics.html**.

EXHIBIT 6.2

NAICS Two-Digit Codes and Corresponding Economic Sectors

NAICS Code	Economic Sector
11	Agriculture, forestry, and fishing
21	Mining
22	Utilities
23	Construction
31–33	Manufacturing
43	Wholesale trade
44–45	Retail trade
47–48	Transportation
51	Information
52	Finance and insurance
53	Real estate and rental and leasing
56	Professional and technical services
57	Management and support services
61	Education services
62	Health and social assistance
71	Arts, entertainment, and recreation
72	Food services, drinking places, and accommodations
81	Other services, except public administration
93	Public administration
98	Estates and trusts
99	Nonclassifiable

EXHIBIT 6.3

Examples of NAICS Hierarchy

NAICS Level	Example 1 NAICS Code	Example 1 Description	Example 2 NAICS Code	Example 2 Description
Sector	31–33	Manufacturing	51	Information
Subsector	334	Computer and electronic product manufacturing	513	Broadcasting and telecommunications
Industry group	3346	Manufacturing and reproduction of magnetic and optical media	5133	Telecommunications
Industry	33461	Manufacturing and reproduction of magnetic and optical media	51332	Wireless telecommunications carriers, except satellite
U.S. industry	334611	Reproduction of software	513321	Paging

SOURCE: U.S. Census Bureau, "New Code System in NAICS," **http://www.census.gov/epcd/www/naics.html**.

5   **Explain the North American Industry Classification System**

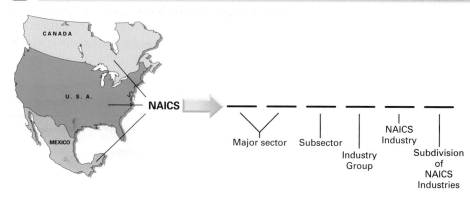

Major sector   Subsector   Industry Group   NAICS Industry   Subdivision of NAICS Industries

6   BUSINESS VERSUS CONSUMER MARKETS

Explain the major differences between business and consumer markets

The basic philosophy and practice of marketing are the same whether the customer is a business organization or a consumer. Business markets do, however, have characteristics different from consumer markets.

DEMAND

Consumer demand for products is quite different from demand in the business market. Unlike consumer demand, business demand is derived, inelastic, joint, and fluctuating.

Derived Demand

FAQs

How can demand for business products be derived and widely fluctuating? Find out by watching the video FAQ on Xtra!

The demand for business products is called **derived demand** because organizations buy products to be used in producing their customers' products. For example, the market for CPUs, hard drives, and CD-ROMs is derived from the demand for personal computers. These items are only valuable as components of computers. Demand for these items rises and falls with the demand for PCs.

Because demand is derived, business marketers must carefully monitor demand patterns and changing preferences in final consumer markets, even though their customers are not in those markets. Moreover, business marketers must carefully monitor their customers' forecasts, because derived demand is based on expectations of future demand for those customers' products.

Some business marketers not only monitor final consumer demand and customer forecasts but also try to influence final consumer demand. Aluminum producers use television and magazine advertisements to point out the convenience and recycling opportunities that aluminum offers to consumers who can choose to purchase soft drinks in either aluminum or plastic containers.

Inelastic Demand

The demand for many business products is inelastic with regard to price. *Inelastic demand* means that an increase or decrease in the price of the product will not significantly affect demand for the product. This will be discussed further in Chapter 17.

The price of a product used in the production of or as part of a final product is often a minor portion of the final product's total price. Therefore, demand for the final consumer product is not affected. If the price of automobile paint or spark plugs rises significantly, say, 200 percent in one year, do you think the number of new automobiles sold that year will be affected? Probably not.

derived demand
The demand for business products.

Joint Demand

Joint demand occurs when two or more items are used together in a final product. For example, a decline in the availability of memory chips will slow production of microcomputers, which will in turn reduce the demand for disk drives. Likewise, the demand for Apple operating systems exists as long as there is demand for Apple computers. Sales of the two products are directly linked.

Fluctuating Demand

The demand for business products—particularly new plants and equipment—tends to be less stable than the demand for consumer products. A small increase or decrease in consumer demand can produce a much larger change in demand for the facilities and equipment needed to make the consumer product. Economists refer to this phenomenon as the **multiplier effect** (or **accelerator principle**).

Cummins Engine Company, a producer of heavy-duty diesel engines, uses sophisticated surface grinders to make parts. Suppose Cummins is using 20 surface grinders. Each machine lasts about ten years. Purchases have been timed so two machines will wear out and be replaced annually. If the demand for engine parts does not change, two grinders will be bought this year. If the demand for parts declines slightly, only 18 grinders may be needed and Cummins won't replace the worn ones. However, suppose that next year demand returns to previous levels plus a little more. To meet the new level of demand, Cummins will need to replace the two machines that wore out in the first year, the two that wore out in the second year, plus one or more additional machines. The multiplier effect works this way in many industries, producing highly fluctuating demand for business products.

joint demand
The demand for two or more items used together in a final product.

multiplier effect (accelerator principle)
Phenomenon in which a small increase or decrease in consumer demand can produce a much larger change in demand for the facilities and equipment needed to make the consumer product.

© AP WIDE/WORLD PHOTOS

One industry with very few customers is the airplane manufacturing industry. When Lockheed won the U.S Air Force contract for the Joint Striker Fighter aircraft, Boeing had to layoff employees. Now the companies are locked in fierce competition over a contract to build marine-patrol planes for the U.S. Navy. If Boeing wins, its planes will be built on a new 737 commercial platform, shown here.

PURCHASE VOLUME

Business customers buy in much larger quantities than consumers. Just think how large an order Kellogg typically places for the wheat bran and raisins used to manufacture Raisin Bran. Imagine the number of tires that Daimler-Chrysler buys at one time.

NUMBER OF CUSTOMERS

Business marketers usually have far fewer customers than consumer marketers. The advantage is that it is a lot easier to identify prospective buyers, monitor current customers' needs and levels of satisfaction, and personally attend to existing customers. The main disadvantage is that each customer becomes crucial—especially for those manufacturers that have only one customer. In many cases, this customer is the U.S. government. The success or failure of one bid can make the difference between prosperity and bankruptcy. After five years of development, testing, and politicking, the Pentagon awarded Lockheed Martin a multidecade contract to build 3,000 jet fighter airplanes.[22] Boeing Aircraft Company, the only other bidder on the $200 billion contract, immediately announced plans for substantial layoffs.

LOCATION OF BUYERS

Business customers tend to be much more geographically concentrated than consumers. For instance, more than half the nation's business buyers are located in New York, California, Pennsylvania, Illinois, Ohio, Michigan, and New Jersey. The aircraft and microelectronics industries are concentrated on the West Coast, and many of the firms that supply the automobile manufacturing industry are located in and around Detroit.

DISTRIBUTION STRUCTURE

Many consumer products pass through a distribution system that includes the producer, one or more wholesalers, and a retailer. In business marketing, however, because of many of the characteristics already mentioned, channels of distribution are typically shorter. Direct channels, where manufacturers market directly to users, are much more common. The use of direct channels has increased dramatically in the past decade with the introduction of various Internet buying and selling schemes. For example, Exostar, the aerospace industry's on-line exchange, has over 12,000 participating suppliers and conducts more than 20,000 transactions each week.[23] Exchanges such as Exostar facilitate direct channel relationships between producers and their customers.

NATURE OF BUYING

Unlike consumers, business buyers usually approach purchasing rather formally. Businesses use professionally trained purchasing agents or buyers who spend their entire career purchasing a limited number of items. They get to know the items and the sellers well. Some professional purchasers earn the designation of Certified Purchasing Manager (CPM) after participating in a rigorous certification program.

NATURE OF BUYING INFLUENCE

Typically, more people are involved in a single business purchase decision than in a consumer purchase. Experts from fields as varied as quality control, marketing, and finance, as well as professional buyers and users, may be grouped in a buying center (discussed later in this chapter).

TYPE OF NEGOTIATIONS

Consumers are used to negotiating price on automobiles and real estate. In most cases, however, American consumers expect sellers to set the price and other conditions of sale, such as time of delivery and credit terms. In contrast, negotiating is common in business marketing. Buyers and sellers negotiate product specifications, delivery dates, payment terms, and other pricing matters. Sometimes these negotiations occur during many meetings over several months. Final contracts are often very long and detailed.

USE OF RECIPROCITY

reciprocity
A practice where business purchasers choose to buy from their own customers.

Business purchasers often choose to buy from their own customers, a practice known as **reciprocity**. For example, General Motors buys engines for use in its automobiles and trucks from Borg Warner, which in turn buys many of the automobiles and trucks it needs from GM. This practice is neither unethical nor illegal unless one party coerces the other and the result is unfair competition. Reciprocity is generally considered a reasonable business practice. If all possible suppliers sell a similar product for about the same price, doesn't it make sense to buy from those firms that buy from you?

USE OF LEASING

Consumers normally buy products rather than lease them. But businesses commonly lease expensive equipment such as computers, construction equipment and vehicles, and automobiles. Leasing allows firms to reduce capital outflow, acquire a seller's latest products, receive better services, and gain tax advantages.

The lessor, the firm providing the product, may be either the manufacturer or an independent firm. The benefits to the lessor include greater total revenue from leasing compared to selling and an opportunity to do business with customers who cannot afford to buy.

PRIMARY PROMOTIONAL METHOD

Business marketers tend to emphasize personal selling in their promotion efforts, especially for expensive items, custom-designed products, large-volume purchases, and situations requiring negotiations. The sale of many business products requires a great deal of personal contact. Personal selling is discussed in more detail in Chapter 16.

REVIEW LEARNING OBJECTIVE 6

| 6 | Explain the major differences between business and consumer markets |

Characteristic	Business Market	Consumer Market
Demand	Organizational	Individual
Purchase volume	Larger	Smaller
Number of customers	Fewer	Many
Location of buyers	Geographically concentrated	Dispersed
Distribution structure	More direct	More indirect
Nature of buying	More professional	More personal
Nature of buying influence	Multiple	Single
Type of negotiations	More complex	Simpler
Use of reciprocity	Yes	No
Use of leasing	Greater	Lesser
Primary promotional method	Personal selling	Advertising

7 TYPES OF BUSINESS PRODUCTS

Describe the seven types of business goods and services

Business products generally fall into one of the following seven categories, depending on their use: major equipment, accessory equipment, raw materials, component parts, processed materials, supplies, and business services.

MAJOR EQUIPMENT

major equipment (installations)
Capital goods such as large or expensive machines, mainframe computers, blast furnaces, generations, airplanes, and buildings.

Major equipment includes such capital goods as large or expensive machines, mainframe computers, blast furnaces, generators, airplanes, and buildings. (These items are also commonly called **installations**.) Major equipment is depreciated over time rather than charged as an expense in the year it is purchased. In addition, major equipment is often custom-designed for each customer. Personal selling is an important part of the marketing strategy for major equipment because distribution channels are almost always direct from the producer to the business user.

ACCESSORY EQUIPMENT

Accessory equipment is generally less expensive and shorter-lived than major equipment. Examples include portable drills, power tools, microcomputers, and fax machines. Accessory equipment is often charged as an expense in the year it is bought rather than depreciated over its useful life. In contrast to major equipment, accessories are more often standardized and are usually bought by more customers. These customers tend to be widely dispersed. For example, all types of businesses buy microcomputers.

Local industrial distributors (wholesalers) play an important role in the marketing of accessory equipment because business buyers often purchase accessories from them. Regardless of where accessories are bought, advertising is a more vital promotional tool for accessory equipment than for major equipment.

RAW MATERIALS

Raw materials are unprocessed extractive or agricultural products—for example, mineral ore, lumber, wheat, corn, fruits, vegetables, and fish. Raw materials become part of finished products. Extensive users, such as steel or lumber mills and food canners, generally buy huge quantities of raw materials. Because there is often a large number of relatively small sellers of raw materials, none can greatly influence price or supply. Thus, the market tends to set the price of raw materials, and individual producers have little pricing flexibility. Promotion is almost always via personal selling, and distribution channels are usually direct from producer to business user.

COMPONENT PARTS

Component parts are either finished items ready for assembly or products that need very little processing before becoming part of some other product. Caterpillar diesel engines are component parts used in heavy-duty trucks. Other examples include spark plugs, tires, and electric motors for automobiles. A special feature of component parts is that they can retain their identity after becoming part of the final product. For example, automobile tires are clearly recognizable as part of a car. Moreover, because component parts often wear out, they may need to be replaced several times during the life of the final product. Thus, there are two important markets for many component parts: the original equipment manufacturer (OEM) market and the replacement market.

Many of the business features listed on page 209 in the review for Learning Objective 6 characterize the OEM market. The difference between unit costs and selling prices in the OEM market is often small, but profits can be substantial because of volume buying.

The replacement market is composed of organizations and individuals buying component parts to replace worn-out parts. Because components often retain their identity in final products, users may choose to replace a component part with the same brand used by the manufacturer—for example, the same brand of automobile tires or battery. The replacement market operates differently from the OEM market, however. Whether replacement buyers are organizations or individuals, they tend to demonstrate the characteristics of consumer markets that were shown in Review 6. Consider, for example, an automobile replacement part. Purchase volume is usually small and there are many customers, geographically dispersed, who typically buy from car dealers or parts stores. Negotiations do not occur, and neither reciprocity nor leasing is usually an issue.

Manufacturers of component parts often direct their advertising toward replacement buyers. Cooper Tire & Rubber, for example, makes and markets component parts—automobile and truck tires—for the replacement market only. General Motors and other car makers compete with independent firms in the market for replacement automobile parts.

accessory equipment
Goods, such as portable tools and office equipment, that are less expensive and shorter-lived than major equipment.

raw materials
Unprocessed extractive or agricultural products, such as mineral ore, lumber, wheat, corn, fruits, vegetables, and fish.

component parts
Either finished items ready for assembly or products that need very little processing before becoming part of some other product.

© AP/WIDE WORLD PHOTOS

Supplies are consumable. And even though the Internet has greatly affected the consumption of many supplies, like envelopes, paper is still in high demand. In fact, computer technology has increased the demand for paper rather than squelched it. As a result, paper companies, like Boise, are developing different types of paper for different types of printing devices.

PROCESSED MATERIALS

Processed materials are products used directly in manufacturing other products. Unlike raw materials, they have had some processing. Examples include sheet metal, chemicals, specialty steel, lumber, corn syrup, and plastics. Unlike component parts, processed materials do not retain their identity in final products.

Most processed materials are marketed to OEMs or to distributors servicing the OEM market. Processed materials are generally bought according to customer specifications or to some industry standard, as is the case with steel and lumber. Price and service are important factors in choosing a vendor.

SUPPLIES

Supplies are consumable items that do not become part of the final product—for example, lubricants, detergents, paper towels, pencils, and paper. Supplies are normally standardized items that purchasing agents routinely buy. Supplies typically have relatively short lives and are inexpensive compared to other business goods. Because supplies generally fall into one of three categories—maintenance, repair, or operating supplies—this category is often referred to as MRO items.

Competition in the MRO market is intense. Bic and Paper Mate, for example, battle for business purchases of inexpensive ballpoint pens.

BUSINESS SERVICES

Business services are expense items that do not become part of a final product. Businesses often retain outside providers to perform janitorial, advertising, legal, management consulting, marketing research, maintenance, and other services. Hiring an outside provider makes sense when it costs less than hiring or assigning an employee to perform the task and when an outside provider is needed for particular expertise.

REVIEW LEARNING OBJECTIVE 7

7 **Describe the seven types of business goods and services**

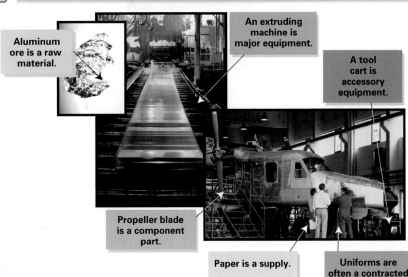

Aluminum ore is a raw material.

An extruding machine is major equipment.

A tool cart is accessory equipment.

Propeller blade is a component part.

Paper is a supply.

Uniforms are often a contracted service.

processed materials
Products used directly in manufacturing other products.

supplies
Consumable items that do not become part of the final product.

business services
Expense items that do not become part of a final product.

Discuss the unique aspects of
business buying behavior

As you probably have already concluded, business buyers behave differently from consumers. Understanding how purchase decisions are made in organizations is a first step in developing a business selling strategy. Business buying behavior has five important aspects: buying centers, evaluative criteria, buying situations, business ethics, and customer service.

BUYING CENTERS

A **buying center** includes all those persons in an organization who become involved in the purchase decision. Membership and influence vary from company to company. For instance, in engineering-dominated firms like Bell Helicopter, the buying center may consist almost entirely of engineers. In marketing-oriented firms like Toyota and IBM, marketing and engineering have almost equal authority. In consumer goods firms like Procter & Gamble, product managers and other marketing decision makers may dominate the buying center. In a small manufacturing company, almost everyone may be a member.

The number of people involved in a buying center varies with the complexity and importance of a purchase decision. The composition of the buying group will usually change from one purchase to another and sometimes even during various stages of the buying process. To make matters more complicated, buying centers do not appear on formal organization charts.

For example, even though a formal committee may have been set up to choose a new plant site, it is only part of the buying center. Other people, like the company president, often play informal yet powerful roles. In a lengthy decision-making process, such as finding a new plant location, some members may drop out of the buying center when they can no longer play a useful role. Others whose talents are needed then become part of the center. No formal announcement of "who is in" and "who is out" is ever made.

FAQs

If buying center members change so often, how can salespeople know who to contact? Find out by watching the video FAQ on Xtra!

Roles in the Buying Center

As in family purchasing decisions, several people may play a role in the business purchase process:

- *Initiator:* the person who first suggests making a purchase.
- *Influencers/evaluators:* people who influence the buying decision. They often help define specifications and provide information for evaluating options. Technical personnel are especially important as influencers.
- *Gatekeepers:* group members who regulate the flow of information. Frequently, the purchasing agent views the gatekeeping role as a source of his or her power. A secretary may also act as a gatekeeper by determining which vendors get an appointment with a buyer.
- *Decider:* the person who has the formal or informal power to choose or approve the selection of the supplier or brand. In complex situations, it is often difficult to determine who makes the final decision.
- *Purchaser:* the person who actually negotiates the purchase. It could be anyone from the president of the company to the purchasing agent, depending on the importance of the decision.
- *Users:* members of the organization who will actually use the product. Users often initiate the buying process and help define product specifications.

An example illustrating these basic roles is shown in Exhibit 6.4.

buying center
All those persons in an organization who become involved in the purchase decision.

EXHIBIT 6.4

Buying-Center Roles for Computer Purchases

Role	Illustration
Initiator	Division general manager proposes to replace company's computer network.
Influencers/evaluators	Corporate controller's office and vice president of data processing have an important say about which system and vendor the company will deal with.
Gatekeepers	Corporate departments for purchasing and data processing analyze company's needs and recommend likely matches with potential vendors.
Decider	Vice president of administration, with advice from others, selects vendor the company will deal with and system it will buy.
Purchaser	Purchasing agent negotiates terms of sale.
Users	All division employees use the computers.

Implications of Buying Centers for the Marketing Manager

Successful vendors realize the importance of identifying who is in the decision-making unit, each member's relative influence in the buying decision, and each member's evaluative criteria. Successful selling strategies often focus on determining the most important buying influences and tailoring sales presentations to the evaluative criteria most important to these buying-center members.

For example, Loctite Corporation, the manufacturer of Super Glue and industrial adhesives and sealants, found that engineers were the most important influencers and deciders in adhesive and sealant purchase decisions. As a result, Loctite focused its marketing efforts on production and maintenance engineers.

EVALUATIVE CRITERIA

Business buyers evaluate products and suppliers against three important criteria: quality, service, and price—in that order.

Quality

In this case, quality refers to technical suitability. A superior tool can do a better job in the production process, and superior packaging can increase dealer and consumer acceptance of a brand. Evaluation of quality also applies to the salesperson and the salesperson's firm. Business buyers want to deal with reputable salespeople and companies that are financially responsible. Quality improvement should be part of every organization's marketing strategy.

Service

Almost as much as they want satisfactory products, business buyers want satisfactory service. A purchase offers several opportunities for service. Suppose a vendor is selling heavy equipment. Prepurchase service could include a survey of the buyer's needs. After thorough analysis of the survey findings, the vendor could prepare a report and recommendations in the form of a purchasing proposal. If a purchase results, postpurchase service might consist of installing the equipment and training those who will be using it. Postsale services may also include maintenance and repairs. Another service that business buyers seek is dependability of supply. They must be able to count on delivery of what was ordered when it is scheduled to be delivered. Buyers also welcome services that help them sell their finished products. Services of this sort are especially appropriate when the seller's product is an identifiable part of the buyer's end product.

Marketing... in Entertainment

Business Buying at Movie Studios

Like any other industry, the entertainment industry uses all types of business equipment, from major installations like camera cranes to more banal office supplies. Industrial Light and Magic (ILM), the special effects arm of Lucas Digital, is the leading special effects provider in Hollywood and has won more visual effects awards than any of its competitors. To stay on top, ILM needs equipment that runs well and doesn't break down. When the company invested $300,000 in a Northlight film scanner manufactured by FilmLight, Ltd., the decision maker was Neil Robinson, ILM's senior software engineer. He compared the Northlight with a competing machine, called Imagica, and found that the quality of their output was nearly identical. But, unlike the Imagica, the Northlight was designed as a production machine rather than a fine engineering solution. Since ILM runs several projects simultaneously—and has never been late on one of them, ever—having a production-grade machine is critical. In fact, ILM is considering purchasing two more Northlight scanners.[24]

Customer service is not just an issue for retailers of consumer products and services. CDW pairs its 360,000 business customers each to an experienced account manager who can match the right technology products to the right needs. CDW sells more technology products from more manufacturers than anyone.

new buy
A situation requiring the purchase of a product for the first time.

modified rebuy
A situation where the purchaser wants some change in the original good or service.

straight rebuy
A situation in which the purchaser reorders the same goods or services without looking for new information or investigating other suppliers.

Price

Business buyers want to buy at low prices—at the lowest prices, under most circumstances. However, a buyer who pressures a supplier to cut prices to a point where the supplier loses money on the sale almost forces shortcuts on quality. The buyer also may, in effect, force the supplier to quit selling to him or her. Then a new source of supply will have to be found.

BUYING SITUATIONS

Often business firms, especially manufacturers, must decide whether to make something or buy it from an outside supplier. The decision is essentially one of economics. Can an item of similar quality be bought at a lower price elsewhere? If not, is manufacturing it in-house the best use of limited company resources? For example, Briggs & Stratton Corporation, a major manufacturer of four-cycle engines, might be able to save $150,000 annually on outside purchases by spending $500,000 on the equipment needed to produce gas throttles internally. Yet Briggs & Stratton could also use that $500,000 to upgrade its carburetor assembly line, which would save $225,000 annually. If a firm does decide to buy a product instead of making it, the purchase will be a new buy, a modified rebuy, or a straight rebuy.

New Buy

A **new buy** is a situation requiring the purchase of a product for the first time. For example, suppose a manufacturing company needs a better way to page managers while they are working on the shop floor. Currently, each of the several managers has a distinct ring, for example, two short and one long, that sounds over the plant intercom whenever he or she is being paged by anyone in the factory. The company decides to replace its buzzer system of paging with handheld wireless radio technology that will allow managers to communicate immediately with the department initiating the page. This situation represents the greatest opportunity for new vendors. No long-term relationship has been established for this product, specifications may be somewhat fluid, and buyers are generally more open to new vendors.

If the new item is a raw material or a critical component part, the buyer cannot afford to run out of supply. The seller must be able to convince the buyer that the seller's firm can consistently deliver a high-quality product on time.

Modified Rebuy

A **modified rebuy** is normally less critical and less time-consuming than a new buy. In a modified-rebuy situation, the purchaser wants some change in the original good or service. It may be a new color, greater tensile strength in a component part, more respondents in a marketing research study, or additional services in a janitorial contract.

Because the two parties are familiar with each other and credibility has been established, buyer and seller can concentrate on the specifics of the modification. But in some cases, modified rebuys are open to outside bidders. The purchaser uses this strategy to ensure that the new terms are competitive. An example would be the manufacturing company buying radios with a vibrating feature for managers who have trouble hearing the ring over the factory noise. The firm may open the bidding to examine the price/quality offerings of several suppliers.

Straight Rebuy

A **straight rebuy** is a situation vendors prefer. The purchaser is not looking for new information or other suppliers. An order is placed and the product is provided as in previous orders. Usually, a straight rebuy is routine because the terms of the purchase have been agreed to in earlier negotiations. An example would be the manufacturing company previously cited purchasing additional radios for new managers from the same supplier on a regular basis.

One common instrument used in straight-rebuy situations is the purchasing contract. Purchasing contracts are used with products that are bought often andin high volume. In essence, the purchasing contract makes the buyer's decision making routine and promises the salesperson a sure sale. The advantage to the buyer is a quick, confident decision and, to the salesperson, reduced or eliminated competition.

Suppliers must remember not to take straight-rebuy relationships for granted. Retaining existing customers is much easier than attracting new ones.

National Association of Purchasing Management
Familiarize yourself with the National Association of Purchasing Management (NAPM) by reading about the organization on its Web site. Based on what you read, do you think a purchasing manager can be effective without being certified by the NAPM? How does the NAPM help its members with ethical dilemmas?

http://www.napm.org

Online

BUSINESS ETHICS

As we noted in Chapter 3, ethics refers to the moral principles or values that generally govern the conduct of an individual or a group. Ethics can also be viewed as the standard of behavior by which conduct is judged.

Many companies have codes of ethics that help guide buyers and sellers. Lockheed Martin, the global aircraft company, has such a code. It deals both with "doing things right" and "the right thing to do." The company strives to achieve ethical conduct in accordance with six virtues: honesty, integrity, respect, trust, responsibility, and citizenship.[25]

Although we have heard a lot about corporate misbehavior in recent years, most people, and most companies, follow ethical practices. To help achieve this, over half of all major corporations offer ethics training to employees.

CUSTOMER SERVICE

Business marketers are increasingly recognizing the benefits of developing a formal system to monitor customer opinions and perceptions of the quality of customer service. Companies like McDonald's, L.L. Bean, and Lexus build their strategies not only around products but also around a few highly developed service skills. These companies understand that keeping current customers satisfied is just as important as attracting new ones, if not more so. These leading-edge firms are obsessed not only with delivering high-quality customer service, but also with measuring satisfaction, loyalty, relationship quality, and other indicators of nonfinancial performance.

Most firms find it necessary to develop measures unique to their own strategy, value propositions, and target market. For example, Anderson Corporation assesses the loyalty of its trade customers by their willingness to continue carrying its windows and doors, recommend its products to colleagues and customers, increase their volume with the company, and put its products in their own homes. In contrast, leading power company Salt River Project looks at whether customers buy its noncommodity offerings, support its stance on public issues, and accept the company's advice and referrals.[26] Basically, each firm's measures should not only ask "what are your expectations?" and "how are we doing?" but should also reflect what the firm wants its customers to do.

REVIEW LEARNING OBJECTIVE 8

| 8 | **Discuss the unique aspects of business buying behavior** |

Buying Center
Initiator
Influencer
Decider   Gatekeeper
Purchaser
User

Evaluative Criteria
✓ Quality
✓ Service
✓ Price

Buying Situations
New buy
Straight rebuy
Modified rebuy

Customer Service

LOOKING BACK

Look back at the story about W. W. Grainger at the beginning of the chapter. You now know that the Internet plays an important role in the strategies of many business marketers, including W. W. Grainger. Visit

http://www.grainger.com to see the special services that Grainger offers on its Web site. While visiting the site, select a particular item and see how much information is available. You will recall that product descriptions in the company's

220,000-item catalog are limited to a couple of lines. By providing additional information the Web site clearly makes it easier for customers to evaluate alternative items—and for Grainger to provide enhanced customer service.

USE IT NOW

EXPLORE THE POSSIBILITIES

Starting a business at home is one of the easiest ways to become self-employed. Using the Home Office Association of America (HOAA) Web site (**http://www.hoaa.com**) for ideas, choose a possible business opportunity that interests you and that has business marketing possibilities. Then explore both the HOAA site and the American Association of Home-Based Businesses Web site (**http://www.aahbb.org**) to learn more about how to set up your business.

LEARN FROM AN ENTREPRENEUR

What does it really take to become an entrepreneur? Find out by interviewing a local entrepreneur or researching an entrepreneur you've read about in this book or in the

business press. Get answers to the following questions, as well as any others you'd like to ask:

- How did you develop your vision for the company?
- What are the most important entrepreneurial characteristics that helped you succeed?
- Where did you learn the business skills you needed to run and grow the company?
- How did you research the feasibility of your idea? Prepare your business idea?
- What were the biggest challenges you had to overcome?
- Where did you obtain financing for the company?
- How do you market your products and services to other businesses?
- What are the most important lessons you learned by starting this company?
- What advice do you have for would-be entrepreneurs?

REVIEW AND APPLICATIONS

1 **Describe business marketing.** Business marketing provides goods and services that are bought for use in business rather than for personal consumption. Intended use, not physical characteristics, distinguishes a business product from a consumer product.

1.1   As the marketing manager for Huggies diapers made by Kimberly-Clark, you are
WRITING constantly going head-to-head with Pampers, produced by rival Procter & Gamble. You are considering unlocking the potential of the business market to increase your share of the disposable diaper market, but how? Write an outline of several ways you could transform this quintessentially consumer product into a successful business product as well.

2 **Describe the role of the Internet in business marketing.** The rapid expansion and adoption of the Internet have made business markets more competitive than ever before. The number of business buyers and sellers using the Internet is rapidly increasing. Firms are seeking new and better ways to expand markets and sources of supply, increase sales and decrease costs, and better serve customers. With the Internet, every business in the world is potentially a local competitor.

2.1   How could you use the Web site **http://www.business2business.on.ca** to helpdefine a target market and develop a marketing plan?

2.2   Reconsider question 1.1. How could you use the Internet in your business marketing of Huggies diapers?

3 **Discuss the role of relationship marketing and strategic alliances in business marketing.** Relationship marketing entails seeking and establishing long-term alliances or partnerships with customers. A strategic alliance is a cooperative agreement between business firms. Firms form alliances to leverage what they do well by partnering with others that have complementary skills.

3.1   Why is relationship or personal selling the best way to promote in business marketing?

4 **Identify the four major categories of business market customers.** Producer markets consist of for-profit organizations and individuals that buy products to use in producing other products, as components of other products, or in facilitating business operations. Reseller markets consist of wholesalers and retailers that buy finished products to resell for profit. Government markets include federal, state, county, and city governments that buy goods and services to support their own operations and serve the needs of citizens. Institutional markets consist of very diverse nonbusiness institutions whose main goals do not include profit.

4.1   INFOTRAC COLLEGE EDITION   Understanding businesses is key to business marketing. Use InfoTrac (**http://www.infotrac-college.com**) to learn more about a variety of industries. Publications like *Manufacturing Automation, Computer Weekly, Power Generation Technology & Markets*, and *Biotech Equipment Update* can give you insights into many business marketing concepts. Research the industrial publications to find an article on a business marketer that interests you. Write a description of the company using as many concepts from the chapter as possible. What major category or categories of business market customers does this firm serve?

5 **Explain the North American Industry Classification System.** The NAICS provides a way to identify, analyze, segment, and target business and government markets. Organizations can be identified and compared by a numeric code indicating business sector, subsector, industry group, industry, and country industry. NAICS is a valuable tool for analyzing, segmenting, and targeting business markets.

5.1   Explain how a marketer can use the Web site **http://www.census. gov/epcd/www/naics.html** to convert SIC data to the NAICS.

5.2   Pick a product and determine its NAICS code. How easy was it to trace the groups and sectors?

6 **Explain the major differences between business and consumer markets.** In business markets, demand is derived, price-inelastic, joint, and fluctuating. Purchase volume is much larger than in consumer markets, customers are fewer in number and more geographically concentrated, and distribution channels are more direct. Buying is approached more formally using professional purchasing agents, more people are involved in the buying process, negotiation is more complex, and reciprocity and leasing are more common. And, finally, selling strategy in business markets normally focuses on personal contact rather than on advertising.

6.1   How might derived demand affect the manufacturing of an automobile?

6.2   Your boss has just asked you, the company purchasing manager, to buy new computers for an entire department. Since you have just recently purchased a new home computer, you are well-educated about the various products available. How will your buying process for the company differ from your recent purchase for yourself?

7 **Describe the seven types of business goods and services.** Major equipment includes capital goods, such as heavy machinery. Accessory equipment is typically less expensive and shorter-lived than major equipment. Raw materials are extractive or agricultural products that have not been processed. Component parts are finished or near-finished items to be used as parts of other products. Processed materials are used to manufacture other products. Supplies are consumable and not used as part of a final product. Business services are intangible products that many companies use in their operations.

7.1 **WRITING TEAM** In small groups, brainstorm examples of companies that feature the products in different business categories. (Avoid examples already listed in the chapter.) Compile a list of ten specific business products including at least one in each category. Then match up with another group. Have each group take turns naming a product and have the other group identify its appropriate category. Try to resolve all discrepancies by discussion. Some identified products may appropriately fit into more than one category.

8 **Discuss the unique aspects of business buying behavior.** Business buying behavior is distinguished by five fundamental characteristics. First, buying is normally undertaken by a buying center consisting of many people who range widely in authority level. Second, business buyers typically evaluate alternative products and suppliers based on quality, service, and price—in that order. Third, business buying falls into three general categories: new buys, modified rebuys, and straight rebuys. Fourth, the ethics of business buyers and sellers are often scrutinized. Fifth, customer service before, during, and after the sale plays a big role in business purchase decisions.

8.1 **WRITING** A colleague of yours has sent you an e-mail seeking your advice as he attempts to sell a new voice-mail system to a local business. Send him a return e-mail describing the various people who might influence the customer's buying decision. Be sure to include suggestions for dealing with the needs of each of these individuals.

8.2 Intel Corporation supplies microprocessors to Hewlett-Packard for use in its computers. Describe the buying situation in this relationship, keeping in mind the rapid advance of technology in this industry.

8.3 Review the "Marketing in Entertainment" box on Industrial Light and Magic (ILM). How would you categorize the purchase of the Northlight film scanner? Outline how ILM's purchase followed the unique aspects of buying behavior. How many concepts from the chapter can you identify in the ILM example?

TERMS

APPLICATION EXERCISE

Purchasing agents are often offered gifts and gratuities. Increasingly, though, companies are restricting the amount and value of gifts that their purchasing managers can accept from vendors. The idea is that purchasing managers should consider all qualified vendors during a buying decision instead of only those who pass out great event tickets. This exercise asks you to consider whether accepting various types of gifts is ethical.[27]

Activities

1. Review the following list of common types of gifts and favors. Put a checkmark next to the items that you think it would be acceptable for a purchasing manager to receive from a vendor.

   —Advertising souvenirs   —Automobiles

   —Clothing   —Dinners

   —Discounts on personal purchases   —Food and liquor

   —Golf outings   —Holiday gifts

   —Large appliances   —Loans of money

   —Lunches   —Small-value appliances

   —Tickets (sports, theater, amusement parks, etc.)   —Trips to vendor plants

   —Vacation trips

2. Now look at your list of acceptable gifts through various lenses. Would your list change if the purchasing manager's buying decision involved a low-cost item (say, pens)? Why or why not? What if the decision involved a very expensive purchase (like a major installation)?

3. Form a team and compare your lists. Discuss (or debate) any discrepancies.

ETHICS EXERCISE

 Cameron Stock, purchasing manager for a sports equipment manufacturer, is responsible for buying $5 million of supplies every year. He has a preferred list of certified suppliers, who are awarded a large percentage of his business. Cameron has been offered a paid weekend for two in Las Vegas as a Christmas present from a supplier with whom he has done business for a decade and built a very good relationship.

Questions

1. Would it be legal and ethical for Cameron Stock to accept this gift?

2. How is this addressed in the AMA Code of Ethics? Go to the AMA Web site at **http://www.marketingpower.com** and reread the Code of Ethics. Write a brief paragraph summarizing where the AMA stands on the issue of supplier gifts.

CAREER EXERCISE

Opportunities for business marketing can be found in nearly all industries and companies.

Activities

1. Looking for a career in this area may involve investigating the institutional arms of consumer-products companies. For example, Procter & Gamble operates a business-to-business site at **http://www.pgbrands.com** and a consumer-products site at **http://www.pg.com**. The same is true of Oneida, the silverware manufacturer.

2. Another avenue to explore is the Institute for Supply Management, formerly the National Association of Purchasing Managers. Its career site includes a resources page that lists over 40 links relevant to a business marketing job search. Go to **http://www.napm.org** for more information.

© A/P/WIDE WORLD PHOTOS

THE SEGWAY COMPANY: REINVENTING THE WHEEL

After months of fevered speculation, Dean Kamen, the award-winning inventor, revealed his innovation: a two-wheeled battery-powered device designed for a single standing rider.[28] The device, the Segway Human Transporter, can go up to 17 miles per hour.

The speed and direction of the Segway are controlled by the rider's shifting weight and one of the handlebars. Demonstrating the device, Kamen said, "Think forward," and inclined his head ever so slightly and zoomed ahead. "Think back," he continued, effortlessly reversing direction. You turn by twisting the handlebar mechanism and stop by simply thinking about stopping. A finely tuned gyroscopic balancing mechanism intuits where its rider wants to go.

Kamen, a college dropout and self-taught physicist and mechanical engineer, has made millions of dollars creating new medical devices, including the first portable dialysis machine, the first insulin pump, and an array of widely used heart stents. The idea for the Segway grew out of his work on a novel motorized wheelchair that can climb stairs. Typically, Kamen directs his attention to research and development with his company, DEKA Research and Development. He then licenses his inventions to other firms to market. But given the dramatic potential that he believes the Segway presents, Kamen decided to form his own company to produce and market it. One venture capital firm has invested $38 million in the project, the largest single investment in the firm's history. Other investors have also provided start-up funds, but Kamen retains majority control of Segway.

Kamen envisions many potential uses of the Segway, developed at a cost of more than $100 million. Initially, the firm concentrated on the business market, namely corporate and government customers, before rolling out a consumer version. The 80-pound industrial version of the Segway is priced at $5,000, while the 70-pound consumer model costs about $4,000. The first business market customers to test the Segway were the U.S. Postal Service, General Electric, and Amazon. Mail carriers are using the Segway on mail routes in selected cities, and Amazon employees use them to navigate around the warehouse fulfilling customer orders. The Department of Defense is also intrigued about the possibility of equipping its special forces units with Segways.[28]

Questions

1. What type of business product is the Segway? Explain.

2. Describe the buying process that you would expect the U.S. Postal Service to use. Include references to the buying behavior roles of various buying-center participants. Do the same thing for Amazon and briefly summarize the differences you would expect to find.

WATCH IT

SmallBusiness**School** ■
the Series on PBS stations and the Web

FEATURE PRESENTATION

Café Pilon

To give you insight into Chapter 6, Small Business School introduces you to the Souto family and the business marketing strategy of their company, Café Pilon, a coffee business that began in Cuba as Rowland Roasters. The Souto family, who established the company in 1856, has since immigrated to Miami, Florida, and their coffee roasting business has grown to 175 employees with $70 million in annual sales. Roasting and selling packaged grinds of Cuban espresso is the company's core business, and Café Pilon was the first to sell brick packs, or vacuum-packed coffee. The Soutos have put the company online, and they are exploring many ideas they hope will someday make them the Starbucks of the business market.

What to Watch for and Ask Yourself

1. Have students think about the evolving role and importance of brand in business marketing.
2. What type of business customer is Café Pilon? What type of business customers does Café Pilon sell to?
3. Explain how the concept of derived demand applies to Café Pilon's business.
4. What types of business products does Café Pilon use? What types of business products does Café Pilon sell?

ENCORE PRESENTATION

Bowfinger

Think more metaphorically about business marketing by watching a clip from *Bowfinger*, starring Steve Martin (Bowfinger), Eddie Murphy (Kit Ramsey), and Robert Downey, Jr., (Jerry Renfro). In this funny look at Hollywood filmmaking, Bobby Bowfinger wants to make a movie featuring action star Kit Ramsey, but the film budget is paltry at best. The selected scene shows you how Bowfinger works to get a deal with a producer.

As you watch the scene, think of it as a buying situation. What kind of buy is it? For what kind of product? What kind of business relationship do you think Bowfinger wants? What about Renfro, the producer? If you haven't already seen the movie, you might want to rent it to see how the product and the business relationship change over the course of the film.

STILL SHAKY?

If you're having trouble with the concepts in this chapter, consider using some of the following study resources. You can review the videos, or test yourself with materials designed for all kinds of learning styles.

☑ **Xtra! (http://lambxtra.swlearning.com)**

| ☑ Quiz | ☑ Feature Videos | ☑ Encore Videos | ☑ FAQ Videos |
| ☑ Exhibit Worksheets | ☑ Marketing Plan Worksheets | ☐ Content | |

☑ **http://lamb.swlearning.com**

| ☑ Quiz | ☑ PowerPoint slides | ☑ Marketing News | ☑ Review Exercises |
| ☑ Links | ☑ Marketing Plan Contest | ☑ Career Exercise | ☑ Use It Now |

☑ **Study guide**

| ☑ Outline | ☑ Vocab Review | ☑ Test Questions | ☑ Marketing Scenario |

Need More? Here's a tip. Find a study partner and have him or her quiz you using the end-of-chapter materials and the quizzes on Xtra! Try to give the rationale for each of your answers.

7

Segmenting and Targeting Markets

LEARNING OBJECTIVES

1. Describe the characteristics of markets and market segments

2. Explain the importance of market segmentation

3. Discuss criteria for successful market segmentation

4. Describe the bases commonly used to segment consumer markets

5. Describe the bases for segmenting business markets

6. List the steps involved in segmenting markets

7. Discuss alternative strategies for selecting target markets

8. Explain one-to-one marketing

9. Discuss the forces that have influenced the emergence of one-to-one marketing

10. Discuss privacy issues related to one-to-one marketing

11. Explain how and why firms implement positioning strategies and how product differentiation plays a role

JCPenney surprised the fashion world recently by signing an exclusive deal with French fashion designer Michele Bohbot, the talent behind the Bisou Bisou brand, whose clothing is sold in chic boutiques and upscale department stores. Now the retail chain whose name evokes visions of polyester pantsuits will be the nation's only distributor of the Bisou Bisou line. Michele's cargo pants, which used to sell for $118, go for $29.99 off the rack at Penney's. When the line was introduced at the 500 largest Penney stores, some items sold out in a few days.

When first approached, Michele Bohbot and her husband, Marc, who markets the line, were aghast at the idea of selling their clothing at Penney's. Meanwhile, the line between high fashion and mass retail began to crack. Target forged partnerships with designers Mossimo and Todd Oldham, and even Kmart got into the game with Joe Boxer. The Bohbots were getting calls from other big-name mall retailers. Soon the idea started to appeal to the Bohbots.

Squeezed between Wal-Mart's everyday low prices and Target's trendiness, Penney is trying to carve out its own niche in the crowded fashion-to-the-masses field. If it was hard to convince the

Bohbots on this idea, it will be even harder to convince the hipster-wannabe shoppers. JCPenney's CEO Allen Questrom recognizes that the chain has a huge image problem to overcome. "Customers see us as that store from their childhood that their grandma dragged them to when the family had no money," he says. But with his new focus on fashion, Questrom insists, "We're not your granny's store anymore."

Penney is also in discussions with several runway designers and is recruiting new designers to improve its own private-label brands. The hope is that with chic designer clothes and revived house brands, Penney will be able to attract the holy grail of retail: women between the ages of 25 and 35 who spend almost $15 billion a year on clothes. The average Penney's customer today? A very uncool 46.

Questrom isn't trying to transform Penney's into Saks; after all, its average shopper, with a household income between $30,000 and $80,000, is looking for a bargain. But he knows his customers would shop at Saks if they could.

The chain has also hired trend expert David Hacker, who scouts out European runways for tips and is always thumbing

through *Vogue* to make sure that the stores are ready to, say, stock the next hot color for spring. The results are getting noticed by fashion bibles, like *Cosmopolitan* and *In Style*, where Penney's affordable merchandise has been featured alongside the likes of DKNY and Armani.

Jeff Bergus, who previously held design posts at Geoffrey Beene and Izod, has taken over Penney's Arizona brand. He did some research and found that the average Arizona customer was actually between 44 and 46—not the 17- to 24-year-old Penney's executives had envisioned. Bergus has transformed the line and is now sending designers to Avril Lavigne concerts to scan the audience for inspiration. A new television ad campaign featured young models wearing strategically placed denim and barely buttoned blouses.[1]

Based on this story, how would you define market segmentation and targeting? What type of targeting strategy is JCPenney using? Do you think this market is a viable segment for the company to target? Explain your answer. This chapter will help you answer these questions about segmentation and more.

Online

JCPenney
Target
Compare the presentation of women's fashions at the Web sites for Target and JCPenney. What are the major differences? Which site is more designer focused, and which is more brand focused? Which company's approach do you think will appeal more to the "holy grail" target market of 25- to 35-year-old women?

http://www.jcpenney.com
http://www.target.com

MARKET SEGMENTATION

market
People or organizations with needs
or wants and the ability and willingness to buy.

market segment
A subgroup of people or organizations sharing one or more characteristics that cause them to have similar
product needs.

market segmentation
The process of dividing a market into
meaningful, relatively similar, and
identifiable segments or groups.

R**EVIEW** L**EARNING** O**BJECTIVE** 1

 Describe the characteristics of markets and market segments

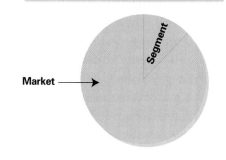

The term *market* means different things to different people. We are all familiar with the supermarket, stock market, labor market, fish market, and flea market. All these types of markets share several characteristics. First, they are composed of people (consumer markets) or organizations (business markets). Second, these people or organizations have wants and needs that can be satisfied by particular product categories. Third, they have the ability to buy the products they seek. Fourth, they are willing to exchange their resources, usually money or credit, for desired products. In sum, a **market** is (1) people or organizations with (2) needs or wants and with (3) the ability and (4) the willingness to buy. A group of people or an organization that lacks any one of these characteristics is not a market.

Within a market, a **market segment** is a subgroup of people or organizations sharing one or more characteristics that cause them to have similar product needs. At one extreme, we can define every person and every organization in the world as a market segment because each is unique. At the other extreme, we can define the entire consumer market as one large market segment and the business market as another large segment. All people have some similar characteristics and needs, as do all organizations.

From a marketing perspective, market segments can be described as somewhere between the two extremes. The process of dividing a market into meaningful, relatively similar, and identifiable segments or groups is called **market segmentation**. The purpose of market segmentation is to enable the marketer to tailor marketing mixes to meet the needs of one or more specific segments.

Exhibit 7.1 illustrates the concept of market segmentation. Each box represents a market consisting of seven persons. This market might vary as follows: one homogeneous market of seven people, a market consisting of seven individual segments, a market composed of two segments based on gender, a market composed of three age segments, or a market composed of five age and gender market segments. Age and gender and many other bases for segmenting markets are examined later in this chapter.

E**XHIBIT** 7.1

Concept of Market Segmentation

No market segmentation

Fully segmented market

Market segmentation
by gender: M, F

Market segmentation
by age group: 1, 2, 3

Market segmentation
by gender and age group

THE IMPORTANCE OF MARKET SEGMENTATION

2

Explain the importance of market segmentation

Until the 1960s, few firms practiced market segmentation. When they did, it was more likely a haphazard effort than a formal marketing strategy. Before 1960, for example, the Coca-Cola Company produced only one beverage and aimed it at the entire soft drink market. Today, Coca-Cola offers over a dozen different products to market segments based on diverse consumer preferences for flavors and calorie and caffeine content. Coca-Cola offers traditional soft drinks, energy drinks (such as Powerade), flavored teas, fruit drinks (Fruitopia), and water (Dasani).

Market segmentation plays a key role in the marketing strategy of almost all successful organizations and is a powerful marketing tool for several reasons. Most importantly, nearly all markets include groups of people or organizations with different product needs and preferences. Market segmentation helps marketers define customer needs and wants more precisely. Because market segments differ in size and potential, segmentation helps decision makers more accurately define marketing objectives and better allocate resources. In turn, performance can be better evaluated when objectives are more precise.

Chico's, a successful women's fashion retailer, thrives by marketing to women aged 35 to 55 who like to wear comfortable, yet stylish clothing. It sells private-label clothing that comes in just a few nonjudgmental sizes: zero (regular sizes 4–6), one (8–10), two (10–12), and three (14–16). The Chico's look, built mainly around wash-and-wear fabrics, is loose and colorful. Prices are moderate, ranging from $20 to $150. Chico's has developed a loyal base of customers and is a fast-growing retailer.[2]

REVIEW LEARNING OBJECTIVE 2

2 | Explain the importance of market segmentation

Market segmentation → More precise definition of consumer needs and wants → More accurate marketing objectives → Improved resource allocation → Better marketing results

CRITERIA FOR SUCCESSFUL SEGMENTATION

3

Discuss criteria for successful market segmentation

Marketers segment markets for three important reasons. First, segmentation enables marketers to identify groups of customers with similar needs and to analyze the characteristics and buying behavior of these groups. Second, segmentation provides marketers with information to help them design marketing mixes specifically matched with the characteristics and desires of one or more segments. Third, segmentation is consistent with the marketing concept of satisfying customer wants and needs while meeting the organization's objectives.

To be useful, a segmentation scheme must produce segments that meet four basic criteria:

- *Substantiality:* A segment must be large enough to warrant developing and maintaining a special marketing mix. This criterion does not necessarily mean that a segment must have many potential customers. Marketers of custom-designed homes and business buildings, commercial airplanes, and large computer systems typically develop marketing programs tailored to each potential customer's needs. In most cases, however, a market segment needs many potential customers to make commercial sense. In the 1980s, home banking failed because not enough people owned personal computers. Today, a larger number of people own computers, and home banking is a growing industry.
- *Identifiability and measurability:* Segments must be identifiable and their size measurable. Data about the population within geographic boundaries, the number of people in various age categories, and other social and demographic

REVIEW LEARNING OBJECTIVE 3

3 | **Discuss criteria for successful market segmentation**

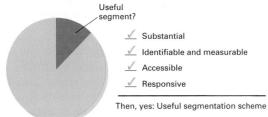

Useful segment?

✓ Substantial
✓ Identifiable and measurable
✓ Accessible
✓ Responsive

Then, yes: Useful segmentation scheme

characteristics are often easy to get, and they provide fairly concrete measures of segment size. Suppose that a social service agency wants to identify segments by their readiness to participate in a drug and alcohol program or in prenatal care. Unless the agency can measure how many people are willing, indifferent, or unwilling to participate, it will have trouble gauging whether there are enough people to justify setting up the service.

- *Accessibility:* The firm must be able to reach members of targeted segments with customized marketing mixes. Some market segments are hard to reach—for example, senior citizens (especially those with reading or hearing disabilities), individuals who don't speak English, and the illiterate.
- *Responsiveness:* As Exhibit 7.1 illustrates, markets can be segmented using any criteria that seem logical. Unless one market segment responds to a marketing mix differently from other segments, however, that segment need not be treated separately. For instance, if all customers are equally price-conscious about a product, there is no need to offer high-, medium-, and low-priced versions to different segments.

4 BASES FOR SEGMENTING CONSUMER MARKETS

Describe the bases commonly used to segment consumer markets

Marketers use **segmentation bases**, or **variables**, which are characteristics of individuals, groups, or organizations, to divide a total market into segments. The choice of segmentation bases is crucial because an inappropriate segmentation strategy may lead to lost sales and missed profit opportunities. The key is to identify bases that will produce substantial, measurable, and accessible segments that exhibit different response patterns to marketing mixes.

Markets can be segmented using a single variable, such as age group, or several variables, such as age group, gender, and education. Although it is less precise, single-variable segmentation has the advantage of being simpler and easier to use than multiple-variable segmentation. The disadvantages of multiple-variable segmentation are that it is often harder to use than single-variable segmentation; usable secondary data are less likely to be available; and as the number of segmentation bases increases, the size of individual segments decreases. Nevertheless, the current trend is toward using more rather than fewer variables to segment most markets. Multiple-variable segmentation is clearly more precise than single-variable segmentation.

Consumer goods marketers commonly use one or more of the following characteristics to segment markets: geography, demographics, psychographics, benefits sought, and usage rate.

GEOGRAPHIC SEGMENTATION

Geographic segmentation refers to segmenting markets by region of a country or the world, market size, market density, or climate. Market density means the number of people within a unit of land, such as a census tract. Climate is commonly used for geographic segmentation because of its dramatic impact on residents' needs and purchasing behavior. Snowblowers, water and snow skis, clothing, and air-conditioning and heating systems are products with varying appeal, depending on climate.

Consumer goods companies take a regional approach to marketing for four reasons. First, many firms need to find new ways to generate sales because of sluggish and intensely competitive markets. Second, computerized checkout stations with scanners enable retailers to assess accurately which brands sell best in their region. Third, many packaged-goods manufacturers are introducing

segmentation bases (variables)
Characteristics of individuals, groups, or organizations.

geographic segmentation
Segmenting markets by region of a country or the world, market size, market density, or climate.

new regional brands intended to appeal to local preferences. Fourth, a more regional approach allows consumer goods companies to react more quickly to competition. For example, Cracker Barrel, a restaurant known in the South for home-style cooking, is altering its menu outside its core southern market to reflect local tastes. Customers in upstate New York can order Reuben sandwiches, and those in Texas can get eggs with salsa. Miller Lite developed the "Miller Lite True to Texas" marketing program, a statewide campaign targeting Texas beer drinkers. The "Global Perspectives" box provides another example of geographic market segmentation.

DEMOGRAPHIC SEGMENTATION

demographic segmentation
Segmenting markets by age, gender, income, ethnic background, and family life cycle.

Marketers often segment markets on the basis of demographic information because it is widely available and often related to consumers' buying and consuming behavior. Some common bases of **demographic segmentation** are age, gender, income, ethnic background, and family life cycle. The discussion here provides some important information about the main demographic segments.

Global Perspectives Global Perspectives

GLOBAL PERSPECTIVES

> AMERICA ADDS SALSA TO ITS BURGERS AND FRIES

McDonald's and Kentucky Fried Chicken long ago conquered Latin America. Now, some of the best-known Latin American fast-food chains plan to invade the United States. Chains from Brazil, Mexico, and Venezuela offering everything from pork tacos to fried sugared dough, called churro, are planning to expand in the U.S. market, often with U.S. franchises. They're betting their success on the power of nostalgia among Latino immigrants and the potential appeal to Americans who want something other than burgers and fries.

The trend also reflects the maturation of Latin American restaurant groups, which previously lacked the size, brand recognition, and capital to expand outside their home markets. But in the past few years, a handful of fast-food chains in the region have branched out to neighboring countries after putting down strong enough roots at home.

U.S. consumers' tastes are also maturing, giving Latino chains a strong chance to prosper in the competitive world of low-priced fast food. It's a good time for Latino chains to woo Americans. Vendors of traditional fast food like burgers and pizzas have shown only modest growth in recent years, while chains serving Mexican food have grown rapidly. Sales of Baja Fresh, a Mexican quick-casual chain bought by Wendy's International, grew 64 percent to $177 million in 2001, says industry consultant Technomic, Inc. The far-bigger Wendy's itself grew 6.5 percent to $1.92 billion in the same period.

Among new Latin-food sellers in the United States is Pollo Campero, a Guatemala City–based seller of spicy fried chicken. Three years ago, Grupo TACA, a Central American airline, asked the company to use sealed, odorless packaging. Why? Because passengers flying back to the United States were bringing on board just-cooked chicken bought at a stand in the airport and the food's pungent aroma lingered in the cabin. A big percentage of the chicken sold annually by Campero at its outlets at airports in Guatemala City and San Salvador, El Salvador, makes its way into the United States on TACA flights in the hands of nostalgic Central Americans.

Executives at Campero found that the chain had big brand recognition in Los Angeles and other U.S. cities, even among non-Central Americans. Having already expanded to neighboring Central and South American countries, the chain signed up with Adir Restaurants Corporation to open a franchise restaurant in a Los Angeles neighborhood that is home to the largest concentration of Guatemalans outside Guatemala City. When it opened, the outlet sold $1 million in food in its first seven weeks. On some days, the lines were so long that some customers waited more than nine hours for their chicken. Within five years, Campero plans to have 200 outlets in the United States, expanding from California to large cities such as Houston and Dallas, Washington, D.C., Chicago, and Salt Lake City.

Campero's menu in the United States won't be identical to its offerings in Latin America to cater to U.S. eating habits. For example, Latin Americans generally eat a more substantial morning meal and expect a wide-ranging breakfast menu. Americans eat lighter breakfast fare, typically on the run or in their cars commuting to work, so Campero plans to offer a slimmed-down breakfast menu.[3]

What market segmentation variables are Latin American fast-food restaurants like Campero using? Explain your answer. Evaluate Campero's targeting strategy.

Age Segmentation

Attracting children is a popular strategy for many companies because they hope to instill brand loyalty early. Furthermore, children influence a great deal of family consumption. There are three subsegments in the children's market: young children (under age 9), tweens (ages 9 to 12), and teens (ages 13 to 19).

The U.S. Census projects there will be more than 38 million children under age nine in the United States in 2005. High-end playthings like luxurious playhouses and BMW skateboards are gaining in popularity with children.[4] Nickelodeon, once simply a television network for kids, now publishes three magazines for this target market: *Nickelodeon*, an entertainment and humor book; *Rugrats Comic Adventures*, a comic book spun off from the popular TV show; and *Crayola Kids*, aimed at kids and their parents.

Older children, dubbed "tweens," number about 20 million and have an estimated spending power of $20 billion.[5] Tweens desire to be kids, but also want some of the fun and glamour of being a teenager. The Disney Channel has developed a successful strategy to capture the tween market by re-creating the old Hollywood star system with its tween actors and actresses, such as Hillary Duff and the Cheetah Girls. Disney makes little-known kids into big names and then directs their talents into every corner of its empire—from TV shows to movies to records to merchandise. The Disney Channel is the corporation's fastest-growing component, accounting for half of the Disney cable network's $1 billion operating income, even though it brings in only about a fifth of the network's $5 billion revenues.[6] Many retailers, such as Limited Too and Abercrombie, are targeting tweens by selling clothing that is similar in style to the more teen- and young adult-oriented stores Limited and Abercrombie & Fitch.

Avon, a brand most associated with older generations, is attempting to break into a more youthful market with its Mark brand of beauty products. Carleigh Krubiner, a sophomore at the University of Pennsylvania and sales representative for Mark, holds a sample of the new products. She sells the brightly colored makeup in funky packaging from her dorm room.

© AP/WIDE WORLD PHOTOS

Teens, sometimes referred to as Generation Y, number 60 million, and represent approximately $170 billion in spending power.[7] Teens spend most of their money on clothing, entertainment, and food. Teens can be loyal to companies that reach them, and they seem to prefer smaller, niche brands, such as Burton Snowboards, Femme Arsenal (a cosmetics firm), and Razor USA (markets push scooters and apparel).[8] The dairy industry is trying to make drinking milk cool among teenagers by selling 16-ounce bottles of milk in vending machines decorated with large pictures of the famous "Got Milk?" ads featuring skateboarder Tony Hawk and other young celebrities wearing milk mustaches.[9] As the chapter-opening vignette in Chapter 5 described, Boost Mobile and Virgin Mobile USA are marketing cell phone services to teens. The handsets come in funky colors or are cobranded with edgy companies such as women's surf-gear maker Roxy. Both Boost and Virgin avoid traditional distribution channels, focusing instead on selling in surf shops, record stores, and other places where teens hang out. No credit checks or binding contracts are used—the company relies on pay-as-you-go plans. Rather than receive a monthly bill, customers can purchase prepaid chunks of airtime, in increments ranging from $20 to $50, at places like 7-Eleven and Target.[10]

Other age segments are also appealing targets for marketers. The approximately 58 million people classified as young adults, between 20 and 34 years of age, are being targeted by many beer, wine, and spirits companies. For example, Bacardi, Ltd. hired a young marketing team to develop ads for Dewars Scotch. The team dropped the "mixability" angle stressed in previous ads and revived the famous Dewars profiles campaign, showing adventure-seeking 25- to 34-year olds. The campaign appeals to Generation X by focusing on people following their dreams and not just evoking money and success.[11] In the United States and the United Kingdom, the average

Bordeaux wine drinker is between 35 and 45 years of age. This region's wine association would like to target drinkers as young as 25, says the president of Sopexa, the trade association for French food and wine. The group is backing fashion shows in Los Angeles, London, and Paris and organizing wine tasting courses, called "Wine Uncorked," for law and business school students at Ivy League universities. It has also launched an ad campaign featuring attractive young guests at a cocktail party with the slogan "Be Seduced" that is running in women's magazines such as *Harper's Bazaar*.[12]

Condé Nast

How many ways can you categorize Condé Nast's publications? How many market segments is the company serving? Do you see any potential overlap between segments (i.e., a segment that may be interested in multiple publications)?

http://www.condenast.com

Online

The baby boom generation, born between 1946 and 1964, comprises the largest age segment—about 30 percent of the entire U.S. population. Households headed by Americans 45 to 64 years old posted faster growth between 1994 and 2002 than other age groups and enjoy far higher wealth and income. In addition, the number of these relatively affluent middle-aged households is still growing rapidly. They already account for 42 percent of U.S. households, and 47 percent of them have incomes above $50,000.[13] Many in this group are approaching (or past) 50 years of age and are continuing to lead active, fully involved lifestyles. Now that many in this group are in or headed toward their fifties, they are changing the way people look at aging, which presents an opportunity for brands to reposition themselves and to be more lifestyle oriented. Starwood Hotels, for instance, designed its W chain to appeal to a young, hip crowd. But the company has been surprised at how much the hotels are attracting baby boomers.[14] Walgreen is opening many new drugstores in Sun Belt states, such as Florida, Texas, California, and Arizona, because that is where the baby boomers will retire and prescription sales will soar.[15]

Seniors (aged 65 and over) are especially attracted to companies that build relationships by taking the time to get to know them and their preferences. As an example, older customers say they prefer catalog shopping to retail outlets because of dissatisfaction with customer service at retail stores. People of this age group are more likely than most to have the combination of free time, money, and health that lets them pursue leisure-time activities, especially education and travel. Boston-based Elderhostel, a large education organization for older adults, enrolled 250,000 students last year in about 10,000 courses worldwide. And travelers 55 and older took nearly a third of the trips made within the United States in 1999.[16] In addition, though the senior audience may be coming online later than their younger counterparts, it is a large audience—one that is driven by a desire to stay in touch and stay connected.[17]

Gender Segmentation

Marketers of products such as clothing, cosmetics, personal-care items, magazines, jewelry, and footwear commonly segment markets by gender. Men aged 18 to 49 are the segment most likely to purchase goods online. Many Internet companies have advertised to this group to build their brands and get exposure for their sites. For example, Blue Nile, one of the most successful online jewelry retailers, targets men who dislike jewelry stores, even though most of the jewelry it sells is for women. Sports Clips is a hair salon designed to appeal to men and boys. The waiting room features a TV with a 52-inch screen, and customers can buy sports memorabilia, pro team caps, and college charcoal grills as well as hair-care products.[18] The wedding industry has started to target grooms as well as brides. For example, several Internet sites provide guidance for grooms; weddingchannel.com's groom-centric content includes proposal dos and don'ts, and groomsline.com offers information on cigars, tuxes, "monster-truck" limos, and other groom-related topics.[19]

Numerous companies offer special products for women. The Consumer Electronics Council introduced a "Technology is a girl's best friend" campaign

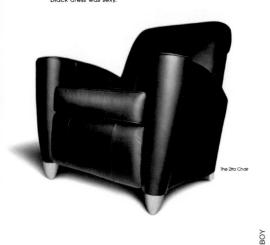

And you thought that little black dress was sexy.

The Zita Chair

The new look of comfort

Z-Boy Incorporated www.lazboy.com

COURTESY OF LA-Z-BOY

Industries like personal-care, clothing, cosmetics, and magazines typically segment their markets by gender. But that can also be said of the furniture industry. Some styles, like soft couches covered in floral chintz, are designed to appeal to women, while the recliner is perceived to be more masculine. La-Z-Boy (even the name is masculine) has, however, designed a line of recliners to appeal to women.

and advertised technology gift ideas for women at Christmas in women's magazines such as *Marie Claire, Cosmopolitan,* and *Redbook.*[20] Procter & Gamble launched a toothpaste designed for women with its Crest brand's "Rejuvenating Effects." A shimmery box and a hint of vanilla and cinnamon flavoring are the product's feminine touches.[21] The London on Park Lane became the first British hotel to reserve a floor of suites for women only. The block of executive suites opened in response to requests from female guests for more security and gender-appropriate services including new room-service menu selections delivered by female staff.[22]

Brands that have traditionally been targeted to men, such as Gillette razors and Rogaine baldness remedy, are increasing their efforts to attract women. La-Z-Boy designed a chair for women after interviewing thousands of them about what their ideal reclining chair would be like. The chair has hidden reclining mechanisms, an optional attached worktable that swivels, a built-in bud vase, and a tailored pocket on the side for storage.[23] Lowe's home improvement stores appeal to women who want to shop for big-ticket appliances and high-margin home furnishings. Presentation counts at Lowe's, which has wide aisles and carries merchandise like Laura Ashley paints and Jenn-Air stainless steel grills.[24] Conversely, "women's" products such as cosmetics, household products, and furniture are being marketed to men. For example, men are the fastest-growing market for Botox antiwrinkle shots.[25] Saturn's latest marketing strategy aims at making the brand less of a "chick's car" by offering versions of the car with more power and "speed-enhancing accessories" that will appeal to men.[26]

Income Segmentation

Income is a popular demographic variable for segmenting markets because income level influences consumers' wants and determines their buying power. Many markets are segmented by income, including the markets for housing, clothing, automobiles, and food. For example, wholesale clubs Costco and Sam's Club appeal to different income segments. Costco attracts more upscale customers with warehouse prices for gourmet foods and upscale brands like Waterford crystal, Raymond Weil watches, and Ralph Lauren clothing. Sam's Club, on the other hand, originally focused more on members' business needs, offering bulk packages of the kinds of items sold in Wal-Mart's discount stores and supercenters. Sam's Club is trying to win more upscale customers by adding items like jewelry and gourmet food. The "Ethics in Marketing" box describes how banks are using income and credit information to identify risky customers.

Ethnic Segmentation

Many companies are segmenting their markets by ethnicity. The three largest ethnic markets are the Hispanic American, African American, and Asian American. These three groups collectively are projected to make up one-third of the country's population by 2010, and they have a combined buying power of more than $1 trillion. Ethnic communities also make up significant portions of many major metropolitan areas, including New York, Chicago, Los Angeles, and Miami.[28]

Hispanic Americans Hispanic Americans are the largest minority group in the United States. The U.S. Hispanic population numbers 38 million, accounting for around 13 percent of the total population. By 2020, Hispanic Americans will comprise almost 19 percent of the population. This group also has substantial buying power, estimated at about $531 billion.[31]

Companies are increasingly directing marketing efforts at Hispanic Americans. Bank of America predicts that 80 percent of the future growth of its retail banking will be in the Hispanic market. Consequently, it is adding Spanish-speaking tellers

cs in MarketingEthics in Marketing Ethics in Marketing Ethics in MarketingEthics in Marketin
Ethics in MarketingEthics in Marketing Ethics in Marketing Ethics in Marketing Ethics in Marketing
cs in MarketingEthics in Marketing **ETHICS IN MARKETING** Marketing Ethics in Marketin
cs in Marketing Ethics in Marketing Ethics in Marketing Ethics in Marketing Ethics in Marketin
cs in Marketing Ethics in Marketing Ethics in Marketing
Ethics in Marketing

> CAREFUL, YOUR BANK IS WATCHING

For years, credit card issuers have quietly checked the credit reports of their customers from time to time to make sure they hadn't run up huge new debts elsewhere. If they found black marks, the companies would often charge those customers a higher interest rate or lower their credit limit. Now banks have the ability to check up on their customers on a daily basis. The three big credit bureaus—Experian Information Solutions, Inc., Marmon Group's TransUnion LLC, and Equifax, Inc.—have introduced new technology that can recognize so-called triggers: signs that tip off card issuers that it is time to rein in a risky customer. If a customer declares bankruptcy today, a card issuer can find out about it the day after and cut off charging privileges the day after that.

Lenders are using these tools to do more than just the traditional review of risk factors. They are also literally watching their customers shop. Experian, for example, is selling banks a daily peek at current customers' credit reports. That way, banks can see if customers are looking to refinance their mortgage with a rival. Bank One Corporation used triggers to identify home-equity-loan holders who are shopping around. If it discovered another lender had pulled a credit report on a customer—a sign the customer was looking for a new loan—Bank One would swoop in and make its own cut-rate offer to keep the customer from bolting.

It is legal to track customers' credit histories and adjust the terms of their loans accordingly. Until recently, however, it was too expensive or complicated to get this information—whether credit blemishes or loan applications—on a daily basis. But new, more powerful computers and databases have changed that. The kind of information tracked includes updates on bankruptcy filings or judgments against a cardholder, information on late payments to other billers, plus data on how much credit they are using. In addition, when consumers apply for new credit cards, a notice of each application appears on their credit report.

J.P. Morgan Chase & Company notified customers whose credit card terms changed for the worse and provided an explanation upon request. It also told cardholders they could get a free copy of their credit report because of the repricing. The company also used triggering information to identify customers whose credit had improved, so it could give them a better deal on their credit cards.

The use of credit reports is drawing scrutiny now that parts of the Fair Credit Reporting Act, which sets rules on how companies use personal data, are up for renewal in Congress. Some consumer advocates and members of Congress would like to restrict the ability of companies to use data from a credit report to change the terms of a credit card. This is known as "risk-based repricing," which often means raising the interest rate on a card held by someone deemed a credit risk.[27]

Discuss the ethical implications of the bank industry's use of credit information. Do you think banks should be allowed to use triggering information to determine risk-based repricing? Defend your answer.

at its branches and learning to write mortgages secured by the credit of extended family members.[32] The Minnesota Twins broadcast two baseball games in Spanish over a Twin Cities radio station in the summer of 2003. The team markets to Hispanic Americans by emphasizing a love of baseball, as well as family and group involvement—all themes that run deep in Latin culture.[33] It is important for organizations to tailor their marketing programs to fit the needs and wants of the Hispanic American audience. For example, a U.S. telecom company attempted to market a Caller ID feature to Hispanics as a way of screening incoming calls—the same way the company marketed the product to its local customers. However, Hispanics see screening calls as one of the rudest things you can do to your family and friends. By changing the message to stress that Caller ID connects people with their family and friends, the company developed a campaign that was more inviting to Hispanic Americans.[34]

African Americans The African American population is expected to grow to more than 45 million by 2020. They spend more than whites on luxury items such as cars, clothing, and home furnishings. Consequently, a number of companies market specifically to African Americans. PepsiCo's Urban Development program combines marketing strategy with outreach by working with community leaders to focus on consumers in minority neighborhoods. For example, after the Greater Grace Temple in Detroit agreed to buy a specified amount of PepsiCo's products, the church received a promotional donation. The money was used to purchase a van to transport the senior members of the church for shopping and banking trips, medical and social appointments, and other needs.[29] As part of its sponsorship of the National Association of Black Journalists convention, DaimlerChrysler AG offers a "Ride & Drive" program that provides cars to attendees so that they can visit local attractions.[30]

 The Internet is of growing importance as a medium to reach the African American consumer. Though Net use among this group lags behind that of the white population, African Americans who are online are younger, more affluent, and better educated than African Americans who do not use the Internet. Web sites such as **http://www.netnoir. com** and **http://www.afronet.com** attract thousands of African Americans with news, information, entertainment, and products of interest to their audiences.

Asian Americans   Asian Americans are a diverse group with 13 submarkets. The five largest are Chinese, Filipino, Japanese, Asian Indian, and Korean. This fast-growing market of 10.2 million is younger and better educated than the general market and has the highest average household income in the United States. Asian Americans spend more time online than any other ethnic group. They are also more likely to research and purchase products online than African Americans and Hispanic Americans.[35]

Family Life-Cycle Segmentation

The demographic factors of gender, age, and income often do not sufficiently explain why consumer buying behavior varies. Frequently, consumption patterns among people of the same age and gender differ because they are in different stages of the family life cycle. The **family life cycle (FLC)** is a series of stages determined by a combination of age, marital status, and the presence or absence of children.

The life-cycle stage consisting of the married-couple household, used to be considered the traditional family in the United States. Today, however, married couples make up just 50.7 percent of households, down from nearly 80 percent in the 1950s. This means that the 86 million single adults in the United States could soon define the new majority. Already, unmarried Americans make up 42 percent of the workforce, 40 percent of home buyers and one of the most potent consumer groups on record.[36] Charles Schwab Corporation, the San Francisco financial-services firm, ran a television ad featuring Sarah Ferguson, the Duchess of York and a divorced mom. The ad shows Ferguson telling a bedtime story to a little girl, and the story ends with the importance of girls understanding their financial choices. Schwab is eager to reach single women because they have a heightened interest in financial strategies.[37]

Exhibit 7.2 on page 233 illustrates numerous FLC patterns and shows how families' needs, incomes, resources, and expenditures differ at each stage. The horizontal flow shows the traditional family life cycle. The lower part of the exhibit gives some of the characteristics and purchase patterns of families in each stage of the traditional life cycle. The exhibit also acknowledges that about half of all first marriages end in divorce. When young marrieds move into the young divorced stage, their consumption patterns often revert back to those of the young single stage of the cycle. About four out of five divorced persons remarry by middle age and reenter the traditional life cycle, as indicated by the "recycled flow" in the exhibit.

Consumers are especially receptive to marketing efforts at certain points in the life cycle. Soon-to-be-married couples are typically considered to be most receptive because they are making brand decisions about products that could last longer than their marriages. To illustrate, research shows that 67 percent of women wear the same fragrance they wore when they got married, 96 percent shop at the same stores they used when engaged, and 81 percent are using the same brands.[38] Furthermore, U.S. newlyweds spend a total of $70 billion in the first year after marriage.

family life cycle (FLC)
A series of stages determined by a combination of age, marital status, and the presence or absence of children.

EXHIBIT 7.2

Family Life Cycle

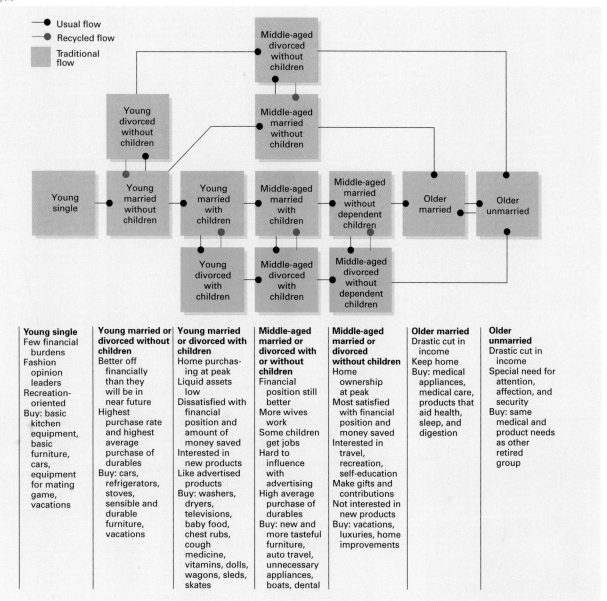

Young single	Young married or divorced without children	Young married or divorced with children	Middle-aged married or divorced with or without children	Middle-aged married or divorced without children	Older married	Older unmarried
Few financial burdens	Better off financially than they will be in near future	Home purchasing at peak	Financial position still better	Home ownership at peak	Drastic cut in income	Drastic cut in income
Fashion opinion leaders	Highest purchase rate and highest average purchase of durables	Liquid assets low	More wives work	Most satisfied with financial position and money saved	Keep home	Special need for attention, affection, and security
Recreation-oriented	Buy: cars, refrigerators, stoves, sensible and durable furniture, vacations	Dissatisfied with financial position and amount of money saved	Some children get jobs	Interested in travel, recreation, self-education	Buy: medical appliances, medical care, products that aid health, sleep, and digestion	Buy: same medical and product needs as other retired group
Buy: basic kitchen equipment, basic furniture, cars, equipment for mating game, vacations		Interested in new products	Hard to influence with advertising	Make gifts and contributions		
		Like advertised products	High average purchase of durables	Not interested in new products		
		Buy: washers, dryers, televisions, baby food, chest rubs, cough medicine, vitamins, dolls, wagons, sleds, skates	Buy: new and more tasteful furniture, auto travel, unnecessary appliances, boats, dental	Buy: vacations, luxuries, home improvements		

PSYCHOGRAPHIC SEGMENTATION

Age, gender, income, ethnicity, family life-cycle stage, and other demographic variables are usually helpful in developing segmentation strategies, but often they don't paint the entire picture. Demographics provides the skeleton, but psychographics adds meat to the bones. **Psychographic segmentation** is market segmentation on the basis of the following variables:

- *Personality:* Personality reflects a person's traits, attitudes, and habits. Porsche Cars North America understood well the demographics of the Porsche owner: a 40-something male college graduate earning over $200,000 per year. However, research discovered that this general demographic category included five personality types that more effectively segmented Porsche buyers. Porsche refined its marketing as a result of the study, and the company's U.S. sales rose 48 percent, reversing a seven-years slump.[40]

psychographic segmentation
Market segmentation on the basis of personality, motives, lifestyles, and geodemographics.

Marketing... in Entertainment

Two Products, One Mind?

Volkswagen has always successfully leveraged its folksy image. The groundbreaking design of the Beetle has garnered a large and distinct following. Who can forget the ad in which two guys pick up a recliner set out with the garbage, put it in their car, and drive around San Francisco, only to return it to the same curb at the end of the 30-second spot? To reinforce its specific marketing segment, VW has paired with Apple to offer a free iPod digital music player inside every new Beetle. The marketing director at Volkswagen explains that Apple and VW have very similar audiences, characterizing them as "a group that embraces something different, simple, and unconventional" and "like-minded brands." For both companies, this alliance represents a positioning based on the product user, whom both Apple and VW regard as being a bit funkier and a bit hipper than the general market.[39]

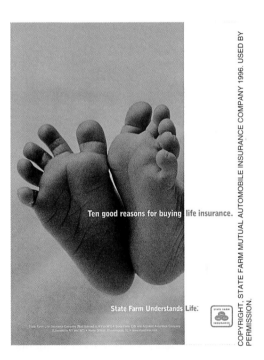

COPYRIGHT, STATE FARM MUTUAL AUTOMOBILE INSURANCE COMPANY 1996. USED BY PERMISSION.

This ad for State Farm clearly appeals to consumers' emotional motives by associating the purchase of life insurance with the caring and responsibility of parenting.

geodemographic segmentation
Segmenting potential customers into neighborhood lifestyle categories.

- *Motives:* Marketers of baby products and life insurance appeal to consumers' emotional motives—namely, to care for their loved ones. Using appeals to economy, reliability, and dependability, carmakers like Subaru and Suzuki target customers with rational motives. Carmakers like Mercedes-Benz, Jaguar, and Cadillac appeal to customers with status-related motives.

- *Lifestyles:* Lifestyle segmentation divides people into groups according to the way they spend their time, the importance of the things around them, their beliefs, and socioeconomic characteristics such as income and education. For example, a recent study of the women's market places women into four categories based on lifestyle distinctions that drive their behavior. *Explorers* are comfortable with themselves and are not obsessed with physical appearance. They also express strong or old-fashioned values such as admiring classical art, literature, and history. *Achievers* care about balance in their lives as much as they do about achieving their goals. They care much more about their own individual view of what success means than about society's expectations. *Builders* struggle between their need for material possessions to support their lives and the desire for simplicity and balance. They also take more time for themselves, even with families to care for. *Masters* are living simplified lives but are not internally settled. They have an active interest in health and beauty, but don't want to be told how they can stay young; they want support in being beautiful and living life to the fullest.[41]

- *Geodemographics:* **Geodemographic segmentation** clusters potential customers into neighborhood lifestyle categories. It combines geographic, demographic, and lifestyle segmentations. Geodemographic segmentation helps marketers develop marketing programs tailored to prospective buyers who live in small geographic regions, such as neighborhoods, or who have very specific lifestyle and demographic characteristics. Central Market, an upscale H-E-B Company food store that sells groceries and prepared foods, has several locations in Texas, and the merchandise mix varies according to the location. In Fort Worth there is a strong Western influence, so the company installed a smoker at that store to smoke beef and poultry—something its other stores do not have. The Hispanic market is strong in San Antonio and Fort Worth, so those stores stock a wide selection of fresh and dried peppers, avocados, and tomatoes.[42]

Psychographic variables can be used individually to segment markets or be combined with other variables to provide more detailed descriptions of market segments. One combination approach is the Claritas PRIZM Lifestyle software program that divides Americans into 62 "clusters," or consumer types, all with catchy names. The clusters combine basic demographic data such as age, ethnicity, and income with lifestyle information, such as magazine and sports preferences, taken from consumer surveys. For example, the "Kids and Cul-de-Sacs" group are upscale, suburban families with a median household income of $68,900 who tend to shop online and visit Disney theme parks. The "Bohemian Mix" cluster are professionals aged 25 to 44 with a median income of $38,500 who are likely to shop at Gap and read *Elle* magazine. The program also predicts to which neighborhoods across the country the clusters are likely to gravitate. Using PRIZM, Hyundai chose ZIP codes with a high percentage of promising clusters and sent test-drive offers only to those areas (instead of blanketing entire cities with the offer). In those markets, Hyundai not only increased the number of people showing up for a test-drive but also increased its sales and cut its costs per vehicle sold in half.[43]

Claritas
See a profile of your neighborhood at Claritas's Web site. Compare your ZIP code clusters in PRIZM and in MicroVision 5.0 by following the "You Are Where You Live" link. Which do you think is more accurate? Are you actually described by one of the groups the software identifies?

http://www.claritas.com

Online

BENEFIT SEGMENTATION

Benefit segmentation is the process of grouping customers into market segments according to the benefits they seek from the product. Most types of market segmentation are based on the assumption that this variable and customers' needs are related. Benefit segmentation is different because it groups potential customers on the basis of their needs or wants rather than some other characteristic, such as age or gender. The snack-food market, for example, can be divided into six benefit segments, as shown in Exhibit 7.3.

Customer profiles can be developed by examining demographic information associated with people seeking certain benefits. This information can be used to match marketing strategies with selected target markets. Procter & Gamble introduced Pampers Rash Guard, a diaper designed to combat diaper rash. The many different types of performance energy bars with various combinations of nutrients are aimed at consumers looking for different benefits. For example, PowerBar is

benefit segmentation
The process of grouping customers into market segments according to the benefits they seek from the product.

EXHIBIT 7.3

Lifestyle Segmentation of the Snack-Food Market

	Nutritional Snackers	Weight Watchers	Guilty Snackers	Party Snackers	Indiscriminate Snackers	Economical Snackers
% of Snackers	22%	14%	9%	15%	15%	18%
Lifestyle Characteristics	Self-assured, controlled	Outdoorsy, influential, venturesome	Highly anxious, isolated	Sociable	Hedonistic	Self-assured, price-oriented
Benefits Sought	Nutritious, without artificial ingredients, natural	Low in calories, quick energy	Low in calories, good tasting	Good to serve guests, served with pride, go well with beverages	Good tasting, satisfies hunger	Low in price, best value
Consumption Level of Snacks	Light	Light	Heavy	Average	Heavy	Average
Type of Snacks Usually Eaten	Fruits, vegetables, cheese	Yogurt, vegetables	Yogurt, cookies, crackers, candy	Nuts, potato chips, crackers, pretzels	Candy, ice cream, cookies, potato chips, pretzels, popcorn	No specific products
Demographics	Better educated, have younger children	Younger, single	Younger or older, female, lower socio-economic status	Middle-aged, nonurban	Teenager	Have large family, better educated

Good *for you* Snacks

Benefit in every way with EDEN® Healthy Snacks. From our sweet-tart Montmorency Dried Cherries, and Organic Almonds, to Snack Mixes, these six EDEN foods are full of flavor and loaded with nutrients and antioxidants. Good for anyone, anytime! Experience Goodness.

Great Taste & Nourishment
The Smart Way to Snack

EDEN®

Eden Foods, Inc., Clinton, Michigan • 888-424-EDEN • www.edenfoods.com

Ads for nutritious snacks are good examples of benefit segmentation. This ad for Eden Foods also plays to some age and FLC segmentation variables by depicting the young boy.

FAQs

How do marketers decide which variables to use to segment a market? Find out the answer by watching the video FAQ on Xtra!

designed for athletes looking for long-lasting fuel, while PowerBar Protein Plus in aimed at those who want extra protein for replenishing muscles after strength training. Carb Solutions High Protein Bars are for those on low-carb diets; Luna Bars are targeted to women who want a bar with fewer calories, soy protein, and calcium; and Clif Bars are for people who want a natural bar with ingredients like rolled oats, soybeans, and organic soy flour.[44]

USAGE-RATE SEGMENTATION

Usage-rate segmentation divides a market by the amount of product bought or consumed. Categories vary with the product, but they are likely to include some combination of the following: former users, potential users, first-time users, light or irregular users, medium users, and heavy users. Segmenting by usage rate enables marketers to focus their efforts on heavy users or to develop multiple marketing mixes aimed at different segments. Because heavy users often account for a sizable portion of all product sales, some marketers focus on the heavy-user segment.

The **80/20 principle** holds that 20 percent of all customers generate 80 percent of the demand. Although the percentages usually are not exact, the general idea often holds true. For example, in the fast-food industry, the heavy user accounts for only one of five fast-food patrons, but makes about 60 percent of all visits to fast-food restaurants. Using this definition, the heavy user (who is most often a single male) accounted for roughly $66 billion of the $110 billion the National Restaurant Association said was spent on fast food in 1999.[45]

Developing customers into heavy users is the goal behind many frequency/loyalty programs like the airlines' frequent flyer programs. Many supermarkets and other retailers have also designed loyalty programs that reward the heavy-user segment with deals available only to them, such as in-store coupon dispensing systems, loyalty card programs, and special price deals on selected merchandise.

REVIEW LEARNING OBJECTIVE 4

4   **Describe the bases commonly used to segment consumer markets**

Geography	Demographics	Psychographics	Benefits	Usage Rate
• Region • Market size • Market density • Climate	• Age • Gender • Income • Race/Ethnicity • Family life cycle	• Personality • Motives • Lifestyle • Geodemographics	• Benefits sought	• Former • Potential • 1st time • Light or irregular • Medium • Heavy

usage-rate segmentation
Dividing a market by the amount of product bought or consumed.

80/20 principle
A principle holding that 20 percent of all customers generate 80 percent of the demand.

The business market consists of four broad segments: producers, resellers, government, and institutions (for a detailed discussion of the characteristics of these segments, see Chapter 6). Whether marketers focus on only one or on all four of these segments, they are likely to find diversity among potential customers. Thus, further market segmentation offers just as many benefits to business marketers as it does to consumer-product marketers.

COMPANY CHARACTERISTICS

Company characteristics, such as geographic location, type of company, company size, and product use, can be important segmentation variables. Some markets tend to be regional because buyers prefer to purchase from local suppliers, and distant suppliers may have difficulty competing in terms of price and service. Therefore, firms that sell to geographically concentrated industries benefit by locating close to their markets.

Segmenting by customer type allows business marketers to tailor their marketing mixes to the unique needs of particular types of organizations or industries. Many companies are finding this form of segmentation to be quite effective. For example, Home Depot, one of the largest do-it-yourself retail businesses in the United States, has targeted professional repair and remodeling contractors in addition to consumers.

Volume of purchase (heavy, moderate, light) is a commonly used basis for business segmentation. Another is the buying organization's size, which may affect its purchasing procedures, the types and quantities of products it needs, and its responses to different marketing mixes. Banks frequently offer different services, lines of credit, and overall attention to commercial customers based on their size.

Many products, especially raw materials like steel, wood, and petroleum, have diverse applications. How customers use a product may influence the amount they buy, their buying criteria, and their selection of vendors. For example, a producer of springs may have customers that use the product in applications as diverse as making machine tools, bicycles, surgical devices, office equipment, telephones, and missile systems.

BUYING PROCESSES

Many business marketers find it helpful to segment customers and prospective customers on the basis of how they buy. For example, companies can segment some business markets by ranking key purchasing criteria, such as price, quality, technical support, and service. Atlas Corporation developed a commanding position in the industrial door market by providing customized products in just 4 weeks, which was much faster than the industry average of 12 to 15 weeks. Atlas's primary market is companies with an immediate need for customized doors.

The purchasing strategies of buyers may provide useful segments. Two purchasing profiles that have been identified are satisficers and optimizers. **Satisficers** contact familiar suppliers and place the order with the first one to satisfy product and delivery requirements. **Optimizers** consider numerous suppliers (both familiar and unfamiliar), solicit bids, and study all proposals carefully before selecting one.

The personal characteristics of the buyers themselves (their demographic characteristics, decision style, tolerance for risk, confidence level, job responsibilities, etc.) influence their buying behavior and thus offer a viable basis for segmenting some business markets. IBM computer buyers, for example, are sometimes characterized as being more risk averse than buyers of less expensive computers that perform essentially the same functions. In advertising, therefore, IBM stressed its reputation for high quality and reliability.

satisficers
Business customers who place an order with the first familiar supplier to satisfy product and delivery requirements.

optimizers
Business customers who consider numerous suppliers, both familiar and unfamiliar, solicit bids, and study all proposals carefully before selecting one.

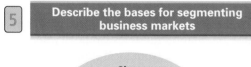

5 **Describe the bases for segmenting business markets**

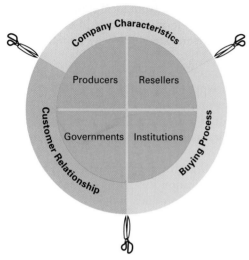

CUSTOMER RELATIONSHIP

More and more, companies are beginning to go beyond the traditional segmentation variables by focusing on the type of relationship they have with their customers. For example, Cable & Wireless, a British telephone company, had traditionally segmented customers based on size. This meant that a *Fortune* 500 organization would have priority over a midsize customer, even if the midsize client accounted for more business. Recently, the company reevaluated this method and began using other factors, such as revenue generated by each customer, and how cost-effective and efficient it is for Cable & Wireless to serve particular customers.[46]

The Chapman Group, a Columbia, Maryland company that specializes in sales and marketing process improvement, has designed a segmentation strategy based on types of relationships companies have with their customers. It developed three segments of relationships: client accounts, customer accounts, and buyer accounts. Clients collaborate with the organization on attaining mutual goals of profitability. They appreciate support, consistently offer profitable revenue, and have reasonable expectations of services for the prices they pay. They are willing to work on teams and expand relationships between both organizations. Customers are less interested in building a relationship network, are indifferent about mutual profitability, want most goods and services for lower-than-market prices, and are more costly to service. Buyers focus on price only. Value, relationships, and services typically do not offset pricing differences in this segment. Companies using this segmentation strategy can then offer different service approaches for each segment.[47]

6 STEPS IN SEGMENTING A MARKET

List the steps involved in segmenting markets

The purpose of market segmentation, in both consumer and business markets, is to identify marketing opportunities.

1. *Select a market or product category for study:* Define the overall market or product category to be studied. It may be a market in which the firm already competes, a new but related market or product category, or a totally new one. For instance, Anheuser-Busch closely examined the beer market before introducing Michelob Light and Bud Light. Anheuser-Busch also carefully studied the market for salty snacks before introducing the Eagle brand.

2. *Choose a basis or bases for segmenting the market:* This step requires managerial insight, creativity, and market knowledge. There are no scientific procedures for selecting segmentation variables. However, a successful segmentation scheme must produce segments that meet the four basic criteria discussed earlier in this chapter.

3. *Select segmentation descriptors:* After choosing one or more bases, the marketer must select the segmentation descriptors. Descriptors identify the specific segmentation variables to use. For example, if a company selects demographics as a basis of segmentation, it may use age, occupation, and income as descriptors. A company that selects usage segmentation needs to decide whether to go after heavy users, nonusers, or light users.

4. *Profile and analyze segments:* The profile should include the segments' size, expected growth, purchase frequency, current brand usage, brand loyalty, and long-term sales and profit potential. This information can then be used to rank potential market segments by profit opportunity, risk, consistency with organizational mission and objectives, and other factors important to the firm.

5. *Select target markets:* Selecting target markets is not a part of but a natural outcome of the segmentation process. It is a major decision that influences and often directly determines the firm's marketing mix. This topic is examined in greater detail later in this chapter.

6. *Design, implement, and maintain appropriate marketing mixes:* The marketing mix has been described as product, place (distribution), promotion, and pricing strategies intended to bring about mutually satisfying exchange relationships with target markets. Chapters 9 through 18 explore these topics in detail.

Markets are dynamic, so it is important that companies proactively monitor their segmentation strategies over time. Often, once customers or prospects have been assigned to a segment, marketers think their task is done. Once customers are assigned to an age segment, for example, they stay there until they reach the next age bracket or category, which could be ten years in the future. Thus, the segmentation classifications are static, but the customers and prospects are changing. Dynamic segmentation approaches adjust to fit the changes that occur in customers' lives. Tesco, a British supermarket company, has a frequent shopper card that gathers data and tracks the purchases of 7 million customers on every shopping occasion. Using these data, Tesco can reclassify every customer every week. Some customers move to different segments, and some don't, but all are evaluated, allowing the company to understand changes in customer behavior on a real-time, ongoing basis. Based on these changes, Tesco can continuously update its marketing programs to accommodate customers' behaviors. Tesco has become number one in food store sales in the United Kingdom primarily by knowing more about its customers than its competitors do.[48]

REVIEW LEARNING OBJECTIVE 6

6 | **List the steps involved in segmenting markets**

1 Select a market or product category for study.

2 Choose a basis or bases for segmenting the market.

3 Select segmentation descriptors.

4 Profile and analyze segments.

5 Select target markets.

6 Design, implement, and maintain appropriate marketing mixes.

Note that steps 5 and 6 are actually marketing activities that follow market segmentation (steps 1 through 4).

7 STRATEGIES FOR SELECTING TARGET MARKETS

Discuss alternative strategies for selecting target markets

So far this chapter has focused on the market segmentation process, which is only the first step in deciding whom to approach about buying a product. The next task is to choose one or more target markets. A **target market** is a group of people or organizations for which an organization designs, implements, and maintains a marketing mix intended to meet the needs of that group, resulting in mutually satisfying exchanges. Because most markets will include customers with different lifestyles, backgrounds, and income levels, it is unlikely that a single marketing mix will attract all segments of the market. Thus, the target market is the specific market segment most likely to purchase the product. For example, JCPenney's target market for women's fashion described in this chapter's opening vignette consists of women who are between 25 and 35 years old, have income between $30,000 and $80,000, and are looking for a bargain. The three general strategies for selecting target markets—undifferentiated, concentrated, and multisegment targeting—are illustrated in Exhibit 7.4. Exhibit 7.5 illustrates the advantages and disadvantages of each targeting strategy.

target market
A group of people or organizations for which an organization designs, implements, and maintains a marketing mix intended to meet the needs of that group, resulting in mutually satisfying exchanges.

EXHIBIT 7.4

Three Strategies for Selecting Target
Markets

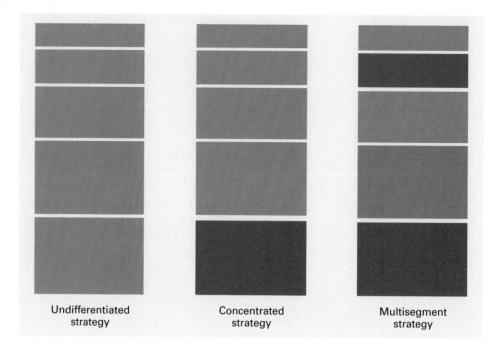

| Undifferentiated strategy | Concentrated strategy | Multisegment strategy |

EXHIBIT 7.5

Advantages and Disadvantages of Target Marketing Strategies

Targeting Strategy	Advantages	Disadvantages
Undifferentiated Targeting	• Potential savings on production/ marketing costs • Company more susceptible to competition	• Unimaginative product offerings
Concentrated Targeting	• Concentration of resources • Can better meet the needs of a narrowly defined segment • Allows some small firms to better compete with larger firms • Strong positioning	• Segments too small, or changing • Large competitors may more effectively market to niche segment
Multisegment Targeting	• Greater financial success • Economies of scale in producing/marketing	• High costs • Cannibalization

UNDIFFERENTIATED TARGETING

A firm using an **undifferentiated targeting strategy** essentially adopts a mass-market philosophy, viewing the market as one big market with no individual segments. The firm uses one marketing mix for the entire market. A firm that adopts an undifferentiated targeting strategy assumes that individual customers have similar needs that can be met with a common marketing mix.

The first firm in an industry sometimes uses an undifferentiated targeting strategy. With no competition, the firm may not need to tailor marketing mixes to the preferences of market segments. Henry Ford's famous comment about the Model T is a classic example of an undifferentiated targeting strategy: "They can have their car in any color they want, as long as it's black." At one time, Coca-Cola used this strategy with a single product and a single size of its familiar green bottle. Marketers of commodity products, such as flour and sugar, are also likely to use an undifferentiated targeting strategy.

undifferentiated targeting strategy
A marketing approach that views the market as one big market with no individual segments and thus uses a single marketing mix.

One advantage of undifferentiated marketing is the potential for saving on production and marketing. Because only one item is produced, the firm should be able to achieve economies of mass production. Also, marketing costs may be lower when there is only one product to promote and a single channel of distribution. Too often, however, an undifferentiated strategy emerges by default rather than by design, reflecting a failure to consider the advantages of a segmented approach. The result is often sterile, unimaginative product offerings that have little appeal to anyone.

Another problem associated with undifferentiated targeting is that it makes the company more susceptible to competitive inroads. Hershey lost a big share of the candy market to Mars and other candy companies before it changed to a multisegment targeting strategy. Coca-Cola forfeited its position as the leading seller of cola drinks in supermarkets to Pepsi-Cola in the late 1950s, when Pepsi began offering several sizes of containers.

You might think a firm producing a standard product like toilet tissue would adopt an undifferentiated strategy. However, this market has industrial segments and consumer segments. Industrial buyers want an economical, single-ply product sold in boxes of a hundred rolls. The consumer market demands a more versatile product in smaller quantities. Within the consumer market, the product is differentiated with designer print or no print, cushioned or noncushioned, and economy priced or luxury priced. Fort Howard Corporation, the market share leader in industrial toilet paper, does not even sell to the consumer market.

CONCENTRATED TARGETING

Pottery Barn
What segmentation strategy does Pottery Barn employ on its Web site? Why do you think as you do?
http://www.potterybarn.com

Online

© AP/WIDE WORLD PHOTOS

Starbucks deploys a very concentrated marketing strategy by focusing on gourmet coffee drinkers. How serious is the company about its strategy? Senior Vice President Mary Williams, pictured here, slurps more than 300 cups of coffee a day. She is in charge of coffee tasting, buying, and education for the company.

concentrated targeting strategy
A strategy used to select one segment of a market for targeting marketing efforts.

niche
One segment of a market.

With a **concentrated targeting strategy**, a firm selects a market **niche** (one segment of a market) for targeting its marketing efforts. Because the firm is appealing to a single segment, it can concentrate on understanding the needs, motives, and satisfactions of that segment's members and on developing and maintaining a highly specialized marketing mix. Some firms find that concentrating resources and meeting the needs of a narrowly defined market segment is more profitable than spreading resources over several different segments.

For example, Starbucks became successful by focusing on consumers who want gourmet coffee products. America Online (AOL) became one of the worlds' leading Internet providers by targeting Internet newcomers. By making the Internet interface easy to use, AOL was able to attract millions of people who otherwise might not have subscribed to an online service. Hot Topic, a chain store found almost exclusively in suburban malls, is aimed at teens who wear alternative-fashion clothing. These teens, who are turned off by more mainstream stores like Abercrombie & Fitch and Wet Seal, buy products such as blue hair dye, rock-band T-shirts, and black gothic platform boots. Hot Topic's sales were increasing as other teen retailers' sales were flat or declining.[49]

Small firms often adopt a concentrated targeting strategy to compete effectively with much larger firms. For example, Enterprise Rent-A-Car rose to number

FAQs

How do firms decide which markets *not* to target? Find out the answer by watching the video FAQ on Xtra!

one in the car rental industry by catering to people with cars in the shop. It has now expanded into the airport rental market.

Some firms, on the other hand, use a concentrated strategy to establish a strong position in a desirable market segment. Porsche, for instance, targets an upscale automobile market through "class appeal, not mass appeal."

Concentrated targeting violates the old adage "Don't put all your eggs in one basket." If the chosen segment is too small or if it shrinks because of environmental changes, the firm may suffer negative consequences. For instance, OshKosh B'Gosh, Inc., was highly successful selling children's wear in the 1980s. It was so successful, however, that the children's line came to define OshKosh's image to the extent that the company could not sell clothes to anyone else. Attempts at marketing older children's clothing, women's casual clothes, and maternity wear were all abandoned. Recognizing it was in the children's-wear business, the company expanded into products such as kids' shoes, children's eyewear, and plush toys.

Mattel targets multiple markets with its Barbie doll. In addition to multicultural Barbies, Mattel has rolled out "Generation" dolls, a new line, which includes a doll with a nose ring and one with a butterfly tattoo on her stomach. Barbie is hoping to deflect the serious competition it faces from Bratz dolls, targeted at the 8- to 12-year old market.

© AP/WIDE WORLD PHOTOS

A concentrated strategy can also be disastrous for a firm that is not successful in its narrowly defined target market. Before Procter & Gamble introduced Head and Shoulders shampoo, several small firms were already selling antidandruff shampoos. Head and Shoulders was introduced with a large promotional campaign, and the new brand captured over half the market immediately. Within a year, several of the firms that had been concentrating on this market segment went out of business.

MULTISEGMENT TARGETING

A firm that chooses to serve two or more well-defined market segments and develops a distinct marketing mix for each has a **multisegment targeting strategy**. Stouffer's, for example, offers gourmet entrées for one segment of the frozen dinner market and Lean Cuisine for another. Hershey offers premium candies like Golden Almond chocolate bars, packaged in gold foil, that are marketed to an adult audience. Another chocolate bar, called RSVP, is targeted toward consumers who crave the taste of Godiva chocolates at the price of a Hershey bar. Cosmetics companies seek to increase sales and market share by targeting multiple age and ethnic groups. Maybelline and Cover Girl, for example, market different lines to teenage women, young adult women, older women, and African American women. PepsiCo has introduced a number of new brands to target different market segments. Its Sierra Mist is aimed at the youth market; Code Red is purchased by urbanites, women, and African Americans; and Pepsi Blue is teen oriented.[50] CitiCard offers its Upromise Card to those who want to earn money to save for college, its Platinum Select Card to those who want no annual fee and a competitive interest rate, its Diamond Preferred Rewards Card to customers who want to earn free rewards like travel and brand-name merchandise, and its Citi AAdvantage Card to those who want to earn American Airlines AAdvantage frequent flyer miles to redeem for travel.

Sometimes organizations use different promotional appeals, rather than completely different marketing mixes, as the basis for a multisegment strategy. Beer marketers such as Adolph Coors and Anheuser-Busch advertise and promote special events targeted toward African American, Hispanic American, and Asian American market segments. The beverages and containers, however, do not differ by ethnic market segment.

multisegment targeting strategy
A strategy that chooses two or more well-defined market segments and develops a distinct marketing mix for each.

cannibalization
A situation that occurs when sales of a new product cut into sales of a firm's existing products.

Multisegment targeting offers many potential benefits to firms, including greater sales volume, higher profits, larger market share, and economies of scale in manufacturing and marketing. Yet it may also involve greater product design, production, promotion, inventory, marketing research, and management costs. Before deciding to use this strategy, firms should compare the benefits and costs of multisegment targeting to those of undifferentiated and concentrated targeting.

Another potential cost of multisegment targeting is **cannibalization**, which occurs when sales of a new product cut into sales of a firm's existing products. In many cases, however, companies prefer to steal sales from their own brands rather than lose sales to a competitor. Also, in today's fast-paced world of Internet business, some companies are willing to cannibalize existing business to build new business. Code Red, mentioned above as part of PepsiCo's multisegmentation approach, gets a quarter of its volume from existing Mountain Dew drinkers.[51]

REVIEW LEARNING OBJECTIVE 7

| 7 | **Discuss alternative strategies for selecting target markets** |

Undifferentiated   Multisegment   Concentrated

8 ONE-TO-ONE MARKETING

Explain one-to-one marketing

FAQs

Is one-to-one marketing really realistic for most businesses? Find out by watching the video FAQ on Xtra!

Most businesses today use a mass-marketing approach designed to increase *market share* by selling their products to the greatest number of people. For many businesses, however, it is more efficient and profitable to use one-to-one marketing to increase *share of customer*—in other words, to sell more products to each customer. **One-to-one marketing** is an individualized marketing method that utilizes customer information to build long-term, personalized, and profitable relationships with each customer. The goal is to reduce costs through customer retention and increase revenue through customer loyalty.

CVS Pharmacy has built customer loyalty through its ExtraCare program. Over 33 million ExtraCare cards have been issued to the company's best customers. While ExtraCare mailings alert cardholders to member discounts, the program helps clerks greet customers by name and provides the pharmacy chain with the information necessary to mail customer coupons based upon each recipient's prescription and nonprescription drug history.[52] CVS maintains a high degree of loyalty among its ExtraCare members.

The difference between one-to-one marketing and the traditional mass-marketing approach can be compared to shooting a rifle and a shotgun. If you have good aim, a rifle is the most efficient weapon to use. A shotgun, on the other hand, increases your odds of hitting the target when it is more difficult to focus. Instead of scattering messages far and wide across the spectrum of mass media (the shotgun approach), one-to-one marketers look for opportunities to communicate with each individual customer (the rifle approach).

As one-to-one marketing continues to spread, it will no longer be sufficient to understand customers and prospects by aggregate profiles. The one-to-one future requires that marketers understand their customers and collaborate with them, rather than use them as targets. In fact, many early one-to-one marketing efforts failed because marketers bombarded customers with irrelevant, one-to-one communications before making an effort to understand the customers. The fundamental challenge of one-to-one marketing today is to combine the customer

How serious are companies about giving customers individualized attention? Levi Strauss has a shrink tub in its San Francisco megastore so that customers can shrink their jeans to fit. After the shrink tub, they pass through the human dryer before leaving the store.

one-to-one marketing
An individualized marketing method that utilizes customer information to build long-term, personalized, and profitable relationships with each customer.

© REUTERS NEWMEDIA INC./CORBIS

REVIEW LEARNING OBJECTIVE 8

8 **Explain one-to-one marketing**

information gleaned from database technology with compelling marketing communications.[53]

The one-to-one future is still a goal, not a reality, for most companies. But progress toward one-to-one marketing is evident in the increase in personalized communications and product customization. The battle for customers will be won by marketers who understand why and how their customers buy their products and who will win them over one customer at a time.

New technology allows businesses to personalize messages to their customers. For example, a user of MyYahoo.com is greeted by name and presented with information in which the user has expressed interest. Similarly, RedEnvelope.com helps customers keep track of special occasions and offers personalized gift recommendations. Best-known examples of one-to-one product customization are Dell, Inc. and Starbucks, but more and more companies are making it possible for customers to customize their purchases. For example, Reflect.com creates customized skin-care products for more than 400,000 customers monthly.[54] With the help of database technology, which is discussed in detail in Chapter 20, one-to-one marketers can track their customers as individuals, even if they number in the millions.

 FORCES INFLUENCING ONE-TO-ONE MARKETING

Discuss the forces that have influenced the emergence of one-to-one marketing

Several forces have helped shape this new one-to-one focus on customers. They include a more diverse society, more demanding and time-poor consumers, a decline in brand loyalty, the explosion of new media alternatives, and demand for marketing accountability.[55]

INCREASING DIVERSITY

In the 1950s and 1960s, Americans strove for the *Leave It to Beaver* and *Dick and Jane* ideal of the perfect lifestyle. The ideal family was Caucasian and lived in a comfortable suburban house, the father worked to support the family, and mom stayed home to keep a tidy house and raise the children. Life was simple. Dad came home from work at five o'clock, the family ate dinner together, and later they gathered around the one television set to watch *Milton Berle*. Although not everyone of that era lived this lifestyle, nearly everybody agreed that it was the ideal.

Today, less than 7 percent of households fit this profile. Modern families are split into many smaller segments, such as unmarried couples living together, fathers or mothers heading households alone, married couples without children, homosexual couples, singles living alone or with roommates, older "empty nesters," and many other profiles. Even more important than the diversity of today's household, however, is society's acceptance of that diversity. Today, people acknowledge and accept diversity, and society's definition of what is acceptable has changed as the family has changed.

MORE DEMANDING, TIME-POOR CONSUMERS

Consumers today are more time-poor than any previous generation. Although the continuing rise in the number of women in the workforce, the increase in working mothers, and the rise in single-parent households mostly headed by women are not new trends, women now constitute the majority of American workers for the first time. As a result, consumers have less and less time to spend on anything but the most pressing details of their lives. This is having a profound impact on consumers' buying behavior. Consumers are becoming more demanding, more impatient, and much less likely to spend time agonizing over small purchases or driving across town to the mall. This is evident in the statistics showing that over 128 million Americans—more than two-thirds of the population—order goods or services by phone, mail, or online each year. The growth of Internet commerce also attests to Americans' lack of time. Thirty-one percent of Americans are "highly tech savvy" people, for whom the Internet and cell phones are more indispensable than televisions or land-line telephones.[56] The number of Internet users worldwide was expected to exceed 709 million in 2004.[57]

DECREASING BRAND LOYALTY

In a 1975 survey of male and female heads of households, over three-quarters agreed with the statement "I try to stick to well-known brand names." Ten years later, only a little over half agreed with the same statement. This trend has continued through the 1990s and into the new century. Consumers are now more likely to experiment with generics or switch back and forth between major brands in a category. They are also more likely to shop for discounts and, if presented with two comparable brands, will likely choose based on price.

The decline in brand loyalty can be attributed in part to the excessive couponing, trade deals, and deep price promotions by manufacturers and retailers that have accustomed consumers to look for the best deal. Brand loyalty has also wavered due to the proliferation of brands available, with thousands more being introduced annually. With so many product choices, consumers often become confused about product differences or lack the time to learn about each new brand. As a result, consumers often resort to basing their purchases on price.

EMERGENCE OF NEW MEDIA ALTERNATIVES

Three decades ago, most Americans spent their evenings in front of their television set, watching network programming on NBC, CBS, or ABC. They were also more likely to read the newspaper and subscribe to a general news magazine such as *Life* or *Time*. Marketers reached consumers by blanketing mass media with image advertising.

Today's busy consumers are not at all likely to be found spending their evenings watching the latest sitcom on network television. Instead, they are probably surfing the hundreds of channels available through their direct satellite system, watching a rented movie, or visiting their favorite game or news site on the Internet. Newspapers and general-interest magazines have given way to an abundance of specialty publications that cater to a wide range of interests.

With the emergence of new and varied media alternatives, mass-media advertising will never be the same. Marketers must increasingly divide their marketing dollars among the various media available, concentrating on those that will bring them the most impact. Although mass-media advertising on network television or through general-interest magazines will continue to play an important role in communicating brand messages, it will never again be the dominant force it once was.

DEMAND FOR ACCOUNTABILITY

The impact of mass-media advertising on sales has always been difficult to measure. Generations of marketers have quoted the comment of John Wanamaker, a late-nineteenth-century American merchant: "I know half of my advertising is wasted. I just don't know which half." Historically, the results of a newspaper or television advertising expenditure could be measured only through future sales of the advertised offering, its increase in market share, or the increase in store traffic. Even sales promotional tactics, which provide more measurability than mass-media efforts, have come under attack. For instance, coupons distributed through the free-standing inserts found in the Sunday paper are just as much a form of mass-media advertising as a full-page image ad in the same paper and, therefore, largely unaccountable. Manufacturers today are under pressure to maintain growth and profits for stockholders. It is no longer acceptable to say that sales increased after an advertising campaign. Management now wants proof that monies spent on advertising and marketing will deliver results.

HOW HAVE THESE TRENDS INFLUENCED ONE-TO-ONE MARKETING?

What are these forces telling marketers? How are they pushing forward the market-oriented philosophy of one-to-one marketing?

For starters, a more diverse society has ruled that the one-size-fits-all marketing of yesteryear no longer fits. Consumers do not want to be treated like the masses. Instead, they want to be treated as the individuals they are, with their own unique sets of needs and wants. By its personalized nature, one-to-one marketing can fulfill this desire.

Second, more direct and personal marketing efforts will continue to grow to meet the needs of consumers who no longer have the time to spend shopping and making purchase decisions. With the personal and targeted nature of one-to-one marketing, consumers can spend less time making purchase decisions and more time doing the things that are important.

Third, consumers will be loyal only to those companies and brands that have earned their loyalty and reinforced it at every purchase occasion. One-to-one marketing techniques focus on finding a firm's best customers, rewarding them for their loyalty, and thanking them for their business.

Fourth, mass-media approaches will decline in importance as advances in market research and database technology allow marketers to collect detailed information on their customers, not just the approximation offered by demographics but the specific names and addresses. One-to-one marketing will increase in importance and offer marketers a more cost-effective avenue to reach customers. Finally, the demand for accountability will drive the growth of one-to-one marketing and justify its continued existence.

One-to-one marketing is a huge commitment and often requires a 180-degree turnaround for marketers who spent the last half of the twentieth century developing and implementing mass-marketing efforts. Although mass marketing will probably continue to be used, especially to create brand awareness or to remind consumers of a product, the advantages of one-to-one marketing cannot be ignored.

REVIEW LEARNING OBJECTIVE 9

9 | **Discuss the forces that have influenced the emergence of one-to-one marketing**

PRIVACY CONCERNS WITH ONE-TO-ONE MARKETING

Discuss privacy issues related to one-to-one marketing

Federal Trade Commission
What is the current status of consumer privacy in politics and regulation? Visit the FTC Web site and read about privacy initiatives for consumers and businesses alike. Did anything you read surprise you? What and why?

http://www.ftc.gov

Online

Before rushing out to invest in computer hardware and software to build a database, marketers should heed consumer reaction to the growing use of databases. One-to-one marketing concerns many Americans because of the potential for invasion of privacy, specifically the sheer volume of information that is aggregated in databases and the vulnerability of this information to unauthorized access and use. A fundamental aspect of one-to-one marketing is providing valuable services to customers based on knowledge of what customers really value. However, it is critical that marketers remember that these relationships should be built on trust. While database technology allows marketers to compile ever-richer information about their customers to build and manage relationships, if these customers feel their privacy is being violated, they are likely to terminate the relationship.

The popularity of the Internet for direct marketing, for consumer data collection, and as a repository of sensitive consumer data has alarmed privacy-minded consumers. So many online users have complained about "spam," the Internet's equivalent of junk mail, that in 2003 the U.S. Congress passed the CAN-SPAM Act in an attempt to regulate it. The act, which took effect on January 1, 2004, does not ban spam, but it does prohibit the use of a false return address and the use of false or misleading information. It also requires commercial e-mailers to provide a way for recipients to "opt out" of receiving further e-mail from the sender.[58]

Another problem is that Web surfers, including children who are using the Internet, are routinely asked to divulge personal information in order to access certain screens or purchase goods or services online. Internet users who once felt fairly anonymous when using the Web are now disturbed by the amount of information marketers collect on them as they visit various sites in cyberspace.

Most consumers are unaware of how personal information is collected, used, and distributed, and they are unaware of how technology helps in collecting personal data. The government actively sells huge amounts of personal information to list compilers. State motor vehicle bureaus sell names and addresses of individuals who get driver's licenses. Hospitals sell the names of women who just gave birth on their premises. Consumer credit databases, developed and maintained by large providers such as Equifax Marketing Services and TransUnion, are often used by credit card marketers to prescreen the targets for solicitations. And, America Online, for instance, keeps records on more than 21 million subscribers, including names, addresses, and credit card numbers. The online service also tracks the movements of subscribers within its proprietary service where users spend over 80 percent of their time, including chat rooms, e-mail, news services, and other content. AOL sells names and addresses of subscribers to direct mailers and also buys information about its members, such as the type of computer owned, from outside data suppliers. It then uses this information to target advertising when a subscriber comes online.[59]

© PHOTODISC/GETTY/IMAGES

Protecting children on the Internet is of prime concern to parents and children's sites. Many ISPs are now marketing their ability to filter out inappropriate sites before children happen upon them.

Further, there is widespread misunderstanding among consumers about existing privacy laws and regulations. Frustrated by their lack of control, consumers want more opportunities to determine how their personal information will be used. According to a recent poll by Forrester Research, Inc., 70 percent of Americans would like Congress to pass legislation protecting privacy on the Internet. Currently, only financial institutions, doctors, and insurance companies are prohibited from revealing certain information such as credit card numbers and medical records to third-party organizations. Therefore, privacy advocates are lobbying Congress to enact more federal regulations.[60]

While regulators have been debating Internet privacy protection legislation, federal law to date is limited to the Children's Online Privacy Protection Act of 1998 (COPPA), which went into effect in 2000 and bars sites from collecting personal information from children under 13 without parental consent. The act does not, however, prohibit the anonymous collection of data about children's Internet activity, a fact that alarmed privacy advocates when N2H2 proposed the sale of data collected from school computers using its Web filter system.[61]

As a result of the Federal Trade Commission's interest in Web privacy, many Internet companies have now adopted privacy policies, and many are now giving Web users the ability to opt out of data collection in an effort to avert federal legislation. The Direct Marketing Association has published new guidelines for its member companies to help assure consumers that their privacy is being respected (see Exhibit 7.6).[62]

 While privacy policies for companies in the United States are largely voluntary and regulations on how personal data are collected and used are practically nonexistent, collecting data about consumers outside the United States is a different matter. Database marketers venturing into new data territories must carefully navigate foreign privacy laws. The European Union's *European Data Protection Directive*, for instance, states that any business that trades with a European organization must comply with the EU's rules for handling information about individuals, or risk prosecution. This directive prohibits the export of personal data to countries not doing enough to protect privacy, in particular, the United States.

More than 50 nations have, or are developing, privacy legislation. Europe has the strictest legislation regarding the collection and use of consumer data, and other countries look to that legislation when formulating their policies. Australia, for instance, recently introduced legislation that would require private companies to follow a set of guidelines regarding the collection, storage, use, and transfer of personal information about individuals. Common privacy rules include obtaining data fairly and lawfully, using the information only for the original purpose specified, making sure it is accurate and up-to-date, and destroying data after the purpose for collection is completed. The EU requires that consumers be presented with an opt-out provision at the point of data collection.

EXHIBIT 7.6

The Direct Marketing Association Privacy Promise

In July, 2002, the Direct Marketing Association made a Privacy Promise to American consumers as a public assurance that all members of the DMA will follow certain specific practices to protect consumer privacy. These practices were designed to have a major impact on those consumers who wish to receive fewer advertising solicitations. Specifically, members of the DMA must abide by the following four privacy protection practices.

1. Provide customers with annual notice of their ability to opt out of information exchanges. For online marketing, provide notice to both customers and prospects in each solicitation;

2. Honor customer opt-out requests not to have their contact information transferred to others for marketing purposes;

3. Accept and maintain consumer requests to be on an in-house suppress file to stop receiving solicitations from your company; and,

4. Use the DMA Preference Service suppression files for mail, telephone, and e-mail lists.

REVIEW LEARNING OBJECTIVE 10

10 **Discuss privacy issues related to one-to-one marketing**

Personal Information
Age
Income
Medical history
Spending habits
Children

Privacy Concerns
Misuse of personal information
Spam
Marketing to children

11 POSITIONING

Explain how and why firms implement positioning strategies and how product differentiation plays a role

FAQs

What is the difference between a market segment, a target market, and positioning? Find out the answer by watching the video FAQ on Xtra!

The development of any marketing mix depends on **positioning**, a process that influences potential customers' overall perception of a brand, product line, or organization in general. **Position** is the place a product, brand, or group of products occupies in consumers' minds relative to competing offerings. Consumer goods marketers are particularly concerned with positioning. Procter & Gamble, for example, markets 11 different laundry detergents, each with a unique position, as illustrated in Exhibit 7.7.

Positioning assumes that consumers compare products on the basis of important features. Marketing efforts that emphasize irrelevant features are therefore likely to misfire. For example, Crystal Pepsi and a clear version of Coca-Cola's Tab failed because consumers perceived the "clear" positioning as more of a marketing gimmick than a benefit.

Effective positioning requires assessing the positions occupied by competing products, determining the important dimensions underlying these positions, and choosing a position in the market where the organization's marketing efforts will have the greatest impact. For example, Ford Motor Company styled the new Taurus models with conventional lines and installed new high-tech protection features. It positioned the Taurus as a safe, family sedan, based on marketing research that revealed consumers view safety as a top priority in automobiles.

As the previous example illustrates, **product differentiation** is a positioning strategy that many firms use to distinguish their products from those of competitors. The distinctions can be either real or perceived. Tandem Computer designed machines with two central processing units and two memories for computer systems that can never afford to be down or lose their databases

EXHIBIT 7.7

Positioning of Procter & Gamble Detergents

Brand	Positioning	Market Share
Tide	Tough, powerful cleaning	31.1%
Cheer	Tough cleaning and color protection	8.2%
Bold	Detergent plus fabric softener	2.9%
Gain	Sunshine scent and odor-removing formula	2.6%
Era	Stain treatment and stain removal	2.2%
Dash	Value brand	1.8%
Oxydol	Bleach-boosted formula, whitening	1.4%
Solo	Detergent and fabric softener in liquid form	1.2%
Dreft	Outstanding cleaning for baby clothes, safe for tender skin	1.0%
Ivory Snow	Fabric and skin safety on baby clothes and fine washables	0.7%
Ariel	Tough cleaner, aimed at Hispanics	0.1%

positioning
Developing a specific marketing mix to influence potential customers' overall perception of a brand, product line, or organization in general.

position
The place a product, brand, or group of products occupies in consumers' minds relative to competing offerings.

product differentiation
A positioning strategy that some firms use to distinguish their products from those of competitors.

perceptual mapping
A means of displaying or graphing, in two or more dimensions, the location of products, brands, or groups of products in customers' minds.

(for example, an airline reservation system). In this case, Tandem used product differentiation to create a product with very real advantages for the target market. However, many everyday products, such as bleaches, aspirin, unleaded regular gasoline, and some soaps, are differentiated by such trivial means as brand names, packaging, color, smell, or "secret" additives. The marketer attempts to convince consumers that a particular brand is distinctive and that they should demand it over competing brands.

Some firms, instead of using product differentiation, position their products as being similar to competing products or brands. Artificial sweeteners advertised as tasting like sugar or margarine tasting like butter are two examples.

PERCEPTUAL MAPPING

Perceptual mapping is a means of displaying or graphing, in two or more dimensions, the location of products, brands, or groups of products in customers' minds. For example, after several years of decreasing market share and the perception of teenagers that Levi's were not "cool," Levi Strauss developed a number of youth-oriented fashions, as well as apparel appealing to adults by extending the Dockers and Slates casual-pants brands. To target high-end

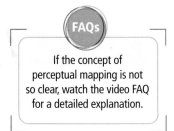

If the concept of perceptual mapping is not so clear, watch the video FAQ for a detailed explanation.

customers, Levi offers styles such as its Vintage line. These jeans sell for $85 to $220 in stores like Neiman Marcus.[63] The perceptual map in Exhibit 7.8 shows Levi's dozens of brands and subbrands, from cheap basics to high-priced fashion.

POSITIONING BASES

Firms use a variety of bases for positioning, including the following:

- *Attribute:* A product is associated with an attribute, product feature, or customer benefit. Rockport shoes are positioned as an always comfortable brand that is available in a range of styles from working shoes to dress shoes.
- *Price and quality:* This positioning base may stress high price as a signal of quality or emphasize low price as an indication of value. Neiman Marcus uses the high-price strategy; Wal-Mart has successfully followed the low-price and value strategy. The mass merchandiser Target has developed an interesting position based on price and quality. It is an "upscale discounter," sticking to low prices but offering higher quality and design than most discount chains.
- *Use or application:* Stressing uses or applications can be an effective means of positioning a product with buyers. Kahlúa liqueur used advertising to point out 228 ways to consume the product. Snapple introduced a new drink called "Snapple a Day" that is intended for use as a meal replacement.[64]
- *Product user:* This positioning base focuses on a personality or type of user. Zale Corporation has several jewelry store concepts, each positioned to a different user. The Zale stores cater to middle-of-the-road consumers with traditional styles. Its Gordon's stores appeal to a slightly older clientele with a contemporary look. Guild is positioned for the more affluent 50-plus consumer.
- *Product class:* The objective here is to position the product as being associated with a particular category of products; for example, positioning a margarine brand with butter. Alternatively, products can be disassociated with a category; for example, the "We're not your father's Oldsmobile" ad campaign.
- *Competitor:* Positioning against competitors is part of any positioning strategy. The Avis rental car positioning as number two exemplifies positioning against specific competitors.
- *Emotion:* Positioning using emotion focuses on how the product makes customers feel. A number of companies use this approach. For example, Nike's "Just Do It" campaign doesn't tell consumers what "it" is, but most get the emotional message of achievement and courage. Budweiser's advertising featuring talking frogs and lizards emphasizes fun. Kodak has long used emotional positioning revolving around family and memories when advertising its cameras and film.[65]

EXHIBIT 7.8

Perceptual Map and Positioning Strategy for Levi Strauss Products

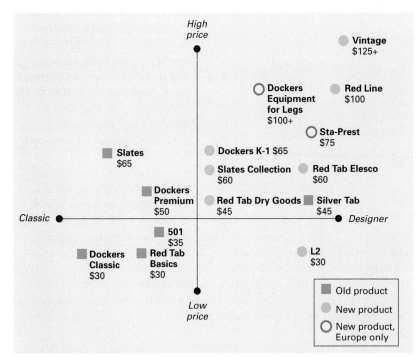

SOURCE: Nina Munk, "How Levi's Trashed a Great American Brand," *Fortune*, April 12, 1999, p. 84.

Companies often use a mix of positioning bases to reach their target audience. Mountain Dew is one of these products. This ad combines the elements of youth, outdoor fun, and even irreverence.

It is not unusual for a marketer to use more than one of these bases. A print ad in the "Got Milk?" campaign featuring Joan Lunden sporting a milk mustache read as follows:

Most people think I must drink at least 10 cups of coffee to be so perky in the morning. But the truth is, I like skim milk first thing. It has all the same nutrients as whole milk without all the fat. And, besides, my husband got the coffee maker.

This ad reflects the following positioning bases:

- *Product attribute/benefit:* The "same nutrients as whole milk without all the fat" describes a product attribute, and that skim milk makes her "perky" is a benefit.
- *Use or application:* Lunden drinks milk first thing in the morning.
- *Product user:* The use of Lunden, a successful, independent woman, shows that milk is not just for kids.
- *Product class (disassociation):* The ad differentiates skim milk from whole milk, showing skim milk is healthier.
- *Competitor (indirect):* She drinks milk instead of coffee.
- *Emotion:* The ad conveys an upbeat, contemporary attitude.[66]

REPOSITIONING

It is not uncommon for food manufacturers to reposition their products, particularly when new research indicates increased health benefits. This ad for almonds, repositions almonds from a snack food to a cholesterol-lowering health food.

Repositioning
Changing consumers' perceptions of a brand in relation to competing brands.

Sometimes products or companies are repositioned in order to sustain growth in slow markets or to correct positioning mistakes. **Repositioning** is changing consumers' perceptions of a brand in relation to competing brands. One of the most successful product repositioning campaigns ever was the National Pork Board's repositioning of pork as "the other white meat." In the late 1980s, when consumers became more health-conscious, pork producers were making changes in response to the demand for a leaner, higher quality product, but few people knew about it. While poultry sales were increasing, sales of pork products declined by more than 20 percent. The Pork Board launched the "Pork: The Other White Meat" campaign, which highlighted pork's convenience and nutritional benefits. By 1996, almost 90 percent of consumers surveyed recognized the slogan—up from 64 percent four years earlier. In 2000, new print, television, and Internet campaigns were introduced, and the slogan was named the fifth most memorable tag line in contemporary advertising by Northwestern University. Since the start of the campaign, pork production has increased nearly 40 percent, and pork is now the most eaten meat in the world.[67] Another company that has capitalized on the trend of health-consciousness in an effort to target baby boomers is Johnson & Johnson. The company repositioned St. Joseph baby aspirin as a low-dose aspirin for adults who want to reduce the risk of heart attack and stroke.[68] Taco Bell, best known for selling tacos and burritos for less than $1, started offering more upscale items such as a $2.99 Chicken Caesar Grilled Stuffed Burrito and a Southwest Steak Border Bowl for $3.49. The company's goal was to reposition itself in the fast-food market as a chain with cleaner, nicer-looking restaurants and higher priced items with better ingredients.[69]

Visit the Web sites where Motorola and Nokia pitch their cell phones and examine the Web pages designed to target customers in the United States, South Korea, and at least one Latin American or European country. Explore some of the links and determine if they use different segmentation strategies. Who do they appear to target? How do you think consumer preferences vary by country or culture?

http://www.hellomoto.com

http://www.nokia.com

Online

REVIEW LEARNING OBJECTIVE 11

Explain how and why firms implement positioning strategies and how product differentiation plays a role

Each car occupies a position in consumers' minds.
Cars can be positioned according to attribute (sporty, conservative, etc.),
to price/quality (affordable, classy, etc.) or other bases.
Cadillac has repositioned itself as a car for younger drivers with edgier ads.

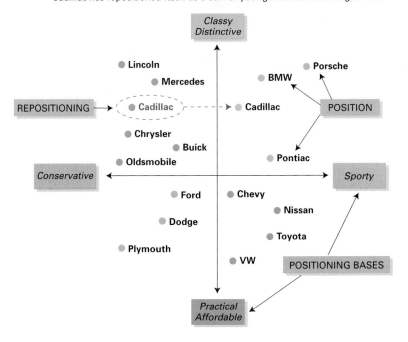

LOOKING BACK

As you read at the beginning of this chapter, market segmentation refers to the process of dividing a market into meaningful, relatively similar, and identifiable segments or groups. Targeting is selecting one or more market segments and designing, implementing, and maintaining distinctive marketing mixes for those segments. JCPenney is using a niche strategy, attempting to target women between the ages of 25 and 35 who are interested in affordable "high" fashion. This market segment is viable according to at least three of the four criteria for successful segmentation. It is substantial, identifiable, and accessible. The critical question for Penney's is whether this segment will be responsive to its marketing efforts.

Although Penney's is not known for its high-fashion women's clothing, women may buy its new designer and revamped private-label clothing lines if they perceive them to represent high fashion at an affordable price. Penney's shift in strategy represents an attempt to reposition its product offering.

USE IT NOW

POSITIONING YOURSELF

The principles of positioning discussed in this chapter do not apply solely to products that you buy. Many people position themselves in different "marketplaces" based on how they present themselves through the clothing they choose, the hairstyles they wear, and the activities they engage in. For example, a young woman may position herself in the dating market by wearing short skirts, sporting a trendy hairstyle, and spending time at night clubs. Another woman may dress modestly, wear a conservative hairstyle, and attend single events at her church. These two women are positioning themselves to attract different kinds of men.

Apply what you have learned in this chapter about positioning by developing a written strategy for a female friend who is interviewing for a job in two different industries: banking and advertising. How would you suggest this friend dress and wear her hair for each of the two interviews? What activities should she stress on her résumé for the bank interview and the advertising agency interview? How would you advise a male friend?

PROTECT YOUR PRIVACY ONLINE

Many Internet surfers don't realize that online companies can track their movements on the Web through the use of "cookie" files. To help maintain your anonymity on the Web refrain from answering online questionnaires, entering sweepstakes or divulging information to Web sites that do not post a privacy policy. Also, check out each site's privacy policy to learn what it does or might do with your personal information. It's also a good idea to periodically purge or clean out your cookie file on your hard drive. Keep only those cookie files for the sites you want to recognize you the next time you visit. To learn more about protecting your personal information as you surf, visit **http://www.junkbusters.com**. Become informed about your rights as a consumer by visiting the Direct Marketing Association at **http://www.the-dma.org**.

REVIEW AND APPLICATIONS

1 **Describe the characteristics of markets and market segments.** A market is composed of individuals or organizations with the ability and willingness to make purchases to fulfill their needs or wants. A market segment is a group of individuals or organizations with similar product needs as a result of one or more common characteristics.

1.1 Mercedes-Benz is thinking about advertising its cars to college students. Do you think that college students are a viable potential market for Mercedes? Why or why not?

1.2 How are visitors to the following Web site segmented when seeking relevant job openings? Try this search engine and report your results: **http://www.careermag.com**.

2 **Explain the importance of market segmentation.** Before the 1960s, few businesses targeted specific market segments. Today, segmentation is a crucial marketing strategy for nearly all successful organizations. Market segmentation enables marketers to tailor marketing mixes to meet the needs of particular population segments. Segmentation helps marketers identify consumer needs and preferences, areas of declining demand, and new marketing opportunities.

2.1 Describe market segmentation in terms of the historical evolution of marketing.

3 **Discuss criteria for successful market segmentation.** Successful market segmentation depends on four basic criteria: (1) a market segment must be substantial and have enough potential customers to be viable; (2) a market segment must be identifiable and measurable; (3) members of a market segment must be accessible to marketing efforts; and (4) a market segment must respond to particular marketing efforts in a way that distinguishes it from other segments.

3.1 As a marketing consultant for a chain of hair salons, you have been asked to evaluate the kids' market as a potential segment for the chain to target. Write a memo to your client discussing your evaluation of the kids' segment in terms of the four criteria for successful market segmentation.

4 **Describe the bases commonly used to segment consumer markets.** Five bases are commonly used for segmenting consumer markets. Geographic segmentation is based on region, size, density, and climate characteristics. Demographic segmentation is based on age, gender, income level, ethnicity, and family life-cycle characteristics. Psychographic segmentation includes personality, motives, and lifestyle characteristics. Benefits sought is a type of segmentation that identifies customers according to the benefits they seek in a product. Finally, usage segmentation divides a market by the amount of product purchased or consumed.

4.1 Choose magazine ads for five different consumer products. For each ad, write a description of what you think the demographic characteristics of the targeted market are.

4.2 Investigate how Delta Airlines (**http://www.delta.com**) uses its Web site to cater to its market segments.

4.3 Review the "Marketing in Entertainment" box on Apple and Volkswagen. Is it possible to identify a single market for two distinctly different products? In other words, how substantial is the market comprised of consumers who use Apple *and* who drive Volkswagens? Can you think of other product combinations that would interest a single market? (Do not use products that are complementary, like a bike and a bike helmet. Think of products, like the iPod and the car, that are very different.) Complete the following sentences and describe the market for each set of products you pair together.

Consumers of:

Propel fitness water could also be a target market for_____.

Proactiv Solution skin care products could also be a target market for_____.

Alienware computers could also be a target market for_____.

Specialty luggage tags could also be a target market for_____.

5 **Describe the bases for segmenting business markets.** Business markets can be segmented on three general bases. First, businesses segment markets based on company characteristics, such as customers' geographic location, type of company, company size, and product use. Second, companies may segment customers based on the buying processes those customers use. Third, companies are increasingly basing market segmentation on the type of relationship they have with their customers.

5.1 Choose five ads from business publications such as the *Wall Street Journal, Fortune,* and *BusinessWeek.* For each ad, write a description of how you think the company has segmented its business market.

6 **List the steps involved in segmenting markets.** Six steps are involved when segmenting markets: (1) selecting a market or product category for study; (2) choosing a basis or bases for segmenting the market; (3) selecting segmentation descriptors; (4) profiling and evaluating segments; (5) selecting target markets; and (6) designing, implementing, and maintaining appropriate marketing mixes.

6.1 Write a letter to the president of your bank suggesting ideas for increasing profits and enhancing customer service by improving segmentation and targeting strategies.

7 **Discuss alternative strategies for selecting target markets.** Marketers select target markets using three different strategies: undifferentiated targeting, concentrated targeting, and multisegment targeting. An undifferentiated targeting strategy assumes that all members of a market have similar needs that can be met with a single marketing mix. A concentrated targeting strategy focuses all marketing efforts on a single market segment. Multisegment targeting is a strategy that uses two or more marketing mixes to target two or more market segments.

7.1 **TEAM** Form a team with two or three other students. Create an idea for a new product. Describe the segment (or segments) you are going to target with the product, and explain why you chose the targeting strategy you did.

8 **Explain one-to-one marketing.** One-to-one marketing is an individualized marketing method that utilizes customer information to build long-term, personalized, and profitable relationships with each customer. Successful one-to-one marketing comes from understanding customers and collaborating with them, rather than using them as targets for generic messages. Database technology makes it possible for companies to interact with customers on a personal, one-to-one basis.

8.1 You are the marketing manager for a specialty retailer that sells customized handbags. Write a memo to your boss describing how the company could benefit from one-to-one marketing.

9 **Discuss the forces that have influenced the emergence of one-to-one marketing.** Forces that have helped shape one-to-one marketing include a more diverse society, more demanding and time-poor consumers, a decline in brand loyalty, the explosion of new media alternatives, and demand for marketing accountability. Consumers no longer want to be treated like the masses. One-to-one marketing allows consumers to be treated as individuals with their own unique sets of needs and wants.

9.1 Review the Marketing in Entertainment box from Chapter 1, found on page 13. Outline the forces that you think have influenced the development of the Pal Mickey. Do you think Pal Mickey will be successful? Why or why not?

10 **Discuss privacy issues related to one-to-one marketing.** One-to-one marketing concerns many Americans because of the potential for invasion of privacy, specifically the sheer volume of information that is aggregated in databases and the vulnerability of this information to unauthorized access and use. Most consumers are unaware of how personal information is collected, used, and distributed, and they are unaware of how technology helps in collecting personal data. Additionally, there is widespread misunderstanding among consumers about existing privacy laws and regulations. Frustrated by their lack of control, consumers want more opportunities to determine how their personal information will be used. The popularity of the Internet for direct marketing, consumer data collection, and as a repository of sensitive consumer data has also alarmed privacy-minded consumers.

10.1 INFOTRAC COLLEGE EDITION Use InfoTrac (**http://www.infotrac-college.com**) to read how the Internet industry is taking privacy issues into its own hands. Conduct a keyword search to find current discussions about consumer privacy in general and online privacy in particular. Read a sampling of articles and write a summary of your findings.

11 **Explain how and why firms implement positioning strategies and how product differentiation plays a role.** Positioning is used to influence consumer perceptions of a particular brand, product line, or organization in relation to competitors. The term *position* refers to the place that the offering occupies in consumers' minds. To establish a unique position, many firms use product differentiation, emphasizing the real or perceived differences between competing offerings. Products may be differentiated on the basis of attribute, price and quality, use or application, product user, product class, or competitor.

11.1 Choose a product category (e.g., pick-up tracks), and identify at least three different brands and their respective positioning strategies. How is each position communicated to the target audience?

TERMS

benefit segmentation 235
cannibalization 242
concentrated targeting strategy 241
demographic segmentation 227
80/20 principle 236
family life cycle (FLC) 232
geodemographic segmentation 234
geographic segmentation 226
market 224

market segment 224
market segmentation 224
multisegment targeting strategy 242
niche 241
one-to-one marketing 243
optimizers 237
perceptual mapping 249
position 249
positioning 249

product differentiation 249
psychographic segmentation 233
repositioning 251
satisficers 237
segmentation bases (variables) 226
target market 239
undifferentiated targeting strategy 240
usage-rate segmentation 236

EXERCISES

APPLICATION EXERCISE

How tightly do you fit into a particular market segment? Do you think you can be neatly classified? If you think your purchasing habits make you an enigma to marketers, you may need to think again.[70]

Activities

1. Go to the Claritas Web site (**http://www.claritas.com**) and use its VALS survey online to find out what your ZIP code says about you. The database will generate many cluster descriptions based on your ZIP code. Depending on the functionality of the Web site at the time you access the database, you may need to reenter your ZIP code multiple times if you want to read all the cluster descriptions.

2. Now pick a product category, like automobiles, athletic shoes, beverages, or health and beauty products. Then think about which products in that category would appeal to each of the clusters generated by your ZIP code search. For example, a car that appeals to a cluster titled "Young Bohemians" may not be the car of choice for the cluster "Pools and Patios." If your search generated only one cluster type, you may wish to enter other ZIP codes for your area of town or for your region.

3. Create a perceptual map for the product you chose. Write a short statement that describes the overall position of each product with an explanation of why you located it where you did on the perceptual map.

ETHICS EXERCISE

Tobacco companies are frequently criticized for targeting potential customers below the legal age to purchase and use their products. Critics cite Joe Camel and the Marlboro man as images meant to make smoking appealing to young people. If tobacco companies are actually following this particular demographic targeting strategy, most would agree that it is unethical if not illegal.

Questions

1. Is marketing tobacco products to younger consumers unethical?

2. Many are beginning to argue that fast-food companies, such as McDonald's and Burger King, are knowingly marketing unhealthy food to consumers. Is it unethical for fast-food companies to market kids' meals to children?

3. What does the AMA Code of Ethics have to say about marketing unhealthy or harmful products to consumers, particularly children and young adults? Go to the AMA Web site at **http://www.marketingpower.com** to review the code. Write a brief paragraph summarizing where the AMA stands on this important issue.

CAREER EXERCISE

Finding a career in market segmentation is not necessarily as difficult as it might sound. One easy way is to use "segmentation" in the keyword search of your favorite career site, such as Monster.com. Go to the Web site of the American Marketing Association, Monster, or the Vault.com and see what job listings contain the word "segmentation" or "targeting."

Activities

1. For a closer look at companies that specialize in segmentation, start by going to **http://www.claritas.com**. You can play with Claritas's geodemographic search engine by entering your ZIP code (if you have already done this in the Application Exercise, go on to the next part of the activity). What clusters are identified for your home address ZIP code? Do any seem to match your family perfectly, or are you best described by a mix of the clusters? Now enter your college address ZIP code. What cluster descriptions appear? Compare them to your home address clusters. How valid do you think Claritas's clusters are?

2. If the idea of breaking market segments into geodemographic clusters is appealing, visit the career page of Claritas's Web site and see what opportunities there are. You may also want to try the careers page at SRI-VALS.

3. Review your findings from activity 1. Then go to the site of a British company that specializes almost exclusively in market segmentation, **http://www.marketsegmentation.co.uk**. There, you can get a detailed look at how things like market mapping, niche marketing, target marketing, and marketing planning work in the real world. How do you think a career in segmentation would differ in the United Kingdom compared to the United States?

ENTREPRENEURSHIP CASE

© ROYALTY-FREE/CORBIS

VIVA LAS VEGAS

In 2003, more than 35.5 million travelers made Las Vegas their destination of choice. It was the second largest volume of visitors the city has ever entertained, lagging just slightly behind the 35.8 million recorded for the year 2000. Those numbers are remarkable given the recent slump in the travel industry, and the city has the Las Vegas Convention and Visitors Authority to thank. For almost 50 years, the LVCVA has been promoting Las Vegas in an effort to maximize occupancy for the city's hoteliers who suffer from the cyclical demand in the travel industry. The authority's marketing of the city's convention, lodging, and entertainment facilities to convention organizers, meeting planners, and leisure travelers plays an integral role in keeping hotel rooms and convention facilities occupied during off-peak times of the year.

Many types of visitors go to Las Vegas for a variety of reasons, and the LVCVA uses a multilevel promotions strategy to reach them all. The organization's promotional mix includes national television advertising, grassroots marketing, and relationship building with a variety of organizations. Each element is specifically designed to address issues within particular segments of its growing target market, such as changes in the composition of the visitor pool, shifts in visitors' travel preferences, the emergence of potentially lucrative metropolitan markets, and trends in foreign visitors.

An LVCVA study of the area's visitors for 2001, for example, found that African Americans, Hispanics, and Asian Americans accounted for 9, 5, and 4 percent, respectively, of the total visitor pool. The same study also revealed that the number of visitors from each of those groups had been steadily rising and that all U.S. visitors were beginning to prefer two- or three-day stays to weeklong vacations. With those data in hand, the LVCVA produced its award-winning "Vegas Stories" series of TV commercials for 2003 and 2004. The irreverent ads poke fun at the sticky situations travelers may find themselves in as a result of too much revelry in the desert.

Using the tagline, "What happens here, stays here," the spots from the "Vegas Stories" campaign include an older Asian woman trying to alter an after-the-trip love letter while Roy Orbison's "Only the Lonely" plays in the background and a bachelorette party of African American women riding quietly in a limousine until the group is slowly overcome with sheepish laughter. Other commercials depict elderly couples, businesswomen, and young professional males. The LVCVA also produced its first-ever commercial recorded entirely in Spanish, which was written specifically to appeal to Hispanics' historical preference for family or group activities for vacations. Additionally, the authority's director of diversity began promoting Las Vegas to ethnic chambers of commerce and organizations like the International Association of Hispanic Meeting Planners and the National Coalition of Black Meeting Planners.

Other research performed by the LVCVA identified Portland, Oregon, and Atlanta as emerging regional markets based on the their median household incomes, their available flights to Las Vegas, the cost of advertising in those markets, and the propensity of their citizens to gamble. The LVCVA then bought billboards in each city, cruised the towns in a specially prepared van featuring an Elvis impersonator and a traditional Vegas showgirl, and promoted special travel deals to promote the entertainment options that Las Vegas offers in addition to gambling.

The authority's message carries beyond the borders of the United States, too. When it noticed significant drops in the visitor volume from Canada—Las Vegas's leading source of international travelers—the LVCVA sent an official delegation to Toronto. The group canvassed Toronto's Canadian Meeting & Incentive Travel Symposium & Trade Show to persuade convention operators to host their future productions in the desert. Representatives also met with private convention and leisure travel planners and attended events in Montreal and Vancouver to promote their cause.

Las Vegas is clearly on the rise again thanks to the tireless work of the LVCVA, and the authority has the hard data to prove it. As long as the LVCVA continues to understand its many diverse customers and communicate with them appropriately, the city of lights should continue to shine brightly for many years to come.[71]

Questions

1. What bases does the LVCVA use for segmenting its target market?

2. Does the LVCVA use an undifferentiated, a concentrated, or a multisegment targeting strategy? Why? Should the LVCVA be concerned with cannibalization?

3. Think of the many reasons a person might want to travel to Las Vegas. Given a target market of all U.S. citizens aged 18 to 75, speculate how you might segment that market by lifestyle.

4. What do you think makes the LVCVA so successful?

WATCH IT

FEATURE PRESENTATION

Le Travel Store

SmallBusinessSchool
the Series on PBS stations and the Web

To give you insight into Chapter 7, Small Business School introduces you to Joan and Bill Keller, owners of Le Travel Store. The company has been serving the independent overseas traveler for over 20 years, and from the humble origins of selling charter flights on a college campus, it has become a thriving travel services and supplies merchant. Though the Kellers moved from a small office to an upscale, theatrical mill location and again to a warehouse-style outlet in a historical part of San Diego, they have always stayed in touch with their target customer. Over the years, they have added backpacks, travel agency services, and a complete line of travel products to their original service of selling airplane tickets. Much change has brought much success, but one thing has remained constant: The Kellers have always been true to their core customer, the independent international traveler.

What to Watch For and Ask Yourself

1. What was Bill Keller's original strategy for selecting a target market? On what kind of segmentation variable(s) was that based? How has that evolved over time? Has there been any change?

2. How does the location and type of retail space of Le Travel Store reflect its positioning?

3. Describe the positioning bases used by Le Travel Store for its luggage products.

ENCORE PRESENTATION

The Breakfast Club

Carefully review this chapter's discussion of segmenting and targeting markets, especially noting Exhibit 7.1, "Concept of Market Segmentation." The scene is an edited version of the "Lunchtime" sequence that appears in the first third of the film. John Hughes's careful look at teenage culture in a suburban Chicago High School focuses on a group of teenagers from the school's different subcultures. View this film scene as a metaphor for market segmentation. What market segments can you identify in the scene? What are your criteria or bases for those segments or divisions? Why would market segmentation be important if you were marketing products or services to the people shown in the scene?

STILL SHAKY?

If you're having trouble with the concepts in this chapter, consider using some of the following study resources. You can review the videos, or test yourself with materials designed for all kinds of learning styles.

☑ **Xtra! (http://lambxtra.swlearning.com)**

☑ Quiz	☑ Feature Videos	☑ Encore Videos	☑ FAQ Videos
☑ Exhibit Worksheets	☑ Marketing Plan Worksheets	☐ Content	

☑ **http://lamb.swlearning.com**

☑ Quiz	☑ PowerPoint slides	☑ Marketing News	☑ Review Exercises
☑ Links	☑ Marketing Plan Contest	☑ Career Exercise	☑ Use It Now

☑ **Study guide**

☑ Outline	☑ Vocab Review	☑ Test Questions	☑ Marketing Scenario

Need More? Here's a tip. The list of key terms on page 256 can be a valuable study aid. Write down the definition of each term on a separate piece of paper, and without consulting the margin terms in the chapter. Cement your understanding by also writing an example if possible.

Decision Support Systems and Marketing Research

LEARNING OBJECTIVES

1. Explain the concept and purpose of a marketing decision support system

2. Define marketing research and explain its importance to marketing decision making

3. Describe the steps involved in conducting a marketing research project

4. Discuss the profound impact of the Internet on marketing research

5. Discuss the growing importance of scanner-based research

6. Explain the concept of competitive intelligence

Lew Frankfort's goal out of school wasn't to become America's most successful purse salesman. The chief executive of Coach wanted to use his MBA to improve society. He spent ten years in New York City government, eventually running the city's HeadStart programs. In 1979 he was introduced to Miles Cahn, the founder of Coach, who was looking for a protégé. Frankfort has been with the accessory maker ever since.

Coach was known for making classic, high-quality purses and handbags, but in the 1990s that image started to become a hindrance. Gucci and Prada offered more stylish products, while Nine West was introducing Euro knockoffs in its shoe stores. Frankfort brought in a designer from Tommy Hilfiger, remodeled stores,

and farmed out production to factories abroad. Coach's new models attracted the fashion-conscious without alienating women who just wanted a classic Coach purse. Since spinning off from Sara Lee in October 2000, Coach has doubled its profits, and its stock has jumped threefold.

It's not just the hipper designs that make Coach tick. Frankfort is an ardent believer in finding out what customers think about Coach in general and its products in particular. The firm interviews up to 5,000 current and potential customers each year. In Frankfort's words, it's the logic behind the magic, and it has helped keep sales soaring even during the economic downturn.

Frankfort was asked "Why so much marketing research?" He replied, "We're

marketing a discretionary product. People don't need to buy Coach. They have to buy toothpaste and cereal. I opened the first Coach store in 1981. I spent the early days speaking to customers about how they purchased handbags, what roles do accessories play in their wardrobes. The better we understand what they're thinking and how they make a purchase decision, the better job we do. We spend over $3 million on research each year."[1]

What are the various techniques for conducting marketing research? Should managers always conduct marketing research before making a decision? How does marketing research relate to decision support systems? We will explore all these topics and others in Chapter 8.

1 MARKETING DECISION SUPPORT SYSTEMS

Explain the concept and purpose of a marketing decision support system

Accurate and timely information is the lifeblood of marketing decision making. Good information can help an organization maximize sales and efficiently use scarce company resources. To prepare and adjust marketing plans, managers need a system for gathering everyday information about developments in the marketing environment—that is, for gathering **marketing information**. The system most commonly used these days for gathering marketing information is called a *marketing decision support system.*

A marketing **decision support system (DSS)** is an interactive, flexible computerized information system that enables managers to obtain and manipulate information as they are making decisions. A DSS bypasses the information-processing specialist and gives managers access to useful data from their own desks.

These are the characteristics of a true DSS:

FAQs

What is the relationship between marketing research and the marketing concept? Find out by watching the video FAQ on Xtra!

- *Interactive:* Managers give simple instructions and see immediate results. The process is under their direct control; no computer programmer is needed. Managers don't have to wait for scheduled reports.
- *Flexible:* A DSS can sort, regroup, total, average, and manipulate the data in various ways. It will shift gears as the user changes topics, matching information to the problem at hand. For example, the CEO can see highly aggregated figures, and the marketing analyst can view very detailed breakouts.
- *Discovery-oriented:* Managers can probe for trends, isolate problems, and ask "what if" questions.
- *Accessible:* Managers who aren't skilled with computers can easily learn how to use a DSS. Novice users should be able to choose a standard, or default, method of using the system. They can bypass optional features so they can work with the basic system right away while gradually learning to apply its advanced features.

marketing information
Everyday information about developments in the marketing environment that managers use to prepare and adjust marketing plans.

decision support system (DSS)
An interactive, flexible computerized information system that enables managers to obtain and manipulate information as they are making decisions.

database marketing
The creation of a large computerized file of customers' and potential customers' profiles and purchase patterns.

As a hypothetical example of how a DSS can be used, consider Renee Smith, vice president and manager of new products for Central Corporation. To evaluate sales of a recently introduced product, Renee can "call up" sales by the week, then by the month, breaking them out at her option by, say, customer segments. As she works at her desktop computer, her inquiries can go in several directions, depending on the decision at hand. If her train of thought raises questions about monthly sales last quarter compared to forecasts, she can use her DSS to analyze problems immediately. Renee might see that her new product's sales were significantly below forecasts. Were her forecasts too optimistic? She compares other products' sales to her forecasts and finds that the targets were very accurate. Was something wrong with the product? Is her sales department getting insufficient leads, or is it not putting leads to good use? Thinking a minute about how to examine that question, she checks ratios of leads converted to sales, product by product. The results disturb her. Only 5 percent of the new product's leads generated orders, compared to the company's 12 percent all-product average. Why? Renee guesses that the sales force is not supporting the new product vigorously enough. Quantitative information from the DSS could perhaps provide more evidence to back that suspicion. But already having enough quantitative knowledge to satisfy herself, the VP acts on her intuition and experience and decides to have a chat with her sales manager.

Perhaps the fastest-growing use of DSSs is for **database marketing**, which is the creation of a large computerized file of customers' and potential customers' profiles and purchase patterns. It is usually the key tool for successful one-to-one marketing, which relies on very specific information about a market.

REVIEW LEARNING OBJECTIVE 1

1 **Explain the concept and purpose of a marketing decision support system**

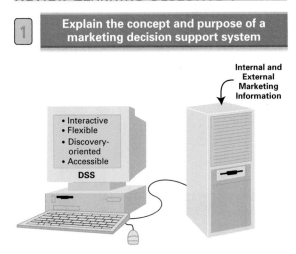

Internal and External Marketing Information

- Interactive
- Flexible
- Discovery-oriented
- Accessible

DSS

Define marketing research and explain its importance to marketing decision making

Marketing research is the process of planning, collecting, and analyzing data relevant to a marketing decision. The results of this analysis are then communicated to management. Marketing research plays a key role in the marketing system. It provides decision makers with data on the effectiveness of the current marketing mix and also with insights for necessary changes. Furthermore, marketing research is a main data source for both management information systems and DSS. In other words, the findings of a marketing research project become data in a DSS.

Marketing research has three roles: descriptive, diagnostic, and predictive. Its *descriptive* role includes gathering and presenting factual statements. For example, what is the historic sales trend in the industry? What are consumers' attitudes toward a product and its advertising? Its *diagnostic* role includes explaining data. For instance, what was the impact on sales of a change in the design of the package? Its *predictive* function is to address "what if" questions. For example, how can the researcher use the descriptive and diagnostic research to predict the results of a planned marketing decision?

MANAGEMENT USES OF MARKETING RESEARCH

Marketing research can help managers in several ways. It improves the quality of decision making and helps managers trace problems. Most important, sound marketing research helps managers focus on the paramount importance of keeping existing customers, aids them in better understanding the marketplace, and alerts them to marketplace trends. Marketing research helps managers gauge the perceived value of their goods and services as well as the level of customer satisfaction. For example, research revealed which brands of plumbing fixtures were traditional to New York City. This helped the Brooklyn Home Depot's store manager Rich Kantor to arrange his small pilot store so that it was designed to meet the needs of urban communities.

Marketing research can help managers in several ways. For example, research revealed which brands of plumbing fixtures were traditional to New York City. This helped the Brooklyn Home Depot's store manager Rich Kantor to arrange his small pilot store so that it was designed to meet the needs of urban communities.

AP/WIDE WORLD PHOTOS

Improving the Quality of Decision Making

Managers can sharpen their decision making by using marketing research to explore the desirability of various marketing alternatives. For example, on the heels of the successful launch of its Young & Tender line of bagged spinach, NewStar, a Salinas, California–based produce firm, was wondering what to do for an encore. A line of salad kits featuring spinach in combination with a dressing and/or other ingredients seemed like a natural idea. But rather than introducing a me-too product to the already-crowded salad kit market, the company wanted to add a gourmet twist.

The process began with an idea generation phase, says Christie Hoyer, vice president of product development and evaluation at the National Food Laboratory (NFL). Sessions were conducted with NFL chefs, food technologists, and other culinary arts workers. "We did a number of brainstorming sessions, game-playing, and other, more coordinated exercises. From that we came up with numerous flavor concepts for the salads and the sauté mixes."

Next came the first round of consumer testing. At this stage, Hoyer says, NFL wanted to validate the product concepts and also gauge reactions to them.

marketing research
The process of planning, collecting, and analyzing data relevant to a marketing decision.

A four-phase process was conducted with male and female consumers ages 21 to 64 who were their family's primary grocery shopper and were positive toward spinach salad and cooked fresh spinach.

The first phase gathered reactions to the concept of a line of gourmet salad and sauté kits and determined purchase intent for each flavor (based on descriptions of the flavors, not actual tasting). Next the respondents tried the product prototypes, which were rotated so that half of the group tried the sautés first and half tried the salads first.

The third phase was a test of packaging. Respondents were taken to a separate area featuring a mock store display of three packaging concepts and asked to rank their preferences for the different graphics. In the fourth phase, the consumers viewed a large copy of the nutritional information for a salad kit and a sauté kit. "Without specifically asking about it, we were interested in their reaction to things such as fat content," Hoyer says.

Since the salad and sauté mixes were introduced, they have been a hit with retailers and with consumers. Marketing research paved the way![2]

Tracing Problems

Another way managers use marketing research is to find out why a plan backfired. Was the initial decision incorrect? Did an unforeseen change in the external environment cause the plan to fail? How can the same mistake be avoided in the future?

Keebler introduced Sweet Spots, a shortbread cookie with a huge chocolate drop on it. It has had acceptable sales and is still on the market, but only after the company used marketing research to overcome several problems. Soon after the cookie's introduction, Keebler increased the box size from 10 ounces at $2.29 to 15 ounces at $3.19. Demand immediately fell. Market research showed that Sweet Spots were now considered more of a luxury than an everyday item. Keebler lowered the price and went back to the 10-ounce box. Even though Sweet Spots originally was aimed at upscale adult females, the company also tried to appeal to kids. In subsequent research, Keebler found that the package graphics appealed to mothers but not to children.

Focusing on the Paramount Importance of Keeping Existing Customers

An inextricable link exists between customer satisfaction and customer loyalty. Long-term relationships don't just happen but are grounded in the delivery of service and value by the firm. Customer retention pays big dividends for organizations. Powered by repeat sales and referrals, revenues and market share grow. Costs fall because firms spend less money and energy attempting to replace defectors. Steady customers are easy to serve because they understand the modus operandi and make fewer demands on employees' time. Increased customer retention also drives job satisfaction and pride, which lead to higher employee retention. In turn, the knowledge employees acquire as they stay longer increases productivity.

The ability to retain customers is based on an intimate understanding of their needs. Sometimes companies think that they are meeting customer needs when they are not. UPS, Inc., for example, had always assumed that on-time delivery was the paramount concern of its customers. Consequently, UPS's definition of quality centered almost exclusively on the results of time-and-motion studies. Knowing the average time elevator doors took to open on a certain city block and figuring how long people took to answer their doorbells were critical parts of the customer satisfaction equation. So was pushing drivers to meet exacting schedules. The problem was that UPS's marketing research survey was asking the wrong questions. It asked customers if they were pleased with delivery times and whether they thought delivery could be even faster.

When UPS began asking broader questions about how it could improve service, it discovered that its customers weren't as obsessed with on-time delivery as the company had thought. The biggest surprise was that customers wanted more interaction with drivers, who provided the only face-to-face contact customers had with the company. Less harried drivers who were more willing to chat could offer customers some practical advice on shipping.

UPS

What evidence can you find at the UPS Web site that the company is responding to the customer needs revealed by its marketing research? In your opinion, what makes the site consumer-centric? Are there any ways UPS could improve its Web site? Specifically, how?

http://www.ups.com

Online

In a sharp departure from tradition, the company now encourages its 62,000 delivery drivers to get out of their trucks and go along with salespeople to visit customers. It also allows drivers an additional 30 minutes a week to spend at their discretion to strengthen ties with customers and perhaps bring in new sales. Drivers use the Internet to report customer needs to the sales team. If a salesperson makes a sale based on that lead, the driver is given points on a debit card that can be used as cash. This has increased sales and encourages drivers to become more aware of customer needs. Using marketing research to understand its customers has enabled UPS to achieve consistently high customer satisfaction scores on the University of Michigan's 200-company Customer Satisfaction Index.[3]

Understanding the Ever-Changing Marketplace

Marketing research also helps managers understand what is going on in the marketplace and take advantage of opportunities. Historically, marketing research has been practiced for as long as marketing has existed. The early Phoenicians carried out market demand studies as they traded in the various ports of the Mediterranean Sea. Marco Polo's diary indicates he was performing marketing research as he traveled to China. There is even evidence that the Spanish systematically conducted "market surveys" as they explored the New World, and there are examples of marketing research conducted during the Renaissance.

A good example of the changing marketplace is the increase in female sports-fans. The percentage of women aged 18 or older who are loyal sports fans doubled from 29 percent in 1998 to 60 percent in 2004. According to a national study by Scarborough Sports Marketing in New York, 50 million women report that they are very or somewhat interested in professional hockey, football, golf, basketball, soccer, baseball, or NASCAR.

The study revealed that Major League Baseball is the biggest hit among women 18 and over. Women are also watching pro football in record numbers, with 31 percent reporting they are loyal National Football League fans. Other professional sports organizations that have demonstrated measurable growth among women include NASCAR, the Professional Golfers' Association, the National Basketball Association, and the National Hockey League (NHL).

The study also offered insight into the demographic profile, socioeconomic characteristics, and lifestyle activities of these sports enthusiasts. For example, female NHL fans are 34 percent more likely than the average woman to be age 18 to 34 and 23 percent more likely to be single; 70 percent of them have purchased sports apparel in the past 12 months. When they're not following the NHL, they are more than twice as likely as the average woman to go in-line skating, 76 percent more likely to participate in team sports, and 44 percent more likely to go camping.

Denver and Minneapolis (both at 69 percent) have the largest percentage of female sports fans. Other high-ranking markets include Buffalo and Cleveland (both at 66 percent) and Jacksonville, Florida, St. Louis, and Atlanta (all at

Define marketing research and explain its importance to marketing decision making

Why marketing research?

☑ Improve quality of decision making

☑ Trace problems

☑ Focus on keeping existing customers

☑ Understand changes in marketplace

65 percent). Meanwhile, female residents of Fresno, California, El Paso, Texas, Los Angeles, and Wichita, Kansas, are the least likely to get in the game.[4] Such information about demographics and the size of the market is important for professional sports organizations and even equipment manufacturers.

 ## STEPS IN A MARKETING RESEARCH PROJECT

Describe the steps involved in conducting a marketing research project

Virtually all firms that have adopted the marketing concept engage in some marketing research because it offers decision makers many benefits. Some companies spend millions on marketing research; others, particularly smaller firms, conduct informal, limited-scale research studies. For example, when Eurasia restaurant, serving Eurasian cuisine, first opened along Chicago's ritzy Michigan Avenue, it drew novelty seekers. But it turned off the important business lunch crowd, and sales began to decline. The owner surveyed several hundred businesspeople working within a mile of the restaurant. He found that they were confused by Eurasia's concept and wanted more traditional Asian fare at lower prices. In response, the restaurant altered its concept; it hired a Thai chef, revamped the menu, and cut prices. The dining room was soon full again.

Whether a research project costs $200 or $2 million, the same general process should be followed. The marketing research process is a scientific approach to decision making that maximizes the chance of getting accurate and meaningful results. Exhibit 8.1 traces the steps: (1) identifying and formulating the problem/opportunity, (2) planning the research design and gathering primary data, (3) specifying the sampling procedures, (4) collecting the data, (5) analyzing the data, (6) preparing and presenting the report, and (7) following up.

The research process begins with the recognition of a marketing problem or opportunity. As changes occur in the firm's external environment, marketing managers are faced with the questions, "Should we change the existing marketing mix?" and, if so, "How?" Marketing research may be used to evaluate product, promotion, distribution, or pricing alternatives.

For example, why has British Airways (BA) beaten American Airlines for years in the highly lucrative business of flying customers between New York and London in first class—using the same kind of aircraft between the same airports? BA understands that success depends fundamentally on the profits it earns from customers—and on management's ability to improve that profitability by creating competitively dominant customer experiences, or *value propositions*. A winning value proposition is the one that best meets the full set of customer needs, including price. That is, certain critical elements of the experience must deliver on the customers' most important needs better than the competition. This creates differentia-

180° flat beds | gracious service | privacy | a better sleep in business class | **BRITISH AIRWAYS**

The red-eye has been replaced by the shut-eye.

COURTESY BRITISH AIRWAYS

British Airways refined its First Class service based on marketing research that revealed travelers often wanted to sleep during long-haul flights. BA created the world's first fully flat bed in business class (Club World) as shown above.

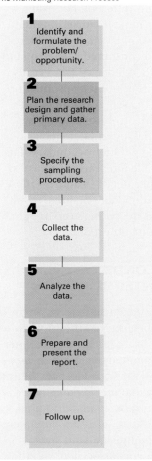

EXHIBIT 8.1

The Marketing Research Process

1 Identify and formulate the problem/opportunity.

2 Plan the research design and gather primary data.

3 Specify the sampling procedures.

4 Collect the data.

5 Analyze the data.

6 Prepare and present the report.

7 Follow up.

marketing research problem
Determining what information is needed and how that information can be obtained efficiently and effectively.

marketing research objective
The specific information needed to solve a marketing research problem; the objective should be to provide insightful decision-making information.

management decision problem
A broad-based problem that uses marketing research in order for managers to take proper actions.

secondary data
Data previously collected for any purpose other than the one at hand.

---

tion and the potential for superior customer profitability—a mutually beneficial value exchange.

To create the right value proposition, BA had to understand its customers' needs. The BA story illustrates an important point about problem/opportunity definition. The **marketing research problem** is information oriented. It involves determining what information is needed and how that information can be obtained efficiently and effectively. The **marketing research objective**, then, is to provide insightful decision-making information. This requires specific pieces of information needed to answer the marketing research problem. Managers must combine this information with their own experience and other information to make a proper decision.

Imagine a lawyer, investment banker, or senior executive who frequently needs to fly from New York after a full workday for meetings the next morning in London, then return to New York for an evening board meeting. The needs of any customer in this segment are quite specific and similar: saving time and getting rest. BA and American Airlines both offer value propositions—which consultant Michael J. Lanning has elegantly defined as complete experiences—for these customers.[5] The experience starts when the customer realizes the need for the trip and comprises each interaction with the airline: making the reservation, arriving at the airport, checking in, clearing security, boarding, eating, sleeping, deplaning, and going through customs in London, with most of the process repeated on the return flight. The experience concludes when the mileage is posted to the customer's frequent flyer statement and the cost is charged to his or her credit card.

The marketing research objective was to determine the common critical needs of this elite group of consumers. In contrast, the **management decision problem** is action oriented. Management problems tend to be much broader in scope and far more general than marketing research problems, which must be narrowly defined and specific if the research effort is to be successful. Sometimes several research studies must be conducted to solve a broad management problem. BA's marketing analysts had already determined that the most profitable 10 percent of its customers are heavily populated by frequent first-class passengers on the New York-to-London route. This group is profitable because its members travel often and pay the full first-class fare. Further analysis showed that these customers frequently depart from New York in the evening and return late the following afternoon; often they don't even stay in a hotel. Demographic analysis indicated that these travelers are senior business executives concentrated in a handful of industries. Interviews with customers revealed common critical needs: saving time on departure and arrival, and maximizing restful sleep on the plane.[6] Armed with this marketing research information, management was able to convert this knowledge to a winning value proposition.

SECONDARY DATA

A valuable tool throughout the research process but particularly in the problem/opportunity identification stage is **secondary data**—data previously collected for any purpose other than the one at hand. Secondary information originating within the company includes documents such as annual reports, reports to stockholders, product testing results perhaps made available to the news media, and house periodicals composed by the company's personnel for communication to employees, customers, or others. Often this information is incorporated into a company's internal database. Recall that British Airways identified its most profitable customers from secondary data.

Innumerable outside sources of secondary information also exist, principally in the forms of government (federal, state, and local) departments and agencies that compile and publish summaries of business data. Trade and industry associations also publish secondary data. Still more data are available in business periodicals and other news media that regularly publish studies and articles on the economy, specific industries, and even individual companies. The unpublished summarized secondary information from these sources corresponds to internal reports, memos, or special-purpose analyses with limited circulation. Economic considerations or priorities in the organization may preclude publication of these summaries. Most of the sources listed above can be found on the Internet.

Secondary data save time and money if they help solve the researcher's problem. Even if the problem is not solved, secondary data have other advantages. They can aid in formulating the problem statement and suggest research methods and other types of data needed for solving the problem. In addition, secondary data can pinpoint the kinds of people to approach and their locations and serve as a basis of comparison for other data. The disadvantages of secondary data stem mainly from a mismatch between the researcher's unique problem and the purpose for which the secondary data were originally gathered, which are typically different. For example, a major consumer-products manufacturer wanted to determine the market potential for a fireplace log made of coal rather than compressed wood by-products. The researcher found plenty of secondary data about total wood consumed as fuel, quantities consumed in each state, and types of wood burned. Secondary data were also available about consumer attitudes and purchase patterns of wood by-product fireplace logs. The wealth of secondary data provided the researcher with many insights into the artificial log market. Yet nowhere was there any information that would tell the firm whether consumers would buy artificial logs made of coal.

The quality of secondary data may also pose a problem. Often secondary data sources do not give detailed information that would enable a researcher to assess their quality or relevance. Whenever possible, a researcher needs to address these important questions: Who gathered the data? Why were the data obtained? What methodology was used? How were classifications (such as heavy users versus light users) developed and defined? When was the information gathered?

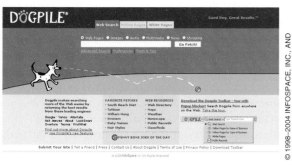

The Internet has eliminated much of the drudgery associated with secondary research. Search engines and meta-search engines, like Dogpile, allow researchers to identify sources of information in an instant. Still, Internet searches can be tedious if you are looking for something uncommon.

THE NEW AGE OF SECONDARY INFORMATION: THE INTERNET

Gathering secondary data, while necessary in almost any research project, has traditionally been a tedious and boring job. The researcher often had to write to government agencies, trade associations, or other secondary data providers and then wait days or weeks for a reply that might never come. Often, one or more trips to the library were required and the researcher might find that needed reports were checked out or missing. With the rapid development of the Internet and World Wide Web in the last few years, however, much of the drudgery associated with the collection of secondary data has been eliminated.

Finding Secondary Data on the Internet

If you know the address of a particular Web site that contains the secondary data that you are searching for, you can type a description of what you are looking for directly into your Web browser (such as Microsoft Internet Explorer).

Search Engines Sites such as Yahoo, All the Web, and Google have become popular with researchers looking for information on the Web. These organizations offer *search engines* that scan the Web looking for sites on a designated topic. Each search engine uses its own indexing system to locate relevant information. All of them allow users to enter one or more keywords that will initiate a search of the databases of Web sites for all occurrences of those words. They then return listings that allow users to go immediately to the sites described.

Metasearch engines are search engines of search engines. This means that they make informational queries to many search engines simultaneously. Two popular metasearch engines are Dogpile and Netcrawler.

Remember that the Internet is a self-publishing medium. Your visits to search engines will yield files with a wide range of quality from a variety of sources. Try out multiple sites when you are investigating a topic.

Directories In addition to search engines, you can use subject directories on the Web to explore a subject. There are two basic types of directories: (1) academic and professional directories, often created and maintained by subject experts to support the needs of researchers, and (2) commercial portals, which cater to the general public and are competing for traffic. Directories depend upon people to compile their listings.

- *Academic and professional directories* are created by librarians or subject experts and tend to be associated with libraries and academic institutions. These collections are created to enhance the research process and help users find high-quality sites of interest. A careful selection process is applied, and links to the selected resources are usually annotated. These collections are often created to serve an institution's constituency but may be useful to any researcher. As a rule, these sites do not generate income or carry advertising. INFOMINE, from the University of California, is an example of an academic directory.
- *Commercial portals* are created to generate income and serve the general public. These services link to a wide range of topics and often emphasize entertainment, commerce, hobbies, sports, travel, and other interests not necessarily covered by academic directories. These sites seek to draw traffic in order to support advertising. As a part of this goal, the directory is offered in conjunction with a number of additional customer services. Yahoo! is an example of a commercial portal.

The lines between directories and search engines are blurring. Directories are present at some search engine sites, and sometimes their contents are searched along with content from the general Web. For example, AltaVista offers the Look-Smart directory; Infoseek shares the screen with the directory at the Go Network; Excite has its own directory; and Lycos offers the directory contents from the Netscape Open Directory. Directory results are sometimes placed before search results to steer users to the directory's content. This can be a useful way of getting at substantive content relating to your query. Most subject directories offer a search engine mechanism to query the database.

Internet Discussion Groups and Special Interest Groups as Sources of Secondary Data

A primary means of communicating with other professionals and special interest groups on the Internet is through newsgroups. With an Internet connection and newsreader software, you can visit any newsgroup supported by your service provider. If your service provider does not offer newsgroups or does not carry the group in which you are interested, you can find one of the publicly available newsgroup servers that does carry the group you would like to read.

Newsgroups function much like bulletin boards for a particular topic or interest. A newsgroup is established to focus on a particular topic. Readers stop by that newsgroup to read messages left by other people, post responses to others' questions, and send rebuttals to comments with which they disagree. Generally,

metasearch engines
Search engines that make informational queries to many search engines simultaneously; search engines of search engines.

newsgroups
Function like bulletin boards on the Internet. They are established to focus on a particular topic.

there is some management of the messages to keep discussions within the topic area and to remove offensive material. However, readers of a newsgroup are free to discuss any issue and communicate with anyone in the world who visits that newsgroup. Images and data files can be exchanged in newsgroups, just as they can be exchanged via e-mail.

With hundreds of thousands of newsgroups currently in existence and more being added every day, there is a newsgroup for nearly every hobby, profession, and lifestyle. Newsgroup messages look like e-mail messages. They contain a subject title, author, and message body. Unlike normal e-mail messages, though, newsgroup messages are threaded discussions. This means that any reply to a previous message will appear linked to that message. Therefore, you can follow a discussion between two or more people by starting at the original message and following the links (or threads) to each successive reply. You can send images, sound files, and video clips attached to your message for anyone to download and examine.

PLANNING THE RESEARCH DESIGN AND GATHERING PRIMARY DATA

Good secondary data can help researchers conduct a thorough situation analysis. With that information, researchers can list their unanswered questions and rank them. Researchers must then decide the exact information required to answer the questions. The **research design** specifies which research questions must be answered, how and when the data will be gathered, and how the data will be analyzed. Typically, the project budget is finalized after the research design has been approved.

Sometimes research questions can be answered by gathering more secondary data; otherwise, primary data may be needed. **Primary data**, or information collected for the first time, is used for solving the particular problem under investigation. The main advantage of primary data is that they will answer a specific research question that secondary data cannot answer. For example, suppose Pillsbury has two new recipes for refrigerated dough for sugar cookies. Which one will consumers like better? Secondary data will not help answer this question. Instead, targeted consumers must try each recipe and evaluate the taste, texture, and appearance of each cookie. Moreover, primary data are current and researchers know the source. Sometimes researchers gather the data themselves rather than assign projects to outside companies. Researchers also specify the methodology of the research. Secrecy can be maintained because the information is proprietary. In contrast, much secondary data is available to all interested parties for relatively small fees or free.

Gathering primary data is expensive; costs can range from a few thousand dollars for a limited survey to several million for a nationwide study. For instance, a nationwide, 15-minute telephone interview with 1,000 adult males can cost $50,000 for everything, including a data analysis and report. Because primary data gathering is so expensive, firms may cut back on the number of in-person interviews to save money. Larger companies that conduct many research projects use another cost-saving technique. They piggyback studies, or gather data on two different projects using one questionnaire. The drawback is that answering questions about, say, dog food and gourmet coffee may be confusing to respondents. Piggybacking also requires a longer interview (sometimes a half hour or longer), which tires respondents. The quality of the answers typically declines, with people

research design
Specifies which research questions must be answered, how and when the data will be gathered, and how the data will be analyzed.

primary data
Information collected for the first time. Is used for solving the particular problem under investigation.

giving curt replies and thinking, "When will this end!" A lengthy interview also makes people less likely to participate in other research surveys.

Nevertheless, the disadvantages of primary data gathering are usually offset by the advantages. It is often the only way of solving a research problem. And with a variety of techniques available for research—including surveys, observations, and experiments—primary research can address almost any marketing question.

Survey Research

The most popular technique for gathering primary data is **survey research**, in which a researcher interacts with people to obtain facts, opinions, and attitudes. Exhibit 8.2 summarizes the characteristics of traditional forms of survey research.

In-Home Personal Interviews   Although in-home personal interviews often provide high-quality information, they tend to be very expensive because of the interviewers' travel time and mileage costs. Therefore, they are rapidly disappearing from the marketing researcher's survey toolbox.

Mall Intercept Interviews   The **mall intercept interview** is conducted in the common area of a shopping mall or in a market research office within the mall. It is the economy version of the door-to-door interview with personal contact between interviewer and respondent, minus the interviewer's travel time and mileage costs. To conduct this type of interview, the research firm rents office space in the mall or pays a significant daily fee. One drawback is that it is hard to get a representative sample of the population.

However, an interviewer can also probe when necessary—a technique used to clarify a person's response. For example, an interviewer might ask, "What did you like best about the salad dressing you just tried?" The respondent might reply, "Taste." This answer doesn't provide a lot of information, so the interviewer could probe by saying, "Can you tell me a little bit more about taste?" The respondent then elaborates: "Yes, it's not too sweet, it has the right amount of pepper, and I love that hint of garlic."

survey research
The most popular technique for gathering primary data, in which a researcher interacts with people to obtain facts, opinions, and attitudes.

mall intercept interview
A survey research method that involves interviewing people in the common areas of shopping malls.

EXHIBIT 8.2

Characteristics of Traditional Forms of Survey Research

Characteristic	In-Home Personal Interviews	Mall Intercept Interviews	Central-Location Telephone Interviews	Self-Administered and One-Time Mail Surveys	Mail Panel Surveys	Executive Interviews	Focus Groups
Cost	High	Moderate	Moderate	Low	Moderate	High	Low
Time span	Moderate	Moderate	Fast	Slow	Relatively slow	Moderate	Fast
Use of interviewer probes	Yes	Yes	Yes	No	Yes	Yes	Yes
Ability to show concepts to respondent	Yes (also taste tests)	Yes (also taste tests)	No	Yes	Yes	Yes	Yes
Management control over interviewer	Low	Moderate	High	n/a	n/a	Moderate	High
General data quality	High	Moderate	High to moderate	Moderate to low	Moderate	High	Moderate
Ability to collect large amounts of data	High	Moderate	Moderate to low	Low to moderate	Moderate	Moderate	Moderate
Ability to handle complex questionnaires	High	Moderate	High if computer-aided	Low	Low	High	N/A

Mall intercept interviews must be brief. Only the shortest ones are conducted while respondents are standing. Usually, researchers invite respondents to their office for interviews, which are still generally less than 15 minutes long. The researchers often show respondents concepts for new products or a test commercial or have them taste a new food product. The overall quality of mall intercept interviews is about the same as telephone interviews.

Marketing researchers are applying computer technology in mall interviewing. The first technique is **computer-assisted personal interviewing**. The researcher conducts in-person interviews, reads questions to the respondent off a computer screen, and directly keys the respondent's answers into the computer. A second approach is **computer-assisted self-interviewing**. A mall interviewer intercepts and directs willing respondents to nearby computers. Each respondent reads questions off a computer screen and directly keys his or her answers into a computer. The third use of technology is fully automated self-interviewing. Respondents are guided by interviewers or independently approach a centrally located computer station or kiosk, read questions off a screen, and directly key their answers into the station's computer.

Telephone Interviews Compared to the personal interview, the telephone interview costs less, but cost is rapidly increasing due to respondent refusals to participate. Most telephone interviewing is conducted from a specially designed phone room called a **central-location telephone (CLT) facility**. A phone room has many phone lines, individual interviewing stations, sometimes monitoring equipment, and headsets. The research firm typically will interview people nationwide from a single location. The federal "Do Not Call" law does not apply to survey research.

Many CLT facilities offer computer-assisted interviewing. The interviewer reads the questions from a computer screen and enters the respondent's data directly into the computer. The researcher can stop the survey at any point and immediately print out the survey results. Thus, a researcher can get a sense of the project as it unfolds and fine-tune the research design as necessary. An online interviewing system can also save time and money because data entry occurs as the response is recorded rather than as a separate process after the interview. Hallmark Cards found that an interviewer administered a printed questionnaire for its Shoebox Greeting cards in 28 minutes. The same questionnaire administered with computer assistance took only 18 minutes.

Mail Surveys Mail surveys have several benefits: relatively low cost, elimination of interviewers and field supervisors, centralized control, and actual or promised anonymity for respondents (which may draw more candid responses). Some researchers feel that mail questionnaires give the respondent a chance to reply more thoughtfully and to check records, talk to family members, and so forth. A disadvantage is that mail questionnaires usually produce low response rates.

Low response rates pose a problem because certain elements of the population tend to respond more than others. The resulting sample may therefore not represent the surveyed population. For example, the sample may have too many retired people and too few working people. In this instance, answers to a question about attitudes toward Social Security might indicate a much more favorable overall view of the system than is actually the case. Another serious problem

Canadian Astronaut Chris Hadfield tests some rehydrated chocolate cake with journalists as NASA Food Scientist Vickie Kloeris, back, waits for a reaction in the Space Food Systems Laboratory at Johnson Space Center. Taste test results are a type of primary data.

computer-assisted personal interviewing
An interviewing method in which the interviewer reads the questions from a computer screen and enters the respondent's data directly into the computer.

computer-assisted self-interviewing
An interviewing method in which a mall interviewer intercepts and directs willing respondents to nearby computers where the respondent reads questions off a computer screen and directly keys his or her answers into a computer.

central-location telephone (CLT) facility
A specially designed phone room used to conduct telephone interviewing.

COURTESY OF OMAHA STEAKS

Omaha Steaks Senior Vice President Todd Simon smiles amid a sea of more than 10,000 mail response cards from the company's Dad's Choice survey. Omaha steaks came in as the Father's Day favorite.

with mail surveys is that no one probes respondents to clarify or elaborate on their answers.

Mail panels like those operated by Market Facts, National Family Opinion Research, and NPD Research offer an alternative to the one-shot mail survey. A mail panel consists of a sample of households recruited to participate by mail for a given period. Panel members often receive gifts in return for their participation. Essentially, the panel is a sample used several times. In contrast to one-time mail surveys, the response rates from mail panels are high. Rates of 70 percent (of those who agree to participate) are not uncommon.

Executive Interviews Marketing researchers use **executive interviews** to conduct the industrial equivalent of door-to-door interviewing. This type of survey involves interviewing businesspeople, at their offices, concerning industrial products or services. For example, if Dell wanted information regarding user preferences for different features that might be offered in a new line of computer printers, it would need to interview prospective user-purchasers of the printers. It is appropriate to locate and interview these people at their offices.

This type of interviewing is very expensive. First, individuals involved in the purchase decision for the product in question must be identified and located. Sometimes lists can be obtained from various sources, but more frequently screening must be conducted over the telephone. A particular company is likely to have individuals of the type being sought, but locating those people within a large organization can be expensive and time-consuming. Once a qualified person is located, the next step is to get that person to agree to be interviewed and to set a time for the interview. This is not as hard as it might seem because most professionals seem to enjoy talking about topics related to their work.

Finally, an interviewer must go to the particular place at the appointed time. Long waits are frequently encountered; cancellations are not uncommon. This type of survey requires the very best interviewers because they are frequently interviewing on topics that they know very little about. Executive interviewing has essentially the same advantages and disadvantages as in-home interviewing.

Focus Groups A **focus group** is a type of personal interviewing. Often recruited by random telephone screening, seven to ten people with certain desired characteristics form a focus group. These qualified consumers are usually offered an incentive (typically $30 to $50) to participate in a group discussion. The meeting place (sometimes resembling a living room, sometimes featuring a conference table) has audiotaping and perhaps videotaping equipment. It also likely has a viewing room with a one-way mirror so that clients (manufacturers or retailers) may watch the session. During the session, a moderator, hired by the research company, leads the group discussion.

Focus groups are much more than question-and-answer interviews. Market researchers draw a distinction between "group dynamics" and "group interviewing." The interaction provided in **group dynamics** is essential to the success of focus-group research; this interaction is the reason for conducting group rather than individual research. One of the essential postulates of group-session usage is

executive interviews
A type of survey that involves interviewing businesspeople at their offices concerning industrial products or services.

focus group
Seven to ten people who participate in a group discussion led by a moderator.

group dynamics
Group interaction essential to the success of focus-group research.

the idea that a response from one person may become a stimulus for another, thereby generating an interplay of responses that may yield more information than if the same number of people had contributed independently.

Focus groups are occasionally used to brainstorm new product ideas or to screen concepts for new products. Ford Motor Company, for example, asked consumers to drive several automobile prototypes. These "test drivers" were then brought together in focus groups. During the discussions, consumers complained that they were scuffing their shoes because the rear seats lacked foot room. In response, Ford sloped the floor underneath the front seats, widened the space between the seat adjustment tracks, and made the tracks in the Taurus and Sable models out of smooth plastic instead of metal.

A new system by Focus Vision Network allows client companies and advertising agencies to view live focus groups in Chicago, Dallas, Boston, and 15 other major cities. For example, the private satellite network lets a General Motors researcher observing a San Diego focus group control two cameras in the viewing room. The researcher can get a full-group view or a close-up, zoom, or pan the participants. The researcher can also communicate directly with the moderator using an ear receiver. Ogilvy & Mather (a large New York advertising agency whose clients include StarKist Sea Foods, Seagram's, MasterCard, and Burger King) has installed the system.

Increasingly, focus groups are being conducted online. Cyber focus groups are examined in detail later in the chapter.

Questionnaire Design

All forms of survey research require a questionnaire. Questionnaires ensure that all respondents will be asked the same series of questions. Questionnaires include three basic types of questions: open-ended, closed-ended, and scaled-response (see Exhibit 8.3). An **open-ended question** encourages an answer phrased in the respondent's own words. Researchers get a rich array of information based on the respondent's frame of reference. In contrast, a **closed-ended question** asks the respondent to make a selection from a limited list of responses. Traditionally, marketing researchers separate the two-choice question (called *dichotomous*) from the many-item type (often called *multiple choice*). A **scaled-response question** is a closed-ended question designed to measure the intensity of a respondent's answer.

Closed-ended and scaled-response questions are easier to tabulate than open-ended questions because response choices are fixed. On the other hand, unless the researcher designs the closed-ended question very carefully, an important choice may be omitted.

For example, suppose a food study asked this question: "Besides meat, which of the following items do you normally add to a taco that you prepare at home?"

Avocado	1	Olives (black/green)	6
Cheese (Monterey Jack/cheddar)	2	Onions (red/white)	7
Guacamole	3	Peppers (red/green)	8
Lettuce	4	Pimento	9
Mexican hot sauce	5	Sour cream	0

The list seems complete, doesn't it? However, consider the following responses: "I usually add a green, avocado-tasting hot sauce"; "I cut up a mixture of lettuce and spinach"; "I'm a vegetarian; I don't use meat at all. My taco is filled only with guacamole." How would you code these replies? As you can see, the question needs an "other" category.

A good question must also be clear and concise, and ambiguous language must be avoided. Take, for example, the question "Do you live within ten minutes of here?" The answer depends on the mode of transportation (maybe the person walks), driving speed, perceived time, and other factors. Instead, respondents

open-ended question
An interview question that encourages an answer phrased in the respondent's own words.

closed-ended question
An interview question that asks the respondent to make a selection from a limited list of responses.

scaled-response question
A closed-ended question designed to measure the intensity of a respondent's answer.

EXHIBIT 8.3

Types of Questions Found on Questionnaires for National Market Research

Open-Ended Questions	Closed-Ended Questions Dichotomous	Scaled-Response Question

Open-Ended Questions

1. What advantages, if any, do you think ordering from a mail-order catalog offers compared to shopping at a local retail outlet?
   (*Probe:* What else?)

2. Why do you have one or more of your rugs or carpets professionally cleaned rather than having you or someone else in the household clean them?

3. What is there about the color of the eye shadow that makes you like it the best?

Dichotomous

1. Did you heat the Danish product before serving it?
   Yes 1
   No 2

2. The federal government doesn't care what people like me think.
   Agree 1
   Disagree 2

Multiple choice

1. I'd like you to think back to the last footwear of any kind that you bought. I'll read you a list of descriptions and would like for you to tell me which category they fall into. *(Read list and circle proper category.)*
   Dress and/or formal 1
   Casual 2
   Canvas/trainer/gym shoes 3
   Specialized athletic shoes 4
   Boots 5

2. In the last three months, have you used Noxzema skin cream . . .
   (Circle all that apply.)
   As a facial wash .1
   For moisturizing the skin 2
   For treating blemishes 3
   For cleansing the skin 4
   For treating dry skin 5
   For softening skin 6
   For sunburn 7
   For making the facial skin smooth 8

Scaled-Response Question

Now that you have used the rug cleaner, would you say that you . . . *(Circle one.)*
Would definitely buy it 1
Would probably buy it 2
Might or might not buy it 3
Probably would not buy it 4
Definitely would not buy it 5

should see a map with certain areas highlighted and be asked whether they live in one of those areas.

Clarity also implies using reasonable terminology. A questionnaire is not a vocabulary test. Jargon should be avoided, and language should be geared to the target audience. A question such as "What is the level of efficacy of your preponderant dishwasher powder?" would probably be greeted by a lot of blank stares. It would be much simpler to say "Are you (1) very satisfied, (2) somewhat satisfied, or (3) not satisfied with your current brand of dishwasher powder?"

Stating the survey's purpose at the beginning of the interview also improves clarity. The respondents should understand the study's intentions and the interviewer's expectations. Sometimes, of course, to get an unbiased response, the interviewer must disguise the true purpose of the study. If an interviewer says, "We're conducting an image study for American National Bank" and then proceeds to ask a series of questions about the bank, chances are the responses will be biased. Many times respondents will try to provide answers that they believe are "correct" or that the interviewer wants to hear.

Finally, to ensure clarity, the interviewer should avoid asking two questions in one; for example, "How did you like the taste and texture of the Pepperidge Farm coffee cake?" This should be divided into two questions, one concerning taste and the other texture.

A question should also be unbiased. A question such as "Have you purchased any quality Black & Decker tools in the past six months?" biases respondents to think of the topic in a certain way (in this case, to link quality and Black & Decker tools). Questions can also be leading: "Weren't you pleased with the good service you received last night at the Holiday Inn?" (The respondent is all but instructed to say yes.) These examples are quite obvious; unfortunately, bias is usually more subtle. Even an interviewer's clothing or gestures can create bias.

Observation Research

In contrast to survey research, **observation research** depends on watching what people do. Specifically, it can be defined as the systematic process of recording the behavioral patterns of people, objects, and occurrences without questioning or with them. A market researcher using the observation technique witnesses and records information as events occur or compiles evidence from records of past events. Carried a step further, observation may involve watching people or phenomena and may be conducted by human observers or machines. Examples of these various observational situations are shown in Exhibit 8.4.

Two common forms of people-watching-people research are mystery shoppers and one-way mirror observations. **Mystery shoppers** are researchers posing as customers who gather observational data about a store (i.e., are the shelves neatly stocked?) and collect data about customer/employee interactions. In the latter case, of course, there is communication between the mystery shopper and the employee. The mystery shopper may ask, "How much is this item?" "Do you have this in blue?" or "Can you deliver this by Friday?" The interaction is not an interview, and communication occurs only so that the mystery shopper can observe the actions and comments of the employee. Mystery shopping is, therefore, classified as an observational marketing research method even though communication is often involved. Conducted on a continuous basis, mystery shopping can motivate and recognize service performance. Used as a benchmark, mystery shopping can pinpoint strengths and weaknesses for training operations and policy refinements.

At the Fisher-Price Play Laboratory, children are invited to spend 12 sessions playing with toys. Toy designers watch through one-way mirrors to see how children react to Fisher-Price's and other makers' toys. Fisher-Price, for example, had

observation research
A research method that relies on four types of observation: people watching people, people watching an activity, machines watching people, and machines watching an activity.

mystery shoppers
Researchers posing as customers who gather observational data about a store.

Exhibit 8.4

Observational Situations

Situation	Example
People watching people	Observers stationed in supermarkets watch consumers select frozen Mexican dinners; the purpose is to see how much comparison shopping people do at the point of purchase.
People watching phenomena	Observer stationed at an intersection counts traffic moving in various directions.
Machines watching people	Movie or videotape cameras record behavior as in the people-watching-people example above.
Machines watching phenomena	Traffic-counting machines monitor traffic flow.

One interesting observation situation is toy-testing day camp. Pictured here, Fama Ana tries on a pair of "spy glasses" at Durcell Toy Testing Camp. In one week, over a thousand children in 15 U.S. cities test 25 different toys while marketers look on.

difficulty designing a toy lawn mower that children would play with. A designer, observing behind the mirror, noticed the children's fascination with soap bubbles. He then created a lawn mower that spewed soap bubbles. It sold over a million units in the first year.

Experiments

An **experiment** is a method a researcher can use to gather primary data. The researcher alters one or more variables—price, package design, shelf space, advertising theme, advertising expenditures—while observing the effects of those alterations on another variable (usually sales). The best experiments are those in which all factors are held constant except the ones being manipulated. The researcher can then observe that changes in sales, for example, result from changes in the amount of money spent on advertising.

Holding all other factors constant in the external environment is a monumental and costly, if not impossible, task. Such factors as competitors' actions, weather, and economic conditions are beyond the researcher's control. Yet market researchers have ways to account for the ever-changing external environment. Mars, the candy company, was losing sales to other candy companies. Traditional surveys showed that the shrinking candy bar was not perceived as a good value. Mars wondered whether a bigger bar sold at the same price would increase sales enough to offset the higher ingredient costs. The company designed an experiment in which the marketing mix stayed the same in different markets but the size of the candy bar varied. The substantial increase in sales of the bigger bar quickly proved that the additional costs would be more than covered by the additional revenue. Mars increased the bar size—and its market share and profits.

SPECIFYING THE SAMPLING PROCEDURES

Once the researchers decide how they will collect primary data, their next step is to select the sampling procedures they will use. A firm can seldom take a census of all possible users of a new product, nor can they all be interviewed. Therefore, a firm must select a sample of the group to be interviewed. A **sample** is a subset from a larger population.

Several questions must be answered before a sampling plan is chosen. First, the population, or **universe,** of interest must be defined. This is the group from which the sample will be drawn. It should include all the people whose opinions, behavior, preferences, attitudes, and so on are of interest to the marketer. For example, in a study whose purpose is to determine the market for a new canned dog food, the universe might be defined to include all current buyers of canned dog food.

After the universe has been defined, the next question is whether the sample must be representative of the population. If the answer is yes, a probability sample is needed. Otherwise, a nonprobability sample might be considered.

Probability Samples

A **probability sample** is a sample in which every element in the population has a known statistical likelihood of being selected. Its most desirable feature is that scientific rules can be used to ensure that the sample represents the population.

experiment
A method a researcher uses to gather primary data.

sample
A subset from a larger population.

universe
The population from which a sample will be drawn.

probability sample
A sample in which every element in the population has a known statistical likelihood of being selected.

One type of probability sample is a **random sample**—a sample arranged in such a way that every element of the population has an equal chance of being selected as part of the sample. For example, suppose a university is interested in getting a cross section of student opinions on a proposed sports complex to be built using student activity fees. If the university can acquire an up-to-date list of all the enrolled students, it can draw a random sample by using random numbers from a table (found in most statistics books) to select students from the list. Common forms of probability and nonprobability samples are shown in Exhibit 8.5.

Nonprobability Samples

Any sample in which little or no attempt is made to get a representative cross section of the population can be considered a **nonprobability sample**. Therefore the probability of selection of each sampling unit is not known. A common form of a nonprobability sample is the **convenience sample**, which uses respondents who are convenient or readily accessible to the researcher—for instance, employees, friends, or relatives.

Nonprobability samples are acceptable as long as the researcher understands their nonrepresentative nature. Because of their lower cost, nonprobability samples are the basis of much marketing research.

Types of Errors

Whenever a sample is used in marketing research, two major types of error may occur: measurement error and sampling error. **Measurement error** occurs when there is a difference between the information desired by the researcher and the information provided by the measurement process. For example, people may tell an interviewer that they purchase Coors beer when they do not. Measurement error generally tends to be larger than sampling error.

random sample
A sample arranged in such a way that every element of the population has an equal chance of being selected as part of the sample.

nonprobability sample
Any sample in which little or no attempt is made to get a representative cross section of the population.

convenience sample
A form of nonprobability sample using respondents who are convenient or readily accessible to the researcher—for example, employees, friends, or relatives.

measurement error
An error that occurs when there is a difference between the information desired by the researcher and the information provided by the measurement process.

EXHIBIT 8.5

Types of Samples

	Probability Samples
Simple Random Sample	Every member of the population has a known and equal chance of selection.
Stratified Sample	The population is divided into mutually exclusive groups (such as gender or age); then random samples are drawn from each group.
Cluster Sample	The population is divided into mutually exclusive groups (such as geographic areas); then a random sample of clusters is selected. The researcher then collects data from all the elements in the selected clusters or from a probability sample of elements within each selected cluster.
Systematic Sample	A list of the population is obtained—i.e., all persons with a checking account at XYZ Bank—and a *skip interval* is obtained by dividing the sample size by the population size. If the sample size is 100 and the bank has 1,000 customers, then the skip interval is 10. The beginning number is randomly chosen within the skip interval. If the beginning number is 8, then the skip pattern would be 8, 18, 28, ...
	Nonprobability Samples
Convenience Sample	The researcher selects the easiest population members from which to obtain information.
Judgment Sample	The researcher's selection criteria are based on personal judgment that the elements (persons) chosen will likely give accurate information.
Quota Sample	The researcher finds a prescribed number of people in several categories—i.e., owners of large dogs versus owners of small dogs. Respondents are not selected on probability sampling criteria.
Snowball Sample	Additional respondents are selected on the basis of referrals from the initial respondents. This method is used when a desired type of respondent is hard to find—i.e., persons who have taken round-the-world cruises in the last three years. This technique employs the old adage "Birds of a feather flock together."

Sampling error occurs when a sample somehow does not represent the target population. Sampling error can be one of several types. Nonresponse error occurs when the sample actually interviewed differs from the sample drawn. This error happens because the original people selected to be interviewed either refused to cooperate or were inaccessible. For example, people who feel embarrassed about their drinking habits may refuse to talk about them.

Frame error, another type of sampling error, arises if the sample drawn from a population differs from the target population. For instance, suppose a telephone survey is conducted to find out Chicago beer drinkers' attitudes toward Coors. If a Chicago telephone directory is used as the *frame* (the device or list from which the respondents are selected), the survey will contain a frame error. Not all Chicago beer drinkers have a phone, and many phone numbers are unlisted. An ideal sample (for example, a sample with no frame error) matches all important characteristics of the target population to be surveyed. Could you find a perfect frame for Chicago beer drinkers?

Random error occurs when the selected sample is an imperfect representation of the overall population. Random error represents how accurately the chosen sample's true average (mean) value reflects the population's true average (mean) value. For example, we might take a random sample of beer drinkers in Chicago and find that 16 percent regularly drink Coors beer. The next day we might repeat the same sampling procedure and discover that 14 percent regularly drink Coors beer. The difference is due to random error.

Error is common to all surveys, yet it is often not reported or is underreported. Typically, the only error mentioned in a written report is sampling error. When errors are ignored, misleading results can result in poor information and, perhaps, bad decisions. The "Ethics in Marketing" box on the next page examines some potential problems with errors in survey research.

COLLECTING THE DATA

Marketing research field service firms collect most primary data. A **field service firm** specializes in interviewing respondents on a subcontracted basis. Many have offices throughout the country. A typical marketing research study involves data collection in several cities, requiring the marketer to work with a comparable number of field service firms. To ensure uniformity among all subcontractors, detailed field instructions should be developed for every job. Nothing should be open to chance; no interpretations of procedures should be left to subcontractors.

Besides conducting interviews, field service firms provide focus-group facilities, mall intercept locations, test product storage, and kitchen facilities to prepare test food products. They also conduct retail audits (counting the amount of a product sold off retail shelves).

ANALYZING THE DATA

After collecting the data, the marketing researcher proceeds to the next step in the research process: data analysis. The purpose of this analysis is to interpret and draw conclusions from the mass of collected data. The marketing researcher tries to organize and analyze those data by using one or more techniques common to marketing research: one-way frequency counts, cross-tabulations, and more sophisticated statistical analysis. Of these three techniques, one-way frequency counts are the simplest. One-way frequency tables record the responses to a question. For example, the answers to the question "What brand of microwave popcorn do you buy most often?" would provide a one-way frequency distribution. One-way

sampling error
An error that occurs when a sample somehow does not represent the target population.

frame error
An error that occurs when a sample drawn from a population differs from the target population.

random error
An error that occurs when the selected sample is an imperfect representation of the overall population.

field service firm
A firm that specializes in interviewing respondents on a subcontracted basis.

Ethics in Marketing Ethics in Marketing Ethics in Marketing
Ethics in Marketing Ethics in Marketing Ethics in Marketing Ethics in Marketing Ethics in Marke
Ethics in Marketing Ethics in Marketing Ethics in Marketing **ETHICS IN MARKETING** Ethics in Marketing Ethics in Marke
Ethics in Marketing Ethics in Marketing Ethics in Marketing Marketing Ethics in Marketing Ethics in Marke
Ethics in Marketing Ethics in Marketing Ethics in Marketing Ethics in Marketing
Ethics in Marketing

> WHAT'S IN A CAR-QUALITY SCORE?

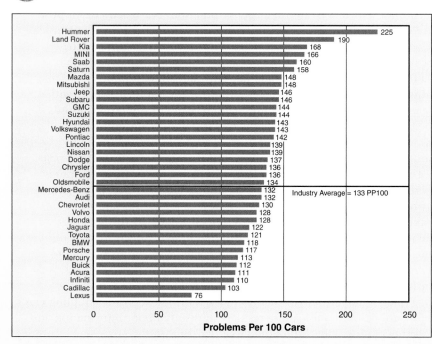

When the J.D. Power & Associates new-car quality study ratings come out, consumers can get ready for a lot of hype and advertising.

What the initial-quality survey does is measure how cars perform in the first 90 days of ownership. The survey is based on 65,000 responses to a questionnaire randomly mailed to nearly 200,000 new-car buyers by J.D. Power, with a payment of $1. The primary audience of the survey is the auto industry itself—not the public. Indeed, the publicly released data from the survey won't tell consumers much about the performance of car models across the board or their long-term reliability.

If the car you've got your heart set on didn't land in the top three in its market segment, you won't get much information from J.D. Powers on how it fared in the survey. The company's Web site doesn't include model scores but carries rankings on a four-point scale, from "among the best" to "the rest."

And even if the model is a top scorer, J.D. Power usually doesn't disclose exactly how well it did or whether the difference between its score and that of the next best fell within the margin of error of the study. General Motors, for example, scored only one point behind Nissan Motor Company in a recent ranking, a gap that was within the margin of error, but J.D. Power still ranked Nissan third and GM fourth, industry officials say.

J.D. Power sells all of the data in a 2,000-page report to the automakers, which also pay J.D. Power handsomely to use its ratings in their ads. J.D. Power spokesman John Tews says the company doesn't release exact results of its surveys because

"we're not going to air [the automakers'] dirty laundry." Instead, J.D. Power offers consumers the general ranking system on its Web site to "put it all together and give them a 30,000-foot picture." Although J.D. Power requires that automakers sign agreements not to make the data public when they buy the results, some usually leaks out.

But even if consumers can figure out how a car did in the study, there's still the question of just what the initial-quality results tell about how the car will hold up over the long haul, which in many cases is of more concern to consumers. "We think our customers weigh us much more on the dependability and durability of our vehicles long term," says Emil Hassan, senior vice president of North American manufacturing, purchasing, quality, and logistics for Nissan's North American arm.

Although J.D. Power highlights the defects, the fact is that most cars don't have significant problems in the first 90 days of ownership. About half of the people who fill out the firm's questionnaires check none of the 135 boxes for possible problems. The rest identify only a few. And the top complaints aren't catastrophic failures: wind noise, loud brakes, and excessive fuel consumption (primarily an issue on fuel-thirsty SUVs and pickups).

In fact, some in the industry argue that the survey is too subjective. "If you are driving with a headache, any little problem will put you in a real grumpy mood," says Koko Hirashima, Honda's manufacturing chief in North America. "When you're having fun driving with your girlfriend next to you, you won't notice a thing even if a wheel cap falls off or the car rattles and squeaks. That's the kind of difference in perceptions that causes a big gap in scores." J.D. Powers says its sample size, usually 250 responses per model or more, ensures the data are objective.

After a few years, the biggest problems tend to be much more serious, according to industry officials. Things like dead batteries, worn-out starters and alternators, and malfunctioning brakes are the main issues after a few years on the road. Those problems rarely turn up in the first few months.[8]

What types of error might be found in the initial-quality survey? Is the initial-quality survey beneficial to consumers or simply a source of advertising hype? Is it unethical for J.D. Power and Associates to charge the survey winners for the right to advertise its ratings? Why? Is it unethical not to make the total survey findings available to consumers?

3 **Describe the steps involved in conducting a marketing research project**

1 Identify problem
- Management decision → Action
- Marketing research (research secondary data) → Information

2 Plan research design

3 Select sampling procedures
- Probability (measure sampling error)
- Non-probability

4 Collect data
- Primary data → • survey • observation • experiment
- Secondary data → • traditional • Internet

5 Analyze data
- Frequency counts Cross-tabulation
- Advanced Statistical analysis

6 Prepare and present the report

7 Follow up

cross-tabulation
A method of analyzing data that lets the analyst look at the responses to one question in relation to the responses to one or more other questions.

frequency tables are always done in data analysis, at least as a first step, because they provide the researcher with a general picture of the study's results.

A **cross-tabulation**, or "cross-tab," lets the analyst look at the responses to one question in relation to the responses to one or more other questions. For example, what is the association between gender and the brand of microwave popcorn bought most frequently? Hypothetical answers to this question are shown in Exhibit 8.6. Although the Orville Reddenbacher brand was popular with both males and females, it was more popular with females. Compared with women, men strongly preferred Pop Rite, whereas women were more likely than men to buy Weight Watchers popcorn.

Researchers can use many other more powerful and sophisticated statistical techniques, such as hypothesis testing, measures of association, and regression analysis. A description of these techniques goes beyond the scope of this book but can be found in any good marketing research textbook. The use of sophisticated statistical techniques depends on the researchers' objectives and the nature of the data gathered.

PREPARING AND PRESENTING THE REPORT

After data analysis has been completed, the researcher must prepare the report and communicate the conclusions and recommendations to management. This is a key step in the process. If the marketing researcher wants managers to carry out the recommendations, he or she must convince them that the results are credible and justified by the data collected.

Researchers are usually required to present both written and oral reports on the project. Today, the written report is no more than a copy of the PowerPoint slides used in the oral presentation. Both reports should be tailored to the audience. They should begin with a clear, concise statement of the research objectives, followed by a complete, but brief and simple, explanation of the research design or methodology employed. A summary of major findings should come next. The conclusion of the report should also present recommendations to management.

Most people who enter marketing will become research users rather than research suppliers. Thus, they must know what to notice in a report. As with many other items we purchase, quality is not always readily apparent. Nor does a high price guarantee superior quality. The basis for measuring the quality of a marketing research report is the research proposal. Did the report meet the objectives established in the proposal? Was the methodology outlined in the

EXHIBIT 8.6

Hypothetical Cross-Tabulation between Gender and Brand of Microwave Popcorn Purchased Most Frequently

Brand	Purchase by Gender	
	Male	Female
Orville Reddenbacher	31%	48%
T.V. Time	12	6
Pop Rite	38	4
Act Two	7	23
Weight Watchers	4	18
Other	8	0

proposal followed? Are the conclusions based on logical deductions from the data analysis? Do the recommendations seem prudent, given the conclusions?

FOLLOWING UP

The final step in the marketing research process is to follow up. The researcher should determine why management did or did not carry out the recommendations in the report. Was sufficient decision-making information included? What could have been done to make the report more useful to management? A good rapport between the product manager, or whoever authorized the project, and the market researcher is essential. Often they must work together on many studies throughout the year.

4 THE PROFOUND IMPACT OF THE INTERNET ON MARKETING RESEARCH

Discuss the profound impact of the Internet on marketing research

EXHIBIT 8.7

Internet Users Worldwide (in millions), 2000–2004

	2000	2004
North America	108.1	184.5
Europe	100.9	221.1
Asia-Pacific	123.3	232.1
Latin America	15.8	60.6
Africa	4.1	10.9
TOTAL	352.2	709.2

SOURCE: http://www.eMarketer.com.

 The way survey research is conducted has changed forever because of the Internet. In 2005 online research accounted for about 50 percent of all marketing research revenue.[9]

A 2003 survey of marketing research firms found that 73 percent were currently conducting Internet survey research.[10] One reason for the mushrooming growth of Internet research is that the online population now closely mirrors the general population. For example:

- The gender distribution of online users is identical to that of the general population (as reported by the U.S. Census).
- Marital status along all dimensions is identical to the general population.
- The age distribution of online individuals is also approaching that of the general population.
- The average online household income is rapidly approaching that of the general population.

These fundamental demographic shifts, in combination with higher respondent cooperation and survey completion rates, make it feasible to transfer research applications from traditional methodologies to the online environment—with impressive results.[11]

Moreover, the number of Internet users around the world continues to explode as shown in Exhibit 8.7. As the number of users grows worldwide, the characteristics of a country's population and of Internet users tend to meld.

There are several other reasons for the success of Internet marketing research:

- It allows for better and faster decision making through much more rapid access to business intelligence.
- It improves the ability to respond quickly to customer needs and market shifts.
- It makes follow-up studies and tracking research much easier to conduct and more fruitful.
- It slashes labor- and time-intensive research activities (and associated costs), including mailing, telephone solicitation, data entry, data tabulation, and reporting.

It is not surprising that a recent study of research clients (users) and research suppliers found that 93 percent predicted their organizations would be using online research more extensively in the future.[12] The reason for the phenomenal growth of online research is straightforward: the advantages far outweigh the disadvantages.

ADVANTAGES OF INTERNET SURVEYS

The huge growth in the popularity of Internet surveys is the result of the many advantages offered by the Internet. The specific advantages of Internet surveys are related to many factors:

- *Rapid development, real-time reporting:* Internet surveys can be broadcast to thousands of potential respondents simultaneously. Respondents complete surveys simultaneously; then results are tabulated and posted for corporate clients to view as the returns arrive. The result: survey results can be in a client's hands in significantly less time than would be required for traditional surveys.
- *Dramatically reduced costs:* The Internet can cut costs by 25 to 40 percent and provide results in half the time it takes to do traditional telephone surveys. Data-collection costs account for a large proportion of any traditional market research budget. Telephone surveys are labor-intensive efforts incurring training, telecommunications, and management costs. Electronic methods eliminate these completely. While costs for traditional survey techniques rise proportionally with the number of interviews desired, electronic solicitations can grow in volume with little increase in project costs.
- *Personalized questions and data:* Internet surveys can be highly personalized for greater relevance to each respondent's own situation, thus speeding the response process. Respondents enjoy a personalized survey because they are asked to answer only pertinent questions, can pause and resume the survey as needed, and can see previous responses and correct inconsistencies.
- *Improved respondent participation:* Busy respondents may be growing increasingly intolerant of "snail mail" or telephone-based surveys. Internet surveys take half as much time to complete as phone interviews, can be accomplished at the respondent's convenience (after work hours), and are much more stimulating and engaging. Graphics, interactivity, links to incentive sites and real-time summary reports make the interview enjoyable. The result? Much higher response rates.
- *Contact with the hard-to-reach:* Certain groups—doctors, high-income professionals, top management in Global 2000 firms—are among the most surveyed on the planet and the most difficult to reach. Many of these groups are well represented online. Internet surveys provide convenient anytime/anywhere access that makes it easy for busy professionals to participate.

The Internet is becoming a powerful tool in marketing research as more and more Americans get online. *Inc. Magazine* is one of a growing number of companies turning to the Internet to gather data about customers and their opinions.

Lee Smith, the chief operating officer of Insight Express, conducted a side-by-side comparison of online research and mail surveys. He found that online research delivered data of the same quality as mail surveys in one-eighth the time and at one-eighth the cost.[13] Other research has shown that in most countries

Global Perspectives
Global Perspectives
Global Perspectives Global Perspectives
Global Perspectives Global Perspectives Global Perspectives Global Perspectives Global Perspec
Global Perspectives Global Perspectives Global Perspectives Global Perspectives Global Perspec
Global Perspectives Global Perspectives **GLOBAL PERSPECTIVES** Global Perspectives Global Perspec
Global Perspectives Global Perspectives Global Perspectives Global Perspectives Global Perspectives
Global Perspectives
Global Perspectives Global Perspectives
Global Perspectives

> THE GLOBALIZATION OF BUSINESS HAS PUT NEW DEMANDS ON THE MARKETING RESEARCH INDUSTRY

The globalization of business is redefining what a client wants and expects from market research efforts. Challenges notwithstanding, at a fundamental level, global manufacturers and retailers want:

- to be able to compare results between countries using consistent methods and assumptions;
- to achieve enterprise-wide understanding of geographically dispersed consumers; and
- to develop work processes that enable faster global innovation.

The evolution of the market research industry, as driven by internal and external forces, continues to be played out on an emerging global landscape. Based on today's unique convergence of trends and pressures, it is possible to fast-forward to a market research industry that displays the following characteristics:

- Internet-based market research will be the standard for managing and deploying quantitative multicountry consumer research.

- The analysis of multicountry results will be conducted via Web-based applications rather than desktop PCs.
- Consumer research data will be closely integrated into global enterprise computing systems.
- Large portions of all research will be conducted using Internet panels.

To see the transformation in the architecture made possible by the Internet, consider the comparative case study of a global market research firm conducting a 10-country study requiring 1,000 15-minute quantitative interviews in each country. The online research, with or without a panel, was significantly cheaper and faster.[15]

Panels consist of prerecruited respondents that have given both demographic and psychographic data on the initial survey. Thus, since this information has already been gathered subsequent questionnaires are shorter. Do you think that panels will dominate Internet survey research? Will Internet survey research be effective in all countries? Explain your answers.

Research Design	CATI (computer-assisted telephone interviewing)	Online with Lists	Online with Panel (A group of individuals that have agreed to participate in a series of studies)
Data collection	CATI from 6 call centers in 4 countries	Online self-administered interview	Online/self-administered interview
Sampling method	Random Digit Dialing	Purchased list of names	Panel
Notification method	Telephone	E-mail	E-mail to panel
Incentive	None	Sweepstakes	Points program
Productivity			
Cooperation rate	24%	3%	50%
% of respondents eligible	30%	30%	95%
Required number of respondent contacts	138,889	1,111,111	17,544
Person-hours elapsed including call center and customer service	11,574	60	10
Data-processing hours	170	10	5
Budget*			
Data collection	$173,611	$35,000	$14,947
Data processing	$10,200	$600	$300
Telecom/IT costs	$34,722	$1,500	$600
Prerecruitment/list	$4,166	$33,333	$15,790
Timeline			
• Top-line results to client	8–10 weeks	2–5 days	2–4 days
• Clean data	9–12 weeks	3–7 days	3–5 days
Respondent incentives	Negligible	$15,000	$67,544
Total research cost	$222,699	$85,433	$99,181
Methodology risk			
• Representativeness	Low risk	Medium/high risk	Low risk
• Interviewer bias	Moderate risk	None	None

*Data-collection costs only. Analysis excludes project management and translation costs that are assumed to be roughly equivalent in each example.

where the Internet penetration rate exceeds 20 percent, online surveys tend to yield very similar results to those found in traditional forums such as telephone or paper and pencil survey research.[14]

In the "Global Perspectives" box, Raymond Pettit, president of ERP Associates and Robert Monster, CEO of Global Market Insite, discuss how the Internet is helping to globalize marketing research.

USES OF THE INTERNET BY MARKETING RESEARCHERS

Marketing researchers are using the Internet to administer surveys, conduct focus groups, and perform a variety of other types of marketing research.

Internet Samples

Internet samples may be classified as unrestricted, screened, or recruited. In an **unrestricted Internet sample**, anyone who desires can complete the questionnaire. It is fully self-selecting and probably representative of nothing except Web surfers. The problem is exacerbated if the same Internet user can access the questionnaire repeatedly. For example, *InfoWorld*, a computer user magazine, decided to conduct its Readers Choice survey for the first time on the Internet. The results were so skewed by repeat voting for one product that the entire survey was publicly abandoned and the editor asked for readers' help to avoid the problem again. A simple solution to repeat respondents is to lock respondents out of the site after they have filled out the questionnaire.

Screened Internet samples adjust for the unrepresentativeness of the self-selected respondents by imposing quotas based on some desired sample characteristics. These are often demographic characteristics such as gender, income, and geographic region, or product-related criteria such as past purchase behavior, job responsibilities, or current product use. The applications for screened samples are generally similar to those for unrestricted samples.

Screened sample questionnaires typically use a branching or skip pattern for asking screening questions to determine whether the full questionnaire should be presented to a respondent. Some Web survey systems can make immediate market segment calculations that first assign a respondent to a particular segment based on screening questions and then select the appropriate questionnaire to match the respondent's segment.

Alternatively, some Internet research providers maintain a "panel house" that recruits respondents who fill out a preliminary classification questionnaire. This information is used to classify respondents into demographic segments. Clients specify the desired segments, and the respondents who match the desired demographics are permitted to fill out the questionnaires of all clients who specify that segment.

Recruited Internet samples are used for targeted populations in surveys that require more control over the makeup of the sample. Respondents are recruited by telephone, mail, e-mail, or in person. After qualification, they are sent the questionnaire by e-mail or are directed to a Web site that contains a link to the questionnaire. At Web sites, passwords are normally used to restrict access to the questionnaire to the recruited sample members. Since the makeup of the sample is known, completions can be monitored, and the participation rate can be improved by sending follow-up messages to those who do not complete the questionnaire.

Recruited respondents often agree to participate in a series of interviews over time. Thus, these individuals become members of an Internet panel. Typically, the more surveys in which the respondents take part, the higher the pay or the bigger the prize. As in traditional mail panels, demographics and psychographic data are gathered from all panel members in the initial survey. This results in shorter interviews in subsequent studies because personal data about the respondents have already been gathered. Internet panels are huge. Harris Interactive, a

unrestricted Internet sample
A survey in which anyone with a computer and modem can fill out the questionnaire.

screened Internet sample
An Internet sample with quotas based on desired sample characteristics.

recruited Internet sample
A sample in which respondents are prerecruited and must qualify to participate. They are then e-mailed a questionnaire or directed to a secure Web site.

marketing research firm, has an Internet panel of 6.5 million respondents that cost over $50 million to create.[16]

Renting Internet Panels   Very few marketing research companies build their own Internet panels because of the huge expense involved. Instead, they rent a sample from an established panel provider. The largest and oldest sample provider in the nation is Survey Sampling, Inc. Today, it offers a huge Internet panel to the marketing research industry called Survey Spot. As with its other (non-Internet) panels, Survey Sampling offers subsets of its main panel, which is balanced demographically. In other words, its panel looks exactly like the U.S. population in terms of demographics, based on the 2000 U.S. Census.

Online Focus Groups

The newest development in qualitative research is the online or cyber focus group. A number of organizations are currently offering this new means of conducting focus groups. The process is fairly simple.

- The research firm builds a database of respondents via a screening questionnaire on its Web site.
- When a client comes to a firm with a need for a particular focus group, the firm goes to its database and identifies individuals who appear to qualify. It sends an e-mail message to these individuals, asking them to log on to a particular site at a particular time scheduled for the group. The firm pays them an incentive for their participation.
- The firm develops a discussion guide similar to the one used for a conventional focus group.
- A moderator runs the group by typing in questions online for all to see. The group operates in an environment similar to that of a chat room so that all participants see all questions and all responses.
- The firm captures the complete text of the focus group and makes it available for review after the group has finished.

The Moderator's Role   The basic way the moderator communicates with respondents in an online focus group is "freestyle" or "on the fly." That is, the moderator types in all questions, instructions, and probes into the text-entry area of the chat room in real-time (live, on-the-spot). In a variation on this method, the moderator copies and pastes questions from an electronic version of the guide into the text-entry area. Here, the moderator will toggle back and forth between the document and the chat room. An advantage of the freestyle method is that it forces the moderator to adapt to the group rather than use a series of canned questions. A disadvantage is that typing everything freestyle (or even copying and pasting from a separate document) takes time.

One way respondents can see stimuli (e.g., a concept statement, a mockup of a print ad, or a short product demonstration on video) is for the moderator to give the respondents a URL. Respondents then copy the URL from the chat stream, open another browser window, paste in the URL, and view it. An advantage of this approach is its simplicity. However, there are several disadvantages. First, if the respondents do not copy the URL correctly, they will not see it. Another disadvantage is that once respondents open another browser, they have "left the room" and the moderator has lost their attention; researchers must hope that respondents will return within the specified amount of time.

More advanced virtual focus group software reserves a frame (section) of the screen for stimuli to be shown. Here, the moderator has control over what is shown in the stimulus area. The advantage of this approach is that the respondent does not have to do any work to see the stimuli.

One of the biggest challenges an online moderator faces is maintaining control of the discussion—keeping it focused on the topic. Sometimes even the most skilled online moderator encounters a respondent exhibiting counterproductive behavior (e.g., refusing to stay on topic, constantly joking, using offensive language). Since most virtual facilities offer instant messaging capabilities between the moderator and individual respondents, the moderator can try to work with the respondent, asking him or her to curb the disruptive behavior. Usually, this will work. In rare instances, however, the only alternative is to remove the problem respondent from the room to salvage the group.

Hershey
Go to Hershey's Web site and read its Idea Submission Policy under Consumer Info. Do you think the policy is a good idea? Why or why not?
http://www.hersheys.com

Online

Types of Online Focus Groups   Decision Analysts, one of America's most progressive firms in applying Internet technology to marketing research, offers two types of online focus groups:

1. *Real-time online focus groups:* These are live, interactive sessions with four to six participants and a moderator in a chat room format. The typical session does not last longer than 45 to 50 minutes. The technique is best for simple, straightforward issues that can be covered in limited time. The results tend to be superficial compared to in-person focus groups—but this is acceptable for certain types of projects. Typically, three to four groups are recommended as a minimum. Clients can view the chat room as the session unfolds and communicate with the moderator.
2. *Time-extended online focus groups:* These sessions follow a message board format and usually last five to ten days. The 15 to 20 participants must comment at least two or three times per day and spend 15 minutes a day logged in to the discussion. The moderator reviews respondents' comments several times per day (and night) and probes or redirects the discussion as needed. This technique provides three to four times as much content as the average in-person focus group. Time-extended online focus groups give participants time to reflect, talk to others, visit a store, or check the pantry. This extra time translates into richer content and deeper insights. Clients can view the online content as it is posted and may communicate with the moderator at any time.[17]

Advantages of Online Focus Groups   Many advantages are claimed for cyber groups. Cyber Dialogue, a marketing research company specializing in cyber groups, lists the following benefits of on-line focus groups on its Web site:

- *Speed:* Typically, focus groups can be recruited and conducted, with delivery of results, within five days of client approval.
- *Cost-effectiveness:* Off-line focus groups incur costs for facility rental, airfare, hotel, and food. None of these costs is incurred with online focus groups.
- *Broad geographic scope:* In a given focus group, you can speak to people in Boise, Idaho, and Miami, Florida, at the same time.
- *Accessibility:* Online focus groups give you access to individuals who otherwise might be difficult to recruit (e.g., business travelers, doctors, mothers with infants).
- *Honesty:* From behind their screen names, respondents are anonymous to other respondents and tend to talk more freely about issues that might create inhibitions in a face-to-face group.

Cyber Dialogue charges $3,000 for its focus groups. This compares very favorably to a cost in the range of $7,000 without travel costs for conventional focus groups.

Online Focus Groups versus Traditional Focus Groups   To determine whether online and traditional focus groups product different results, academic researchers

conducted nine focus groups using three different modalities (in-person focus groups, online focus groups, and telephone focus groups) and compared the results. Three main research findings stood out and dispelled certain misconceptions regarding online groups. First, although the researchers observed differences across modalities in the speech segments in which participants interacted with each other, these differences were not statistically significant. Second, the proportion of strong (positive or negative) words was significantly higher for the online groups. Finally, there were no significant differences in responses to the specific sensitive questions—for example, on personal hygiene—presented to these groups. The interaction that occurred depended more on the people involved in the discussion than on the type of focus group. The online dynamics differed, but that was because group members were less influenced by others' opinions and had a more equal opportunity to respond rather than having to wait their turn to speak.[18]

Other Uses of the Internet by Marketing Researchers

The Internet revolution in marketing research has had an impact on more than just the way surveys and focus groups are conducted. The management of the research process and the dissemination of information have also been greatly enhanced by the Internet. Several key areas have been affected by the Internet:

- *The distribution of requests for proposals (RFPs) and proposals:* Companies can now quickly and efficiently send RFPs to a select e-mail list of research suppliers. In turn, research suppliers can develop proposals and e-mail them back to clients. A process that used to take days using snail mail now occurs in a matter of hours.
- *Collaboration between the client and the research supplier in the management of a research project:* Now a researcher and client may both be looking at a proposal, RFP, report, or some type of statistical analysis at the same time on their respective computer screens while discussing it over the telephone. This is very powerful and efficient. Changes in the sample size, quotas, and other aspects of the research plan can be discussed and made immediately.
- *Data management and online analysis:* Clients can access their survey via the research supplier's secure Web site and monitor the data gathering in real time. The client can use sophisticated tools to actually do data analysis as the survey develops. This real-time analysis may result in changes in the questionnaire, sample size, or the types of respondents being interviewed. The research supplier and the client become partners in "just-in-time" marketing research.
- *Publication and distribution of reports:* Reports can be published to the Web directly from programs such as PowerPoint and all the latest versions of leading word-processing, spreadsheet, and presentation software packages. This means that results are available to appropriate managers worldwide on an almost instantaneous basis. Reports can be searched for the content of interest using the same Web browser used to view the report.
- *Viewing of oral presentations of marketing research surveys by widely scattered audiences:* By placing oral presentations on password-protected Web sites, managers throughout the world can see and hear the actual client presentation. This saves time and money by avoiding the need for the managers to travel to a central meeting site.[19]

REVIEW LEARNING OBJECTIVE 4

4 | **Discuss the profound impact of the Internet on marketing research**

By driving down time and cost of collecting data, Internet has increased in popularity, become easier to use and therefore is used in a growing number of research applications.

5 SCANNER-BASED RESEARCH

Scanner-based research is a system for gathering information from a single group of respondents by continuously monitoring the advertising, promotion, and pricing they are exposed to and the things they buy. The variables measured are advertising campaigns, coupons, displays, and product prices. The result is a huge database of marketing efforts and consumer behavior. Scanner-based research is bringing ever closer the Holy Grail of marketing research: an accurate, objective picture of the direct causal relationship between different kinds of marketing efforts and actual sales.

The two major scanner-based suppliers are Information Resources. Inc. (IRI) and the A. C. Nielsen Company. Each has about half the market. However, IRI is the founder of scanner-based research.

IRI's first product is called **BehaviorScan**. A household panel (a group of 3,000 long-term participants in the research project) has been recruited and maintained in each BehaviorScan town. Panel members shop with an ID card, which is presented at the checkout in scanner-equipped grocery stores and drugstores, allowing IRI to track electronically each household's purchases, item by item, over time. It uses microcomputers to measure TV viewing in each panel household and can send special commercials to panel member television sets. With such a measure of household purchasing, it is possible to manipulate marketing variables, such as TV advertising or consumer promotions, or to introduce a new product and analyze real changes in consumer buying behavior.

IRI's most successful product is **InfoScan**—a scanner-based sales-tracking service for the consumer packaged-goods industry. Retail sales, detailed consumer purchasing information (including measurement of store loyalty and total grocery basket expenditures), and promotional activity by manufacturers and retailers are monitored and evaluated for all bar-coded products. Data are collected weekly from more than 31,000 supermarkets, drugstores, and mass merchandisers.

IRI's BehaviorScan product allows IRI to track individual household purchases over time. Participants in the household panel present an ID card at the checkout of a scanner-equipped grocery store.

© PHOTODISC/GETTY IMAGES

REVIEW LEARNING OBJECTIVE 5

5 Discuss the growing importance of scanner-based research

BehaviorScan

Panel-information from specific groups of people, enables researchers to manipulate variables and see real results

InfoScan

Aggregate consumer information on all bar-coded products

WHEN SHOULD MARKETING RESEARCH BE CONDUCTED?

scanner-based research
A system for gathering information from a single group of respondents by continuously monitoring the advertising, promotion, and pricing they are exposed to and the things they buy.

When managers have several possible solutions to a problem, they should not instinctively call for marketing research. In fact, the first decision to make is whether to conduct marketing research at all.

Some companies have been conducting research in certain markets for many years. Such firms understand the characteristics of target customers and their likes and dislikes about existing products. Under these circumstances, further research would be repetitive and waste money. Procter & Gamble, for example, has extensive knowledge of the coffee market. After it conducted initial taste tests with Folgers Instant Coffee, P&G went into national distribution without further research. Consolidated Foods Kitchen of Sara Lee followed the same strategy with its frozen croissants, as did Quaker Oats with Chewy Granola Bars. This tactic, however, does not always work. P&G marketers thought they understood the pain reliever market thoroughly, so they bypassed market research for Encaprin aspirin in capsules. Because it lacked a distinct competitive advantage over existing products, however, the product failed and was withdrawn from the market.

Managers rarely have such great trust in their judgment that they would refuse more information if it were available and free. But they might have enough confidence that they would be unwilling to pay very much for the information or to wait a long time to receive it. The willingness to acquire additional decision-making information depends on managers' perceptions of its quality, price, and timing. Of course, if perfect information were available—that is, the data conclusively showed which alternative to choose—decision makers would be willing to pay more for it than for information that still left uncertainty. In summary, research should be undertaken only when the expected value of the information is greater than the cost of obtaining it.

FAQs

Are there ever conflicts between marketing researchers and product managers? Find out by watching the video FAQ on Xtra!

6 COMPETITIVE INTELLIGENCE

Explain the concept of competitive intelligence

Derived from military intelligence, competitive intelligence is an important tool for helping a firm overcome a competitor's advantage. Specifically, competitive intelligence can help identify the advantage, play a major role in determining how the advantage was achieved, and then provide insights on how it was achieved.

Competitive intelligence (CI) is the creation of a system that helps managers assess their competitors and their vendors in order to become a more efficient and effective competitor. Intelligence is analyzed information. It becomes decision-making intelligence when it has implications for the organization. For example, a primary competitor may have plans to introduce a product with performance standards equal to ours but with a 15 percent cost advantage. The new product will reach the market in eight months. This intelligence has important decision-making and policy consequences for management. Competitive intelligence and environmental scanning (where management gathers data about the external environment—see Chapter 2) combine to create marketing intelligence. Marketing intelligence is then used as input into a marketing decision support system. Nine out of ten large companies have employees dedicated to the CI function. Many firms spend several million dollars a year on the function.[20]

The top corporate CI officer at a multibillion-dollar global technology company claims that competitive intelligence helped his company recover after it began losing market share to a competitor. The rival, after competing directly with the company for years, had figured out its bidding strategy. Instead of competing on price with an off-the-shelf offering, the rival was beginning to offer prospects a customized solution—and it was winning. When the CI officer's company changed to a customized approach, it won hundreds of millions of dollars in new business the following year. At Pergo, Inc., a maker of laminate flooring, CI helped win a major contract. When Pergo told a national retailer what it had learned from a mutual supplier—that the rival would not be able to launch a new product when it said it would—the retailer signed with Pergo instead.

Competitive intelligence can also help companies avoid unnecessary costs. At Phoenix-based electronics distributor Avnet, Inc., in-house analysts predicted—correctly—that four of its rivals in the server industry would soon be out of business. So when two of them began offering special financing deals to build market

BehaviorScan
A scanner-based research program that tracks the purchases of 3,000 households through store scanners in each research market.

InfoScan
A scanner-based sales-tracking service for the consumer packaged-goods industry.

competitive intelligence (CI)
An intelligence system that helps managers assess their competition and vendors in order to become more efficient and effective competitors.

share, Avnet stayed on the side-lines. Intelligence developed by Avnet's analysts allowed company managers to avoid a potentially crippling fight and to compete forcefully with the rivals that remained.[21]

Society for Competitive Intelligence Professionals
Find out more about competitive intelligence at the Society for Competitive Intelligence Professionals Web site. Research a career in CI by checking out the job marketplace at SCIP.
http://www.scip.org

Online

SOURCES OF COMPETITIVE INTELLIGENCE

 The Internet and its databases are a great source of CI. A CI researcher can use Internet databases to answer these and other questions:

- What articles were written about this market?
- What companies are associated with this product group?
- What patents have been filed for this technology?
- What are the major magazines or texts in this industry?
- What are the chances that I will find something in print on the target company?
- How many companies are in the same industry as the target company?
- Who are the reporters studying this industry?
- How can I be updated on industry and company events without having to constantly request the information?
- How can I compile a list of the leading experts in the industry and the key institutions they are associated with?

Non-computer-based sources of CI can be found in a variety of areas:

- A company's salespeople, who can directly observe and ask questions about the competition.
- Experts with in-depth knowledge of a subject or activity.
  - CI consultants, who can use their knowledge and experience to gather needed information quickly and efficiently.
  - Government agencies, a valuable source of all types of data.
  - Uniform Commercial Code (UCC) filings, a system that identifies goods that are leased or pledged as collateral. This is an excellent source for learning about a company's latest additions to plant assets.
  - Suppliers, a group that may offer information on products shipped to a competitor.
  - Periodicals, a good source for timely articles on successes, failures, opportunities, and threats.
  - The Yellow Pages, which often provide data on number of competitors, trading areas, and special offerings.
  - Trade shows, official gatherings where competitors display their latest offerings.

This list is not exhaustive, but it does provide an idea of how CI can be gathered.

 Read more about competitive intelligence in the supplemental module on Xtra!

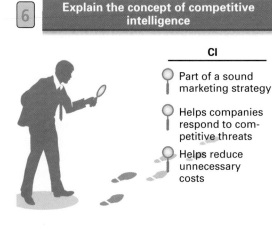

REVIEW LEARNING OBJECTIVE 6

6 Explain the concept of competitive intelligence

CI

- Part of a sound marketing strategy
- Helps companies respond to competitive threats
- Helps reduce unnecessary costs

LOOKING BACK

Look back at the story about Coach at the beginning of this chapter. A company can use survey research, observations, or experiments to conduct marketing research.

Unless a company has extensive knowledge, based on research, of the problem at hand, it should probably conduct marketing research. Yet managers should also be reasonably sure that the cost of gathering the information will be less than the value of the data gathered.

Key marketing data often come from a company's own decision support system, which continually gathers data from a variety of sources and funnels the information to decision makers. They then manipulate the data to make better decisions. DSS data are often supplemented by marketing research information.

USE IT NOW

As a consumer, you participate in shaping consumer products by the choices you make and the products and services you buy. You can become a better consumer by actively participating in marketing surveys and learning more about the products you buy.

PARTICIPATE IN MARKETING RESEARCH SURVEYS

All of us get tired of telephone solicitations where people try to sell us everything from new carpet to chimney cleaning. Recognize that marketing research surveys are different. A true marketing research survey will *never* involve a sales pitch nor will the research firm sell your name to a database marketer. The purpose of marketing research is to build better goods and services for you and me. If you help out such researchers, you ultimately help yourself. The Council for Marketing and Opinion Research (CMOR) is an organization of hundreds of marketing research professionals that is dedicated to preserving the integrity of the research industry. If you receive a call from someone who tries to sell you something under the guise of marketing research, get the name and address of the organization. Call CMOR at 1 (800) 887-CMOR and report the abuse.

REVIEW AND APPLICATIONS

1 **Explain the concept and purpose of a marketing decision support system.** A decision support system (DSS) makes data instantly available to marketing managers and allows them to manipulate the data themselves to make marketing decisions. Four characteristics make DSSs especially useful to marketing managers: They are interactive, flexible, discovery oriented, and accessible. Decision support systems give managers access to information immediately and without outside assistance. They allow users to manipulate data in a variety of ways and to answer "what if" questions. And, finally, they are accessible to novice computer users.

1.1 In the absence of company problems, is there any reason to develop a marketing DSS?

1.2 Explain the difference between marketing research and a DSS.

2 **Define marketing research and explain its importance to marketing decision making.** Marketing research is a process of collecting and analyzing data for the purpose of solving specific marketing problems. Marketers use marketing research to explore the profitability of marketing strategies. They can examine why particular strategies failed and analyze characteristics of specific market segments. Managers can use research findings to help keep current customers. Moreover, marketing research allows management to behave proactively, rather than reactively, by identifying newly emerging patterns in society and the economy.

2.1 The task of marketing is to create exchanges. What role might marketing research play in the facilitation of the exchange process?

2.2 Marketing research has traditionally been associated with manufacturers of consumer goods. Today, however, an increasing number of organizations, both profit and nonprofit, are using marketing research. Why do you think this trend exists? Give some examples of specific reasons why organizations might use marketing research.

2.3 *WRITING* Write a reply to the following statement: "I own a restaurant in the downtown area. I see customers every day whom I know on a first-name basis. I understand their likes and dislikes. If I put something on the menu and it doesn't sell, I know that they didn't like it. I also read the magazine *Modern Restaurants*, so I know what the trends are in the industry. This is all of the marketing research I need to do."

2.4 Give an example of (a) the descriptive role of marketing research, (b) the diagnostic role, and (c) the predictive function of marketing research.

2.5 Review the "Marketing in Entertainment" box on PBS. Companies, like PBS, commission surveys to find out about themselves. How can these surveys aid management decision making? Can these surveys be conducted efficiently over the Internet? How important is image to an organization like PBS? Can marketing research help PBS understand its image?

2.6 *WRITING* *INFOTRAC COLLEGE EDITION* A new (and expensive) trend in marketing research is ethnographic research. Use InfoTrac (**http://www. infotrac-college.com**) to find an article titled "Every Move You Make" written by Linda Tischler for the April 2004 issue of *Fast Company*. Read and summarize the article. What is your opinion of ethnographic research? Do you think it will be the wave of the future? Explain your reasoning.

3 **Describe the steps involved in conducting a marketing research project.** The marketing research process involves several basic steps. First, the researcher and the decision maker must agree on a problem statement or set of research objectives. The researcher then creates an overall research design to specify how primary data will be gathered and analyzed. Before collecting data, the researcher decides whether the group to be interviewed will be a probability or nonprobability sample. Field service firms are often hired to carry out data collection. Once data have been collected, the researcher analyzes them using statistical analysis. The researcher then prepares and presents oral and written reports, with conclusions and recommendations, to management. As a final step, the researcher determines whether the recommendations were implemented and what could have been done to make the project more successful.

3.1 Critique the following methodologies and suggest more appropriate alternatives:

a. A supermarket was interested in determining its image. It dropped a short questionnaire into the grocery bag of each customer before putting in the groceries.

b. To assess the extent of its trade area, a shopping mall stationed interviewers in the parking lot every Monday and Friday evening. Interviewers walked up to people after they had parked their cars and asked them for their ZIP codes.

c. To assess the popularity of a new movie, a major studio invited people to call a 900 number and vote yes, they would see it again, or no, they would not. Each caller was billed a $2 charge.

3.2 *WRITING* You have been charged with determining how to attract more business majors to your school. Write an outline of the steps you would take, including the sampling procedures, to accomplish the task.

3.3 Why are secondary data sometimes preferable to primary data?

3.4 Discuss when focus groups should and should not be used.

3.5 *TEAM* Divide the class into teams of eight persons. Each group will conduct a focus group on the quality and number of services that your college is providing to its students. One person from each group should be chosen to act as moderator.

Remember, it is the moderator's job to facilitate discussion, not to lead the discussion. These groups should last approximately 45 minutes. If possible, the groups should be videotaped or recorded. Upon completion, each group should write a brief report of its results. Consider offering to meet with the dean of students to share the results of your research.

4 **Discuss the profound impact of the Internet on marketing research.** The Internet has vastly simplified the secondary data search process, placing more sources of information in front of researchers than ever before. Internet survey research is surging in popularity. Internet surveys can be created rapidly and reported in real time. They are also relatively inexpensive and can easily be personalized. Often researchers can use the Internet to contact respondents who are difficult to reach by other means. The Internet can also be used to conduct focus groups, to distribute research proposals and reports, and to facilitate collaboration between the client and the research supplier. Clients can access real-time data and analyze the information as the collection process continues.

4.1 Use the Internet and a Web browser, such as Google or Yahoo!, and type "marketing research." You will then have thousands of options. Pick a Web site that you find interesting and report on its content to the class.

4.2 Why has the Internet been of such great value to researchers seeking secondary data?

4.3 Do you see traditional forms of marketing research disappearing?

5 **Discuss the growing importance of scanner-based research.** A scanner-based re search system enables marketers to monitor a market panel's exposure and reaction to such variables as advertising, coupons, store displays, packaging, and price. By analyzing these variables in relation to the panel's subsequent buying behavior, marketers gain useful insight into sales and marketing strategies.

5.1 Why has scanner-based research been seen as "the ultimate answer" for marketing researchers? Do you see any disadvantages of this methodology?

5.2 Detractors claim that scanner-based research is like "driving a car down the road looking only in the rearview mirror." What does this mean? Do you agree?

6 **Explain the concept of competitive intelligence.** Competitive intelligence (CI) is the creation of an intelligence system that helps managers assess their competition and their vendors in order to become more efficient and effective competitors. Intelligence is analyzed information, and it becomes decision-making intelligence when it has implications for the organization.

By helping managers assess their competition and vendors, CI leads to fewer surprises. CI allows managers to predict changes in business relationships, guard against threats, forecast a competitor's strategy, and develop a successful marketing plan.

The Internet and databases accessed via the Internet offer excellent sources of CI. Company personnel, particularly sales and service representatives, are usually good sources of CI. Many companies require their salespersons to routinely fill out CI reports. Other external sources of CI include experts, CI consultants, government agencies, UCC filings, suppliers, newspapers and other publications, Yellow Pages, and trade shows.

6.1 Why do you think that CI is so hot in today's environment?

6.2 Prepare a memo to your boss at JetBlue Airlines and outline why the organization needs a CI unit.

6.3 Form a team with three other students. Each team must choose a firm in the PC manufacturing industry and then go to the Web site of the firm and acquire as much CI as possible. Each team will then prepare a five-minute oral presentation on its findings.

TERMS

EXERCISES

APPLICATION EXERCISE

Often students think marketing research is hard and unnecessary, but nothing could be further from the truth. The following activities will help you see how vital research is to all marketing activities and at the same time will help you review the basic functions of marketing.[22]

Activities

1. Make a two-column table on a sheet of paper, and in the left column, list the basic functions of marketing. Refer to past chapters if necessary. If you have trouble coming up with more than one or two items, think of a particular product or service (like cars, shoes, carbonated beverages, or haircuts). What functions should be performed to successfully market this product or service?

2. In the right column of your table, identify all of the potential research activities that are needed to support each marketing function. For example, for the function of promotion planning, you might list learning more about types of media (e.g., availability, effectiveness, cost) as a research activity.

ETHICS EXERCISE

John Michael Smythe owns a small marketing research firm in Cleveland, Ohio, which employs 75 people. Most employees are sole breadwinners in their families. John's firm has not fared well for the past two years and is on the verge of bankruptcy. The company recently surveyed over 2,500 people in Ohio about new-car purchase plans for the Ohio Department of Economic Development. Because the study identified many hot prospects for new cars, a car dealer has offered John $8,000 for the names and phone numbers of people saying they are "likely" or "very likely" to buy a new car within the next 12 months. John needs the money to avoid laying off a number of employees.

Questions

1. Should John Smythe sell the names?

2. Does the AMA Code of Ethics address this issue? Go to **http://www.marketingpower.com** and review the code. Then, write a brief paragraph on what the AMA Code of Ethics contains that relates to John Smythe's dilemma.

CAREER EXERCISE

A great resource for learning more about marketing research is the Marketing Research Association at **http://www.mra-net.org**. A student membership costs $50, but the site includes information, job postings, and internship resources for free.

Another good place to find out more about a career in marketing research is *Quirk's Marketing Research Review*, available online at **http://www.quirks.com**. Quirk's lists marketing research providers and abundant job postings for the marketing research profession.

Activities

1. The Who's Who of marketing research suppliers is the Greenbook, located online at **http://www.greenbook.org**. To learn more about what marketing researchers actually do, take a virtual tour of a marketing research facility. Greenbook online has several tours available. Once you finish the tour, write a few sentences about whether the tour differed from what you expected.

2. Stay at Greenbook online and locate marketing research suppliers in the area where you would like to live after college. Visit a handful of company Web sites, review their job postings, and determine if the geographic area seems to have a concentration of suppliers with a particular specialty (e.g., numerous focus-group centers or survey researchers).

3. Using any of the resources listed in this exercise, find a job listing that interests you and compare the requirements to your current résumé. Would you be able to get the job right out of college? If not, would taking some different courses fill out your résumé, or would you need to work in the industry for a while before being qualified?

ENTREPRENEURSHIP CASE

COURTESY LOOK-LOOK, INC.

COOL AND HOW TO FIND IT: LOOK-LOOK

You can't always believe what you hear, particularly in the fast-moving world of youth trends. That is, unless you listen to Sharon Lee and DeeDee Gordon, founders of Look-Look, the most accurate information resource on the global youth culture. The pair founded the company in 1999, determined to find whatever makes the cultural spider-sense tingle—music, shoes, clothes, games, makeup, food, and technology. Lee and Gordon took Look-Look online in 2000, and the company has since risen to be the paragon of trend forecasting in the youth market. How?

When Sharon Lee needs to know what's cool, she taps into a network of experts the CIA would envy. It's a Web-linked weave of nearly 10,000 volunteers and part-timers, aged 14 to 30, recruited over several years at clubs and hangouts around the country, from New York to Los Angeles and points in between, to report on their world.

Look-Look's multilevel database is populated with thousands of prescreened recruits who log on to answer surveys and polls, register opinions, and communicate for points that can lead to cash, digital cameras, and other techie toys. Some of the recruits, armed with digital cameras, can photograph their world, then upload the pictures, send e-mail reports, and use Look-Look's Intranet message boards. The young field agents might snap anything from a rave to their bedroom walls. Look-Look relies on "early adopters" and "influencers" to provide the layers of information that traditional research only skims.

Look-Look is a cool seeker, paid by major marketers to get the first bead on what's next on the horizon. With a cool seeker's expertise, even the most staid company can be on the razor's edge: Look-Look ferreted out the then-uncharted popularity of under-a-dollar stores, fold-up scooters, and over-the-shoulder bags.

Cornerstone Promotion, a Look-Look rival, was behind Microsoft's successful launch of the Xbox video-gaming system. "Seventy kids got units," said Cornerstone's president. "They were plugged into the local clubs and set up gaming parties with music giveaways from our record label clients. They'd do it in campus rec centers or at night clubs or on radio shows." By the time Xbox made its debut, "we created a huge frenzy." Microsoft was no longer stodgy compared to Sega or PlayStation.

In addition to youth market environmental scanning, a client might ask Look-Look to check the coolness quotient of a product. After the small army is canvassed with online polls and surveys, the results are arranged into categories. "The turnaround," says Lee, "can be as little as 48 hours." Look-Look categorizes information into ten channels: fashion, entertainment, technology, activities, eating and drinking, health and beauty, mood of culture (how kids feel about life), spirituality, city guide, and Look Out (a "best of" findings in a snapshot). The information is put through rigorous paces. "Methodology is crucial, especially with the quantity and quality of the sample," says Lee. "We can take a sample of 300 or thousands. That's up to Gallup standards."

To ensure the most accurate information, Look-Look steers away from focus groups because peer pressure is a factor at this age; teens are more likely to bend to pressure and follow the leader of a peer group. One-on-one interviews are, therefore, preferred. They keep the responses truer and uninfluenced by external pressures. To get to cool, Look-Look has to keep its sources cool.

And what is cool, anyway? Says Lee, "For young people now it's pure raw emotion—it's anything that inspires you to think 'I want that because it fits me so well.' It can be a person, a product, a place, anything." According to Que Gaskins, the chief marketing officer of Ad*itive, a multicultural marketing firm, cool really starts with the "what if" factor: " 'What if I wore that hat or that jersey?' Then you give it your own twist, the way African American males sport Asian tattoos or middle-class white kids wear dreadlocks or cornrows. But there's just no formula for cool."

"Cool burns out so fast that by the time companies know it's cool, it's not cool anymore," says Lee. "The old-time corporate methodology was to treat it like the annual report for shareholders—going out and testing a sample size of a few hundred people, then retesting it again the next year. But a year in youth culture is like a year in dog years."

Still, cool is as hard to pin down as a weather forecast for next week. But the real arbiters of cool are those who can afford to lead. "Ultimately," says Gaskins, "the future of cool belongs to whoever has the most buying power."[23]

Questions

1. What is Look-Look offering businesses that traditional market research firms cannot offer?

2. Describe the role of the Internet in youth trend spotting. Do you think a research firm can accurately forecast youth trends without an online component to its research plan?

3. Go to Look-Look's Web site at **http://www.look-look.com** and check out some of the free information in each category. How accurate do you find the information? Have you seen any of these trends in your city or region, or among your friends and classmates?

4. Make a list of products or companies that you think could benefit from Look-Look's form of predictive market research. Next to each item, write a brief reason why and how you think cool seeking would benefit the company or product.

WATCH IT

SmallBusinessSchool ▣
the Series on PBS stations and the Web

FEATURE PRESENTATION

Specialty Cheese Company

To give you insight into Chapter 8, Small Business School will introduce you to Vicki and Paul Scharfman, owners of the oldest continuously running cheese factory in the state of Wisconsin. Their company, Specialty Cheese Company, has used savvy marketing research strategy to breathe new life into a very old business. By studying what American consumers want in a cheese and identifying the needs of particular ethnic groups, the Scharfmans now produce cheeses that are market-driven in concept and execution. The key has been unfailing attention to market research, especially at the ground level. The Scharfmans talk to the people who eat and work with their cheeses, both consumers and cooks, to learn their specific wants and needs. Using marketing research, Paul and Vicki have transformed what has long been a production-driven, commodity-type market into a market where cheese products, specialized in their appearance, texture, and cooking tendencies, reflect the varying needs of a very diverse market.

What to Watch For and Ask Yourself

1. Did the Scharfmans begin their marketing research efforts in response to a problem or in hopes of recognizing an opportunity?

2. Which steps of the marketing research process did you hear mentioned in the video (i.e., that the Scharfmans use in their business)?

3. Discuss the role of competitive intelligence in the small business environment.

ENCORE PRESENTATION

Apollo 13

Now that you have read about how critical information is to good marketing decision making, watch this clip from *Apollo 13*. This scene shows a crisis in space which the astronauts and mission control need to work out in order to avoid catastrophe. What evidence of a decision support system do you see in the clip? What kind of information do the astronauts use to assess their situation (akin to identifying the research problem)? Can you draw parallels between what you see in the clip and the job of a market researcher?

STILL SHAKY?

If you're having trouble with the concepts in this chapter, consider using some of the following study resources. You can review the videos, or test yourself with materials designed for all kinds of learning styles.

☑ **Xtra! (http://lambxtra.swlearning.com)**

| ☑ Quiz | ☑ Feature Videos | ☑ Encore Videos | ☑ FAQ Videos |
| ☑ Exhibit Worksheets | ☑ Marketing Plan Worksheets | ☑ Content | |

☑ **http://lamb.swlearning.com**

| ☑ Quiz | ☑ PowerPoint slides | ☑ Marketing News | ☑ Review Exercises |
| ☑ Links | ☑ Marketing Plan Contest | ☑ Career Exercise | ☐ Use It Now |

☑ **Study guide**

| ☑ Outline | ☑ Vocab Review | ☑ Test Questions | ☑ Marketing Scenario |

Need More? Here's a tip. Review your class notes. Do they give you enough information? If they are lacking, visit your campus study center to learn how to take good notes.

MARKETING MISCUE

Remembering *The Alamo* May Be Painful for Disney

The rallying cry "Remember the Alamo" has survived many generations. Unfortunately, Disney's 2004 movie, *The Alamo*, was unlikely to have a comparably long life. After costing over $100 million to produce, the Disney film took in a meager $9.2 million on its opening weekend. Interestingly, the movie also angered many in its target audience.

Some Americans felt that the movie desecrated the memory of American heroes like Davy Crockett, Jim Bowie, and Sam Houston. Mexican audiences were not excited to have one of the country's most reviled traitors, Santa Anna, depicted on the big screen, nor were they happy to have the Battle of San Jacinto as the closing scene of the movie. Viewers from Mexico felt that the movie was filmed from an American point of view even though part of the movie was in Spanish with English subtitles. Viewers from the United States dubbed the movie another Disney fairy tale.

The movie was based on the 1836 story of how Texans (Anglo immigrants to Texas, which was then a part of Mexico) and Tejanos (people of Mexican descent in Texas) defended the Alamo for 13 days until its fall to Mexican troops led by General Santa Anna. Rather than ending the movie with the fall of the Alamo (a win for the Mexican forces), the movie closes with the Battle of San Jacinto one month later. Mexico lost this battle and, with it, lost Texas to the United States. The May 2002 announcement of the upcoming movie was an attempt to capitalize on the post–September 11 surge in patriotism. Presenting both the American and Mexican sides of the extended battle was an attempt to present a politically correct version of the tale.

With a star-studded lineup of Patrick Wilson as William Travis, Jason Patric as James Bowie, Billy Bob Thornton as Davy Crockett, Dennis Quaid as Sam Houston, and Emilio Echevarria as Santa Anna, the movie was scheduled to open on Christmas Day 2003. After spending approximately $130,000 to promote the Christmas Day opening with billboards and a DVD trailer attached to the front cover of *Daily Variety*, Disney pulled the movie from the release schedule for further editing. Disney went on to spend around $35 million in promoting a 2004 Easter weekend release.

Changing the December release date was just one more fiasco in a long line of production problems for the film. The film was originally to be directed by Ron Howard in 2002 on a $125 million budget with an R rating for violence. Disney then switched gears, hiring John Lee Hancock (a less experienced director and a native of the Lone Star state), cutting the budget to $75 million and reducing the violence so as to appeal to a broader audience with a PG-13 rating. Heavy on history, however, the movie came in at three hours (resulting in much cutting, editing, and a delayed release) and $25 million over budget.

On its Easter weekend debut, *The Alamo* tied for third place at the box office with Fox Searchlight's comedy *Johnson Family Vacation*. Mel Gibson's *The Passion of the Christ* was in first place, with Sony Pictures Entertainment's *Hellboy* coming in second. Market research was not offering a positive long-term outlook for *The Alamo*. Given the historical connections between box-office performance and company performance, financial analysts were expected to lower their estimates for the company as a whole.

The dismal box-office showing was just one more problem trial for Disney and its chief executive officer, Michael Eisner. Unfortunately for Eisner, the fact that *The Alamo* tanked in its debut added fuel to a shareholder revolt. Moviegoers have to wonder if Disney ever considered market desires in developing and producing *The Alamo* or even if the company had any idea as to who might be its target audience.[1]

Questions

1. What is the role of the consumer decision-making process in the movie industry?

2. Describe segmentation processes within the film marketplace.

3. Can you think of other movies that flopped because of an unclear target market?

Tall Magazine Debuts to the Vertically Gifted Crowd

Towering overhead at 6 feet 9 inches tall, Everard Strong thought he had heard every tall pun and suffered through innumerable physical discomforts in his life. For almost five years, Strong mulled over the idea for a niche magazine devoted to tall people. A prototype of Strong's magazine, Tall Magazine, debuted in July 2003 with a motto of "Life may be short, but we're not." The target market for Tall is the 12.3 million men who are 6 feet 2 inches or taller and the 7.5 million women 5 feet 9 inches or taller. Tall is the only consumer magazine targeting this particular market profile. The jury is still out, however, as to whether this lifestyle segmentation approach can be successful long term since succeeding with a niche publication is a daunting feat in even the best of economic times.

Niche Marketing

The Web site of one magazine superstore, **http://www. bluedolphin.com**, offers the following niche categories: African American, Animals, Antiques, Art, Astrology, Auto Racing, Beer/Wine/Spirits, Best Sellers, Boating & Sailing, Cars, Children's, Collectibles, Comics, Computers & Internet, Crafts, En Español, Entertainment, Fashion, Fishing, Flying, Food & Cooking, Gambling, Gardening, Gift Ideas, Golf, Health & Fitness, Healthy Eating, History, Home Decorating, Home Electronics, Home Improvement, Hunting & Shooting, Literature, Magazine of the Month, Mature Living, Men's Living, Money & Business, Motorcycles, Movies & TV, Music, News & Politics, Outdoor Adventure, Parenting & Family, Photography, Professional & Trade, Puzzles & Games, Radio Control Models, Regional & International, Religion & Spirituality, Science, Sports, Teens, Travel, Trucks & Off-Road, Video Games, and Women's Living. This abundance of niche publications has been made feasible by a combination of technology and the decreased cost of publishing.

With Tall Magazine, Strong is hoping to form a community voice and inspire a culture of height. He thinks that the public as a whole does not recognize the problems that tall people encounter in their daily lives. Indeed, tall people have to counter the perception that there is bias toward height, that was reinforced by a segment on ABC's 20/20 that pointed to research showing that women, corporations, and children all prefer tall people. Thus, the magazine was launched to address the dilemmas that tall people encounter on a day-to-day basis and serve as a voice for this segment of the population.

Initial Publications

In July 2003, Tall Magazine printed a 24-page prototype issue to test the waters for advertising support and to provide a sneak preview to members of the target audience. With celebrity profiles on actor Donald Sutherland, basketball twins Heather and Heidi Burge, and villain Roger Morrissey from Buffy the Vampire Slayer and columns about back care, proper exercise techniques, and the world's tallest chair, the magazine elicited considerable reader and advertising support. The editorial plan was to include celebrity features, service/social articles (e.g., chronic back pain, the Fair Air Coalition, Marfan syndrome), and regular editorial fixtures focused on tall things and tall talk in each bimonthly issue.

The official first issue of Tall Magazine was released in February 2004. This 64-page issue featured the Grammy Award–winning Eroica Trio, as well as celebrity profiles on members of the Improv Allstars and the James Bond villain Richard Kiel. Additional columns were devoted to automobiles, top fashions, workout routines, and product reviews. The magazine included a tribute to Robert Wadlow, the tallest man who ever lived (8 feet 11 inches).

The May 2004 issue featured actor, director, and writer Ron Perlman, the man behind Hellboy. Other celebrity featured in the issue were NBA All-Star Bill Walton and Olympic swimmer Michael Phelps. Keeping with the plan to include service-related articles in each issue, a feature article was devoted to Marfan syndrome (a connective tissue disorder that affects the skeleton, lungs, eyes, heart, and blood vessels, with a major symptom being disproportionate growth that usually results in tall stature). Other editorial fixtures included columns on the big man scooter club and fashions.

Retail and Advertising Support

By early 2004, Tall Magazine had signed a contract to be available in Books-A-Million bookstores and Tattered Cover bookstores in the Colorado area. Other retail outlets under consideration were Barnes & Noble, newsstands, and boutique stores such as Big & Tall stores. The magazine did not see itself going into the mass market via outlets such as Walgreens and Wal-Mart in the near future. The single-issue purchase price was $5.95; a six-issue subscription to U.S. addresses cost $24.95. International subscriptions were also welcome, at a higher price to cover mailing expenses. Online ordering was possible, with payment via Paypal, credit card, or personal check. PDF versions of the magazine were available online, with the July 2003 prototype offered for $1.99 and regular issues at $3.95. Advertisers interested in Tall Magazine included companies offering clothing, car accessories, cabinetry, mattresses, and golf club extensions.

Challenges Ahead

The staff at Tall Magazine recognizes that writing for a highly specialized niche market will not be easy and that finding something to talk about every two months will be a challenge. Nevertheless, the magazine's Web site has already become a favorite destination for the tall community due, in part, to its launch of a Personals (matchmaking) portal. This portal allows members of the tall community to find people with similar interests by offering free opportunities to post and browse.[2]

Questions

1. Does Tall's market profile fit the basic criteria for market segmentation?

2. What kind of market research does *Tall Magazine* need?

3. In which niche category at bluedolphin.com would one find *Tall Magazine*?

CROSS-FUNCTIONAL CONNECTIONS SOLUTIONS

Part 2: Information Integration Facilitates Market Knowledge

Questions

1. Why has information historically been perceived as "owned" by the marketing department?

   There are probably a few general answers to this question. One is that because information is referred to as "marketing research" rather than "market" or "marketplace," it automatically denotes that it is part of the marketing department. Also, the research has traditionally been conducted by the marketing department—reinforcing the notion that the marketing department owns it. Additionally, prior to the 1990s, the marketing department was the only formal link between the company and the customer. Because a primary focus of marketing research is the customer, the information was always owned by the marketing department.

2. What data differences exist across functions?

   The historical data debate between marketing and other business functions centers on the qualitative-versus-quantitative format of the data. The data collected by marketers are perceived to be "touchy-feely" data when compared to the "hard" data utilized by other functional areas. In addition to unit sales and competitive offerings, marketing data look at customers' perceptions—something very "soft" when compared to other functional data. For example, manufacturing can cite exact production output, cost, and cycle data, and R&D has precise specifications for tensile strength, electrical usage, and battery power. Add accounting data with its general accounting standards to the "hard" data side of the picture, and it's not surprising that data differences cause cross-functional conflict within a firm.

3. What is the job of a chief knowledge officer?

   The chief knowledge officer is a company executive who manages institutional learning. CKOs are responsible for integrating internal and external knowledge into their companies. In addition to monitoring this information, the CKO creates and propagates new knowledge based on industry observations, best practices, and benchmarking studies. The CKO shares the collected knowledge with all members of firm, thereby providing them with consistently important and relevant information.

Suggested Readings

Edward F. McQuarrie, *Customer Visits: Building a Better Market Focus* (Thousand Oaks, CA: Sage Publications, 1998).

Rick Whiting, "Hidden Value in Customer Calls," *Information Week,* August 12, 2002, online (http://www.informationweek.com).

Product

Decisions

CROSSING FUNCTIONAL LINES IN SPEEDING PRODUCTS TO MARKET

Historically, marketers focused on the company's products or services from a *demand-side* perspective. Using marketing research, marketers determined customers' current and future wants and needs. Once these wants and needs were determined, marketing then expected research and development to develop a device that would satisfy customer demands. Once the device was developed, the expectation was that manufacturing would produce it. The device became a true product with the development of a marketing program that added value in the customers' minds.

On the flip side, the manufacturing and R&D departments traditionally viewed products from a *supply-side* perspective. In this framework, new-product conception was the job of the R&D group for design; the device would then be produced by the manufacturing group. The supply-side role of marketing was to entice the marketplace to want the product. From this perspective, marketing was the functional group that told the marketplace about the product's performance but had no input as to what actually went into the product or service.

Many businesspeople have suggested that whether a company or product is driven by a demand-side or a supply-side focus depends on the nature of the product. For example, highly technological entertainment-oriented products, such as Smart Watches by Fossil and Suunto, are based more on supply-side thinking. These highly sophisticated watches utilize Microsoft's Smart Personal Objects Technology (SPOT) to deliver customized infobits wirelessly. These bulky watches were not designed for those seeking fashionable styling. Rather, the watch design was driven by Microsoft's SPOT capabilities, with Fossil and Suunto expecting at least some level of acceptance from technology-seeking early adopters.

Consumer-oriented electronic entertainment products, however, appear to be examples of demand-side product concepts. For example, Apple focused on consumers' interest in portability and mobility when it designed the iPod. Steve Jobs has a track record of providing consumers with entertainment products. The development of his company's products is driven by an understanding of consumers' wants and needs—wants and needs that can be satisfied by Apple's technological capabilities.

Demand-side versus supply-side thinking has resulted in three major areas of conflict between marketing and R&D/manufacturing: managing variety, managing availability, and managing reliability. Generally, marketing has wanted a large variety of high-quality products for customers to choose from and will promise the shortest delivery time necessary to get the order. In contrast, R&D and manufacturing have preferred fewer models so that they can concentrate on a smaller number of projects, thereby achieving high quality without having to hold too many products in inventory.

Research and development and manufacturing functional groups have become quite efficient at working together using processes such as "design-factory fit," "concurrent engineering," "design for manufacturability and assembly," and "early manufacturing involvement." Basically, all of these concepts refer to advance linkage between a product's design and its manufacturing needs so that the manufacturing group will be ready to make the product once it has been designed.

Companies have been quite successful at implementing various versions of these general cross-functional concepts. FutureLogic, the gaming industry's top producer of thermal printers used inside the new wave of slot machines, utilized its technology and printing knowledge in a concurrent engineering project with International Game Technology (IGT). The result of the partnership was a first-generation thermal printer for slot machines. FutureLogic introduced its second-generation thermal printer soon thereafter, after soliciting feedback from the casino operations staff on the floor. This customer interaction enabled the company to develop and manufacture the best product possible to fill the staff's needs. In essence, FutureLogic built the initial printing product using manufacturing and R&D expertise and then found that it could create a better printer by building customers' desires into the printer.

The efficient coordinating processes developed on the technical side of business have been meshed with customers' demands for high-quality, highly customized products that can be delivered immediately. Such expectations are in direct contrast to traditional thinking. Traditionally, companies made standardized products available immediately, and customers understood that customization would result in delays in delivery. Today's marketplace is increasingly demanding that companies compete on both time and customization.

The key to providing customized products quickly is a multidisciplinary approach to business. Marketplace demands for immediacy and customization have focused attention on marketing, R&D, and manufacturing. Traditionally, products were conceptualized by one function, given to another function to produce, and then handed over to another function to sell. Now, however, the need to compete on time when developing new products has done away with such a linear product development process. Today, the expectation is that the final product is high quality and has moved through the company's functional processes in at least half the time of the traditional linear process.

Harley-Davidson's Web site tells readers that its motorcycles are "about riding." Motorcycle enthusiasts confirm that by spending countless hours riding the open road just for the thrill of riding. It is the company's behind-the-scenes management processes that make it possible for bikers to ride the high-quality machine that Harley-Davidson produces. The company uses cross-functional teams from concept to market. Implementing the cross-functional team approach helped save the company from possible demise in the latter half of the twentieth century. The general idea is that a company can design a product that simultaneously satisfies customers' demands and is quicker and easier to assemble. This type of design and assembly requires a high level of coordination among marketing, R&D, and manufacturing.

Cross-functional teams are at the heart of decision making at Wizards of the West Coast, the maker of entertainment trading card games such as Magic, Dungeons & Dragons, Alternity, Pokemon, Major League Baseball, Legend of the Five Rings, and WCW Wrestling. To develop all of its roleplaying games, Wizards utilizes cross-functional teams with representatives from all the Wizards divisions that have to work together to design, produce, market, and sell the products. Not only do these teams develop new products, but they also determine when it is time to remove a product from the mix.

Companies also have focused on meeting customization and speed-to-market demands with "modularization." A consumer-products company that has been extremely successful with modularity is Build-A-Bear Workshops. Using modular components, the company can construct a stuffed toy exactly to the customer's specifications. Though modularity might not seem at first to apply to stuffed animals, it enables the company to sell individually customized stuffed toys, as well as offer entertainment opportunities such as birthday parties. In technical terms, modularity reduces the number of individual parts, allowing Build-A-Bear Workshop to quickly customize a product beyond the core architecture of a stuffed toy.

The finance and accounting areas have been particularly thorny areas concerning both new and existing products. Financial managers often complain that marketers are not held to the same financial standards as the rest of the company, particularly when rolling out a new product. In turn, marketers feel the need to justify each expenditure—even though the payback on marketing allocations, such as advertising, is not immediate and/or always easily discernible. This type of friction, referred to as "creative friction" at Harley-Davidson, between marketing and finance/accounting can slow the development cycle and be in direct conflict with the speed-to-market initiatives the company may be taking.

Typically, we think of new products in terms of tangible items, but cross-functional coordination is particularly important when a new or existing service is being introduced and delivered. Since the production and marketing of a service happen simultaneously, it is imperative that these two functions be closely integrated. The service imperative spotlights another vital business function—human resources. Employees are at the heart of customer service. Front-line employees play a pivotal role in delivering high-quality service. A service provider's profitability and growth are driven by customer loyalty, which is in turn driven by customer satisfaction, which is the direct result of the human interaction with the service provider.

Whether it is developing a new product/service or managing the existing product line or service offerings, cross-functional teamwork is necessary for company-wide success. Successful interaction between marketing and all other business functions is imperative for competitive advantage in today's rapidly changing marketplace.

Questions

1. What is the difference between the demand-side perspective and the supply-side perspective to doing business? Is either perspective more appropriate?

2. What are some of the popular business terms used to describe cross-functional integration?

3. Why are employees (whether marketing or not) at the heart of customer service?

9

Product Concepts

LEARNING OBJECTIVES

1   Define the term *product*

2   Classify consumer products

3   Define the terms *product item, product line,* and *product mix*

4   Describe marketing uses of branding

5   Describe marketing uses of packaging and labeling

6   Discuss global issues in branding and packaging

7   Describe how and why product warranties are important marketing tools

Private-label products from laundry detergent to jam have received an eager reception from some American consumers, but similarly marketed beers typically have not been a success. Although private-label beers claim only 0.1 percent of sales, 7-Eleven has decided to introduce its own Latin-style brew to compete head-to-head with the nation's—and its own—best-selling import: Mexican-made Corona.

Cerveseria La Constancia, a 97-year-old brewery in San Salvador, will brew the 7-Eleven beer, to be called Santiago. A six-pack will sell for $5.99, more than inexpensive domestic beers but less than Corona's $7.49 to $7.99. Constancia can sell the private-label beer cheaper because the brewery, not a household name, spends nothing on Swedish Bikini teams, all-women mud fights, wisecracking reptile mascots, or any other advertising beyond the store. And the house brands fetch a higher margin than more expensive name-brand beers. Two rows of Santiago will be placed in coolers next to one row of six-packs of Corona at many

7-Elevens. The stores will tout Santiago through in-store promotions, including large banners.

Traditionally, the three major U.S. brewers have shied away from the generic or private-label field, instead spending millions building up "brand equity" for their top beers. But the game apparently changed when South African Breweries became SABMiller through a merger with Milwaukee-based Miller in 2002. South African had already ventured into private-label territory with Corona look-alikes for several national supermarket chains.

The big question is whether consumers will forsake Corona, the country's most popular import with $360 million in annual sales, for an unknown house brand that's cheaper. Suzanne McDonald, 7-Eleven's category manager for beer and wine, predicts that Santiago will attract import buyers looking for a bargain and domestic beer drinkers desiring something new. Yet Harry Snyder of Latin Brews Sales Company, a marketing company and importer, argues that Corona drinkers probably won't change.

He believes that Santiago is most likely to appeal to those who are "trading up from the domestic beers. We want to have a beer that the Bud, Miller, or Coors drinker will try at $5.99 but would find the Corona too high."

As with other private-label items, including its flavored-ice Slurpees, 7-Eleven aims to use beer to build customer loyalty. The theory is that if buyers are pleased, they will return to the only stores that sell what is perceived as an exclusive brand. Santiago has undergone a "tweakage" at the brewer to differentiate itself from other Constancia private-label beers that are sold by three U.S. grocers. Each lager and light lager is identical to corresponding house brands at the competing supermarkets. Constancia's export manager says Santiago will have a "mouth feel" that's distinct from the other Constancia beers.[1]

What is the difference between brand equity and brand loyalty? What are the advantages and disadvantages of private-label branding? Do you think Santiago will be successful? Explain your answer.

1 WHAT IS A PRODUCT?

Define the term *product*

REVIEW LEARNING OBJECTIVE 1

1 Define the term *product*

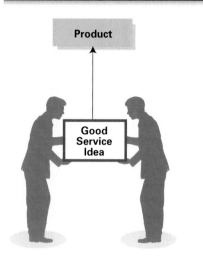

The product offering, the heart of an organization's marketing program, is usually the starting point in creating a marketing mix. A marketing manager cannot determine a price, design a promotion strategy, or create a distribution channel until the firm has a product to sell. Moreover, an excellent distribution channel, a persuasive promotion campaign, and a fair price have no value when the product offering is poor or inadequate.

A **product** may be defined as everything, both favorable and unfavorable, that a person receives in an exchange. A product may be a tangible good like a pair of shoes, a service like a haircut, an idea like "don't litter," or any combination of these three. Packaging, style, color, options, and size are some typical product features. Just as important are intangibles such as service, the seller's image, the manufacturer's reputation, and the way consumers believe others will view the product.

To most people, the term *product* means a tangible good. However, services and ideas are also products. (Chapter 11 focuses specifically on the unique aspects of marketing services.) The marketing process identified in Chapter 1 is the same whether the product marketed is a good, a service, an idea, or some combination of these.

2 TYPES OF CONSUMER PRODUCTS

Classify consumer products

Products can be classified as either business (industrial) or consumer products, depending on the buyer's intentions. The key distinction between the two types of products is their intended use. If the intended use is a business purpose, the product is classified as a business or industrial product. As explained in Chapter 6, a **business product** is used to manufacture other goods or services, to facilitate an organization's operations, or to resell to other customers. A **consumer product** is bought to satisfy an individual's personal wants. Sometimes the same item can be classified as either a business or a consumer product, depending on its intended use. Examples include lightbulbs, pencils and paper, and computers.

We need to know about product classifications because business and consumer products are marketed differently. They are marketed to different target markets and tend to use different distribution, promotion, and pricing strategies.

Chapter 6 examined seven categories of business products: major equipment, accessory equipment, component parts, processed materials, raw materials, supplies, and services. The current chapter examines an effective way of categorizing consumer products. Although there are several ways to classify them, the most popular approach includes these four types: convenience products, shopping products, specialty products, and unsought products (see Exhibit 9.1). This approach classifies products according to how much effort is normally used to shop for them.

CONVENIENCE PRODUCTS

A **convenience product** is a relatively inexpensive item that merits little shopping effort—that is, a consumer is unwilling to shop extensively for such an item. Candy, soft drinks, combs, aspirin, small hardware items, dry cleaning, and car washes fall into the convenience product category.

Consumers buy convenience products regularly, usually without much planning. Nevertheless, consumers do know the brand names of popular convenience products, such as Coca-Cola, Bayer aspirin, and Right Guard deodorant. Convenience products normally require wide distribution in order to sell sufficient

product
Everything, both favorable and unfavorable, that a person receives in an exchange.

business product (industrial product)
A product used to manufacture other goods or services, to facilitate an organization's operations, or to resell to other customers.

consumer product
A product bought to satisfy an individual's personal wants.

convenience product
A relatively inexpensive item that merits little shopping effort.

EXHIBIT 9.1

Classification of Consumer Products

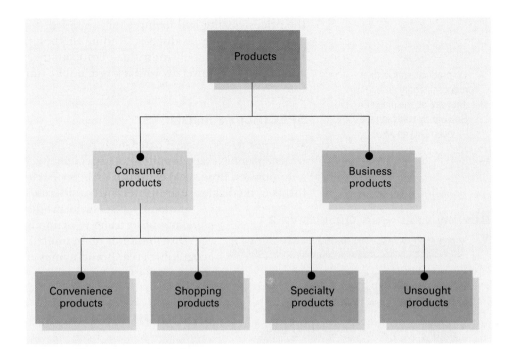

```
                          ┌──────────┐
                          │ Products │
                          └──────────┘
                 ┌────────────┴────────────┐
         ┌──────────────┐          ┌──────────────┐
         │  Consumer    │          │  Business    │
         │  products    │          │  products    │
         └──────────────┘          └──────────────┘
     ┌─────────┬─────────┴─────────┬─────────┐
┌─────────┐ ┌─────────┐ ┌─────────┐ ┌─────────┐
│Convenience│ │Shopping │ │Specialty│ │Unsought │
│ products │ │products │ │products │ │products │
└─────────┘ └─────────┘ └─────────┘ └─────────┘
```

shopping product
A product that requires comparison shopping because it is usually more expensive than a convenience product and is found in fewer stores.

quantities to meet profit goals. For example, the gum Dentyne Ice is available everywhere, including Wal-Mart, Walgreens, Shell gas stations, newsstands, and vending machines.

It's **OK** to fall in **love**
with your washer **AND** dryer
Really. Perfectly normal.

The LG Tromm Front Panel Washer and Dryer.
Introducing the newest laundry combination from LG. Incredible style and performance to match. Features convenient upfront electronic control panels and a Sensor Dry system for intelligent fabric care and energy efficiency. Easy to use side by side, or stack them to save space. Either way, you'll not only like it, you'll love it. Don't be surprised if you look for excuses to do the wash! Great design. Great technology. Great for the way you live. Discover the full line of LG premium home appliances at www.LGusa.com, or call 1-800-243-0000.

Life's Good
LG

© 2004 LG Electronics, Inc. LG Design and Life's Good are trademarks of LG Electronics, Inc.

© COURTESY OF LG APPLIANCES

SHOPPING PRODUCTS

A **shopping product** is usually more expensive than a convenience product and is found in fewer stores. Consumers usually buy a shopping product only after comparing several brands or stores on style, practicality, price, and lifestyle compatibility. They are willing to invest some effort into this process to get the desired benefits.

There are two types of shopping products: homogeneous and heterogeneous. Consumers perceive *homogeneous* shopping products as basically similar—for example, washers, dryers, refrigerators, and televisions. With homogeneous shopping products, consumers typically look for the lowest-priced brand that has the desired features. For example, they might compare Kenmore, Whirlpool, and General Electric refrigerators.

In contrast, consumers perceive *heterogeneous* shopping products as essentially different—for example, furniture, clothing, housing, and universities. Consumers often have trouble comparing heterogeneous shopping products because

Although major appliances, like washers and dryers, are usually considered homogeneous shopping products, the high-efficiency, front-loaders that boast many more features than standard machines are gaining in popularity. Do you think high-efficiency technology is enough to make washers and dryers heterogeneous shopping products?

Do products stay in their product category as long as they are on the market? Find out by watching the video FAQ on Xtra!

the prices, quality, and features vary so much. The benefit of comparing heterogeneous shopping products is "finding the best product or brand for me"; this decision is often highly individual. For example, it would be difficult to compare a small, private university with a large, public university.

SPECIALTY PRODUCTS

When consumers search extensively for a particular item and are very reluctant to accept substitutes, that item is a **specialty product**. Rolex watches, Rolls Royce automobiles, Bose speakers, Ruth's Chris steakhouse, and highly specialized forms of medical care are generally considered specialty products.

Marketers of specialty products often use selective, status-conscious advertising to maintain their product's exclusive image. Distribution is often limited to one or a very few outlets in a geographic area. Brand names and quality of service are often very important.

UNSOUGHT PRODUCTS

A product unknown to the potential buyer or a known product that the buyer does not actively seek is referred to as an **unsought product**. New products fall into this category until advertising and distribution increase consumer awareness of them.

Some goods are always marketed as unsought items, especially needed products we do not like to think about or care to spend money on. Insurance, burial plots, encyclopedias, and similar items require aggressive personal selling and highly persuasive advertising. Salespeople actively seek leads to potential buyers. Because consumers usually do not seek out this type of product, the company must go directly to them through a salesperson, direct mail, or direct-response advertising.

REVIEW LEARNING OBJECTIVE 2

2 Classify consumer products

---

3 PRODUCT ITEMS, LINES, AND MIXES

Define the terms *product item, product line,* and *product mix*

Rarely does a company sell a single product. More often, it sells a variety of things. A **product item** is a specific version of a product that can be designated as a distinct offering among an organization's products. Gillette's MACH3 razor is an example of a product item (see Exhibit 9.2).

A group of closely related product items is a **product line**. For example, the column in Exhibit 9.2 titled "Blades and Razors" represents one of Gillette's product lines. Different container sizes and shapes also distinguish items in a product line. Diet Coke, for example, is available in cans and various plastic containers. Each size and each container are separate product items.

An organization's **product mix** includes all the products it sells. All Gillette's products—blades and razors, toiletries, writing instruments, and lighters—constitute its product mix. Each product item in the product mix may require a separate marketing strategy. In some cases, however, product lines and even entire product mixes share some marketing strategy components. Nike promoted all of its product items and lines with the theme "Just Do It."

Organizations derive several benefits from organizing related items into product lines, including the following:

* *Advertising economies:* Product lines provide economies of scale in advertising. Several products can be advertised under the umbrella of the line. Campbell's can talk about its soup being "m-m-good" and promote the entire line.

specialty product
A particular item that consumers search extensively for and are very reluctant to accept substitutes.

unsought product
A product unknown to the potential buyer or a known product that the buyer does not actively seek.

product item
A specific version of a product that can be designated as a distinct offering among an organization's products.

product line
A group of closely related product items.

product mix
All products that an organization sells.

EXHIBIT 9.2

Gillette's Product Lines and Product Mix

Width of the Product Mix			
Blades and Razors	Toiletries	Writing Instruments	Lighters
MACH 3	Series	Paper Mate	Cricket
Sensor	Adorn	Flair	S.T. Dupont
Trac II	Toni		
Atra	Right Guard		
Swivel	Silkience		
Double-Edge	Soft and Dri		
Lady Gillette	Foamy		
Super Speed	Dry Look		
Twin Injector	Dry Idea		
Techmatic	Brush Plus		

(Row label spanning left side: **Depth of the Product Lines**)

Marriott

Does Marriott's use its product lines to organize its Web site? Why not? Compare the sites for the different hotels listed under the About Brands link. Why do you think Marriot chooses to focus overwhelmingly on the Marriot brand on its home page? Of what benefit is that strategy to Marriot?

http://www.marriott.com

Online

- *Package uniformity:* A product line can benefit from package uniformity. All packages in the line may have a common look and still keep their individual identities. Again, Campbell's soup is a good example.
- *Standardized components:* Product lines allow firms to standardize components, thus reducing manufacturing and inventory costs. For example, many of the components Samsonite uses in its folding tables and chairs are also used in its patio furniture. General Motors uses the same parts on many automobile makes and models.
- *Efficient sales and distribution:* A product line enables sales personnel for companies like Procter & Gamble to provide a full range of choices to customers. Distributors and retailers are often more inclined to stock the company's products if it offers a full line. Transportation and warehousing costs are likely to be lower for a product line than for a collection of individual items.
- *Equivalent quality:* Purchasers usually expect and believe that all products in a line are about equal in quality. Consumers expect that all Campbell's soups and all Mary Kay cosmetics will be of similar quality.

Product mix width (or breadth) refers to the number of product lines an organization offers. In Exhibit 9.2, for example, the width of Gillette's product mix is four product lines. **Product line depth** is the number of product items in a product line. As shown in Exhibit 9.2, the blades and razors product line consists of ten product items; the toiletries product line also includes ten product items.

Firms increase the *width* of their product mix to diversify risk. To generate sales and boost profits, firms spread risk across many product lines rather than depend on only one or two. Firms also widen their product mix to capitalize on established reputations. By introducing new product lines, Levi's Dockers brand capitalized on its image of casual style and comfort. Dockers started as a casual apparel brand for men, but extended into women's apparel with Dockers for Her in 1988. Recently, Dockers moved its comfort proposition from clothing to bedroom and bath products with its Dockers Home line.[2] The Oreo Cookie brand has been extended to include items such as breakfast cereal, ice cream, Jell-O pudding, and cake mix.

Firms increase the *depth* of product lines to attract buyers with different preferences, to increase sales and profits by further segmenting the market, to capitalize on economies of scale in production and marketing, and to even out seasonal sales patterns. Marriott International has 14 different lodging brands that are divided into three groups. The full-service group includes flagship Marriott, upscale Renaissance Hotels and Resorts, and Marriott Conference Centers. The select service group includes Courtyard, Spring Hill Suites, and Fairfield Inn. The extended stay group includes Residence Inn and ExecuStay. As another example, Oreo Cookies now come in a variety of flavors, including Double Delight Mint Creme, Chocolate Creme, Uh-Oh Oreos (vanilla cookie, chocolate filling), and Double Delight Peanut Butter and Chocolate.

FAQs

Do you need another explanation of product mix, product line depth, and product mix width? Then watch the video FAQ on Xtra!

product mix width
The number of product lines an organization offers.

product line depth
The number of product items in a product line.

EVERY KID GOES THROUGH STAGES.
FORTUNATELY, SO DO OUR NEW BRUSHES.

INTRODUCING NEW
Oral-B
Stages

COURTESY THE GILLETTE COMPANY

Oral-B's Stages toothbrushes represent a functional modification to adult toothbrushes. Numerous colors and designs of a single stage toothbrush would be a style modification.

FAQs

Is planned obsolescence always due to style changes? Find out by watching the video FAQ on Xtra!

product modification
Changing one or more of a product's characteristics.

planned obsolescence
The practice of modifying products so those that have already been sold become obsolete before they actually need replacement.

ADJUSTMENTS TO PRODUCT ITEMS, LINES, AND MIXES

Over time, firms change product items, lines, and mixes to take advantage of new technical or product developments or to respond to changes in the environment. They may adjust by modifying products, repositioning products, or extending or contracting product lines.

Product Modification

Marketing managers must decide if and when to modify existing products. **Product modification** changes one or more of a product's characteristics:

- *Quality modification:* change in a product's dependability or durability. Reducing a product's quality may let the manufacturer lower the price and appeal to target markets unable to afford the original product. Conversely, increasing quality can help the firm compete with rival firms. Increasing quality can also result in increased brand loyalty, greater ability to raise prices, or new opportunities for market segmentation. Inexpensive ink-jet printers have improved in quality to the point that they produce photo-quality images. These printers are now competing with camera film. To appeal to a more upscale market, Robert Mondavi Winery introduced a high-end wine called Twin Oaks to prestige restaurants and hotels. This wine is positioned as a higher quality wine than the one Mondavi sells in supermarkets.
- *Functional modification:* change in a product's versatility, effectiveness, convenience, or safety. Oral-B introduced Stages toothbrushes, a line of toothbrushes for children. For example, Stage 2, designed for toddlers, has an easy-to-grip handle and a narrow brush that makes it easier to reach all teeth.[3] Lea & Perrins offers its steak sauce in a value-priced squeeze bottle with a "no mess, stay clean" cap.
- *Style modification:* aesthetic product change, rather than a quality or functional change. Pontiac modified the style of its Aztec car based on focus-group results after initial sales were weak. The original two-tone color scheme with gray trim was replaced by a monochromatic color scheme, and the small wheels were replaced with 16-inch cast aluminum wheels. A spoiler was also added to soften some of the car's sharp lines.[4] Clothing and auto manufacturers also commonly use style modifications to motivate customers to replace products before they are worn out. **Planned obsolescence** is a term commonly used to describe the practice of modifying products so that those that have already been sold become obsolete before they actually need replacement. Some argue that planned obsolescence is wasteful; some claim it is unethical. Marketers respond that consumers favor style modifications because they like changes in the appearance of goods like clothing and cars. Marketers also contend that consumers, not manufacturers and marketers, decide when styles are obsolete.

Repositioning

Repositioning, as Chapter 7 explained, involves changing consumers' perceptions of a brand. For example, Tommy Hilfiger started out offering classic, preppy clothing. During the 1990s, Hilfiger was repositioned as a hipper, more urban brand to appeal to a younger audience. In the early 2000s, to combat decreasing sales and regain its core market, Hilfiger once again repositioned itself and returned to its clean-cut image.[5]

Changing demographics, declining sales, or changes in the social environment often motivate firms to reposition established brands. The clothing retailer Banana Republic started out selling safari-style clothing, but the concept soon became outdated. Gap acquired the chain and repositioned it as a more upscale retailer offering business casual clothing.[6] Lava soap had a reputation as a harsh, men's soap, but was repositioned as a heavy-duty hand cleaner for both men and women.[7]

Unilever
Can Unilever delete anything from its product lines? Visit the company's product category pages on its "Brands" Web page to see the number of existing products and new products planned. Write a proposal for contracting one of Unilever's product lines.

http://www.unilever.com

Online

Product Line Extensions

A **product line extension** occurs when a company's management decides to add products to an existing product line in order to compete more broadly in the industry. Minute Maid has added two calcium-fortified juices—Premium Home-Squeezed Style orange juice and Ruby Red Grapefruit Blend—to attract health-conscious baby boomers.[8] Jolly Rancher launched Fruit Chews to compete in the chewy candy product category.[9] Procter & Gamble has developed numerous extensions of its Tide laundry detergent, including Tide with Bleach, Tide Free (which has no fragrance), Tide WearCare (which claims to keep fabrics brighter longer), Tide HE (for front-loading washers), and Tide Kick (whose package has a nozzle to rub detergent directly into fabrics).[10]

© AP/WIDE WORLD PHOTOS

Companies extend their brands to compete more broadly in a market. Starkist first added tuna packed in water to its line, then albacore-only canned tuna, vacuum packed tuna, single-serve packages of tuna, and now flavored tuna.

Product Line Contraction

Does the world really need 31 varieties of Head and Shoulders shampoo? Or 52 versions of Crest? Black & Decker has decided the answer is no. The company has deleted a number of household products—Dustbusters, SnakeLight flashlights, and toaster ovens—and is concentrating on power tools. Symptoms of product line overextension include the following:

- Some products in the line do not contribute to profits because of low sales or cannibalize sales of other items in the line.
- Manufacturing or marketing resources are disproportionately allocated to slow-moving products.
- Some items in the line are obsolete because of new product entries in the line or new products offered by competitors.

Three major benefits are likely when a firm contracts overextended product lines. First, resources become concentrated on the most important products. Second, managers no longer waste resources trying to improve the sales and profits of poorly performing products. Third, new product items have a greater chance of being successful because more financial and human resources are available to manage them.

product line extension
Adding additional products to an existing product line in order to compete more broadly in the industry.

3 | Define the terms *product item, product line,* and *product mix*

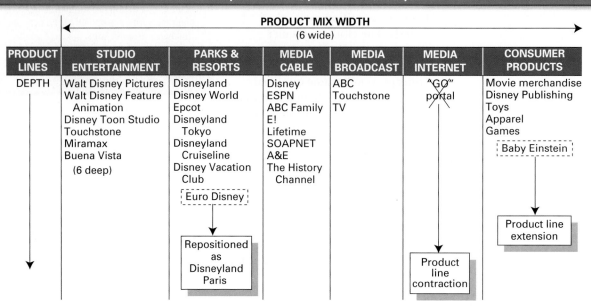

PRODUCT LINES	STUDIO ENTERTAINMENT	PARKS & RESORTS	MEDIA CABLE	MEDIA BROADCAST	MEDIA INTERNET	CONSUMER PRODUCTS

DEPTH	Walt Disney Pictures
	Walt Disney Feature
	  Animation
	Disney Toon Studio
	Touchstone
	Miramax
	Buena Vista
	  (6 deep)
		Disneyland
		Disney World
		Epcot
		Disneyland
		  Tokyo
		Disneyland
		  Cruiseline
		Disney Vacation
		  Club
			Disney
			ESPN
			ABC Family
			E!
			Lifetime
			SOAPNET
			A&E
			The History
			  Channel
				ABC
				Touchstone
				TV
					"GO"
					portal
						Movie merchandise
						Disney Publishing
						Toys
						Apparel
						Games

PRODUCT MIX WIDTH (6 wide)

- Euro Disney → Repositioned as Disneyland Paris
- Media Internet "GO" portal → Product line contraction
- Baby Einstein → Product line extension

---

4 BRANDING

Describe marketing uses of branding

The success of any business or consumer product depends in part on the target market's ability to distinguish one product from another. Branding is the main tool marketers use to distinguish their products from the competition's.

A **brand** is a name, term, symbol, design, or combination thereof that identifies a seller's products and differentiates them from competitors' products. A **brand name** is that part of a brand that can be spoken, including letters (GM, YMCA), words (Chevrolet), and numbers (WD-40, 7-Eleven). The elements of a brand that cannot be spoken are called the **brand mark**—for example, the well-known Mercedes-Benz and Delta Airlines symbols.

BENEFITS OF BRANDING

Branding has three main purposes: product identification, repeat sales, and new-product sales. The most important purpose is *product identification*. Branding allows marketers to distinguish their products from all others. Many brand names are familiar to consumers and indicate quality.

 The term **brand equity** refers to the value of company and brand names. A brand that has high awareness, perceived quality, and brand loyalty among customers has high brand equity. Starbucks, Volvo, and Dell are companies with high brand equity. A brand with strong brand equity is a valuable asset.

The term **global brand** has been used to refer to brands where at least 20 percent of the product is sold outside the home country or region. "A strong global brand acts as an ambassador when companies enter new markets or offer new products." It also helps guide corporate strategy decisions by indicating which new ideas fit within the brand concept and which do not.[11] Yum Brands, which owns Pizza Hut, KFC, and Taco Bell, is a good example of a company that has developed strong global brands. Yum believes that it has to adapt its restaurants to local tastes and different cultural and political climates. In Japan, for instance,

brand
A name, term, symbol, design, or combination thereof that identifies a seller's products and differentiates them from competitors' products.

brand name
That part of a brand that can be spoken, including letters, words, and numbers.

brand mark
The elements of a brand that cannot be spoken.

brand equity
The value of company and brand names.

global brand
A brand where at least 20 percent of the product is sold outside its home country or region.

KFC sells tempura crispy strips. In northern England, KFC focuses on gravy and potatoes, and in Thailand it offers rice with soy or sweet chili sauce. In China, the company recruits employees who balance an understanding of the Chinese mind-set with Western business training.[12] The "Global Perspectives" box focuses on companies that have been successful in global markets by marketing locally. Exhibit 9.3 lists the world's ten most valuable brands.

The best generator of *repeat sales* is satisfied customers. Branding helps consumers identify products they wish to buy again and avoid those they do not. **Brand loyalty**, a consistent preference for one brand over all others, is quite high in some product categories. Over half the users in product categories such as cigarettes, mayonnaise, toothpaste, coffee, headache remedies, photographic film, bath soap, and ketchup are loyal to one brand. Many students come to college and are not "price" buyers. Instead, they purchase the same brands they used at home. Brand identity is essential to developing brand loyalty.

brand loyalty
A consistent preference for one brand over all others.

Hormel
How does Hormel use its Web site to promote its store brands? Is the site designed more to promote the company or its brands? Check out the Spam Web site. How do you think Hormel is able to successfully sustain this brand that is often the punch line to a joke?
http://www.hormel.com
http://www.spam.com

Online

GLOBAL PERSPECTIVES

> THINK GLOBALLY, MARKET LOCALLY

Increasingly, consumer-products companies are finding their brands under attack because of their home countries' foreign policies. When American consumers and restaurateurs boycotted French wines after France refused to support the U.S. military campaign in Iraq, it was serious business for winemakers in Bordeaux and Burgundy. What can firms do? In essence: localize. Firms can build a strong national and regional presence by producing, distributing, packaging, branding, and communicating on a local basis. Many companies that are successful in international markets are now using this strategy.

In Saudi Arabia, where many American products currently are threatened by boycotts, Procter & Gamble changed the packaging for Tide, its leading detergent brand. Now the words "Made in Saudi Arabia" appear prominently, and the brand name itself is written in Arabic on one side of the package. Journalists and consumers have also been invited to visit the plant. Even though Tide has been produced locally for decades by a Saudi company, few Saudis knew it. Algida (Unilever) customizes its brands in each market and disassociates them from its corporate name. In Europe, General Motors uses its Opel brand, which has strong German connotations, instead of its global brand.

Multinationals that get involved with local communities effectively reduce risk. Consumers are more likely to overlook foreign ownership if a company plays a positive role in local development. In China, for example, Seattle-based Starbucks positions its coffee

shops as members of the local neighborhood. It has developed affordable snacks for local celebrations, like the annual midautumn Moon Festival. When protests broke out in 1999 in response to a mistaken U.S. bombing of a Chinese embassy in Belgrade, Beijing protesters took a short cut through a Starbucks to the U.S. embassy—and bought coffee en route.

Companies also bring genuine value, especially in developing countries, by transferring technical skills and training employees. In India, for example, PepsiCo's agriscientists have helped contract potato farmers to improve their yields from 9 tons per acre to 20 tons, boosting their incomes and PepsiCo's supply.

Finally, multinationals need to address their local communications directly to the local audience. It would be naive today for any brand to have a single, global advertising campaign. Instead, companies need to understand what is relevant to their target markets and to hire excellent local communicators to get this across.

Marketing locally works. Although French wine sales in the United States were predicted to drop by more than 10 percent in 2003, there was no evidence that American consumers cut their wine consumption of California labels owned by French companies.[13]

Can you think of any recent examples of brands that have suffered because of their home countries' foreign policies? Alternatively, can you think of any examples, besides those mentioned here, of brands that have continued to be successful despite opposition to their home countries' policies?

EXHIBIT 9.3

The World's Ten Most Valuable Brands

Rank	Brand	2003 Brand Value ($ billions)	Country of Ownership
1	Coca-Cola	67	U.S.
2	Microsoft	61	U.S.
3	IBM	54	U.S.
4	GE	44	U.S.
5	Intel	33	U.S.
6	Disney	27	U.S.
7	McDonald's	25	U.S.
8	Nokia	24	Finland
9	Toyota	23	Japan
10	Marlboro	22	U.S.

SOURCE: "The 100 Top Brands," *BusinessWeek*, August 2, 2004, 68–71.

The third main purpose of branding is to *facilitate new-product sales*. Company and brand names like those listed in Exhibit 9.3 are extremely useful when introducing new products.

 The Internet provides firms a new alternative for generating brand awareness, promoting a desired brand image, stimulating new and repeat brand sales, and enhancing brand loyalty and building brand equity. Nearly all packaged-goods firms have a presence online. Tide.com offers a useful feature called Stain Detective, a digital tip sheet on how to remove almost any substance from almost any fabric. Reflect.com lets women mix and match various options to create their own "brands" of makeup, perfume, and other beauty-care products.[14]

BRANDING STRATEGIES

Firms face complex branding decisions. As Exhibit 9.4 illustrates, the first decision is whether to brand at all. Some firms actually use the lack of a brand name as a selling point. These unbranded products are called generic products. Firms that decide to brand their products may choose to follow a policy of using manufacturers' brands, private (distributor) brands, or both. In either case, they must then decide among a policy of individual branding (different brands for different products), family branding (common names for different products), or a combination of individual branding and family branding.

Generic Products versus Branded Products

generic product
A no-frills, no-brand-name, low-cost product that is simply identified by its product category.

A **generic product** is typically a no-frills, no-brand-name, low-cost product that is simply identified by its product category. (Note that a generic product and a brand name that becomes generic, such as cellophane, are not the same thing.) Generic products have captured significant market shares in some product

EXHIBIT 9.4

Major Branding Decisions

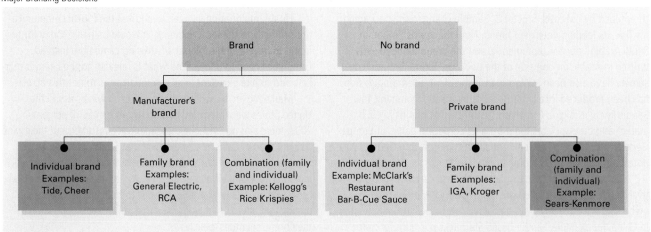

© AP/WIDE WORLD PHOTOS

categories, such as canned fruits, canned vegetables, and paper products. These unbranded products are frequently identified only by black stenciled lettering on white packages.

The main appeal of generics is their low price. Generic grocery products are usually 30 to 40 percent less expensive than manufacturers' brands in the same product category and 20 to 25 percent less expensive than retailer-owned brands.

Pharmaceuticals are another product category where generics have made inroads. When patents on successful pharmaceutical products expire, low-cost generics rapidly appear on the market. For example, when the patent on Merck's popular antiarthritis drug Clinoril expired, sales declined by 50 percent almost immediately.

Part of Target's amazing success as an upscale discount retailer has been its branding of products designed by cutting-edge designers, like Mossimo, pictured here, Isaac Mizrahi, and Michael Graves. Each designer creates a line specially for Target that cannot be found anywhere else. Can these designer lines, found exclusively at Target, be considered private brands if Target does not produce them?

Manufacturers' Brands versus Private Brands

The brand name of a manufacturer—such as Kodak, La-Z-Boy, and Fruit of the Loom—is called a **manufacturer's brand**. Sometimes "national brand" is used as a synonym for "manufacturer's brand." This term is not always accurate, however, because many manufacturers serve only regional markets. Using "manufacturer's brand" more precisely defines the brand's owner.

A **private brand**, also known as a private label or store brand, is a brand name owned by a wholesaler or a retailer. Private brands include Wal-Mart's Ol' Roy dog food, which has surpassed Nestlé's Purina as the world's top-selling dog food, and the George line of apparel, which has knocked Liz Claiborne's clothing out of Wal-Mart. Private brands now account for over 20 percent of sales at all U.S. mass merchandisers, drugstores, and supermarkets. At some stores, the penetration is much higher. At Target, for example, more than 50 percent of the merchandise is exclusive to the store. And across the board, store brands are growing faster than national brands. According to A.C. Nielsen, unit sales of store-brand goods grew 8.6 percent during a recent two-year period in which national brands grew only 1.5 percent. A 2001 Gallup poll found that 45 percent of shoppers were likely to switch to a store brand, up from only 31 percent in 1996.[15]

Retailers love consumers' greater acceptance of private brands. Because overhead is low and there are no marketing costs, private-label products bring 10 percent higher margins, on average, than manufacturers' brands. More than that, a trusted store brand can differentiate a chain from its competitors. For example, many shoppers will drive the extra mile to Costco, a wholesale club, to buy the store's Kirkland brands and will also buy other goods while they are there.[16] Exhibit 9.5 illustrates key issues that wholesalers and retailers should consider in deciding whether to sell manufacturers' brands or private brands. Many firms offer a combination of both. In fact, JCPenney and Sears have turned their low-priced, private-label jeans into some of the most popular brands around, thanks to hip marketing campaigns that feature rock bands, Web sites, and imagery targeted at teens.

Individual Brands versus Family Brands

Many companies use different brand names for different products, a practice referred to as **individual branding**. Companies use individual brands when their products vary greatly in use or performance. For instance, it would not make

manufacturer's brand
The brand name of a manufacturer.

private brand
A brand name owned by a wholesaler or a retailer.

individual branding
Using different brand names for different products.

EXHIBIT 9.5

Comparing Manufacturers' and Private Brands from the Reseller's Perspective

Key Advantages of Carrying Manufacturers' Brands	Key Advantages of Carrying Private Brands
• Heavy advertising to the consumer by manufacturers like Procter & Gamble helps develop strong consumer loyalties.	• A wholesaler or retailer can usually earn higher profits on its own brand. In addition, because the private brand is exclusive, there is less pressure to mark the price down to meet competition.
• Well-known manufacturers' brands, such as Kodak and Fisher-Price, can attract new customers and enhance the dealer's (wholesaler's or retailer's) prestige.	• A manufacturer can decide to drop a brand or a reseller at any time or even to become a direct competitor to its dealers.
• Many manufacturers offer rapid delivery, enabling the dealer to carry less inventory.	• A private brand ties the customer to the wholesaler or retailer. A person who wants a Die-Hard battery must go to Sears.
• If a dealer happens to sell a manufacturer's brand of poor quality, the customer may simply switch brands and remain loyal to the dealer.	• Wholesalers and retailers have no control over the intensity of distribution of manufacturers' brands. Wal-Mart store managers don't have to worry about competing with other sellers of Sam's American Choice products or Ol' Roy dog food. They know that these brands are sold only in Wal-Mart and Sam's Wholesale Club stores.

where's the one place all our brands hang out together?

introducing the **PG.com** network

The new pg.com lets you **do more**, **learn more** and **get more** from P&G and our brands than ever before...

| Discover the surprising number of online resources our brands have to offer. | Try and buy products before they're available in stores. | Share your ideas for improving our products and creating new ones. | and coming soon... Take advantage of new tools to help manage your P&G shareholders account. |

w w w . p g . c o m

Procter & Gamble has many Web sites that market and support the company's individual brands and categories. These consumer-targeted sites, as well as sites for business and corporate partners, come together as a network under PG.com. PG.com is managed as the "one-stop connection to P&G and our brands," making it easy for users to find their favorite product sites and learn more about the corporate brand, P&G.

family brand
Marketing several different products under the same brand name.

cobranding
Placing two or ore brand names on a product or its package.

sense to use the same brand name for a pair of dress socks and a baseball bat. Procter & Gamble targets different segments of the laundry detergent market with Bold, Cheer, Dash, Dreft, Era, Gain, Ivory Snow, Oxydol, Solo, and Tide. Marriott International also targets different market segments with Courtyard by Marriott, Residence Inn, and Fairfield Inn.

In contrast, a company that markets several different products under the same brand name is using a **family brand**. Sony's family brand includes radios, television sets, stereos, and other electronic products. A brand name can only be stretched so far, however. Do you know the differences among Holiday Inn, Holiday Inn Express, Holiday Inn Select, Holiday Inn Sunspree Resort, Holiday Inn Garden Court, and Holiday Inn Hotel & Suites? Neither do most travelers.

Cobranding

Cobranding entails placing two or more brand names on a product or its package. Three common types of cobranding are ingredient branding, cooperative branding, and complementary branding. *Ingredient branding* identifies the brand of a part that makes up the product. Examples of ingredient branding are Intel (a microprocessor) in a personal computer, such as Dell, or a premium leather interior (Coach) in an automobile (Lincoln). *Cooperative branding* occurs when two brands receiving equal treatment (in the context of an advertisement) borrow on each other's brand equity. A promotional contest jointly sponsored by Ramada Inns, American Express, and Continental Airlines is an example of cooperative branding. Guests at Ramada who paid with an American Express card were automatically entered in the contest and were eligible to win more than a hundred getaways for two at any Ramada in the continental United States and round-trip airfare from Continental. Finally, with *complementary branding*, products are advertised or marketed together to suggest usage, such as a spirits brand (Seagram's) and a compatible mixer (7-Up).

Cobranding is a useful strategy when a combination of brand names enhances the prestige or perceived value of a product or when it benefits brand owners and users. Starbucks' deal with United Airlines put Starbucks coffee on United flights worldwide and allowed both companies to achieve important brand objectives.[17]

Cobranding may be used to increase a company's presence in markets where it has little or no market share. For example, Disney is attempting to increase its share of the food and beverage market by developing cobranding deals with Minute Maid for an 18-variety line of Disney Xtreme! Coolers based on Mickey and Friends and with Kellogg for cobranded cereals.[18] Georgia-Pacific's Dixie unit has teamed up with Coca-Cola to make a new line of Coke-themed cups. Dixie's marketing group has succeeded in placing the products in the soft-drink section of supermarkets, which could be important in the fight for shelf space and marketing allies. Coca-Cola also has customers that Dixie wants, such as McDonald's, which will sell Coke fountain drinks in a Dixie collectible cup similar to a glass bottle.[19]

Bose

Many automobile manufacturers tout the fact that their cars include audio systems engineered by Bose. Visit the Bose Web site and search for the list of vehicles that offer Bose stereos as standard or optional equipment. What types of brands are they? How do the relationships benefit Bose? What is the payoff for the auto manufacturers?

http://www.bose.com

Online

European firms have been slower to adopt cobranding than U.S. firms have. One reason is that European customers seem to be more skeptical than U.S. customers about trying new brands. European retailers also typically have less shelf space than their U.S. counterparts and are less willing to give new brands a try.

TRADEMARKS

A **trademark** is the exclusive right to use a brand or part of a brand. Others are prohibited from using the brand without permission. A **service mark** performs the same function for services, such as H&R Block and Weight Watchers. Parts of a brand or other product identification may qualify for trademark protection. Some examples are

- Shapes, such as the Jeep front grille and the Coca-Cola bottle
- Ornamental color or design, such as the decoration on Nike tennis shoes, the black-and-copper color combination of a Duracell battery, Levi's small tag on the left side of the rear pocket of its jeans, or the cutoff black cone on the top of Cross pens
- Catchy phrases, such as Prudential's "Own a piece of the rock," Merrill Lynch's "We're bullish on America," and Budweiser's "This Bud's for you"
- Abbreviations, such as Bud, Coke, or The Met
- Sounds, such as General Electric Broadcasting Company's ship's bell clock sound and the MGM lion's roar.

The Trademark Revision Act of 1988 allows organizations to register trademarks based on a bona fide intention to use them (normally, within six months following the issuance of the trademark) for ten years. To renew the trademark, the company must prove it is using the mark. Rights to a trademark last as long as the mark is used. Normally, if the firm does not use it for two years, the trademark is considered abandoned, and a new user can claim exclusive ownership of the mark.

 In November 1999, legislation went into effect that explicitly applies trademark law to the online world. This law includes financial penalties for those who violate trademarked products or register an otherwise trademarked term as a domain name.[21]

Companies that fail to protect their trademarks face the possibility that their product names will become generic. A **generic product name** identifies a product

trademark
The exclusive right to use a brand or part of a brand.

service mark
A trademark for a service.

generic product name
Identifies a product by class or type and cannot be trademarked.

by class or type and cannot be trademarked. Former brand names that were not sufficiently protected by their owners and were subsequently declared to be generic product names by U.S. courts include aspirin, cellophane, linoleum, thermos, kerosene, monopoly, cola, and shredded wheat.

Companies like Rolls Royce, Cross, Xerox, Levi Strauss, Frigidaire, and McDonald's aggressively enforce their trademarks. Rolls Royce, Coca-Cola, and Xerox even run newspaper and magazine ads stating that their names are trademarks and should not be used as descriptive or generic terms. Some ads threaten lawsuits against competitors that violate trademarks.

Despite severe penalties for trademark violations, trademark infringement lawsuits are not uncommon. One of the major battles is over brand names that closely resemble another brand name. Donna Karan filed a lawsuit against Donnkenny Inc., whose Nasdaq trading symbol—DNKY—was too close to Karan's DKNY trademark.

Companies must also contend with fake or unauthorized brands, such as fake Levi's jeans, Microsoft software, Rolex watches, Reebok and Nike footwear, and Louis Vuitton handbags. Knockoffs of Burberry's trademarked tan, black, white, and red plaid are easy to find in cheap shops all over the world, and loose imitations are found in some reputable department stores as well. One Web site sells a line of plaid bags, hats, and shoes that it says are "inspired by Burberry." Burberry says it spends a couple million pounds a year running ads in trade publications and sending letters to trade groups, textile manufacturers, and retailers reminding them about its trademark rights. It also works with customs officials and local law enforcement to seize fakes, sues infringers, and scans the Internet to pick up online chatter about counterfeits.[22]

 In Europe, you can sue counterfeiters only if your brand, logo, or trademark is formally registered. Until recently, formal registration was required in each country in which a company sought protection. A company can now register its trademark in all European Union (EU) member countries with one application.

REVIEW LEARNING OBJECTIVE 4

4 | **Describe marketing uses of branding**

Brand name: MGM

Brand mark:

TRADE MARK

BRANDING

Benefits	Strategies
Brand equity (from being able to identify product)	
Brand loyalty (from repeat sales)	Generic Brand Trademark → Manufacturer → Individual / Family / Combination; Private
Brand recognition (to generate new product sales)	

5 PACKAGING

Describe marketing uses of packaging and labeling

Packages have always served a practical function—that is, they hold contents together and protect goods as they move through the distribution channel. Today, however, packaging is also a container for promoting the product and making it easier and safer to use.

PACKAGING FUNCTIONS

The three most important functions of packaging are to contain and protect products, promote products, and facilitate the storage, use, and convenience of products. A fourth function of packaging that is becoming increasingly important is to facilitate recycling and reduce environmental damage.

Containing and Protecting Products

The most obvious function of packaging is to contain products that are liquid, granular, or otherwise divisible. Packaging also enables manufacturers, wholesalers, and retailers to market products in specific quantities, such as ounces.

Physical protection is another obvious function of packaging. Most products are handled several times between the time they are manufactured, harvested, or otherwise produced and the time they are consumed or used. Many products are shipped, stored, and in-

spected several times between production and consumption. Some, like milk, need to be refrigerated. Others, like beer, are sensitive to light. Still others, like medicines and bandages, need to be kept sterile. Packages protect products from breakage, evaporation, spillage, spoilage, light, heat, cold, infestation, and many other conditions.

Promoting Products

Packaging does more than identify the brand, list the ingredients, specify features, and give directions. A package differentiates a product from competing products and may associate a new product with a family of other products from the same manufacturer. Welch's repackaged its line of grape juice–based jams, jellies, and juices to unify the line and get more impact on the shelf.

Packages use designs, colors, shapes, and materials to try to influence consumers' perceptions and buying behavior. For example, marketing research shows that health-conscious consumers are likely to think that any food is probably good for them as long as it comes in green packaging. Two top brands of low-fat foods—SnackWell's and Healthy Choice—use green packaging. Sunsweet Growers, appealing to baby boomers' interest in health foods, used the theme "Be good to yourself" on new packages for its line of prune products.

Packaging has a measurable effect on sales. Quaker Oats revised the package for Rice-a-Roni without making any other changes in marketing strategy and experienced a 44 percent increase in sales in one year.

Facilitating Storage, Use, and Convenience

Wholesalers and retailers prefer packages that are easy to ship, store, and stock on shelves. They also like packages that protect products, prevent spoilage or breakage, and extend the product's shelf life.

Consumers' requirements for storage, use, and convenience cover many dimensions. Consumers are constantly seeking items that are easy to handle, open, and reclose, although some consumers want packages that are tamperproof or childproof. Consumers also want reusable and disposable packages. Surveys conducted by *Sales & Marketing Management* magazine revealed that consumers dislike—and avoid buying—leaky ice cream boxes, overly heavy or fat vinegar bottles, immovable pry-up lids on glass bottles, key-opener sardine cans, and hard-to-pour cereal boxes. Such packaging innovations as zipper tear strips, hinged lids, tab slots, screw-on tops, and pour spouts were introduced to solve these and other problems. H.J. Heinz developed a new container for ketchup designed to fit the hands of children and encourage

One way marketers design packaging is to facilitate use of the product. Recent innovations in this area include Hungry Jack's microwaveable syrup bottle, Pringles' lunch buddies single-serving containers, and now lightweight, easy-to-carry, plastic paint cans with a pourable spout by Sherwin Williams.

Food and Drug Administration
Just what does the label on your snack foods have to say? What about your makeup? Go to the Food and Drug Administration's Web site to read the exact requirements for labeling various products. Pick a product and report back to the class.

http://www.fda.gov

Online

extra squeezing, which facilitates use for this target market.[23] Another package design that was developed for kids—the tube, exemplified by GoGurt yogurt—has decreased in popularity. Retailers say consumers find tubes inconvenient, messy, and even dangerous as they often need to be opened with scissors.[24]

Some firms use packaging to segment markets. For example, a C&H sugar carton with an easy-to-pour, reclosable top is targeted to consumers who don't do a lot of baking and are willing to pay at least 20 cents more for the package. Different-size packages appeal to heavy, moderate, and light users. Salt is sold in package sizes ranging from single serving to picnic size to giant economy size. Campbell's soup is packaged in single-serving cans aimed at the elderly and singles market segments. Beer and soft drinks are similarly marketed in various package sizes and types. Packaging convenience can increase a product's utility and, therefore, its market share and profits. To appeal to women, Dutch Boy designed a square plastic paint container with a side handle and a spout to replace the traditional wire-handled round metal paint can. Women make up a large part of the interior paint customer base, thanks to popular do-it-yourself television programs, such as *Decorating Cents* and *Trading Spaces*.[25]

 The Internet will soon give consumers more packaging options. Indeed, the Internet may significantly change the purpose and appearance of packaging. Packaging for products sold on the Internet will be more under the customer's control and will be customized by consumers to fit their

ETHICS IN MARKETING

 IS FAT THE NEXT TOBACCO?

Although some claim that junk food is not addictive, rates of overweight among small children—to whom junk-food companies aggressively market their products—have doubled since 1980, while rates among adolescents have tripled. In 1999, physicians began reporting an alarming rise of obesity-linked type 2 diabetes in children. Once an obese youngster develops diabetes, he or she will never get rid of it.

New York City attorney Sam Hirsch filed a class-action lawsuit against McDonald's on behalf of obese and overweight children. He alleged that the fast-food chain "negligently, recklessly, carelessly, and/or intentionally" markets to children food products that are "high in fat, salt, sugar, and cholesterol" while failing to warn of those ingredients' links to "obesity, diabetes, coronary heart disease, high blood pressure, strokes, elevated cholesterol intake, related cancers" and other conditions. McDonald's fought the lawsuit, arguing that it has long made nutritional information available to consumers upon request.

Though many people recoil from the idea of obesity suits—eating habits are a matter of personal responsibility, they protest—the tobacco precedents show that such qualms can be overcome. Most people know that eating a Big Mac isn't the same as eating a spinach salad, but most people knew that smoking was bad for them, too. Diet is only one of many risk factors that contribute to obesity, but smoking is also just one risk factor for diseases for which the tobacco companies were forced to fork

over reimbursement to Medicaid. The tobacco companies eventually agreed to pay $246 billion to the states, and juries are now ordering them to pay individual smokers large sums as well.

By the U.S. Surgeon General's estimate, public health costs attributable to overweight and obesity now come to about $117 billion a year—fast approaching the $140 billion stemming from smoking. Suing Big Food offers incentives to contingency-fee lawyers that rival those of Big Tobacco, and the implications are pretty easy to foresee. While the food industry is unlikely to face anything like the penalties that hit tobacco, companies will face consumer-protection suits that might cost them many tens of millions of dollars and force them to significantly change their marketing practices.

For the past 50 years, public health officials have encouraged the American people to eat less. But food companies advertise that their products can be "part of a balanced and nutritional diet," even though they know that their products typically are not consumed that way. Any food can theoretically be part of a balanced diet if you keep the portions tiny enough and eat lots of fruits, vegetables, and whole grains. Advertising claims that are literally true, but misleading when viewed in a real-world context, can violate state consumer-protection laws.[27]

Debate the issue of whether food companies should be held responsible for the growing rate of childhood obesity.

needs. Some designers are already offering to personalize, for a fee, packages such as wine bottle labels.[26]

Facilitating Recycling and Reducing Environmental Damage

One of the most important packaging issues today is compatibility with the environment. Some firms use their packaging to target environmentally concerned market segments. Brocato International markets shampoo and hair conditioner in bottles that are biodegradable in landfills. Procter & Gamble markets Sure Pro and Old Spice in "eco-friendly" pump-spray packages that do not rely on aerosol propellants. Other firms that have introduced pump sprays include S.C. Johnson (Pledge furniture polish) and Reckitt & Coleman Household Products (Woolite rug cleaner).

LABELING

An integral part of any package is its label. Labeling generally takes one of two forms: persuasive or informational. **Persuasive labeling** focuses on a promotional theme or logo, and consumer information is secondary. Price Pfister developed a new, persuasive label—featuring a picture of a faucet, the brand name, and the logo—with the goal of strengthening brand identity and becoming known as a brand instead of as a manufacturer. Note that the standard promotional claims— such as "new," "improved," and "super"—are no longer very persuasive. Consumers have been saturated with "newness" and thus discount these claims.

Informational labeling, in contrast, is designed to help consumers make proper product selections and lower their cognitive dissonance after the purchase. Sears attaches a "label of confidence" to all its floor coverings. This label gives such product information as durability, color, features, cleanability, care instructions, and construction standards. Most major furniture manufacturers affix labels to their wares that explain the products' construction features, such as type of frame, number of coils, and fabric characteristics. The Nutritional Labeling and Education Act of 1990 mandated detailed nutritional information on most food packages and standards for health claims on food packaging. An important outcome of this legislation has been guidelines from the Food and Drug Administration for using terms like *low fat, light, reduced cholesterol, low sodium, low calorie,* and *fresh.* The "Ethics in Marketing" box describes ethical issues related to food labeling.

UNIVERSAL PRODUCT CODES

The **universal product codes** (**UPCs**) that appear on most items in supermarkets and other high-volume outlets were first introduced in 1974. Because the numerical codes appear as a series of thick and thin vertical lines, they are often called *bar codes.* The lines are read by computerized optical scanners that match codes with brand names, package sizes, and prices. They also print information on cash register tapes and help retailers rapidly and accurately prepare records of customer purchases, control inventories, and track sales. The UPC system and scanners are also used in single-source research (see Chapter 8).

persuasive labeling
A type of package labeling that focuses on a promotional theme or logo and consumer information is secondary.

informational labeling
A type of package labeling designed to help consumers make proper product selections and lower their cognitive dissonance after the purchase.

universal product codes (UPCs)
A series of thick and thin vertical lines (bar codes), readable by computerized optical scanners, that represent numbers used to track products.

REVIEW LEARNING OBJECTIVE 5

5 | Describe marketing uses of packaging and labeling

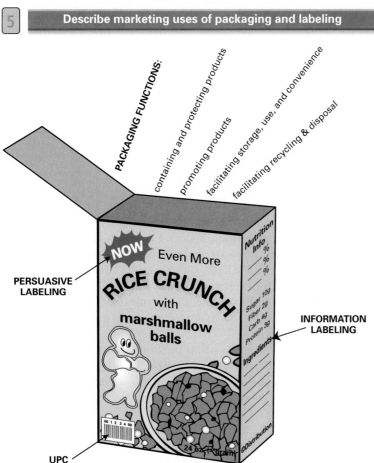

PACKAGING FUNCTIONS:
containing and protecting products
promoting products
facilitating storage, use, and convenience
facilitating recycling & disposal

PERSUASIVE LABELING

NOW Even More
RICE CRUNCH
with marshmallow balls

Nutrition Info
%
%
%
Sugar 10g
Fiber 2g
Carb 4g
Protein 3g
Ingredients

INFORMATION LABELING

UPC

24 oz (1 gram)
©Distribution

Discuss global issues in branding and packaging

International marketers must address several concerns regarding branding and packaging.

BRANDING

 When planning to enter a foreign market with an existing product, a firm has three options for handling the brand name:

- *One brand name everywhere:* This strategy is useful when the company markets mainly one product and the brand name does not have negative connotations in any local market. The Coca-Cola Company uses a one-brand-name strategy in 195 countries around the world. The advantages of a one-brand-name strategy are greater identification of the product from market to market and ease of coordinating promotion from market to market.

- *Adaptations and modifications:* A one-brand-name strategy is not possible when the name cannot be pronounced in the local language, when the brand name is owned by someone else, or when the brand name has a negative or vulgar connotation in the local language. The Iranian detergent "Barf," for example, might encounter some problems in the U.S. market.

- *Different brand names in different markets:* Local brand names are often used when translation or pronunciation problems occur, when the marketer wants the brand to appear to be a local brand, or when regulations require localization. Gillette's Silkience hair conditioner is called Soyance in France and Sientel in Italy. The adaptations were deemed to be more appealing in the local markets. Coca-Cola's Sprite brand had to be renamed Kin in Korea to satisfy a government prohibition on the unnecessary use of foreign words. Snuggle fabric softener is called FaFa in Japan, Cajoline in France, and other cuddly names elsewhere in the world.

Coca-Cola uses a one-brand-name strategy in 195 countries around the world. Its product and positive image are recognizable almost everywhere.

PACKAGING

 Three aspects of packaging that are especially important in international marketing are labeling, aesthetics, and climate considerations. The major *labeling* concern is properly translating ingredient, promotional, and instructional information on labels. In Eastern Europe, packages of Ariel detergent are printed in 14 languages, from Latvian to Lithuanian. Care must also be employed in meeting all local labeling requirements. Several years ago, an Italian judge ordered that all bottles of Coca-Cola be removed from retail shelves because the ingredients were not properly labeled. Labeling is also harder in countries like Belgium and Finland, which require it to be bilingual.

Package *aesthetics* may also require some attention. The key is to stay attuned to cultural traits in host countries. For example, colors may have different connotations. Red is associated with witchcraft in some countries, green may be a sign of danger, and white may be symbolic of death. Aesthetics also influence package size. Soft drinks are not sold in six-packs in countries that lack refrigeration. In some countries, products like detergent may be bought only in small quantities because of a lack of storage space. Other products, like cigarettes, may be bought in small quantities, and even single units, because of the low purchasing power of buyers.

On the other hand, simple visual elements of the brand, such as a symbol or logo, can be a standardizing element across products and countries. For example, when Scott Paper wanted to establish a global brand identity for its product line, it used a single brand mark for all product lines that had the flexibility to accommodate such variables as country-specific product names.

Extreme *climates* and long-distance shipping necessitate sturdier and more durable packages for goods sold overseas. Spillage, spoilage, and breakage are all more important concerns when products are shipped long distances or frequently handled during shipping and storage. Packages may also have to ensure a longer product life if the time between production and consumption lengthens significantly.

REVIEW LEARNING OBJECTIVE 6

6 Discuss global issues in branding and packaging

Branding choices:	Packaging considerations:
1 name	Labeling
Modify or adapt 1 name	Aesthetics
Different names in different markets	Climate

7 PRODUCT WARRANTIES

Describe how and why product warranties are important marketing tools

warranty
A confirmation of the quality or performance of a good or service.

express warranty
A written guarantee.

implied warranty
An unwritten guarantee that the good or service is fit for the purpose for which it was sold.

Just as a package is designed to protect the product, a **warranty** protects the buyer and gives essential information about the product. A warranty confirms the quality or performance of a good or service. An **express warranty** is a written guarantee. Express warranties range from simple statements—such as "100 percent cotton" (a guarantee of quality) and "complete satisfaction guaranteed" (a statement of performance)—to extensive documents written in technical language. In contrast, an **implied warranty** is an unwritten guarantee that the good or service is fit for the purpose for which it was sold. All sales have an implied warranty under the Uniform Commercial Code.

Congress passed the Magnuson-Moss Warranty–Federal Trade Commission Improvement Act in 1975 to help consumers understand warranties and get action from manufacturers and dealers. A manufacturer that promises a full warranty must meet certain minimum standards, including repair "within a reasonable time and without charge" of any defects and replacement of the merchandise or a full refund if the product does not work "after a reasonable number of attempts" at repair. Any warranty that does not live up to this tough prescription must be "conspicuously" promoted as a limited warranty.

REVIEW LEARNING OBJECTIVE 7

7 Describe how and why product warranties are important marketing tools

Express warranty = written guarantee

Implied warranty = unwritten guarantee

LOOKING BACK

Look back to the chapter-opening story about 7-Eleven's new private-label Santiago beer. *Brand equity* refers to the value of brand names to the company. A brand that has high awareness, perceived quality, and brand-loyal customers has

high brand equity. *Brand loyalty* is the customer's consistent preference for one brand over competing brands. The advantages and disadvantages of private-label branding were listed in Exhibit 9.5. Santiago's success will depend on whether

it meets the needs and desires of the target market—import buyers looking for a bargain and domestic beer drinkers looking for something new.

USE IT NOW

As a student, you are required to hand in written assignments, such as papers and group projects. Have you ever thought about these class projects as a product that you exchange for a grade? Maybe not, but some of the product concepts discussed in this chapter are as applicable to class projects as they are to products. One of the most applicable product concepts in this context is that of packaging. Think about the four functions of packaging, and how they might apply to class projects. How could you more effectively package your class projects to contain and protect the project? As a tool for promotion, packaging is not only important for identification purposes, but also serves the critical function of differentiating your project from the competition (other students' projects). It is also important to facilitate storage, use, and convenience of the project for your customer—the instructor! What are some things you could do to make your project more convenient for the instructor to read and to grade? Finally, packaging facilitates recycling. How might you facilitate the environmental recycling of your project?

REVIEW AND APPLICATIONS

1 **Define the term *product*.** A product is anything, desired or not, that a person or organization receives in an exchange. The basic goal of purchasing decisions is to receive the tangible and intangible benefits associated with a product. Tangible aspects include packaging, style, color, size, and features. Intangible qualities include service, the retailer's image, the manufacturer's reputation, and the social status associated with a product. An organization's product offering is the crucial element in any marketing mix.

1.1 Form a team of four or five members. Have the team determine what the tangible and intangible benefits are for a computer, a tube of toothpaste, a beauty salon, and a dentist.

2 **Classify consumer products.** Consumer products are classified into four categories: convenience products, shopping products, specialty products, and unsought products. Convenience products are relatively inexpensive and require limited shopping effort. Shopping products are of two types: homogeneous and heterogeneous. Because of the similarity of homogeneous products, they are differentiated mainly by price and features. In contrast, heterogeneous products appeal to consumers because of their distinct characteristics. Specialty products possess unique benefits that are highly desirable to certain customers. Finally, unsought products are either new products or products that require aggressive selling because they are generally avoided or overlooked by consumers.

2.1 Break into groups of four or five. Have the members of the group classify each of the following products into the category (convenience, shopping, specialty, unsought) that they think fits best from their perspective as consumers (i.e., if they were buying the product): Coca-Cola (brand), car stereo, winter coat, pair of shoes, life insurance, blue jeans, fast-food hamburgers, shampoo, canned vegetables, curtains.

3 **Define the terms *product item, product line,* and *product mix*.** A product item is a specific version of a product that can be designated as a distinct offering among an organization's products. A product line is a group of closely related products offered by an organization. An organization's product mix includes all the products it sells. Product mix width refers to the number of product lines an organization offers. Product line depth is the number of product items in a product line. Firms modify existing products by changing their quality, functional characteristics, or style. Product line extension occurs when a firm adds new products to existing product lines.

3.1 A local civic organization has asked you to give a luncheon presentation about planned obsolescence. Rather than pursuing a negative approach by talking about how businesses exploit customers through planned obsolescence, you have decided to talk about the benefits of producing products that do not last forever. Prepare a one-page outline of your presentation.

3.2 Review the "Marketing in Entertainment" box on *Law and Order* television shows. Identify Dick Wolf's product mix, product mix width, and product line depth. Use Exhibit Worksheet 9.2 as a template. How long do you think Dick Wolf can keep extending his *Law and Order* product mix? What will be the effects of overextending the *Law and Order* brand?

4 **Describe marketing uses of branding.** A brand is a name, term, or symbol that identifies and differentiates a firm's products. Established brands encourage customer loyalty and help new products succeed. Branding strategies require decisions about individual, family, manufacturers', and private brands.

4.1 WRITING A local supermarket would like to introduce its own brand of paper goods (i.e., paper towels, facial tissue, etc.) to sell alongside its current inventory. The company has hired you to generate a report outlining the advantages and disadvantages of doing so. Write the report.

5 **Describe marketing uses of packaging and labeling.** Packaging has four functions: containing and protecting products; promoting products; facilitating product storage, use, and convenience; and facilitating recycling and reducing environmental damage. As a tool for promotion, packaging identifies the brand and its features. It also serves the critical function of differentiating a product from competing products and linking it with related products from the same manufacturer. The label is an integral part of the package, with persuasive and informational functions. In essence, the package is the marketer's last chance to influence buyers before they make a purchase decision.

5.1 WRITING Find a product at home that has a distinctive package. Write a paragraph evaluating that package based on the four functions of packaging discussed in the chapter.

6 **Discuss global issues in branding and packaging.** In addition to brand piracy, international marketers must address a variety of concerns regarding branding and packaging, including choosing a brand-name policy, translating labels and meeting host-country labeling requirements, making packages aesthetically compatible with host-country cultures, and offering the sizes of packages preferred in host countries.

6.1 ONLINE List the countries to which Levi Strauss & Company markets through the Web site **http://www.levi.com**. How do the product offerings differ between the U.S. and European selections?

7 **Describe how and why product warranties are important marketing tools.** Product warranties are important tools because they offer consumers protection and help them gauge product quality.

7.1 INFOTRAC COLLEGE EDITION Learn more about how product warranties are handled worldwide. Using InfoTrac (**http://infotrac-college.com**), run a keyword search for "warranty" or "guarantee" and a country of interest. For example, search for "warranty" and "Germany" or "guarantee" and "Mexico." Write a paragraph about what you discover.

7.2 ONLINE Lands' End and L.L. Bean are renowned for their product guarantees. Find and read the exact wording of their guarantees on their Web sites (**http://www. landsend.com** and **http://www.llbean.com**). Do you think a company could successfully compete against either without offering the same guarantee?

TERMS

EXERCISES

APPLICATION EXERCISE

What is your favorite brand of sandwich cookie? If you're like most Americans, chances are it's Oreo. In fact, Oreos are so popular that many people think Oreo was the original sandwich cookie. But they're wrong. Sunshine first marketed its Hydrox sandwich cookie in 1908. Hydrox thrived until 1912, when Nabisco (now part of Kraft) launched Oreo. With Nabisco's superior distribution and advertising, Hydrox was soon outmatched. By 1998, Hydrox sales totaled $16 million, while Oreo's revenues were at $374 million. Hydrox has been purchased by Keebler (subsequently purchased by Kellogg), whose elves are trying to give the cookie a major facelift. You are part of the Keebler team deciding what to do with the Hydrox brand.[28]

Activities

1. Can you re-create Hydrox through a name change? What kind of brand name could go head-to-head with Oreo? (Most people unfamiliar with Hydrox think it is a cleaning product.) Make a list of three to five possibilities.

2. How can you package your renewed sandwich cookie to make it more attractive on the shelf than Oreo? What about package size? Draft a brief packaging plan for the new Hydrox (or whatever name you chose).

3. Can you modify the original formula to make something new and more competitive? Will a brand extension work here? Why or why not?

4. INFOTRAC COLLEGE EDITION After you complete the entire exercise, use InfoTrac to research the current state of affairs at Oreo and Hydrox. The search terms "Oreo sales" and "Hydrox cookie" will probably generate the most successful search results.

ETHICS EXERCISE

A product that a potential buyer knows about but is not actively seeking is called an unsought product. Is the marketing of unsought products unethical? Discuss your answer in terms of the AMA Code of Ethics, found at **http://www.marketingpower.com**.

CAREER EXERCISE

Careers in brand management are probably most easily pursued at large consumer-products companies like Procter & Gamble, Unilever, Johnson & Johnson, Valvoline, and Drackett. Such companies have more brands and, therefore, more brand teams and more positions for brand-related employment. Think creatively about brands; Marvel Comics regards its characters (such as Superman, Spiderman, and the Hulk) as brands.

Another way to explore a career in brand management is to use "brand" as the keyword at your favorite job search site (like Monster, Vault, or JobTrak/MonsterTrak). If you type only the word "brand," you are more likely to find specific jobs with responsibilities in areas of branding than if you type "brand management."

Activities

1. Visit the Web site of a company or brand you like and locate job opportunities on the brand team. What are the requirements of the job?

2. One way to prepare for working on the product side of marketing is to familiarize yourself with the actual production of products. What is involved in making your favorite product? To find out, take a factory tour. Many U.S. companies, including Kellogg, Hershey, Corning, and perhaps even your local newspaper, open their doors to visitors. Taking a factory tour will help you understand what goes into the manufacture of products and will also help you better understand some of the cross-functional friction between marketing and manufacturing (see Cross-Functional Connections on page 304). If you can't take a real tour, check out a virtual tour, like the one at Coca-Cola's Web site. It's an animated tour of the manufacture and bottling of Coke.

ENTREPRENEURSHIP CASE

FINALLY, A GARAGEBAND THAT REALLY ROCKS

Steve Jobs's keynote address at the 2004 MacWorld conference was roundly criticized for being blasé and void of any exciting new developments. It did, however, have one major and perhaps easily overlooked bright spot—the unveiling of the latest version of Apple's iLife software. The standard suite of iLife products includes the popular and much heralded iTunes music management software, as well as a digital photograph manipulator and organizer called iPhoto, a digital video-editing program named iMovie, and a DVD mastering program called iDVD. The big news at MacWorld was that Apple has added a new program to iLife '04 called GarageBand. Complete with Garage-Band, iLife '04 comes free on all new Apple computers and is available as an upgrade to owners of older systems for a mere $49.

That $49 buys more than a thousand prerecorded Apple loops (or riffs), over 50 virtual instruments, and a virtual recording engineer (which performs over 200 effects). Put simply, GarageBand helps any aspiring musician or hobbyist compose music, and all of those features turn any owner's computer into a pretty substantial home recording studio. Whether the musician needs a drumbeat to back up an external electric guitar for a jam session or a full range of orchestral instruments to provide the background to a keyboard solo, GarageBand makes sure that all selected loops come together on time and in key. The user can even manipulate loops to create an entire song without using any instruments at all. The loops are royalty-free, so new songwriters don't have to worry about paying licensing fees to loop creators if they happen to make the next Hip Hop chart topper.

The software provides a synthesizer-like keyboard that displays on the screen for those who wish to play the plethora of virtual instruments via their computer keyboards, but plugging in an external keyboard allows the aspiring or accomplished musician to seriously expand his or her range. Whether the user selects a Stratocaster guitar, a Steinway piano, a pop organ, or a big-band bass from the library of virtual instruments, the keyboard assumes its identity. Any notes or chords played on it will produce the exact sounds that would emulate from the original version of the virtual instrument. To the delight of guitar players, GarageBand also offers virtual amplifiers that allow them to extract the sounds of the British invasion, arena rock, or cool jazz from their axes.

GarageBand comes with a vast array of effects that composers can apply to their arrangements, too. Loops and any recorded pieces can be faded, reverberated, brightened, echoed, compressed, or tweaked in any number of ways to obtain just the right sound. When masterpieces are finished, GarageBand automatically exports them to iTunes where they are filed in a play list under the composer's name. The program also integrates new compositions with the rest of the iLife programs so that users can match soundtracks to their slide shows and movies. In fact, the programs are so well integrated that Apple is advertising them as "just like Microsoft Office, for the rest of your life."

GarageBand is the latest push by Jobs and Apple to make its computers the hubs of digital home entertainment centers. Unlike iTunes, GarageBand is compatible only with Apple computers. Jobs is betting that with an active musician in one of every two U.S. households, Garage-Band will draw a virtually untapped market of more than a hundred million amateur musicians to Apple computers. Considering that iTunes' music store owns 70 percent of the legal music download market and that the iPod is the best-selling digital music playback device, that bet looks like a sound one.[29]

Questions

1. What type of product is GarageBand?

2. To which of Apple's product lines does GarageBand belong?

3. Is GarageBand a new product or a modification of an existing product? If it is a modification, what type of modification is it? Explain.

WATCH IT

SmallBusinessSchool ▣
the Series on PBS stations and the Web

FEATURE PRESENTATION

Fluker Cricket Farms

To give you insight into Chapter 9, Small Business School introduces you to the Fluker family and their business, Fluker Cricket Farms, located in Baton Rouge, Louisiana. Fluker Cricket Farms started as a small bait shop, but the owners have used clever product expansion to grow their business. Once just a specialist in live bait products for regional fishermen, the Fluker family now has multiple product lines, some of which they export to places as far away as Spain and Japan. They even sell gourmet chocolate-covered crickets. Richard Fluker slowly grew his business by finding a variety of customers who needed live crickets for several reasons—bait, food for captive animals, and research studies. After turning the company over to his children, he watched them take the business from a half-million dollar lifestyle business to a $5 million enterprise. The younger generation accomplished that feat by using cost-effective promotions tactics, exploring new markets, and developing new and expanded product lines.

What to Watch for and Ask Yourself

1. 1. Do the Flukers sell consumer products, business products, or both? Explain.

2. Crickets were the Flukers' original product. Discuss the addition of the company's other products. Was each an extension of the product mix width or product line depth?

3. One employee said, "We guarantee 'em live." Is this an express or implied warranty?

ENCORE PRESENTATION

Josie and the Pussycats

Now that you understand product concepts, watch the clip from *Josie and the Pussycats*, a film based on the cartoon show and comic book. The little-known, teen rock and roll trio, "The Pussycats," gets an unexpected career boost from a record executive who embeds subliminal advertising into the groups' recordings. The fiendish executive plans to use the altered recordings to control the minds, product choices, and spending habits of the nation's teenagers.

The edited scene is a montage of many different product placements throughout the film. As you watch the clip the first time, try to remember all the brands you see. Do some appear more than once? Even if you can't see what's in the shopping bags, can you make assumptions about the types of products they contain (i.e., convenience, shopping, specialty, unsought)? How well do the brands in the clip match what you perceive to be the wants and needs of teenagers?

STILL SHAKY?

If you're having trouble with the concepts in this chapter, consider using some of the following study resources. You can review the videos, or test yourself with materials designed for all kinds of learning styles.

☑ **Xtra! (http://lambxtra.swlearning.com)**

| ☑ Quiz | ☑ Feature Videos | ☑ Encore Videos | ☑ FAQ Videos |
| ☑ Exhibit Worksheets | ☑ Marketing Plan Worksheets | ☐ Content | |

☑ **http://lamb.swlearning.com**

| ☑ Quiz | ☑ PowerPoint slides | ☑ Marketing News | ☑ Review Exercises |
| ☑ Links | ☑ Marketing Plan Contest | ☐ Career Exercises | ☐ Use It Now |

☑ **Study guide**

| ☑ Outline | ☑ Vocab Review | ☑ Test Questions | ☑ Marketing Scenario |

Need More? Here's a tip. Pick up a recent copy of the *Wall Street Journal* at a newsstand or library and read several articles in the Marketplace section (section B). What product issues are facing the companies you read about? Make two lists: one of marketing concepts you read about and one of product topics.

10

Developing and Managing Products

LEARNING OBJECTIVES

1. Explain the importance of developing new products and describe the six categories of new products

2. Explain the steps in the new-product development process

3. Explain why some products succeed and others fail

4. Discuss global issues in new-product development

5. Explain the diffusion process through which new products are adopted

6. Explain the concept of product life cycles

In 1999, Schick-Wilkinson Sword held employee conferences around the world to talk about how women shave. At the time, women's razors were essentially men's razors with a pink handle. But Schick's research showed that women wanted a product designed specifically for shaving legs in the shower or bath.

Back in her room one evening after a session in Greenwich, Connecticut, Glennis Orloff, a Schick razor engineer, saw a small bar of hotel soap on the edge of the tub and wondered if she could figure out a way to lather up and shave at the same time. Orloff took the bar back to the lab, carved a hole in it, and stuck a razor cartridge in the hole. "It worked really well considering how crude it was," she said.

The concept emerged in 2003 as Intuition, with the soap dressed up and dubbed a "skin conditioning solid." In retail outlets tracked by researcher Information Resources, Inc., Intuition racked up $27.5 million in sales in the first six months following its introduction. Since IRI's data don't include giant Wal-Mart Stores or warehouse or club outlets, total sales probably were closer to $40 million.

With Intuition and Quattro, a four-bladed men's razor also introduced in 2003, Schick, a unit of Energizer Holdings, Inc., has jolted industry behemoth Gillette and altered the competitive landscape in razors in ways that some analysts believe may be permanent.

Gillette still dominates the worldwide razor market. It holds a two-thirds share in the U.S. market and an even stronger position in the high-end, high-margin, replaceable-cartridge razors that it pioneered. It has also perfected a "trade-up" strategy that has made the daily act of shaving steadily more costly; the company waits roughly eight years before rolling out a new system, promising revolutionary improvements in shaving performance, albeit at a higher price.

The time gap puts distance between razor launches, which require heavy capital spending—Gillette shelled out $750 million to develop MACH3, a 1998 launch—and allows time to reap the rewards of the steep investment. MACH3, which followed the spring-mounted Sensor by eight years, is the best-selling razor brand of all time.

As it pulls up the price of its new razors, Gillette also lifts prices on older lines. MACH3 Turbo cartridges today can cost more than $2 each. Two-bladed Sensor cartridges of the previous generation, meanwhile, are more than 25 percent more expensive today than at the time of MACH3's launch. The increase gives consumers more reason to move up to the new brand.

But analysts say the new competition from Schick could throw a wrench into that plan. Bill Pecoriello, an analyst at Morgan Stanley, argues that Gillette will need to speed up its product launches and trim its cycle times now that premium-priced Schick razors are appearing on shelves. Gillette, he says, can't risk having older razors on the market for too long. A Gillette spokeswoman, Michele Szynal, says the time between major product launches won't be influenced by Schick. "Our product life cycles have historically been driven by internal forces, not external forces," she says. "And we don't see any changes in that."[1]

What is a product life cycle? How do you think the marketing strategy for a brand such as MACH3 might change over its product life cycle?

1 THE IMPORTANCE OF NEW PRODUCTS

Explain the importance of developing new products and describe the six categories of new products

Why are such a small portion of new products new-to-the-world products? Find out by watching the video FAQ on Xtra!

New products are important to sustain growth, increase revenues and profits, and replace obsolete items. According to Leslie Moeller, vice president at the global management consulting firm Booz, Allen, & Hamilton, "innovation is the engine powering long-term value."[2] His research indicates that companies that focus on product innovation can boost revenues and profitability as much as 1,000 percent . When Procter & Gamble launched Crest Whitestrips in 2001, it created a new market of 10 million users with nearly $300 million in sales.[3] Since its introduction in 2001, the Listerine Powerpak has become the leading seller in the gum/mint product category with retail sales of over $175 million in 2002 alone.[4]

According to ProductScan Online, there were 33,678 new food, beverage, health and beauty, household, and pet products introduced in 2003, up 6 percent from 2002. The popularity of the Atkins and South Beach diets led to a near doubling of no- and low-carbohydrate food products.[5] Many of the other new products focused on saving time and making everyday life simpler and easier.

CATEGORIES OF NEW PRODUCTS

The term **new product** is somewhat confusing because its meaning varies widely. Actually, the term has several "correct" definitions. A product can be new to the world, to the market, to the producer or seller, or to some combination of these. There are six categories of new products:

New product lines are a type of new product that allows a company to enter an established market. With its Ready Brush toilet cleaning system, Lysol is entering the market for cleaning tools (toilet brushes, sponges, mops, etc.), which is dominated by companies like Ocello and Quickie.

new product
A product new to the world, the market, the producer, the seller, or some combination of these.

- *New-to-the-world products* (also called *discontinuous innovations*): These products create an entirely new market. New-to-the-world products represent the smallest category of new products. Ten of the most important new-to-the-world products introduced in the past 100 years are:[6]
  1. Penicillin
  2. Transistor radio
  3. Polio vaccine
  4. Mosaic (the first graphic Web browser)
  5. Microprocessor
  6. Black and white television
  7. Plain paper copier
  8. Alto personal computer (prototype of today's PCs)
  9. Microwave oven
  10. Arpanet network (the groundwork for the Internet)
  New-to-the-world products represent the smallest category of new products.
- *New product lines:* These products, which the firm has not previously offered, allow it to enter an established market. Heinz Frozen Foods introduced a new product line called Boston Market Home Style following a ten-year licensing deal with Boston Chicken, Inc. The new line anchors the premium end of three Heinz lines that include Budget Gourmet (a value product line) and Smart Ones (a nutritionally oriented product line).
- *Additions to existing product lines:* This category includes new products that supplement a firm's established line. Examples of product line additions include Huggies Pull-Ups and Pampers Easy-Ups brands of disposable training pants. This product category accounts for $1 billion in sales in the United States alone.[7]
- *Improvements or revisions of existing products:* The "new and improved" product may be significantly or slightly changed. Schick

Quattro and Intuition razors, discussed at the beginning of this chapter, and new formulations of Tide such as Tide With Bleach, Tide Free (which has no fragrance), Tide Wear Care (that purports to keep fabrics vibrant longer), and Tide With Bleach Powder are examples of improvements or revisions of existing products.[8] Another type of revision is package improvement. The Heinz EZ Squirt Ketchup bottle is short and made from easy-to-squeeze plastic; its needle-shaped nozzle lets small hands use it to decorate food. Tide Kick's package includes a nozzle so that detergent can be rubbed directly into a stain. Most new products fit into the revision or improvement category.

- *Repositioned products:* These are existing products targeted at new markets or market segments. General Motors has done the seemingly impossible, taking a tired, defeated luxury brand two decades past its peak and repositioning it as a direct competitor to European brands such as BMW and Lexus.[9] Cadillac Escalade sport-utility vehicles and CTS sedans are showing up in Miami's trendy South Beach district and similar locations. The average age of Cadillac buyers has dropped from 64 in 1999 to 59 in 2003. The new XLR, SRX, and STS models are all aimed at a younger, "hipper" target market.[10]

- *Lower-priced products:* This category refers to products that provide performance similar to competing brands at a lower price. Hewlett-Packard Laser Jet 3100 is a scanner, copier, printer, and fax machine combined. This new product is priced lower than many conventional color copiers and much lower than the combined price of the four items purchased separately. Wal-Mart is making headway penetrating the low-price fashion market dominated by Target. Despite a nationwide apparel slump, Wal-Mart was able to increase sales by double-digit figures in a recent six-month period.[11]

REVIEW LEARNING OBJECTIVE 1

1 **Explain the importance of developing new products and describe the six categories of new products**

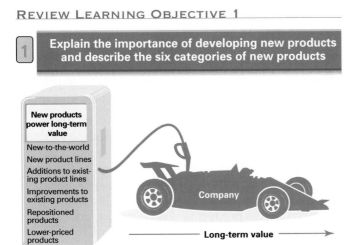

New products power long-term value

New-to-the-world
New product lines
Additions to existing product lines
Improvements to existing products
Repositioned products
Lower-priced products

Company

Long-term value →

2 THE NEW-PRODUCT DEVELOPMENT PROCESS

Explain the steps in the new-product development process

The management consulting firm Booz, Allen, & Hamilton has studied the new-product development process for over 30 years. Analyzing five major studies undertaken during this period, the firm has concluded that the companies most likely to succeed in developing and introducing new products are those that take the following actions:

- Make the long-term commitment needed to support innovation and new-product development
- Use a company-specific approach, driven by corporate objectives and strategies, with a well-defined new-product strategy at its core
- Capitalize on experience to achieve and maintain competitive advantage
- Establish an environment—a management style, organizational structure, and degree of top-management support—conducive to achieving company-specific new-product and corporate objectives.

Most companies follow a formal new-product development process, usually starting with a new-product strategy. Exhibit 10.1 traces the seven-step process, which is discussed in detail in this section. The exhibit is funnel-shaped to highlight the fact that each stage acts as a screen. The purpose is to filter out unworkable ideas.

FAQs

What kind of companies are particularly successful in developing and introducing new products? Find out by watching the video FAQ on Xtra!

NEW-PRODUCT STRATEGY

A **new-product strategy** links the new-product development process with the objectives of the marketing department, the business unit, and the corporation.

new-product strategy
A plan that links the new-product development process with the objectives of the marketing department, the business unit, and the corporation.

EXHIBIT 10.1

New-Product Development Process

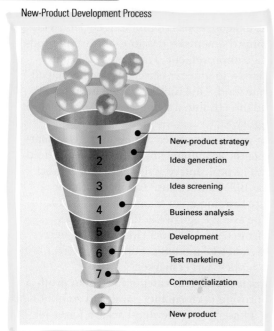

1	New-product strategy
2	Idea generation
3	Idea screening
4	Business analysis
5	Development
6	Test marketing
7	Commercialization
	New product

A new-product strategy must be compatible with these objectives, and in turn, all three objectives must be consistent with one another.

A new-product strategy is part of the organization's overall marketing strategy. It sharpens the focus and provides general guidelines for generating, screening, and evaluating new-product ideas. The new-product strategy specifies the roles that new products must play in the organization's overall plan and describes the characteristics of products the organization wants to offer and the markets it wants to serve.

Many companies are under pressure to bring new products to market more and more quickly. These pressures are especially intense in fast-paced markets, such as those for high-tech and medical products, and in competitive markets for complex products that require large investments and long development times, such as automobiles and airplanes.[12]

IDEA GENERATION

New-product ideas come from many sources, including customers, employees, distributors, competitors, vendors, research and development (R&D), and consultants.

- *Customers:* The marketing concept suggests that customers' wants and needs should be the springboard for developing new products. Thermos, the vacuum bottle manufacturer, provides an interesting example of how companies tap customers for ideas. The company's first step in developing an innovative home barbecue grill was to send ten members of its interdisciplinary new-product team into the field for about a month. Their assignment was to learn all about people's cookout needs and to invent a product to meet them. In various cities including Boston, Los Angeles, and Columbus, Ohio, the team conducted focus groups, visited people's homes, and even videotaped barbecues.

- *Employees:* Marketing personnel—advertising and marketing research employees, as well as salespeople—often create new-product ideas because they analyze and are involved in the marketplace. The very successful introduction of Post-it Notes started with an employee's idea. In 1974, the R&D department of 3M's commercial tape division developed and patented the adhesive component of Post-it Notes. However, it was a year before an employee of the commercial tape division, who sang in a church choir, identified a use for the adhesive. He had been using paper clips and slips of paper to mark places in hymn books. But the paper clips damaged his books, and the slips of paper fell out. The solution, as we now all know, was to apply the adhesive to small pieces of paper and sell them in packages.

- *Distributors:* A well-trained sales force routinely asks distributors about needs that are not being met. Because they are closer to end users, distributors are often more aware of customer needs than are manufacturers. The inspiration for Rubbermaid's litter-free lunch box, named Sidekick, came from a distributor. The distributor suggested that Rubbermaid place some of its plastic containers inside a lunch box and sell the box as an alternative to plastic wrap and paper bags.

- *Competitors:* No firms rely solely on internally generated ideas for new products. A big part of any organization's marketing intelligence system should be monitoring the performance of competitors' products. One purpose of competitive monitoring is to determine which, if any, of the competitors' products should be copied.

There is plenty of information about competitors on the World Wide Web. For example, AltaVista (**http://www.altavista.digital.com**) is a powerful index tool that can be used to locate information about products and companies. Fuld & Company's competitive intelligence guide provides links to a variety of market intelligence sites.

- *Vendors:* 7-Eleven regularly forges partnerships with vendors to create proprietary products such as Candy Gulp (a plastic cup filled with gummies) and Blue Vanilla Laffy Taffre Rope candy developed by Nestlé's Wonka division exclusively for 7-Eleven. In other cases, 7-Eleven's agreements with its vendor partners call for exclusive distribution rights for 30 to 90 days following joint development.[13]

- *Research and development:* R&D is carried out in four distinct ways. Basic research is scientific research aimed at discovering new technologies. Applied research takes these new technologies and tries to find useful applications for them. **Product development** goes one step further by converting applications into marketable products. *Product modification* makes cosmetic or functional changes in existing products. Many new-product breakthroughs come from R&D activities. Ynjö Neuvo, head of R&D at Nokia, offers five tips for successful new-product development:[14]

  - Don't locate your R&D in a single place, especially not near the smothering influence of headquarters. Disperse R&D around the globe.
  - Keep teams small—no larger than 50 if possible—and give individual engineers and their managers a lot of power and authority.
  - Flatten hierarchy and stay as close as possible to your engineers. Hierarchy dissipates energy.
  - Encourage engineers to generate crazy new ideas outside their official work assignments by celebrating secret tinkering and side projects—and get innovations into production with rocket speed.
  - Welcome mistakes. If you're not making them, you're not pushing the envelope hard enough.

  With an annual research budget of $3 billion, Nokia has more than 20,000 employees in R&D. In 2001, Nokia's Mobile Phone division launched 15 new products. In 2002, it doubled that to 30. These numbers are expected to keep rising.[15]

- *Consultants:* Outside consultants are always available to examine a business and recommend product ideas. Examples include the Weston Group; Booz, Allen, & Hamilton; and Management Decisions. Traditionally, consultants determine whether a company has a balanced portfolio of products and, if not, what new-product ideas are needed to offset the imbalance. For instance, an outside consultant conceived Airwick's highly successful Carpet Fresh carpet cleaner.

Creativity is the wellspring of new-product ideas, regardless of who comes up with them. A variety of approaches and techniques have been developed to stimulate creative thinking. The two considered most useful for generating new-product ideas are brainstorming and focus-group exercises. The goal of **brainstorming** is to get a group to think of unlimited ways to vary a product or solve a problem. Group members avoid criticism of an idea, no matter how ridiculous it may seem. Objective evaluation is postponed. The sheer quantity of ideas is what matters. As noted in Chapter 8, an objective of focus-group interviews is to stimulate insightful comments through group interaction. Focus groups usually consist of seven to ten people. Sometimes consumer focus groups generate excellent new-product ideas—for example, Cycle dog food, Stick-Up room deodorizers, Dustbuster vacuum cleaners, and Wendy's salad bar. In the industrial market, machine tools, keyboard designs, aircraft interiors, and backhoe accessories have evolved from focus groups. Leverage Marketing Corporation of America uses high-IQ Mensa Society members in its focus groups to generate new-product ideas.[16]

IDEA SCREENING

After new ideas have been generated, they pass through the first filter in the product development process. This stage, called **screening**, eliminates ideas that are inconsistent with the organization's new-product strategy or are obviously inap-

product development
A marketing strategy that entails the creation of marketable new products; the process of converting applications for new technologies into marketable products.

brainstorming
The process of getting a group to think of unlimited ways to vary a product or solve a problem.

screening
The first filter in the product development process, which eliminates ideas that are inconsistent with the organization's new-product strategy or are obviously inappropriate for some other reason.

propriate for some other reason. The new-product committee, the new-product department, or some other formally appointed group performs the screening review. General Motors' Advanced Portfolio Exploration Group (APEx) knows that only one out of every 20 new car concepts developed by the group will ever become a reality. That's not a bad percentage. In the pharmaceutical business, one new product out of 5,000 ideas is not uncommon.[17] Most new-product ideas are rejected at the screening stage.

Concept tests are often used at the screening stage to rate concept (or product) alternatives. A **concept test** evaluates a new-product idea, usually before any prototype has been created. Typically, researchers get consumer reactions to descriptions and visual representations of a proposed product.

Concept tests are considered fairly good predictors of success for line extensions. They have also been relatively precise predictors of success for new products that are not copycat items, are not easily classified into existing product categories, and do not require major changes in consumer behavior—such as Betty Crocker Tuna Helper, Cycle dog food, and Libby Fruit Float. However, concept tests are usually inaccurate in predicting the success of new products that create new consumption patterns and require major changes in consumer behavior—such as microwave ovens, videocassette recorders, computers, and word processors.

BUSINESS ANALYSIS

New-product ideas that survive the initial screening process move to the **business analysis** stage, where preliminary figures for demand, cost, sales, and profitability are calculated. For the first time, costs and revenues are estimated and compared. Depending on the nature of the product and the company, this process may be simple or complex.

The newness of the product, the size of the market, and the nature of the competition all affect the accuracy of revenue projections. In an established market like soft drinks, industry estimates of total market size are available. Forecasting market share for a new entry is a bigger challenge.

Analyzing overall economic trends and their impact on estimated sales is especially important in product categories that are sensitive to fluctuations in the business cycle. If consumers view the economy as uncertain and risky, they will put off buying durable goods like major home appliances, automobiles, and homes. Likewise, business buyers postpone major equipment purchases if they expect a recession.

These questions are commonly asked during the business analysis stage:

- What is the likely demand for the product?
- What impact would the new product probably have on total sales, profits, market share, and return on investment?
- How would the introduction of the product affect existing products? Would the new product cannibalize existing products?
- Would current customers benefit from the product?
- Would the product enhance the image of the company's overall product mix?
- Would the new product affect current employees in any way? Would it lead to hiring more people or reducing the size of the workforce?
- What new facilities, if any, would be needed?
- How might competitors respond?
- What is the risk of failure? Is the company willing to take the risk?

Marketing... in Entertainment

Nonmedia Entertainment Growing

One way Americans entertain themselves is by tailgating. A marketing research study conducted by Synovate for Weber Stephen, one of the leading manufacturers of outdoor grills, found that one out of six adults attended a tailgating party in the previous six months. The survey also revealed that 70 percent of tailgaters like to grill as a pregame activity. This information prompted Weber to develop a new style of grill more suitable for tailgating. Since 62 percent of tailgate grillers use charcoal, the company designed a portable charcoal grill that is much flatter than its hallmark kettle-shaped grill. Dubbed the Baby Q, the new grill is targeted at the tailgating and recreational vehicle markets. Along with tailgating, traveling in an RV is becoming an increasingly popular type of nonmedia entertainment.[18]

concept test
A test to evaluate a new-product idea, usually before any prototype has been created.

business analysis
The second stage of the screening process where preliminary figures for demand, cost, sales, and profitability are calculated.

New-product development is the lifeblood of many companies. IBM is working on a flexible panel/e-newspaper device that will allow users to download news services through wireless access.

Answering these questions may require studies of markets, competition, costs, and technical capabilities. But at the end of this stage, management should have a good understanding of the product's market potential. This understanding is important as costs increase dramatically once a product idea enters the development stage.

DEVELOPMENT

In the early stage of **development**, the R&D or engineering department may develop a prototype of the product. During this stage, the firm should start sketching a marketing strategy. The marketing department should decide on the product's packaging, branding, labeling, and so forth. In addition, it should map out preliminary promotion, price, and distribution strategies. The feasibility of manufacturing the product at an acceptable cost should be thoroughly examined.

The development stage can last a long time and thus be very expensive. Crest toothpaste was in the development stage for 10 years. It took 18 years to develop Minute Rice, 15 years to develop the Polaroid Colorpack camera, 15 years to develop the Xerox copy machine, and 51 years to develop television. The "Ethics in Marketing" box in this chapter examines both sides of a debate between pharmaceutical manufacturers and their critics who argue that drug prices are too high and should be regulated. A key issue is the cost of developing new drugs and the extent to which regulated prices would stifle R&D.

The development process works best when all the involved areas (R&D, marketing, engineering, production, and even suppliers) work together rather than sequentially, a process called **simultaneous product development**. This approach allows firms to shorten the development process and reduce costs. With simultaneous product development, all relevant functional areas and outside suppliers participate in all stages of the development process. Rather than proceeding through highly structured stages, the cross-functional team operates in unison. Involving key suppliers early in the process capitalizes on their knowledge and enables them to develop critical component parts. General Motors expects simultaneous product development to cut several months from the vehicle design process.[20]

ONLINE The Internet is a useful tool for implementing simultaneous product development. On the Net, multiple partners from a variety of locations can meet regularly to assess new-product ideas, analyze markets and demographics, and review cost information. Ideas judged to be feasible can quickly be converted into new products. For example, by using the Web, Mattel's designers and licensees in far-flung locales can collaborate on toy designs. The company estimates that this has cut the time it takes to develop new products by 20 percent. Lockheed Martin expects to save $25 million a year over the next decade by linking 80 major suppliers that will participate in the development and testing of a new stealth fighter plane.[21]

Laboratory tests are often conducted on prototype models during the development stage. User safety is an important aspect of laboratory testing, which actually subjects products to much more severe treatment than is expected by end users. The Consumer Product Safety Act of 1972 requires manufacturers to conduct a "reasonable testing program" to ensure that their products conform to established safety standards.

Many products that test well in the laboratory are also tried out in homes or businesses. Examples of product categories well suited for such use tests include human and pet food products, household cleaning products, and industrial

development
The stage in the product development process in which a prototype is developed and a marketing strategy is outlined.

simultaneous product development
A team-oriented approach to new-product development.

> SHOULD DRUG PRICES BE REGULATED?

Consumers keep hearing that laws to lower prescription drug prices would harm research, stifle innovation, and, ultimately, wreck hopes of cures for major diseases. Critics call this argument the drugmakers' "scare card," accusing them of using it whenever their bottom line is threatened.

It's certainly a scary idea. Most people are thankful for the medicines the drug industry has produced over the past 20 years. Most look forward to more drugs for diseases that as yet can't be treated.

But is it true that we can kiss such hopes goodbye if drug prices are lowered? That's what the industry claims. When Maine legislators were debating a tough law to curb drug prices, the Pharmaceutical Research and Manufacturers of America (PhRMA) ran full-page ads in Maine newspapers showing an old lady looking frail and wistful. The headline: "She'll Just Have to *Wait*."

According to PhRMA, the United States leads the world in bringing out new drugs because the U.S. free market rewards innovation. It says that R&D is costly and high risk and that high profits are needed to attract investment that allows research to continue.

"We need to make sure that incentives for pharmaceutical innovation remain strong," said PhRMA President Alan Holmer in a recent speech. Critics, however, say drug R&D is neither as risky nor as costly as the industry claims. The debate focuses on three questions:

- *Do price cuts harm research?* According to Uwe Reinhardt, an expert on health policy at Princeton University, "R&D spending [as a percentage of revenue] is equal or higher in Europe than here," yet European countries all control drug prices. The

top 10 American drug companies plow back an average of 12.5 percent of their sales revenue into R&D, according to company reports. PhRMA disputes this figure, saying that spending on R&D for prescription drugs alone is 17.7 percent. In contrast, the price-controlled British drug industry says it spends about 20 percent of sales revenue on R&D.

- *How much do drugmakers spend on research?* PhRMA estimates that bringing a new drug to market costs $800 million on average. The watchdog group Public Citizen disputes this figure—arguing that, for example, it does not take into account the large tax deductions companies can claim for R&D.

- *How innovative are American drugs?* PhRMA says that eight of the world's ten best-selling drugs originated in this country. However, only about one-third of new American drugs are truly innovative in that they provide new treatments or are safer or more effective than existing drugs, according to a study by the National Institute for Health Care Management, which relied on classifications made by the FDA for more than 1,000 new drugs introduced from 1988 to 2000. "In this period of incredible growth in research spending and profitability, the drug companies have not demonstrated any significant increase in innovation," says Nancy Chockley, the institute's president. "The numbers just don't show it."[19]

Do you think drug prices should be regulated? If so, by whom? Explain your answer.

---

chemicals and supplies. These products are all relatively inexpensive, and their performance characteristics are apparent to users. For example, Procter & Gamble tests a variety of personal and home-care products in the community around its Cincinnati, Ohio headquarters. One recent study used 105 subjects to see how sensitive skin reacts to a new product ingredient. Subjects were paid $55 to wear patches, which were replaced every other day, for one week.[22] Red Lobster's Southlake, Texas restaurant, known within the corporation as a model "M7," is a working consumer-testing ground that auditions trial recipes to the dining public.[23]

Most products require some refinement based on the results of laboratory and use tests. General Mills tested various package prototypes of Go-Gurt with mothers and their children. "If you could squeeze it, push it, pump it, peel it, or sip it, we tried it."[24] A second stage of development often takes place before test marketing.

test marketing
The limited introduction of a product and a marketing program to determine the reactions of potential customers in a market situation.

TEST MARKETING

After products and marketing programs have been developed, they are usually tested in the marketplace. **Test marketing** is the limited introduction of a product and a marketing program to determine the reactions of potential customers in a market situation. Test

AP/WIDE WORLD PHOTOS

Before rolling out its "Go Active! Happy Meal," McDonald's test marketed the idea in Indianapolis because central Indiana is considered a good test market for many types of product. The new meal includes a premium salad, bottled water (or medium drink), a pedometer, and an exercise guide on how to increase physical activity.

marketing allows management to evaluate alternative strategies and to assess how well the various aspects of the marketing mix fit together. Quaker Oats test marketed the Take Heart line of food products including ready-to-eat cereals, snack bars, and fruit juice beverages in selected markets in the New York State area before introducing the line nationwide.[25] Even established products are test marketed to assess new marketing strategies. One-dollar bottles of chocolate, strawberry, and coffee-flavored milk, distributed through vending machines, were offered in schools in Texas, California, Massachusetts, Nebraska, and Florida to assess this alternative distribution strategy. Initial weekly sales ran about 200 bottles per machine.[26]

The cities chosen as test sites should reflect market conditions in the new product's projected market area. Yet no "magic city" exists that can universally represent market conditions, and a product's success in one city doesn't guarantee that it will be a nationwide hit. When selecting test market cities, researchers should therefore find locations where the demographics and purchasing habits mirror the overall market. The company should also have good distribution in test cities. Moreover, test locations should be isolated from the media. If the TV stations in a particular market reach a very large area outside that market, the advertising used for the test product may pull in many consumers from outside the market. The product may then appear more successful than it really is. Exhibit 10.2 provides a useful checklist of criteria for selecting test markets.

EXHIBIT 10.2

Checklist for Selecting Test Markets

In choosing a test market, many criteria need to be considered, especially the following:
Similarity to planned distribution outlets
Relative isolation from other cities
Availability of advertising media that will cooperate
Diversified cross section of ages, religions, cultural-societal preferences, etc.
No atypical purchasing habits
Representative population size
Typical per capita income
Good record as a test city, but not overly used
Not easily "jammed" by competitors
Stability of year-round sales
No dominant television station; multiple newspapers, magazines, and radio stations
Availability of research and audit services
Availability of retailers that will cooperate
Freedom from unusual influences, such as one industry's dominance or heavy tourism

The High Costs of Test Marketing

Test marketing frequently takes one year or longer, and costs can exceed $1 million. Some products remain in test markets even longer. McDonald's spent 12 years developing and testing salads before introducing them. Despite the cost, many firms believe it is a lot better to fail in a test market than in a national introduction.

Because test marketing is so expensive, some companies do not test line extensions of well-known brands. For example, because the Folgers brand is well known, Procter & Gamble faced little risk in distributing its instant decaffeinated version nationally. Consolidated Foods Kitchen of Sara Lee followed the same approach with its frozen croissants. Other products introduced without being test marketed include General Foods' International Coffees, Quaker Oats' Chewy Granola Bars and Granola Dipps, and Pillsbury's Milk Break Bars.

The high cost of test marketing is not just financial. One unavoidable problem is that test marketing exposes the new product and its marketing mix to competitors before its introduction. Thus, the element of surprise is lost. Hamilton Beach sued both Honeywell and Holmes Products for copying its TrueAir odor eliminator. The device in question, about the size of a hardcover book, claims to eliminate odors within a six-foot radius by pulling air through a filter.[27] Competitors can also sabotage or "jam" a testing program by introducing their own sales promotion, pricing, or advertising campaign. The purpose is to hide or distort the normal conditions that the testing firm might expect in the market.

Alternatives to Test Marketing

Many firms are looking for cheaper, faster, safer alternatives to traditional test marketing. In the early 1980s, Information Resources, Inc., pioneered one alternative: single-source research using supermarket scanner data (discussed in Chapter 8). A typical supermarket scanner test costs about $300,000. Another alternative to traditional test marketing is **simulated (laboratory) market testing**. Advertising and other promotional materials for several products, including the test product, are shown to members of the product's target market. These people are then taken to shop at a mock or real store, where their purchases are recorded. Shopper behavior, including repeat purchasing, is monitored to assess the product's likely performance under true market conditions. Research firms offer simulated market tests for $25,000 to $100,000, compared to $1 million or more for full-scale test marketing.

Online Test Marketing

Despite these alternatives, most firms still consider test marketing essential for most new products. The high price of failure simply prohibits the widespread introduction of most new products without testing. Many firms are finding that the Internet offers a fast, cost-effective way to conduct test marketing.

Procter & Gamble is an avid proponent of using the Internet as a means of gauging customer demand for potential new products. The company reportedly conducts 40 percent of its product tests and other studies online and hopes to cut its $140 million annual research budget in half by shifting efforts to the Internet.[28]

Many products that are not available in grocery stores or drugstores can be sampled or purchased from P&G's corporate Web site **http://pg.com**. The company's home tooth-bleaching kit Crest Whitestrips provides an illustration. When the company was ready to launch Crest Whitestrips, management wasn't sure that consumers would be willing to pay the proposed $44 retail price. P&G then began an eight-month campaign offering the strips exclusively on **http://whitestrips.com**. TV spots and magazine ads were run to promote the online sale. In eight months, 144,000 whitening kits were sold online. The product was then introduced in retail outlets, and $50 million worth of kits were sold in the first three months at the initial $44 per kit price.[29]

Other consumer goods firms that have recently begun online test marketing include General Mills and Quaker Oats. Other sites have appeared that offer consumers prototype products developed by all sizes of firms.

COMMERCIALIZATION

The final stage in the new-product development process is **commercialization**, the decision to market a product. The decision to commercialize the product sets several tasks in motion: ordering production materials and equipment, starting production, building inventories, shipping the product to field distribution points,

simulated (laboratory) market testing
The presentation of advertising and other promotion materials for several products, including a test product, to members of the product's target market.

commercialization
The decision to market a product.

FAQs

Why do so many new products fail? Find out by watching the video FAQ on Xtra!

3

Explain why some products succeed and others fail

FAQs

What factors increase the chances of new-to-the-world product success? Find out by watching the video FAQ on Xtra!

AP/WIDE WORLD PHOTOS

training the sales force, announcing the new product to the trade, and advertising to potential customers.

The time from the initial commercialization decision to the product's actual introduction varies. It can range from a few weeks for simple products that use existing equipment to several years for technical products that require custom manufacturing equipment.

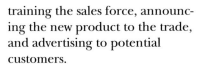

New Product Works

Not all new products are well received in the marketplace. Go to New Product Works' Web site and read the polls for an overview of products the company expects to "hit" and some it expects to "miss." What is your opinion of the products listed?

http://www.newproductworks.com

Online

The total cost of development and initial introduction can be staggering. Gillette spent $750 million developing MACH3, and the first-year marketing budget for the new three-bladed razor was $300 million.

For some products, a well-planned Internet campaign can provide new-product information for people who are looking for the solutions that a particular new product offers. Attempting to reach customers at the point in time when they need a product is much more cost-effective and efficient than communicating with a target market that may eventually have a need for the product.

Despite the high cost of developing and testing new products, a large proportion of all new-product introductions fail. Products fail for a number of reasons. One common reason is that they simply do not offer any discernible benefit compared to existing products. Another commonly cited factor in new-product failures is a poor match between product features and customer desires. For example, there are telephone systems on the market with over 700 different functions, although the average user is happy with just 10 functions. Other reasons for failure include overestimation of market size, incorrect positioning, a price too high or too low, inadequate distribution, poor promotion, or simply an inferior product compared to those of competitors.

Failure can be a matter of degree. Absolute failure occurs when a company cannot recoup its development, marketing, and production costs. The product actually loses money for the company. A relative product failure results when the product returns a profit but fails to achieve sales, profit, or market share goals.

High costs and other risks of developing and testing new products do not stop many companies, such as Rubbermaid, Colgate-Palmolive, Campbell's Soup, 3M Company, and Procter & Gamble, from aggressively developing and introducing new products.

The most important factor in successful new-product introduction is a good match between the product and market needs—as the marketing concept would predict. Successful new products deliver a meaningful and perceivable benefit to a sizable number of people or organizations and are different in some meaningful way from their intended substitutes. Firms that routinely experience success in new-product introductions tend to share the following characteristics:

In the commercialization phase, companies decide to produce the product. But this does not mean the product will be available everywhere all at once. Coca-Cola decided to launch its new Barq's Floatz in just two southern states, hoping to create buzz in Barq's home territory before going nationwide. Barq's Floatz is touted to taste like a root-beer float.

- A history of carefully listening to customers
- An obsession with producing the best product possible
- A vision of what the market will be like in the future
- Strong leadership
- A commitment to new-product development
- A project-based team approach to new-product development
- Getting every aspect of the product development process right

2 **Explain the steps in the new-product development process**

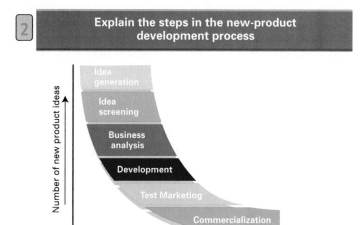

3 **Explain why some products succeed and others fail**

Good match leads to success

4 GLOBAL ISSUES IN NEW-PRODUCT DEVELOPMENT

Discuss global issues in new-product development

Increasing globalization of markets and of competition provides a reason for multinational firms to consider new-product development from a worldwide perspective. A firm that starts with a global strategy is better able to develop products that are marketable worldwide. In many multinational corporations, every product is developed for potential worldwide distribution, and unique market requirements are built in whenever possible. Procter & Gamble introduced Pampers Phases into global markets within one month of introducing the product in the United States. P&G's goal was to have the product on the shelf in 90 countries within one year. The objective was to establish brand loyalty among dealers and consumers before foreign competitors could react.

Some global marketers design their products to meet regulations in their major markets and then, if necessary, meet smaller markets' requirements country by country. Nissan develops lead-country car models that, with minor changes, can be sold in most markets. With this approach, Nissan has been able to reduce the number of its basic models from 48 to 18.

Some products, however, have little potential for global market penetration without modification. Russia and China represent two huge automobile markets but not at prevailing international prices. General Motors, Ford Motor Company, Fiat, Renault, and others are working with Russian partners to produce cars that can retail for $15,000 or less. GM, Toyota, and Volkswagen AG are focusing on China.

Coca-Cola is a company that seems to need little help with global penetration of its product. In fact, despite adapting its product formula and product mix to various cultures, Coke is one of the world's most recognized brands.

We often hear about how popular American products are in foreign countries. Recently, U.S. companies such as Levi Strauss, Coca-Cola, RJR Nabisco, and Nike have been finding that products popular in foreign markets can become hits in the United States. Häagen-Dazs' ice cream flavor *dulce de leche,* named after a caramelized milk drink that is popular in Argentina, was originally introduced in Buenos Aires in 1997. Enova, a cooking oil that helps cut body weight and fat, was the top-selling brand in Japan before it was introduced in the United States in 2003.[30]

 Other companies are applying a new twist on the popular international business aphorism, "think global, act local." At Coca-Cola, this means giving country managers more autonomy in new-product development.[31] The idea has resulted in seven new brands of energy drinks, waters, and teas being introduced in various Asian countries. More are planned to diversify beyond colas. Results have been impressive. Approximately 90 percent of Coca-Cola's worldwide sales come from traditional brands such as Coke and Sprite. In Japan, it's more like one-third. Xing Mu (Smart), a Coca-Cola brand, has become the fourth-most-popular carbonated soft drink in China in just four years.[32]

Coca-Cola also follows a one product–one message strategy in some markets. It markets Powerade, an American brand of sport drink, the same way in Europe as in the United States. It also markets a popular European after-exercise drink called Aquarius.[33] The "Global Perspectives" box describes an interesting method of testing and marketing new products in Brazil.

REVIEW LEARNING OBJECTIVE 4

4 | Discuss global issues in new-product development

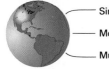

— Single product worldwide

— Modification of products

— Multiple products in multiple countries

Global Perspectives

GLOBAL PERSPECTIVES

Global Perspectives Global Perspectives

> FUEL AND FREEBIES

 In a suburb of São Paulo, Brazil, Adam Pereira drives his Volkswagen truck up and down the streets blaring out tunes like an ice cream van. But the truck is packed with canisters of gas, a blend of propane and butane, used widely as cooking fuel. Pereira stops to chat with many customers, and like hundreds of other gas-balloon deliverymen, Pereira is at the very heart of Brazilian town life.

These days, he is also central to the marketing efforts of multinational companies. His rapport with customers makes him an extremely valuable tool for introducing new products. Pereira has distributed packets of Nestlé flavorings, Johnson floor wax, and both Procter & Gamble and Unilever laundry detergents to thousands of households.

In Brazil, where stoves run on gas rather than electricity, the gas balloon is a kitchen fixture. Ultragaz SA, the firm that employs Pereira, distributes gas to about 15 percent of all Brazilian homes, or about 18 million households, each month. The company's national reach and rich database enable food, household goods, and toiletries makers to test products on a mass scale or to target consumers by income group or geographic area.

Brazil's gas deliverymen provide a crucial personal link to consumers. Because they are usually assigned to the same district for several years, employees like Pereira command the trust of entire communities. Sara Lee enlisted Ultragaz to distribute samples of two new fragrances of Phebo bath soap, part of an effort to revitalize the 70-year-old Brazilian brand that it recently acquired.

During his rounds recently, Pereira stops at the gate of Adelia Goncalves, who smiles broadly at the sight of him. "Hey princess, how are you doing?" he says. "Need some gas today?" After sharing details of her home renovation with Pereira, the housewife informs him that she hasn't run out of fuel. No matter. Pereira tucks his hand into his blue uniform's shirt pocket, produces a small blue box. "Here's a little gift for you, it's a marvelous new Phebo product," says the man, who has been delivering gas balloons for 21 years.

Ultragaz was the first gas company to do product samplings, though a local unit of Royal Dutch/Shell Group has also joined the fray. Ultragaz started teaming up with multinationals in 1995. It charges companies just five cents to distribute each unit of a product. Delivering the samples doesn't require additional staff, and indeed, people like Pereira aren't paid extra for their added service.

For a multinational, distributing samples of new and established products through a gas company isn't just effective, it's economical. Indeed, marketers agree that there is no sampling mechanism in Brazil that comes close to gas-balloon delivery.

It is hard to gauge the gas deliverer's direct impact on sales of a product, however, since the sampling exercise is usually part of a broader strategy that involves advertising and promotional activities. Since starting its Phebo soap campaign early this year in the interior of São Paulo state, Sara Lee reports that its market share has increased by as much as 13 percent in that region. The company aims to distribute about five million samples through Ultragaz by year's end.[34]

Why is this method of introducing new products so successful in Brazil? How might the advantages of this approach be transferred to countries that do not use this form of heating fuel distribution? Sampling as a sales promotion tool is discussed in Chapter 16.

Explain the diffusion process through which new products are adopted

Managers have a better chance of successfully marketing products if they understand how consumers learn about and adopt products. A person who buys a new product never before tried may ultimately become an **adopter**, a consumer who was happy enough with his or her trial experience with a product to use it again.

DIFFUSION OF INNOVATION

An **innovation** is a product perceived as new by a potential adopter. It really doesn't matter whether the product is "new to the world" or some other category of new product. If it is new to a potential adopter, it is an innovation in this context. **Diffusion** is the process by which the adoption of an innovation spreads.

Five categories of adopters participate in the diffusion process:

- *Innovators:* the first 2.5 percent of all those who adopt the product. Innovators are eager to try new ideas and products, almost as an obsession. In addition to having higher incomes, they are more worldly and more active outside their community than noninnovators. They rely less on group norms and are more self-confident. Because they are well educated, they are more likely to get their information from scientific sources and experts. Innovators are characterized as being venturesome.

- *Early adopters:* the next 13.5 percent to adopt the product. Although early adopters are not the very first, they do adopt early in the product's life cycle. Compared to innovators, they rely much more on group norms and values. They are also more oriented to the local community, in contrast to the innovators' worldly outlook. Early adopters are more likely than innovators to be opinion leaders because of their closer affiliation with groups. The respect of others is a dominant characteristic of early adopters. According to a new book by Ed Keller and Jon Berry, one American in ten tells the other nine how to vote, where to eat, and what to buy.[35] These people are clearly opinion leaders.

- *Early majority:* the next 34 percent to adopt. The early majority weighs the pros and cons before adopting a new product. They are likely to collect more information and evaluate more brands than early adopters, therefore extending the adoption process. They rely on the group for information but are unlikely to be opinion leaders themselves. Instead, they tend to be opinion leaders' friends and neighbors. The early majority is an important link in the process of diffusing new ideas because they are positioned between earlier and later adopters. A dominant characteristic of the early majority is deliberateness. Most of the first residential broadband users were classic early adopters—white males, well educated and wealthy, with a great deal of Internet experience. In 2003, *eMarketer* reported that high-speed access had moved to the early majority stage of the diffusion process.[36]

- *Late majority:* the next 34 percent to adopt. The late majority adopts a new product because most of their friends have already adopted it. Because they also rely on group norms, their adoption stems from pressure to conform. This group tends to be older and below average in income and education. They depend mainly on word-of-mouth communication rather than on the mass media. The dominant characteristic of the late majority is skepticism. According to *eMarketer*, both Hispanics and African Americans are late adopters of the Internet compared to their Caucasian and Asian American counterparts.[37]

- *Laggards:* the final 16 percent to adopt. Like innovators, laggards do not rely on group norms. Their independence is rooted in their ties to tradition. Thus, the past heavily influences their decisions. By the time laggards adopt an innovation, it has probably been outmoded and replaced by something else. For example, they may have bought their first black-and-white TV set after color television was already widely diffused. Laggards have the longest adoption time and

adopter
A consumer who was happy enough with his or her trial experience with a product to use it again.

innovation
A product perceived as new by a potential adopter.

diffusion
The process by which the adoption of an innovation spreads.

the lowest socioeconomic status. They tend to be suspicious of new products and alienated from a rapidly advancing society. The dominant value of laggards is tradition. Marketers typically ignore laggards, who do not seem to be motivated by advertising or personal selling.

Note that some product categories, such as monochrome televisions, may never be adopted by 100 percent of the population. The adopter categories refer to all of those who will eventually adopt a product, not the entire population.

PRODUCT CHARACTERISTICS AND THE RATE OF ADOPTION

Five product characteristics can be used to predict and explain the rate of acceptance and diffusion of a new product:

- *Complexity:* the degree of difficulty involved in understanding and using a new product. The more complex the product, the slower is its diffusion. For instance, DVD recorders have been around for a few years, but they have been bought mostly by early adopters willing to go to the trouble of linking the gadgets to their PCs or to pay high prices for the first stand-alone machines that connect to a TV.
- *Compatibility:* the degree to which the new product is consistent with existing values and product knowledge, past experiences, and current needs. Incompatible products diffuse more slowly than compatible products. For example, the introduction of contraceptives is incompatible in countries where religious beliefs discourage the use of birth control techniques.
- *Relative advantage:* the degree to which a product is perceived as superior to existing substitutes. For example, because it reduces cooking time, the microwave oven has a clear relative advantage over a conventional oven.
- *Observability:* the degree to which the benefits or other results of using the product can be observed by others and communicated to target customers. For instance, fashion items and automobiles are highly visible and more observable than personal-care items.
- *"Trialability":* the degree to which a product can be tried on a limited basis. It is much easier to try a new toothpaste or breakfast cereal than a new automobile or microcomputer. Demonstrations in showrooms and test-drives are different from in-home trial use. To stimulate trials, marketers use free-sampling programs, tasting displays, and small package sizes.

Exhibit 10.3 shows the rate of adoption of 5 audio products introduced in the last 25 years. Satellite radio has been adopted more quickly than any other innovative audio product.

EXHIBIT 10.3

Sales of New Audio Products

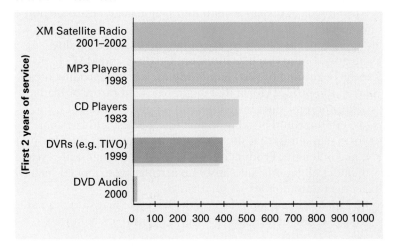

(First 2 years of service)

XM Satellite Radio 2001–2002	
MP3 Players 1998	
CD Players 1983	
DVRs (e.g. TIVO) 1999	
DVD Audio 2000	

0 100 200 300 400 500 600 700 800 900 1000

MARKETING IMPLICATIONS OF THE ADOPTION PROCESS

Two types of communication aid the diffusion process: *word-of-mouth communication* among consumers and communication from marketers to consumers. Word-of-mouth communication within and across groups speeds diffusion. Opinion leaders discuss new products with their followers and with other opinion leaders. Marketers must therefore ensure that opinion leaders have the types of information desired in the media that they use. Suppliers of some products, such as professional and health-care services, rely almost solely on word-of-mouth communication for new business.

The second type of communication aiding the diffusion process is *communication directly from the marketer to potential adopters.* Messages directed toward early adopters should normally use different appeals than messages directed toward the early majority, the late majority, or the laggards. Early adopters are more important than innovators because they make up a larger group, are more socially active, and are usually opinion leaders.

As the focus of a promotional campaign shifts from early adopters to the early majority and the late majority, marketers should study the dominant characteristics, buying behavior, and media characteristics of these target markets. Then they should revise messages and media strategy to fit. The diffusion model helps guide marketers in developing and implementing promotion strategy.

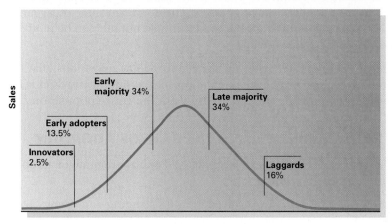

5 Explain the diffusion process through which new products are adopted

Percentage of total adoptions by category

Product Characteristics (Influence Rate of Adoption)

- Complexity
- Compatibility
- Relative Advantage
- Observability
- "Trialability"

 6 PRODUCT LIFE CYCLES

Explain the concept of product life cycles

product life cycle (PLC)
A concept that provides a way to trace the stages of a product's acceptance, from its introduction (birth) to its decline (death).

product category
All brands that satisfy a particular type of need.

The **product life cycle (PLC)** is one of the most familiar concepts in marketing. Few other general concepts have been so widely discussed. Although some researchers have challenged the theoretical basis and managerial value of the PLC, most believe it has great potential as a marketing management tool.

The product life cycle is a concept that provides a way to trace the stages of a product's acceptance, from its introduction (birth) to its decline (death). As Exhibit 10.4 shows, a product progresses through four major stages: introduction, growth, maturity, and decline.

The product life cycle concept can be used to analyze a brand, a product form, or a product category. Brands such as Intuition, Quattro, and MACH3 discussed in the story at the beginning of this chapter will each have a product life cycle. They all are part of the product form that might be called razors or blade shaving systems. The PLC for a product form is usually longer than the PLC for any one brand. The exception would be a brand that was the first and last competitor in a product form market. In that situation, the brand and product form life cycles would be equal in length. Product categories have the longest life cycles. A **product category** includes all brands that satisfy a particular type of need such as shaving products, passenger automobiles, or soft drinks.

The time a product spends in any one stage of the life cycle may vary dramatically. Some products, such as fad items, move through the entire cycle in weeks.

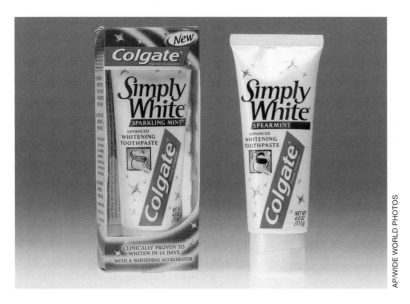

Development and use of tooth-whitening products have exploded in recent years. Crest Whitestrips, Colgate Simply White Gel, and now Colgate's new Simply White Whitening toothpaste are some of the big products in this market. Do you think tooth-whitening is a style, fashion, or fad?

Others, such as electric clothes washers and dryers, stay in the maturity stage for decades. Exhibit 10.4 illustrates the typical life cycle for a consumer durable good, such as a washer or dryer. In contrast, Exhibit 10.5 illustrates typical life cycles for styles (such as formal, business, or casual clothing), fashions (such as miniskirts or baggy jeans), and fads (such as leopard-print clothing). Changes in a product, its uses, its image, or its positioning can extend that product's life cycle.

The product life cycle concept does not tell managers the length of a product's life cycle or its duration in any stage. It does not dictate marketing strategy. It is simply a tool to help marketers forecast future events and suggest appropriate strategies. Look at Exhibit 10.6 on page 350. What conclusions can you draw about the product life cycle of non-digital TVs, digital TVs, and flat panel TVs based on four and a half years of sales data?

INTRODUCTORY STAGE

The **introductory stage** of the product life cycle represents the full-scale launch of a new product into the marketplace. Computer databases for personal use, room-deodorizing air-conditioning filters, and wind-powered home electric generators are all product categories that have recently entered the product life cycle. A high failure rate, little competition, frequent product modification, and limited distribution typify the introductory stage of the PLC.

Marketing costs in the introductory stage are normally high for several reasons. High dealer margins are often needed to obtain adequate distribution, and incentives are needed to get consumers to try the new product. Advertising expenses are high because of the need to educate consumers about the new product's benefits. Production costs are also often high in this stage, as product and manufacturing flaws are identified and corrected and efforts are undertaken to develop mass-production economies.

As Exhibit 10.4 illustrates, sales normally increase slowly during the introductory stage. Moreover, profits are usually negative because of R&D costs, factory tooling, and high introduction costs. The length of the introductory phase is largely determined by product characteristics, such as the product's advantages over substitute products, the educational

introductory stage
The full-scale launch of a new product into the marketplace.

EXHIBIT 10.4

Four Stages of the Product Life Cycle

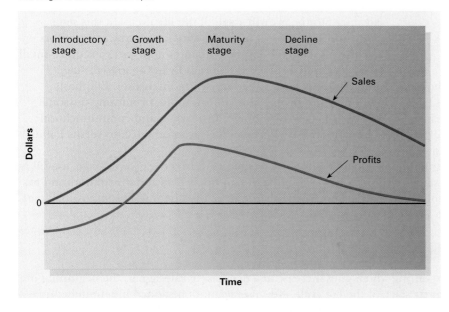

EXHIBIT 10.5

Product Life Cycles for Styles, Fashions, and Fads

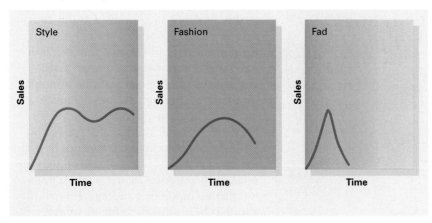

EXHIBIT 10.6

U.S. Sales of Televisions, in Billions:

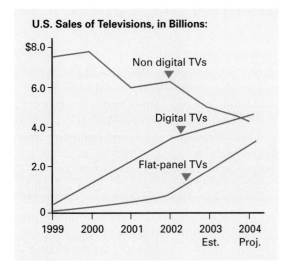

SOURCE: Consumer Electronics Association as seen in Evan Ramstad, "Flat-Panel, Plasma TV Sets Bring a Flood of New Brands," *Wall Street Journal*, January 13, 2004, B1.

growth stage
The second stage of the product life cycle when sales typically grow at an increasing rate, many competitors enter the market, large companies may start acquiring small pioneering firms, and profits are healthy.

maturity stage
A period during which sales increase at a decreasing rate.

effort required to make the product known, and management's commitment of resources to the new item. A short introductory period is usually preferred to help reduce the impact of negative earnings and cash flows. As soon as the product gets off the ground, the financial burden should begin to diminish. Also, a short introduction helps dispel some of the uncertainty as to whether the new product will be successful.

Promotion strategy in the introductory stage focuses on developing product awareness and informing consumers about the product category's potential benefits. At this stage, the communication challenge is to stimulate primary demand—demand for the product in general rather than for a specific brand. Intensive personal selling is often required to gain acceptance for the product among wholesalers and retailers. Promotion of convenience products often requires heavy consumer sampling and couponing. Shopping and specialty products demand educational advertising and personal selling to the final consumer.

Interestingly, the introductory stage of the PLC seems to vary among European countries. As Exhibit 10.7 shows, the average introductory stage ranges from just under 4 years in Denmark to about 9 years in Greece. Cultural factors seem to be largely responsible for these differences. Scandinavians are often more open to new ideas than people in other European countries.[39]

GROWTH STAGE

If a product category survives the introductory stage, it advances to the **growth stage** of the life cycle. In this stage, sales typically grow at an increasing rate, many competitors enter the market, and large companies may start to acquire small pioneering firms. Profits rise rapidly in the growth stage, reach their peak, and begin declining as competition intensifies. Emphasis switches from primary demand promotion (for example, promoting personal digital assistants [PDAs]) to aggressive brand advertising and communication of the differences between brands (for example, promoting Casio versus Palm and Visor).

Distribution becomes a major key to success during the growth stage, as well as in later stages. Manufacturers scramble to sign up dealers and distributors and to build long-term relationships. Without adequate distribution, it is impossible to establish a strong market position.

MATURITY STAGE

A period during which sales increase at a decreasing rate signals the beginning of the **maturity stage** of the life cycle. New users cannot be added indefinitely, and sooner or later the market approaches saturation. Normally, this is the longest

The European Divide

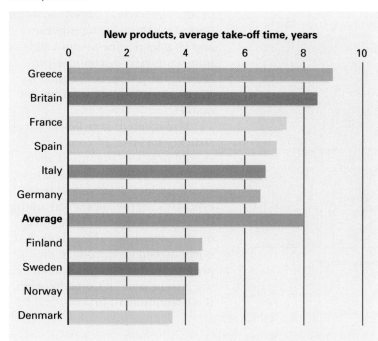

New products, average take-off time, years

Country	Years
Greece	~8.7
Britain	~8.5
France	~7.3
Spain	~7.0
Italy	~6.6
Germany	~6.5
Average	~8.0
Finland	~4.5
Sweden	~4.4
Norway	~4.0
Denmark	~3.7

SOURCE: Tellis, Stremersch, and Yin. Reprinted from "When Will It Fly?" *The Economist*, August 9, 2003, 332.

Coffee is an example of a product in the maturity stage where niche marketers have emerged. Starbucks, for example, targets its gourmet products at newer, younger, more affluent coffee drinkers.

decline stage
A long-run drop in sales.

Cheerios
What is Cheerios doing to compete successfully in the maturity stage? Go to its Web site to find out.

http://www.cheerios.com

Online

stage of the product life cycle. Many major household appliances are in the maturity stage of their life cycles.

For shopping products and many specialty products, annual models begin to appear during the maturity stage. Product lines are lengthened to appeal to additional market segments. Service and repair assume more important roles as manufacturers strive to distinguish their products from others. Product design changes tend to become stylistic (How can the product be made different?) rather than functional (How can the product be made better?).

As prices and profits continue to fall, marginal competitors start dropping out of the market. Dealer margins also shrink, resulting in less shelf space for mature items, lower dealer inventories, and a general reluctance to promote the product. Thus, promotion to dealers often intensifies during this stage in order to retain loyalty.

Heavy consumer promotion by the manufacturer is also required to maintain market share. Consider these well-known examples of competition in the maturity stage: the "cola war" featuring Coke and Pepsi, the "beer war" featuring Anheuser-Busch's Budweiser brands and Philip Morris's Miller brands, and the "burger wars" pitting leader McDonald's against challengers Burger King and Wendy's.

Another characteristic of the maturity stage is the emergence of "niche marketers" that target narrow, well-defined, underserved segments of a market. Starbucks Coffee targets its gourmet line at the only segment of the coffee market that is growing: new, younger, more affluent coffee drinkers.

DECLINE STAGE

A long-run drop in sales signals the beginning of the **decline stage**. The rate of decline is governed by how rapidly consumer tastes change or substitute products are adopted. Many convenience products and fad items lose their market overnight, leaving large inventories of unsold items, such as designer jeans. Others die more slowly, like citizen band (CB) radios, black-and-white console television sets, and typewriters.

EXHIBIT 10.8

Relationship between the diffusion process and the product life cycle

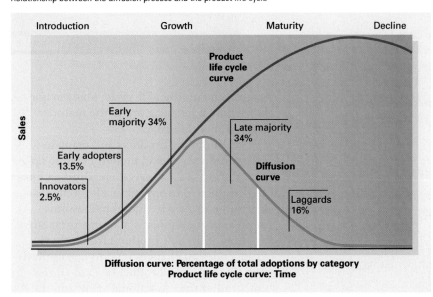

Diffusion curve: Percentage of total adoptions by category
Product life cycle curve: Time

Some firms have developed successful strategies for marketing products in the decline stage of the product life cycle. They eliminate all nonessential marketing expenses and let sales decline as more and more customers discontinue purchasing the products. Eventually, the product is withdrawn from the market.

Management sage Peter Drucker says that all companies should practice "organized abandonment," which entails reviewing every product, service, and policy every two or three years and asking the critical question, "If we didn't do this already, would we launch it now?" Would we introduce the product, service, or policy now? If the answer is no, it's time to begin the abandonment process.[40]

REVIEW LEARNING OBJECTIVE 6

6 | **Explain the concept of product life cycles**

Product Life Cycle Stage

Marketing Mix Strategy	Introductory	Growth	Maturity	Decline
Product Strategy	Limited number of models; frequent product modifications	Expanded number of models; frequent product modifications	Large number of models	Elimination of unprofitable models and brands
Distribution Strategy	Distribution usually limited, depending on product; intensive efforts and high margins often needed to attract wholesalers and retailers	Expanded number of dealers; intensive efforts to establish long-term relationships with wholesalers and retailers	Extensive number of dealers; margins declining; intensive efforts to retain distributors and shelf space	Unprofitable outlets phased out
Promotion Strategy	Develop product awareness; stimulate primary demand; use intensive personal selling to distributors; use sampling and couponing for consumers	Stimulate selective demand; advertise brand aggressively	Stimulate selective demand; advertise brand aggressively; promote heavily to retain dealers and customers	Phase out all promotion
Pricing Strategy	Prices are usually high to recover development costs (see Chapter 17)	Prices begin to fall toward end of growth stage as result of competitive pressure	Prices continue to fall	Prices stabilize at relatively low level; small price rises are possible if competition is negligible

Sales

Time

IMPLICATIONS FOR MARKETING MANAGEMENT

The product life cycle concept encourages marketing managers to plan so that they can take the initiative instead of reacting to past events. The PLC is especially useful as a predicting or forecasting tool. Because products pass through distinctive stages, it is often possible to estimate a product's location on the curve using historical data. Profits, like sales, tend to follow a predictable path over a product's life cycle.

Exhibit 10.8 shows the relationship between the adopter categories and stages of the PLC. Note that the various categories of adopters first buy products in different stages of the life cycle. Almost all sales in the maturity and decline stages represent repeat purchasing.

LOOKING BACK

Look back at the story at the beginning of this chapter about the introduction of Schick-Wilkinson Sword's Intuition and Quattro razors, as well as Gillette's MACH3. You now know that the product life cycle is a concept that provides a way to trace the stages of a product's acceptance from its introduction to its decline. You also learned in Review 6 that different marketing strategies are needed in different stages of the PLC. Remember that the PLC concept can be used to analyze brands, product forms, or product categories and help marketers identify appropriate marketing strategies at various times throughout the cycle.

USE IT NOW

STAY INFORMED

 To keep current with the changing trends and new products in the financial-services industry, arm yourself with information. A banking Web site that will help you make informed decisions is **http://www. bankrate.com**. It has a How-to section that teaches the basics of banking and helps you calculate your payment on loans. The site's collection of interest rate information covers everything from car loans to money market accounts and enables you to compare rates from financial institutions in all 50 states. You can also check the fees different banks charge for their services and compare them to online banking service charges.

LOCATE LENDERS

More and more financial institutions are expanding their lending to entrepreneurs and small-business owners. The following Web sites help start-ups and small businesses find financing:

- **http://quicken.com** and **http://intuit.com** Both of these sites offer numerous tools for small business and personal finance. Lending Tree offers access to several financial institutions through its site. You can fill out a single loan application at its Web site, **http://lendingtree.com**, and you will receive quotes from various lenders.
- **http://www.icba.org** The Web site of the Independent Community Bankers of America provides leads to all U.S. community banks.
- **http://www.Yahoo.com** This site links to various sources of financial information, news, and advice.

1 **Explain the importance of developing new products and describe the six categories of new products.** New products are important to sustain growth and profits and to replace obsolete items. New products can be classified as new-to-the-world products (discontinuous innovations), new product lines, additions to existing product lines, improvements or revisions of existing products, repositioned products, or lower-priced products. To sustain or increase profits, a firm must innovate.

1.1 How many new products can you identify? Visit the supermarket and make a list of at least 15 items with the word "New" on the label. Include on your list anything that looks like a new product. Next to each item on your list, write the category of new product that best describes the item. Share your results with the class.

1.2 New entertainment products aren't necessarily media products. Review the "Marketing in Entertainment" box on the Weber Baby Q. Form a team of 3 to 4 students and brainstorm new non-media entertainment products. Try to identify one item for each of the categories of new products discussed in the chapter.

2 **Explain the steps in the new-product development process.** First, a firm forms a new-product strategy by outlining the characteristics and roles of future products. Then new-product ideas are generated by customers, employees, distributors, competitors, vendors, and internal R&D personnel. Once a product idea has survived initial screening by an appointed screening group, it undergoes business analysis to determine its potential profitability. If a product concept seems viable, it progresses into the development phase, in which the technical and economic feasibility of the manufacturing process is evaluated. The development phase also includes laboratory and use testing of a product for performance and safety. Following initial testing and refinement, most products are introduced in a test market to evaluate consumer response and marketing strategies. Finally, test market successes are propelled into full commercialization. The commercialization process involves starting up production, building inventories, shipping to distributors, training a sales force, announcing the product to the trade, and advertising to consumers.

2.1 List the advantages of simultaneous product development.

2.2 You are a marketing manager for Nike. Your department has come up with the idea of manufacturing a baseball bat for use in colleges around the nation. Assuming you are in the business analysis stage, write a brief analysis based on the questions in the "Business Analysis" section of the chapter.

2.3 What are the major disadvantages to test marketing, and how might they be avoided?

2.4 How could information from customer orders at **http://www.pizzahut.com** help the company's marketers plan new-product developments?

3 **Explain why some products succeed and others fail.** The most important factor in determining the success of a new product is the extent to which the product matches the needs of the market. Good matches are frequently successful. Poor matches are not.

3.1 In small groups, brainstorm ideas for a new wet-weather clothing line. What type of product would potential customers want and need? Prepare and deliver a brief presentation to your class.

4 **Discuss global issues in new-product development.** A marketer with global vision seeks to develop products that can easily be adapted to suit local needs. The goal is not simply to develop a standard product that can be sold worldwide. Smart global marketers also look for good product ideas worldwide.

4.1 Visit **http://pg.com** and look at the brands it offers around the world. What conclusions can you draw about Procter & Gamble's global new-product development strategy?

5 **Explain the diffusion process through which new products are adopted.** The diffusion process is the spread of a new product from its producer to ultimate adopters. Adopters in the diffusion process belong to five categories: innovators, early adopters, the early majority, the late majority, and laggards. Product characteristics that affect the rate of adoption include product complexity, compatibility with existing social values, relative advantage over existing substitutes, visibility, and "trialability." The diffusion process is facilitated by word-of-mouth communication and communication from marketers to consumers.

5.1 Describe some products whose adoption rates have been affected by complexity, compatibility, relative advantage, observability, and/or "trialability."

5.2 What type of adopter behavior do you typically follow? Explain.

5.3 *WRITING* Review Exhibit 10.3. Analyze each product on the graph according to the characteristics that influence the rate of adoption. For example, what can you conclude from the data about the relative advantage of DVD Audio? Write 1 to 2 pages explaining your analysis.

6 **Explain the concept of product life cycles.** All brands and product categories undergo a life cycle with four stages: introduction, growth, maturity, and decline. The rate at which products move through these stages varies dramatically. Marketing managers use the product life cycle concept as an analytical tool to forecast a product's future and devise effective marketing strategies.

6.1 *INFOTRAC COLLEGE EDITION* *ONLINE* Place the personal computer on the product life cycle curve, and give reasons for placing it where you did. Use InfoTrac (**http://www.infotrac-college.com**) to consult publications like *Technology Review*, *Computer World*, and *Computer Weekly* to help support your position.

TERMS

adopter 346
brainstorming 337
business analysis 338
commercialization 342
concept test 338
decline stage 351
development 339

diffusion 346
growth stage 350
innovation 346
introductory stage 349
maturity stage 350
new product 334
new-product strategy 335

product category 348
product development 337
product life cycle (PLC) 348
screening 337
simulated (laboratory) market testing 342
simultaneous product development 339
test marketing 340

EXERCISES

APPLICATION EXERCISE

A simple statistical analysis will help you better understand the types of new products. As in the Application Exercise in Chapter 5, you will be using print advertisements, but you will also be adding information from other sources (TV ads, trips to the store, and the like).[41]

Activities

1. Compile a list of 100 new products. If you are building a portfolio of ads (see the Application Exercise in Chapter 5), you can generate part of this list as you collect print advertisements for the topics in this chapter. Consider tabulating television ads for new products that are aired during programs you normally watch. A trip to the grocery could probably yield your entire list, but then your list would be limited to consumer products.

2. Make a table with six columns labeled as follows: new-to-the-world products, new product line, addition to existing product line, improvement/revision of existing product line, repositioned product, and lower-priced product.

3. Place each of your 100 new products into one of the six categories. Tabulate your results at the bottom of each column. What conclusions can you draw from the distribution of your products? Consider adding your results together with the rest of the class to get a larger and more random sample.

ETHICS EXERCISE

One source of new-product ideas is competitors. Steven Fischer recently joined Frankie and Alex Specialty Products as a brand manager. His new boss told him, "We don't have a budget for new-product development. We just monitor our competitors' new-product introductions and offer "knockoffs" or copies of any that look like they will be successful."

Questions

1. Is this practice ethical?
2. Does the AMA Code of Ethics address this issue? Go to **http://www.marketingpower.com** and review the code. Then, write a brief paragraph on what the AMA Code of Ethics contains that relates to knockoff products.

CAREER EXERCISE

New-product development is undertaken by third-party providers on behalf of companies as well as by companies themselves.

Activities

1. Companies like IDEO (**http://www.ideo.com**) and New Product Innovations (**http://www.npi.com**) provide new-product development services to companies like Procter & Gamble, Motorola, Bausch & Lomb, TaylorMade Golf, Handspring, and others. Research these and other similar companies for job opportunities.
2. A site called "ExpertsOn" collects numerous resources on a variety of topics together in one place. Go to **http://www.expertson.com** and follow the link to New Product Development to find resources that will enrich your job search for a job in this field.

ENTREPRENEURSHIP CASE

COURTESY OF THE VALVOLINE COMPANY

VALVOLINE: COMING TO A PEP RALLY NEAR YOU

Be prepared for surprises at Valvoline's research and development lab in Lexington, Kentucky. You might picture lab director Fran Lockwood poring over bottles of colored fluids or frowning over mathematical equations. But recently, she was touching up a picture she'd drawn on the wall by her desk with a can of black Spirit Foam.

The foam, a decorative spray that will not drip, was developed by Lockwood's crew of scientists. Lockwood had drawn a pumpkin, a lopsided one with two bats—not birds, she insisted—flying overhead. She wasn't happy with the way the eyes on the pumpkin had turned out.

This is not what you'd expect from the top scientist at Valvoline, a chemist who runs a $4.9 million lab. But then, Spirit Foam isn't the kind of product you'd expect from a company like Valvoline, the world's oldest premium motor oil brand.

During three years of research, testing, and tweaking, Lockwood's scientists revved up their creative engines to create Spirit Foam. Valvoline is taking the product, its first nonautomotive invention brought to market in its 108-year history, for a test-drive at Wal-Mart stores across the nation.

Analysts are applauding Valvoline's move, one the company's competitors have also made in recent years. Pennzoil–Quaker State introduced Glass Chalk, a chalk that can be used to write on glass, about two years ago, and its Medo division makes air fresheners for the home. Industry observers think it is time Valvoline stepped out, too.

"They're pretty well-known, so it makes sense for them to spin into other products to take advantage of that," says Mike Beall of Davenport & Company LLC in Richmond, Virginia. "It's clever of them to try it. They have the maturity to carry it out."

Spirit Foam has sold beyond the company's expectations. The product contributed about $500,000 in profits to the company in its first month on the shelf. Wal-Mart quickly asked Valvoline to move the product out of testing mode and into full production.

According to Jim O'Brien, the company's president, Valvoline wanted its first steps out of its motor oil box to be made with a product that would easily capture the public's attention: "We wanted to prove that we can call on customers we don't normally call on and be welcomed in, and have an audience." O'Brien says that while the motor oil market will be a profitable market for Valvoline for many years, it is growing at only 1 to 2 percent per year. This means that new-product development can play a large role in the company's future. Plans for other products are already in the works. Lockwood has formed a strategic group dedicated to exploring new-project areas, and she plans to have a new-product idea every year.

"We're not going to leave our core business to chase a few whiffs," O'Brien says. "We were feeling around outside the box, but we're not jumping out. This is more of an evolution than a revolution."[42]

Questions

1. How you think Spirit Foam's characteristics will affect its rate of adoption?

2. What advantages does Valvoline have when introducing a new product into a new marketplace?

3. Why is a new product like Spirit Foam so important to Valvoline's future? What kind of marketing strategy is Valvoline following?

4. To what category of new products does Spirit Foam belong? Why is this an advantage for Valvoline? Explain.

WATCH IT

FEATURE PRESENTATION

Ping

SmallBusinessSchool ▣
the Series on PBS stations and the Web

To give you insight into the concepts in Chapter 10, Small Business School introduces you to Karsten Manufacturing, the company famous for producing Ping Golf clubs. From the humble beginnings of his own garage, Karsten Solheim, the father of Ping Golf clubs, built one of the most recognized manufacturing companies the sports world has ever known. Solheim's company is most famous for its putters, clubs that, when first introduced, met with much speculation from consumers and, at one point, an outright ban from the United States Golf Association (USGA). More importantly, however, opinion leaders and leading professional golfers, Jack Nicklaus and Gary Player, greeted the clubs with enthusiasm. As televised golf grew in popularity, players at all levels saw repeatedly that professional tournament winners were using the radical new putter and decided to give it a try. Eventually, Karsten Manufacturing worked with the USGA to certify its clubs for USGA-sanctioned play, and the rest is history.

big brown bag

What to Watch For and Ask Yourself

1. In which category of new products does the Ping putter fit? What about Ping's other golf clubs?
2. Discuss the product development process for the Ping putter.
3. Discuss the product characteristics of the Ping putter and their effect on the rate of adoption.
4. Place Ping Golf clubs in the product life cycle. What is Ping doing to address this current position?

ENCORE PRESENTATION

October Sky

Watch the *October Sky* film scenes after you have studied the discussion of developing and managing products in Chapter 10. The film tells the true story of Homer Hickam's (Jake Gylenhaal) rise from a West Virginia coal-mining town to becoming a NASA engineer. The scenes are an edited composite of parts of the "Rocket Roulette" and "Splitting the Sky" sequences that appear a third of the way into the film. Although the Homer and his friends are not developing a new product for sale, the process they use to develop their rocket has many characteristics of the new-product development process described in this chapter. Which process characteristics do you see in these scenes? Are there examples of idea generation and idea screening in the scenes? What are they? Companies develop new products to sustain their profits and growth. What motivates Homer and his friends to solve their rocket functioning problem? Which new product category discussed in the beginning of this chapter best fits the result of their efforts?

STILL SHAKY?

If you're having trouble with the concepts in this chapter, consider using some of the following study resources. You can review the videos, or test yourself with materials designed for all kinds of learning styles.

☑ **Xtra! (http://lambxtra.swlearning.com)**

- ☑ Quiz
- ☑ Feature Videos
- ☑ Encore Videos
- ☑ FAQ Videos
- ☑ Exhibit Worksheets
- ☐ Marketing Plan Worksheets
- ☐ Content

☑ **http://lamb.swlearning.com**

- ☑ Quiz
- ☑ PowerPoint slides
- ☑ Marketing News
- ☑ Review Exercises
- ☑ Links
- ☑ Marketing Plan Contest
- ☑ Career Exercise
- ☑ Use It Now

☑ **Study guide**

- ☑ Outline
- ☑ Vocab Review
- ☑ Test Questions
- ☑ Marketing Scenario

Need More? Here's a tip. The main diagrams in this chapter are Exhibits 10.1, 10.4, 10.5, and 10.8. On a separate sheet, write the titles of these exhibits. Then, with your book closed, try to reproduce the diagrams exactly as they are in the book. Write a short description of what the diagram depicts, and open your book to check your work.

Services and Nonprofit Organization Marketing

11

LEARNING OBJECTIVES

1. Discuss the importance of services to the economy

2. Discuss the differences between services and goods

3. Describe the components of service quality and the gap model of service quality

4. Develop marketing mixes for services

5. Discuss relationship marketing in services

6. Explain internal marketing in services

7. Discuss global issues in services marketing

8. Describe nonprofit organization marketing

Few businesses are as adept at fulfilling their customers' every need as the world-famous Inn at Little Washington in Washington, Virginia. In fact, the 2003 *Zagat's* hotel survey ranked the inn's 100-seat dining room as America's best. The restaurant has a five-part system for delivering the superior service experience.

First, it is important to measure the customers' mood before they dine. When a new party arrives in the dining room, the captain assigns a number from 1 (low) to 10 (high) that assesses the guests' apparent state of mind. The mood rating is typed into a computer, written on the dinner order, and placed on a spool in the kitchen where the entire staff can see it. Whatever the circumstances, the goal of the staff is that no one should leave below a 9. Nothing is spared in the attempt to raise the number—be it complimentary champagne, extra desserts, a tableside visit from one of the owners, even a kitchen tour. "Consciousness to the extreme is great customer service," notes Chef Patrick O'Connell.

Second, the staff must go beyond being courteous and convey an extraordinary degree of competence. Employees are encouraged never to stop learning about their job, the inn, and anything else that might take the team closer to perfection. In line with that philosophy, all employees—from managers to waiters to hosts—are assigned research projects and expected to become the resident expert on their subject, which can range from wild mushrooms to French merlots and vintage port wines. And staff members demonstrate their expertise by giving presentations to their coworkers.

Third, failure is tolerated—once. Creating a great experience for customers requires everyone to be "on" all the time and to practice impeccable follow-through. If employees make mistakes by, say, pouring water the wrong way or removing a plate at an inappropriate time, the experience is tarnished. When such mistakes occur, O'Connell lets the offenders know immediately—a practice he calls "instant correction." "It sounds rough, but it actually reduces the employees' anxiety by letting them know what is expected," he says. "Plus, bad habits aren't allowed to form."

Fourth, hire for attitude. Talent means little if an employee has a lousy attitude, especially in the hospitality business. O'Connell has found that "over time, nice people can be taught almost anything." During the hiring process, potential employees are placed into two distinct groups: those who liked their past bosses and those who didn't. In nearly all cases, applicants who have positive things to say about previous jobs make better employees. In an industry known for its high employee turnover, the Inn at Little Washington manages to keep employees on board for years.

Finally, staffers are forbidden to say "no." If a guest asks if an appetizer is sweet, a waiter won't answer no—even if it's very spicy. Instead, the waiter describes the ingredients that make up the dish so diners can understand exactly what they're ordering and make their own informed decision. The phrase "I don't know" is also discouraged. Following several months of apprenticeship and training, all new waiters undergo a rigorous test, in which veteran staffers ask every imaginable question, from when the inn was built to peculiarities on the menu. Only after passing the test are waiters considered "full cut," meaning worthy of a portion of the significant tip pool. A monthly newsletter keeps everyone up-to-date, and a list is passed around enumerating the 12 most-asked questions and how they're to be answered.

O'Connell's perspective is that being in a service business requires a shift in your staff's mentality. "All of these policies help convey to our people that they don't deal in financial transactions, but rather financial dependencies—we owe our business to the customer and great service comes from showing incredible gratitude for precisely that."[1]

How does a service, like a restaurant, differ from goods—for example, soft drinks, automobiles, or blue jeans? What components of service quality, as presented in the gap model, are exemplified by the Inn at Little Washington?

1 THE IMPORTANCE OF SERVICES

 Discuss the importance of services to the economy

FAQs

Find out more about why service companies comprise such a large percentage of the GDP by watching the video FAQ on Xtra!

service
The result of applying human or mechanical efforts to people or objects.

A **service** is the result of applying human or mechanical efforts to people or objects. Services involve a deed, a performance, or an effort that cannot be physically possessed. Today, the service sector substantially influences the U.S. economy. The service sector accounts for 76 percent of the U.S. gross domestic product and 79 percent of employment.[2] In 2002, 64 of *Fortune*'s top 100 companies were service companies.[3] The demand for services is expected to continue. According to the Bureau of Labor Statistics, service occupations will be responsible for nearly all net job growth through the year 2012, as can be seen in Exhibit 11.1. Much of this demand results from demographics. An aging population will need nurses, home health care, physical therapists, and social workers. Two-earner families need child-care, housecleaning, and lawn-care services. Also increasing will be the demand for information managers, such as computer engineers and systems analysts. There is also a growing market for service companies worldwide. U.S. service exports are expected to reach $650 billion by 2010—about the same value as current U.S. exports of farm and manufactured goods.[4]

The marketing process described in Chapter 1 is the same for all types of products, whether they are goods or services. Many ideas and strategies discussed throughout this book have been illustrated with service examples. In many ways, marketing is marketing, regardless of the product's characteristics. In addition, although a comparison of goods and services marketing can be beneficial, in reality it is hard to distinguish clearly between manufacturing and service firms. Indeed, many manufacturing firms can point to service as a major factor in their success. For example, maintenance and repair services offered by the manufacturer are important to buyers of copy machines. General Electric makes most of its revenues from finance operations rather than from products.[5] Nevertheless, services have some unique characteristics that distinguish them from goods, and marketing strategies need to be adjusted for these characteristics.

REVIEW LEARNING OBJECTIVE 1

1 Discuss the importance of services to the economy

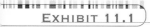

Services ⟶ Deed / Performance / Effort

Services as a percentage of GDP

10% 20% 30% 40% 50% 60% 70% 80% 90% 100%
76%

Services as a percentage of employment

10% 20% 30% 40% 50% 60% 70% 80% 90% 100%
79%

EXHIBIT 11.1

Service-Producing Industries and Job Growth

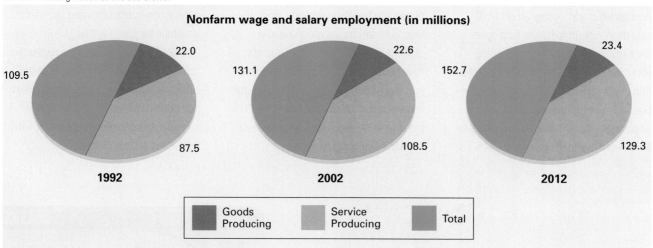

Nonfarm wage and salary employment (in millions)

1992	2002	2012
109.5 / 22.0 / 87.5	131.1 / 22.6 / 108.5	152.7 / 23.4 / 129.3

Goods Producing / Service Producing / Total

SOURCE: Bureau of Labor Statistics, http://www.bls.gov, February 1, 2004.

Discuss the differences between services and goods

Services have four unique characteristics that distinguish them from goods. Services are intangible, inseparable, heterogeneous, and perishable.

Web MD
What elements of the Web MD Web site communicate search, experience, and credence qualities of the services offered by the online medical consultant?
http://www.webmd.com

Online

intangibility
The inability of services to be touched, seen, tasted, heard, or felt in the same manner that goods can be sensed.

search quality
A characteristic that can be easily assessed before purchase.

experience quality
A characteristic that can be assessed only after use.

credence quality
A characteristic that consumers may have difficulty assessing even after purchase because they do not have the necessary knowledge or experience.

inseparability
The inability of the production and consumption of a service to be separated. Consumers must be present during the production.

INTANGIBILITY

The basic difference between services and goods is that services are intangible performances. Because of their **intangibility**, they cannot be touched, seen, tasted, heard, or felt in the same manner that goods can be sensed. Services cannot be stored and are often easy to duplicate.

Evaluating the quality of services before or even after making a purchase is harder than evaluating the quality of goods because, compared to goods, services tend to exhibit fewer search qualities. A **search quality** is a characteristic that can be easily assessed before purchase—for instance, the color of an appliance or automobile. At the same time, services tend to exhibit more experience and credence qualities. An **experience quality** is a characteristic that can be assessed only after use, such as the quality of a meal in a restaurant or the actual experience of a vacation. A **credence quality** is a characteristic that consumers may have difficulty assessing even after purchase because they do not have the necessary knowledge or experience. Medical and consulting services are examples of services that exhibit credence qualities.

These characteristics also make it harder for marketers to communicate the benefits of an intangible service than to communicate the benefits of tangible goods. Thus, marketers often rely on tangible cues to communicate a service's nature and quality. For example, Travelers' Insurance Company's use of the umbrella symbol helps make tangible the benefit of protection that insurance provides.

The facilities that customers visit, or from which services are delivered, are a critical tangible part of the total service offering. Messages about the organization are communicated to customers through such elements as the decor, the clutter or neatness of service areas, and the staff's manners and dress. The Sheraton Hotel chain replaced its outdated shag carpeting and flowered bedspreads with pin stripes and sleigh beds. Its goal was to restore a reputation for reliability and comfort and to avoid scaring off travelers with tacky accommodations. The new design features clubby library-like furnishings and practical amenities like ergonomic desk chairs and two-line phones. The remodeling is also a part of the strategy followed by Sheraton's parent company, Starwood Hotels & Resorts Worldwide, to differentiate the company's hotel brands aesthetically. For example, it wants its Sheratons to attract conservative business travelers, while its Westin Hotels are targeting younger, hipper, and somewhat richer overnighters.[6]

Even though you may initially think of goods and services as being distinctly different enterprises, many companies offer both. For example, a hair salon will often sell hair care products. Big hardware stores, like Home Depot, will often install the products they sell. Pictured here, trainer Steve Mraz explains a typical wiring circuit to attendees at a "Do It Herself" clinic at the Home Depot.

© AP/WIDE WORLD PHOTOS

INSEPARABILITY

Goods are produced, sold, and then consumed. In contrast, services are often sold, produced, and consumed at the same time. In other words, their production and consumption are inseparable activities. This **inseparability** means that,

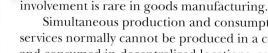

because consumers must be present during the production of services like haircuts or surgery, they are actually involved in the production of the services they buy. That type of consumer involvement is rare in goods manufacturing.

Simultaneous production and consumption also means that services normally cannot be produced in a centralized location and consumed in decentralized locations, as goods typically are. Services are also inseparable from the perspective of the service provider. Thus, the quality of service that firms are able to deliver depends on the quality of their employees.

FAQs

Is it really meaningful to distinguish between goods and services, since often they are interrelated? Find out the answer by watching the video FAQ on Xtra!

heterogeneity
The variability of the inputs and outputs of services, which cause services to tend to be less standardized and uniform than goods.

perishability
The inability of services to be stored, warehoused, or inventoried.

HETEROGENEITY

One great strength of McDonald's is consistency. Whether customers order a Big Mac and french fries in Fort Worth, Tokyo, or Moscow, they know exactly what they are going to get. This is not the case with many service providers. Because services have greater **heterogeneity** or variability of inputs and outputs, they tend to be less standardized and uniform than goods. For example, physicians in a group practice or barbers in a barber shop differ within each group in their technical and interpersonal skills. A given physician's or barber's performance may even vary depending on time of day, physical health, or some other factor. Because services tend to be labor-intensive and production and consumption are inseparable, consistency and quality control can be hard to achieve.

Standardization and training help increase consistency and reliability. Limited-menu restaurants like Pizza Hut and KFC offer customers high consistency from one visit to the next because of standardized preparation procedures. Another way to increase consistency is to mechanize the process. Banks have reduced the inconsistency of teller services by providing automated teller machines (ATMs). Automatic coin receptacles on toll roads have replaced human collectors.

REVIEW LEARNING OBJECTIVE 2

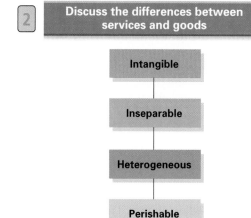

2 | **Discuss the differences between services and goods**

Intangible

Inseparable

Heterogeneous

Perishable

PERISHABILITY

The fourth characteristic of services is their **perishability**, which means that they cannot be stored, warehoused, or inventoried. An empty hotel room or airplane seat produces no revenue that day. The revenue is lost. Yet service organizations are often forced to turn away full-price customers during peak periods.

One of the most important challenges in many service industries is finding ways to synchronize supply and demand. The philosophy that some revenue is better than none has prompted many hotels to offer deep discounts on weekends and during the off-season and has prompted airlines to adopt similar pricing strategies during off-peak hours. Car rental agencies, movie theaters, and restaurants also use discounts to encourage demand during nonpeak periods.

3 SERVICE QUALITY

Describe the components of service quality and the gap model of service quality

Because of the four unique characteristics of services, service quality is more difficult to define and measure than is the quality of tangible goods. Business executives rank the improvement of service quality as one of the most critical challenges facing them today.

Research has shown that customers evaluate service quality by the following five components:[7]

- *Reliability:* the ability to perform the service dependably, accurately, and consistently. Reliability is performing the service right the first time. This component has been found to be the one most important to consumers.
- *Responsiveness:* the ability to provide prompt service. Examples of responsiveness include calling the customer back quickly, serving lunch fast to someone who is in a hurry, or mailing a transaction slip immediately. The ultimate in responsiveness is offering service 24 hours a day, seven days a week. For example, customer service representatives answer calls round the clock at Relocation Management Resources, Inc., which arranges all the details of transporting household goods for companies that are relocating their employees. Even the company's president invites customers to call his cell phone at all hours.[8]
- *Assurance:* the knowledge and courtesy of employees and their ability to convey trust. Skilled employees who treat customers with respect and make customers feel that they can trust the firm exemplify assurance.
- *Empathy:* caring, individualized attention to customers. Firms whose employees recognize customers, call them by name, and learn their customers' specific requirements are providing empathy. Union Square Hospitality Group, owner of several popular New York City restaurants, returns items customers have left behind by messenger or FedEx so that the customers do not have to come back to retrieve their belongings.[9]
- *Tangibles:* the physical evidence of the service. The tangible parts of a service include the physical facilities, tools, and equipment used to provide the service, such as a doctor's office or an ATM, and the appearance of personnel. For example, Enterprise Rent-A-Car has strict dress codes for its employees. Female employees have 30 guidelines including that pants must be creased, skirts must not be shorter than two inches above the knee, and legs must be in stockings. Male employees have to follow 26 dress rules, including dress shirts with coordinated ties and no beards. In fact, "distinctive professional dress" is mentioned in Enterprise's written founding values.[10] Hospitals have found that improving their layouts and looks can translate into better health for their patients. After the Barbara Ann Karmanos Cancer Institute in Detroit was renovated, using soft colors, warm indirect lighting, wider hallways and doors, and pullout sofas for visitors, hospital administrators found that patients dealt more effectively with their pain than they had before the remodeling.[11]

Overall service quality is measured by combining customers' evaluations for all five components.

THE GAP MODEL OF SERVICE QUALITY

A model of service quality called the **gap model** identifies five gaps that can cause problems in service delivery and influence customer evaluations of service quality.[12] These gaps are illustrated in Exhibit 11.2:

reliability
The ability to perform a service dependably, accurately, and consistently.

responsiveness
The ability to provide prompt service.

assurance
The knowledge and courtesy of employees and their ability to convey trust.

empathy
Caring, individualized attention to customers.

tangibles
The physical evidence of a service, including the physical facilities, tools, and equipment used to provide the service.

gap model
A model identifying five gaps that can cause problems in service delivery and influence customer evaluations of service quality.

EXHIBIT 11.2

Gap Model of Service Quality

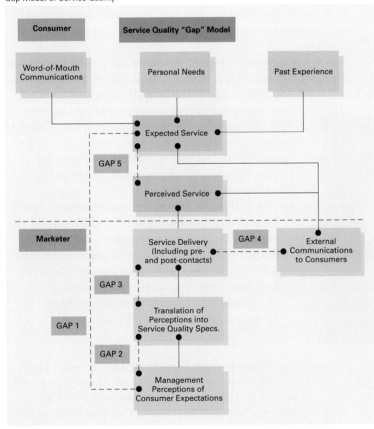

SOURCE: Valarie A. Zeithaml, A. Parasuraman, and Leonard L. Berry, "A Conceptual Model of Service Quality and Its Implications for Future Research," *Journal of Marketing*, 49 (fall) 1985, 41–50.

Plate Inflation

There really is no sure way to determine the quality of a service before you experience it, but the *Zagat Survey* helps to minimize your chances, say, of having an unexpectedly bad meal. The guide started 25 years ago when Tim and Nina Zagat informally polled a group of friends about their experiences at New York eateries. Today, *Zagat Survey* is the world's leading provider of consumer survey–based leisure guides for restaurants, hotels, nightlife, movies, shopping, and a range of other entertainment services, now including music. The guides include the reviews and ratings of over 250,000 surveyors and are available in print and online, Palm and Pocket PC formats, mobile phones, television, and radio. *Zagat's* differentiates itself from the local newspaper critic this way: those reviews are enjoyable, entertaining even, but *Zagat* reviews help you make a decision. Some who have used the guide since its inception, however, are beginning to doubt that distinction. When the guide began, the mean score for all New York restaurants was 16.5 out of 30, or at the low end of the good/very good range of 16–20. Last year, however, the mean had risen to 19.93, or over 30 percent, probably much like the prices at the restaurants the guide reviews.[14]

- *Gap 1:* the gap between what customers want and what management thinks customers want. This gap results from a lack of understanding or a misinterpretation of the customers' needs, wants, or desires. A firm that does little or no customer satisfaction research is likely to experience this gap. An important step in closing gap 1 is to keep in touch with what customers want by doing research on customer needs and customer satisfaction. Every year, Susquehanna Health System looks at its own as well as national surveys of patient satisfaction to determine what patients really want.[13]

- *Gap 2:* the gap between what management thinks customers want and the quality specifications that management develops to provide the service. Essentially, this gap is the result of management's inability to translate customers' needs into delivery systems within the firm. For example, Kentucky Fried Chicken once rated its managers' success according to "chicken efficiency," or how much chicken they threw away at the end of the night. Consumers who came in late at night would either have to wait for chicken to be cooked or settle for chicken several hours old. The "chicken efficiency" measurement did not take customers into account.

- *Gap 3:* the gap between the service quality specifications and the service that is actually provided. If both gaps 1 and 2 have been closed, then gap 3 is due to the inability of management and employees to do what should be done. Poorly trained or poorly motivated workers can cause this gap. Management needs to ensure that employees have the skills and the proper tools to perform their jobs. Other techniques that help to close gap 3 are training employees so they know what management expects and encouraging teamwork.

- *Gap 4:* the gap between what the company provides and what the customer is told it provides. This is clearly a communication gap. It may include misleading or deceptive advertising campaigns promising more than the firm can deliver or doing "whatever it takes" to get the business. To close this gap, companies need to create realistic customer expectations through honest, accurate communication about what the firms can provide.

  - *Gap 5:* the gap between the service that customers receive and the service they want. This gap can be positive or negative. For example, if a patient expects to wait 20 minutes in the physician's office before seeing the physician but waits only 10 minutes, the patient's evaluation of service quality will be high. However, a 40-minute wait would result in a lower evaluation.

    When any one or more of these gaps are large, service quality is perceived as low. As the gaps shrink, service quality improves. For instance, Ritz-Carlton has excelled in closing gap 3. This hotel firm puts potential employees through a comprehensive screening process to match their skills with positions for which they are naturally inclined. Ritz-Carlton also sponsors one

© STEVE DUNWELL/CORBIS

Ritz-Carlton works hard to close any gaps in service its customers might experience. The Baldrige National Quality Award winner trains its employees to give superior service in one of the most thorough training programs in the business world.

of the most thorough training programs in the business world. Its frontline employees undergo 300 hours of training their first year and 120 hours per year thereafter. They learn how all the areas in the hotel work together to provide customer satisfaction. They also learn about the company's vision and the high service standards it aims to achieve with each guest experience. When they first report to their jobs, they are paired with a trainer, who is an experienced coworker. Ritz-Carlton employees are authorized to spend up to $2,000 on the spot to make sure a customer's needs are met. For example, a couple mentioned to their bellhop in passing that they were on their honeymoon. He sent them champagne and flowers, creating a lasting, positive impression. The company also recognizes and rewards employee contributions by listing them in its weekly newsletter, paying spot cash bonuses, and mentioning great acts of service during each hotel's daily morning meeting.[15] The result has been consistently superior service delivery—so superior that Ritz-Carlton has twice won the Baldrige National Quality Award.

REVIEW LEARNING OBJECTIVE 3

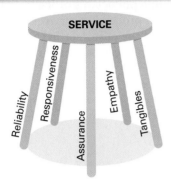

3 Describe the components of service quality and the gap model of service quality

SERVICE

Reliability | Responsiveness | Assurance | Empathy | Tangibles

4 MARKETING MIXES FOR SERVICES

Develop marketing mixes for services

Services' unique characteristics—intangibility, inseparability of production and consumption, heterogeneity, and perishability—make marketing more challenging. Elements of the marketing mix (product, place, promotion, and pricing) need to be adjusted to meet the special needs created by these characteristics.

PRODUCT (SERVICE) STRATEGY

A product, as defined in Chapter 9, is everything a person receives in an exchange. In the case of a service organization, the product offering is intangible and consists in large part of a process or a series of processes. Product strategies for service offerings include decisions on the type of process involved, core and supplementary services, standardization or customization of the service product, and the service mix.

Service as a Process

Two broad categories of things get processed in service organizations: people and objects. In some cases, the process is physical, or tangible, while in others the process is intangible. Based on these characteristics, service processes can be placed into one of four categories:[16]

Dry cleaning is an example of possession processing services. These types of services require less focus on attractive physical environments and customer service training than people processing services like hairdressers and airlines.

© THE RITZ-CARLTON HOTEL COMPANY, L.L.C.

- *People processing* takes place when the service is directed at a customer. Examples are transportation services, hairstyling, health clubs, and dental and health care.
- *Possession processing* occurs when the service is directed at customers' physical possessions. Examples are lawn care, car repair, dry cleaning, and veterinary services.
- *Mental stimulus processing* refers to services directed at people's minds. Examples are entertainment, spectator sports events, theater performances, and education.

EXHIBIT 11.3

Core and Supplementary Services for FedEx

SOURCE: From *Services Marketing,* 3rd ed., by Christopher H. Lovelock, © 1996. Reprinted by permission of Prentice-Hall, Inc., Upper Saddle River, NJ.

- *Information processing* describes services that use technology or brainpower directed at a customer's assets. Examples are insurance, banking, and consulting.

Because customers' experiences and involvement differ for each of these types of services, marketing strategies may also differ. For example, people processing services require customers to enter the *service factory*, which is a physical location, such as an aircraft, a physician's office, or a hair salon. In contrast, possession processing services typically do not require the presence of the customer in the service factory; the customer may simply leave the car at the garage for repairs, for example. Marketing strategies for the former would therefore focus more on an attractive, comfortable physical environment and employee training on employee-customer interaction issues than would strategies for the latter.

Core and Supplementary Service Products

The service offering can be viewed as a bundle of activities that includes the **core service**, which is the most basic benefit the customer is buying, and a group of **supplementary services** that support or enhance the core service. Exhibit 11.3 illustrates these concepts for FedEx. The core service is overnight transportation and delivery of packages, which involves possession processing. The supplementary services, some of which involve information processing, include problem solving, advice and information, billing statements, and order taking. Starbucks has added a wireless Internet service called "T-Mobile HotSpot" that enhances its core offering—the Starbucks' experience of high-quality coffee served in a coffeehouse atmosphere. Starbucks is not trying to become an Internet coffeehouse, but to become the "other place" where people want to be connected to the Internet.[17]

In many service industries, the core service becomes a commodity as competition increases. Thus, firms usually emphasize supplementary services to create a competitive advantage. Virgin Atlantic, Malaysia Airlines, and Japan Airlines provide complimentary limo service to and from the airport. Virgin's chauffeurs check in passengers en route. In some cities, United Airlines delivers passengers' luggage to their hotels so that they can go straight to business meetings.[18] On the other hand, some firms are positioning themselves in the marketplace by greatly reducing supplementary services. For example, Microtel Inn is an amenity-free hotel concept known as "fast lodging." These low-cost hotels have one- and two-bedroom accommodations and a swimming pool, but no meeting rooms or other services.

Customization/Standardization

An important issue in developing the service offering is whether to customize or standardize it. Customized services are more flexible and respond to individual customers' needs. They also usually command a higher price. The traditional law firm, which treats each case differently according to the client's situation, offers customized services. Standardized services are more efficient and cost less. Unlike the traditional law firm, for example, Hyatt Legal Services offers low-cost, standardized service "packages" for those with uncomplicated legal needs, such as drawing up a will or mediating an uncontested divorce.

Instead of choosing to either standardize or customize a service, a firm may incorporate elements of both by adopting an emerging strategy called **mass customization**. Mass customization uses technology to deliver customized services on a mass basis, which results in giving each customer whatever she or he asks for.

core service
The most basic benefit the consumer is buying.

supplementary services
A group of services that support or enhance the core service.

mass customization
A strategy that uses technology to deliver customized services on a mass basis.

For example, a feature on Lands' End Web site allows women to define their figures online, receive advice on what swimsuits will flatter their shapes, and mix and match more than 216 combinations of colors and styles. Several airlines are designing services to cater to travelers' individual needs and preferences. Some will serve dinner to passengers when they want to eat it, rather than when the airline wants to serve it. More airlines are offering video-on-demand systems, which let passengers start or stop their movie anytime they want. British Airlines predicts that there will be airline seats that will read passengers' shapes and program their seat-position preferences into smart cards.[19]

Making services more personalized is the goal of mass customization. For example, airlines are rolling out personal interactive entertainment systems on airplanes so that passengers can watch movies when they want, rather than only at a set time during the flight.

The Service Mix

Most service organizations market more than one service. For example, ChemLawn offers lawn care, shrub care, carpet cleaning, and industrial lawn services. Each organization's service mix represents a set of opportunities, risks, and challenges. Each part of the service mix should make a different contribution to achieving the firm's goals. To succeed, each service may also need a different level of financial support.

Designing a service strategy therefore means deciding what new services to introduce to which target market, what existing services to maintain, and what services to eliminate. For example, to increase membership, AAA added financial services, credit cards, and travel perks. Organic, a San Francisco–based company that designs Web sites for clients, has set up two new service divisions: Organic Communications, a full-service public relations department; and Organic Logistics, which helps clients figure out how to get products ordered online into customers' hands.[20]

PLACE (DISTRIBUTION) STRATEGY

Distribution strategies for service organizations must focus on such issues as convenience, number of outlets, direct versus indirect distribution, location, and scheduling. A key factor influencing the selection of a service provider is *convenience*. Therefore, service firms must offer convenience. Many banks have opened small branches in supermarkets and discount stores like Wal-Mart to make it more convenient for customers to use their services. Restaurants such as Chili's and Macaroni Grill deliver take-out food to customers waiting in their cars. Some doctors are even starting to make house calls to elderly and infirm patients.[21]

An important distribution objective for many service firms is the *number of outlets* to use or the number of outlets to open during a certain time. Generally, the intensity of distribution should meet, but not exceed, the target market's needs and preferences. Having too few outlets may inconvenience customers; having too many outlets may boost costs unnecessarily. Intensity of distribution may also depend on the image desired. Having only a few outlets may make the service seem more exclusive or selective.

The next service distribution decision is whether to distribute services to end users *directly* or *indirectly* through other firms. Because of the intangible nature of services, many service firms have to use direct distribution or franchising. Examples include legal, medical, accounting, and personal-care services. The newest form of direct distribution is the Internet. Most of the major airlines are now using online services to sell tickets directly to consumers, which results in lower distribution costs for the airline companies. Merrill Lynch offers Merrill Lynch OnLine, an Internet-based service that connects clients with company representatives. Other firms with standardized service packages have developed indirect channels using independent intermediaries. For example, Bank of America is offering teller services and loan services to customers in small satellite facilities located in Albertson's grocery stores in Texas.

The *location* of a service most clearly reveals the relationship between its target market strategy and distribution strategy. Reportedly, Conrad Hilton claimed that the three most important factors in determining a hotel's success are "location, location, and location." An interesting location trend has started in the banking industry. In the past few years, banks aggressively directed customers away from branches and toward ATMs and the Internet. In a recent about-face, banks are trying to entice customers back into the branches. For example, Washington Mutual, Inc., based in Seattle, is designing new branches and remodeling old ones to resemble a Gap store. Each branch employs a concierge who greets customers. Tellers and managers in khakis and casual shirts walk the floor offering traditional bank services as well as products such as insurance and mutual funds. Customers can also buy products such as colorful calculators, pens, and piggy banks.[22]

For time-dependent service providers like airlines, physicians, and dentists, scheduling is often a more important factor. Scheduling is sometimes the most important factor in a customer's choice of airline.

PROMOTION STRATEGY

Consumers and business users have more trouble evaluating services than goods because services are less tangible. In turn, marketers have more trouble promoting intangible services than tangible goods. Here are four promotion strategies they can try:

- *Stressing tangible cues:* A tangible cue is a concrete symbol of the service offering. To make their intangible services more tangible, hotels turn down the bedcovers and put mints on the pillows. Insurance companies use symbols like rocks, blankets, umbrellas, and hands to help make their intangible services appear tangible. Merrill Lynch uses a bull to help give its services substance.
- *Using personal information sources:* A personal information source is someone consumers are familiar with (such as a celebrity) or someone they know or can relate to personally. Celebrity endorsements are sometimes used to reduce customers' perceived risk in choosing a service. Service firms may also seek to simulate positive word-of-mouth communication among present and prospective customers by using real customers in their ads.
- *Creating a strong organizational image:* One way to create an image is to manage the evidence, including the physical environment of the service facility, the appearance of the service employees, and the tangible items associated with a service (like stationery, bills, and business cards). For example, McDonald's has created a strong organizational image with its Golden Arches, relatively standardized interiors, and employee uniforms. Another way to create an image is through branding. Disney brands include Disneyland, Disney World, the Disney Channel, and Disney Stores. The "Global Perspectives" box describes how Disney has been able to extend its brand internationally.
- *Engaging in postpurchase communication:* Postpurchase communication refers to the follow-up activities that a service firm might engage in after a customer transaction. Postcard surveys, telephone calls, brochures, and various other types of follow-up show customers that their feedback matters and their patronage is appreciated.

PRICE STRATEGY

Considerations in pricing a service are similar to the pricing considerations to be discussed in Chapters 17 and 18. However, the unique characteristics of services present two special pricing challenges.

First, in order to price a service, it is important to define the unit of service consumption. For example, should pricing be based on completing a specific service task

> A CERTAIN "JE NE SAIS QUOI" AT DISNEY'S NEW PARK

When visitors take a tram ride through the Walt Disney Studios' theme park in Marne la Vallée, France, their virtual tour guides won't be Hollywood stars like Bruce Willis. Instead, European actors like Jeremy Irons, Isabella Rossellini, and Natassja Kinski will be speaking—and in their native tongues.

A decade after being slammed for its alleged ignorance of European ways with Disneyland Paris, Disney is trying to prove it has gotten things right the second time around. Disneyland Paris, was considered a flop for years after its 1992 opening. Disney was criticized for creating a mere outpost of American cultural imperialism, even failing to include such basic local customs as serving wine with meals.

Over time, Disney added more local flourishes and food options that seems to have quieted critics and improved business. Small details reflect the cultural lessons learned. For example, food venues now have covered seating. When Disneyland Paris first opened, open-air restaurants offered no protection from the rain that ails the park for long stretches of the year.

Today Disneyland Paris is Europe's biggest tourist attraction—even more popular than the Eiffel Tower—a turnaround that showed the park operators' ability to learn from their mistakes.

A second park intends to capitalize on that by getting visitors from around Europe to stay an extra day at the resort. The hope is to boost attendance to 17 million visitors a year. The second park's general layout is modeled after an old Hollywood studio complex, and some of the rides and shows are near replicas of Disney–MGM Studios in Orlando, Florida with some noteworthy exceptions. A show celebrating the history of animation involves a montage of Disney characters speaking six different languages. A big stunt show, designed by French stuntman Remy Julienne, features cars and motorcycles that race through a village modeled after the French resort town of St. Tropez.

Disney sells the new park through travel agents, whom Disney initially left out of the loop in promoting Disneyland Paris. Travel operators control a large portion of the market, so one of seven new hotels being built at the resort—all in partnership with major hotel operators like Marriott International—is a joint venture with Airtours, PLC, the biggest tour operator in the United Kingdom.[23]

Explain the advantages to Disney of having international theme parks. What marketing elements might the company have to adjust in different countries?

The owner of 112 McDonald's restaurants in Switzerland leveraged the company's strong organizational image (quality, service, cleanliness, and hygiene) and created a hotel. The four-star Golden Arch Hotel is extremely modern in its design, offers wireless Internet connections through the television, and is priced as if it were a two-star hotel: only around $90 per night.

(cutting a customer's hair), or should it be time based (how long it takes to cut a customer's hair)? Some services include the consumption of goods, such as food and beverages. Restaurants charge customers for food and drink rather than the use of a table and chairs. Some transportation firms charge by distance; others charge a flat rate.

Second, for services that are composed of multiple elements, the issue is whether pricing should be based on a "bundle" of elements or whether each element should be priced separately. A bundled price may be preferable when consumers dislike having to pay "extra" for every part of the service (for example, paying extra for baggage or food on an airplane), and it is simpler for the firm to administer. For instance, MCI offered a basic communications package that included 30 minutes of telephone time, five hours of Internet access, a personal number that could route calls to several locations, and a calling card all for one price. Alternatively, customers may not want to pay for service elements they do not use. Many furniture stores now have "unbundled" delivery charges from the price of the furniture. Customers who wish to can pick up the furniture at the store, saving on the delivery fee.

Marketers should set performance objectives when pricing each service. Three categories of pricing objectives have been suggested:[24]

- *Revenue-oriented pricing* focuses on maximizing the surplus of income over costs. A limitation of this approach is that determining costs can be difficult for many services.
- *Operations-oriented pricing* seeks to match supply and demand by varying prices. For example, matching hotel demand to the number of available rooms can be achieved by raising prices at peak times and decreasing them during slow times.
- *Patronage-oriented pricing* tries to maximize the number of customers using the service. Thus, prices vary with different market segments' ability to pay, and methods of payment (such as credit) are offered that increase the likelihood of a purchase.

A firm may need to use more than one type of pricing objective. In fact, all three objectives probably need to be included to some degree in a pricing strategy, although the importance of each type may vary depending on the type of service provided, the prices that competitors are charging, the differing ability of various customer segments to pay, or the opportunity to negotiate price. For customized services (for example, legal services and construction services), customers may also have the ability to negotiate a price.

REVIEW LEARNING OBJECTIVE 4

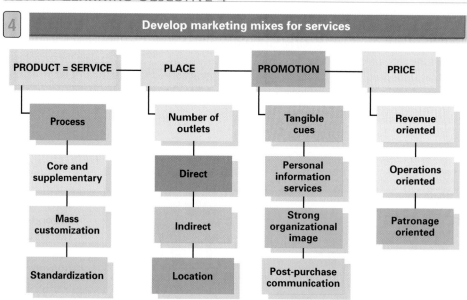

5 RELATIONSHIP MARKETING IN SERVICES

Discuss relationship marketing in services

Many services involve ongoing interaction between the service organization and the customer. Thus, they can benefit from relationship marketing, the strategy described in Chapter 1, as a means of attracting, developing, and retaining customer relationships. The idea is to develop strong loyalty by creating satisfied customers who will buy additional services from the firm and are unlikely to switch to a competitor. Satisfied customers are also likely to engage in positive word-of-mouth communication, thereby helping to bring in new customers.

Many businesses have found that it is more cost-effective to hang on to the customers they have than to focus only on attracting new ones. A bank executive, for example, found that increasing customer retention by 2 percent can have the same effect on profits as reducing costs by 10 percent.

Services that purchasers receive on a continuing basis (for example, cable TV, banking, insurance) can be considered membership services. This type of service naturally lends itself to relationship marketing. When services involve discrete transactions (for example, a movie theater, a restaurant, public transportation), it may be more difficult to build membership-type relationships with customers. Nevertheless, services involving discrete transactions may be transformed into membership relationships using marketing tools. For example, the service could be sold in bulk (for example, a theater series subscription or a commuter pass on public transportation). Or a service firm could offer special benefits to customers who choose to register with the firm (for example, loyalty programs for hotels, airlines, and car rental firms). The service firm that has a more formalized relationship with its customers has an advantage because it knows who its customers are and how and when they use the services offered.[25]

It has been suggested that relationship marketing can be practiced at three levels:[26]

- *Level 1:* The firm uses pricing incentives to encourage customers to continue doing business with it. Examples include the frequent flyer programs offered by many airlines and the free or discounted travel services given to frequent hotel guests. This level of relationship marketing is the least effective in the long term because its price-based advantage is easily imitated by other firms.

- *Level 2:* This level of relationship marketing also uses pricing incentives but seeks to build social bonds with customers. The firm stays in touch with customers, learns about their needs, and designs services to meet those needs. 1-800-FLOWERS, for example, developed an online Gift Reminder Program. Customers who reach the company via its Web site can register unlimited birthdays, anniversaries, or other special occasions. Five days before each occasion and at their request, 1-800-FLOWERS sends them an e-mail reminder. Level 2 relationship marketing has a higher potential for keeping the firm ahead of the competition than does level 1 relationship marketing.

- *Level 3:* At this level, the firm again uses financial and social bonds but adds structural bonds to the formula. Structural bonds are developed by offering value-added services that are not readily available from other firms. Hertz's #1 Club Gold program allows members to call and reserve a car, board a courtesy bus at the airport, tell the driver their name, and get dropped off in front of their car. Hertz also starts up the car and turns on the air conditioning or heat, depending on the temperature. Marketing programs like this one have the strongest potential for sustaining long-term relationships with customers.

Building relationships with customers sometimes depends on using data collected by the service organization. However, this practice may not be welcomed by customers, as the "Ethics in Marketing" box illustrates.

REVIEW LEARNING OBJECTIVE 5

5 | **Discuss relationship marketing in services**

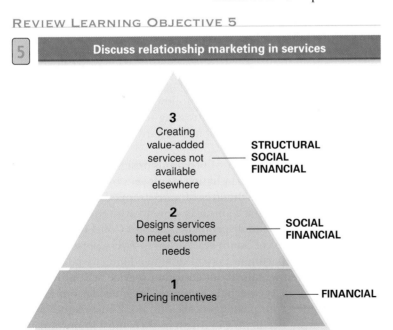

3
Creating value-added services not available elsewhere
— **STRUCTURAL** **SOCIAL** **FINANCIAL**

2
Designs services to meet customer needs
— **SOCIAL** **FINANCIAL**

1
Pricing incentives
— **FINANCIAL**

Ethics in Marketing Ethics in Marketing Ethics in Marketing Ethics in Marketing Ethics in Marketing Ethics in Marke
Ethics in MarketingEthics in MarketingEthics in Marketing Ethics in MarketingEthics in Marketing Ethics in Marke
Ethics in MarketingEthics in Marketing Ethics in Marketing Ethics in MarketingEthics in Marketing Ethics in Marke
Ethics in Marketing **ETHICS IN MARKETING** MarketingEthics in Marketing Ethics in Marke
Ethics in MarketingEthics in Marketing Ethics in Marketing Ethics in Marketing Ethics in Marke
Ethics in Marketing Ethics in Marketing
Ethics in Marketing

> SOON, THE DESK CLERK WILL KNOW ALL ABOUT YOU

Hilton Hotels has developed a sophisticated customer and hotel-management system in its 2,100 hotels. The $50 million network will amass a sizable marketing database of customers' habits and spending, in addition to everything from running the hotels' reservations systems to tracking inventory and room-cleaning schedules. The system will extend across all of Hilton's chains and will set the company apart from other big hotel companies. But the new technology also means that guests will have a bit less privacy.

The system ranks customers in order of their value to Hilton—how often they stay with the company and how much they spend. Once guests are identified at the front desk, the clerk will be prompted with the correct way to greet them: "I see this is your first time at an Embassy Suites. Let me tell you about our made-to-order breakfast," for instance. A clerk may be prompted to apologize that a guest's room wasn't made up on time during a trip to a Hampton Inn in Orlando, Florida, last year. The clerk will be only a few mouse clicks away from seeing the guests' bar bill last week at the Hilton Garden Inn in Cleveland and whether they used the

high-speed Internet there. All that information gets collected, and could be used to tailor marketing offers in the future.

Many travelers mistakenly think that hotels know more about them than they really do. In fact, such personalized data about preferences are often maintained by a general manager at a particular hotel but not shared with other properties in a chain. That's particularly true for big companies that have bought up chains and patched together inherited computer systems. For example, Hilton's Doubletree hotels, acquired in 1999, have had a hard time sharing information with Hilton Garden Inns, a homegrown chain.

Hilton expects the new technology will help it market more accurately to its 15 million customers by sharing more information between hotels. It also hopes to make its hotels operate more efficiently and to cut down on billing errors when data get lost in the patchwork of computer systems. The network is already reducing the frequency with which Hilton loses room deposits paid in advance of a stay.[27]

Is it ethical to collect and use database information to customize service?

6 INTERNAL MARKETING IN SERVICE FIRMS

Explain internal marketing in services

Services are performances, so the quality of a firm's employees is an important part of building long-term relationships with customers. Employees who like their jobs and are satisfied with the firm they work for are more likely to deliver superior service to customers. In other words, a firm that makes its employees happy has a better chance of keeping its customers coming back. Studies show that replacing an employee costs roughly 1.5 times a year's pay. Also, companies with highly committed employees have been found to post sharply higher shareholder returns.[28] Thus, it is critical that service firms practice **internal marketing**, which means treating employees as customers and developing systems and benefits that satisfy their needs. Internal marketing involves the following activities: competing for talent, offering a vision, training employees, stressing teamwork, giving employees more freedom to make decisions, measuring and rewarding good service performance, and knowing employees' needs.[29]

FAQs

Learn some specific examples of how companies practice internal service marketing by watching the video FAQ on Xtra!

Companies have instituted a wide variety of programs designed to satisfy employees. Some companies are trying to retain happy employees by offering concierges who run errands to help ease the lives of time-strapped, stressed-out workers.[30] Marriott International set up a 24-hour hotline to answer questions from employees having personal and family problems.[31] Notes Colleen Barrett, president and chief operating officer of Southwest Airlines, "Every person we hire, even if it's a back-room finance department person or a mechanic, we talk to them about customer service. And when we talk about customer service at Southwest, we're talking about internal as well as external customers. We consider our employees to be our No. 1 customers; our passengers are our No. 2 customers."[32] These examples illustrate how service firms can invest in their most important resource—their employees.

internal marketing
Treating employees as customers and developing systems and benefits that satisfy their needs.

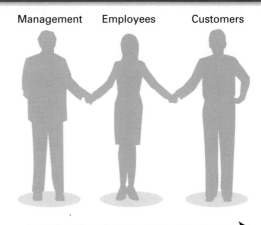

6 | Explain internal marketing in services

Management Employees Customers

Good service flows from management
to customers through employees.

7 GLOBAL ISSUES IN SERVICES MARKETING

Discuss global issues in services
marketing

The international marketing of services is a major part of global business, and the United States has become the world's largest exporter of services. Competition in international services is increasing rapidly, however.

To be successful in the global marketplace, service firms must first determine the nature of their core product. Then the marketing mix elements (additional services, place, promotion, pricing, distribution) should be designed to take into account each country's cultural, technological, and political environment.

REVIEW LEARNING OBJECTIVE 7

7 | Discuss global issues in services marketing

United States
is world's largest
exporter of
services.

Because of their competitive advantages, many U.S. service industries have been able to enter the global marketplace. U.S. banks, for example, have advantages in customer service and collections management. The field of construction and engineering services offers great global potential; U.S. companies have vast experience in this industry, so economies of scale are possible for machinery and materials, human resource management, and project management. The U.S. insurance industry has substantial knowledge about underwriting, risk evaluation, and insurance operations that it can export to other countries.

8 NONPROFIT ORGANIZATION MARKETING

Describe nonprofit organization
marketing

A **nonprofit organization** is an organization that exists to achieve some goal other than the usual business goals of profit, market share, or return on investment. Nonprofit organizations share important characteristics with private-sector service firms. Both market intangible products. Both often require the customer to be present during the production process. Both for-profit and nonprofit services vary greatly from producer to producer and from day to day, even from the same producer. Neither for-profit nor nonprofit services can be stored in the way that tangible goods can be produced, saved, and sold at a later date.

nonprofit organization
An organization that exists to achieve some goal other than the usual business goals of profit, market share, or return on investment.

Few people realize that nonprofit organizations account for over 20 percent of the economic activity in the United States. The cost of government (i.e., taxes), the predominant form of nonprofit organization, has become the biggest single item in the American family budget—more than housing, food, or health care. Together, federal, state, and local governments collect tax revenues that amount to more than a third of the U.S. gross domestic product. Moreover, they employ nearly one of every five nonagricultural civilian workers. In addition to government entities, nonprofit organizations include hundreds of thousands of private museums, theaters, schools, and churches.

WHAT IS NONPROFIT ORGANIZATION MARKETING?

Nonprofit organization marketing is the effort by nonprofit organizations to bring about mutually satisfying exchanges with target markets. Although these organizations vary substantially in size and purpose and operate in different environments, most perform the following marketing activities:

- Identify the customers they wish to serve or attract (although they usually use another term, such as *clients, patients, members,* or *sponsors*)
- Explicitly or implicitly specify objectives
- Develop, manage, and eliminate programs and services
- Decide on prices to charge (although they use other terms, such as *fees, donations, tuition, fares, fines,* or *rates*)
- Schedule events or programs, and determine where they will be held or where services will be offered
- Communicate their availability through brochures, signs, public service announcements, or advertisements

Often, the nonprofit organizations that carry out these functions do not realize they are engaged in marketing.

UNIQUE ASPECTS OF NONPROFIT ORGANIZATION MARKETING STRATEGIES

Like their counterparts in business organizations, nonprofit managers develop marketing strategies to bring about mutually satisfying exchanges with target markets. However, marketing in nonprofit organizations is unique in many ways—including the setting of marketing objectives, the selection of target markets, and the development of appropriate marketing mixes.

Objectives

In the private sector, the profit motive is both an objective for guiding decisions and a criterion for evaluating results. Nonprofit organizations do not seek to make a profit for redistribution to owners or shareholders. Rather, their focus is often on generating enough funds to cover expenses. The Methodist Church does not gauge its success by the amount of money left in offering plates. The Museum of Science and Industry does not base its performance evaluations on the dollar value of tokens put into the turnstile.

Most nonprofit organizations are expected to provide equitable, effective, and efficient services that respond to the wants and preferences of multiple constituencies. These include users, payers, donors, politicians, appointed officials, the media, and the general public. Nonprofit organizations cannot measure their success or failure in strictly financial terms.

The lack of a financial "bottom line" and the existence of multiple, diverse, intangible, and sometimes vague or conflicting objectives make prioritizing objectives, making decisions, and evaluating performance hard for nonprofit managers. They must often use approaches different from the ones commonly used in the private sector. For example, Planned Parenthood has devised a system for basing salary increases on how employees perform in relation to the objectives they set each year.

nonprofit organization marketing
The effort by nonprofit organizations to bring about mutually satisfying exchanges with target markets.

Target Markets

Three issues relating to target markets are unique to nonprofit organizations:

- *Apathetic or strongly opposed targets:* Private-sector organizations usually give priority to developing those market segments that are most likely to respond to particular offerings. In contrast, nonprofit organizations must often target those who are apathetic about or strongly opposed to receiving their services, such as vaccinations, family-planning guidance, help for problems of drug or alcohol abuse, and psychological counseling.
- *Pressure to adopt undifferentiated segmentation strategies:* Nonprofit organizations often adopt undifferentiated strategies (see Chapter 7) by default. Sometimes they fail to recognize the advantages of targeting, or an undifferentiated approach may appear to offer economies of scale and low per capita costs. In other instances, nonprofit organizations are pressured or required to serve the maximum number of people by targeting the average user. The problem with developing services targeted at the average user is that there are few "average" users. Therefore, such strategies typically fail to fully satisfy any market segment.
- *Complementary positioning:* The main role of many nonprofit organizations is to provide services, with available resources, to those who are not adequately served by private-sector organizations. As a result, the nonprofit organization must often complement, rather than compete with, the efforts of others. The positioning task is to identify underserved market segments and to develop marketing programs that match their needs rather than to target the niches that may be most profitable. For example, a university library may see itself as complementing the services of the public library, rather than as competing with it.

Product Decisions

There are three product-related distinctions between business and nonprofit organizations:

The Texas department of transportation used Santa Claus as a spokesperson to remind its target (Texas motorists) not to drink and drive. During a holiday season known for festive parties, being a designated driver can represent a high-involvement product for some.

- *Benefit complexity:* Rather than simple product concepts, like "Fly the friendly skies" or "We earn money the old-fashioned way," nonprofit organizations often market complex behaviors or ideas. Examples include the need to exercise or eat right, not to drink and drive, and not to smoke tobacco. The benefits that a person receives are complex, long term, and intangible and therefore are more difficult to communicate to consumers.
- *Benefit strength:* The benefit strength of many nonprofit offerings is quite weak or indirect. What are the direct, personal benefits to you of driving 55 miles per hour, donating blood, or asking your neighbors to contribute money to a charity? In contrast, most private-sector service organizations can offer customers direct, personal benefits in an exchange relationship.
- *Involvement:* Many nonprofit organizations market products that elicit very low involvement ("Prevent forest fires" or "Don't litter") or very high involvement ("Join the military" or "Stop smoking"). The typical range for private-sector goods is much narrower. Traditional promotional tools may be inadequate to motivate adoption of either low- or high-involvement products.

Place (Distribution) Decisions

A nonprofit organization's capacity for distributing its service offerings to potential customer groups when and where they want them is typically a key variable in determining the success of those service offerings. For example, most state land-grant universities offer extension programs throughout their state to reach the general public. Many large universities have one or more satellite campus locations to provide easier access for students in other areas. Some educational institutions also offer classes to students at off-campus locations via interactive video technology.

The extent to which a service depends on fixed facilities has important implications for distribution decisions. Obviously, services like rail transit and lake fishing can be delivered only at specific points. Many nonprofit services, however, do not depend on special facilities. Counseling, for example, need not take place in agency offices; it may occur wherever counselors and clients can meet. Probation services, outreach youth programs, and educational courses taught on commuter trains are other examples of deliverable services.

Promotion Decisions

Many nonprofit organizations are explicitly or implicitly prohibited from advertising, thus limiting their promotion options. Most federal agencies fall into this category. Other nonprofit organizations simply do not have the resources to retain advertising agencies, promotion consultants, or marketing staff. However, nonprofit organizations have a few special promotion resources to call on:

Cause-related marketing can be a controversial marketing technique because not all companies are as scrupulous as they should be about their intentions. A company like Newman's Own, however, which donates all after-tax profits to charity, is clear in its mission. By not profiting from using causes as a marketing tool, its motives are beyond reproach.

public service advertisement (PSA)

An announcement that promotes a program of a federal, state, or local government or of a non-profit organization.

- *Professional volunteers:* Nonprofit organizations often seek out marketing, sales, and advertising professionals to help them develop and implement promotion strategies. In some instances, an advertising agency donates its services in exchange for potential long-term benefits. One advertising agency donated its services to a major symphony because the symphony had a blue-ribbon board of directors. Donated services create goodwill, personal contacts, and general awareness of the donor's organization, reputation, and competency.

- *Sales promotion activities:* Sales promotion activities that make use of existing services or other resources are increasingly being used to draw attention to the offerings of nonprofit organizations. Sometimes nonprofit charities even team up with other companies for promotional activities. For example, in a number of large cities including Dallas, Chicago, and Denver, local charities lined up retailers such as Crate & Barrel and Polo Ralph Lauren to offer 20 percent discounts for a limited time to shoppers who purchased a special $50 card from the charity. To get the discount, the shopper simply showed the participating store the card.[33]

- *Public service advertising:* A **public service advertisement (PSA)** is an announcement that promotes a program of a federal, state, or local government or of a nonprofit organization. Unlike a commercial advertiser, the sponsor of the PSA does not pay for the time or space. Instead, it is donated by the medium. The Advertising Council has developed PSAs that are some of the most memorable advertisements of all time. For example, Smokey the Bear reminded everyone to be careful not to start forest fires.

Pricing Decisions

Five key characteristics distinguish the pricing decisions of nonprofit organizations from those of the profit sector:

- *Pricing objectives:* The main pricing objective in the profit sector is revenue or, more specifically, profit maximization, sales maximization, or target return on sales or investment. Many nonprofit organizations must also be concerned about revenue. Often, however, nonprofit organizations seek to either partially or fully defray costs rather than to achieve a profit for distribution to stockholders. Nonprofit organizations also seek to redistribute income—for instance, through taxation and sliding-scale fees. Moreover, they strive to allocate resources fairly among individuals or households or across geographic or political boundaries.
- *Nonfinancial prices:* In many nonprofit situations, consumers are not charged a monetary price but instead must absorb nonmonetary costs. The importance of those costs is illustrated by the large number of eligible citizens who do not take advantage of so-called free services for the poor. In many public assistance programs, about half the people who are eligible don't participate. Nonmonetary costs consist of the opportunity cost of time, embarrassment costs, and effort costs.
- *Indirect payment:* Indirect payment through taxes is common to marketers of "free" services, such as libraries, fire protection, and police protection. Indirect payment is not a common practice in the profit sector.
- *Separation between payers and users:* By design, the services of many charitable organizations are provided for those who are relatively poor and largely paid for by those who are better off financially. Although examples of separation between payers and users can be found in the profit sector (such as insurance claims), the practice is much less prevalent.
- *Below-cost pricing:* An example of below-cost pricing is university tuition. Virtually all private and public colleges and universities price their services below full cost.

REVIEW LEARNING OBJECTIVE 8

8   **Describe nonprofit organization marketing**

Nonprofit Organization Marketing

LOOKING BACK

Look back at the story about the Inn at Little Washington at the beginning of this chapter. After reading the chapter, you should be able to answer the questions posed at the end of the story. A service, like a restaurant, differs from goods on four basic characteristics. Compared to goods, services are intangible performances, are produced and consumed simultaneously, have greater heterogeneity, and are perishable. The components of service quality exemplified by the Inn at Little Washington are reliability (failure only tolerated once), assurance (staff must be courteous, display a high level of competence, and be able to describe the food in detail), and empathy (measure customers' moods before dining, and hire for attitude).

USE IT NOW

Have you ever wanted to provide feedback to your college or university about the quality of the services that you, as a student, receive? Choose a department or function within your college or university (for example, the registrar, advising office, bursar, financial-aid office) with which you have had a negative service quality experience. Write a letter to the department/function and suggest ways it can improve its service quality. Use what you have learned about the components of service quality (tangibles, reliability, responsiveness, empathy, and assurance) to help you think about what needs to be improved. You may also use the gap model of service quality to guide your thoughts and suggestions about how to make improvements. For example, you might suggest that a department needs to conduct research to find out what kind of service students expect.

REVIEW IT

1 **Discuss the importance of services to the economy.** The service sector plays a crucial role in the U.S. economy, employing about three-quarters of the workforce and accounting for more than 70 percent of the gross domestic product.

1.1 What services does the Web site **http://www.travelweb.com** offer? How do visitors use the Special Offer List?

2 **Discuss the differences between services and goods.** Services are distinguished by four characteristics. Services are intangible performances in that they lack clearly identifiable physical characteristics, making it difficult for marketers to communicate their specific benefits to potential customers. The production and consumption of services occur simultaneously. Services are heterogeneous because their quality depends on such elements as the service provider, individual consumer, location, and so on. Finally, services are perishable in the sense that they cannot be stored or saved. As a result, synchronizing supply with demand is particularly challenging in the service industry.

2.1 Assume that you are a manager of a bank branch. Write a list of the implications of intangibility for your firm.

2.2 Review the "Marketing in Entertainment" box on the *Zagat* surveys. In your opinion, are *Zagat* survey guides goods or services? Explain your reasoning.

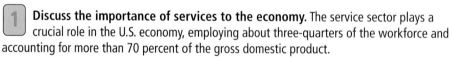

3 **Describe the components of service quality and the gap model of service quality.** Service quality has five components: reliability (ability to perform the service dependably, accurately, and consistently), responsiveness (providing prompt service), assurance (knowledge and courtesy of employees and their ability to convey trust), empathy (caring, individualized attention), and tangibles (physical evidence of the service).

The gap model identifies five key discrepancies that can influence customer evaluations of service quality. When the gaps are large, service quality is low. As the gaps shrink, service quality improves. Gap 1 is found between customers' expectations and management's perceptions of those expectations. Gap 2 is found between management's perception of what the customer wants and specifications for service quality. Gap 3 is found between service quality specifications and delivery of the service. Gap 4 is found between service delivery and what the company promises to the customer through external communication. Gap 5 is found between customers' service expectations and their perceptions of service performance.

3.1 Analyze a recent experience that you have had with a service business (for example, hairdresser, movie theater, dentist, restaurant, car repair) in terms of your expectations and perceptions about each of the five components of service quality.

4 **Develop marketing mixes for services.** "Product" (service) strategy issues include what is being processed (people, possessions, mental stimulus, information), core and supplementary services, customization versus standardization, and the service mix or portfolio. Distribution decisions involve convenience, number of outlets, direct versus indirect distribution, and scheduling. Stressing tangible cues, using personal sources of information, creating strong organizational images, and engaging in postpurchase communication are effective promotion strategies. Pricing objectives for services can be revenue oriented, operations oriented, patronage oriented, or any combination of the three.

4.1 TEAM Form a team with at least two other classmates, and come up with an idea for a new service. Develop a marketing mix strategy for the new service.

5 **Discuss relationship marketing in services.** Relationship marketing in services involves attracting, developing, and retaining customer relationships. There are three levels of relationship marketing: level 1 focuses on pricing incentives; level 2 uses pricing incentives and social bonds with customers; and level 3 uses pricing, social bonds, and structural bonds to build long-term relationships.

5.1 TEAM For the new service developed for question 4.1, have the members of the team discuss how they would implement a relationship marketing strategy.

6 **Explain internal marketing in services.** Internal marketing means treating employees as customers and developing systems and benefits that satisfy their needs. Employees who like their jobs and are happy with the firm they work for are more likely to deliver good service. Internal marketing activities include competing for talent, offering a vision, training employees, stressing teamwork, giving employees freedom to make decisions, measuring and rewarding good service performance, and knowing employees' needs.

6.1 WRITING Choose a service firm with which you do a lot of business. Write a memo to the manager explaining the importance of internal marketing and outlining the factors internal marketing includes.

6.2 ONLINE If you didn't answer question 2.2, review the "Marketing in Entertainment" box on the *Zagat* surveys. Go to **http://www.zagat.com** and investigate what the site offers. How does *Zagat* propose to help companies do internal services marketing?

7 **Discuss global issues in services marketing.** The United States has become the world's largest exporter of services. Although competition is keen, the United States has a competitive advantage because of its vast experience in many service industries. To be successful globally, service firms must adjust their marketing mix for the environment of each target country.

7.1 What issues would you have to think about in going global with the new service that you developed in the questions above? How would you change your marketing mix to address those issues?

 8 **Describe nonprofit organization marketing.** Nonprofit organizations pursue goals other than profit, market share, and return on investment. Nonprofit organization marketing facilitates mutually satisfying exchanges between nonprofit organizations and their target markets. Several unique characteristics distinguish nonbusiness marketing strategy, including a concern with services and social behaviors rather than manufactured goods and profit; a difficult, undifferentiated, and in some ways marginal target market; a complex product that may have only indirect benefits and elicit very low involvement; a short, direct, immediate distribution channel; a relative lack of resources for promotion; and prices only indirectly related to the exchange between the producer and the consumer of services.

8.1 Form a team with two or three classmates. Using the promotion strategies discussed in the nonprofit section of this chapter, develop a promotion strategy for your college or university.

TERMS

assurance 365
core service 368
credence quality 363
empathy 365
experience quality 363
gap model 365
heterogeneity 364

inseparability 363
intangibility 363
internal marketing 374
mass customization 368
nonprofit organization 375
nonprofit organization marketing 376
perishability 364

public service advertisement (PSA) 378
reliability 365
responsiveness 365
search quality 363
service 362
supplementary services 368
tangibles 365

EXERCISES

APPLICATION EXERCISE

 All people know quality when they see it—or do they? Let's take a look at some goods and services and then think about assessing their quality. For this exercise, work in teams of two to three and discuss each item before determining its final placement.[34]

Activities

1. Using the abbreviations in parentheses, place each of the following products and services along the continuum below: a new car (C), designer jeans (J), car oil change (O), dress dry cleaning (D), haircut (H), tax preparation software (T), college education (E).

100% physical good _____ 100% service

2. Once you have placed the items along the continuum, consider how easy it is to assess the quality of each item.

Easy to assess quality _____ Difficult to assess quality

3. What assumptions can you make about the ability to assess the quality of goods compared to services? Is it easier to assess the quality of some goods than others? What about for services?

ETHICS EXERCISE

Web sites such as Oncology.com, cancerpage.com, and CancerSource.com offer cancer patients sophisticated medical data and advice in exchange for personal information that is then sold to advertisers and business partners and used by the Web sites to create products to sell back to patients. Some argue that cancer patients visiting these sites are willingly exchanging their personal information for the sites' medical information. Others contend that this kind of exchange is unethical.

Questions

1. Is this practice ethical?

2. Does the AMA Code of Ethics have anything to say about this issue? Go to **http://www.marketingpower.com** and review the code. Then, write a brief paragraph on what the AMA Code of Ethics contains that relates to this situation.

CAREER EXERCISE

If the topics in this chapter sound interesting to you, you may want to find a marketing position at a services company or a nonprofit organization. If you are pulled to the latter, start by identifying a cause you feel passionate about. It can be difficult to convince people to donate to a charity if you are not thoroughly supportive of the work it is doing. Once you have identified an organization that you feel strongly about, see if it has a Web site. If it does, you can do some preliminary research there; if not, you will need to write for information regarding job opportunities. For the activities below, you will need to select a nonprofit organization as the basis of your work.

Activities

1. GuideStar (**http://www.guidestar.org**) is a database containing over 850,000 listings for IRS-recognized nonprofit, charitable organizations. Consult the list to verify that the organization that interests you is bona fide. Also consult the IRS Web site at **http://www.irs.gov** to check out the financial information on the charity.

2. The Better Business Bureau operates a separate division for charities, called the BBB Wise Giving Alliance. Its Web site (**http://www.give.org**) has information on charity standards, donor complaints, and so forth. Research the resources at Give.org, then compare what you know about your charity to the standards listed at the site. Does your charity seem well run?

3. To get an inside glimpse of work at a nonprofit, volunteer to help your charity of choice with its marketing efforts for a special event, a fundraising campaign, or even its day-to-day marketing activities. Keep a journal of your experience.

ENTREPRENEURSHIP CASE

© ADAM WOOLFITT/CORBIS

CAST IN THE LEADING ROLE, PLAYBILL SHINES

Anyone who has ever attended live theater has probably, at some point, flipped through a copy of *Playbill*. Established in New York City in 1884 as the program of choice for Broadway and off-Broadway theaters, Playbill the company publishes and distributes the near-ubiquitous black and white program with the familiar yellow and black cover to theaters in almost every major and medium-sized city in the United States. Over 3 million theatergoers read the programs every month.

Complete with cast rosters and biographies, show synopses, lists of prominent theater sponsors, insider gossip columns, and various feature articles on nationally known actors and theater personalities, *Playbill* provides its readers with a panoramic view of the performing arts. Playbill distributes its programs free to theaters, which, in turn, give them to show attendees as a complimentary item included with the price of their tickets. Like most magazine publishers, Playbill earns revenue simply by selling the advertising space—a lot of it—within its pages. Thanks to its broad distribution network and its wealth of proprietary and nationally oriented editorial content, Playbill is able to extend its revenue base with a mix of local, regional, and national advertisers.

Although the audiences at the many performing arts centers represent a highly coveted and affluent consumer demographic, Playbill's competition has been limited to one national and several regional program publishers. To establish itself as the lone national brand, Playbill purchased its primary rival, Stagebill, which publishes *Performing Arts* magazine, in 2002. Though Playbill's purchase of Stagebill could be interpreted as a move to exert its dominance, closer inspection of the deal and the state of the industry reveals that Playbill was motivated simply by survival. Program publishers suffer from exceptionally low profit margins, and continual pressure to cut costs left Playbill with the ability to supply programs to only a select few of Stagebill's most lucrative former customers.

Though Playbill has eliminated its most serious rival, fallout from the takeover emboldened the theater owners who were left behind. Consequently, demand for locally published programs has increased. Sizable theater consortiums in major markets such as San Francisco, Chicago, Seattle, and Los Angeles now work with local publishers who afford them more editorial control over their programs' content. To venue owners in those markets, providing locally focused news, information, and personal profiles is the key to building audience support for live theater in their particular market. To help offset their publishing costs, some even assume responsibility for selling advertising space in their programs in exchange for a share of the ad revenue they generate.

In addition to effectively monopolizing the national market for printed programs, Playbill has further extended its appeal to advertisers by forming the necessary business partnerships to take its product to the airwaves and into cyberspace. Recently, Playbill and Sirius Satellite Radio formed a strategic alliance to provide daily news features, live programming, music, special programming, and information from the world of Broadway for Sirius Radio's Broadway's Best channel. In return for the increased brand exposure, Playbill will promote Sirius in printed editions of *Playbill* and through Playbill On-Line, at Playbill.com.

Playbill.com uses a mix of exclusive content, feature articles pulled from the printed *Playbill*, show schedules, and seating charts for all of Playbill's partner theaters around the world to generate 20 million hits each month. Playbill has used the Web site to coordinate partnerships with ticket agencies, restaurants, and hotels that offer discounts to the hundreds of thousands of subscribers to Playbill On-Line's Playbill Club. Consumers can join the club for free, and it offers tremendous exposure for Playbill's business partners who are able to place their products or services directly in front of individuals with an average yearly income of $80,000.

Clearly, Playbill is on solid ground. Nevertheless, it still faces the challenge of finding innovative ways to earn a profit from a product that doesn't cost its end customers a single cent.[35]

Questions

1. Is *Playbill* a good, a service, or both? Explain.

2. Using the material in learning objective 4 as a template, outline Playbill's marketing mix. Discuss its product, core and supplementary services, mass customization, service mix, distribution, promotion, and pricing.

3. What role does the alliance with Sirius play in Playbill's marketing mix? Do you think the alliance will enhance demand for Playbill's services? Explain.

WATCH IT

SmallBusinessSchool
the Series on PBS stations and the Web

FEATURE PRESENTATION

Texas Jet

To give you insight into Chapter 11, Small Business School will take you inside the Texas Jet terminal at Meacham Field, just outside of Fort Worth, Texas, where you'll meet entrepreneur Reed Pigman. When Reed realized that he couldn't compete with other private jet companies on price, he decided he was really in the service business. That realization helped Reed turn a struggling airplane transportation business into a thriving refueling service station. Texas Jet specializes in refueling jets flown for private use, but what sets it apart from the competition is its unfailing attention to customer service. It all starts when a customer's jets lands and Texas Jet rolls out the red carpet (literally). Inside the terminal are waiting areas complete with Internet access; sleep rooms;

complimentary drinks and snacks; showers; and recreation, fitness, and banquet facilities. The company can also arrange for rental cars, limousines, and catering services. Customers can even use company cars (for free) to head out to lunch for the afternoon or to the hotel for the night. Passengers who will be returning can park in a covered lot, and pilots can use Texas Jet's air-conditioning units to cool their jets parked in the sweltering Texas sun. Texas Jet does far more than supply jet fuel for airplanes: What it really sells is an exemplary care-taking service for pilots and passengers.

What to Watch for and Ask Yourself

1. Does Texas Jet sell goods, services, or both? Do you think the company can be successful doing just one or the other?

2. Discuss whether Texas Jet satisfies the five requirements of service quality. Does it meet all five? If not, where does it fall short?

3. What is the target market for Texas Jet's product (service)? Based on the video, do you think the market is growing or shrinking?

4. Describe the service marketing mix for Texas Jet.

ENCORE PRESENTATION

Intolerable Cruelty

Now that you have worked through this chapter, you will be able to see the concepts in a more nuanced situation. As an encore to your study, watch the film clip from *Intolerable Cruelty*, starring George Clooney (Miles Massey), Stacey Travis (Mrs. Donaly), and Catherine Zeta-Jones (Marylin Rexroth). The selected scene shows the introductory interview between Mr. Massey and Mrs. Donaly. Mrs. Donaly is hiring Mr. Massey as her divorce attorney. As you watch the clip, think about what Massey is communicating about his service. How is his service customized? How is it standardized? What is your assessment of how Mrs. Donaly is evaluating the service she is buying (i.e., does she seem satisfied, dissatisfied, or ambivalent by the end of the clip)? What other service concepts from the chapter can you relate to the film clip?

STILL SHAKY?

If you're having trouble with the concepts in this chapter, consider using some of the following study resources. You can review the videos, or test yourself with materials designed for all kinds of learning styles.

☑ **Xtra! (http://lambxtra.swlearning.com)**

| ☑ Quiz | ☑ Feature Videos | ☑ Encore Videos | ☑ FAQ Videos |
| ☑ Exhibit Worksheets | ☑ Marketing Plan Worksheets | ☐ Content | |

☑ **http://lamb.swlearning.com**

| ☑ Quiz | ☑ PowerPoint slides | ☑ Marketing News | ☑ Review Exercises |
| ☑ Links | ☑ Marketing Plan Contest | ☑ Career Exercise | ☐ Use It Now |

☑ **Study guide**

| ☑ Outline | ☑ Vocab Review | ☑ Test Questions | ☑ Marketing Scenario |

Need More? Here's a tip. Take advantage of all the review opportunities on the Marketing Web site at **http://lamb. swlearning.com**. Write up a list of questions you have about concepts you don't understand and visit your professor or TA during office hours.

MARKETING MISCUE

The Boston Ballet Gets Evicted

The Boston Ballet's *Nutcracker* is one of the longest running shows in North America. The seasonal offering plays about 40 performances in a seven-week period each year and attracts over 100,000 fans. Almost 30 percent of the Boston Ballet's $20 million annual budget comes from *Nutcracker* performances. For 35 years, the ballet has been performed at the Wang Center for the Performing Arts, a nonprofit facility located in the heart of Boston's Theater District. In October 2003, however, Valerie Wilder, executive director of the Boston Ballet, was shocked to find out that the 2003 performances of the *Nutcracker* would be the last at the Wang Center.

The Wang Center's Story

In the face of an uncertain economy and commercial competition, Josiah Spaulding Jr, the Wang Center's president and CEO, decided to replace the *Nutcracker* with Cablevision's *Radio City Christmas Spectacular.* A New York company, Cablevision owns Madison Square Garden, the New York Knicks, and the New York Rangers. Its *Radio City Christmas Spectacular* is often promoted by Clear Channel Entertainment—a media outlet that allows promoters to literally dominate a region's advertising market.

From an economic perspective, theater attendance has dropped since the terrorist attacks on September 11, 2001. Broadway attendance dropped to 11.2 million in 2003, down from 11.41 million in 2002. While high-ticket prices have kept Broadway revenues increasing annually, the Wang Center has not been as lucky. The Wang Center ended 1999 and 2000 with operating surpluses of around $2 million, but lost $500,000 in each subsequent year. Attendance at the *Nutcracker* dropped 12 percent in 2002. Overall, paid attendance at *Nutcracker* performances across the United States has dropped 10 percent since 2000.

The Wang Center also faced new competition. Broadway in Boston, a division of Clear Channel Entertainment, had refurbished the 2,500-seat Boston Opera House and was scheduled to debut with *The Lion King* in July 2004. Clear Channel, owner of 1,225 radio stations, 750,000 billboards, and 135 theaters, had already purchased two popular theaters in Boston, the Wilbur and the Colonial. Historically, Disney shows would have premiered at the Wang Center.

Given the declining attendance at the *Nutcracker* and stiffer competition, Spaulding announced that he could no longer afford to keep the Boston Ballet since the group paid a lower rental rate than a commercial touring show.

The Boston Ballet's Story

Supporters of the Boston Ballet argued that the purpose of the ballet company and the Wang, as nonprofit organizations, was to bring culture to the Boston area—not to generate profits. Ballet supporters charged that the Wang Center existed to promote the kind of high culture that the *Nutcracker* represented. By not doing this, the Wang Center would become a piece of rental property going for the highest bid.

Valerie Wilder chose to fight the eviction publicly by focusing on the sudden notice. She criticized Spaulding for not telling her until October. Historically, the Boston Ballet announced its new season in February, with preseason ticket sales starting at that time. With the October notice, Wilder said that she could not have a new venue by the February announcement.

While ballet supporters were bemoaning the loss of its 35-year venue, another endangered party was the Boston Ballet Orchestra. The orchestra pit at the Wang Center had been renovated to the exact specifications of the orchestra's music director, Jonathan McPhee. McPhee was concerned that the ballet would not be able to find a theater with a comparable orchestra pit and acoustics. He expressed fear that *Nutcracker* performances would have to resort to a prerecorded soundtrack.

Budget Woes

Both parties were facing budget woes. Only time will tell whether ousting a Boston institution for a marquee production will be acceptable in a community steeped in tradition. The local and national media, however, were clearly in favor of the Boston Ballet and condemned the Wang Center.

Questions

1. What is the product in this situation?

2. What are the unique aspects of marketing in this environment?

CRITICAL THINKING CASE

Twister Moves—The Cool Hip Dance Version of the Classic Game of Twister

Founded in 1923 in Providence, Rhode Island, by brothers, Henry and Helal Hassenfeld, as Hassenfeld Brothers, the company we know as Hasbro, Inc. originally sold textile remnants. By the 1940s, Hasbro had begun its entry into the toy and game marketplace. Now a worldwide leader in children and family leisure-time, entertainment products, the company is involved in the design, manufacture, and marketing of games ranging from traditional to high tech. Company names like Milton Bradley, Playskool, Parker Brothers, Tonka Corporation, Kenner Products, Tiger Electronics, and Wizards of the Coast are all part of the Hasbro family.

Toys offered in the Hasbro line of toy products include:

- Easy-Bake Oven
- Mr. Potato Head
- Play-Doh
- Tinkertoy
- G.I. Joe (the world's first action figure)
- Star Wars action figures
- My Little Pony
- Transformers
- Nerf
- Furby
- Beyblade

Games offered by the Hasbro family include:

- Twister
- Clue
- The Game of Life
- Monopoly
- Scrabble
- Sorry
- Operation
- Battleship
- Yahtzee
- Candy Land
- Chutes and Ladders
- Risk
- Connect Four
- Jenga
- Trivial Pursuit (distributed under exclusive license from Horn Abbot, Ltd.),
- Big Ben puzzles

Believing that playing games is still an important part of our culture, Hasbro Games entered the twenty-first century by delivering a contemporary twist to the company's all-time favorite games. In 2003, Hasbro Games introduced Twister Moves, Deluxe Yahtzee, and Jenga Extreme.

Twister

The "Twister" brand was introduced in 1966 and was the first game in history to use the human body as a full-fledge playing piece. The product's debut took place on the *Tonight Show* with Johnny Carson playing the game with Skitch Henderson. On May 3, 1966, the Twister game was back on the *Tonight Show,* with Carson and the show's guest, Eva Gabor, playing the game. The game was a huge hit, selling more than 2 million copies during its first year of release.

In 1987, the University of Massachusetts at Amherst set the Guinness World Record for the largest Twister game with 4,160 students playing the game at one time. With household brand awareness of 81 percent, it is estimated that 65 million people, in 34 countries, have played the game. Twister is licensed to appear on:

- Slippers
- Beach sandals
- Men's boxers
- Lounge pants
- Camp shirts
- Beach towels
- Slumber bags
- Bedding ensembles
- Pillows
- Inflatable furniture
- Chocolates
- Novelty pens
- Key chains

Twister Moves

Brand management at Hasbro Games wanted to build on the popularity of Twister by extending the experience with a new play pattern, all the while capitalizing on the popularity of club-style dance simulation. Utilizing the cultural insight that children express their individuality through dance, music, and social interaction, Twister brand management combined all three cultural elements into game play via Twister Moves.

At a retail price of around $19.99, the Twister Moves game package consists of three 60-minute dance-style music CDs and a game mat. When the game is played, two recorded DJs call out directions. The DJs (a male directing the left side and a female directing the right) engage in comedic banter as they provide directions to the players. First, players listen for the dance sequence as called out by the DJs; then they follow the moves with their feet on the game mat.

The grassroots launch effort for Twister Moves included product sampling during spring break in 2003. The objective of this sampling initiative was to generate trial among college-age students and to get media coverage on the Twister Moves craze. The 2003 spring break event took place at the Holiday Inn Sunspree Hotel in Panama City Beach, Florida, and included both individual demonstrations and stage competitions. The grassroots effort also included a summer dance tour. In this marketing effort, professional dancers traveled up and down the eastern coast of the United States appearing at various summer camps and programs.

A key component of the Twister Moves' marketing program was its celebrity partnership with recording artists Aaron and Nick Carter. The agreement among Hasbro Games, Jive Records, and the Carters resulted in a game-compatible music track CD (featuring the Carters) packaged with the game. Marking only the third time these siblings had performed on the same recording, the CD included an exclusive single, "She Wants Me." The Carters were featured in the fall television and print advertising for Twister Moves and also served as hosts of the Twister Moves kick-off event in New York City in September 2003. The promotional program integrating the Carters achieved 26 million television impressions and 9 million print impressions. Additionally, the exclusive Carters' single went platinum.

Hasbro is the largest toy company in the world, and the promotional events for Twister Moves enabled the game to become one of the top selling games at retail in 2003. With some of the best-selling toys and board games in the marketplace, the company has to wonder, however, if brand extensions are its key to long-term success.[2]

Questions

1. What role does an understanding of consumer behavior play in the toy and game industry?

2. Describe Hasbro's brand extension methodology.

3. What does the term *brand equity* mean in relation to Hasbro, Inc.?

CROSS-FUNCTIONAL SOLUTIONS

Questions

1. What is the difference between the demand-side perspective and the supply-side perspective to doing business? Is either perspective more appropriate?

   The demand-side perspective focuses upon determining, via marketing research, the customer's wants and needs. Products/services are then developed that satisfy these wants and needs. Once the products/services are developed, marketing adds the finishing touches by positioning them in such a manner that customers recognize that the products/services will fulfill their needs. The demand side starts with the customer and ends with the customer, with marketing and the other business functions working in the middle.

   The supply-side perspective takes the position that engineers should develop and manufacture leading-edge products. Once a product is developed and manufactured, marketing then introduces it to the customer by telling the customer about the product's performance. The supply side tends to start with the research and development group, move to the manufacturing group, then move to marketing, and end with the customer.

   As marketers, we believe that the demand-side perspective is the best approach to doing business. Some argue, however, that the supply-side perspective is more appropriate for high-tech products—that if we had waited for the customer, we would not yet have call-waiting, microwave ovens, or video games.

2. What are some of the popular business terms used to describe cross-functional integration?

   - Design-factory fit
   - Concurrent engineering
   - Design for manufacturability and assembly
   - Early manufacturing involvement
   - Modularization

3. Why are employees (whether involved in marketing or not) at the heart of customer service?

   A customer generally does not work directly with the marketing department when purchasing a product or service. Instead, the customer may be asking questions of someone on the store floor who was hired to stock shelves, work the cash register, or sweep the floor. The responses that the customer receives from these employees tend to shape the customer's image of the company. Also, when a customer calls to check on the status of a repair, the customer is speaking with someone who may have been hired to answer the telephone. Nevertheless, this receptionist is the customer's first contact with the organization and provides a lasting impression of the way the company treats its customers. The way all employees treat the customer becomes intermingled with the product's quality and can drive the customer's perception of quality either up or down.

Suggested Readings

Christopher M. Barlow, "Deliberate Insight in Team Creativity," *Journal of Creative Behavior* 34, no. 2 (2000): 101, 117.

Geoffrey A. Moore, *Crossing the Chasm* (New York: HarperBusiness, 1999).

Distribution
Decisions

CROSS-FUNCTIONAL COLLABORATION IN MANAGING DISTRIBUTION

Achieving customer satisfaction means that the company must have the right product at the right place at the right time (and at the right price). The need for cross-functional coordination in developing and producing a high-quality product is clear. Getting the product to the consumer at the right place and time is also a result of considerable interaction among marketing and its internal and external partners. Once the product is designed, developed, and produced, marketing and its partners must get it from the factory to the end user using the best methods.

Considerable costs are associated with getting a high-quality product out the door, and manufacturing has been a key marketing partner in making the delivery process successful. Advanced manufacturing systems (AMS) have been developed that not only reduce costs (ultimately affecting the price charged to the customer), but also allow faster product delivery. Two popular advanced manufacturing systems are just-in-time (JIT) and electronic data interchange (EDI).

A JIT manufacturing system allows a product to be produced as needed, instead of being produced for stock. Ultimately, such a manufacturing system can change the structure of the distribution channel. Customers may be able to receive products directly from the manufacturer rather than via a longer distribution channel. Not only are products available faster, but with fewer channel members, costs are lowered, achieving the ultimate in efficient operations. Marketing must make sure, however, that the change in the channel structure is more effective as well as more efficient. That is, marketing must determine whether the eliminated channel intermediary provided a service that will be unavailable if the product is shipped directly to the customer from the manufacturer.

The use of electronic data interchange can significantly increase the efficiency of operations between the shop floor and distribution of the product. EDI permits the exchange of information electronically, using data collected at the point of sale and transmitted automatically to the manufacturing department. Thus, manufacturing knows the exact number of available units at any point in time, allowing the manufacturing group to time its production and delivery to meet the customer's specific needs.

KOCH Entertainment Distribution is the leading independent music company in the United States. The company's state-of-the-art distribution center is at the heart of its distribution network, which is the best independent distribution network in North America. The National Association of Recording Merchandisers named KOCH the "Distributor of the Year" in 2001, 2002, and 2003, largely because of its patented robotic order-picking system. Named Amadeus, the automated storage and retrieval system allows KOCH to utilize its coordinated, technology-driven distribution system as a competitive advantage.

In some instances, retail sales data transmitted electronically to the manufacturing group start the machines on the shop floor. Such quick response to channel needs can dramatically reduce the time from order entry to delivery. Many companies have seen the cycle time from order entry to delivery cut in half due to direct (and immediate) interactions between channel members and the manufacturing function in a firm. This reduction in cycle time also allows retailers to limit the amount of inventory they need to warehouse, which, in turn, lowers cost and, ultimately, price.

In today's converging entertainment marketplace, Alliance Entertainment Corporation is known as a total solution provider of infrastructure services. Understanding the importance of distribution efficiency and immediacy in the world of entertainment, Alliance hosts an extensive product inventory (e.g., CDs, cassettes, DVDs, videos, video games) and utilizes cutting-edge technology to enable retailers to have the right product at the right time. In addition to its inventory and quick delivery, Alliance has also become a service provider by licensing databases and developing proprietary music, movie, and game Web sites.

As these examples illustrate, operational efficiencies in linking marketing's distribution to manufacturing's production processes are the result of well-thought-out cross-functional plans. Such plans have to be developed in conjunction with both marketing and manufacturing functional groups. Benefits to consumers appear in both dollar savings and improved customer service.

One important aspect of the distribution channel is the actual delivery of the company's products. The equipment used to make deliveries is an important decision that the company faces. Decisions regarding the type of transportation equipment (from aircraft to rail cars) receive considerable input from both the marketing and the finance/accounting groups. For example, marketing might prefer that its perishable product be delivered by air to avoid any spoilage. From a cost-effectiveness viewpoint, however, the financial group might determine that the product should be shipped via truck because the savings would offset the costs associated with any spoiled product. The two functional groups have to balance customer demands with the relative costs of shipment. The manufacturing group must be involved as well to ensure that appropriate and cost-effective packaging is used for the transportation method ultimately selected.

A cross-functional area within entertainment distribution that often generates conflict is the delivery of foreign DVDs. Under U.S. law, consumers can import DVDs (including ordering a movie online) for personal use, but retailers cannot sell a foreign film in the United States if a studio (e.g., Miramax) has purchased the distribution rights. Although the studio may not have produced the film, purchasing the distribution rights gives it copyright ownership in the United States. Thus, a retailer (online or brick and mortar) can no longer sell and deliver the film even for a consumer's personal use unless, of course, it has been designated by the studio as an authorized distributor.

A functional department that cannot be overlooked in a company's distribution process is the human resources department. This is particularly important for a service provider since the people are the ones who actually make the logistical process work appropriately. An interesting aspect of a service provider is that production and delivery of the company's product (service) take place simultaneously. Therefore, functional integration has to occur at the point of delivery. The customer's perception of quality delivery is determined both by the actual tasks performed and by the way employees talk, look, and act. This makes it imperative that marketing and human resources work together to hire and train the right people. As a service provider, DigitalBang LLC is involved in marketing sports-related products and services and knows firsthand the importance of the employee in the service encounter. The company offers online sports games that customers can play at company Web sites, so it must respond quickly if there is an error in delivery (e.g., posting the wrong online score).

Coordination between marketing and other business functions is necessary to get a high-quality, competitively priced product or service to the end user in a timely manner. Companies, such as Radio Shack and Blockbuster, that draw from the same customer base have become experts at developing channel systems that utilize all functional components of the organization in getting the right product/service to the right customer at just the right time. Radio Shack has attempted to position itself as America's home connectivity store by partnering with Blockbuster to sell its broadband services and related products at Blockbuster's brick

and mortar locations. Since the adoption of broadband will be driven largely by entertainment products, locating in Blockbuster stores allows Radio Shack direct access to entertainment customers. Strategically, for both companies, adding hardware and services within an entertainment retailer is expected to facilitate the customer's understanding of entertainment content and technology, thus speeding adoption.

Technology is a powerful force behind improvements in distribution. In the future, more and more companies will be combining cross-functional skills with information technology infrastructures to better serve customers.

Questions

1. What are the popular advanced manufacturing systems, and how do they interact with marketing?

2. What is an enterprise-wide integrated distribution system? What is marketing's role in such a system?

3. How do production and delivery happen simultaneously in the service sector? What other functional areas are important partners in the service arena?

12

Marketing Channels and Supply Chain Management

LEARNING OBJECTIVES

1. Explain what a marketing channel is and why intermediaries are needed

2. Define the types of channel intermediaries and describe their functions and activities

3. Describe the channel structures for consumer and business products and discuss alternative channel arrangements

4. Define supply chain management and discuss its benefits

5. Discuss the issues that influence channel strategy

6. Explain channel leadership, conflict, and partnering

7. Describe the logistical components of the supply chain

8. Discuss new technology and emerging trends in supply chain management

9. Discuss channels and distribution decisions in global markets

10. Identify the special problems and opportunities associated with distribution in service organizations

© AP / WIDE WORLD PHOTO

Starbucks, the number one coffee retailer in the world and a *Fortune* 500 company, wants to become the most recognized brand in the world. To accomplish this Starbucks engages in multichannel distribution, product innovation, and extensive marketing that reaches customers in more than 25 countries including Japan, Kuwait, and Lebanon. Starbucks' products, which can be purchased at over 7,000 locations, account for yearly sales exceeding $4 billion.

How did Starbucks become so successful? In 1971, Starbucks opened its first store in Pikes Place Market in Seattle. By the early 1990s, it had 120 stores in the western United States and southern Canada. After Starbucks' IPO (initial public offering) in 1992, it began opening stores across the United States at nearly a 100 percent growth rate for the next four years. Along with its domestic growth, Starbucks began pursuing international contracts in countries such as Japan and the Philippines. After 1996, Starbucks began to capitalize on wholesale distribution channels that previously were used only on a limited basis. As a result, Starbucks created Frappuccino, an iced coffee beverage, and Starbucks Ice Cream, both of which were sold at over 9,000 grocery and convenience stores.

Other product innovations such as Tiazzi, a blended juice and tea drink, were introduced to reach consumers who do not drink coffee. These products increased Starbucks' customer base and are now a mainstay of its corporate strategy.

Starbucks' core business is purchasing and roasting high-quality whole coffee beans that are used to create brewed coffee, espresso, ice cream, and ready-to-drink beverages. The beverages are distributed through a variety of channels including Starbucks-owned retail stores, licensed vendors (grocery stores, offices and educational institutions, airlines, and health-care facilities), and wholesale distributors such as Pepsi, Dreyer's, and Kraft.

Starbucks has increased its stores' market share by creating loyalty in existing customers and obtaining new customers in untapped markets. To increase brand loyalty, Starbucks recently launched the Starbucks Card Duetto Visa, which rewards customers for purchases, makes buying coffee easier, and helps the community. The card functions as a dual Visa credit card and reloadable Starbucks drink card. Cardholders are rewarded based on usage with Duetto dollars, coffee beans, and gift certificates. The Starbucks Foundation also receives funds based on the cards' use.

In addition to building loyalty, Starbucks also focuses on garnering new market share by selecting prime retail locations convenient for automobile and pedestrian traffic. It also attempts to make Starbucks brand coffee available wherever consumers may wish to purchase it. In conjunction with its prime locations, Starbucks creates beverages that appeal to a variety of tastes and offers food items and seasonal drinks. In addition to beverages, Starbucks sells coffee-making equipment, CDs, games, and novelty items. By offering a wide variety of products in every feasible location, Starbucks will continue to build market share and brand awareness.

Even though Starbucks owns all of its U.S. stores, it always seeks a local business partner when expanding into new overseas markets. In Japan, Starbucks has partnered with Sazaby, Inc., and in Korea with Shinsegae Company. Each partner has special capabilities in food distribution.[1]

Do you think Starbucks' marketing strategy has been effective? Does Starbucks face any major competitors? What would you do to make Starbucks better?

Online

Starbucks

What elements of Starbucks' supply chain are evident on the company's Web site? Do you think Starbucks' "coffee education" builds loyalty for its brand? Why or why not?

http://www.starbucks.com

MARKETING CHANNELS

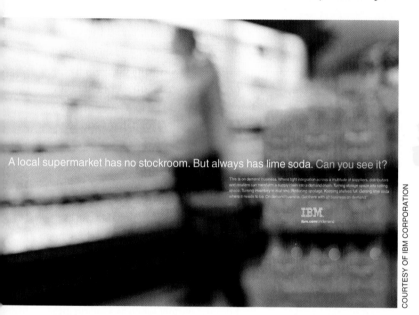

A local supermarket has no stockroom. But always has lime soda. Can you see it?

This is on demand business. Where tight integration across a multitude of suppliers, distributors and retailers can transform a supply chain into a demand chain. Turning storage space into selling space. Turning inventory in real time. Reducing spoilage. Keeping shelves full. Getting lime soda where it needs to be. On demand business. Get there with i/t business on demand.

IBM

ibm.com/ondemand

COURTESY OF IBM CORPORATION

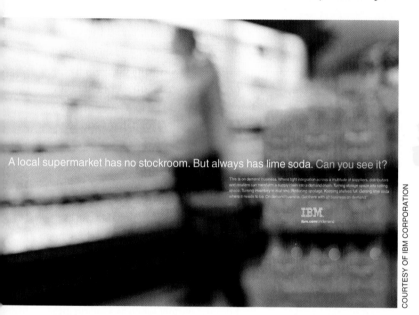

Marketing channels aid in overcoming discrepancies of quantity, like the one suggested by this ad for IBM supply chain management software.

marketing channel (channel of distribution)
A set of interdependent organizations that ease the transfer of ownership as products move from producer to business user or consumer.

channel members
All parties in the marketing channel that negotiate with one another, buy and sell products, and facilitate the change of ownership between buyer and seller in the course of moving the product from the manufacturer into the hands of the final consumer.

supply chain
The connected chain of all of the business entities, both internal and external to the company, that perform or support the logistics function.

The term *channel* is derived from the Latin word *canalis*, which means canal. A marketing channel can be viewed as a large canal or pipeline through which products, their ownership, communication, financing and payment, and accompanying risk flow to the consumer. Formally, a **marketing channel** (also called a **channel of distribution**) is a business structure of interdependent organizations that reach from the point of product origin to the consumer with the purpose of moving products to their final consumption destination. Marketing channels facilitate the physical movement of goods through the supply chain, representing "place" or "distribution" in the marketing mix (product, price, promotion, and place) and encompassing the processes involved in getting the right product to the right place at the right time.

Many different types of organizations participate in marketing channels. **Channel members** (also called *intermediaries*, *resellers*, and *middlemen*) negotiate with one another, buy and sell products, and facilitate the change of ownership between buyer and seller in the course of moving the product from the manufacturer into the hands of the final consumer. An important aspect of marketing channels is the joint effort of all channel members to create a continuous and seamless supply chain. The **supply chain** is the connected chain of all of the business entities, both internal and external to the company, that perform or support the marketing channel functions. As products move through the supply chain, channel members facilitate the distribution process by providing specialization and division of labor, overcoming discrepancies, and providing contact efficiency.

PROVIDING SPECIALIZATION AND DIVISION OF LABOR

According to the concept of *specialization and division of labor*, breaking down a complex task into smaller, simpler ones and allocating them to specialists will create greater efficiency and lower average production costs. Manufacturers achieve economies of scale through the use of efficient equipment capable of producing large quantities of a single product.

Marketing channels can also attain economies of scale through specialization and division of labor by aiding producers who lack the motivation, financing, or expertise to market directly to end users or consumers. In some cases, as with most consumer convenience goods, such as soft drinks, the cost of marketing directly to millions of consumers—taking and shipping individual orders—is prohibitive. For this reason, producers hire channel members, such as wholesalers and retailers, to do what the producers are not equipped to do or what channel members are better prepared to do. Channel members can do some things more efficiently than producers because they have built good relationships with their customers. Therefore, their specialized expertise enhances the overall performance of the channel.

OVERCOMING DISCREPANCIES

Marketing channels also aid in overcoming discrepancies of quantity, assortment, time, and space created by economies of scale in production. For example, assume that Pillsbury can efficiently produce its Hungry Jack instant pancake mix only at a rate of 5,000 units in a typical day. Not even the most ardent pancake fan could consume that amount in a year, much less in a day. The quantity produced to achieve low unit costs has created a **discrepancy of quantity**, which is the difference between the amount of product produced and the amount an end user wants to buy. By storing the product and distributing it in the appropriate amounts, marketing channels overcome quantity discrepancies by making products available in the quantities that consumers desire.

Mass production creates not only discrepancies of quantity but also discrepancies of assortment. A **discrepancy of assortment** occurs when a consumer does not have all of the items needed to receive full satisfaction from a product. For pancakes to provide maximum satisfaction, several other products are required to complete the assortment. At the very least, most people want a knife, fork, plate, butter, and syrup. Others might add orange juice, coffee, cream, sugar, eggs, and bacon or sausage. Even though Pillsbury is a large consumer-products company, it does not come close to providing the optimal assortment to go with its Hungry Jack pancakes. To overcome discrepancies of assortment, marketing channels assemble in one place many of the products necessary to complete a consumer's needed assortment.

A **temporal discrepancy** is created when a product is produced but a consumer is not ready to buy it. Marketing channels overcome temporal discrepancies by maintaining inventories in anticipation of demand. For example, manufacturers of seasonal merchandise, such as Christmas or Halloween decorations, are in operation all year even though consumer demand is concentrated during certain months of the year.

Furthermore, because mass production requires many potential buyers, markets are usually scattered over large geographic regions, creating a **spatial discrepancy**. Often global, or at least nationwide, markets are needed to absorb the outputs of mass producers. Marketing channels overcome spatial discrepancies by making products available in locations convenient to consumers. For example, if all the Hungry Jack pancake mix is produced in Boise, Idaho, then Pillsbury must use an intermediary to distribute the product to other regions of the United States. Consumers elsewhere would be unwilling to drive to Boise to purchase pancake mix.

PROVIDING CONTACT EFFICIENCY

The third need fulfilled by marketing channels is that they provide contact efficiency. Consider your extra costs if supermarkets, department stores, and shopping centers or malls did not exist. Suppose you had to buy your milk at a dairy and your meat at a stockyard. Imagine buying your eggs and chicken at a hatchery and your fruits and vegetables at various farms. You would spend a great deal of time, money, and energy just shopping for a few groceries. Supply chains simplify distribution by cutting the number of transactions required to get products from manufacturers to consumers and making an assortment of goods available in one location.

Consider the example illustrated in Exhibit 12.1 on page 396. Four consumers each want to buy a television set. Without a retail intermediary like Circuit City, television manufacturers JVC, Zenith, Sony, Toshiba, and RCA would each have to make four contacts to reach the four buyers who are in the target market, for a total of 20 transactions. However, when Circuit City acts as an intermediary between the producer and consumers, each producer has to make only one contact, reducing the number of transactions to 9. Each producer sells to one retailer rather than to four consumers. In turn, consumers buy from one retailer instead of from five producers.

discrepancy of quantity
The difference between the amount of product produced and the amount an end user wants to buy.

discrepancy of assortment
The lack of all the items a customer needs to receive full satisfaction from a product or products.

temporal discrepancy
A situation that occurs when a product is produced but a customer is not ready to buy it.

spatial discrepancy
The difference between the location of a producer and the location of widely scattered markets.

EXHIBIT 12.1

How Marketing Channels Reduce the Number of Required Transactions

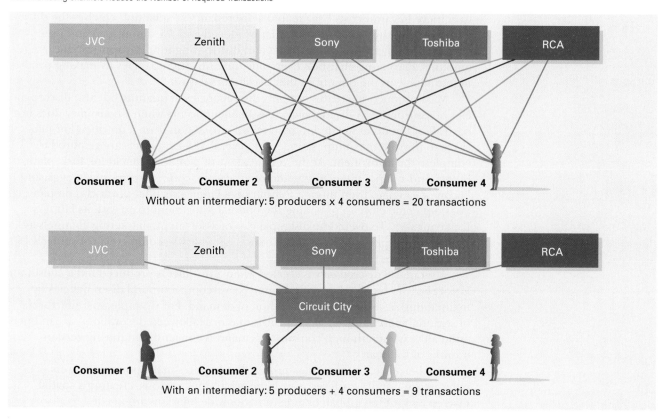

Without an intermediary: 5 producers x 4 consumers = 20 transactions

With an intermediary: 5 producers + 4 consumers = 9 transactions

REVIEW LEARNING OBJECTIVE 1

1 | **Explain what a marketing channel is and why intermediaries are needed**

Marketing channel

Providing Specialization and Division of Labor

Overcoming Discrepancies

Providing Contact Efficiency

Supply chain

Define the types of channel intermediaries and describe their functions and activities

Intermediaries in a channel negotiate with one another, facilitate the change of ownership between buyers and sellers, and physically move products from the manufacturer to the final consumer. The most prominent difference separating intermediaries is whether they take title to the product. *Taking title* means they own the merchandise and control the terms of the sale—for example, price and delivery date. Retailers and merchant wholesalers are examples of intermediaries that take title to products in the marketing channel and resell them. **Retailers** are firms that sell mainly to consumers. Retailers will be discussed in more detail in Chapter 13.

Merchant wholesalers are those organizations that facilitate the movement of products and services from the manufacturer to producers, resellers, governments, institutions, and retailers. All merchant wholesalers take title to the goods they sell, and most of them operate one or more warehouses where they receive goods, store them, and later reship them. Customers are mostly small- or moderate-sized retailers, but merchant wholesalers also market to manufacturers and institutional clients.

Other intermediaries do not take title to goods and services they market but do facilitate the exchange of ownership between sellers and buyers. **Agents and brokers** simply facilitate the sale of a product from producer to end user by representing retailers, wholesalers, or manufacturers. Title reflects ownership, and ownership usually implies control. Unlike wholesalers, agents or brokers only facilitate sales and generally have little input into the terms of the sale. They do, however, get a fee or commission based on sales volume. For example, when selling a home, the owner usually hires a real estate agent who then brings potential buyers to see the house. The agent facilitates the sale by bringing the buyer and owner together, but never actually takes ownership of the home.

Variations in channel structures are due in large part to variations in the numbers and types of wholesaling intermediaries. Generally, product characteristics, buyer considerations, and market conditions determine the type of intermediary the manufacturer should use.

FAQs

Wouldn't it be better for a company to have its own sales force than using distributors? Find out the answer by watching the Video FAQ on Xtra!

- *Product characteristics* that may dictate a certain type of wholesaling intermediary include whether the product is standardized or customized, the complexity of the product, and the gross margin of the product. For example, a customized product such as insurance is sold through an insurance agent or broker who may represent one or multiple companies. In contrast, a standardized product such as gum is sold through a merchant wholesaler that takes possession of the gum and reships it to the appropriate retailers.
- *Buyer considerations* affecting the wholesaler choice include how often the product is purchased and how long the buyer is willing to wait to receive the product. For example, at the beginning of the school term, a student may be willing to wait a few days for a textbook to get a lower price by ordering online. Thus, this type of product can be distributed directly. But, if the student waits to buy the book until right before an exam and needs the book immediately, it will have to be purchased at the school bookstore.
- *Market characteristics* determining the wholesaler type include how many buyers are in the market and whether they are concentrated in a general location or are widely dispersed. Gum and textbooks, for example, are produced in one location and consumed in many other locations; therefore, a merchant wholesaler is needed to distribute the products. In contrast, in a home sale, the buyer and seller are localized in one area, which facilitates the use of an agent/broker relationship.

retailer
A channel intermediary that sells mainly to consumers.

merchant wholesaler
An institution that buys goods from manufacturers and resells them to businesses, government agencies, and other wholesalers or retailers and that receives and takes title to goods, stores them in its own warehouses, and later ships them.

agents and brokers
Wholesaling intermediaries who do not take title to a product but facilitate its sale from producer to end user by representing retailers, wholesalers, or manufacturers.

Exhibit 12.2 shows the factors determining the type of wholesaling intermediary.

EXHIBIT 12.2

Factors Suggesting Type of Wholesaling Intermediary to Use

Factor	Merchant Wholesalers	Agents or Brokers
Nature of Product	Standard	Nonstandard, custom
Technicality of Product	Complex	Simple
Product's Gross Margin	High	Low
Frequency of Ordering	Frequent	Infrequent
Time between Order and Receipt of Shipment	Buyer desires shorter lead time	Buyer satisfied with long lead time
Number of Customers	Many	Few
Concentration of Customers	Dispersed	Concentrated

SOURCE: Reprinted by permission of the publisher. From Donald M. Jackson and Michael F. D'Amico, "Products and Markets Served by Distributors and Agents," 27–33 in *Industrial Marketing Management*. Copyright 1989 by Elsevier Science Inc.

logistics
The process of strategically managing the efficient flow and storage of raw materials, in-process inventory, and finished goods from point of origin to point of consumption.

EXHIBIT 12.3

Marketing Channel Functions Performed by Intermediaries

CHANNEL FUNCTIONS PERFORMED BY INTERMEDIARIES

Retailing and wholesaling intermediaries in marketing channels perform several essential functions that make the flow of goods between producer and buyer possible. The three basic functions that intermediaries perform are summarized in Exhibit 12.3.

Transactional functions involve contacting and communicating with prospective buyers to make them aware of existing products and explain their features, advantages, and benefits. Intermediaries in the supply chain also provide *logistical* functions. **Logistics** is the process of strategically managing the efficient flow and storage of raw materials, in-process inventory, and finished goods from point of origin to point of consumption. Logistical functions include transporting, storing, sorting out, accumulating, allocating, and assorting products into either homogeneous or heterogeneous collections. For example, grading agricultural products typifies the sorting-out process while consolidation of many lots of grade A eggs from different sources into one lot illustrates the accumulation process. Supermarkets or other retailers perform the assorting function by assembling thousands of different items that match their customers' desires. Similarly, while large companies typically have direct channels, many small companies depend on wholesalers to champion and distribute their products. For example, small beverage manufacturers like Jones Soda, Honest Tea, and Energy Brands depend on wholesalers to distribute their products in a marketplace dominated by large competitors like Coca-Cola and Pepsi.

Type of Function	Description
Transactional Functions	**Contacting and promoting:** Contacting potential customers, promoting products, and soliciting orders
	Negotiating: Determining how many goods or services to buy and sell, type of transportation to use, when to deliver, and method and timing of payment
	Risk taking: Assuming the risk of owning inventory
Logistical Functions	**Physically distributing:** Transporting and sorting goods to overcome temporal and spatial discrepancies
	Storing: Maintaining inventories and protecting goods
	Sorting: Overcoming discrepancies of quantity and assortment by
	Sorting out: Breaking down a heterogeneous supply into separate homogeneous stocks
	Accumulation: Combining similar stocks into a larger homogeneous supply
	Allocation: Breaking a homogeneous supply into smaller and smaller lots ("breaking bulk")
	Assortment: Combining products into collections or assortments that buyers want available at one place
Facilitating Function	**Researching:** Gathering information about other channel members and consumers
	Financing: Extending credit and other financial services to facilitate the flow of goods through the channel to the final consumer

The third basic channel function, *facilitating*, includes research and financing. Research provides information about channel members and consumers by getting answers to key questions: Who are the buyers? Where are they located? Why do they buy? Financing ensures that channel members have the money to keep products moving through the channel to the ultimate consumer.

A single company may provide one, two, or all three functions. Consider Kramer Beverage Company, a Coors beer distributor. As a beer distributor, Kramer provides transactional, logistical, and facilitating channel functions. Sales representatives contact local bars and restaurants to negotiate the terms of the sale, possibly giving the customer a discount for large purchases, and arrange for delivery of the beer. At the same time, Kramer also provides a facilitating function by extending credit to the customer. Kramer merchandising representatives, meanwhile, assist in promoting the beer on a local level by hanging Coors beer signs and posters. Kramer also provides logistical functions by accumulating the many types of Coors beer from the Coors manufacturing plant in Golden, Colorado, and storing them in its refrigerated warehouse. When an order needs to be filled, Kramer then sorts the beer into heterogeneous collections for each particular customer. For example, the local Chili's Grill & Bar may need two kegs of Coors, three kegs of Coors Light, and two cases of Killian's Red in bottles. The beer will then be loaded onto a refrigerated truck and transported to the restaurant. Upon arrival, the Kramer delivery person will transport the kegs and cases of beer into the restaurant's refrigerator and may also restock the coolers behind the bar.

Although individual members can be added to or deleted from a channel, someone must still perform these essential functions. They can be performed by producers, end users, or consumers, channel intermediaries such as wholesalers and retailers, and sometimes nonmember channel participants. For example, if a manufacturer decides to eliminate its private fleet of trucks, it must still have a way to move the goods to the wholesaler. This task may be accomplished by the wholesaler, which may have its own fleet of trucks, or by a nonmember channel participant, such as an independent trucking firm. Nonmembers also provide many other essential functions that may at one time have been provided by a channel member. For example, research firms may perform the research function; advertising agencies, the promotion function; transportation and storage firms, the physical distribution function; and banks, the financing function.

REVIEW LEARNING OBJECTIVE 2

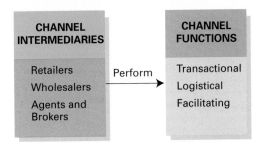

2 Define the types of channel intermediaries and describe their functions and activities

CHANNEL INTERMEDIARIES		CHANNEL FUNCTIONS
Retailers	Perform →	Transactional
Wholesalers		Logistical
Agents and Brokers		Facilitating

3 CHANNEL STRUCTURES

Describe the channel structures for consumer and business products and discuss alternative channel arrangements

A product can take many routes to reach its final consumer. Marketers search for the most efficient channel from the many alternatives available. Marketing a consumer convenience good like gum or candy differs from marketing a specialty good like a Mercedes-Benz. The two products require very different distribution channels. Likewise, the appropriate channel for a major equipment supplier like Boeing Aircraft would be unsuitable for an accessory equipment producer like Black & Decker. To illustrate the differences in typical marketing channels for consumer and business-to-business products like these, the next sections discuss the structures of marketing channels for each product type. Alternative channel structures are also discussed.

What kind of marketing channel functions can be performed over the Internet? Why do you think so?

Online

CHANNELS FOR CONSUMER PRODUCTS

Exhibit 12.4 illustrates the four ways manufacturers can route products to consumers. Producers use the **direct channel** to sell directly to consumers. Direct marketing activities—including telemarketing, mail-order and catalog shopping, and forms of electronic retailing like online shopping and shop-at-home television networks—are a good example of this type of channel structure. For example, home computer users can purchase Dell computers directly over the telephone or directly from Dell's Internet Web site. There are no intermediaries. Producer-owned stores and factory outlet stores—like Sherwin-Williams, Polo Ralph Lauren, Oneida, and West Point Pepperel—are other examples of direct channels. Farmers' markets are also direct channels. Direct marketing and factory outlets are discussed in more detail in Chapter 13.

At the other end of the spectrum, an *agent/broker channel* involves a fairly complicated process. Agent/broker channels are typically used in markets with many small manufacturers and many retailers that lack the resources to find each other. Agents or brokers bring manufacturers and wholesalers together for negotiations, but they do not take title to merchandise. Ownership passes directly to one or more wholesalers and then to retailers. Finally, retailers sell to the ultimate consumer of the product. For example, a food broker represents buyers and sellers of grocery products. The broker acts on behalf of many different producers and negotiates the sale of their products to wholesalers that specialize in foodstuffs. These wholesalers in turn sell to grocers and convenience stores.

Most consumer products are sold through distribution channels similar to the other two alternatives: the retailer channel and the wholesaler channel. A *retailer channel* is most common when the retailer is large and can buy in large quantities directly from the manufacturer. Wal-Mart, Sears, and car dealers are examples of retailers that often bypass a wholesaler. A *wholesaler*

direct channel
A distribution channel in which producers sell directly to consumers.

EXHIBIT 12.4

Marketing Channels for Consumer Products

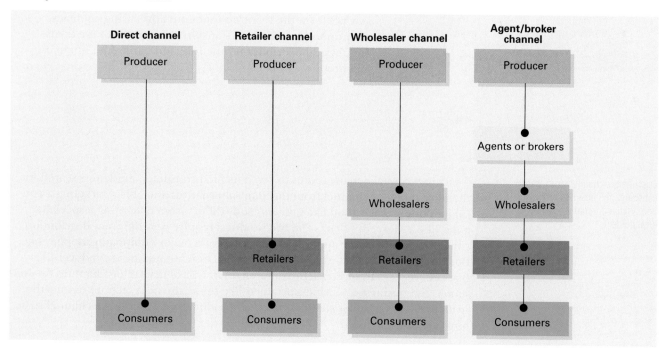

Marketing... in Entertainment

New Venues for New Films

Perhaps the most daunting part of filmmaking is finding a distributor for the finished product. This is particularly true for smaller and nontraditional films. Sundance, the creative enclave founded by Robert Redford, is helping to minimize this problem through its annual Sundance Film Festival and its online venue, the Sundance Online Film Festival (SOFF). SOFF is divided into three categories: animation, short subject, and new forms (multimedia). SOFF runs in January during the regular Sundance Film Festival in Park City, Utah, and even has its own digital center equipped with 15 computers with exclusive access to SOFF. One 2004 entry came from Jibjab.com, an Internet filmmaker. Jibjab has nearly 300,000 subscribers and exhibits more than 20 short animation projects, including one awarded a place at SOFF titled *Ahhhhnold for Governor.* To maintain the integrity of its artists and ensure that the quality of the work is not compromised by technology, Jibjab will only stream video of its films for broadband users. For many unconventional filmmakers like Jibjab, using a direct channel is the first step to obtaining a legitimate place in a recognized and highly competitive market.[2]

channel is commonly used for low-cost items that are frequently purchased, such as candy, cigarettes, and magazines. For example, M&M/Mars sells candies and chocolates to wholesalers in large quantities. The wholesalers then break these quantities into smaller quantities to satisfy individual retailer orders.

CHANNELS FOR BUSINESS AND INDUSTRIAL PRODUCTS

As Exhibit 12.5 illustrates, five channel structures are common in business and industrial markets. First, direct channels are typical in business and industrial markets. For example, manufacturers buy large quantities of raw materials, major equipment, processed materials, and supplies directly from other manufacturers. Manufacturers that require suppliers to meet detailed technical specifications often prefer direct channels. The direct communication required between DaimlerChrysler and its suppliers, for example, along with the tremendous size of the orders, makes anything but a direct channel impractical. The channel from producer to government buyers is also a direct channel. Since much government buying is done through bidding, a direct

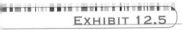

EXHIBIT 12.5

Channels for Business and Industrial Products

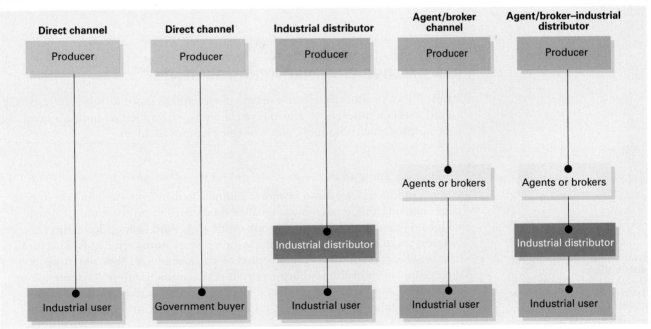

channel is attractive. Dell, for example, the top seller of desktop computers to federal, state, and local government agencies in the United States, sells the computers through direct channels.

Companies selling standardized items of moderate or low value often rely on *industrial distributors*. In many ways, an industrial distributor is like a supermarket for organizations. Industrial distributors are wholesalers and channel members that buy and take title to products. Moreover, they usually keep inventories of their products and sell and service them. Often small manufacturers cannot afford to employ their own sales force. Instead, they rely on manufacturers' representatives or selling agents to sell to either industrial distributors or users. A variation of a traditional industrial distributor relationship is created when companies form partnerships. For example, IBM partners with software vendors to distribute products. Both companies benefit from the alliance because the software vendor uses IBM's marketing and distribution channels to get the product to the market and IBM offers a more comprehensive software package for its customers. In one case, IBM used its popular database, DB2, to partner with Siebel, a CRM software developer. The result was a superior customer database that enabled clients to better manage customer relationships.[3]

Increasingly, companies are using the Internet to create more direct and efficient business channels. Currently, three major forms of business-to-business exchanges are taking place on the Internet. The first and smallest sector is made up of new Internet companies that have been developed to link buyers and sellers. These companies act as agents and charge a service fee. For example, Expedia.com links business travelers to airlines, hotels, and car rental companies. A second form of marketplace has been developed by existing companies looking for a way to drop the intermediary from the supply chain. For example, the Worldwide Retail Exchange is a marketplace created by more than 50 major retailers including Target, JCPenney, and Safeway. Retailers use the exchange to make purchases that in the past would have required telephone, fax, or face-to-face sales calls. Retailers using the exchange estimate they have saved approximately 15 percent in their purchasing costs. Finally, the third type of Internet marketplace is a "private exchange." Private exchanges allow companies to automate their supply chains while sharing information only with select suppliers. Ace Hardware and Hewlett-Packard, for example, use private exchanges to manage their inventory supplies.[4] Another example is I-textile, which enables companies in the textile business to communicate over a secure online platform to place orders, update information, and standardize transactions.[5]

ALTERNATIVE CHANNEL ARRANGEMENTS

Rarely does a producer use just one type of channel to move its product. It usually employs several different or alternative channels, which include multiple channels, nontraditional channels, and strategic channel alliances.

Multiple Channels

When a producer selects two or more channels to distribute the same product to target markets, this arrangement is called **dual distribution** (or **multiple distribution**). For example, since Sears took over Lands' End (a traditional direct business-to-consumer clothing manufacturer), Sears stores sell Lands' End products, and Sears credit cards are accepted on the Lands' End Web site. Avon, a direct supplier of health and beauty products for women, offers consumers four alternatives for purchasing products. They can contact a representative in person (the original business model), purchase on the Web, order direct from the

dual distribution (multiple distribution)
The use of two or more channels to distribute the same product to target markets.

FAQs

What do you have to consider when choosing a distribution channel? Find out the answer by watching the Video FAQ on Xtra!

company, or pick up products at an Avon Salon & Spa. With both Sears/Lands' End and Avon, identical products are being distributed to existing markets using more than one channel of distribution.[6]

Nontraditional Channels

Often nontraditional channel arrangements help differentiate a firm's product from the competition. For example, manufacturers may decide to use nontraditional channels such as the Internet, mail-order channels, or infomercials, to sell products instead of going through traditional retailer channels. Although nontraditional channels may limit a brand's coverage, they can give a producer serving a niche market a way to gain market access and customer attention without having to establish channel intermediaries. Nontraditional channels can also provide another avenue of sales for larger firms. For example, a London publisher sells short stories through vending machines in the London Underground. Instead of the traditional book format, the stories are printed like folded maps making them an easy-to-read alternative for commuters.

Kiosks, long a popular method for ordering and registering for wedding gifts, dispersing cash through ATMs, and facilitating airline check-in, are finding new uses. Ethan Allen furniture stores use kiosks as a product locator tool for consumers and salespeople. Kiosks on the campuses of Cheney University allow students to register for classes, see their class schedule and grades, check account balances, and even print transcripts. The general public, when it has access to the kiosks, can use them to gather information about the university.[7]

Strategic Channel Alliances

Producers often form **strategic channel alliances**, which enable the producers to use another manufacturer's already-established channel. Alliances are used most often when the creation of marketing channel relationships may be too expensive and time-consuming. Amazon and Circuit City have a multiyear agreement to expand the selection of electronics available on Amazon.com. Under the agreement, Amazon.com customers have the option of purchasing items from Amazon's inventory of electronic items or from the broader selection offered by Circuit City. The arrangement benefits both companies: It allows Amazon.com to deepen its selection without increasing its own inventory expense, and it increases sales for Circuit City. Similarly, Amazon.com and Target formed an alliance involving the customer service and distribution operations for Target.com.

The deal increases Target's online selection of books, music, and entertainment while adding clothing, jewelry, and other products to Amazon's selection.[8]

Strategic channel alliances are proving to be more successful for growing businesses than mergers and acquisitions. This is especially true in global markets where cultural differences, distance, and other barriers can prove challenging. For example, Heinz has a strategic alliance with Kagome, one of Japan's largest food companies. The companies are working together to find ways to reduce operating costs while expanding both brands' market presence globally.[9]

strategic channel alliance
A cooperative agreement between business firms to use the other's already established distribution channel.

REVIEW LEARNING OBJECTIVE 3

3	Describe the channel structures for consumer and business products and discuss alternative channel arrangements

CONSUMER CHANNELS	BUSINESS CHANNELS	ALTERNATIVE CHANNELS
• Direct • Retail • Wholesaler • Agent/broker	• Direct • Industrial • Agent/broker • Agent/broker industrial	• Multiple • Nontraditional • Strategic alliances

Define supply chain management and discuss its benefits

In today's sophisticated marketplace, many companies are turning to supply chain management for competitive advantage. The goal of **supply chain management** is to coordinate and integrate all of the activities performed by supply chain members into a seamless process from the source to the point of consumption, ultimately giving supply chain managers "total visibility" of the supply chain both inside and outside the firm. The philosophy behind supply chain management is that by visualizing the entire supply chain, supply chain managers can maximize strengths and efficiencies at each level of the process to create a highly competitive, customer-driven supply system that is able to respond immediately to changes in supply and demand.

An important element of supply chain management is that it is completely customer driven. In the mass-production era, manufacturers produced standardized products that were "pushed" down through the supply channel to the consumer. In contrast, in today's marketplace, products are being driven by customers, who expect to receive product configurations and services matched to their unique needs. For example, Dell only builds computers according to its customers' precise specifications, such as the amount of RAM memory; type of monitor, modem, or CD drive; and amount of hard disk space. Similarly, car companies offer customers the option to customize even economy-priced cars. For less than $20,000, customers can order a Mitsubishi Lancer with spoilers and flashy colors or a Mazda Protégé with a faster engine, special transmission, and 280-watt MP3 sound system. The focus is on pulling products into the marketplace and partnering with members of the supply chain to enhance customer value. Customizing an automobile is now possible because of new supply chain relationships between the automobile manufacturers and the after-market auto-parts industry.[10]

Dreyer's Ice Cream's successful logistics systems starts with its state-of-the-art manufacturing facility. The return on investment the company experienced subsequent to its supply chain upgrades was extremely impressive.

AP/WIDE WORLD PHOTOS

This reversal of the flow of demand from a "push" to a "pull" has resulted in a radical reformulation of both market expectations and traditional marketing, production, and distribution functions. Through the channel partnership of suppliers, manufacturers, wholesalers, and retailers along the entire supply chain who work together toward the common goal of creating customer value, supply chain management allows companies to respond with the unique product configuration and mix of services demanded by the customer. Today, supply chain management plays a dual role: first, as a *communicator* of customer demand that extends from the point of sale all the way back to the supplier, and second, as a *physical flow process* that engineers the timely and cost-effective movement of goods through the entire supply pipeline.

Accordingly, supply chain managers are responsible for making channel strategy decisions, coordinating the sourcing and procurement of raw materials, scheduling production, processing orders, managing inventory, transporting and storing supplies and finished goods, and coordinating customer service activities. Supply chain managers are also responsible for the management of information that flows through the supply chain. Coordinating the relationships between the company and its external partners, such as vendors, carriers, and third-party companies, is also a critical function of supply chain management. Because supply chain managers play such a major role in both cost control and customer satisfaction, they are more valuable than ever. In fact, demand

supply chain management
A management system that coordinates and integrates all of the activities performed by supply chain members into a seamless process, from the source to the point of consumption, resulting in enhanced customer and economic value.

for supply chain managers has increased substantially in recent years.

In summary, supply chain managers are responsible for directing raw materials and parts to the production department and the finished or semifinished product through warehouses and eventually to the intermediary or end user. Above all, supply chain management begins and ends with the customer. Instead of forcing into the market a product that may or may not sell quickly, supply chain managers react to actual customer demand. By doing so, they minimize the flow of raw materials, finished product, and packaging materials at every point in the supply chain, resulting in lower costs and increased customer value. Exhibit 12.6 depicts the supply chain process.

Nash Finch
What role does Nash Finch play in the supply chain?
http://www.nashfinch.com

Online

BENEFITS OF SUPPLY CHAIN MANAGEMENT

Supply chain management is a key means of differentiation for a firm and a critical component in marketing and corporate strategy. Companies that focus on supply chain management commonly report lower inventory, transportation, warehousing, and packaging costs; greater supply chain flexibility; improved customer service; and higher revenues. Research has shown a clear relationship between supply chain performance and profitability. Leaders in supply chain management report a 5 percent increase in revenue due to reducing supply chain costs, a 65

FAQs

Why should managers be concerned with supply chain management? Find out the answer by watching the Video FAQ on Xtra!

EXHIBIT 12.6

The Supply Chain Process

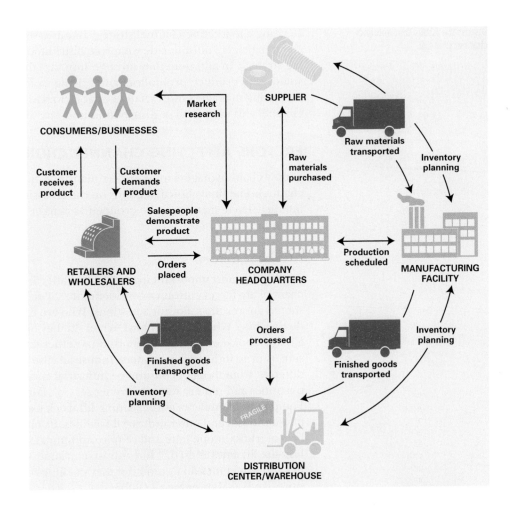

Define supply chain management and discuss its benefits

Well-managed supply chains . . .

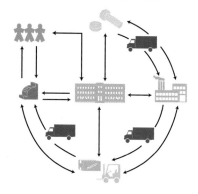

lead to . . .

 reduced costs

✓ increased flexibility

✓ improved customer service

✓ greater revenue

percent increase in supply chain flexibility, and an 18 percent improvement in cash flow.[11]

Dreyer's as a maker of ice cream, has built its success on its logistics system. The company recently invested $150 million in a new fleet of trucks, manufacturing centers, additional employees, and a computerized delivery system that enables dispatchers to design delivery routes around sales volume, mileage, traffic patterns, road tolls, and a store's hours of operation. As a return on its investment, the company has experienced a 33 percent increase in sales accounts, eliminated more than 42,000 unnecessary stops, saved $11 million in gas and labor hours, and increased its net income. In fact, the system provides such strong customer service capability and cost savings that nearly one-third of Dreyer's revenue comes from deals to distribute its competitors' brands such as Häagen-Dazs and Ben & Jerry's.[12] On a more individual level, one materials analyst for a company that produces seat belts reported that when her company began focusing on supply chain management, it shortened her workweek by 15 to 20 hours and reduced her inventory costs by 75 percent.[13]

5 MAKING CHANNEL STRATEGY DECISIONS

Discuss the issues that influence channel strategy

Devising a marketing channel strategy requires several critical decisions. Supply chain managers must decide what role distribution will play in the overall marketing strategy. In addition, they must be sure that the channel strategy chosen is consistent with product, promotion, and pricing strategies. In making these decisions, marketing managers must analyze what factors will influence the choice of channel and what level of distribution intensity will be appropriate.

FACTORS AFFECTING CHANNEL CHOICE

Supply chain managers must answer many questions before choosing a marketing channel. The final choice depends on the analysis of several factors, which often interact. These factors can be grouped as market factors, product factors, and producer factors.

Market Factors

Among the most important market factors affecting the choice of distribution channel are target customer considerations. Specifically, supply chain managers should answer the following questions: Who are the potential customers? What do they buy? Where do they buy? When do they buy? How do they buy? Additionally, the choice of channel depends on whether the producer is selling to consumers or to industrial customers. Industrial customers' buying habits are very different from those of consumers. Industrial customers tend to buy in larger quantities and require more customer service. For example, Toyota Industrial Equipment manufactures the leading lift truck used to move materials in and out of warehouses and other industrial facilities. Its business customers buy large numbers of trucks at one time and require additional services such as data tracking on how the lift truck is used.[14] In contrast, consumers usually buy in very small quantities and sometimes do not mind if they get little or no service, such as in a discount store like Wal-Mart or Sam's Club.

The geographic location and size of the market are also important to channel selection. As a rule, if the target market is concentrated in one or more specific areas, then direct selling through a sales force is appropriate. When markets are more widely dispersed, intermediaries would be less expensive. The size of the market also influences channel choice. Generally, larger markets require more intermediaries. For instance, Procter & Gamble has to reach millions of consumers with its many brands of household goods. It needs many intermediaries, including wholesalers and retailers.

Product Factors

Products that are more complex, customized, and expensive tend to benefit from shorter and more direct marketing channels. These types of products sell better through a direct sales force. Examples include pharmaceuticals, scientific instruments, airplanes, and mainframe computer systems. On the other hand, the more standardized a product is, the longer its distribution channel can be and the greater the number of intermediaries that can be involved. For example, with the exception of flavor and shape, the formula for chewing gum is about the same from producer to producer. Chewing gum is also very inexpensive. As a result, the distribution channel for gum tends to involve many wholesalers and retailers.

The product's life cycle is also an important factor in choosing a marketing channel. In fact, the choice of channel may change over the life of the product.

Vending machines are becoming a popular way to sell everything from boxer shorts to cameras. Kodak teamed up with Maytag to roll out thousands of camera-and-film vending machines. Kodak wants to satisfy instant cravings for a must-have snapshot in places like amusement parks, ski resorts, and the beach.

For example, when photocopiers were first available, they were typically sold by a direct sales force. Now, however, photocopiers can be found in several places, including warehouse clubs, electronics superstores, and mail-order catalogs. As products become more common and less intimidating to potential users, producers tend to look for alternative channels. Gatorade was originally sold to sports teams, gyms, and fitness clubs. As the drink became more popular, mainstream supermarket channels were added, followed by convenience stores and drugstores. Now Gatorade can be found in vending machines and even in some fast-food restaurants.

Another factor is the delicacy of the product. Perishable products like vegetables and milk have a relatively short life span. Fragile products like china and crystal require a minimum amount of handling. Therefore, both require fairly short marketing channels. eBay facilitates the sale of unusual or difficult-to-find products that benefit from a direct channel.

Producer Factors

Several factors pertaining to the producer itself are important to the selection of a marketing channel. In general, producers with large financial, managerial, and marketing resources are better able to use more direct channels. These producers have the ability to hire and train their own sales force, warehouse their own goods, and extend credit to their customers. For example, variety store Dollar Tree distributes products through retail locations at low prices. To increase cost-efficiency, Dollar Tree built two distribution centers to service its 2,400 stores.[15] Smaller or weaker firms, on the other hand, must rely on intermediaries to provide these services for them. Compared to producers with only one or two product lines, producers that sell several products in a related area are able to choose channels that are more direct. Sales expenses then can be spread over more products.

A producer's desire to control pricing, positioning, brand image, and customer support also tends to influence channel selection. For instance, firms that sell products with exclusive brand images, such as designer perfumes and clothing, usually avoid channels in which discount retailers are present. Manufacturers of upscale products, such as Gucci (handbags) and Godiva (chocolates), may sell their wares only in expensive stores in order to maintain an image of exclusivity. Many producers have opted to risk their image, however, and test sales in discount channels. Levi Strauss expanded its distribution to include JCPenney and Sears. JCPenney is now Levi Strauss's biggest customer.

LEVELS OF DISTRIBUTION INTENSITY

Organizations have three options for intensity of distribution: intensive distribution, selective distribution, or exclusive distribution (see Exhibit 12.7).

Intensive Distribution

Intensive distribution is a form of distribution aimed at maximum market coverage. The manufacturer tries to have the product available in every outlet where potential customers might want to buy it. If buyers are unwilling to search for a product (as is true of convenience goods and operating supplies), the product must be very accessible to buyers. A low-value product that is purchased frequently may require a lengthy channel. For example, candy, chips, and other snack foods are found in almost every type of retail store imaginable. These foods typically are sold to retailers in small quantities by food or candy wholesalers. The Wrigley Company could not afford to sell its gum directly to every service station, drugstore, supermarket, and discount store. The cost would be too high. Similarly, Sysco delivers food and related products to restaurants and other food service companies that prepare meals for customers dining out. It is not economically feasible for restaurants to go to individual vendors for each product. Therefore, Sysco serves as an intermediary by delivering all products necessary to fulfill restaurants' needs.[16]

Most manufacturers pursuing an intensive distribution strategy sell to a large percentage of the wholesalers willing to stock their products. Retailers' willingness (or unwillingness) to handle items tends to control the manufacturer's ability to achieve intensive distribution. For example, a retailer already carrying ten brands of gum may show little enthusiasm for one more brand.

intensive distribution
A form of distribution aimed at having a product available in every outlet where target customers might want to buy it.

EXHIBIT 12.7

Intensity of Distribution Levels

Intensity Level	Distribution Intensity Objective	Number of Intermediaries in Each Market	Examples
Intensive	Achieve mass-market selling; popular with health and beauty aids and convenience goods that must be available everywhere	Many	Pepsi-Cola, Frito-Lay potato chips, Huggies diapers, Alpo dog food, Crayola crayons
Selective	Work closely with selected intermediaries who meet certain criteria; typically used for shopping goods and some specialty goods	Several	Donna Karan clothing, Hewlett-Packard printers, Burton snowboards, Aveda aromatherapy products
Exclusive	Work with a single intermediary for products that require special resources or positioning; typically used for specialty goods and major industrial equipment	One	BMW cars, Rolex watches

Selective Distribution

Selective distribution is achieved by screening dealers and retailers to eliminate all but a few in any single area. Because only a few are chosen, the consumer must seek out the product. For example, when Heeling Sports Ltd. launched Heelys, thick-soled sneakers with a wheel embedded in each heel, the company hired a group of 40 teens to perform Heelys exhibitions in targeted malls, skate parks, and college campuses across the country to create demand. Then the company made the decision to avoid large stores like Target and to distribute the shoes only through selected mall retailers and skate and surf shops in order to position the product as "cool and kind of irreverent."[17]

Selective distribution strategies often hinge on a manufacturer's desire to maintain a superior product image so as to be able to charge a premium price. DKNY clothing, for instance, is sold only in select retail outlets, mainly full-price department stores. Likewise, premium pet food brands such as Hill's Pet Nutrition and Ralston-Purina's ProPlan are distributed chiefly through specialty pet food stores and veterinarians, rather than mass retailers like Wal-Mart, so that a premium price can be charged. Procter & Gamble, which purchased rival premium pet food brand Iams, recently expanded Iams's selective distribution strategy to include mass retailers like Target. The strategy has created channel conflict with the breeders and veterinarians who have been the brand's primary source of strength over the years.[18]

Exclusive Distribution

The most restrictive form of market coverage is **exclusive distribution**, which entails only one or a few dealers within a given area. Because buyers may have to search or travel extensively to buy the product, exclusive distribution is usually confined to consumer specialty goods, a few shopping goods, and major industrial equipment.

Products such as Rolls Royce automobiles, Chris-Craft power boats, and Pettibone tower cranes are distributed under exclusive arrangements. Sometimes exclusive territories are granted by new companies (such as franchisers) to obtain market coverage in a particular area. Limited distribution may also serve to project an exclusive image for the product.

Retailers and wholesalers may be unwilling to commit the time and money necessary to promote and service a product unless the manufacturer guarantees them an exclusive territory. This arrangement shields the dealer from direct competition and enables it to be the main beneficiary of the manufacturer's promotion efforts in that geographic area. With exclusive distribution, channels of communication are usually well established because the manufacturer works with a limited number of dealers rather than many accounts.

Exclusive distribution also takes place within a retailer's store rather than a geographic area—for example, when a retailer agrees not to sell a manufacturer's competing brands. Mossimo, traditionally an apparel wholesaler, developed an agreement with Target to design clothing and related items sold exclusively at Target stores. Other exclusive distributors involved in this successful model include Michael Graves (architect) housewares, Sonia Kashuk makeup, Eddie Bauer camping goods, Todd Oldham home furnishings for the college student, and the Swell line by Cynthia Rowley and Ilene Rosenzweig.[19]

Target.com

How does Target use its Web site to promote its exclusive distribution of the products listed on this page? Do Mossimo, Michael Graves, Sonia Kashuk, Eddie Bauer, Todd Oldham, and Swell by Cynthia Rowley and Ilene Rosenzweig reciprocate? Discuss what you discover.

http://www.target.com

http://www.mossimo.com

http://www.michaelgraves.com

http://www.soniakashuk.com

http://www.eddiebauer.com

http://toddoldhamstudio.com

http://www.cynthiarowley.com

Online

selective distribution
A form of distribution achieved by screening dealers to eliminate all but a few in any single area.

exclusive distribution
A form of distribution that establishes one or a few dealers within a given area.

REVIEW LEARNING OBJECTIVE 5

5 Discuss the issues that influence channel strategy

Factors	Distribution
Market	Intensive
Product	Selective
Producer	Exclusive

Channel Strategy

Explain channel leadership, conflict, and partnering

A marketing channel is more than a set of institutions linked by economic ties. Social relationships play an important role in building unity among channel members. A critical aspect of supply chain management, therefore, is managing the social relationships among channel members to achieve synergy. The basic social dimensions of channels are power, control, leadership, conflict, and partnering.

CHANNEL POWER, CONTROL, AND LEADERSHIP

Channel power is a channel member's capacity to control or influence the behavior of other channel members. **Channel control** occurs when one channel member affects another member's behavior. To achieve control, a channel member assumes channel leadership and exercises authority and power. This member is termed the **channel leader**, or **channel captain**. In one marketing channel, a manufacturer may be the leader because it controls new-product designs and product availability. In another, a retailer may be the channel leader because it wields power and control over the retail price, inventory levels, and postsale service.

The exercise of channel power is a routine element of many business activities in which the outcome is often more efficient operations and cost savings. Lancôme, which traditionally sold its makeup in upscale department stores, encountered channel control issues when the department stores launched their own Web sites and wanted Lancôme to sell its makeup online. Lancôme's managers held off initially because they wanted to have control over how the makeup was "presented" to the consumer. Rather than grouping all products together, Lancôme wanted its promotional messages displayed with each product. Using iChannel software, Lancôme was able to control the presentation of the brand by controlling content delivery, thereby delivering a consistent customer experience online and off-line.[20]

CHANNEL CONFLICT

Inequitable channel relationships often lead to **channel conflict**, which is a clash of goals and methods among the members of a distribution channel. In a broad context, conflict may not be bad. Often it arises because staid, traditional channel members refuse to keep pace with the times. Removing an outdated intermediary may result in reduced costs for the entire supply chain. The Internet has forced many intermediaries to offer services such as merchandise tracking and inventory availability online.

Conflicts among channel members can be due to many different situations and factors. Oftentimes, conflict arises because channel members have conflicting goals. For instance, athletic footwear retailers want to sell as many shoes as possible in order to maximize profits, regardless of whether the shoe is manufactured by Nike, adidas, or Saucony. But the Nike manufacturer wants a certain sales volume and market share in each market.

Conflict can also arise when channel members fail to fulfill expectations of other channel members—for example, when a franchisee does not follow the rules set down by the franchiser, or when communications channels break down between channel members. As another example, if a manufacturer reduces the length of warranty coverage and fails to communicate this change to dealers, then conflict may occur when dealers make repairs with the expectation that they will be reimbursed by the manufacturer. Further, ideological differences and different perceptions of reality can also cause conflict among channel members. For instance, retailers may believe "the customer is always right" and offer a very liberal return policy. Wholesalers and manufacturers may feel that people "try to get something for nothing" or don't follow product instructions carefully.

channel power
The capacity of a particular marketing channel member to control or influence the behavior of other channel members.

channel control
A situation that occurs when one marketing channel member intentionally affects another member's behavior.

channel leader (channel captain)
A member of a marketing channel that exercises authority and power over the activities of other channel members.

channel conflict
A clash of goals and methods between distribution channel members.

Their differing views of allowable returns will undoubtably conflict with those of retailers.

Conflict within a channel can be either horizontal or vertical. **Horizontal conflict** occurs among channel members on the same level, such as two or more different wholesalers or two or more different retailers, that handle the same manufacturer's brands. This type of channel conflict is found most often when manufacturers practice dual or multiple distribution strategies. For instance, there was considerable channel conflict after computer manufacturers began to go beyond the traditional computer resellers and distribute their computers through discount stores, department stores, warehouse clubs, and giant electronic superstores, such as Circuit City and Comp-USA. Horizontal conflict can also occur when channel members on the same level feel they are being treated unfairly by the manufacturer. For example, the American Booksellers Association, a group representing small independent booksellers, filed a lawsuit against bookstore giants Barnes & Noble and Borders, claiming they had violated antitrust laws by using their buying power to demand "illegal and secret" discounts from publishers. These deals, the association contended, put independent booksellers at a serious competitive disadvantage.

Many regard horizontal conflict as healthy competition. Much more serious is **vertical conflict**, which occurs between different levels in a marketing channel, most typically between the manufacturer and wholesaler or the manufacturer and retailer. Producer-versus-wholesaler conflict occurs when the producer chooses to bypass the wholesaler and deal directly with the consumer or retailer. For example, conflict arose when several producers agreed to Wal-Mart's request to deal with it directly, bypassing intermediaries altogether.

Dual distribution strategies can also cause vertical conflict in the channel. For example, high-end fashion designers traditionally sold their products through luxury retailers such as Neiman Marcus and Saks Fifth Avenue. Interested in increasing sales and gaining additional presentation control, many designers such as Giorgio Armani, Donna Karan, and Louis Vuitton began opening their own boutiques in the same shopping centers anchored by the luxury retailers. As a result, the retailers lost substantial revenues on the designers' items. Similarly, manufacturers experimenting with selling to customers directly over the Internet are creating conflict with their traditional retailing intermediaries. For example, Baby Jogger worked closely with retailers to build a business with $15 million in sales. But when numerous look-alike products began appearing on the market, the company decided to try to increase sales by selling directly to consumers on the Internet. Angry retailers responded by promoting other brands. Recognizing how important the retailers were to its success, Baby Jogger halted Internet sales in 2001.[21]

Producers and retailers may also disagree over the terms of the sale or other aspects of the business relationship. When Procter & Gamble introduced "everyday low pricing" to its retail channel members, a strategy designed to standardize wholesale prices and eliminate most trade promotions, many retailers retaliated. Some cut the variety of P&G sizes they carried or eliminated marginal brands. Others moved P&G brands from prime shelf space to less visible shelves.

© AP/WIDE WORLD PHOTO

Louis Vuitton opened a store of its own on Madison Avenue in New York. The new location will be the world's largest Louis Vuitton store and will definitely affect sales of Vuitton products at the city's luxury department stores like Saks and Bergdorf Goodman.

horizontal conflict
A channel conflict that occurs among channel members on the same level.

vertical conflict
A channel conflict that occurs between different levels in a marketing channel, most typically between the manufacturer and wholesaler or between the manufacturer and retailer.

EXHIBIT 12.8

Transaction- versus Partnership-Based Firms

	Transaction-Based	Partnership-Based
Relationships between Manufacturer and Supplier	• Short-term • Adversarial • Independent • Price more important	• Long-term • Cooperative • Dependent • Value-added services more important
Number of Suppliers	Many	Few
Level of Information Sharing	Minimal	High
Investment Required	Minimal	High

SOURCE: David Frederick Ross, *Competing Through Supply Chain Management: Creating Market-Winning Strategies Through Supply Chain Partnerships* (New York: Chapman & Hall, 1998), 61.

CHANNEL PARTNERING

Regardless of the locus of power, channel members rely heavily on one another. Even the most powerful manufacturers depend on dealers to sell their products; even the most powerful retailers require the products provided by suppliers. In sharp contrast to the adversarial relationships of the past between buyers and sellers, contemporary management thought emphasizes the development of close working partnerships among channel members. **Channel partnering**, or **channel cooperation**, is the joint effort of all channel members to create a supply chain that serves customers and creates a competitive advantage. Channel partnering is vital if each member is to gain something from other members. By cooperating, retailers, wholesalers, manufacturers, and suppliers can speed up inventory replenishment, improve customer service, and reduce the total costs of the marketing channel.

Channel alliances and partnerships help supply chain managers create the parallel flow of materials and information required to leverage the supply chains' intellectual, material, and marketing resources. The rapid growth in channel partnering is due to new enabling technology and the need to lower costs. A comparison between companies that approach the marketplace unilaterally and those that engage in channel cooperation and form partnerships is detailed in Exhibit 12.8.

Collaborating channel partners meet the needs of consumers more effectively by ensuring that the right products are available at the right time and for a lower cost, thus boosting sales and profits. Forced to become more efficient, many companies are turning formerly adversarial relationships into partnerships. For example, Kraft is the largest coffee purchaser in the world. Rather than clash with coffee bean growers, Kraft partners with them to help build customer demand and develop "sustainable" coffee production (growing coffee in a way that reduces the impact on the environment, provides quality ingredients for manufacturers to meet consumer needs, and is more valuable to the farmer).[22]

REVIEW LEARNING OBJECTIVE 6

6 Explain channel leadership, conflict, and partnering

Channel power, control, leadership

Channel partnering

Channel relationship synergy

Channel conflict

horizontal   vertical

7 MANAGING THE LOGISTICAL COMPONENTS OF THE SUPPLY CHAIN

Describe the logistical components of the supply chain

Now that you are familiar with the structure and strategy of marketing channels and the role of supply chain management, it is important to also understand the physical means through which products move through the supply chain. As mentioned earlier, supply chain management coordinates and integrates all of the activities performed by supply chain members into a seamless process. The supply chain consists of several interrelated and integrated logistical components: (1) sourcing and procurement of raw materials and supplies, (2) production scheduling, (3) order processing, (4) inventory control, (5) warehousing and materials-handling, and (6) transportation.

channel partnering (channel cooperation)
The joint effort of all channel members to create a supply chain that serves customers and creates a competitive advantage.

Integrating and linking all of the logistics components of the supply chain is the **logistics information system**. Today's supply chain logisticians are at the forefront of information technology, which is not just a functional affiliate of supply chain management. Rather it is the enabler, the facilitator, the linkage that connects the various components and partners of the supply chain into an integrated whole. Electronic data interchange, on-board computers, RFID chips, satellite and cellular communications systems, materials-handling and warehouse-management software, enterprise-wide systems solutions, and the Internet are among the information enablers of successful supply chain management.

The **supply chain team**, in concert with the logistics information system, orchestrates the movement of goods, services, and information from the source to the consumer. Supply chain teams typically cut across organizational boundaries, embracing all parties who participate in moving the product to market. The best supply chain teams also move beyond the organization to include the external participants in the chain, such as suppliers, transportation carriers, and third-party logistics suppliers. Members of the supply chain communicate, coordinate, and cooperate extensively.

Today's corporate supply chain logisticians have become so efficient that the U.S. Marine Corps is now consulting with companies like Wal-Mart, UPS, and Unilever to improve its own supply chain efficiency. The Marine Corps's goal is to reduce the time it takes to deliver supplies to the front lines from one week to 24 hours and lower costs by cutting inventories in half.

SOURCING AND PROCUREMENT

One of the most important links in the supply chain is that between the manufacturer and the supplier. Purchasing professionals are on the front lines of supply chain management. Purchasing departments plan purchasing strategies, develop specifications, select suppliers, and negotiate price and service levels.

The goal of most sourcing and procurement activities is to reduce the costs of raw materials and supplies. Purchasing professionals have traditionally relied on tough negotiations to get the lowest price possible from suppliers of raw materials, supplies, and components. Perhaps the biggest contribution purchasing can make to supply chain management, however, is in the area of vendor relations. Companies can use the purchasing function to strategically manage suppliers in order to reduce the total cost of materials and services. Through enhanced vendor relations, buyers and sellers can develop cooperative relationships that reduce costs and improve efficiency with the aim of lowering prices and enhancing profits. By integrating suppliers into their companies' businesses, purchasing managers have become better able to streamline purchasing processes, manage inventory levels, and reduce overall costs of the sourcing and procurement operations.

PRODUCTION SCHEDULING

In traditional mass-market manufacturing, production begins when forecasts call for additional products to be made or inventory control systems signal low inventory levels. The firm then makes a product and transports the finished goods to its own warehouses or those of intermediaries, where the goods wait to be ordered by retailers or customers. For example, many types of convenience goods, such as toothpaste, deodorant, and detergent, are manufactured based on past sales and demand and then sent to retailers to resell. Production scheduling based on pushing a product down to the consumer obviously has its disadvantages, the most notable being that companies risk making products that may become obsolete or that consumers don't want in the first place.

In a customer "pull" manufacturing environment, which is growing in popularity, production of goods or services is not scheduled until an order is placed by the customer specifying the desired configuration. As you read in Chapter 11, this process, known as **mass customization**, or **build-to-order**, uniquely tailors mass-market

logistics information system
Information technology that integrates and links all of the logistics functions of the supply chain.

supply chain team
An entire group of individuals who orchestrate the movement of goods, services, and information from the source to the consumer.

mass customization (build-to-order)
A production method whereby products are not made until an order is placed by the customer; products are made according to customer specifications.

goods and services to the needs of the individuals who buy them.
Companies as diverse as BMW, Dell, Levi Strauss, Mattel, and a slew
of Web-based businesses are adopting mass customization to maintain or obtain a competitive edge.

As more companies move toward mass customization—and
away from mass marketing—of goods, the need to stay on top of
consumer demand is forcing manufacturers to make their supply
chains more flexible. Flexibility is critical to a manufacturer's success when dramatic swings in demand occur. For example, M&M launched color-
works.com where consumers can create custom color combinations of its chocolate
candies. The site offers 21 different colors that can be ordered in any combination
in eight-ounce or five-pound bags. Similarly, Procter & Gamble launched
Reflect.com where consumers create beauty products tailored specifically to their
needs. Yankee Candle Company offers customers the opportunity to create a customized candle. Staples office supply allows consumers to custom pick the color of
their chairs. To meet consumers' demand for customized products, companies are
forced to adapt their manufacturing approach or even create a completely new process. Reflect.com has patented its production process featuring modular vats that
can be switched around as needed for individual recipes.[23]

Just-in-Time Manufacturing

An important manufacturing process common today among manufacturers
is just-in-time manufacturing. Borrowed from the Japanese, **just-in-time production** (**JIT**), sometimes called *lean production*, requires manufacturers to
work closely with suppliers and transportation providers to get necessary items to the
assembly line or factory floor at the precise time they are needed for production. For
the manufacturer, JIT means that raw materials arrive at the assembly line in guaranteed working order "just in time" to be installed, and finished products are generally
shipped to the customer immediately after completion. For the supplier, JIT means
supplying customers with products in just a few days, or even a few hours, rather than
weeks. For the ultimate consumer, JIT means lower costs, shorter lead times, and
products that more closely meet the consumer's needs. For example, Zara, a European clothing manufacturer and retailer, has begun using the JIT process to ensure
that its stores are stocked with the latest fashion trends. Using its salespeople to track
which fashions are selling fastest, the company can increase production of hot items
and ship them to its stores in just a few days. Because Zara stores do not maintain
large inventories, they can respond quickly to fashion trends and offer their products
for less, giving Zara a distinct advantage over more traditional retailers like Gap that
place orders months in advance.[24]

JIT benefits manufacturers most by reducing their raw materials inventories.
For example, at Dell's Texas plant, computer components often are delivered just
minutes before they are needed. Chips, boards, and drives are kept in trucks
backed into bays located 50 feet from the beginning of the production line. On average, Dell takes only about a week from buying parts to selling them as a finished
product. Similarly, Customized Transportation, Inc., works with General Motors to
coordinate delivery of interior door panels at the moment they are needed for
production. CTI also helps GM manage its supply chain by issuing purchase orders, buying the raw materials from vendors, assembling the components, and
packaging them for delivery.

Additionally, JIT shortens lead times—the time it takes to get parts from a supplier after an order has been placed. Manufacturers also enjoy better relationships
with suppliers and can decrease their production and storeroom costs. Because
there is little safety stock, and therefore no margin for error, the manufacturer
cannot afford to make a mistake. As a result, a manufacturer using JIT must be
sure it receives high-quality parts from all vendors, be confident that the supplier
will meet all delivery commitments, and have a crisis management plan to handle
any disruptions. Finally, JIT tends to reduce the amount of paperwork.

just-in-time production (JIT)
A process that redefines and
simplifies manufacturing by reducing
inventory levels and delivering raw
materials just when they are needed
on the production line.

ORDER PROCESSING

The order is often the catalyst that sets the supply chain in motion, especially in the build-to-order environments of leading computer manufacturers such as Dell. The **order processing system** processes the requirements of the customer and sends the information into the supply chain via the logistics information system. The order goes to the manufacturer's warehouse. If the product is in stock, the order is filled and arrangements are made to ship it. If the product is not in stock, it triggers a replenishment request that finds its way to the factory floor.

The role of proper order processing in providing good service cannot be overemphasized. As an order enters the system, management must monitor two flows: the flow of goods and the flow of information. Often the best-laid plans of marketers can get entangled in the order processing system. Obviously, good communication among sales representatives, office personnel, and warehouse and shipping personnel is essential to correct order processing. Shipping incorrect merchandise or partially filled orders can create just as much dissatisfaction as stockouts or slow deliveries. The flow of goods and information must be continually monitored so that mistakes can be corrected before an invoice is prepared and the merchandise shipped.

Order processing is becoming more automated through the use of computer technology known as **electronic data interchange (EDI)**. The basic idea of EDI is to replace the paper documents that usually accompany business transactions, such as purchase orders and invoices, with electronic transmission of the needed information. A typical EDI message includes all the information that would traditionally be included on a paper invoice such as product code, quantity, and transportation details. The information is usually sent via private networks, which are more secure and reliable than the networks used for standard e-mail messages. Most importantly, the information can be read and processed by computers, significantly reducing costs and increasing efficiency. Companies that use EDI can reduce inventory levels, improve cash flow, streamline operations, and increase the speed and accuracy of information transmission. EDI is also believed to create a closer relationship between buyers and sellers.

It should not be surprising that retailers have become major users of EDI. For Wal-Mart, Target, and the like, logistics speed and accuracy are crucial competitive tools in an overcrowded retail environment. Many big retailers are helping their suppliers acquire EDI technology so that they can be linked into the system. EDI works hand in hand with retailers' *efficient consumer response* programs, which are designed to have the right products on the shelf, in the right styles and colors, at the right time, through improved inventory, ordering, and distribution techniques. (See Chapter 13 for more discussion of retailers' use of EDI techniques.)

INVENTORY CONTROL

Closely interrelated with the procurement, manufacturing, and ordering processes is the **inventory control system**—a method that develops and maintains an adequate assortment of materials or products to meet a manufacturer's or a customer's demands.

Inventory decisions, for both raw materials and finished goods, have a big impact on supply chain costs and the level of service provided. If too many products are kept in inventory, costs increase—as do risks of obsolescence, theft, and damage. If too few products are kept on hand, then the company risks product shortages and angry customers, and ultimately lost sales. For example, negative sales forecasts for the Christmas buying season in the past few years caused many retailers to cut back on orders because they were afraid of having to discount large end-of-the-year inventories. As a result, many companies including Panasonic and Lands' End lost sales due to inventory shortages on popular items. The goal of inventory management, therefore, is to keep inventory levels as low as possible

order processing system
A system whereby orders are entered into the supply chain and filled.

electronic data interchange (EDI)
Information technology that replaces the paper documents that usually accompany business transactions, such as purchase orders and invoices, with electronic transmission of the needed information to reduce inventory levels, improve cash flow, streamline operations, and increase the speed and accuracy of information transmission.

inventory control system
A method of developing and maintaining an adequate assortment of materials or products to meet a manufacturer's or a customer's demand.

Build-to-order computers are more than commonplace today, thanks to Dell's direct selling model. The company allows customers to track their orders throughout manufacturing and shipping.

materials requirement planning (MRP) (materials management)
An inventory control system that manages the replenishment of raw materials, supplies, and components from the supplier to the manufacturer.

distribution resource planning (DRP)
An inventory control system that manages the replenishment of goods from the manufacturer to the final consumer.

while maintaining an adequate supply of goods to meet customer demand.

Managing inventory from the supplier to the manufacturer is called **materials requirement planning (MRP)**, or **materials management**. This system also encompasses the sourcing and procurement operations, signaling purchasing when raw materials, supplies, or components will need to be replenished for the production of more goods. The system that manages the finished goods inventory from manufacturer to end user is commonly referred to as **distribution resource planning (DRP)**. Both inventory systems use various inputs, such as sales forecasts, available inventory, outstanding orders, lead times, and mode of transportation to be used, to determine what actions must be taken to replenish goods at all points in the supply chain. Demand in the system is collected at each level in the supply chain, from the retailer back up the chain to the manufacturer. With the use of electronic data interchange, the information can be transmitted much faster to meet the quick-response needs of today's competitive marketplace. Exhibit 12.9 provides an example of inventory replenishment using DRP from the retailer to the manufacturer.

Just-in-time manufacturing processes have had a significant impact on reducing inventory levels. Since JIT requires supplies to be delivered at the time they are needed on the factory floor, little inventory is needed. With JIT the purchasing firm can reduce the amount of raw materials and parts it keeps on hand by ordering more often and in smaller amounts. And lower inventory levels due to JIT can give firms a competitive edge through the flexibility to halt production of existing products in favor of those gaining popularity with consumers. Savings also come from having less capital tied up in inventory and from the reduced need for storage facilities.

EXHIBIT 12.9

Inventory Replenishment Example

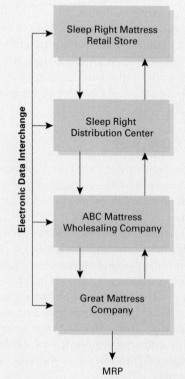

Sleep Right Mattress Retail Store

Sleep Right is planning a promotion on the Great Mattress Company's Gentle Rest mattress. Sales forecast is for 50 units to be sold. Sleep Right has 10 open Gentle Rest orders with its distribution center. New mattresses must be delivered in two weeks in time for the promotion.

Sleep Right Distribution Center

Sleep Right's Distribution Center is electronically notified of the order of 50 new Gentle Rest mattresses. It currently has 20 Gentle Rest mattresses in inventory and begins putting together the transportation plans to deliver these to the Sleep Right Store. Delivery takes one day. It orders 40 new mattresses from its mattress wholesaler to make up the difference.

ABC Mattress Wholesaling Company

ABC Mattress Wholesaling Company is electronically notified of Sleep Right DC's order of 40 new Gentle Rest mattresses. It currently does not have any of these in stock but electronically orders 40 from the Great Mattress Company's factory. Once it receives the new mattresses, it can have them delivered to the Sleep Right DC in two days.

Great Mattress Company

The Great Mattress Company electronically receives ABC's order and forwards it to the factory floor. Production of a new mattress takes 20 minutes. The total order of 40 mattresses can be ready to be shipped to ABC in two days. Delivery takes one day. Raw material supplies for this order are electronically requested from Great Mattress's supply partners, who deliver the needed materials just-in-time to its stitching machines.

MRP

WAREHOUSING AND MATERIALS-HANDLING

Supply chain logisticians oversee the constant flow of raw materials from suppliers to manufacturer and finished goods from the manufacturer to the ultimate consumer. Although JIT manufacturing processes may eliminate the need to warehouse many raw materials, manufacturers may often keep some safety stock on hand in the event of an emergency, such as a strike at a supplier's plant or a catastrophic event that temporarily stops the flow of raw materials to the production line. Likewise, the final user may not need or want the goods at the same time the manufacturer produces and wants to sell them. Products like grain and corn are produced seasonally, but consumers demand them year-round. Other products, such as Christmas ornaments and turkeys, are produced year-round, but consumers do not want them until autumn or winter. Therefore, management must have a storage system to hold these products until they are shipped.

Storage is what helps manufacturers manage supply and demand, or production and consumption. It provides time utility to buyers and sellers, which means that the seller stores the product until the buyer wants or needs it. Even when products are used regularly, not seasonally, many manufacturers store excess products in case the demand surpasses the amount produced at a given time. Storing additional product does have disadvantages, however, including the costs of insurance on the stored product, taxes, obsolescence or spoilage, theft, and warehouse operating costs. Another drawback is opportunity costs—that is, the opportunities lost because money is tied up in stored product instead of being used for something else.

Because businesses are focusing on cutting supply chain costs, the warehousing industry is also changing to better serve its customers. For example, many warehouses are putting greater emphasis on more efficient unloading and reloading layouts and customized services that move merchandise through the warehouse faster, often in the same day. They also are investing in services using sophisticated tracking technology such as materials-handling systems.

A **materials-handling system** moves inventory into, within, and out of the warehouse. Materials-handling includes these functions:

- Receiving goods into the warehouse or distribution center
- Identifying, sorting, and labeling the goods
- Dispatching the goods to a temporary storage area
- Recalling, selecting, or picking the goods for shipment (may include packaging the product in a protective container for shipping)

The goal of the materials-handling system is to move items quickly with minimal handling. With a manual, nonautomated materials-handling system, a product may be handled more than a dozen times. Each time it is handled, the cost and risk of damage increase; each lifting of a product stresses its package. Consequently, most manufacturers today have moved to automated systems. Scanners quickly identify goods entering and leaving a warehouse through bar-coded labels affixed to the packaging. Automatic storage and retrieval systems automatically store and pick goods in the warehouse or distribution center. Automated materials-handling systems decrease product handling, ensure accurate placement of product, and improve the accuracy of order picking and the rates of on-time shipment.

At Dell the OptiPlex system runs the factory. The computer software receives orders, sends requests for parts to suppliers, orders components, organizes assembly of the product, and even arranges for it to be shipped. Thus, instead of hundreds of workers, often fewer than six are working at one time. An order for a few hundred computers can be filled in less than eight hours using the automated system. With the OptiPlex system, productivity has increased 160 percent per person per hour.[25]

TRANSPORTATION

materials-handling system
A method of moving inventory into, within, and out of the warehouse.

Transportation typically accounts for 5 to 10 percent of the price of goods. Supply chain logisticians must decide which mode of transportation to use to move

EXHIBIT 12.10

Criteria for Ranking Modes of Transportation

	Highest				Lowest
Relative Cost	Air	Truck	Rail	Pipe	Water
Transit Time	Water	Rail	Pipe	Truck	Air
Reliability	Pipe	Truck	Rail	Air	Water
Capability	Water	Rail	Truck	Air	Pipe
Accessibility	Truck	Rail	Air	Water	Pipe
Traceability	Air	Truck	Rail	Water	Pipe

products from supplier to producer and from producer to buyer. These decisions are, of course, related to all other logistics decisions. The five major modes of transportation are railroads, motor carriers, pipelines, water transportation, and airways. Supply chain managers generally choose a mode of transportation on the basis of several criteria:

- *Cost:* The total amount a specific carrier charges to move the product from the point of origin to the destination
- *Transit time:* The total time a carrier has possession of goods, including the time required for pickup and delivery, handling, and movement between the point of origin and the destination
- *Reliability:* The consistency with which the carrier delivers goods on time and in acceptable condition
- *Capability:* The ability of the carrier to provide the appropriate equipment and conditions for moving specific kinds of goods, such as those that must be transported in a controlled environment (for example, under refrigeration)
- *Accessibility:* A carrier's ability to move goods over a specific route or network
- *Traceability:* The relative ease with which a shipment can be located and transferred

The mode of transportation used depends on the needs of the shipper, as they relate to these six criteria. Exhibit 12.10 compares the basic modes of transportation on these criteria.

In many cases, especially in a JIT manufacturing environment, the transportation network replaces the warehouse or eliminates the expense of storing inventories as goods are timed to arrive the moment they're needed on the assembly line or for shipment to customers. In fact, Toyota is so committed to JIT that has no parts warehouses in the United States. Instead, it works closely with its suppliers to make sure that parts will be delivered on time even during a crisis. For example, Continental Teves, Inc., supplies Toyota with German-made steering sensors for its Sequoia SUV. Traditionally, the parts were flown from Germany and delivered to Toyota when they were needed for installation. Since the September 11 terrorist attacks, however, Continental has been shipping the parts via ship to ensure that they will arrive on time even if U.S. airspace is shut down. Although the change has increased Continental's costs, the company realizes it is necessary to meet Toyota's needs.

REVIEW LEARNING OBJECTIVE 7

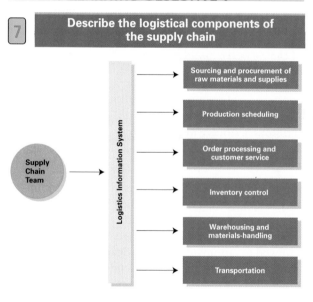

7 | Describe the logistical components of the supply chain

8 TRENDS IN SUPPLY CHAIN MANAGEMENT

Discuss new technology and emerging trends in supply chain management

Several technological advances and business trends are affecting the job of the supply chain manager today. Three of the most important trends are advanced computer technology, outsourcing of logistics functions, and electronic distribution.

ADVANCED COMPUTER TECHNOLOGY

Advanced computer technology has boosted the efficiency of logistics dramatically with tools such as automatic identification systems (auto ID) using bar coding and radio frequency technology, communications technology, and supply chain software systems that help synchronize the flow of

goods and information with customer demand. Amazon.com's state-of-the-art distribution centers, for instance, use sophisticated order picking systems that utilize computer terminals to guide workers through the picking and packing process. Radio frequency technology, which uses radio signals that work with scanned bar codes to identify products, directs Amazon's workers to the exact locations in the warehouse where the product is stored. Warehouse management software examines pick rates, location, and picking and storage patterns, and builds combinations of customer orders for shipping. After installing these supply chain technology tools, Amazon saw a 70 percent improvement in operational efficiency.[26]

Procter & Gamble and many other companies use radio-frequency identification tags (RFID) in shipments to Wal-Mart stores. RFID are chips attached to a pallet of goods that allow the goods to be tracked from the time they are packed at the manufacturing plant until the consumer purchases them. Benefits include increased revenue for Wal-Mart because the shelves are always full and reduced inventory management costs because time spent counting items and overstocking are minimized. Wal-Mart requires all vendors to use RFID technology.[27]

One of the major goals of technology is to bring up-to-date information to the supply chain manager's desk. The transportation system has long been referred to as a "black hole," where products and materials fall out of sight until they reappear some time later in a plant, store, or warehouse. Now carriers have systems that track freight, monitor the speed and location of carriers, and make routing decisions on the spur of the moment. Roadway Express, named one of the "Top 100 U.S. Motor Carriers" by Inbound Logistics, handles more than 70,000 shipments a day, many for large retailers like Wal-Mart, Target, and Home Depot. Information technology systems enable each package to be tracked from the minute it is received at one of Roadway's terminals until it is delivered. Customers can check on the progress of their shipment anytime by logging on to Roadway's Web site and entering the tracking number. Companies needing trucking services can go to the Inbound Logistics Web site and use their Trucking Decision Support Tool to identify motor carriers that can meet their service needs.[28] Swedish-based communications giant Ericsson, whose operations span the globe, uses specialized supply chain software to gain visibility over the 50,000 outbound shipments it makes a year. As products leave its manufacturing facilities, transportation providers transmit status information at specified intervals to Ericsson's information system, which is accessible to management using a standard Web browser. The company has benefited greatly from the increased visibility of shipments the system has provided. Ericsson's management is now in a position to identify bottlenecks and respond before a crisis occurs, as well as measure the performance of its supply chain at different checkpoints.[29]

OUTSOURCING LOGISTICS FUNCTIONS

External partners are becoming increasingly important in the efficient deployment of supply chain management. **Outsourcing**, or **contract logistics**, is a rapidly growing segment of the distribution industry in which a manufacturer or supplier turns over the entire function of buying and managing transportation or another function of the supply chain, such as warehousing, to an independent third party. Many manufacturers are turning to outside partners for their logistics expertise in an effort to focus on the core competencies that they do best. Partners create and manage entire solutions for getting products where they need to be, when they need to be there. Logistics partners offer staff, an infrastructure, and services that reach consumers virtually anywhere in the world. Because a logistics provider is focused, clients receive service in a timely, efficient manner, thereby increasing customers' level of satisfaction and boosting their perception of added value to a company's offerings. The trend is so strong that the supply chain outsourcing industry is expected to generate almost $1.8 billion in revenue by 2005.[30]

outsourcing (contract logistics)
A manufacturer's or supplier's use of an independent third party to manage an entire function of the logistics system, such as transportation, warehousing, or order processing.

GLOBAL Third-party contract logistics allow companies to cut inventories, locate stock at fewer plants and distribution centers, and still provide the same service level or even better. The companies then can refocus investment on

Electronic distribution has become a viable channel for many products, including tax preparation software, postage stamps, and even movie tickets, which can be purchased over the Internet prior to a show.

their core business. Ford Motor Company uses third-party logistics provider UPS Worldwide Logistics Group to manage the delivery of Ford, Lincoln, and Mercury cars and trucks in the United States, Canada, and Mexico. The alliance between Ford and UPS has substantially reduced the time it takes to move vehicles from Ford's assembly plants to dealers and customers. Moreover, the Web-based system enables Ford and its dealers to track an individual vehicle's location from production through delivery to the final destination.[31]

Many firms are taking outsourcing one step further by allowing business partners to take over the final assembly of their product or its packaging in an effort to reduce inventory costs, speed up delivery, or meet customer requirements better. Ryder Truck Lines assembles and packages 22 different combinations of shrink-wrapped boxes that contain the ice trays, drawers, shelves, doors, and other accessories for the various refrigerator models Whirlpool sells. Similarly, outsourcing firm, StarTek, Inc., packages and ships products for Microsoft, provides technical support to customers of America Online, and maintains AT&T communication systems.[32]

ELECTRONIC DISTRIBUTION

Electronic distribution is the most recent development in the logistics arena. Broadly defined, **electronic distribution** includes any kind of product or service that can be distributed electronically, whether over traditional forms such as fiber-optic cable or through satellite transmission of electronic signals. For instance, instead of buying and installing software from stores, computer users purchase software over the Internet and download it electronically to their personal computers or rent the same software from Internet services that have the program available for use on their servers. For example, Intuit, Inc., allows people to fill out their tax returns on its Web site rather than buying its TurboTax software. Postage stamps can be purchased online through E-Stamp, which uses a silver-dollar size "vault" attached to the purchaser's computer to keep track of postage purchases. Similarly, consumers can purchase tickets to sporting events, concerts, and movies via the Internet from online ticket companies and movie theaters and print the tickets at home.

Hollywood movie studios are preparing to deliver their products directly to consumers through digital pipelines.[33] Consumers can already download digital files of their favorite music, movies, and television shows to be played on their computers, portable players, and televisions.

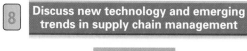

REVIEW LEARNING OBJECTIVE 8

8 **Discuss new technology and emerging trends in supply chain management**

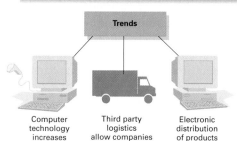

| Computer technology increases efficiency. | Third party logistics allow companies to focus on core business functions. | Electronic distribution of products and services collapse the supply chain. |

CHANNELS AND DISTRIBUTION DECISIONS FOR
9 GLOBAL MARKETS

Discuss channels and distribution decisions in global markets

With the spread of free-trade agreements and treaties, such as the European Union and the North American Free Trade Agreement (NAFTA) in recent decades, global marketing channels and management of the supply chain have become increasingly important to U.S. corporations that export their products or manufacture abroad.

DEVELOPING GLOBAL MARKETING CHANNELS

Executives should recognize the unique cultural, economic, institutional, and legal aspects of each market before trying to design marketing channels in foreign countries. Manufacturers introducing products in global

electronic distribution
A distribution technique that includes any kind of product or service that can be distributed electronically, whether over traditional forms such as fiber-optic cable or through satellite transmission of electronic signals.

markets face a tough decision: what type of channel structure to use. Specifically, should the product be marketed directly, mostly by company salespeople, or through independent foreign intermediaries, such as agents and distributors? Using company salespeople generally provides more control and is less risky than using foreign intermediaries. However, setting up a sales force in a foreign country also entails a greater commitment, both financially and organizationally.

Marketers should be aware that channel structures and types abroad may differ from those of channels in the United States. For instance, the more highly developed a nation is economically, the more specialized its channel types. Therefore, a marketer wishing to sell in Germany or Japan will have several channel types to choose from. Conversely, developing countries like India, Ethiopia, and Venezuela have limited channel types available; there are typically few mail-order channels, vending machines, or specialized retailers and wholesalers.

 Marketers must also be aware that many countries have "gray" marketing channels in which products are distributed through unauthorized channel intermediaries. It is estimated that sales of counterfeit luxury items like Prada handbags and Big Bertha golf clubs have reached almost $2 billion a year. The new fakes are harder to detect and hit the market almost instantly. For instance, a fake Christian Dior saddlebag was available just weeks after the original arrived on retailers' shelves. Similarly, Chinese companies are producing so many knockoffs of Yamaha, Honda, and Suzuki motorcycles that the Japanese companies are seeing a drop in sales. What's more, many companies are getting so good at design piracy that they are beginning to launch their own new products.[34] The "Ethics in Marketing" box explores the issue of piracy further.

Ethics in Marketing Ethics in Marketing Ethics in Marketing Ethics in Marketing Ethics in Marketing Ethics in Marketing Ethics in Marketing Ethics in Marketing Ethics in Marketing Ethics in Marketing Ethics in Marketing Ethics in Marketing Ethics in Marketing Ethics in Marketing Ethics in Marketing Ethics in Marketing Ethics in Marketing

ETHICS IN MARKETING

> PIRACY AND PURSE PARTIES

 Have you ever bought a fake? The International Chamber of Commerce estimates that sales of counterfeit goods amount to more than $500 billion annually, of which about $200 billion affects the U.S. economy.

The most recent trend in counterfeiting is the "purse party." Purse parties follow the Tupperware home party concept but feature top-quality knockoff purses and accessories such as scarves, belts, and jewelry by hot designers such as Prada, Burberry, Louis Vuitton, and Kate Spade. For example, you might be able to buy an $800 Louis Vuitton purse for a mere $75. Sometimes the counterfeit designs are available before the new design is released by the fashion designer. The parties are illegal and have sparked a series of arrests across the country. Usually, young urban adults and suburban moms are the culprits. They are charged with distribution of counterfeit merchandise, a felony.

The effect of the imitation brands on the legitimate brand has aroused some debate. Some argue that an imitation brand will not harm the legitimate brand because it is a form of "flattery" and will not affect the brand's bottom line. Leading industry experts discount this theory, however, arguing that brands are hurt considerably because they are "cheapened." Kate Spade attributes losses of about $70 million a year to counterfeit products.

Putting an end to counterfeits is almost impossible, however. The police often can provide little help, so companies hire private investigators to find the counterfeiters and then threaten to sue them unless they shut down. Counterfeiters barely flinch, however: the style is usually obsolete long before the litigation is completed. Furthermore, fashion designers do not have copyright protection under the U.S. Copyright Act. Thus, counterfeiters are able to introduce a "creative interpretation" of an existing product. Consequently, even if designers decide to sue, there is no guarantee that they will win.[35]

Although stopping consumers from buying counterfeits has always been difficult, some local law enforcement groups are beginning to take an interest because the money is known to fund terrorist activities, drugs, and prostitution. A problem for authorities, however, is that it is only illegal to sell counterfeits, not to buy them.

Do you think buying a "fake" purse should be illegal? Do you think "imitation" brands cheapen the value of the "legitimate" brand? What do you think companies should do to fight off counterfeiters?

World Trade Organization
Learn more about how globalization affects supply chain management as well as other aspects of business at the World Trade Organization's Web site.

http://www.wto.org

Online

The Internet has also proved to be a way for pirates to circumvent authorized distribution channels, especially in the case of popular prescription drugs. In recent years, the U.S. Customs Service has seized millions of dollars worth of prescription drugs, most of which were purchased from foreign Internet sites. Some were seized because they had not been approved for use in the United States, others because they did not comply with U.S. labeling laws. Most sites offer just a handful of the most popular drugs, such as Viagra and the diet drug Xenical; consumers can get the drugs after obtaining the approval of a doctor who is affiliated with the site and who never sees the patient.

GLOBAL LOGISTICS AND SUPPLY CHAIN MANAGEMENT

 As global trade becomes a more decisive factor in success or failure for firms of all sizes, a well-thought-out global logistics strategy becomes more important.

One of the most critical global logistical issues for importers of any size is coping with the legalities of trade in other countries. Shippers and distributors must be aware of the permits, licenses, and registrations they may need to acquire and, depending on the type of product they are importing, the tariffs, quotas, and other regulations that apply in each country. This multitude of different rules is why multinational companies like Eastman Kodak are so committed to working through the

Global Perspectives

GLOBAL PERSPECTIVES

 OUTSOURCING AND GLOBAL SUPPLY CHAIN MANAGEMENT

Many products bought in the United States are manufactured in countries abroad and resold to Americans under "Made in Taiwan" labels (China and India, too). The United States is not the only nation that relies on products from other countries. England's national flower is the rose, but 80 percent of the roses sold in England aren't grown there. They come from England's former colony Kenya. Given the extent of world trade, global supply chain efficiency is essential. Without it many products either would not be available or would be too expensive.

The Internet, just-in-time technology, international trade agreements, cheap labor, and overnight delivery facilitate global supply chains, which are bringing the world's businesses closer together. Today, sourcing and procurement needs for both large multinational corporations and small businesses are being met by businesses around the world. A survey by the consulting firm Accenture revealed that 80 percent of executives were able "to cut costs, improve efficiencies, enhance customer service and revenues, or improve competitiveness with supply chain management initiatives" in their companies by outsourcing supply chain functions. Seventy percent of the same executives said the Internet was a vital factor in facilitating supply chain management.

As an example of how global supply chains are changing, consider that Italy, famous for leather shoes by designers like Manolo Blahnik and Prada, used to be the largest *exporter* of expensive designer shoes. Now Italy has been replaced by China because shoes, which are extremely expensive to produce, can be produced by cheap Chinese labor. Italy is now the largest *importer* of shoes and shoe components. Therefore, the shoes you buy in the United States may have a "Made in Italy" label, but they are made from shoe components produced in a number of countries across Europe and Asia.

As another example, K2, the number one ski brand in the United States, recently marketed itself as an "American Class." But the company manufactures its skis in China, not the United States. The company claims the workmanship in China is "Better. Not the same," and says this quality is the reason the K2 5500 was voted the Best Value Ski of the Year for two years in a row. K2 also sells the Rawlings baseballs and equipment that are used by Major League Baseball. They are made in Asia and Costa Rica.[36]

Do you think companies should reveal more information when products are manufactured outside the United States? Do you think greater supply chain efficiencies justify the lower prices, or would you be willing to pay higher prices for products produced in the United States?

World Trade Organization to develop a global set of rules and to encourage countries to participate. Other goals for these companies include reducing trade barriers such as tariffs. As these barriers fall, the flow of merchandise across borders is increasing as more companies are sourcing from multiple countries. For instance, a Kodak camera sold in France may have been assembled there, but the camera mechanism probably came from China and the film from the United States. The "Global Perspectives" box discusses some of these outsourcing issues further.

The presence of different rules hasn't slowed the spread of supply chain globalization, however. In spite of the added costs associated with importing and exporting goods, many companies are looking to other countries for their sourcing and procurement needs. For example, Applica, Inc., a U.S. maker of small appliances, is committed to using technology to improve its relationships with suppliers in Mexico. The company has linked its suppliers directly to sales data from Wal-Mart stores to help manage production and inventory costs.[37]

Transportation can also be a major issue for companies dealing with global supply chains. Uncertainty regarding shipping usually tops the list of reasons why companies, especially smaller ones, resist international markets. Even companies that have scored overseas successes often are vulnerable to logistical problems. Large companies have the capital to create global logistics systems, but smaller companies often must rely on the services of carriers and freight forwarders to get their products to overseas markets.

In some instances, poor infrastructure makes transportation dangerous and unreliable. And the process of moving goods across the borders of even the most industrialized nations can still be complicated by government regulations. For example, NAFTA was supposed to improve the flow of goods across the continent, but moving goods across the border still requires approvals from dozens of government agencies, broker intervention, and hours spent at border checks. Shipping companies like Ryder are working to make the process easier. Currently, Ryder operates a cross-border facility in San Antonio to help clients like General Motors and Xerox with customs and logistics costs. The company also is part of a pilot project to automate border crossings with technology similar to that of an E-Z pass. The new system sends and receives short-range radio signals containing information on the load to toll booths, weigh stations, and border crossings. If the cargo meets requirements, the truck or train receives a green light to go ahead. Questionable cargo is set aside for further inspection. Transportation industry experts say the system can reduce delivery times by more than three hours.[38]

REVIEW LEARNING OBJECTIVE 9

9 Discuss channels and distribution decisions in global markets

— Distribute directly or through foreign partners

— Different channel structures than in domestic markets

— Illegitimate 'gray' marketing channels

— Legal and infrastructure differences

CHANNELS AND DISTRIBUTION DECISIONS FOR SERVICES

10 Identify the special problems and opportunities associated with distribution in service organizations

The fastest-growing part of our economy is the service sector. Although distribution in the service sector is difficult to visualize, the same skills, techniques, and strategies used to manage inventory can also be used to manage service inventory—for instance, hospital beds, bank accounts, or airline seats. The quality of the planning and execution of distribution can have a major impact on costs and customer satisfaction.

One thing that sets service distribution apart from traditional manufacturing distribution is that, in a service environment, production and consumption are simultaneous. In manufacturing, a production setback can often be remedied by using safety stock or a faster mode of transportation. Such substitution is not possible with a service. The benefits of a service are also relatively intangible—that is, you normally can't see the benefits of a service, such as a doctor's physical exam. But a consumer can normally see the benefits provided by a product—for example, a vacuum cleaner removing dirt from the carpet.

Does your bank deliver any of its services online? Visit its Web site to find out. Which online services would you be inclined to use? Are there any that you would definitely *not* use? Why not?

Online

Because service industries are so customer oriented, customer service is a priority. To manage customer relationships, many service providers, such as insurance carriers, physicians, hair salons, and financial services, use technology to schedule appointments, manage accounts, and disburse information. Service distribution focuses on three main areas:

- *Minimizing wait times:* Minimizing the amount of time customers wait in line to deposit a check, wait for their food at a restaurant, or wait in a doctor's office for an appointment is a key factor in maintaining the quality of service. People tend to overestimate the amount of time they spend waiting in line, researchers report, and unexplained waiting seems longer than explained waits. To reduce anxiety among waiting customers, some restaurants give patrons pagers that allow them to roam around or go to the bar. Banks sometimes install electronic boards displaying stock quotes or sports scores. Car rental companies reward repeat customers by eliminating their waits altogether. Airports have designed comfortable sitting areas with televisions and children's play areas for those waiting to board planes. Some service companies are using sophisticated technology to further ease their customers' waiting time. Similarly, many hotels and airlines are using electronic check-in kiosks. Travelers can insert their credit cards to check in upon arrival to receive their room key, get directions and print maps to area restaurants and attractions, and print out their hotel bills.

- *Managing service capacity:* For product manufacturers, inventory acts as a buffer, enabling them to provide the product during periods of peak demand without extraordinary efforts. Service firms don't have this luxury. If they don't have the capacity to meet demand, they must either turn down some prospective customers, let service levels slip, or expand capacity. For instance, at tax time a tax preparation firm may have so many customers desiring its services that it has to either turn business away or add temporary offices or preparers. Popular restaurants risk losing business when seating is unavailable or the wait is too long. To manage their capacity, travel Web sites allow users to find last-minute deals to fill up empty airline seats and hotel rooms.

Keller Williams Realty has changed the distribution channel for its real estate services by opening a storefront in a shopping mall. The Showcase of Homes store includes a kiosk where potential customers can browse the multiple listing service database for homes of interest.

AP/WIDE WORLD PHOTO

- *Improving service delivery:* Like manufacturers, service firms are now experimenting with different distribution channels for their services. Choosing the right distribution channel can increase the times that services are available (such as using the Internet to disseminate information and services 24/7) or add to customer convenience (like pizza delivery, walk-in medical clinics, or a dry cleaner located in a supermarket). The airline industry has found that using the Internet for ticket sales both reduces distribution costs and raises the level of customer service by making it easier for customers to plan their own travel. Cruise lines, on the other hand, have found that travel agents add value by helping customers sort through the abundance of information and complicated options available when booking a cruise. In the real estate industry, realtors are placing kiosks in local malls that enable consumers to directly access listings.

10 Identify the special problems and opportunities associated with distribution in service organizations

 Minimizing wait times is a key factor in maintaining service quality.

 Managing service capability is critical to successful service distribution.

KIOSK Improving service delivery makes it easier and more convenient for consumers to use the service.

 The Internet is fast becoming an alternative channel for delivering services. Consumers can now purchase plane tickets, plan a vacation cruise, reserve a hotel room, pay bills, purchase mutual funds, and receive electronic newspapers in cyberspace. Insurance giant Allstate, for instance, now sells auto and home insurance directly to consumers in some states through the Internet in addition to its traditional network of agents. The effort reduces costs so that Allstate can stay competitive with rival insurance companies Progressive and Geico that already target customers directly. Similarly, several real estate Web sites are making it easier for customers to shop for a new home on the Web. Traditionally, the only way for customers to gain access to realtors' listings was to work through a real estate agent who would search the listings and then show customers homes that met their requirements. The new companies offer direct access to the listings, enabling customers to review properties for sale on their own, and choose which ones they would like to visit.

LOOKING BACK

As you complete this chapter, you should be able to see how marketing channels operate and how supply chain management is necessary to move goods from the manufacturer to the final consumer.

Companies can choose from several different marketing channels to sell their products. For example, the opening story discussed how Starbucks is using multi-channel distribution, product innovation,

and channel partnering to reach customers in 25 countries and over 7,000 locations. This strategy has made the company the most widely known coffee brand in the world.

USE IT NOW

BUY YOUR TEXTBOOKS THROUGH A DIRECT MARKETING CHANNEL

 Save money and valuable loafing or study time by buying your textbooks from online textbook sellers, such as Big Words (**bigwords.com**), **ecampus.com**, or **VarsityBooks.com.** These sites provide students with the right textbooks, at the right price, right in time for classes to begin. And, instead of having to wait in line at the bookstore with your course curriculum, you can zap your book list to any of the cyber-bookstores that work with your school and then have them delivered directly to your dorm room. Since approximately nine out of ten of the 15 million students enrolled in higher-education institutions use the Internet, buying textbooks online is a natural fit.

HAVE A PRODUCT YOU WANT TO SELL ON THE WEB?

 Specialized Web sites can help you set up an e-commerce site with minimal effort and cost. Sites such as **BizLand.com, Bigstep.com,** and **Go2Net** help small-business owners create e-commerce Web sites where purchases can be accepted online with a credit card. BizLand's site, for instance, provides free online storefronts and shopping carts, custom domain names, e-mail, business promotional tools, site monitoring, plus lots more. Easy-to-use software helps merchants build and maintain catalogs of products and services to sell over the Internet. The sites are becoming very popular; Bizland's membership swelled to over 500,000 small-business owners from all 50 states plus 150 countries in just one year.

REVIEW AND APPLICATIONS

1 **Explain what a marketing channel is and why intermediaries are needed.** A marketing channel is a business structure of interdependent organizations that reach from the point of product origin to the consumer with the purpose of physically moving products to their final consumption destination, representing "place" or "distribution" in the marketing mix and encompassing the processes involved in getting the right product to the right place at the right time. Members of a marketing channel create a continuous and seamless supply chain that performs or supports the marketing channel functions. Channel members provide economies to the distribution process in the form of specialization and division of labor; overcoming discrepancies in quantity, assortment, time, and space; and providing contact efficiency.

1.1 Your family runs a specialty ice cream parlor, Graeter's, that manufactures its own ice cream in small batches and sells it only in pint-sized containers. After someone not affiliated with the company sent six pints of its ice cream to Oprah Winfrey, she proclaimed on her national TV show that it was the best ice cream she had ever eaten. Immediately after the broadcast, orders came flooding in, overwhelming your small-batch production schedule and your rudimentary distribution system. The company's shipping manager thinks she can handle it, but you disagree. List the reasons why you need to restructure your supply chain.[39]

1.2 *INFOTRAC COLLEGE EDITION* *ONLINE* The "Marketing in Entertainment" box in this chapter dealt with the topic of movie distribution. To better appreciate how novel Sundance and the SOFF are, you need to understand how traditional movie distribution channels work. Use InfoTrac (**http://infotrac.college.swlearning.com**) to research "movie distribution" or "film distribution." You may also benefit from a keyword search in your favorite search engine. Once you have read enough material, draw a sketch of the traditional movie distribution process.

2 **Define the types of channel intermediaries and describe their functions and activities.** The most prominent difference separating intermediaries is whether they take title to the product. Retailers and merchant wholesalers take title, but agents and brokers do not. Retailers are firms that sell mainly to consumers. Merchant wholesalers are those organizations that facilitate the movement of products and services from the manufacturer to producers, resellers, governments, institutions, and retailers. Agents and brokers do not take title to the goods and services they market, but do they facilitate the exchange of ownership between sellers and buyers. Channel intermediaries perform three basic types of functions. Transactional functions include contacting and promoting, negotiating, and risk taking. Logistical functions performed by channel members include physical distribution, storing, and sorting functions. Finally, channel members may perform facilitating functions, such as researching and financing.

2.1 *INFOTRAC COLLEGE EDITION* *ONLINE* Recently, the business and popular presses ran articles on the souring relationship between Pixar Studios (maker of animated blockbusters *Toy Story*, *Bug's Life*, and *Finding Nemo*) and Disney, which distributes Pixar's creations. Use InfoTrac (**http://infotrac.college.swlearning.com**) and your favorite search engine to research the tensions between the two companies. What kind of channel intermediary is Disney and what functions does it provide for Pixar? Describe the channel conflict in this relationship (see review 6).

3 **Describe the channel structures for consumer and business products and discuss alternative channel arrangements.** Marketing channels for consumer and business products vary in degree of complexity. The simplest consumer-product channel involves direct selling from producers to consumers. Businesses may sell directly to business or government buyers. Marketing channels grow more complex as intermediaries become involved. Consumer-product channel intermediaries include agents, brokers, wholesalers, and retailers. Business-product channel intermediaries include agents, brokers, and industrial distributors. Marketers often use alternative channel arrangements to move their products to the consumer. With dual distribution or multiple distribution, they choose two or more different channels to distribute the same product. Nontraditional channels help differentiate a firm's product from the competitor's or provide a manufacturer with another avenue for sales. Finally, strategic channel alliances are arrangements that use another manufacturer's already established channel.

3.1 Describe the most likely marketing channel structure for each of these consumer products: candy bars, Tupperware products, nonfiction books, new automobiles, farmers' market produce, and stereo equipment. Now, construct alternative channels for these same products.

3.2 INFOTRAC COLLEGE EDITION Dell successfully uses a direct channel to sell computers and equipment it manufactures to consumers over the telephone and Internet. How has Dell affected traditional computer retailers with brick-and-mortar buildings? How have other computer manufacturers, such as Hewlett-Packard and IBM, countered Dell's competitive advantage in its direct channel? Use InfoTrac (**http://www.infotrac-college.com**) to search for articles on this topic. You may also need to consult your campus library's databases on companies and articles to search for this information.

3.3 WRITING You have been hired to design an alternative marketing channel for a firm specializing in the manufacturing and marketing of novelties for college student organizations. In a memo to the president of the firm, describe how the channel operates.

3.4 WRITING Building on question 1.1, determine a new channel structure for Graeter's. Write a proposal to present to your key managers.

4 **Define supply chain management and discuss its benefits.** Supply chain management coordinates and integrates all of the activities performed by supply chain members into a seamless process from the source to the point of consumption. The responsibilities of a supply chain manager include developing channel design strategies, managing the relationships of supply chain members, sourcing and procurement of raw materials, scheduling production, processing orders, managing inventory and storing product, and selecting transportation modes. The supply chain manager is also responsible for managing customer service and the information that flows through the supply chain. The benefits of supply chain management include reduced costs in inventory management, transportation, warehousing, and packaging; improved service through techniques like time-based delivery and make-to-order; and enhanced revenues, which result from such supply chain–related achievements as higher product availability and more customized products.

4.1 Discuss the benefits of supply chain management. How does the implementation of supply chain management result in enhanced customer value?

5 **Discuss the issues that influence channel strategy.** When determining marketing channel strategy, the supply chain manager must determine what market, product, and producer factors will influence the choice of channel. The manager must also determine the appropriate level of distribution intensity. Intensive distribution is distribution aimed at maximum market coverage. Selective distribution is achieved by screening dealers to eliminate all but a few in any single area. The most restrictive form of market coverage is exclusive distribution, which entails only one or a few dealers within a given area.

5.1 Decide which distribution intensity level—intensive, selective, or exclusive—is used for each of the following products, and explain why: Rolex watches, Land Rover sport utility vehicles, M&Ms, special edition Barbie dolls, Crest toothpaste.

5.2 TEAM Now that you have a basic channel structure for Graeter's (from question 3.4), form a team of three to four students and list the market, product, and producer factors that will affect your final channel structure.

6 Explain channel leadership, conflict, and partnering. Power, control, leadership, conflict, and partnering are the main social dimensions of marketing channel relationships. Channel power refers to the capacity of one channel member to control or influence other channel members. Channel control occurs when one channel member intentionally affects another member's behavior. Channel leadership is the exercise of authority and power. Channel conflict occurs when there is a clash of goals and methods among the members of a distribution channel. Channel conflict can be either horizontal, between channel members at the same level, or vertical, between channel members at different levels of the channel. Channel partnering is the joint effort of all channel members to create a supply chain that serves customers and creates a competitive advantage. Collaborating channel partners meet the needs of consumers more effectively by ensuring that the right products reach shelves at the right time and at a lower cost, boosting sales and profits.

6.1 Procter & Gamble and Wal-Mart are key partners in a shared supply chain. P&G is one of Wal-Mart's biggest suppliers, and Wal-Mart provides extremely detailed scanner data about customer purchases of P&G products. Wal-Mart has begun selling its own brand of Sam's Choice laundry detergent in bright orange bottles alongside P&G's Tide but for a greatly reduced price. What do you think will be the impact of this new product on what has been a stable channel relationship?

7 Describe the logistical components of the supply chain. The logistics supply chain consists of several interrelated and integrated logistical components: (1) sourcing and procurement of raw materials and supplies, (2) production scheduling, (3) order processing, (4) inventory control, (5) warehousing and materials-handling, and (6) transportation. Integrating and linking all of the logistics functions of the supply chain is the logistics information system. Information technology connects the various components and partners of the supply chain into an integrated whole. The supply chain team, in concert with the logistics information system, orchestrates the movement of goods, services, and information from the source to the consumer. Supply chain teams typically cut across organizational boundaries, embracing all parties who participate in moving product to market. Procurement deals with the purchase of raw materials, supplies, and components according to production scheduling. Order processing monitors the flow of goods and information (order entry and order handling). Inventory control systems regulate when and how much to buy (order timing and order quantity). Warehousing provides storage of goods until needed by the customer while the materials-handling system moves inventory into, within, and out of the warehouse. Finally, the major modes of transportation include railroads, motor carriers, pipelines, waterways, and airways.

7.1 Discuss the impact of just-in-time production on the entire supply chain. Specifically, how does JIT affect suppliers, procurement planning, inventory levels, mode of transportation selected, and warehousing? What are the benefits of JIT to the end consumer?

7.2 Assume that you are the supply chain manager for a producer of expensive, high-tech computer components. Identify the most suitable method(s) of transporting your product in terms of cost, transit time, reliability, capability, accessibility, and traceability. Now, assume you are the supply chain manager for a producer of milk. How does this change your choice of transportation?

8 Discuss new technology and emerging trends in supply chain management. Several emerging trends are changing the job of today's supply chain manager. Technology and automation are bringing up-to-date distribution information to the decision maker's desk. Technology is also linking suppliers, buyers, and carriers for joint decision making, and it has created a new electronic distribution channel. Many companies are saving money and time by outsourcing third-party carriers to handle some or all aspects of the distribution process.

8.1 Visit the Web site of Menlo Logistics at **http://www.menlolog.com**. What logistics functions can this third-party logistics supplier provide? How does its mission fit in with the supply chain management philosophy?

9 Discuss channels and distribution decisions in global markets. Global marketing channels are becoming more important to U.S. companies seeking growth abroad. Manufacturers introducing products in foreign countries must decide what type of channel structure to use—in particular, whether the product should be marketed through direct channels or through foreign intermediaries. Marketers should be aware that channel structures in foreign markets may be very different from those they are accustomed to in the United States. Global distribution expertise is also emerging as an important skill for supply chain managers as many countries are removing trade barriers.

9.1 *INFOTRAC COLLEGE EDITION* How are transportation and logistics issues handled around the world? To find out, consult the *Transportation Journal* using InfoTrac (**http://www.infotrac-college.com**). Create a grid comparing at least two countries according to standard procedures, particular challenges faced, and creative solutions to problems they have encountered.

10 Identify the special problems and opportunities associated with distribution in service organizations. Managers in service industries use the same skills, techniques, and strategies to manage logistics functions as managers in goods-producing industries. The distribution of services focuses on three main areas: minimizing wait times, managing service capacity, and improving service delivery.

10.1 *WRITING* Assume that you are the marketing manager of a hospital. Write a report indicating the distribution functions that concern you. Discuss the similarities and dissimilarities of distribution for services and for goods.

TERMS

agents and brokers 397
channel conflict 410
channel control 410
channel leader (channel captain) 410
channel members 394
channel partnering (channel cooperation) 412
channel power 410
direct channel 400
discrepancy of assortment 395
discrepancy of quantity 395
distribution resource planning (DRP) 416
dual distribution (multiple distribution) 402

electronic data interchange (EDI) 415
electronic distribution 420
exclusive distribution 409
horizontal conflict 411
intensive distribution 408
inventory control system 415
just-in-time production (JIT) 414
logistics 398
logistics information system 413
marketing channel (channel of distribution) 394
mass customization (build-to-order) 413
materials-handling system 417

materials requirement planning (MRP) (materials management) 416
merchant wholesaler 397
order processing system 415
outsourcing (contract logistics) 419
retailer 397
selective distribution 409
spatial discrepancy 395
strategic channel alliance 403
supply chain 394
supply chain management 404
supply chain team 413
temporal discrepancy 395
vertical conflict 411

EXERCISES

APPLICATION EXERCISE

It may be easy to understand how supply chain management works just from reading, but you may still not appreciate the scope of distribution channels. This exercise will help you see for yourself how deep and complex a single distribution channel is. Then, when you think of the number of products and services available on the market at any one time, you will understand how tremendous the national (and international) distribution network actually is.[40]

Activities

1. Pick a product with which you are familiar or that you anticipate being able to research easily. You may want to consult family members, relatives, or even a former or current employer who can give you details of the business.

2. Trace the distribution network of your product as far back as is feasible. A simple example is a diamond sold by a local jewelry store, purchased direct from diamond wholesalers in the Netherlands, bought by wholesalers from diamond centers in South Africa, brought out of mines owned by a company in South Africa. Identify participants in the channel by company name and location as much as possible.

3. Identify the mode of transportation used between each stage in the channel.

4. Identify by name and location the component parts of the product, if any. For example, let's expand the diamond example from a single diamond to a diamond necklace. You would need to trace the distribution history of the chain until the point at which the diamond and chain are combined to form the diamond necklace.

ETHICS EXERCISE

Wholesome Snacks, Inc., the maker of a variety of cookies and crackers, has just created a new vitamin-packed cookie. The new cookie has the potential to combat many of the health problems caused by malnutrition in children throughout poverty-stricken areas of the world. To date, however, many of the larger developing markets have resisted opening distribution channels to Wholesome's products. Wholesome realizes that its new cookie could also help open the door for the company to sell its less nutritious products in these markets. Therefore, the company is offering the new cookie at a low cost to government relief programs in exchange for the long-sought distribution channels. The company feels the deal is good for business, but the countries feel it is corporate bullying.

Questions

1. What do you think about Wholesome's idea for opening a new distribution channel?

2. Does the AMA Code of Ethics address this issue? Go to **http://www.marketingpower.com** and review the code. Then, write a brief paragraph stating what the AMA Code of Ethics contains that relates to distribution channels in developing nations.

CAREER EXERCISE

There are numerous avenues to pursue in a career in supply chain management and logistics. In fact, your college or university may even offer separate courses in transportation and logistics management.

The following resources are a good starting point:

*   **http://www.jobsinlogistics.com** Offers numerous job listings in the field of logistics

*   **http://www.supplychainrecruit.com** Allows you to search for jobs globally, a plus if you would like to work abroad

*   **http://www.supplychaintoday.com** Job listings are only one of the many resources on this site dedicated to supply chain management. Most resources involve industry analysis, company-specific information, and a discussion forum.

Activity

1. To get a glimpse of how a third-party logistics firm works, consider taking a "factory" tour of a UPS or FedEx distribution center. If the center is not open to the public, explain that you are researching a career in logistics and ask for a special tour.

AP/WIDE WORLD PHOTOS

CARSDIRECT.COM: DRIVING CAR BUYERS TO THE INTERNET

CarsDirect.com is heating up the new car industry.[41] The country's first direct broker of cars on the Internet has sent automakers, online-buying services, and dealer groups scrambling to control the growing number of customers going online to shortcut the traditional process of shopping for new and used vehicles. The Internet start-up sparked a flurry of copycat Web sites dedicated to the direct-to-consumer purchase of cars, like CarOrder.com, DriveOff.com, Carpoint.com, Autobytel.com, Cars.com, and Greenlight.com. But several have now gone out of business.

Backed by Michael Dell's personal investment firm, CarsDirect.com was conceived by Bill Gross, chairman of Idealab, a venture incubator that has also launched other Internet businesses, such as eToys, Tickets.com, and Cooking.com. After becoming frustrated with his own efforts at buying an auto online, Gross realized that current Internet options for car buying were not only inadequate but did nothing to leverage available technology on behalf of the consumer. At the time of his search, online car sites functioned only as lead generators for local dealers, requiring him to close the sale of his car the old-fashioned way: haggling at the dealership with the untrustworthiest of people—a car salesperson.

His vision, CarsDirect.com, sells cars entirely through the Internet, allowing consumers to bypass traditional car dealers in their negotiations. As a car broker, CarsDirect.com offers Web buyers a car at a fixed price based on recent average selling prices. Then, CarsDirect.com works through its network of existing dealers to get the car at that price. Since CarsDirect.com doesn't hold franchise agreements with any car manufacturers, consumers enjoy an impartial and unbiased shopping experience as well as an unrivaled selection. In contrast, buying cars the old-fashioned way forces consumers to travel from car dealer to car dealer looking for the models they are interested in or the best price.

Car buyers visiting CarsDirect.com can research a car by searching the site's extensive database, which provides objective information on price, performance, and options for more than 2,500 different makes and models—virtually every production vehicle available in the United States. CarsDirect.com's research tools let buyers compare the features of vehicles and see in seconds the manufacturer's suggested retail price, the invoice, and, most importantly, the price CarsDirect.com can get for them. If a consumer wants to buy, payment is arranged completely online to close the deal. Financing options are provided through CarsDirect.com's financial partners. Then, the buyer can arrange for delivery of the vehicle at home or the office or pick it up from a local automotive retailer.

With online auto sales expected to exceed 5 percent of total sales soon, there are still big hurdles ahead for car brokers like CarsDirect.com. General Motors, for instance, recently warned its 7,700 dealers to cease and desist from using online car-buying sites like CarsDirect.com. The largest obstacle, however, is the myriad of state franchise laws that protect car dealers and restrict direct sales of automobiles. Car brokers have found that no two states' franchise laws are the same, and many include rules that are arcane or impractical. Texas, the nation's second biggest automotive market, has the most restrictive dealer-protection laws in the country. There, only state-licensed dealers can sell cars. Brokering of cars to consumers by anyone other than a dealer is strictly prohibited. As a result, car brokers have had to redesign their direct-sales model around Texas laws. CarsDirect.com, for instance, currently does not offer cars to residents of Texas. Often, instead of trying to bypass dealers, Internet car brokers are forming alliances with dealers or reworking their strategies to become more dealer-friendly to comply with state law.

Questions

1. Explain how CarsDirect.com fits into the channel structure for car retailing to consumers.

2. How has CarsDirect.com's selling model caused channel conflict?

3. Visit CarsDirect.com's Web site at **http://www.carsdirect.com**. Give examples of how its Web site simplifies the car-buying process for consumers.

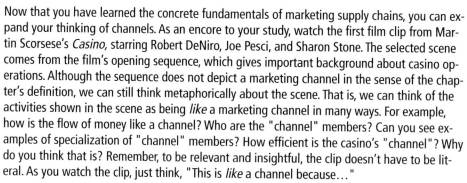

FEATURE PRESENTATION

Ping

To give you insight into Chapter 12, Small Business School takes you back to Karsten Manufacturing in Phoenix, Arizona, to see how this company manages its supply chain. Although you saw the same segment in Chapter 10, this time concentrate on issues like channel structure, channel relationships, and the logistical components of Karsten's supply chain. From the humble beginnings of his own garage, Karsten Solheim, the father of Ping Golf clubs, built one of the most recognized manufacturing companies the sports world has ever known. One of the underpinnings of Ping's success is the company's unique distribution strategy. What started as a club used exclusively by golf professionals has become product highly sought after by golf amateurs and dilettantes as well.

What to Watch For and Ask Yourself

1. Through what type of channel intermediary are Ping clubs sold? Through what type of marketing channel are Ping clubs distributed?

2. What are the key factors in the determination of Ping's channel choice?

3. What is the intensity level of their distribution?

4. How would you describe Ping's channel relationship management?

ENCORE PRESENTATION

Casino

Now that you have learned the concrete fundamentals of marketing supply chains, you can expand your thinking of channels. As an encore to your study, watch the first film clip from Martin Scorsese's *Casino,* starring Robert DeNiro, Joe Pesci, and Sharon Stone. The selected scene comes from the film's opening sequence, which gives important background about casino operations. Although the sequence does not depict a marketing channel in the sense of the chapter's definition, we can still think metaphorically about the scene. That is, we can think of the activities shown in the scene as being *like* a marketing channel in many ways. For example, how is the flow of money like a channel? Who are the "channel" members? Can you see examples of specialization of "channel" members? How efficient is the casino's "channel"? Why do you think that is? Remember, to be relevant and insightful, the clip doesn't have to be literal. As you watch the clip, just think, "This is *like* a channel because…"

CASINO/CORBIS

If you're having trouble with the concepts in this chapter, consider using some of the following study resources. You can review the videos, or test yourself with materials designed for all kinds of learning styles.

☑ **Xtra! (http://lambxtra.swlearning.com)**

☑ Quiz   ☑ Feature Videos   ☑ Encore Videos   ☑ FAQ Videos

☑ Exhibit Worksheets   ☑ Marketing Plan Worksheets   ☐ Content

☑ **http://lamb.swlearning.com**

☑ Quiz   ☑ PowerPoint slides   ☑ Marketing News   ☑ Review Exercises

☑ Links   ☑ Marketing Plan Contest   ☑ Career Exercise   ☑ Use It Now

☑ **Study guide**

☑ Outline   ☑ Vocab Review   ☑ Test Questions   ☑ Marketing Scenario

Need More? Here's a tip. In the margin next to each paragraph or section in the chapter, write the question that the section answers. For example, "What discrepancies do marketing channels aid in overcoming?" could go on page 395. Once you have questions throughout the chapter, you can quiz yourself by using a blank piece of paper to cover the content. To check yourself, reveal each paragraph after you have answered the corresponding question.

13

Retailing

LEARNING OBJECTIVES

1 Discuss the importance of retailing in the U.S. economy

2 Explain the dimensions by which retailers can be classified

3 Describe the major types of retail operations

4 Discuss nonstore retailing techniques

5 Define franchising and describe its two basic forms

6 List the major tasks involved in developing a retail marketing strategy

7 Describe new developments in retailing

© MARIANNA DAY / ZUMA / CORBIS

Krispy Kreme has been a successful, specialty manufacturer and retailer of the "Hot Original Glazed" doughnut since 1937. Krispy Kreme's signature product, the "Hot Original Glazed," is sold along with two dozen other doughnut varieties through Krispy Kreme retail stores, gas stations, convenience stores, grocery stores, and campus cafeterias. System-wide sales at Krispy Kreme are almost $800 million, which translates into over 5 million doughnuts sold every day or more than 1.8 billion doughnuts per year. Krispy Kreme strives to offer customers affordable, tasty, high-quality doughnuts.

Krispy Kreme uses an original secret recipe to create a great tasting doughnut. To ensure consistency, Krispy Kreme uses a vertically integrated supply chain. The supply chain's success begins in the manufacturing plant where top-quality ingredients are mixed to form batches of dough. Once a batch is created, it is quality tested in a Krispy Kreme lab. The manufacturing plant is not the only location that produces doughnuts, however. Local Krispy Kreme retailers also make doughnuts, which are sold on and off the premises. To ensure standardization of the process outside the manufacturing plant, each retail outlet uses customized doughnut-making equipment to produce 4,000 to 10,000 dozen doughnuts each day.

The one-of-a-kind doughnut is not the only aspect of the Krispy Kreme brand. Krispy Kreme's on-premise retailers differentiate themselves from traditional doughnut shops by offering a unique buying experience called "doughnut theater," which allows consumers to watch the doughnuts being made while making purchases. Another unique aspect of Krispy Kreme retailers is the "Hot Doughnuts Now" sign, which stimulates impulse purchasing. When the sign is on, customers know the signature doughnut is being made and that hot, fresh doughnuts will be available shortly.

In fact, Krispy Kreme retailers have been so successful that they do not even have to advertise store openings. Typically, Krispy Kreme sends free doughnuts to politicians, radio stations, newspapers, TV stations, local schools, and sports teams to create a word-of-mouth buzz about the doughnuts. Once the media receive doughnuts and a press release, they often promote the product for free by announcing and broadcasting opening-related events. Krispy Kreme also hands out free doughnuts to the general public on opening day. Sometimes customers camp out for days before an opening. Although Krispy Kreme does not initiate the campouts, it does accommodate the campers by showing movies and putting up tents. An opening in Oregon was a televised event with a beauty queen, business leaders, and campers.

Another facet of Krispy Kreme's success is its franchising business. Approximately 500 people request information about Krispy Kreme franchises each week. But not many people can afford to own one at about $2 million per store (compared to about $750,000 for a McDonald's franchise). A Krispy Kreme franchise must pay $40,000 for 15-year rights to a location, plus 4.5 percent of sales for royalty fees and an additional 2 percent for branding and promotional expenditures. Although these fees are relatively close to the industry standard, investors must meet other stringent requirements, such as having a net worth of $5 million and experience in "multi-unit food-service operations." Franchisees also must commit to open approximately ten stores in a region. Once approved, franchisees will pay about $1.35 million in operational expenses (about five times the industry average); of that amount, $350,000 goes toward the doughnut machine. In addition, franchisees pay another $500,000 for the real estate. But once the store is open, revenues quickly exceed expenses. One store in Washington brought in $450,000 in the first week. The company average is about $43,000 per week ($2.2 million per year compared to $1.5 million per year for McDonald's).[1]

So, have you tried a Krispy Kreme donut? What are the major factors that have made Krispy Kreme successful? Do you think Krispy Kreme can continue to grow as it has in the past few years? What will its major challenges be?

THE ROLE OF RETAILING

Discuss the importance of retailing in the U.S. economy

Retailing—all the activities directly related to the sale of goods and services to the ultimate consumer for personal, nonbusiness use—has enhanced the quality of our daily lives. When we shop for groceries, hair styling, clothes, books, and many other products and services, we are involved in retailing. The millions of goods and services provided by retailers mirror the needs and styles of U.S. society.

Retailing affects all of us directly or indirectly. The retailing industry is one of the largest employers; over 1 million U.S. retailers employ more than 15 million people. Retail trade accounts for 11.7 percent of U.S. employment, and nearly 13 percent of all business are considered retail under NAICS. At the store level, retailing is still considered a mom-and-pop business. Almost nine out of ten retail companies employ fewer than 20 employees, and, according to the National Retail Federation, 95 percent of all retailers operate just one store.[2]

The U.S. economy is heavily dependent on retailing. Retailers ring up over $3.75 trillion in sales annually, nearly 40 percent of the gross domestic product (GDP).[3] Although most retailers are quite small, a few giant organizations dominate the industry, most notably Wal-Mart, whose annual U.S. sales alone account for about 5 percent of all retail sales. Who are these giants? Exhibit 13.1 lists the ten largest U.S. retailers.

EXHIBIT 13.1

Ten Largest U.S. Retailers

2003 Rank	Company	Retailing Formats	2003 Revenues (in billions)	2003 Number of Stores
1	**Wal-Mart** Bentonville, Arkansas	Discount stores, super-centers, and warehouse clubs	$258.6	4,906
2	**The Home Depot** Atlanta, Georgia	Home centers	$64.8	1,707
3	**Kroger** Cincinnati, Ohio	Supermarkets and convenience stores	$53.7	3,774
4	**Target Corporation*** Minneapolis, Minnesota	Discount stores and department stores	$48.1	1,553
5	**Costco** Issaquah, Washington	Warehouse clubs	$42.5	420
6	**Sears, Roebuck** Hoffman Estates, Illinois	Department stores, catalogs, home centers, and specialty	$41.1	1,970
7	**Safeway** Pleasanton, California	Supermarkets	$35.6	1,817
8	**Albertson's** Boise, Idaho	Supermarkets	$35.4	2,305
9	**Walgreen** Deerfield, Ill.	Drug stores	$32.5	4,227
10	**Lowe's** Mooresville, North Carolina	Home centers	$30.8	952

* Renamed Target Corporation in January 2000; formerly was Dayton Hudson Corporation.
SOURCE: STORES, July 2004, **http://www.stores.org**. Sales figures include international sales.

REVIEW LEARNING OBJECTIVE 1

1 | **Discuss the importance of retailing in the U.S. economy**

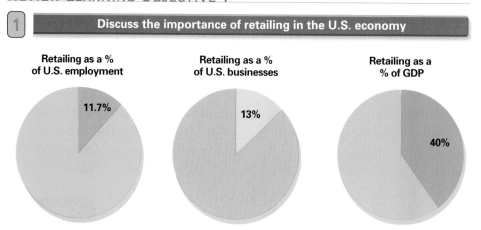

retailing
All the activities directly related to the sale of goods and services to the ultimate consumer for personal, nonbusiness use.

Explain the dimensions by which retailers can be classified

A retail establishment can be classified according to its ownership, level of service, product assortment, and price. Specifically, retailers use the latter three variables to position themselves in the competitive marketplace. (As noted in Chapter 7, positioning is the strategy used to influence how consumers perceive one product in relation to all competing products.) These three variables can be combined in several ways to create distinctly different retail operations. Exhibit 13.2 lists the major types of retail stores discussed in this chapter and classifies them by level of service, product assortment, price, and gross margin.

OWNERSHIP

Retailers can be broadly classified by form of ownership: independent, part of a chain, or franchise outlet. Retailers owned by a single person or partnership and not operated as part of a larger retail institution are **independent retailers**. Around the world, most retailers are independent, operating one or a few stores in their community. Local florists, shoe stores, and ethnic food markets typically fit this classification.

Chain stores are owned and operated as a group by a single organization. Under this form of ownership, many administrative tasks are handled by the home office for the entire chain. The home office also buys most of the merchandise sold in the stores. Gap and Starbucks are examples of chains.

Franchises are owned and operated by individuals but are licensed by a larger supporting organization, such as Krispy Kreme. Franchising combines the advantages of independent ownership with those of the chain store organization. Franchising is discussed in more detail later in the chapter.

EXHIBIT 13.2

Types of Stores and Their Characteristics

Type of Retailer	Level of Service	Product Assortment	Price	Gross Margin
Department store	Moderately high to high	Broad	Moderate to high	Moderately high
Specialty store	High	Narrow	Moderate to high	High
Supermarket	Low	Broad	Moderate	Low
Convenience store	Low	Medium to narrow	Moderately high	Moderately high
Drugstore	Low to moderate	Medium	Moderate	Low
Full-line discount store	Moderate to low	Medium to broad	Moderately low	Moderately low
Discount specialty store	Moderate to low	Medium to broad	Moderately low to low	Moderately low
Warehouse clubs	Low	Broad	Low to very low	Low
Off-price retailer	Low	Medium to narrow	Low	Low
Restaurant	Low to high	Narrow	Low to high	Low to high

LEVEL OF SERVICE

The level of service that retailers provide can be classified along a continuum, from full service to self-service. Some retailers, such as exclusive clothing stores, offer high levels of service. They provide alterations, credit, delivery, consulting, liberal return policies, layaway, gift wrapping, and personal shopping. Discount stores usually offer fewer services. Retailers like factory outlets and warehouse clubs offer virtually no services.

independent retailers
Retailers owned by a single person or partnership and not operated as part of a larger retail institution.

chain stores
Stores owned and operated as a group by a single organization.

franchise
The right to operate a business or to sell a product.

PRODUCT ASSORTMENT

The third basis for positioning or classifying stores is by the breadth and depth of their product line. Specialty stores—for example, Hallmark card stores, Lady Foot Locker, and TCBY yogurt shops—have the most concentrated product assortments, usually carrying single or narrow product lines but in considerable depth. On the other end of the spectrum, full-line discounters typically carry broad assortments of merchandise with limited depth. For example, Target carries automotive supplies, household cleaning products, and pet food. Typically, though, it carries only four or five brands of dog food. In contrast, a specialty pet store, such as Petsmart, may carry as many as 20 brands in a large variety of flavors, shapes, and sizes.

Other retailers, such as factory outlet stores, may carry only part of a single line. Nike stores sell only certain items of its own brand. Discount specialty stores like Home Depot or Toys "R" Us carry a broad assortment in concentrated product lines, such as building and home supplies or toys.

PRICE

Price is a fourth way to position retail stores. Traditional department stores and specialty stores typically charge the full "suggested retail price." In contrast, discounters, factory outlets, and off-price retailers use low prices as a major lure for shoppers.

The last column in Exhibit 13.2 shows the typical **gross margin**—how much the retailer makes as a percentage of sales after the cost of goods sold is subtracted. The level of gross margin and the price level generally match. For example, a traditional jewelry store has high prices and high gross margins. A factory outlet has low prices and low gross margins. Markdowns on merchandise during sale periods and price wars among competitors, in which stores lower prices on certain items in an effort to win customers, cause gross margins to decline. When Wal-Mart entered the grocery business in a small Arkansas community, a fierce price war ensued. By the time the price war was in full swing, the price of a quart of milk had plummeted by more than 50 percent (below the price of a pint) and a loaf of bread sold for only 9 cents—prices at which no retailer could make a profit.

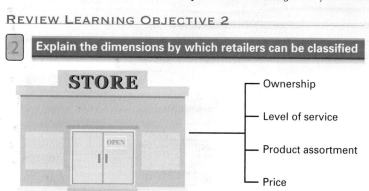

REVIEW LEARNING OBJECTIVE 2

2 Explain the dimensions by which retailers can be classified

STORE

— Ownership

— Level of service

— Product assortment

— Price

3 MAJOR TYPES OF RETAIL OPERATIONS

Describe the major types of retail operations

Traditionally, there have been several distinct types of retail stores, with each offering a different product assortment, type of service, and price level, according to its customers' shopping preferences.

In a recent trend, however, retailers are experimenting with alternative formats that make it harder to classify them. For instance, supermarkets are expanding their nonfood items and services, discounters are adding groceries, drugstores are becoming more like convenience stores, and department stores are experimenting with smaller stores. Nevertheless, many stores still fall into the basic types.

DEPARTMENT STORES

gross margin
The amount of money the retailer makes as a percentage of sales after the cost of goods sold is subtracted.

department store
A store housing several departments under one roof.

buyer
A department head who selects the merchandise for his or her department and may also be responsible for promotion and personnel.

A **department store** carries a wide variety of shopping and specialty goods, including apparel, cosmetics, housewares, electronics, and sometimes furniture. Purchases are generally made within each department rather than at one central checkout area. Each department is treated as a separate buying center to achieve economies in promotion, buying, service, and control. Each department is usually headed by a **buyer**, a department head who not only selects the merchandise for his or her department but may also be responsible for promotion and for personnel. For a consistent, uniform store image, central management sets broad policies about the types of merchandise carried and price ranges. Central management is also responsible for the overall advertising program, credit policies, store expansion, customer service, and so on.

Large independent department stores are rare today. Most are owned by national chains. Among the largest U.S. department store chains are Sears, JCPenney, Federated Department Stores, and May Department Stores. All operate more than one chain of retail stores, from discount chains to upscale clothiers. Two newer department store chains are Dillard's and Nordstrom. Dillard's is known for its distribution expertise. Nordstrom offers innovative customer service.

In recent years, consumers have become more cost conscious and value oriented. Specialty retailers, discounters, catalog outlets, and even online Internet shopping alternatives are offering superior merchandise selection and presentation, sharper pricing, and greater convenience to take sales away from department stores. They have also been quicker to adopt new technology and invest in labor-saving strategies. In addition, their leaner cost structure translates into lower prices for the customer. Meanwhile, manufacturers like Bass, Calvin Klein, Guess, and Polo/Ralph Lauren have opened outlet stores of their own, and discount stores such as Wal-Mart and Target have upgraded their apparel assortments, taking more sales away from department stores.

SPECIALTY STORES

Specialty store formats allow retailers to refine their segmentation strategies and tailor their merchandise to specific target markets. A **specialty store** is not only a type of store but also a method of retail operations—namely, specializing in a given type of merchandise. Examples include children's clothing, men's clothing, candy, baked goods, gourmet coffee, sporting goods, and pet supplies. A typical specialty store carries a deeper but narrower assortment of specialty merchandise than does a department store. Generally, specialty stores' knowledgeable sales clerks offer more attentive customer service. The format has become very powerful in the apparel market and other areas. In fact, according to recent studies, consumers buy more clothing from specialty stores than from any other type of retailer.[4] The Disney Store, Gadzooks, Williams-Sonoma, Foot Locker, and Tower Records are examples of successful chain specialty retailers.

Consumers usually consider price to be secondary in specialty outlets. Instead, the distinctive merchandise, the store's physical appearance, and the caliber of the staff determine its popularity. For example, Sharper Image, a national retail chain, has grown quickly by offering high-tech gadgets for consumers. Gadgets are created either by the in-house design department or by independent innovators who sell ideas to Sharper Image. The retailer avoids price wars by packing products with distinguishing features, creating all-in-one product combinations, and keeping pace with demand for innovative gizmos.[5] Because of their attention to the customer and limited product line, manufacturers often favor introducing new products in small specialty stores before moving on to larger retail and department stores.

Small specialty stores also provide a low-risk testing ground for many new products. Nike, for instance, often uses athletic footwear retailer Foot Locker as its venue for new shoe introductions. As an example, Nike introduced its $130 Tuned Air running shoe exclusively at Foot Locker shoe outlets. While the arrangement protected Foot Locker from price competition from other retailers, allowing it to charge full retail price, it also created an image of exclusivity for Nike.

SUPERMARKETS

U.S. consumers spend about a tenth of their disposable income in **supermarkets**. Supermarkets are large, departmentalized, self-service retailers that specialize in food and some nonfood items. Supermarkets have experienced declining sales in recent years. Some of this decline has been the result of increased competition from discounter Wal-Mart and Sam's Clubs. But demographic and lifestyle changes have also affected the supermarket industry.

FAQs

How can small companies compete with giants like Wal-Mart? Find out the answer by watching the Video FAQ on Xtra!

specialty store
A retail store specializing in a given type of merchandise.

supermarket
A large, departmentalized, self-service retailer that specializes in food and some nonfood items.

One major change has been the increase in dual-income and single-parent families that eat out more or are just too busy to prepare meals at home. According to the U.S. Department of Agriculture, Americans spend about 60 percent of their food money in retail grocery stores, with 40 percent spent for food away from home. In comparison, Americans spent over three-fourths of their food money in grocery stores in 1950.[6] The growth in the away-from-home food market has been driven by the entry of more women into the workforce and their need for convenience and time-saving products. Working couples need one-stop shopping, and the growing number of affluent customers are willing to pay for specialty and prepared foods.

As stores seek to meet consumer demand for one-stop shopping, conventional supermarkets are being replaced by bigger *superstores,* which are usually twice the size of supermarkets. Superstores meet the needs of today's customers for convenience, variety, and service. Superstores offer one-stop shopping for many food and nonfood needs, as well as many services—including pharmacies, flower shops, salad bars, in-store bakeries, takeout food sections, sit-down restaurants, health food sections, video rentals, dry-cleaning services, shoe repair, photo processing, and banking. Some even offer family dentistry or optical shops. **This tendency to offer a wide variety of nontraditional goods and services under one roof is called scrambled merchandising.** Albertson's supermarkets are a good example of scrambled merchandising. In addition to including an Albertson's branded liquor store, floral department, and pharmacy, they also lease space to Starbucks and local banks. Under recent partnerships with Toys "R" Us and Office Depot, the retailers supply Albertson's with products that are managed by employees.[7]

A recent trend in supermarket diversification is the addition of store-owned gas stations. The gas stations are not only a new revenue source for the supermarkets and a convenience for customers, but they also attract customers to the location by offering lower prices than can usually be found at a traditional gas station. Experts expect the trend will continue and that by 2005 supermarkets will account for 15 percent of overall gasoline sales.

Another demographic trend affecting supermarkets is expanding ethnicity. If current trends in shopping patterns among ethnic groups continue, demographic changes promise to have a vast impact on supermarket retailers. For example, both African American and Hispanic households now outspend white American households on weekly grocery shopping. In terms of shopping habits, African Americans and Hispanics tend to be conservative, looking for products and brands they know and trust and shopping at stores that reliably meet their needs. It will also be increasingly important for supermarkets to tailor their stores' product mix to reflect the demographics of the population they serve. For example, thousands of retailers carry Hispanic-owned Goya Foods.[8]

To stand out in an increasingly competitive marketplace, many supermarket chains are tailoring marketing strategies to appeal to specific consumer segments. Most notable is the shift toward *loyalty marketing programs* that reward loyal customers carrying frequent shopper cards with discounts or gifts. Once scanned at the checkout, frequent shopper cards help supermarket retailers electronically track shoppers' buying habits. Sixty percent of customers who shop at the 110 stores operated by South Carolina–based Piggly Wiggly, for instance, carry the Pig's Favorite loyalty card. Customers use their card each time they shop to get special discounts on items. Piggly Wiggly also uses consumer purchase data stored in its database to determine customer preferences. If management sees that a customer buys flowers regularly,

© ALAN LEVENSON/GETTY IMAGES/STONE

Recent trends in retailing are making it increasingly difficult to classify retailers, as stores are crossing into each other's domains. This woman is purchasing computer software in her grocery store.

scrambled merchandising
The tendency to offer a wide variety of nontraditional goods and services under one roof.

then it sends that customer a coupon redeemable in its floral department.[9]

DRUGSTORES

Drugstores stock pharmacy-related products and services as their main draw. Consumers are most often attracted to a drugstore by its pharmacy or pharmacist, its convenience, or because it honors their third-party prescription drug plan. Drugstores also carry an extensive selection of over-the-counter (OTC) medications, cosmetics, health and beauty aids, seasonal merchandise, specialty items such as greeting cards and a limited selection of toys, and some nonrefrigerated convenience foods. As competition has increased from mass merchandisers and supermarkets with their own pharmacies, as well as from direct-mail prescription services, drugstores have added value-added services such as 24-hour operations and drive-through pharmacies in many locations.

Demographic trends in the United States look favorable for the drugstore industry. As the baby boom population continues to age, they will spend an increasing percentage of their disposable income on health care and wellness. This is good news for the drugstore industry, as the average 60-year-old purchases 15 prescriptions per year, nearly twice as many as the average 30-year-old. Because baby boomers are attentive to their health and keenly sensitive about their looks, the increased traffic at the pharmacy counter in the future should also spur sales in other traditionally strong drugstore merchandise categories, most notably OTC drugs, vitamins, and health and beauty aids.

CONVENIENCE STORES

A **convenience store** can be defined as a miniature supermarket, carrying only a limited line of high-turnover convenience goods. These self-service stores are typically located near residential areas and are open 24 hours, seven days a week. Convenience stores offer exactly what their name implies: convenient location, long hours, fast service. However, prices are almost always higher at a convenience store than at a supermarket. Thus, the customer pays for the convenience.

When the original convenience stores added self-service gas pumps, full-service gas stations fought back by closing service bays and opening miniature stores of their own, selling convenience items like cigarettes, sodas, and snacks. Supermarkets and discount stores also wooed customers with one-stop shopping and quick checkout. To combat the gas stations' and supermarkets' competition, convenience store operators have changed their strategy. They have expanded their offerings of nonfood items with video rentals and health and beauty aids and added upscale sandwich and salad lines and more fresh produce. Some convenience stores are even selling Pizza Hut, Subway, and Taco Bell products prepared in the store. For example, Exxon on the Run features Mountain Coffee Roasters, Blimpies Subs and Salads, and an On the Run Café that offers everything from fresh sandwiches and fresh fruits to a grilled hamburger and french fries.[10]

DISCOUNT STORES

A **discount store** is a retailer that competes on the basis of low prices, high turnover, and high volume. Discounters can be classified into four major categories: full-line discount stores, specialty discount stores, warehouse clubs, and off-price discount retailers.

Walgreen's
Do you think drugstore Web sites add value for the consumer? What services on Walgreen's site would you be most likely to use? Would Internet selling be a factor in your choice of pharmacy? To what group of consumers might selling items over the Internet be the most appealing? Why?
http://www.walgreens.com

Online

drugstore
A retail store that stocks pharmacy-related products and services as its main draw.

convenience store
A miniature supermarket, carrying only a limited line of high-turnover convenience goods.

discount store
A retailer that competes on the basis of low prices, high turnover, and high volume.

Full-Line Discount Stores

Compared to traditional department stores, **full-line discount stores** offer consumers very limited service and carry a much broader assortment of well-known, nationally branded "hard goods," including housewares, toys, automotive parts, hardware, sporting goods, and garden items, as well as clothing, bedding, and linens. Some even carry limited nonperishable food items, such as soft drinks, canned goods, and potato chips. As with department stores, national chains dominate the discounters. Full-line discounters are often called mass merchandisers. **Mass merchandising** is the retailing strategy whereby retailers use moderate to low prices on large quantities of merchandise and lower service to stimulate high turnover of products.

 Wal-Mart is the largest full-line discount store in terms of sales. Wal-Mart initially expanded rapidly by locating on the outskirts of small towns and absorbing business for miles around. In recent years, most of its growth has come in larger cites. Today, it has over 4,000 stores. Much of Wal-Mart's success has been attributed to its merchandising foresight, cost consciousness, efficient communication and distribution systems, and involved, motivated employees. Wal-Mart is credited with pioneering the retail strategy of "everyday low pricing," a strategy now widely copied by retailers the world over. Besides expanding throughout all 50 states and Puerto Rico, Wal-Mart has expanded globally into Mexico, Canada, Brazil, Argentina, China, Germany, Korea, and the United Kingdom. Wal-Mart has also become a formidable retailing giant in online shopping, concentrating on toys and electronics. With tie-ins to its stores across the country, Wal-Mart offers online shopping with in-store kiosks linking to the site and the ability to handle returns and exchanges from Internet sales at its physical stores.[11]

Supercenters combine a full line of groceries and general merchandise with a wide range of services, including pharmacy, dry cleaning, portrait studios, photo finishing, hair salons, optical shops, and restaurants—all in one location. For supercenter operators like Wal-Mart, food is a customer magnet that sharply increases the store's overall volume, while taking customers away from traditional supermarkets. Wal-Mart now operates over 1,000 supercenters and plans to keep opening them at a rate of more than 150 a year for the near future. Although Target was the last major discounter to embrace the supercenter concept, it recently doubled the number of Super Target stores and is investing in the development of private-label grocery products.[12]

Supercenters are also threatening to push Europe's traditional small and medium-sized food stores into extinction. Old-fashioned corner stores and family businesses are giving way to larger chains that offer food, drugs, services, and general merchandise all in one place. Many European countries are passing legislation to make it more difficult for supercenters to open. In France, for example, laws were passed that banned authorizations for new supercenters over 1,000 square meters (10,800 square feet). Belgium and Portugal have passed similar bans. In Britain and the Netherlands, areas outside towns and cities are off limits to superstores. By imposing planning and building restrictions for large stores, these countries are trying to accommodate environmental concerns, movements to revive city centers, and the worries of small shopkeepers.

An increasingly popular variation of off-price retailing at full-line discount stores is *extreme-value retailing,* the most notable examples being Dollar General and Family Dollar. Extreme-value retailers have grown in popularity as major discounters continue to shift toward the supercenter format, broadening their customer base and increasing their offerings of higher priced goods aimed at higher income consumers. This has created an opening for extreme-value retailers to entice shoppers from the low-income segment. Low- and fixed-income customers are drawn to extreme-value retailers, whose stores are located within their communities. Extreme-value retailers also build smaller stores (a typical store is about the size of one department in a Wal-Mart superstore) with a narrower selection of

full-line discount stores
A retailer that offers consumers very limited service and carries a broad assortment of well-known, nationally branded "hard goods."

mass merchandising
A retailing strategy using moderate to low prices on large quantities of merchandise and lower service to stimulate high turnover of products.

supercenter
A retail store that combines groceries and general merchandise goods with a wide range of services.

merchandise emphasizing day-to-day necessities. Rock-bottom prices are also key to their success. With the average transaction under $10, extreme-value retailers have found low price to be far more critical to building traffic and loyalty than any other retailing format.[13]

Specialty Discount Stores

Another discount niche includes the single-line **specialty discount stores**—for example, stores selling sporting goods, electronics, auto parts, office supplies, housewares or toys. These stores offer a nearly complete selection of single-line merchandise and use self-service, discount prices, high volume, and high turnover to their advantage. Specialty discount stores are often termed **category killers** because they so heavily dominate their narrow merchandise segment. Examples include Toys "R" Us in toys, Circuit City and Best Buy in electronics, Staples and Office Depot in office supplies, Home Depot and Lowe's in home improvement supplies, IKEA in home furnishings, Bed, Bath & Beyond in kitchen and bath accessories, and Linens N Things in bedding.

  Toys "R" Us was the first category killer, offering a giant selection of toys, usually over 15,000 different items per store, at prices usually 10 to 15 percent less than competitors'. When Toys "R" Us came on the retail scene, department stores were generally limiting their toy assortments to the Christmas season. Toys "R" Us offered a broad assortment of inventory all year long. Additionally, the playing field was scattered with many small toy chains or mom-and-pop stores. With its bright warehouse-style stores, Toys "R" Us gobbled up market share, and many small toy stores failed and department stores eliminated their toy departments. The Toys "R" Us chain—currently an $11.3 billion company with more than 1,600 stores worldwide—now commands about a quarter of the U.S. retail toy business. Toys "R" Us first went international in 1984 with stores in Canada and Singapore. Since then, the company has opened over 500 stores in more than two dozen foreign countries, the most recent being Japan. Toys "R" Us has also expanded its category-killer retailing concept to include over 200 Kids "R" Us children's clothing stores and 160 Babies "R" Us product stores. In addition, the company's Web site garnered more than $200 million in sales last year thanks in part to an alliance with Amazon.com. The company plans to build on its momentum by also enhancing its Web sites for Babies "R" Us and Imaginarium.com.[14]

Other specialty segments have followed the lead of Toys "R" Us, hoping to build similar retailing empires in highly fragmented mom-and-pop markets. For instance, the home improvement industry, which for years was served by professional builders and small hardware stores, is now dominated by Home Depot and Lowe's. Similarly, prior to the creation of Petsmart and Petco pet supplies chains, the pet industry was dominated by thousands of independent neighborhood pet stores. Another industry that was very fragmented was the office products industry. As more people began to work from home, replacing their typewriters with personal computers and purchasing fax machines, the local stationery store, with its limited selection of paper and writing materials, quickly became obsolete. The industry is now dominated by Office Depot, Staples, and OfficeMax, each stocking 5,000 to 7,000 different types of products. Category-dominant retailers like these serve their customers by offering a large selection of merchandise, stores that make shopping easy, and low prices every day, which eliminates the need for time-consuming comparison shopping.

Warehouse Membership Clubs

Warehouse membership clubs sell a limited selection of brand-name appliances, household items, and groceries. These are usually sold in bulk from warehouse outlets on a cash-and-carry basis to members only. Individual members of warehouse clubs are charged low or no membership fees. Currently, the leading stores in this category are Wal-Mart's Sam's Club, Costco, and BJ's Wholesale Club.

specialty discount store
A retail store that offers a nearly complete selection of single-line merchandise and uses self-service, discount prices, high volume, and high turnover.

category killers
Specialty discount stores that heavily dominate their narrow merchandise segment.

warehouse membership clubs
A limited-service merchant wholesaler that sells a limited selection of brand-name appliances, household items, and groceries on a cash-and-carry basis to members, usually small businesses and groups.

Warehouse clubs, like Costco, are growing in popularity as they continue to offer savings on everyday items and luxury products. Costco only marks up its inventory 10 percent, whether it's a case of toothpaste or a case of Dom Perignon champagne.

Warehouse clubs have had a major impact on supermarkets. With 90,000 square feet or more, warehouse clubs offer 60 to 70 percent general merchandise and health- and beauty-care products, with grocery-related items making up the difference. Warehouse club members tend to be more educated and more affluent and have a larger household than regular supermarket shoppers. These core customers use warehouse clubs to stock up on staples; then they go to specialty outlets or food stores for perishables.

Off-Price Retailers

An **off-price retailer** sells at prices 25 percent or more below traditional department store prices because it pays cash for its stock and usually doesn't ask for return privileges. Off-price retailers buy manufacturers' overruns at cost or even less. They also absorb goods from bankrupt stores, irregular merchandise, and unsold end-of-season output. Nevertheless, much off-price retailer merchandise is first-quality, current goods. Because buyers for off-price retailers purchase only what is available or what they can get a good deal on, merchandise styles and brands often change monthly. Today there are hundreds of off-price retailers, the best known being T. J. Maxx, Ross Stores, Marshall's, HomeGoods, and Tuesday Morning.

Factory outlets are an interesting variation on the off-price concept. A **factory outlet** is an off-price retailer that is owned and operated by a manufacturer. Thus, it carries one line of merchandise—its own. Each season, from 5 to 10 percent of a manufacturer's output does not sell through regular distribution channels because it consists of closeouts (merchandise being discontinued), factory seconds, and canceled orders. With factory outlets, manufacturers can regulate where their surplus is sold, and they can realize higher profit margins than they would by disposing of the goods through independent wholesalers and retailers. Factory outlet malls typically locate in out-of-the-way rural areas or near vacation destinations. Most are situated at least 30 miles from urban or suburban shopping areas so that manufacturers don't alienate their department store accounts by selling the same goods virtually next door at a discount.

Manufacturers reaping the benefits of outlet mall popularity include Gap, J. Crew, and Calvin Klein clothiers; West Point Pepperel textiles; Pottery Barn and Crate & Barrel home products; Oneida silversmiths; and Dansk kitchenwares. Top-drawer department stores—including Neiman Marcus—have also opened outlet stores to sell hard-to-move merchandise. Dillard Department Stores has opened a series of clearance centers to make final attempts to move merchandise that failed to sell in the department store. To move their clearance items, Nordstrom's operates Nordstrom Rack, Saks Fifth Avenue has Off Fifth, and Boston's Filene's has Filene's Basement.

RESTAURANTS

Restaurants straddle the line between retailing establishments and service establishments. Restaurants do sell tangible products, food and drink, but they also provide a valuable service for consumers in the form of food preparation and food service. Most restaurants could even fall into the definition of a specialty retailer given that most concentrate their menu offerings on a distinctive type of cuisine—for example, Olive Garden Italian restaurants, Starbucks coffeehouses, Popeye's Fried Chicken, and Pizza Hut pizza restaurants.

As a retailing institution, restaurants must deal with many of the same issues as a more traditional retailer, such as personnel, distribution, inventory management, promotion, pricing, and location. Restaurants and food-service retailers run the

off-price retailer
A retailer that sells at prices 25 percent or more below traditional department store prices because it pays cash for its stock and usually doesn't ask for return privileges.

factory outlet
An off-price retailer that is owned and operated by a manufacturer.

spectrum from those offering limited service and inexpensive food, such as fast-food chains or the local snack bar or coffeehouse, to those that offer sit-down service and moderate to high prices, such as the Outback Steakhouse & Saloon chain or a local trendy Italian bistro.

Eating out is an important part of Americans' daily activities and is growing in strength. According to the National Restaurant Association, more than 70 billion meals are eaten in restaurants or cafeterias annually. This means that Americans consume an average of 4.8 commercially prepared meals per week. Food away from home accounts for about 25 percent of the household food budget for lower income families and as much as 50 percent for those with higher incomes. The trend toward eating out has been fueled by the increase in working mothers and dual-income families who have more money to eat out and less time to prepare meals at home. Money spent on food away from home is expected to grow from 46 percent of household food budgets in 2004 to 53 percent by 2010.[15]

The restaurant industry is one of the most entrepreneurial of businesses and one of the most competitive. Because barriers to entering the restaurant industry are low, the opportunity appeals to many people. The risks, however, are great. About 50 percent of all new restaurants fail within the first year of operation. Restaurants face competition not only from other restaurants but also from the consumer who can easily choose to cook at home. Competition has fostered innovation in the restaurant industry, such as Pizza Hut's introduction of the Pzone—a combination of a pizza and a calzone—and the ever-changing menus at fast-food restaurants. Seeking out and targeting underserved distribution niches is another way restaurants are competing with one another to reach consumers. Fast-food operators are increasingly looking to provide service at locations such as hospitals, airports, schools, and highway rest stops. Companies like Subway, Dunkin' Donuts, and Church's Fried Chicken also are partnering with branded service stations to offer customers one-stop shopping. These partnerships save money on leases, lure more customers, and foster innovation. And, more restaurants are now competing directly with supermarkets by offering takeout and delivery in an effort to capture more of the home meal replacement market.

REVIEW LEARNING OBJECTIVE 3

3 | **Describe the major types of retail operations**

Department Stores	Specialty Stores	Supermarket	Drugstores	Convenience Stores	Discount Stores	Restaurants

Scrambled merchandising

- Full-line
  - hypermarket
  - supercenter
  - extreme-value
- Specialty
  - category killer
- Warehouse
- Off-price
  - factory outlet

4 NONSTORE RETAILING

Discuss nonstore retailing techniques

The retailing methods discussed so far have been at the origin in-store methods, in which customers must physically shop at stores. In contrast, **nonstore retailing** is shopping without visiting a store. Because consumers demand convenience, nonstore retailing is currently growing faster than in-store retailing. The major forms of nonstore retailing are automatic vending, direct retailing, direct marketing, and electronic retailing.

AUTOMATIC VENDING

A low-profile yet important form of retailing is **automatic vending**, the use of machines to offer goods for sale—for example, the cola, candy, or snack vending machines found in college cafeterias and office buildings. Vending is the most pervasive retail business in the United States, with about six million vending machines selling $40 billion annually. Food and beverages account for about 85 percent of all sales

nonstore retailing
Shopping without visiting a store.

automatic vending
The use of machines to offer goods for sale.

from vending machines. Due to the convenience, consumers are willing to pay higher prices for products from a vending machine than for the same products in traditional retail settings.

Retailers are constantly seeking new opportunities to sell via vending. For example, United Artists Theaters offer moviegoers the option of purchasing hot popcorn, Tombstone pizza, Kraft macaroni-and-cheese, and chicken fingers from a vending machine instead of waiting in line at the concession stand.[16] Many vending machines today also sell nontraditional kinds of merchandise, such as videos, toys, stickers, and sports cards. Vending machines in college libraries sell computer diskettes, pens and highlighters, and other office-type supplies. Tourists can purchase film and disposable cameras from vending machines in many popular destinations. And Joe Boxer underwear can be purchased with a credit card from vending machines in selected department stores.

Of course, vending machines are also an important tool in the ongoing cola wars between Coca-Cola and Pepsi. Both companies are constantly looking for new ways to improve vending machine sales. For example, Coca-Cola is implementing Intelligent Vending, a "cashless" payment system. Vending machines with this system accept credit cards, RFID devices, and hotel room keys and can be accessed via cell phone (mobile e-commerce, or m-commerce, as discussed later in this chapter).[17]

McDonald's pushed the limits of vending with its Redbox concept, a convenient market in a vending machine. Redbox machines sold a wide variety of convenience foods and groceries (including milk, eggs, and toiletries) and accepted credit cards. Although the concept did not succeed in the United States, automated convenience stores are still used in Europe in places like train stations and bus depots.

DIRECT RETAILING

In **direct retailing**, representatives sell products door-to-door, office-to-office, or at home sales parties. Companies like Avon, Mary Kay Cosmetics, The Pampered Chef, Usbourne Books, and World Book Encyclopedia have used this approach for years. But recently direct retailers' sales have suffered as women have entered the workforce. Working women are not home during the day and have little time to attend selling parties. Although most direct sellers like Avon and Tupperware still advocate the party plan method, the realities of the marketplace have forced them to be more creative in reaching their target customer. Direct sales representatives now hold parties in offices, parks, and even parking lots. Others hold informal gatherings where shoppers can drop in at their convenience or offer self-improvement classes. Many direct retailers are also turning to direct mail, telephone, or more traditional retailing venues to find new avenues to their customers and increase sales. Avon, for instance, has begun opening cosmetic kiosk counters, called Avon Beauty Centers, in malls and strip centers. Avon has also launched a new brand—Mark, a beauty "experience" for young women. Most Mark representatives are students who typically sell the product as an afterschool part-time job. Prospective representatives and consumers can buy products or register to be a representative in person, online, or over the phone.[18]

Direct retailers are also using the Internet as a channel to reach more customers and increase sales. Amway launched Quixtar.com, an online channel for its products that generated over $1 billion in revenues in 2003. Customers access the site using a unique referral number for each Amway rep, a system that ensures that the reps earn their commissions. Best known for its health and beauty offerings, Quixtar features hundreds of products from leading brand-name companies in many categories, including apparel, athletic gear, photography, electronics, appliances, and furniture. Avon, Tupperware, and Mary Kay also have Internet retail sites. At Avon's site, individual reps have their own home pages that link from Avon's home page so that sales are credited to them.

direct retailing
The selling of products by representatives who work door-to-door, office-to-office, or at home parties.

In response to the decline in U.S. sales, many direct retailers are exploring opportunities in other countries. For example, Mary Kay, Avon, and Amway have started successful operations in China by adapting their business models to China's laws. Mary Kay agents in China do not purchase and resell the products but are paid a sales commission instead. The company also changed its slogan from "God First, Family Second, Career Third," to "Faith First, Family Second, Career Third."[19]

Avon
What advantages do you think the Avon site has over a visit from an Avon representative? Can you get the same amount of product information from each? Does Avon offer any products that you would prefer to order from a representative?

http://www.avon.com

Online

DIRECT MARKETING

Direct marketing, sometimes called **direct-response marketing**, refers to the techniques used to get consumers to make a purchase from their home, office, or other nonretail setting. Those techniques include direct mail, catalogs and mail order, telemarketing, and electronic retailing. Shoppers using these methods are less bound by traditional shopping situations. Time-strapped consumers and those who live in rural or suburban areas are most likely to be direct-response shoppers because they value the convenience and flexibility that direct marketing provides.

Direct Mail

Direct mail can be the most efficient or the least efficient retailing method, depending on the quality of the mailing list and the effectiveness of the mailing piece. According to the Direct Marketing Association, direct mail typically generates over $600 billion in revenue a year. With direct mail, marketers can precisely target their customers according to demographics, geographics, and even psychographics. Good mailing lists come from an internal database or are available from list brokers for about $35 to $150 per thousand names.

Direct mailers are becoming more sophisticated in targeting the "right" customers. Using statistical methods to analyze census data, lifestyle and financial information, and pastpurchase and credit history, direct mailers can pick out those most likely to buy their products. For example, Range Rover recently launched a direct-mail campaign that invited 150,000 potential customers to one of six test-drive events. Approximately 1,000 people attended each event, and of those approximately 12 people bought the new SUV at each event. Overall, a total of 775 new SUVs were sold to those who received the mailer. To compile the list, Range Rover used current customers, subscribers of selected Condé Nast magazines, and American Express platinum cardholders. By targeting the solicitation to only the best prospects, the company could save millions in postage while still generating new sales. For more expensive products, direct mailers are using videocassettes in place of letters and brochures to deliver their sales messages.[20]

Catalogs and Mail Order

Consumers can now buy just about anything through the mail, from the mundane like books, music, and polo shirts to the outlandish, such as the $5 million diamond-and-ruby-studded bra available through the Victoria's Secret catalog. Although women make up the bulk of catalog shoppers, the percentage of male catalog shoppers has recently soared. As changing demographics have shifted more of the shopping responsibility to men, they are viewing shopping via catalog, mail order, and the Internet as more sensible than a trip to the mall.

 Successful catalogs usually are created and designed for highly segmented markets. For example, Schwan Food Company recently launched Impromptu Gourmet, which offers convenient gourmet and

**direct marketing
(direct-response marketing)**
Techniques used to get consumers to make a purchase from their home, office, or other nonretail setting.

fine dining frozen foods. Certain types of retailers are using mail order successfully. For example, computer manufacturers have discovered that mail order is a lucrative way to sell computers to home and small-business users, evidenced by the huge successes of Dell and Gateway. Dell has used its direct business model to become a 41 billion-dollar company that is number one in global market share. It sells over $50 million worth of computers and computer equipment online every day.[21]

Improved customer service and quick delivery policies have boosted consumer confidence in mail order. L.L. Bean and Lands' End are two catalog companies known for their excellent customer service. Shoppers can order 24 hours a day and return merchandise for any reason for a full refund. Other successful mail-order catalogs—including Talbots, Frontgate, and Lillian Vernon—target hardworking, home-oriented baby boomers who don't have time to visit or would rather not visit a retail store. To remain competitive and save time for customers, catalog companies have computer databases containing customer information so they do not have to repeatedly give their addresses, credit card information, and so on. They also are working with overnight shippers such as UPS and FedEx to speed up deliveries. Indeed, some products can be ordered as late at 12:30 A.M. and still arrive the same day by 10:30 A.M.

Telemarketing

Telemarketing is the use of the telephone to sell directly to consumers. It consists of outbound sales calls, usually unsolicited, and inbound calls—that is, orders through toll-free 800 numbers or fee-based 900 numbers.

Outbound telemarketing is an attractive direct-marketing technique because of rising postage rates and decreasing long-distance phone rates. Skyrocketing field sales costs have also put pressure on marketing managers to use outbound telemarketing. Searching for ways to keep costs under control, marketing managers are discovering how to pinpoint prospects quickly, zero in on serious buyers, and keep in close touch with regular customers. Meanwhile, they are reserving expensive, time-consuming, in-person calls for closing sales. In 2003, however, the large number of complaints about outbound telemarketing calls led Congress to pass legislation establishing a national "do not call" list of consumers who do not want to receive unsolicited telephone calls. In addition, Congress passed laws requiring e-mail marketers to allow recipients to opt out of mass e-mails (spam). The laws also prohibit marketers from camouflaging their identity through false return addresses and misleading subject lines. A problem with the telemarketing law, however, is that it exempted nonprofits, so some companies have set up nonprofit subsidiaries to continue their calling activities. Some industry experts say the lists help them by eliminating nonbuyers, but others believe this legislation could have a long-term negative effect on telemarketing sales.[22]

Inbound telemarketing programs, which use 800 and 900 numbers, are mainly used to take orders, generate leads, and provide customer service. Inbound 800 telemarketing has successfully supplemented direct-response TV, radio, and print advertising for more than 25 years. The more recently introduced 900 numbers, which customers pay to call, are gaining popularity as a cost-effective way for companies to target customers. One of the major benefits of 900 numbers is that they allow marketers to generate qualified responses. Although the charge may reduce the total volume of calls, the calls that do come are from customers who have a true interest in the product.

ELECTRONIC RETAILING

Electronic retailing includes the 24-hour, shop-at-home television networks and online retailing.

telemarketing
The use of the telephone to sell directly to consumers.

The Benefit
of
Fashion.

QVC Presents "FFANY Shoes On Sale"
Beautiful Shoes at Half Price, Benefiting Breast Cancer Research

Over 100,000 pairs of designer and brand-name shoes will be sold at half price, with net proceeds
benefiting The Fashion Footwear Charitable Foundation, which supports breast cancer research and
education programs. Tune in live from New York's Chelsea Piers and just imagine what you'll save.

Watch Wednesday, October 16; 7–10pm ET on QVC

Shop-at-home networks are incredibly successful. By mixing show business and commerce, companies like Home Shopping Network (HSN) and QVC have hit upon an extremely successful retailing strategy. HSN has been in business over 25 years and has annual sales in the $2 billion range. QVC was launched in the fall of 1987. In 2003, QVC achieved $4.89 billion in sales. 2003 marked the 10th Annual "Shoes on Sale" event.

online retailing
A type of shopping available to consumers with personal computers and access to the Internet.

Gap
J. Crew
Do you think it's harder for a retailer that sells primarily through its catalog (like J. Crew) or one that sells primarily through its retail outlets (like Gap) to make the transition to successful e-tailing? Check out the two Web sites and compare how they present their products, their site functionality, and the integration of all their retail venues.

http://www.gap.com

http://www.jcrew.com

Online

Shop-at-Home Networks

The shop-at-home television networks are specialized forms of direct-response marketing. These shows display merchandise, with the retail price, to home viewers. Viewers can phone in their orders directly on a toll-free line and shop with a credit card. The shop-at-home industry has quickly grown into a billion-dollar business with a loyal customer following. Shop-at-home networks have the capability of reaching nearly every home that has a television set.

The best-known shop-at-home networks are the Home Shopping Network and the QVC (Quality, Value, Convenience) Network. Home shopping networks attract a broad audience through diverse programming and product offerings and are now adding new products to appeal to more affluent audiences. For instance, on QVC, cooking programs attract both men and women, fashion programs attract mostly women, and the NFL Team Shop attracts primarily men. Since it began broadcasting, the channel has sold everything from Sony electronics to Bugs Bunny to Gucci. The company typically ships more than 100 million packages worldwide annually to 6.8 million customers and exceeds $4.5 billion in sales. Its success is partially based on a customer file of more than 20 million people in 40 countries.[23]

Online Retailing

For years, shopping at home meant looking through catalogs and then placing an order over the telephone. For many people today, however, it now means turning on a computer, surfing retail Web sites, and selecting and ordering products online with the click of a mouse. **Online retailing**, or *e-tailing*, is a type of shopping available to consumers with personal computers and access to the Internet. Over 65 percent of Americans have Internet access either at home or at work.

Online retailing has exploded in the last several years as consumers have found this type of shopping convenient and, in many instances, less costly. Consumers can shop without leaving home, choose from a wide selection of merchants, use shopping comparison services to search the Web for the best price, and then have the items delivered to their doorsteps. As a result, online shopping continues to grow at a rapid pace, with online sales representing almost 5 percent of total retail sales. In fact, according to the National Retail Federation, e-retailers' sales increased by over 48 percent in 2002 to $76 billion, and 2003 projected sales were expected to reach almost $100 billion.[24] Online retailing is also increasing in popularity outside the United States. Read more about e-tailing worldwide in the "Global Perspectives" box.

Amazon.com, an e-commerce leader, and CDNOW, a premier online music retailer, have partnered to create a better online shopping experience. The success of both companies is attributed to product selection, customer service, one-click payment methods, and reliable shipping and delivery. Amazon.com, founded in 1995, aims to offer "the Earth's Biggest Selection and to be the Earth's most customer-centric company, where customers can find and discover anything they might want to buy online" while selling at the lowest possible price. Amazon has

Global Perspectives Global Perspectives Global Perspectives
Global Perspectives Global Perspectives Global Perspectives Global Perspectives Global Perspe
Global Perspectives Global Perspectives **GLOBAL PERSPECTIVES** ectives Global Perspectives Global Perspe
Global Perspectives Global Perspectives Global Perspectives Global Perspectives Global Perspe
Global Perspectives Global Perspectives
Global Perspectives

> ONLINE RETAILING GROWS WORLDWIDE

Consumers and marketers around the world are embracing the Internet and online retailing (both e-commerce and m-commerce). According to Nielsen/NetRatings, over 173 million Americans, 34 million Britons, 17 million Canadians, 17 million Indians, 13 million Austrians, and 3 million South Africans are using the Internet. Marketers definitely are vying for Internet consumers' attention, with online advertising in recent years surpassing experts' estimates. Approximately $7 billion was spent on Internet ads in the United States in 2003, and online ad spending in the United Kingdom was about £300 million (U.S. $550 million).

Given the dramatic increases in the number of Web surfers and online advertising spending, online retailers have consistently enjoyed big payoffs during holiday shopping season. Nearly half of the over $17 billion holiday shopping revenues in the United States are generated by online merchants. Global online spending is also increasing, though not as fast. One problem, though, is that the number of online fraud claims is keeping pace with the growth in spending. VeriSign estimates that over 6 percent of online transactions are fraudulent and that 52 percent of those take place outside the United States.

Amazon.com is the best example of a successful global e-commerce business model. Amazon believes that it is very important to reach customers throughout the world. Therefore, it has five separate Web sites, each directed to a different nationality. The Web sites include a British site Amazon.co.uk, a French-language site Amazon.fr, a German-language site Amazon.de, and a Japanese-language site Amazon.co.jp. Each Web site is tailored to its country of origin and helps Amazon remain the leading online global retailer. In addition to online ads, such as pop-ups and banner ads, Amazon uses print media such as direct mail and newspaper inserts to encourage online purchasing.

In global online retailing, a multichannel approach is essential to reaching consumers because they want to shop both online and in stores. Most consumers prefer to use both channels of distribution rather than just one, and they expect identical product selection and customer service online and in stores. About half of online shoppers research purchases off-line, using catalogs and stores, and then make the purchase online.[25]

As Internet usage around the world increases, so will the number of online shoppers. How do you think that will affect traditional retailers? Will they learn to operate in the cyberworld, or will they try to compete against their online counterparts? Do you think the Internet will create a truly global retail marketplace?

become a $4.5 billion business selling millions of products to customers all over the world.[26]

Most traditional retailers have now jumped on the Internet bandwagon, allowing shoppers to purchase the same merchandise found in their stores from their Web site. Online retailing also fits well with traditional catalog companies, such as Lands' End and Eddie Bauer that already have established distribution networks. In a drastic turnabout in its retail strategy, computer software retailer Egghead recently closed all of its brick-and-mortar stores, moved its entire business onto the Web, and added ".com" to the end of its name. Software purchased at the company's site, **http://www.egghead.com**, can be downloaded directly to the purchaser's computer.

As the popularity of online retailing grows, it is becoming critical that retailers be online and that their stores, Web sites, and catalogs be integrated. Customers expect to find the same brands, products, and prices whether they purchase online, on the phone, or in a store. Therefore, retailers are increasingly using in-store kiosks to help tie the channels together for greater customer service. Retailer and cataloger Williams-Sonoma, for example, recently linked its store gift registry to its Web site, allowing brides to see who has bought what in real time. Banana Republic stores in New York and Santa Monica, California, have kiosks where customers can order items that aren't on the shelves. Kiosks are even more popular among retailers that target younger, more computer-oriented customers. For example, Van's operates eight skate parks, which are a combination retail store, entertainment venue, and alternative sports arena. In addition to the skating rink, each park has a lounge area where customers can hang out, watch customized videos, and surf Van's Web site at a bank of kiosks. Each kiosk not only offers a complete selection of Van's footwear, apparel, and accessories, but also includes a

4 | **Discuss nonstore retailing techniques**

Nonstore Retailing

Vending

Direct retailing

Direct marketing
- direct mail
- catalogs
- telemarketing

Electronic retailing
- online
- shop at home

full-service pro shop that sells over 500 skateboards, bicycles, helmets, and other equipment and an information center with the latest tour, special event, and contest information.[27]

Online auctions run by Internet companies such as eBay and Amazon.com have enjoyed phenomenal success in recent years. With more than two million items for sale each day, ranging from antique clocks to car stereos, eBay is the leader in cyberspace auctions. Internet auction services like eBay run the Web service and collect a listing fee, plus a commission of 1 to 5 percent when a sale is completed. They also host auctions for other companies. For example, eBay and Sotheby's have a joint venture that offers fine art, rare coins, sports collectibles, jewelry, and antiques online. Each item carries a stamp of authenticity from Sotheby's or one of the 2,800 art and antiques dealers worldwide who have signed exclusive agreements with Sotheby's. The joint venture supports eBay's fine arts and antiques division and enables Sotheby's to offer online sales without the overhead expense of managing its own site.[28]

5 FRANCHISING

Define franchising and describe its two basic forms

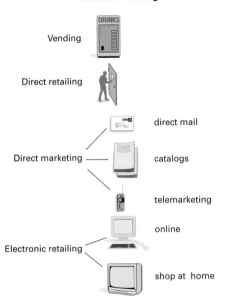

Franchising is usually associated with restaurants, but some of the most successful franchises of late are not even food related. Sylvan Learning Systems is an example.

franchiser
The originator of a trade name, product, methods of operation, and so on, that grants operating rights to another party to sell its product.

franchisee
An individual or business that is granted the right to sell another party's product.

A *franchise* is a continuing relationship in which a franchiser grants to a franchisee the business rights to operate or to sell a product. The **franchiser** originates the trade name, product, methods of operation, and so on. The **franchisee**, in return, pays the franchiser for the right to use its name, product, or business methods. A franchise agreement between the two parties usually lasts for 10 to 20 years, at which time the agreement can be renewed if both parties are agreeable.

To be granted the rights to a franchise, a franchisee usually pays an initial, one-time franchise fee. The amount of this fee depends solely on the individual franchiser, but it generally ranges from $5,000 to $150,000. In addition to this initial franchise fee, the franchisee is expected to pay royalty fees, usually in the range of 3 to 7 percent of gross revenues. The franchisee may also be expected to pay advertising fees, which usually cover the cost of promotional materials and, if the franchise organization is large enough, regional or national advertising. A McDonald's franchise, for example, costs an initial $45,000 per store plus a monthly fee based upon the restaurant's sales performance and base rent. In addition, a new McDonald's franchisee can expect start-up costs for equipment and pre-opening expenses to range from $466,000 to $955,500. The size of the restaurant facility, area of the country, inventory, selection of kitchen equipment, signage, and style of decor and landscaping affect new restaurant costs.[29] Though the dollar amount will vary depending on the type of franchise, fees such as these are typical for all major franchisers, including Burger King, Jani-King, Athlete's Foot, Sonic, and Subway.

Franchising is not new. General Motors has used this approach since 1898, and Rexall drugstores, since 1901. Today, there are over half a million franchised establishments in the United States, with combined sales approaching $1 trillion,

EXHIBIT 13.3

Largest U.S. Franchisers

Franchiser	Type of Business	Total Units	Initial Investment
McDonald's	Fast food	Franchised units: 18,551 Company-owned units: 10,983	$408,600–$687,000
Southland (7-Eleven)	Convenience stores	Franchised units: 15,572 Company-owned units: 2,666	$83,000
Subway	Fast food	Franchised units: 18,594 Company-owned units: 0	$69,300–$191,000
Burger King	Fast food	Franchised units: 10,348 Company-owned units: 1,053	$294,000–$825,000
KFC	Fast food	Franchised units: 3,255 Company-owned units: 1,759	Not available
Pizza Hut	Pizza	Franchised units: 4,200 Company-owned units: 2,800	Not available
Tandy (Radio Shack)	Consumer electronics	Franchised units: 2,052 Company-owned units: 5,161	$60,000+
Jani-King	Janitorial cleaning	Franchised units: 9,500 Company-owned units: 32	$8,170–$74,000
Taco Bell	Fast food	Franchised units: 4,132 Company-owned units: 1,264	$200,000+
Dairy Queen	Ice cream, etc.	Franchised units: 5,969 Company-owned units: 51	$212,000–$952,750
Dunkin' Donuts	Coffee & donuts	Franchised units: 5,000+ Company-owned units: 0	$200,000–$400,000

SOURCE: http://www.franchise.org.

EXHIBIT 13.4

Sources of Franchise Information

Some Web sites where people with francising-related questions can find answers:

■ **Federal Trade Commission**

http://www.ftc.gov
Has a host of information consumers looking to buy a franchise might need. Click on the "for consumers" link and then on "Franchise & Business Opportunities." Contains information on FTC regulation as well as contact information for state regulators.

■ **North American Securities Administrators Association**

http://www.nasaa.org
The umbrella group for state securities regulators offers links to find regulators and also has links to other governmental agencies.

■ **International Franchise Association**

http://www.franchise.org
Contains information on such topics as buying a franchise and government relations. The site's FAQ section deals with some issues of franchise regulation.

■ **American Franchise Association**

http://www.franchisee.org
Offers information on legal resources, FTC regulations, and state law.

■ **American Association of Franchisees & Dealers**

http://www.aafd.org
Has information on finding a franchise lawyer.

SOURCE: *Wall Street Journal*, December 15, 2003.

or about 40 percent of all retail trade. Although franchised restaurants attract most of those dollars, hundreds of retail and service franchises, such as Alphagraphics Printshops, Supercuts, and Sylvan Learning Systems, also are thriving. Indeed, there are over 320,000 franchises in 75 industries. Industries expected to see real growth in franchising include home repair, business support services, automotive repairs, hair salons, children's services, and telecommunications.[30] Exhibit 13.3 lists some facts about some of the largest and best-known U.S. franchisers. Exhibit 13.4 lists some Web sites that provide information about franchises.

Two basic forms of franchises are used today: product and trade name franchising and business format franchising. In *product and trade name franchising*, a dealer agrees to sell certain products provided by a manufacturer or a wholesaler. This approach has been used most widely in the auto and truck, soft drink bottling, tire, and gasoline service industries. For example, a local tire retailer may hold a franchise to sell Michelin tires. Likewise, the Coca-Cola bottler in a particular area is a product and trade name franchisee licensed to bottle and sell Coca-Cola's soft drinks.

Business format franchising is an ongoing business relationship between a franchiser and a franchisee. Typically, a franchiser "sells" a franchisee the rights to use the franchiser's format or approach to doing business. This form of franchising has rapidly expanded since the 1950s through retailing, restaurant, food-service, hotel and motel, printing, and real estate franchises.

FAQs

If you want to run your own business, is it better to start your own, or buy a franchise? Find out the answer by watching the Video FAQ on Xtra!

Fast-food restaurants like McDonald's, Wendy's, and Burger King use this kind of franchising, as do other companies such as Hyatt Corporation, Unocal Corporation, and ExxonMobil Corporation. To be eligible to be a Domino's Pizza franchisee, you must have worked in a Domino's pizza store for at least one year. The company believes that after working in an existing location, you will have a better understanding of the company and its values and standards. Then potential franchisees must participate in a series of career development, franchise orientation, presentation skills, and franchise development programs.[31]

Like other retailers, franchisers are seeking new growth abroad. Hundreds of U.S. franchisers have begun international expansion and are actively looking for foreign franchisees to open new locations. KFC operates approximately 5,000 restaurants in the United States and 6,000 abroad in more than 80 countries around the world including Japan, Australia, China, Indonesia, and Saudi Arabia. An additional 1,000 overseas locations are planned for the near future. KFC's parent company attributes the franchise's success to its ability to adapt to local cultures and tastes without losing control of quality and brand image.[32] The International Franchise Association now lists over 50 national franchise organizations in countries from Argentina to Zimbabwe.

Franchisers usually allow franchisees to alter their business format slightly in foreign markets. For example, some McDonald's franchisees in Germany sell beer, and in Japan they offer food items that appeal to Japanese tastes, such as steamed dumplings, curry with rice, and roast pork cutlet burgers with melted cheese. McDonald's franchisees in India serve mutton instead of beef because most Indians are Hindu, a religion whose followers believe cows are a sacred symbol of the source of life. The menu also features rice-based Vegetable Burgers made with peas, carrots, red pepper, beans, and Indian spices as well as Vegetable McNuggets. But, in spite of menu differences, McDonald's foreign franchisees still maintain the company's standards of service and cleanliness.

REVIEW LEARNING OBJECTIVE 5

5 **Define franchising and describe its two basic forms**

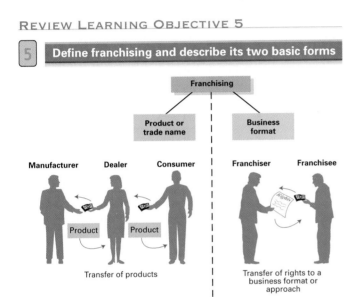

6 RETAIL MARKETING STRATEGY

List the major tasks involved in developing a retail marketing strategy

Retailers must develop marketing strategies based on overall goals and strategic plans. Retailing goals might include more traffic, higher sales of a specific item, a more upscale image, or heightened public awareness of the retail operation. The strategies that retailers use to obtain their goals might include a sale, an updated decor, or a new advertisement. The key tasks in strategic retailing are defining and selecting a target market and developing the retailing mix to successfully meet the needs of the chosen target market.

DEFINING A TARGET MARKET

The first and foremost task in developing a retail strategy is to define the target market. This process begins with market segmentation, the topic of Chapter 7. Successful retailing has always been based on knowing the customer. Sometimes retailing chains flounder when management loses sight of the customers the stores should be serving. For example, during the 1990s Gap built a retail empire by offering updated, casual classics like white shirts and khaki pants that appealed to everyone from high school through middle age. But the company began losing customers when it shifted toward trendier fashions with a limited appeal. Analysts blame the chain's problems on losing focus and touch with its customers.

When Beth McLaughlin launched a line of clothing stores, Torrid, aimed exclusively at teenaged girls sizes 12 to 26, she clearly identified her target. Her product offering was tailored to meet that target, as were her choices of location, pricing, and promotion. Torrid has expanded from six to 33 stores, with plans for another 19, as a result of McLaughlin's successful strategy.

© DOROTHY LOW PHOTOGRAPHY

EXHIBIT 13.5

The Retailing Mix

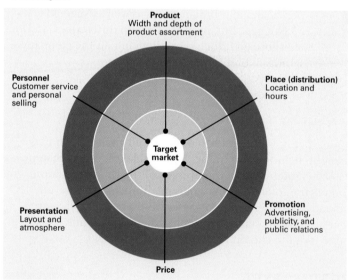

retailing mix
A combination of the six Ps—product, place, promotion, price, presentation, and personnel—to sell goods and services to the ultimate consumer.

product offering
The mix of products offered to the consumer by the retailer; also called the *product assortment* or *merchandise mix*.

Target markets in retailing are often defined by demographics, geographics, and psychographics. For instance, Bluefly.com, a discount fashion e-tailer, targets both men and women in their thirties, who have a higher-than-average income, read fashion magazines, and favor high-end designers. By understanding who its customers are, the company has been able to tailor its Web site to appeal specifically to its audience. The result is a higher sales rate than most e-tailers.[33]

Determining a target market is a prerequisite to creating the retailing mix. For example, Target's merchandising approach for sporting goods is to match its product assortment to the demographics of the local store and region. The amount of space devoted to sporting goods, as well as in-store promotions, also varies according to each store's target market. Similarly, American Eagle Outfitters offers fashionable, high-quality clothing at reasonable prices. AE is a lifestyle retailer that designs casual clothing such as jeans, pants, graphic T-shirts, outerwear, footwear, swimwear, and accessories that appeal to the 20-year-old with a hip, youthful, active attitude.[34]

CHOOSING THE RETAILING MIX

Retailers combine the elements of the retailing mix to come up with a single retailing method to attract the target market. The **retailing mix** consists of six Ps: the four Ps of the marketing mix (product, place, promotion, and price) plus presentation and personnel (see Exhibit 13.5).

The combination of the six Ps projects a store's image, which influences consumers' perceptions. Using these impressions of stores, shoppers position one store against another. A retail marketing manager must make sure that the store's positioning is compatible with the target customers' expectations. As discussed at the beginning of the chapter, retail stores can be positioned on three broad dimensions: service provided by store personnel, product assortment, and price. Management should use everything else—place, presentation, and promotion—to fine-tune the basic positioning of the store.

The Product Offering

The first element in the retailing mix is the **product offering**, also called the *product assortment* or *merchandise mix*. Retailers decide what to sell on the basis of what their target market wants to buy. They can base their decision on market research, past sales, fashion trends, customer requests, and other sources. A recent approach, called data mining, uses complex mathematical models to help retailers make better product mix decisions. Early users of the approach, such as Dillard's, Target, and Wal-Mart, are using data mining to determine which products to stock at what price, how to manage markdowns, and how to advertise to draw target customers.

Developing a product offering is essentially a question of the width and depth of the product assortment. *Width* refers to the assortment of products offered; *depth* refers to the number of different brands offered within each assortment. Price, store design, displays, and service are important to consumers in determining where to shop, but the most critical factor is merchandise selection. This reasoning also holds true for online retailers. Amazon.com, for instance, is building the world's biggest online department store so that shoppers can get whatever they want with one click on their Web browsers. Like a traditional department store or mass merchandiser, Amazon offers considerable width in its product assortment with millions of different items, including books, music, toys, videos, tools and hardware, health and beauty aids, electronics, and software. Conversely, online specialty retailers, such as 1-800-Flowers.com, gloss.com makeup, and polo.com clothing, focus on a single category of merchandise, hoping to attract loyal customers with a larger depth of products at lower prices and better customer service. Many online retailers purposely focus on single product line niches that could never garner enough foot traffic to support a traditional brick-and-mortar store. For instance, Mustardstore.com, now operated by **http://www.thebestofchicago.com**, offers hundreds of different gourmet mustards, along with information on mustard and recipes. Similarly, Fridgedoor.com claims to be the single largest stop for all things magnetic: novelty magnets, custom magnets, and magnetic supplies. It is the Web's largest refrigerator magnet retailer, with over 1,500 different types of magnets for sale.[35]

Publix

What brand name does Publix use for its private label? How extensive is the grocer's private-label product mix? Assess the growth potential for the private-label brand and propose other types of products that Publix could put under thet label.

http://www.publix.com

Online

After determining what products will satisfy target customers' desires, retailers must find sources of supply and evaluate the products. When the right products are found, the retail buyer negotiates a purchase contract. The buying function can either be performed in-house or be delegated to an outside firm. The goods must then be moved from the seller to the retailer, which means shipping, storing, and stocking the inventory. The trick is to manage the inventory by cutting prices to move slow goods and by keeping adequate supplies of hot-selling items in stock. As in all good systems, the final step is to evaluate the entire process to seek more efficient methods and eliminate problems and bottlenecks.

As margins drop and competition intensifies, retailers are becoming ever more aware of the advantages of *private brands,* or those brands that are designed and developed using the retailer's name. Because the cost of goods typically makes up between 70 and 85 percent of a retailer's expenses, eliminating intermediaries can shave costs. As a result, prices of private-label goods are typically lower than for national brands, giving customers greater value. Private-label branding is not new. For decades, Sears has fashioned its Kenmore, Craftsman, and DieHard brands into household names. Wal-Mart has several successful private-label brands such as White Cloud paper products, Spring Valley nutritional supplements, Sam's American Choice laundry detergent, EverActive alkaline batteries, and EverStart auto batteries. Its Ol' Roy dog food and Sam's American Choice garden fertilizer are now the best-selling brands in their categories.

As the world's largest retailer, Wal-Mart's foray into private labels worries many brand marketers, such as Procter & Gamble, which manufactures Tide laundry detergent. Whereas Wal-Mart was once its biggest customer, the giant retailer is transforming itself into P&G's biggest competitor with the introduction of Sam's American Choice laundry soap that sells for 25 to 30 percent lower. And while Wal-Mart's private labels may not steal significant sales away from popular brands like Tide, in the long run smaller second- and third-tier brands that don't bring consumers to the shelves may have a difficult time surviving.

Promotion Strategy

Retail promotion strategy includes advertising, public relations and publicity, and sales promotion. The goal is to help position the store in consumers' minds. Retailers design intriguing ads, stage special events, and develop promotions aimed at their target markets. Today's grand openings are a carefully orchestrated blend of advertising, merchandising, goodwill, and glitter. All the elements of an opening—press coverage, special events, media advertising, and store displays—are carefully planned. For example, when Victoria's Secret recently opened its third megastore in Dallas, the opening featured a $150 gift with a $50 purchase and free makeovers from a Victoria's Secret Fashion Show leading makeup artist. In addition, consumers received $10 gift cards that could be redeemed in the store, and Heidi Klum, an international supermodel, made an in-store appearance.

Retailers' advertising is carried out mostly at the local level. Local advertising by retailers usually provides specific information about their stores, such as location, merchandise, hours, prices, and special sales. In contrast, national retail advertising generally focuses on image. For example, Target has used its "sign of the times" advertising campaign to effectively position itself as the "chic place to buy cheap."

Target's advertising campaign also takes advantage of cooperative advertising, another popular retail advertising practice. Traditionally, marketers would pay retailers to feature their products in store mailers, or a marketer would develop a TV campaign for the product and simply tack on several retailers' names at the end. But Target's advertising makes use of a more collaborative trend in cooperative advertising by integrating products such as Tide laundry detergent, Tums antacids, or Coca-Cola into the actual campaign. Another common form of cooperative advertising involves promotion of exclusive products. For example, Target hires famous designers to develop reasonably priced product lines available exclusively at Target stores. One recent campaign featured women's clothing designer Isaac Mizrahi.

Many retailers are forgoing media advertising these days in favor of direct-mail or frequent shopper programs. Direct-mail and catalog programs are luring many retailers, which hope they will prove to be a cost-effective means of increasing brand loyalty and spending by core customers. Nordstrom, for example, mails catalogs featuring brand-name and private-brand clothing, shoes, and accessories to target the shop-at-home crowd. Home repair outlets such as Lowe's and Home Depot also use direct mail, often around holidays when people have time off to complete needed repairs. Restaurants and small retailers have successfully used frequent diner or frequent shopper programs for years. Now many retail chains, like Gap, Victoria's Secret, and Eddie Bauer, are offering frequent shopper programs with perks ranging from gift certificates to special "members only" sale prices. For example, customers with a Victoria's Secret Angel credit card are offered monthly specials on store merchandise, including items that generally are not put on sale to the public.

The Proper Location

The retailing axiom "location, location, location" has long emphasized the importance of place to the retail mix. The location decision is important first because the retailer is making a large, semipermanent commitment of resources that can reduce its future flexibility. Second, the location will affect the store's future growth and profitability.

Marketing... in Entertainment

One Store Really Is for Your Entertainment

For Your Entertainment, one of the country's leading specialty retailers of movies, music, and games, regularly invites artists to perform in its stores: FYE, Strawberries, Coconuts, Spec's Music, and Planet Music. Performers may be local favorites or national superstars like Ziggy Marley and Michael Bolton. FYE is so committed to bringing live entertainment to its customers and creating opportunities for them to meet well-known recording artists that it dedicates part of its Web site to a state-by-state touring schedule. It also allows local performers to sign up to play at its stores. Fans can request to see a local group perform at an FYE store or ask the stores to stock recordings by their local favorites. Visit FYE's Web site and check out a show near you![36]

FAQs

What should be considered when developing a strategy for retailing business? Find out the answer by watching the Video FAQ on Xtra!

Site location begins by choosing a community. Important factors to consider are the area's economic growth potential, the amount of competition, and geography. For instance, retailers like T. J. Maxx, Wal-Mart, and Toys "R" Us build stores in areas where the population is growing. Often these large retailers will build stores in new communities that are still under development. On the other hand, while population growth is an important consideration for fast-food restaurants, most also look for an area with other fast-food restaurants because being located in clusters helps to draw customers for each restaurant. Finally, for many retailers geography remains the most important factor in choosing a community. For example, Starbucks coffee looks for densely populated urban communities for its stores, Talbots looks for locations near upper-class neighborhoods, and Buckle stores look for locations in small, underserved cities.

After settling on a geographic region or community, retailers must choose a specific site. In addition to growth potential, the important factors are neighborhood socioeconomic characteristics, traffic flows, land costs, zoning regulations, and public transportation. A particular site's visibility, parking, entrance and exit locations, accessibility, and safety and security issues are other variables contributing to site selection success. Additionally, a retailer should consider how its store would fit into the surrounding environment. Retail decision makers probably would not locate a Dollar General store next door to a Neiman Marcus department store.

One final decision about location faces retailers: whether to have a freestanding unit or to become a tenant in a shopping center or mall.

Freestanding Stores An isolated, freestanding location can be used by large retailers like Wal-Mart or Target and sellers of shopping goods like furniture and cars because they are "destination" stores. **Destination stores** are stores consumers seek out and purposely plan to visit. An isolated store location may have the advantages of low site cost or rent and no nearby competitors. On the other hand, it may be hard to attract customers to a freestanding location, and no other retailers are around to share costs.

Freestanding units are increasing in popularity as retailers strive to make their stores more convenient to access, more enticing to shop, and more profitable. Freestanding sites now account for more than half of all retail construction starts in the United States as more and more retailers are deciding not to locate in pedestrian malls. Perhaps the greatest reason for developing a freestanding site is greater visibility. Retailers often feel they get lost in huge centers and malls, but freestanding units can help stores develop an identity with shoppers. The ability to grow at faster rates through freestanding buildings has also propelled the surge toward stand-alone units. Retailers like The Sports Authority, Linens N Things, Best Buy, and Bed, Bath & Beyond choose to be freestanding to achieve their expansion objectives. An aggressive expansion plan may not allow time to wait for shopping centers to be built. Similarly, drugstore chains like Walgreens and Rite-Aid have been aggressively relocating their existing mall and shopping center stores to freestanding sites, especially street corner sites for drive-through accessibility.

Shopping Centers Shopping centers began in the 1950s when the U.S. population started migrating to the suburbs. The first shopping centers were *strip centers*, typically located along busy streets. They usually included a supermarket, a variety store, and perhaps a few specialty stores. Then *community shopping centers* emerged, with one or two small department stores, more specialty stores, a couple of restaurants, and several apparel stores. These community shopping centers provided off-street parking and a broader variety of merchandise.

Regional malls offering a much wider variety of merchandise started appearing in the mid-1970s. Regional malls are either entirely enclosed or roofed to allow shopping in any weather. Most are landscaped with trees, fountains, sculptures,

destination stores
Stores that consumers purposely plan to visit.

PHOTO COURTESY OF MALL OF AMERICA

In addition to being commercial centers, shopping malls were once a hub of community social activity. Lately, however, malls have struggled to compete against newer lifestyle centers and freestanding stores. Even with 520 stores, Mall of America regularly adds rides to its entertainment section to attract shoppers.

and the like to enhance the shopping environment. They have acres of free parking. The *anchor stores* or *generator stores* (JCPenney, Sears, or major department stores) are usually located at opposite ends of the mall to create heavy foot traffic. Las Vegas's Fashion Show Mall takes the concept to the extreme. The mall has 2 million square feet of retail space and boasts over 250 stores, eight of which are anchor stores, including Neiman Marcus, Saks Fifth Avenue, Macy's, Bloomingdale Home, and Nordstrom.[37]

According to shopping center developers, *lifestyle centers* are now emerging as the newest generation of shopping centers offering time-pressed consumers a more convenient alternative to malls. These new open-air shopping centers are targeted to upper-income shoppers with an aversion for "the mall" and seek to create an atmosphere that is part neighborhood park and part urban shopping center. Lifestyle centers have upscale retail space occupied by trendy restaurants, such as PF Chang's and Chinese Bistro, and specialty retailers like Pottery Barn and Williams-Sonoma. Other attractions include expensive landscaping and convenient parking.

Locating in a community shopping center or regional mall offers several advantages. First, the facilities are designed to attract shoppers. Second, the shopping environment, anchor stores, and "village square" activities draw customers. Third, ample parking is available. Fourth, the center or mall projects a unified image. Fifth, tenants also share the expenses of the mall's common area and promotions for the whole mall. Finally, malls can target different demographic groups. Some malls are considered upscale; others are aimed at people shopping for bargains.

Locating in a shopping center or mall does have disadvantages. These include expensive leases, the chance that common promotion efforts will not attract customers to a particular store, lease restrictions on merchandise carried and hours of operation, the anchor stores' domination of the tenants' association, and the possibility of having direct competitors within the same facility. Consumers have also become more pressed for time in recent years and have decreased the number of visits and the time they spend in malls in favor of more convenient stand-alone stores and neighborhood centers. Faced with this trend, mall developers have improved the layout of many malls to make it more convenient for customers to shop. For instance, the RiverTown Crossings center in Grandville, Michigan, clusters competing stores, like Abercrombie Kids, GapKids, Gymboree, and other kids' clothing stores in one section of the mall to accommodate time-strapped parents.[38]

Retail Prices

Another important element in the retailing mix is price. Retailing's ultimate goal is to sell products to consumers, and the right price is critical in ensuring sales. Because retail prices are usually based on the cost of the merchandise, an essential part of pricing is efficient and timely buying.

Price is also a key element in a retail store's positioning strategy. Higher prices often indicate a level of quality and help reinforce the prestigious image of retailers, as they do for Lord & Taylor, Saks Fifth Avenue, Gucci, Cartier, and Neiman Marcus. On the other hand, discounters and off-price retailers, such as Target and T. J. Maxx, offer a good value for the money. There are even stores, such as Dollar Tree, where everything costs one dollar. Dollar Tree's single-price-point strategy is aimed at getting customers to make impulse purchases through what analysts call the "wow factor"—the excitement of discovering that an item costs only a dollar.

A pricing trend among American retailers that seems to be here to stay is *everyday low pricing,* or EDLP. Introduced to the retail industry by Wal-Mart, EDLP offers consumers a low price all the time rather than holding periodic sales on merchandise. Even large retail giants, like Federated Department Stores, parent of Macy's and Bloomingdale's, have phased out deep discounts and sales in favor of lower prices every day. Similarly, Gap reduced prices on denim jeans, denim shirts, socks, and other items to protect and broaden the company's share of the casual clothes market. Supermarkets such as Albertson's and Winn Dixie have also found success in EDLP.

How can a company create an atmosphere on its Web site? Visit the pages of some of your favorite retailers to see if they have been able to re-create the store atmosphere on the Internet.

Online

Presentation of the Retail Store

The presentation of a retail store helps determine the store's image and positions the retail store in consumers' minds. For instance, a retailer that wants to position itself as an upscale store would use a lavish or sophisticated presentation.

The main element of a store's presentation is its **atmosphere**, the overall impression conveyed by a store's physical layout, decor, and surroundings. The atmosphere might create a relaxed or busy feeling, a sense of luxury or of efficiency, a friendly or cold attitude, a sense of organization or of clutter, or a fun or serious mood. For example, Wolfgang Puck restaurants feature tiles in the shape of a pizza on the floors, walls, and counter tops. Urban Outfitters stores, targeted to Generation Y consumers, use raw concrete, original brick, rusted steel, and unfinished wood to convey an urban feel. Likewise, REI sporting-goods stores feature indoor rock-climbing walls, bike test trails, and rain rooms for testing outdoor gear.

More often these days retailers are adding an element of entertainment to their store atmosphere. The Nike Town store in Chicago looks more like a museum than a traditional retail store. The three-story space displays products amid life-size Michael Jordan statues and glassed-in relics like baseball legend Nolan Ryan's shoes. A History of Air exhibit explains the pockets of air on the bottom of some Nike shoes. A video theater plays Nike commercials and short films featuring Nike gear.

The layout of retail stores is a key factor in their success. Layout is planned so that all space in the store is used effectively, including aisles, fixtures, merchandise displays, and nonselling areas. Effective store layout ensures the customer's shopping ease and convenience, but it also has a powerful influence on customer traffic patterns and purchasing behavior. For instance, Kohl's is known for its unique circular store layout, which encourages customers to pass all of a store's departments to reach the checkout lanes. The stores are smaller than most department stores but have a wide aisle designed to allow plenty of room for customers and shopping carts. Each department is limited to five display racks on the main aisle. Displays are spaced widely apart and are set at varying heights so that a customer can see everything in the department, including wall displays, from the main aisle. To further enhance the store's clean crisp presentation, merchandise is displayed from light to dark, which research suggests is most pleasing to the eye. Finally, to encourage last-minute, impulse purchases, Kohl's displays low-cost items at the checkout register. The result of the store layout is a $300 sales per square foot average (sales per square foot is a standard industry measurement).[39]

Layout also includes where products are placed in the store. Many technologically advanced retailers are using a technique called *market-basket analysis* to analyze the huge amounts of data collected through their point-of-purchase scanning equipment. The analysis looks for products that are commonly purchased together to help retailers remerchandise their stores to place products in the right places. Wal-Mart uses market-basket analysis to determine where in the store to stock

atmosphere
The overall impression conveyed by a store's physical layout, decor, and surroundings.

products for customer convenience. Bananas are placed not only in the produce section but also in the cereal aisle. Kleenex tissues are in the paper-goods aisle and also mixed in with the cold medicines. Measuring spoons are in the housewares and also hanging next to Crisco shortening. During October, flashlights are with the Halloween costumes as well as in the hardware aisle.

These are the most influential factors in creating a store's atmosphere:

- *Employee type and density:* Employee type refers to an employee's general characteristics—for instance, neat, friendly, knowledgeable, or service oriented. Density is the number of employees per thousand square feet of selling space. A discounter like Kmart has a low employee density that creates a "do-it-yourself," casual atmosphere. In contrast, Neiman Marcus's density is much higher, denoting readiness to serve the customer's every whim. Too many employees and not enough customers, however, can convey an air of desperation and intimidate customers.

- *Merchandise type and density:* The type of merchandise carried and how it is displayed add to the atmosphere the retailer is trying to create. A prestigious retailer like Saks or Marshall Field's carries the best brand names and displays them in a neat, uncluttered arrangement. Discounters and off-price retailers, such as Marshall's and T. J. Maxx, may sell some well-known brands. But many carry seconds or out-of-season goods. Their merchandise is crowded into small spaces and hung on long racks by category—tops, pants, skirts, etc.—so that it almost falls into the aisles, helping create the impression that "We've got so much stuff, we're practically giving it away."

- *Fixture type and density:* Fixtures can be elegant (rich woods), trendy (chrome and smoked glass), or consist of old, beat-up tables, as in an antiques store. The fixtures should be consistent with the general atmosphere the store is trying to create. Gap creates a relaxed and uncluttered atmosphere by displaying its merchandise on tables and shelves, rather than on traditional pipe racks, allowing customers to see and touch the merchandise more easily. Adding technology as a fixture is a recent successful trend in many retail stores. For example, Apple Computer's stores offer free interactive workshops where consumers can see product demonstrations on a 10-foot diagonal screen and try new products. Customers can ask questions about their Apple products at the "genius bar."[40]

- *Sound:* Sound can be pleasant or unpleasant for a customer. Classical music at a nice Italian restaurant helps create ambience, just as country-and-western music does at a truck stop. Music can also entice customers to stay in the store longer and buy more or eat quickly and leave a table for others. For instance, rapid music tends to make people eat more, chew less, and take bigger bites whereas slow music prompts people to dine more leisurely and eat less. Retailers can tailor their musical atmosphere to their shoppers' demographics and the merchandise they're selling. Music can control the pace of the store traffic, create an image, and attract or direct the shopper's attention. For example, Harrods in London features music by live harpists, pianists, and marching bagpipers to create different atmospheres in different departments. Coffee shops are also getting into the music business as are theme restaurants like Hard Rock Cafe, Planet Hollywood, Harley-Davidson Cafe, and Rainforest Cafe, which turn eating a hamburger and fries into an experience. Au Bon Pain, Starbucks, and Victoria's Secret have all sold copies of their background music, hoping that the music will remind consumers of the feeling of being in their stores.

- *Odors:* Smell can either stimulate or detract from sales. The wonderful smell of pastries and breads entices bakery customers. Conversely, customers can be repulsed by bad odors such as cigarette smoke, musty smells, antiseptic odors, and overly powerful room deodorizers. If a grocery store pumps in the smell of baked goods, sales in that department increase threefold. Department stores have pumped in fragrances that are pleasing to their target market, and the response has been favorable. Not surprisingly, retailers are increasingly using fragrance as a key design element, as important as layout, lighting, and background music. Research suggests that people evaluate merchandise more positively, spend more time shopping, and are generally in a better mood when an agreeable odor is present. Retailers use fragrances as an extension of their retail strategy. The Rainforest Cafe, for instance, pumps fresh-flower extracts into its retail sections. Similarly, the Christmas Store at Disney World, which is open year-round, is infused with the scents of evergreen and spiced apple cider. Jordan's Furniture in Massachusetts and New Hampshire uses the scent of pine in its country-style sections to make the environment more interesting and encourage customers to linger longer.

- *Visual factors:* Colors can create a mood or focus attention and therefore are an important factor in atmosphere. Red, yellow, and orange are considered warm colors and are used when a feeling of warmth and closeness is desired. Cool colors like blue, green, and violet are used to open up closed-in places and create an air of elegance and cleanliness. For example, Starbucks Coffee uses an eggplant, golden yellow, and dark olive color combination so that customers will feel comfortable yet sophisticated. Some colors are better for display. For instance, diamonds appear most striking against black or dark blue velvet. Lighting can also have an important effect on store atmosphere. Jewelry is best displayed under high-intensity spotlights and cosmetics under more natural lighting. Many retailers have found that natural lighting, either from windows or skylights, can lead to increased sales. Outdoor lighting can also affect consumer patronage. Consumers often are afraid to shop after dark in many areas and prefer strong lighting for safety. The outdoor facade of the store also adds to its ambience and helps create favorable first impressions. For example, on the top of the roof over the door at Cup o' Joe specialty coffee shop in Lennox Town Square, Columbus, Ohio, sits a 12-foot-wide by 6-foot-tall coffee mug. The coffee shop's designers used the exaggerated storefront to call attention to its site, which would otherwise have gotten lost amid its big-box neighbors Old Navy, Target, and an AMC Theater.[41]

Personnel and Customer Service

People are a unique aspect of retailing. Most retail sales involve a customer–salesperson relationship, if only briefly. When customers shop at a grocery store, the cashiers check and bag their groceries. When customers shop at a prestigious clothier, the salesclerks may help select the styles, sizes, and colors. They may also assist in the fitting process, offer alteration services, wrap purchases, and even offer a glass of champagne. Sales personnel provide their customers with the amount of service prescribed in the retail strategy of the store. (A store's strategy should not include questionable hiring practices, however, as the "Ethics in Marketing" box explains.)

Retail salespeople serve another important selling function: They persuade shoppers to buy. They must therefore be able to persuade customers that what they are selling is what the customer needs. Salespeople are trained in two common selling techniques: trading up and suggestion selling. Trading up means persuading customers to buy a higher-priced item than they originally intended to buy. To avoid selling customers something they do not need or want, however, salespeople should take care when practicing trading-up techniques. Suggestion selling, a common practice among most retailers, seeks to broaden customers' original purchases with related items. For example, if you buy a new printer at Office Depot, the sales representative will ask if you would like to purchase paper, a USB cable, and/or extra ink cartridges. Similarly, McDonald's cashiers are trained to ask customers if they would like a hot apple pie with their hamburger and fries. Suggestion selling and trading up should always help shoppers recognize true needs rather than sell them unwanted merchandise. To learn about problems retailers sometimes have with overzealous employees, read about racial profiling by retailers in the "Ethics in Marketing" box.

Ethics in Marketing Ethics in Marketing Ethics in Marketing Ethics in Marketing Ethics in Marketing Ethics in Marketing Ethics in Mark
Ethics in Marketing Ethics in Marketing Ethics in Marketing Ethics in Marketing Ethics in Mark
ETHICS IN MARKETING Marketing Ethics in Marketing Ethics in Mark
Ethics in Marketing Ethics in Marketing Ethics in Marketing Ethics in Marketing
Ethics in Marketing

> ## DISCRIMINATION AT ABERCROMBIE & FITCH?

As pointed out in this chapter, in most cases retailers rely on their salespeople to represent the company to the customer. Therefore, to make customers feel welcome and appreciated, retailers hire salespeople who are courteous and outgoing. But what if some customers don't feel welcome? Many African Americans, Hispanics, and Asian Americans say they often feel unwelcome in retail stores and restaurants. This perception can be detrimental to a business, as a major retailer has learned.

Recently, the Mexican American Legal Defense and Educational Fund, the Asian Pacific American Legal Center, and the NAACP Legal Defense and Educational Fund filed a class-action lawsuit against Abercrombie & Fitch, accusing the retailer of employment discrimination. The Equal Employment Opportunity Commission supports the lawsuit, saying that "evidence . . . revealed that Latinos and blacks as a class were denied permanent positions, denied good assignments, and treated in an unfair manner with regard to recruitment based on race and national origin." One African American woman claims she was not hired because of her race. She says that a company representative told her "she didn't represent the image the company wanted to portray." A

Latina woman claims she worked 30 hours a week for three years, but was fired because she wasn't "American" enough. Allegedly, a corporate representative informed her manager that the store needed more people who looked like the (predominantly white) models. The suit also alleges that A&F recruits and hires a disproportionate number of white employees and that minority employees are assigned to work in nonvisible locations such as the stockroom or in overnight positions.

The suit has attracted national media attention including stories in the *Wall Street Journal* and *New York Times* and on *60 Minutes*. With at least one in five Gen Yers being Hispanic and one in three describing themselves as "non-Caucasian," such publicity can create considerable problems for A&F with its target market even if the suit is ultimately resolved in its favor.[42]

If Abercrombie & Fitch is hiring employees with an "American" look that it defines as "white," do you think this would alienate its target market? What do you think would happen to the company over time? Do you think Gen Yers would purchase a brand that they perceive as alienating their friends? What policies should A&F implement to project a more "American" workforce?

---

6 | **List the major tasks involved in developing a retail marketing strategy**

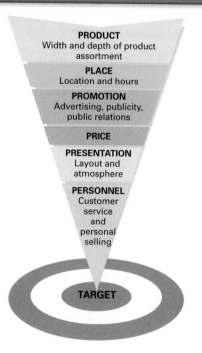

Providing great customer service is one of the most challenging elements in the retail mix because customer expectations for service are so varied. What customers expect in a department store is very different from their expectations for a discount store. Customer expectations also change. Ten years ago, shoppers wanted personal one-on-one attention. Today, most customers are happy to help themselves as long as they can easily find what they need. For example, Home Depot has always had a reputation for great customer service. Shoppers enjoy talking to the store's knowledgeable staff in the busy, do-it-yourself, warehouse atmosphere. But as store sales increased, the company began receiving customer feedback that the salespeople seemed too busy to help and the stores were too cluttered. To meet customers' new expectations, the company recently changed its store policy to free up staff time to help customers and has eliminated merchandise displays from the aisles.

Customer service is also critical for online retailers. Online shoppers expect a retailer's Web site to be easy to use, products to be available, and returns to be simple. Therefore, customer-friendly retailers like Bluefly.com design their sites to give their customers the information they need such as what's new and what's on sale. Other companies like Amazon.com and LandsEnd.com offer product recommendations and personal shoppers. Many on-line retailers have also begun including a return envelope with orders to make returns easier for the customer.

7 NEW DEVELOPMENTS IN RETAILING

Describe new developments in retailing

In an effort to better serve their customers and attract new ones, retailers are constantly adopting new strategies. Two recent developments are interactivity and m-commerce.

INTERACTIVITY

Adding interactivity to the retail environment is one of the most popular strategies in retailing in the past few years. Small retailers as well as national chains are using interactivity in stores to differentiate themselves from the competition. For some time, retailers have used "entertainment" retailing in the form of playing music, showing videos, hosting special events, and sponsoring guest appearances, but the new interactive trend gets customers involved rather than just catching their eye. For example, Central Market food stores sell mostly organic, natural, whole foods. To get customers involved in the process, Central Market allows them to weigh, price, and bag their own fruits and vegetables. It also offers the typical grocery store samples, but involves customers by offering preparation details.

M-COMMERCE

M-commerce (mobile e-commerce) enables consumers using wireless mobile devices to connect to the Internet and shop. M-commerce enjoyed early success overseas, but recently has been gaining acceptance and popularity in the United States. Essentially, m-commerce goes beyond text message advertisements to allow consumers to purchase goods and services using wireless mobile devices, such as mobile telephones, pagers, personal digital assistants (PDAs), and handheld computers. For example, Coca-Cola drinkers in Europe just dial a phone number on their mobile device, and the machine will signal them to select a drink; the transaction appears on the next phone bill. M-commerce users adopt the new technology because it saves time and offers more convenience in a greater number of locations. One study of m-commerce users who use Web-enabled devices to conduct transactions found that they consider relevant content, easy site navigation, and mobile device compatibility to be very important.[43]

© DAVID SAMUEL ROBBINS/CORBIS

Retailers use the physical space of the store to entice customers to buy merchandise. REI encourages customers to try out the rock-climbing wall at its flagship store in Seattle, Washington.

REVIEW LEARNING OBJECTIVE 7

7 Describe new developments in retailing

Interactivity gets consumers involved in retail experience.

M-commerce is purchasing goods through mobile devices.

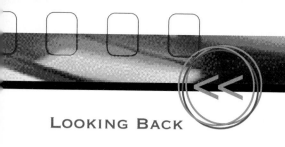

LOOKING BACK

Think back to the opening story about Krispy Kreme's phenomenal success as a doughnut retailer. The chain's retailing strategy, which combines affordable, tasty, high-quality doughnuts at a low price with a "doughnut theater" in-store entertainment concept, has led to an almost cult-like following among its most loyal consumers. All elements in Krispy Kreme's retailing mix, from product assortment to pricing, customer service, atmosphere, and location, must be carefully considered to provide its customers with the products and experience they desire.

This is no easy feat for retailers, but discovering the right combination often means the difference between success and failure. To maintain its success, Krispy Kreme will need to keep adjusting its mix as the marketing environment changes.

USE IT NOW

STUDY FRANCHISE OPPORTUNITIES

Franchising offers an alternative to starting a business on your own. But which franchise is a good match for your interests and skills? Narrow the field of the thousands of different franchise opportunities by visiting the Franchise Handbook Online at **http://www.franchise1.com**. There you will find articles with checklists to help you thoroughly research a franchise and its industry, as well as a directory of franchise opportunities. Armed with this information, you can develop a questionnaire to evaluate a prospective franchise. Also visit the International Franchise Association, a Washington, D.C., trade group, at **http://www.franchise.org** to find more information about franchising and learn if it's right for you.

STOP JUNK MAIL

If you are upset about junk mail, contact the Direct Marketing Association and have your name removed from mailing lists. The e-mail address is **http://www.the-dma.org.** You can also join an umbrella organization dedicated to stopping the flood of junk e-mail, intrusive telemarketing calls, and junk mail.

REVIEW AND APPLICATIONS

1 **Discuss the importance of retailing in the U.S. economy.** Retailing plays a vital role in the U.S. economy for two main reasons. First, retail businesses contribute to our high standard of living by providing a vast number and diversity of goods and services. Second, retailing employs a large part of the U.S. working population—over 20 million people.

1.1 **INFOTRAC** COLLEGE EDITION In order to fully appreciate the role retailing plays in the U.S. economy, it may be helpful to review a selection of press articles related to the retailing industry. Using InfoTrac (**http://www.infotrac-college.com**), run a keyword search for articles pertaining to retailing. Read a selection of articles, and report your findings to the class.

2 **Explain the dimensions by which retailers can be classified.** Many different kinds of retailers exist. A retail establishment can be classified according to its ownership, level of service, product assortment, and price. On the basis of ownership, retailers can be broadly differentiated as independent retailers, chain stores, or franchise outlets. The level of service retailers provide can be classified along a continuum of high to low. Retailers also classify themselves by the breadth and depth of their product assortments; some retailers have concentrated product assortments, whereas others have extensive product assortments. Last, general price levels also classify a store, from discounters offering low prices to exclusive specialty stores where high prices are the norm. Retailers use these latter three variables to position themselves in the marketplace.

2.1 Form a team of three classmates to identify different retail stores in your city where pet supplies are sold. Include nonstore forms of retailing, such as catalogs, the Internet, or the local veterinarian. Team members should divide up and visit all the different retailing outlets for pet supplies. Prepare a report describing the differences in brands and products sold at each of the retailing formats and the differences in store characteristics and service levels. For example, which brands are sold via mass merchandiser, independent specialty store, or other venue? Suggest why different products and brands are distributed through different types of stores.

2.2 Review the "Marketing in Entertainment" box on For Your Entertainment. What kind of retailer is FYE? Make a list of other entertainment retailers, and then classify them according to the dimensions discussed in the chapter. Do any trends emerge? What conclusions can you draw about entertainment and retailing, if any?

3 **Describe the major types of retail operations.** The major types of retail stores are department stores, specialty retailers, supermarkets, drugstores, convenience stores, discount stores, and restaurants. Department stores carry a wide assortment of shopping and specialty goods, are organized into relatively independent departments, and offset higher prices by emphasizing customer service and decor. Specialty retailers typically carry a narrower but deeper assortment of merchandise, emphasizing distinctive products and a high level of customer service. Supermarkets are large self-service retailers that offer a wide variety of food products and some nonfood items. Drugstores are retail formats that sell mostly prescription and over-the-counter medications, health and beauty aids, cosmetics, and specialty items. Convenience stores carry a limited line of high-turnover convenience goods. Discount stores offer low-priced general merchandise and consist of four types: full-line discounters, specialty discount retailers, warehouse clubs, and off-price retailers. Finally, restaurants straddle the line between the retailing and services industries; although restaurants sell a product, food and drink, to final consumers, they can also be considered service marketers because they provide consumers with the service of preparing food and providing table service.

3.1 Discuss the possible marketing implications of the recent trend toward supercenters, which combine a supermarket and a full-line discount store.

3.2 Explain the function of warehouse clubs. Why are they classified as both wholesalers and retailers?

4 **Discuss nonstore retailing techniques.** Nonstore retailing, which is shopping outside a store setting, has three major categories. Automatic vending uses machines to offer products for sale. In direct retailing, the sales transaction occurs in a home setting, typically through door-to-door sales or party plan selling. Direct marketing refers to the techniques used to get consumers to buy from their homes or place of business. Those techniques include direct mail, catalogs and mail order, telemarketing, and electronic retailing, such as home shopping channels and online retailing using the Internet.

4.1 Go to the Gift Shop at online wine retailer Wine.com's Web site at **http://www.wine.com/**. How does this site help shoppers select gifts?

4.2 How much does the most powerful computer with the fastest modem, most memory, largest monitor, biggest hard drive, and all the available peripherals cost at **http://www.dell.com**? Then visit a store like Best Buy or Circuit City and price a comparable computer. How can you explain any price differences between the two retail operations? Explain any differences in features that you encountered. What conclusions can you draw from your research?

4.3 Why should retailers market their printed catalogs online? Look at Web site **http://www.catalogsite.com**.

Define franchising and describe its two basic forms. Franchising is a continuing relationship in which a franchiser grants to a franchisee the business rights to operate or to sell a product. Modern franchising takes two basic forms. In product and trade name franchising, a dealer agrees to buy or sell certain products or product lines from a particular manufacturer or wholesaler. Business format franchising is an ongoing business relationship in which a franchisee uses a franchiser's name, format, or method of business in return for several types of fees.

5.1   What advantages does franchising provide to franchisers as well as franchisees?

List the major tasks involved in developing a retail marketing strategy. Retail management begins with defining the target market, typically on the basis of demographic, geographic, or psychographic characteristics. After determining the target market, retail managers must develop the six variables of the retailing mix: product, promotion, place, price, presentation, and personnel.

6.1   Identify a successful retail business in your community. What marketing strategies have led to its success?

6.2    You want to convince your boss, the owner of a retail store, of the importance of store atmosphere. Write a memo citing specific examples of how store atmosphere affects your own shopping behavior.

Describe new developments in retailing. Two major trends are evident in retailing today. First, adding interactivity to the retail environment is one of the most popular strategies in retailing in recent years. Small retailers as well as national chains are using interactivity to involve customers and set themselves apart from the competition. Second, m-commerce (mobile e-commerce) is gaining in popularity. M-commerce enables consumers to purchase goods and services using wireless mobile devices, such as mobile telephones, pagers, PDAs, and handheld computers.

7.1   WRITING   INFOTRAC COLLEGE EDITION   You have been asked to write a brief article about the way m-commerce is influencing the future of retailing. Write the outline for your article. Once you have written your outline, use InfoTrac (**http://www.infrotrac-college.com**) to locate several articles on m-commerce. Read a sampling and draft your article.

TERMS

atmosphere 459
automatic vending 445
buyer 438
category killers 443
chain stores 437
convenience store 441
department store 438
destination stores 457
direct marketing (direct-response marketing) 447
direct retailing 446
discount store 441

drugstore 441
factory outlet 444
franchise 437
franchisee 451
franchiser 451
full-line discount store 442
gross margin 438
independent retailers 437
mass merchandising 442
nonstore retailing 445
off-price retailer 444
online retailing 449

product offering 454
retailing 436
retailing mix 454
scrambled merchandising 440
specialty discount store 443
specialty store 439
supercenter 442
supermarket 439
telemarketing 448
warehouse membership clubs 443

APPLICATION EXERCISE

After reading the chapter, you can see that differences in retailing are the result of strategy. To better understand the relationship between strategic retailing factors and consumer perceptions, you can conduct a simple observation exercise. First, pick a product to shop for, and then identify two stores where you have *never* shopped as places to look for your product. The two stores must be different types of retailers. For example, you can shop for a video game at Toys "R" Us (category killer) and at Hollywood Video (specialty retailer). Once you have identified what you are looking for and where you're going to look, visit each store and record your observations of specific strategic retailing factors.[44]

Activities

1. Go through each store and make careful observations on the following:

    *   *Location:* Where is each store? How congested is the area of town where each store is located? What influence does the neighborhood have on your impression of the store? Would you travel to this store under normal circumstances to shop? Write a detailed paragraph on the location of each store.
    *   *Exterior atmosphere:* How convenient is parking (is there even parking?)? Is parking adequate? Other issues about parking (cleanliness and size of the lot, size of spaces, well-lit, etc.)? What kinds of stores are around the store you are visiting? Do you think being located next to them increases traffic at your store? Are direct competitors nearby? Is the building modern, historic, attractive, clean, and appealing? Is the entrance inviting to shoppers?
    *   *Interior atmosphere:* Compare the following attributes at each store: aisle width; lighting; number of customers; noise (background music, loudspeakers, etc.); store layout; signage; accessibility of the cashier; number of products available (depth and width of assortment); ability to inspect the product before purchase; quality of the fixtures (shelves, lights, etc.); availability of salespeople and their knowledge about the product; willingness of salespeople to help.
    *   *Product:* Is your product available? If not, is there a satisfactory substitute? What is your perception of the quality of goods offered? Why do you think as you do?
    *   *Price:* What is the price of the product/brand at this store? Is the price prominently marked? How do the prices at the two stores compare? How does the price compare to your expectations?

2. From which of these two stores would you actually purchase the item? Why, specifically? List the factors that played a role in your decision. Which factor is most important to you? If you would not purchase the item at either store, why not?

3. What are the three most important differences you observed between the stores?

4. Using the results of your research, write a short paper that outlines your observations. Conclude your paper with your answers to questions 2 and 3.

ETHICS EXERCISE

A–Z Grocery Company is well known for offering quality grocery products at the lowest prices in the market. When the company applied for a zoning change to build a new store in a middle-class neighborhood, several members of the city council objected because the company has no stores in low-income neighborhoods, where they argue the low prices are needed most. The company contends that it cannot operate profitably in these neighborhoods because of higher security and operating costs.

Questions

1. Should low-cost retailers be required to locate near low-income customers? Why or why not?

2. Does the AMA Code of Ethics address this issue? Go to **http://www.marketingpower.com** and review the code. Then, write a brief paragraph on how the AMA Code of Ethics relates to retailing locations.

CAREER EXERCISE

As you might expect, resources for finding a retail job are numerous. In fact, retail jobs may be well represented in your local newspaper classifieds. The following Web resources give you access to retail job information across the country:

- **http://www.allretailjobs.com**
- **http://www.retailjobmart.com**
- **http://www.retailjobs.com**
- **http://www.retail-recruiter.com**
- **http://www.retailnetwork.com**

Different sites may feature different retailers, so you may want to visit several sites for better coverage of openings in the industry as a whole. Another good resource for information on the industry is the National Retail Federation (**http://www.nrf.com**). Although the site doesn't provide job listings, it does give ample information on the status of the industry so that you are better prepared to make wise selections from the job listings you locate at other sites and through other media.

Activities

1. Most students have worked in some kind of retail job. If you haven't, but want to, then research opportunities with companies that have established and thorough initiation periods. One example is Gap, which has a 60-day training period—even the current CEO spent his first 60 days folding inventory, straightening dressing rooms, and helping customers. The detailed training period will give you a good foundation for understanding retailing and help you as you move up in your retailing career.

2. If you can't find a job at a bigger retailer with a well-established training program, consider applying for an entry-level job at a small retailer in your area. Due to the nature of small businesses, you will most likely have a wide range of responsibilities (rather than just being, say, a cashier at a big box retailer). This may help you decide if a longer career in retailing is for you.

ENTREPRENEURSHIP CASE

© 2004 BEST BUY PHOTOGRAPHER/MOSHE BRAKHA

BEST BUY GIVES A WHOLE NEW MEANING TO "THOUSANDS OF POSSIBILITIES. GET YOURS."

The promise of the long awaited digital revolution has finally been fulfilled. Flat-panel televisions, MP3 players, wireless laptops, cell phones with Internet browsing capability, wirelessly networked computing devices for the home, digitally controlled home appliances, and more are no longer the toys of a future generation. They are here today, and Best Buy wants to sell them—all of them—to anyone with the money to burn on such luxury items. In addition to all the gee-whiz electronic merchandise, the company still sells coffee makers, vacuum cleaners, and washing machines, albeit slightly more expensive ones than before.

The new digital gadgets, however, are fast crossing the threshold from expensive luxury items to affordable common electronics. The upside is that more customers are able to buy such products; the downside is the negative pressure put on prices and revenues. If any retailer can find a way to survive and turn a profit in the fiercely competitive electronics and home appliance industry, it's Best Buy. Twenty years ago, when it operated under the name Sound of Music, a tornado ripped through its flagship store, and the company held a "best buy" sale to liquidate its merchandise and cover the costs of repairs. The success of the sale was the impetus for the name change to Best Buy, and the opening of its first superstore in 1984 marked the beginning of "big box" retailing as it is known today. Nine years later, the new-look national chain surpassed Circuit City as the number one retailer in the segment.

Best Buy's stores offer a dizzying array of products (its stores have nearly 25,000 separate items) at affordable prices. Usually located in a small- or medium-sized outdoor shopping centers with other "big box" retailers, an average 40,000-square-foot Best Buy store is large enough to hold ample stock of all available items while still comfortably accommodating customers. Bright lights, concrete floors, wide and easily navigated aisles, oversize shopping carts, and a helpful but unobtrusive staff dressed in blue shirts and khaki pants have put Best Buy at the head of the retail class when it comes to customer satisfaction surveys. Best Buy's television commercials, which feature the tag line, "Thousands of Possibilities. Get Yours," communicate an accurate picture of the customer experience. Inside every Best Buy store, a canned deejay plays the latest popular music over the public address system; recently released DVDs play on big-screen TVs; and personal computers, video game modules, home stereo systems, and more are turned on and available for customers to tinker with.

The ability to connect with its customers has brought Best Buy a 16 percent share of the $130 billion North American market for electronics and related devices. It now operates 600 stores in the United States and plans to open 60 or so new stores each year for the near future. Competition, however, is stiffening. Best Buy's main threat now comes from discount super-store Wal-Mart, whose share of the market has climbed rapidly to just 5 percentage points behind Best Buy's. That development, combined with a downward pressure on prices for electronic devices similar to the pressures in the PC industry, has forced Best Buy to explore new and more profitable ways of meeting the needs of the market.

The firm's latest initiatives include selling more upscale and higher margin merchandise, hiring highly trained sales "consultants" to assist with more complex and expensive purchases, staying open for longer hours on weekends, outsourcing lower end items to China, and selling installation and connection services for its products. Those who prefer to shop in their pajamas can check out the possibilities online at BestBuy.com. Best Buy is also selling home entertainment packages direct to upscale homebuilders in cities such as Minneapolis, Dallas, and Las Vegas. For a nominal surcharge as low as $1,000, Best Buy will install, connect, and integrate the system while the house is being constructed, leaving the home's new owner to sit back and enjoy the show.[46]

Questions

1. What type of retailer is Best Buy?

2. Describe the six components of Best Buy's retailing mix. Is there anything you would change? Explain.

3. Do you agree with the strategy Best Buy has adopted to respond to its competition? Why or why not?

WATCH IT

SmallBusinessSchool ▣
the Series on PBS stations and the Web

FEATURE PRESENTATION

The Art Store

To give you insight into Chapter 13, Small Business School introduces you to George Granoff and his company, The Art Store. The Art Store is a small chain of stores that sells art supplies. Its locations in New York City, Berkeley, Pasadena, Oakland, and San Diego stock, on average, 17,000 items and rarely go out of stock in a single item. When George bought the business, its sales were slumping. Now, armed with a unique warehouse format, Granoff can showcase his incredible product assortment. Employees are trained to help fellow artists pinpoint exactly what their needs are, and a well-managed targeted mailing campaign brings in new and repeat customers. All of these marketing efforts have made the store an unmitigated success. The video explains the thinking behind The Art Store's retailing mix and reveals how the owner plans to continue growing the business.

What to Watch for and Ask Yourself

1. What was the key change George Granoff made after acquiring The Art Store?

2. To paraphrase, the owner says that in order to be successful, a retailer has to excel in at least two of the following three areas: 1) assortment, 2) price, and 3) service. In which two areas has The Art Store concentrated its efforts?

3. What type of retail operation is The Art Store?

4. Discuss the product, presentation and personnel strategies of The Art Store.

ENCORE PRESENTATION

Man's Favorite Sport

Now that you understand retailing, you can appreciate the changes that retailing has experienced over the years. As an encore to your study, watch the film clip from *Man's Favorite Sport*, starring Rock Hudson as a salesman (Roger Willoughby) at Abercrombie & Fitch. In this scene, Roger enters his department and greets Major Phipps (Roscoe Karns), who is looking for a new fly rod to use in a local fishing competition. The scene shows an Abercrombie & Fitch of the 1960's, when the store was an upscale outdoor sporting-goods retailer, much like Orvis, Cabelas, and Galyan's. Now, however, the retailing mix for Abercrombie & Fitch is quite different. If you are unfamiliar with the 21st century Abercrombie & Fitch, visit the company's Web site at **http://www.abercrombie.com**. How has the company changed its target market and its retailing mix? Even though the market and strategy have changed, is Abercrombie & Fitch the same type of retailer today as it was in the 1960's? Explain.

If you're having trouble with the concepts in this chapter, consider using some of the following study resources. You can review the videos, or test yourself with materials designed for all kinds of learning styles.

☑ **Xtra! (http://lambxtra.swlearning.com)**

- ☑ Quiz
- ☑ Feature Videos
- ☑ Encore Videos
- ☑ FAQ Videos
- ☑ Exhibit Worksheets
- ☑ Marketing Plan Worksheets
- ☐ Content

☑ **http://lamb.swlearning.com**

- ☑ Quiz
- ☑ PowerPoint slides
- ☑ Marketing News
- ☑ Review Exercises
- ☑ Links
- ☑ Marketing Plan Contest
- ☑ Career Exercise
- ☑ Use It Now

☑ **Study guide**

- ☑ Outline
- ☑ Vocab Review
- ☑ Test Questions
- ☑ Marketing Scenario

Need More? Here's a tip. Make up a crossword puzzle using the key terms in this chapter. Writing the clues will help you remember the definition and the context of each concept. Make photocopies for exam time and for your study group.

MARKETING MISCUE

Comic Book Distribution Methods Define (and Shrink) Audience

The big question for publishers of comic books is "Why aren't kids reading comic books?" The answer to this question, as well as the reason for the publishers' depressed sales, may lie at the feet of these same publishing houses. The problem is that they have failed to make their comic books accessible to youth. The distribution system they created omitted a direct channel to the younger audience.

The major players in the comic book publishing industry are as follows:

- Marvel Enterprises, Inc. (with Spider-Man, X-Men, Hulk).
- DC Comics (with Superman, Batman, Orion).
- Image Comics (with Spawn, Powers, Normalman).
- Dark Horse (with Star Wars, Conan, Buffy the Vampire Slayer).
- Crossgen (with Sojourn, Ruse, Way of the Rat).

These publishers rely upon the world's largest distributor of English-language comic books, Diamond Comic Distributors, to get comic books into readers' hands. Founded in 1982 by Steve Geppi, Diamond has a network of affiliated companies that provide a wide variety of entertainment opportunities. These affiliates include Alliance Game Distributors, Diamond Book Distributors, Diamond International Galleries, Diamond Select Toys & Collectibles, Diamond UK, E. Gerber Products LLC, Game Trade Magazine, and Gemstone Publishing.

A comic book enters the retail marketplace through a rather straightforward distribution process, with the ordering occurring significantly ahead of the consumer purchase. Basically, the retailer is solicited with previews three months prior to shipping, orders are due two months prior to shipping, and comic book publishers print only to fulfill these orders (which are nonreturnable and nonrefundable).

Comic books are no longer available at general merchandise stores or even bookstores. Instead, comic books are now found only in specialty comic shops. Herein lies the heart of the distribution problem. These shops tend to be occupied by adolescent and teenage boys. Thus, younger children, teenage girls, and adult shoppers may tend to avoid browsing there. If comic books are available only in comic shops, then several potential target markets are not being accessed via any distribution methods. The snowball effect is that younger potential readers are never introduced to comic books and, thus, never become comic book fans. The female and adult shoppers who might have had an interest in comic books turn to other reading genres.

This endless, downward spiraling distribution cycle has resulted in sales of individual issues of comic books dropping dramatically in recent decades. In the mid-1990s, an individual issue might have a circulation of around 1 million copies. By the mid-2000s, an individual issue might have a circulation of only 100,000. If kids do not know where to get comic books, they do not buy them. Once kids do not buy comic books, they do not become adult collectors. If the comic book industry does not have readers and collectors, then it will cease to be an industry.

The comic book industry has inadvertently built a multitude of distribution barriers into its readership program. By relying upon one major distributor, publishers and retailers have shifted the balance of power to this distributor. Adding to this power imbalance, the number of comic specialty shops has diminished over time. Thus, even this limited channel has become less available. The remaining comic specialty shops tend to be widely dispersed geographically, making it difficult for new, or even devoted, readers to obtain a comic book.

The decline in comic book readership is attributed to a lack of availability. Industry experts suggest that a change in distribution is the only way to see a change in readership. Something has to be done if the comic book industry is to survive in today's marketplace; if the system has to be changed, it needs to be done quickly before the decline in readership dips too much further.[1]

Questions

1. Describe the channel of distribution for comic books.

2. How can comic book publishers use the channel of distribution to rejuvenate the industry?

CRITICAL THINKING CASE

Hollywood Refuses easy Cinema's Distributions Request

Six months after easyCinema opened for business, movie giants were still refusing its requests to run new releases. Since major movie studios use distribution fees to offset production costs, easyCinema's cheap early-bird ticket prices would contribute very little to a studio's bottom line. Can easyCinema survive in an industry in which suppliers (Hollywood production studios) have all of the power?

The "Easy" Moniker

EasyCinema is one of many businesses owned by Stelios Haji-Ioannou, a self-styled entrepreneur who operates a no-frills business model. The heart of this business model is easyGroup's no-frills, demand-led pricing; that is, the price of a service depends on demand, resulting in lower prices at off-peak times or for advance purchases.

Other businesses in the easyGroup include easyCar, easyInternetCafe, easyBus, easyPizza, easyDorm, easyCruise, and easyJet. EasyJet is the only easyGroup business to have achieved success. The easyCar and easyInternetCafe businesses have run into numerous management problems. The company plans to implement its demand-led pricing with easyPizza (pizza delivery), easyDorm (budget hotel company), and easyBus (inter-city coach operation) in 2004. Plans for easyCruise are in the works for 2005.

Although Haji-Ioannou is no longer on easyJet's board, he owns 20 percent of the company's shares and uses money from this cash cow to fund his other no-frills ideas. His objective is to use easyGroup, a private holding company, as an incubator for new distribution ideas. He believes that there are many distribution opportunities for his demand management model.

easyCinema

In the summer of 2003, Haji-Ioannou launched easyCinema. Located in Milton Keynes, in the United Kingdom, this no-frills, ten-screen cinema does not have a box office or a food counter. Moviegoers book movie tickets online, with prices controlled by the yield management techniques (that is, prices vary with demand) that made easyJet so successful. A customer who makes reservations well in advance could pay as little as 20 pence (about 40 cents) for a seat. Seat prices can rise as high as 3.5 pounds (about $6.50), however, as the cinema fills.

With its bring-your-own food concept (and what moviegoer likes paying the high prices for popcorn and soda?) and cheap seats, one has to wonder why easyCinema is floundering. Unfortunately, easyCinema failed to take into account the balance of power in its business model. Movie theaters can show only movies that are provided by the studios. If a Hollywood distributor does not think that a cinema chain is first rate, it does not have to license first-run movies to that chain. EasyCinema's problem is that U.S. film distributors have refused to allow it to show new releases.

After six months, easyCinema had shown only one new release, *Down with Love*. This movie, produced by 20th Century Fox and starring Ewan McGregor and Renee Zellweger, was pegged as a less-than-successful romantic comedy. Without first-run movies, the easyCinema in Milton Keynes has been operating at only about 20 percent of its seating capacity. Haji-Ioannou offered Hollywood studios a flat fee for the rights to show newly released films. Hollywood, however, traditionally receives its payment in royalties or a percentage of attendance revenue. Thus, a highly successful movie can recoup its production costs very quickly.

By the end of 2003, Haji-Ioannou had decided to open a second multiplex cinema in a central London suburb. Though Milton Keynes was operating at a loss, he felt that the customer side of the relationship was working and that customers enjoyed using easyCinema's Web-based, yield management system. He was convinced that it was the distributor side of the relationship that was causing problems for easyCinema. To solve the problem, he placed an advertisement in *Variety*, the entertainment industry magazine, announcing that easyCinema was seeking a CEO who could help convince movie distributors to license first-run movies to the chain. The ad said the starting salary was $500,000.

This could prove to be a challenging task for any new CEO, particularly since movie distributors have worked hard in the past to build strong relationships with cinema groups in Britain. Both Odeon and United Cinemas International are big cinema companies in the United Kingdom. Why would Hollywood movie distributors risk these strong relationships by opening the market to a new, upstart rival?[2]

Questions

1. Describe the balance of power in the movie distribution marketplace.

2. What is the relationship between easyCinema's yield management system and movie distributors?

3. How is the yield management system different from other online ticket ordering systems?

CROSS-FUNCTIONAL SOLUTIONS

Questions

1. What are the popular advanced manufacturing systems, and how do they interact with marketing?

   Advanced manufacturing systems include just-in-time (JIT) and electronic data interchange (EDI).
   Advanced manufacturing systems allow a firm to compete on both time and quality. The systems allow for a quicker response to customers' demands and shorten the new-product production cycle. The systems allow firms to produce a large variety of high-quality products in a reduced cycle time. Thus, such systems result in more timely deliveries.

2. What is an enterprise-wide integrated distribution system? What is marketing's role in such a system?

   Simply put, an enterprise-wide integrated distribution system brings together all aspects of the business in order to get products to customers in a timely manner. Such a system generally relies heavily upon automated exchanges among various channel parties. The marketing function's role in such a system is varied and may include channel selection strategies, automatic customer data transmission to the shop floor, wireless tracking of a customer's order, and/or customer satisfaction measures.

3. How do production and delivery happen simultaneously in the service sector? What other functional areas are important partners in the service arena?

   A unique characteristic of a service is its inseparability; that is, services are generally sold, produced, and consumed at the same time. Consumers must be present during the production and delivery of a service. For example, a consumer receives a haircut at the same time as the haircut is being produced. This inseparability means that the service cannot be produced in one location and delivered at another location. Thus, the quality of the service depends upon the quality of the employee, making human resources a very important cross-functional partner.

Suggested Readings

Alexander E. Ellinger, "Improving Marketing/Logistics Cross-Functional Collaborations in the Supply Chain," *Industrial Marketing Management*, January 2000, 85–96.

John J. Lee, Jr., *The Producer's Business Handbook* (Oxford: UK: Elsevier, 2000).

INTEGRATING MARKETING COMMUNICATIONS FOR INCREASED FIRM VALUE

When purchasing a product or service, a customer does not think in terms of advertising, sales promotion, public relations, and personal selling; nor does he or she think in terms of marketing, manufacturing, accounting, finance, research and development, and human resources. Rather, the product or service received by the customer is the sum of all of the internal processes, just as the communications message is the sum of all of the communications vehicles available to the firm. It is the company's responsibility to make certain that the product/service received by the customer is consistent with the message that the customer has received via the firm's integrated marketing communications.

For example, World Wrestling Entertainment, Inc. (WWE) was experiencing dwindling live audiences, declining TV ratings, and a slew of lackluster talent. The WWE's turnaround was due to a change in its production strategy (dividing shows into two separate entities), the acquisition of a large library of wrestling tapes, and considerable cost-cutting efforts. While these behind-the-scenes movies were being made, the WWE was using its integrated marketing communications efforts to create positive "buzz" about its future. The average consumer was unaware of the internal changes that were making this comeback possible. Nonetheless, it was the interactions among various functional areas that led to the organization's improved ratings and stronger advertising revenue.

Product quality is an issue at the heart of a firm's operational processes, and the WWE was working hard to boost its product quality in terms of talent and offerings. Marketers love to tout a product's superior quality when communicating with potential customers. When a company's communications strategy focuses on promoting quality features, pressure is placed on R&D, manufacturing, and human resources to deliver on quality. Unfortunately, what a scientist or an engineer in manufacturing or R&D perceives as quality may not be perceived the same way by the customer. Companies that offer wireless communications technology, for example, must deal with these differences in perception of quality. Many purchasers of a wireless router for a video game system view quality in terms of ease of home installation. Within the organization, however, quality may be viewed in terms of the reliability of wireless transmission.

If a firm's communications program entices the consumer to try a product or service, the product or service must then be consistent with the consumer's expectations of quality. In the wireless router example, consumers need only look at the package to read how easy it is to hook up the router and begin playing games online. Unfortunately, the number of telephone calls to technical support suggests that the packaging communication made the installation appear easier than the average consumer's experience.

With more and more products requiring technical support just for installation and use, R&D engineers and manufacturing specialists can no longer work only within their limited domains. Many firms are now insisting that R&D and manufacturing employees talk directly with customers. Not surprisingly, such an external emphasis is in direct contrast with the technical orientation of R&D and manufacturing employees. Studies have shown that these employees are inherently more introverted than their marketing counterparts.

Addressing this introverted-extroverted dichotomy, firms such as Motorola and Intuit expect their engineers to go on sales calls, as well as provide telephone technical support. These engineers may visit customers with a marketing person as part of a sales call or separately to watch the customer use the product. These companies have found that the best way to develop and manufacture innovative, cutting-edge products is to have the people who work directly with the product also work closely with the end user.

Companies should also include salespeople on cross-functional new-product development teams. Salespeople are out in the field where they see how customers use the company's products on a daily basis and hear what their preferences are. Thus, salespeople can bring the voice of the customer into the firm. Additionally, salespeople are great sources of competitive intelligence as they are often the first to hear (from a customer) about a competitor's new product.

Personal selling is a component of integrated marketing communications where considerable interaction among functions has been occurring and where expenses tend to be viewed as investments since human capital is involved. It is no longer sufficient for a salesperson to have good personal interaction skills to be successful. Now, salespeople have to possess intimate knowledge of the products they present to potential consumers. For example, a salesperson for South-Western College Publishing has to understand the topics covered in a particular text in order to talk knowledgeably to professors in the area.

The sales area is also beginning to work closely with finance, accounting, and human resources with regard to compensation systems. Firms are beginning to move from sales objectives (volume and/or revenue) to financial objectives (profit). By linking sales commissions to profit-related objectives, firms stress the importance of understanding the firm's margin rather than focusing solely upon product revenue. While finance and accounting will generally be focused on the profit aspect of the salesperson's objectives, human resources will have to work closely with the salesperson to develop the most appropriate compensation system for the types of accounts in the salesperson's territory. Additionally, the human resources staff is trained to help the salesperson clarify individual goals for responsibilities and desired accomplishments that will be consistent with company-wide strategic goals. In today's business environment of teamwork and cross-selling, the human resources department may also be asked to help interview and train potential sales personnel.

Unfortunately, advertising and other promotional efforts still tend to be a source of friction between marketing and financial managers. Oddly, advertising and promotional expenditures are generally viewed as cost elements rather than investments in the product or brand. Marketers view these expenditures as investments in building the business, much as companies invest in personnel in order to have a well-managed organization. Customer satisfaction and repeat business depend upon constant maintenance by the marketing department. In contrast, accountants often view advertising and promotional expenses as variable costs. Unfortunately, when viewed as variable costs, advertising expenses are tied directly to sales increases and decreases, so marketing budgets are often cut when they are needed most.

As a global brand, Coca-Cola is attempting to change this view of promotional efforts. The company has now moved into experiential promotion with its Coke Red Lounge. Located in malls, the lounge was invented as a gathering place for mall rats, providing a way for Coke to reach this youth audience. Though purchase intent has risen, Coca-Cola's bottom line has not improved. This creates an interesting conundrum in which the marketing group has achieved success via improved purchase intentions, yet has not satisfied the financial side of the business. The bottom line for analysts is that the promotional expense is not increasing sales revenue, at least in the short term.

The clear linkage among finance, accounting, human resources, and marketing is evident in a company's focus on both profit and customer satisfaction. A successful integrated marketing communications program is dependent upon marketing working closely with R&D and manufacturing in regard to quality and product availability. Simultaneously, marketing has to interact closely with finance, accounting, and human resources to establish appropriate goals and objectives for its marketing communications programs. It is the sum of the external messages and internal operations that produces a satisfied customer.

Questions

1. Why are the company's marketing communications of particular concern to research and development and manufacturing?

2. Why do financial managers view advertising and promotional expenditures as costs?

3. How has personal selling become functionally integrated?

14

Integrated Marketing Communications

LEARNING OBJECTIVES

1. Discuss the role of promotion in the marketing mix

2. Discuss the elements of the promotional mix

3. Describe the communication process

4. Explain the goals and tasks of promotion

5. Discuss the AIDA concept and its relationship to the promotional mix

6. Describe the factors that affect the promotional mix

7. Discuss the concept of integrated marketing communications

Michael Jordan's name is synonymous with basketball. But Jordan is also a leading sports endorser of consumer products who could bring in $50 million a year during his peak. Today, he is still on the Burns Sports & Celebrities list of the top ten sports endorsers. In fact, he was number two behind Tiger Woods (number one) in 2003. Jordan's contracts to be a spokesperson for Nike, Gatorade, Hanes, Ball Park Franks, McDonald's, MCI, and Rayovac have led to phenomenal financial success off the court. Jordan parlayed that success into a business venture with Nike in which Nike created a premium footwear and apparel brand called Jordan. The brand has been very successful and features endorsements from "Team Jordan" athletes such as Michael Finley of the Dallas Mavericks, Donovan McNabb of the Philadelphia Eagles, and Roy Jones Jr., a boxing champion, among others. The Jordan brand offers products ranging from the ever-popular Air Jordan shoes to jackets, shorts, jerseys, jeans, parkas, caps, and even an MP3 player.

The brand also sponsors an interactive Web site, **http://www.jumpman23. com**, which gives consumers a behind-the-scenes look at pictures and commercials. In addition, the site offers exclusive interviews with "Team Jordan" athletes. At the "Jordan College Program" area of the site, Web surfers have an opportunity to win shoes from the college of their choice.

In conjunction with Jordan's retirement in 2003, Nike debuted a "Love" Campaign in February 2003 to promote the Jordan brand. The campaign utilized an integrated marketing communications strategy to reach its target audience. The "Love" campaign had at least five different love-related facets including *Spontaneous Love, Love Submissions, Love: In Concert, Love Truck*, and *Love Stories. Spontaneous Love* was a grassroots campaign in which "Team Jordan" athletes surprised local communities by making appearances at sporting venues, college campuses, and other community locations to participate in sports clinics, mentoring, and other special events. *Love Submissions* was a one-to-one marketing campaign that asked fans to send in answers to the question "What Do You Love?" Responses were not limited to a written essay—Nike received e-mails, mail, videos, and artwork from fans showing what they loved. The best submissions were featured on the Web site www.jumpman23.com. *Love: In Concert* was a rock concert featuring popular artists such as Ja Rule, Eve, The Roots, and Jurassic 5. Proceeds directly benefited the Greater Atlanta Inner-City Games organization, which brings sporting, education, and cultural opportunities to at-risk youth in Atlanta. *Love Truck*, an 18-wheeler covered in Jordan graphics, went on a four-city tour to promote the brand. The *Love Truck* representatives hosted special events, gave away prizes, and featured athlete appearances. *Love Stories* was a series of 5- to 60-minute documentary-style short films aired in a variety of places to promote the brand. In addition, Nike Jordan heavily supported the integrated marketing communications campaign through print advertising to capitalize even further on the "love" theme.[1]

As you can see, Nike Jordan places considerable emphasis on promotion in its marketing mix. What types of promotional tools are available to companies, and what factors influence the choice of tool? Why is consistent integrated marketing important to the promotional plan? These questions and others will be answered as you read this chapter.

Online

Jumpman

Nike

Visit Nike's Web site and explore the various areas. How does Nike use its Web site as part of its integrated marketing communications strategy? How is Nike Jordan using the Jumpman site to create more interactivity among its users? Are there references to any outside advertising or promotions activities? Is the presentation of the product and information at Nike site consistent with what it promotes at its stores or in its advertisements? What role does the jumpman23 site play? Explain.

http://www.jumpman23.com

http://www.nike.com

THE ROLE OF PROMOTION IN THE MARKETING MIX

Discuss the role of promotion in the marketing mix

Few goods or services, no matter how well developed, priced, or distributed, can survive in the marketplace without effective **promotion**—communication by marketers that informs, persuades, and reminds potential buyers of a product in order to influence their opinion or elicit a response.

Promotional strategy is a plan for the optimal use of the elements of promotion: advertising, public relations, personal selling, and sales promotion. As Exhibit 14.1 shows, the marketing manager determines the goals of the company's promotional strategy in light of the firm's overall goals for the marketing mix—product, place (distribution), promotion, and price. Using these overall goals, marketers combine the elements of the promotional strategy (the promotional mix) into a coordinated plan. The promotion plan then becomes an integral part of the marketing strategy for reaching the target market.

The main function of a marketer's promotional strategy is to convince target customers that the goods and services offered provide a differential advantage over the competition. A **competitive advantage** is the set of unique features of a company and its products that are perceived by the target market as significant and superior to the competition. Such features can include high product quality, rapid delivery, low prices, excellent service, or a feature not offered by the competition. For example, fast-food restaurant Subway promises fresh sandwiches that are better for you than a hamburger or pizza. Subway effectively communicates its competitive advantage through advertising featuring longtime "spokes-eater" Jared Fogle, who lost weight by eating Subway every day.[2] Thus, promotion is a vital part of the marketing mix, informing consumers of a product's benefits and thereby positioning the product in the marketplace.

EXHIBIT 14.1

Role of Promotion in the Marketing Mix

REVIEW LEARNING OBJECTIVE 1

1	Discuss the role of promotion in the marketing mix

Promotional Strategy

promotion
Communication by marketers that informs, persuades, and reminds potential buyers of a product in order to influence an opinion or elicit a response.

promotional strategy
A plan for the optimal use of the elements of promotion: advertising, public relations, personal selling, and sales promotion.

competitive advantage
One or more unique aspects of an organization that cause target consumers to patronize that firm rather than competitors.

Discuss the elements of the promotional mix

Most promotional strategies use several ingredients—which may include advertising, public relations, sales promotion, and personal selling—to reach a target market. That combination is called the **promotional mix**. The proper promotional mix is the one that management believes will meet the needs of the target market and fulfill the organization's overall goals. The more funds allocated to each promotional ingredient and the more managerial emphasis placed on each technique, the more important that element is thought to be in the overall mix.

ADVERTISING

Almost all companies selling a good or a service use some form of advertising, whether it be in the form of a multimillion-dollar campaign or a simple classified ad in a newspaper. **Advertising** is any form of paid communication in which the sponsor or company is identified. Traditional media—such as television, radio, newspapers, magazines, books, direct mail, billboards, and transit cards (advertisements on buses and taxis and at bus stops)—are most commonly used to transmit advertisements to consumers. With the increasing fragmentation of traditional media choices, marketers are sending their advertisements to consumers in many new and innovative ways, such as with interactive video technology located in department stores and supermarkets and through Internet Web sites and electronic mail.

One of the primary benefits of advertising is its ability to communicate to a large number of people at one time. Cost per contact, therefore, is typically very low. Advertising has the advantage of being able to reach the masses (for instance, through national television networks), but it can also be microtargeted to small groups of potential customers, such as television ads on a targeted cable network or through print advertising in a trade magazine.

Although the cost per contact in advertising is very low, the total cost to advertise is typically very high. This hurdle tends to restrict advertising on a national basis to only those companies that are financially able to do so. For instance, when Degree antiperspirant introduced its new line of clear gel products aimed at men, the company spent $25 to $30 million on media advertising alone.[3] Few small companies can match this level of spending for a national campaign. Chapter 15 examines advertising in greater detail.

 Many companies are including Internet advertising as a vital component in their marketing mix. Banner ads, viral marketing, and interactive promotions are all ways that marketers utilize the Internet to try and reach their target audience. But some consumers and lawmakers feel that privacy issues are being violated. Read about this issue in the "Ethics in Marketing" box.

PUBLIC RELATIONS

Concerned about how they are perceived by their target markets, organizations often spend large sums to build a positive public image. **Public relations** is the marketing function that evaluates public attitudes, identifies areas within the organization the public may be interested in, and executes a program of action to earn public understanding and acceptance. Public relations helps an organization communicate with its customers, suppliers, stockholders, government officials, employees, and the community in which it operates. Marketers use public relations not only to maintain a positive image but also to educate the public about the company's goals and objectives, introduce new products, and help support the sales effort.

Cirque du Soleil, a world-famous circus company created by a Canadian acrobatic troupe, tours the globe performing shows featuring acrobats, singers, dancers, musicians, clowns, and actors. Almost every event is sold out because the company offers a limited number of tickets and uses a savvy marketing campaign that relies on public relations and heavy print advertising to introduce the Cirque

promotional mix
The combination of promotional tools—including advertising, public relations, personal selling, and sales promotion—used to reach the target market and fulfill the organization's overall goals.

advertising
Impersonal, one-way mass communication about a product or organization that is paid for by a marketer.

public relations
The marketing function that evaluates public attitudes, identifies areas within the organization the public may be interested in, and executes a program of action to earn public understanding and acceptance.

Ethics in Marketing Ethics in Marketing Ethics in Marketing Ethics in Marketing Ethics in Marketing Ethics in Marketing Ethics in Mark
Ethics in Marketing Ethics in Marketing Ethics in Marketing Ethics in Marketing Ethics in Marketing Ethics in Mark
Ethics in Marketing Ethics in Marketing **ETHICS IN MARKETING** Ethics in Marketing Ethics in Marketing Ethics in Mark
Ethics in Marketing Ethics in Marketing Ethics in Marketing Ethics in Mark
Ethics in Marketing

CAN SPAM LEGISLATION HELP?

Most Americans are familiar with the ever-present spam filling our in-boxes in the form of e-mail offering herbal supplements, prescription drugs, low-interest loans, and free money. The term *spam* came originally from the name of the canned meat product, but it is now used to refer to unwanted e-mails because of a 1970 Monty Python skit in which a customer is urged to order Spam repeatedly until she screams "I don't want any Spam!"—which is how many of us feel today about the useless products we are exposed to in our e-mail. Aside from its humorous side, spam raises serious moral issues, especially when it exposes children to pornography.

In December 2003, Congress approved "can-spam" legislation that was designed to curtail the flood of unsolicited commercial e-mails. This antispam law is the most comprehensive measure taken thus far. The law encourages the Federal Trade Commission to create a do-not-spam list of e-mail addresses. Marketers sending unsolicited commercial e-mails are prohibited from (1) using a false return address or subject line that conceals their identity and (2) harvesting addresses from Web sites. In addition, all e-mails must have a functioning opt-out mechanism that recipients can use to prevent future e-mails. Marketers who fail to comply can be imprisoned for up to five years.

Although the law is expected to curtail some spamming, it will not stop all spam because much of the spam in our in-boxes originates outside the United States. Critics of the legislation such as the Coalition Against Unsolicited Commercial E-mails describe the law as "really disappointing" and argue that marketers should have to obtain the recipient's permission before sending any e-mail at all.

Technology may provide other solutions. Microsoft has introduced a new e-mail filter called SmartScreen. It uses complicated mathematical formulas to screen e-mails and discard junk mail (spam). Several e-mail programs such as Yahoo! have launched filters that send spam to a separate in-box.[5]

Unsolicited e-mail is a huge inconvenience to consumers. Companies that employ this practice should worry about consumer backlash. Marketers have an ethical obligation to be sensitive to privacy concerns when using e-mail campaigns.

Do you think spam or unsolicited commercial e-mail is an effective marketing tool? When does e-mail become spamming? Do you think the government should be passing stronger measures to prevent spamming? Is spam even preventable?

One way that the Cirque du Soleil generates publicity is by sending performers to venues where passers by can stop to enjoy the acrobats in a street-performance setting. In addition to being public relations, could this also be considered sampling?

© BLAKE LITTLE/THE IMAGE BANK/GETTY IMAGES

publicity
Public information about a company, good, or service appearing in the mass media as a news item.

show in each city. To gain public exposure, Cirque performers arrive a few weeks before the show to host media events, which include the raising of the circus tent. In addition to airing live performances on television, Cirque prepared an award-winning documentary that focuses on how a Cirque show is created. Cirque also offers corporate sponsorships, has a fan club called Cirque Club, and features an interactive Web site.[4]

A solid public relations program can generate favorable **publicity**—public information about a company, good, or service appearing in the mass media as a news item. The organization generally is not identified as the source of the information. The soy industry received favorable publicity and an increase in sales after the Food and Drug Administration (FDA) approved a health claim for food labeling suggesting a link between soy protein and the reduced risk of coronary heart disease.[6] This incident underscores a peculiar reality of marketing: No matter how many millions are spent on advertising, nothing sells a product better than free publicity.

Although an organization does not pay for this kind of mass-media exposure, publicity should not be viewed as free. Preparing news releases, staging special events, and persuading media personnel to print or broadcast them costs money. During the year-and-a-half it took the FDA to approve the soy claim, meatless burger marketer Gardenburger was busy capitalizing on the pre-approval buzz on soy and readying a public relations plan to put its brand at the forefront should

Nabisco
What is the primary vehicle Nabisco uses to promote its products at its Web site? What do you think the advantages and disadvantages of this technique are? What changes, if any, would you suggest?
http://www.nabiscoworld.com

Online

the FDA approve the claim. While the FDA was mulling its final decision, Gardenburger used interim packaging touting its soy burgers as "great-tasting and packed with soy protein" to spark interest among those who were hearing about soy's health attributes in the press. Gardenburger also provided footage of its factory lines to major media outlets. These tactics proved quite beneficial for the soy marketer: Seventy-five newspapers and 100 television stations used Gardenburger's packaging and production line footage in their coverage of the soy story, reaching some 35 million consumers. Two months after the FDA's approval, Gardenburger's sales had risen 25 percent.[7] Public relations and publicity are examined further in Chapter 15.

Trade shows are an example of sales promotion. At the International Consumer Electronics Show, approximately 300 models, dressed in evening attire, walked through the crowd passing out cards with cryptic messages in one of seven different languages. The models were part of an effort by Bluetooth Special Interest Group to drive traffic to its trade booth promoting Bluetooth technology as a global standard.

sales promotion
Marketing activities—other than personal selling, advertising, and public relations—that stimulate consumer buying and dealer effectiveness.

SALES PROMOTION

Sales promotion consists of all marketing activities—other than personal selling, advertising, and public relations—that stimulate consumer purchasing and dealer effectiveness. Sales promotion is generally a short-run tool used to stimulate immediate increases in demand. Sales promotion can be aimed at end consumers, trade customers, or a company's employees. Sales promotions include free samples, contests, premiums, trade shows, vacation giveaways, and coupons. A major promotional campaign might use several of these sales promotion tools. For example, Motorola, a sponsor of a mountain bike event called "24 Hours of Adrenaline," teamed up recently with Canadian Future Shop to debut the Motorola Gear Grab. This promotion gave ten people 24 seconds to grab as much Motorola gear as they could in a Future Shop store. Contestants worked in pairs and used Motorola two-way radios so that one partner could provide the other with the name, description, and location of a Motorola product—including cell phones and messaging devices—within the store. Contestants were also eligible for a grand prize of various Motorola and mountain biking gear. Besides the Gear Grab, Motorola sponsored several mini–Gear Grabs during mountain bike event weekends in different cities.[8]

Often marketers use sales promotion to improve the effectiveness of other ingredients in the promotional mix, especially advertising and personal selling. Research shows that sales promotion complements advertising by yielding faster sales responses. Jose Cuervo International, a Mexican tequila manufacturer, launched the online marketing campaign "Endless Summer." The campaign asked tequila drinkers to register online to sign a petition asking Congress to change Labor Day from the first Monday in September to the last day of summer. As incentives for registration, Jose Cuervo offered a party pack, including margarita mix, a blender, a portable grill, a portable stereo, and a $250 party supplies gift certificate. Registered users were asked to forward e-mails and information about the petition to their friends.[9] Sales promotion is discussed in more detail in Chapter 16.

PERSONAL SELLING

Personal selling is a purchase situation in which two people communicate in an attempt to influence each other. In this dyad, both the buyer and the seller have specific objectives they wish to accomplish. The buyer may need to minimize cost or assure a quality product, for instance, while the salesperson may need to maximize revenue and profits.

Traditional methods of personal selling include a planned presentation to one or more prospective buyers for the purpose of making a sale. Whether it takes place face-to-face or over the phone, personal selling attempts to persuade the buyer to accept a point of view or convince the buyer to take some action. For example, a car salesperson may try to persuade a car buyer that a particular model is superior to a competing model in certain features, such as gas mileage, roominess, and interior styling. Once the buyer is somewhat convinced, then the salesperson may attempt to elicit some action from the buyer, such as a test-drive or a purchase. Frequently, in this traditional view of personal selling, the objectives of the salesperson are at the expense of the buyer, creating a win-lose outcome.

More current notions on personal selling emphasize the relationship that develops between a salesperson and a buyer. Initially, this concept was more typical in business-to-business selling situations, involving the sale of products like heavy machinery or computer systems. More recently, both business-to-business and business-to-consumer selling focus on building long-term relationships rather than on making a one-time sale. Relationship selling emphasizes a win-win outcome and the accomplishment of mutual objectives that benefit both buyer and salesperson in the long term. Rather than focusing on a quick sale, relationship selling attempts to create a long-term, committed relationship based on trust, increased customer loyalty, and a continuation of the relationship between the salesperson and the customer. Personal selling and relationship selling are discussed in Chapter 16.

REVIEW LEARNING OBJECTIVE 2

2 | Discuss the elements of the promotional mix

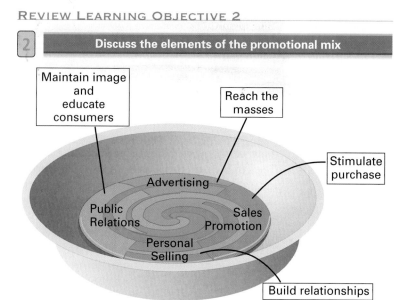

3 MARKETING COMMUNICATION

Describe the communication process

Promotional strategy is closely related to the process of communication. As humans, we assign meaning to feelings, ideas, facts, attitudes, and emotions. **Communication** is the process by which we exchange or share meanings through a common set of symbols. When a company develops a new product, changes an old one, or simply tries to increase sales of an existing good or service, it must communicate its selling message to potential customers. Marketers communicate information about the firm and its products to the target market and various publics through its promotion programs. Neiman Marcus, for example, set out to capture as many e-mail addresses as possible for its recent holiday promotions campaign. The focus of the campaign was "There is something for everyone at Neiman's." To build the database that launched the holiday campaign, Neiman's mailed print catalogs, sent over 750,000 e-mails, bought online ads, and hosted a

personal selling
A purchase situation in which two people communicate in an attempt to influence each other.

communication
The process by which we exchange or share meanings through a common set of symbols.

"fantasy gift" press event. As an incentive for registration, Neiman's automatically entered all registered subscribers in its holiday sweepstakes, which awarded two Hummer 24-speed mountain bikes valued at $745. The press event and catalog featured everything from fantasy gifts—a Learjet valued at $7.7 to $12.7 million and a $27,000 luxury ice fishing house—to gifts under $100. Although official numbers were not released, Neiman's e-mails typically have an "extremely high" response rate.[10]

Communication can be divided into two major categories: interpersonal communication and mass communication. **Interpersonal communication** is direct, face-to-face communication between two or more people. When communicating face-to-face, people see the other person's reaction and can respond almost immediately. A salesperson speaking directly with a client is an example of marketing communication that is interpersonal.

Mass communication refers to communicating a concept or message to large audiences. A great deal of marketing communication is directed to consumers as a whole, usually through a mass medium such as television or newspapers. When a company advertises, it generally does not personally know the people with whom it is trying to communicate. Furthermore, the company is unable to respond immediately to consumers' reactions to its message. Instead, the marketing manager must wait to see whether people are reacting positively or negatively to the mass-communicated promotion. Any clutter from competitors' messages or other distractions in the environment can reduce the effectiveness of the mass-communication effort.

THE COMMUNICATION PROCESS

Marketers are both senders and receivers of messages. As *senders*, marketers attempt to inform, persuade, and remind the target market to adopt courses of action compatible with the need to promote the purchase of goods and services. As *receivers*, marketers attune themselves to the target market in order to develop the appropriate messages, adapt existing messages, and spot new communication opportunities. In this way, marketing communication is a two-way, rather than one-way, process. The two-way nature of the communication process is shown in Exhibit 14.2.

The Sender and Encoding

The **sender** is the originator of the message in the communication process. In an interpersonal conversation, the sender may be a parent, a friend, or a salesperson. For an advertisement or press release, the sender is the company or organization itself. For example, McDonald's fast-food restaurants launched a marketing campaign using the theme "I'm lovin' it." The objective of the campaign was to increase purchases of traditional menu items by children, teenagers, and young adults. To appeal to this market, McDonald's signed Justin Timberlake to sing a "hip-pop" jingle and do a voice-over in the commercial.

Encoding is the conversion of the sender's ideas and thoughts into a message, usually in the form of words or signs. Thus, to promote the message that a meal at McDonald's "is one of the simplest pleasures of daily life," the ad featured a mohawked dad with his mohawked child singing the jingle "I'm lovin it." Marketers encoded the message by using the dad and child "lovin' it" at McDonald's.

A basic principle of encoding is that what matters is not what the source says but what the receiver hears. One way of conveying a message that the receiver will hear properly is to use concrete words and pictures. For example, in addition to

---

interpersonal communication
Direct, fact-to-face communication between two or more people.

mass communication
The communication of a concept or message to large audiences.

sender
The originator of the message in the communication process.

encoding
The conversion of a sender's ideas and thoughts into a message, usually in the form of words or signs.

EXHIBIT 14.2

Communication Process

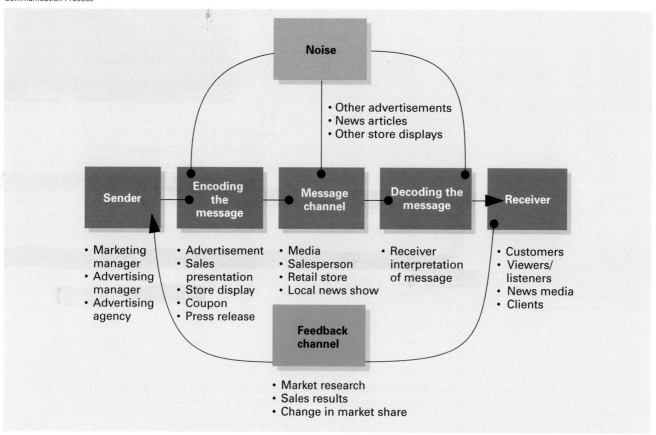

visual images, the McDonald's "I'm lovin it" jingle sung by Justin Timberlake explicitly conveyed the message:

> I'm lovin' it. Is this the place to eat? Since I don't cook, I'll just rock to the beat. I'm lovin' it. At the end of the day, to relieve the stress, we add a little play. I'm lovin' it. Sometimes we have mishaps. You just overcome it, adapt to setback. I'm lovin' it. I'm lovin' it.[11]

Message Transmission

Transmission of a message requires a **channel**—a voice, radio, newspaper, or other communication medium. A facial expression or gesture can also serve as a channel.

Reception occurs when the message is detected by the receiver and enters his or her frame of reference. In a two-way conversation such as a sales pitch given by a sales representative to a potential client, reception is normally high. In contrast, the desired receivers may or may not detect the message when it is mass communicated because most media are cluttered by **noise**—anything that interferes with, distorts, or slows down the transmission of information. In some media overcrowded with advertisers, such as newspapers and television, the noise level is high and the reception level is low. For example, competing network advertisements, other entertainment option advertisements, or other programming on the network itself might hamper reception of the McDonald's "I'm lovin it" advertising campaign message. Transmission can also be hindered by situational factors such as physical surroundings like light, sound, location, and weather; the presence of other people; or the temporary moods consumers might bring to the situation. Mass communication may not even reach all the right consumers. Some members of the target audience may have been watching television when McDonald's advertisements were shown, but others may not have been.

channel
A medium of communication—such as a voice, radio, or newspaper—for transmitting a message.

noise
Anything that interferes with, distorts, or slows down the transmission of information.

The Receiver and Decoding

Marketers communicate their message through a channel to customers, or **receivers**, who will decode the message. **Decoding** is the interpretation of the language and symbols sent by the source through a channel. Common understanding between two communicators, or a common frame of reference, is required for effective communication. Therefore, marketing managers must ensure a proper match between the message to be conveyed and the target market's attitudes and ideas.

Even though a message has been received, it will not necessarily be properly decoded—or even seen, viewed, or heard—because of selective exposure, distortion, and retention (refer to Chapter 5). Even when people receive a message, they tend to manipulate, alter, and modify it to reflect their own biases, needs, knowledge, and culture. Factors that can lead to miscommunication include differences in age, social class, education, culture, and ethnicity. Further, because people don't always listen or read carefully, they can easily misinterpret what is said or written. In fact, researchers have found that a large proportion of both printed and televised communications are misunderstood by consumers. Bright colors and bold graphics have been shown to increase consumers' comprehension of marketing communication. Even these techniques are not foolproof, however. A classic example of miscommunication occurred when Lever Brothers mailed out samples of its then new dishwashing liquid, Sunlight, which contains real lemon juice. The package clearly stated that Sunlight was a household cleaning product. Nevertheless, many people saw the word *sunlight*, the large picture of lemons, and the phrase "with real lemon juice" and thought the product was lemon juice.

Marketers targeting consumers in foreign countries must also worry about the translation and possible miscommunication of their promotional messages by other cultures. An important issue for global marketers is whether to standardize or customize the message for each global market in which they sell. For instance, when using the "I'm lovin it" advertising message in other countries, McDonald's might choose to use the same commercials featuring Justin Timberlake as well as the selling points that it uses in the United States. But it might decide to develop unique ads with a different celebrity for each country or culture. Read about how some global marketers have adapted their marketing mix to appeal to consumers in different cultures in the "Global Perspectives" box.

McDonald's new food packaging supports the company's new "I'm lovin' it" promotional message. The company has also ensured that the campaign has global reach by translating the phrase into numerous languages. The packaging depicts people enjoying the simple pleasures of life and furthers McDonald's creative intent to connect with customers worldwide in fresh and relevant ways.

© AP/WIDE WORLD PHOTOS

Feedback

In interpersonal communication, the receiver's response to a message is direct **feedback** to the source. Feedback may be verbal, as in saying "I agree," or nonverbal, as in nodding, smiling, frowning, or gesturing.

Because mass communicators like McDonald's are often cut off from direct feedback, they must rely on market research or analysis of viewer responses for indirect feedback. McDonald's might use such measurements as the percentage of television viewers who recognized, recalled, or stated that they were exposed to the McDonald's messages. Indirect feedback enables mass communicators to decide whether to continue, modify, or drop a message.

receiver
The person who decodes a message.

decoding
Interpretation of the language and symbols sent by the source through a channel.

feedback
The receiver's response to a message.

> THE CHALLENGES OF GLOBAL MARKETING

Global marketing—selling your products and services worldwide—is a huge undertaking. Marketing products or services overseas requires both cultural sensitivity and an understanding of the consumers in diverse markets.

Philips wanted to increase sales and brand-name recognition of its electronic products among affluent young people and executives in Argentina, Uruguay, and Chile. To accomplish this, Philips launched an interactive 12-city tour in South America with a "circus" theme, called the "Philips Electronic Circus."

The objective of the "circus" promotion was to convey the product attributes—functional, dynamic, innovative, and stimulating—in not only a circus setting, but in everyday life. The Philips products featured ranged from stereos to televisions and video products. The circus included three tents inside which consumers could try the different products and watch an almost four-hour "show" featuring an actual circus. The circus was not live, but was shown using Philips technology. For example, one plasma TV played a ringmaster taming animals, another showed a knife thrower, and yet another showed a magician cutting a woman into three parts. The circus was promoted using "fire-themed" ads in local magazines and on TV. Invitations were sent by local sporting clubs and cosponsors to club members.

Coca-Cola has gone beyond just building brand awareness in foreign countries. It has developed products made with native ingredients in an effort to expand market share. For example, in Argentina Coke launched Nativa, a soft drink made with yerba maté herbal tea, which is a national icon in that country.

To launch Nativa, Coke used a combination of print, radio, outdoor, and TV ads, as well as sampling. The TV commercial was filmed in two locations: the tropical northern region where yerba maté grows and the snowy southern region. Marketers were attempting to show the versatility of the drink in the extreme regions of Argentina. The ad shows a boy drinking Nativa in the rain while his girlfriend lies by a sunny creek. The tagline is "Refresh your day with a flavor that is very much ours." The packaging, which has little yerba maté leaves encircling the bottle, also reflects the herb. After the launch, Coke polled Argentinians and found that 87 percent said they would be willing to buy the product.

When advertising abroad, companies do more than just adjust messages. Individual country messages often are tailored to local tastes, languages, and other cultural influences. For example, Comcast, a high-speed Internet service provider, ran a series of "Asian American" print ads in Asian-language newspapers in San Francisco. The message it wanted to convey is that Comcast cable modems are faster and cheaper than digital modems. One ad, aimed at the Chinese target market, showed a tombstone with DSL engraved at the top, with the remainder of the ad in Chinese. Another showed DSL painted in large letters on a road, but the letters were covered by tire tracks; the remainder of the ad was in Vietnamese.[12]

What challenges do you think Philips, Coke, and Comcast faced as they developed the campaigns described above? What can marketers do as they enter new cultural markets? What kinds of research could marketers utilize when entering new countries? Can you think of other barriers that could hinder a company's entry into another country?

THE COMMUNICATION PROCESS AND THE PROMOTIONAL MIX

The four elements of the promotional mix differ in their ability to affect the target audience. For instance, promotional mix elements may communicate with the consumer directly or indirectly. The message may flow one way or two ways. Feedback may be fast or slow, a little or a lot. Likewise, the communicator may have varying degrees of control over message delivery, content, and flexibility. Exhibit 14.3 outlines differences among the promotional mix elements with respect to mode of communication, marketer's control over the communication process, amount and speed of feedback, direction of message flow, marketer's control over the message, identification of the sender, speed in reaching large audiences, and message flexibility.

From Exhibit 14.3, you can see that most elements of the promotional mix are indirect and impersonal when used to communicate with a target market, providing only one direction of message flow. For example, advertising, public relations, and sales promotion are generally impersonal, one-way means of mass communication. Because they provide no opportunity for direct feedback, they cannot easily adapt to consumers' changing preferences, individual differences, and personal goals.

Personal selling, on the other hand, is personal, two-way communication. The salesperson is able to receive immediate feedback from the consumer and adjust the message in response. Personal selling, however, is very slow in dispersing the marketer's message to large audiences. Because a salesperson can only communicate to one person or a small group of persons at one time, it is a poor choice if the marketer wants to send a message to many potential buyers.

EXHIBIT 14.3

Characteristics of the Elements in the Promotional Mix

	Advertising	Public Relations	Sales Promotion	Personal Selling
Mode of Communication	Indirect and nonpersonal	Usually indirect and nonpersonal	Usually indirect and nonpersonal	Direct and face-to-face
Communicator Control over Situation	Low	Moderate to low	Moderate to low	High
Amount of Feedback	Little	Little	Little to moderate	Much
Speed of Feedback	Delayed	Delayed	Varies	Immediate
Direction of Message Flow	One-way	One-way	Mostly one-way	Two-way
Control over Message Content	Yes	No	Yes	Yes
Identification of Sponsor	Yes	No	Yes	Yes
Speed in Reaching Large Audience	Fast	Usually fast	Fast	Slow
Message Flexibility	Same message to all audiences	Usually no direct control over message	Same message to varied target audiences	Tailored to prospective buyer

REVIEW LEARNING OBJECTIVE 3

3 | Describe the communication process

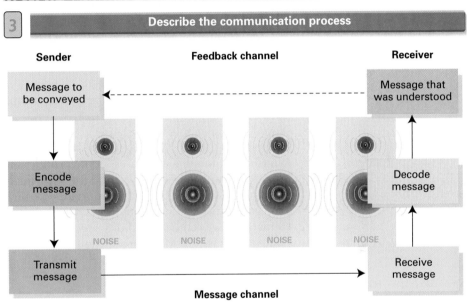

4 THE GOALS AND TASKS OF PROMOTION

Explain the goals and tasks of promotion

People communicate with one another for many reasons. They seek amusement, ask for help, give assistance or instructions, provide information, and express ideas and thoughts. Promotion, on the other hand, seeks to modify behavior and thoughts in some way. For example, promoters may try to persuade consumers to drink Pepsi rather than Coke, or to eat at Burger King rather than at McDonald's. Promotion also strives to reinforce existing behavior—for instance, getting consumers to continue dining at Burger King once they have switched. The source (the seller) hopes to project a favorable image or to motivate purchase of the company's goods and services.

Promotion can perform one or more of three tasks: *inform* the target audience, *persuade* the target audience, or *remind* the target audience. Often a marketer will try to accomplish two or more of these tasks at the same time.

INFORMING

Informative promotion seeks to convert an existing need into a want or to stimulate interest in a new product. It is generally more prevalent during the early stages of the product life cycle. People typically will not buy a product service or support a nonprofit organization until they know its purpose and its benefits to them. Informative messages are important for promoting complex and technical products such as automobiles, computers, and investment services. For example, Philips's original advertisement for the Magnavox flat-screen television showed young, urban consumers trying the flat-screen TV all over the house, including the ceiling. The ad focused on "how to" use the flat-screen TV rather than the Philips Magnavox brand or the technological capabilities.[13] Informative promotion is also important for a "new" brand being introduced into an "old" product class—for example, a new brand of frozen pizza entering the frozen pizza industry, which is dominated by well-known brands like Kraft's DiGiorno and Schwan's Grocery Products' Red Baron. The new product cannot establish itself against more mature products unless potential buyers are aware of it, understand its benefits, and understand its positioning in the marketplace.

PERSUADING

Persuasive promotion is designed to stimulate a purchase or an action—for example, to eat more Doritos or use Verizon wireless mobile phone service. Persuasion normally becomes the main promotion goal when the product enters the growth stage of its life cycle. By this time, the target market should have general product awareness and some knowledge of how the product can fulfill their wants. Therefore, the promotional task switches from informing consumers about the product category to persuading them to buy the company's brand rather than the competitor's. At this time, the promotional message emphasizes the product's real and perceived competitive advantages, often appealing to emotional needs such as love, belonging, self-esteem, and ego satisfaction. For example, the latest advertisement for the Philips Magnavox flat-screen television still features young, urban consumers. But the ad focuses on the product's benefits such as lifestyle enhancements, technological features, and the superiority of the brand.[14]

Persuasion can also be an important goal for very competitive mature product categories such as many household items, soft drinks, beer, and banking services. In a marketplace characterized by many competitors, the promotional message often encourages brand switching and aims to convert some buyers into loyal users. For example, to persuade new customers to switch their checking accounts, a bank's marketing manager may offer a year's worth of free checks with no fees.

Critics believe that some promotional messages and techniques can be too persuasive, causing consumers to buy products and services they really don't need.

REMINDING

Reminder promotion is used to keep the product and brand name in the public's mind. This type of promotion prevails during the maturity stage of the life cycle. It assumes that the target market has already been persuaded of the good's or service's merits. Its purpose is simply to trigger a memory. Crest toothpaste, Tide laundry detergent, Miller beer, and many other consumer products often use reminder promotion. Similarly, Philips Magnavox could advertise just the brand rather than the benefits of the product.

REVIEW LEARNING OBJECTIVE 4

 Explain the goals and tasks of promotion

- **Informative promotion**
  Increasing the awareness of a new brand, product class, or product attribute
  Explaining how the product works
  Suggesting new uses for a product
  Building a company image
- **Persuasive promotion**
  Encouraging brand switching
  Changing customers' perceptions of product attributes
  Influencing customers to buy now
  Persuading customers to call
- **Reminder promotion**
  Reminding consumers that the product may be needed in the near future
  Reminding consumers where to buy the product
  Maintaining consumer awareness

5 PROMOTIONAL GOALS AND THE AIDA CONCEPT

Discuss the AIDA concept and its relationship to the promotional mix

Kohler

How does a Web site's ease of use affect its ability to create attention, interest, desire, and action? Visit the kitchen and bath pages of Kohler's Web site and determine how successful the company is at moving consumers through the AIDA process.

http://www.kohler.com

Online

The ultimate goal of any promotion is to get someone to buy a good or service or, in the case of nonprofit organizations, to take some action (for instance, donate blood). A classic model for reaching promotional goals is called the **AIDA concept.**[15] The acronym stands for *attention, interest, desire,* and *action*—the stages of consumer involvement with a promotional message.

This model proposes that consumers respond to marketing messages in a cognitive (thinking), affective (feeling), and conative (doing) sequence. First, the promotion manager attracts a person's *attention* by (in personal selling) a greeting and approach or (in advertising and sales promotion) loud volume, unusual contrasts, bold headlines, movement, bright colors, and so on. Next, a good sales presentation, demonstration, or advertisement creates *interest* in the product and then, by illustrating how the product's features will satisfy the consumer's needs, arouses *desire*. Finally, a special offer or a strong closing sales pitch may be used to obtain purchase *action*.

The AIDA concept assumes that promotion propels consumers along the following four steps in the purchase-decision process:

AIDA concept
A model that outlines the process for achieving promotional goals in terms of stages of consumer involvement with the message; the acronym stands for *attention, interest, desire,* and *action*.

1. *Attention:* The advertiser must first gain the attention of the target market. A firm cannot sell something if the market does not know that the good or service exists. Imagine that Acme Company, a pet food manufacturer, is introducing a new brand of cat food called Stripes, specially formulated for finicky cats. To increase the general awareness of its new brand, Acme heavily publicizes the introduction and places several ads on TV and in consumer magazines.

2. *Interest:* Simple awareness of a brand seldom leads to a sale. The next step is to create interest in the product. A print ad or TV commercial can't actually tell pet owners whether their cats will like Stripes. Thus, Acme might send samples of the new cat food to cat owners to create interest in the new brand.

3. *Desire:* Even though owners (and their cats) may like Stripes, they may not see any advantage over competing brands, especially if owners are brand loyal. Therefore, Acme must create brand preference by explaining the product's differential advantage over the competition. Specifically, Acme has to show that cats want to eat nothing else. Advertising at this stage claims that Stripes will satisfy "even the pickiest of the litter." Although pet owners may come to prefer Stripes to other brands, they still may not have developed the desire to buy the new brand. At this stage Acme might offer the consumer additional reasons to buy Stripes, such as easy-to-open, zip-lock packaging that keeps the product fresh; additional vitamins and minerals that healthy cats need; or feline taste-test results.

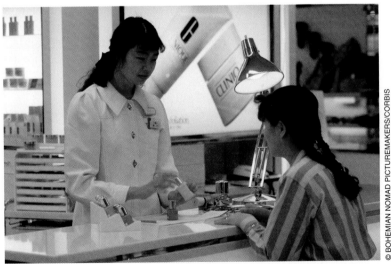

This cosmetics saleswoman at Clinique can create desire for her line of products by showing her potential customer how wonderful she looks after using them. Salespeople are very effective at creating desire, particularly in this type of situation.

Sex in the City and Manolo Blahnik

The AIDA concept is not something initiated uniquely by marketers. Believe it or not, television plays a large role in unleashing the AIDA model. Nowhere is that more obvious than in the high-end fashion industry, which saw drastic changes in its marketing environment with the unbridled success of HBO's original series *Sex in the City*. Over time, fashion became a critical element in the show's atmosphere and in the characters' personalities. In fact, the show legitimized women's obsession with shoes and clothes and introduced them to a slate of smaller, exclusive, and expensive designers. Shoe designer Manolo Blahnik experienced the results of that budding awareness firsthand. In a period of stagnant fashion industry retail sales, he has enjoyed amazing growth. Some of his shoe styles sold out almost immediately after they were featured on *Sex in the City*. (A pair of Manolo Blahnik's retails in the $600 range.) By drawing women's attention to designer fashion and introducing them to names like Dolce & Gabbana, Jimmy Choo, Manolo Blahnik, and Marc Jacobs, *Sex in the City* fired an intense interest, which became a deep desire and, ultimately, an (un)heavenly expenditure for many. (Recall Chapter 5 and think about how this relates to consumer behavior.)[17]

4. *Action:* Some members of the target market may now be convinced to buy Stripes but have yet to make the purchase. Displays in grocery stores, coupons, premiums, and trial-size packages can often push the complacent shopper into purchase.

Most buyers involved in high-involvement purchase situations pass through the four stages of the AIDA model on the way to making a purchase. The promoter's task is to determine where on the purchase ladder most of the target consumers are located and design a promotion plan to meet their needs. For instance, if Acme has determined that about half its buyers are in the preference or conviction stage but have not bought Stripes cat food for some reason, the company may mail cents-off coupons to cat owners to prompt them to buy.

The AIDA concept does not explain how all promotions influence purchase decisions. The model suggests that promotional effectiveness can be measured in terms of consumers progressing from one stage to the next. However, the order of stages in the model, as well as whether consumers go through all steps, has been much debated. For example, a purchase can occur without interest or desire, perhaps when a low-involvement product is bought on impulse. Regardless of the order of the stages or consumers' progression through these stages, the AIDA concept helps marketers by suggesting which promotional strategy will be most effective.[16]

AIDA AND THE PROMOTIONAL MIX

Exhibit 14.4 depicts the relationship between the promotional mix and the AIDA model. It shows that, although advertising does have an impact in the later stages, it is most useful in gaining attention for goods or services. In contrast, personal selling reaches fewer people at first. Salespeople are more effective at creating customer interest for merchandise or a service and at creating desire. For example, advertising may help a potential computer purchaser gain knowledge and information about competing brands,

EXHIBIT 14.4

When the Elements of Promotion Are Most Useful

	Attention	Interest	Desire	Action
Advertising	●	●	○	⬤
Public Relations	●	●	●	⬤
Sales Promotion	○	○	●	○
Personal Selling	○	●	●	●

● Very effective   ○ Somewhat effective   ⬤ Not effective

but the salesperson in an electronics store may be the one who actually encourages the buyer to decide a particular brand is the best choice. The salesperson also has the advantage of having the computer physically there to demonstrate its capabilities to the buyer.

Public relations has its greatest impact in gaining attention for a company, good, or service. Many companies can attract attention and build goodwill by sponsoring community events that benefit a worthy cause such as antidrug and antigang programs. Such sponsorships project a positive image of the firm and its products into the minds of consumers and potential consumers. Good publicity can also help develop consumer desire for a product. Washington Mutual Financial Services invited 50,000 people to "Teacherpalooza: The World's Biggest Barbeque for the World's Greatest Teachers" in Chicago. The goal was to honor teachers and set a Guinness world record for the "World's Largest Barbeque." The barbeque featured performances by local teachers who competed for $15,000 prizes for the school they represented and live entertainment by Tim McGraw and Michelle Branch. A "Teacher Pavilion" described teacher-oriented financial services provided by Washington Mutual. Local news media cosponsored the event and were on hand to provide media coverage.[18] Book publishers push to get their titles on the best-seller lists of major publications, such as *Publishers Weekly*, the *New York Times*, or the *Wall Street Journal*. Book authors also make appearances on talk shows and at bookstores to personally sign books and speak to fans. Similarly, movie marketers use prerelease publicity to raise the profile of their movies and to increase initial box-office sales. For example, most major motion picture studios have their own Web sites with multimedia clips and publicity photos of their current movies to attract viewers. Furthermore, movie promoters include publicity gained from reviewers' quotes and Academy Award nominations in their advertising.

Sales promotion's greatest strength is in creating strong desire and purchase intent. Coupons and other price-off promotions are techniques used to persuade customers to buy new products. Frequent buyer sales promotion programs, popular among retailers, allow consumers to accumulate points or dollars that can later be redeemed for goods. Frequent buyer programs tend to increase purchase intent and loyalty and encourage repeat purchases. Many supermarket chains have developed loyalty programs patterned after the airlines' frequent flyer programs. Kroger's Plus Card members can go online and choose the coupons they want. The coupons are then downloaded to the member's Plus Card, and the savings can be redeemed when the member goes shopping with the card.

© AP/WIDE WORLD PHOTOS

Washington Mutual's Teacherpalooza in Chicago was successful in drawing attention to the company as a member of the Chicagoland community. With over 50,000 people attending, the public relations event also doubled as an attempt at entering the Guinness Book of World Records.

Discuss the AIDA concept and its relationship to the promotional mix

Attention	Interest	Desire	Action

	Attention	Interest	Desire	Action
Advertising	✓+	✓+	✓	✓−
Public Relations	✓+	✓+	✓+	✓−
Sales Promotion	✓	✓	✓+	✓
Personal Sell	✓	✓+	✓+	✓+

6 FACTORS AFFECTING THE PROMOTIONAL MIX

Describe the factors that affect the promotional mix

Promotional mixes vary a great deal from one product and one industry to the next. Normally, advertising and personal selling are used to promote goods and services, supported and supplemented by sales promotion. Public relations helps develop a positive image for the organization and the product line. However, a firm may choose not to use all four promotional elements in its promotional mix, or it may choose to use them in varying degrees. The particular promotional mix chosen by a firm for a product or service depends on several factors: the nature of the product, the stage in the product life cycle, target market characteristics, the type of buying decision, funds available for promotion, and whether a push or a pull strategy will be used.

NATURE OF THE PRODUCT

Characteristics of the product itself can influence the promotional mix. For instance, a product can be classified as either a business product or a consumer product (refer to Chapters 6 and 9). As business products are often custom-tailored to the buyer's exact specifications, they are often not well suited to mass promotion. Therefore, producers of most business goods, such as computer systems or industrial machinery, rely more heavily on personal selling than on advertising. Informative personal selling is common for industrial installations, accessories, and component parts and materials. Advertising, however, still serves a purpose in promoting business goods. Advertisements in trade media may be used to create general buyer awareness and interest. Moreover, advertising can help locate potential customers for the sales force. For example, print media advertising often includes coupons soliciting the potential customer to "fill this out for more detailed information."

In contrast, because consumer products generally are not custom-made, they do not require the selling efforts of a company representative who can tailor them to the user's needs. Thus, consumer goods are promoted mainly through advertising to create brand familiarity. Broadcast advertising, newspapers, and consumer-oriented magazines are used extensively to promote consumer goods, especially nondurables. Sales promotion, the brand name, and the product's packaging are about twice as important for consumer goods as for business products. Persuasive personal selling is important at the retail level for shopping goods such as automobiles and appliances.

The costs and risks associated with a product also influence the promotional mix. As a general rule, when the costs or risks of using a product increase, personal selling becomes more important. Items that are a small part of a firm's budget (supply

 FAQs

Which factors influence the promotional mix and how? Find out more by watching the video FAQ on Xtra!

Kellogg has launched a new public relations campaign featuring the Tonymobile, which will be touring the United States (re)introducing families to Kellogg's family of characters: Toucan Sam, Dig 'Em, Snap!Crackle! and Pop! Competition in the breakfast food market is fierce, and Kellogg is using the Tonymobile to remind consumers about its cereals and cereal products.

© AP/WIDE WORLD PHOTOS

items) or of a consumer's budget (convenience products) do not require a salesperson to close the sale. In fact, inexpensive items cannot support the cost of a salesperson's time and effort unless the potential volume is high. On the other hand, expensive and complex machinery, new buildings, cars, and new homes represent a considerable investment. A salesperson must assure buyers that they are spending their money wisely and not taking an undue financial risk.

Social risk is an issue as well. Many consumer goods are not products of great social importance because they do not reflect social position. People do not experience much social risk in buying a loaf of bread or a candy bar. However, buying some shopping products and many specialty products such as jewelry and clothing does involve a social risk. Many consumers depend on sales personnel for guidance and advice in making the "proper" choice.

STAGE IN THE PRODUCT LIFE CYCLE

The product's stage in its life cycle is a big factor in designing a promotional mix (see Exhibit 14.5). During the *introduction stage*, the basic goal of promotion is to inform the target audience that the product is available. Initially, the emphasis is on the general product class—for example, personal computer systems. This emphasis gradually changes to gaining attention for a specific brand, such as IBM, Apple, or Hewlett-Packard. Typically, both extensive advertising and public relations inform the target audience of the product class or brand and heighten awareness levels. Sales promotion encourages early trial of the product, and personal selling gets retailers to carry the product.

When the product reaches the *growth stage* of the life cycle, the promotion blend may shift. Often a change is necessary because different types of potential buyers are targeted. Although advertising and public relations continue to be major elements of the promotional mix, sales promotion can be reduced because consumers need fewer incentives to purchase. The promotional strategy is to emphasize the product's differential advantage over the competition. Persuasive promotion is used to build and maintain brand loyalty to support the product during the growth stage. By this stage, personal selling has usually succeeded in getting adequate distribution for the product.

As the product reaches the *maturity stage* of its life cycle, competition becomes fiercer, and thus persuasive and reminder advertising are more strongly emphasized. Sales promotion comes back into focus as product sellers try to increase their market share.

All promotion, especially advertising, is reduced as the product enters the *decline stage*. Nevertheless, personal selling and sales promotion efforts may be maintained, particularly at the retail level.

EXHIBIT 14.5

Product Life Cycle and the Promotional Mix

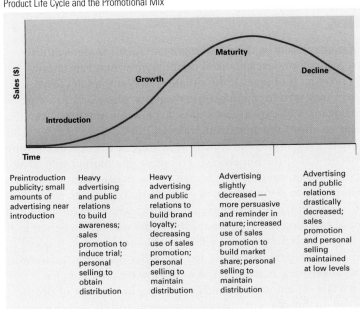

TARGET MARKET CHARACTERISTICS

A target market characterized by widely scattered potential customers, highly informed buyers, and brand-loyal repeat purchasers generally requires a promotional mix with more advertising and sales promotion and less personal selling. Sometimes, however, personal selling is required even when buyers are well informed and geographically dispersed. Although industrial installations and component parts may be sold to extremely competent people with extensive education and work experience, salespeople must still be present to explain the product and work out the details of the purchase agreement.

Often firms sell goods and services in markets where potential customers are hard to locate. Print advertising can be used to find them. The reader is invited to call for more information or to mail in a reply card for a detailed brochure. As the calls or cards are received, salespeople are sent to visit the potential customers.

TYPE OF BUYING DECISION

The promotional mix also depends on the type of buying decision—for example, a routine decision or a complex decision. For routine consumer decisions like buying toothpaste or soft drinks, the most effective promotion calls attention to the brand or reminds the consumer about the brand. Advertising and, especially, sales promotion are the most productive promotion tools to use for routine decisions.

If the decision is neither routine nor complex, advertising and public relations help establish awareness for the good or service. Suppose a man is looking for a bottle of wine to serve to his dinner guests. As a beer drinker, he is not familiar with wines, yet he has seen advertising for Robert Mondavi wine and has also read an article in a popular magazine about the Robert Mondavi winery. He may be more likely to buy this brand because he is already aware of it.

In contrast, consumers making complex buying decisions are more extensively involved. They rely on large amounts of information to help them reach a purchase decision. Personal selling is most effective in helping these consumers decide. For example, consumers thinking about buying a car usually depend on a salesperson to provide the information they need to reach a decision. Print advertising may also be used for high-involvement purchase decisions because it can often provide a large amount of information to the consumer.

AVAILABLE FUNDS

Money, or the lack of it, may easily be the most important factor in determining the promotional mix. A small, undercapitalized manufacturer may rely heavily on free publicity if its product is unique. If the situation warrants a sales force, a financially strained firm may turn to manufacturers' agents, who work on a commission basis with no advances or expense accounts. Even well-capitalized organizations may not be able to afford the advertising rates of publications like *Better Homes and Gardens, Reader's Digest,* and the *Wall Street Journal,* or the cost of running television commercials on *CSI* or the Superbowl. The price of a high-profile advertisement in these media could support a salesperson for an entire year.

When funds are available to permit a mix of promotional elements, a firm will generally try to optimize its return on promotion dollars while minimizing the *cost per contact,* or the cost of reaching one member of the target market. In general, the cost per contact is very high for personal selling, public relations, and sales promotions like sampling and demonstrations. On the other hand, for the number of people national advertising reaches, it has a very low cost per contact.

Usually, there is a trade-off among the funds available, the number of people in the target market, the quality of communication needed, and the relative costs

EXHIBIT 14.6

Push Strategy versus Pull Strategy

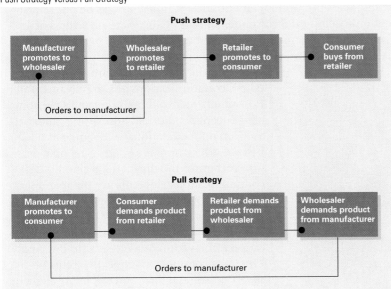

Push strategy

Manufacturer promotes to wholesaler → Wholesaler promotes to retailer → Retailer promotes to consumer → Consumer buys from retailer

Orders to manufacturer

Pull strategy

Manufacturer promotes to consumer — Consumer demands product from retailer — Retailer demands product from wholesaler — Wholesaler demands product from manufacturer

Orders to manufacturer

push strategy
A marketing strategy that uses aggressive personal selling and trade advertising to convince a wholesaler or a retailer to carry and sell particular merchandise.

pull strategy
A marketing strategy that stimulates consumer demand to obtain product distribution.

REVIEW LEARNING OBJECTIVE 6

6 | **Describe the factors that affect the promotional mix**

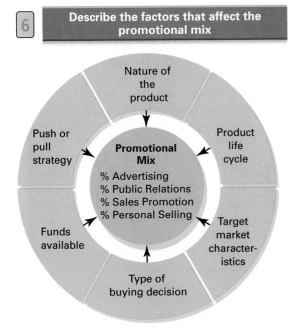

of the promotional elements. A company may have to forgo a full-page, color advertisement in *People* magazine in order to pay for a personal selling effort. Although the magazine ad will reach more people than personal selling, the high cost of the magazine space is a problem.

PUSH AND PULL STRATEGIES

The last factor that affects the promotional mix is whether a push or a pull promotional strategy will be used. Manufacturers may use aggressive personal selling and trade advertising to convince a wholesaler or a retailer to carry and sell their merchandise. This approach is known as a **push strategy** (see Exhibit 14.6). The wholesaler, in turn, must often push the merchandise forward by persuading the retailer to handle the goods. The retailer then uses advertising, displays, and other forms of promotion to convince the consumer to buy the "pushed" products. This concept also applies to services. For example, the Jamaican Tourism Board targets promotions to travel agencies, which, in turn, tell their customers about the benefits of vacationing in Jamaica.

At the other extreme is a **pull strategy**, which stimulates consumer demand to obtain product distribution. Rather than trying to sell to the wholesaler, the manufacturer using a pull strategy focuses its promotional efforts on end consumers or opinion leaders. For example, BriteSmile Professional Teeth Whitening Centers sent office merchandising displays to dentists across the country to create a buzz and generate demand for its after-care whitening maintenance products, such as the Sonicare sonic toothbrush, toothpaste, mouthwash, and mint gum.[19] As consumers begin demanding the product, the retailer orders the merchandise from the wholesaler. The wholesaler, confronted with rising demand, then places an order for the "pulled" merchandise from the manufacturer. Consumer demand pulls the product through the channel of distribution (see Exhibit 14.6). Heavy sampling, introductory consumer advertising, cents-off campaigns, and couponing are part of a pull strategy. For example, Smirnoff Ice sold almost 11 million cases in its first six months of national distribution. Contributing to those unprecedented numbers were extensive sampling, on-premise promotions, and $25 million in advertising.[20] Similarly, Splenda No Calorie Sweetner offered free samples, recipes, and a coupon to potential consumers who tried the product.[21]

Rarely does a company use a pull or a push strategy exclusively. Instead, the mix will emphasize one of these strategies. For example, pharmaceutical companies generally use a push strategy, through personal selling and trade advertising, to promote their drugs and therapies to physicians. Sales presentations and advertisements in medical journals give physicians the detailed information they need to prescribe medication to their patients. Most pharmaceutical companies supplement their push promotional strategy with a pull strategy targeted directly to potential patients through advertisements in consumer magazines and on television.

Discuss the concept of integrated marketing communications

Ideally, marketing communications from each promotional mix element (personal selling, advertising, sales promotion, and public relations) should be integrated—that is, the message reaching the consumer should be the same regardless of whether it is from an advertisement, a salesperson in the field, a magazine article, or a coupon in a newspaper insert.

From the consumer's standpoint, a company's communications are already integrated. Consumers do not think in terms of the four elements of promotion: advertising, sales promotion, public relations, and personal selling. Instead, everything is an "ad." The only people who recognize the distinctions among these communications elements are the marketers themselves. Unfortunately, many marketers neglect this fact when planning promotional messages and fail to integrate their communication efforts from one element to the next. The most common rift typically occurs between personal selling and the other elements of the promotional mix.

This unintegrated, disjointed approach to promotion has propelled many companies to adopt the concept of **integrated marketing communications (IMC)**. IMC is the careful coordination of all promotional messages—traditional advertising, direct marketing, interactive, public relations, sales promotion, personal selling, event marketing, and other communications—for a product or service to assure the consistency of messages at every contact point where a company meets the consumer. Following the concept of IMC, marketing managers carefully work out the roles that various promotional elements will play in the marketing mix. Timing of promotional activities is coordinated, and the results

Movies are often very successful at implementing integrated marketing campaigns. *The Lord of the Rings* was able to parlay huge box-offices successes into merchandising successes—not to mention great anticipation for sequels.

© AP/WIDE WORLD PHOTOS

of each campaign are carefully monitored to improve future use of the promotional mix tools. Typically, a marketing communications director is appointed who has overall responsibility for integrating the company's marketing communications.

Movie marketing campaigns benefit greatly from an IMC approach. Those campaigns that are most integrated generally have more impact and make a deeper impression on potential moviegoers, leading to higher box-office sales. New Line Cinema used an integrated marketing approach when it released the first installment of *The Lord of the Rings: The Fellowship of the Ring*. Excitement about the release of the film gathered momentum a full year in advance as the trailer was shown on the Internet (the trailer received 62 million hits the first week online). A partnership with Burger King gave consumers the opportunity to buy *The Fellowship of the Ring* glass goblets with the purchase of a Whopper sandwich value meal. Consumers could also buy a Burger King Big Kids Meal to receive one of 19 premiums featuring characters from the movie. One hundred selected bookstores around the country sponsored lunchtime events featuring a 20-minute video that included never-before-seen interviews, behind-the-scenes footage, and conversations with director Peter Jackson and other stars from the movie. The bookstores were also given in-store event kits to supplement the showing with a trivia contest, in-store readings by fans of favorite scenes,

integrated marketing communications (IMC)
The careful coordination of all promotional messages for a product or a service to assure the consistency of messages at every contact point where a company meets the consumer.

Online

Hallmark
What do you think is the role of Hallmark's Web site in the company's integrated marketing communications plan? What seems to be the marketing function of the site? Do you think the site is effective?

http://www.hallmark.com

or other activities. Cobranded DVD players and VCR packages loaded with movie trailers, behind-the-scenes footage, and stickers hit shelves a couple of months before the movie premiered. Through an agreement with the New York Times Company, both the *Times* and NYTimes.com promoted the film. Praised by critics and audiences alike, *The Fellowship of the Ring* surpassed the $100 million mark on its opening weekend and was named the top movie of the year by *Entertainment Weekly* and *Rolling Stone.*[22] The second and third installments of *The Lord of the Rings* trilogy also used IMC approaches to achieve successful launches and box office results.

The IMC concept has been growing in popularity for several reasons. First, the proliferation of thousands of media choices beyond traditional television has made promotion a more complicated task. Instead of promoting a product just through mass-media options, like television and magazines, promotional messages today can appear in many varied sources. Further, the mass market has also fragmented— more selectively segmented markets and an increase in niche marketing have replaced the traditional broad market groups that marketers promoted to in years past. For instance, many popular magazines now have Spanish-language editions targeted toward America's growing Hispanic population. Finally, marketers have slashed their advertising spending in favor of promotional techniques that generate immediate sales responses and those that are more easily measured, such as direct marketing. Thus, the interest in IMC is largely a reaction to the scrutiny that marketing communications has come under and, particularly, to suggestions that uncoordinated promotional activity leads to a strategy that is wasteful and inefficient.

REVIEW LEARNING OBJECTIVE 7

7 | **Discuss the concept of integrated marketing communications**

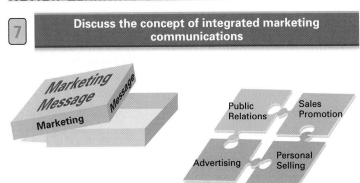

LOOKING BACK

Nike Jordan employs many different elements of the promotional mix to promote its products. Grassroots marketing tactics, public relations, celebrity endorsements, and publicity are important elements of the integrated marketing communications strategic plan. The promotion plan utilized more than five different facets to deliver a clear, consistent, unified message about the Jordan brand, which is crucial to its success in the footwear and athletic clothing market. As you read the next two chapters, keep in mind that marketers try to choose the mix of promotional elements that will best promote their good or service. Marketers seldom rely on just one method of promotion.

USE IT NOW

LEARN A NEW FORM OF COMMUNICATION

 Learn American Sign Language and communicate through your hands, gestures, and body movements. Visit HandSpeak at **http://www.handspeak.com** for a practical visual dictionary of sign language for everyday life. More information is available at **http://www.deafresources.com**.

BECOME A MARKETING GUERRILLA

 Entrepreneurs and small businesses don't always have big promotional budgets. For hundreds of low-cost promotional ideas, turn to the Guerrilla Marketing Web page at **http://www.gmarketing.com**. Find out how to promote effectively for a fraction of what the big guys spend.

1 **Discuss the role of promotion in the marketing mix.** Promotion is communication by marketers that informs, persuades, and reminds potential buyers of a product in order to influence an opinion or elicit a response. Promotional strategy is the plan for using the elements of promotion—advertising, public relations, sales promotion, and personal selling—to meet the firm's overall objectives and marketing goals. Based on these objectives, the elements of the promotional strategy become a coordinated promotion plan. The promotion plan then becomes an integral part of the total marketing strategy for reaching the target market along with product, distribution, and price.

1.1 What is a promotional strategy? Explain the concept of a competitive advantage in relation to promotional strategy.

2 **Discuss the elements of the promotional mix.** The elements of the promotional mix include advertising, public relations, sales promotion, and personal selling. Advertising is a form of impersonal, one-way mass communication paid for by the source. Public relations is the function of promotion concerned with a firm's public image. Firms can't buy good publicity, but they can take steps to create a positive company image. Sales promotion is typically used to back up other components of the promotional mix by stimulating immediate demand. Finally, personal selling typically involves direct communication, in person or by telephone; the seller tries to initiate a purchase by informing and persuading one or more potential buyers.

2.1 **WRITING** As the promotional manager for a new line of cosmetics targeted to preteen girls, you have been assigned the task of deciding which promotional mix elements—advertising, public relations, sales promotion, and personal selling— should be used in promoting it. Your budget for promoting the preteen cosmetics line is limited. Write a promotional plan explaining your choice of promotional mix elements given the nature of the product, the stage in the product life cycle, the target market characteristics, the type of buying decision, available funds, and the use of a pull or push strategy.

3 **Describe the communication process.** The communication process has several steps. When an individual or organization has a message it wishes to convey to a target audience, it encodes that message using language and symbols familiar to the intended receiver and sends the message through a channel of communication. Noise in the transmission channel distorts the source's intended message. Reception occurs if the message falls within the receiver's frame of reference. The receiver decodes the message and usually provides feedback to the source. Normally, feedback is direct for interpersonal communication and indirect for mass communication.

3.1 Why is understanding the target market a crucial aspect of the communication process?

4 **Explain the goals and tasks of promotion.** The fundamental goals of promotion are to induce, modify, or reinforce behavior by informing, persuading, and reminding. Informative promotion explains a good's or service's purpose and benefits. Promotion that informs the consumer is typically used to increase demand for a general product category or to introduce a new good or service. Persuasive promotion is designed to stimulate a purchase or an action. Promotion that persuades the consumer to buy is essential during the growth stage of the product life cycle, when competition becomes fierce. Reminder promotion is used to keep the product and brand name in the public's mind. Promotions that remind are generally used during the maturity stage of the product life cycle.

4.1 Why might a marketing manager choose to promote his or her product using persuasion? Give some current examples of persuasive promotion.

4.2 **TEAM WRITING** Choose a partner from class and go together to interview the owners or managers of several small businesses in your city. Ask them what their promotional objectives are and why. Are they trying to inform, persuade, or remind customers to do business with them? Also determine whether they believe they have an awareness problem or whether they need to persuade customers to come to them instead of to competitors. Ask them to list the characteristics of their primary market, the strengths and weaknesses of their direct competitors, and how they are positioning their store to compete. Prepare a report to present in class summarizing your findings.

5 **Discuss the AIDA concept and its relationship to the promotional mix.** The AIDA model outlines the four basic stages in the purchase decision-making process, which are initiated and propelled by promotional activities: (1) attention, (2) interest, (3) desire, and (4) action. The components of the promotional mix have varying levels of influence at each stage of the AIDA model. Advertising is a good tool for increasing awareness and knowledge of a good or service. Sales promotion is effective when consumers are at the purchase stage of the decision-making process. Personal selling is most effective in developing customer interest and desire.

5.1 Discuss the AIDA concept. How do these different stages of consumer involvement affect the promotional mix?

5.2 As you read in the "Marketing in Entertainment" box on *Sex in the City*, the entertainment media can be a powerful force in marketing, particularly when it comes to setting fashion styles and trends. Can you think of other entertainment programs, besides *Sex in the City*, that shined a spotlight on previously obscure products and services? Make a list of all you can recall. Did the products receive only fleeting consumer interest, or were the results of the media attention longer lasting?

6 **Describe the factors that affect the promotional mix.** Promotion managers consider many factors when creating promotional mixes. These factors include the nature of the product, product life-cycle stage, target market characteristics, the type of buying decision involved, availability of funds, and feasibility of push or pull strategies. Because most business products tend to be custom-tailored to the buyer's exact specifications, the marketing manager may choose a promotional mix that relies more heavily on personal selling. On the other hand, consumer products are generally mass produced and lend themselves more to mass promotional efforts such as advertising and sales promotion. As products move through different stages of the product life cycle, marketers will choose to use different promotional elements. For example, advertising is emphasized more in the introductory stage of the product life cycle than in the decline stage. Characteristics of the target market, such as geographic location of potential buyers and brand loyalty, influence the promotional mix as does whether the buying decision is complex or routine. The amount of funds a firm has to allocate to promotion may also help determine the promotional mix. Small firms with limited funds may rely more heavily on public relations, whereas larger firms may be able to afford broadcast or print advertising. Last, if a firm uses a push strategy to promote the product or service, the marketing manager may choose to use aggressive advertising and personal selling to wholesalers and retailers. If a pull strategy is chosen, then the manager often relies on aggressive mass promotion, such as advertising and sales promotion, to stimulate consumer demand.

6.1 Explain the difference between a "pull" and a "push" promotional strategy. Under what conditions should each strategy be used?

6.2 *INFOTRAC COLLEGE EDITION* Choose two companies, one a consumer-products company and the other an online retailer. Conduct some research on these two companies in terms of their promotional practices by observation (such as looking in magazines, the newspaper, television, Web site, etc.) and searching at your campus library. You may also use InfoTrac (**http://www.infotrac-college.com**) to locate any articles written on the promotional activities of the companies you select. Describe some of the types of promotions that these companies have engaged in during the last year—for example, ran television ads, sponsored an event, held a sweepstakes, or expanded sales force. To the best of your abilities, determine the objective of each promotion in relation to the AIDA model. For example, the objective of a magazine ad might be to gain attention or to create interest, while the objective of a coupon might be to stimulate the action of purchase. Also note if the companies' promotions are integrated or not.

6.3 Visit **http://www.teenresearch.com**. What research can this company offer about the size and growth of the teen market, the buying power of teenagers, and their buying habits? Why might these statistics be important to a company targeting teenagers in terms of marketing communications and promotion strategy?

7 **Discuss the concept of integrated marketing communications.** Integrated marketing communications is the careful coordination of all promotional messages for a product or service to assure the consistency of messages at every contact point where a company meets the consumer—advertising, sales promotion, personal selling, public relations, as well as direct marketing, packaging, and other forms of communication. Marketing managers carefully coordinate all promotional activities to ensure that consumers see and hear one message. Integrated marketing communications has received more attention in recent years due to the proliferation of media choices, the fragmentation of mass markets into more segmented niches, and the decrease in advertising spending in favor of promotional techniques that generate an immediate sales response.

7.1 Discuss the importance of integrated marketing communications. Give some current examples of companies that are and are not practicing IMC.

TERMS

advertising 481
AIDA concept 491
channel 486
communication 484
competitive advantage 480
decoding 487
encoding 485
feedback 487

integrated marketing communications (IMC) 498
interpersonal communication 485
mass communication 485
noise 486
personal selling 484
promotion 480
promotional mix 481
promotional strategy 480

publicity 482
public relations 481
pull strategy 497
push strategy 497
receiver 487
sales promotion 483
sender 485

EXERCISES

APPLICATION EXERCISE 1

Many people are not aware of the rationale behind certain advertising messages. "Why do Infiniti ads show rocks and trees instead of automobiles?" "If car safety is so important, why do automobile ads often show cars skidding on wet, shiny surfaces?" "Target's ads are funky, with all the bright colors and product packaging, but what's the message?"

One way to understand the vagaries of the encoding process is to think of the popular board game *Taboo* by Hasbro. In this game, each team tries to get its members to guess a word without using obvious word clues. For example, to get the team to guess "apple," you may not say such words as *red, fruit, pie, cider*, or *core*. Sometimes advertising is like *Taboo* in that advertisers are not allowed to use certain words or descriptions. For example, pharmaceutical companies are not permitted to make certain claims or to say what a drug treats unless the ad also mentions the potential side effects. Language choices are also limited in advertising. To appreciate this, you can apply the *Taboo* game rules in an advertising format.[23]

Activities

1. Select a product from the list below, and then create a print advertisement or a television storyboard for that product. As part of the exercise, give your product a brand name. Taboo words, visuals, and concepts are given for each product type. Taboo items cannot be present in your work.

Product	Taboo Words, Visuals, and Concepts
Deodorant	Odor, underarm, perspiration, smell, sweat
Toothpaste	Teeth, smile, breath, clean, plaque
Pain reliever	Pain, aches, fever, child-proof cap, gel
Soft drinks	Sugar-free, refreshing, thirst, swimwear, any celebrity

2. Now create a second ad or storyboard for your product. This time, however, you must use all the words, visuals, and concepts that are listed in the right column.

Product	Must-Use Words, Visuals, and Concepts
Deodorant	A romantic couple, monster trucks
Toothpaste	Lips, tongue, flowers
Pain reliever	A mother and child, oatmeal, homework
Soft drinks	A cup of coffee, cookies, birthday cake, wine

APPLICATION EXERCISE 2

An important concept in promotion is semiotics, or the study of meaning and meaning-producing events. An understanding of semiotics can help you not only to identify objects (denotation) but also to grasp the utility of images and associations (connotation). By manipulating connotations of objects in advertising, you can create, change, or reinforce images for products. Thus, semiotics is a powerful tool for brand management and promotion.[24]

Activities

1. Make a list of ten images and associations that come to mind for each of the following items: baseball, vinyl record album, spoon, rubber band.

2. Look through magazines in the periodical section of the campus library and see if you can find print advertisements that include each of the items (baseball, vinyl record album, spoon, rubber band) in a supporting role. What seems to be the message of each ad? How does the item help create or reinforce an image for the product being sold in the ad?

3. Think of an everyday object of your own. If you can't decide, write down a number of objects on slips of paper, and draw one at random from a box. Once you have selected an object, think of its likely connotations. For example, a dog in a car might signal a family vehicle, but a dog also connotes loyalty, "man's best friend," dependability, and so forth. What images and associations are likely with your item? Make a list of as many as you can.

4. Now use your object and list of associations to create an image for another product. Think of the likely connotations your object will have for a certain target market and how such connotations can support a brand image. For example, if your everyday object is a candle, you might choose lingerie for your product, based on a candle's romantic connotations.

ETHICS EXERCISE

Integrated Marketing Solutions is a consumer-products marketing services firm. Currently, the firm is handling the launch of a new book for one of its publishing clients. The campaign includes advance review copies for key book reviewers, "Coming Soon" posters for booksellers, an author book-signing tour, and several television interviews. Everything has been produced and scheduled for release next week. Today, Jane Kershaw, the account executive, has learned that although the book received numerous favorable reviews, the review quoted on all of the promotional materials is fabricated.

Questions

1. What should Jane do? Why?

2. What does the AMA Code of Ethics say about accuracy in promotional materials? Go to **http://www.marketingpower.com** and review the code. Then, write a brief paragraph describing how the AMA Code of Ethics relates to this issue.

Marketing communication is something that all companies do at some level, so you may think that finding a job in this area will be easier than in other marketing fields.

Activities

1. MarcommWise (**http://www.marcommwise.com**) has a wonderful job listings function that allows you to search its database by selecting more than one variable. For example, you can look for all jobs in event marketing, public relations, and media buying. There are more than 35 variables in sales, marketing, advertising, sales management, marketing management, and advertising management.

2. Another resource is Media Recruiter (**http://www.mediarecruiter.com**). Media Recruiter is smaller than MarcommWise, but it allows you to select the geographic regions where you want to search for job postings. This is helpful if you want to stay in a certain area. Media Recruiter is designed as a career recruitment program for all media professionals, including marketing, so you may find some job postings not specifically targeted to marketers. Still, it can be a valuable tool.

ENTREPRENEURSHIP CASE

PHOTO COURTESY OF NANTUCKET NECTARS.

NANTUCKET NECTARS: BLENDING MARKETING METHODS FOR A JUICY SUCCESS

After graduating from Brown University in the spring of 1989, college friends Tom First and Tom Scott moved to Nantucket Island, Massachusetts, determined to make it on their own and avoid the inevitable coat-and-tie corporate life. There, the two friends opened a boat-based delivery business in Nantucket Harbor to service the visiting yachts that came to the remote island in the warmer months. Having the summer of their lives, the pair delivered coffee, muffins, laundry, and other necessities to well-to-do island visitors and worked other odd jobs, such as shelling scallops, washing dogs, and pumping sewage, to earn money. Then Nantucket's ferocious winter kicked in, and their business slowed to a crawl.

One night during their first winter, the Toms started mixing fruit in a blender, trying to re-create a peach nectar that First had tasted during his travels to Spain. When they stumbled on some flavorful concoctions, their entrepreneurial spirits took over, and First and Scott decided to hand-bottle their juices in recycled wine bottles and sell them off their boat when the yachts returned with the warmer weather. They called their juices Nantucket Nectars and sold 2,000 bottles at $1 apiece the next summer. Encouraged by their initial sales, First and Scott decided to go into the juice business.

In the beginning, the pair targeted New England colleges close to Nantucket Island and Boston, thinking that the young adults there would most likely be receptive to their anti-establishment and underdog image. They pitched a big purple tent at football games and other college events and handed out juice and T-shirts with the distinctive Nantucket Nectars' logo. Their low-cost, grassroots marketing early on helped position Nantucket Nectars as the youthful, natural, and independent alternative to larger juice and beverage companies.

They also stumbled upon an effective radio advertising campaign. After booking a recording session, the Toms never got around to actually writing a script for their ad. Instead, they persuaded the radio producer to just record them talking. First and Scott "shot the breeze" for a couple of hours, reminiscing about their early days as "Juice Guys," and then edited the conversation for a radio spot. What resulted was an off-the-cuff, down-to-earth radio ad that ended up winning an award for excellence in radio advertising.

Nantucket Nectars still prefers such homespun techniques to promote its many juice flavors. The company uses "mobile marketing squads" that drive purple Winnebagos to outdoor events frequented by the company's coveted consumers—18- to 35-year-olds. Members of the company's high-energy, purple-shirted juice squad hand out free samples of the company's flavorful juices to sports fans, marathoners, and concertgoers. Mobile squads will also swap any competitor's product for a new cold bottle of Nantucket Nectars.

To introduce its latest Squeezed Nectars line of juice teas and lemonades packaged in distinctive wide-mouthed glass canning jars, the company relied heavily on sampling and promotions to create a buzz. In addition, the Toms decided to invite their grandmothers to promote the new line. In radio spots, the grandmothers chat with Scott and First about a wide range of topics, but mostly about how lemonade was made long ago, reinforcing the idea that Nantucket Nectars' lemonades taste just like grandma's.

From its humble beginnings, Nantucket Nectars has grown to be a major player in the premium juice drink category with a loyal following. While "Juice Guys" First and Scott have had their share of bumps along the way, their once tiny company now employs over 100 people, and revenues top $80 million. Their evolving juice lineup—50 different flavors in all—are sold in about 40 states and in Britain, France, Korea, the Caribbean, South and Central America, and Canada. The Toms still consider themselves the underdog in the premium juice industry. But no matter how much Nantucket Nectars grows, Scott says, he will always be looking for ways to change since the only way to succeed in this competitive environment is to be entrepreneurial.[25]

Questions

1. What elements of the promotional mix does Nantucket Nectars utilize to promote its juice line?

2. Where would you place Nantucket Nectars in the product life cycle? How does this affect the company's choice of promotional mix elements?

3. Visit the company's Web site at **http://www.juiceguys.com**. Give examples of how its Web site conveys its folksy, down-to-earth image.

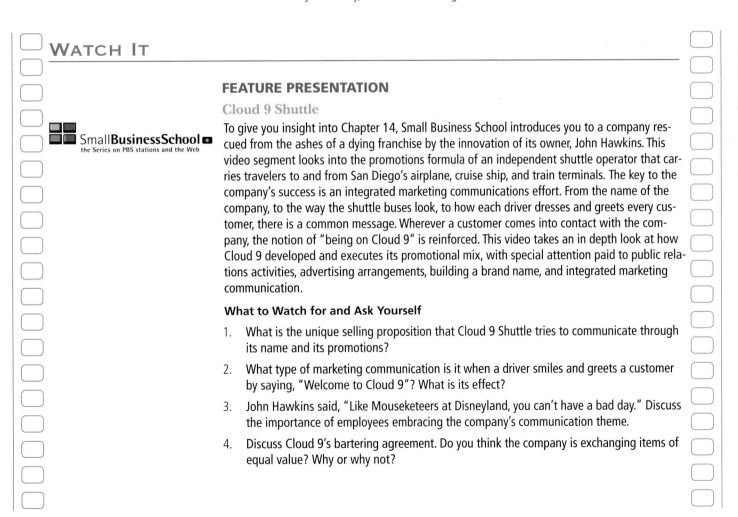

WATCH IT

SmallBusinessSchool ▪
the Series on PBS stations and the Web

FEATURE PRESENTATION

Cloud 9 Shuttle

To give you insight into Chapter 14, Small Business School introduces you to a company rescued from the ashes of a dying franchise by the innovation of its owner, John Hawkins. This video segment looks into the promotions formula of an independent shuttle operator that carries travelers to and from San Diego's airplane, cruise ship, and train terminals. The key to the company's success is an integrated marketing communications effort. From the name of the company, to the way the shuttle buses look, to how each driver dresses and greets every customer, there is a common message. Wherever a customer comes into contact with the company, the notion of "being on Cloud 9" is reinforced. This video takes an in depth look at how Cloud 9 developed and executes its promotional mix, with special attention paid to public relations activities, advertising arrangements, building a brand name, and integrated marketing communication.

What to Watch for and Ask Yourself

1. What is the unique selling proposition that Cloud 9 Shuttle tries to communicate through its name and its promotions?

2. What type of marketing communication is it when a driver smiles and greets a customer by saying, "Welcome to Cloud 9"? What is its effect?

3. John Hawkins said, "Like Mouseketeers at Disneyland, you can't have a bad day." Discuss the importance of employees embracing the company's communication theme.

4. Discuss Cloud 9's bartering agreement. Do you think the company is exchanging items of equal value? Why or why not?

ENCORE PRESENTATION

About a Boy

Now that you have a better grasp of marketing communications, you understand how messages can be designed to produce desired results. As an encore to your study, watch the film clip from *About a Boy*, starring Hugh Grant as happy, self-absorbed bachelor Will Lightman, who joins a support group for single parents as a way to meet women. Although Will has no children of his own, he finds himself inventing a son named Ned at his first Single Parents Alone Together (SPAT) meeting. Watching the clip, think about the communication process. How is Will's monologue like a promotional message? How is the AIDA concept at work in this scene? Explain. What other chapter concepts can you see in the clip if you think of it as a metaphor for marketing promotion?

STILL SHAKY?

If you're having trouble with the concepts in this chapter, consider using some of the following study resources. You can review the videos, or test yourself with materials designed for all kinds of learning styles.

☑ **Xtra! (http://lambxtra.swlearning.com)**

☑ Quiz   ☑ Feature Videos   ☑ Encore Videos   ☑ FAQ Videos

☑ Exhibit Worksheets   ☑ Marketing Plan Worksheets   ☐ Content

☑ **http://lamb.swlearning.com**

☑ Quiz   ☑ PowerPoint slides   ☑ Marketing News   ☑ Review Exercises

☑ Links   ☑ Marketing Plan Contest   ☑ Career Exercise   ☑ Use It Now

☑ **Study guide**

☑ Outline   ☑ Vocab Review   ☑ Test Questions   ☑ Marketing Scenario

Need More? Here's a tip. Use the learning objectives list on page 478 as a study tool. After reading the whole chapter, return to the beginning and write the summary for each objective. Check your work by reading the actual summary points on pages 500–502. If you are a visual learner, meaning you understand better and faster if you can see a picture, then try to draw your own set of visual summaries (similar to the ones throughout the chapter).

15

Advertising and Public Relations

LEARNING OBJECTIVES

1. Discuss the effects of advertising on market share and consumers

2. Identify the major types of advertising

3. Discuss the creative decisions in developing an advertising campaign

4. Describe media evaluation and selection techniques

5. Discuss the role of public relations in the promotional mix

ular games is *Madden NFL 2004*.

Madden NFL 2004 was designed to appeal to 16- to 34-year-olds. The game features real-life NFL teams playing each other. In the first three weeks after release, two million copies were sold for $50 each. Sales were expected to reach $200 million in the first year (for comparison, *Chicago*, which won the Oscar for Best Picture, brought in $171 million at the box office). Furthermore, unlike movie watchers, who often view a one and a half-hour movie only once, game players spend about 100 hours playing, watching, and listening to the same thing.

Madden NFL 2004 is not the only popular video game. Analysts expect Americans to spend about 75 hours per year playing video games. In a recent survey of college students, all of them had

played a video game before, and 70 percent said that they play occasionally. Thus, video games are an excellent medium for ~hing Gen Yers.

~e entire entertainment industry has ~d to the surge in online gaming. ~om movies stars to athletes ~s is trying to be featured in a video game. Movie stars are even signing up to record voice-overs or submit additional filming for some games. The recording industry is taking advantage of this opportunity by including new releases from big-name artists who reach the same demographic as the game. For example, *Madden NFL 2004* features Blink 182, The Roots, and Adema. The sports industry supports video gaming by providing information on athletes and teams. *Madden NFL 2004* provides players with information on what happened in training camp, relevant stats, and draft day. Game covers no longer feature animated figures; instead, they show the recording artist or real-life athlete featured in the game. For example, *Madden NFL 2004* features Michael Vick, the quarterback for the Atlanta Falcons, on the cover.

The latest video game offering is an online service where players compete against each other or on teams in cyberspace. The online service features tournaments, leagues, stats, and rankings. To encourage more game usage, EA Sports, the parent company of *Madden NFL 2004*, tracks gamers' bios. When they win, it gives them access to additional game secrets, athletes, uniforms, teams, stadiums, and gaming modes—the objective is to interest gamers in other games the company offers, such as *FIFA Soccer 2004*. To effectively reach the target market, EA Sports advertises heavily during *NFL Monday Night Football* on ABC and on Comedy Central.[1]

How do marketers of video games like *Madden NFL 2004* decide what type of advertising message should be used to appeal to prospective customers? How do marketers decide what media to use? How do public relations and publicity benefit a marketer's promotional plan? Answers to these questions and many more will be found as you read through this chapter.

1 THE EFFECTS OF ADVERTISING

Discuss the effects of advertising on market share and consumers

Advertising is defined in Chapter 14 as any form of impersonal, paid communication in which the sponsor or company is identified. It is a popular form of promotion, especially for consumer packaged goods and services. Advertising spending increases annually and is expected to reach nearly $300 billion per year in the United States by 2006.[2] The top 200 brands account for approximately 37 percent of all media spending. Some of those brands include Ford Motor Company, Sony, L'Oréal (cosmetics), and Verizon Communications.[3]

EXHIBIT 15.1

Top Ten Leaders by U.S. Advertising Spending

Rank	Advertiser	Total U.S. Ad Spending In 2003 (in millions)
1	General Motors Corporation	$3,429.9
2	Procter & Gamble	$3,322.7
3	Time Warner	$3,097.3
4	Pfizer	$2,838.5
5	DaimlerChrysler	$2,317.5
6	Ford Motor, Dearborn	$2,233.8
7	Walt Disney	$2,129.3
8	Johnson & Johnson	$1,995.7
9	Sony Corporation	$1,814.8
10	Toyota Motor Corporation	$1,682.7

(Chart axis: 0, 500, 1000, 1500, 2000, 2500, 3000, 3500, 4000)

SOURCE: Computed from data obtained in R. Craig Endicott, "Leading National Advertisers Report," *Advertising Age,* June 28, 2004.

Although total advertising expenditures seem large, the industry itself is small. Only about 140,000 people are employed in the advertising departments of manufacturers, wholesalers, and retailers and in the 13,000 or so advertising agencies.[4] This figure also includes people working in media services, such as radio and television, magazines and newspapers, and direct-mail firms.

The amount of money budgeted for advertising by some firms is staggering (see Exhibit 15.1). General Motors, Procter & Gamble and Time Warner each spend over $3 billion annually in the United States on national advertising alone. That's approximately $9 million a day on national advertising. If local advertising, sales promotion, and public relations are included, this figure rises much higher. Almost 100 additional companies spend over $200 million each.

Spending on advertising varies by industry. For example, the game and toy industry has one of the highest ratios of advertising dollars to sales. For every dollar of merchandise sold in the toy industry, about 12 to 15 cents is spent on advertising the toy to consumers. Book publishers spend roughly 27 cents on advertising for every dollar of book revenue. Other consumer goods manufacturers that spend heavily on advertising in relation to total sales include sugar and confectionery products manufacturers, leather manufacturers, watchmakers, perfume and cosmetic manufacturers, detergent makers, and wine and liquor companies.[5]

FAQs

How do businesses decide how much to advertise? Find out the answer by watching the video FAQ on Xtra!

ADVERTISING AND MARKET SHARE

Today's most successful brands of consumer goods, like Ivory soap and Coca-Cola, were built by heavy advertising and marketing investments long ago. Today's advertising dollars are spent on maintaining brand awareness and market share.

New brands with a small market share tend to spend proportionately more for advertising and sales promotion than those with a large market share, typically for two reasons. First, beyond a certain level of spending for advertising and sales promotion, diminishing returns set in. That is, sales or market share begins to decrease no matter how much is spent on advertising and sales promotion. This phenomenon is called the **advertising response function**. Understanding the advertising response function helps marketers use budgets wisely. A market leader like Johnson & Johnson's Neutrogena typically spends proportionately less on advertising than a newcomer like Jergens' Naturally Smooth Shave Minimizing Moisturizer brand. Jergens spends more on its brand to gain attention and increase market share. Neutrogena, on the other hand, spends only as much as is needed to maintain market share; anything more would produce diminishing benefits. Neutrogena has already captured the attention of the majority of its target market. It only needs to remind customers of its product.

advertising response function
A phenomenon in which spending for advertising and sales promotion increases sales or market share up to a certain level but then produces diminishing returns.

The second reason that new brands tend to require higher spending for advertising and sales promotion is that a certain minimum level of exposure is needed to measurably affect purchase habits. If Jergens advertised Naturally Smooth Shave Minimizing Moisturizer in only one or two publications and bought only one or two television spots, it certainly would not achieve the exposure needed to penetrate consumers' perceptual defenses, gain attention, and ultimately affect purchase intentions. Instead, Naturally Smooth Shave Minimizing Moisturizer was advertised in many different media for a sustained time.

THE EFFECTS OF ADVERTISING ON CONSUMERS

Advertising affects consumers' daily lives, informing them about products and services and influencing their attitudes, beliefs, and ultimately their purchases. The average U.S. citizen is exposed to hundreds of advertisements a day from all types of advertising media. In the television medium alone, researchers estimate that the average viewer watches at least six hours of commercial television messages a week. In addition, that person is exposed to countless print ads and promotional messages seen in other places. Advertising affects the TV programs people watch, the content of the newspapers they read, the politicians they elect, the medicines they take, and the toys their children play with. Consequently, the influence of advertising on the U.S. socioeconomic system has been the subject of extensive debate among economists, marketers, sociologists, psychologists, politicians, consumerists, and many others.

Though advertising cannot change consumers' deeply rooted values and attitudes, advertising may succeed in transforming a person's negative attitude toward a product into a positive one. For instance, serious or dramatic advertisements are more effective at changing consumers' negative attitudes. Humorous ads, on the other hand, have been shown to be more effective at shaping attitudes when consumers already have a positive image of the advertised brand.[6] For this reason, beer marketers often use humorous ads, such as those featuring the Budweiser frogs, to communicate with their core market of young adults.

Advertising also reinforces positive attitudes toward brands. When consumers have a neutral or favorable frame of reference toward a product or brand, advertising often positively influences them. When consumers are already highly loyal to a brand, they may buy more of it when advertising and promotion for that brand increase.[7] This is why market leaders like General Motors and Procter & Gamble spend billions of dollars annually to reinforce and remind their loyal customers about the benefits of their cars and household products.

Advertising can also affect the way consumers rank a brand's attributes, such as color, taste, smell, and texture. For example, in years past car ads emphasized such brand attributes as roominess, speed, and low maintenance. Today, however, car marketers have added safety, versatility, and customization to the list. Safety features like antilock brakes, power door locks, and front and side air bags are now a standard part of the message in many carmakers' ads. Moreover, Toyota Scion appeals to consumers' sense of individuality by allowing purchasers to custom-design their cars by selecting features such as the steering wheel color, multishade illuminated cup holders, and "sport" pedals.[8]

REVIEW LEARNING OBJECTIVE 1

1 | **Discuss the effects of advertising on market share and consumers**

Advertising can:
- ✓ change negative attitude to positive
- ✓ reinforce positive attitude
- ✓ affect how consumers rank brand attributes

Ford Motor Company's 100th anniversary gave the company a unique opportunity for institutional advertising. Ford capitalized on the event to promote updates and reintroductions of classic models.

100 years. The sheet metal anniversary.

Ford
100 YEARS

© COURTESY OF FORD MOTOR

services. For example, when Time Warner dropped AOL from the company's corporate brand name, it hired a branding agency to develop institutional advertising to reposition the brand without the Internet unit and refocus the image on Time Warner as a media giant. In designing the "rebranding," executives did not want a radical change. Rather they wanted to "freshen" the previous image and maintain its favorable status. The logo itself changed in texture, color, and typeface. In addition to changing the logo on buildings, business cards, and stationary, the company changed its stock ticker symbol to reflect the new image.[9]

A form of institutional advertising called **advocacy advertising** is typically used to safeguard against negative consumer attitudes and to enhance the company's credibility among consumers who already favor its position. Often corporations use advocacy advertising to express their views on controversial issues. At other times, firms' advocacy campaigns react to criticism or blame, some in direct response to criticism by the media. Other advocacy campaigns may try to ward off increased regulation, damaging legislation, or an unfavorable outcome in a lawsuit. The tobacco companies have utilized "good citizen campaigns" in the United States and around the world in an effort to create a positive public image for themselves after losing several class-action suits and being accused of targeting children with their marketing campaigns. In an effort to improve public opinion, Philip Morris has been pouring $100 million a year into feel-good ads promoting corporate good deeds such as donations to food banks and shelters for battered women.[10]

PRODUCT ADVERTISING

Unlike institutional advertising, product advertising promotes the benefits of a specific good or service. The product's stage in its life cycle often determines which type of product advertising is used: pioneering advertising, competitive advertising, or comparative advertising.

Pioneering Advertising

Pioneering advertising is intended to stimulate primary demand for a new product or product category. Heavily used during the introductory stage of the product life cycle, pioneering advertising offers consumers in-depth information about the benefits of the product class. Pioneering advertising also seeks to create interest. Microsoft

institutional advertising
A form of advertising designed to enhance a company's image rather than promote a particular product.

product advertising
A form of advertising that touts the benefits of a specific good or service.

advocacy advertising
A form of advertising in which an organization expresses its views on controversial issues or responds to media attacks

pioneering advertising
A form of advertising designed to stimulate primary demand for a new product or product category.

used pioneering advertising to introduce its new Windows and Office software products. In a move to reposition the products as more "user-friendly," the software giant renamed its flagship products by adding "XP"—short for "Experience"—to the Windows and Office

Pizza Hut
Papa John's
Can you find evidence of comparative advertising on either Pizza Hut's or Papa John's Web site?
http://www.pizzahut.com
http://www.papajohns.com

Online

upgrades.[11] Microsoft's $200 million four-month launch phase kicked off with two 15-second TV teaser spots, plus one 60-second and two 30-second TV spots that featured the Madonna song "Ray of Light." The print, outdoor, TV, and online campaign carries the tagline "Yes, you can" and features XP's signature look—blue skies with white clouds over a green field. The goal of Microsoft's pioneering campaign was to convince PC users to buy the upgrade because of the more intuitive interfaces and abilities to work seamlessly and easily with digital photographs, music files, and video.[12]

Competitive Advertising

Firms use competitive or brand advertising when a product enters the growth phase of the product life cycle and other companies begin to enter the marketplace. Instead of building demand for the product category, the goal of **competitive advertising** is to influence demand for a specific brand. Often promotion becomes less informative and appeals more to emotions during this phase. Advertisements may begin to stress subtle differences between brands, with heavy emphasis on building recall of a brand name and creating a favorable attitude toward the brand. Automobile advertising has long used very competitive messages, drawing distinctions based on such factors as quality, performance, and image. Similarly, in an effort to obtain market share from competitors and build brand awareness in the wireless industry, Nextel Communications signed a ten-year title sponsorship agreement with NASCAR. NASCAR executives, interested in building a younger fan base, consider the telecom industry to be one of the best ways to reach younger consumers because they always have a cell phone "stuck" to their ear.[13]

Comparative Advertising

Comparative advertising directly or indirectly compares two or more competing brands on one or more specific attributes. Some advertisers even use comparative advertising against their own brands. Products experiencing sluggish growth or those entering the marketplace against strong competitors are more likely to employ comparative claims in their advertising. For instance, Miller Lite implemented a comparative advertising campaign in an attempt to regain market share from Bud Light. The focus of the campaign was that Miller Lite has the fewest simple carbohydrates of the leading light beers. The ads ended by stating that "Miller Lite has half the carbs of Bud Light."[14]

Before the 1970s, comparative advertising was allowed only if the competing brand was veiled and unidentified. In 1971, however, the Federal Trade Commission (FTC) fostered the growth of comparative advertising by saying that it provided information to the customer and that advertisers were more skillful than the government in communicating this information. Federal rulings prohibit advertisers from falsely describing competitors' products and allow competitors to sue if ads show their products or mention their brand names in an incorrect or false manner.

FTC rules also apply to advertisers making false claims about their own products. Recently, a physicians' group filed false advertising complaints against the popular and long-lasting "milk mustache" ad campaign. The physicians said the ads, featuring sports figures, falsely claimed to enhance sports performances. In response to the physicians' petition, a federal panel was formed to determine whether there was a scientific consensus regarding the range of benefits attributed to milk. The panel's report supported most of the physicians' complaints and was turned over to the FTC for investigation.[15] In a case against computer maker

competitive advertising
A form of advertising designed to influence demand for a specific brand.

comparative advertising
A form of advertising that compares two or more specifically named or shown competing brands on one or more specific attributes.

perceived to produce a higher quality vodka than that made from potatoes. Rival distributor Aosta Company, noting that two of its products were made from grain, filed a complaint against Absolut's Italian distributor, Seagram Italia.[18] Although comparative advertising has been legal in Italy since 1999, ads cannot make unsubstantiated claims. So authorities ordered the campaign stopped and Seagram Italia had to

ETHICS IN MARKETING

> WHAT IS DECEPTIVE ADVERTISING?

A class-action suit has been filed against Bacardi, Heineken, Coors, and other alcohol producers that mirrors the claims against tobacco company ads. The suit charges that the marketers of alcohol products are attempting to establish brand loyalty among younger consumers by using devices such as code words and video games in a variety of advertising media. For example, the suit alleges that the "Bacardi by Night" advertising series features "wild, raucous, irresponsible, and immature behavior by models chosen to appeal to underage consumers." The print ad shows a young guy taking a "body shot" off a younger woman's bare midriff. In addition to the print ads, the Web site uses cartoon characters. The ads ran in magazines such as *Stuff, FHM*, and *Spin* that are read by a large number of young consumers. A Heineken ad came under fire for showing two beers duct taped to a Nintendo Gamecube controller with the heading "It's Game Day," followed by the caption "Add two more to your controller." Coors came under heavy criticism for using tie-ins with the PG 13–rated *Scary Movie*. Coors used cooperative advertising with the Disney film in the form of TV commercials and in-store displays. Coors also used product placement with the Coors twins making a cameo appearance in the film. The companies deny all of the claims and say their ads reach only consumers of legal age.

Kentucky Fried Chicken received a complaint from the Federal Trade Commission alleging that its advertising campaign portrayed fried chicken as part of a healthy diet. KFC originally developed the campaign because it felt "consumers should no longer feel guilty about eating fried chicken." To convey this idea, KFC used a TV commercial in which a wife brings a bucket of fried chicken to her husband and tells him they are going to start eating better. Then the voice-over says "Two Original Recipe chicken breasts have less fat than a BK [Burger King] Whopper. Or go skinless for 3 grams of fat per piece. . . . For a fresh way to eat better, you gotta KFC what's cookin'!" The commercial shows consumers peeling the skin off the chicken, which lowers its fat content to only 3 grams. Complaints about this advertising campaign arose in the wake of studies attributing the obesity epidemic to fast-food restaurants.

Issues with deceptive or unethical advertising extend beyond U.S. borders. One of Honda's ads was pulled from Australian TV because it "trivialized suicide." The ad showed a driver of an old model Honda Accord ogling a new model Accord. The old Accord then locks its own doors and drives over a cliff without the driver. A local Australian activist group said the ad targeted young people who are often victims of suicide.[17]

Do you think these ads are deceptive or unethical? Can you recall other advertisements that you think were questionable?

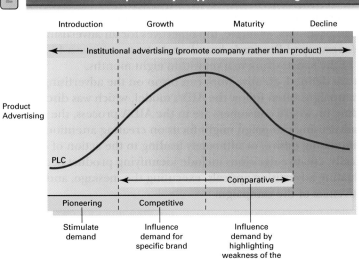

2 | Identify the major types of advertising

pull all ads. Finally, in South Korea, where comparative advertising is banned, ads for the domestic search engine Empas proclaim, "Empas Is No. 1, Yahoo! Is No. 6," and "If you can't find it with Yahoo!, try Empas." Yahoo! filed a complaint with Korea's Fair Trade Commission requesting that the ads be stopped.[19]

In other countries, hard-hitting comparative advertising will not be effective because it offends cultural values. For example, Arabic culture generally encourages people not to compete with one another, and the sharing of wealth is common practice. Therefore, comparative advertising is not consistent with social values in these countries. Japanese advertisers are also reluctant to use comparative advertising because it is considered confrontational and doesn't promote the respectful treatment of consumers or portray a company in a respectful light. Nevertheless, although the Japanese have traditionally favored soft-sell advertising approaches, consumers are witnessing a trend toward comparative ads.

3 CREATIVE DECISIONS IN ADVERTISING

 Discuss the creative decisions in developing an advertising campaign

Advertisements that are seen on television, in magazines, and on the Internet are typically the result of an **advertising campaign**—a series of related advertisements focusing on a common theme, slogan, and set of advertising appeals. It is a specific advertising effort for a particular product that extends for a defined period of time. For example, XM Satellite Radio, the first subscription-based, digital-quality, satellite-transmitted radio service, developed an introductory advertising campaign around the theme "Radio to the Power of X." The company was attempting to persuade consumers to pay $10 a month for what has always been free. Launched in movie theaters followed by TV, the $100 million ad campaign featured musicians and objects crashing to earth, each highlighting a different genre of satellite programming. B. B. King, Snoop Dogg, and David Bowie made appearances as they tumbled toward the ground. Other spots showed records raining on kids in a parking lot and a truck driver caught in a storm of cellos, trombones, and pianos. At the end of each spot, an XM tuner cycled through the channels until it rested on the appropriate genre. The idea was to convey the endless variety of programming offered on XM Satellite Radio and to set XM apart from its competitor, Sirius.[20]

Before any creative work can begin on an advertising campaign, it is important to determine what goals or objectives the advertising should achieve. An **advertising objective** identifies the specific communication task that a campaign should accomplish for a specified target audience during a specified period. The objectives of a specific advertising campaign often depend on the overall corporate objectives and the product being advertised. For example, McIlhenny Company's Tabasco Hot Sauce launched a print advertising campaign with the objective of educating consumers about how to use the product and the variety of flavors offered. The ads featured product information embedded in the label, which was blown up to cover the entire page. The ad copy for the Garlic Pepper Sauce read: "The only one potent enough to ward off both hypothermia and vampires at once." The original Tabasco Pepper Sauce ad copy read: "It's like love, you always want more no matter how badly you got burned last time." The ad campaign increased sales by more over 11 percent in the first four weeks. The print medium was also supported by participation in special events, such as *ESPN the Magazine* and the National Collegiate Tailgate Tour.[21]

advertising campaign
A series of related advertisements focusing on a common theme, slogan, and set of advertising appeals.

advertising objective
A specific communication task that a campaign should accomplish for a specified target audience during a specified period.

steak"—that is, in advertising the goal is to sell the benefits of the product, not its attributes. An attribute is simply a feature of the product such as its easy-open package or special formulation. A benefit is what consumers will receive or achieve by using the product. A benefit should answer the consumer's question "What's in it for me?" Benefits might be such things as convenience, pleasure, savings, or relief. A quick test to determine whether you are offering attributes or benefits in your advertising is to ask "So?" Consider this example:

Attribute: "Powerade's new line has been reformulated to combine the scientific benefits of sports drinks with B vitamins and to speed up energy metabolism." "So . . . ?" *Benefit:* "So, you'll satisfy your thirst with a great-tasting drink that will power you throughout the day."

Marketing research and intuition are usually used to unearth the perceived benefits of a product and to rank consumers' preferences for these benefits. Coke's rival, PepsiCo, has its own sports drink, Gatorade. Already positioned as *the* thirst-quencher, Gatorade's advertising touts its refueling benefits to serious athletes of mainstream sports. When Hollywood chewing gum lost its market leader status in France, the company conducted extensive research and development and identified several functional benefits for the "flavor" positioned gum such as fresh breath, white teeth, an energy boost, and decongestant. After repositioning the gum's functional benefits, sales increased by 28 percent.[22]

Verizon has created a strong advertising appeal with its "Do you hear me now?" campaign. The company's unique selling proposition of nationwide wireless phone service has become its slogan: "We never stop working for you."

© BILL ARON/PHOTO EDIT

DEVELOPING AND EVALUATING ADVERTISING APPEALS

An **advertising appeal** identifies a reason for a person to buy a product. Developing advertising appeals, a challenging task, is typically the responsibility of the creative people in the advertising agency. Advertising appeals typically play off of consumers' emotions, such as fear or love, or address some need or want the consumer has, such as a need for convenience or the desire to save money.

advertising appeal
A reason for a person to buy a product.

Advertising campaigns can focus on one or more advertising appeals. Often the appeals are quite general, thus allowing the firm to develop a number of sub-themes or minicampaigns using both advertising and sales promotion. Several possible advertising appeals are listed in Exhibit 15.2.

Choosing the best appeal from those developed normally requires market research. Criteria for evaluation include desirability, exclusiveness, and believability. The appeal first must make a positive impression on and be desirable to the target market. It must also be exclusive or unique; consumers must be able to distinguish the advertiser's message from competitors' messages. Most important, the appeal should be believable. An appeal that makes extravagant claims not only wastes promotional dollars but also creates ill will for the advertiser.

The advertising appeal selected for the campaign becomes what advertisers call its **unique selling proposition**. The unique selling proposition usually becomes the campaign's slogan. For example, Unilever's Degree antiperspirant, targeted at males aged 18 to 25, attempted to convey the brand's "never say die" personality by partnering with Ironman and NBC to create a TV special "Degree Road to the Ironman." The TV special was to correspond with the ad campaign carrying the slogan "Kicks in the Clutch," which was also Degree's unique selling proposition.[23] Similarly, Powerade's advertising campaign aimed at the nontraditional sports enthusiast carries the slogan "Very Real Power." This is also Powerade's unique selling proposition, implying that you can push yourself to the limit because the drink offers more "power" through carbonated fuel.[24]

Effective slogans often become so ingrained that consumers can immediately conjure up images of the product just by hearing the slogan. For example, most consumers can easily name the companies and products behind these memorable slogans or even hum the jingle that goes along with some of them: "Have it your way," "Tastes great, less filling," "Ring around the collar," and "Tum te Tum Tum." Advertisers often revive old slogans or jingles in the hope that the nostalgia will create good feelings with consumers. In 2003, Maytag Corporation refreshed its campaign featuring its appliance pitchman by changing the actor who plays him and by giving him a helper—the third change since the ads originated in 1967. And Hershey Foods' Kit Kat bar's ten-year old jingle "Gimme a Break" is so etched in consumers' minds that recently the agency hired a film crew to walk around and ask people on the street to sing the jingle for use in future spots.[25]

EXECUTING THE MESSAGE

Message execution is the way an advertisement portrays its information. In general, the AIDA (see Chapter 14) plan is a good blueprint for executing an advertising

unique selling proposition
A desirable, exclusive, and believable advertising appeal selected as the theme for a campaign.

Common Advertising Appeals

Profit	Lets consumers know whether the product will save them money, make them money, or keep them from losing money
Health	Appeals to those who are body-conscious or who want to be healthy
Love or Romance	Is used often in selling cosmetics and perfumes
Fear	Can center around social embarrassment, growing old, or losing one's health; because of its power, requires advertiser to exercise care in execution
Admiration	Is the reason that celebrity spokespeople are used so often in advertising
Convenience	Is often used for fast-food restaurants and microwave foods
Fun and Pleasure	Are the key to advertising vacations, beer, amusement parks, and more
Vanity and Egotism	Are used most often for expensive or conspicuous items such as cars and clothing
Environmental Consciousness	Centers around protecting the environment and being considerate of others in the community

cated. Humorous ads are typically used for lower risk, routine purchases such as candy, cigarettes, and soft drinks than for higher risk purchases or those that are expensive, durable, or flamboyant.[26] Anheuser-Busch's consistent humorous approach to its Budweiser and Bud Light advertising campaigns has been credited with giving Bud a competitive edge in an image-conscious category that traditionally prefers upscale imports. Frogs, lizards, a ferret and, of course, the "Whassup?" guys resonate with the core 21- to 27-year-old target market and have also secured a place in American pop culture.[27] But the situation must be considered before using a humorous

EXHIBIT 15.3

Ten Common Executional Styles for Advertising

Slice-of-Life	Depicts people in normal settings, such as at the dinner table or in their car. McDonald's often uses slice-of-life styles showing youngsters munching french fries and Happy Meals on family outings.
Lifestyle	Shows how well the product will fit in with the consumer's lifestyle. As their Volkswagen Jetta moves through the streets of the French Quarter, the Gen X drivers plug in a techno music CD and marvel at how the rhythms of the world mimic the ambient vibe inside their vehicle.
Spokesperson/ Testimonial	Can feature a celebrity, company official, or typical consumer making a testimonial or endorsing a product. Sarah Michelle Gellar, star of *Buffy the Vampire Slayer,* endorses Maybelline cosmetics while country singer Shania Twain introduced Revlon's ColorStay Liquid Lip. Dell Computer founder Michael Dell touts his vision of the customer experience via Dell in television ads.
Fantasy	Creates a fantasy for the viewer built around use of the product. Carmakers often use this style to let viewers fantasize about how they would feel speeding around tight corners or down long country roads in their cars.
Humorous	Advertisers often use humor in their ads, such as Snickers' "Not Going Anywhere for a While" campaign featuring hundreds of souls waiting, sometimes impatiently, to get into heaven.
Real/Animated Product Symbols	Creates a character that represents the product in advertisements, such as the Energizer bunny, Starkist's Charlie the Tuna, or General Mills' longtime icon, Betty Crocker, redesigned for the new millennium.
Mood or Image	Builds a mood or image around the product, such as peace, love, or beauty. DeBeers ads depicting shadowy silhouettes wearing diamond engagement rings and diamond necklaces portray passion and intimacy while extolling that a "diamond is forever."
Demonstration	Shows consumers the expected benefit. Many consumer products use this technique. Laundry-detergent spots are famous for demonstrating how their product will clean clothes whiter and brighter. Fort James Corporation recently demonstrated in television commercials how its Dixie Rinse & ReUse disposable stoneware product line can stand up to the heat of a blowtorch and survive a cycle in a clothes washer.
Musical	Conveys the message of the advertisement through song. For example, Nike's recent ads depicting a marathoner's tortured feet, skier Picabo Street's surgery-scarred knee, and a surfer's thigh scarred by a shark attack while strains of Joe Cocker's "You Are So Beautiful" are heard in the background.
Scientific	Uses research or scientific evidence to give a brand superiority over competitors. Pain relievers like Advil, Bayer, and Excedrin use scientific evidence in their ads.

EXHIBIT 15.4

Dreamful Attraction: Shaquille O'Neal's Thoughts on Marketing and Advertising

While on the outside looking in, I did not realize that marketing was so complicated. I never knew that a person, such as an athlete, could have such a powerful effect on peoples' thought processes and purchasing behavior. The use of a well-known athlete in marketing a product or service can have a great impact on the sales of that product or service. Look at Michael Jordan. Almost overnight most every kid either was wearing or wanted to wear Air Jordan shoes.

Why does this happen? Is it the appeal of a great athlete or is it great marketing? The answer is "none of the above." It's both. In my years as a professional basketball player, I have seen firsthand the dramatic appeal that athletes have for the fans and public in general. Top-name athletes are like E. F. Hutton—when they talk, people listen. But why do they listen? I believe they listen to us, the athletes, because we have credibility. The effectiveness of celebrity endorsements depends largely on how credible and attractive the spokesperson is and how familiar people are with him or her. Companies sometimes use sports figures and other celebrities to promote products hoping they are appropriate opinion leaders.

Because of an athlete's fame and fortune, or attraction, the athlete can often have the right credibility to be a successful spokesperson. The best definition of credibility that I could find was by James Gordon in his book, *Rhetoric of Western Thought.* He said that attraction "can come from a person's observable talents, achievements, occupational position or status, personality and appearance, and style."* That may be why a famous athlete's personality and position can help him or her communicate more effectively than a not-so-famous athlete.

Credibility is a positive force in the persuasive promotion used predominantly by cola marketers like Pepsi because of what I like to call "dreamful attraction." For example, when I was young, I dreamed that I was like Dr. J., the famous basketball player for the Philadelphia 76ers. I would take his head off a poster and put my head on it. I wanted to be Dr. J. That is dreamful attraction. The youth of today are no different. Just the other day a kid stopped me and told me that he wanted to be like me. He had a dreamful attraction. This dreamful attraction can help sell products. In my case, Pepsi, Spalding, Kenner, and Reebok are hoping that they are able to package properly and market whatever dreamful attraction I might have for their target audience—kids.

There are many ways to communicate to my target audience. I find that the most effective way for me is through television commercials. This avenue gives me a chance to express myself and show my real feelings about a message we are trying to communicate—either visually or vocally. I feel that I have what Clint Eastwood has—"Sudden Impaq." My impact is revealed through my sense of humor and my nonverbal communication.

Why does Shaq sell? Communication. Although the verbal communication in many of my commercials is slim, the impact is still there. This makes me believe even more in the quote that who you are can almost be as important as what you say. But if you can blend the two together—who you are and what you have to say—then imagine how much more successful the communication message can be in the marketing process. Andre Agassi's favorite quote from his Canon commercial is "Image is everything." If it is not everything, it is almost everything. If you have the right image, match it with the right product, and market it properly, then success should follow.

I have been involved in commercials and the marketing of products for only a short time, but I have learned a great deal. If there is one formula for success in selling products, it would be this: Marketing plus credibility and image plus effective communications equals increase in sales—hopefully.

Now, you can call me Dr. Shaq, M.E. (Marketing Expert).

*James Gordon, *Rhetoric of Western Thought* (Dubuque, Iowa: Kendall-Hunt Publishing Co., 1976), 207.

An advertising appeal identifies a reason for a person to buy a product. This ad for Crest Whitestrips uses a vanity appeal by conveying the idea of looking better and younger. The scientific executional style cites research that supports the ad with the language "clinically proven."

approach in advertising. After the September 11 terrorist attacks on the Pentagon and the World Trade Center, many shell-shocked consumers felt that some advertising campaigns were no longer appropriate. And participants in nationwide focus groups felt that marketers should consider using sentimental messages or even reviving nostalgic campaigns.[28]

Executional styles for foreign advertising are often quite different from those we are accustomed to in the United States. Sometimes they are sexually oriented or aesthetically imaginative. For example, the *Financial Times* created the world's biggest newspaper by covering Hong Kong's tallest skyscraper in fabric that showed the front page. The skyscraper is also home to the newspaper's Asian headquarters. The outdoor advertising space is worth about $6 million.[29] European advertising avoids the direct-sell approaches common in U.S. ads and instead is more indirect, more symbolic, and, above all, more visual. Nike, known in the United States for "in-your-face" advertising and irrever-

Vietnam, India, and China was designed to show consumers how a mobile phone can improve their lifestyles. The campaign, titled "We Never Stop Challenging the Future," was supported through TV, print, outdoor, and online advertising. One print ad showed a person stranded on a dirt road with the possibility of going in four different directions. The caption read "You could call for directions. Or use your phone to download maps. What if it could actually guide you home?" Another ad emphasized the phone's technological capabilities by showing a phone embedded in a man's hand. The copy read

Subsequent 2-page print ads featured a picture of a VW car and a poem about the feelings associated with a VW automobile. The intent was that consumers viewing these ads would identify with the emotions that support their beliefs about the company.[31]

These examples illustrate how companies are using advertising to reach consumers in markets outside the United States. How do the domestic advertising campaigns by the same companies differ? Compare the advertisements and consider the similarities and differences.

ent slogans such as "Just Do It," discovered that its brash advertising did not appeal to Europeans.

 Japanese advertising is known for relying on fantasy and mood to sell products. Ads in Japan notoriously lack the emphatic selling demonstrations found in U.S. advertising, limit the exposure of unique product features, and avoid direct comparisons to competitors' products. Japanese ads often feature cartoon characters or place the actors in irrelevant situations. For example, one advertisement promotes an insect spray while showing the actor having teeth extracted at the dentist's office. One explanation of Japan's preference for soft-sell advertising is cultural: Japanese consumers are naturally suspicious of someone who needs to extol the virtues of a product. Additionally, unlike advertising agencies in the United States, which consider working for competing companies to be unethical, Japan's larger ad agencies customarily maintain business relationships with competing advertisers. Ads are less hard-hitting so as not to offend other clients.[30] See the "Global Perspectives" box in this chapter for some other examples of advertising around the world.

Determining how consumers will react to advertising can be a difficult proposition. During the 2004 Super Bowl, ad agency McKee Wallwork Henderson launched AdBowl IV. Viewers judged the commercials aired during the game and rated them on a scale of 1 (fumble) to 5 (touchdown).

POSTCAMPAIGN EVALUATION

Evaluating an advertising campaign can be the most demanding task facing advertisers. How do advertisers know whether the campaign led to an increase in sales or market share or elevated awareness of the product? Most advertising campaigns aim to create an image for the good or service instead of asking for action, so their real effect is unknown. So many variables shape the effectiveness of an ad that, in many cases, advertisers must guess whether their money has been well spent. Despite this gray area, marketers spend a considerable amount of time studying advertising effectiveness and its probable impact on sales, market share, or awareness.

Testing ad effectiveness can be done either before or after the campaign. Before a campaign is released, marketing managers use pretests to determine the best advertising appeal, layout, and media vehicle. After advertisers implement a campaign, they often conduct tests to measure its effectiveness. Several monitoring techniques can be used to determine whether the campaign has met its original goals. Even if a campaign has been highly successful, advertisers still typically do a postcampaign analysis. They assess how the campaign might have been more efficient and what factors contributed to its success. For example, Hallmark's market researchers wanted to capitalize on aging baby boomers. Research indicated that baby boomers do not want to age, but since that is inevitable, boomers want to see the positive side of aging. Therefore, Hallmark created the "Time of Your Life" series that flattered their egos. The cards were not successful, however, because they were placed in the "over 50" section of the store and baby boomers do not want to shop in that section.[32]

3 Discuss the creative decisions in developing an advertising campaign

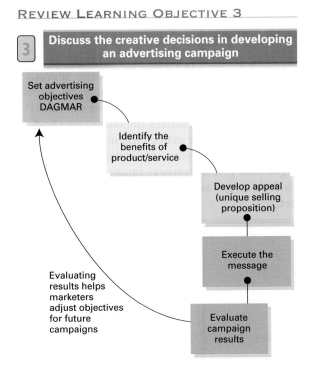

Set advertising objectives DAGMAR

Identify the benefits of product/service

Develop appeal (unique selling proposition)

Execute the message

Evaluate campaign results

Evaluating results helps marketers adjust objectives for future campaigns

4 MEDIA DECISIONS IN ADVERTISING

Describe media evaluation and selection techniques

A major decision for advertisers is the choice of **medium**—the channel used to convey a message to a target market. **Media planning**, therefore, is the series of decisions advertisers make regarding the selection and use of media, allowing the marketer to optimally and cost-effectively communicate the message to the target audience. Specifically, advertisers must determine which types of media will best communicate the benefits of their product or service to the target audience and when and for how long the advertisement will run.

Promotional objectives and the appeal and executional style of the advertising strongly affect the selection of media. It is important to understand that both creative and media decisions are made at the same time. Creative work cannot be completed without knowing which medium will be used to convey the message to the target market. For instance, creative planning will likely differ for an ad to be displayed on an outdoor billboard versus that placed in a print medium, such as a newspaper or magazine. In many cases, the advertising objectives dictate the medium and the creative approach to be used. For example, if the objective is to demonstrate how fast a product operates, a TV commercial that shows this action may be the best choice.

U.S. advertisers spend about $300 billion on media advertising annually. Almost one-half of that is spent on media monitored by national reporting services—newspapers, magazines, Yellow Pages, Internet, radio, television, and outdoor media. The remainder is spent on unmonitored media, such as direct mail, trade exhibits, cooperative advertising, brochures, coupons, catalogs, and special events. Exhibit 15.5 shows how monitored advertising is spent by media type. As you can see, more than 40 percent of every dollar spent in monitored

medium
The channel used to convey a message to a target market.

media planning
The series of decisions advertisers make regarding the selection and use of media, allowing the marketer to optimally and cost-effectively communicate the message to the target audience.

http://www.adage.com.

EXHIBIT 15.6

Advantages and Disadvantages of Major Advertising Media

Medium	Advantages	Disadvantages
Newspapers	Geographic selectivity and flexibility; short-term advertiser commitments; news value and immediacy; year-round readership; high individual market coverage; co-op and local tie-in availability; short lead time	Little demographic selectivity; limited color capabilities; low pass-along rate; may be expensive
Magazines	Good reproduction, especially for color; demographic selectivity; regional selectivity; local market selectivity; relatively long advertising life; high pass-along rate	Long-term advertiser commitments; slow audience buildup; limited demonstration capabilities; lack of urgency; long lead time
Radio	Low cost; immediacy of message; can be scheduled on short notice; relatively no seasonal change in audience; highly portable; short-term advertiser commitments; entertainment carryover	No visual treatment; short advertising life of message; high frequency required to generate comprehension and retention; distractions from back-ground sound; commercial clutter
Television	Ability to reach a wide, diverse audience; low cost per thousand; creative opportunities for demonstration; immediacy of messages; entertainment carryover; demographic selectivity with cable stations	Short life of message; some consumer skepticism about claims; high campaign cost; little demographic selectivity with network stations; long-term advertiser commitments; long lead times required for production; commercial clutter
Outdoor media	Repetition; moderate cost; flexibility; geographic selectivity	Short message; lack of demographic selectivity; high "noise" level distracting audience
Internet	Fastest growing medium; ability to reach a narrow target audience; relatively short lead time required for creating Web-based advertising; moderate cost	Difficult to measure ad effectiveness and return on investment; ad exposure relies on "click-through" from banner ads; not all consumers have access to the Internet

Newspapers

The advantages of newspaper advertising include geographic flexibility and time-liness. Because copywriters can usually prepare newspaper ads quickly and at a reasonable cost, local merchants can reach their target market almost daily. Because newspapers are generally a mass-market medium, however, they may not be the best vehicle for marketers trying to reach a very narrow market. For example, local news-papers are not the best media vehicles for reaching purchasers of specialty steel products or even tropical fish. These target consumers make up very small, special-ized markets. Newspaper advertising also encounters a lot of distractions from com-peting ads and news stories; thus, one company's ad may not be particularly visible.

The main sources of newspaper ad revenue are local retailers, classified ads, and cooperative advertising. In **cooperative advertising**, the manufacturer and the retailer split the costs of advertising the manufacturer's brand. One reason manufacturers use cooperative advertising is the impracticality of listing all their dealers in national advertising. Also, co-op advertising encourages retailers to devote more effort to the manufacturer's lines.

Magazines

Compared to the cost of other media, the cost per contact in magazine advertising is usually high. The cost per potential customer may be much lower, however, because magazines are often targeted to specialized audiences and thus reach more potential customers. The types of products most frequently advertised in magazines include automobiles, apparel, computers, and cigarettes.

One of the main advantages of magazine advertising is its market selectivity. Magazines are published for virtually every market segment. For instance, *Lucky* "The Magazine About Shopping" is a leading fashion magazine; *ESPN the Magazine* is a successful sports magazine; *Essence* is targeted toward African American women; *Marketing News* is a trade magazine for the marketing professional; and *The Source* is a niche publication geared to young urbanites with a passion for hip-hop music.

Radio

Radio has several strengths as an advertising medium: selectivity and audience segmentation, a large out-of-home audience, low unit and production costs, timeliness, and geographic flexibility. Local advertisers are the most frequent users of radio advertising, contributing over three-quarters of all radio ad revenues. Like newspapers, radio also lends itself well to cooperative advertising.

Long merely an afterthought to many advertisers, radio advertising is enjoying a resurgence in popularity. As Americans become more mobile and pressed for time, other media such as network television and newspapers struggle to retain viewers and readers. Radio listening, however, has grown in step with population increases mainly because its immediate, portable nature meshes so well with a fast-paced lifestyle. The ability to target specific demographic groups is also a major selling point for radio stations, attracting advertisers who are pursuing narrowly defined audiences that are more likely to respond to certain kinds of ads and products. Moreover, radio listeners tend to listen habitually and at predictable times, with the most popular being "drive time," when commuters form a vast captive audience.

Television

Because television is an audiovisual medium, it provides advertisers with many creative opportunities. Television broadcasters include network television, independent stations, cable television, and a relative newcomer, direct broadcast satellite television. ABC, CBS, NBC, and the Fox Network dominate network television, which reaches a wide and diverse market. Conversely, cable television and direct broadcast satellite systems, such as DirecTV and PrimeStar, offer consumers a multitude of channels devoted exclusively to particular audiences—for example, women, children, African Americans, nature lovers, senior citizens, Christians, Hispanics, sports fans, and fitness enthusiasts. Recent niche market entries include TFN (The Football Network) and the NFL Network—focused exclusively on the football enthusiast—and the casino and gambling channel. Because of its targeted channels, cable television is often characterized as "narrowcasting" by media buyers. More businesses are including cable buys in their marketing mix. For instance, Novell, a marketer of Internet software, found that consumers who were exposed to its ads several times on cable were more familiar with its story and had an increasingly favorable view of the company. Even better, viewers of its spots on cable were found to be more likely to buy or recommend a Novell product.[34]

cooperative advertising
An arrangement in which the manufacturer and the retailer split the costs of advertising the manufacturer's brand.

The genesis of any television commercial is the storyboard, which is a collection of images and text that tells the story of the advertisement. Shown here is the storyboard for one of Hanes' commercials in which Michael Jordan is the spokesperson.

cated information to potential customers, which other advertising vehicles typically don't allow time to do. Infomercials are rapidly gaining favor with some of the more mainstream marketers. In the last few years, several companies including Philips Electronics, Apple, Nissan, Mercedes, Nikon, and Microsoft have bought infomercial airtime. And a growing number of businesses are adding to the legitimacy of the medium by producing infomercials with a more polished look. For example, Callaway Golf used an infomercial to pitch its expensive new Rule 35 ball to upscale golfers. A higher production budget was established to allow for a lot of graphic detail with a rich feel to enhance the perceived quality of the product and the medium. Hollywood is even cashing in on infomercials. Universal Pictures released a 30-minute infomercial for its Jurassic Park franchise hosted by E! Entertainment's Steve Kmetko. The actual offer—a boxed DVD/video set of the movie's first two installments—aired periodically during the glossy, behind-the-scenes footage, which included interviews with the stars of *Jurassic Park III*. With the polished look of a behind-the-scenes special, it felt more like 30 minutes of programming than an infomercial.[38]

Outdoor Media

Outdoor or out-of-home advertising is a flexible, low-cost medium that may take a variety of forms. Examples include billboards, skywriting, giant inflatables, mini-billboards in malls and on bus stop shelters, signs in sports arenas, lighted moving signs in bus terminals and airports, and ads painted on the sides of cars, trucks, buses, water towers, and even people, called "living advertising." This recent experiment in London used students, who "rented" their foreheads for temporary tattoos of brands and then walked around specified areas of the city.[39] Marketers have even begun utilizing the plywood scaffolding that often rings downtown construction sites. Manhattan's Times Square, with an estimated 1.5 million daily pedestrians and recent construction projects, for example, has been a popular area for outdoor advertising using scaffolding.

Outdoor advertising reaches a broad and diverse market and is, therefore, ideal for promoting convenience products and services as well as directing consumers to local businesses. One of outdoor's main advantages over other media is

infomercial
A 30-minute or longer advertisement that looks more like a TV talk show than a sales pitch.

that its exposure frequency is very high, yet the amount of clutter from competing ads is very low. Outdoor advertising also has the ability to be customized to local marketing needs. For these reasons, local business establishments, such as local services and amusements, retailers, public transportation, and hotels and restaurants, are the leading outdoor advertisers. Outdoor advertising categories on the rise include telecommunications with a heavy emphasis on wireless services, financial services, and packaged goods.

Outdoor advertising continues to become more innovative. For instance, Absolut Vodka teamed up with Ikea furniture to produce a 19-by-49-foot billboard in Manhattan's SoHo district. The billboard shows a life-size studio apartment in the shape of an Absolut bottle that is filled with furniture from Ikea. The billboard is basically a fully furnished apartment with everything glued to the board and then turned on its side.

Unusual outdoor advertising campaigns are not limited to the United States. Snapple's launch in Mexico featured a giant street ad campaign with people going about their regular routines dressed as giant pieces of fruit, such as bananas and strawberries.[40] Adidas Japan created a "living billboard" in the form of a vertical soccer field on the side of a skyscraper. The billboard featured live players and a ball attached by ropes to the side of the building.[41]

The Internet

The Internet had definitely changed the advertising industry. With ad revenues exceeding $6 billion in 2003, the Internet has established itself as a solid advertising medium.[42] Online advertising has made significant gains in recent years and represents an ever-larger portion of companies' total advertising budgets. By 2006, Internet advertising is expected to exceed $25 billion and represent close to 10 percent of total media spending. Popular Internet sites and search engines, such as Google and Yahoo!, as well as online service providers like America Online, generally sell advertising space, called "banners," to marketers to promote their goods and services. Internet surfers click on these banners to be linked to more information about the advertised product or service.

Advertising executives and academicians have hotly debated the effectiveness of banner ads. Early research indicated that banner ads were generating response rates as high as 30 percent.[43] But other industry observers feel that banner ads have been largely ineffective, with low click-through rates and recall. Consumers today are more Web savvy and often ignore banner advertising, to the point where the click-through rate is less than 1 percent. Marketers are recognizing, however, that banner ads can build brand awareness, so banners are being produced that don't actually link to anything. Initial studies indicate that brand awareness increases by 5 percent and that the association between the brand and its tagline increases by an average of 16 percent with banner advertising.[44] With over 65 percent of the U.S. population now online, marketers are looking for new approaches to online advertising. Some marketers are offering a variety of content-sponsorship deals, video ads that pop up in another window, and online and off-line cross-promotions. They are also developing new ad formats with big, hard-to-miss shapes. The new formats include the *skyscraper*, a tall, skinny oblong at the side of a Web page, and the *rectangle*, a box much larger than a banner. These new formats are large enough for marketers to include their entire message so that users don't have to click through to another site.

One of the most popular Internet advertising options utilizes search engines. Overture, now part of Yahoo!, initiated the business model in which advertisers bid on "keywords" entered by online surfers. When the keyword combination is entered, the ad shows up next to the search results on the Web page.[45] Advergaming, another popular Internet advertising format, appears on Web sites as pop-ups and banner ads. The format encourages users to register for a sweepstakes and then play a game. For example, on the discount designer retailer site Bluefly.com, shoppers can register to win a pair of Manolo Blahnik shoes (value approximately

To cut through the clutter of traditional advertising media, advertisers are creating new media vehicles to advertise their products, some ordinary and others quite innovative. Alternative media vehicles can include shopping carts in grocery stores, computer screen savers, CD-ROMs, interactive kiosks in department stores, advertisements run before movies at the cinema and on rented videocassettes, and "advertainments"—"mini movies" that promote a product and are shown via the Internet. For example, BMW shows films by recognized directors that run six to eight minutes and feature the cars in extreme situations.[46] Coca-Cola recently sponsored a 25-minute advertainment program called "Sound Check" that was available only on TiVo. The program featured exclusive interviews, music videos, live shows, behind-the-scenes filming, and recordings by artists such as Ashanti, Sting, and Mary J. Blige.[47]

Indeed, almost anything can become a vehicle for displaying advertising. For instance, supermarkets have begun using "Flooranimation"—ads that are animated with graphics and sounds and installed on supermarket floors. Unanimated floor ads have been in use for some time, and research shows that they increase sales 15 to 30 percent. Marketers are hoping that with animation and sound, sales will increase even more.[48] Video Venue recently unveiled plans to install ten-inch, wireless, high-resolution screens at gas pumps to run six-minute cycles of full-motion video and sound ads. Marketers are hoping to capitalize on the four to six minutes it takes for consumers to pump gas and will advertise products available right there in the store.[49] Marketers are also looking for more innovative ways to reach captive and often bored commuters. For instance, subway systems are now showing ads via lighted boxes installed along tunnel walls. As a train passes through the tunnel, the passengers view the illuminated boxes, which create the same kind of illusion as a child's flip book, in which the images appear to move as the pages are flipped rapidly, as with the odd pages in this book.

MEDIA SELECTION CONSIDERATIONS

An important element in any advertising campaign is the **media mix**, the combination of media to be used. Media mix decisions are typically based on several factors: cost per contact, reach, frequency, target audience considerations, flexibility of the medium, noise level, and the life span of the medium.

Cost per contact is the cost of reaching one member of the target market. Naturally, as the size of the audience increases, so does the total cost. Cost per contact enables an advertiser to compare media vehicles, such as television versus radio or magazine versus newspaper, or more specifically *Newsweek* versus

media mix
The combination of media to be used for a promotional campaign.

cost per contact
The cost of reaching one member of the target market.

Lunch hour elevator passengers follow the stock market through a wireless Internet device installed by the elevator door. Otis Elevator, Captivate, and eBillboards are entering this alternative media space and bringing weather, news, sports, and stock market data to elevator riders in many of the largest cities in the United States.

Time. An advertiser debating whether to spend local advertising dollars for TV spots or radio spots could consider the cost per contact of each. The advertiser might then pick the vehicle with the lowest cost per contact to maximize advertising punch for the money spent.

Reach is the number of different target consumers who are exposed to a commercial at least once during a specific period, usually four weeks. Media plans for product introductions and attempts at increasing brand awareness usually emphasize reach. For example, an advertiser might try to reach 70 percent of the target audience during the first three months of the campaign. Reach is related to a medium's ratings, generally referred to in the industry as *gross ratings points*, or GRP. A television program with a higher GRP means that more people are tuning in to the show and the reach is higher. Accordingly, as GRP increases for a particular medium, so does cost per contact.

Because the typical ad is short-lived and because often only a small portion of an ad may be perceived at one time, advertisers repeat their ads so that consumers will remember the message. **Frequency** is the number of times an individual is exposed to a message during a specific period. Advertisers use average frequency to measure the intensity of a specific medium's coverage. For example, Coca-Cola might want an average exposure frequency of five for its Powerade television ads. That means that each of the television viewers who saw the ad saw it an average of five times.

Media selection is also a matter of matching the advertising medium with the product's target market. If marketers are trying to reach teenage females, they might select *Seventeen* magazine. If they are trying to reach consumers over 50 years old, they may choose *Modern Maturity* magazine. A medium's ability to reach a precisely defined market is its **audience selectivity**. Some media vehicles, like general newspapers and network television, appeal to a wide cross section of the population. Others—such as *Brides, Popular Mechanics, Architectural Digest, Lucky,* MTV, ESPN, and Christian radio stations—appeal to very specific groups.

The *flexibility* of a medium can be extremely important to an advertiser. In the past, because of printing timetables, pasteup requirements, and so on, some magazines required final ad copy several months before publication. Therefore, magazine advertising traditionally could not adapt as rapidly to changing market conditions. While this is fast changing due to computer technology that creates electronic ad images and layouts, the lead time for magazine advertising is still considerably longer. Radio and Internet advertising, on the other hand, provide maximum flexibility. Usually, the advertiser can change a radio ad on the day it is aired, if necessary. Similarly, advertisements on the Internet can be changed in minutes with the click of a few buttons.

Noise level is the level of distraction to the target audience in a medium. For example, to understand a televised promotional message, viewers must watch and listen carefully. But they often watch television with others, who may well provide distractions. Noise can also be created by competing ads, as when a street is lined with billboards or when a television program is cluttered with competing ads. About two-thirds of a newspaper's pages are now filled with advertising. A recent Sunday issue of the *Los Angeles Times* contained over one thousand ads, not counting the small classifieds. Even more space is dedicated to ads in magazines. For example, 85 percent of the space in the February/March issue of *Brides* magazine

reach
The number of target consumers exposed to a commercial at least once during a specific period, usually four weeks.

frequency
The number of times an individual is exposed to a given message during a specific period.

audience selectivity
The ability of an advertising medium to reach a precisely defined market.

Additionally, media planners have hundreds more media options today than they had 40 years ago when network television reigned. For instance, there are over 1,600 television stations across the country. In the Los Angeles market alone, there are now 79 radio stations, with seven offering an "adult contemporary" format. The number of unique magazine titles has more than doubled over the last decade, with publications now targeting every target market possible. Satellite television can now bring hundreds of channels into viewers' homes. The Internet provides media planners with even more targeted choices in which to send their messages. And alternative media choices are popping up in some very unlikely places. *Media fragmentation* is forcing media planners to pay as much attention to where they place their advertising, as to how often the advertisement is repeated. Indeed, experts recommend evaluating reach along with frequency in assessing the effectiveness of advertising. That is, in certain situations it may be important to reach potential consumers through as many media vehicles as possible. When this approach is considered, however, the budget must be large enough to achieve sufficient levels of frequency to have an impact. In evaluating reach versus frequency, therefore, the media planner ultimately must select an approach that is most likely to result in the ad being understood and remembered when a purchase decision is being made.

Advertising researchers are also discussing the qualitative factors that should be present during media selection. These qualitative factors include such things as attention to the commercial and the program, involvement, program liking, lack of distractions, and other audience behaviors that affect the likelihood that a commercial message is being seen and, hopefully, absorbed. While advertisers can advertise their product in as many media as possible and repeat the ad as many times as they like, the ad still may not be effective if the audience is not paying attention. Research on audience attentiveness for television, for example, shows that the longer viewers stay tuned to a particular program, the more memorable they find the commercials. The study suggests that "holding power," is more important than ratings (the number of people tuning in to any part of the program) when selecting media vehicles, challenging the long-held assumption that the higher the rating of a program, the higher the cost to advertise during the program. For instance, the television program *ER*, which is one of the top-rated shows among 25- to 54-year-olds and costs over $400,000 for a 30-second spot, measures relatively lower for holding power than the low-rated program *Candid Camera*, which ranks high in holding power, but costs only $55,000 for a 30-second spot.[50]

MEDIA SCHEDULING

media schedule
Designation of the media, the specific publications or programs, and the insertion dates of advertising.

continuous media schedule
A media scheduling strategy in which advertising is run steadily throughout the advertising period; used for products in the latter stages of the product life cycle.

flighted media schedule
A media scheduling strategy in which ads are run heavily every other month or every two weeks, to achieve a greater impact with an increased frequency and reach at those times.

pulsing media schedule
A media scheduling strategy that uses continuous scheduling throughout the year coupled with a flighted schedule during the best sales periods.

seasonal media schedule
A media scheduling strategy that runs advertising only during times of the year when the product is most likely to be used.

After choosing the media for the advertising campaign, advertisers must schedule the ads. A **media schedule** designates the medium or media to be used (such as magazines, television, or radio), the specific vehicles (such as *People* magazine, the show *Survivor* on TV, or Howard Stern's national radio program), and the insertion dates of the advertising.

There are three basic types of media schedules:

- Products in the latter stages of the product life cycle, which are advertised on a reminder basis, use a **continuous media schedule**. A continuous schedule allows the advertising to run steadily throughout the advertising period. Examples include Ivory soap, Tide detergent, Bounty paper towels, and Charmin toilet tissue, which may have an ad in the newspaper every Sunday and a TV commercial on NBC every Wednesday at 7:30 P.M. over a three-month time period.
- With a **flighted media schedule**, the advertiser may schedule the ads heavily every other month or every two weeks to achieve a greater impact with an increased frequency and reach at those times. Movie studios might schedule television advertising on Wednesday and Thursday nights, when moviegoers are deciding which films to see that weekend. A variation is the **pulsing media schedule**, which combines continuous scheduling with flighting. Continuous advertising is simply heavier during the best sale periods. A retail department store may advertise on a year-round basis but place more advertising during certain sale periods such as Thanksgiving, Christmas, and back-to-school.
- Certain times of the year call for a **seasonal media schedule**. Products like Contac cold tablets and Coppertone suntan lotion, which are used more during certain times of the year, tend to follow a seasonal strategy. Advertising for champagne is concentrated during the weeks of Christmas and New Year's, whereas health clubs concentrate their advertising in January to take advantage of New Year's resolutions.

New research comparing continuous media schedules versus flighted ones finds that continuous schedules for television advertisements are more effective than flighting in driving sales. The research suggests that it may be more important to get exposure as close as possible to the time when someone is going to make a purchase. For example, if a consumer shops on a weekly basis, the best time to reach that person is right before he or she shops. Therefore, the advertiser should maintain a continuous schedule over as long a period of time as possible. Often called *recency planning*, this theory of scheduling is now commonly used for scheduling television advertising for frequently purchased products, such as Coca-Cola or Tide detergent. Recency planning's main premise is that advertising works by influencing the brand choice of people who are ready to buy.

REVIEW LEARNING OBJECTIVE 4

 4 Describe media evaluation and selection techniques

Media Choices

Type:

Magazine, Radio, Television, Newspaper, Outdoor, Alternative, Internet

Considerations:
Mix	**(How much of each?)**
Cost per contact	**(How much per person?)**
Reach	**(How many people?)**
Frequency	**(How often?)**
Audience selectivity	**(How targeted is audience?)**

flexibility
noise
life span
fragmentation

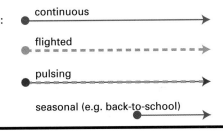

Scheduling:
continuous
flighted
pulsing
seasonal (e.g. back-to-school)

Winter Spring Summer Fall

story will be published or broadcast. Savvy publicity can often create overnight sensations.

SK Telecom developed a guerrilla marketing campaign to secure its position as the mobile communications leader in Korea. During the FIFA World Cup held in Korea, SK Telecom launched a campaign called "Be the Reds" named after Korean national soccer team, the Red Devils. The company invited sports fans to join the Red Devil's fan club and learn two new special team cheers. SK Telecom then distributed millions of free "Be the Reds" t-shirts. It sponsored TVs in commuter trains and massive television screens in highly populated public areas, all blazoned with the SK telecom logo. Marketing activities were not permitted inside the stadium, but fans wearing their "Be the Reds" t-shirts blanketed the stands and screamed SK's team cheers. Recognition of the SK Telecom brand skyrocketed past that of the official sponsor. During the FIFA World Cup, SK Telecom signed up 96,000 new customers and increased its market share of Korean mobile communications service by 22 percent.[51]

Corporate donations and sponsorships can also create favorable publicity. When two high school seniors wanted to go to college in California, but couldn't afford the tuition, they set out to find corporate sponsors to pay for their education. The young entrepreneurs set up a Web site offering their services as "spokesguys" and posted photos of themselves wearing T-shirts and carrying surfboards inscribed with the message YOUR LOGO HERE. They got the attention of First USA, the country's largest Visa issuer, which decided to lend a hand. In exchange for the boys promoting fiscal responsibility to other college kids, First USA paid for their tuition and room and board. As a public relations investment, it's already paid off with the kind of publicity that money can't buy, including a story in the *New York Times*.[52]

Public relations departments may perform any or all of the following functions:

- *Press relations:* placing positive, newsworthy information in the news media to attract attention to a product, a service, or a person associated with the firm or institution
- *Product publicity:* publicizing specific products or services
- *Corporate communication:* creating internal and external messages to promote a positive image of the firm or institution
- *Public affairs:* building and maintaining national or local community relations
- *Lobbying:* influencing legislators and government officials to promote or defeat legislation and regulation
- *Employee and investor relations:* maintaining positive relationships with employees, shareholders, and others in the financial community
- *Crisis management:* responding to unfavorable publicity or a negative event

MAJOR PUBLIC RELATIONS TOOLS

Public relations professionals commonly use several tools, including new-product publicity, product placement, consumer education, event sponsorship, issue sponsorship, and Web sites. Although many of these tools require an active role on the part of the public relations professional, such as writing press releases and engaging in proactive media relations, many of these techniques create their own publicity.

New-Product Publicity

Publicity is instrumental in introducing new products and services. Publicity can help advertisers explain what's different about their new product by prompting free news stories or positive word of mouth about it. During the introductory period, an especially innovative new product often needs more exposure than conventional, paid advertising affords. Public relations professionals write press releases or develop videos in an effort to generate news about their new product. They also jockey for exposure of their product or service at major events, on popular television and news shows, or in the hands of influential people. The chairman of Virgin Group, Richard Branson, recently helped promote a new line of consumer electronics, Virgin Pulse, distributed by Target. To get free publicity, Branson attended the release party wearing skin-colored leggings and a ripped T-shirt and holding a CD player over his private parts. Free publicity is one of the mainstays of the Virgin marketing approach. Branson has also made guest appearances on *Friends* and *Baywatch* and ridden down Fifth Avenue in a tank.[53]

Product Placement

Marketers can also garner publicity by making sure their products appear at special events or in movies or television shows. Absolut Vodka set a new standard in product placement when a fake Absolut ad called "Absolut Hunk" was included in a *Sex in the City* story line. The ad featuring actor Jason Lewis generated a lot of publicity and talk on HBO's Web site for the show. Absolut capitalized on the publicity by creating recipe cards for the "Absolut Hunk" cocktail.[54] And best-selling author Fay Weldon caused quite a stir in literary circles with her novel *The Bulgari Connection.* The Italian jewelry company reportedly paid an undisclosed amount of money to be prominently featured in the novel. Public relations experts predict that books are the next wave of product placement.[55]

Companies reap invaluable product exposure through product placement, usually at a fraction of the cost of paid-for advertising. Often the fee for exposure is in merchandise. Fashion designer Georgio Armani, for example, uses celebrities to burnish his brand in the eyes of the public. Armani clothed Samuel L. Jackson for his role in the movie *Shaft.* The designer then marketed a line of *Shaft*-inspired clothes and featured Jackson in fashion shows in Milan, Italy. Armani also provides select Hollywood stars and celebrities with free gowns and tuxedos for personal appearances. For example, Christina Aguilera was featured in almost all of Armani's fall 2003 fashion ads.

© AP/WIDE WORLD PHOTOS

Cause-related marketing efforts usually rely heavily on public relations. One example is the Susan G. Komen Breast Cancer Foundation, which among other things, sponsors Race for the Cure marathons around the country. In preparation for the New York City race and in conjunction with the city's annual City in Pink lighting campaign, a ten-story-high pink ribbon was affixed to the Westin Hotel on Times Square.

such as tie-ins with schools, charities, and other community service organizations. For example, NBC, Mongoose, Sobe, Cingular, Lego, Slim Jim, and Toyota Supra sponsored the 2003 Gravity Games extreme sporting event that competes with ESPN's highly successful X Games. Some 200,000 spectators, a large majority of them young males between the ages of 12 and 24, descended on Cleveland, Ohio, for the eight-day festival. Sponsors gave away free samples, hosted extreme athlete autograph sessions and sports demonstrations, and organized alternative music concerts.[56]

Marketers can also create their own events tied around their product. The state of Hawaii organized its own mall touring event, titled "Experience Aloha: Hawaii on Tour," to promote the islands as a tourist destination. The tour traveled to 22 U.S. cities for weekend mall visits that included hula dancers, chefs cooking Hawaiian cuisine, lei-making demonstrations, and a virtual reality film simulating a helicopter ride over Hawaii's islands. Many other states also sponsor events to promote tourism.

Issue Sponsorship

Corporations can build public awareness and loyalty by supporting their customers' favorite issues. Education, health care, and social programs get the largest share of corporate funding. Firms often donate a percentage of sales or profits to a worthy cause their target market is likely to favor. For example, Gap hoped to break through the holiday advertising clutter by focusing on a simple theme of "Give your gift" reinforced by corporate donations. The company made donations to charities on behalf of the celebrities appearing in the commercials and print ads, including the singers Sheryl Crow and Alanis Morissette and the cast of *The Producers*. In an unusual example of issue sponsorship, local advertisers purchased ad space on police vehicle bumpers. When the police department in Ashland, Nebraska, could not afford new police cars, Government Acquisitions, Inc. found local sponsors for the vehicles and sold them to the police department for a dollar each.[59]

"Green marketing" has also become an important way for companies to build awareness and loyalty by promoting a popular issue. By positioning their brands as ecologically sound, marketers can convey concern for the environment and society as a whole. Burger King and McDonald's no longer use styrofoam cartons to package their burgers in an effort to decrease waste in landfills. In a similar effort, Toyota is working with the Japanese government to implement a program where people purchase "transportation" without owning a car. Consumers can buy access to Toyota's electronic fleet of automobiles to travel for short distances. Thus, Toyota is both establishing itself as the leader in electronic-combustion automobiles and reducing a negative environmental impact.[60]

Volkswagen
General Motors
How effective do you think the Internet is at achieving new product publicity? Compare how Volkswagen and General Motors use the Internet to advertise their new models, the Phaeton and the Chevy SSR. Does the primary function of each Web site seem to be advertising, publicity, or something else?

http://www.vw.com

http://www.chevrolet.com

Online

Internet Web Sites

Public relations professionals use Internet Web sites as a vehicle to post news releases on products, product enhancements, strategic relationships, and financial earnings. Corporate press releases, technical papers and articles, and product news help inform the press, customers, prospects, industry analysts, stockholders, and others of the firm's products and services and their applications. The Web site is also an open forum for new-product ideas, product improvements, and customer feedback. Online reviews from opinion leaders and other consumers also help marketers sway shopping decisions in their favor. When Sony redesigned Playstation.com, it incorporated message boards where its game-playing community could post notes. Players discuss techie topics like "Desperately Seeking Playstation2," review and exchange tips on games, and even vote on lifestyle issues such as music and personal taste.[61]

Several marketers also use the Web to try new products and gather more consumer data. Through research, Volkswagen knew that over 60 percent of its customers use the Internet. So, when the company wanted to attract a different, "funkier" audience for its new Beetle and test out new car colors, it employed a special online marketing promotion. Volkswagen made a limited-edition model of its Beetle available exclusively online, in two limited-edition colors: Vapor Blue and Reflex Yellow. The company got the word out about the promotion through traditional advertising methods including print, TV, and radio advertisements. Consumers then signed up to learn more via e-mail. On being admitted to a special section of the VW site, consumers learned more about the car, viewed photos, checked the availability, picked a dealer, and considered financing and a purchase date. The online promotion was a huge success, and Volkswagen sold out of all 4,000 limited-edition Beetles.[62]

U.S. beverage giants Coke and Pepsi have been facing very unfavorable publicity in India, where an independent Indian environmental watchdog reported elevated levels of pesticides in soda manufactured by these companies and sold in India. The backlash included a push for drinking natural beverages, like coconut water and sugar cane juice.

© INDRANIL MUKHERJEE/AFP/GETTY IMAGES

MANAGING UNFAVORABLE PUBLICITY

Although marketers try to avoid unpleasant situations, crises do happen. Coca-Cola had to issue an official apology to Chinese basketball star Yao Ming after Coke used his logo on its

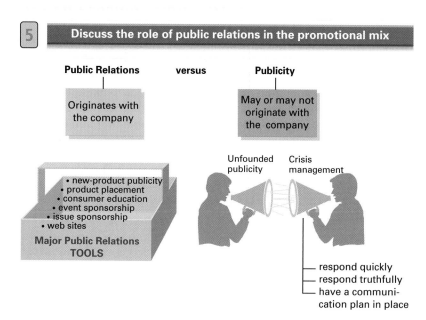

Discuss the role of public relations in the promotional mix

Public Relations   versus   **Publicity**

Originates with the company

May or may not originate with the company

Unfounded publicity   Crisis management

• new-product publicity
• product placement
• consumer education
• event sponsorship
• issue sponsorship
• web sites

Major Public Relations TOOLS

— respond quickly
— respond truthfully
— have a communi-
    cation plan in place

McDonald's awarded $10 million in prizes to customers to make up for the prizes that had been wrongfully awarded.[64]

A good public relations and crisis management plan helped Internet auctioneer eBay climb its way out of a public relations mess after a computer crash halted its bidding operations for 22 hours. The outage left nearly 2.3 million auctions stranded in the middle of bids, infuriating customers and sellers. To soothe users' frustrations, eBay sent messages apologizing for the disruption and promising to aggressively hire more computer-network experts. The company also refunded users' listing fees totaling close to $5 million.[65]

LOOKING BACK

As you finish reading this chapter, think back to the opening story about the *Madden NFL 2004* video game. Consider how EA Sports uses advertising and public relations to dominate the video game industry.

To advertise its products, the EA Sports promotional team went through the same creative steps as other marketers—from determining what appeal to use to choosing the appropriate execution style. Great

effort was also spent on deciding which medium would best reach the desired target market. Public relations and publicity played a significant role in making the *Madden NFL* video game a success.

USE IT NOW

BECOMING A MEDIA EXPERT

 Find the perfect magazine to advertise your product or service. Visit the MediaFinder Web site at **http://www.mediafinder.com**. The site has a searchable database of thousands of magazines. Or visit Channel Seven at **http://www.channelseven.com** to find news and views on hot new advertising media.

TICKED OFF ABOUT THAT AD?

File a complaint with the Better Business Bureau. See which companies get the most complaints about their advertising at the Better Business

Bureau's Web site at **http://www.bbb.org.** Want to avoid legal problems with your advertising campaign? Find detailed information about advertising law and Federal Trade Commission regulations at **http://www.advertisinglaw.com**.

HOW TO WRITE A PRESS RELEASE

Visit **http://www.press-release-writing.com** to learn the right way to get publicity for your product or service. This Web site offers sample press releases, templates, formatting suggestions, and basic information that should always be included. The service also helps you distribute your press release to thousands of different media outlets.

REVIEW AND APPLICATIONS

1 **Discuss the effects of advertising on market share and consumers.** Advertising helps marketers increase or maintain brand awareness and, subsequently, market share. Typically, more is spent to advertise new brands with a small market share than to advertise older brands. Brands with a large market share use advertising mainly to maintain their share of the market. Advertising affects consumers' daily lives as well as their purchases. Although advertising can seldom change strongly held consumer attitudes and values, it may transform a consumer's negative attitude toward a product into a positive one. Additionally, when consumers are highly loyal to a brand, they may buy more of that brand when advertising is increased. Last, advertising can also change the importance of a brand's attributes to consumers. By emphasizing different brand attributes, advertisers can change their appeal in response to consumers' changing needs or try to achieve an advantage over competing brands.

1.1 Discuss the reasons why new brands with a smaller market share spend proportionately more on advertising than brands with a larger market share.

1.2 **TEAM** Form a three-person team. Divide the responsibility for getting newspaper advertisements and menus for several local restaurants. While you are at the restaurants to obtain copies of their menus, observe the atmosphere and interview the manager to determine what he or she believes are the primary reasons people choose to dine there. Pool your information and develop a table comparing the restaurants in terms of convenience of location, value for the money, food variety and quality, atmosphere, and so on. Rank the restaurants in terms of their appeal to college students. Explain the basis of your rankings. What other market segment would be attracted to the restaurants and why? Do the newspaper advertisements emphasize the most effective appeal for a particular restaurant? Explain.

2 **Identify the major types of advertising.** Advertising is any form of nonpersonal, paid communication in which the sponsor or company is identified. The two major types of advertising are institutional advertising and product advertising. Institutional advertising is not product oriented; rather, its purpose is to foster a positive company image among the general public, investment community, customers, and employees. Product advertising is designed mainly to promote goods and services, and it is classified into three main categories: pioneering, competitive, and comparative. A product's place in the product life cycle is a major determinant of the type of advertising used to promote it.

4 **Describe media evaluation and selection techniques.** Media evaluation and selection make up a crucial step in the advertising campaign process. Major types of advertising media include newspapers, magazines, radio, television, outdoor advertising such as billboards and bus panels, and the Internet. Recent trends in advertising media include fax, video shopping carts, computer screen savers, and cinema and video advertising. Promotion managers choose the advertising campaign's media mix on the basis of the following variables: cost per contact, reach, frequency, characteristics of the target audience, flexibility of the medium, noise level, and the life span of the medium. After choosing the media mix, a media schedule designates when the advertisement will appear and the specific vehicles it will appear in.

4.1 What are the advantages of radio advertising? Why is radio expanding as an advertising medium?

4.2 **WRITING** You are the advertising manager of a sailing magazine, and one of your biggest potential advertisers has questioned your rates. Write the firm a letter explaining why you believe your audience selectivity is worth the extra expense for advertisers.

4.3 Identify an appropriate media mix for the following products:

   a. Chewing tobacco

   b. *People* magazine

   c. Weed-Eaters

   d. Foot odor killers

   e. "Drink responsibly" campaigns by beer brewers

5 **Discuss the role of public relations in the promotional mix.** Public relations is a vital part of a firm's promotional mix. A company fosters good publicity to enhance its image and promote its products. Popular public relations tools include new-product publicity, product placement, consumer education, event sponsorship, issue sponsorship, and Internet Web sites. An equally important aspect of public relations is managing unfavorable publicity in a way that is least damaging to a firm's image.

5.1 How can advertising and publicity work together? Give an example.

5.2 **WRITING** As the new public relations director for a sportswear company, you have been asked to set public relations objectives for a new line of athletic shoes to be introduced to the teen market. Draft a memo outlining the objectives you propose for the shoe's introduction and your reasons for them.

5.3

WRITING As you read in the "Marketing in Entertainment" box on LG, event sponsorship is a good way to garner publicity, particularly when entering new markets. This type of public relations is not just for national companies and national events. In fact, there are probably numerous events in your city or region that are sponsored by local, regional, and national brands. Review the newspapers in your area for one week. Try to review several and varied newspapers (local, campus, cultural, countercultural, etc.) During this period, cut out all the event advertisements that list sponsors. Once you have your collection, spread them out so you can see them all at once. Identify any patterns or connections between the type of event and its sponsors. Identify companies that sponsor more than one event. What do sponsors tell you about target markets? After analyzing the ads, write a brief paragraph summarizing your discoveries.

TERMS

EXERCISES

APPLICATION EXERCISE 1

You may think that creating advertising is easy. After all, you have a lot of experience with advertising, having been bombarded with advertisements since you were a child. But creating advertising presents real challenges. In this exercise, you will be challenged to create an ad for a new product for animal use that is based on a product used by humans. Some examples include bras for cows, claw polish for tigers, and "Minute Mice" for cats. You can pick any product and any animal, but the combination must make sense.[66]

Activities

1. You have been hired by the purveyor of your chosen product to create a print advertisement. Lay out your ad on a piece of paper that is no smaller than 8.5 by 11 inches and no larger than 11 by 14 inches. Include a headline, illustration, logo, and body copy. Your illustration may be either hand-drawn or clipped from a magazine.

2. Include the copy for your ad directly on the front of the ad unless your copy blocks are too large for you to be legible or neat. If that is the case, then label your copy blocks with letters, put them on the back of your ad, and write the corresponding letter in the appropriate place on the front of the ad.

3. Don't forget to pick your own brand name for the product or service (like "Minute Mice").

APPLICATION EXERCISE 2

In this age of 24-hour cable news channels, tabloid news shows, and aggressive local and national news reporters intent on exposing corporate wrongdoing, one of the most important skills for a manager to learn is how to deal effectively with the press. Test your ability to deal effectively with the press by putting yourself in the following situation. To make the situation more realistic read the scenario and then give yourself two minutes to write a response to each question.[67]

porter), how can your customers know whether the food that you serve is healthy for them?

3. "These new studies were based on lunches and dinners sampled from Chinese restaurants across the nation. A local company, Huntington Labs, has agreed to test foods from local restaurants so that we can provide accurate information to our viewers. Would you agree to let us sample the main dishes in your restaurant to test the level of calories, calories from fat, and cholesterol? Furthermore, can we take the cameras into your restaurant so that we can get your customers' reactions to these studies?"

ETHICS EXERCISE

Creative Advertising Agency has been asked to help its largest client improve its corporate image after a highly publicized product recall. The client requests a television advertisement highlighting the company's generous donation of products to low-income families. The only such donation the company has made, however, is a donation of the recalled products. The account executive fears promoting the donation could cause further consumer backlash, but the client continues to press for the spot.

Questions

1. Should Creative Advertising meet the client's expectations (i.e., create the promotional spot) or risk losing the account? Explain your reasoning.

2. What does the AMA Code of Ethics say about truth in advertising? Go to **http://www. marketingpower.com** and review the code. Then, write a brief paragraph describing how the AMA Code of Ethics relates to this issue.

CAREER EXERCISE

If you are not reticent to register at Web sites, you might find what you need at the Advertising Media Internet Center (**http://www.amic.com**). This resource page includes advertising news, links to professional associations, and links to affiliate programs.

AdJobsInc.com is another job listings site. If you have a good idea of where you want to live and work, you can search for specific types of jobs in specific metro areas. This can be beneficial if you want to focus on a particular location; if you want to cast a wider net, however, it might be frustrating.

Workinpr.com is a Web site dedicated to public relations jobs. You have to register, however, to gain access to the listings. Another resource is **Online-pr.com**. This site links out to numerous career resources and contains job listings as well. The "Advertising and Public Relations" page of **Careers-in-Marketing.com** also provides general resources for finding advertising and public relations jobs.

THE MOVE FROM TV TO TIVO

In the late 1990s, Silicon Graphics employees Mike Ramsay and Jim Barton were working together on the *Full-Service Network Project* in Orlando, Florida, a joint venture between Time Warner and Silicon Graphics to create the first large-scale interactive television system, when they hit upon an idea. They could build a system that would give viewers control over their television programming and their time, but with far greater intelligence and ease-of-use than anything previously designed at a price the average customer could afford.

Their idea was the genesis of TiVo, a revolutionary new service that puts viewers in control of their television-viewing experience in a way never before possible. TiVo's service uses an electronic device called a digital video recorder (DVR). Its newest set top box, the Series2, can digitally save up to 60 hours of television programs to its hard disk. But instead of punching in times and channels one at a time to record a show on a videocassette tape, as with a VCR, the DVR uses a telephone connection to download television program schedules that pop up on the TV screen. TiVo subscribers then click on any shows they want to select and digitally record them. What's more, the Series2 has the ability to deliver digital music and photo files, video party games, Internet radio, and broadband video.

With TiVo, viewers get more control than ever over what they want to watch on television. Subscribers can digitally record their favorite shows, creating and organizing their own programming schedule to watch when they want, not bound by the timetable of any network schedule. Some of TiVo's television network partners even allow subscribers to select shows as they are advertised in televised promotions. For instance, if a subscriber sees a promo for an upcoming show to be aired on Showtime, she can click the remote when a small icon appears in the corner of her television screen during the promo to automatically record it when the program is aired. No longer do viewers have to remember when the desired show will come on in order to watch it—TiVo records properly even if the network changes its schedule! TiVo can also automatically record subscribers' favorite shows every week or suggest other shows that they might want to see based on what they've recorded in the past.

Ranging in cost from $299 for the 40-hour version available for AT&T Broadband customers to $399 for the 60-hour version, the digital video recorders provide several features that are superior to a conventional VCR and its limited recording capabilities. During live programs, for example, viewers can pause during a broadcast while the DVR keeps recording. DVRs can also provide instant replay and slow motion features so avid sports fans will never miss a play again. Additionally, TiVo DVRs include a fast-forward button so viewers can bypass television commercials or catch up with live programming that they have paused.

TiVo, based in Alviso, California, currently has over 422,000 subscribers, with projections of continued growth. While analysts expect DVRs to take several years to reach the market penetration of the ubiquitous VCR, DVRs are projected to be in 14 million homes by 2005, possibly making them the fastest growing consumer electronics product in history. If this prediction pans out, the impact on television from DVRs and TiVo-like services could be enormous. For instance, since TiVo subscribers can create their own programming schedule, prime time could become increasingly irrelevant as more shows get recorded for later viewing. Additionally, viewers armed with the ability to fast-forward through commercials will see less of them; analysts estimate that the viewing of commercials will decrease by 50 percent by 2009 with increased market penetration of DVRs.

Not surprisingly, TiVo and DVRs have most advertising and television executives watching carefully to see how the technology develops. TiVo believes its technology is actually an opportunity for advertisers to target their audiences more directly. Best Buy was the first consumer electronics retailer to work with TiVo to deliver customized advertising to TiVo subscribers. As an extension of its national "Go Mobile" advertising campaign, Best Buy provided an electronic tag for commercials that appeared to TiVo subscribers. Simply clicking their remote control while the ads were on their television screen transported TiVo subscribers to a "Video Showcase" area where they could view innovative Best Buy branded entertainment.

digital video recording services. Entertainment giants like Time Warner, DirecTV, AT&T, RealNetworks, Blockbuster, Cox Communications, Showtime Networks, HBO, and others have partnered with TiVo to develop programming and advertising solutions. Additionally, entertainment companies including Interscope Geffen A&M, New Line Cinema, Sony Pictures, and PBS have partnered with TiVo to produce entertainment Showcases similar to the Best Buy campaign that will extend their advertising campaigns and appeal to the entertainment enthusiasts within TiVo's subscriber base.[68]

Questions

1. If the majority of TiVo viewers fast-forward through commercials, advertisers will essentially be wasting the millions of dollars they spend on them. What solutions might you suggest to advertisers as TiVo gains in popularity?

2. How might TiVo and DVRs affect traditional television networks that rely on advertising revenue to support original programming?

3. How might the popularity of TiVo's service affect traditional media selection criteria like reach and frequency?

WATCH IT

FEATURE PRESENTATION

Zubi Advertising

SmallBusinessSchool
the Series on PBS stations and the Web

To deepen your understanding of the concepts in Chapter 15, Small Business School introduces you to Teresa Zubizarreta, the founder and president of Miami, Florida-based Zubi Advertising. Zubi has concentrated its efforts on serving the burgeoning Hispanic-American market, and with hard work and exceptional insight, the company has won contracts for such prestigious accounts as American Airlines, Ford Motor Company, and S.C. Johnson, maker of Windex, Ziploc, and Pledge products. Hispanics are the largest minority group and the fastest growing population in the United States; and Miami is one of the top ten cities for Hispanic-American population growth. Zubi takes a partnering approach to working with its customers, because in addition to providing the base logistics of advertising work, Zubi positions itself as a valuable source of knowledge, insight, and innovation for reaching an often misunderstood market.

What to Watch for and Ask Yourself

1. What type of advertising does Zubi use for the Ford account?

2. What is the advertising objective for the Ford Motor campaign?

3. Discuss the Erase Stereotypes tool. What does it accomplish for Zubi Advertising?

ENCORE PRESENTATION

Ed TV

After working through the advertising and public relations concepts in Chapter 15, you can see that promotional elements are often intertwined. As an encore to your study, watch the film clip from *Ed TV,* starring Rob Reiner (Whitaker), Ellen DeGeneres, and Matthew McConaughey as the star of a reality television series. The scene is taken from the film's opening sequence, in which Whitaker shows the advertising for "True TV" to an audience of press reporters. Watch the opening advertisement carefully. What kind of ad is it? Can you identify one (or more) exe-cutional styles or appeals? Could the advertisement be considered public relations? Why? What kind of public relations could it be? Can you envision other ways in which advertising and public relations could be intertwined?

STILL SHAKY?

If you're having trouble with the concepts in this chapter, consider using some of the following study resources. You can review the videos, or test yourself with materials designed for all kinds of learning styles.

☑ **Xtra! (http://lambxtra.swlearning.com)**

☑ Quiz	☑ Feature Videos	☑ Encore Videos	☑ FAQ Videos
☑ Exhibit Worksheets	☑ Marketing Plan Worksheets	☐ Content	

☑ **http://lamb.swlearning.com**

☑ Quiz	☑ PowerPoint slides	☑ Marketing News	☐ Review Exercises
☑ Links	☑ Marketing Plan Contest	☑ Career Exercise	☑ Use It Now

☑ **Study guide**

☑ Outline	☑ Vocab Review	☑ Test Questions	☑ Marketing Scenario

Need More? Here's a tip. Close your book and write a list of the key concepts in this chapter. Or create flashcards for key concepts (concept on one side, explanation and example on the other). Flashcards are great portable study aids that you can use over and over, in a group, with a partner, or on your own.

Sales Promotion and Personal Selling

LEARNING OBJECTIVES

1. Define and state the objectives of sales promotion

2. Discuss the most common forms of consumer sales promotion

3. List the most common forms of trade sales promotion

4. Describe personal selling

5. Discuss the key differences between relationship selling and traditional selling

6. List the steps in the selling process

7. Describe the functions of sales management

LOOKING FORWARD

What is satellite radio? This relatively new service is commercial-free (almost) radio that is beamed down from satellites that reach across the entire United States. Listeners on the West Coast and those on the East Coast hear the same radio station. Imagine listening to the same radio station as you drive across the entire country. Other advantages are the number and variety of stations offered. You can choose from nearly 100 stations broadcasting everything from sports and talk radio to entertainment and news. The genres may be as general as country or pop or as specific as big band–swing, reggae, and Broadway show tunes. Though satellite radio is a relatively new enterprise, it is taking off quickly; the two companies offering this service (XM Satellite Radio and Sirius) have over one million subscribers between them.

XM Satellite Radio costs $9.99 per month and features 70 music stations (35 are commercial-free) and 31 entertainment, comedy, news, and sports stations. XM competes head-to-head with Sirius, which offers 60 commercial-free music stations and 40 talk and sports stations for $12.95 per month. Both companies have exclusive contracts with major

automakers and are fighting for market share of American drivers. Though XM Satellite Radio has the first mover advantage, Sirius is catching up quickly by offering unique features such as in-studio performances and live interviews.

Recently, XM Satellite Radio launched a new satellite radio system for vehicles and homes called the Roady. The Roady was developed to appeal to a younger target market that wants value in terms of affordability and style. It was positioned as one of the top holiday gifts for the 2003 holiday season. The radio is produced by Delphi, known for top-quality, mobile audio products.

The Roady receiver is customizable to user preferences with a choice of seven different display colors, three interchangeable colored faceplates, and a variety of display screen options. For example, a user can choose a red faceplate with a blue display that shows the artist, radio station, and song title; another possibility is to have a blue faceplate with a green display that shows just the song title. At only five ounces and half the size of previous "portable" receivers, the pocket-sized receiver is extremely portable. It can even be taken from the vehicle to a home base

for extended listening options. The Roady offers maximum convenience because it allows for easy scrolling between stations and direct programming of up to 30 channels. Another distinguishing feature is the Micro Antenna, which is the smallest available in the satellite radio market. The most unique feature is TuneSelect, which remembers the songs you hear and alerts you when one of those songs is playing on a different channel. The $120 package includes the Micro Antenna, mounting accessories, and a cassette adaptor. Salespersons at dealerships and in retail outlets are given extensive training on these features as well as incentives for selling the Roady.

XM offers a variety of sales promotions to encourage users to purchase its receivers. For example, during the 2003 holiday season XM offered a "free home kit" valued at $40 with the purchase of an XM satellite receiver. The kit included a base, antenna, a/c adaptor, and cables.[1]

Why has satellite radio been so successful? What are the most important features? Which market segments are likely to be most interested in satellite radio? What is the best way to sell satellite radio—sales promotions or personal selling?

Online

XM Satellite Radio
How many promotions is XM currently offering on its Web site? Do you see evidence of targeted promotions? In other words, do some promotions seem to be geared to certain target segments? After researching the Web site, would you be interested in XM radio? Why or why not?

http://www.xmradio.com

Trade sales promotion is directed to members of the marketing channel, such as wholesalers and retailers. Sales promotion has become an important element in a marketer's integrated marketing communications program (see Chapter 14). Sales promotion expenditures have been steadily increasing over the last several years as a result of increased competition, the ever-expanding array of available media choices, consumers and retailers demanding more deals from manufacturers, and the continued reliance on accountable and measurable marketing strategies. In addition, product and service marketers that have traditionally ignored sales promotion activities, such as power companies and restaurants, have discovered the marketing power of sales promotion. In fact, *PROMO Magazine* estimates that promotion marketing in the United States now exceeds $288 billion a year.[2]

THE OBJECTIVES OF SALES PROMOTION

Sales promotion usually has more effect on behavior than on attitudes. Immediate purchase is the goal of sales promotion, regardless of the form it takes. Therefore, it seems to make more sense when planning a sales promotion campaign to target customers according to their general behavior. For instance, is the consumer loyal to your product or to your competitor's? Does the consumer switch brands readily in favor of the best deal? Does the consumer buy only the least expensive product, no matter what? Does the consumer buy any products in your category at all?

The objectives of a promotion depend on the general behavior of target consumers (see Exhibit 16.1). For example, marketers who are targeting loyal users of their product actually don't want to change behavior. Instead, they need to reinforce existing behavior or increase product usage. An effective tool for strengthening brand loyalty is the *frequent buyer program* that rewards consumers for repeat purchases. Other types of promotions are more effective with customers prone to brand switching or with those who are loyal to a competitor's product. A cents-off coupon, free sample, or eye-catching display in a store will often entice shoppers to try a different brand. Consumers who do not use the product may be enticed to try it through the distribution of free samples.

Once marketers understand the dynamics occurring within their product category and have determined the particular consumers and consumer behaviors they want to influence, they can then go about selecting promotional tools to achieve these goals.

consumer sales promotion
Sales promotion activities targeting the ultimate consumer.

trade sales promotion
Sales promotion activities targeting a channel member, such as a wholesaler or retailer.

EXHIBIT 16.1

Types of Consumers and Sales Promotion Goals

Type of Buyer	Desired Results	Sales Promotion Examples
Loyal customers People who buy your product most or all of the time	Reinforce behavior, increase consumption, change purchase timing	• Loyalty marketing programs, such as frequent buyer cards or frequent shopper clubs • Bonus packs that give loyal consumers an incentive to stock up or premiums offered in return for proofs of purchase
Competitor's customers People who buy a competitor's product most or all of the time	Break loyalty, persuade to switch to your brand	• Sampling to introduce your product's superior qualities compared to their brand • Sweepstakes, contests, or premiums that create interest in the product
Brand switchers People who buy a variety of products in the category	Persuade to buy your brand more often	• Any promotion that lowers the price of the product, such as coupons, price-off packages, and bonus packs • Trade deals that help make the product more readily available than competing products
Price buyers People who consistently buy the least expensive brand	Appeal with low prices or supply added value that makes price less important	• Coupons, price-off packages, refunds, or trade deals that reduce the price of the brand to match that of the brand that would have been purchased

SOURCE: From *Sales Promotion Essentials*, 2nd ed., by Don E. Schultz, William A. Robinson, and Lisa A. Petrison. Reprinted by permission of NTC Publishing Group, 4255 Touhy Ave., Lincolnwood, IL 60048.

REVIEW LEARNING OBJECTIVE 1

1 **Define and state the objectives of sales promotion**

Goal = Drive immediate purchase

= Influence <u>Behavior</u> not A~~ttit~~ude

2 TOOLS FOR CONSUMER SALES PROMOTION

Discuss the most common forms of consumer sales promotion

Marketing managers must decide which consumer sales promotion devices to use in a specific campaign. The methods chosen must suit the objectives to ensure success of the overall promotion plan. Popular tools for consumer sales promotion are coupons and rebates, premiums, loyalty marketing programs, contests and sweepstakes, sampling, and point-of-purchase promotion. Consumer sales promotion tools have also been easily transferred to online versions to entice Internet users to visit sites, purchase products, or use services on the Web. This chapter's "Global Perspectives" box offers some insight into how domestic brands are promoted abroad.

With approximately 33,000 stores, Yum! Brands is the world's largest restaurant company. Yum! Brands' restaurants include KFC, Pizza Hut, Taco Bell, Long John Silver's, and A&W. Some restaurants offer one brand, while others offer a multibrand store concept with two or more brands housed under one roof. For example, one restaurant might serve a combo meal that includes an A&W root beer float, KFC chicken strips, a Taco Bell taco, and Pizza Hut pizza.

To ensure rapid global growth, Yum! opens nearly 1,100 overseas stores a year of which 250 are in China. In China alone, more than two million consumers visit a KFC restaurant every day. Yum!'s products, branding, and advertising strategies are tailored to meet

ing the coupon to any KFC for instant redemption.

Yum! was able to multiply the number of participants by awarding points to customers who forwarded the coupon to friends and family. Yum! assigned a personal ID number to each entrant, which allowed customers to access their point balances online. Each week, customers who forwarded the most coupons received additional m-coupons for KFC food prizes. The results were impressive. Over 20,000 people downloaded the m-coupon during the month-long campaign, and 63 percent of those redeemed the coupon![3]

Why do you think Yum! chose KFC for satellite messaging promotions? Can you think of ways that Yum! could expand its satellite messaging promotions to other marketing campaigns, restaurants, or countries?

COUPONS AND REBATES

A **coupon** is a certificate that entitles consumers to an immediate price reduction when they buy the product. Coupons are a particularly good way to encourage product trial and repurchase. They are also likely to increase the amount of a product bought.

Coupon distribution has been steadily declining in recent years as packaged-goods marketers attempt to wean consumers off coupon clipping. Although approximately $258 billion in coupons are distributed each year, only about 1.4 percent, or about $3.6 billion, are actually redeemed by consumers.[4] Part of the problem is that coupons are often wasted on consumers who have no interest in the product, such as pet food or feminine products coupons that reach the petless or men. This is due mainly to the typical distribution of coupons in mass-media newspaper Sunday inserts. Additionally, coupons are more likely to encourage repeat purchase by regular users, customers who would have purchased the product regardless, than to stimulate product trial by nonusers.

Because of the high cost and disappointing redemption rates, many marketers are reevaluating their use of coupons. By shortening the time the coupon can be redeemed, some marketers have increased redemption rates by creating a greater sense of urgency to redeem the coupon. Other marketers are de-emphasizing their use of coupons in favor of everyday low pricing, while others are distributing single, all-purpose coupons that can be redeemed for several brands.

coupon
A certificate that entitles consumers to an immediate price reduction when they buy the product.

In-store coupons have become popular because they are more likely to influence customers' buying decisions. Instant coupons on product packages, coupons distributed from on-shelf coupon-dispensing machines, and electronic coupons issued at the checkout counter are achieving much higher redemption rates. Indeed, instant coupons are redeemed more than 15 times more frequently than traditional newspaper coupons, indicating that consumers are making more in-store purchase decisions.

Starbucks has taken in-store coupons to a new level by installing interactive units on grocery store shelves. Each unit provides consumers with product information related to brewing, coffee education, and a taste matcher. In one test the units resulted in a 200 percent increase in sales. Internet coupons are also gaining in popularity. For example, Kroger has launched "Coupons that you click. Not clip." on Kroger.com. Registered Kroger Plus Shoppers card members just log on to the Web site and click on the coupons they want. Coupons are automatically loaded on to the Kroger Plus card and redeemed at checkout when the shopper's Kroger Plus card is scanned.[5]

As marketing tactics grow more sophisticated, coupons are no longer viewed as a stand-alone tactic, but as an integral component of a larger promotional campaign. For example, Domino's Pizza teamed with eBay to launch a "Back to School" campaign focused on building the Domino's brand and driving consumers to **http://www.ebay.com**. The coupons arrive on pizza boxes. Customers then log on to eBay for a chance to win one million eBay points (a cash value of $10,000) to be spent on eBay.com, textbook discounts, and Domino's gift certificates.[6]

Rebates are similar to coupons in that they offer the purchaser a price reduction; however, because the purchaser must mail in a rebate form and usually some proof of purchase, the reward is not as immediate. Traditionally used by food and cigarette manufacturers, rebates now appear on all types of products, from computers and software to film and cell phones. Consumers purchasing one of the new varieties of Vlasic pickles receive a rebate form to mail in for a discount off the purchase price. As an incentive to mail in the rebate, consumers are entered into a sweepstakes for a Ford SUV.[7]

Manufacturers prefer rebates for several reasons. Rebates allow manufacturers to offer price cuts to consumers directly. Manufacturers have more control over rebate promotions because they can be rolled out and shut off quickly. Further, because buyers must fill out forms with their names, addresses, and other data, manufacturers use rebate programs to build customer databases. Perhaps the best reason of all to offer rebates is that although rebates are particularly good at enticing purchase, most consumers never bother to redeem them. Studies have found that as few as 2 percent of consumers eligible for rebates apply for them.[8]

PREMIUMS

A **premium** is an extra item offered to the consumer, usually in exchange for some proof that the promoted product has been purchased. Premiums reinforce the consumer's purchase decision, increase consumption, and persuade nonusers to switch brands. Premiums like telephones, tote bags, and umbrellas are given away when consumers buy cosmetics, magazines, bank services, rental cars, and so on. Probably the best example of the use of premiums is McDonald's Happy Meal, which rewards children with a small toy. The fast-food marketer's promotions in partnership with companies like Disney make its Happy Meals highly popular with children.[9]

On-shelf coupon-dispensing machines make coupon usage more convenient for consumers, the majority of whom are not regular coupon clippers.

© JEFF GREENBERG/PHOTO EDIT

rebate
A cash refund given for the purchase of a product during a specific period.

premium
An extra item offered to the consumer, usually in exchange for some proof of purchase of the promoted product.

consumer loyalty is on the decline. Forrester Research found that the percentage of consumers ranking price as more important than brand rose from 41 to 47 percent over three years. According to research conducted by Gartner, more than 75 percent of consumers have more than one loyalty card that rewards them with redeemable points. Furthermore, U.S. companies spent over $1.2 billion on loyalty programs in 2003, a figure that is expected to rise in the future.[11]

The objective of loyalty marketing programs is to build long-term, mutually beneficial relationships between a company and its key customers. Frequent shopper card programs offered by many supermarkets and other retailers have exploded in popularity. Research from Forrester shows that 54 percent of primary grocery shoppers belong to two or more supermarket loyalty programs. Although this speaks to the popularity of loyalty cards, it also shows that customers are pledging "loyalty" to more than one store: 15 percent of primary grocery shoppers are cardholders in at least three programs, and 4 percent participate in four or five programs.[12] Combined with the statistics on the growing importance of price over brands, frequent shopper programs need to offer something more than just discounts to build customer loyalty. One of the more successful recent premium promotions is Starbucks' Duetto Card, which combines a Visa credit card with a reloadable Starbucks card. The card allows members to collect "Duetto Dollars" that can be redeemed for anything they want to purchase at a Starbucks location. Starbucks also sends members quarterly opportunities based on usage, such as product samples and previews.[13]

Indeed, cobranded credit cards are an increasingly popular loyalty marketing tool. Over 263 million Americans received a pitch for a cobranded credit card in the last quarter of 2003 alone, an increase of 35 percent over the same period the previous year. Target, Gap, Sony, and Delta are only a few examples of companies sponsoring cobranded Visa or Master Cards. American Express has a program with Space Adventures, a company that offers simulated space flight experiences.[14]

One unique frequent buyer program is called Stratus, which is promoted as a gateway to a more glamorous lifestyle. The Stratus Visa card is underwritten by U.S. Bank and available only by invitation. Stratus cardholders pay an annual fee of $1,500 and are required to spend at least $100,000 per year on the card. Stratus partners include luxury catalog Vivre, luxury travel company Abercrombie and Kent, MarquisJet, Sony Cierge, and YachtStore, among others. Cardholders can redeem points for dinner at the Louvre, a private tour of the pyramids, a yoga class with Gwyneth Paltrow, or even trips in a private jet (furnished by MarquisJet, of course).[15]

Through loyalty programs, shoppers receive discounts, alerts on new products, and other types of enticing offers. In exchange, retailers are able to build customer databases that help them better understand customer preferences. Verizon

loyalty marketing program
A promotional program designed to build long-term, mutually beneficial relationships between a company and its key customers.

frequent buyer program
A loyalty program in which loyal consumers are rewarded for making multiple purchases of a particular good or service.

Wireless builds loyalty with its "New Every Two" program. Consumers who have been Verizon customers for two years are eligible for a $100 credit toward a new digital phone.[16]

Sweepstakes On-line

How do online sweepstakes sites compare with the kind of sweepstakes entries you receive in the mail? Visit the popular sweepstakes site Sweepstakesonline.com. Do any of the contests interest you? Do you think the online pitches are ethical? Why or why not?

http://www.sweepstakesonline.com

Online

CONTESTS AND SWEEPSTAKES

Contests and sweepstakes are generally designed to create interest in a good or service, often to encourage brand switching. *Contests* are promotions in which participants use some skill or ability to compete for prizes. A consumer contest usually requires entrants to answer questions, complete sentences, or write a paragraph about the product and submit proof of purchase. Winning a *sweepstakes*, on the other hand, depends on chance or luck, and participation is free. Sweepstakes usually draw about ten times more entries than contests do.

While contests and sweepstakes may draw considerable interest and publicity, generally they are not effective tools for generating long-term sales. To increase their effectiveness, sales promotion managers must make certain the award will appeal to the target market. For example, Home & Garden Television Network's annual "Dream Home Giveaway" sweepstakes awards a fully furnished, custom-built home to one lucky viewer. The promotion is cosponsored by Sears, which stocks the home with Kenmore appliances, a Craftsman workshop, home fashions, lawn and garden equipment, and home electronics, and General Motors, which fills the garage with a new sport utility vehicle. The annual sweepstakes typically draws over four million entries.[17] Offering several smaller prizes to many winners instead of one huge prize to just one person often will increase the effectiveness of the promotion, but there's no denying the attractiveness of a jackpot-type prize.

Marketers have recently launched some of the biggest and most outrageous promotions ever. PepsiCo hosted a sweepstakes that featured a $1 billion giveaway. The winner was announced on a Warner Brothers television special hosted by Drew Carey. Pepsi also partnered with Apple Computer to give away 100 million free music downloads from iTunes.com. United Airlines launched a "Ticket to the World" that gives away free international travel tickets (previously only domestic tickets were given away), and Volkswagen launched a promotion that gave an Apple Computer iPod to anyone who purchased a Beetle.[18]

Marketing... in Entertainment

Enter Now for Your Chance to Win

Among the most popular sales promotion tools in the entertainment industry are the contest and the sweepstakes, or giveaway. Offering opportunities to win prizes ranging from backstage passes to see the band to dream homes, sweepstakes appeal to many marketing segments. The sweepstakes may, in fact, be the sales promotion tool best suited to attracting a wide audience. It may also have been the genesis of the reality TV genre. *Survivor, The Bachelor, My Big, Fat, Obnoxious Fiancé, The Apprentice*, and even shows like *Fear Factor* and *American Idol* attract contestants (and viewers) with the lure of winning a tremendous prize (millions of dollars, a recording contract, a dream job). Certainly, reality shows dominate a large portion of network programming and are widely watched. And much like sales promotions, the results of reality TV programs (in other words, the ratings) are easily measured. So, are reality TV shows really just marketing promotions? If so, what are they promoting? What do you think?

SAMPLING

Consumers generally perceive a certain amount of risk in trying new products. Many are afraid of trying something they will not like (such as a new food item) or spending too much money and getting little reward. **Sampling** allows the customer to try a product risk-free. Sampling can increase retail sales by as much as 40 percent.[19] It is no surprise, therefore, that product sampling has increased by more than 8 percent annually in recent years and has reached $1.5 billion per year.[20]

Sampling can be accomplished by directly mailing the sample to the customer, delivering the sample door-to-door, packaging the sample with another product, or demonstrating or sampling the product at a retail store or service outlet.

sampling
A promotional program that allows the consumer the opportunity to try a product or service for free.

and festivals, beach events, and chili cook-offs. For example, product sampling during tailgating at college and professional football stadiums allows marketers to reach anywhere from 10,000 to 50,000 consumers in a single afternoon. H.J. Heinz tests products such as new barbecue sauces and ketchups to get immediate feedback about what consumers like and dislike about the products.[23]

Distributing samples to specific location types where consumers regularly meet for a common objective or interest, such as health clubs, churches, or doctors' offices, is one of the most efficient methods of sampling. What better way to get consumers to try a product than to offer a sample exactly when it is needed most? If someone visits a health club regularly, chances are he or she is a good prospect for a health-food product or vitamin supplement. Health club instructors are handing out not only these products but also body wash, deodorant, and face cloths to sweating participants at the end of class, and makers of stain removers and hand cleansers are giving away samples in mall food courts and petting zoos. Likewise, pharmaceutical companies offer free samples of new and expensive drugs as a tactic to entice doctors and consumers to become loyal to a product. This method of distributing samples is working. In fact, one recent study found that sampling events produced an average 36 percent increase in sales soon afterward.[24]

POINT-OF-PURCHASE PROMOTION

Point-of-purchase (P-O-P) promotion includes any promotional display set up at the retailer's location to build traffic, advertise the product, or induce impulse buying. Point-of-purchase promotions include shelf "talkers" (signs attached to store shelves), shelf extenders (attachments that extend shelves so products stand out), ads on grocery carts and bags, end-aisle and floor-stand displays, television monitors at supermarket checkout counters, in-store audio messages, and audiovisual displays. One big advantage of P-O-P promotion is that it offers manufacturers a captive audience in retail stores. Another advantage is that between 70 and 80 percent of all retail purchase decisions are made in-store, so P-O-P promotions can be very effective. One study found that properly displayed P-O-P promotions boosted sales anywhere from 2 to 65 percent, depending on the brand and P-O-P mix. Signs such as header or riser cards increased weekly store sales 6 percent for one brand; base or case wraps boosted total sales 12 percent; standees, 2 percent; inflatable or mobile displays, 40 percent; and signs that advertised a brand's sports, movie, or charity tie-in, 65 percent.[25] When Hershey Foods launched its new Swoops, a "chip" version of popular candy bars such as Almond Joy, Reese's, and Hershey Bars, it successfully used in-store displays to stimulate in-store, impulse purchases of the new candy.[26]

point-of-purchase display
A promotional display set up at the retailer's location to build traffic, advertise the product, or induce impulse buying.

Corporations are cashing in on in-store purchasing decisions through more sophisticated P-O-P promotions. For example, MasterCard International sent 300,000 of its merchant and restaurant partners across the country with P-O-P kits containing window clings, tent cards, employee buttons, register decals, coupons, and check presenter inserts customized by retail category. The promotion program, called Priceless P-O-P, awarded one cardholder five "prizes of a lifetime": an African safari, a visit from a celebrity chef, a behind-the-scenes tour of Space Center Houston, a trip to a racing school in England, and VIP passes to the My VH-1 Music Awards. MasterCard encouraged compliance among retailers with a mystery shopper program that sent teams into stores to award $50 gift cards to store employees whenever they encountered a Priceless P-O-P. Five random participants won $2,500 gift cards, and the staff at the store that produced the grand-prize winner earned a Major League Baseball prize package.[27]

Upromote.com

How can Upromote.com help you with your sales promotions efforts? What kind of marketing budget would you need to take advantage of its services? What kind of company would be best served by Upromote.com?

http://www.upromote.com

Online

ONLINE SALES PROMOTION

Online sales promotions have been booming in recent years. Marketers are now spending billions of dollars annually on such promotions. Sales promotions online have proved effective and cost-efficient, generating response rates three to five times higher than those of their off-line counterparts. The most effective types of online sales promotions are free merchandise, sweepstakes, free shipping with purchases, and coupons.

Eager to boost traffic, Internet retailers are busy giving away free services or equipment, such as personal computers and travel, to lure consumers not only to their own Web sites but to the Internet in general. Another goal is to add potential customers to their databases. For example, Heineken USA, Inc. launched the "Headline Hoax" online promotional campaign in which consumers (hoaxers) trick a friend (victim). The hoax is a fake headline with a photograph that looks as though it is on the front page of a major Web page such as Maximonline.com. The hoaxer can choose from a selection of pictures and headlines. One photo shows two football players attacking one another and the tackler has one hand inside the other's shirt and another hand pulling on his shorts; the headline reads "[Person's Name] is too touchy at touch football game." Once the victim opens this e-mail, other friends on the hoaxer's list are alerted to the joke. At the start of the campaign, Heineken had only 5,000 e-mail addresses in its database. Within six months, it had collected an additional 95,000 e-mail addresses.[28]

After several years of declining coupon distribution due to high cost and low redemption rates, many marketers are now distributing coupons online. Even after the dot-com bust, online coupons benefit from a redemption rate of over 3 percent, or more than double the redemption rate for traditional coupons. In fact, nearly 50 percent of consumers who purchase something online use a coupon or discount promotional code. According to CMS, a coupon-management company in Winston-Salem, North Carolina, over 7.9 million electronic coupons were redeemed in 2003.[29] In addition, e-coupons can help marketers lure new customers. For example, Staples.com jumped from 23rd to 14th among retail Web sites with the most buyers through an e-coupon promotion that offered $25 off on purchases of $75 or more.[30]

REVIEW LEARNING OBJECTIVE 2

2   **Discuss the most common forms of consumer sales promotion**

CONSUMER SALES PROMOTION

- Coupons and rebates
- Premiums
- Loyalty marketing program
- Contests and sweepstakes
- Sampling
- P-O-P
- Online

- *Push money:* Intermediaries receive **push money** as a bonus for pushing the manufacturer's brand through the distribution channel. Often the push money is directed toward a retailer's salespeople. LinoColor, the leading high-end scanner company, produces a Picture Perfect Rewards catalog filled with merchandise retailers can purchase with points accrued for every LinoColor scanner they sell. The cover of the catalog features a wave runner that was brought to three industry trade shows and given away in a sweepstakes to one of the dealers who had visited all the product displays and passed a quiz. The program resulted in a 26 percent increase in LinoColor sales, and the manufacturer recruited 32 new dealers to carry the product line.[31]
- *Training:* Sometimes a manufacturer will train an intermediary's personnel if the product is rather complex—as frequently occurs in the computer and telecommunication industries. For example, representatives of a TV manufacturer like Toshiba may train salespeople in how to demonstrate the new features of the latest models of TVs to consumers. This is particularly helpful when salespeople must explain the features to older consumers who are less technology oriented.
- *Free merchandise:* Often a manufacturer offers retailers free merchandise in lieu of quantity discounts. For example, a breakfast cereal manufacturer may throw in one case of free cereal for every 20 cases ordered by the retailer. Occasionally, free merchandise is used as payment for trade allowances normally provided through other sales promotions. Instead of giving a retailer a price reduction for buying a certain quantity of merchandise, the manufacturer may throw in extra merchandise "free" (that is, at a cost that would equal the price reduction).
- *Store demonstrations:* Manufacturers can also arrange with retailers to perform an in-store demonstration. Food manufacturers often send representatives to grocery stores and supermarkets to let customers sample a product while shopping. Cosmetic companies also send their representatives to department stores to promote their beauty aids by performing facials and makeovers for customers.
- *Business meetings, conventions, and trade shows:* Trade association meetings, conferences, and conventions are an important aspect of sales promotion and a growing, multibillion-dollar market. At these shows, manufacturers, distributors, and other vendors have the chance to display their goods or describe their services to customers and potential customers. A recent study reported that, on average, the cost of closing a lead generated at an exhibition is 56 percent of the cost of closing a lead generated in the field—$625 versus $1,117.[32] Trade shows have been uniquely effective in introducing new products; they can establish products in the marketplace more quickly than can advertising,

trade allowance
A price reduction offered by manufacturers to intermediaries, such as wholesalers and retailers.

push money
Money offered to channel intermediaries to encourage them to "push" products—that is, to encourage other members of the channel to sell the products.

3 List the most common forms of trade sales promotion

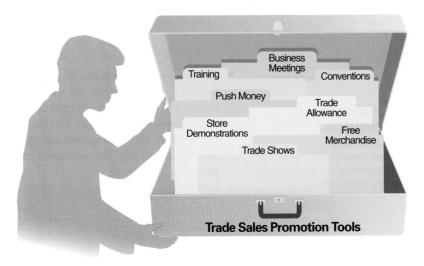

Training

Business Meetings

Conventions

Push Money

Trade Allowance

Store Demonstrations

Free Merchandise

Trade Shows

Trade Sales Promotion Tools

direct marketing, or sales calls. Companies participate in trade shows to attract and identify new prospects, serve current customers, introduce new products, enhance corporate image, test the market response to new products, enhance corporate morale, and gather competitive product information.

Trade promotions are popular among manufacturers for many reasons. Trade sales promotion tools help manufacturers gain new distributors for their products, obtain wholesaler and retailer support for consumer sales promotions, build or reduce dealer inventories, and improve trade relations. Car manufacturers annually sponsor dozens of auto shows for consumers. Many of the displays feature interactive computer stations where consumers enter vehicle specifications and get a printout of prices and local dealer names. In return, the local car dealers get the names of good prospects. The shows attract millions of consumers, providing dealers with increased store traffic as well as good leads.

4 PERSONAL SELLING

Describe personal selling

As mentioned in Chapter 15, *personal selling* is direct communication between a sales representative and one or more prospective buyers in an attempt to influence each other in a purchase situation.

In a sense, all businesspeople are salespeople. An individual may become a plant manager, a chemist, an engineer, or a member of any profession and yet still have to sell. During a job search, applicants must "sell" themselves to prospective employers in an interview. To reach the top in most organizations, individuals need to sell ideas to peers, superiors, and subordinates. Most important, people must sell themselves and their ideas to just about everyone with whom they have a continuing relationship and to many other people they see only once or twice. Chances are that students majoring in business or marketing will start their professional careers in sales. Even students in nonbusiness majors may pursue a sales career.

Personal selling offers several advantages over other forms of promotion:

- Personal selling provides a detailed explanation or demonstration of the product. This capability is especially needed for complex or new goods and services.
- The sales message can be varied according to the motivations and interests of each prospective customer. Moreover, when the prospect has questions or raises objections, the salesperson is there to provide explanations. In contrast, advertising and sales promotion can only respond to the objections the copywriter thinks are important to customers.
- Personal selling can be directed only to qualified prospects. Other forms of promotion include some unavoidable waste because many people in the audience are not prospective customers.

Customers are concentrated.	Customers are geographically dispersed.
Examples: insurance policies, custom windows, airplane engines	**Examples:** soap, magazine subscriptions, cotton T-shirts

4 **Describe personal selling**

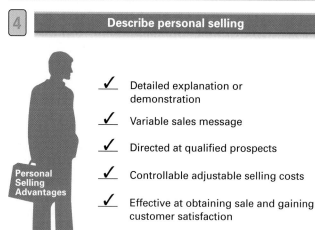

Personal Selling Advantages

✓ Detailed explanation or demonstration

✓ Variable sales message

✓ Directed at qualified prospects

✓ Controllable adjustable selling costs

✓ Effective at obtaining sale and gaining customer satisfaction

Perhaps the most important advantage is that personal selling is considerably more effective than other forms of promotion in obtaining a sale and gaining a satisfied customer.

Personal selling might work better than other forms of promotion given certain customer and product characteristics. Generally speaking, personal selling becomes more important as the number of potential customers decreases, as the complexity of the product increases, and as the value of the product grows (see Exhibit 16.2). When there are relatively few potential customers and the value of the good or service is relatively sufficient, the time and travel costs of personally visiting each prospect are justifiable. For highly complex goods, such as business jets or private communication systems, a salesperson is needed to determine the prospective customer's needs, explain the product's basic advantages, and propose the exact features and accessories that will meet the client's needs.

5 RELATIONSHIP SELLING

Discuss the key differences between relationship selling and traditional selling

Until recently, marketing theory and practice concerning personal selling focused almost entirely on a planned presentation to prospective customers for the sole purpose of making the sale. Marketers were most concerned with making a one-time sale and then moving on to the next prospect. Whether the presentation took place face-to-face during a personal sales call or over the telephone (telemarketing), traditional personal selling methods attempted to persuade the buyer to accept a point of view or convince the buyer to take some action. Once the customer was somewhat convinced, then the salesperson used a variety of techniques in an attempt to elicit a purchase. Frequently, the objectives of the salesperson were at the expense of the buyer, creating a win-lose outcome. Although this type of sales approach has not disappeared entirely, it is being used less and less often by professional salespeople.

In contrast, modern views of personal selling emphasize the relationship that develops between a salesperson and a buyer. **Relationship selling**, or **consultative selling**, is a multistage process that emphasizes personalization and empathy as key ingredients in identifying prospects and developing them as long-term, satisfied customers. The old way was to sell a product, but with relationship selling, the objective is to build long-term branded relationships with consumers/buyers. Thus, the focus is on building mutual trust between the buyer and seller through the delivery of anticipated, long-term, value-added benefits to the buyer.

Relationship or consultative salespeople, therefore, become consultants, partners, and problem solvers for their customers. They strive to build long-term relationships with key accounts by developing trust over time. The emphasis shifts from a one-time sale to a long-term relationship in which the salesperson works with the customer to develop solutions for enhancing the customer's bottom line. Moreover, research has shown that positive customer-salesperson relationships contribute to trust, increased customer loyalty, and the intent to continue the relationship with the salesperson.[33] Thus, relationship selling promotes a win-win situation for both buyer and seller.

The end result of relationship selling tends to be loyal customers who purchase from the company time after time. A relationship selling strategy focused on retaining customers costs a company less than constantly prospecting and selling to new customers. Companies that focus on customer retention through high customer service gain 6 percent market share per year, while companies that offer low customer service lose 2 percent market share per year.[34] In fact, it costs businesses six times more to gain a new customer than to retain a current one.[35]

Relationship selling is more typical with selling situations for industrial-type goods, such as heavy machinery or computer systems, and services, such as airlines and insurance, than for consumer goods. For example, Kinko's has built a long-term business relationship with PeopleSoft. The software maker now gives many of its training and educational materials printing jobs to Kinko's—a deal worth close to $5 million in revenues. Kinko's has forged such a close relationship with the company that Kinko's representatives are even invited to sit in on internal planning meetings in PeopleSoft's human resources department at the company's headquarters.

"Webinars" (online seminars lasting about an hour) are becoming an increasingly popular way to support relationship selling tasks like lead generation, client support, sales training, and corporate meetings. For example, 3Com, a computer data networking system, held a webinar that was attended by 1,300 executives in 80 countries; the session generated 60 percent of 3Com's five-month lead generation goals. Similarly, SpectraLink, a provider of wireless phone and text messaging systems to Verizon and SBC, uses webinars to give new-product demonstrations so that channel managers can focus on other tasks.[36]

Exhibit 16.3 lists the key differences between traditional personal selling and relationship or consultative selling. These differences will become more apparent as we explore the personal selling process later in the chapter.

relationship selling (consultative selling)
A sales practice that involves building, maintaining, and enhancing interactions with customers in order to develop long-term satisfaction through mutually beneficial partnerships.

REVIEW LEARNING OBJECTIVE 5

5 | Discuss the key differences between relationship selling and traditional selling

Sales Increases Result from Creating Value

| Initial Sale | Repeat Sale | Successive Sales |

Traditional Sales

Relationship Selling

STEPS IN THE SELLING PROCESS

List the steps in the selling process

Although personal selling may sound like a relatively simple task, completing a sale actually requires several steps. The **sales process**, or **sales cycle**, is simply the set of steps a salesperson goes through to sell a particular product or service. The sales process or cycle can be unique for each product or service, depending on the features of the product or service, characteristics of customer segments, and internal processes in place within the firm, such as how leads are gathered.

Some sales take only a few minutes, but others may take much longer to complete. Sales of technical products like a Boeing or Airbus airplane and customized goods and services typically take many months, perhaps even years, to complete. On the other end of the spectrum, sales of less technical products like copy machines or office supplies are generally more routine and may take only a few days. Whether a salesperson spends a few minutes or a few years on a sale, these are the seven basic steps in the personal selling process:

1. Generating leads
2. Qualifying leads
3. Approaching the customer and probing needs
4. Developing and proposing solutions
5. Handling objections
6. Closing the sale
7. Following up

Like other forms of promotion, these steps of selling follow the AIDA concept discussed in Chapter 14. Once a salesperson has located a prospect with the authority to buy, he or she tries to get the prospect's attention. A thorough needs assessment turned into an effective sales proposal and presentation should generate interest. After developing the customer's initial desire (preferably during the presentation of the sales proposal), the salesperson seeks action in the close by trying to get an agreement to buy. Follow-up after the sale, the final step in the selling process, not only lowers cognitive dissonance (refer to Chapter 5) but also may open up opportunities to discuss future sales. Effective follow-up will also lead to repeat business in which the process may start all over again at the needs assessment step.

Traditional selling and relationship selling follow the same basic steps. They differ in the relative importance placed on key steps in the process (see Exhibit 16.4). Traditional selling efforts are transaction oriented, focusing on generating as

sales process (sales cycle)
The set of steps a salesperson goes through in a particular organization to sell a particular product or service.

EXHIBIT 16.4

Relative Amount of Time Spent in Key Steps of the Selling Process

Key Selling Steps	Traditional Selling	Relationship/Consultative Selling
Generating leads	High	Low
Qualifying leads	Low	High
Approaching the customer and probing needs	Low	High
Developing and proposing solutions	Low	High
Handling objections	High	Low
Closing the sale	High	Low
Following up	Low	High

many leads as possible, making as many presentations as possible, and closing as many sales as possible. Minimal effort is placed on asking questions to identify customer needs and wants or matching these needs and wants to the benefits of the product or service. In contrast, the salesperson practicing relationship selling emphasizes an up-front investment in the time and effort needed to uncover each customer's specific needs and wants and matching to them, as closely as possible, the product or service offering. By doing the homework up front, the salesperson creates the conditions necessary for a relatively straightforward close. Let's look at each step of the selling process individually.

GENERATING LEADS

Initial groundwork must precede communication between the potential buyer and the salesperson. **Lead generation**, or **prospecting**, is the identification of those firms and people most likely to buy the seller's offerings. These firms or people become "sales leads" or "prospects."

Sales leads can be obtained in several different ways, most notably through advertising, trade shows and conventions, or direct-mail and telemarketing programs. One accounting firm used direct mail, telephone, sales visits, and seminars in a four-step process aimed at generating business-to-business leads. The initial step was a direct-mail piece, in the form of an introductory letter from a firm partner. The second piece, sent one month later, was a black and white direct-mail circular with company contact information. The third step was a follow-up call from a firm partner to arrange a meeting. In the last stage, partners contacted prospects who had initially declined appointments and invited them to attend a free tax seminar the following month. Of the 1,100 businesses targeted, 200 prospects set up meetings. Favorable publicity also helps to create leads. Company records of past client purchases are another excellent source of leads. Many sales professionals are also securing valuable leads from their firm's Internet Web site. For example, Ford Motor Company's drive to reach consumers online is paying off. Recently, the company's combination of Web sites and other online ventures sent an estimated half-million leads—60 percent of them in the United States—to its dealers. In the future, more than half of all sales leads likely will come from the Internet.[37]

Another way to gather a lead is through a **referral**—a recommendation from a customer or business associate. The advantages of referrals over other forms of prospecting include highly qualified leads, higher closing rates, larger initial transactions, and shorter sales cycles. Simply put, the salesperson and the company can earn more money in less time when prospecting using referrals. Referrals typically are as much as ten times more productive in generating sales than are cold calls. Unfortunately, although most clients are willing to give referrals, many salespeople do not ask for them. Effective sales training can help to overcome this reluctance to ask for referrals. To increase the number of referrals they receive, some companies even pay or send small gifts to customers or suppliers who provide referrals.

Networking is using friends, business contacts, coworkers, acquaintances, and fellow members in professional and civic organizations to identify potential clients. Indeed, a number of national networking clubs have been started for the sole purpose of generating leads and providing valuable business advice. The networking clubs usually have between 15 and 30 members in

lead generation (prospecting)
Identification of those firms and people most likely to buy the seller's offerings.

referral
A recommendation to a salesperson from a customer or business associate.

networking
A process of finding out about potential clients from friends, business contacts, coworkers, acquaintances, and fellow members in professional and civic organizations.

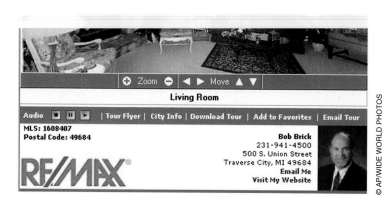

Realtors are consumer marketing salespeople, and as such, they follow the same steps in the sales process as a salesperson working in business markets. One way real estate agents can generate leads is through the ubiquitous MLS (multiple listing service), which allows people shopping for a house to view various properties and their features online before scheduling a tour.

needle in a haystack." Passing the job of cold calling to a lower-cost employee, typically an internal sales support person, allows salespeople to spend more time and use their relationship-building skills on prospects who have already been identified. Sales experts note that the days of cold calls and unannounced office visits have given way to referral-based and relationship selling.

QUALIFYING LEADS

When a prospect shows interest in learning more about a product, the salesperson has the opportunity to follow up, or qualify, the lead. Personally visiting unqualified prospects wastes valuable salesperson time and company resources. Often many leads go unanswered because salespeople are given no indication as to how qualified the leads are in terms of interest and ability to purchase. Unqualified prospects give vague or incomplete answers to a salesperson's specific questions, try to evade questions on budgets, and request changes in standard procedures like prices or terms of sale. In contrast, qualified leads who represent real prospects answer questions, value your time, and are realistic about money and when they are prepared to buy. Salespersons who are given accurate information on qualified leads are more than twice as likely to follow up.[39]

Lead qualification involves determining whether the prospect has three things:

- *A recognized need:* The most basic criterion for determining whether someone is a prospect for a product is a need that is not being satisfied. The salesperson should first consider prospects who are aware of a need but should not discount prospects who have not yet recognized that they have one. With a little more information about the product, they may decide they do have a need for it. Preliminary interviews and questioning can often provide the salesperson with enough information to determine whether there is a need.
- *Buying power:* Buying power involves both authority to make the purchase decision and access to funds to pay for it. To avoid wasting time and money, the salesperson needs to identify the purchasing authority and the ability to pay before making a presentation. Organizational charts and information about a

cold calling
A form of lead generation in which the salesperson approaches potential buyers without any prior knowledge of the prospects' needs or financial status.

lead qualification
Determination of a sales prospect's (1) recognized need, (2) buying power, and (3) receptivity and accessibility.

firm's credit standing can provide valuable clues.

- *Receptivity and accessibility:* The prospect must be willing to see the salesperson and be accessible to the salesperson. Some prospects simply refuse to see salespeople. Others, because of their stature in their organization, will see only a salesperson or sales manager with similar stature.

Often the task of lead qualification is handled by a telemarketing group or a sales support person who *prequalifies* the lead for the salesperson. Prequalification systems free sales representatives from the time-consuming task of following up on leads to determine need, buying power, and receptiveness. Prequalification systems may even set up initial appointments with the prospect for the salesperson. The result is more time for the sales force to spend in front of interested customers. Software is increasingly being utilized in lead qualification. For example, one janitorial company initially considered anyone with a minimum of 75,000 square feet to be a prospect. But often properties are already under contract or have been contacted. Using software, the company was able to create a "smart" list that included only true prospects.[40]

Companies are increasingly using their Web sites to qualify leads. When qualifying leads online, companies want visitors to register, indicate the products and services they are interested in, and provide information on their time frame and resources. Leads from the Internet can then be prioritized (those indicating a short time frame, for instance, given a higher priority) and then transferred to salespeople. Often Web site visitors can be enticed to answer questions with offers of free merchandise or information. Enticing visitors to register also enables companies to customize future electronic interactions—for example, by giving prospects who visit the Web site their choice from a menu of products tailored specifically to their needs.

APPROACHING THE CUSTOMER AND PROBING NEEDS

Before approaching the customer, the salesperson should learn as much as possible about the prospect's organization and its buyers. This process, called the **preapproach**, describes the "homework" that must be done by the salesperson before contacting the prospect. This may include consulting standard reference sources, such as Moody's, Standard & Poor's, or Dun & Bradstreet, or contacting acquaintances or others who may have information about the prospect. Another preapproach task is to determine whether the actual approach should be a personal visit, a phone call, a letter, or some other form of communication.

During the sales approach, the salesperson either talks to the prospect or secures an appointment for a future time in which to probe the prospect further as to his or her needs. Relationship selling theorists suggest that salespeople should begin developing mutual trust with their prospect during the approach. Salespeople should use the approach as a way of introducing themselves and their company and products. They must sell themselves before they can sell the product. Small talk that projects sincerity and some suggestion of friendship is encouraged to build rapport with the prospect, but remarks that could be construed as insincere should be avoided.

The salesperson's ultimate goal during the approach is to conduct a **needs assessment** to find out as much as possible about the prospect's situation. This involves interviewing the customer to determine his or her specific needs and wants and the range of options the customer has for satisfying them. The salesperson should be determining how to maximize the fit between what he or she can

preapproach
A process that describes the "homework" that must be done by a salesperson before he or she contacts a prospect.

needs assessment
A determination of the customer's specific needs and wants and the range of options the customer has for satisfying them.

Hoover's Online

son doesn't just sell products. He or she brings to each client business-building ideas and solutions to problems. For the customer, consulting a professional salesperson is like having another vital person on the team at no cost. For example, if the Xerox salesperson is asking the "right" questions, then he or she should be able to identify copy-related areas where the doctor's office is losing or wasting money. By being familiar with the Xerox product lines and discovering the doctor's needs, in terms of copying capability, the Xerox salesperson can act as a "consultant" on how the doctor's office can save money and time, rather than just selling a copier.

- *The competition:* The salesperson must know as much about the competitor's company and products as he or she knows about his or her own company. *Competitive intelligence* includes many factors: who the competitors are and what is known about them; how their products and services compare; advantages and disadvantages; and strengths and weaknesses. In this case, the Xerox salesperson must be familiar with the products of competitors, such as Canon and Minolta. For example, if the Canon copy machine is less expensive than the Xerox copier, the doctor's office may be leaning toward purchasing the Canon. But if the Xerox salesperson can point out that the cost of long-term maintenance and toner cartridges is lower for the Xerox copier, offsetting its higher initial cost, the salesperson may be able to persuade the doctor's office to purchase the Xerox copier because of the long-term savings.

- *The industry:* Knowing the industry involves active research on the part of the salesperson. This means attending industry and trade association meetings, reading articles published in industry and trade journals, keeping track of legislation and regulation that affect the industry, awareness of product alternatives and innovations from domestic and foreign competition, and having a feel for economic and financial conditions that may affect the industry. Thus, the Xerox salesperson should stay on top of emerging technological innovations so that he or she can better serve customers looking for the latest and greatest technology. It is also important to be aware of economic downturns because businesses may be looking for less expensive financing options. In either case, the Xerox salesperson will be able to provide better service by knowing how industry trends may affect customers' office purchases.

Creating a *customer profile* during the approach helps salespeople optimize their time and resources. This profile is then used to help develop an intelligent analysis of the prospect's needs in preparation for the next step, developing and proposing solutions. Customer profile information is typically stored and manipulated using sales force automation software packages designed for use on laptop computers. Sales force automation software provides sales reps with a computerized and efficient method of collecting customer information for use during the entire sales process. Further, customer and sales data stored in a computer database can be easily shared among sales team members. The information can also be appended with industry statistics, sales or meeting notes, billing data, and other information that may be pertinent to the prospect or the prospect's company. The more salespeople know about their prospects, the better they can meet their needs.

Salespeople should wrap up their sales approach and need-probing mission by summarizing the prospect's need, problem, and interest. The salesperson should also get a commitment from the customer to some kind of action, whether it's reading promotional material or agreeing to a demonstration. This commitment helps qualify the prospect further and justify additional time invested by the salesperson. The salesperson should reiterate the action he or she promises to take, such as sending information or calling back to provide answers to questions. The date and time of the next call should be set at the conclusion of the sales approach as well as an agenda for the next call in terms of what the salesperson hopes to accomplish, such as providing a demonstration or presenting a solution.

DEVELOPING AND PROPOSING SOLUTIONS

Once the salesperson has gathered the appropriate information about the client's needs and wants, the next step is to determine whether his or her company's products or services match the needs of the prospective customer. The salesperson then develops a solution, or possibly several solutions, in which the salesperson's product or service solves the client's problems or meets a specific need.

These solutions are typically presented to the client in the form of a sales proposal presented at a sales presentation. A **sales proposal** is a written document or professional presentation that outlines how the company's product or service will meet or exceed the client's needs. The **sales presentation** is the formal meeting in which the salesperson has the opportunity to present the sales proposal. The presentation should be explicitly tied to the prospect's expressed needs. Further, the prospect should be involved in the presentation by being encouraged to participate in demonstrations or by exposure to computer exercises, slides, video or audio, flipcharts, photographs, and so on.

Technology has become an important part of presenting solutions for many salespeople. Pen manufacturer BIC uses the Internet to connect with its wholesale and convenience store customers. Before launching BIClink.com, BIC received 80 percent of its order volume by fax. Processing these orders was time-consuming, and the orders often were filled with errors. BIClink.com has eliminated the potential for errors and made it easier and faster to validate purchase order numbers, ship dates, case quantities, and pricing. When customers sign on (through a secure, password-protected system), the welcome screen is personalized with their company's name and the name of their BIC rep. On placing an order, customers receive both a hard copy and e-mail confirmation statement with the salesperson's name and contact information including e-mail, voice mail, phone, and fax numbers. Virtually all of BIC's customers now order online.[41]

Because the salesperson often has only one opportunity to present solutions, the quality of both the sales proposal and presentation can make or break the sale. Salespeople must be able to present the proposal and handle any customer

sales proposal
A formal written document or professional presentation that outlines how the salesperson's product or service will meet or exceed the prospect's needs.

sales presentation
A formal meeting in which the salesperson presents a sales proposal to a prospective buyer.

Part of the selling process involves proposing solutions to resolve difficulties customers are having. BIC utilized the Internet to streamline the order process for its wholesale and convenience store customers. The result was BIClink.com.

language, voice patterns, dress, and body type. Often customers are more likely to remember how salespeople present themselves than what they say.

HANDLING OBJECTIONS

Rarely does a prospect say "I'll buy it" right after a presentation. Instead, the prospect often raises objections or asks questions about the proposal and the product. The potential buyer may insist that the price is too high, that he or she does not have enough information to make a decision, or that the good or service will not satisfy the present need. The buyer may also lack confidence in the seller's organization or product.

One of the first lessons that every salesperson learns is that objections to the product should not be taken personally as confrontations or insults. Rather, a salesperson should view objections as requests for information. A good salesperson considers objections a legitimate part of the purchase decision. To handle objections effectively, the salesperson should anticipate specific objections such as concerns about price, fully investigate the objection with the customer, be aware of what the competition is offering, and, above all, stay calm. When Dell introduced its direct selling model, salespeople anticipated that customers would worry that they would not receive the same level of service and dedication as they would get from a reseller. As a result, the salespeople included assurances about service and support following the sale in their sales presentations.

Zig Ziglar, a renowned sales trainer, created a popular method for handling objections: "When an objection occurs, always use the fundamentals of FEEL, FELT, FOUND. It gives you an extra cushion of time and allows the prospect to identify with others." For example: "I see how you FEEL! Others have FELT the same way too until they FOUND. . . ." In the Xerox copier example, the doctor might say, "The copy machine seems to be very expensive." Using the Zig Ziglar method the salesperson would respond, "I see how you *feel*. Other doctors have *felt* the same way until they *found* out how much money they were saving after the first year."[43]

Often the salesperson can use the objection to close the sale. If the customer tries to pit suppliers against each other to drive down the price, the salesperson should be prepared to point out weaknesses in the competitor's offer and stand by the quality in his or her own proposal.

CLOSING THE SALE

At the end of the presentation, the salesperson should ask the customer how he or she would like to proceed. If the customer exhibits signs that he or she is ready to purchase and all questions have been answered and objections have been met, then the salesperson can try to close the sale. Customers often give signals during or after the presentation that they are ready to buy or are not interested. Examples include changes in facial expressions, gestures, and questions asked. The salesperson should look for these signals and respond appropriately.

Closing requires courage and skill. Naturally, the salesperson wants to avoid rejection, and asking for a sale carries with it the risk of a negative answer. A salesperson should keep an open mind when asking for the sale and be prepared for either a yes or a no. Rarely is a sale closed on the first call. In fact, the typical salesperson makes several hundred sales calls a year, many of which are repeat calls to the same client in an attempt to make a sale. Some salespeople may negotiate with large accounts for several years before closing a sale. As you can see, building a good relationship with the customer is very important. Often, if the salesperson has developed a strong relationship with the customer, only minimal efforts are needed to close a sale.

Negotiation often plays a key role in the closing of the sale. **Negotiation** is the process during which both the salesperson and the prospect offer special concessions in an attempt to arrive at a sales agreement. For example, the salesperson may offer a price cut, free installation, free service, or a trial order. Effective negotiators, however, avoid using price as a negotiation tool because cutting price directly affects a company's profitability. Because companies spend millions on advertising and product development to create value, when salespeople give in to price negotiations too quickly, it decreases the value of the product. Instead, effective salespeople should emphasize value to the customer, rendering price a nonissue. Salespeople should also be prepared to ask for trade-offs and try to avoid giving unilateral concessions. If you're making only a 50 percent margin on a product, and you need at least a 60 percent margin, raise your prices or drop the product. Moreover, if the customer asks for a 5 percent discount, the salesperson should ask for something in return, such as higher volume or more flexibility in delivery schedules.

More and more U.S. companies are expanding their marketing and selling efforts into global markets. Salespeople selling in foreign markets should tailor their presentation and closing styles to each market. Different personalities and skills will be successful in some countries and absolute failures in others. For instance, if a salesperson is an excellent closer and always focuses on the next sale, doing business in Latin America might be difficult. The reason is that in Latin America people want to take a long time building a personal relationship with their suppliers.

FOLLOWING UP

Unfortunately, many salespeople have the attitude that making the sale is all that's important. Once the sale is made, they can forget about their customers. They are wrong. Salespeople's responsibilities do not end with making the sales and placing the orders. One of the most important aspects of their jobs is **follow-up**—the final step in the selling process, in which they must ensure that delivery schedules are met, that the goods or services perform as promised, and that the buyers' employees are properly trained to use the products.

In the traditional sales approach, follow-up with the customer is generally limited to successful product delivery and performance. A basic goal of relationship selling is to motivate customers to come back, again and again, by developing and nurturing long-term relationships. Most businesses depend on repeat sales, and repeat sales depend on thorough and continued follow-up by the salesperson.

negotiation
The process during which both the salesperson and the prospect offer special concessions in an attempt to arrive at a sales agreement.

follow-up
The final step of the selling process, in which the salesperson ensures that delivery schedules are met, that the goods or services perform as promised, and that the buyers' employees are properly trained to use the products.

6 List the steps in the selling process

Closing the Sale
Handling objections
Developing and proposing solutions
Approach customer
Qualifying leads
Generating leads

Follow Up

A Continuing Process

personalized e-mail over a period of time. College-Recruiter.com is one company taking advantage of this technology. The company posts ads for businesses recruiting recent college graduates on its Web site and has seen phenomenal results from autoresponse marketing. Prospects start receiving a series of e-mails once they have visited the site and requested advertising rates. The first message goes out immediately. The next two go out in 4 to 11 days. From there, e-mails go out monthly. The average sale for CollegeRecruiter.com is $375, and the company gets $4,000 to $5,000 in additional sales from new customers each month just from the automated follow-ups.[45]

7 SALES MANAGEMENT

Describe the functions of sales management

There is an old adage in business that nothing happens until a sale is made. Without sales there is no need for accountants, production workers, or even a company president. Sales provide the fuel that keeps the corporate engines humming. Companies like Cisco Systems, International Paper, and Johnson Controls, and several thousand other manufacturers would cease to exist without successful salespeople. Even companies like Procter & Gamble and Kraft General Foods that mainly sell consumer goods and use extensive advertising campaigns still rely on salespeople to move products through the channel of distribution. Thus, sales management is one of marketing's most critical specialties. Effective sales management stems from a highly success-oriented sales force that accomplishes its mission economically and efficiently. Poor sales management can lead to unmet profit objectives or even to the downfall of the corporation.

Just as selling is a personal relationship, so is sales management. Although the sales manager's basic job is to maximize sales at a reasonable cost while also maximizing profits, he or she also has many other important responsibilities and decisions:

1. Defining sales goals and the sales process
2. Determining the sales force structure
3. Recruiting and training the sales force

4. Compensating and motivating the sales force
5. Evaluating the sales force

DEFINING SALES GOALS AND THE SALES PROCESS

Effective sales management begins with a determination of sales goals. Without goals to achieve, salesperson performance would be mediocre at best, and the company would likely fail. Like any marketing objective, sales goals should be stated in clear, precise, and measurable terms and should always specify a time frame for their fulfillment. Overall sales force goals are usually stated in terms of desired dollar sales volume, market share, or profit level. For example, a life insurance company may have a goal to sell $50 million in life insurance policies annually, to attain a 12 percent market share, or to achieve $1 million in profits. Individual salespeople are also assigned goals in the form of quotas. A **quota** is simply a statement of the salesperson's sales goals, usually based on sales volume alone but sometimes including key accounts (those with greatest potential), new accounts, repeat sales, and specific products.

Great sales managers focus not only on sales goals but also on the entire process that drives their sales organizations to reach those goals. Without a keen understanding of the sales process, a manager will never be successful—no matter how defined the sales goals or how great the sales reps. An important responsibility of the sales manager, therefore, is to determine the most effective and efficient sales process to follow in selling each different product and service. Although the basic steps of the sales process are the same as discussed earlier in the chapter (i.e., lead generation and qualification, approach and needs assessment, proposal creation and presentation, handling objections, closing, and follow-up), a manager must formally define the specific procedures salespeople go through to do their jobs—for example, where leads are generated, how they are qualified, what the best way is to approach potential clients, and what terms can be negotiated during closing. General Electric, for example, focuses on attracting, hiring, and keeping the right salespeople through continuous training and the development of an effective sales process for its sales force. GE has an excellent performance management program that gives an employee concrete goals to meet in order to receive a promotion. The company performs formal reviews three or four times a year and also provides an extensive product- and skills-training program that can last anywhere from one to two years. Salespeople are also rotated through up to five assignments before being placed in a permanent position to see what best suits the individual sales rep. When a GE rep finally makes a call, he or she is completely knowledgeable about the product being sold.[46]

DETERMINING THE SALES FORCE STRUCTURE

Because personal selling is so costly, no sales department can afford to be disorganized. Proper design helps the sales manager organize and delegate sales duties and provide direction for salespeople. Sales departments are most commonly organized by geographic regions, by product line, by marketing function performed (such as account development or account maintenance), by market or industry, or by individual client or account. The sales force for IBM could be organized into sales territories covering New England, the Midwest, the South, and the West Coast or into distinct groups selling personal computer systems and mainframe computer systems. IBM salespeople may also be assigned to a specific industry or market, for example, the telecommunications industry, or to key clients such as AT&T and Sprint.

 Market- or industry-based structures and key account structures are gaining popularity in today's competitive selling environment, especially with the emphasis on relationship selling. Being familiar with one industry

quota
A statement of the individual salesperson's sales objectives, usually based on sales volume alone but sometimes including key accounts (those with greatest potential), new accounts, repeat sales, and specific products.

recruits over 1,000 students on 100 college campuses across the United States for entry-level, internship, and co-op positions. Its Web site provides prospective salespeople with explanations of different career entry paths and video accounts of what it is like to have a career at GE. Aside from the usual characteristics such as level of experience or education, what traits should sales managers look for in applicants? One of the most important traits of top performers is ego strength, or having a strong, healthy self-esteem and the ability to bounce back from rejection. Great salespeople also have a sense of urgency and competitiveness that pushes their sales to completion. Moreover, they have a desire to persuade people and close the sale. Effective salespeople are also assertive; they have the ability to be firm in one-to-one negotiations, to lead the sales process, and to get their point across confidently, without being overbearing or aggressive. They are sociable, willing to take risks, and capable of understanding complex concepts and ideas. Additionally, great salespeople are creative in developing client solutions, and they possess empathy—the ability to place oneself in someone else's shoes. Not surprisingly, virtually all successful salespeople say their sales style is relationship oriented rather than transaction oriented.[48]

After the sales recruit has been hired and given a brief orientation, training begins. A new salesperson generally receives instruction in company policies and practices, selling techniques, product knowledge, industry and customer characteristics, and nonselling duties such as filling out sales and market information reports or using a sales automation computer program. Firms that sell complex products generally offer the most extensive training programs. Once applicants are hired at General Electric, they enter one of the many "rotational" training programs depending on their interest and major. For example, the Communications Leadership Development Program (CDLP) is geared toward public

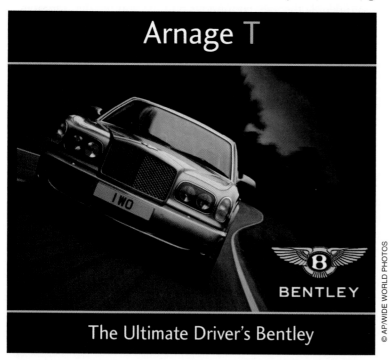

Bentley Motors produced a film and DVD training tool for its worldwide dealer network. The film also serves as an in-store infomercial showcasing the world's most powerful production sedan, the Bentley Arnage T. The film can be seen at http://www.executivevisions.com/projectdetails.asp?ProjectID=9e.

relations, marketing, communications, and organizational development. It is a 21-month program that includes three 6-month rotations and a project. When they have completed the program, the new employees can decide whether they want to enter GE's sales force. At this point, they will be better able to sell GE products because of their high level of product knowledge.[49]

Most successful sales organizations have learned that training is not just for newly hired salespeople. Instead, training is offered to all salespeople in an ongoing effort to hone selling skills and relationship building. In pursuit of solid salesperson-client relationships, training programs now seek to improve salespeople's consultative selling and listening skills and to broaden their product and customer knowledge. In addition, training programs stress the interpersonal skills needed to become the contact person for customers. Because negotiation is increasingly important in closing a sale, salespeople are also trained to negotiate effectively without risking profits.

COMPENSATING AND MOTIVATING THE SALES FORCE

Compensation planning is one of the sales manager's toughest jobs. Only good planning will ensure that compensation attracts, motivates, and retains good salespeople. Generally, companies and industries with lower levels of compensation suffer higher turnover rates, which increase costs and decrease effectiveness. Therefore, compensation needs to be competitive enough to attract and motivate the best salespeople. Firms sometimes take profit into account when developing their compensation plans. Instead of paying salespeople on overall volume, they pay according to the profitability achieved from selling each product. Still other companies tie a part of the salesperson's total compensation to customer satisfaction assessed through periodic customer surveys.

The three basic compensation methods for salespeople are commission, salary, and combination plans. A typical commission plan gives salespeople a specified percentage of their sales revenue. A **straight commission** system compensates the salesperson only when a sale is made. On the other end of the spectrum, a **straight salary** system compensates a salesperson with a stated salary regardless of sales productivity. Most companies, however, offer a compromise between straight commission and straight salary plans. A *combination system* offers a base salary plus an incentive—usually a commission or a bonus. Combination systems have benefits for both the sales manager and the salesperson. The salary portion of the plan helps the manager control the sales force; the incentive provides motivation. For the salesperson, a combination plan offers an incentive to excel while minimizing the extremely wide swings in earnings that may occur when the economy surges or contracts too much. General Electric, Procter & Gamble, and Xerox are among the many large corporations that offer a base salary plus commission for sales representatives.

As the emphasis on relationship selling increases, many sales managers feel that tying a portion of a salesperson's compensation to a client's satisfaction with the salesperson and the company encourages relationship building. To determine this, sales managers can survey clients on a salesperson's ability to create realistic expectations and his or her responsiveness to customer needs. At PeopleSoft, the world's second largest applications software company, structure, culture, and strategies are built around customer satisfaction. Sales force compensation is

straight commission
A method of compensation in which the salesperson is paid some percentage when a sale is made.

straight salary
A method of compensation in which the salesperson receives a salary regardless of sales productivity.

add new accounts, improve morale and goodwill, move slow items, and bolster slow sales. They can also be used to achieve long-term or short-term objectives, such as unloading overstocked inventory and meeting a monthly or quarterly sales goal.

Motivation also takes the form of effective sales leadership on the part of the sales manager. An effective sales manager is inspirational to his or her salespeople, encouraging them to achieve their goals through clear and enthusiastic communications. He or she has a clear vision and commitment to the mission of the organization and the ability to instill pride and earn the respect of employees. Effective sales leaders continuously increase their knowledge and skill base while also encouraging others to do so. A recent study that assessed the attributes of sales leaders found that the best sales leaders share a number of key personality traits (see Exhibit 16.5), such as a sense of urgency, openness to new ideas, and a desire to take risks. These traits separate motivational sales leaders from mere sales managers. In motivating their sales force, sales managers must be careful not to encourage unethical behavior, as the "Ethics in Marketing" box explains.

EXHIBIT 16.5

Seven Key Leadership Traits of Effective Sales Leaders

Effective sales leaders . . .	
Are assertive	Assertive sales leaders know when and how to get tough and how to assert their authority.
Possess ego drive	Sales leaders with ego drive have the desire and ability to persuade their reps to take action.
Possess ego strength	Sales leaders with ego strength are able to make sure not only that they bounce back from rejection but also that their reps rebound, too.
Take risks	Risk-taking sales leaders are willing to go out on a limb in an effort to make a sale or enhance a relationship.
Are innovative	Innovative sales leaders stay open to new ideas and new ways of conducting business.
Have a sense of urgency	Urgent sales leaders understand that getting things done now is critical to winning and keeping business.
Are empathetic	Empathetic sales leaders help their reps grow by listening and understanding.

SOURCE: Table adapted from "The 7 Traits of Great Sales Leaders" by Geoffrey Brewer, *Sales & Marketing Management*, July 1997, 38–46. Reprinted with permission.

PROMOTING ETHICAL BEHAVIOR IN BUSINESS

It is important for all companies to monitor their corporate cultures. This is especially true when salespeople are motivated by sales incentives. Salespeople's behavior often reflects the company's sales management program.

To develop a training program that will produce an ethical and successful sales force, sales managers should consider the company's mission statement, employee incentives, and compensation. When developing or modifying the mission statement, managers and employees should consider their customers' needs and wants. Salespeople who must try to sell unnecessary or unwanted products are more likely to cross ethical boundaries.

Sales managers should also consider what motivates employees to sell the company's product or service. Aside from compensation, many companies offer some type of incentive package, such as a trip, merchandise, or extra vacation time, that is based on the volume or dollars sold. Sales managers must also guard against unintended negative consequences of the incentives they offer.

Compensation policies are a major ethical issue for many sales-motivated organizations and must be designed to discourage unethical behavior.

Finally, sales managers should regularly evaluate and review the performance of their salespeople to make sure that they are not engaging in unethical behavior. In their book *The Psychology of Sales Call Reluctance*, George Dudley and Shannon Goodson include a list labeled "How to Spot Unethical Self-Promoters." It provides a good guide to unethical salesperson behaviors, like:

1. *Compulsive name-dropping:* Unethical salespeople know everybody you need them to know in order to impress you with their social network, contacts, and connections.

2. *Unshakable:* They are inappropriately calm and poised—even when you catch them in a lie.

3. *Dismissive:* When caught lying and confronted, they explain deception as a "harmless misunderstanding."

4. *Camouflage:* Their air of confidence and superiority conceals a history of legal problems and "misunderstandings."

5. *Fakes sincerity:* They tenaciously project phony sincerity because in their view, "everyone else is doing it."

6. *Mirror:* They repeatedly say whatever is necessary to make you think they acknowledge and closely identify with your values, interests, ambitions, and objectives.

7. *Aggressively advertise personal virtues:* They habitually package self-presentation with words like *integrity, openness, trust, principles,* and *honesty.*

Sales managers can use guidelines like these to identify individuals who may be using unethical approaches. By carefully reviewing performance and developing an incentive and compensation program that properly motivates employees, sales mangers can help to ensure that their company has an ethical sales force.[53]

EVALUATING THE SALES FORCE

The final task of sales managers is evaluating the effectiveness and performance of the sales force. To evaluate the sales force, the sales manager needs feedback—that is, regular information from salespeople. Typical performance measures include sales volume, contribution to profit, calls per order, sales or profits per call, or percentage of calls achieving specific goals such as sales of products that the firm is heavily promoting.

Performance information helps the sales manager monitor a salesperson's progress through the sales cycle and pinpoint where breakdowns may be occurring. For example, by knowing the number of prospects an individual salesperson has in each step of the sales cycle process and determining where prospects are falling out of the sales cycle, a manager can determine how effective a salesperson may be at lead generation, needs assessment, proposal generation, presenting, closing, and follow-up stages. This information can then tell a manager what sales skills may need to be reassessed or retrained. For example, if a sales manager notices that a sales rep seems to be letting too many prospects slip away after presenting proposals, it may mean he or she needs help with developing proposals, handling objections, or closing sales.

FAQs

Has the Internet really reduced the need for salespeople? Find out the answer by watching the video FAQ on Xtra!

Just as technology is affecting other areas of marketing, it is also a factor in personal selling. Although at first it was thought that technology would replace salespeople, it is now clear that sales support technology can enhance sales force productivity, as this ad for SanDisk makes apparent.

E-business, or buying, selling, marketing, collaborating with partners, and servicing customers electronically using the Internet, has had a significant impact on personal selling. Virtually all large companies and most medium and small companies are involved in e-commerce and consider it to be necessary to compete in today's marketplace. For customers, the Web has become a powerful tool to get accurate and up-to-date information on products, pricing, and order status. The Internet also cost-effectively processes orders and services requests. Although on the surface the Internet might look like a threat to the job security of salespeople, the Web is actually freeing sales reps from tedious administrative tasks, like shipping catalogs, placing routine orders, or tracking orders. This leaves them more time to focus on the needs of their clients.

REVIEW LEARNING OBJECTIVE 7

7 | **Describe the functions of sales management**

Results help in setting new goals or revising prior goals.

5 Evaluate
4 Compensate & Motivate
3 Recruit & Train
2 Create sales force structure
1 Set sales goals

As a sales tool, technology can:

✓ Ease administration burden

✓ Arm salespeople with valuable information

✓ Track sales performance individually and company-wide

✓ Enable collaboration

✓ Make sales management more effective

LOOKING BACK

As you think back to the opening story, recall how satellite radio is beginning to penetrate the market. The small size of the receivers as well as the flexibility to be used at home and in the car is increasing their popularity. But the personal selling efforts and the sales promotions have also been important. With its personal selling program and appealing new features, the Roady has made strong inroads into this new market. An aggressive sales and promotional program is very a effective competitive tool for sales managers.

USE IT NOW

GET FREE PRODUCT SAMPLES ONLINE

Receive free samples of consumer products by registering online at **http://www.FreeSamples. com** and **http://www.StartSampling.com**. There you can choose from a variety of free products, such as beauty aids, pet food, and new food products. In exchange, you provide marketers with feedback on what you liked and didn't like about the product.

SELL YOURSELF

Go to Amazon.com and under the search engine, type "selling yourself." Order one or more books to improve your selling skills. Also, consider a Dale

Carnegie training course. For more information, go to **http://www.dale-carnegie.com/**.

LOOKING FOR A SALES JOB?

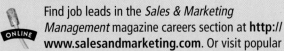
Find job leads in the *Sales & Marketing Management* magazine careers section at **http:// www.salesandmarketing.com**. Or visit popular employment site Monster.com (**http://www. monster.com**) and use its searchable database to search for sales opportunities in a specific geographic area. You can also post your résumé at these and a number of other employment sites.

REVIEW AND APPLICATIONS

1 **Define and state the objectives of sales promotion.** Sales promotion consists of those marketing communication activities, other than advertising, personal selling, and public relations, in which a short-term incentive motivates consumers or members of the distribution channel to purchase a good or service immediately, either by lowering the price or by adding value. The main objectives of sales promotion are to increase trial purchases, consumer inventories, and repeat purchases. Sales promotion is also used to encourage brand switching and to build brand loyalty. Sales promotion supports advertising activities.

1.1 **WRITING** You have recently been assigned the task of developing promotional techniques to introduce your company's new product, a Cajun chicken sandwich. Advertising spending is limited, so the introduction will include only some low-budget sales promotion techniques. Write a sales promotion plan that will increase awareness of your new sandwich and allow your customer base to try it risk-free.

2 **Discuss the most common forms of consumer sales promotion.** Consumer forms of sales promotion include coupons and rebates, premiums, loyalty marketing programs, contests and sweepstakes, sampling, and point-of-purchase displays. Coupons

sales promotion are more effective at persuading consumers to switch brands?

2.3 [TEAM] Form a three-person team. Go to the local grocery store and write down all of the forms of sales promotion you see, including company name, product being promoted, form of promotion, and objective. Also, make a note of the sales promotion's message or offer, such as "two-for-one" or "cents off." Create a table that lists this information; then rate the effectiveness of each one, in your opinion, on a scale from 1 to 5 where 1 is "poor" and 5 is "excellent." Present a summary of your findings to the class. What kind of conclusions can you draw about product type and promotion?

2.4 [ONLINE] Not everyone thinks supermarket shopper cards are a bargain. Go to **http://www.nocards.org** and read several pages. Is the information on the site compelling? What do you think of shopper cards? You may want to use the Internet to research shopper cards in more detail before forming an opinion.

2.5 As you read in the "Marketing in Entertainment" box on reality television programming, contests and sweepstakes are very common in the entertainment industry. Radio stations have contests almost weekly (some daily); local television morning shows quiz viewers on trivia; even movies offer sweepstakes in conjunction with film previews and premiere nights. Think of a television or radio program unlikely to have contests or sweepstakes (things like *Cops, The View, Scooby Doo,* or your local classical music radio station, for example). Once you have chosen your program, design a contest or sweepstake to promote the show or the channel on which it airs. List the objectives and describe the rationale behind each part of your promotion.

3 **List the most common forms of trade sales promotion.** Manufacturers use many of the same sales promotion tools used in consumer promotions, such as sales contests, premiums, and point-of-purchase displays. In addition, manufacturers and channel intermediaries use several unique promotional strategies: trade allowances, push money, training programs, free merchandise, store demonstrations, and meetings, conventions, and trade shows.

3.1 How does trade sales promotion differ from consumer sales promotion? How is it the same?

3.2 [TEAM] Form a team of three to five students. As marketing managers, you are in charge of selling Dixie cups. Design a consumer sales promotion plan and trade sales promotion plan for your product. Incorporate at least three different promotion tools into each plan. Share your results with the other teams in the class.

4 **Describe personal selling.** Personal selling is direct communication between a sales representative and one or more prospective buyers in an attempt to influence each other in a purchase situation. Broadly speaking, all businesspeople use personal selling to promote themselves and their ideas. Personal selling offers several advantages over other forms of promotion. Personal selling allows salespeople to thoroughly explain and demonstrate a product. Salespeople have the flexibility to tailor a sales proposal to the needs and preferences of individual customers. Personal selling is more efficient than other forms of promotion because salespeople target qualified prospects and avoid wasting efforts on unlikely buyers. Personal selling affords greater managerial control over promotion costs. Finally, personal selling is the most effective method of closing a sale and producing satisfied customers.

4.1 Discuss the role of personal selling in promoting products. What advantages does personal selling offer over other forms of promotion?

5 **Discuss the key differences between relationship selling and traditional selling.** Relationship selling is the practice of building, maintaining, and enhancing interactions with customers in order to develop long-term satisfaction through mutually beneficial partnerships. Traditional selling, on the other hand, is transaction focused. That is, the salesperson is most concerned with making one-time sales and moving on to the next prospect. Salespeople practicing relationship selling spend more time understanding a prospect's needs and developing solutions to meet those needs.

5.1 What are the key differences between relationship selling and traditional methods of selling? What types of products or services do you think would be conducive to relationship selling?

6 **List the steps in the selling process.** The selling process is composed of seven basic steps: (1) generating leads, (2) qualifying leads, (3) approaching customer and probing needs, (4) developing and proposing solutions, (5) handling objections, (6) closing the sale, and (7) following up.

6.1 WRITING You are a new salesperson for a well-known medical software company, and one of your clients is a large group of physicians. You have just arranged an initial meeting with the office manager. Develop a list of questions you might ask at this meeting to uncover the group's specific needs.

6.2 What does sales follow-up entail? Why is it an essential step in the selling process, particularly from the perspective of relationship selling? How does it relate to cognitive dissonance?

7 **Describe the functions of sales management.** Sales management is a critical area of marketing that performs several important functions. Sales managers set overall company sales goals and define the sales process most effective for achieving those goals. They determine sales force structure based on geographic, product, functional, or customer variables. Managers develop the sales force through recruiting and training. Sales management motivates the sales force through compensation planning, motivational tools, and effective sales leadership. Finally, sales managers evaluate the sales force through salesperson feedback and other methods of determining their performance.

7.1 TEAM With two classmates, select a company or business near campus that has a sales force. Using York's article (from question 7.1) as a starting point, list all the things the company would need to do to create an e-savvy sales force.

7.2 INFOTRAC COLLEGE EDITION Without revenue, a company cannot survive, and sales is the means to that end. How important is the effectiveness of a company's sales force? Use InfoTrac (**http://www.infotrac-college.com**) to run a keyword search for "sales force" or "sales force automation." Skim six to ten articles and write down all the automation tools (software and hardware) that you discover.

have you ever waited forever to get a fast-food hamburger? Have you even been left to languish in a dressing room by a salesperson who left for a coffee break? If so, you already know that sales and customer service are integral parts of marketing. While you are working on this chapter, keep a journal of your personal sales and/or customer service experiences with local merchants. Don't ignore the details. Even such things as how crowded a store or restaurant is when you visit may affect your perceptions of the service you received.[55]

Activities

1. Keep your journal for a week, recording all sales and service transactions, if possible, on the day they occur.

2. At the end of the week, examine your journal, and pick the most noteworthy entry. Provide the basic information about the transaction: company where it occurred, type of transaction (purchase, return, complaint, etc.), type of good or service involved, and so forth.

3. Once you have the outlined the situation, evaluate the experience. Use the information about selling in this chapter as support for your evaluation. For example, did the salesperson seem to treat the situation as an individual, discrete transaction, or did he or she seem interested in building a relationship?

4. Finally, make recommendations as to how the company can improve its sales and/or service. Suggestions should be logical and achievable (meaning you have to consider the cost of implementing your suggestion).

ETHICS EXERCISE

Bruce Jackson sells air conditioners for Comfort Heating and Air Conditioning. He is having a very good year and hopes to win the incentive trip his company awards the top salesperson each year. With one quarter in the year left to go, Bruce learns that another salesperson has slightly higher sales. He also learns that the other salesperson is exaggerating product benefits in his sales pitch but company officials seem to be looking the other way.

Questions

1. What should Bruce do?

2. Does the AMA Code of Ethics address this issue in its Code of Ethics? Go to **http://www.marketingpower.com** and review the code. Then, write a brief paragraph describing how the AMA Code of Ethics relates to this issue.

CAREER EXERCISE

The best avenue for exploring jobs in sales promotion and personal selling is through the major job listing sites, such as Monster and Vault. By typing "promotions" into the keyword search, you can retrieve a huge assortment of job postings across the nation and in all industries.

For an outlook on occupations in sales promotion, advertising, public relations, and selling, go to the U.S. Department of Commerce, Bureau of Labor Statistics for an occupational outlook handbook (**http://stats.bls.gov/oco/ocos020.htm**).

Activities

1. If you are interested in marcomm (jargon for marketing communication), you may benefit from taking a personality assessment to determine how introverted or extroverted you are. Typically, extroverted personalities are associated more with sales and public relations. But that does not mean that there are no opportunities for introverts in marketing communication. Visit your campus career center and ask about personality assessment tools.

2. Recall your last big purchase (car, computer, expensive formal outfit, stereo, etc.) and the salesperson who assisted you. Outline the sales process and compare it to the process outlined in the book. If you were the salesperson in this situation, would you have done anything differently?

ENTREPRENEURSHIP CASE

© BOB KRIST/CORBIS

VARSITY GROUP: THE CAMPUS BOOKSTORE ALTERNATIVE

The U.S. market for educational textbooks is roughly an $8 billion industry, with U.S. college students spending $4 to 5 billion each year purchasing over 70 million textbooks needed for classes. With the industry averaging 7 percent annual growth, the marketing implications—and opportunities—can be huge, but so can the challenges. Varsity Group knows this probably better than most.

The company burst onto the college campus scene in 1998 ready to turn what is now a $10 billion-a-year campus store retail business on its ear by providing an online store where college students could buy their books and supplies at a discount. When the company first launched its online storefront, VarsityBooks.com, only about 1 percent of college textbooks were sold via the Web. But with close to 100 percent of college students using the Internet and over 70 percent logging on daily, the potential for Varsity Group and other online textbook retailers to make it big was enormous. Online textbook retailers offered all the conveniences of Internet shopping, such as round-the-clock service and a wider selection than the campus bookstore could offer. And because Varsity Group had no brick-and-mortar storefront and few storage costs, it could sell some textbooks for as much as 40 percent less than traditional textbook sellers.

Initially, Varsity Group succeeded in the online textbook market because of its highly creative, albeit unusual, promotional tactics. Instead of putting its entire promotional budget into buying ads in the campus newspaper or on local radio stations, Varsity Group would recruit college students to help promote its Web site on college campuses and to persuade their classmates to purchase their textbooks from the company's Web site instead of at inconvenient campus bookstores where prices are higher. At one point, close to 3,000 students on 600 U.S. campuses signed on to become representatives for Varsity Group. Campus reps received hourly and commission-based wages and the freedom to execute their own campaigns. Lead campus reps enjoyed business cards, stock options, a PalmPilot, and a flexible budget. Student reps also attended biannual training programs to listen to speakers on marketing best practices, case studies, codes of conduct, and team management skills.

Some of the more interesting grassroots promotional and sales techniques the student reps used to promote VarsityBooks.com included sponsoring parties, dressing local bands in VarsityBooks.com T-shirts, and handing out candy bars, granola bars, and lollipops with VarsityBooks.com coupons. At Florida State University, campus reps used sidewalk chalk to pen messages such as "Smashing Savings" on sidewalks around campus. At Stanford University, Varsity reps passed out coupons at a nearby movie theater. Other reps distributed price comparisons for books for particular courses at classroom doorways.

months or longer. Since the target customer has changed from the student buying the book to the school providing the service of a bookstore, the sales force has taken a more consultative approach to its sales strategy. The in-house sales reps spend more time building relationships with Varsity Group's eduPartners, listening to their needs and developing solutions to match them: eduPartners receive a high level of service at a reasonable price and lose all the hassles of managing and financing a campus store.

Although Varsity Group has changed its sales strategy from a customer focus to an institutional focus, the company continues to look for unique market segments and opportunities by leveraging a novel approach in its marketing efforts.[56]

Questions

1. What can you deduce about the textbook market from Varsity Group's new sales strategy?

2. What can you deduce about Varsity Group's promotional goals from the changes it has made to its business model?

3. You are a sales rep for Varsity Group and are working with potential clients, who are not entirely convinced that eduPartners will work for their campus. Anticipate objections that they may raise and address them positively. You may consult the VarsityBooks.com Web site at **http://www.varsitybooks.com** as a resource.

WATCH IT

FEATURE PRESENTATION

AMCI

SmallBusinessSchool
the Series on PBS stations and the Web

For Chapter 16, Small Business School takes you inside the world of Ann and Michael McGilvray, founders of AMCI, a manufacturers' rep company that specializes in novelty and other fun goods. Have you ever bought a rubber bug? If you have, chances are that it was sold to the store where you bought it by Ann McGilvray or one of her reps. AMCI represents over 200 manufacturers and gets their products into the hands of over 65,000 retailers, most of which are individual stores or small retail chains. AMCI relies on a sales force of 90 reps to do the job, and it has taken the lead in utilizing technology to enhance the efficiency and effectiveness of its operation. Watch this segment to see what the woman who has sold everything from greeting cards to glow-in-the-dark cockroaches has to say about personal selling and sales management.

What to Watch for and Ask Yourself

1. What kinds of product does AMCI represent? Why, then, is personal selling the appropriate approach for AMCI?

2. How does AMCI approach recruiting and training the sales force?

3. Discuss the role technology plays in supporting the sales force. How does it benefit AMCI, its vendors, and its customers?

ENCORE PRESENTATION

Family Man (II)

Now that you have a better understanding of personal selling, you can see how selling techniques extend beyond the world of marketing. As an encore to your study, watch the second clip from *The Family Man,* starring Nicolas Cage as confirmed Wall Street bachelor Jack Campbell. After doing a good deed one Christmas, Jack wakes up to find himself married to his high-school sweetheart and leading a very different life. Jack meets his former employer, Peter Lassiter, at his father-in-law's tire store where he now works. In this scene, Jack is trying to convince Lassiter to give him a job. Is Jack using a traditional or relationship selling approach? What makes you say so? Even though Jack is not selling a product, you can still see evidence of the personal selling process throughout the scene. Identify the steps of the selling process that you see in the clip. Does Jack execute them in order, or does he deviate from the process order?

STILL SHAKY?

If you're having trouble with the concepts in this chapter, consider using some of the following study resources. You can review the videos, or test yourself with materials designed for all kinds of learning styles.

☑ **Xtra! (http://lambxtra.swlearning.com)**

☑ Quiz ☑ Feature Videos ☑ Encore Videos ☑ FAQ Videos

☑ Exhibit Worksheets ☑ Marketing Plan Worksheets ☐ Content

☑ **http://lamb.swlearning.com**

☑ Quiz ☑ PowerPoint slides ☑ Marketing News ☑ Review Exercises

☑ Links ☑ Marketing Plan Contest ☐ Career Exercise ☑ Use It Now

☑ **Study guide**

☑ Outline ☑ Vocab Review ☑ Test Questions ☑ Marketing Scenario

Need More? Here's a tip. If your instructor did not assign all the "Review and Applications" and "Exercises," do them all anyway. Then visit your professor or TA during office hours for any solutions you need.

depicted as a big baseball fan) in either of the movies, but baseball is not a noticeable pastime for this superhero. As it turned out, using the sacred ground of the baseball diamonds as a marketing tool was not popular with baseball fans.

The *Spider-Man 2* and MLB promotion scenario played out over a few days in early May of 2004. The promotion announcement was made on one day, baseball fans went berserk the next day, and day three saw the promotion cancelled. The scenario played out so quickly that marketers may have had little idea as to what transpired.

In an attempt to develop a splashier national marketing image, while reaching out to children and families, MLB formed a marketing partnership with the Columbia TriStar Motion Picture Group. During MLB's *Spider-Man 2* weekend, ballparks were to be transformed into a promotional medium with in-park signs, *Spider-Man 2* promotional giveaways (masks, foam fingers), movie trailers on scoreboards, and fields decorated with the *Spider-Man 2* logo. It was the field decoration that drew the fans' fury. The plan was to place a four-by-four inch *Spider-Man 2* logo (black and yellow webbing on a red background) on first, second, and third bases, with a similar logo on the on-deck circles. The logo would also have adorned home plate and the pitching rubber, but would have been removed from these areas before the first pitch.

sion. The Yankees, who would be hosting the San Diego Padres on the promotional weekend, said that they would allow the on-base ads only during pregame batting practice. The promotions would be removed before the start of the game. The lack of full support from one of baseball's premier teams, in conjunction with the public outcry, resulted in the cancellation of the on-base ads, although the other aspects of the promotional plan were to be carried out as planned.

Columbia TriStar had expected to spend between $3 million and $4 million on the baseball promotion. Advertising benefits to the movie were obvious, and the company would be the first to have ads embedded on a baseball field. Baseball fans wondered, however, how logos on bases would promote baseball. If this was truly a partnership, what was in it for MLB except money? According to baseball fans, the baseball diamond is hallowed ground and should not be for sale.

Questions

1. How could a promotional partnership between a motion picture company and MLB attract younger fans to baseball?

2. Was the controversy beneficial to Columbia TriStar?

Adidas Takes Human Billboards to New Heights

For decades, advertisers have hung billboards on humans by having people wear costumes or sandwich boards to present messages to passersby. Adidas, however, has taken human billboards to a new height by hanging humans on its billboards. In a marketplace crowded with advertising messages, what's next in the battle for consumer awareness?

Adidas in Japan

In Tokyo, where it is not unusual to have a 70-minute commute to work, advertisers allocate 9 to 12 percent of total ad spending to outdoor media. They spend about $4.4 billion, or three to four times as much as in the United States, on giant billboards, neon signs, electronic video billboards, and other creative challenge efforts to attract the Japanese commuter's attention.

To celebrate the start of the soccer season, TBWA Japan, a unit of Omnicom Group, Inc. developed the vertical soccer billboard concept for Adidas. At each Adidas billboard site around Tokyo and Osaka, two players, suspended from ropes with a tethered ball hanging between them, played 15-minute soccer matches five times a day (weather permitting). They played at a 90-degree angle to a vertical soccer field displayed behind them with the Adidas headline, "Own the passion and you own the game."

Adidas and its advertising agency have taken human billboards in a new direction. One has to wonder, however, whether it is the actual message or the method that is building brand awareness. Regardless, advertisers have moved rapidly to come up with creative methods to foster word-of-mouth communications for clients.

Living Advertising

In early 2003, Cunning Stunts Communications, a small advertising agency in London, began recruiting students to be human message carriers. The agency had the idea to use college students' foreheads as an advertising medium. It tested the idea around London, by having students wearing temporary brand logo tattoos for the men's magazine *FHM* and for cable channel CNX. The students earned 6.33 euros an hour for displaying the logos three or four hours a day in designated locations. The logos, which were henna transfer tattoos, remained on a student's forehead for about a week and then would be washed off. Assuming that the ads would be a big hit with clients, the agency posted "casting living advertising calls" on college campus bulletin boards.

Other designers have used similar methods Reebok utilized what its agency, Bennett Global, referred to as "head advertising" at the 2003 Boston Marathon. At $50 a head, Reebok plastered its promotional slogan, "The Pain Train Is Coming," on the foreheads of 100 Boston area college stu-

dents on the day of the marathon. In turn, these students distributed temporary Reebok tattoos and T-shirts to other college students. Although Adidas is an official sponsor of the Boston Marathon, Reebok was able to extend its brand into the event via these forehead advertisers. A team of students from the University of Wales at Swansea were recruited to promote a regional rugby match. The students' foreheads were branded with washable ink that said, "Ospreys v Connacht @ St Helen's Oct 31." The goal was to reach a wider and younger audience than usually attends rugby matches.

In another twist on the human billboard, an Illinois man auctioned off the back of his head for advertising purposes. A Texas-based Web hosting company, C I Host, which is known for its unique promotional efforts, including having its name on the back of Evander Holyfield's boxing shorts, won the auction. It took four hours to tattoo the company logo and its phrase, "Managed Web Hosting," on the back of the man's head. As part of his five-year contract with C I Host, the living billboard must keep the tattoo visible on his head at all times and distribute company flyers and business cards when he is outside his home.

Wearing a company's logo and message is not the only approach that has been tried in living advertising. In late 2002, Acclaim UK turned humans into living advertisements when five Britons legally changed their names to live for a year as a dinosaur hunter named Turok. Turok is a video game series about a time-traveling Indian who slays bionically enhanced dinosaurs. For undergoing the identity change, the human advertisers were paid 500 pounds and were given a Microsoft X-Box and a copy of the company's new Turok Evolution game. Because their names were changed legally, everything from passports to driver's licenses carried the name Turok. More than 10,000 people applied for the chance to live as Turok for a year.

Extreme Marketing

Guerrilla marketing emerged as a grassroots way to attract consumers' attention. Yet, even guerrilla tactics appear mild compared to the living billboards used by Adidas. With name changes, headliner billboards, and soccer players suspended in air, marketing communications efforts are fighting advertising clutter with new and exciting forms of entertainment phenomena. One has to wonder, however, what Adidas can do as a follow-up.

Questions

1. Compare human billboards to traditional forms of integrated marketing communications.

2. What are the pros and cons of extreme marketing communications tactics?

low quality product.

2. Why do financial managers view advertising and promotional expenditures as costs?

   Financial managers believe there is a direct correlation between advertising and promotional expenditures and sales. In recognizing this relationship, financial managers view these expenditures as variable costs, thinking that one directly affects the other. Financial analysts are result oriented and ultimately will base their allocation of funds on whether the product is selling; they view an increase in sales as "money well spent." Unfortunately, viewing the relationship in this way can be detrimental to the product; advertising budgets may be cut, based on low sales numbers,

other major area of integration has been the involvement of R&D and manufacturing in customer visits. Finance, accounting, and human resources are taking a much stronger role in the sales process with regard to compensation systems, cross-selling, and teamwork.

Suggested Readings

"The Mirage of Integration," *Advertising Age*, June 4, 2001, 16.

Victoria L. Crittenden and William F. Crittenden, "Developing the Sales Force and Growing the Business: The Direct Selling Industry Experience," *Business Horizons*, September/October 2004.

Pricing

Decisions

number of internal and external parties have an interest in ticket-pricing practices. They include performers, agents, promoters, ticket agencies, and venues, as well as the customers who actually utilize the entertainment seats.

Marketing is interested in pricing to provide value to the customer while meeting competitors' prices. Since costs determine the floor on prices, the accounting group has traditionally identified with a cost-plus pricing approach. Naturally, finance has a keen interest in the pricing process in relation to its targets for return on investment. The relationship between price and demand has downstream effects on the manufacturing process, bringing production capabilities (seating capacity in terms of entertainment venues) into the pricing decisions, particularly in relation to the company's ability to produce the number of units (or fill the number of seats) needed to break even. Research and development pays close attention to the introductory price of the product since this is considered to be the point at which development costs are recouped. With all of these interested parties, it is hard to say if any one particular functional group is actually in charge of the final pricing decision!

The pricing decision must be viewed as an interactive process. There is a strong need for cross-functional interaction. For example, if marketing identifies an initial price as too high to capture customer interest, R&D and manufacturing must be consulted to see if product features, product materials, or assembly processes can be modified to decrease costs. Finance and accounting must be involved in reevaluating appropriate margins. The Boston Red Sox baseball team took customer interest, capacity, and development costs into consideration in developing the pricing strategy for its new Green Monster seats. Using a variable pricing scheme, Monster seat prices are higher for popular games and lower for less popular games. In this way, the club can avoid deadwood (unsold seats) and still make the highest possible margin when possible.

market segmentation approach based on customer needs. Activity-based costing allows the company to determine what will have to be done to satisfy customers' needs and assign a cost to each activity. In this way, companies can distinguish between the truly profitable customers and those who may purchase in volume but require so much work (activities) that they are actually unprofitable. Party planners (entertainment professionals) have become quite astute at using ABC in pricing their offerings. Estimates are that at least 75 percent of the cost of a wedding is attributable to entertainment expenses. With an average wedding costing $20,000, these entertainment professionals have to understand clearly the cost of various components of a party and what clients are willing to pay for these events.

Marketers have long recognized the importance of accounting information in the pricing process. Tactically, marketers recognize that accurate cost data are needed to make good pricing decisions, but traditional accounting methods were criticized for being too production oriented. Nonetheless, it is this cost information that points to the lowest possible price that can be charged for a product without losing money on a per item basis (considering traditional accounting methods). The activity-based system goes beyond the cost of production and looks at how much it costs to maintain individual customer accounts. Ultimately, ABC allows marketers to price products/services to individual consumers based upon the total cost of providing the product or service. From a marketer's perspective, for example, travel time to visit with a customer would be included as a cost and could be reflected in the price charged to that particular customer.

Products such as CDs, video games, and software, however, do not fit easily within an activity-based pricing process. The pricing of such products extends the pricing initiative into functional areas that include engineers, developers, and the legal department. It is very difficult to determine the actual costs involved in developing these types of products. Burning a new CD, making copies of video games, or making duplicates of software is unlikely to correlate with the price of the product. Rather, it is the human investment, time, and legal maneuvering that go into the development of these types of products that have to be considered. Production costs do not accurately reflect the firm's investment expenses.

Additionally, some products are in the category of "better than, but not as good as" competitive products. Video game peripherals such as game controllers, adapters, and memory cards fall into this category. Such new products have to be priced higher than the "better than" competitive products and lower than the "not as good as" competitive products. By relying solely on the accountants and their pure cost data, a product might be priced too close to the high-end competitor (with better capabilities) or too close to the low-end competitor (therefore not conveying the value added of the new product offering).

The marketing function is generally the driver in day-to-day price decisions. Although marketers try to think about the overall organizational impact of their daily pricing decisions, minor changes can have a ripple effect in the organization. Price promotions are an example of the downstream effects of day-to-day pricing decisions. A major objective of a price promotion campaign is stimulating increased demand for the firm's product. Studies show that the sales rate changes during and immediately after the campaign. Such fluctuating sales have a dual effect upon the manufacturer.

For example, an electronics store will increase the quantity ordered of video players so that it will have inventory on hand during a promotion. But the store may order more than it expects to sell so that it can sell the discounted players at the regular price (i.e., greater margin) after the promotion ends. This reduces normal delivery after the promotion and puts the store in the comfortable position of waiting until the next deal to repurchase. This sort of buying behavior disrupts the production and delivery cycle and may also mean that employees will have to work extra shifts (thus increasing manufacturing costs due to overtime pay) to help meet demand. Decreased purchasing after the price promotion has the opposite effect. Manufacturing may need to build excess inventory in order to maintain a stable production flow, thus driving up inventory costs.

The relative importance of marketing's internal partners in the pricing process relates closely to the product life cycle. Accounting, finance, and R&D have particular interests that appear to be addressed during the introductory stage of the life cycle. Manufacturing is especially interested in the pricing process during the growth stage when the production facility is attempting to reach economies of scale. Once the product reaches maturity, all competitive manufacturers are operating with similar cost structures, and pricing is most clearly driven by the external environment. However, overall monitoring of product revenue is important throughout a product's life cycle.

Too many variables are at play in the pricing decision to say that the decision is the responsibility of any particular function. Rather, all functions have a need for functional-level input. Nonetheless, it is safe to say that marketing has the broadest perspective on pricing since it is the function that looks at both internal cost issues and external demand pressures.

Questions

1. Should marketing play the lead role in coordinating the pricing decision? Why or why not?

2. How is activity-based costing more market oriented than traditional accounting methods?

3. What kinds of internal problems are caused by price promotions?

Pricing Concepts

LEARNING OBJECTIVES

1   Discuss the importance of pricing decisions to the economy and to the individual firm

2   List and explain a variety of pricing objectives

3   Explain the role of demand in price determination

4   Understand the concept of yield management systems

5   Describe cost-oriented pricing strategies

6   Demonstrate how the product life cycle, competition, distribution and promotion strategies, customer demands, the Internet and extranets, and perceptions of quality can affect price

A few years ago, Goodyear's main North American rival, Bridgestone Corporation's Firestone unit, nearly had a credibility meltdown when it had to recall 6.5 million tires linked to fatal accidents, mostly on Ford Explorers. As people scrambled for other brands, Goodyear, the largest tire maker in the United States, ought to have benefited most. On top of that, Goodyear was selling into the greatest U.S. car-buying binge in recent history. Instead of seizing the moment, though, Goodyear missed a golden opportunity.

Goodyear misjudged its core customers. The Firestone recall briefly swamped Goodyear with more business than it could handle. It also convinced Goodyear executives that their brand carried a certain cachet and a reassurance of safety for which Americans would pay a premium price. Goodyear executives described the phenomenon as a "flight to quality." But once the Firestone recall fell out of the headlines, the public did what it has increasingly been doing: buying whatever was on sale.

Goodyear's biggest mistake appears to have been its effort to capitalize on the Firestone recall by raising its prices. Starting in January 2001, Goodyear boosted prices on its passenger and light-truck tires by up to 7 percent and followed up with another hefty increase the following June. Partly, the company saw itself asserting its right to charge prices closer to those of Michelin, which generally are the highest in the market.

But in the eyes of many customers, Goodyear failed to justify the increases. To charge a premium, a tire maker has to offer some advantage, even if it's just an aura of quality—which Michelin has historically promoted. Though it's difficult to measure, Michelin also has a reputation among consumers for safety. The U.S. government sets minimum standards for tire safety, but it doesn't rate the safety of specific brands.

Goodyear's huge $60 million advertising campaign, launched in 2001, apparently didn't help. In the commercials, parents in different parts of the world—Russia, Tibet, and Africa—are shown enduring children whining in their respective native tongues: "Are we there yet?"

"It didn't address the issue that's in the top of the mind of the retail consumer—some combination of price and value," said Tom Geiger Jr. of Capital Tire in Toledo, Ohio, a major Goodyear dealer and distributor for 56 years. "I didn't have people coming in and saying, 'I saw that cute commercial, let me see some of them tires.'" He added, "Goodyear got this idea of a flight to quality, but when the economy goes south, the flight stops."[1]

What determines price in the marketplace? How are costs, revenues, and profits related? Can price influence perceived quality of a product? What happened to the demand for Goodyear tires after the price increase?

Consumers are interested in obtaining a "reasonable price." "Reasonable price" really means "perceived reasonable value" at the time of the transaction. One of the authors of this textbook bought a fancy European-designed toaster for about $45. The toaster's wide mouth made it possible to toast a bagel, warm a muffin, and, with a special $15 attachment, make a grilled sandwich. The author felt that a toaster with all these features surely must be worth the total price of $60. But after three months of using the device, toast burned around the edges and raw in the middle lost its appeal. The disappointed buyer put the toaster in the attic. Why didn't he return it to the retailer? Because the boutique had gone out of business, and no other local retailer carried the brand. Also, there was no U.S. service center. Remember, the price paid is based on the satisfaction consumers *expect* to receive from a product and not necessarily the satisfaction they *actually* receive.

Price can relate to anything with perceived value, not just money. When goods and services are exchanged, the trade is called *barter*. For example, if you exchange this book for a chemistry book at the end of the term, you have engaged in barter. The price you paid for the chemistry book was this textbook.

THE IMPORTANCE OF PRICE TO MARKETING MANAGERS

Prices are the key to revenues, which in turn are the key to profits for an organization. **Revenue** is the price charged to customers multiplied by the number of units sold. Revenue is what pays for every activity of the company: production, finance, sales, distribution, and so on. What's left over (if anything) is **profit**. Managers usually strive to charge a price that will earn a fair profit.

To earn a profit, managers must choose a price that is not too high or too low, a price that equals the perceived value to target consumers. If, in consumers' minds, a price is set too high, the perceived value will be less than the cost, and sales opportunities will be lost. Many mainstream purchasers of cars, sporting goods, CDs, tools, wedding gowns, and computers are buying "used or preowned" items to get a better deal. Pricing a new product too high may give some shoppers an incentive to go to a "preowned" or consignment retailer. Lost sales mean lost revenue. Conversely, if a price is too low, the consumer may perceive it as a great value, but the firm loses revenue it could have earned.

FAQs

Why do managers claim that "setting the right price" is the most difficult aspect of creating a marketing mix? Find out the answer by watching the video FAQ on Xtra!

price
That which is given up in an exchange to acquire a good or service.

revenue
The price charged to customers multiplied by the number of units sold.

profit
Revenue minus expenses.

Setting the right price on a product is extremely critical and so is a source of much stress for the marketing manager. Part of the reason is the continuous flood of new products that encourages shoppers to carefully compare prices.

Trying to set the right price is one of the most stressful and pressure-filled tasks of the marketing manager, as trends in the consumer market attest:

- Confronting a flood of new products, potential buyers carefully evaluate the price of each one against the value of existing products.
- The increased availability of bargain-priced private and generic brands has put downward pressure on overall prices.
- Many firms are trying to maintain or regain their market share by cutting prices. For example, Dell has gained PC market share by aggressively cutting prices.

In the organizational market, where customers include both governments and businesses, buyers are also becoming more price sensitive and better informed. In the consumer market, consumers are using the Internet to make wiser purchasing decisions. Computerized information systems enable the organizational buyer to compare price and performance with great ease and accuracy. Improved communication and the increased use of direct marketing and computer-aided selling have also opened up many markets to new competitors. Finally, competition in general is increasing, so some installations, accessories, and component parts are being marketed like indistinguishable commodities.

REVIEW LEARNING OBJECTIVE 1

 1 | **Discuss the importance of pricing decisions to the economy and to the individual firm**

Price × Sales Units = Revenue

Revenue − Costs = Profit

Profit drives growth, salary increases, and corporate investment

2 PRICING OBJECTIVES

List and explain a variety of pricing objectives

To survive in today's highly competitive marketplace, companies need pricing objectives that are specific, attainable, and measurable. Realistic pricing goals then require periodic monitoring to determine the effectiveness of the company's strategy. For convenience, pricing objectives can be divided into three categories: profit oriented, sales oriented, and status quo.

PROFIT-ORIENTED PRICING OBJECTIVES

Profit-oriented objectives include profit maximization, satisfactory profits, and target return on investment. A brief discussion of each of these objectives follows.

Profit Maximization

Profit maximization means setting prices so that total revenue is as large as possible relative to total costs. (A more theoretically precise definition and explanation of profit maximization appear later in the chapter.) Profit maximization does not always signify unreasonably high prices, however. Both price and profits depend on the type of competitive environment a firm faces, such as whether it is in a monopoly position (being the only seller) or in a much more competitive situation. Also, remember that a firm cannot charge a price higher than the product's perceived value. Many firms do not have the accounting data they need for maximizing profits. It is easy to say that a company should keep producing and selling goods or services as long as revenues exceed costs. Yet it is often hard to set up an accounting system that can accurately determine the point of profit maximization.

ENTREPRENEUR maximizing profits, many organizations strive for profits that are satisfactory to the stockholders and management—in other words, a level of profits consistent with the level of risk an organization faces. In a risky industry, a satisfactory profit may be 35 percent. In a low-risk industry, it might be 7 percent. To maximize profits, a small-business owner might have to keep his or her store open seven days a week. However, the owner might not want to work that hard and might be satisfied with less profit.

Target Return on Investment

The most common profit objective is a target **return on investment (ROI),** sometimes called the firm's return on total assets. ROI measures management's overall effectiveness in generating profits with the available assets. The higher the firm's ROI, the better off the firm is. Many companies—including DuPont, General Motors, Navistar, ExxonMobil, and Union Carbide—use a target ROI as their main pricing goal. In summary, ROI is a percentage that puts a firm's profits into perspective by showing profits relative to investment.

Return on investment is calculated as follows:

$$\text{Return on investment} = \frac{\text{Net profits after taxes}}{\text{Total assets}}$$

Assume that in 2005 Johnson Controls had assets of \$4.5 million, net profits of \$550,000, and a target ROI of 10 percent. This was the actual ROI:

$$\text{ROI} = \frac{\$550,000}{\$4,500,000}$$

$$= 12.2 \text{ percent}$$

As you can see, the ROI for Johnson Controls exceeded its target, which indicates that the company prospered in 2005.

Comparing the 12.2 percent ROI with the industry average provides a more meaningful picture, however. Any ROI needs to be evaluated in terms of the competitive environment, risks in the industry, and economic conditions. Generally speaking, firms seek ROIs in the 10 to 30 percent range. For example, General Electric seeks a 25 percent ROI, whereas Alcoa, Rubbermaid, and most major pharmaceutical companies strive for a 20 percent ROI. In some industries such as the grocery industry, however, a return of under 5 percent is common and acceptable.

A company with a target ROI can predetermine its desired level of profitability. The marketing manager can use the standard, such as 10 percent ROI, to determine whether a particular price and marketing mix are feasible. In addition,

return on investment (ROI)
Net profit after taxes divided by total assets.

however, the manager must weigh the risk of a given strategy even if the return is in the acceptable range.

SALES-ORIENTED PRICING OBJECTIVES

Sales-oriented pricing objectives are based either on market share or on dollar or unit sales. The effective marketing manager should be familiar with these pricing objectives.

Market Share

Market share is a company's product sales as a percentage of total sales for that industry. Sales can be reported in dollars or in units of product. It is very important to know whether market share is expressed in revenue or units because the results may be different. Consider four companies competing in an industry with 2,000 total unit sales and total industry revenue of $4 million (see Exhibit 17.1). Company A has the largest unit market share at 50 percent, but it has only 25 percent of the revenue market share. In contrast, company D has only a 15 percent unit share but the largest revenue share: 30 percent. Usually, market share is expressed in terms of revenue and not units.

Many companies believe that maintaining or increasing market share is an indicator of the effectiveness of their marketing mix. Larger market shares have indeed often meant higher profits, thanks to greater economies of scale, market power, and ability to compensate top-quality management. Conventional wisdom also says that market share and return on investment are strongly related. For the most part they are; however, many companies with low market share survive and even prosper. To succeed with a low market share, companies need to compete in industries with slow growth and few product changes—for instance, industrial component parts and supplies. Otherwise, they must vie in an industry that makes frequently bought items, such as consumer convenience goods.

The early 2000s proved that the conventional wisdom about market share and profitability isn't always reliable. Because of extreme competition in some industries, many market share leaders either did not reach their target ROI or actually lost money. Freightliner, DaimlerChrysler's U.S. heavy-truck unit, aggressively fought for market share gains during the past decade.

market share
A company's product sales as a percentage of total sales for that industry.

© MICHAEL NEWMAN/PHOTO EDIT

For over a decade, Folgers and Maxwell House have been locked in a struggle to dominate the coffee market. Numerous product extensions and modifications have been tried to persuade coffee-drinkers to switch brands (or stay with their current brand). Now, however, both companies face a new and increasingly formidable competitor for market share: Starbucks.

EXHIBIT 17.1

Two Ways to Measure Market Share (Units and Revenue)

Company	Units Sold	Unit Price	Total Revenue	Unit Market Share	Revenue Market Share
A	1,000	$1.00	$1,000,000	50%	25%
B	200	4.00	800,000	10	20
C	500	2.00	1,000,000	25	25
D	300	4.00	1,200,000	15	30
Total	2,000		$4,000,000		

share of industry profit, not in share of sales volume.

Still, the struggle for market share can be all-consuming for some companies. For over a decade, Maxwell House and Folgers, the biggest U.S. coffee brands, have been locked in a struggle to dominate the market. Their weapons have been advertising, perpetual rounds of price cutting, and millions upon millions of cents-off coupons. At this point, Maxwell House, a unit of Kraft General Foods, has regained a few drops of market share that it had lost to Folgers, a unit of Procter & Gamble, earlier in the war. Maxwell House's strategy has been to advertise heavily (spending over $100 million a year) and to introduce new products that lure consumers with taste rather than price. Examples include ready-made coffee in refrigerator cartons and coffee syrup, both designed for consumers to pour and microwave as needed. Nevertheless, Folgers is still the nation's best-selling coffee, although the Kraft General Foods brands, which include Yuban and Sanka, account for a 35 percent market share. P&G has 32 percent of the U.S. coffee market.

Research organizations like A. C. Nielsen and Information Resources, Inc., provide excellent market share reports for many different industries. These reports enable companies to track their performance in various product categories over time.

Sales Maximization

Rather than strive for market share, sometimes companies try to maximize sales. A firm with the objective of maximizing sales ignores profits, competition, and the marketing environment as long as sales are rising.

If a company is strapped for funds or faces an uncertain future, it may try to generate a maximum amount of cash in the short run. Management's task when using this objective is to calculate which price-quantity relationship generates the greatest cash revenue. Sales maximization can also be effectively used on a temporary basis to sell off excess inventory. It is not uncommon to find Christmas cards, ornaments, and so on discounted at 50 to 70 percent off retail prices after the holiday season. In addition, management can use sales maximization for year-end sales to clear out old models before introducing the new ones.

Maximization of cash should never be a long-run objective because cash maximization may mean little or no profitability. Without profits, a company cannot survive.[4]

STATUS QUO PRICING OBJECTIVES

status quo pricing
A pricing objective that maintains existing prices or meets the competition's prices.

Status quo pricing seeks to maintain existing prices or to meet the competition's prices. This third category of pricing objectives has the major advantage of requiring little planning. It is essentially a passive policy.

Often firms competing in an industry with an established price leader simply meet the competition's prices. These industries typically have fewer price wars than those with direct price competition. In other cases, managers regularly shop competitors' stores to ensure that their prices are comparable. Target's middle managers must visit competing Wal-Mart stores weekly to compare prices and then make adjustments. In response to MCI's claims that its long-distance service is overpriced, AT&T struck back with advertisements showing that its rates are essentially equal to competitors'. AT&T was attempting to convince target consumers that it follows a status quo pricing strategy.

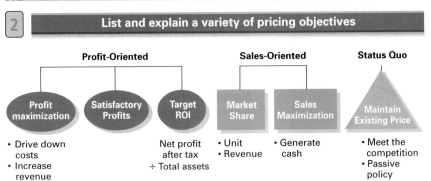

2 List and explain a variety of pricing objectives

Profit-Oriented
- Profit maximization
- Satisfactory Profits
- Target ROI

Sales-Oriented
- Market Share
- Sales Maximization

Status Quo
- Maintain Existing Price

- Drive down costs
- Increase revenue

Net profit after tax ÷ Total assets

- Unit
- Revenue

- Generate cash

- Meet the competition
- Passive policy

---

3 # THE DEMAND DETERMINANT OF PRICE

Explain the role of demand in price determination

After marketing managers establish pricing goals, they must set specific prices to reach those goals. The price they set for each product depends mostly on two factors: the demand for the good or service and the cost to the seller for that good or service. When pricing goals are mainly sales oriented, demand considerations usually dominate. Other factors, such as distribution and promotion strategies, perceived quality, demands of large customers, the Internet, and stage of the product life cycle, can also influence price.

demand
The quantity of a product that will be sold in the market at various prices for a specified period.

THE NATURE OF DEMAND

Demand is the quantity of a product that will be sold in the market at various prices for a specified period. The quantity of a product that people will buy depends on its price. The higher the price, the fewer goods or services consumers will demand. Conversely, the lower the price, the more goods or services they will demand.

This trend is illustrated in Exhibit 17.2(a), which graphs the demand per week for gourmet popcorn at a local retailer at various prices. This graph is called a *demand curve*. The vertical axis of the graph shows different prices of gourmet popcorn, measured in dollars per package. The horizontal axis measures the quantity of gourmet popcorn that will be demanded per week at each price. For example, at a price of $2.50, 50 packages will be sold per week; at $1.00, consumers will demand 120 packages—as the *demand schedule* in Exhibit 17.2(b) shows.

The demand curve in Exhibit 17.2 slopes downward and to the right, which indicates that more gourmet popcorn is demanded as the price is lowered. In other words, if popcorn manufacturers put a greater quantity on the market, then their hope of selling all of it will be realized only by selling it at a lower price.

EXHIBIT 17.2

Demand Curve and Demand Schedule for Gourmet Popcorn

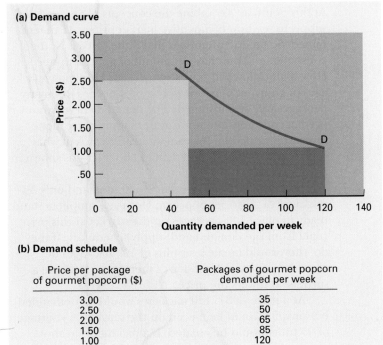

(a) Demand curve

(b) Demand schedule

Price per package of gourmet popcorn ($)	Packages of gourmet popcorn demanded per week
3.00	35
2.50	50
2.00	65
1.50	85
1.00	120

(b) Supply schedule

Price per package of gourmet popcorn ($)	Packages of gourmet popcorn supplied per week
3.00	140
2.50	130
2.00	110
1.50	85
1.00	25

Unlike the falling demand curve, the supply curve for gourmet popcorn slopes upward and to the right. At higher prices, gourmet popcorn manufacturers will obtain more resources (popcorn, flavorings, salt) and produce more gourmet popcorn. If the price consumers are willing to pay for gourmet popcorn increases, producers can afford to buy more ingredients.

Output tends to increase at higher prices because manufacturers can sell more packages of gourmet popcorn and earn greater profits. The *supply schedule* in Exhibit 17.3(b) shows that at $2 suppliers are willing to place 110 packages of gourmet popcorn on the market, but that they will offer 140 packages at a price of $3.

How Demand and Supply Establish Prices

At this point, let's combine the concepts of demand and supply to see how competitive market prices are determined. So far, the premise is that if the price is X, then consumers will purchase Y amount of gourmet popcorn. How high or low will prices actually go? How many packages of gourmet popcorn will be produced? How many packages will be consumed? The demand curve cannot predict consumption, nor can the supply curve alone forecast production. Instead, we need to look at what happens when supply and demand interact—as shown in Exhibit 17.4.

At a price of $3, the public would demand only 35 packages of gourmet popcorn. However, suppliers stand ready to place 140 packages on the market at this price (data from the demand and supply schedules). If they do, they would create a surplus of 105 packages of gourmet popcorn. How does a merchant eliminate a surplus? It lowers the price.

At a price of $1, 120 packages would be demanded, but only 25 would be placed on the market. A shortage of 95 units would be created. If a product is in short supply and consumers want it, how do they entice the

EXHIBIT 17.4

Equilibrium Price for Gourmet Popcorn

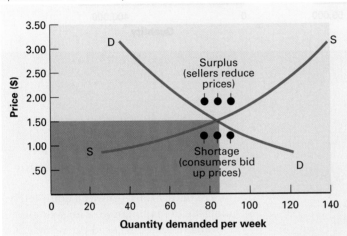

dealer to part with one unit? They offer more money—that is, pay a higher price.

Now let's examine a price of $1.50. At this price, 85 packages are demanded and 85 are supplied. When demand and supply are equal, a state called **price equilibrium** is achieved. A temporary price below equilibrium—say, $1.00—results in a shortage because at that price the demand for gourmet popcorn is greater than the available supply. Shortages put upward pressure on price. As long as demand and supply remain the same, however, temporary price increases or decreases tend to return to equilibrium. At equilibrium, there is no inclination for prices to rise or fall.

An equilibrium price may not be reached all at once. Prices may fluctuate during a trial-and-error period as the market for a good or service moves toward equilibrium. Sooner or later, however, demand and supply will settle into proper balance.

ELASTICITY OF DEMAND

To appreciate demand analysis, you should understand the concept of elasticity. **Elasticity of demand** refers to consumers' responsiveness or sensitivity to changes in price. **Elastic demand** occurs when consumers buy more or less of a product when the price changes. Conversely, **inelastic demand** means that an increase or a decrease in price will not significantly affect demand for the product.

Elasticity over the range of a demand curve can be measured by using this formula:

$$\text{Elasticity } (E) = \frac{\text{Percentage change in quantity demanded of good A}}{\text{Percentage change in price of good A}}$$

If E is greater than 1, demand is elastic.
If E is less than 1, demand is inelastic.
If E is equal to 1, demand is unitary.

Unitary elasticity means that an increase in sales exactly offsets a decrease in prices, so total revenue remains the same.

Elasticity can be measured by observing these changes in total revenue:

If price goes down and revenue goes up, demand is elastic.
If price goes down and revenue goes down, demand is inelastic.
If price goes up and revenue goes up, demand is inelastic.
If price goes up and revenue goes down, demand is elastic.
If price goes up or down and revenue stays the same, elasticity is unitary.

Exhibit 17.5(a) shows a very elastic demand curve. Decreasing the price of a Sony DVD player from $300 to $200 increases sales from 18,000 units to

supply
The quantity of a product that will be offered to the market by a supplier at various prices for a specified period.

price equilibrium
The price at which demand and supply are equal.

elasticity of demand
Consumers' responsiveness or sensitivity to changes in price.

elastic demand
A situation in which consumer demand is sensitive to changes in price.

inelastic demand
A situation in which an increase or a decrease in price will not significantly affect demand for the product.

unitary elasticity
A situation in which total revenue remains the same when prices change.

59,000 units. Revenue increases from $5.4 million ($300 × 18,000) to $11.8 million ($200 × 59,000). The price decrease results in a large increase in sales and revenue.

Exhibit 17.5(b) shows a completely inelastic demand curve. The state of Nevada dropped its used-car vehicle inspection fee from $20 to $10. The state continued to inspect about 400,000 used cars annually. Decreasing the price (inspection fee) 50 percent did not cause people to buy more used cars. Demand is completely inelastic for inspection fees, which are required by law. Thus, it also follows that Nevada could double the original fee to $40 and double the state's inspection revenues. People won't stop buying used cars if the inspection fee increases—within a reasonable range.

Exhibit 17.6 presents the demand curve and demand schedule for three-ounce bottles of Spring Break suntan lotion. Let's follow the demand curve from the highest price to the lowest and examine what happens to elasticity as the price decreases.

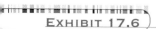

EXHIBIT 17.6

Demand for Three-Ounce Bottles of Spring Break Suntan Lotion

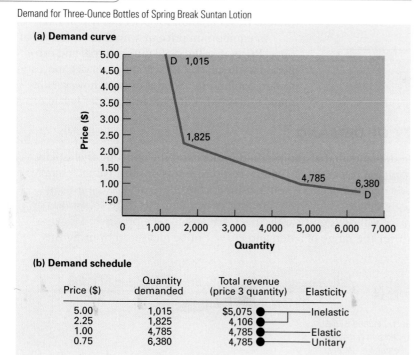

(a) Demand curve

(b) Demand schedule

Price ($)	Quantity demanded	Total revenue (price 3 quantity)	Elasticity
5.00	1,015	$5,075	Inelastic
2.25	1,825	4,106	
1.00	4,785	4,785	Elastic
0.75	6,380	4,785	Unitary

Inelastic Demand

The initial decrease in the price of Spring Break suntan lotion, from $5.00 to $2.25, results in a decrease in total revenue of $969 ($5,075 − $4,106). When price and total revenue fall, demand is inelastic. The decrease in price is much greater than the increase in suntan lotion sales (810 bottles). Demand is therefore not very flexible in the price range $5.00 to $2.25.

When demand is inelastic, sellers can raise prices and increase total revenue. Often items that are relatively inexpensive but convenient tend to have inelastic demand.

Elastic Demand

In the example of Spring Break suntan lotion, shown in Exhibit 17.6, when the price is dropped from $2.25 to $1.00, total revenue increases by $679 ($4,785 − $4,106). An increase in total revenue when price falls indicates that demand is elastic. Let's measure Spring Break's elasticity of demand when the price drops from $2.25 to $1.00 by applying the formula presented earlier:

$$E = \frac{\text{Change in quantity}/(\text{Sum of quantities}/2)}{\text{Change in price}/(\text{Sum of prices}/2)}$$

$$= \frac{(4,785 - 1,825)/[(1,825 + 4,785)/2]}{(2.25 - 1.00)/[(2.25 + 1.00)/2]}$$

$$= \frac{2,960/3,305}{1.25/1.63}$$

$$= \frac{.896}{.767}$$

$$= 1.17$$

Because *E* is greater than 1, demand is elastic.

Factors That Affect Elasticity

Several factors affect elasticity of demand, including the following:

FAQs

What is the relationship between substitute and complementary products and the elasticity of demand? Find out the answer by watching the video FAQ on Xtra!

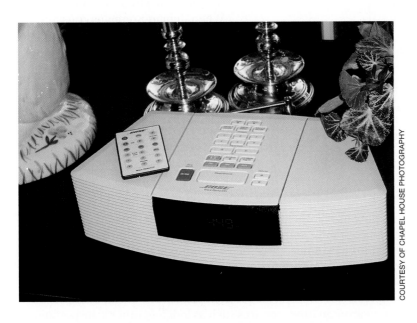

One factor affecting price elasticity is the availability of substitutes. For example, many consumers do not consider there to be a substitute for Bose radio and stereo products. As a result, the price on Bose products is inelastic, even priced at 300 to 500 percent above other stereo manufacturer's brands.

COURTESY OF CHAPEL HOUSE PHOTOGRAPHY

- *Availability of substitutes:* When many substitute products are available, the consumer can easily switch from one product to another, making demand elastic. The same is true in reverse: A person with complete renal failure will pay whatever is charged for a kidney transplant because there is no substitute. Interestingly, Bose Stereo equipment is priced 300 to 500 percent higher than other stereo brands. Yet consumers are willing to pay the price because they perceive the equipment as being so superior to other brands that there is no acceptable substitute.
- *Price relative to purchasing power:* If a price is so low that it is an inconsequential part of an individual's budget, demand will be inelastic. For example, if the price of salt doubles, consumers will not stop putting salt and pepper on their eggs because salt is cheap anyway.
- *Product durability:* Consumers often have the option of repairing durable products rather than replacing them, thus prolonging their useful life. If a person plans to buy a new car and prices suddenly begin to rise, he or she may elect to fix the old car and drive it for another year. In other words, people are sensitive to the price increase, and demand is elastic.
- *A product's other uses:* The greater the number of different uses for a product, the more elastic demand tends to be. If a product has only one use, as may be true of a new medicine, the quantity purchased probably will not vary as price varies.

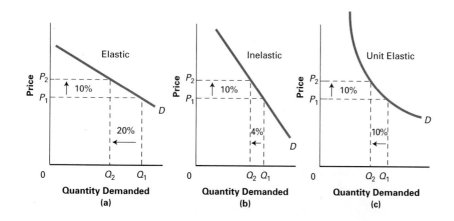

What affects elasticity?
• Availability of subtitutes
• Price relative to purchasing power
• Product durability
• Product's other uses

much more elastic.

As another example of supply and demand at work, consider that when car manufacturers began offering zero percent financing, sales of new vehicles jumped 35 percent over the same period a year earlier. Sales of so many new cars resulted in a huge surplus of used vehicles. When demand remains constant and supply increases, prices fall. In this case, the price of a used Lexus fell 12 percent from the price for a comparable vehicle a year earlier; the price of a used Chevrolet Tahoe fell 14 percent, and the price of used Ford F-series pickup trucks fell 11 percent.[7]

Understand the concept of yield management systems

THE POWER OF YIELD MANAGEMENT SYSTEMS

When competitive pressures are high, a company must know when it can raise prices to maximize its revenues. More and more companies are turning to yield management systems to help adjust prices. First developed in the airline industry, **yield management systems** (**YMS**) use complex mathematical software to profitably fill unused capacity. The software employs techniques such as discounting early purchases, limiting early sales at these discounted prices, and overbooking capacity. YMS now are appearing in other services such as lodging, other transportation forms, rental firms, retailers, and even hospitals.[8]

Yield management systems are spreading beyond service industries as their popularity increases. The lessons of airlines and hotels aren't entirely applicable to other industries, however, because plane seats and hotel beds are perishable—if they go empty, the revenue opportunity is lost forever. So it makes sense to slash prices to move toward capacity if it's possible to do so without reducing the prices that other customers pay. Cars and steel aren't so perishable. Still, the capacity to make these goods is perishable. An underused factory or mill is a lost revenue opportunity. So it makes sense to cut prices to use up capacity if it's possible to do so while getting other customers to pay full price.

yield management systems (YMS)
A technique for adjusting prices that uses complex mathematical software to profitably fill unused capacity by discounting early purchases, limiting early sales at these discounted prices, and overbooking capacity.

ProfitLogic has helped customers such as JCPenney, Gymboree, Ann Taylor, and Gap determine the best markdown price. The software has boosted profit margins from 5 to 18 percent. KhiMetrics, used by Buy.com and others, analyzes dozens of factors such as a product's life cycle, competitors' prices, and past sales data at various price points before churning out a list of possible prices and calculating the best ones. New sales data are fed back into the formulas daily to refine the process. Systems such as this aren't cheap, however, costing from $200,000 to $500,000.[9]

Yield management software is the reason that consumers now find prices at the 390 Longs Drug Stores in amounts like $2.07 or $5.84 instead of the traditional price-ending digits of .95 or .99. The company says the software has triggered a "category-by-category increase in sales and profit margins."[10] That's the main reason that DemandTec's YMS algorithms, and not manufacturers' suggested retail prices, now govern pricing in all Longs' stores in the continental United States.

With its lower cost structure and massive buying power, Wal-Mart has put pressure on everyone. Many retailers have fought back by slashing prices across the board—a foolhardy move, as many retailers have found out (think of Kmart). "You can't out-Wal-Mart Wal-Mart," says Terry Burnside, CEO of Longs Drug Stores. "We'd lose that game."[11]

All the more reason, argues DemandTec's founder Michael Neal, to focus on better pricing. Neal explains that one DemandTec client, a retailer, began bargain pricing what it thought was a very price-sensitive product—diapers—to generate store traffic. But after running sales data through the pricing software, the client discovered that was not the case. Most price-conscious diaper shoppers had long since abandoned the store for bulk purchases at discounters such as Wal-Mart. As a result, the client raised prices on diapers, increasing margins without hurting sales or traffic.

Is there just one acceptable price that people are willing to pay? Find out the answer by watching the video FAQ on Xtra!

 REVIEW LEARNING OBJECTIVE 4

4 Understand the concept of yield management systems

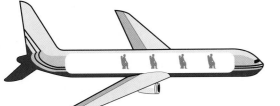

Price = $x

YMS varies price to fill capacity
(adjusts price to increase demand to meet supply)

Discounted Price = $x − y%

 5 THE COST DETERMINANT OF PRICE

Describe cost-oriented pricing strategies

Sometimes companies minimize or ignore the importance of demand and decide to price their products largely or solely on the basis of costs. Prices determined strictly on the basis of costs may be too high for the target market, thereby reducing or eliminating sales. On the other hand, cost-based prices may be too low, causing the firm to earn a lower return than it should. Nevertheless, costs should generally be part of any price determination, if only as a floor below which a good or service must not be priced in the long run.

The idea of cost may seem simple, but it is actually a multifaceted concept, especially for producers of goods and services. A **variable cost** is a cost that varies with changes in the level of output; an example of a variable cost is the cost of materials. In contrast, a **fixed cost** does not change as output is increased or decreased. Examples include rent and executives' salaries.

To compare the cost of production to the selling price of a product, it is helpful to calculate costs per unit, or average costs. **Average variable cost (AVC)** equals total variable costs divided by quantity of output. **Average total cost (ATC)** equals total costs divided by output. As the graph in Exhibit 17.7(a) shows, AVC and ATC

variable cost
A cost that varies with changes in the level of output.

fixed cost
A cost that does not change as output is increased or decreased.

average variable cost (AVC)
Total variable costs divided by quantity of output.

average total cost (ATC)
Total costs divided by quantity of output.

(b) Cost schedule

	Total-cost data, per week			Average-cost data, per week			
(1) Total product (Q)	(2) Total fixed cost (TFC)	(3) Total variable cost (TVC)	(4) Total cost (TC)	(5) Average fixed cost (AFC)	(6) Average variable cost (AVC)	(7) Average total cost (ATC)	(8) Marginal cost (MC)
			$TC = TFC + TVC$	$AFC = \dfrac{TFC}{Q}$	$AVC = \dfrac{TVC}{Q}$	$ATC = \dfrac{TC}{Q}$	$(MC) = \dfrac{\text{change in TC}}{\text{change in Q}}$
0	$100	$ 0	$ 100	—	—	—	—
1	100	90	190	$100.00	$90.00	$190.00	$ 90
2	100	170	270	50.00	85.00	135.00	80
3	100	240	340	33.33	80.00	113.33	70
4	100	300	400	25.00	75.00	100.00	60
5	100	370	470	20.00	74.00	94.00	70
6	100	450	550	16.67	75.00	91.67	80
7	100	540	640	14.29	77.14	91.43	90
8	100	650	750	12.50	81.25	93.75	110
9	100	780	880	11.11	86.67	97.78	130
10	100	930	1,030	10.00	93.00	103.00	150

are basically U-shaped curves. In contrast, average fixed cost (AFC) declines continually as output increases because total fixed costs are constant.

Marginal cost (MC) is the change in total costs associated with a one-unit change in output. Exhibit 17.7(b) shows that when output rises from seven to eight units, the change in total cost is from $640 to $750; therefore, marginal cost is $110.

All the curves illustrated in Exhibit 17.7(a) have definite relationships:

- AVC plus AFC equals ATC.
- MC falls for a while and then turns upward, in this case with the fourth unit. At that point diminishing returns set in, meaning that less output is produced for every additional dollar spent on variable input.
- MC intersects both AVC and ATC at their lowest possible points.

marginal cost (MC)
The change in total costs associated with a one-unit change in output

TIMEPIECES
INTERNATIONAL

KLAUS KOBEC
DIAMOND
MASTERPIECE

EXQUISITE
BRILLIANT CUT DIAMONDS
SET IN SOLID
STAINLESS STEEL

RETAIL PRICE $1055. ON YOUR WRIST $289. IN YOUR POCKET $766.

The Klaus Kobec Charisma Diamond a stunning timepiece created from solid stainless steel inlaid with exquisite Brilliant Cut diamonds accented by a cabochon sapphire crown. An elegant and stylish timepiece with a refined Swiss movement, now available direct from the manufacturer at the astonishingly low price of $289. A saving of $766 on the retail price of $1055. So how can we make an offer like this? The answer is beautifully simple. We have no middleman to pay. No retail overheads to pay. And not the usual mark-up to make, which on luxury items (including watches) can be enormous. We just make beautiful watches, beautifully simple to buy.

30 DAY MONEY BACK GUARANTEE

LADIES RETAIL PRICE $1055 DIRECT PRICE $289, GENTS RETAIL PRICE $1280 DIRECT PRICE $339. LADIES INLAID WITH 14 BRILLIANT CUT DIAMONDS, GENTLEMENS WATCH INLAID WITH 18 BRILLIANT CUT DIAMONDS. SET IN HIGHLY POLISHED STAINLESS STEEL CASE. FEATURES INCLUDE: GENUINE CABOCHON SAPPHIRE CROWN, BLUE STEELED HANDS. WATER RESISTANT TO 3 ATM. 5 YEAR WARRANTY ON THE QUALITY SWISS MOVEMENT.

Shipping/ Handling $12.95 FL Res add 6% Sales Tax total charge

CREDIT CARD HOTLINE 1-800-733-TIME (1-800-733-8463), 24 HOURS A DAY, SEVEN DAYS A WEEK. PLEASE QUOTE CODE MSL/43CDS.
TIMEPIECES INTERNATIONAL, 3580 NORTH WEST 56TH STREET, FORT LAUDERDALE, FLORIDA 33309. FAX: 1 888 675 3045 www.timepiecesusa.com

© COURTESY OF TIMEPIECES INTERNATIONAL

It is not uncommon for specialty retailers to markup their merchandise by 100 percent, even more in industries like high fashion. This ad for Timepieces International touts the fact that by selling direct, it can does not have "the usual mark-up to make" and so can offer this luxury watch at over 70 percent off the retail price.

markup pricing
The cost of buying the product from the producer plus amounts for profit and for expenses not otherwise accounted for.

- When MC is less than AVC or ATC, the incremental cost will continue to pull the averages down. Conversely, when MC is greater than AVC or ATC, it pulls the averages up, and ATC and AVC begin to rise.
- The minimum point on the ATC curve is the least cost point for a fixed-capacity firm, although it is not necessarily the most profitable point.

Costs can be used to set prices in a variety of ways. The first two methods discussed here, markup pricing and formula pricing, are relatively simple. The other three—profit maximization pricing, break-even pricing, and target-return pricing—make use of the more complicated concepts of cost.

MARKUP PRICING

Markup pricing, the most popular method used by wholesalers and retailers to establish a selling price, does not directly analyze the costs of production. Instead, **markup pricing** uses the cost of buying the product from the producer, plus amounts for profit and for expenses not otherwise accounted for. The total determines the selling price.

A retailer, for example, adds a certain percentage to the cost of the merchandise received to arrive at the retail price. An item that costs the retailer $1.80 and is sold for $2.20 carries a markup of 40 cents, which is a markup of 22 percent of the cost ($.40 ÷ $1.80). Retailers tend to discuss markup in terms of its percentage of the retail price—in this example, 18 percent ($.40 ÷ $2.20). The difference between the retailer's cost and the selling price (40 cents) is the gross margin, as Chapter 13 explained.

The formula for calculating the retail price given a certain desired markup is as follows:

$$\text{Retail price} = \frac{\text{Cost}}{1 - \text{Desired return on sales}}$$
$$= \frac{\$1.80}{\$1.00 - \$.18}$$
$$= \$2.20$$

If the retailer wants a 30 percent return, then:

$$\text{Retail price} = \frac{\$1.80}{\$1.00 - \$.30}$$
$$= \$2.57$$

The reason that retailers and others speak of markups on selling price is that many important figures in financial reports, such as gross sales and revenues, are sales figures, not cost figures.

To use markup based on cost or selling price effectively, the marketing manager must calculate an adequate gross margin—the amount added to cost to determine price. The margin must ultimately provide adequate funds to cover selling expenses and profit. Once an appropriate margin has been determined, the markup technique has the major advantage of being easy to employ. Wal-Mart, for example, strives for a gross margin of around 16 percent.[12] Because supermarket chains, such as Safeway and Kroger, have typically had gross margins of 24 percent,

Point of Profit Maximization

Quantity	Marginal Revenue (MR)	Marginal Cost (MC)	Cumulative Total Profit
0	—	—	—
1	$140	$90	$50
2	130	80	100
3	105	70	135
4	95	60	170
5	85	70	185
*6	80	80	185
7	75	90	170
8	60	110	120
9	50	130	40
10	40	150	(70)

*Profit maximization.

is the extra revenue associated with selling an extra unit of output. As long as the revenue of the last unit produced and sold is greater than the cost of the last unit produced and sold, the firm should continue manufacturing and selling the product.

Exhibit 17.8 shows the marginal revenues and marginal costs for a hypothetical firm, using the cost data from Exhibit 17.7(b). The profit-maximizing quantity, where MR = MC, is six units. You might say, "If profit is zero, why produce the sixth unit? Why not stop at five?" In fact, you would be right. The firm, however, would not know that the fifth unit would produce zero profits until it determined that profits were no longer increasing. Economists suggest producing up to the point where MR = MC. If marginal revenue is just one penny greater than marginal costs, it will still increase total profits.

BREAK-EVEN PRICING

Now let's take a closer look at the relationship between sales and cost. **Break-even analysis** determines what sales volume must be reached before the company breaks even (its total costs equal total revenue) and no profits are earned.

The typical break-even model assumes a given fixed cost and a constant average variable cost. Suppose that Universal Sportswear, a hypothetical firm, has fixed costs of $2,000 and that the cost of labor and materials for each unit produced is 50 cents. Assume that it can sell up to 6,000 units of its product at $1 without having to lower its price.

Exhibit 17.9(a) illustrates Universal Sportswear's break-even point. As Exhibit 17.9(b) indicates, Universal Sportswear's total variable costs increase by 50 cents every time a new unit is produced, and total fixed costs remain constant at $2,000 regardless of the level of output. Therefore, for 4,000 units of output, Universal Sportswear has $2,000 in fixed costs and $2,000 in total variable costs (4,000 units × $.50), or $4,000 in total costs.

Revenue is also $4,000 (4,000 units × $1), giving a net profit of zero dollars at the break-even point of 4,000 units. Notice that once the firm gets past the break-even

keystoning
The practice of marking up prices by 100 percent, or doubling the cost.

profit maximization
A method of setting prices that occurs when marginal revenue equals marginal cost.

marginal revenue (MR)
The extra revenue associated with selling an extra unit of output or the change in total revenue with a one-unit change in output.

break-even analysis
A method of determining what sales volume must be reached before total revenue equals total costs.

EXHIBIT 17.9

Costs, Revenues, and Break-Even Point for Universal Sportswear

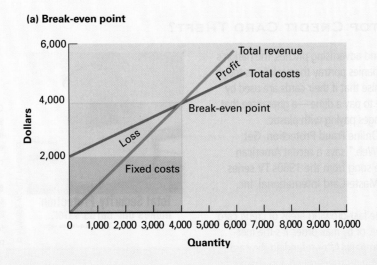

(a) Break-even point

(b) Costs and revenues

Output	Total fixed costs	Average variable costs	Total variable costs	Average total costs	Average revenue (price)	Total revenue	Total costs	Profit or loss
500	$2,000	$0.50	$ 250	$4.50	$1.00	$ 500	$2,250	($1,750)
1,000	2,000	0.50	500	2.50	1.00	1,000	2,500	(1,500)
1,500	2,000	0.50	750	1.83	1.00	1,500	2,750	(1,250)
2,000	2,000	0.50	1,000	1.50	1.00	2,000	3,000	(1,000)
2,500	2,000	0.50	1,250	1.30	1.00	2,500	3,250	(750)
3,000	2,000	0.50	1,500	1.17	1.00	3,000	3,500	(500)
3,500	2,000	0.50	1,750	1.07	1.00	3,500	3,750	(250)
*4,000	2,000	0.50	2,000	1.00	1.00	4,000	4,000	(0)
4,500	2,000	0.50	2,250	.94	1.00	4,500	4,250	250
5,000	2,000	0.50	2,500	.90	1.00	5,000	4,500	500
5,500	2,000	0.50	2,750	.86	1.00	5,500	4,750	750
6,000	2,000	0.50	3,000	.83	1.00	6,000	5,000	1,000

*Break-even point

point, the gap between total revenue and total costs gets wider and wider because both functions are assumed to be linear.

The formula for calculating break-even quantities is simple:

$$\text{Break-even quantity} = \frac{\text{Total fixed costs}}{\text{Fixed cost contribution}}$$

Fixed cost contribution is the price minus the average variable cost. Therefore, for Universal Sportswear,

$$\text{Break-even quantity} = \frac{\$2,000}{(\$1.00 - \$.50)} = \frac{\$2,000}{\$.50}$$

$$= 4,000 \text{ units}$$

The advantage of break-even analysis is that it provides a quick estimate of how much the firm must sell to break even and how much profit can be earned if a

holder's money, credit card companies turn around and charge the retailers for the loss. The merchants are also often charged additional fees that can range from $10 to $100 per transaction. The merchants argue that these fees—which generate $500 million in yearly revenue for the card industry—eliminate much of the card companies' incentive to pursue fraud.

When fraud occurs in a face-to-face transaction—at a department store or gas station, for instance—the credit card issuer shoulders the loss. Police say many card issuers find it easier and more cost-effective simply to write off such losses than to spend the time and resources pursuing the culprit, especially if the amount is less than $2,000.

As credit card fraud continues to escalate, the question of who should bear the cost of controlling it remains unresolved. Across the spectrum of the credit card industry, there appears to be little incentive or willingness to pick up the tab. Credit card companies and merchants point the finger at each other. Consumers, typically told they will be reimbursed for fraudulent charges, are lulled into complacency.[13]

Why do you think credit card companies are not doing more to prevent fraud? Are they making money off of fraud? Who ultimately pays for credit card fraud?

REVIEW LEARNING OBJECTIVE 5

 Describe cost-oriented pricing strategies

Markup: Cost + x% = Price

Profit Maximization: Price set at point where MR = MC

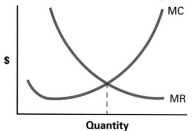

Break-even: Price set at point where total cost = total revenue

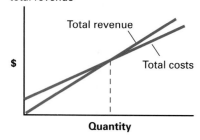

higher sales volume is obtained. If a firm is operating close to the break-even point, it may want to see what can be done to reduce costs or increase sales. Moreover, in a simple break-even analysis, it is not necessary to compute marginal costs and marginal revenues because price and average cost per unit are assumed to be constant. Also, because accounting data for marginal cost and revenue are frequently unavailable, it is convenient not to have to depend on that information.

Break-even analysis is not without several important limitations. Sometimes it is hard to know whether a cost is fixed or variable. If labor wins a tough guaranteed-employment contract, are the resulting expenses a fixed cost? Are middle-level executives' salaries fixed costs? More important than cost determination is the fact that simple break-even analysis ignores demand. How does Universal Sportswear know it can sell 4,000 units at $1? Could it sell the same 4,000 units at $2 or even $5? Obviously, this information would profoundly affect the firm's pricing decisions.

The break-even point can always be lowered by lowering costs. But before costs can be lowered, the question of "whose cost is it?" may have to be addressed. The "Ethics in Marketing" box explains who bears the cost of credit card fraud.

Demonstrate how the product life cycle, competition, distribution and promotion strategies, customer demands, the Internet and extranets, and perceptions of quality can affect price

Other factors besides demand and costs can influence price. For example, the stages in the product life cycle, the competition, product distribution strategy, promotion strategy, and perceived quality can all affect pricing.

STAGES IN THE PRODUCT LIFE CYCLE

As a product moves through its life cycle (see Chapter 10), the demand for the product and the competitive conditions tend to change:

- *Introductory stage.* Management usually sets prices high during the introductory stage. One reason is that it hopes to recover its development costs quickly. In addition, demand originates in the core of the market (the customers whose needs ideally match the product's attributes) and thus is relatively inelastic. On the other hand, if the target market is highly price sensitive, management often finds it better to price the product at the market level or lower. For example, when Kraft General Foods brought out Country Time lemonade, it was priced like similar products in the highly competitive beverage market because the market was price sensitive.

- *Growth stage.* As the product enters the growth stage, prices generally begin to stabilize for several reasons. First, competitors have entered the market, increasing the available supply. Second, the product has begun to appeal to a broader market, often lower income groups. Finally, economies of scale are lowering costs, and the savings can be passed on to the consumer in the form of lower prices.

- *Maturity stage.* Maturity usually brings further price decreases as competition increases and inefficient, high-cost firms are eliminated. Distribution channels become a significant cost factor, however, because of the need to offer wide product lines for highly segmented markets, extensive service requirements, and the sheer number of dealers necessary to absorb high-volume production. The manufacturers that remain in the market toward the end of the maturity stage typically offer similar prices. Usually, only the most efficient remain, and they have comparable costs. At this stage, price increases are usually cost initiated, not demand initiated. Nor do price reductions in the late phase of maturity stimulate much demand. Because demand is limited and producers have similar cost structures, the remaining competitors will probably match price reductions.

- *Decline stage.* The final stage of the life cycle may see further price decreases as the few remaining competitors try to salvage the last vestiges of demand. When only one firm is left in the market, prices begin to stabilize. In fact, prices may eventually rise dramatically if the product survives and moves into the specialty goods category, as horse-drawn carriages and vinyl records have.

THE COMPETITION

Competition varies during the product life cycle, of course, and so at times it may strongly affect pricing decisions. Although a firm may not have any competition at first, the high prices it charges may eventually induce another firm to enter the market. Several Internet auto sellers, such as Autobytel.com, have sprung up in response to the perceived high profit margins earned by car dealers.

On the other hand, intense competition can sometimes lead to price wars. One company recently took action to avoid a calamitous price war by outsmarting its competition. A company (call it Acme) heard that its competitor was trying to steal some business by offering a low price to one of its best customers. Instead of immediately cutting prices, Acme reps visited three of its competitor's best clients and said they figured the client was paying *x*, the same price that the competitor had quoted to Acme's own customer. Within days, the competitor had retracted its

brand. They place well-known brands on the shelves at high prices while offering other brands—typically, their private-label brands, such as Craftsman tools, Kroger canned pears, or Cost Cutter paper towels—at lower prices. Of course, sales of the higher priced brands decline.

Wholesalers and retailers may also go outside traditional distribution channels to buy gray-market goods. As explained previously, distributors obtain the goods through unauthorized channels for less than they would normally pay, so they can sell the goods with a bigger-than-normal markup or at a reduced price. Imports seem to be particularly susceptible to gray marketing. Porsches, JVC stereos, and Seiko watches are among the brand-name products that have experienced this problem. Although consumers may pay less for gray-market goods, they often find that the manufacturer won't honor the warranty.

Manufacturers can regain some control over price by using an exclusive distribution system, by franchising, or by avoiding doing business with price-cutting discounters. Manufacturers can also package merchandise with the selling price marked on it or place goods on consignment. The best way for manufacturers to control prices, however, is to develop brand loyalty in consumers by delivering quality and value.

In some cases, such as in the pharmaceutical industry, government actions have caused companies to lose channel pricing control, as the "Global Perspectives" box explains.

THE IMPACT OF THE INTERNET AND EXTRANETS

The Internet, corporate networks, and wireless setups are linking people, machines, and companies around the globe—and connecting sellers and buyers as never before. This link is enabling buyers to quickly and easily compare products and prices, putting them in a better bargaining position. At the same time, the technology allows sellers to collect detailed data about customers' buying habits, preferences, and even spending limits so that they can tailor their products and prices. For a time, all of these developments raised hopes of a more efficient marketplace.

Unfortunately, the promise of pricing efficiencies for Internet retailers and lower costs for consumers has run headlong into reality. Flawed pricing strategies have taken much of the blame for the implosion of many dot-coms. Too many merchants offered deep discounts that made profits all but impossible to achieve. Other e-retailers have felt the consumer backlash against price discrimination, as the Internet has given shoppers the ability to better detect price discrepancies and bargains. The dot-com survivors must now figure out if it is even possible to take

selling against the brand
Stocking well-known branded items at high prices in order to sell store brands at discounted prices.

Global Perspectives Global Perspectives Global Perspectives Global Perspectives Global Perspectives Global Perspectives
Global Perspectives Global Perspectives Global Perspectives Global Perspectives Global Perspectives Global Perspectives
GLOBAL PERSPECTIVES
bal Perspectives Global Perspectives Global Perspectives Global Perspectives Global Perspectives Global Perspectives
bal Perspectives Global Perspectives Global Perspectives Global Perspectives Global Perspectives
Global Perspectives
Global Perspectives

> THE EUROPEAN UNION HOLDS THE PRICING HAMMER OVER DRUG MANUFACTURERS

At the heart of the pharmaceutical industry's problem in Europe is the market's inability to "liberate the value" from drug products. Unlike free markets, in which companies set their own prices, Europe is beset by a complex maze of government-enforced pricing and reimbursement controls. Those controls have depressed pharmaceutical prices to the point where some companies now believe it is just not economical to launch new products in certain European countries. Marion Bamberger, senior director for Bristol-Myers Squibb, hit the nail on the head at a recent European pricing conference. She joked, with more than a hint of gallows humor, that she often has to explain to her U.S. colleagues that "the words *price increase* do not exist in France."

"Europe is becoming more and more unattractive," says Franz Humer, chairman of Roche, the Swiss pharmaceuticals giant. Perhaps the biggest drain for the industry in Europe is the growth of the so-called parallel trade in drugs. Although the European Union's single market rules strongly defend the free flow of goods between member countries, national governments have held on to the power to set their own prices for pharmaceuticals.

The result is a huge arbitrage opportunity for wholesalers who buy drugs in low-price countries such as Spain and Greece and then resell them in high-price Germany. The European Federation of Pharmaceutical Industry Associations, the industry's lobby group in Brussels, estimates that this parallel trade accounts for 3.5 billion euros of revenues a year. "The companies are playing with one hand behind their backs," says Rob Whewell from PA Consulting Group. "These distributors are extracting a large chunk of value from the chain without adding anything back."

Profit margins are also being squeezed by efforts by European governments to reduce their spending. In a bid to keep budget deficits within the Eurozone's fiscal rules, countries such as Germany, Italy, and France have all taken steps to rein in drug costs. These plans have taken a number of forms. In Germany, the government required a 6 percent rebate from drug makers and enacted a "pharmacy substitution" law, which requires pharmacists to substitute generic drugs if certain prescription drugs are above a threshold price. Italy, meanwhile, has introduced a 5 percent across-the-board price cut and set up a system of reference prices in which the government will not pay the full price for some products if their price is above a certain level. France has also opted for a reference pricing system.

Generics have never played as large a role in the European market as they have in the United States, but their use is expanding rapidly in a number of countries. And companies can still face long waits after a drug is approved by regulators before European governments agree to pay for it. According to Efpia, Belgium takes nearly two years on average to agree on the reimbursement for new drugs.

According to Lehman Brothers, the U.S. investment bank, the total cost to the pharmaceutical industry of all these cost-cutting efforts by European governments will be $2.2 billion in annual revenues.[15]

Should the EU ban "parallel trade" in drugs? Should the EU prohibit individual countries from controlling drug prices? Drug companies say that new drug research will decline because of European government actions. Do you agree? What do you think should be done about drug pricing?

---

advantage of the Internet's unique capabilities to set dynamic prices, which would better reflect a customer's willingness to pay more under different circumstances.

"Before the Internet existed, retail was a very competitive, difficult, low-margin business," says Austan Goolsbee, an economist at the University of Chicago. "With the advent of Internet retailers, there was a brief moment in which they and others believed they had broken the iron chain of low margins and high competition in retail by introducing the Internet. Now, retail online is starting to look like retail off-line—very competitive, profit margins squeezed. In all, a very tough place to be."[16]

Setting prices on the Internet was expected to offer retailers a number of advantages. To begin with, it would be far easier to raise or lower prices in response to demand, without the need for a clerk to run through a store with a pricing gun. Online prices could be changed in far smaller increments—even by just a penny or two—as frequently as a merchant desired, making it possible to fine-tune pricing strategies.

But the real payoff was supposed to be better information on exactly how price-conscious customers are. For instance, knowing that customer A doesn't care whether an Oscar-nominated DVD in her shopping basket costs $21.95 or $25.95 would leave an enterprising merchant free to charge the higher price on the spot. By contrast, knowing that customer B is going to put author John Le Carré's latest thriller back on the shelf unless it's priced at $20, instead of $28, would open an

2007.[17] If so, that will make Amazon one of the most profitable companies around.

While the Internet helps drive down prices by making it easier for consumers to shop for the best bargain, it also makes it possible for online merchants to monitor each other's prices—whether higher or lower—and to adjust them in concert without overtly colluding. As long as the number of retailers in a given market is relatively small, it is now much simpler for merchants to signal each other by changing prices for short periods—long enough for their competitors to notice, but not so long that consumers do. Airlines have long used online reservation systems to signal fare changes to each other.

Online price-comparison engines, known as shopbots, were supposed to make it easy for consumers to find the lowest prices for any goods. But making effective use of competitive price information has been more difficult for consumers than retailers and economists originally thought. For one thing, price comparisons, which must include a range of shipping options and fees, state-based sales taxes, and any special offers from individual merchants, are far from straightforward. And the time it takes to look up the best prices for a collection of items—say, books or DVDs—can outweigh price savings of a dollar or two.

"Shopbots are tedious to use," says Karen Clay, a Carnegie Mellon economist, who notes that consumers also tend to be willing to pay more for goods from familiar online retailers. Since trying a new retailer always involves uncertainty as to whether goods will arrive on time, whether customer service is satisfactory, and even whether the merchant has honestly posted its prices, she says, "that uncertainty can easily outweigh what you could save by shopping somewhere else."[18]

One area where the Internet is having, and will continue to have, a major impact on pricing is the bargaining power between buyers and sellers. For example, a group of 40-plus retailers, with nearly three and a half times the buying power of Wal-Mart, have formed the WorldWide Retail Exchange. On the manufacturing side, Procter & Gamble, Kraft Foods, and 50 others have invested more than $250 million to build business-to-business (B2B) megamarket Transora. Whatever the outcome of these markets, suppliers will soon be facing a world in which there are no more weak customers. Every buyer will wield Wal-Mart's bargaining power.

As bargaining power evens out, companies are reaching price agreements more quickly and then disseminating this information throughout the channel of distribution. Manufacturers are creating private networks, or **extranets**, that link them with their suppliers and customers. These systems make it possible to get a precise handle on inventory, costs, and demand at any given moment—and, after bargaining with suppliers, adjust prices instantly. In the past, a significant cost, known as the "menu cost," was associated with changing prices. For a company

extranet
A private electronic network that links a company with its suppliers and customers.

with a large product line, it could take months for price adjustments to filter down to distributors, retailers, and salespeople. Streamlined networks reduce menu cost and time to near zero.

Internet Auctions

The Internet auction business is huge. Part of the lure of buying online is that shoppers don't have to go to a flea market or use up a coveted weekend day or worry about the weather. Plus, bidding itself can be fun and exciting. Among the most popular consumer auction sites are the following:

- **http://www.auctions.amazon.com:** Links to Sotheby's for qualified sellers of high-end items.
- **http://www.ebay.com:** The most popular auction site.
- **http://www.auctions.yahoo.com:** Free listings and numerous selling categories including international auctions.

Even though consumers are spending billions on Internet auctions, B2B auctions are likely to be the dominant form in the future. FreeMarkets, Inc., a publicly traded B2B exchange based in Pittsburgh, has hosted online reverse auctions—in which suppliers bid for a factory's component order—involving $5.4 billion of transactions. Among the companies using FreeMarkets are Owens Corning, GlaxoSmithKline PLC, and Visteon Corporation, the auto-parts unit spun off by Ford Motor Company.[19] As an example of the benefits of using FreeMarkets.com, a company paid $175,000 for a batch of plastic auto parts—before using auctions. With an auction, in 33 minutes of frenzied bidding by 25 competing suppliers, the price came down to $118,000. In fact, FreeMarkets has helped companies in the automotive industry source over $20 billion in products and realize savings estimated at more than $3.5 billion. This success enabled FreeMarkets to acquire the auction assets of Covisint, the exchange started by Ford, General Motors, and DaimlerChrysler. The acquisition makes FreeMarkets the leading provider of sourcing technologies services to the automotive industry.[20]

FreeMarkets has quickly moved beyond selling metal and plastic parts and is auctioning tax preparation services, relocation services, temporary help, and other services. Retailers have created the Worldwide Retail Exchange and Global Net Xchange; and dozens of similar services are running or in the works.

Recently, Whirlpool began holding online auctions. Participants bid on the price of the items that they would supply to Whirlpool, but with a twist: They had to include the date when Whirlpool would have to pay for the items. The company wanted to see which suppliers would offer the longest grace period before requiring payment. Five auctions held over five months helped Whirlpool uncover savings of close to $2 million and more than doubled the grace period.

Whirlpool's success is a sign that the B2B auction world is shifting from haggling over prices to niggling over parameters of the deal. Warranties, delivery dates, transportation methods, customer support, financing options, and quality have all become bargaining chips.

There is also a dark side to Internet auctions, however, especially those where most participants are consumers. Every day crooks lure hundreds of unsuspecting users with auctions that appear legitimate but are really a hollow shell. They hop from user ID to user ID, feeding the system with fake information and stolen credit cards so that the auction site can't tell who they are. In response to a dramatic increase in auction-fraud complaints, the Federal Trade Commission banded together with the National Association of Attorneys General to conduct Operation Bidder Beware, a nationwide crackdown and consumer-education campaign. In 2004, the FTC logged 23,000 auction-fraud complaints, triple the number in 2001. "It's one of our top priorities," says Barbara Anthony, Northeast regional director at the FTC. "It jeopardizes the e-commerce marketplace and the confidence consumers have in the Internet." These numbers include auctions on Yahoo.com and other sites, but the bulk of them are on eBay, which boasts 85 percent of the online auction market.[21]

Crested Butte Resort no longer loses money during this time of the year.

Pricing can be a tool for trade promotions as well. For example, Levi's Dockers (casual men's pants) are very popular with white-collar men ages 25 to 45, a growing and lucrative market. Sensing an opportunity, rival pants-maker Bugle Boy began offering similar pants at cheaper wholesale prices, which gave retailers a bigger gross margin than they were getting with Dockers. Levi Strauss had to either lower prices or risk its $400 million annual Docker sales. Although Levi Strauss intended its cheapest Dockers to retail for $35, it started selling Dockers to retailers for $18 a pair. Retailers could then advertise Dockers at a very attractive retail price of $25.

Hair-care products benefit from the customer perception that higher prices mean higher quality. Salon products, like Bed Head and Paul Mitchell, convey the message of quality through high prices and exclusive distribution. In fact, customers may assume that the products are better because of the expertise of the hairdresser in whose salon the products are sold.

DEMANDS OF LARGE CUSTOMERS

Large customers of manufacturers such as Wal-Mart, JCPenney, and other department stores often make specific pricing demands that the suppliers must agree to. Department stores are making greater-than-ever demands on their suppliers to cover the heavy discounts and markdowns on their own selling floors. They want suppliers to guarantee their stores' profit margins, and they insist on cash rebates if the guarantee isn't met. They are also exacting fines for violations of ticketing, packing, and shipping rules. Cumulatively, the demands are nearly wiping out profits for all but the very biggest suppliers, according to fashion designers and garment makers.

With annual sales of over $240 billion and 1.3 million "associates" (employees), Wal-Mart is the world's largest company. Its sales on one day in 2004 were $2.17 billion.[23] That is more than the gross domestic product of 36 countries! Wal-Mart is the largest customer of Disney brands, Procter & Gamble, Kraft, Gillette, Campbell Soups, and most of America's other leading branded manufacturers. Wal-Mart expects suppliers to offer their best price, period. There is no negotiation or raising prices later. When suppliers have raised prices, Wal-Mart has been known to keep sending the old amount.[24]

THE RELATIONSHIP OF PRICE TO QUALITY

When a purchase decision involves great uncertainty, consumers tend to rely on a high price as a predictor of good quality. Reliance on price as an indicator of quality seems to occur for all products, but it reveals itself more strongly for some items than for others.[25]

Among the products that benefit from this phenomenon are coffee, stockings, aspirin, salt, floor wax, shampoo, clothing, furniture, perfume, whiskey, and many services. In the absence of other information, people typically assume that prices are higher because the products contain better materials, because they are made more carefully, or, in the case of professional services, because the provider has more expertise. In other words, consumers assume that "You get what you pay for."

Research has found that products that are perceived to be of high quality tend to benefit more from price promotions than products perceived to be of lower quality.[26] However, when perceived high- and lower-quality products are offered in settings where consumers have difficulty making comparisons, then price promotions have an equal effect on sales. Comparisons are more difficult in end-of-aisle displays, feature advertising, and the like.

Knowledgeable merchants take these consumer attitudes into account when devising their pricing strategies. **Prestige pricing** is charging a high price to help promote a high-quality image. A successful prestige pricing strategy requires a retail price that is reasonably consistent with consumers' expectations. No one goes shopping at a Gucci's shop in New York and expects to pay $9.95 for a pair of loafers. In fact, demand would fall drastically at such a low price. Bayer aspirin would probably lose market share over the long run if it lowered its prices. A new mustard packaged in a crockery jar was not successful until its price was doubled.

Some of the latest research on price-quality relationships has focused on consumer durable goods. The researchers first conducted a study to ascertain the dimensions of quality. These are (1) ease of use; (2) versatility (the ability of a product to perform more functions, e.g., special stitch types on sewing machines, or be more flexible, e.g., continuous temperature controls on microwave ovens); (3) durability; (4) serviceability (ease of obtaining quality repairs); (5) performance; and (6) prestige. The researchers found that when consumers focused on prestige and/or durability to assess quality, price was a strong indicator of perceived overall quality. Price was less important as an indicator of quality if the consumer was focusing on one of the other four dimensions of quality.[27]

prestige pricing
Charging a high price to help promote a high-quality image.

REVIEW LEARNING OBJECTIVE 6

6 — Demonstrate how the product life cycle, competition, distribution and promotion strategies, customer demands, the Internet and extranets, and perceptions of quality can affect price

Price/quality relationship
– Uncertain consumers tend to rely on price to indicate quality ("You get what you pay for.")

PLC
Introduction
Growth
Maturity
Decline

Competition
– Other firms enter market
– Price wars

Demands of large customers
– Large customers pressure suppliers for price reductions and guaranteed margins

Price

– Convenience
– Selling against the brand
– Exclusive distribution

Distribution

Promotion strategy
Price used as a promotional tool

– Not as easy to use variable pricing
– Consumers shop hard for bargains
– Increased competition

Internet and extranets

USE IT NOW

Here is a seller's guide to Internet auctions. Online auctions bring out the competitive nature in bidders, especially as the clock runs out. Bidding wars are a seller's dream; to make sure your auction gets significant play, follow these steps.

- Include specifics, such as manufacturer or product name, in both the title and the description. Don't include asterisks in your descriptions, as many newbies do in a misguided attempt to draw attention to their listings—the search engine reads "*" as a wild card, so your auction may not come up.
- Be honest in describing imperfections. This gives buyers comfort that you're acting on the up-and-up, and could head off conflicts when it's time to close the deal.
- Set a low initial bid amount to attract more bidders. The mere *possibility* of getting a great deal encourages competition and increases the likelihood of rival bidders driving up the price. This can also save you money, since eBay's listing fees are based on the minimum bid you set.
- Set a "buy it now" price, which allows buyers to subvert the bidding process and nab an item outright for a predetermined amount.

- Don't set a "reserve" price, which requires bidders to meet or exceed a certain minimum. Since bidders can't see this minimum price, many avoid such auctions altogether out of fear that they'll be wasting their time.
- Accept multiple forms of payment, which increases the likelihood that interested buyers will place bids.
- Pay attention to when your auction is scheduled to end. eBay auctions run 3, 5, 7, or 10 days; to get the most traffic, make sure that yours includes a full weekend and ends at a time when people will be around to bid up the price (in other words, don't close your auction at 2:30 A.M. on a Wednesday). **Tip:** Peak traffic on eBay tends to be at about 6 P.M. Pacific on weekends, when both East and West Coast bidders are still online.
- Consider paying a little more for special treatment. eBay offers extras like highlighting ($5 for a colored band around your item in both category listings and search results pages) and featured placement on its home page ($99.95), which will get your auction noticed.[28]

REVIEW AND APPLICATIONS

1 **Discuss the importance of pricing decisions to the economy and to the individual firm.** Pricing plays an integral role in the U.S. economy by allocating goods and services among consumers, governments, and businesses. Pricing is essential in business because it creates revenue, which is the basis of all business activity. In setting prices, marketing managers strive to find a level high enough to produce a satisfactory profit.

1.1 Why is pricing so important to the marketing manager?

1.2 How does price allocate goods and services?

2 **List and explain a variety of pricing objectives.** Establishing realistic and measurable pricing objectives is a critical part of any firm's marketing strategy. Pricing objectives are commonly classified into three categories: profit oriented, sales oriented, and status quo. Profit-oriented pricing is based on profit maximization, a satisfactory level of profit, or a target return on investment. The goal of profit maximization is to generate as much revenue as possible in relation to cost. Often, a more practical approach than profit maximization is setting prices to produce profits that will satisfy management and stockholders. The most common profit-oriented strategy is pricing for a specific return on investment relative to a firm's assets. The second type of pricing objective is sales oriented, and it focuses on either maintaining a percentage share of the market or maximizing dollar or unit sales. The third type of pricing objective aims to maintain the status quo by matching competitors' prices.

2.1 Give an example of each major type of pricing objective.

2.2 Why do many firms not maximize profits?

3 **Explain the role of demand in price determination.** Demand is a key determinant of price. When establishing prices, a firm must first determine demand for its product. A typical demand schedule shows an inverse relationship between quantity demanded and price: When price is lowered, sales increase; and when price is increased, the quantity demanded falls. For prestige products, however, there may be a direct relationship between demand and price: The quantity demanded will increase as price increases.

Marketing managers must also consider demand elasticity when setting prices. Elasticity of demand is the degree to which the quantity demanded fluctuates with changes in price. If consumers are sensitive to changes in price, demand is elastic; if they are insensitive to price changes, demand is inelastic. Thus, an increase in price will result in lower sales for an elastic product and little or no loss in sales for an inelastic product.

3.1 Explain the role of supply and demand in determining price.

3.2 If a firm can increase its total revenue by raising its price, shouldn't it do so?

3.3 Explain the concepts of elastic and inelastic demand. Why should managers understand these concepts?

3.4 As you read in the "Marketing in Entertainment" box, EasyCinema leverages the principle of supply and demand in the movie ticket market. That is, people willing to reserve early pay less. Online movie ticket purchase is not new, however. Go to movietickets.com and research a film and cinema in your area. How much is a ticket for a matinée? A ticket for an 8:00 P.M. show? Once you have the prices, call or visit the cinema you chose. How do the prices compare? If there is a difference in price, how can you account for it?

4 **Understand the concept of yield management systems.** Yield management systems use complex mathematical software to profitably fill unused capacity. The software uses techniques such as discounting early purchases, limiting early sales at these discounted prices, and overbooking capacity. These systems are used in service and retail businesses and are substantially raising revenues.

4.1 Why are so many companies adopting yield management systems?

4.2 I N F O T R A C° COLLEGE EDITION How is yield management helping companies achieve competitive advantage? Use InfoTrac to find out (**http://www.infotrac-college.com**). Run a keyword search for "yield management" and read through the headlines to see what industries are profiled most often. What industries seem to be good candidates for yield management?

agement often sets a high price at the introductory stage, and the high price tends to attract competition. The competition usually drives prices down because individual competitors lower prices to gain market share.

Adequate distribution for a new product can sometimes be obtained by offering a larger-than-usual profit margin to wholesalers and retailers. The Internet enables consumers to compare products and prices quickly and efficiently. Extranets help control costs and lower prices. Price is also used as a promotional tool to attract customers. Special low prices often attract new customers and entice existing customers to buy more. Large buyers can extract price concessions from vendors. Such demands can squeeze the profit margins of suppliers.

Perceptions of quality can also influence pricing strategies. A firm trying to project a prestigious image often charges a premium price for a product. Consumers tend to equate high prices with high quality.

6.1   **TEAM**   Divide the class into teams of five. Each team will be assigned a different grocery store from a different chain. (An independent is fine.) Appoint a group leader. The group leaders should meet as a group and pick 15 nationally branded grocery items. Each item should be specifically described as to brand name and size of the package. Each team will then proceed to its assigned store and collect price data on the 15 items. The team should also gather price data on 15 similar store brands and 15 generics, if possible.

Each team should present its results to the class and discuss why there are price variations between stores, national brands, store brands, and generics.

As a next step, go back to your assigned store and share the overall results with the store manager. Bring back the manager's comments and share them with the class.

6.2   How does the stage of a product's life cycle affect price? Give some examples.

6.3   **ONLINE**   Go to Priceline.com. Can you research a ticket's price before purchasing it? What products and services are available for purchasing? How comfortable are you with naming your own price? Relate the supply and demand curves to customer-determined pricing.

Go to one of the Internet auction sites listed in this chapter. Report to the class on how the auction process works and the items being auctioned.

6.4   **INFOTRAC COLLEGE EDITION**   How important is pricing when a company is entering new markets? The article in *Across the Board* titled "Is the Price Right?" by Peter Meyer can tell you. Print out the article using InfoTrac (**http://www.infotrac-college.com**) and then underline all of the chapter concepts that it discusses. What issues does the article address that the chapter does not? What issues does the chapter address that are not included in the article?

TERMS

average total cost (ATC) 597
average variable cost (AVC) 597
break-even analysis 600
demand 591
elastic demand 593
elasticity of demand 593
extranet 606
fixed cost 597
inelastic demand 593

keystoning 600
marginal cost (MC) 598
marginal revenue (MR) 600
market share 589
markup pricing 599
prestige pricing 609
price 586
price equilibrium 593
profit 586

profit maximization 600
return on investment (ROI) 588
revenue 586
selling against the brand 604
status quo pricing 590
supply 593
unitary elasticity 593
variable cost 597
yield management systems (YMS) 596

EXERCISES

APPLICATION EXERCISE

Reliance on price as a predictor of quality seems to occur for all products. Does this mean that high-priced products are superior? Well, sometimes. Price can be a good predictor of quality for some products, but for others, price is not always the best way to determine the quality of a product or service before buying it. This exercise (and worksheet) will help you examine the price-quality relationship for a simple product: canned goods.[29]

Activities

1. Take a trip to a local supermarket where you are certain to find multiple brands of canned fruits and vegetables. Pick a single type of vegetable or fruit you like, such as cream corn or peach halves, and list five or six brands in the worksheet below:

(1) Brand	(2) Quality Rank (y)	Price			(6) d (y − x)	(7) d²
		(3) Price/ Weight	(4) Price per Ounce	(5) Price Rank (x)		
TOTAL						

2. Before going any further, rank the brands according to which you think is the highest quality (1) to the lowest quality (5 or 6, depending on how many brands you find). This ranking will be y.

3. Record the price and the volume of each brand. For example, if a 14-ounce can costs $.89, you would list $.89/14 oz.

4. Translate the price per volume into price per ounce. Our 14-ounce can costs $.064 per ounce.

5. Now rank the price per ounce (we'll call it x) from the highest (1) to the lowest (5 or 6, again depending on how many brands you have).

6. We'll now begin calculating the coefficient of correlation between the price and quality rankings. The first step is to subtract x from y. Enter the result, d, in column 6.

7. Now calculate d² and enter the value in column 7. Write the sum of all the entries in column 7 in the final row.

8. The formula for calculating a price-quality coefficient r is as follows:

$$r_s = 1 - \frac{6 \sum d^2}{(n^3 - n)}$$

and review the code. Then, write a brief paragraph on what the AMA Code of Ethics contains that relates to ABM's dilemma.

CAREER EXERCISE

There are no specific career resources for pricing per se because pricing is not a function separate from other marketing activities. In fact, marketers in careers such as brand management, sales, marketing communications, and new-product development have a hand in making pricing decisions about their companies' products or services.

Activity

1. One way to investigate pricing is as a responsibility under a larger umbrella. Go to one of your favorite online (or off-line) career resources, and read several job descriptions for a variety of marketing positions. Keep a list of openings that specifically mention pricing as one of the general responsibilities.

ENTREPRENEURSHIP CASE

HDNET AIMS TO REDEFINE TELEVISION

If billionaire entrepreneur Mark Cuban had his way, the future would be today. The Web broadcasting pioneer earned nearly $2 billion when he and his partner sold their Broadcast.com business to Yahoo! for the princely sum of $5.7 billion at the height of the Internet frenzy in 2000. While looking to spend some of his newly found wealth on the latest and greatest in home entertainment systems, Cuban had his first experience with high-definition television. High-definition TV is a digital format that produces a picture resolution that can be up to ten times sharper than that of standard TVs (depending on screen pixel count), and it is typically presented in a wide-screen format along with digital surround sound. Cuban was so captivated by the amazing resolution on his new 100-inch projection set that he decided to start his own high-definition television network.

With a $100 million investment from Cuban, HDNet—the first-ever all-high-definition network—was off and running less than a year later. Three years later, HDNet boasts over 1,200 hours of original programming. In addition to the shows it produces, it has licensing contracts that double its programming inventory. HDNet also has broadcasting agreements that allow it to carry live sporting events from the National Hockey League, Major League soccer, and the NCAA. The company also operates HDNetMovies, which has scored deals with several major movie studios to convert their 35-millimeter films to a high-definition format.

Though HDNet's current subscriber base is estimated at around 1 million, industry statistics suggest that 60 million U.S. homes have television sets capable of delivering high-definition programming. With prices that started near $5,000 a couple of years ago, the prohibitive cost of the special television sets required to transmit high-definition programming was one of the company's major early hurdles. The other was the lack of available programming. High-definition shows must be produced on special equipment, and only a few major networks, such as NBC, CBS, ABC, HBO, Showtime, and the Discovery channel, have made the investment to do so.

Cuban has stayed the course, patiently waiting for prices of high-definition TV sets to drop to where they would have mass-market appeal. As with his Internet business, his timing appears to be perfect. Electronics retailer Best Buy now sells 27-inch high-definition TV sets for as low as $500. Of course, the discerning customer can spend as much as $9,000 in the same store for a top-of-the-line 60-inch model; but now that the television sets are affordable, adoption rates could be on the verge of exploding. Cuban, therefore, has turned his attention to securing distribution deals with major cable operators and satellite programmers.

His company has already locked in deals with all but three of the nation's largest cable television providers and with satellite broadcasters DirecTV and DISHNET. Both satellite programmers and the heavyweight cable-operating trio of Time Warner, Charter Communications, and Adelphia have begun to sell subscriptions to HDNet, which comes packaged with HDNet-Movies. Those companies pay an as yet undisclosed amount of money back to Cuban for the rights to carry the channel and license HDNet's exclusive content. To reduce some of the technical confusion for customers, the satellite companies offer subscribers package deals. DirecTV's includes a dish, a high-definition receiver (required to transmit the signal to the high-definition TV), professional installation, and a year's worth of high-definition programming for $399. DISHNET offers a similar package, but throws in a TV for a total start-up cost of $1,000. Its subscriptions are priced separately and start at $110 per year. Cable operators charge a premium for HDNet and include it only with their high-end digital offerings, which generally cost around $100 per month. To entice skeptical consumers into signing up, some cable companies are offering 30-day free trials.

Mark Cuban truly believes that the story of high-definition television services will someday mirror that of FM radio or basic cable television. Of course, only time will tell if he is right, but one thing is for sure—with high-definition television, the future certainly *appears* brighter.[30]

Questions

1. Based on how resellers are pricing HDNet for their subscribers, how would you characterize HDNet's pricing objectives?

2. How will demand and supply trends in the high-definition industry affect the price for HDNet's programming?

3. From what you can discern about HDNet's stage in the product life cycle, competition, distribution, resellers' sales promotion strategies, customer demands, and perception of quality, submit a projection of what you think HDNet should charge carriers for access to its channels and original programming. Defend your answer.

WATCH IT

SmallBusinessSchool
the Series on PBS stations and the Web

FEATURE PRESENTATION

Texas Jet

To give you insight into the concepts in Chapter 17, Small Business School returns to the terminal of Texas Jet, founded by entrepreneur Reed Pigman. When Reed realized that he couldn't compete with other private jet companies on price, he decided he was really in the service business. This realization helped Reed turn a struggling airplane transportation business into a thriving refueling service station. Texas Jet specializes in refueling jets flown for private use, and what sets it apart from the competition is its unfailing attention to customer service. It all starts when a customer's jet lands and Texas Jet rolls out the red carpet (literally). Inside the terminal

ENCORE PRESENTATION

The Money Pit

Now that you have a basic understanding of the issues affecting price, you can see why pricing is the most flexible—and difficult—element of the marketing mix. As an encore to your study, watch the film clip from *The Money Pit,* starring Tom Hanks (Walter Fielding) and Shelley Long (Anna Crowley) as new homeowners. Problems with their dream home's plumbing, electricity, roof, and general structure force the owners to make a series of expensive repairs. However, Walter has tremendous difficulty finding contractors to make the needed repairs. In this scene, a plumber visits the house on the recommendation of his brother, a carpenter, who has put in a bid to do woodworking repairs. What chapter concepts can you identify in the scene? How do supply and demand determine the price the homeowners are willing to pay for the plumber's services? Based on what you see of the plumber, how elastic are his prices?

THE MONEY PIT/CORBIS

STILL SHAKY?

If you're having trouble with the concepts in this chapter, consider using some of the following study resources. You can review the videos, or test yourself with materials designed for all kinds of learning styles.

☑ **Xtra! (http://lambxtra.swlearning.com)**

☑ Quiz	☑ Feature Videos	☑ Encore Videos	☑ FAQ Videos
☑ Exhibit Worksheets	☑ Marketing Plan Worksheets	☐ Content	

☑ **http://lamb.swlearning.com**

☑ Quiz	☑ PowerPoint slides	☑ Marketing News	☑ Review Exercises
☐ Links	☑ Marketing Plan Contest	☐ Career Exercise	☐ Use It Now

☑ **Study guide**

☑ Outline	☑ Vocab Review	☑ Test Questions	☑ Marketing Scenario

Need More? Here's a tip. Your professor and TA are the most valuable resources in your course. If you have questions on the fundamentals of pricing, go to office hours. Report back to your study partner or group.

Setting the
Right Price

LEARNING OBJECTIVES

1 Describe the procedure for setting the right price

2 Identify the legal and ethical constraints on pricing decisions

3 Explain how discounts, geographic pricing, and other pricing tactics can be used to fine-tune the base price

4 Discuss product line pricing

5 Describe the role of pricing during periods of inflation and recession

With his twinkly eyes and durable smile, Wendelin Wiedeking doesn't look like a fighter. But the Porsche CEO loves a good scrap. Taking principled but unpopular positions, then defending them to the death, is his nature. When the German government offered $97.5 million in subsidies in 1999 to help Porsche build a new assembly plant, for example, Wiedeking turned it down. He said he wanted to protect Porsche customers from complaints that taxpayers were subsidizing their expensive tastes.

Recently, Wiedeking got into an unseemly public disagreement with one of his own executives. When he heard that Porsche's U.S. sales arm was offering cash rebates, he turned—while at a public event—to the executive who had authorized the offer and declared, "It won't happen again." Indeed it won't. The executive recently retired.

Speaking his mind and following his instincts—regardless of where they lead—have been the keys to Wiedeking's success at Porsche. "Those who make concessions will lose," he observes. "If we were just a small copy of a major player, our continued existence would certainly be unjustified." Instead he has justified Porsche's existence to investors in the most compelling way possible: by making money. Porsche made profits of around $850 million on sales of approximately $5 billion in 2003.

Wiedeking's insistence on following his own road got a huge test in 2003. He launched a Porsche that sent the company in a new direction. The Cayenne is a four-door, four-wheel-drive off-road vehicle—in short, an SUV. Named after the pepper, the Cayenne was the subject of intense debate within the company, and loyal Porsche owners have screamed in protest. They fear that Porsche is compromising its heritage as a maker of exclusive sports cars.

Wiedeking is unmoved. "It was not easy to make the decision, but now everybody [at Porsche] is happy with the Cayenne. It rides like a Porsche and drives like a Porsche. It is 100 percent Porsche." The Cayenne was launched in Europe in December 2002 and went on sale in the United States a few months later, and Wiedeking notes that the first year's production of 25,000 vehicles quickly sold out. If the Cayenne's appeal proves lasting, Wiedeking will have succeeded in broadening Porsche's sporty image and boosting its annual sales by half, to 80,000 cars a year. That would still leave the company less than a tenth the size of BMW, but it would nevertheless constitute an important step toward securing Porsche's future. "Porsche wants to grow, and we want to have only exclusive products," he says. "That means we will keep following the niche strategy. We want to stay independent."

The Cayenne is engineered for financial performance too. Porsche needs just 300 workers at its Leipzig plant to assemble 25,000 Cayennes annually. That has allowed Wiedeking to anticipate handsome profit margins. Analysts at Deutsche Bank estimate that the Cayenne will produce an overall operating profit of 19 percent. The price for the 450-horsepower Turbo model starts at $88,900; it is expected to account for 20 percent or more of sales, generating a handsome 26 percent operating return, compared with 16 percent for the 911 and 10 percent for the Boxter.

Demand for the Cayenne is likely to remain strong for several years, as curiosity seekers and Porsche sports-car owners snap up early models. Some critics say its exterior and interior design are inferior to the Volkswagen's entry, the Touareg. But the two vehicles are unlikely to cannibalize each other because they compete in different segments; the V-8 version of the Touareg will be $15,000 cheaper than the comparable Cayenne.[1]

What type of basic price strategy is Porsche following? What are some of the ways to fine-tune the strategy? What kinds of discounts could Porsche offer?

than attempting to be a market leader, may establish a status quo goal. This company is simply trying to preserve its position in the marketplace. Finally, a company committed to maximizing shareholder value will establish aggressive profit-oriented pricing goals.

A good understanding of the marketplace and of the consumer can sometimes tell a manager very quickly whether a goal is realistic. For example, if firm A's objective is a 20 percent target return on investment (ROI), and its product development and implementation costs are $5 million, the market must be rather large or must support the price required to earn a 20 percent ROI. Assume that company B has a pricing objective that all new products must reach at least 15 percent market share within three years after their introduction. A thorough study of the environment may convince the marketing manager that the competition is too strong and the market share goal can't be met.

All pricing objectives have trade-offs that managers must weigh. A profit maximization objective may require a bigger initial investment than the firm can commit or wants to commit. Reaching the desired market share often means sacrificing short-term profit because without careful management, long-term profit goals may not be met. Meeting the competition is the easiest pricing goal to implement. But can managers really afford to ignore demand and costs, the life-cycle stage, and other considerations? When creating pricing objectives, managers must consider these trade-offs in light of the target customer, the environment, and the company's overall objectives.

EXHIBIT 18.1

Steps in Setting the Right Price on a Product

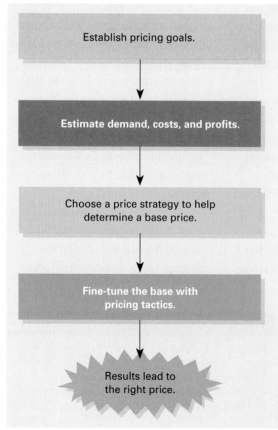

Establish pricing goals.

↓

Estimate demand, costs, and profits.

↓

Choose a price strategy to help determine a base price.

↓

Fine-tune the base with pricing tactics.

↓

Results lead to the right price.

ESTIMATE DEMAND, COSTS, AND PROFITS

Chapter 17 explained that total revenue is a function of price and quantity demanded and that quantity demanded depends on elasticity. After establishing pricing goals, managers should estimate total revenue at a variety of prices. Next, they should determine corresponding costs for each price. They are then ready to estimate how much profit, if any, and how much market share can be earned at each possible price. These data become the heart of the developing price policy.

Managers can study the options in light of revenues, costs, and profits. In turn, this information can help determine which price can best meet the firm's pricing goals.

CHOOSE A PRICE STRATEGY

The basic, long-term pricing framework for a good or service should be a logical extension of the pricing objectives. The marketing manager's chosen **price strategy** defines the initial price and gives direction for price movements over the product life cycle.

The price strategy sets a competitive price in a specific market segment, based on a well-defined positioning strategy. Changing a price level from premium to superpremium may require a change in the product itself, the target customers served, the promotional strategy, or the distribution channels. Thus, changing a price strategy can require dramatic alterations in the marketing mix. A carmaker cannot successfully compete in the superpremium category if the car looks and drives like an economy car.

A company's freedom in pricing a new product and devising a price strategy depends on the market conditions and the other elements of the marketing mix. If a firm launches a new item resembling several others already on the market, its pricing freedom will be restricted. To succeed, the company will probably have to charge a price close to the average market price. In contrast, a firm that introduces a totally new product with no close substitutes will have considerable pricing freedom.

Most companies do not do a good job of doing research to create a price strategy. A recent study found that only about 8 percent of the companies surveyed conducted serious pricing research to support the development of an effective pricing strategy. In fact, 88 percent of them did little or no serious pricing research. McKinsey & Company's Pricing Benchmark Survey estimated that only about 15 percent of companies do serious pricing research. A Coopers & Lybrand study found that 87 percent of the surveyed companies had changed prices in the previous year. Only 13 percent of the price changes, however, came after a scheduled review of pricing strategy.[2]

These numbers indicate that strategic pricing decisions tend to be made without an understanding of the likely buyer or the competitive response. Further, the research shows that managers often make tactical pricing decisions without reviewing how they may fit into the firm's overall pricing or marketing strategy. The data suggest that many companies make pricing decisions and changes without an existing process for managing the pricing activity. As a result, many of them do not have a serious pricing strategy and do not conduct pricing research to develop their strategy.[3]

Companies that do serious planning for creating a price strategy can select from three basic approaches: price skimming, penetration pricing, and status quo pricing. A discussion of each type follows.

Price Skimming

Price skimming is sometimes called a "market-plus" approach to pricing because it denotes a high price relative to the prices of competing products. BMW, like Porsche, has focused almost exclusively on premium cars. In contrast, Daimler-Chrysler management is convinced that the company can be competitive only by combining luxury and mass-market brands such as its Mercedes-Benz and Chrysler units. BMW's focus on premium vehicles enables it to use a skimming strategy in the overall automobile market.

The term **price skimming** is derived from the phrase "skimming the cream off the top." Companies often use this strategy for new products when the product is perceived by the target market as having unique advantages. For example, Caterpillar sets premium prices on its construction equipment to support and capture its high perceived value. Genzyme Corporation introduced Ceredase as the first effective treatment for Gaucher's disease. The pill allows patients to avoid years of painful physical deterioration and lead normal lives. The cost of a year's supply for one patient can exceed $300,000.

price strategy
A basic, long-term pricing framework, which establishes the initial price for a product and the intended direction for price movements over the product life cycle.

price skimming
A pricing policy whereby a firm charges a high introductory price, often coupled with heavy promotion.

competitors. Managers may follow a skimming strategy when production cannot be expanded rapidly because of technological difficulties, shortages, or constraints imposed by the skill and time required to produce a product. As long as demand is greater than supply, skimming is an attainable strategy.

A successful skimming strategy enables management to recover its product development or "educational" costs quickly. (Often consumers must be "taught" the advantages of a radically new item, such as high-definition TV.) Even if the market perceives an introductory price as too high, managers can easily correct the problem by lowering the price. Firms often feel it is better to test the market at a high price and then lower the price if sales are too slow. They are tacitly saying, "If there are any premium-price buyers in the market, let's reach them first and maximize our revenue per unit." Successful skimming strategies are not limited to products. Well-known athletes, entertainers, lawyers, and hairstylists are experts at price skimming. Naturally, a skimming strategy will encourage competitors to enter the market.

Penetration Pricing

Penetration pricing is at the opposite end of the spectrum from skimming. **Penetration pricing** means charging a relatively low price for a product as a way to reach the mass market. The low price is designed to capture a large share of a substantial market, resulting in lower production costs. If a marketing manager has made obtaining a large market share the firm's pricing objective, penetration pricing is a logical choice.

Penetration pricing does mean lower profit per unit, however. Therefore, to reach the break-even point, it requires a higher volume of sales than would a skimming policy. If reaching a high volume of sales takes a long time, then the recovery of product development costs will also be slow. As you might expect, penetration pricing tends to discourage competition.

Procter & Gamble examined the electric toothbrush market and noted that most electric brushes cost over $50. The company brought out the Crest Spin-Brush that works on batteries and sells for just $5. It is now the nation's best-selling toothbrush, manual or electric, and has helped the Crest brand of products become P&G's twelfth billion-dollar brand.[5]

A penetration strategy tends to be effective in a price-sensitive market. Price should decline more rapidly when demand is elastic because the market can be expanded through a lower price. Also, price sensitivity and greater competitive pressure should lead to a lower initial price and a relatively slow decline in the price later. Southwest Airlines' success is based on penetration pricing. By flying only the

penetration pricing
A pricing policy whereby a firm charges a relatively low price for a product initially as a way to reach the mass market.

Boeing 737, it realizes efficiencies in stocking parts and training pilots and mechanics. It also saves by avoiding a costly computer reservation system, such as Apollo or SABRE, and by not serving meals. Southwest has one of the lowest cost per seat mile in the industry. The value of Southwest's stock is greater than that of all other U.S. airlines combined.

If a firm has a low fixed cost structure and each sale provides a large contribution to those fixed costs, penetration pricing can boost sales and provide large increases in profits—but only if the market size grows or if competitors choose not to respond. Low prices can attract additional buyers to the market. The increased sales can justify production expansion or the adoption of new technologies, both of which can reduce costs. And, if firms have excess capacity, even low-priced business can provide incremental dollars toward fixed costs.

Southwest Airlines

It's no secret that Southwest Airlines has some of the cheapest fares around the nation. But just how much cheaper are they? The next time you travel, take the time to compare Southwest's prices with another carrier's. Has your regular airline met the challenge of Southwest's penetration pricing strategy? If so, how?

http://www.iflyswa.com

Online

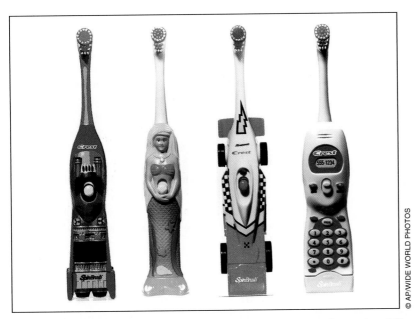

Although the Crest Spinbrush for kids is a low-priced electric toothbrush, it costs about 200 percent more than a traditional kid's tootbrush. Do you think that is penetration pricing or price skimming? Why?

Penetration pricing can also be effective if an experience curve will cause costs per unit to drop significantly. The experience curve proposes that per-unit costs will go down as a firm's production experience increases. On average, for each doubling of production, a firm can expect per-unit costs to decline by roughly 20 percent. Cost declines can be significant in the early stages of production. Manufacturers that fail to take advantage of these effects will find themselves at a competitive cost disadvantage relative to others that are further along the curve.

The big advantage of penetration pricing is that it typically discourages or blocks competition from entering a market. The disadvantage is that penetration means gearing up for mass production to sell a large volume at a low price. What if the volume fails to materialize? The company will face huge losses from building or converting a factory to produce the failed product. Skimming, in contrast, lets a firm "stick its toe in the water" and see if limited demand exists at the high price. If not, the firm can simply lower the price. Skimming lets a company start out with a small production facility and expand it gradually as price falls and demand increases.

Penetration pricing can also prove disastrous for a prestige brand that adopts the strategy in an effort to gain market share and fails. When Omega—once a more prestigious brand than Rolex—was trying to improve the market share of its watches, it adopted a penetration pricing strategy that succeeded in destroying the watches' brand image by flooding the market with lower priced products. Omega never gained sufficient share on its lower priced/lower image competitors to justify destroying its brand image and high-priced position with upscale buyers. Lacoste clothing experienced a similar outcome from a penetration pricing strategy.

Sometimes marketers in other countries adapt price strategies to meet the unique needs of their target markets. Such was the case when Casas Bahia stores modified their penetration pricing strategy to include installment buying. The concept is explained in the "Global Perspectives" box.

FAQs

How does competitive-bid pricing differ from traditional pricing? Find out the answer by watching the video FAQ on Xtra!

customers to return to the store each month to pay, he induces two-thirds of them to make another purchase. About 90 percent of sales are on credit. Klein's closely held Casas Bahia chain is Brazil's biggest nonfood retailer, selling about $1.5 billion annually of furniture, household goods, and appliances—including one-third of all new TV sets sold in Brazil each year.

While most mainstream Brazilian retailers shun the poor, the former salesman courts them assiduously. Klein's stripped-down stores are located in some of the most deprived neighborhoods of São Paulo and Rio de Janeiro. His clients include freelance masons, hot-dog vendors, and blue-collar workers whose average monthly income is $190, below the national average of $290. Surprisingly, their default rates are lower than the market average, too, and their loyalty is intense—a combination that has turned Klein into a

The average monthly installment at Casas Bahia is about $14. Only a permanent mailing address is required to get credit approval, though about one-tenth of applicants are rejected, usually because their names appear on a federal list of defaulters.

Many customers say they are aware they may pay more at Casas Bahia. But "here the terms are good for me," says Maria Nogueira, a building superintendent, after depositing a $13 installment on a $200 sofa. Plus, she notes, Casas Bahia gives a five-day grace period and marginally discounts early installment payments.[6]

Is Klein serving the poor or taking advantage of them? If his target market didn't buy from Casas Bahia, where would they shop? Would they have a higher or lower standard of living? Would this concept work in the United States? Why or why not? Would it be better for the poor to save their money and just pay cash?

REVIEW LEARNING OBJECTIVE 1

1   **Describe the procedure for setting the right price**

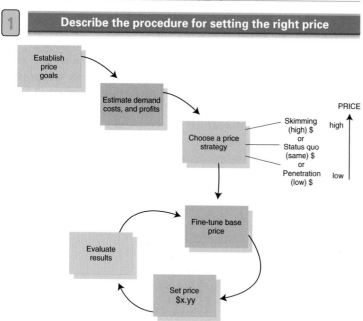

Status Quo Pricing

The third basic price strategy a firm may choose is status quo pricing, also called meeting the competition or going rate pricing (see also Chapter 17). It means charging a price identical to or very close to the competition's price. JCPenney, for example, makes sure it is charging comparable prices by sending representatives to shop at Sears stores.

Although status quo pricing has the advantage of simplicity, its disadvantage is that the strategy may ignore demand or cost or both. If the firm is comparatively small, however, meeting the competition may be the safest route to long-term survival.

THE LEGALITY AND ETHICS OF PRICE STRATEGY

Identify the legal and ethical constraints on pricing decisions

As we mentioned in Chapter 3, some pricing decisions are subject to government regulation. Before marketing managers establish any price strategy, they should know the laws that limit their decision making. Among the issues that fall into this category are unfair trade practices, price fixing, price discrimination, and predatory pricing.

UNFAIR TRADE PRACTICES

In over half the states, **unfair trade practice acts** put a floor under wholesale and retail prices. Selling below cost in these states is illegal. Wholesalers and retailers must usually take a certain minimum percentage markup on their combined merchandise cost and transportation cost. The most common markup figures are 6 percent at the retail level and 2 percent at the wholesale level. If a specific wholesaler or retailer can provide "conclusive proof" that operating costs are lower than the minimum required figure, lower prices may be allowed.

The intent of unfair trade practice acts is to protect small local firms from giants like Wal-Mart and Target, which operate very efficiently on razor-thin profit margins. State enforcement of unfair trade practice laws has generally been lax, however, partly because low prices benefit local consumers.

PRICE FIXING

Price fixing is an agreement between two or more firms on the price they will charge for a product. Suppose two or more executives from competing firms meet to decide how much to charge for a product or to decide which of them will submit the lowest bid on a certain contract. Such practices are illegal under the Sherman Act and the Federal Trade Commission Act. Offenders have received fines and sometimes prison terms. Price fixing is one area where the law is quite clear, and the Justice Department's enforcement is vigorous.

In the past several years, the Justice Department has vigorously pursued price-fixing cases. ISK Japan, a Japanese manufacturer of a coating for videotape, was fined $5 million for its role in a conspiracy to fix the prices of and allocate customers for video magnetic iron oxide (MIO) particles in the United States. Gemstar–TV Guide International paid $5.67 million in civil penalties and agreed to certain restrictions to resolve federal charges that Gemstar and TV Guide had fixed prices. Also, Hoechst AG, an international chemical conglomerate based in Germany, was fined $12 million for participating in a conspiracy to suppress competition in the world markets for an industrial chemical used in the production of various products, including pharmaceuticals, herbicides, and plastic additives.[7]

Recently, the Justice Department investigated five global paint manufacturers, including DuPont, Sherwin-Williams, and PPG Industries in the United States, for price fixing in the automotive refinishing industry. Concurrently, the Justice

In a scandal that rocked the art world, Sotheby's and Christie's, two of the industry's most venerable auction houses, were caught in a price-fixing scheme. The CEOs of both companies received substantial fines and prison time.

unfair trade practice acts
Laws that prohibit wholesalers and retailers from selling below cost.

price fixing
An agreement between two or more firms on the price they will charge for a product.

AP/WIDE WORLD PHOTOS

prices to different customers for the same product.

- The transaction must occur in interstate commerce.
- The seller must discriminate by price among two or more purchasers; that is, the seller must make two or more actual sales within a reasonably short time.
- The products sold must be commodities or other tangible goods.
- The products sold must be of like grade and quality, not necessarily identical. If the goods are truly interchangeable and substitutable, then they are of like grade and quality.
- There must be significant competitive injury.

The Robinson-Patman Act provides three defenses for the seller charged with price discrimination (in each case the burden is on the defendant to prove the defense):

- *Cost:* A firm can charge different prices to different customers if the prices represent manufacturing or quantity discount savings.
- *Market conditions:* Price variations are justified if designed to meet fluid product or market conditions. Examples include the deterioration of perishable goods, the obsolescence of seasonal products, a distress sale under court order, and a legitimate going-out-of-business sale.
- *Competition:* A reduction in price may be necessary to stay even with the competition. Specifically, if a competitor undercuts the price quoted by a seller to a buyer, the law authorizes the seller to lower the price charged to the buyer for the product in question.

PREDATORY PRICING

 Predatory pricing is the practice of charging a very low price for a product with the intent of driving competitors out of business or out of a market. Once competitors have been driven out, the firm raises its prices. This practice is illegal under the Sherman Act and the Federal Trade Commission Act. Proving the use of the practice is difficult and expensive, however. The Justice Department must show that the predator, the destructive company, explicitly tried to ruin a competitor and that the predatory price was below the predator's average variable cost.

Prosecutions for predatory pricing suffered a major setback recently when a federal judge threw out a predatory pricing suit filed by the Justice Department against American Airlines. Instead of using the traditional predatory pricing definition of pricing below average variable cost, the Justice Department had argued

predatory pricing
The practice of charging a very low price for a product with the intent of driving competitors out of business or out of a market.

that the definition should be updated and that the test should be whether there was any business justification, other than driving away competitors, for American's aggressive pricing. Under that definition, the Justice Department attorneys thought they had a great case. Whenever a fledgling airline tried to get a toehold in the Dallas market, American would meet its fares and add flights. As soon as the rival retreated, American would jack its fares back up.

Under the average variable cost definition, however, the case would have been almost impossible to win. The reason is that like the high-tech industry, the airline industry has high fixed costs and low marginal costs. An airline's biggest expense is buying airplanes and labor. Once a flight is scheduled, the marginal cost of providing a seat for an additional passenger is almost zero. Thus, it is very difficult to prove that an airline is pricing below its average variable cost. The judge was not impressed by the Justice Department's argument, however, and stuck to the average variable cost definition of predatory pricing. The ruling likely marks the end of predatory pricing lawsuits for the foreseeable future, and it may well open the door for dominant companies to use predatory pricing to destroy smaller competitors, at least in industries with cost structures similar to those of the airline industry's.[10]

STATE EFFORTS TO DRIVE DOWN DRUG PRICES

 A recent development in pricing strategies with both legal and ethical implications is occurring throughout the United States at the state government level. In a serious challenge to the U.S. pharmaceutical industry, state governments are taking steps to cut the prices of prescription drugs. Florida became the first state since federal Medicaid laws were overhauled in 1990 to extract additional price concessions from drugmakers. Under federal law, pharmaceutical companies that sell to state Medicaid programs must offer them the same prices they give their most-favored customers. Florida took this a step further, generally requiring companies to offer rebates averaging around 6 percent on top of the already-discounted prices.

Michigan's experiment is potentially even more far-reaching because it extends well beyond Medicaid-funded drugs and takes aim at drug companies' freedom to set prices. Instead of using the prices offered to companies' most-favored customers as a starting point, Michigan is trying to drive all prices down to a low common denominator. A similar movement in Europe, known as "reference pricing," has severely hurt drug company profits there.[11]

In Michigan, a committee of 11 doctors and pharmacists chose the best-in-class drugs in 40 categories. These drugs are guaranteed a large portion of the $1.1 billion the state spends each year on prescription medicines for both Medicaid and a state-funded program for the elderly.[12] Doctors can prescribe drugs that aren't on the list but only after justifying their decision in a call to a phone bank of pharmacy technicians—a requirement that is expected to discourage use of unlisted drugs. Thus, all companies wanting to sell drugs under these programs risk losing market share unless they agree to slash prices to win a spot on the preferred list.

In a related case, in the summer of 2003, the United States Supreme Court approved the state of Maine's plan for cutting drug prices. The state will negotiate prescription prices on behalf of its residents, thereby giving 300,000 Maine citizens who currently lack drug insurance the clout of group buying power. Drug companies argue that giving discounts to those paying full price now will drive up costs for everyone else.[13]

As expected, the pharmaceutical companies are filing lawsuits against the states. The companies claim that federal law allows states to limit access to Medicaid-funded drugs only if they offer no clinical benefit, not merely because the manufacturer doesn't offer a large enough price cut. The cases were still pending at the publication of this text.

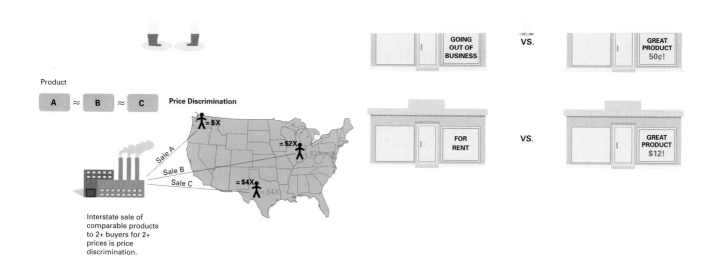

Product

A ≈ B ≈ C

Price Discrimination

Interstate sale of comparable products to 2+ buyers for 2+ prices is price discrimination.

Sale A = $X
Sale B = $2X
Sale C = $4X

GOING OUT OF BUSINESS vs. GREAT PRODUCT 50¢!

FOR RENT vs. GREAT PRODUCT $12!

3 TACTICS FOR FINE-TUNING THE BASE PRICE

Explain how discounts, geographic pricing, and other pricing tactics can be used to fine-tune the base price

After managers understand both the legal and the marketing consequences of price strategies, they should set a **base price**, the general price level at which the company expects to sell the good or service. The general price level is correlated with the pricing policy: above the market (price skimming), at the market (status quo pricing), or below the market (penetration pricing). The final step, then, is to fine-tune the base price.

Fine-tuning techniques are short-run approaches that do not change the general price level. They do, however, result in changes within a general price level. These pricing tactics allow the firm to adjust for competition in certain markets, meet ever-changing government regulations, take advantage of unique demand situations, and meet promotional and positioning goals. Fine-tuning pricing tactics include various sorts of discounts, geographic pricing, and other pricing tactics.

DISCOUNTS, ALLOWANCES, REBATES, AND VALUE-BASED PRICING

base price
The general price level at which the company expects to sell the good or service.

A base price can be lowered through the use of discounts and the related tactics of allowances, rebates, low or zero percent financing, and value-based pricing.

Managers use the various forms of discounts to encourage customers to do what they would not ordinarily do, such as paying cash rather than using credit, taking delivery out of season, or performing certain functions within a distribution channel.[14] The following are some of the most common tactics:

- *Quantity discounts:* When buyers get a lower price for buying in multiple units or above a specified dollar amount, they are receiving a **quantity discount**. A **cumulative quantity discount** is a deduction from list price that applies to the buyer's total purchases made during a specific period; it is intended to encourage customer loyalty. In contrast, a **noncumulative quantity discount** is a deduction from list price that applies to a single order rather than to the total volume of orders placed during a certain period. It is intended to encourage orders in large quantities.

- *Cash discounts:* A **cash discount** is a price reduction offered to a consumer, an industrial user, or a marketing intermediary in return for prompt payment of a bill. Prompt payment saves the seller carrying charges and billing expenses and allows the seller to avoid bad debt.

- *Functional discounts:* When distribution channel intermediaries, such as wholesalers or retailers, perform a service or function for the manufacturer, they must be compensated. This compensation, typically a percentage discount from the base price, is called a **functional discount** (or **trade discount**). Functional discounts vary greatly from channel to channel, depending on the tasks performed by the intermediary.

- *Seasonal discounts:* A **seasonal discount** is a price reduction for buying merchandise out of season. It shifts the storage function to the purchaser. Seasonal discounts also enable manufacturers to maintain a steady production schedule year-round.

- *Promotional allowances:* A **promotional allowance** (also known as a **trade allowance**) is a payment to a dealer for promoting the manufacturer's products. It is both a pricing tool and a promotional device. As a pricing tool, a promotional allowance is like a functional discount. If, for example, a retailer runs an ad for a manufacturer's product, the manufacturer may pay half the cost. If a retailer sets up a special display, the manufacturer may include a certain quantity of free goods in the retailer's next order.[15]

- *Rebates:* A **rebate** is a cash refund given for the purchase of a product during a specific period. The advantage of a rebate over a simple price reduction for stimulating demand is that a rebate is a temporary inducement that can be taken away without altering the basic price structure. A manufacturer that uses a simple price reduction for a short time may meet resistance when trying to restore the price to its original, higher level.

  Ford spends about $300 less on rebates per vehicle than does General Motors. Ford collects sales data daily from dealerships and feeds the data into computer models that predict which incentives will spark the best results. The output also shows marketers which cars need an incentive and in which regional markets—and which cars don't. Why waste cash on vehicles that sell well without it? Ford used a $1,000 rebate on the popular Escape, a small SUV, but offered $3,000 on the slower-selling Explorer.

- *Zero percent financing:* During the recession of the early 2000s, new-car sales plummeted. To get people back into the automobile showrooms, manufacturers offered zero percent financing, which enabled purchasers to borrow money to pay for new cars with no interest charge. The tactic created a huge increase in sales but not without cost to the manufacturers. A five-year interest-free car

quantity discount
A price reduction offered to buyers buying in multiple units or above a specified dollar amount.

cumulative quantity discount
A deduction from list price that applies to the buyer's total purchases made during a specific period.

noncumulative quantity discount
A deduction from list price that applies to a single order rather than to the total volume of orders placed during a certain period.

cash discount
A price reduction offered to a consumer, an industrial user, or a marketing intermediary in return for prompt payment of a bill.

functional discount (trade discount)
A discount to wholesalers and retailers for performing channel functions.

seasonal discount
A price reduction for buying merchandise out of season.

promotional allowance (trade allowance)
A payment to a dealer for promoting the manufacturer's products.

rebate
A cash refund given for the purchase of a product during a specific period.

cent, or even more. One benefit of doing this is that it allows the retailer to use heavy discounting as a promotional tool. Bluefly.com regularly offers designer apparel at lower-than-retail prices, and at the end of the season, puts its samples on sale at its New York City outlet.

very few firms operate in a pure monopoly, however, a marketer using value-based pricing must also determine the value of competitive offerings to customers. Customers determine the value of a product (not just its price) relative to the value of alternatives. In value-based pricing, therefore, the price of the product is set at a level that seems to the customer to be a good price compared with the prices of other options.

When two Wal-Mart supercenters and a rival regional grocery opened near a Kroger supermarket in Houston, the Kroger's sales dropped 10 percent. The store manager moved quickly to slash some prices and cut labor costs, for example, by buying ready-made cakes instead of baking them in-house and ordering precut salad-bar items from suppliers. Kroger employees used to stack displays by hand; now fruit and vegetables arrive stacked for display.

Such moves have helped Kroger cut worker-hours by 30 to 40 percent over the last four years and lower the prices of staples such as cereal, bread, milk, eggs, and disposable diapers. If Wal-Mart's supercenters continue to expand at their current pace, however, within this decade, more than three-quarters of the nation's Kroger's and Albertson's stores and more than half the Safeway outlets could be within ten miles of a Wal-Mart supercenter.

The fight for the minds of customers is already having an impact. Shoppers in competitive markets are seeing prices fall as Wal-Mart pushes rivals to match its value prices. The chains are using various tactics including improving their inventory-tracking systems, doubling or tripling discount coupons, and boosting customer loyalty with discount cards.

As with its other merchandise, Wal-Mart is aggressive on cutting costs. To simplify inventory, suppliers are being asked to pack fresh chicken trays in uniform weights to make it easier for the store to restock and price the poultry. A machine, rather than a person, fries and flips doughnuts. Produce is stacked in reusable plastic containers to cut labor costs. Meanwhile, a central office at Wal-Mart's Arkansas headquarters monitors the stores' heating and cooling systems and refrigerated cases to control utility bills.

Studies show that items cost 8 to 27 percent less at Wal-Mart than at Kroger, Albertson's, or Safeway, even when discounts from these competitors' loyalty cards and specials are included.[16] Wal-Mart is the king of value pricing.

Discount cards aren't always the great value that they seem. The "Ethics in Marketing" box explores this issue.

value-based pricing
Setting the price at a level that seems to the customer to be a good price compared to the prices of other options.

Ethics in Marketing Ethics in Marketing
Ethics in Marketing Ethics in Marketing Ethics in Marketing Ethics in Marketing
Ethics in Marketing Ethics in Marketing Ethics in Marketing Ethics in Marketing Ethics in Marketing Ethics in Marketing
cs in Marketing Ethics in Marketing Ethics in Marketing Ethics in Marketing Ethics in Marketing Ethics in Marketing
cs in Marketing Ethics in Marketing **ETHICS IN MARKETING** Marketing Ethics in Marketing
cs in Marketing Ethics in Marketing Ethics in Marketing Ethics in Marketing Ethics in Marketing
cs in Marketing Ethics in Marketing Ethics in Marketing
Ethics in Marketing

❯ GET A DISCOUNT CARD AND SPEND MORE MONEY

They are the three words supermarket shoppers love to hear: "You just saved." These days that is the phrase increasingly being chirped by grocery-store clerks amid the rapid proliferation of supermarket club cards. These programs are calculated to appeal directly to your inner penny-pincher: Swipe your membership card in the checkout line, and the next thing you know a receipt prints out saying something like, "You just saved $21.83." Message: You are being rewarded with deals so special, they are reserved for members only.

The programs, with names such as the Kroger Plus Savings card and Dominick's Fresh Values Club, are spreading quickly. Even Albertson's—which previously marketed itself with the slogan "no card, no hassle"—now has its own Preferred Savings Card. Today, more than three-quarters of Americans have club cards. But how much cash are you really saving by shopping at a supermarket that has a card, instead of a noncard store? To find out, two *Wall Street Journal* reporters went shopping at both types of stores and talked to a range of card experts. They found that, most likely, you are saving no money at all. In fact, if you are shopping at a store using a card, you may be spending more money than you would down the street at a grocery store that doesn't have a discount card.

They learned this the hard way—by going on a five-city, shop-till-you-drop grocery spree. In each city, they shopped first at a store using its discount card and then bought the same things at a nearby grocery store that doesn't have a card. Then they rolled up their sleeves, unrolled their receipts, and crunched the numbers.

In all five of their comparisons, the reporters wound up spending less money in a supermarket that doesn't offer a card, in one case 29 percent less. Supermarkets strongly defend their programs. The cards let stores "target savings" to loyal customers, says Ertharin Cousin of Albertson's. In addition, some card stores aren't competing solely on price, but on things like selection and store cleanliness. Several chains also pointed out that their cards offer more than discounts. Safeway, for example, lets shoppers earn airline frequent flyer miles; Albertson's new program makes donations to local schools.[17]

Should discount cards be outlawed? Are they deceptive? Why do you think that Albertson's finally decided to offer a discount card? Are card programs unfair to shoppers who don't use the cards?

Pricing Products Too Low

Sometimes managers price their products too low, thereby reducing company profits.[18] This seems to happen for two reasons. First, managers attempt to buy market share through aggressive pricing. Usually, however, these price cuts are quickly met by competitors. Thus, any gain in market share is short-lived, and overall industry profits end up falling. Second, managers have a natural tendency to want to make decisions that can be justified objectively. The problem is that companies often lack hard data on the complex determinants of profitability, such as the relationship between price changes and sales volumes, the link between demand levels and costs, and the likely responses of competitors to price changes. In contrast, companies usually have rich, unambiguous information on costs, sales, market share, and competitors' prices. As a result, managers tend to make pricing decisions based on current costs, projected short-term share gains, or current competitor prices rather than on long-term profitability.

The problem of "underpricing" can be solved by linking information about price, cost, and demand within the same decision support system. The demand data can be developed via marketing research. This will enable managers to get the hard data they need to calculate the effects of pricing decisions on profitability.

GEOGRAPHIC PRICING

Because many sellers ship their wares to a nationwide or even a worldwide market, the cost of freight can greatly affect the total cost of a product. Sellers may use

area—may modify the base price with a zone-pricing tactic. **Zone pricing** is a modification of uniform delivered pricing. Rather than using a uniform freight rate for the entire United States (or its total market), the firm divides it into segments or zones and charges a flat freight rate to all customers in a given zone. The U.S. Postal Service's parcel post rate structure is probably the best-known zone-pricing system in the country.

- *Freight absorption pricing:* In **freight absorption pricing**, the seller pays all or part of the actual freight charges and does not pass them on to the buyer. The manager may use this tactic in intensely competitive areas or as a way to break into new market areas.

- *Basing-point pricing:* With **basing-point pricing**, the seller designates a location as a basing point and charges all buyers the freight cost from that point, regardless of the city from which the goods are shipped. Thanks to several adverse court rulings, basing-point pricing has waned in popularity. Freight fees charged when none were actually incurred, called *phantom freight*, have been declared illegal.

OTHER PRICING TACTICS

Unlike geographic pricing, other pricing tactics are unique and defy neat categorization. Thus, we simply call this group "other." Managers use these tactics for various reasons—for example, to stimulate demand for specific products, to increase store patronage, and to offer a wider variety of merchandise at a specific price point. "Other" pricing tactics include a single-price tactic, flexible pricing, professional services pricing, price lining, leader pricing, bait pricing, odd–even pricing, price bundling, and two-part pricing. A brief overview of each of these tactics follows, along with a manager's reasons for using that tactic or a combination of tactics to change the base price.

Single-Price Tactic

A merchant using a **single-price tactic** offers all goods and services at the same price (or perhaps two or three prices). Retailers using this tactic include One Price Clothing Stores, Dre$$ to the Nine$, Your $10 Store, and Fashions $9.99. One Price Clothing Stores, for example, tend to be small, about 3,000 square feet. Their goal is to offer merchandise that would sell for at least $15 to $18 in other stores. The stores carry pants, shirts, blouses, sweaters, and shorts for juniors, misses, and large-sized women. The stores do not feature any seconds or irregular items, and everything is sold for $6.

FOB origin pricing
A price tactic that requires the buyer to absorb the freight costs from the shipping point ("free on board").

uniform delivered pricing
A price tactic in which the seller pays the actual freight charges and bills every purchaser an identical, flat freight charge.

zone pricing
A modification of uniform delivered pricing that divides the United States (or the total market) into segments or zones and charges a flat freight rate to all customers in a given zone.

freight absorption pricing
A price tactic in which the seller pays all or part of the actual freight charges and does not pass them on to the buyer.

basing-point pricing
A price tactic that charges freight from a given (basing) point, regardless of the city from which the goods are shipped.

single-price tactic
A price tactic that offers all goods and services at the same price (or perhaps two or three prices).

KeepMedia is a Web site that offers consumers unlimited access to a database of magazine articles for a flat monthly rate of $4.95. In addition to using a single-price tactic, KeepMedia's pricing strategy represents penetration pricing in a market where online articles regularly cost around $3 per article. Pictured here is KeepMedia Chairman, Louis Borders.

FAQs

Which pricing tactics are most effective? Find out the answer by watching the video FAQ on Xtra!

flexible pricing (variable pricing)
A price tactic in which different customers pay different prices for essentially the same merchandise bought in equal quantities.

price lining
The practice of offering a product line with several items at specific price points.

Single-price selling removes price comparisons from the buyer's decision-making process. The consumer just looks for suitability and the highest perceived quality. The retailer enjoys the benefits of a simplified pricing system and minimal clerical errors. However, continually rising costs are a headache for retailers following this strategy. In times of inflation, they must frequently raise the selling price.

Flexible Pricing

Flexible pricing (or **variable pricing**) means that different customers pay different prices for essentially the same merchandise bought in equal quantities. This tactic is often found in the sale of shopping goods, specialty merchandise, and most industrial goods except supply items. Car dealers, many appliance retailers, and manufacturers of industrial installations, accessories, and component parts commonly follow the practice. It allows the seller to adjust for competition by meeting another seller's price. Thus, a marketing manager with a status quo pricing objective might readily adopt the tactic. Flexible pricing also enables the seller to close a sale with price-conscious consumers. If buyers show promise of becoming large-volume shoppers, flexible pricing can be used to lure their business.

The obvious disadvantages of flexible pricing are the lack of consistent profit margins, the potential ill will of high-paying purchasers, the tendency for salespeople to automatically lower the price to make a sale, and the possibility of a price war among sellers. The disadvantages of flexible pricing have led the automobile industry to experiment with one price for all buyers. General Motors has used a one-price tactic for some of its models, including the Saturn and the Buick Regal.

Professional Services Pricing

Professional services pricing is used by people with lengthy experience, training, and often certification by a licensing board—for example, lawyers, physicians, and family counselors. Professionals sometimes charge customers at an hourly rate, but sometimes fees are based on the solution of a problem or performance of an act (such as an eye examination) rather than on the actual time involved. A surgeon may perform a heart operation and charge a flat fee of $5,000. The operation itself may require only four hours, resulting in a hefty $1,250 hourly rate. The physician justifies the fee because of the lengthy education and internship required to learn the complex procedures of a heart operation. Lawyers also sometimes use flat-rate pricing, such as $500 for completing a divorce and $50 for handling a traffic ticket.

Those who use professional pricing have an ethical responsibility not to overcharge a customer. Because demand is sometimes highly inelastic, such as when a person requires heart surgery or a daily insulin shot to survive, there may be a temptation to charge "all the traffic will bear."

Price Lining

When a seller establishes a series of prices for a type of merchandise, it creates a price line. **Price lining** is the practice of offering a product line with several items at specific price points. For example, Hon, an office furniture manufacturer, may offer its four-drawer file cabinets at $125, $250, and $400. The Limited may offer women's dresses

quality merchandise at each price point. Second, sellers can change the prices, although frequent price line changes confuse buyers. Third, sellers can accept lower profit margins and hold quality and prices constant. This third alternative has short-run benefits, but its long-run handicaps may drive sellers out of business.

Leader Pricing

Leader pricing (or **loss-leader pricing**) is an attempt by the marketing manager to attract customers by selling a product near or even below cost in the hope that shoppers will buy other items once they are in the store. This type of pricing appears weekly in the newspaper advertising of supermarkets, specialty stores, and department stores. Leader pricing is normally used on well-known items that consumers can easily recognize as bargains at the special price. The goal is not necessarily to sell large quantities of leader items, but to try to appeal to customers who might shop elsewhere.[19]

Leader pricing is not limited to products. Health clubs offer a one-month free trial as a loss leader. Lawyers give a free initial consultation. And restaurants distribute two-for-one coupons and "welcome to the neighborhood" free meal coupons.

Bait Pricing

In contrast to leader pricing, which is a genuine attempt to give the consumer a reduced price, bait pricing is deceptive. **Bait pricing** tries to get the consumer into a store through false or misleading price advertising and then uses high-pressure selling to persuade the consumer to buy more expensive merchandise. You may have seen this ad or a similar one:

> REPOSSESSED . . . Singer slant-needle sewing machine . . . take over 8 payments of $5.10 per month . . . ABC Sewing Center.

This is bait. When a customer goes in to see the machine, a salesperson says that it has just been sold or else shows the prospective buyer a piece of junk no one would buy. Then the salesperson says, "But I've got a really good deal on this fine new model." This is the switch that may cause a susceptible consumer to walk out with a $400 machine. The Federal Trade Commission considers bait pricing a deceptive act and has banned its use in interstate commerce. Most states also ban bait pricing, but sometimes enforcement is lax.

Odd–Even Pricing

Odd–even pricing (or **psychological pricing**) means pricing at odd-numbered prices to connote a bargain and pricing at even-numbered prices to imply quality. For

---

leader pricing (loss-leader pricing)
A price tactic in which a product is sold near or even below cost in the hope that shoppers will buy other items once they are in the store.

bait pricing
A price tactic that tries to get consumers into a store through false or misleading price advertising and then uses high-pressure selling to persuade consumers to buy more expensive merchandise.

odd–even pricing (psychological pricing)
A price tactic that uses odd-numbered prices to connote bargains and even-numbered prices to imply quality.

Wyndham Hotels and Resorts uses its e-mail newsletter to advertise an inclusive weekend getaway from $136 a night. Price bundling is common in the hospitality industry.

years, many retailers have priced their products in odd numbers—for example, $99.95 or $49.95—to make consumers feel they are paying a lower price for the product.

Some retailers favor odd-numbered prices because they believe that $9.99 sounds much less imposing to customers than $10.00. Other retailers believe that an odd-numbered price signals to consumers that the price is at the lowest level possible, thereby encouraging them to buy more units. Neither theory has ever been conclusively proved.

Even-numbered pricing is sometimes used to denote quality. Examples include a fine perfume at $100 a bottle, a good watch at $500, or a mink coat at $3,000. The demand curve for such items would also be sawtoothed, except that the outside edges would represent even-numbered prices and, therefore, elastic demand.

Price Bundling

Price bundling is marketing two or more products in a single package for a special price. Examples include the sale of maintenance contracts with computer hardware and other office equipment, packages of stereo equipment, packages of options on cars, weekend hotel packages that include a room and several meals, and airline vacation packages. Microsoft offers "suites" of software that bundle spreadsheets, word processing, graphics, electronic mail, Internet access, and groupware for networks of microcomputers. Price bundling can stimulate demand for the bundled items if the target market perceives the price as a good value.

Services like hotels and airlines sell a perishable commodity (hotel rooms and airline seats) with relatively constant fixed costs. Bundling can be an important income stream for these businesses because the variable cost tends to be low—for instance, the cost of cleaning a hotel room or putting one more passenger on an airplane. Therefore, most of the revenue can help cover fixed costs and generate profits.

The automobile industry has a different motive for bundling. People buy cars only every three to five years. Thus, selling options is a somewhat rare opportunity for the car dealer. Price bundling can help the dealer sell a maximum number of options.

Bundling has also been used in the telecommunications industry. Companies offer local service, long distance, DSL Internet service, wireless, and even cable TV in various menus of bundling. Such bundling is not necessarily consumer focused. Telecom companies use bundling as a way to protect their market share and fight off competition by locking customers into a group of services. For consumers, comparison shopping may be difficult since they may not be able to determine how much they are really paying for each component of the bundle.

A related price tactic is **unbundling**, or reducing the bundle of services that comes with the basic product. Rather than raise the price of hotel rooms, some hotel chains have started charging registered guests for parking. To help hold the line on costs, some stores require customers to pay for gift wrapping.

Clearly, price bundling—for example, a theater series pass or a vacation package that combines airfare, lodging, and meals—can influence consumers' purchase

Marketing... in Entertainment

Theme Parks Face Tough Times

Amusement parks around the country are facing a pricing crisis. Over the years, parks have raised admission prices each year, but they are now finding themselves at a pricing limit. For example, over the past seven years, Cedar Point in Sandusky, Ohio, has raised the price of admission a total of $15, or 50 percent, to $44. But this year, the park has chosen to hold prices steady and eliminate some discount options rather than lose potential visitors. This, according to the retired general manager of Legoland California, is because people no longer want a $50 experience buffet. People have less time and are increasingly reluctant to pay an elevated flat entrance fee when they will not be able to spend the entire day at the park. Parks are hitting the upper limits of what people will pay, and when people perceive decreasing value for what they are spending, the result is price resistance. In response, some parks are considering alternative pay-as-you-go pricing strategies, or variable, modular pricing. Such à la carte pricing might actually take the industry back to the strategies it used when it began, like the coupon books that Walt Disney parks used until the early 1980s.[20]

price bundling
Marketing two or more products in a single package for a special price.

unbundling
Reducing the bundle of services that comes with the basic product.

one payment, one benefit), the costs and benefits of that transaction are tightly coupled, resulting in strong sunk cost pressure to consume the pending benefit. In other words, "I bought this ticket, now I've got to use it."

In practice, these findings mean that a theater manager might expect a no-show rate of 20 percent when the percentage of season ticket holders is high, but a no-show rate of only 5 percent when the percentage of season ticket holders is low. With a high number of season ticket holders, a manager could oversell performances and maximize the revenue for the theater. Airlines routinely overbook in anticipation of a predictable percentage of no-shows.

The physical format of the transaction also figures in. A ski lift pass in the form of a booklet of tickets strengthens the cost-benefit link for consumers, whereas a single pass for multiple ski lifts weakens that link. Thus, the skier with a booklet of tickets is likely to use the ski lift more often than the skier who has just one pass, even though both paid the same amount at the outset.

Though price bundling of services can result in a lower rate of total consumption of that service, the same is not necessarily true for products. Consider the purchase of an expensive bottle of wine, which can be inventoried until needed. When the wine is purchased as a single unit, its cost and eventual benefit are tightly coupled. As a result, the cost of the wine will be quite important, and a person will likely reserve that wine for a special occasion. When purchased as part of a bundle (e.g., as part of a case of wine), however, the cost and benefit of that individual bottle of wine will likely become decoupled, reducing the impact of the cost on eventual consumption. As a result, a person will likely find the wine appropriate for many more (not-so-special) occasions. Thus, in contrast to the price bundling of services, the price bundling of physical goods could lead to an increase in product consumption.

AP/WIDE WORLD PHOTOS

In order to maximize revenue, managers could oversell tickets to an event for which season ticket subscriptions are high. This is because people who buy season tickets for an event, like these students from the University of Mississippi, holding their just-purchased season basketball tickets, are less likely to use all the tickets they purchase.

Two-Part Pricing

Two-part pricing means establishing two separate charges to consume a single good or service. Tennis clubs and health clubs charge a membership fee and a flat fee each time a person uses certain equipment or facilities. In other cases they charge a base rate for a certain level of usage, such as ten racquetball games per month, and a surcharge for anything over that amount.

Consumers sometimes prefer two-part pricing because they are uncertain about the number and the types of activities they might use at places like an amusement park. Also, the people who use a service most often pay a higher total price. Two-part pricing can increase a seller's revenue by attracting consumers who would not pay a high fee even for unlimited use. For example, a health club might be able to sell only 100 memberships at $700 annually with unlimited use of facilities, for total revenue of $70,000. However, perhaps it could sell 900 memberships at $200 with a guarantee of using the racquetball courts ten times a month. Every use over ten would require the member to pay a $5 fee. Thus, membership revenue would provide a base of $180,000, with some additional usage fees coming in throughout the year.

two-part pricing
A price tactic that charges two separate amounts to consume a single good or service.

consumer penalty
An extra fee paid by the consumer for violating the terms of the purchase agreement.

Princess Cruises
Carnival Cruises

How up-front are companies about their pricing penalties? Compare what you find out at Princess Cruises' Web page (type "penalties" into the search box) with what you find on Carnival Cruises' page. From a marketing standpoint, do you think it is better to hide penalties in the fine print or to clearly let the customer know in advance?

http://www.princesscruises.com
http://www.carnival.com

Online

CONSUMER PENALTIES

More and more businesses are adopting **consumer penalties**—extra fees paid by consumers for violating the terms of a purchase agreement (see Exhibit 18.2).

EXHIBIT 18.2

Common Consumer Penalties

1. Airlines
- Some airlines charge a penalty of $100 for changing reservations on discount tickets.

2. Automobiles
- Penalties are imposed for early terminations of car leases. In some cases, deposits on canceled leases can be subject to penalties.
- Car owners in England pay penalties, administration fees, and commissions if they cancel an insurance policy early.

3. Banks
- Penalties are often associated with early withdrawal of certificates of deposit.
- Some banks charge penalties for too many withdrawals in a month.
- Some have monthly penalties of $5 to $10 if a client's balance falls below a minimum level.
- Banks can charge late fees, in addition to interest, for tardy payments.

4. Car Rentals
- Rental companies often have $25 to $100 penalties for no-shows for specialty vehicles. Budget, National, and Dollar/Thrifty are experimenting with no-show fees on all rentals.

5. Child Day Care
- Many day-care centers charge a penalty of up to $5 a minute when parents are late in picking up their children.

6. Cellular Phones
- Companies have cancellation penalties, often in the small print on the back of a contract, that can run as high as $525.

7. Credit and Debit Cards
- Some vendors now charge late fees (beyond normal interest). Lenders collect about $2 billion in late charges each year.
- GE Rewards MasterCard charges $25 a year for those who pay their bill each month, in full, on time. Advanta credit card company may charge $25 for six-month inactivity on an account and $25 to close an account.

8. Cruises
- If a cruise is sailing, even though there are hurricane warnings, some cruise lines will assess penalties if a passenger cancels.
- Even trip cancellation insurance will not ensure a refund if the traveler has embarked on the trip.
- Britain is trying to crack down on executive cancellation penalties on package holidays.
- The *Carnival Paradise* will disembark passengers found smoking.

9. Hotels
- Some hotels require 72 hours' cancellation notice, or the client must pay a penalty of one day's room cost.
- Most hotels have high charges for using in-room long-distance service.
- Hilton, Hyatt, and Westin have early departure fees ranging from $25 to $50.

10. Restaurants
- Some now charge up to $50 per person for no-show parties.

11. Retail Stores
- Circuit City and Best Buy are leading others in charging a 15 percent restocking fee on some items. A restocking fee is for putting a returned item back in inventory.

12. Trains
- Amtrak has a $20 penalty for a returned ticket and charges the same fee for changing a ticket.

13. Universities
- Universities will give only a partial tuition refund if a student becomes ill after a course begins.

SOURCE: Eugene Fram and Michael McCarthy, "The True Price of Penalties," *Marketing Management,* Fall 1999, 51.

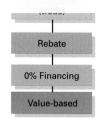

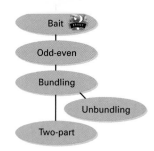

Rebate

0% Financing

Value-based

Freight absorption

Basing-point

Bait

Odd-even

Bundling

Unbundling

Two-part

may affect some consumers' willingness to patronize a business in the future.

Discuss product line pricing

4   PRODUCT LINE PRICING

Product line pricing is setting prices for an entire line of products. Compared to setting the right price on a single product, product line pricing encompasses broader concerns. In product line pricing, the marketing manager tries to achieve maximum profits or other goals for the entire line rather than for a single component of the line.

RELATIONSHIPS AMONG PRODUCTS

The manager must first determine the type of relationship that exists among the various products in the line:

- If items are *complementary*, an increase in the sale of one good causes an increase in demand for the complementary product, and vice versa. For example, the sale of ski poles depends on the demand for skis, making these two items complementary.
- Two products in a line can also be *substitutes* for each other. If buyers buy one item in the line, they are less likely to buy a second item in the line. For example, if someone goes to an automotive supply store and buys paste Turtle Wax for a car, it is very unlikely that he or she will buy liquid Turtle Wax in the near future.
- A *neutral* relationship can also exist between two products. In other words, demand for one of the products is unrelated to demand for the other. For instance, Ralston Purina sells chicken feed and Wheat Chex, but the sale of one of these products has no known impact on demand for the other.

JOINT COSTS

Joint costs are costs that are shared in the manufacturing and marketing of several products in a product line. These costs pose a unique problem in product pricing.

product line pricing
Setting prices for an entire line of products.

joint costs
Costs that are shared in the manufacturing and marketing of several products in a product line.

In oil refining, for example, fuel oil, gasoline, kerosene, naphtha, paraffin, and lubricating oils are all derived from a common production process. Another example is the production of compact discs that combine photos and music.

Any assignment of joint costs must be somewhat subjective because costs are actually shared. Suppose a company produces two products, X and Y, in a common production process, with joint costs allocated on a weight basis. Product X weighs 1,000 pounds, and product Y weighs 500 pounds. Thus, costs are allocated on the basis of $2 for X for every $1 for Y. Gross margins (sales less the cost of goods sold) might then be as follows:

	Product X	Product Y	Total
Sales	$20,000	$6,000	$26,000
Less: cost of goods sold	15,000	7,500	22,500
Gross margin	$ 5,000	($1,500)	$ 3,500

This statement reveals a loss of $1,500 on product Y. Is that important? Yes, any loss is important. However, the firm must realize that overall it earned a $3,500 profit on the two items in the line. Also, weight may not be the right way to allocate the joint costs. Instead, the firm might use other bases, including market value or quantity sold.

REVIEW LEARNING OBJECTIVE 4

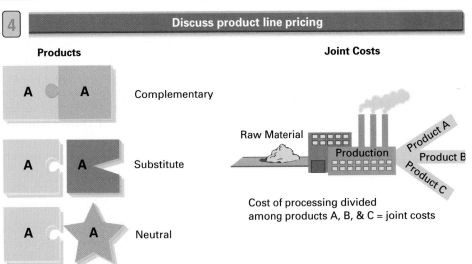

5 PRICING DURING DIFFICULT ECONOMIC TIMES

Describe the role of pricing during periods of inflation and recession

Pricing is always an important aspect of marketing, but it is especially crucial in times of inflation and recession. The firm that does not adjust to economic trends may lose ground that it can never make up.

INFLATION

When the economy is characterized by high inflation, special pricing tactics are often necessary. They can be subdivided into cost-oriented and demand-oriented tactics.

Cost-Oriented Tactics

One popular cost-oriented tactic is *culling products with a low profit margin* from the product line. However, this tactic may backfire for three reasons:

however. Often it is used only for extremely complex products that take a long time to produce or with new customers.

Any cost-oriented pricing policy that tries to maintain a fixed gross margin under all conditions can lead to a vicious circle. For example, a price increase will result in decreased demand, which in turn increases production costs (because of lost economies of scale). Increased production costs require a further price increase, leading to further diminished demand, and so on.

Demand-Oriented Tactics

Demand-oriented pricing tactics use price to reflect changing patterns of demand caused by inflation or high interest rates. Cost changes are considered, of course, but mostly in the context of how increased prices will affect demand.

Price shading is the use of discounts by salespeople to increase demand for one or more products in a line. Often shading becomes habitual and is done routinely without much forethought. Ducommun, a metals producer, is among the major companies that have succeeded in eliminating the practice. Ducommun has told its salespeople, "We want no deviation from book price" unless authorized by management.

To make the demand for a good or service more inelastic and to create buyer dependency, a company can use several strategies:

- *Cultivate selected demand:* Marketing managers can target prosperous customers who will pay extra for convenience or service. Neiman Marcus, for example, stresses quality. As a result, the luxury retailer is more lenient with suppliers and their price increases than is Dollar's Stores, a discounter. In cultivating close relationships with affluent organizational customers, marketing managers should avoid putting themselves at the mercy of a dominant firm. They can more easily raise prices when an account is readily replaceable. Finally, in companies where engineers exert more influence than purchasing departments do, performance is favored over price. Often a preferred vendor's pricing range expands if other suppliers prove technically unsatisfactory.
- *Create unique offerings:* Marketing managers should study buyers' needs. If the seller can design distinctive goods or services uniquely fitting buyers' activities, equipment, and procedures, a mutually beneficial relationship will evolve. Buyers would incur high changeover costs in switching to another supplier. By satisfying targeted buyers in a superior way, marketing managers can make them dependent. Cereal manufacturers have skirted around passing on costs by marketing unique value-added or multi-ingredient cereals, increasing the per-

delayed-quotation pricing
A price tactic used for industrial installations and many accessory items, in which a firm price is not set until the item is either finished or delivered.

escalator pricing
A price tactic in which the final selling price reflects cost increases incurred between the time the order is placed and the time delivery is made.

price shading
The use of discounts by salespeople to increase demand for one or more products in a line.

Kellogg is no stranger to creating unique offerings to stimulate demand. It has extended many of its brands by creating cereal bars based on popular boxed cereals, and it has created new, boxed cereals designed to appeal to a variety of markets. One new cereal is Smorz. In order to create demand for Smorz, Kellogg hosted a summer kick-off even with one hundred third-graders, who participated in a Smores-making contest.

Although Wendy's launched its Super Value menu during the recession of the early 1990s, it took competitors nearly a decade to respond to Wendy's successful price strategy. McDonald's and Burger King also now have low-cost menus, and all three fast-food chains have retained these menus through economic recoveries and boom times.

ceived quality of cereals and allowing companies to raise prices. These cereals include General Mills' Basic 4, Clusters, and Oatmeal Crisp; Post's Banana Nut Crunch and Blueberry Morning; and Kellogg's Mueslix, Nutri-Grain, and Temptations.

- *Change the package design:* Another way companies pass on higher costs is to shrink product sizes but keep prices the same. Scott Paper Company reduced the number of sheets in the smallest roll of Scott Clean paper towels from 96 to 60 and actually lowered the price by 10 cents a roll. The increases in costs for paper towels were tied to a 50 to 60 percent increase in the cost of pulp paper. The company also changed the names of the sizes to de-emphasize the magnitude of the rolls.
- *Heighten buyer dependence:* Owens-Corning Fiberglass supplies an integrated insulation service (from feasibility studies to installation) that includes commercial and scientific training for distributors and seminars for end users. This practice freezes out competition and supports higher prices.

RECESSION

A recession is a period of reduced economic activity. Reduced demand for goods and services, along with higher rates of unemployment, is a common trait of a recession. Yet astute marketers can often find opportunity during recessions. A recession is an excellent time to build market share because competitors are struggling to make ends meet.

Two effective pricing tactics to hold or build market share during a recession are value-based pricing and bundling. *Value-based pricing*, discussed earlier in the chapter, stresses to customers that they are getting a good value for their money. Charles of the Ritz, usually known for its pricey products, introduced the Express Bar during a recession. A collection of affordable cosmetics and skin treatment products, the Express Bar sold alongside regular Ritz products in department stores. Although lower priced products offer lower profit margins, Ritz found that increases in volume can offset slimmer margins. For example, the company found that consumers will buy two or three Express Bar lipsticks at a time.

Bundling or *unbundling* can also stimulate demand during a recession. If features are added to a bundle, consumers may perceive the offering as having greater value. For example, suppose that Hyatt offers a "great escape" weekend for $119. The package includes two nights' lodging and a continental breakfast. Hyatt could add a massage and a dinner for two to create more value for this price. Conversely, companies can unbundle offerings and lower base prices to stimulate demand. A furniture store, for example, could start charging separately for design consultation, delivery, credit, setup, and hauling away old furniture.

Recessions are a good time for marketing managers to study the demand for individual items in a product line and the revenue they produce. Pruning unprofitable items can save resources to be better used

5 | **Describe the role of pricing during periods of inflation and recession**

prices 10 percent or risk losing GE's business. Honeywell, Dow Chemical, General Motors, and DuPont made similar demands of their suppliers. Specific strategies that companies use with suppliers include the following:

- *Renegotiating contracts:* Sending suppliers letters demanding price cuts of 5 percent or more; putting out for rebid the contracts of those that refuse to cut costs.
- *Offering help:* Dispatching teams of experts to suppliers' plants to help reorganize and suggest other productivity-boosting changes; working with suppliers to make parts simpler and cheaper to produce.
- *Keeping the pressure on:* To make sure that improvements continue, setting annual, across-the-board cost reduction targets, often of 5 percent or more a year.
- *Paring down suppliers:* To improve economies of scale, slashing the overall number of suppliers, sometimes by up to 80 percent, and boosting purchases from those that remain.

Tough tactics like these help keep companies afloat during economic downturns.

Porsche, as described at the beginning of the chapter, is using a skimming price strategy. The company can fine-tune the base price with discounts, rebates, odd-even pricing, bundling, FOB pricing, or other geographic pricing tactics. Porsche can offer several discounts including cash and seasonal discounts. While all of these are available to Porsche, it is likely that it will use few, if any, of the above. This is because Porsche's CEO is strongly opposed to any form of discounting. He believes that discounting cheapens the Porsche image.

USE IT NOW

PARTICIPATING IN CLINICAL TRIALS

Some of the best medical care in the country is free. The price is unbeatable. Doctors and researchers around the country are providing free stop-smoking and weight-loss programs, physicals, vitamins, and even yoga and massage therapy. The giveaways are available through a variety of clinical research studies that focus on preventing disease or treating everyday health problems.

The range of benefits on offer may come as a surprise, given the common belief that clinical trials are for desperate patients seeking experimental therapies. But clinical trials represent a remarkable opportunity for the rest of us to gain access to top doctors and care that might not otherwise be available.

Not only do doctors doing clinical research pay fastidious attention to every complaint and comment of the study subject, but they also often conduct comprehensive health screenings with far more follow-up than many patients get from their family physicians. To be sure, any student thinking about taking part in a clinical trial needs to assess the risk of the study and the credibility of the researchers involved. Participants in trials should be given detailed informed-consent statements and have the opportunity to ask as many questions as they like. Credible research studies are conducted in obvious health-care or university settings. Any trial that uses experimental treatments or drugs or seems to carry even a minimal risk should be examined carefully by a trusted health professional who doesn't have a personal stake in the research.

Clinical trials aren't a substitute for regular medical care, and they don't solve the problems of people who don't have health insurance. "People have access to health care at no cost to them, but it's finite," says Diana Anderson, chairwoman of the Association of Clinical Research Professionals.

Another downside is that patients who sign up for clinical research may end up in the control group, meaning they get the basic health evaluation and access to top doctors, but they won't always get all the perks of the trial. In addition, clinical trials may also require a bigger time commitment than traditional care so that researchers can get answers to all their questions.

The best way to find a clinical trial is through your own doctor, particularly those who are affiliated with medical schools and teaching hospitals. Ask your doctor if he or she knows of any research studies on a particular health topic or simply mention that you're open to the idea of taking part in clinical research. Some studies are advertised in newspapers and on the radio.

If you're interested in a particular type of study—for instance smoking cessation or weight loss—a few clicks on the Internet may turn up dozens of opportunities. The National Institutes of Health sponsors **http://www.clinicaltrials.gov**, which lists NIH-funded trials around the country. Another site, **http://www.centerwatch.com**, is a clearinghouse for both public and privately funded health studies.[24]

USING COUPONS

You can also save some money by using coupons. Whether you're shopping online or heading to the mall, make a pit stop at UltimateCoupons.com. The site features coupons from more than a hundred major retailers (mostly on the Web) in categories such as groceries and electronics. It also searches through offers on other coupon Web sites, so you'll get the best deals. One recent bargain: Save $10 when you spend $75 or more at Amazon.com. Printable coupons are available for brick-and-mortar stores; discount codes are provided for orders at e-tailers. For online coupons, go to **http://www.smartsource.com**, **http://www.hotcoupons.com**, **http://www.VAlPAK.com**, or **http://www.coolsavings.com**. Excellent deals that change daily are available at **http://www.slickdeals.net**.

Compare prices before you buy. Rely on price comparison services like My Simon (**http://www.mysimon.com**) or Price Scan (**http://www.pricescan.com**). Perhaps the best is **http://froogle.google.com**.

just charge what my competitors charge. I'm happy because I'm making money." React to Janet's statement.

1.3   What is the difference between a price policy and a price tactic? Give an example.

2   **Identify the legal and ethical constraints on pricing decisions.** Government regulation helps monitor four major areas of pricing: unfair trade practices, price fixing, predatory pricing, and price discrimination. Many states have enacted unfair trade practice acts that protect small businesses from large firms that operate efficiently on extremely thin profit margins; the acts prohibit charging below-cost prices. The Sherman Act and the Federal Trade Commission Act prohibit both price fixing, which is an agreement between two or more firms on a particular price, and predatory pricing, in which a firm undercuts its competitors with extremely low prices to drive them out of business. Finally, the Robinson-Patman Act makes it illegal for firms to discriminate between two or more buyers in terms of price.

2.1   INFOTRAC COLLEGE EDITION   What kind of factors can push a respectable firm to enter a price-fixing arrangement with a competitor? Using InfoTrac (**http://www.infotrac-college.com**), read about the price-fixing scandals that rocked the art auction industry or the Hollywood movie studios and Blockbuster Video. If there are more current scandals, read a selection of articles on a particular industry. Then compile a list of business practices and pricing issues that are present in the reports of each scandal. Is each scandal unique, or are there overlapping characteristics? What conclusion can you draw about price fixing from the articles you read? How does the federal government deal with price fixing?

3   **Explain how discounts, geographic pricing, and other pricing tactics can be used to fine-tune the base price.** Several techniques enable marketing managers to adjust prices within a general range in response to changes in competition, government regulation, consumer demand, and promotional and positioning goals. Techniques for fine-tuning a price can be divided into three main categories: discounts, allowances, rebates, and value-based pricing; geographic pricing; and other pricing tactics.

The first type of tactic gives lower prices to those that pay promptly, order a large quantity, or perform some function for the manufacturer. Value-based pricing starts with the customer, considers the competition and costs, and then determines a price. Additional tactics in this category include seasonal discounts, promotion allowances, and rebates (cash refunds).

Geographic pricing tactics—such as FOB origin pricing, uniform delivered pricing, zone pricing, freight absorption pricing, and basing-point pricing—are ways of moderating the impact of shipping costs on distant customers.

A variety of "other" pricing tactics stimulate demand for certain products, increase store patronage, and offer more merchandise at specific prices.

More and more customers are paying price penalties, which are extra fees for violating the terms of a purchase contract. The perceived fairness or unfairness of a penalty may affect some consumers' willingness to patronize a business in the future.

3.1   You are contemplating a price change for an established product sold by your firm. Write a memo analyzing the factors you need to consider in your decision.

3.2   Columnist Dave Barry jokes that federal law requires this message under the sticker price of new cars: "Warning to stupid people: Do not pay this amount." Discuss why the sticker price is generally higher than the actual selling price of a car. Tell how you think car dealers set the actual prices of the cars they sell.

3.3   Divide into teams of four persons. Each team should choose one of the following topics: skimming, penetration pricing, status quo pricing, price fixing, geographic pricing, adopting a single-price tactic, flexible pricing, or professional services pricing. Each team should then pick a retailer that it feels most closely follows the team's chosen pricing strategy. Go to the store and write down examples of the strategy. Interview the store manager and get his or her views on the advantages and disadvantages of the strategy. Each team should then make an oral report in class.

3.4   The U.S. Postal Service regularly raises the price of a first-class stamp but continues to operate in the red year after year. Is uniform delivered pricing the best choice for first-class mail? Explain your reasoning.

3.5   How is the "information age" changing the nature of pricing?

3.6   Have you ever paid a price penalty? How did it affect your attitude toward that company?

3.7   Imagine that you are a marketing manager for a mid-sized amusement park. You have attended an industry-wide meeting where a colleague gave a talk about new pricing strategies for amusement parks. You were very motivated by the seminar. Upon your return to work, write a memo to your boss outlining the pros and cons of the new pricing strategy. End your memo with a recommendation either for or against à la carte pricing of attractions. (You may want to reread in the "Marketing in Entertainment" box on amusement parks before you begin this exercise.)

4   **Discuss product line pricing.** Product line pricing maximizes profits for an entire product line. When setting product line prices, marketing managers determine what type of relationship exists among the products in the line: complementary, substitute, or neutral. Managers also consider joint (shared) costs among products in the same line.

4.1   Develop a price line strategy for each of these firms:

   a. a college bookstore

   b. a restaurant

   c. a video-rental firm

5   **Describe the role of pricing during periods of inflation and recession.** Marketing managers employ cost-oriented and demand-oriented tactics during periods of economic inflation. Cost-oriented tactics include dropping products with a low profit margin, delayed-quotation pricing, and escalator pricing. Demand-oriented pricing methods include price shading and increasing demand through cultivating selected customers, creating unique offerings, changing the package size, and heightening buyer dependence.

To stimulate demand during a recession, marketers use value-based pricing, bundling, and unbundling. Recessions are also a good time to prune unprofitable items from product lines. Managers strive to cut costs during recessions in order to maintain profits as revenues decline. Implementing new technology, cutting payrolls, and pressuring suppliers for reduced prices are common techniques used to cut costs. Companies also create new value-added products.

5.1   During a recession, what pricing strategies would you consider using to gain or maintain market share? Explain your answer.

EXERCISES

APPLICATION EXERCISE

You read in the chapter about the dangers of pricing products too low. It seems so obviously wrong, but do companies really price their products so low that they won't make any money? After all, companies are in business to make money, and if they don't, they're probably not in business for very long. Let's take a deeper look at the effects of pricing products too low or creating too deep discounts during sale periods.[25]

Activity

1. The average markup for a produce department is 28 percent on selling price. When sold at 28 percent markup on selling price, bananas usually account for 25 percent of department sales and 25 percent of department markup. This week, because bananas were on special sale at the retailer's cost, the department sold twice as many pounds of bananas as usual. However, they were sold at zero markup. If all other things remain the same, what is the average markup on selling price for the entire produce department this week?

ETHICS EXERCISE

People feel better when they think they are getting a great bargain when they shop. Knowing this, some retailers mark up items above the traditional retail price and then offer a 60 percent discount. If they had simply discounted the normal retail price by 20 percent the resulting "sale price" would have been the same. One retailer says that he is just making shoppers happy that they got a great deal when he inflates the retail price before discounting.

Questions

1. What do you think?

2. Does the AMA Code of Ethics address this issue? Go to **http://www.marketingpower.com** and review the code. Then, write a brief paragraph summarizing what the AMA Code of Ethics contains that relates to retail pricing.

CAREER EXERCISE

Recall from Chapter 17 that marketers in careers such as brand management, sales, marketing communications, and new-product development have a hand in pricing decisions made about their companies' products or services. To get more experience with pricing, do the activities below.

Activities

1. To get some experience with setting prices, offer to help a student group to which you belong set prices for fundraising activities. For example, you could help determine the pricing for the T-shirts sold to support a specific event or cause, for tickets to a function, or even for food and beverages at an event. Likewise, if you have the opportunity to help a friend or family member with a garage or yard sale, offer to help price the merchandise. You can experiment with different pricing strategies during the sale as you negotiate with potential buyers. Doing so will help you get a feel for the intricacies of setting prices.

2. To experiment with pricing, you can also pretend to sell your belongings. Imagine that you will be moving overseas at the end of the semester and will be able to take only one suitcase with you. You will need to "liquidate" your possessions. Think about your belongings. How much could you get for them? Could you offer some kind of price bundling, such as selling all of your stereo components as a unit? What about discounts close to the end of your sale? Be creative. Then write up a brief outline of your sales plan (products, prices, pricing strategies). If you do end up going abroad, or even cross-country, you may already have a plan in place!

ENTREPRENEURSHIP CASE

DISCONNECTING CABLE CHANNELS FROM PRICING BUNDLES

When people go shopping, the grocery store doesn't make them buy broccoli if they are buying milk. Why then do cable and satellite TV companies make people pay for channels they don't watch, for example, highly targeted channels like Home and Garden Television (HGTV), Spike, and ESPN? Congressional lawmakers are interested in the cable industry's answer to this question. Several lawmakers are pushing for legislation that would prevent the cable industry from forcing consumers to buy a prix fixe menu of channels and would require the industry instead to offer à la carte service, or individual channels, in lieu of traditional packages. And the idea is gaining popularity.

This idea, and complaints about cable television service and rising rates, emerged at a Senate subcommittee hearing where legislators pilloried the cable industry for being unresponsive to consumers. One senator went so far as to say that cable subscribers "are being force-fed channels and features they don't want," and encouraged the industry to give consumers a choice. Another warned, "Do something about your rising rates or you're going to have trouble." The senators aren't alone in their frustration. Bipartisan members of the Federal Communications Commission have also signaled support for more personalized cable options. The industry, however, insists that such options will end up costing consumers more.

Fueling the debate is the spiraling price of cable TV service. According to a recent General Accounting Office study, cable programming rates jumped at least 34 percent during a recent three-year period, far outpacing the general rate of inflation. The report attributed higher cable rates at least partially to billions of dollars of investments made by cable companies in original programming and upgraded technology. Cable companies are also paying more for sports programming; such fees rose 59 percent during the same period because of the higher prices being paid to sports teams and leagues to carry games.

Unbundling cable channels appeals to some consumers who hope it would lower monthly bills and give them more control over what their families are watching. Besides, the idea of paying for an individual channel isn't altogether new in the cable industry: plenty of consumers already pay extra for commercial-free channels such as HBO and Showtime. Proponents of the à la carte plan say most cable subscribers watch the same channels all the time, so why should they pay for all the others? "The average household watches no more than a dozen to 17

*As of February.
Source: Bureau of Labor Statistics.

distribution drop dramatically because of an a la carte system, the network would be making less money to put back into programming. Unbundling cable packages could have some serious unforeseen consequences.

"It could really destroy a business that is monumentally successful," adds Andy Heller, president of distribution for Time Warner's Turner Broadcasting, parent of TNT, the Cartoon Network, and CNN. He notes that the average monthly cable bill is less than the cost for a family of four to go to a baseball game nowadays.

Ironically, a cable operator in the New York City area tried to offer a channel on an à la carte basis but was not allowed to do so. An arbitration panel ruled against Cablevision Systems Corporation's effort to offer the New York sports channel YES individually to subscribers. YES challenged Cablevision's original decision not to bundle the channel with its basic service. The cable operator had said the YES channel, which carries Yankees games, was too costly.

Cable operators also say that selling channels separately presents technological problems. Only one-third of the country gets digital cable. The rest of the nation has older, analog systems in which it is more difficult to break down individual channel signals for each household. Given the technological costs of implementing an individualized system and the likelihood that fees would increase to make up for lost subscribers, subscribers could end up getting only a dozen or so channels for the same price they currently pay for a bundle.[26]

Questions

1. What other pricing strategies could cable operators use that would maintain their revenue stream and check the escalating price of cable service?

2. Is it legal for the government to intervene in industries whose prices outpace inflation? Is it appropriate?

3. What would happen to the cable industry if it was deregulated in the same way as the telecommunications industry?

4. Would you prefer an à la carte or a bundle pricing strategy for your cable service?

WATCH IT

SmallBusinessSchool
the Series on PBS stations and the Web

FEATURE PRESENTATION

Nicole Miller Fashion House

To give you insight into Chapter 18, Small Business School returns to New York City and the Nicole Miller Fashion House. Founders Bud Konheim and Nicole have devised a strategy to target the company's products toward a very specific market: Nicole and her designers create clothes and accessories for women who want to cultivate a stylish and youthful look, but who don't want to pay premium prices for high-end couture. Even though Bud and Nicole use a value pricing technique for their lines, Nicole's signature clothes and accessories have a unique, upscale appeal.

In order to best understand her customers, Nicole started offering her full line of fashions exclusively through Nicole Miller Boutiques. There are thirty Nicole Miller Boutiques in all, fifteen owned by Nicole Miller Company and fifteen owned by licensees. This distribution strategy has exposed the full range of Nicole's designs to potential customers, and it has given the brand the strength it needed to later stand alongside major fashion labels offered in luxury department stores like Neiman Marcus, Saks Fifth Avenue, and Nordstrom.

This is the same feature video as for Chapter 2, but when you watch this time, focus on what influences Konheim and Miller as they try to set the right price for their products.

What to Watch for and Ask Yourself

1 When Bud Konheim says, "We have runway shows just like everybody who charges 50 times the price. But, it's got to work for her the way she expects it," what is he talking about? Explain.

2 Who determines price for Nicole Miller fashions?

3 What is the customer's role in setting the right price?

ENCORE PRESENTATION

Fast Times at Ridgemont High

Review this chapter's discussion of setting the right price and then watch the scene from *Fast Times at Ridgemont High*. This iconic teen film is set at a southern California high school. This scene comes from "The Dudes" sequence early in the film. Mike Damone (Robert Romanus) has some Van Halen concert tickets for sale. Does Mike follow the steps for setting a price described earlier in this chapter? For example, does he have a pricing goal or a price strategy? If *yes*, what are they? This chapter emphasizes the importance of legal and ethical issues in price strategy. Does either of these issues apply to the behavior shown in the scene? Review the section "Special Pricing Tactics" earlier in this chapter. Did Mike use any of the tactics?

STILL SHAKY?

If you're having trouble with the concepts in this chapter, consider using some of the following study resources. You can review the videos, or test yourself with materials designed for all kinds of learning styles.

☑ **Xtra! (http://lambxtra.swlearning.com)**

| ☑ Quiz | ☑ Feature Videos | ☑ Encore Videos | ☑ FAQ Videos |
| ☑ Exhibit Worksheets | ☑ Marketing Plan Worksheets | ☐ Content | |

☑ **http://lamb.swlearning.com**

| ☑ Quiz | ☑ PowerPoint slides | ☑ Marketing News | ☑ Review Exercises |
| ☑ Links | ☑ Marketing Plan Contest | ☐ Career Exercise | ☑ Use It Now |

☑ **Study guide**

| ☑ Outline | ☑ Vocab Review | ☑ Test Questions | ☑ Marketing Scenario |

Need More? Here's a tip. Chapter 18 is a good place to revisit study tips from Chapters 5, 7, and 12 (pages 194, 263, and 433). Try to find additional examples for each pricing technique described in the chapter.

drawn to southern California, the theme parks then compete with each other and with other Southern attractions (beaches, Hollywood) for visitors. Popular theme park destinations in southern California include Disneyland, Six Flags, SeaWorld, Universal Studios, and Knott's Berry Farm.

Historically, theme parks have used new rides or attractions as the major competitive weapon. The assumption is that visitors choosing between two parks will select the park with the newest attractions. Thus, theme parks in southern California constantly update their product offerings, with most having a goal of opening one new attraction every year. Consistent with this goal, Knott's Berry Farm, which is owned by Cedar Fair and located in Buena Park, California, has opened both new rides and new parks. Newer rides include GhostRider[SM], the longest and highest-rated wooden roller coaster in the western United States; Supreme Scream[SM], the world's tallest descending thrill ride; and Edison International Electric Nights[SM], a nighttime laser extravaganza. In 2004, Silver Bullet, a world-class inverted roller coaster, is the newest ride at Knott's Berry Farm. Costing $16 million, the Silver Bullet is the park's seventh coaster. One of the newest parks at Knott's Berry Farm is Soak City U.S.A. The 13-acre water park has more than 20 separate water rides that cater to families and preteens.

Southern California theme park pricing has tended to be in the $30–$40 range for children and $40–$50 range for adults. Six Flags had the highest posted children's gate ad-

the discount price that had been offered during the park's summer co-promotions with local supermarkets. A spokesperson for the park said that the new price would not pose a revenue risk for Knott's Berry Farm because most children were admitted at a discount anyway. The park did not change to its adult admission price of $43.

Knott's Berry Farm finished 2003 with attendance of 3.5 million, down 4 percent from the previous year. Competing theme parks in southern California had the following attendance figures for 2003: Disneyland, 12.7 million (flat); Universal Studios, 4.5 million (down 12 percent); SeaWorld, 4 million (flat); and Six Flags, 3 million (down 2 percent). With decreased tourism and stagnant attendance at theme parks, is Knott's Berry Farm instigating a price war in its local market? The park already had the lowest gate admission price in the area and still experienced a drop in attendance. What signal has its dramatically decreased price sent to local consumers?[1]

Questions

1. What non-theme park companies offer an "everyday low price"?

2. How will this everyday low price affect Knott's Berry Farm's break-even point?

CRITICAL THINKING CASE

Apple Bites Into Online Music Sales

Based in Cupertino, California, Apple has been at the forefront in innovative computer design. The company ignited the computer revolution in the 1970s with the Apple II and then reenergized the personal computer market in the 1980s with the Macintosh. Now, in the twenty-first century, Apple is emerging as a leading innovator in the music industry with its iTunes music store.

Like most Apple product launches, iTunes was rolled out in spectacular fashion. Taking the stage at San Francisco's Moscone Center to the sound of David Bowie's "Changes," Apple CEO Steve Jobs announced the iTunes music store, along with improvements to the company's iTunes software and iPod personal music player. Apple has managed to fashion a near-perfect retail outlet on the Web, clearly taking cues from Amazon and, more subtly, from Starbucks, Crate & Barrel, and a few other vanguard retailers. A multimillion dollar television advertising campaign followed the iTunes store launch. Chiat-Day created ads that featured unknowns warbling hit songs while listening to their iPods with the tag line, "Your favorite songs. 99 cents."

iTunes does what Napster and Kazaa were unable to do: legally distribute music electronically. After numerous meetings with over 150 music label executives, Jobs assembled a database of around 250,000 songs from all five major record labels, including some artists who had previously resisted online distribution, such as Eminem, U2, and the Eagles. Music lovers can easily search iTunes' broad catalog of songs and then listen to a 30-second clip before deciding whether to buy the track. On average, people listen to about ten sample clips before buying a single track. After making a selection (or selections), a customer can download singles—or entire albums—at the price of 99 cents per track with no subscription fee, and the cover art is included. Once downloaded, the AAC file format song is automatically stored in the iTunes library on the customer's Macintosh computer. Purchased tracks are the permanent property of the customer. They can be shared among as many as three other Macs, transferred onto an Ipod, or burned to CD. The only restriction is that each playlist can be burned no more than ten times.

Initially, only users of Apple's Mas OS X operating system could shop at the store. Even with the small (some would say minuscule) market, iTunes sold over 5 million songs in its first eight weeks, and over 80 percent of the songs in the database were purchased at least once. Surprisingly, 45 percent of all songs are purchased as part of an album, not as single tracks. The initial success of iTunes signals the likelihood of a shootout over the real money—the much bigger Microsoft-driven PC market. As existing and upstart competitors begin to capitalize on Apple's success, a floodgate could open for new sales, as thousands of previously unavailable songs go on-line legally.

Despite the healthy start, industry analysts are concerned about the 99-cent price. Major labels are charging Apple approximately 70 cents per download, so launching at a lower price is not a viable option. Considering the other costs associated with individual transactions, not to mention maintaining the site, Apple is making only cents on the dollar from iTunes.

Questions

1. Will iTunes change the way major record labels promote their music? How?
2. How does the supply and demand relationship work in Apple's iTune model?
3. What is Apple's pricing strategy with iTunes? How can it fine-tune its base price of 99 cents per song?

company.

2. How is activity-based costing more market oriented than traditional accounting methods?

Traditional accounting methods do not make it easy to track marketing costs. Thus, the floor on price is determined by manufacturing's variable costs. Activity-based costing focuses upon *all* costs related to bringing a product to market; thus, it allows marketers to more accurately utilize cost as the floor in the pricing process for individual customers. For example, activity-based costing would include travel time to visit a customer as a customer-related cost, which would be reflected in the pricing for that particular customer.

ramifications. If a retailer purchases more of the product than can be sold during the promotion, normal shipments to the retailer will be reduced until the retailers inventory is back to normal levels. The manufacturing group often finds itself struggling to maintain stability in its production processes.

Suggested Readings

Pascal Courty, "An Economic Guide to Ticket Pricing in the Entertainment Industry," *Louvain Economic Review* 66, no. 1 (2000): 167–192.

Thomas Nagle and Reed Holden, *The Strategy and Tactics of Pricing: A Guide to Profitable Decision Making*, 3d ed. (Upper Saddle River, NJ: Prentice Hall, 2002).

PART 7

Technology-Driven Marketing

ness Systems, Inc. to discover why some callers buy tickets and others do not. Internet provider EarthLink, Inc. uses call-monitoring software from Nice Systems to better understand both its satisfied and its dissatisfied customers. Some industry experts predict that call-monitoring software will replace focus groups in the future.

In the same fashion, online gaming companies obtain customer information when users subscribe to online gaming services. By utilizing this demographic information, along with usage data, a company can better profile its current customers and predict a customer's next level of gaming. Since the installation of online gaming software utilizes online registration, a wealth of customer information can be assembled.

To help companies gather current and future customer information, ePrize has produced decoder technology that businesses can use to drive customers to their Web sites. To learn more about its customers, the Michigan International Speedway used the decoder, whose message is descrambled online, to learn more about its customers via an online contest. The decoders were distributed at retail sponsorship outlets and an amusement park complex. More than one-fourth of the initial one million decoder recipients provided preference information on the Speedway's contest Web site as part of the company's online contest. The decoder technology allows for a powerful combination of marketing and technology—a combination that facilitates the marketer's quest for customer information.

Without a doubt, today's marketers are expected to respond quickly to customer demands, and technology has enabled this rapid response. Entertainment service facilitators like Priceline.com and Amazon.com have been able to meet consumers' demands for immediate service and need fulfillment and, in doing so, have transformed industries. By bringing the pricing process into the consumer's home, Priceline has changed the way customers think about travel-related purchases. Amazon was one of the first

that keeps customers returning to these companies as loyal and repeat users.

Understanding the marketplace and responding to marketplace demands require internal technological linkages unheard of only a few decades ago. Today, advances in computer technology link marketing and its functional counterparts, making it possible for all functions to have access to the same valuable market information. While the benefits of networking functional departments, customers, and suppliers are vast, the process of bringing all of these groups together has not been without problems.

Internet marketing is leading to vast changes in the way all functional areas do business. Probably one of the major points of contention within an organization has been the necessary interaction between marketing and the information technology group. Information technologists generally have backgrounds in areas such as computer science, mathematics, and engineering, which put little emphasis on interactions with customers. Nonetheless, these same information technologists may now be charged with developing the company's Web site.

Traditionally, the marketing group was in charge of developing the marketing communications program that reached the potential customer. Now, the nature of a firm's marketing communications has changed dramatically. Today, a Web site may be the customer's first and only contact with a company. What was once a brochure or print ad is now on the consumer's computer screen. The responsibility for the actual development and functional capabilities of a company's Web site, a major element of the firm's marketing communications program, is in the hands of information technology experts.

Companies often refer to marketers as the site/content *strategists* and information technologists as the site/content *implementers*. Unfortunately, the separation into strategy and implementation has tended to exacerbate the conflict between marketing and information technology. The information technologists do not like "taking orders" from marketers about something that comes under their purview of computer expertise. Likewise, marketers fear that letting information technologists build the Web site will result in a site that is too technologically advanced and not visually appealing to the average customer.

Not only must technologists and marketers work together in developing a company's Web page, but the legal department must also be intimately involved in the process. Domain registration (similar to trademarks and trade names), intellectual property rights, hidden language (called metatext), taxation, and privacy policies are all areas in which legal assistance is of utmost importance. The marketing and information technology departments have to develop legally and ethically appropriate material that will also be interesting and easy to navigate. Having a cyberlaw expert working in tandem with marketing and information technology is extremely important.

Once the marketers and information technologists have gotten past their functional biases and the lawyers have determined that the Web site is legally and ethically appropriate, doing business on the Internet begins to highlight necessary interactions between marketing and other business functions. For example, fulfilling customer requests for technical support electronically can dramatically improve customer satisfaction. Technicians are able to respond much more quickly to requests, bringing positive results to marketing in the form of satisfied customers and to engineering in that the number of engineers needed for product support is reduced. Customers, however, now expect 24/7 service and want to receive responses to e-mail inquiries within six hours. Thus, technicians and support providers have begun suggesting that marketers are creating unreasonable expectations among customers.

Marketing direct to the consumer also provides manufacturing rewards. Network capabilities and/or personal digital assistants can lead to little or no inventory requirements. When a consumer places an order, advanced technological capabilities enable suppliers to receive electronic messages indicating the raw materials that will be needed to satisfy the customer's product demands. Raw materials can be shipped directly to the manufacturing facility. The manufacturing facility, having received the order transmission at the same time as its suppliers, will begin production immediately upon receipt of the necessary supplies. Marketing on the Net also allows customers to receive their orders more quickly. No longer does the order have to work its way through various steps before finally reaching the production people. Electronic order taking transmits the customer's order directly to the order fulfillment center, highlighting the need for close relations with the logistics and transportation people.

E-commerce does entail considerable start-up costs, however. For example, the firm's security expenses increase when it becomes involved in Internet marketing. Additionally, the initial financial investment for marketing on the Internet can be very high, and customer relationship management (CRM) database systems can be expensive. Like many marketing initiatives, technology is treated by many companies as a cost center rather than an investment. This tends to create tension among marketing, information technologists, and accountants.

Technology is changing the way we market our products. It is also expected to have long-term implications for a company's organizational structure and management processes. Changes in the way consumers interact with companies will no doubt lead to greater challenges in cross-functional coordination.

Questions

1. How has today's technology altered the role of marketing both internally and externally?

2. What are some of the benefits of networking functional departments, customers, and suppliers?

3. Which functional areas are actively involved in making e-commerce a success? How?

Internet Marketing

LEARNING OBJECTIVES

1 Explain how the Internet affects the traditional marketing mix

2 Describe how marketers are leveraging the power of online technology

3 Discuss the legal and privacy issues surrounding Internet-based commerce

4 Name the critical factors marketers face when measuring online success

5 Discuss the effects of the Internet on marketing objectives and strategy

LOOKING FORWARD

Find the whole chapter online at
http://lamb.swlearning.com

Customer Relationship Management (CRM)

LEARNING OBJECTIVES

1 Define customer relationship management

2 Explain how to identify customer relationships with the organization

3 Understand interactions with the current customer base

4 Outline the process of capturing customer data

5 Describe the use of technology to store and integrate customer data

6 Describe how to identify the best customers

7 Explain the process of leveraging customer information throughout the organization

LOOKING FORWARD

The music industry claims that consumers downloading free music caused it to lose $3.5 billion in recent years. In response, industry executives sued the free online file-sharing networks such as Napster. But subsequent lawsuits against Morpheus and Grokster were not successful because they only provide software and do not store shared tracks (as Napster did). The recording industry then began suing individuals, but this tactic also presented a problem—these individuals were also the industry's customers.

Now, to capitalize on the gap between what the recording industry was offering and what consumers were seeking, several companies have developed pay models that allow consumers to download individual songs for a nominal fee or subscribe to streaming music services. Among the leaders are Apple's iTunes Online Music Store, Listen.com's Rhapsody player, and Roxio's PressPlay, which was relaunched as a Napster pay-per-download model.

Listen.com's digital music service features the Rhapsody player, which provides subscribers with broadband-quality music at dial-up rates. Music from companies like Listen.com is of higher quality because the songs do not drop out or have to rebuffer, which compromises listening quality. For $9.95 per month, Rhapsody subscribers have access to over 330,000

full songs, 200,000 of which can be burned to CD. Each download costs 79 cents. One drawback to the Listen.com model is that songs cannot be downloaded to a hard drive. For the same price, the Roxio model offers access to only 300,000 songs, but 270,000 of those are available for burning. To download songs on the Roxio site, consumers must pay an additional $17.95 for ten songs, and downloaded songs disappear when a subscription is canceled. The most recent entry into this market is Apple's iTunes, which allows customers only to download songs—no streaming music. iTunes sold more than 70 million songs in its first year and boasts the largest legal download catalog in the industry. Thirty-second samples of the more than 700,000 burnable songs are available. Apple charges 99 cents per download.

Thus far, the pay-per-track model and subscription model combination from Listen.com seems to be the most successful. *PC World* voted it the "Best Streaming Audio Service" in June 2003 and "Best Buy, Online Music" in September 2003. It offers consumers the most control over the music because they are not forced to download a certain number of songs per month, nor are they limited to listening only to songs that are downloaded. Listen.com has introduced several value-added services, such as listening to the Rhapsody

player through a home stereo or mobile phone, sharing a customized playlist and favorite songs via e-mail, and listening to the Rhapsody player on any connected PC.

Rhapsody, Listen.com's streaming audio player, has also revolutionized the type of consumer data a company can collect. Since users must log in to use the services, every song played is recorded in the database. As a result, Rhapsody can make recommendations about other artists the listener may be interested in (much like the current Amazon.com model). Once users are logged in, they can choose to listen to an artist, album, track, playlist, or radio station. Selections can also be tracked. This information is useful for marketers. For example, by tracking playlists, they can determine which genres or artists are often listened to at the same time and use that information to make better music recommendations. In addition, the Rhapsody player provides links to the Web sites of artists, biographies, and featured music mixes. By using these links, consumers can purchase band-related merchandise such as CDs or T-shirts.[1]

How do you think marketers could use the information collected by Listen.com to sell related products to consumers? What additional information could marketers collect to help them develop advertising campaigns for users?

Online

Roxio
Listen.com
iTunes
How familiar are you with downloading music? How robust do you think a music site should be (meaning how many other things besides music should it offer)? Go to Roxio, Listen.com, and iTunes and compare how the companies present their products and the information they require from you in return.

http://www.roxio.com
http://www.listen.com
http://www.itunes.com

CRM is a strategy designed to optimize business performance by focusing on highly defined customer groups. This Surado ad for SCM SQL is a perfect example of what CRM systems seek to know: The real customer.

What exactly is CRM and how can I use it in my business? Find out the answer by watching the video on Xtra!

customer relationship management (CRM)
A company-wide business strategy designed to optimize profitability, revenue, and customer satisfaction by focusing on highly defined and precise customer groups.

customer-satisfying behaviors, and linking all processes of the company from its customers through its suppliers. For example, Listen.com's Rhapsody player targets consumers who listen to streaming audio. Then, by requiring users to log in, Rhapsody tracks their musical preferences and usage. Listen.com can leverage this information to offer special promotions and make recommendations to specific target markets and individuals.

The difference between CRM and traditional mass marketing can be compared to shooting a rifle and a shotgun. If you have good aim, a rifle is the most efficient weapon to use. A shotgun, on the other hand, increases your odds of hitting the target when it is more difficult to focus. Instead of scattering messages far and wide across the spectrum of mass media (the shotgun approach), CRM marketers now are homing in on ways to effectively communicate with each individual customer (the rifle approach).

THE CUSTOMER RELATIONSHIP MANAGEMENT CYCLE

On the surface, CRM may appear to be a rather simplistic customer service strategy. But, though customer service is part of the CRM process, it is only a small part of a totally integrated approach to building customer relationships. CRM is often described as a closed-loop system that builds relationships with customers. Exhibit 20.1 illustrates this closed-loop system, one that is continuous and circular with no predefined starting or end point.[2]

To initiate the CRM cycle, a company must first *identify customer relationships with the organization*. This may simply entail learning who the customers are or where they are located, or it may require more detailed information on the products and services they are using. Bridgestone/Firestone, a tire manufacturer and tire service company, uses a CRM system called NuEdge.[3] NuEdge initially gathers information from a point-of-sale interaction. The types of information gathered include basic demographic information, how frequently consumers purchase goods, how much they purchase, and how far they drive.

Next, the company must *understand the interactions with current customers*. Companies accomplish this by collecting data on all types of communications a customer has with the company. Using its NuEdge system, Bridgestone/Firestone can add information based on additional interactions with the consumer such as multiple visits to a physical store location and purchasing history. In this phase, companies build on the initial information collected and develop a more useful database.

Using this knowledge of its customers and their interactions, the company then *captures relevant customer data on interactions.* As an example, Bridgestone/Firestone can collect such relevant information as the date of the last communication with a customer, how often the customer makes purchases, and whether the customer redeemed coupons sent through direct mail.

How can marketers realistically analyze and communicate with individual customers? How can huge corporations like FedEx and Williams-Sonoma manage relationships with each and every one of their millions of customers on a personal level? The answer lies in how information technology is used to implement the CRM system. Fundamentally, a CRM approach is no more than the relationship cultivated by a salesperson with the customer. A successful salesperson builds a relationship over time, constantly thinks about what the customer needs and wants, and is mindful of the trends and patterns in the customer's purchase history. A good salesperson often knows what the customer needs even before the customer knows. The salesperson may also inform, educate, and instruct the customer about new products, technology, or applications in anticipation of the customer's future needs or requirements.

This kind of thoughtful attention is the basis of successful CRM systems. Information technology is used not only to enhance the collection of customer data, but also to *store and integrate customer data* throughout the company and, ultimately, to "get to know" customers on a personal basis. Customer data are the first-hand responses that are obtained from customers through investigation or by asking direct questions. These initial data, which might include individual answers to questionnaires, responses on warranty cards, or lists of purchases recorded by electronic cash registers, have not yet been analyzed or interpreted.

EXHIBIT 20.1

A Simple Flow Model of the Customer Relationship Management System

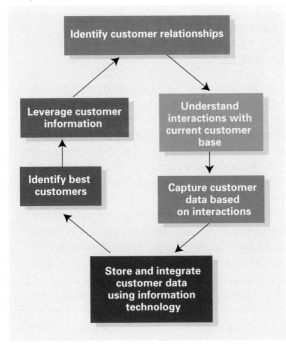

The value of customer data depends on the system that stores the data and the consistency and accuracy of the data captured. Obtaining high-quality, actionable data from various sources is a key element in any CRM system. Bridgestone/Firestone accomplishes this by managing all information in a central database accessible by marketers. Different kinds of database management software are available, from extremely high-tech, expensive, custom-designed databases to standardized programs. NetERP, for example, offers users database technology in a standardized rather than a customized format and is available at a much lower cost.[4]

Every customer wants to be a company's main priority. Yet not all customers are equally important in the eyes of a business. Some customers are simply more profitable for the company than others. Consequently, the company must identify *its profitable and unprofitable customers.* Data mining is an analytical process that compiles actionable data about the purchase habits of a firm's current and potential customers. Essentially, data mining transforms customer data into customer information a company can use to make managerial decisions. The NetERP software allows managers to customize their "dashboard" to obtain real-time reports on top-selling items and gross sales over a given time period.

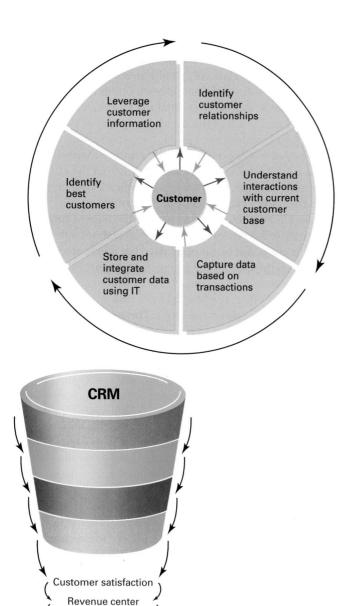

IMPLEMENTING A CUSTOMER RELATIONSHIP MANAGEMENT SYSTEM

Our discussion of a CRM system has assumed two key points. First, customers take center stage in any organization. Second, the business must manage the customer relationship across all points of customer contact throughout the entire organization. The Seattle Mariners baseball team took proactive steps to increase customer attendance at games based on these two points. The team implemented a loyalty card program to help the Mariners "better understand the fans." By collecting information from every interaction a customer has with the Mariners, from visiting concession stands to purchasing online tickets and even frequenting retail stores that sell Mariner merchandise, marketers were able to track the number of games consumers were attending. They sent reminder e-mails if a fan was close to achieving "season-ticket holder" status, and they also monitored complaints. For example, when the CRM system identified a complaint from a fan about the smell of garlic fries, the organization moved the fan to an area where there were no frequent consumers of garlic fries.[6]

Charles Schwab also understands these two key points about CRM. According to vice chairman and CIO Dawn Lepore, "Our mission is to delight our most demanding customers in the busiest hour of the busiest day. The most demanding customers are great for our business. They're like our toughest competitors. They push us to do things we haven't thought about before."[7]

In the next sections, we examine how a CRM system is implemented and follow the progression depicted in Exhibit 20.1 as we explain each step in greater detail.

2 IDENTIFY CUSTOMER RELATIONSHIPS

Explain how to identify customer relationships with the organization

Companies that have a CRM system follow a customer-centric focus or model. **Customer-centric** is an internal management philosophy similar to the marketing concept discussed in Chapter 1. Under this philosophy, the company customizes its product and service offering based on data generated through interactions between the customer and the company. This philosophy transcends all functional areas of the business (production, operations, accounting, etc.), producing an internal system where all of the company's decisions and actions are a direct result of customer information.

 A customer-centric company builds long-lasting relationships by focusing on what satisfies and retains valuable customers. For example, Sony's Web site (**http://www.playstation.com**) focuses on learning, customer knowledge management, and empowerment to market its PlayStation gaming computer entertainment system. The PlayStation Web site is designed to create a community of users who can join PlayStation Underground where they will "feel like they belong to a subculture of intense gamers." To achieve this objective, the Web site offers online shopping, opportunities to try new games, customer support, and information on news, events, and promotions. The interactive features include online gaming and message boards.

Online gaming with PlayStation requires users to purchase a Network Adaptor so that they can compete with other players worldwide. The message boards enable players to discuss and debate gaming topics. In addition, when PlayStation users wish to access amenities on the site, they are required to log in and supply information such as their name, e-mail address, and birth date. Furthermore, users can opt to fill out a survey that asks questions about the types of computer entertainment systems they own, how many games are owned for each console, expected future game purchases, time spent playing games, types of games played, and level of Internet connectivity. Armed with this information, Sony marketers are then able to tailor the site, new games, and PlayStation hardware based on players' replies to the survey and use of the Web site.[8]

Customer-centric companies continually learn ways to enhance their product and service offerings. **Learning** in a CRM environment involves collecting customer information through comments and feedback on product and service performance. As just described, Sony uses its PlayStation Web site to gather information from surveys and message boards so that it can offer more customer-friendly products and services.

Each unit of a business typically has its own way of recording what it learns and perhaps even its own customer information system. The departments' different interests make it difficult to pull all of the customer information together in one place using a common format. To overcome this problem, companies using CRM rely on knowledge management. **Knowledge management** is a process by which customer information is centralized and shared in order to enhance the relationship between customers and the organization. Information collected includes experiential observations, comments, customer actions, and qualitative facts about the customer. For example, PlayStation marketers gather survey information and generate a computer file for each customer that is available

Marketing... in Entertainment

Know Your Big Spenders

No one in the gaming industry is as well known for customer relationship management as Harrah's. The company recently added a new clienteling program to its already sophisticated software applications. The new software allows Harrah's 300 salespeople, called hosts, to tailor their interactions with the casino's top 100,000 frequent visitors (VIPs) and to make sure they are interacting with the right customers, in other words, not with customers who are already going to visit the casino. Each host has a personal home page that contains a prioritized list of VIPs. By clicking on a client's name, the host has access to that person's customer history, including the customer's casino activity. Having such information at hand helps the hosts make more successful personal contacts with their clients. And personalizing the interactions seems to be working. Since the complete rollout of the software, Harrah's estimates that it has increased its share of its customers' gaming budgets by 7 percent.[9]

customer-centric
Under this philosophy, the company customizes its product and service offering based on data generated through interactions between the customer and the company.

learning
An informal process of collecting customer data through customer comments and feedback on product or service performance.

knowledge management
The process by which learned information from customers is centralized and shared in order to enhance the relationship between customers and the organization.

...customer loyalty and ensure that the company's products meet the needs and wants of its target market, Sony designed a Web site that feels like an exclusive club for video gamers. And through player feedback, Sony can refine its site to match its customers' exact wants as they evolve.

empowerment
Delegation of authority to solve customers' problems quickly—usually by the first person that the customer notifies regarding the problem.

interaction
The point at which a customer and a company representative exchange information and develop learning relationships.

approval. Usually, organizational representatives are able to make such changes during interactions with customers through phone, fax, e-mail, Web communication, or face-to-face.

An **interaction** is a touch point at which a customer and a company representative exchange information and develop learning relationships. With CRM the customer, and not the organization, defines the terms of the interaction, often by stating his or her preferences. The organization responds by designing products and services around customers' desired experiences. For example, students can purchase the Student Advantage Discount Card for a nominal fee and use it to obtain discounts from affiliated retailers, such as USAirways, Greyhound, and Tower Records. Student Advantage tracks the cardholders' spending patterns and behaviors to gain a better understanding of what the college customer wants. Student Advantage then communicates this information to the affiliated retailers, who can then tailor their discounts to meet college students' needs. Ultimately, everyone benefits from this program: cardholders get relevant discounts, and retailers enjoy increased sales.[11]

The success of CRM—building lasting and profitable relationships—can be directly measured by the effectiveness of the interaction between the customer and the organization. In fact, what further differentiates CRM from other strategic initiatives is the organization's ability to establish and manage interactions with its current customer base. The more latitude (empowerment) a company gives its representatives, the more likely the interaction will conclude in a way that satisfies the customer.

REVIEW LEARNING OBJECTIVE 2

2 Explain how to identify customer relationships with the organization

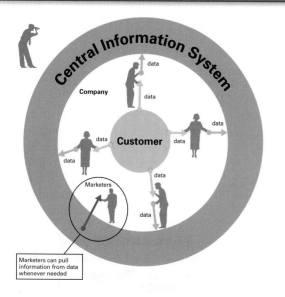

- Interaction, learning
- Knowledge management
- Marketer

3 UNDERSTAND INTERACTIONS OF THE CURRENT CUSTOMER BASE

Understand interactions with the current customer base

Best Buy

What evidence do you see on Best Buy's Web site of the company's behind-the-scenes CRM program? How many touch points can you identify at BestBuy.com?

http://www.bestbuy.com

Online

The *interaction* between the customer and the organization is the foundation on which a CRM system is built. Only through effective interactions can organizations learn about the expectations of their customers, generate and manage knowledge about them, negotiate mutually satisfying commitments, and build long-term relationships.

Exhibit 20.2 illustrates the customer-centric approach for managing customer interactions. Following a customer-centric approach, an interaction can occur through a formal or direct communication channel, such as a phone, the Internet, or a salesperson. Interactions also occur through a previous relationship a customer has had with the organization, such as a past purchase or a survey response, or through some current transaction or request by the customer, such as an actual product purchase, a request for repair service, or a response to a coupon offer. In short, any activity or touch point a customer has with an organization, either directly or indirectly, constitutes an interaction.

EXHIBIT 20.2

Customer-Centric Approach for Managing Customer Interactions

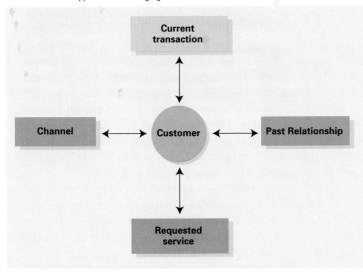

Best Buy, an electronic retail superstore, offers a Performance Service Plan (PSP) on products bought in-store or online. The PSP guarantees products against damage and malfunctioning. If customers need assistance, they can contact the company by mail, phone, in-store, or online. All initial purchase contact information is kept in the customer database, along with copies of the PSP. If a customer calls the Customer Care 1-800 number, the representative will have access to all of this information and can either help the customer or refer him or her to another representative. Thus, any form of communication with Best Buy whether initiated by the customer or by a company representative qualifies as an interaction or touch point.[12]

Companies that effectively manage customer interactions recognize that customers provide data to the organization that affect a wide variety of touch points. In a CRM system, **touch points** are all areas of a business where customers have contact with the company and data might be gathered. Touch points might include a customer registering for a particular service, a customer communicating with customer service for product information, a customer completing and returning the warranty information card for a product, or a customer talking with salespeople, delivery personnel, and product installers. In the Best Buy example, touch points include the initial customer-initiated purchase and the customer-initiated call to the Customer Care line. Data gathered at these touch points, once interpreted, provide information that affects touch points inside the company. For example, interpreted information may be redirected to marketing research, to develop profiles of extended warranty purchasers; to production, to analyze recurring problems and repair components; and to accounting, to establish cost-control models for repair service calls.

Web-based interactions are an increasingly popular touch point for customers to communicate with companies on their own terms. Instead of wasting time with phone numbers and mail surveys, companies are publicizing their Web sites as the first touch point for customer interactions. Web users

touch point
All possible areas of a business where customers communicate with that business.

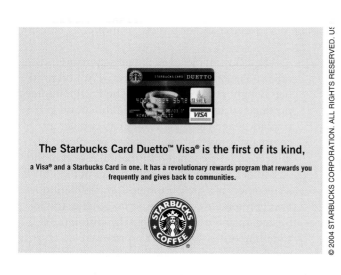

The Starbucks Card Duetto™ Visa® is the first of its kind,

a Visa® and a Starbucks Card in one. It has a revolutionary rewards program that rewards you frequently and gives back to communities.

Point-of-sale interactions help companies design customer recognition programs. The Starbucks Card Duetto Visa functions both as a Visa credit card and a reloadable Starbucks card. For every dollar purchased with a Duetto, customers earn 1 percent in Duetto Dollars, which are transferred directly to the customer's Starbucks card account. Duetto Dollars are redeemable instantly for purchases at Starbucks.

REVIEW LEARNING OBJECTIVE 3

3 | **Understand interactions with the current customer base**

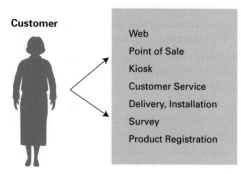

Interactions

Customer

- Web
- Point of Sale
- Kiosk
- Customer Service
- Delivery, Installation
- Survey
- Product Registration

Another touch point is through **point-of-sale interactions** in stores or at information kiosks. Many point-of-sale software packages enable customers to easily provide information about themselves without feeling violated. The information is then used in two ways: for marketing and merchandising activities, and to accurately identify the store's best customers and the types of products they buy. Data collected at point-of-sale interactions is also used to increase customer satisfaction through the development of in-store services and customer recognition promotions. For example, Borders and Waldenbooks have joined together to offer a Platinum Visa Card that allows members to collect points for making purchases and redeem them for an in-store gift certificate. The companies can then track purchases and identify the best customers.[14]

Transaction-based interactions differ from other interactions in that they focus on the exchange of information at the point of the actual transaction. Through the use of optical scanning technology and product bar codes, in conjunction with the payment method used by the customer (credit/debit card or check), retailers can create parallel streams of information on each individual customer. Stores with programs like Borders and Waldenbooks can then track types of purchases, volume, and frequency.

Once a credit card is swiped (or a check is processed for approval), two major streams of information are produced. First, optical scanning and bar coding allow businesses to capture information about which products the customer purchased and in what quantity. Second, by swiping a credit card or processing a bank check, the business can obtain all the information contained in the customer's credit card file or checking account file. Thus, businesses obtain information on both the customer's purchases and the customer's profile.

4 CAPTURE CUSTOMER DATA

Outline the process of capturing customer data

GEICO Insurance

How comfortable are you completing the information form for an online rate quote at GEICO Insurance? Would you be more comfortable talking with a representative on the phone? How effective is the Web as a channel for this type of customer interaction?

http://www.geico.com

Online

Vast amounts of data can be obtained from the interactions between an organization and its customers. Therefore, in a CRM system, the issue is not how much data can be obtained, but rather what types of data should be acquired and how the data can effectively be used for relationship enhancement.

 The traditional approach for acquiring data from customers is through channel interactions. Channel interactions include store visits, conversations with salespeople, interactions via the Web, traditional phone conversations, and wireless communications, such as cell phone conversations and satellite communications. In a CRM system, channel interactions are viewed as prime information sources based on the channel selected to initiate the interaction rather than on the data acquired. For example, if a consumer logs on to the Sony Web site to find out why a Sony device is not functioning properly and the answer is not available online, the consumer is then referred to a page where he or she can describe the problem. The Web site then e-mails the problem description to a company representative, who will research the problem and reply via e-mail. Furthermore, Sony will follow up with a brief satisfaction survey also sent via e-mail. Sony continues to use the e-mail mode of communication because the customer has established this as the preferred method of contact.[15]

Interactions between the company and the customer facilitate collection of large amounts of data. Companies can obtain not only simple contact information (name, address, phone number), but also data pertaining to the customer's current relationship with the organization—past purchase history, quantity and frequency of purchases, average amount spent on purchases, sensitivity to promotional activities, and so forth. GEICO Insurance Company, for example, at the time of policy renewal for its auto insurance customers, requests information pertaining to lifestyles (activities, interests, opinions, etc.), cultural factors (ethnicity, religion, etc.), and customer life stage (family composition, number and age of children, children living at home, etc.) for the purposes of pricing and customizing insurance packages for its customers. These data are also used for planning new product offerings such as vehicle maintenance insurance and gap insurance for lease customers along with cross-selling other GEICO services such as life insurance, home insurance, and marine insurance.[16]

The physical as well as the psychological consumption of the firm's product or service constitutes an additional touch point for customer interaction. As an interaction point, it also represents an opportunity to acquire and capture customer data related to the consumption experience. The unique dimension of the product or service interaction is that it enables customer data to be collected during the actual use of the product. Key customer data that can be captured at this interaction include the various brands and product types (package variations, sizes, colors, etc.) the customer consumes. The average length of time it takes to consume the product along with the volume consumed, price paid, and the preferred transaction method can also be obtained. For example, Avery Dennison, a manufacturer of office products and labeling systems, used its consumer call center, Web site (**http://www.avery.com**), business reply cards, and survey reply cards to collect information about its 8 million customers. Information collected initially includes name, address, values, and needs.

Even more important are data related to the performance of the product and the method customers use to report performance-related issues. Because the customer typically initiates the interaction, these data are extremely valuable for the organization. Customers can call in to a company's knowledge center requesting

point-of-sale interactions
Communications between customers and organizations that occur at the point of sale, normally in a store.

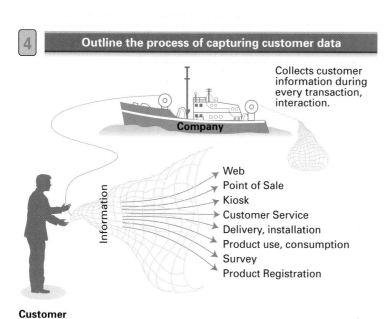

4 **Outline the process of capturing customer data**

Collects customer information during every transaction, interaction.

Company

Information

Web
Point of Sale
Kiosk
Customer Service
Delivery, installation
Product use, consumption
Survey
Product Registration

Customer

registered at its Web site, including children's names and birth dates, to a third party. When the company filed for bankruptcy protection, it said the information collected constituted a company asset that needed to be sold off to pay creditors.[18] Despite the outrage at this announcement, many dot.com companies closing their doors found they had little in the way of assets and followed Toysmart's lead. The attorney general of Delaware filed suit against myseasons.com, a garden products seller, for selling its customer list despite promises to keep that information confidential.[19] The issue was so alarming that North Dakota voters overwhelmingly rejected a state law that would have allowed banks to sell customer information without written permission from the customers. Opponents of the law declared that customer information belongs to the customer, not the company.[20]

 STORE AND INTEGRATE CUSTOMER DATA

Describe the use of technology to store and integrate customer data

data warehouse
A central repository for data from various functional areas of the organization that are stored and inventoried on a centralized computer system so that the information can be shared across all functional departments of the business.

database
A collection of data, especially one that can be accessed and manipulated by computer software.

Customer data are only as valuable as the system in which the data are stored and the consistency and accuracy of the data captured. Gathering data is further complicated by the fact that data needed by one unit of the organization, such as sales and marketing, often are generated by another area of the business or even a third-party supplier, such as an independent marketing research firm. Thus, companies must use information technology to capture, store, and integrate strategically important customer information. This process of centralizing data in a CRM system is referred to as data warehousing.

A **data warehouse** is a central repository (*database*) of customer data collected by an organization. Essentially, it is a large computerized file of all information collected in the previous phase of the CRM process, for example, information collected in channel, transaction, and product/service touch points. The core of the data warehouse is the **database**, "a collection of data, especially one that can be accessed and manipulated by computer software."[21] The CRM database focuses on collecting vital statistics on consumers, their purchasing habits, transactions methods, and product usage in a centralized repository that is accessible by all functional areas of a company. Traditionally, this information was stored in separate computer systems throughout the company. By utilizing a data warehouse, however, marketing managers can quickly access vast amounts of information required to make decisions. For example, Continental Airlines used to store data in a variety of operational systems that could not be integrated. As a result, managers did not have the depth and breadth of information to facilitate their decision-making capabilities. Now the Continental data warehouse centralizes data from 41 sources. The warehouse is accessible by 35 departments and 1,300 employees. The database content includes everything from flight schedules, seat inventory, and customer profiles to employee and crew payroll. Even aircraft parts and maintenance is being added to the system to aid in distribution decision making.[22]

Prior to building the data warehouse, company executives must define their strategic objectives and determine what information must be collected in the database to meet those objectives. At Continental Airlines, strategists initially focused on forecasting passenger bookings. As a result, they needed to collect information related to flight reservations, high-demand destinations, and peak travel times.

The foundation of the data warehouse is the database, which begins with collecting the "right" information. As database marketing experts Rob Jackson and Paul Wang state in their book *Strategic Database Marketing*, "A database is only as powerful as the information it houses."[23] A company can have the most elaborate and expensive database system available and a staff of statistical professionals and marketing experts, but if it does not collect the right data, the other building blocks will never be used to their potential.

The first step is to develop a list. Usually, this is in the form of a **response list**, based on customers who have indicated interest in a product or service, or a compiled list, created by an outside company that has collected names and contact information for potential consumers. Response lists tend to be especially valuable because past behavior is a strong predictor of future behavior and because consumers who have indicated interest in the product or service are more prone to purchase. **Compiled lists** usually are prepared by an outside company and are available for purchase. A compiled list generally includes names and addresses gleaned from telephone directories or membership rosters. Many lists are available, ranging from those owned by large list companies, such as Dun & Bradstreet for business-to-business data and Donnelley and R. L. Polk for consumer lists, to small groups or associations that are willing to sell their membership lists. Data compiled by large data-gathering companies usually are very accurate.

In this phase companies are usually collecting basic channel, transaction, and product/service information such as store, salesperson, communication channel, contact information, relationship, and brands. For example, when Philips wanted to determine how to best sell its CoolSkin Shaver accessories, it used existing information to expand its database. By sending an e-mail to registered users, Philips was able to collect information including whether consumers purchased online; if so, the "landing page" on the Web site; the number of "unsubscribes" when sent an e-mail; and the timeliness of response.[24]

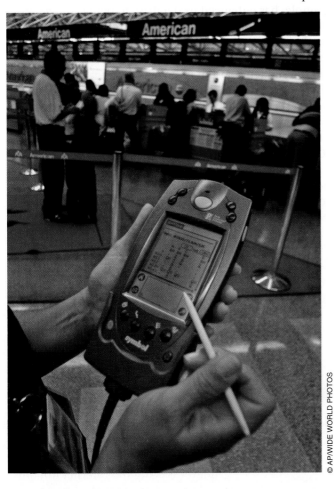

American Airlines uses data warehousing to propel its customer-centric focus. Information collected at multiple touch points is stored and redistributed throughout the organization. Here, gate agent Debbie Bernard uses a Palm device to help a passenger find his seating assignment.

response list
A customer list that includes the names and addresses of individuals who have responded to an offer of some kind, such as by mail, telephone, direct-response television, product rebates, contests or sweepstakes, or billing inserts.

compiled list
A customer list that was developed by gathering names and addresses from telephone directories and membership rosters, usually enhanced with information from public records, such as census data, auto registrations, birth announcements, business start-ups, or bankruptcies.

want. When the company opened one of its upscale Central Market stores in Fort Worth, Texas, customer profiles indicated that Fort Worth residents have a strong sense of Western heritage. The Fort Worth location, therefore, offers customers chipotle-smoked barbecue ribs, game birds, and briskets. The store has also adjusted the way it cuts and sells beef to meet local preferences, and it carries an expanded selection of peppers and fresh tortillas for its Hispanic customers. Once open, the stores continue to use databases to collect information about customer preferences and to tweak product offerings.

Multinational companies building worldwide databases often face difficult problems when pulling together internal data about their customers. Differences in language, computer systems, and data-collection methods can be huge obstacles to overcome. In spite of the challenges, many global companies are committed to building databases. Unilever is using the Internet not only to educate consumers about the brand but also to develop relationships with its customers by providing helpful information. Web site visitors can get information on removing stubborn stains and solving similar consumer problems. They also receive a discount on their next purchase in exchange for completing an online questionnaire. With diligent effort, Unilever has collected information on more than 30 million loyal customers from numerous countries.[26]

REVIEW LEARNING OBJECTIVE 5

5 | **Describe the use of technology to store and integrate customer data**

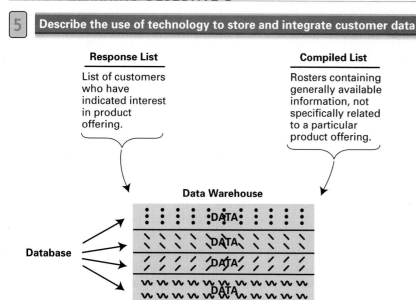

Response List

List of customers who have indicated interest in product offering.

Compiled List

Rosters containing generally available information, not specifically related to a particular product offering.

Data Warehouse

Database

6 | IDENTIFYING THE BEST CUSTOMERS

Describe how to identify the best customers

CRM manages interactions between a company and its customers. To be successful, companies must identify customers who yield high profits or potential profits. To do so, significant amounts of data must be gathered from customers, stored and integrated in the data warehouse, and then analyzed and interpreted for

To be successful, company CRM initiatives cannot only identify customers, but must identify the company's most valuable customers. Many companies rank their customers so as to spend more time on those customers that account for the bulk of revenues and profits. SAS software enables companies to track their customers according to many metrics, including their value.

modeling
The act of building a model in a situation where the answer is known and then applying the model to another situation where the answer is unknown.

common patterns that can identify homogeneous customers who are different from other customer segments. Because all customers are not the same, organizations need to develop interactions that target *individual* customer needs and wants. Likewise, all customers do not generate the same revenue for a company. Recall, from Chapter 7, the 80/20 principle—80 percent of a company's revenue is generated by 20 percent of its customers. Therefore, the question becomes, how do we identify the 20 percent of our customer base that contributes 80 percent of our revenue? In a CRM system, the answer is data mining.

DATA MINING

Data mining is used to find hidden patterns and relationships in the customer data stored in the data warehouse. It is a data analysis approach that identifies patterns of characteristics that relate to particular customers or customer groups. Although businesses have been conducting such analyses for many years, the procedures typically were performed on small data sets containing as few as 300 to 400 customers. Today, with the development of sophisticated data warehouses, millions of customers' shopping patterns can be analyzed. Wal-Mart's data warehouse, believed to be second in size only to the Pentagon's, contains over 200 terabytes (trillions of characters) of customer transaction data. Wal-Mart uses its huge data warehouse to help each of its stores adapt its merchandising mix to local neighborhood preferences.

Using data mining, marketers can search the data warehouse, capture relevant data, categorize significant characteristics, and develop customer profiles. For example, in the Philips razor example, marketers were attempting to build a relationship with consumers through e-mail. By assessing response and nonresponse rates along with online purchases, they developed a profile of consumers likely to purchase CoolSkin accessories over the Internet. Moreover, once Philips was successful with CoolSkin accessories, it used this approach on other product lines.[27]

When using data mining, it is important to remember that the real value is in the company's ability to transform its data from operational bits and bytes into information marketers need for successful marketing strategies. Companies must go beyond merely creating a mailing list. They must analyze the data to identify and profile the best customers, calculate their lifetime value, and ultimately predict purchasing behavior through statistical modeling.

Data mining works through a process known as modeling. **Modeling** involves building a model in a situation where the answer is known and then applying the model to another situation where the answer is unknown. If the necessary information exists in the data warehouse, the data-mining process can model virtually any customer activity. The key is finding relevant patterns. For example, a business could use data mining to address unknown situations such as these: "Which customers are most likely to drop their wireless phone service?" "What is the probability a customer will purchase $100 of merchandise from a particular store location?" "Which potential customers are most likely to respond to a particular coupon?" If the data warehouse contains the "right" information, then it will generate probable answers.

A wide range of companies have used data mining successfully. Albertson's Supermarkets uses data mining to identify commonly purchased items that should be placed together on shelves and to learn what soft drinks sell best in different parts of

customers. Profiles of the best customers can be compared and contrasted with other customer segments. For example, a bank could segment consumers on frequency of usage, credit, age, and turnover. Once a profile of the best customer is developed using these criteria, it can be used to screen other potential consumers. Similarly, customer profiles can be used to introduce customers selectively to specific marketing actions. For example, young customers with an open mind can be introduced to home banking, and older, well-established customers to investment opportunities.[29] See Chapter 7 for a detailed discussion of segmentation.

Recency-Frequency-Monetary Analysis (RFM)

Customers who have purchased recently and often and have spent considerable money are more likely to purchase again. Recency-frequency-monetary analysis (RFM) identifies those customers most likely to purchase again because they have bought recently, bought frequently, or spent a specified amount of money with the firm. Firms develop equations to identify the "best customers" (often the top 20 percent of the customer base) by assigning a score to customer records in the database on how often, how recently, and how much they have spent. Customers are then ranked to determine which ones move to the top of the list and which ones fall to the bottom. The ranking provides the basis for maximizing profits because it enables the firm to use the information in its customer database to select those persons who have proved to be good sources of revenue. As an example of RFM analysis, Exhibit 20.3 depicts the breakdown of customers in categories that describe their value. Casino operator Harrah's Entertainment used RFM analysis to determine that gamblers who spent between $100 and $499 a trip accounted for only about 30 percent of its customer base but generated 80 percent of its revenue and nearly 100 percent of its profits. As a result, the company refocused its marketing efforts on this group, which it calls "avid players."[30]

Many marketers take RFM analysis one step further by introducing *profitability* into the equation. For instance, based on the monetary value of purchases, a customer may float to the top of the RFM list. If this customer only buys items on sale, however, he or she is less

EXHIBIT 20.3

RFM Analysis: All Customers Are Not the Same

Best Customers	Average Customers	Poor Customers
High profit	Average profit	Low profit
Spent >$1,500	Spent approximately $400	Spent < $100
Multiple purchases	Two purchases	One purchase
Purchase in last 6 months	Purchase in last 18 months	Purchase in last two years
Lifetime value = high	Lifetime value = average	Lifetime value = low
N = 2,500 (18.5%)*	N = 4,000 (29.6%)*	N = 7,000 (51.9%)*
Total annual sales = $2.4 million	Total annual sales = $1.1 million	Total annual sales = $800,000

*N = number of customers in a category. The total number of customers is 13,500, and total annual sales are $4.3 million.

lifetime value analysis (LTV)
A data manipulation technique that projects the future value of the customer over a period of years using the assumption that marketing to repeat customers is more profitable than marketing to first-time buyers.

predictive modeling
A data manipulation technique in which marketers try to determine, based on some past set of occurrences, what the odds are that some other occurrence, such as a response or purchase, will take place in the future.

profitable for the firm than a customer who purchases the identical items at full price. For example, a major retailer discovered that 3 percent of shoppers accounted for 40 percent of its sales volume. Using RFM, the retailer determined that each year the "best customers" charged over $1,000 on the private-label credit card and shopped at least five times in at least four product categories. With this analysis, a marketing campaign was designed to reach the "best customers," the top 10 percent of the cardholders. The campaign resulted in a 21 percent increase in the "best customer" retention rate and an annual purchase increase of $100 per customer. In addition, the information was used to move other consumers into the "best customer" category. Each of these factors had a significant impact on increasing the company's profitability.[31]

Lifetime Value Analysis (LTV)

Recency, frequency, and monetary data can also be used to create a lifetime value model on customers in the database. Whereas RFM looks at how valuable a customer currently is to a company, **lifetime value analysis (LTV)** projects the future value of the customer over a period of years. One of the basic assumptions in any lifetime value calculation is that marketing to repeat customers is more profitable than marketing to first-time buyers. That is, it costs more to find a new customer in terms of promotion and gaining trust than to sell more to a customer who is already loyal.

Customer lifetime value has a number of benefits. It shows marketers how much they can spend to *acquire* new customers, it tells them the level of spending to *retain* customers, and it facilitates targeting new customers who look as though they will be profitable customers. Cadillac has calculated the lifetime value of its top customers at $332,000. Similarly, Pizza Hut figures its best customers are worth $8,000 in bottom-line lifetime value.

Predictive Modeling

The ability to reasonably predict future customer behavior gives marketers a significant competitive advantage. Through **predictive modeling**, marketers try to determine, based on some past set of occurrences, what the odds are that some other occurrence, such as an Internet inquiry or purchase, will take place in the future. SPSS Predictive Marketing is one tool marketers can use to answer questions about their consumers. The software requires minimal knowledge of statistical analysis. Users operate from a prebuilt model, which generates profiles in three to four days. SPSS also has an online product that predicts Web site users' behavior. FT.com, the *Financial Times* Web site, uses the software to predict which subscribers may not renew their subscription and to convince users of free content to "subscribe" to FT.com.[32]

REVIEW LEARNING OBJECTIVE 6

6 | **Describe how to identify the best customers**

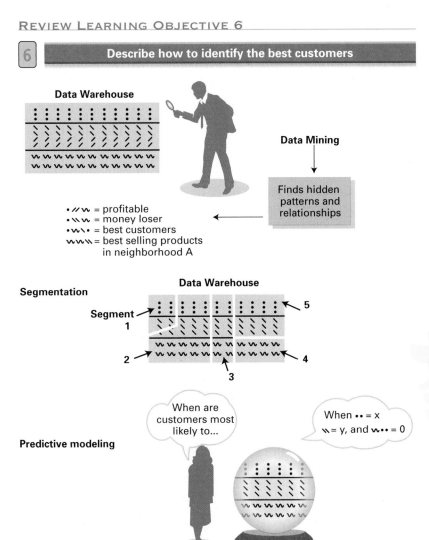

Data Warehouse

Data Mining

Finds hidden patterns and relationships

- //w = profitable
- \\w = money loser
- w• = best customers
- www\ = best selling products in neighborhood A

Segmentation

Data Warehouse

Segment 1
Segment 2
3
4
5

Predictive modeling

When are customers most likely to...

When •• = x
\\ = y, and w•• = 0

Data Warehouse

R-F-M = (How recent, how often, how much)
Can be used for single situations
or to determine
LTV = Lifetime Value

US Airways

How could US Airways use an e-mail program as a CRM initiative? Go to the company's Web site to find out. You may need to navigate to the site or a specific campaign by clicking on a link.

http://www.technology.com

enhancing customer relationships   development of programs targeted to customers. **Campaign management** involves

Global Perspectives
Global Perspectives Global Perspectives
Global Perspectives Global Perspectives Global Perspectives Global Perspectives Global Perspectives Global Perspe
Global Perspectives Global Perspectives Global Perspectives Global Perspectives Global Perspe
Global Perspectives Global Perspectives **GLOBAL PERSPECTIVES** ectives Global Perspectives
Global Perspectives Global Perspectives Global Perspectives Global Perspe
Global Perspectives Global Perspectives Global Perspectives
Global Perspectives

GLOBAL PERSPECTIVES

> CRM ENHANCES GLOBAL MARKETING STRATEGIES

Staples' successful use of CRM technology probably contributed in many ways to the company's recent record earnings. Under CEO Ron Sargent's management, Staples has deployed numerous CRM initiatives and has passed Office Depot as the number one office supply retail chain in the United States.

Adoption of a CRM system in the global marketplace is a challenge for many U.S.-based companies. To create more profitable global marketing campaigns, companies rely heavily on information in their databases that will reveal universal trends rather than country or region-specific trends. For example, Staples, a worldwide, discount office supply retailer, sells office products to 10 million consumers through three channels—the Staples.com Web site, the Staples Direct catalog, and over 1,400 Staples retail locations. The company uses a CRM database to make

decisions involving everything from broad-based marketing programs to promotions for individual products. A single CRM database integrates customer data collected from retail stores, Web site, and catalog transactions. All Staples employees worldwide have access to the same data. Database analysis has increased effiency and effectiveness in the company's worldwide corporate management.

CRM systems aren't used exclusively by American companies. Many foreign-based companies are also using the technology to become more profitable and better manage customer relationships. A CRM system doesn't always have to focus directly on promotions to the consumer to increase profitability. A South African bank, Absa Group, wanted to reduce the number of bank robberies it was experiencing. At the time, Absa was being targeted more frequently than other banks, so it turned to a CRM system to determine how to make its branches less attractive to criminals. Absa was able to use the CRM system to take preventive measures by predicting crime waves, choosing better branch locations, and discovering which locations would be prime targets. Two years after the changes were implemented, Absa saw a 41 percent decline in robberies and a 38 percent decrease in cash losses, compared to an industry increase of 25 to 200 percent in number of robberies and a 50 to 150 percent increase in cash losses. And the company achieved a 9-fold return on its CRM investment. Besides the financial results, 11 percent of customers felt more satisfied and 91 percent felt safer while banking at Absa.[33]

Will CRM give global companies an advantage? Can you think of other uses of CRM that might improve the bottom line?

EXHIBIT 20.4

Common CRM Marketing Database Applications

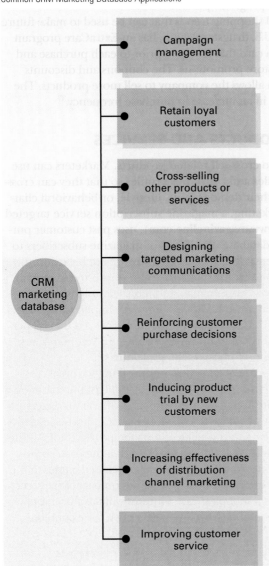

Campaign management

Retain loyal customers

Cross-selling other products or services

Designing targeted marketing communications

CRM marketing database

Reinforcing customer purchase decisions

Inducing product trial by new customers

Increasing effectiveness of distribution channel marketing

Improving customer service

monitoring and leveraging customer interactions to sell a company's products and to increase customer service. Campaigns are based directly on data obtained from customers through various interactions. Campaign management includes monitoring the success of the communications based on customer reactions through sales, orders, callbacks to the company, and the like. If a campaign appears unsuccessful, it is evaluated and changed to better achieve the company's desired objective. Stave Puzzles, the "Rolls Royce" of puzzles, produces handcrafted wood puzzles. Each puzzle is unique and can be customized as the customer desires. Steve Richardson, the company's cofounder, has narrowed his customer base to his "Hot Hundred" most valuable customers. To manage his customer base and ensure they are receiving optimal service, he tracks not only standard information, such as contact data and orders, but also birthdays, anniversaries, relationships between customers, phone conversations, inquiries, and workshop visits.[34]

Campaign management involves developing customized product and service offerings for the appropriate customer segment, pricing these offerings attractively, and communicating these offers in a manner that enhances customer relationships. Customizing product and service offerings requires managing multiple interactions with customers, as well as giving priority to those products and services that are viewed as most desirable for a specifically designated customer. Even within a highly defined market segment, individual customer differences will emerge. Therefore, interactions among customers must focus on individual experiences, expectations, and desires. Stave Puzzles customizes its marketing campaigns by tailoring mailouts to eight different segments. For example, the monthly buyers and top 10 percent of the customers receive individual reminder notes about special occasions and previous purchases. Zanes Cycles (**http://www.zanes.com**) in Branford, Connecticut, successfully uses customized campaigns, too. Every March, Zanes searches its marketing database for customers who bought baby seats three years earlier. Knowing that they may wish to buy a child's bike soon, Zanes sends these customers a postcard showcasing its inventory of children's bicycles and offering a discount on the purchase. About 60 percent of those who receive the postcard return to buy a bike.

RETAINING LOYAL CUSTOMERS

If a company has identified its best customers, then it should make every effort to maintain and increase their loyalty. When a company retains an additional 5 percent of its customers each year, profits will increase by as much as 25 percent. What's more, improving customer retention by a mere 2 percent can decrease costs by as much as 10 percent.[35] For example, The Palace of Auburn Hills, a sporting venue, is home to the NBA Detroit Pistons, the WNBA Detroit Shock, and the Detroit Fury in the Arena Football League. To increase game attendance, the arena developed its MyPal rewards card, which enables fans to receive e-mail updates. As a result, game attendance has increased for all types of consumers.[36]

Loyalty programs reward loyal customers for making multiple purchases. The objective is to build long-term mutually beneficial relationships between a company and its key customers. Marriot, Hilton, and Starwood Hotels, for instance, reward their best customers with special perks not available to customers who stay less frequently. Travelers who spend a specified number of nights per year receive

feature new magazines that may interest the customer. Past purchase behavior may show that subscribers to *Sports Illustrated*, for instance, are also interested in general news magazines such as *Time* and *Newsweek*. Similarly, to increase purchasing across different departments and in different product lines, Wegman's Supermarkets monitors sales using a frequent buyer card. Using data mining, it discovered that 80 percent of shoppers buying baby food also bought flowers. As a result, Wegman's was able to develop a more effective method for cross-selling products.[38]

ONLINE

Internet companies use product and customer profiling to reveal cross-selling opportunities while a customer is surfing their site. Past purchases on a particular Web site and the site a surfer comes from give online marketers clues about the surfer's interests and what items to cross-sell. Fry's Outpost electronics (**http://www.outpost.com**), a computer-goods e-tailer, adjusts the pages visitors see depending on what they click on at the site or what they purchased in the past. For instance, if a surfer always goes to computer game pages or has purchased games in the past, Outpost will automatically place offers for other game titles on part of the screen. Depending on what a shopper puts in a shopping cart, Outpost will flash promotions for related items—a leather case for someone who is buying a PDA, for example.

DESIGNING TARGETED MARKETING COMMUNICATIONS

Using transaction and purchase data, a database allows marketers to track customers' relationships to the company's products and services and modify the marketing message accordingly. For example, Kraft Foods teamed with Wegman's Supermarkets to determine which advertising campaigns were most effective for frequent buyers of Kraft Macaroni & Cheese. Kraft used the results to better reach its frequent buyers in future campaigns.[39]

Customers can also be segmented into infrequent users, moderate users, and heavy users. A segmented communications strategy can then be developed based on which group the customer falls into. Communications to infrequent users might encourage repeat purchases through a direct incentive such as a limited-time price discount for ordering again. Communications to moderate users may use fewer incentives and more reinforcement of past purchase decisions. Communications to heavy users would be designed around loyalty and reinforcement of the purchase rather than price promotions. For example, Nike Store Toronto offers the Air Max Club (AMC), a loyalty club for customers. Club members can collect points and redeem them for gift certificates, movies, and books. Customers considered "most valuable" are identified when they swipe their card to collect points, thereby alerting the salesperson. A message on the salesperson's screen indicates that the customer should receive a special thank-you and possibly a prize.

The system also generates customized coupons based on purchase history. The company has found that club members spend about 50 percent more than the average customer.[40]

Rite Aid Corporation's pharmacy division uses its database to create direct-to-patient targeted information in the form of informational pamphlets that also carry targeted advertising. A consumer filling a prescription for a diabetes medication, for example, will receive a pamphlet with different editorial content and advertising than a consumer filling a prescription for a hypertension drug. Dick's Supermarkets in Wisconsin (**http://www.dickssupermarket.com**) uses transaction data from its loyalty card program to personalize shopping lists that it mails every two weeks to its nearly 30,000 members. The shopping lists contain timed offers based on past purchases. A consumer who bought Tide soap powder or Maxwell House coffee several weeks ago, for instance, may be offered a cents-off coupon to buy again.

REINFORCING CUSTOMER PURCHASE DECISIONS

As you learned in the consumer behavior chapter, cognitive dissonance is the feeling consumers get when they recognize an inconsistency between their values and opinions and their purchase behavior. In other words, they begin to doubt the soundness of their purchase decision and often feel anxious as well. CRM offers marketers an excellent opportunity to reach out to customers to reinforce the purchase decision. By thanking customers for their purchases and telling them they are important, marketers can help cement a long-term, profitable relationship. Guests staying at the quaint Village Country Inn nestled in the Green Mountains of Vermont receive a handwritten thank-you note from the inn's proprietors within a week of their stay. The note thanks the guests for visiting and encourages them to return in the future.

Updating customers periodically about the status of their order reinforces purchase decisions. Postsale e-mails also afford the chance to provide more customer service or cross-sell other products. Minutes after customers order merchandise from Amazon.com's Web site, for example, they receive an e-mail acknowledging their order. Every few days thereafter, customers receive updates that allow them to track the shipment of the order, from ship date to receipt. Similarly, Sumerset Houseboats builds customized, luxury houseboats priced at about $250,000 each. The company uses its Web site to monitor customer profiles, post company information, and communicate with customers. For example, it posts daily pictures of progress on houseboats being built. By reinforcing customers' decisions, Sumerset is able to offset the feeling of cognitive dissonance.[41]

INDUCING PRODUCT TRIAL BY NEW CUSTOMERS

Although significant time and money are expended on encouraging repeat purchases by the best customers, a marketing database is also used to identify new customers. Because a firm using a marketing database already has a profile of its best customers, it can easily use the results of modeling to profile potential customers. EATEL, a regional telecommunications firm, uses modeling to identify prospective residential and commercial telephone customers and successfully attract their business.

Marketing managers generally use demographic and behavioral data overlaid on existing customer data to develop a detailed customer profile that is a powerful tool

Olay, a brand of Procter & Gamble, invites customers to join Club Olay, which offers special discounts, free samples, and the opportunity to purchase products before they're available in stores. But members are also able to communicate with the company by sharing their beauty secrets and entering various sweepstakes.

© THE PROCTER & GAMBLE COMPANY. USED BY PERMISSION.

lose touch with the customer as an individual since the relationship is really between the retailer and the consumer. Marketers in this predicament often view their customers as aggregate statistics because specific customer information is difficult to gather.

With CRM databases, manufacturers now have a tool to gain insight into who is buying their products. Instead of simply unloading products into the distribution channel and leaving marketing and relationship building to dealers, auto manufacturers today are using Web sites to keep in touch with customers and prospects, learn about their lifestyles and hobbies, understand their vehicle needs, and develop relationships in hopes these consumers will reward them with brand loyalty in the future. BMW and Mercedes-Benz USA, as well as other vehicle manufacturers, have databases with names of millions of consumers who have expressed an interest.

With many brick and mortar stores setting up shop online, companies are now challenged to monitor purchases of customers who shop both in-store and online. This concept is referred to as multichannel marketing. After Lands' End determined that multichannel customers are the most valuable, the company targeted marketing campaigns toward retaining these customers and increased sales significantly. Talbot's and Victoria's Secret have also developed successful campaigns to serve multichannel customers.

Companies are also using Radio Frequency Identification (RFID) technology to improve distribution. The technology uses a microchip with an antenna that tracks anything from a soda can to a car. A computer can locate the product anywhere. The main implication of this technology is that companies will enjoy a reduction in theft and loss of merchandise shipments and will always know where merchandise is in the distribution channel.

© AP/WIDE WORLD PHOTOS

American ExpressPay keys contain a radio-frequency identification chip that enables cardholders to make instant purchases at places like Carl's Jr. restaurants. The ExpressPay keys are contactless versions of American Express credit cards, requiring the user to simply tap the card on a special reader to make a purchase.

Moreover, as this technology is further developed, marketers will be able to gather essential information related to product usage and consumption.[42]

IMPROVING CUSTOMER SERVICE

CRM marketing techniques increasingly are being used to improve customer service. Boise Cascade Office Products uses CRM to compete against competitors like Staples and Office Depot. The company recently changed its culture to become more customer-centric. Sales reps are sent out to meet one-to-one with customers, and when customers place orders, either by phone or the Internet, information technology software automatically accesses their transaction history and customizes the response. In another competitive move, Boise Cascade acquired office products retailer OfficeMax. When the merger was announced, the company's chairman stated, "The combined office products business will be strategically stronger and better able to deliver compelling value to its customers through all channels and across all segments of the market."[43]

Many companies are using CRM techniques to service customers better by hosting online feedback forums and chat rooms where users can discuss and debate products. To determine how to better tailor products and services to customer needs, marketers monitor these chat rooms. Additionally, many businesses have expanded their lines of communication, allowing customers much freer access to the company. Gap, for example, uses a database to monitor inventory at individual stores around the country. A sales rep can locate an item of clothing at any store in the surrounding area. Target Stores offers a Target credit card that holds all purchase information in a centralized database. If a customer needs to return merchandise but has lost the receipt, the item can be scanned and purchase information retrieved. The company credits the customer's account instead of issuing credit to the store.

PRIVACY CONCERNS AND CRM

Before rushing out to invest in a CRM system and build a database, marketers should consider consumers' reactions to the growing use of databases. Many Americans and customers abroad are concerned about databases because of the potential for invasion of privacy. The sheer volume of information that is aggregated in databases makes this information vulnerable to unauthorized access and use. A fundamental aspect of marketing using CRM databases is providing valuable services to customers based on knowledge of what customers really value. It is critical, however, that marketers remember that these relationships should be built on trust. Although database technology enables marketers to compile ever-richer information about their customers that can be used to build and manage relationships, if these customers feel their privacy is being violated, then the relationship becomes a liability.

The popularity of the Internet for e-commerce and customer data collection and as a repository for sensitive customer data has alarmed privacy-minded customers. Online users complain loudly about being "spammed," and Web surfers, including children, are routinely asked to divulge personal information to access certain screens or purchase goods or services. Internet users are disturbed by the amount of information businesses collect on them as they visit various sites in cyberspace. Indeed, many users are unaware of how personal information is collected, used, and distributed. The government

- ✔ Designing targeted marketing communications
- ✔ Reinforcing customer purchase decisions
- ✔ Inducing product trial by new customers
- ✔ Increasing effectiveness of distribution channel marketing
- ✔ Improving customer service

More than 50 nations have, or are developing, privacy legislation. Europe has the strictest legislation regarding the collection and use of customer data, and other countries are looking to that legislation when formulating their policies. The "Ethics in Marketing" box provides more perspectives on resolving CRM privacy issues.

Ethics in Marketing Ethics in Marketing Ethics in Marketing Ethics in Marketing Ethics in Marke Ethics in Marketing Ethics in Marketing Ethics in Marketing Ethics in Marketing Ethics in Marketing Ethics in Marke Ethics in Marketing Ethics in Marketing Ethics in Marketing Ethics in Marketing Ethics in Marketing Ethics in Marke Ethics in Marketing Ethics in Marketing Ethics in Marketing Ethics in Marketing

ETHICS IN MARKETING

> PRIVACY ISSUES MUST BE RESOLVED FOR CRM'S SUCCESS

CRM is a hot marketing topic and a popular business tool. But it also sparks hot debates regarding consumers' privacy. American businesses have collected consumer data for years. Policies and laws govern what businesses can do with that information once it is collected. Current laws cover several industries including finance, health care, retail, automotive and transportation, technology, and direct marketing. The Gramm-Leach-Bliley Act enforces privacy guidelines for financial information, the Health Insurance Portability and Accountability Act (HIPAA) regulates medical records, and the National Do-Not-Call list governs telemarketing. Most recently, the CAN-SPAM Act provided guidelines for e-mail.

Companies have taken initiatives, too. Many have developed independent privacy policies designed to govern how they collect, use, share, and protect the personal information of consumers and employees. According to the 2003 Benchmark Study of Corporate Privacy Practices Report, 98 percent of U.S. companies have a privacy policy in effect. Nevertheless, more than half of those companies feel their policy may be difficult to understand. One problem is that only 53 percent require mandatory training for policy enforcement.

Consequently, consumer information is still vulnerable to unethical corporate practices.

Despite consumers' concerns, company executives realize that consumer information is very profitable. Companies can profit by sharing the information with a third party or by purchasing third-party information to build a more comprehensive database. As a result, companies are struggling to balance consumer trust and profitability. For example, the Walt Disney Company had a strict policy that did not allow it to share information collected on its Web site with third parties. Once executives realized the value of the information, however, they amended the privacy policy to enable third-party companies to send promotions to consumers. To ensure continued consumer trust, Disney allows consumers to opt in or opt out of third-party promotions. Additionally, Disney offers consumers updated privacy information on its Web site and sends e-mails to registered users explaining any privacy policy changes.[44]

How does a firm's privacy policy affect your purchasing decisions? Do you think it is ethical for a company to post a privacy policy but not have mandatory enforcement? What are the most important issues in establishing a privacy policy for a business?

The chapter's opening vignette described how Listen.com uses sophisticated marketing approaches to maximize profitability. Among other things, Listen.com has implemented and leveraged a CRM system. By interacting with users through the Rhapsody player, Listen.com is able to highly customize its service offerings. This information then becomes part of a data warehouse maintained by Listen.com to enable it to apply data-mining techniques. Data mining helps Listen.com to make product recommendations and cross-sell products to consumers.

USE IT NOW

Stay up-to-date on the latest developments in the CRM world. Because CRM is technology driven, the ways companies interact, collect customer information, and analyze that information are constantly changing. New and unique methods are being introduced along with new approaches in campaign management. To keep current with such changes and to understand how companies are using CRM, visit the Web site for the *Direct Marketing Review*, **http://www.dmreview.com**. This site provides access to the latest developments in CRM, case histories of companies using CRM, and trends that are shaping the industry.

REVIEW AND APPLICATIONS

1 **Define customer relationship management.** Customer relationship management (CRM) is a company-wide business strategy designed to optimize profitability, revenue, and customer satisfaction by focusing on highly defined and precise customer groups. This is accomplished by organizing the company around customer segments, encouraging and tracking customer interaction with the company, fostering customer-satisfying behaviors, and linking all processes of a company from its customers through its suppliers.

1.1 Identify the six components of the CRM process.

1.2 **TEAM** Form a team and identify several local businesses that would benefit from a CRM strategy. Select one business and outline a plan for implementing a CRM strategy for that business. You may want to visit the company and interview managers about their current initiatives. When you have completed your CRM plan, share it with the class—and the company.

1.3 **ONLINE WRITING** General Motors installs the "On-Star" system in many of its vehicles. On-Star is a location, information, and communication system available to drivers who wish to subscribe to the service. Go to the On-Star Web site, **http://www.onstar.com**, and read about some of the services that are offered to consumers. Based on your discovery, write a short report describing the various ways that On-Star can be used as a CRM tool, specifically in the context of creating interactions, gathering customer data, and customizing service offerings to customers.

unique approaches for establishing interactions specifically for this purpose. They include Web-based interactions, point-of-sale interactions, and transaction-based interactions.

3.1 Develop a plan for establishing and managing interactions with a business's customers. In this plan, identify the key touch points for customers, explain how the data warehouse would be designed, and indicate the main interaction methods that would be promoted to the customer.

4 **Outline the process of capturing customer data.** Based on the interaction between the organization and its customers, vast amounts of information can be obtained. In a CRM system, the issue is not how much data can be obtained, but rather what type of data should be acquired and how those data can be used effectively for relationship enhancement. The channel, transaction, and product or service consumed all constitute touch points between a customer and the organization. These touch points represent possible areas within a business where customer interactions can take place and, hence, the opportunity for acquiring data from the customer.

4.1   Assume you are the manager for a Hard Rock Café. Your boss has asked you to evaluate how the company is using its Web site to gather customer data. Go to the Web site for the Hard Rock (**http://www.hardrock.com**) and provide a detailed critique on how the site is used for capturing customer data. Comment on the types of customer data the Web site is designed to capture, and explain how those data would benefit your local Hard Rock operation.

5 **Describe the use of technology to store and integrate customer data.** Customer data gathering is complicated because information needed by one unit of the organization (e.g., sales and marketing) is often generated by another area of the business or even a third-party supplier (e.g., an independent marketing research firm). Because of the lack of standard structure and interface, organizations rely on technology to capture, store, and integrate strategically important customer information. The process of centralizing data in a CRM system is referred to as data warehousing. A data warehouse is a central repository of customer information collected by an organization.

5.1 Briefly explain the concept of a data warehouse. In the context of a CRM framework, why is a data warehouse such an important tool?

5.2 **WRITING** What is being written about customer data in today's periodicals? Search the InfoTrac database of articles at **http://www.infotrac-college.com** using keywords like "customer data" and "data warehousing." Are certain industries better represented in the citation list generated by your search? Are certain issues more prevalent? Read a selection of at least three to four articles, and write a brief analysis of what is being discussed in the press regarding these CRM topics.

6 **Describe how to identify the best customers.** Customer relationship management, as a process strategy, attempts to manage the interactions between a company and its customers. To be successful, organizations must identify customers who yield high profitability or high potential profitability. To accomplish this task, significant amounts of information must be gathered from customers, stored and integrated in the data warehouse, and then analyzed for commonalities that can produce segments that are highly similar, yet different from other customer segments. A useful approach to identifying the best customers is recency-frequency-monetary (RFM) analysis. Data mining uses RFM, predictive modeling, and other approaches to identify significant relationships among several customer dimensions within vast data warehouses. These significant relationships enable marketers to better define the most profitable customers and prospects.

6.1 Explain the concept of data mining. Provide five examples of companies that are currently using data mining, and explain why each is using it.

7 **Explain the process of leveraging customer information throughout the organization.** One of the benefits of a CRM system is the capacity to share information throughout the organization. This allows an organization to interact with all functional areas to develop programs targeted to its customers. This process is commonly referred to as campaign management. Campaign management involves developing customized product/service offerings for the appropriate customer segment and pricing and communicating these offerings for the purpose of enhancing customer relationships.

7.1 Campaign management is a benefit derived by an organization's ability to leverage and disseminate information throughout the company. Briefly define campaign management and explain how a business may apply it to its daily operations. In your answer, select a particular business as an example of effective campaign management.

TERMS

campaign management 674
compiled list 669
customer-centric 663
customer relationship management (CRM) 660
data warehouse 668

database 668
empowerment 664
interaction 664
knowledge management 663
learning 663
lifetime value analysis (LTV) 673

modeling 671
point-of-sale interactions 667
predictive modeling 673
response list 669
touch point 665

5. Write out an aggregate profile for each address. If you were a direct marketer, what kind of products and services would you market to each? What kind of offers would you create?

ETHICS EXERCISE

By combining several of its databases about parental purchasing behavior and the results of its market research, Maxwell, Inc. believes it has the tools to launch one-to-one marketing messages for the six- to nine-year-old fans of its JoyMax educational toy products without violating the law. In spite of potential parental backlash, the company believes the approach will help to customize new children's products and increase the company's share of these profitable young customers.

Questions

1. What do you think? Should Maxwell use one-to-one marketing tools to communicate with children?

2. Does the AMA Code of Ethics address marketing to children in its Code of Ethics? Go to **http://www.marketingpower.com** and review the code. Then, write a brief paragraph on how the AMA Code of Ethics relates to Maxwell's dilemma.

CAREER EXERCISE

If you are thinking about a career in customer relationship management, a good place to start is the Direct Marketing Association, at **http://www.the-dma.org**, which offers loads of professional development opportunities. Being proactive in developing your marketing portfolio will help you build your résumé and look good to prospective employers. The DMA also has a job bank on its site. You do not have to sign up to use it, and you can search the bank by keyword, career field, and/or location.

Although you may not qualify for many of the jobs at **http://www.brint.com/km/ken/jobs. html**, you will want to keep it in mind later on as you grow in a CRM career. Why? The reason is that it contains executive and professional job postings in the field of knowledge management.

Activity

1. Before looking for CRM openings, you may want to increase your understanding about this topic, even building this part of your marketing experience for your résumé. To do this, go to **http://www.dci.com**. View the listings of trade shows, lectures, seminars, and other resources on this site. Then choose one in your area, and register to attend. After the event, write a paragraph about your experience. How did the event affect your thinking about CRM? Did you leave with more questions or answers?

© GETTY IMAGES/PHOTODISC

GREEN HILLS FARMS: BEATING THE BIG STORES ONE CUSTOMER AT A TIME

ENTREPRENEUR Managing to stay in business for 68 years during the twentieth century was no small feat in any industry, let alone the hypercompetitive market for grocery sales. Everything from the supermarket to the megamarket to the hypermarket has been invented and built in the last 50 years, and most independently run stores have long since gone out of business. Independent grocer Gary Hawkins, however, has bucked the trend. In a neighborhood where the landscape is dominated by the megastores of large regional or national chains, Hawkins's family-run Green Hills Farms supermarket continues to thrive.

Grocery store shoppers are usually mercenaries, skipping from store to store to find the lowest prices on commodity-like goods. Hawkins's strategy has been to identify his customers, learn their shopping habits, and, no matter how much or how often they buy, entice them to return to the store. His program worked so successfully that his store was presented with a 1-to-1 Innovator Award from the prestigious Peppers and Rogers Group. To find the secret to Green Hills' success, one needs to look no farther than the one-to-one marketing tactics Hawkins uses to serve his most valuable customers.

Hawkins launched his frequent shopper rewards program in 1993, long before it was fashionable to collect shopper data. The store managed to sign 70 percent of its customers to the program within the first two years of its existence, and Hawkins then had the ability to identify more than 10,000 of his 15,000 customers by name. After giving cards to customers, Green Hills assigns them to one of five categories according to how much and how frequently they spend at the store.

Gem names—diamond, ruby, pearl, opal, and quartz—are used to describe the five spending segments, which signify a spending range from $100 per week at the diamond level to $10 per week at the quartz. Perks for customers who reach the diamond level include free Thanksgiving turkeys—fresh, not frozen—hand-selected Douglas fir trees at Christmas, $25 coupons for the garden shop in the spring, six coupons distributed throughout the year for 5 percent off a total purchase amount, and many postcard notifications of unadvertised specials.

That might seem rather costly, but Green Hills earns margins for diamond and ruby customers that are 10 percent above the average for the rest of the store's customers. In an industry where 1 percent margins are the norm for almost all stores and chains no matter their size, Hawkins hints that his are conservatively double that. Hawkins and his partners have been able to beat back *six* major competitors in the same neighborhood by making superior use of the data gained at the point of sale.

Lisa Piron, director of information services, applies database information toward promotion development. She targets known customers with customized offers on items in the area of the store that best meet their individual interests. Those promotions are far less costly to run than nontargeted mass-media advertising, and they yield much higher retention rates—96 percent of diamond-level customers, 80 percent of all customers—while satisfying the most valuable customers.

Green Hills has also reduced its weekly marketing costs by 50 percent by targeting its advertising to the zip codes where its most profitable customers live. That kind of commitment to identifying, collecting information, and targeting offers to the right customers in a timely fashion will probably keep Green Hills at the top of the hill for another sixty-eight years.[46]

Questions

1. Explain how database technology makes possible the CRM efforts at Green Hills Farms. Identify specific data that Green Hills is likely to collect and apply.

2. Describe how Green Hills' marketing communications are more effective than traditional methods.

identify any similarities to the modern components of the CRM model.

3. Explain the learning processes at Navarro Discount Pharmacies.

4. How does Navarro manage interactions with its customer base in terms of acquiring and capturing data?

ENCORE PRESENTATION

Casino (II)

Now that you have a basic understanding of customer relationship management, you can see how companies can use it to their advantage. As an encore to your study, watch the second film clip from Martin Scorsese's *Casino*, starring Robert DeNiro (Sam Rothstein), Joe Pesci, and Sharon Stone. The scene for this chapter shows how the casino handles high rollers, or "whales," to attract their business. Even though this scene is not a literal depiction of a customer relationship management system, you can still see how the clip illustrates chapter concepts. For instance, in what way does the narration describe the customer relationship management cycle in Exhibit 20.1? And think about what Sam Rothstein seems to know about his customer. Does this mean he has a customer-centric focus? Why or why not?

If you're having trouble with the concepts in this chapter, consider using some of the following study resources. You can review the videos, or test yourself with materials designed for all kinds of learning styles.

☑ **Xtra! (http://lambextra.swlearning.com)**

☑ Quiz   ☑ Feature Videos   ☑ Encore Videos   ☑ FAQ Videos

☑ Exhibit Worksheets   ☑ Marketing Plan Worksheets   ☐ Content

☑ **http://lamb.swlearning.com**

☑ Quiz   ☑ PowerPoint slides   ☑ Marketing News   ☑ Review Exercises

☐ Links   ☑ Marketing Plan Contest   ☑ Career Exercise   ☑ Use It Now

☑ **Study guide**

☑ Outline   ☑ Vocab Review   ☑ Test Questions   ☑ Marketing Scenario

Need More? Here's a tip. Studying for comprehensive exams doesn't have to be a chore. Form a study group. Photocopy the *Marketing* 8e glossary and cut it into strips, one term per strip. Put all strips into a large bowl. Divide into teams and draw out one strip at a time. Quiz the opposing team and then read the correct answer. You can do the same with the summary sections at the end of each chapter. You can tabulate points, but you'll all win!

tion of the DMCA will dramatically affect Web-based advertising in the future.

With over 40 million unique visitors monthly, Google is one of the most popular search engines on the Internet. Google and its chief competitor Yahoo! have experienced booming online advertising revenue due to keyword advertising. In 2003, keyword advertising accounted for between 50 and 75 percent of Google's $1 billion revenue. Search engines claim that keyword advertising is more effective at reaching consumers than other types of online advertising.

The pay-to-play model in which search engine companies sell keywords to the highest bidders has, however, brought legal troubles to Google. In early 2004, American Blind and Wallpaper Factory, Inc., filed a lawsuit against Google alleging that Google and its partners infringed on the company's trademark by allowing American Blind's competitors to bid on its trademarked keywords. The company wants Google to stop selling keywords such as *American Blind* (and any keyword combinations) since these words are part of its trademark. American Blind claims that any combination of its trademarked words will result in consumer confusion and allow its competitors to capitalize unfairly on American Blind's quality reputation.

American Blind and Wallpaper Factory was not the first company to sue search engines for trademark infringement. Playboy Enterprises filed a lawsuit against Netscape and America Online for infringement based on pop-up and banner ads keyed to words such as *playboy* and *playmate*.

brands. Basically, the company has agreed to halt the sale of keyword ads linked directly to verbatim, trademarked phrases at the request of the copyright holder. However, the company has refused to follow a similar practice for more generic, descriptive words such as *American, wallpaper,* and *blind*.

Although the jury is still out as to whether Google does violate trademarks, a ruling against Google would have a major financial impact on search engines. In the third quarter of 2003 alone, Web advertising was estimated at $1.75 billion with a large amount of that coming from keyword advertising. Regardless of the ruling, Google is finding that its pay-to-play revenue model has raised complex domain issues. Unfortunately, the keyword ad struggle took place at a time when Google was preparing for its highly anticipated initial public offering.

If search engines cannot sell keyword ads or are bound by considerable restrictions, the power of advertising on the Web will be diminished. Naturally, current and potential investors in Internet companies' stock will take this into consideration before making any stock purchases.[1]

Questions

1. Describe keyword advertising and explain how it could positively and negatively affect companies.

2. Conduct a keyword search for "marketing textbooks" on any search engine and identify pay-to-play advertisers.

Will Tickle, Inc. Lead the New Revolution of Internet Social Networking?

In the late 1990s, a group of Pennsylvania college students came up with a game they called "Six Degrees of Kevin Bacon." The game is based on the plot of the 1993 movie *Six Degrees of Separation*, in which a con man managed to convince people that he was the son of actor Sidney Poitier. The idea behind the game and the movie is that every person is separated by only six other people—six degrees of separation between you and everyone on earth.

The object of the game is to connect any film actor to Kevin Bacon with the fewest number of links. For example, suppose that a player is given Elvis Presley as an actor. The player could point out that both Elvis Presley and Edward Asner were in the 1969 movie *Change of Habit* (link 1). Edward Asner was in *JFK* in 1991 with Kevin Bacon (link 2). Thus, Elvis Presley has a Bacon number of two. Although some actors have no connection to Bacon (e.g., Fred Ott acted solo in the two films he appeared in), most actors can be linked to Bacon in six or fewer links.

The concept of the six degrees of separation is at the heart of social network theory. That is, the person you want to date, the person you want to work for or have working for you, the person you want to hang out with, or the person you want to do business with is probably no more than six degrees away from you. Whether for work or play, what better way to connect with people than via an online social network?

Internet-Based Social Networking Services

Social networking services help users expand their network of personal and business relationships. Joining an Internet social networking site is easy, and the idea is that once a person becomes a member, he or she will ask friends to join. These friends will ask friends to join, resulting in a network of personal links. Some network sites allow direct access to anyone in a personal network, while others require an introduction via the chain of acquaintances before personal contact can be made on the network.

By the beginning of 2004, several social networking sites were in beta testing. None of the sites charged a membership fee. Though similar in concept, the sites differed in implementation. Some sites were positioned more for relationships and others for professional contacts. The oldest site was one-year-old Friendster, which was also the largest, with over three million users. Online membership at competitors' sites was well below 500,000.

Friendster (**http://www.friendster.com**) and competitor Friendzy (**http://www.friendzy.com**) were geared for after-hours relationships. LinkedIn (**http://www.linkedin.com**) and Ryze (**http://www.ryze.com**) targeted business users by focusing on building professional relationships, including matching potential employers and employees and business partnering. Tribe (**http://www.tribe.net**) provides the opportunity for personal and/or business networking via the joining of special-interest groups ("tribes").

Social networks can also be formed by a group of strangers with similar interests. By June 2003, close to 800,000 people had signed up to use Meetup (**http://www.meetup.com**) to organize special events involving approximately 2,500 topics in over 600 cities. For example, Meetup was a major source of contact in Howard Dean's campaign for the Democratic presidential nomination in 2003 and 2004. More than 100,000 people linked for Dean meetings via this Internet site.

Emode

Founded in the late 1990s, Emode.com was positioned as one of the top Internet sites for personality quizzes. By 2004, the company was the number one destination for self-discovery and improvement. Tests available to members include quizzes that are primarily for entertainment such as "What's Your Party Style?" "What's Your Comfort Zone?" "What Kind of Kisser Are You?" and "How Obnoxious Are You?" More serious tests include IQ, Career Interest Inventory, the True Talent Test, and the Corporate Culture Test.

With two million registered members, however, the company provides more than entertainment. By aligning with third-party product and service companies, Emode has become a direct marketer capable of targeting advertisements directly to consumers who meet a company's target demographic profile. Additionally, Emode can align with companies to explore the relationships between its members and a company's brand. For example, Emodo created a test called "Which VW Beetle Are You?" The test results match a member's personality with the appropriate Volkswagen Beetle model—and provide Volkswagen with considerable market research.

In late 2003, Emode.com was renamed Tickle, Inc. to reflect the company's fun and intimate personality. At the same time, the company acquired Ringo, Inc., the third largest social networking company in the market. Just prior to the name change and acquisition, Emode had launched a social networking service. The acquisition of Ringo, with its 350,000 members, pushed Tickle's social networking membership to over one million members.

Tickle's goal is to market social marketing as a feature on its site. The company is currently profitable with its fee-based personality quizzes and matchmaking service. With the addition of a social networking offering, the company

Internet has caused the marketing department, which in the past was responsible for creating and developing the entire communications program for products/services, to share its marketing communications responsibilities with other functional groups within the company. Marketing has relinquished sole ownership of the creative process, due to its inability to design a Web site that echoes its vision for the communications program. Marketing must now work closely with information technology, which translates the vision into a visual, interactive Web site. Traditionally, a product was marketed to a mass audience through brochures and/or print ads. Marketing departments created communications campaigns on a grand, informal scale to promote products. Now, with the Internet, companies are marketing their products to consumers directly. Consequently, marketing, along with information technologists, must develop Web sites (which may ultimately replace print ads and brochures) that clearly communicate the company as well as the products to the online user.

2. What are some of the benefits of networking functional departments, customers, and suppliers?

   Very broadly, benefits include:

   - *Facilitation of cross-functional communication:* All functional groups have access to the same information, at the same time.

to get the product to the customer).

   - *Immediate delivery of component parts, materials, etc.:* Suppliers become as aware of the stock level as the customer and ship based on their reporting processes rather than waiting for the customer to place an order.

3. Which functional areas are actively involved in making e-commerce a success? How?

   Marketing, information technology, legal, finance/accounting, and research and development are all functional areas that are involved in making e-commerce a success. Marketing and information technology partner to create a visual communication to the customer while lawyers, specialized in cyber law, analyze the Web site's legal logistics. Finance and accounting evaluate the costs of maintaining the site and determine its budget. Research and development continuously work on improving the product offering. Together, these departments work to create a successful cyber experience.

Suggested Readings

Jerry Luftman and Tom Brier, "Achieving and Sustaining Business-IT Alignment," *California Management Review* (Fall 1999), 109–122.

Roland Rust, Katherine N. Lemon, and Das Narayandas, *Customer Equity Management: Marketing Strategy for Profitable Customer Relationships* (Upper Saddle River, NJ: Pearson Prentice Hall, 2005).

Glossary

A

accessory equipment Goods, such as portable tools and office equipment, that are less expensive and shorter-lived than major equipment.

adopter A consumer who was happy enough with his or her trial experience with a product to use it again.

advertising Impersonal, one-way mass communication about a product or organization that is paid for by a marketer.

advertising appeal A reason for a person to buy a product.

advertising campaign A series of related advertisements focusing on a common theme, slogan, and set of advertising appeals.

advertising objective A specific communication task a campaign should accomplish for a specified target audience during a specified period.

advertising response function A phenomenon in which spending for advertising and sales promotion increases sales or market share up to a certain level but then produces diminishing returns.

advocacy advertising A form of advertising in which an organization expresses its views on controversial issues or responds to media attacks.

agents and brokers Wholesaling intermediaries who do not take title to a product but facilitate its sale from producer to end user by representing retailers, wholesalers, or manufacturers.

AIDA concept A model that outlines the process for achieving promotional goals in terms of stages of consumer involvement with the message; the acronym stands for *attention, interest, desire,* and *action.*

applied research An attempt to develop new or improved products.

aspirational reference group A group that someone would like to join.

assurance The knowledge and courtesy of employees and their ability to convey trust.

ATC. *See* average total cost.

atmosphere The overall impression conveyed by a store's physical layout, decor, and surroundings.

attitude A learned tendency to respond consistently toward a given object.

audience selectivity The ability of an advertising medium to reach a precisely defined market.

automatic vending The use of machines to offer goods for sale.

AVC. *See* average variable cost.

average total cost (ATC) Total costs divided by quantity of output.

average variable cost (AVC) Total variable costs divided by quantity of output.

B

baby boomers People born between 1946 and 1964.

bait pricing A price tactic that tries to get consumers into a store through false or misleading price advertising and then uses high-pressure selling to persuade consumers to buy more expensive merchandise.

base price The general price level at which the company expects to sell the good or service.

basic research Pure research that aims to confirm an existing theory or to learn more about a concept or phenomenon.

basing-point pricing A price tactic that charges freight from a given (basing) point, regardless of the city from which the goods are shipped.

BehaviorScan A scanner-based research program that tracks the purchases of 3,000 households through store scanners in each research market.

belief An organized pattern of knowledge that an individual holds as true about his or her world.

benefit segmentation The process of grouping customers into market segments according to the benefits they seek from the product.

brainstorming The process of getting a group to think of unlimited ways to vary a product or solve a problem.

brand A name, term, symbol, design, or combination thereof that identifies a seller's products and differentiates them from competitors' products.

brand equity The value of company and brand names.

brand loyalty A consistent preference for one brand over all others.

brand mark The elements of a brand that cannot be spoken.

brand name That part of a brand that can be spoken, including letters, words, and numbers.

break-even analysis A method of determining what sales volume must be reached before total revenue equals total costs.

business analysis The second stage of the screening process where preliminary figures for demand, cost, sales, and profitability are calculated.

business marketing The marketing of goods and services to individuals and organizations for purposes other than personal consumption.

business product (industrial product) A product used to manufacture other goods or services, to facilitate an organization's operations, or to resell to other customers.

business services Expense items that do not become part of a final product.

buyer A department head who selects the merchandise for his or her department and may also be responsible for promotion and personnel.

buyer for export An intermediary in the global market that assumes all ownership risks and sells globally for its own account.

buying center All those persons in an organization who become involved in the purchase decision.

C

campaign management Developing product or service offerings customized for the appropriate customer segment and then pricing and communicating these offerings for the purpose of enhancing customer relationships.

cannibalization A situation that occurs when sales of a new product cut into sales of a firm's existing products.

capital-intensive Using more capital than labor in the production process.

cash discount A price reduction offered to a consumer, an industrial user, or

member of a marketing channel that exercises authority and power over the activities of other channel members.

channel members All parties in the marketing channel that negotiate with one another, buy and sell products, and facilitate the change of ownership between buyer and seller in the course of moving the product from the manufacturer into the hands of the final consumer.

channel partnering (channel cooperation) The joint effort of all channel members to create a supply chain that serves customers and creates a competitive advantage.

channel power The capacity of a particular marketing channel member to control or influence the behavior of other channel members.

CLT. *See* central-location telephone facility.

closed-ended question An interview question that asks the respondent to make a selection from a limited list of responses.

cobranding Placing two or more brand names on a product or its package.

code of ethics A guideline to help marketing managers and other employees make better decisions.

cognitive dissonance Inner tension that a consumer experiences after recognizing an inconsistency between behavior and values or opinions.

cold calling A form of lead generation in which the salesperson approaches potential buyers without prior knowledge of the prospects' needs or financial status.

commercialization The decision to market a product.

communication The process by which we exchange or share meanings through a common set of symbols.

hanced with information from public records, such as census data, auto registrations, birth announcements, business start-ups, or bankruptcies.

component lifestyles The practice of choosing goods and services that meet one's diverse needs and interests rather than conforming to a single, traditional lifestyle.

component parts Either finished items ready for assembly or products that need very little processing before becoming part of some other product.

computer-assisted personal interviewing An interviewing method in which the interviewer reads the questions from a computer screen and enters the respondent's data directly into the computer.

computer-assisted self-interviewing An interviewing method in which a mall interviewer intercepts and directs willing respondents to nearby computers where the respondent reads questions off a computer screen and directly keys his or her answers into a computer.

concentrated targeting strategy A strategy used to select one segment of a market for targeting marketing efforts.

concept test A test to evaluate a new-product idea, usually before any prototype has been created.

consumer behavior Processes a consumer uses to make purchase decisions, as well as to use and dispose of purchased goods or services; also includes factors that influence purchase decisions and product use.

consumer decision-making process A five-step process used by consumers when buying goods or services.

consumer penalty An extra fee paid by the consumer for violating the terms of the purchase agreement.

recting actions that do not help the organization reach those objectives within budget guidelines.

convenience product A relatively inexpensive item that merits little shopping effort.

convenience sample A form of nonprobability sample using respondents who are convenient or readily accessible to the researcher—for example, employees, friends, or relatives.

convenience store A miniature supermarket, carrying only a limited line of high-turnover convenience goods.

cooperative advertising An arrangement in which the manufacturer and the retailer split the costs of advertising the manufacturer's brand.

core service The most basic benefit the consumer is buying.

corporate social responsibility Business's concern for society's welfare.

cost competitive advantage Being the low-cost competitor in an industry while maintaining satisfactory profit margins.

cost per contact The cost of reaching one member of the target market.

countertrade A form of trade in which all or part of the payment for goods or services is in the form of other goods or services.

coupon A certificate that entitles consumers to an immediate price reduction when they buy the product.

credence quality A characteristic that consumers may have difficulty assessing even after purchase because they do not have the necessary knowledge or experience.

crisis management A coordinated effort to handle all the effects of unfavorable publicity or of another unexpected, unfavorable event.

cross-tabulation A method of analyzing data that lets the analyst look at the responses to one question in relation to the responses to one or more other questions.

culture The set of values, norms, attitudes, and other meaningful symbols that shape human behavior and the artifacts, or products, of that behavior as they are transmitted from one generation to the next.

cumulative quantity discount A deduction from list price that applies to the buyer's total purchases made during a specific period.

customer-centric Under this philosophy, the company customizes its product and service offering based on data generated through interactions between the customer and the company.

customer relationship management (CRM) A company-wide business strategy designed to optimize profitability, revenue, and customer satisfaction by focusing on highly defined and precise customer groups.

customer satisfaction Customers' evaluation of a good or service in terms of whether it has met their needs and expectations.

customer value The ratio of benefits to the sacrifice necessary to obtain those benefits.

D

data warehouse A central repository for data from various functional areas of the organization that are stored and inventoried on a centralized computer system so that the information can be shared across all functional departments of the business.

database A collection of data, especially one that can be accessed and manipulated by computer software.

database marketing The creation of a large computerized file of customers' and potential customers' profiles and purchase patterns.

decision support system (DSS) An interactive, flexible computerized information system that enables managers to obtain and manipulate information as they are making decisions.

decline stage A long-run drop in sales.

decoding Interpretation of the language and symbols sent by the source through a channel.

delayed-quotation pricing A price tactic used for industrial installations and many accessory items, in which a firm price is not set until the item is either finished or delivered.

demand The quantity of a product that will be sold in the market at various prices for a specified period.

demographic segmentation Segmenting markets by age, gender, income, ethnic background, and family life cycle.

demography The study of people's vital statistics, such as their age, race and ethnicity, and location.

department store A store housing several departments under one roof.

derived demand The demand for business products.

destination stores Stores that consumers purposely plan to visit.

development The stage in the product development process in which a prototype is developed and a marketing strategy is outlined.

diffusion The process by which the adoption of an innovation spreads.

direct channel A distribution channel in which producers sell directly to consumers.

direct foreign investment Active ownership of a foreign company or of overseas manufacturing or marketing facilities.

direct marketing (direct-response marketing) Techniques used to get consumers to make a purchase from their home, office, or other non-retail setting.

direct retailing The selling of products by representatives who work door-to-door, office-to-office, or at home parties.

discount store A retailer that competes on the basis of low prices, high turnover, and high volume.

discrepancy of assortment The lack of all the items a customer needs to receive full satisfaction from a product or products.

discrepancy of quantity The difference between the amount of product produced and the amount an end user wants to buy.

distribution resource planning (DRP) An inventory control system that manages the replenishment of goods from the manufacturer to the final consumer.

diversification A strategy of increasing sales by introducing new products into new markets.

DRP. *See* distribution resource planning.

drugstore A retail store that stocks pharmacy-related products and services as its main draw.

DSS. *See* decision support system.

dual distribution (multiple distribution) The use of two or more channels to distribute the same product to target markets.

dumping The sale of an exported product at a price lower than that charged for the same or a like product in the "home" market of the exporter.

E

EDI. *See* electronic data interchange.

80/20 principle A principle holding that 20 percent of all customers generate 80 percent of the demand.

elastic demand A situation in which consumer demand is sensitive to changes in price.

elasticity of demand Consumers' responsiveness or sensitivity to changes in price.

electronic data interchange (EDI) Information technology that replaces the paper documents that usually accompany business transactions, such as purchase orders and invoices, with electronic transmission of the needed information to reduce inventory levels, improve cash flow, streamline operations, and increase the speed and accuracy of information transmission.

electronic distribution A distribution technique that includes any kind of product or service that can be distributed electronically, whether over traditional forms such as fiber-optic cable or through satellite transmission of electronic signals.

empathy Caring, individualized attention to customers.

empowerment Delegation of authority to solve customers' problems quickly—usually by the first person that the customer notifies regarding a problem.

encoding The conversion of a sender's ideas and thoughts into a message, usually in the form of words or signs.

environmental management When a company implements strategies that attempt to shape the external environment within which it operates.

environmental scanning Collection and interpretation of information about forces, events, and relationships in the external environment that may affect the future of the organization or the implementation of the marketing plan.

escalator pricing A price tactic in which the final selling price reflects cost increases incurred between the time the order is placed and the time delivery is made.

ethics The moral principles or values that generally govern the conduct of an individual.

evaluation Gauging the extent to which the marketing objectives have been achieved during the specified time period.

evoked set (consideration set) A group of brands, resulting from an information search, from which a buyer can choose.

export broker An intermediary who plays the traditional broker's role by bringing buyer and seller together.

exporting Selling domestically produced products to buyers in another country.

express warranty A written guarantee.

extensive decision making The most complex type of consumer decision making, used when buying an unfamiliar, expensive product or an infrequently bought item; requires use of several criteria for evaluating options and much time for seeking information.

external information search The process of seeking information in the outside environment.

extranet A private electronic network that links a company with its suppliers and customers.

F

factory outlet An off-price retailer that is owned and operated by a manufacturer.

family brand Marketing several different products under the same brand name.

family life cycle (FLC) A series of stages determined by a combination of age, marital status, and the presence or absence of children.

Federal Trade Commission (FTC) A federal agency empowered to prevent persons or corporations from using unfair methods of competition in commerce.

feedback The receiver's response to a message.

field service firm A firm that specializes in interviewing respondents on a subcontracted basis.

fixed cost A cost that does not change as output is increased or decreased.

FLC. *See* family life cycle.

follow-up The final step of the selling process, in which the salesperson ensures that delivery schedules are met, that the goods or services perform as promised, and that the buyers' employees are properly trained to use the products.

Food and Drug Administration (FDA) A federal agency charged with enforcing regulations against selling and distributing adulterated, misbranded, or hazardous food and drug products.

four Ps Product, place, promotion, and price, which together make up the marketing mix.

frame error An error that occurs when a sample drawn from a population differs from the target population.

franchise The right to operate a business or to sell a product.

franchisee An individual or business that is granted the right to sell another party's product.

franchiser The originator of a trade name, product, methods of operation, and so on, that grants operating rights to another party to sell its product.

Free Trade Area of the Americas (FTAA) A regional trade agreement that, when signed, will create a regional trading zone encompassing 34 countries in North and South America.

freight absorption pricing A price tactic in which the seller pays all or part of the actual freight charges and does not pass them on to the buyer.

frequency The number of times an individual is exposed to a given message during a specific period.

frequent buyer program A loyalty program in which loyal consumers are rewarded for making multiple

1965 and 1978.

Generation Y People born between 1979 and 1994.

generic product A no-frills, no-brand-name, low-cost product that is simply identified by its product category.

generic product name Identifies a product by class or type and cannot be trademarked.

geodemographic segmentation Segmenting potential customers into neighborhood lifestyle categories.

geographic segmentation Segmenting markets by region of the country or the world, market size, market density, or climate.

global brand A brand where at least 20 percent of the product is sold outside its home country or region.

global marketing Marketing that targets markets throughout the world.

global marketing standardization Production of uniform products that can be sold the same way all over the world.

global vision Recognizing and reacting to international marketing opportunities, being aware of threats from foreign competitors in all markets, and effectively using international distribution networks.

gross margin The amount of money the retailer makes as a percentage of sales after the cost of goods sold is subtracted.

group dynamics Group interaction essential to the success of focus-group research.

growth stage The second stage of the product life cycle when sales typically grow at an increasing rate, many competitors enter the market, large companies may start acquiring small pioneering firms, and profits are healthy.

H

heterogenity The variability of the inputs and outputs of services, which cause services to tend to be less standardized and uniform than goods.

horizontal conflict A channel conflict that occurs among channel members on the same level.

I

ideal self-image The way an individual would like to be.

IMC. *See* integrated marketing communications.

implementation The process that turns marketing plans into action assignments and ensures that these assignments are executed in a way that accomplishes the plans' objectives.

implied warranty An unwritten guarantee that the good or service is fit for the purpose for which it was sold.

independent retailers Retailers owned by a single person or partnership and not operated as part of a larger retail institution.

individual branding Using different brand names for different products.

inelastic demand A situation in which an increase or a decrease in price will not significantly affect demand for the product.

inflation A general rise in prices, often accompanied by a lack of increase in wages, which results in decreased purchasing power.

infomercial A 30-minute or longer advertisement that looks more like a TV talk show than a sales pitch.

informational labeling A type of package labeling designed to help consumers make proper product selections and lower their cognitive dissonance after the purchase.

InfoScan A scanner-based sales-tracking service for the consumer packaged-goods industry.

innovation A product perceived as new by a potential adopter.

inseparability The inability of the production and consumption of a service to be separated. Consumers must be present during the production.

institutional advertising A form of advertising designed to enhance a company's image rather than promote a particular product.

intangibility The inability of services to be touched, seen, tasted, heard, or felt in the same manner that goods can be sensed.

integrated marketing communications (IMC) The careful coordination of all promotional messages for a product or a service to assure the consistency of messages at every contact point where a company meets the consumer.

intensive distribution A form of distribution aimed at having a product available in every outlet where target customers might want to buy it.

interaction The point at which a customer and a company representative exchange information and develop learning relationships.

internal information search The process of recalling past information stored in the memory.

internal marketing Treating employees as customers and developing systems and benefits that satisfy their needs.

International Monetary Fund (IMF) An international organization that acts as a lender of last resort, providing loans to troubled nations, and also works to promote trade through financial cooperation.

interpersonal communication Direct, fact-to-face communication between two or more people.

introductory stage The full-scale launch of a new product into the marketplace.

inventory control system A method of developing and maintaining an adequate assortment of materials or products to meet a manufacturer's or a customer's demand.

involvement The amount of time and effort a buyer invests in the search, evaluation, and decision processes of consumer behavior.

J

JIT. *See* just-in-time production.

joint costs Costs that are shared in the manufacturing and marketing of several products in a product line.

joint demand The demand for two or more items used together in a final product.

joint venture A venture in which a domestic firm buys part of a foreign company or joins with a foreign company to create a new entity.

just-in-time production (JIT) A process that redefines and simplifies manufacturing by reducing inventory levels and delivering raw materials just when they are needed on the production line.

K

keiretsu A network of interlocking corporate affiliates.

keystoning The practice of marking up prices by 100 percent, or doubling the cost.

knowledge management The process by which learned information from customers is centralized and shared in order to enhance the relationship between customers and the organization.

L

lead generation (prospecting) Identification of those firms and people most likely to buy the seller's offerings.

lead qualification Determination of a sales prospect's (1) recognized need, (2) buying power, and (3) receptivity and accessibility.

leader pricing (loss-leader pricing) A price tactic in which a product is sold near or even below cost in the hope that shoppers will buy other items once they are in the store.

learning A process that creates changes in behavior, immediate or expected, through experience and practive.

learning (CRM) An informal process of collecting customer data through customer comments and feedback on product or service performance.

licensing The legal process whereby a licensor agrees to let another firm use its manufacturing process, trademarks, patents, trade secrets, or other proprietary knowledge.

lifestyle A mode of living as identified by a person's activities, interests, and opinions.

lifetime value analysis (LTV) A data manipulation technique that projects the future value of the customer over a period of years using the assumption that marketing to repeat customers is more profitable than marketing to first-time buyers.

limited decision making The type of decision making that requires a moderate amount of time for gathering information and deliberating about an unfamiliar brand in a familiar product category.

logistics The process of strategically managing the efficient flow and storage of raw materials, in-process inventory, and finished goods from point of origin to point of consumption.

logistics information system Information technology that integrates and links all of the logistics functions of the supply chain.

loyalty marketing program A promotional program designed to build long-term, mutually beneficial relationships between a company and its key customers.

LTV. *See* lifetime value analysis.

M

major equipment (installations) Capital goods such as large or expensive machines, mainframe computers, blast furnaces, generators, airplanes, and buildings.

egy that entails attracting new customers to existing products.

market opportunity analysis (MOA) The description and estimation of the size and sales potential of market segments that are of interest to the firm and the assessment of key competitors in these market segments.

market orientation A philosophy that assumes that a sale does not depend on an aggressive sales force but rather on a customer's decision to purchase a product.

market penetration A marketing strategy that tries to increase market share among existing customers.

market segment A subgroup of people or organizations sharing one or more characteristics that cause them to have similar product needs.

market segmentation The process of dividing a market into meaningful, relatively similar, and identifiable segments or groups.

market share A company's product sales as a percentage of total sales for that industry.

marketing An organizational function and a set of processes for creating, communicating, and delivering value to customers and for managing customer relationships in ways that benefit the organization and its stakeholders.

marketing audit A thorough, systematic, periodic evaluation of the objectives, strategies, structure, and performance of the marketing organization.

marketing channel (channel of distribution) A set of interdependent organizations that ease the transfer of ownership as products move from producer to business user or consumer.

marketing concept The idea that the social and economic justification for

marketing objective A statement of what is to be accomplished through marketing activities.

marketing plan A written document that acts as a guidebook of marketing activities for the marketing manager.

marketing planning Designing activities relating to marketing objectives and the changing marketing environment.

marketing research The process of planning, collecting, and analyzing data relevant to a marketing decision.

marketing research objective The specific information needed to solve a marketing research problem; the objective should be to provide insightful decision-making information.

marketing research problem Determining what information is needed and how that information can be obtained efficiently and effectively.

marketing strategy The activities of selecting and describing one or more target markets and developing and maintaining a marketing mix that will produce mutually satisfying exchanges with target markets.

markup pricing The cost of buying the product from the producer plus amounts for profit and for expenses not otherwise accounted for.

Maslow's hierarchy of needs A method of classifying human needs and motivations into five categories in ascending order of importance: physiological, safety, social, esteem, and self-actualization.

mass communication The communication of a concept or message to large audiences.

mass customization (build-to-order) A production method whereby products are not made until an order is

between the information desired by the researcher and the information provided by the measurement process.

media mix The combination of media to be used for a promotional campaign.

media planning The series of decisions advertisers make regarding the selection and use of media, allowing the marketer to optimally and cost-effectively communicate the message to the target audience.

media schedule Designation of the media, the specific publications or programs, and the insertion dates of advertising.

medium The channel used to convey a message to a target market.

merchant wholesaler An institution that buys goods from manufacturers and resells them to businesses, government agencies, and other wholesalers or retailers and that receives and takes title to goods, stores them in its own warehouses, and later ships them.

Mercosur The largest Latin American trade agreement, which includes Argentina, Bolivia, Brazil, Chile, Paraguay, and Uruguay.

metasearch engines Search engines that make informational queries to many search engines simultaneously; search engines of search engines.

mission statement A statement of the firm's business based on a careful analysis of benefits sought by present and potential customers and analysis of existing and anticipated environmental conditions.

modeling The act of building a model in a situation where the answer is known and then applying the model to another situation where the answer is unknown.

modified rebuy A situation where the purchaser wants some change in the original good or service.

morals The rules people develop as a result of cultural values and norms.

motive A driving force that causes a person to take action to satisfy specific needs.

MR. *See* marginal revenue.

MRP. *See* materials requirement planning.

multiculturalism When all major ethnic groups in an area—such as a city, county, or census tract—are roughly equally represented.

multinational corporation A company that is heavily engaged in international trade, beyond exporting and importing.

multiplier effect (accelerator principle) Phenomenon in which a small increase or decrease in consumer demand can produce a much larger change in demand for the facilities and equipment needed to make the consumer product.

multisegment targeting strategy A strategy that chooses two or more well-defined market segments and develops a distinct marketing mix for each.

mystery shoppers Researchers posing as customers who gather observational data about a store.

N

NAICS. *See* North American Industry Classification System.

need recognition Result of an imbalance between actual and desired states.

needs assessment A determination of the customer's specific needs and wants and the range of options the customer has for satisfying them.

negotiation The process during which both the salesperson and the prospect offer special concessions in an attempt to arrive at a sales agreement.

networking A process of finding out about potential clients from friends, business contacts, coworkers, acquaintances, and fellow members in professional and civic organizations.

new buy A situation requiring the purchase of a product for the first time.

new product A product new to the world, the market, the producer, the seller, or some combination of these.

new-product strategy A plan that links the new-product development process with the objectives of the marketing department, the business unit, and the corporation.

newsgroups Function like bulletin boards on the Internet. They are established to focus on a particular topic.

niche One segment of a market.

niche competitive advantage The advantage achieved when a firm seeks to target and effectively serve a small segment of the market.

noise Anything that interferes with, distorts, or slows down the transmission of information.

nonaspirational reference group A group with which an individual does not want to associate.

noncumulative quantity discount A deduction from list price that applies to a single order rather than to the total volume of orders placed during a certain period.

nonmarketing-controlled information source A product information source that is not associated with advertising or promotion.

nonprobability sample Any sample in which little or no attempt is made to get a representative cross section of the population.

nonprofit organization An organization that exists to achieve some goal other than the usual business goals of profit, market share, or return on investment.

nonprofit organization marketing The effort by nonprofit organizations to bring about mutually satisfying exchanges with target markets.

nonstore retailing Shopping without visiting a store.

norm A value or attitude deemed acceptable by a group.

North American Free Trade Agreement (NAFTA) An agreement between Canada, the United States, and Mexico that created the world's largest free trade zone.

North American Industry Classification System (NAICS) A detailed numbering system developed by the United States, Canada, and Mexico to classify North American business establishments by their main production processes.

O

observation research A research method that relies on four types of observation: people watching people, people watching an activity, machines watching people, and machines watching an activity.

odd–even pricing (psychological pricing) A price tactic that uses odd-numbered prices to connote bargains and even-numbered prices to imply quality.

off-price retailer A retailer that sells at prices 25 percent or more below traditional department store prices because it pays cash for its stock and usually doesn't ask for return privileges.

online retailing A type of shopping available to consumers with personal computers and access to the Internet.

one-to-one marketing An individualized marketing method that utilizes customer information to build long-term, personalized, and profitable relationships with each customer.

open-ended question An interview question that encourages an answer phrased in the respondent's own words.

opinion leader An individual who influences the opinions of others.

optimizers Business customers who consider numerous suppliers, both familiar and unfamiliar, solicit bids, and study all proposals carefully before selecting one.

order processing system A system whereby orders are entered into the supply chain and filled.

original equipment manufacturers (OEMs) Individuals and organizations that buy business goods and incorporate them into the products that they produce for eventual sale to other producers or to consumers.

outsourcing (contract logistics) A manufacturer's or supplier's use of an independent third party to manage an entire function of the logistics system, such as transportation, warehousing, or order processing.

P

penetration pricing A pricing policy whereby a firm charges a relatively low price for a product initially as a way to reach the mass market.

perception The process by which people select, organize, and interpret stimuli into a meaningful and coherent picture.

perceptual mapping A means of displaying or graphing, in two or more dimensions, the location of products, brands, or groups of products in customers' minds.

perishability The inability of services to be stored, warehoused, or inventoried.

personality A way of organizing and grouping the consistencies of an individual's reactions to situations.

personal selling A purchase situation in which two people communicate in an attempt to influence each other.

persuasive labeling A type of package labeling that focuses on a promotional theme or logo with consumer information being secondary.

pioneering advertising A form of advertising designed to stimulate primary demand for a new product or product category.

positioning Developing a specific marketing mix to influence potential customers' overall perception of a brand, product line, or organization in general.

preapproach A process that describes the "homework" that must be done by a salesperson before he or she contacts a prospect.

predatory pricing The practice of charging a very low price for a product with the intent of driving competitors out of business or out of a market.

predictive modeling A data manipulation technique in which marketers try to determine, based on some past set of occurrences, what the odds are that some other occurrence, such as a response or purchase, will take place in the future.

premium An extra item offered to the consumer, usually in exchange for some proof of purchase of the promoted product.

prestige pricing Charging a high price to help promote a high-quality image.

price That which is given up in an exchange to acquire a good or service.

price bundling Marketing two or more products in a single package for a special price.

price equilibrium The price at which demand and supply are equal.

price fixing An agreement between two or more firms on the price they will charge for a product.

price lining The practice of offering a product line with several items at specific price points.

price shading The use of discounts by salespeople to increase demand for one or more products in a line.

price skimming A pricing policy whereby a firm charges a high

processed materials Products used directly in manufacturing other products.

product Everything, both favorable and unfavorable, that a person receives in an exchange.

product advertising A form of advertising that touts the benefits of a specific good or service.

product category All brands that satisfy a particular type of need.

product development A marketing strategy that entails the creation of new products for current customers; the process of converting applications for new technologies into marketable products.

product differentiation A positioning strategy that some firms use to distinguish their products from those of competitors.

product item A specific version of a product that can be designated as a distinct offering among an organization's products.

product life cycle (PLC) A concept that provides a way to trace the stages of a product's acceptance, from its introduction (birth) to its decline (death).

product line A group of closely related product items.

product line depth The number of product items in a product line.

product line extension Adding additional products to an existing product line in order to compete more broadly in the industry.

product line pricing Setting prices for an entire line of products.

product mix All products that an organization sells.

product mix width The number of product lines an organization offers.

product modification Changing one or more of a product's characteristics.

uct in order to influence an opinion or elicit a response.

promotional allowance (trade allowance) A payment to a dealer for promoting the manufacturer's products.

promotional mix The combination of promotion tools—including advertising, public relations, personal selling, and sales promotion—used to reach the target market and fulfill the organization's overall goals.

promotional strategy A plan for the optimal use of the elements of promotion: advertising, public relations, personal selling, and sales promotion.

PSA. *See* public service advertisement.

psychographic segmentation Market segmentation on the basis of personality, motives, lifestyles, and geodemographics.

publicity Public information about a company, good, or service appearing in the mass media as a news item.

public relations The marketing function that evaluates public attitudes, identifies areas within the organization the public may be interested in, and executes a program of action to earn public understanding and acceptance.

public service advertisement (PSA) Announcement that promotes a program of a federal, state, or local government or of a nonprofit organization.

pull strategy A marketing strategy that stimulates consumer demand to obtain product distribution.

pulsing media schedule A media scheduling strategy that uses continuous scheduling throughout the year coupled with a flighted schedule during the best sales periods.

purchasing power A comparison of income versus the relative cost of a set standard of goods and services in different geographic areas.

push money Money offered to channel intermediaries to encourage them to "push" products—that is, to encourage other members of the channel to sell the products.

push strategy A marketing strategy that uses aggressive personal selling and trade advertising to convince a wholesaler or a retailer to carry and sell particular merchandise.

pyramid of corporate social responsibility A model that suggests corporate social responsibility is composed of economic, legal, ethical, and philanthropic responsibilities and that the firm's economic performance supports the entire structure.

Q

quantity discount A price reduction offered to buyers buying in multiple units or above a specified dollar amount.

quota A statement of the individual salesperson's sales objectives, usually based on sales volume alone but sometimes including key accounts (those with greatest potential), new accounts, repeat sales, and specific products.

R

random error An error that occurs when the selected sample is an imperfect representation of the overall population.

random sample A sample arranged in such a way that every element of the population has an equal chance of being selected as part of the sample.

raw materials Unprocessed extractive or agricultural products, such as mineral ore, lumber, wheat, corn, fruits, vegetables, and fish.

reach The number of target consumers exposed to a commercial at least once during a specific period, usually four weeks.

real self-image The way an individual actually perceives himself or herself.

rebate A cash refund given for the purchase of a product during a specific period.

receiver The person who decodes a message.

recession A period of economic activity characterized by negative growth, which reduces demand for goods and services.

reciprocity A practice where business purchasers choose to buy from their own customers.

recruited Internet sample A sample in which respondents are prerecruited and must qualify to participate. They are then e-mailed a questionnaire or directed to a secure Web site.

reference group A group in society that influences an individual's purchasing behavior.

referral A recommendation to a salesperson from a customer or business associate.

relationship marketing A strategy that entails forging long-term partnerships with customers.

relationship selling (consultative selling) A sales practice that involves building, maintaining, and enhancing interactions with customers in order to develop long-term satisfaction through mutually beneficial partnerships.

reliability The ability to perform a service dependably, accurately, and consistently.

repositioning Changing consumers' perceptions of a brand in relation to competing brands.

research design Specifies which research questions must be answered, how and when the data will be gathered, and how the data will be analyzed.

response list A customer list that includes the names and addresses of individuals who have responded to an offer of some kind, such as by mail, telephone, direct-response television, product rebates, contests or sweepstakes, or billing inserts.

responsiveness The ability to provide prompt service.

retailer A channel intermediary that sells mainly to consumers.

retailing All the activities directly related to the sale of goods and services to the ultimate consumer for personal, nonbusiness use.

retailing mix A combination of the six Ps—product, place, promotion, price, presentation, and personnel—to sell goods and services to the ultimate consumer.

return on investment (ROI) Net profit after taxes divided by total assets.

revenue The price charged to customers multiplied by the number of units sold.

ROI. *See* return on investment.

routine response behavior The type of decision making exhibited by consumers buying frequently purchased, low-cost goods and services; requires little search and decision time.

S

sales orientation The idea that people will buy more goods and services if aggressive sales techniques are used and that high sales result in high profits.

sales presentation A formal meeting in which the salesperson presents a sales proposal to a prospective buyer.

sales process (sales cycle) The set of steps a salesperson goes through in a particular organization to sell a particular product or service.

sales promotion Marketing activities—other than personal selling, advertising, and public relations—that stimulate consumer buying and dealer effectiveness.

sales proposal A formal written document or professional presentation that outlines how the salesperson's product or service will meet or exceed the prospect's needs.

sample A subset from a larger population.

sampling A promotional program that allows the consumer the opportunity to try the product or service for free.

sampling error An error that occurs when a sample somehow does not represent the target population.

satisficers Business customers who place an order with the first familiar supplier to satisfy product and delivery requirements.

scaled-response question A closed-ended question designed to measure the intensity of a respondent's answer.

scanner-based research A system for gathering information from a single group of respondents by continuously monitoring the advertising, promotion, and pricing they are exposed to and the things they buy.

scrambled merchandising The tendency to offer a wide variety of nontraditional goods and services under one roof.

screened Internet sample An Internet sample with quotas based on desired sample characteristics.

screening The first filter in the product development process, which eliminates ideas that are inconsistent with the organization's new-product strategy or are obviously inappropriate for some other reason.

search quality A characteristic that can be easily assessed before purchase.

seasonal discount A price reduction for buying merchandise out of season.

seasonal media schedule A media scheduling strategy that runs advertising only during times of the year when the product is most likely to be used.

secondary data Data previously collected for any purpose other than the one at hand.

formation that supports his or her personal beliefs.

self-concept How consumers perceive themselves in terms of attitudes, perceptions, beliefs, and self-evaluations.

selling against the brand Stocking well-known branded items at high prices in order to sell store brands at discounted prices.

sender The originator of the message in the communication process.

service The result of applying human or mechanical efforts to people or objects.

service mark A trademark for a service.

shopping product A product that requires comparison shopping because it is usually more expensive than a convenience product and found in fewer stores.

simulated (laboratory) market testing The presentation of advertising and other promotion materials for several products, including a test product, to members of the product's target market.

simultaneous product development A team-oriented approach to new-product development.

single-price tactic A price tactic that offers all goods and services at the same price (or perhaps two or three prices).

social class A group of people in a society who are considered nearly equal in status or community esteem, who regularly socialize among themselves both formally and informally, and who share behavioral norms.

socialization process How cultural values and norms are passed down to children.

societal marketing orientation The idea that an organization exists not only to satisfy customer wants and needs

stimulus Any unit of input affecting one or more of the five senses: sight, smell, taste, touch, hearing.

stimulus discrimination A learned ability to differentiate among similar products.

stimulus generalization A form of learning that occurs when one response is extended to a second stimulus similar to the first.

straight commission A method of compensation in which the salesperson is paid some percentage when a sale is made.

straight rebuy A situation in which the purchaser reorders the same goods or services without looking for new information or investigating other suppliers.

straight salary A method of compensation in which the salesperson receives a salary regardless of sales productivity.

strategic alliance (strategic partnership) A cooperative agreement between business firms.

strategic business unit (SBU) A subgroup of a single business or collection of related businesses within the larger organization.

strategic channel alliance A cooperative agreement between business firms to use the other's already established distribution channel.

strategic planning The managerial process of creating and maintaining a fit between the organization's objectives and resources and evolving market opportunities.

subculture A homogeneous group of people who share elements of the overall culture as well as unique elements of their own group.

supercenter A retail store that combines groceries and general merchandise goods with a wide range of services.

the source to the point of consumption, resulting in enhanced customer and economic value.

supply chain team An entire group of individuals who orchestrate the movement of goods, services, and information from the source to the consumer.

survey research The most popular technique for gathering primary data, in which a researcher interacts with people to obtain facts, opinions, and attitudes.

sustainability The idea that socially responsible companies will outperform their peers by focusing on the world's social problems and viewing them as opportunities to build profits and help the world at the same time.

sustainable competitive advantage An advantage that cannot be copied by the competition.

SWOT analysis Identifying internal strengths (S) and weaknesses (W) and also examining external opportunities (O) and threats (T).

T

tangibles The physical evidence of a service, including the physical facilities, tools, and equipment used to provide the service.

target market A defined group most likely to buy a firm's product; a group of people or organizations for which an organization designs, implements, and maintains a marketing mix intended to meet the needs of that group, resulting in mutually satisfying exchanges.

teamwork Collaborative efforts of people to accomplish common objectives.

telemarketing The use of the telephone to sell directly to consumers.

temporal discrepancy A situation that occurs when a product is produced but a customer is not ready to buy it.

test marketing The limited introduction of a product and a marketing program to determine the reactions of potential customers in a market situation.

touch point All possible areas of a business where customers communicate with that business.

trade allowance A price reduction offered by manufacturers to intermediaries, such as wholesalers and retailers.

trademark The exclusive right to use a brand or part of a brand.

trade sales promotion Sales promotion activities targeting a channel member, such as a wholesaler or retailer.

two-part pricing A price tactic that charges two separate amounts to consume a single good or service.

U

unbundling Reducing the bundle of services that comes with the basic product.

undifferentiated targeting strategy A marketing approach that views the market as one big market with no individual segments and thus uses a single marketing mix.

unfair trade practice acts Laws that prohibit wholesalers and retailers from selling below cost.

uniform delivered pricing A price tactic in which the seller pays the actual freight charges and bills every purchaser an identical, flat freight charge.

unique selling proposition A desirable, exclusive, and believable advertising appeal selected as the theme for a campaign.

unitary elasticity A situation in which total revenue remains the same when prices change.

universal product codes (UPCs) A series of thick and thin vertical lines (bar codes), readable by computerized optical scanners, that represent numbers used to track products.

universe The population from which a sample will be drawn.

unrestricted Internet sample A survey in which anyone with a computer and modem can fill out the questionnaire.

unsought product A product unknown to the potential buyer or a known product that the buyer does not actively seek.

UPCs. *See* universal product codes.

Uruguay Round An agreement to dramatically lower trade barriers worldwide; created the World Trade Organization.

usage-rate segmentation Dividing a market by the amount of product bought or consumed.

V

value The enduring belief that a specific mode of conduct is personally or socially preferable to another mode of conduct.

value-based pricing Setting the price at a level that seems to the customer to be a good price compared to the prices of other options.

variable cost A cost that varies with changes in the level of output.

vertical conflict A channel conflict that occurs between different levels in a marketing channel, most typically between the manufacturer and wholesaler or between the manufacturer and retailer.

W

want Recognition of an unfulfilled need and a product that will satisfy it.

warehouse membership clubs Limited-service merchant wholesalers that sell a limited selection of brand-name appliances, household items, and groceries on a cash-and-carry basis to members, usually small businesses and groups.

warranty A confirmation of the quality or performance of a good or service.

World Bank An international bank that offers low-interest loans, advice, and information to developing nations.

World Trade Organization (WTO) A trade organization that replaced the old General Agreement on Tariffs and Trade (GATT).

WTO. *See* World Trade Organization.

Y

yield management systems (YMS) A technique for adjusting prices that uses complex mathematical software to profitably fill unused capacity by discounting early purchases, limiting early sales at these discounted prices, and overbooking capacity.

Z

zone pricing A modification of uniform delivered pricing that divides the United States (or the total market) into segments or zones and charges a flat freight rate to all customers in a given zone.

Prentice-Hall, 2000), 12.

4. Nora Isaacs, "Crash & Burn," http://www.upsidetoday.com, March 2001, 186–192.

5. David W. Cravens, Charles W. Lamb, Jr., and Victoria Crittenden, *Strategic Marketing Management Cases,* 7th ed. (New York: McGraw-Hill Irwin, 2002), 2.

6. Ibid.

7. Gordon Fairclough, "Some Pharmacies Sell New Nic-Fix Lollipops Laced with Nicotine," *Wall Street Journal,* April 3, 2002, B1, B4. Used with permission.

8. Larry Selden and Geoffrey Colvin, "What Customers Want," *Fortune,* July 7, 2003, 122–127.

9. Lisa Picarille, "It's the Customer, Stupid," *Customer Relationship Management,* July 2002, 20.

10. Isaacs, "Crash & Burn," 190.

11. Sandra Dolbow, "Kmart May Be Down, but Don't Count It Out," *Brandweek,* January 28, 2002, 5.

12. Ibid.

13. Don Peppers and Martha Rogers, "The Seven Habits of Successful Customer-Based Firms," *eMarketer,* May 10, 2002, online.

14. Christopher J. Zane, "Creating Lifetime Customers," *The Retailing Issues Letter,* September 2000, 2.

15. Tony Pachi, "Sublime Service," *Customer Relationship Management,* October 2001, 25–26.

16. "Return to Sender," *Marketing News,* June 18, 2001, 3.

17. Valarie A. Zeithaml and Mary Jo Bitner, *Services Marketing* (New York: McGraw-Hill Irwin, 2003), 86.

18. Robert Bibb and Eric Gehm, "The 360-Degree View," *Customer Relationship Management,* June 2001, 23–24.

19. "Interview with Disney's CIO Roger Berry," *eWeek,* December 23, 2003.

20. Robert Levering and Milton Moskowitz, "100 Best Companies to Work For," *Fortune,* January 20, 2003, 127–152.

21. John Yokoyama and Jim Bergquist, "The World Famous Pike Place Fish Story," *The Retailing Issues Letter,* November 2001, 5.

Teaching Marketing" contest held in conjunction with the publication of the Eighth Edition of *Marketing.* Ideas came from marketing professors across the country, who teach all different sizes and types of marketing courses. Information on ways to implement these great ideas in the classroom can be found in the Instructor Manual that accompanies this text.

25. Joyceann Cooney-Curran, "All About 'Me': Noodé Provides a Fun Yet Effective Skin-Care Line to the 'Generation Me' Demographic," *Global Cosmetic Industry,* November 2000, 62; Andrea Grossman, "It's a Noodé for Skin Care," *WWD,* January 5, 2001, 13; ———, "Noodé Aims to Shield Sun's Rays," *WWD,* January 4, 2002, 10; ———, "Small Firms Win with Samples, Moxie," *WWD,* January 11, 2002, 10; "Noodé for the Me Generation," *Soap & Cosmetics,* November 2000, 72.

CHAPTER 2

1. Mike Steere, "A Timeless Recipe for Success," *Business 2.0,* September 2003, 47–49; Stacy Perman, "Fat Burgers: How the Snyder Family Has Kept In-N-Out Hot for Half a Century," *Los Angeles Magazine,* February 2004, 36.

2. Chris Reidy, "Lands' End To Join Sears Family for $1.9 Billion," *Knight Ridder Tribune Business News,* May 14, 2002, 1.

3. Lisa McLaughlin, "The War of the Low-Carb Colas," *Time,* June 7, 2004, 137.

4. Jennifer Dixon, "Shoppers Abandon Kmart Stores; Wal-Mart, Target Pick Up Business" *Knight Ridder Tribune Business News,* March 30, 2002, 1.

5. Christine Bittar, "S. C. Johnson Flushes Lines with New Wipes," *Brandweek,* January 28, 2002, 4.

6. http://www.benjerry.com/mission.html, November 1, 2003.

7. "Technology Brief—Hewlett-Packard Co.: Officials Don't Get Bonuses Because of Failed Objectives," *Wall Street Journal,* January 30, 2002, B5.

Move to Boost Revenue," *Multichannel News,* January 26, 2004, 26; "A 'Drive-In' 50th for Hallmark Series: Movies Fit for the Family Still Inspire," *Christian Science Monitor,* February 2, 2001, 18; "Hallmark Cards and Crown Media Holdings Launch Hallmark Channel in U.S.; Odyssey Network to Become Hallmark Channel August 6th," *PR Newswire,* March 28, 2001, online.

11. Julia Boorstin, "How Coach Got Hot," *Fortune,* October 28, 2003, 131–134.

12. Alex Taylor, "Bill's Brand New Ford," *Fortune,* July 2004, 68.

13. Paul Gao, Jonathan R. Woetzel, and Yibing Wu, "Can Chinese Brands Make It Abroad?" *The McKinsey Quarterly,* 4, 2003, online.

14. This application exercise is based upon the contribution of Robert O'Keefe, Philip R. Kemp, and J. Steven Kelly, all of DePaul University, to *Great Ideas in Teaching Marketing,* a teaching supplement that accompanies Lamb, Hair, and McDaniel's *Marketing.* Their entry titled "Using Environmental Scan Reports as a Means of Assessing Student Learning" received a first place award in the strategy category of the "Best of the Great Ideas in Teaching Marketing" contest held in conjunction with the publication of the Eighth Edition of *Marketing.*

15. Geoff Keighly, "The Phantasmagoria Factory," *Business 2.0,* January/February 2004, 103; Christopher J. Chipello, "Cirque du Soleil Seeks Partnerships to Create Entertainment Centers," *WSJ.com,* July 18, 2001; Steve Friess, "Cirque Dreams Big," *Newsweek,* July 14, 2003, 42; "Bravo Announces Programming Alliance with Cirque du Soleil; Original Series, Specials, and Documentaries to Air on Bravo, 'The Official U.S. Network of Cirque du Soleil,'" *Business Wire,* June 19, 2000; "Inhibitions Take the Night Off for International Gala Premiere of ZUMANITY(tm); Another Side of Cirque du Soleil(tm) at New York–New York Hotel and Casino," *PR Newswire,* September 21,

2003; Laura Del Rosso, "'O' Dazzles with Air, Underwater Acrobatics," *Travel Weekly*, August 5, 2002; Gigi Berardi, "Circus + Dance = Cirque du Soleil," *Dance Magazine*, September 2002.

CHAPTER 3

1. Marc Gunther, "Tree Huggers, Soy Lovers, and Profits," *Fortune*, June 23, 2003, 98–104.
2. Ibid., 102.
3. Ibid., 104.
4. Ibid., 104.
5. This section is adapted from Archie B. Carroll, "The Pyramid of Corporate Social Responsibility: Toward the Moral Management of Organizational Stakeholders," *Business Horizons*, July/August 1991, 39–48; see also Kirk Davidson, "Marketers Must Accept Greater Responsibilities," *Marketing News*, February 2, 1998, 6.
6. "Survey Rates Companies' Reputations, and Many Are Found Wanting," *Wall Street Journal*, February 7, 2001, B1, B6.
7. Sankar Sen and C. B. Bhattacharya, "Does Doing Good Always Lead to Doing Better? Consumer Reactions to Corporate Responsibility," *Journal of Marketing Research*, May 2001, 225–243.
8. Gunther, "Tree Huggers," 104.
9. "CBS Television Issues First Responsibility Report," *PR Newswire*, October 2, 2003; Mary Ann Watson, "Ethics in Entertainment Television," *Journal of Popular Film and Television*, Winter 2004, 3.
10. Gunther, "Tree Huggers," 104.
11. "Greed, Grasso and a Gilded Age," *Wall Street Journal*, September 18, 2003, A17.
12. Based on Edward Stevens, *Business Ethics* (New York: Paulist Press, 1979). Reprinted with permission. Used with permission of Paulist Press.
13. Anusorn Singhapakdi, Skott Vitell, and Kenneth Kraft, "Moral Intensity and Ethical Decisionmaking of Marketing Professionals," *Journal of Business Research* 36 (March 1996): 245–255; Ishmael Akaah and Edward Riordan, "Judgments of Marketing Professionals about Ethical Issues in Marketing Research: A Replication and Extension," *Journal of Marketing Research*, February 1989, 112–120. See also Shelby Hunt, Lawrence Chonko, and James Wilcox, "Ethical Problems of Marketing Researchers," *Journal of Marketing Research*, August 1984, 309–324; Kenneth Andrews, "Ethics in Practice," *Harvard Business Review*, September/October 1989, 99–104; Thomas Dunfee, Craig Smith, and William T. Ross, Jr., "Social Contracts and Marketing Ethics," *Journal of Marketing*, July 1999, 14–32; Jay Handleman and Stephen Arnold, "The Role of Marketing Actions with a Social Dimension: Appeals to the Institutional Environment," *Journal of Marketing*, July 1999, 33–48; and David Turnipseed, "Are Good Soldiers Good? Exploring the Link between Organizational Citizenship Behavior and Personal Ethics," *Journal of Business Research*, January 2002, 1–16.
14. O. C. Ferrell, Debbie Thorne, and Linda Ferrell, "Legal Pressure for Ethical Compliance in Marketing," *Proceedings of the American Marketing Association*, Summer 1995, 412–413.
15. "Raytheon Teams with LRN to Create Online and Interactive Standards of Business Conduct," *PR Newswire*, November 4, 2002.
16. "Four Businesses Honored with Prestigious International Award for Outstanding Marketplace Ethics," *PR Newswire*, September 23, 2002.
17. Todd Zaun, "For Japanese Girls, Uniforms Are Now Too Cool for School," *Wall Street Journal*, August 5, 2003, A1, A6.
18. "Women-Owned Businesses Booming, but So Are Obstacles," *Associated Press Newswires*, April 11, 2000.
19. "Tech Companies Try Wooing Women with Girlie Marketing," *Wall Street Journal*, August 26, 2003, B1, B4.
20. Ibid.
21. "Tool Sellers Tap Their Feminine Side," *Wall Street Journal*, February 29, 2002, B1.
22. Ibid.
23. Christy Harvey, "A Guide to Who Holds the Purse Strings," *Wall Street Journal*, June 22, 2000, A14.
24. Ibid.
25. Linda Morten, "Targeting Generation Y," *Public Relations Quarterly*, Summer 2002, 46–49.
26. Michael Weiss, "To Be About To Be," *American Demographics*, September 2003, 31.
27. "Hooking Up with Gen Y," *Business 2.0*, October 2003, 49–50.
28. "The Gen X Budget," *American Demographics*, July/August 2002, S5.
29. Pamela Paul, "Meet the Parents," *American Demographics*, January 2002, 47.
30. "The Younger Boomer Budget," *American Demographics*, July/August 2002, S6.
31. Ibid.
32. Ibid.
33. "The Older Boomer Budget," *American Demographics*, July/August 2002, S7.
34. Ibid.
35. "Many Older Workers to Delay Retirement until after the Age of 70," *Wall Street Journal*, September 23, 2003, D2.
36. "The Senior Budget," *American Demographics*, July/August 2002, S10.
37. "The Mighty Mature Market," *American Demographics*, April 2003, 25.
38. "On the Move," *American Demographics*, February 2003, 8.
39. "Diversity in America," *American Demographics*, November 2002, S1–S15.
40. Ibid.
41. "Race, Ethnicity and the Way We Shop," *American Demographics*, February 2003, 30.
42. "Color Blind," *American Demographics*, September 2003, 22–26.
43. Lafayette Jones, "A Sign of the Times," *Promo*, February 2, 2002.
44. "A Multicultural Mecca," *American Demographics*, May 2003, S4–S7.
45. "Buying Power of Hispanics Set to Soar," *Wall Street Journal*, April 18, 2003, B1, B3.
46. "Look Who's Tuned In," *American Demographics*, October 2002, 26–28.
47. Joan Raymond, "The Multicultural Report," *American Demographics*, November 2001, S1–S4.
48. Ibid., S6.
49. Ibid.
50. Jerry Goodbody, "Taking the Pulse of Asian Americans," *Adweek's Marketing Week*, August 12, 2001, 32.
51. "Income Gap Steady, Poverty Spreads," *Wall Street Journal*, September 29, 2003, A14.
52. "The Rich Get Richer and That's OK," *BusinessWeek*, August 26, 2002, 90.
53. "Life below the U.S. Median," *American Demographics*, December 2002/January 2003, 36.
54. U.S. Census Bureau, 2000 U.S. Census.
55. "The Affluent," *American Demographics*, December 2002/January 2003, 42.
56. "The Upper Echelon," *American Demographics*, December 2002/January 2003, 44.
57. "Why for Many This Recovery Feels More Like a Recession," *Wall Street Journal*, May 29, 2003, A1.
58. "A New Picture," *Wall Street Journal*, May 19, 2003, R17.
59. "Productivity: Too Much of a Good Thing," *Wall Street Journal*, December 19, 2003, A2.
60. "Freeze-Dried Berries Heat Up Cereal Duel," *Wall Street Journal*, May 15, 2003, B2.
61. The Tide story is from Katrina Brooker, "A Game of Inches," *Fortune*, February 5, 2001, 98–100.
62. "Money Talks," *American Demographics*, September 2002, 53.
63. "In Age of SARS, Wal-Mart Adjusts Global Buying Machine," *Wall Street Journal*, May 28, 2003, B1
64. This application exercise is based upon the contribution of Mark Andrew Mitchell (University of South Carolina— Spartanburg) to *Great Ideas in Teaching Marketing*, a teaching supplement that accompanies Lamb, Hair, and McDaniel's *Marketing*. Professor Mitchell's entry titled "The Guide to Ethnic Dining" was part of the "Best of the Great Ideas in Teaching Marketing" contest held in conjunction with the publication of the Eighth Edition of *Marketing*.
65. http://www.rocksktargames.com; http://www.take2games.com; Logan Hill, "Why Rockstar Games Rock," *Wired.com*, July 2002; Michael Serazio, "Vice City Confidential: The 'Atari' Generation Grows Up," *Columbia.edu*, March 7, 2003; "The Games Kids Play: Are Mature Video Games Too Violent for Teens?" *Current Events*, February 7, 2003; "Deadly Inspiration? Teens Say Video Game Inspired Them in Deadly Highway Shooting," *ABCnews.com*, September 5, 2003; "Florida Officials Take Aim at Violent Games," *Reuters*, February 6, 2004; Andrew Bushell, "Popular Video Game Instructs Players to 'Shoot the Haitians'—New York AG Takes on *Grand Theft Auto*," *VillageVoice.com*, January 30, 2004; Christopher Byron, "Give Back Take-Two," *New York Post*, December 29, 2003, 29.

tional Center for Policy Analysis, http://www.ncpa.org, October 23, 2003.

9. "Shippers Say New Border Rules Could Delay Just-in-Time Cargo," *Wall Street Journal,* August 29, 2003, A1, A10.

10. "Borders Are So 20th Century," *BusinessWeek,* September 22, 2003, 68.

11. Roger Thurow and Susan Warren, "In War on Poverty, Chad's Pipeline Plays Unusual Role," *Wall Street Journal,* June 24, 2003, A1, A9. Used with permission.

12. Theodore Levitt, "The Globalization of Markets," *Harvard Business Review,* May/June 1983, 92–102.

13. For an excellent article on culture and marketing, see Cheryl Nakata and K. Sivakauar, "Instituting the Marketing Concept in a Multinational Setting: The Role of National Culture," *Journal of the Academy of Marketing Science,* Summer 2001, 255–275.

14. "To Put It in Perspective," *American Demographics,* June 2003, 9.

15. Ibid.

16. "The Driver's Seat Is More Lavish, As Bentley Buyers Grow in China," *Wall Street Journal,* June 11, 2003, B5.

17. "World Bank Faults Tight Regulation," *Wall Street Journal,* October 7, 2003, A2, A10.

18. "Bush's Steely Pragmatism," *BusinessWeek,* March 18, 2002, 44.

19. Don Groves, "Writers Back Oz Trade Plan," *Daily Variety,* October 15, 2003, 4; Lawrie Zion, "Aussies Fear Culture Clash: Exemption Sought in U.S. Trade Pact," *Hollywood Reporter,* October 7, 2003, 4.

20. http://www.wto.org, October 24, 2003.

21. "Cancun: Victory for Whom?" *Wall Street Journal,* September 16, 2003, A4.

22. "After Cancun, WTO Panel Seeks an End to Gridlock," *Wall Street Journal,* September 29, 2003, A16.

23. "Preserving and Expanding Our Important NAFTA Trading Relationships," *Business Credit,* September 2002, 54.

24. "NAFTA's Benefits to Firms in Canada May Top Those for Mexico," *Wall Street Journal,* February 24, 2003, A2.

51–67.

32. "In Europe, Hot New Fashion for Urban Hipsters Comes from Peoria," *Wall Street Journal,* August 28, 2002, B1.

33. http://www.franchise.org, October 30, 2003.

34. http://www.newhorizons.com, October 30, 2003.

35. "A Sneaker Maker Says China Partner Became Its Rival," *Wall Street Journal,* December 14, 2002, A1, A8.

36. For an excellent article on joint ventures, see Mark Houston and Shane Johnson, "Buyer-Supplier Contracts versus Joint Ventures: Determinants and Consequences of Transaction Structure," *Journal of Marketing Research,* February 2000, 1–15.

37. See Debanjan Mitra and Peter Golden, "Whose Culture Matters? Near-Market Knowledge and Its Impact on Foreign Market Entry Timing," *Journal of Marketing Research,* August 2002, 350–365.

38. "Visions of Sugar Plums South of the Border," *Wall Street Journal,* February 13, 2002, A15.

39. "Cracking China's Market," *Wall Street Journal,* January 9, 2003, B1, B4.

40. "Something Fishy Is Going On in Japan in the Ice-Cream Biz," *Wall Street Journal,* September 4, 2002, A1, A10.

41. "Small Is Profitable," *BusinessWeek,* August 26, 2002, 112–114.

42. "A Certain 'Je Ne Sais Quoi' at Disney's New Park," *Wall Street Journal,* March 12, 2002, B1, B4.

43. "Why Corona Is Big Here, and Miller Is So Scarce in Mexico," *Wall Street Journal,* January 17, 2003, B1, B4.

44. "India's Retailing Makeover," *Wall Street Journal,* October 28, 2003, A1, A15.

45. "Amway in China: Once Barred, Now Booming," *Wall Street Journal,* March 12, 2003, B1, B5.

46. "Solving China's Logistics Riddle," *Wall Street Journal,* October 15, 2003, A18, A19.

47. Sarah McBride, "Kia's Audacious Sorento Plan," *Wall Street Journal,* April 8, 2003, A12.

bility," *Billboard,* March 8, 2003, 59; "MTV Announces International Expansion Plans for Europe, Asia and Latin America; Company to Add New Services in Regional Growth Markets Worldwide," *Business Wire,* March 9, 1996; Kerry Cappel, Catherine Belton, Tom Lowry, Manjeet Kripalani, Brian Bremner, and Dexter Roberts, "MTV's World," *BusinessWeek.com,* February 18, 2002.

PART 1

1. "Scholastic Debt Rating Placed on CreditWatch Negative," *BusinessWeek Online,* July 18, 2003, http://www.businessweek.com; "Teaching Reading Is Rocket Science," American Federation of Teachers, June 1999 http://www.aft.org/Edissues/rocketscience.htm; Diane Brady, "Harry Potter and—What Else?" *BusinessWeek Online,* June 30, 2003, http://www.businessweek.com; Britt Erica Tunick, "Is There a Harry Potter Effect? Scholastic's Woes Aren't Offset by Huge Children's Hit," *Investment Dealer's Digest,* June 23, 2003, online; U.S. Department of Education, Office of Educational Research and Improvement, National Center for Education Statistics, 1999.

2. "What's Next for Valve and Half-Life 2?" October 3, 2003, http://www.gamespy.com; Nationwide News Proprietary Ltd, "No Force, No Clues, No Suspect in Game Theft," *The Australian,* November 4, 2003, T31; Kay Randall, "The Status of Online Gaming," The University of Texas at Austin, Feature Story, February 4, 2004, http://www.utexas.edu/features; Suneel Ratan, "Theft Adds to VU Games' Woes," *Wired News,* October 10, 2003, http://www.wired.com/news; David Walsh, Douglas Gentile, Jeremy Gleske, Monica Walsh, and Emily Chasco, "Eighth Annual Mediawise Video Game Report Card," National Institute on Media and the Family, December 8, 2003, http://www.mediafamily.org/research/report.

CHAPTER 5

1. Matthew Maier, "Hooking up with Gen Y," *Business 2.0*, October 2003, 49; http://www.virginmobileusa.com/.

2. Michael Totty, "Information, Please," *Wall Street Journal*, October 29, 2001, R6.

3. Emily Nelson, "P&G Checks Out Real Life," *Wall Street Journal*, May 17, 2001, B1.

4. "What's Hot in the Living Spaces of Young Adults?" *American Demographics*, September 2003, 14.

5. http://www.cingular.com.

6. Lee Gomes, "Download, Downshift and Go: MP3 Takes to the Road," *Wall Street Journal*, February 27, 2001, B1.

7. Suzanne Bidlake, "P&G to Roll Laundry Tablet in Europe," *Advertising Age*, March 1, 1999, 18.

8. Ronald Alsop, "Survey Rates Companies' Reputations, and Many Are Found Wanting," *Wall Street Journal*, February 7, 2001, B1. See also Gordon Fairclough, "Philip Morris Seeks to Mold Its Image into an Altria State," *Wall Street Journal*, November 16, 2001, A3.

9. Ernest Beck, "Boosting Diageo's Sprits," *Wall Street Journal*, February 23, 2001, B1.

10. David P. Hamilton, "Not an Easy Sell: TiVo, ReplayTV and Other 'PVRs' Don't Take Off," *Wall Street Journal*, February 7, 2001, B1.

11. Ronald Alsop, "The Best Corporate Reputations in America: Johnson & Johnson (Think Babies!) Turns Up Tops," *Wall Street Journal*, September 23, 1999, B1. See also Alsop, "Survey Rates Companies' Reputations, and Many Are Found Wanting."

12. Princeton Research Survey Associates, "Consumer Behavior, Experiences and Attitudes: A Comparison by Age Groups," *AARP*, March 1999.

13. Amy Goldwasser, "What Is the Good Life? An A–Z Guide to Living Large," *Inc.*, October 2003, 71.

14. http://www.mystictan.com.

15. Philips Magnavox ad, *Business 2.0*, October 2003, 81.

16. Michael Totty, "Making the Sale," *Wall Street Journal*, September 24, 2001, R6.

17. Stephanie Thompson, "Marketers Embrace Latest Health Claims," *Advertising Age*, February 28, 2000, 20–22.

18. Ibid. See also John Urquhart, "A Health Food Hits Big Time," *Wall Street Journal*, August 3, 1999, B1, B4.

19. Sandra Yin, "Color Bind," *American Demographics*, September 2003, 24, 26.

20. Stephanie Thompson, "Fashion Week Gets TV Channel," *Advertising Age*, September 1, 2003, 3.

21. Cathleen Egan, "Kellogg, General Mills Battle over Bars," *Wall Street Journal*, March 26, 2001, B10.

22. Bill Stoneman, "Beyond Rocking the Ages: An Interview with J. Walker Smith," *American Demographics*, May 1998, 44–49.

23. Pamela Paul, "Getting Inside Gen Y," *American Demographics*, September 2001, 42–49. See also Pooja Bhatia, "Look Who's Reading," *Wall Street Journal*, November 9, 2001, W1.

24. Michael Weiss, "To Be About To Be," *American Demographics*, September 2003, 30–36.

25. Miriam Jordon, "Global Craze for Diet Drugs," *Wall Street Journal*, August 24, 2001, B1. See also Leslie Chang, "Bring Science to Weight Loss in China," *Wall Street Journal*, August 24, 2001, B1.

26. Bill Spindle, "Cowboys and Samurai: The Japanizing of Universal," *Wall Street Journal*, March 22, 2001, B1.

27. "How to Succeed in Multicultural Marketing," *American Demographics*, July 2003, Special Supplement; John Schmid, "American Exporters Struggle to Make Inroads into Chinese Market," *Knight Ridder Tribune Business News*, August 1, 2003, 3C; Christina Hoag, "Barnes & Noble Goes Bilingual," *Knight Ridder Tribune Business News*, September 16, 2003, 2C; Naomi Klein, "The Tyranny of Brands," *Australian Financial Review*, February 11, 2000, 1; Sally Beatty and Carol Hymowitz, "How MTV Stays Tuned In to Teens," *Wall Street Journal*, March 21, 2000, B1, B4.

28. Joshua Harris Prager, "People with Disabilities Are Next Consumer Niche," *Wall Street Journal*, December 15, 1999, B1, B6.

29. Devon Spurgeon, "Hold the Oatmeal! Restaurants Now Court the Breakfast Burger Eater," *Wall Street Journal*, September 4, 2001, B1.

30. http://www.snitch.com; http://www.lexingtonsnitch.com.

31. Eduardo Porter, "For Hispanic Marketers, Census Says It All," *Wall Street Journal*, April 24, 2001, B8. See also Dean Bonham, "Hispanic Fans Make It to Big Leagues," *Rocky Mountain News*, June 23, 2001, 5C.

32. Heidi J. Shrager, "Closed-Circle Commerce," *Wall Street Journal*, November 19, 2001, B1.

33. Ned Potter, "The World's Most Luxurious Car? Mercedes-Benz' Maybach Costs $350,000," *ABC Nightly News*, August 19, 2003.

34. Michael J. Weiss, "A Tale of Two Cheeses," *American Demographics*, February 1998, 16–17.

35. Rich Thomaselli, "James' Coke Deal Sets New Endorser Standard," *Advertising Age*, August 25, 2003, 3.

36. Barbara Cooke, "Radar Fine-Tuned to 'Cool' Sets Some Teens Apart," *Chicago Tribune*, March 5, 2000, 1.

37. Erin White, "Abercrombie Seeks to Send Teeny-Boppers Packing," *Wall Street Journal*, August 30, 2001, B1.

38. Norihiko Shirouzu, "Japan's High-School Girls Excel in Art of Setting Trends," *Wall Street Journal*, April 24, 1998, B1, B6.

39. Thompson, "Fashion Week Gets TV Channel."

40. Kortney Stringer, "Young and Restless," *Wall Street Journal*, September 24, 2001, R8; Nina Munk, "Peddling Cool: How Teens Buy," *Fortune*, April 13, 1998, 28–30.

41. Jason Schrotberger and Mark Turner, "Obesity and Organic Foods: Countervailing Social Trends," January 14, 2003, http://www.turner-invest.com/index.cfm/fuseaction/commentary.detail/ID/913; "Preventing Obesity and Chronic Diseases through Good Nutrition and PhysicalActivity," Centers for Disease Control and Prevention, July 2003, http://www.cdc.gov/nccdphp/pe_factsheets/pe_pa.htm; http://www.corpschoolpartners.org/bev_guidelines.shtm; http://www2.coca-cola.com/ourcompany/hal_schools.html; http://www.pepsico.com/citizenship/healthwellness.shtml; http://www.healthispower.net; http://teenagerstoday.com/resources/articles/overweight.htm; Greg Winter, "States Try to Limit Sales of Junk Food in School Buildings," *New York Times*, September 9, 2001, 1; Betsy McKay, "Coke Finds Its Exclusive School Contracts Aren't So Easily Given Up," *Wall Street Journal*, June 26, 2001, B1; Randy Southerland, "Schools' Soda Deals Losing Fizz? Challenges Mount over Issues of Nutrition, Commercialization," *Atlanta Journal-Constitution*, September 26, 2001, JA1.

42. John Gaffney, "The Kids Are Doing It. Should You?" *Business 2.0*, November 2001, 141.

43. Jonathan Eig, "Edible Entertainment," *Wall Street Journal*, October 24, 2001, B1.

44. *Advertising Age*, December 10, 2003, back cover.

45. Matthew Klein, "He Shops, She Shops," *American Demographics*, March 1998, 34–35.

46. Khanh T. L. Tran, "Women Assert Computer Games Aren't Male Preserve," *Wall Street Journal*, February 26, 2001, B1. See also Meeyoung Song, "Credit-Card Companies Cater to Korean Women," *Wall Street Journal*, June 6, 2001, B4.

47. Emily Nelson, "Forget Super-models—Revlon's New Face Gets Lipstick on Her Teeth," *Wall Street Journal*, March 30, 2001, B1.

48. Rebecca Gardyn, "Almost Adults," *American Demographics*, September 2003, 11.

49. Diane Crispell, "Fruit of the Boom," *Marketing Tools*, April 1998.

50. Vanessa O'Connell and Jon E. Hilsenrath, "Advertisers Are Cautious as Household Makeup Shifts," *Wall Street Journal*, May 15, 2001, B1.

51. Jean Halliday, "$45 Mil Campaign: Nissan Attempts to Sex Up Quest," *Advertising Age*, August 4, 2003, 7.

52. Nora J. Rifon and Molly Catherine Ziske, "Using Weight Loss Products: The Roles of Involvement, Self-Efficacy and Body Image," in *1995 AMA Educators' Proceedings*, ed. Barbara B. Stern and George M. Zinkhan (Chicago: American Marketing Association, 1995), 90–98.

53. Lisa Vickery, Kelly Greene, Shelly Branch, and Emily Nelson, "Marketers Tweak Strategies as Age Groups Realign," *Wall Street Journal*, May 15, 2001, B1.

December 1992, 101–111.

60. Mark Stiving and Russell S. Winer, "An Empirical Analysis of Price Endings with Scanner Data," *Journal of Consumer Research*, June 1997, 57–67. See also Robert M. Schindler and Patrick N. Kirby, "Patterns of Rightmost Digits Used in Advertised Price: Implications for Nine-Ending Effects," *Journal of Consumer Research*, September 1997, 192–201.

61. Sheila Muto, "What's in an Address? Sometimes, a Better Image," *Wall Street Journal*, September 5, 2001, B14.

62. Stuart Elliot, "Growing Number of Airlines Resume Image Advertising," *New York Times* online, November 6, 2001.

63. Kevin Helliker, "How Hardy Are Upscale Gyms?" *Wall Street Journal*, February 9, 2001, B1.

64. Jim Carlton, "Recycling Redefined," *Wall Street Journal*, March 6, 2001, B1.

65. Stephanie Thompson, "Cole Haan Fashions an Effort for Women," *Advertising Age*, August 25, 2003, 6.

66. Miriam Jordan, "Debut of Rival Diet Colas in India Leaves a Bitter Taste," *Wall Street Journal*, July 21, 1999, B1, B4.

67. This application exercise is based on the contribution of Pj Forrest (Mississippi College) to *Great Ideas in Teaching Marketing*, a teaching supplement that accompanies Lamb, Hair, and McDaniel's *Marketing*. Professor Forrest's entry titled "Print Ad Projects for Consumer Behavior" was a winner in the "Best of the Great Ideas in Teaching Marketing" contest held in conjunction with the publication of the eighth edition of *Marketing*.

68. Kevin Coupe, "A Theme Retailing Failure and Some Views on Restaurant and Pub Trends," *Store Equipment & Design*, January 2001, 24. Danielle Furfaro, "Entrepreneur Opens Family-Centered Restaurant in Albany, N.Y.," *Knight-Ridder Tribune Business News*, February 18, 2002. "McDonald's Launches World's First 'Town Center' Restaurant: New Restaurant Is Second Largest in U.S., Features Family 'EduTainment,'" PR *Newswire*, April 30,

space," *Wall Street Journal*, November 20, 2003, B1.

6. "Europe E-Commerce to Grow Fourfold by 2006," *eMarketer*, July 3, 2003, online.

7. Timothy I. Mullaney, Heather Green, Michael Arndt, Robert Hof, and Linda Himelstein, "The EBiz Surprise," *BusinessWeek*, May 12, 2003, 61.

8. Hutt and Speh, *Business Marketing Management*, 117, 122.

9. Paul C. Judge, "How I Saved $100 Million on the Web," *Fast Company*, February 2001, 174–181.

10. Ibid.

11. Ibid.

12. Alex Frangos, "Just One Word: Plastics," *Wall Street Journal*, May 21, 2001, R20.

13. Ibid.

14. Hutt and Speh, *Business Marketing Management*, 118.

15. David Sims, "Bringing Online Help to the B2B World," *Customer Relationship Management*, August 2001, 32–36.

16. Vanessa O'Connell, "Medical Studies, Drug Advertising Get Cozy Online," *Wall Street Journal*, March 28, 2002, B1, B3. Used by permission.

17. William Hoffman, Jennifer Keedy, and Karl Roberts, "The Unexpected Return of B2B," *The McKinsey Quarterly*, no. 3, 2002, online.

18. Ibid.

19. Steve Bodow, "The Care and Feeding of a Killer App," *Business 2.0*, August 2002, 76–78.

20. Gabriel Kahn, "Made to Measure: Invisible Supplier Has Penney's Shirts All Buttoned Up," *Wall Street Journal*, September 11, 2003, online. Used with permission.

21. U.S. Census Bureau, "North American Industry Classification System (NAICS)—United States," http://www.census.gov/epcd/www/naics.html.

22. "Lockheed Wins JSF Contract," *Fort Worth Star-Telegram*, December 30, 2001, 6F.

23. Steve Butler, "B2B Exchanges' Transaction Activity," *eMarketer*, February 18, 2003, online.

permission, Amy Harmon, "An Inventor Unveils His Mysterious Personal Transportation Device," *New York Times*, December 3, 2001, C1, C10; John Heilemann, "Reinventing the Wheel," *TIME.com*, December 2, 2001.

CHAPTER 7

1. Cora Daniels, "J.C. Penney Dresses Up," *Fortune*, June 9, 2003, 127–130.

2. Pamela Sebastian Ridge, "Chico's Scores with Its Nonjudgmental Sizes," *Wall Street Journal*, March 8, 2001, B1, B4.

3. Teresa Bouza and Gabriel Sama, "America Adds Salsa to Its Burgers and Fries," *Wall Street Journal*, January 2, 2003, A9.

4. Nicole L. Torres, "It's Child's Play," *Entrepreneur*, December 2001, 24–26.

5. Heather Landy, "Kiddie Cash," *Fort Worth Star-Telegram*, October 13, 2003, 8C.

6. Julia Boorstin, "Disney's 'Tween Machine," *Fortune*, September 29, 2003, 111–114.

7. Matthew Maier, "Hooking Up with Gen Y," *Business 2.0*, October 2003, 49–52.

8. "Graying Boomers, Booming Teens," *Inc.*, May 15, 2001, 86–87.

9. Meg Jones, "Milking It," *Fort Worth Star-Telegram*, October 29, 2001, 1F, 6F.

10. Maier, "Hooking Up with Gen Y."

11. Lisa Vickery, Kelly Greene, Shelly Branch, and Emily Nelson, "Marketers Tweak Strategies As Age Groups Realign," *Wall Street Journal*, May 15, 2001, B1.

12. Deborah Ball and Christopher Lawton, "Wine Gets Wild and Crazy," *Wall Street Journal*, April 24, 2003, B1, B3.

13. Gene Koretz, "Bless the Baby Boomers," *BusinessWeek*, June 10, 2002, 30.

14. Vickery et al., "Marketers Tweak Strategies As Age Groups Realign."

15. Dave Carpenter, "Fountain of Youth," *Fort Worth Star-Telegram*, January 23, 2001, 1C, 10C.

16. Vickery et al., "Marketers Tweak Strategies As Age Groups Realign."

17. "Mature Audience," *Business 2.0*, April 17, 2001, 59.

18. Ellison Clary, "Tackling the Male Hair Market," *Fort Worth Star-Telegram*, April 19, 2002, 1C, 9C.

19. Rachel Emma Silverman, "The Groom with a View," *Wall Street Journal*, April 16, 2003, D1, D2.

20. Kimberly Palmer, "Tech Companies Try Wooing Women with Girlie Marketing," *Wall Street Journal*, August 26, 2003, B1, B4.

21. Sarah Ellison, "P&G's Latest Growth Strategy: His and Hers Toothpaste," *Wall Street Journal*, September 5, 2002, B1, B5.

22. Kenneth Kiesnoski, "London Unveils Floor for Women Only," *Travel Weekly*, March 31, 2003, 38.

23. Sarah Kickler Kelber, "La-Z-Boy for La-Z-Girls," *Fort Worth Star-Telegram*, January 11, 2003, 3E.

24. Aixa M. Pascual, "Lowe's Is Sprucing Up Its House," *BusinessWeek*, June 3, 2002, 56–58.

25. Kimberly Weisul, "Botox: Now It's a Guy Thing," *BusinessWeek*, May 6, 2002, 40.

26. David Kiley, "Saturn Aims to Ring Up Younger, Male Buyers," *USA Today*, January 21, 2003, 8B.

27. Ron Leiber, "Careful, Your Bank Is Watching," *Wall Street Journal*, July 22, 2003, D1, D2.

28. Chuck Paustian, "Anybody Can Do It," *Marketing News*, March 26, 2001, 23.

29. Christopher Tkaczyk, Ellen Florian, and Jaclyn Stemple, "50 Best Companies for Minorities," *Fortune*, July 7, 2003, 103–119.

30. Paustian, "Anybody Can Do It."

31. Deborah L. Vence, "Win Hispanic Market with Proper Research," *Marketing News*, January 7, 2003, 4, 8.

32. Shawn Tully, "Bank of the Americas," *Fortune*, April 14, 2003, 145–148.

33. Catherine Arnold, "Change-Up Pitch," *Marketing News*, October 13, 2003, 5, 12.

34. Vence, "Win Hispanic Market with Proper Research."

35. Ben Macklin, "Targeting Hispanics and African Americans Online," *eMarketer*, February 13, 2003.

36. Michelle Conlin, "Unmarried America," *BusinessWeek*, October 20, 2003, 106–116.

37. Vanessa O'Connell and Jon E. Hilsenrath, "Advertisers Are Cautious As Household Makeup Shifts," *Wall Street Journal*, May 15, 2001, B1, B4.

38. Sarah Ellison and Carlos Tejada, "Mr., Mrs., Meet Mr. Clean," *Wall Street Journal*, January 30, 2003, B1, B3.

39. Lisa Van der Pool, "Apple iPod, VW Beetle in Promotional Duet," *AdWeek Western Edition*, July 15, 2003.

40. Alex Taylor III, "Porsche Slices Up Its Buyers," *Fortune*, January 16, 1995, 24.

41. "Work That's Never Done," *BrandWeek*, March 2, 2003, 30–36.

42. Beverly Bundy, "Central Market Says It Knows What You Want to Eat, Even if You Don't," *Fort Worth Star-Telegram*, October 10, 2001, 1F, 2F.

43. Amy Merrick, "The 2000 Count: Counting on the Census—New Data Will Let Starbucks Plan Store Openings, Help Blockbuster Stock Its Videos," *Wall Street Journal*, February 14, 2001, B1.

44. Carolyn Poirot, "If It Fuels Good, Eat It," *Fort Worth Star-Telegram*, August 11, 2003, E1.

45. Jennifer Ordonez, "Cash Cows: Hamburger Joints Call Them 'Heavy Users'—But Not to Their Faces," *Wall Street Journal*, January 12, 2000, A1, A10.

46. Ginger Cooper, "Centricity," *Customer Relationship Management*, December 2001, 35–40.

47. Dennis J. Chapman, "Clients, Customers and Buyers," *Customer Relationship Management*, March 2001, 65–71.

48. Don E. Schultz, "Behavior Changes: Do Your Segments?" *Marketing News*, July 22, 2002, 5.

49. Maureen Tkacik, "Hey Dude, This Sure Isn't The Gap," *Wall Street Journal*, February 12, 2002, B1, B4.

50. Gerry Khermouch, "Call It the Pepsi Blue Generation," *BusinessWeek*, February 3, 2003, 96.

51. Ibid.

52. Bob Francis, "After the Sale," *Brandweek*, March 31, 2003, 20–24.

53. J. Walker Smith, "Marketing with Attitude," *Marketing Management*, January/February 2002, 48.

54. Evantheia Schibsted, "Say Goodbye to Mass Selling: Designer Products: Personalized Product Marketing the Net's New Frontier," *National Post*, April 2, 2001, E2.

55. This section is based on Rob Jackson and Paul Wang, *Strategic Database Marketing* (Lincolnwood, IL: NTC Business Books, 1997), 4–11; and Frederick Newell, *The New Rules of Marketing: How to Use One-to-One Relationship Marketing to Be the Leader in Your Industry* (New York: McGraw-Hill, 1997), 10–32.

56. "31% of U.S. Tech Savvy, Finds Study," *Direct Marketing Association*, http://www.the-dma.org, November 25, 2003.

57. "Despite Recession and Terrorism, Internet Growth Continues," *eMarketer*, January 31, 2002, online.

58. "The DMA Supports House Passage of National Anti-Spam Law," *Direct Marketing Association*, http://www.the-dma.org, November 22, 2003; Mylene Mangalindan, "Web Firms File Spam Suit under New Law," *Wall Street Journal*, March 11, 2004, B4, B6.

59. Nick Wingfield and Glenn R. Simpson, "With So Much Subscriber Data, AOL Walks a Cautious Line on Privacy," *Wall Street Journal*, March 15, 2000, B1, B4.

60. Johanna Bennett, "It's My Life," *Wall Street Journal*, October 29, 2001, R9.

61. Jason Anders, "Web Filter Data from Schools Put Up for Sale," *Wall Street Journal*, January 26, 2001, B1.

62. "Privacy Promise Member Compliance Guide," *Direct Marketing Association*, http://www.the-dma.org.

63. Sally Beatty, "Mass Levi's, Class Levi's," *Wall Street Journal*, October 31, 2002, B1, B3.

64. Kenneth Hein, "Snapple Bulks Up Its Beverage Line to Challenge Newest Foe: Slim-Fast," *BrandWeek*, October 7, 2002, 10.

65. Vijay Mahajan and Toram (Jerry) Wind, "Got Emotional Product Positioning?" *Marketing Management*, May/June 2002, 36–41.

66. Ibid.

67. Kim T. Gordon, "Different Strokes," *Entrepreneur*, January 2002, 99.

68. Abbey Klaassen, "St. Joseph: From Babies to Boomers," *Advertising Age*, July 9, 2001,1.

69. Karen Robinson-Jacobs, "More than Tacos," *Fort Worth Star-Telegram*, July 31, 2003, 1C.

70. This application exercise is based upon the contribution of Kim McKeage (University of Maine) to *Great Ideas in Teaching Marketing*, a teaching supplement that accompanies Lamb, Hair, and McDaniel's *Marketing*. Professor McKeage's entry titled "Students Practice Making Market/Product Grids on Themselves" received an Honorable Mention in the "Best of the Great Ideas in Teaching Marketing" contest held in conjunction with the publication of the eighth edition of *Marketing*.

71. "Las Vegas Tourism Agency Announces 1.3 Percent Rise in Visitor Totals for 2003," *Las Vegas Review-Journal*, February 14, 2004; Jennifer Bjorhus, "Las Vegas Tourism Authorities Campaign in Portland, Ore," *Knight Ridder/Tribune Business News*, June 4, 1999; Chris Jones, "Las Vegas Tourism Agency Executive Says Research, Marketing Are Key to Success," *Las Vegas Review-Journal*, April 6, 2003; Chris Jones, "Las Vegas Tourism Chief Opposes Ads; Board Members Object to 'Sin City' Phrase," *Las Vegas Review-Journal*, December 16, 2003; Chris Jones, "Las Vegas Tourism Officials Plan Marketing Blitz to Attract Canadian Tourists," *Las Vegas Review-Journal*, August 19, 2003; "LVCVA Exec Seeks Diversity," *Travel Weekly*, March 3, 2003; Chris Jones, "New Las Vegas Tourism Ads Target Hispanics with Tradition-Focused Messages," *Las Vegas Review-Journal*, July 17, 2003; Chris Jones, "Las Vegas Tourism Authority Unveils Culturally Diverse Television Ads," *Las Vegas Review-Journal*, February 11, 2004.

CHAPTER 8

1. Russel Pearlman, "The Logic behind the Magic," *Smart Money*, June 2003, 34.

2. Joseph Rydholm, "A Natural Extension," *Quirk's Marketing Research Review*, May 2002, 22–23, 69–70.

3. "Couriers Deliver Customer Service," *Information Week*, June 3, 2002, 60.

4. "Percentage of Adult Women Sports Fans Doubles," *Quirk's Marketing Research Review*, January 2003, 58.

5. Larry Selden and Geoffrey Colvin, "What Customers Want," *Fortune*, July 7, 2003, 122–127.

6. Ibid.

7. John Eggerton, "In PBS We Trust, According to PBS Survey," *Broadcasting and Cable*, February 9, 2004, 11.

15. Raymond Pettit and Robert Monster, "Expanding Horizons: Web-Enabled Technologies Helping Globalize Marketing Research," *Quirk's Marketing Research Review*, November 2000, 38–42.

16. HarrisInteractive.com, July 10, 2003.

17. Author discussion with Jerry Thomas, CEO, Decision Analysts, Inc., July 7, 2003.

18. David Bradford, "Successful Online Qualitative Market Research," *Quirk's Marketing Research Review*, July/August 2001, 48–51.

19. Carl McDaniel and Roger Gates, *Contemporary Marketing Research*, 5th ed. (Cincinnati: International Thomson Publishing, 2002).

20. "The Case of the Corporate Spy," *BusinessWeek*, November 26, 2001, 56–58.

21. Adapted from "The Case of the Corporate Spy." See also Mark Peyrot, Nancy Childs, Doris Van Doren, and Kathleen Allen, "An Empirically Based Model of Competitor Intelligence Use," *Journal of Business Research*, September 2002, 747–758.

22. This application exercise is based upon the contribution of Matthew D. Shank and Fred Beasley (Northern Kentucky University) to Great Ideas in Teaching Marketing, a teaching supplement that accompanies Lamb, Hair, and McDaniel's *Marketing*. Their entry titled "Understanding the Importance of Marketing Research (Or Why Do I Have to Take This Class?)" was a Runner-Up in the "Best of the Great Ideas in Teaching Marketing" contest held in conjunction with the publication of the eighth edition of *Marketing*.

23. C. Pappas, "Pop Culture—Where It's All Cool and How to Find It," *Advertising Age*, May 10, 2002, 16; R. A. Jones, "L.A. Duo Serves Fresh Trends Fast," *WWD*, December, 14, 2000, 11; T. Coffey, "Researchers Review Youth Buying Trends," *San Diego Business Journal*, November 13, 2000, 55.

Forward with No Shortage of Vision," *PRWeb*, January 23, 2004, http://www.prweb.com; Jeff Bercovici, "Tall Magazine, for Men Who Are," *Media Life*, August 14, 2003, http://www.medialifemagazine.com; John Leo, "The High and the Mighty," *U.S. News & World Report*, August 18, 2003, 27; Aline Mendelsohn, "Niche Marketing Is More Focused," *Orlando Sentinel*, October 5, 2003, F04; http://www.tallmagazine.com.

CHAPTER 9

1. Barry Shlachter, "Another Beer on the Wall," *Fort Worth Star-Telegram*, May 7, 2003, 1C.

2. Sandra Dolbow, "Beyond Khakis," *BrandWeek*, October 21, 2002, 1.

3. "Oral-B Unveils Age-Pegged Toothbrushes for Kids," *BusinessWeek Online*, October 4, 2001, http://www.businessweek.com/reuters_market/8/REUT-8KW.HTM.

4. "GM Isn't Giving Up On the Pontiac Aztec Yet," *WSJ.com*, November 27, 2001, http://interactive.wsj.com.

5. Teri Agins, "Hilfiger Returns to Preppy Roots, but Sales Slump," *Wall Street Journal*, February 2, 2001, B1, B6.

6. Scott Bedbury, "Nine Ways to Fix a Broken Brand," *Fast Company*, February 2002, 72–77.

7. Kenneth Hein and Christine Bittar, "Lava Looks to Clean Its Image with Women," *BrandWeek*, April 15, 2002, 9.

8. Sonia Reyes, "Minute Maid Juices Up Calcium Fortified Line," *BrandWeek*, March 13, 2000, 323.

9. Mike Beirne, "Hershey Chews on Gum, Mint Plans; Jolly Rancher Eyes Preemptive Strike," *BrandWeek*, February 26, 2001, p. 9.

10. Katrina Brooker, "A Game of Inches," *Fortune*, February 5, 2001, 98–100.

11. Gerry Khermouch, Stanley Holmes, and Moon Ihlwan, "The Best Global Brands," *BusinessWeek*, August 6, 2001, 50–57.

12. Brian O'Keefe, "Global Brands," *Fortune*, November 26, 2001, 102–110.

Schneider, "Nets Catch Franchise Fever. TV Wakes Up to Film's Longtime Game Plan," *Variety*, January 21, 2002, 1; Joe Flint, "NBC's 'Law and Order' Habit Could Spell Trouble Ahead," *Wall Street Journal*, October 27, 2003, B1.

21. James Heckman, "Trademarks Protected through New Cyber Act," *Marketing News*, January 3, 2000, 6.

22. Erin White, "Burberry Wants the Knockoffs to Knock It Off," *Fort Worth Star-Telegram*, May 28, 2003, 6F.

23. Jonathan Eig, "Food Companies Grab Kids' Attention by Packaging Products as Toys, Games," *WSJ.com*, October 26, 2001, http://interactive.wsj.com.

24. Sonia Reyes, "Down with Tubes?" *BrandWeek*, March 3, 2003, 1.

25. Cynthia Arnold, "Way Outside the Box," *Marketing News*, January 23, 2003, 13.

26. Herbert M. Meyers, "The Internet's Threat to Branding," *BrandWeek*, December 4, 2000, 30.

27. Roger Parloff, "Is Fat the Next Tobacco?" *Fortune*, February 3, 2003, 51.

28. This application exercise is based on the contribution of Alice Griswold to *Great Ideas in Teaching Marketing*, a teaching supplement that accompanies Lamb, Hair, and McDaniel's *Marketing*. Professor Griswold's entry titled "The Oreo Debate" received an Honorable Mention in the "Best of the Great Ideas in Teaching Marketing" contest held in conjunction with the publication of the eighth edition of *Marketing*.

29. http://www.apple.com; Riva Richmond, "Apple's New GarageBand Makes Making Music Easy," *Dow Jones Newswires*, January 27, 2004; Walter Mossberg, "How to Become a Rock Star: Apple's Latest Music Offering Lets Closet Crooners Record and Mix Their Own Tunes," *WSJ.com*, February 4, 2004; Bob Massey, "Music-Making Made Slick," *Washington Post*, January 25, 2004, F07; Jonathan Seff, "Center of Attention—iPod Mini, iLife '04 Expand Apple's Digital Hub," *www.macworld.com*, March 2004.

CHAPTER 10

1. Charles Forelle, "Schick Puts a Nick in Gillette's Razor Sales," *Wall Street Journal*, October 3, 2003, B7.
2. Peggy Anne Salz, "The Art of Innovation," *Fortune*, July 23, 2003, 517.
3. Robert D. Hof, "Innovate or Die," *BusinessWeek*, October 6, 2003, 26.
4. Salz, "The Art of Innovation."
5. ProductScan Online, January 2005.
6. "Changing the World," *Entrepreneur*, October 2003, 30.
7. Matthew Boyle, "Dueling Diapers," *Fortune*, February 17, 2003, 115–116.
8. Katrina Brooker, "A Game of Inches," *Fortune*, February 5, 2001, 98–99.
9. David Welch, "The Second Coming of Cadillac," *BusinessWeek*, November 24, 2003, 79–80.
10. Ibid.
11. Ann Zimmerman and Teri Agins, "Pinstripes and Motor Oil?" *Wall Street Journal*, September 3, 2002, B1, B2.
12. Richard Holman, Hans-Werner Kaas, and David Keeling, "The Future of Product Development," *The McKinsey Quarterly*, November 3, 2003, 1.
13. Mary Ellen Kuhn, "Why 7-Eleven Is Leader of the Pack," *Confectioner*, December 2002, 11.
14. Paul Kaihla, "What Works," *Business 2.0*, August 2002, 65–70.
15. Ian Wylie, "Calling for a Renewable Future," *Fast Company*, May 2003, 46–48.
16. Suzanne Vranica, "Mensa Members Find Their Way into Focus Groups for Marketers," *WSJ.com*, February 26, 2002, online.
17. Anna Muoio, "GM Has a New Model for Change," *Fast Company*, December 2000, 62–64.
18. "The Popular Weber Q Grill Becomes Even More Portable," *PR Newswire*, November 4, 2003; "Tailgating Secrets Revealed," *The Channel News NewsFax*, November 3, 2003; "Weber-Stephen Products Co. Reveals Results from First Comprehensive Tailgating Study," *PR Newswire*, October 29, 2003.
19. Patricia Barry, "Drug Profits vs. Research," *AARP Bulletin*, June 2002, 8–10.
20. Michael Ellis, "GM Moves to Cut Months from Vehicle Design Process," *Yahoo.com*, February 1, 2002, online.
21. Charles Haddad, "Collaboration," *BusinessWeek*, November 24, 2003, 84–85.
22. Emily Nelson, "Focus Groupies: P&G Keeps Cincinnati Busy with All Its Studies," *Wall Street Journal*, January 24, 2002, A1, A7.
23. Barry Shlachter, "Entrée Auditioning," *Fort Worth Star-Telegram*, April 2, 2002, C1, C10.
24. Sonia Reyes, "Groove Tube," *BrandWeek*, October 16, 2000, M114.
25. "Phytol Products Take Market Test," *Food Ingredients News*, August 2001, online.
26. Philip Brasher, "Teens Sample Milk from Vending Machines," *Fort Worth Star-Telegram*, April 5, 2001, 10A.
27. Reed Tucker, "Air Purifiers Cause a Stink," *Fortune*, June 10, 2002, 40.
28. John Gaffney, "How Do You Feel about a $44 Tooth-Bleaching Kit?" *Business 2.0*, October 2001, 125–127.
29. Ibid.
30. Sonia Reyes, "ADM Adds Fat to the Fire in Obesity Debate with Oil Touted as Fat Fighter," *BrandWeek*, February 10, 2003, 6.
31. Michael Flagg, "Coca-Cola Is Adopting Strategy in Asia of Inventing Drinks Tied to Local Tastes," *Wall Street Journal*, July 30, 2001, B9C.
32. Ibid.
33. Alessandra Galloni, "Coke to Launch Powerade Drink across Europe," *Wall Street Journal*, October 16, 2001, B11E.
34. Miriam Jordan, "Fuel and Freebies," *Wall Street Journal*, June 10, 2002, B1, B6. Used with permission.
35. Ed Keller and Jon Berry, *The Influentials* (New York: Free Press, 2003), cover.
36. Ben Macklin, "Broadband Moves Beyond Early Adopters," *eMarketer*, January 23, 2003, online.
37. Ben Macklin, "Targeting Hispanics and African Americans Online," *eMarketer*, February 13, 2003, online.
38. "When Will It Fly?" *The Economist*, August 9, 2003, 332.
39. Ibid.
40. James Daly, "Restart, Redo, Recharge," *Business 2.0*, May 1, 2001, 11.
41. This application exercise is based upon the contribution of Karen Stewart (Richard Stockton College of New Jersey) to *Great Ideas in Teaching Marketing*, a teaching supplement that accompanies Lamb, Hair, and McDaniel's *Marketing*. Professor Stewart's entry titled "New-Product Development" was a winner in the "Best of the Great Ideas in Teaching Marketing" contest held in conjunction with the publication of the eighth edition of *Marketing*.
42. Risa Brim, "Lexington, Ky.-Based Motor Oil Producer Steps Out of Mold," *Lexington Herald-Leader*, November 5, 2001, available online at http://www.wsj.com; Lucy May, "Ashland Launches Spirit 3-D Foam," *Business Courier Serving Cincinnati-Northern Kentucky*, October 12, 2001, 13.

CHAPTER 11

1. Tahl Raz, "A Recipe for Perfection," *Inc.*, July 2003, 36.
2. Valarie A. Zeithaml and Mary Jo Bitner, *Services Marketing* (New York: McGraw-Hill, 2003).
3. Cait Murphy, "Fortune 5 Hundred," *Fortune*, April 15, 2002, 95–98.
4. Joel Milliman, "Services May Lead U.S. to Trade Surplus," *Wall Street Journal*, December 14, 2000, A1.
5. Murphy, "Fortune 5 Hundred."
6. Christina Binkley, "From Orange Shag to Pin Stripes: Sheraton Gets a Makeover," *Wall Street Journal*, April 19, 2000, B1, B10.
7. Zeithaml and Bitner, *Services Marketing*.
8. Susan Greco, "Fanatics!" *Inc.*, April 2001, 35–48.
9. Luey McCauley, ed., "Unit of One," *Fast Company*, March 6, 2000, 104.
10. Suein Hwang, "Enterprise Takes Idea of Dresses for Success to a New Extreme," *Wall Street Journal*, November 20, 2002, B1.
11. Montoko Rich, "Healthy Hospital Designs," *Wall Street Journal*, November 27, 2002, B1.
12. Zeithaml and Bitner, *Services Marketing*.
13. "Exceeding Customer Expectations," *Fortune*, March 6, 2000, S3.
14. Mark Gimein, "Table for Mr. Bigfoot," *Fortune*, January 12, 2004, 46; Kate Stroup, "Guides: Everyone's a Critic," *Newsweek*, September 29, 2003, 10; "Zagat Survey Names Longtime Consumer Reports Editorial Director as Vice President for Content: Julia Kagan Tapped to Head Editorial and Product Development for Leading Leisure Guide Publisher," *PR Newswire*, December 9, 2003.
15. Stacey L. Bell, "Puttin' on the Ritz," *Customer Relationship Management*, May 2001, 35–40.
16. Much of the material in this section is based on Christopher H. Lovelock, *Services Marketing* (Upper Saddle River, NJ: Prentice-Hall, 2001), 39–41.
17. Michael Krauss, "Starbucks Adds Value by Taking on Wireless," *Marketing News*, February 3, 2003, 9.
18. Wendy Perrin, "Bells and Whistles," special business supplement 2000 to *Conde Nast Traveler*, 21–22.
19. Ibid.
20. Susan Kuchinskas, "Organic San Francisco," *IQnews*, February 14, 2000, 36.
21. Kelly Greene, "Doctor at the Doorstep," *Fort Worth Star-Telegram*, November 25, 2002, D3.
22. Calmetta Coleman, "Banks Cozy Up to Customers," *Wall Street Journal*, April 26, 2001, B1, B4.
23. Paulo Prada and Bruce Orwall, "A Certain 'Je Ne Sais Quoi' at Disney's New Park," *Wall Street Journal*, March 12, 2002, B1.
24. Lovelock, *Services Marketing*, 262–265.
25. Ibid., 149–150.
26. Much of the material in this section is based on Leonard L. Berry and A. Parasuraman, *Marketing Services* (New York: Free Press, 1991), 132–150.
27. Christina Binkley, "Soon, the Desk Clerk Will Know All About You," *Wall Street Journal*, May 8, 2003, D4.
28. Sue Shellenberger, "To Win the Loyalty of Your Employees, Try a Softer Touch," *Wall Street Journal*, January 26, 2000, B1.
29. Berry and Parasuraman, *Marketing Services*, 151–152.
30. Kirsten Downey Grimsley, "At Your Service," *Fort Worth Star-Telegram*, March 1, 2000, C1.
31. Ellen Graham, "Marriott's Bid to Patch the Child-Care Gap Gets a Reality Check," *Wall Street Journal*, February 2, 2000, B1.
32. James Lardner, "Building a Customer-Centric Company," *Business 2.0*, July 10, 2001, 55–59.

Damage West Coast Arts Coverage?" *Back Stage West*, July 1, 2002, 1; Leonard Jacobs, "Theatre Mag Shake-up: Playbill Buys Stagebill; Show People to Debut," *Back Stage*, June 14, 2002, 2.

PART 3

1. Geoff Edgers, "Can the Center Hold?" *Boston Globe*, November 23, 2003, and "The New York Grinch Who Stole Christmas," *Boston Globe*, November 2, 2003, http://www.boston.com; T. J. Medrek, "'Nutcracker' Eviction Is Pits for Orchestra," *BostonHerald.com*, December 19, 2003, http://theedge.bostonherald.com; "Theatre Should Devote Resources to Keep 'Nutcracker,'" *The Wellesley News Online*, December 6, 2003, http://www.wellesley.edu; Frank Rizzo, "Rockette Raids Crack 'Nut,'" *Variety*, December 15–21, 2003, 60.

2. "Hasbro Signs Pop Music Sensations and Siblings Nick and Aaron Carter to Launch New Twister Moves Game in June 2003," *Business Wire*, May 20, 2003, http://www.businesswire.com; John P. Santanella, Director of Marketing, Hasbro Games; http://www.hasbro.com.

CHAPTER 12

1. http://www.starbucks.com; Starbucks Annual Report, 2002; Scott Donaton, "Starbucks Must Not Forget What Made Success Possible," *www.AdAge.com*, January 13, 2003.

2. Minju Park, "Site of Passage: The Festival's Online Component Offers Filmmakers Yet Another Creative Outlet," *Hollywood Reporter*, January 14, 2004, S-12.

3. David Shook, "IBM: Winning as a Team Player," *BusinessWeek Online*, December 2003.

4. Nicole Harris, "'Private Exchanges' May Allow B-to-B Commerce to Thrive After All," *Wall Street Journal*, March 16, 2001, B1; Michael Totty, "The Next Phase," *Wall Street Journal*, May 21, 2001, R8.

5. http://global.I-textile.com.

10. Jonathan Welsh, "Auto Makers Now 'Slam' Cars Right in the Factory," *Wall Street Journal*, October 30, 2001, B1.

11. Owen Keates, "Flow Control," *Management*, March 2001, 28.

12. Rob Wherry, "Ice Cream Wars: Dreyer's Conquered Supermarket Freezers. Now It's Going After the Corner Store," *Forbes*, May 28, 2001, 160.

13. Karen Lundegaard, "Bumpy Ride," *Wall Street Journal*, May 21, 2001, R21.

14. http://www.toyotaforklift.com; http://www.toyotaforklift.com/about_us/company_profile/toyotaphilosophy.aspx; Elena Eptako Murphy, "Buying on Price Alone Can Lead to High Operating Costs," *Purchasing.com*, September 4, 2003; http://www.manufacturing.net/pur/index.asp?layout-article&articleid=CA319650&industry=Industrial+Markets&industryid-21951.

15. http://www.dollartree.com.

16. http://www.sysco.com.

17. Leigh Muzslay, "Shoes That Morph from Sneakers to Skates Are Flying Out of Stores," *Wall Street Journal*, July 26, 2001, B1.

18. Shelly Branch, "P&G Buys Iams: Will Pet-Food Fight Follow?" *Wall Street Journal*, August 12, 1999, B1, B4.

19. http://www.target.com; http://www.finance.yahoo.com; http://finance.yahoo.com/q/pr?s-MOSS; Robert Berner, "Target's Aim: The Designer's Edge," *BusinessWeek Online*, February 27, 2002; http://www.businessweek.com/bwdaily/dnflash/feb2002/nf20020227_0567.htm.

20. Jessia Davis, "Cutting in the Middleman," *InfoWorld*, January 22, 2001, at http://www.itworld.com.

21. Ellen Neuborne, "Big Brands (Small Companies)," *BusinessWeek*, August 13, 2001, 12.

22. http://www.kraft.com; http://kraft.com/corpresp.html.

23. http://www.colorworks.com; Faith Keenan, Stanley Holmes, Jay Green, and Roger O. Crockett, "A Mass Market of

31. http://www.tord.com.

32. Michael Selz, "Outsourcing Firms Venture Beyond Primary Functions," *Wall Street Journal*, June 26, 2001, B2.

33. Martin Peers, "Video on Demand Arrives—Sort Of," *Wall Street Journal*, January 29, 2001, B1.

34. Ken Bensinger, "Can You Spot the Fake?" *Wall Street Journal*, February 16, 2001, W1; Todd Zaun and Karby Leggett, "Motorcycle Makers from Japan Discover Piracy Made in China," *Wall Street Journal*, July 25, 2001, A1.

35. Diane O'Brien, "When Imposters Knock Off Profits," *brandchannel.com*, December 1, 2003; "Ruth to the Rescue Uncovers Handbag Rip-Offs," *ClickOnDetroit.com*, November 10, 2003.

36. Ron Irwin, "Made Where?" *brandchannel.com*, October 6, 2003; Casey Freymuth, "Feature: Executives Consider Outsourcing Supply-Chain Initiatives, Survey Finds," *eMarketect Magazine*, February 6, 2002, at http://www.emarketect.com.

37. Jon E. Hilsenrath, "Globalization Persists in Precarious New Age," *Wall Street Journal*, December 31, 2001, A1.

38. Kevin Hogan, "Borderline Savings," *Business 2.0*, May 17, 2001, 34.

39. Chuck Martin, "Oprah Fans Scoop Up Graeter's," *Cincinnati Enquirer*, June 4, 2002, online.

40. This application exercise is based upon the contribution of John Beisel (University of Pittsburgh) to *Great Ideas in Teaching Marketing*, a teaching supplement that accompanies Lamb, Hair, and McDaniel's *Marketing*. The entry by Professors Mader and Mader titled "Identifying Channels of Distribution" was a runner-up in the "Best of the Great Ideas in Teaching Marketing" contest held in conjunction with the publication of the eighth edition of *Marketing*.

41. CarsDirect.com Web site at http://www.carsdirect.com; Robert Elder, Jr., and Jonathan Weil, "To Sell Cars in Texas, Online Firms Are Forced to Enter the Real World," *Wall Street Journal*, January 26,

2000, T1, T4; Maynard M. Gordon, "Battle Lines Forming in the Wild World of the Automotive Web Sites," *Ward's Dealer Business*, June 1, 2000, 12; Chris Knap, "Online Car Sales Will Rise, Analysts Say," *KRTBN Knight-Ridder Tribune Business News: The Orange County Register—California*, September 19, 1999; Jennifer Montgomery, "Texas State Law Bars Residents from Buying Cars Online," *KRTBN Knight-Ridder Tribune Business News: Houston Chronicle—Texas*, March 19, 2000; Fara Warner, "Racing for Slice of a $350 Billion Pie, Online Auto-Sales Sites Retool," *Wall Street Journal*, January 24, 2000, B1, B6;———, "New Tactics Shake Up Online Auto Retailing," *Wall Street Journal*, October 18, 1999, B1;———, "CarsDirect.com Bets on One-Stop, Desktop Showroom," *Wall Street Journal*, May 17, 1999, B4; Scott Woolley, "A Car Dealer by Any Other Name," *Forbes*, November 29, 1999, 113–116.

CHAPTER 13

1. Ian Mount, "Krispy Kreme's Secret Ingredient," *Business 2.0 Online*, September 2003; Jason Kelly, "Mmmm . . . Reheated Doughnuts," *Business 2.0 Online*, March 2002; Ryan Frank, "Buzz Is Key Ingredient to Krispy Kreme's Rise," *OregonLive.com*, September 1, 2003; Carlyle Adler, "Would You Pay $2 Million for This Franchise?" *Fortune Online*, http://www.fortune.com/fortune/smallbusiness/articles/0,15114,361359,00.html; http://www.krispykreme.com.
2. Bureau of Labor Statistics, "Industry at a Glance: NAICS 42–45, Wholesale and Retail Trade," online at http://www.bls.gov, May 2004.
3. U.S. Census Bureau, Monthly Retail Trade Report, 2004; Betty W. Su, "The U.S. Economy to 2012: Signs of Growth," *Monthly Labor Review*, February 2004, Vol 127, No. 2, online at http://www.bls.gov.
4. David Schultz, "The Definitive Ranking of the Nation's Biggest Specialty Chains," *Stores* online, August 2001.
5. Johnathan Thaw, "Why Sharper Image Is Playing the Hits Again," *Business 2.0 Online*, November 2003.
6. Maureen C. Carini, "Retailing: Supermarkets and Drugstores," *Standard & Poor's Industry Surveys*, vol. 166, no. 14, sec. 1, April 2, 1998, 12–13.
7. Maria Halkias, "2 Retailers; 1 Roof: A Profitable Trend," *Dallas Morning News*, October 30, 2003, http://www.DallasNews.com.
8. http://www.goya.com.
9. Matt Nannery, "Pigging Out," *Chain Store Age*, July 1999, 77.
10. http://www.exxonmobil.com.
11. http://www.walmart.com.
12. http://www.target.com.
13. Tony Lisanti, "Extreme Segment, Extreme Growth," *Discount Store News*, July 26, 1999, 13.
14. http://www4.toysrus.com.
15. National Restaurant Association, "Industry at a Glance," 2004.
16. Cathleen Egan, "Vending-Machine Technology Matures, Offering Branded Foods, Convenience," *Wall Street Journal*, December 13, 2001, B13.
17. http://www.usatech.com.
18. http://www.meetmark.com.
19. Amy Lo, "Selling Dreams the Mary Kay Way," *AsiaWeek*, June 29, 2001.
20. Mickey Khan, "Pulling People to Test Drive Raised Range Rover Sales," *DM News Online*, November 14, 2003.
21. Dell Web site, http://www.dell.com/us/en/gen/corporate.
22. "New Anti-spam Measure Compels Consumers to Hit 'Reply' to E-mails," http://www.webfin.com, December 9, 2003; http://www.webfin.com/en/news/news.html/?id=43947.
23. Sasha Issenberg, "Getting Ready for Prime Time," *Inc.*, November 2003, 17; http://www.qvc.com.
24. Scott Krugman and Ellen Tolley, "Online Sales Soared 48% in 2002, According to Latest Shop.Org/Forrester Study," *Shop.org*, May 15, 2003.
25. http://www.shop.org; http://www.comScore.com; http://www.nielsen-netratings.com; http://www.amazon.com; http://www.emarketer.com; "Holiday Shopping: Online, Offline or Multichannel?" *eMarketer.com*, December 9, 2003.
26. http://www.amazon.com and 2002 Annual Report.
27. Timothy Henderson, "Multi-Channel Retailers Increasingly Rely on Internet-Based Kiosk to Bridge Gap Between Channels," *Stores* online, October 1, 2001.
28. Alexander Peers and Nick Wingfield, "Sotheby's, eBay Team Up to Sell Fine Art Online," *Wall Street Journal*, January 31, 2002, B8; http//:search.sothbys.com.
29. McDonald's Corporation, Inside the U.S. Franchising Fact Sheet, http://www.mcdonalds/corp/franchise/faqs.html.
30. International Franchise Association Web site, http://www.franchise.org.
31. Domino's Pizza Web site, http://www.dominos.com/Franchise.
32. Brian O'Keefe, "Global Brands," *Fortune*, November 26, 2001, 104.
33. http://www.bluefly.com.
34. http://www.americaneagle.com and 2002 Annual Report.
35. http://www.thebestofchicago.com; http://www.Fridgedoor.com.
36. "Two Time Grammy Winner Michael Bolton Exclusively Touring FYE: For Your Entertainment Stores Nationwide," *PR Newswire*, December 4, 2003; http://www.fye.com.
37. http://www.thefashionshow.com.
38. Calmetta Y. Coleman, "Making Malls (Gasp!) Convenient," *Wall Street Journal*, February 8, 2000, B1, B4.
39. Calmetta Y. Coleman, "Kohl's Retail Racetrack," *Wall Street Journal*, March 13, 2001, B1; http://www.kohls.com.
40. http://www.apple.com.
41. "Playful Touches Dress Up the Box," *Chain Store Age*, June 1998, 110–111.
42. Glenn J. Kalinoski, "A&F Faces Discrimination Suit," *DM News Online*, November 20, 2003; http://www.afjustice.com/; Louis Aguilar, "Hispanics Receiving More Positive Representation in Media," *Knight Ridder Tribune Business News*, August 1, 2003; http://www.onpoint-marketing.com/generation-y.htm.
43. Viswanath Venkatesh, V. Ramesh, and Anne P. Massey, "m-Commerce: Breaking Through the Adoption Barriers," Research at Smith, Fall 2003 vol. 4, no. 1; http://www.bearingpoint.com; http://www.bearingpoint.com/solutions/wireless_internet_solutions/mcommerce.html; "The Swipe and Sip Soda: Pepsi Taste-Tests New Wireless Credit Card System for Vending Machines," *mpulse: A Cooltown Magazine*, November 23, 2003; http://www.cooltown.hp.com.
44. This application exercise is based on the contribution of Amy Hubbert (University of Nebraska at Omaha) to *Great Ideas in Teaching Marketing*, a teaching supplement that accompanies Lamb, Hair, and McDaniel's *Marketing*. Professor Hubbert's entry titled "Discovery of Strategic Retailing Factors" was a winner in the "Best of the Great Ideas in Teaching Marketing" contest conducted in conjunction with the publication of the eighth edition of *Marketing*.
45. http://www.bestbuy.com; Mark Tatge, "Fun and Games," *Forbes*, January 12, 2004, 138; Scott Carlson, "Best Buy Extends Weekend Store Hours," *Saint Paul Pioneer Press*, February 17, 2004; Scott Carlson, "Best Buy, Target Stores Score High in Consumer-Approval Survey," *Saint Paul Pioneer Press*, January 30, 2004; Laura Heller, "Connected Life Blooms in the Desert," *DSN Retailing News*, February 9, 2004, 188.

PART 4

1. Todd Allen, "Comics on the Internet: A Business Primer," http://www.indignantonline.com/clectica/comics_white_paper.htm; Jennifer M. Contino, "Kids, Comics, and the Future," *Sequential Tart*, January 2004, http://www.sequentialtart.com; http://www.comicsetc.com; http://www.diamondcomics.com.
2. James Doran, "Stelios Goes to Hollywood in Search of Cinema Chief," *Times Online*, December 10, 2003, http://business.timesonline.co.uk; Jeremy Hunt, "Easy-Going Guru Accepts Hard Facts," *The Express on Sunday*, December 7, 2003, 6; Angela Jameson, "EasyCinema Will Take Hollywood Fight to EU," *The Times*, January 23, 2004, 38; Robert Lea, "Stelios' Struggling Cinemas Venture to Zoom in on London," *The Evening Standard*, December 9, 2003, 33; Lucy Smy, "EasyJet Founder Plans to Expand by Bus," *Financial Times*, November 24, 2003, 25.

CHAPTER 14

1. "Jordan Spreads Love with New Integrated Brand Marketing Campaign,"

7. Ibid.

8. "Promo Shorts," *Marketing Magazine*, September 3, 2001, P4.

9. Mickey Khan, "Cuervo Works to Change Labor Day," *DM News.com*, August 25, 2003.

10. Mickey Khan, "Neiman Marcus Eyes Fatter Database for Holidays," *DM News.com*, October 23, 2003.

11. Rance Crain, "We're Not Lovin' McDonald's New Strategy Either," *Ad Age Online*, September 22, 2003; Stuart Elliott, "Big New Campaign for McDonald's," *New York Times* (http://nytimes.com), September 3, 2003; Bob Garfield, "Why We're Not Lovin' It," *Ad Age.com*, September 8, 2003.

12. Charles Newberry, "Coke Goes Native with a New Soft Drink," *Advertising Age*, December 1, 2003, 34; Charles Newberry, "Philips under the Big Top," *Advertising Age*, December 1, 2003, 3, 36; "Work," *Advertising Age*, December 1, 2003, 26.

13. http://www.philips.com.

14. Ibid.

15. The AIDA concept is based on the classic research of E. K. Strong, Jr., as theorized in *The Psychology of Selling and Advertising* (New York: McGraw-Hill, 1925) and "Theories of Selling," *Journal of Applied Psychology* 9 (1925), 75–86.

16. Thomas E. Barry and Daniel J. Howard, "A Review and Critique of the Hierarchy of Effects in Advertising," *International Journal of Advertising* 9 (1990), 121–135.

17. Kristin Larson, "Life without Sex: As the Acclaimed HBO Series 'Sex in the City' Comes to a Close, the Fashion World Looks at the Profound Influence the Show Has Had and What—If Anything—Will Replace It," *Footwear News*, February 2, 2004, 36; "A Passion for Fashion: Nameplate Necklaces, Fendi Bags, Drop-Dead Manolos—'Sex in the City' Made Stars of Them All," *People Weekly*, June 23, 2003, 106.

18. Washington Mutual Press Release, "Teacher Talent Competition, Free BBQ and Performances by Tim McGraw and

tion" was a runner-up in the "Best of the Great Ideas in Teaching Marketing" contest held in conjunction with the publication of the eighth edition of *Marketing*.

24. This application exercise is based on the contribution of David M. Blanchette (Rhode Island College) to *Great Ideas in Teaching Marketing*, a teaching supplement that accompanies Lamb, Hair, and McDaniel's *Marketing*. Professor Blanchette's entry titled "Applying Semiotics in Promotion" was a runner-up in the "Best of the Great Ideas in Teaching Marketing" contest held in conjunction with the publication of the eighth edition of *Marketing*.

25. Katrina Burger, "A Drink With an Attitude," *Forbes*, February 10, 1997; Joel Kurtzman, "Advertising for All the Little Guys," *Fortune*, April 12, 2000, 16; Greg Masters, "All Juiced Up," *Discount Merchandiser*, July 1999, 107; Gwen Moran, "Go, Granny, Go," *Entrepreneur Magazine*, March 2000; Nantucket Nectars Web site at http://www.juiceguys.com; "Nantucket Nectars Will Tie Up in Denver," *Denver Rocky Mountain News*, February 14, 1999; Nancy Coltun Webster. "Squeezed Nectars: Chris Testa," *Advertising Age*, June 26, 2000, s4; "What Have You Become?" *Entrepreneur Magazine*, May 2000.

CHAPTER 15

1. Peter Lewis, "The Biggest Game in Town," *Fortune*, September 15, 2003; http://www.marketingpower.com; http://www.easports.com.

2. Robyn Greenspan, "U.S. Online Ad Growth Underway," http://www.cyberatlas.com, July 15, 2003.

3. Mark Schumann, "Top 200 Bolt Ahead, Spend $20 Bil," *Advertising Age*, October 13, 2003, 23.

4. U.S. Department of Commerce, Bureau of the Census, http://www.census.gov.

5. http://www.adage.com.

6. Michael R. Solomon, *Consumer Behavior*, 6th ed. (Upper Saddle River, NJ: Prentice Hall, 2004), 275.

15. Maryann Napoli, *Health Facts*, October 2001, 2.

16. Sebastian Rupley, "No False Ads," *PC Magazine*, July 3, 2001, 64.

17. Ira Teinowitz, "Marketers Blast Charges in Alcohol Suit," *Advertising Age*, December 1, 2003, 10; Christina Berk, "Alcohol Industry Faces Suit Alleging Marketing to Teens," *Wall Street Journal online*, November 26, 2003; "KFC Pulls 'Health' Ads, Prepares Response to FTC," *Advertising Age*, December 1, 2003, 2; Kate MacArthur, "KFC Launches Campaign to Change High-Fat Image," *Ad Age Online*, October 28, 2003; Normandy Madden, "Honda Suicide Car Ad Pulled in Australia," *Ad Age Online*, September 22, 2003; Kate MacArthur, "Coors Slammed for Targeting Kids," *Advertising Age*, November 3, 2003, 1, 59; Bob Garfield, "KFC Serves Big, Fat Bucket of Nonsense in 'Healthy' Spots," *Advertising Age*, November 3, 2003, 61.

18. "Absolut Vodka Must Pull Campaign in Italy," http://www.adageglobal.com, February 2, 2001.

19. "Yahoo! Korea Complains about Comparative Ads," http://www.adageglobal.com, September 21, 2001.

20. "Rainmakers," *Advertising Age's Creativity*, October 2001, 14.

21. Tabasco advertisement, *Advertising Age*, October 13, 2003, 8.

22. Emma Hall, "Case Study," *Advertising Age*, September 22, 2003, 18.

23. Hank Kim, "Unilever, Ironman Link for NBC Reality Special," *Advertising Age*, September 8, 2003, 6.

24. Barbara Lippert, "Power Trips," *Adweek Eastern Edition*, September 3, 2001, 18.

25. Laura Q. Hughes and Wendy Davis, "Revival of the Fittest," *Advertising Age*, March 12, 2001, 18–19.

26. Solomon, *Consumer Behavior*.

27. Mike Beirne, "Can Your Beer Do This?" *Brandweek*, October 15, 2001, M50.

28. Suzanne Vranica, "Focus Groups Favor Nostalgic Messages," *Wall Street Journal*, October 10, 2001, B6.

29. "'FT' Creates World's Biggest Newspaper," *Advertising Age*, October 20, 2003.

30. Duncan, *Integrated Marketing Communications*, 696–697.

31. "China Retailer Bags Spokesman," *Advertising Age*, November 24, 2003, 12; "Spotlight," *Advertising Age*, December 1, 2003, 18; Bill Britt, "Volkswagen Waxes Poetic to Stir Up Emotions and Sales," *Advertising Age*, September 29, 2003.

32. Pamela Paul, "Sell It to the Psyche," *Time*, September 15, 2003, 47; http://www.marketingpower.com.

33. http://www.adage.com.

34. Edmund O. Lawler, "B-to-B Skewed Cable Now Mainstream Buy," *Advertising Age*, May 7, 2001, 32.

35. Dan Lippe, "Fox Tops Twentysomethings' Favorite TV List," *Ad Age Online*, August 4, 2003.

36. Richard Linnett, "TV Show with Highest-Priced Ads: Friends," *Ad Age Online*, September 15, 2003.

37. Richard Linnett, "Super Bowl Ad Prices Set New Record," *Ad Age Online*, January 12, 2004.

38. Jim Edwards, "The Art of the Infomercial," *Brandweek*, September 3, 2001, 14.

39. Erin White, "In-Your-Face Marketing: Ad Agency Rents Foreheads," *Wall Street Journal*, February 11, 2003, B2; http://www.commercialalert.org.

40. "Cadbury Rolls Snapple in Mexico," *Advertising Age*, October 13, 2003, 18.

41. Ryan Woo, "Adidas Wows Japan with Vertical Soccer Field," *Wall Street Journal*, September 22, 2003, B1.

42. Ken Magill, "IAB: Online Ad Spending Still Climbing," *DM News Online*, August 21, 2003.

43. Jennifer Rewick, "Brand Awareness Fuels Strategies for Online Advertisers Next Year," *Wall Street Journal*, December 28, 2000, B2.

44. Ibid.

45. Mary Anne Ostrom, "Yahoo to Buy Online Ad Pioneer," *Knight Ridder Tribune Business News*, July 15, 2003; Tessa Wegert, "Games Pop Up in Ads," http://www.clickz.com, July 17, 2003; Tessa Wegert, "Advergaming Catches On," http://www.clickz.com, July 17, 2003; http://www.candystand.com; http://www.bluefly.com.

46. http://www.bmwfilms.com.

47. Tobi Elkin, "Coca-Cola's First TiVo Advertainment Airs Today," *AdAge.com*, October 9, 2003.

48. Jack Neff, "Floors in Stores Start Moving," *Advertising Age*, August 20, 2001, 15.

49. Cara Beardi, "Video Venue Joins the Line for Gas-Pump Advertising," *Advertising Age*, April 23, 2001, 8.

50. Sally Beatty, "Ogilvy's TV-Ad Study Stresses 'Holding Power' Instead of Ratings," *Wall Street Journal*, June 4, 1999, B2.

51. Marketing Agencies Association (MAA) Worldwide Press Releases, October 27, 2003, http://www.maaw.org; Annie Smith Hughes, "SK Telecom Steals World Cup—and PMAA Grand Prix," *PROMO Magazine*, August 1, 2003, online.

52. Jean Sherman Chatzky, "Whose Name Here? It Seems No Event Is Too Personal to Have a Corporate Sponsor," *Money*, October 1, 2001, 196.

53. Alice Z. Cuneo, "Virgin Mobile Gets Naked," *Advertising Age*, October 27, 2003, 4; Claire Atkinson, "There's a Method to Branson's Madness," *Advertising Age*, October 20, 2003, 3, 54.

54. "Absolut Hunk: Story of a Wildly Successful Product Placement," *Ad Age Online*, January 1, 2003.

55. "The Bulgari Connection," *Natural Life*, November/December 2001, 22.

56. http://www.gravitygames.com.

57. "LG Electronics Digital Display Products Debut at Sundance Film Festival," *PR Newswire*, January 15, 2004.

58. "Modernista! Adds Avon, to Unveil Holiday Gap Ads" *Adweek*, November 12, 2001, 32.

59. Tidd Van Kampen, "Ads Seen as Good Trade-off for Police Cars," *Omaha World-Herald*, July 28, 2003.

60. Michael Jay Polonsky, "Reevaluating Green Marketing: A Strategic Approach," *Business Horizons*, September/October 2001, 21.

61. Kathleen Cholewka, "The 5 Best E-Marketing Campaigns," *Sales & Marketing Management*, January 2001, 53.

62. Ibid.

63. "Coca-Cola Says Sorry to Yao Ming," *PromoXtra Newsletter*, October 23, 2003.

64. Maxine Lans Retsky, "More Steps to Avoid McDonald's Situation," *Marketing News*, November 19, 2001, 11.

65. George Anders, "eBay to Refund Millions after Outrage," *Wall Street Journal*, June 14, 1999, B8; George Anders, "eBay Scrambles to Repair Image after Big Crash," *Wall Street Journal*, June 14, 1999, B1, B4.

66. This application exercise is based on the contribution of S. J. Garner (Eastern Kentucky University) to *Great Ideas in Teaching Marketing*, a teaching supplement that accompanies Lamb, Hair, and McDaniel's *Marketing*. Professor Garner's entry titled "Creating Advertising for Illegal Products/Services" was a runner-up in the "Best of the Great Ideas in Teaching Marketing" contest conducted in conjunction with the publication of the eighth edition of *Marketing*.

67. This application exercise is taken from Chuck Williams, *Management*, 3d ed. (Cincinnati: South-Western, 2005). The idea to include a crisis management exercise in this chapter came from a contribution by Jack K. Mandel (Nassau Community College) to *Great Ideas in Teaching Marketing*, a teaching supplement that accompanies Lamb, Hair, and McDaniel's *Marketing*. Professor Mandel's entry titled "Putting Students in the Line of Fire to Learn Crisis Management Techniques" received an honorable mention in the "Best of the Great Ideas in Teaching Marketing" contest held in conjunction with the publication of the eighth edition of *Marketing*.

68. Bill Carter, "Will This Machine Change Television?" *New York Times*, 5 July 1999, p. 1; Jim Cooper, "Inside the Box," *Brandweek*, 8 May 2000, C32; Marla Matzer Rose, "TV Advertisers Worry About Growth of New PVRs," *Chicago Tribune*, 14 April 2000, 4; Erin Strout, "The End of TV Advertising?" *Sales & Marketing Management*, January 2000, 15; TiVo Web site at http://www.tivo.com "TiVo Signs Showtime," *Advertising Age*, 16 May 2000.

CHAPTER 16

1. Press release, August 11, 2003, http://www.xmradio.com; Undated AP release, "A Free Offer for Satellite Radio," http://www.sirius.com; Barry Willis, "Satellite Radio News," http://www.stereophile.com, August 11, 2003; Elizabeth Boston, "Satellite Radio Signs Up Another Automaker," *Ad Age Online*, April 16, 2003; Tom Jacobs, "XM and Sirius Get Busy," *The Motley Fool* (http://www.fool.com), August 12, 2003; Mike Langberg, "Satellite Radio Is Ready to Go Mainstream," *STLtoday.com*, July 23, 2003; Joseph B. White, "Car Makers Hope to Lure Buyers with Fancy New Audio Options," *Wall Street Journal*, July 21, 2003.

2. "2003 Annual Report: Industry Report 2003," *PROMO Magazine*.

3. Eric Whalgren, "For Yum!, the Whole Apple's World Is Fat City," *Business Week Online*, December 11, 2003, http://www.businessweek.com/bwdaily/dnflash/dec2003/nf20031211_5852_db008.htm; Carlye Adler, "Colonel Sander's March on China," *Time Asia Magazine Online*, November 24, 2003, http://www.time.com/time/asia/magazine/article/0,13673,501031124-543845,00.html; http://www.yumcareers.com; http://www.kfc.com.

4. Carol Agrisani, "Coupon Confidence: Consumers May Not Be Embracing Coupons Like They Used To, But Marketers Remain Committed to the Promotional Tool," *Supermarket News*, April 5, 2004, 22.

5. http://www.kroger.com; Internet Coupons link at http://www.kroger.upons.com.

6. Mickey Kahn, "eBay Offers Will Ride on Domino's Pizza Boxes," *DM News Online*, August 22, 2003; http://www.dominos.com; Joint press release of eBay and Domino's, August 21, 2003.

7. Betsy Spethmann, "Vlasic Spurs Trial with SUV Sweepstakes," *PROMO Xtra Newsletter*, October 23, 2003.

8. Anne Kandra, "Bait and Rebate," *PC World*, September 2001, 45.

9. "REPEAT/Starbucks, Bank One, Visa Launch Starbucks Card Duetto Visa," *Business Wire*, October 13, 2003; http://www.starbucks.com.

10. "Vodka," *PROMO Xtra Newsletter*, October 16, 2003.

11. Elizabeth Millard, "Bets Loyalty Programs on the Internet," *E-Commerce Times*, February 28, 2004, http://www.ecommercetimes.com.

12. Matthew Haeberle, "Loyalty Is Dead: Great Experiences, Not Price, Will Create

pling: The Hidden Opportunity," *Retail Merchandiser*, August 2001, 45.

20. Lorin Cipolla, "Sampling: Instant Gratification," *PROMO Magazine*, April 1, 2004, http://www.promomagazine.com.

21. Stephanie Thompson, "Ben & Jerry's Goes Alternative with New Effort: Marketer Sticks to Its Grassroots Via Print, Radio," *Advertising Age*, May 8, 2000, 111.

22. Stephanie Thompson, "Dove Targets the Chocoholic," *Advertising Age*, September 15, 2003, 45.

23. Andy Cohen, "A Marketing Touchdown," *Sales & Marketing Management*, October 2001, 16.

24. Geoffrey A. Fowler, "When Free Samples Become Saviors," *Wall Street Journal*, August 14, 2001, B1, B4.

25. "Point-of-Purchase: $17 Billion," *PROMO Magazine*, October 29, 2001, 3.

26. Stephanie Thompson, "Hershey Sets $30M Push," *Advertising Age*, September 15, 2003, 3, 45.

27. "MasterCard Unwraps Priceless Holiday Prizes," *PROMO Xtra,* November 5, 2001, 22.

28. Mickey Khan, "Heineken Hoaxes Are Real Deal for Building E-mail Names," *DM News Online*, October 7, 2003.

29. Catherine Seda, "What a Deal! Attract Customers with Online Coupons," *Entrepreneur*, December 2003, 104.

30. Roger O. Crocket, "Penny-Pinchers' Paradise," *BusinessWeek*, January 22, 2001, EB12.

31. Libby Estell, "Economic Incentives," *Sales & Marketing Management*, October 2001, S2–S4.

32. Ben Chapman, "The Trade Show Must Go On," *Sales & Marketing Management*, June 2001, 22.

33. Michael Beverland, "Contextual Influences and the Adoption and Practice of Relationship Selling in a Business-to-Business Setting: An Exploratory Study," *Journal of Personal Selling & Sales Management*, Summer 2001, 207.

34. Richard Morrison, "The Business Process of Customer Retention and Loyalty,"

41. http://www.bicworld.com; http://www.BIClink.com.

42. http://www.presentations.com.

43. http://www.chanimal.com; "chatrooms" link at the "Overcoming Objections" Web page (link to http://www.chanimal.com/html/objections.html).

44. Troy Korsgaden, "Fine-tuning Your Agency's Office Systems," http://www.roughnotes.com/rnmag/june00/06p116.htm.

45. David Garfinkel, "The E-Vangelist: Autoresponse Marketing," *Sales & Marketing Management*, May 2001, 27; http://www.CollegeRecruiter.com.

46. http://www.ge.com.

47. http://www.doubleclick.com.

48. Weitz, Castleberry, and Tanner, *Selling*, 18–20.

49. http://www.ge.com.

50. http://www.peoplesoft.com.

51. http://www.businesswire.com.

52. Kathleen Joyce, "In the Cards," *PROMO Magazine* September 1, 2003, http://www.promomagazine.com.

53. G. Dudley and S. Goodson, *The Psychology of Sales Call Reluctance*, Behavioral Sciences Research Press, Dallas, TX, 1999; http://www.bsrpinc.com/research/unethical_survey_02.htm?Sex=F&Age=27&Country=usa&Education=5&Profession=Academic&Title=Instructor&submit=Continue; "How to Do the Right Thing: The 90-Day Plan," *Optimize*, February 2002, http://www.optimizemag.com; Dwight Ueda, "Sales Compensation," *Salary.com*, http://www.salary.com/advice/layouthtmls/advl_display_Cat14_Ser6_Par23.html.

54. Kathleen Cholewka, "E-Market Stats," *Sales & Marketing Management*, September 2001, 21.

55. This application exercise is based on the contribution of John Ronchetto (University of San Diego) to *Great Ideas in Teaching Marketing*, a teaching supplement that accompanies Lamb, Hair, and McDaniel's *Marketing*. Professor Ronchetto's entry titled "Sales and Customer Service Experi-

PART 5

1. Rob Neyer, "Almighty Buck Doesn't Rule," *ESPN.com*, May 7, 2004, http://sports.espn.go.com; Mike Penner, "Baseball Cancels Plans for Movie Ad on Bases," *Los Angeles Times*, May 7, 2004, http://www.latimes.com; Brian Steinberg and Stefan Fatsis, "With Web on Bases, Baseball Will Push 'Spider-Man 2,'" *Wall Street Journal Online*, May 5, 2004, http://online.wsj.com; Rich Thomaselli, "On-Field Spider-Man Baseball Ads Cancelled," *AdAge.com*, May 7, 2004, http://www.adage.com.

2. "'My Name Is Turok'—UK Human Billboards Announced," *Reuters News*, September 3, 2002, http://global.factiva.com; Greg Gatlin, "Race Ads Go to Head of Class; Tattoo Technique Sneaks Reebok Brand into Rival's Marathon," *Boston Herald*, April 22, 2003, 029; Geoffrey A. Fowler and Sebastian Moffett, "Adidas's Billboard Ads Give Kick to Japanese Pedestrians (Tethered Soccer Players 10 Stories Up)," *Wall Street Journal*, August 29, 2003, B1; Normandy Madden and Laurel Wentz, "Adidas Introduces Human Billboards," *Advertising Age*, September 1, 2003, 11; D. Kent Pingel, "World's First Walking, Talking Advertisement Makes a Big Splash," *PR Newswire*, December 2, 2003, http://www.prnewswire.com; Robin Turner, "It's Written All Over their Faces—Students Turned into Human Billboards," *The Western Mail*, October 30, 2003, 6; Erin White, "Students Recruited to Advertise Brands Via Face Tattoos," *Wall Street Journal Europe*, February 10, 2003, A6.

CHAPTER 17

1. Timothy Aeppel, "How Goodyear Blew Its Chance to Capitalize on a Rival's Woes," *Wall Street Journal*, February, 19, 2003, A1, A10.

2. Roland Rust, Christine Moorman, and Peter R. Dickson, "Getting Return on Quality: Revenue Expansion, Cost Reduction, or Both?" *Journal of Marketing*, October 2002, 7–24.

3. "DaimlerChrysler's Freightliner Puts New Chief at the Wheel," *Wall Street Journal*, May 29, 2001, B4.

4. "Dispel Major Myths about Pricing Strategy," *Marketing News*, February 3, 2003, 10.

5. Andreas Fuchs, "Just the Ticket? A Greek Entrepreneur Is Attempting to Shake Up European Exhibition with a Discount Admission System That Makes Hollywood Nervous," *Hollywood Reporter*, July 8, 2003, 14; Ian Wylie, "In Movieland, Not So Easy," *Fast Company*, October 2003, 35.

6. "Four Biggest Cigarette Makers Can't Raise Prices As They Did," *Wall Street Journal*, October 25, 2002, A1, A8.

7. "Financing Deals for New Cars Shake Up Market for Used Cars," *Wall Street Journal*, November 16, 2001, B1, B4.

8. "The Price Is Really Right," *BusinessWeek*, March 31, 2003, 62–66.

9. Michael Mendano, "Priced to Perfection," *Business2.com*, March 6, 2001, 40–41.

10. "The Power of Optimal Pricing," *Business 2.0*, September 2002, 68–70.

11. Ibid.

12. "Meet Your New Neighborhood Grocer," *Fortune*, May 13, 2002, 93–96.

13. Paul Beckett and Jathon Sapsford, "As Credit-Card Theft Grows, a Tussle over Paying to Stop It," *Wall Street Journal*, May 1, 2003, A1, A15.

14. See Joseph Cannon and Christian Homburg, "Buyer-Supplier Relationships and Customer Firm Costs," *Journal of Marketing*, January 2001, 29–43.

15. Neil Turner, "European Pricing Squeeze," *Pharmaceutical Executive*, October 2002, 84–91; Geoff Dyer, "Why Drugmakers Are Losing Sleep—European Pricing," *Financial Times*, April 16, 2003, 3.

16. Most of this section is taken from David Hamilton, "The Price Isn't Right," *Wall Street Journal*, February 12, 2001, R8, R10. Used with permission.

17. "Amazon Takes Page from Wal-Mart to Prosper on Web," *Wall Street Journal*, November 22, 2002, A1, A6; "Mighty Amazon," *Fortune*, May 26, 2003, 60.

18. Hamilton, "The Price Isn't Right."

19. "Price Buster," *Wall Street Journal*, July 17, 2000, R12.

20. "Value Driven," *Fortune*, May 1, 2000, 74; Press release at FreeMarkets.com, December 31, 2003.

21. "U.S., 29 States Crack Down on Illicit Internet Auctions," *Milwaukee Journal Sentinel*, May 1, 2003, 3A.

22. "eBay's Worst Nightmare," *Fortune*, May 26, 2003, 89–92.

23. "One Nation under Wal-Mart," *Fortune*, March 3, 2003, 65–78.

24. Ibid.

25. R. Chandrashekaran, "The Implications of Individual Differences in Reference to Price Utilization for Designing Effective Price Communications," *Journal of Business Research*, August 2001, 85–92.

26. Katherine Lemon and Stephen Nowlis, "Developing Synergies between Promotions and Brands in Different Price-Quality Tiers," *Journal of Marketing Research*, May 2002, 171–185. Also see Valerie Taylor and William Bearden, "The Effects of Price on Brand Extension Evaluations: The Moderating Role of Extension Similarity," *Journal of the Academy of Marketing Science*, Spring 2002, 131–140; and Raj Sethuraman and V. Srinivasan, "The Asymmetric Share Effect: An Empirical Generalization on Cross-Price Effects," *Journal of Marketing Research*, August 2002, 379–386.

27. Merrie Brucks, Valarie Zeithaml, and Gillian Naylor, "Price and Brand Name as Indicators of Quality Dimensions for Consumer Durables," *Journal of the Academy of Marketing Science*, Summer 2000, 359–374.

28. Matthew Maier, "Making the Most of eBay," *Business 2.0*, June 2002, 130.

29. This application exercise is based on the contribution of Vaughn C. Judd (Auburn University, Montgomery) to *Great Ideas in Teaching Marketing*, a teaching supplement that accompanies Lamb, Hair, and McDaniel's *Marketing*. Professor Judd's entry titled "Analyzing the Price-Quality Relationship" was a winner in the "Best of the Great Ideas in Teaching Marketing" contest held in conjunction with the publication of the eighth edition of *Marketing*.

30. http://www.HDNet.com; http://www.DirectTV.com; http://www.Adephia.com; http://www.timewarner.com; Leigh Gallagher, "The Big Picture," *Forbes*, March 1, 2004, 78; Allison Roman, "All HD All the Time: Mark Cuban's HDNet Is Typically Offered on Operators' Premium Tier," *Broadcasting & Cable*, January 26, 2004, 20; Meredith Amdur, "New Definition at TW: Cuban's HDNet Lands Carriage with Cabler," *Daily Variety*, December 18, 2003, 6.

CHAPTER 18

1. Alex Taylor III, "Porsche's Risky Recipe," *Fortune*, February 17, 2003, 91–94.

2. Kent Monroe and Jennifer Cox, "Pricing Practices That Endanger Profits," *Marketing Management*, September/October 2001, 42–46.

3. Thomas T. Nagle and George Cressman, "Don't, Just Set Prices, Manage Them," *Marketing Management*, November/December 2002, 29–33; Jay Klompmaker, William H. Rogers, and Anthony Nygren, "Value, Not Volume," *Marketing Management*, June 2003, 45–48.

4. Jeff Bailey, "Fat Margins: Market Share, Penetration Score," *Wall Street Journal*, May 13, 2003, B7.

5. "Why P&G's Smile Is So Bright," *BusinessWeek*, August 12, 2002, 58–60.

6. Miriam Jordan, "A Retailer in Brazil Has Become Rich by Courting Poor," *Wall Street Journal*, June 11, 2002, A1, A8.

7. "The Price Fixing Series," *Multinational Monitor* 24, issue 3 (2003): 30.

8. "Five Paint Firms Are Scrutinized for Price Fixing," *Wall Street Journal*, June 4, 2001, A3–4.

9. "Doctor Group Settle Charges," *San Diego Union-Tribune*, May 31, 2003, C-3.

10. Dan Carney, "Predatory Pricing: Cleared for Takeoff," *BusinessWeek*, May 14, 2001, 50.

11. "States Square Off Against Drug Firms in Crusade on Prices," *Wall Street Journal*, December 7, 2001, A1, A13.

12. Ibid.

13. "The Maine Idea—Justices Open the Door to Experiment in Cutting Drug Costs," *The Plain Dealer*, May 26, 2003, B6.

14. Bruce Alford and Abhijit Biswas, "The Effects of Discount Level, Price Consciousness, and Sale Proneness on Consumers' Price Perception and Behavioral Intention," *Journal of Business Research*, September 2002, 775–783.

15. Pradeep Chintagunta, "Investigating Category Pricing Behavior at a Retail Chain," *Journal of Marketing Research*, May 2002, 141–154.

16. "Price War in Aisle 3," *Wall Street Journal*, May 27, 2003, B1, B16.

17. Katy McLaughlin, "The Discount Grocery Cards That Don't Save You Money," *Wall Street Journal Online*, January 21, 2003.

18. Joel Urbany, "Are Your Prices Too Low?" *Harvard Business Review*, October 2001, 26–27.

19. David Bell, Ganesh Iyer, and V. Padmanabhar, "Price Competition under Stockpiling and Flexible Consumption," *Journal of Marketing Research*, August 2002, 292–303.

20. "Owner of Sandusky, Ohio, Amusement Park to Keep General Admission Unchanged," *Toledo Blade*, December 6, 2003; James Zoltack, "Alternative Pricing Strategies Focus of Talk at TEA Summit," *Amusement Business*, October 13, 2003, 5; James Zoltack, "More Parks Mull Flexible Pricing System: Pay As You Go," *Amusement Business*, November 3, 2003, 1.

21. Dilip Soman and John Gourville, "Transaction Decoupling: The Effects of Price Bundling on the Decision to Consume," *MSI Report No. 98-131*, 2002; Stefan Stremersch and Gerard J. Tellis, "Strategic Bundling of Products and Prices: A New Synthesis for Marketing," *Journal of Marketing*, January 2002, 55–72.

22. Dilip Soman and John Gourville, "Transaction Decoupling: How Price Bundling Affects the Decision to Consume," *Journal of Marketing Research*, February 2001, 30–44.

23. "How to Thrive When Prices Fall," *Fortune*, May 12, 2003, 131–134.

24. Tara Parker-Pope, "Lose Weight! Get a Free Massage! The Perks of Becoming a Lab Rat," *Wall Street Journal*, May 6, 2003, B1.

25. This application exercise is based on the contribution of William H. Brannen (Creighton University) to *Great Ideas in Teaching Marketing*, a teaching supplement that accompanies Lamb, Hair, and McDaniel's *Marketing*. Professor Brannen's entry titled "Can Your Marketing Students Solve the Banana Problem? Can You?" was a runner-up in the "Best of the Great Ideas in Teaching Marketing" contest held in conjunction with the

Downloads: Apple to Ship One Millionth iPod This Week," *M2 Presswire,* June 24, 2003; "Leaked iTunes Info Gives Insight into Apple's Success," *TV Meets the Web,* June 11, 2003; Chris Marlowe, "Apple Jams with Music Service: iTunes Music Store Offers 200,000 from All Major Labels," *Hollywood Reporter,* April 29, 2003, 4; Melinda Newman and Brian Garrity, "Apple's Service Tests Music Biz: Can Artists, Industry Capitalize on Digital Bid?" *Billboard,* May 10, 2003, 1; Justin Oppelaar, "Will Apple For-Pay Keep Doldrums Away?" *Variety,* May 12, 2003, 42; Randall Rothenberg, "Plenty to Learn from Apple's 'Near-Perfect' iTunes Store," *Advertising Age,* June 9, 2003, 22.

CHAPTER 20

1. Nick Wingfield and Brian Steinberg, "Ads Aim to Sell That Tune," *Wall Street Journal Online,* November 10, 2003; Katie Dean, "New Napster Off to a Solid Start," *Wired News,* November 3, 2003; Leander Kahney, "Music Biz Buzzing over iTunes," *Wired News,* May 2, 2003; Joanna Glasner, "Dollar Songs: Bargain or Rip Off?" *Wired News,* May 1, 2003; Reuters, "What a Difference 20 Cents Makes," *Wired News,* July 1, 2003, http://www.wired.com; "Online Music Wings Its Way to the Celestial Jukebox," *Marketing @ Wharton,* July 2, 2003, http://www.knowledge.wharton.upenn.edu; Narasu Rebbapragada, "Tune Wars!" *Mac Addict,* August 2003; PR Newswire, "XM Satellite Radio Holdings Inc. Announces Third Quarter 2003 Results," *Satellite Today,* November 6, 2003, http://www.telecomweb.com; Jim Stafford, "Online Music Sales Pose Practical Questions for Traditional Retailers," *Knight Ridder Tribune Business News,* August 2, 2003; http://www.listen.com; http://www.apple.com; http://www.xmradio.com.

2. Joseph Hair, Robert Bush, and David Ortinau, *Marketing Research: Within a Changing Information Environment,* 2d ed. (Burr Ridge, IL: McGraw-Hill/Irwin, 2002), 128.

13. "Heading to the Border: Borders Books and Music Celebrates Three Decades of Prosperity Thanks to Its Successful Retailing Recipe," *Shopping Center World,* December 1, 2001, http://www.scwonline.com; http://www.amazon.com; http://www.firstusa.com (follow link from amazon.com).

14. http://www.firstusa.com.

15. http://www.sony.com.

16. "Group 1 and iWay Software Partner to Enhance Enterprise Wide Data Quality and Customer Data Integration," Press Release: iWay software, January 15, 2002.

17. "Data Management Case Study: Avery Dennison 'Tags' Its CRM Goals," http://www.dataflux.com.

18. Sean Doherty, "Keeping Data Private," *Network Computing,* June 25, 2001, 83.

19. "Attorney General Files Motion to Prevent Bankrupt Company from Selling Customer Information," *M2 Presswire,* December 17, 2001.

20. "North Dakota Voters Reject Referendum to Allow Banks to Sell Customer Information without Written Permission," *Monday Business Briefing,* June 27, 2002.

21. *Random House Webster's Dictionary.*

22. Rick Whiting, "The Data-Warehouse Advantage," *Information Week.com,* July 28, 2003; John Courtmanche, "Continental Is Merging Databases, Testing Operational CRM," *1to1 Magazine,* May/June 2001.

23. Rob Jackson and Paul Wang, *Strategic Database Marketing* (Lincolnwood, IL: NTC Business Books, 1997), 83.

24. "The Key to Effective CRM: Building an Interactive Dialog," http://www.marketing3.nl, presentation in Utrecht, The Netherlands, December 4, 2003.

25. Whiting, "The Data-Warehouse Advantage."

26. http://www.unilever.com.

27. "The Key to Effective CRM: Building an Interactive Dialog."

28. http://www.theknot.com; "TheKnot Ties in Consumers with Personalization," *Consumer-Centric Benchmarks for 2001 & Beyond,* http://www.risnews.com.

June 8, 2004; "Prediction and Prevention," http://www.sas.com/success/absa.html.

34. Jaimie Seaton, "Stave Solves the Relationship Puzzle," *1to1 Magazine,* August 4, 2003, http://www.1to1.com.

35. B. Weitz, S. Castleberry, and J. Tanner, *Selling* (Burr Ridge, IL: McGraw-Hill/Irwin, 2004), 184–85.

36. "The MyPal Rewards Program Scores Big with Fans," *1to1 Magazine,* April 2003.

37. Kim Steffen, "CVS Gives Customers ExtraCare," *1to1 Magazine,* April 2, 2001.

38. Lauren Paul, "Wegman's Proves to Kraft That Customer Differentiation Works," *1to1 Magazine,* November/December 2002.

39. Karen Schwartz, "Kraft Data Mining Transforms Marketing and Margins," *Consumer Goods Magazine,* September 2000, http://www.consumergoods.com.

40. Jane Zarem, "Nike's 'Smart' Loyalty Program," *1to1 Magazine,* March 2002.

41. Christopher Caggiano, "Building Customer Loyalty," *Inc. Magazine Online,* November 2003.

42. Kit Davis, "Track Star, RFID Is Racing to Market," *Consumer Goods Magazine,* June 2003, http://www.consumergoods.com.

43. "Boise Completes OfficeMax Merger," December 9, 2003, http://www.boisecascade.com; Jim Kirk, "Boise Taking Its Business Personally," *Chicago Tribune,* January 6, 2002, C1.

44. Janis Mara, "Companies Alter Privacy Policies," *Internetnews.com,* January 2, 2004, http://www.internetnews.com/IAR/article.php/3294471; "Ponemon Institute, International Association of Privacy Professionals Release Results of Benchmark Privacy Practices Survey," June 4, 2003, http://www.privacyassociation.org/docs/BenchmarkSurvJTH.pdf.

45. The idea for this Application Exercise came from an entry to *Great Ideas in Teaching Marketing* submitted by Professor Kenneth J. Radig of Medaille College. Professor Radig's submission titled "Direct Mail Assignment" was a runner-up in the "Best

of the Great Ideas in Teaching Marketing" contest held in conjunction with the publication of the Eighth Edition of *Marketing* by Lamb, Hair, and McDaniel.

46. "One to One," *Progressive Grocer*, February 15, 2002, 8; S. Mulholland, "Mining for Diamonds: An Upstate New York Independent Is Reaping Rewards through a Multi-Pricing System That Recognizes Its Best Shoppers," *Supermarket News*, February 11, 2002, 17; S. Greco, "Inc. Case Study—Green Hills Farms 67-Year-Old Grocery Store," *Inc.*, June 2001, 54.

PART 7

1. "Handbag Maker Vuitton Sues Google," *CNN.com*, October 24, 2003, http://www.cnn.com; Robert Mullins, "Group Wants Search Engines Freed from Policing Copyrights," *Silicon Valley/San Jose Business Journal*, August 22, 2003, http://www.bizjournals.com/sanjose; Alex Salkever, "Searching for Trouble?" *BusinessWeek Online*, January 22, 2004, http://www.businessweek.com.

2. "Six Degrees of Kevin Bacon: ATL Edition," *Louisville Magazine/Web Edition*,

March 1997, http://www.louisville.com; Matt Hicks, "Renamed Emode.com Acquires Social Networking Web Site," *eWeek*, November 14, 2003, http://www.eweek.com; Chris Metz, "Make Contact," *PC Magazine*, January 20, 2004, http://www.pcmag.com; "Six Degrees of Kevin Bacon" and "Six Degrees of Separation," *Wikipedia*, the free encyclopedia, http://en.wikipedia.org; http://web.tickle.com.

TEXT LEARNING OBJECTIVES

break up the material into manageable portions for students, and provide a structure for self-testing and review.

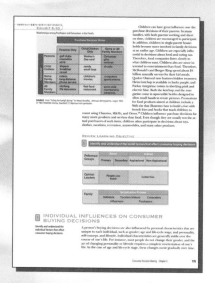

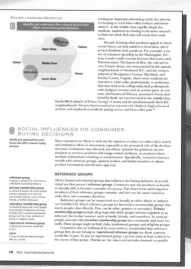

NUMBERED ICONS

in the text margins with their learning objectives mark where each objective is covered.

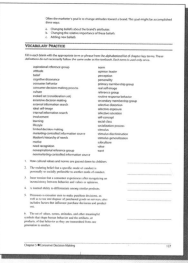

CHAPTER SUMMARIES

in the text are organized by learning objective, so that students can easily check their grasp of each objectives key concepts.

KEY-CONCEPT SUMMARIES, OUTLINE, AND SELF TESTS

for each objective in the Study Guide can help students test their achievement of learning goals. Students can quickly locate all relevant material in the text and Study Guide by looking for the numbered icon.